EIGHTH EDITION

Aging and Society

Canadian Perspectives

EIGHTH EDITION

Aging and Society

Canadian Perspectives

MARK NOVAK
California State University, Bakersfield

HERBERT C. NORTHCOTT
University of Alberta

LORI CAMPBELL
McMaster University

TOP HAT   NELSON

TOP HAT

Aging and Society: Canadian Perspectives, Eighth Edition
by Mark Novak, Herbert C. Northcott, and Lori Campbell

Publisher, Digital and Print Content:
Leanna MacLean

Marketing Manager:
Terry Fedorkiw

Content Manager:
Lisa Peterson

Photo and Permissions Researcher:
Natalie Barrington

Production Project Manager:
Jennifer Hare

Production Service:
SPi Global

Copy Editor:
June Trusty

Proofreader:
SPi Global

Indexer:
SPi Global

Design Director:
Ken Phipps

Higher Education Design PM:
Pamela Johnston

Interior Design:
Ken Cadinouche

Cover Design:
Ken Cadinouche

Compositor:
SPi Global

Cover Image:
Hero Images/Getty Images

**Library and Archives Canada
Cataloguing in Publication Data**

Novak, Mark W., author
   Aging and society : Canadian
perspectives / Mark Novak, California
State University, Bakersfield, Herbert
C. Northcott, University of Alberta,
Lori Campbell, McMaster University.
— Eighth edition.

Includes bibliographical references
and index.
Issued in print and electronic formats.
ISBN 978-0-17-670001-0 (softcover).
—ISBN 978-0-17-684630-5 (PDF)

   1. Aging—Canada—Textbooks.
2. Older people—Canada—Textbooks.
3. Older people—Canada—Social
conditions—Textbooks. I. Campbell,
Lori Anne, 1959-, author II. Northcott,
Herbert C., 1947-, author III. Title.

HQ1064.C2N68 2017   305.260971
C2017-904301-3
C2017-904302-1

ISBN-13: 978-0-17-670001-0
ISBN-10: 0-17-670001-3

I dedicate this edition of Aging and Society
to my wife Mona, my lifelong companion and
support for all that I do.
—**Mark Novak**

BRIEF CONTENTS

Preface xiii
About the Authors xx

PART 1 GERONTOLOGY TODAY 1
CHAPTER 1 *Aging Today 1*
CHAPTER 2 *Theories and Methods 20*

PART 2 SOCIAL CHANGE 45
CHAPTER 3 *Aging in Canada and the World Today 45*
CHAPTER 4 *Aging and Ethnicity 75*

PART 3 MATURATIONAL CHANGE 94
CHAPTER 5 *Personal Health and Illness 94*
CHAPTER 6 *The Psychology of Aging 131*

PART 4 INSTITUTIONAL CHANGE 164
CHAPTER 7 *Healthcare 164*
CHAPTER 8 *Finances and Economics 195*
CHAPTER 9 *Retirement and Work 223*
CHAPTER 10 *Leisure, Recreation, and Service 244*
CHAPTER 11 *Housing and Transportation 265*

PART 5 THE EXPERIENCE OF AGING 291
CHAPTER 12 *Family Life 291*
CHAPTER 13 *Social Support 317*
CHAPTER 14 *Dying, Death, and Bereavement 342*

Glossary 363
References 370
Index 422

CONTENTS

Preface xiii
About the Authors xx

PART 1 GERONTOLOGY TODAY 1

CHAPTER 1 *Aging Today* 1

Learning Objectives 1
Introduction 2
Myths and Realities of Aging 2
Attitudes Toward Old Age 6
Ageism and Discrimination in the Workplace 10
A New View of Old Age 11
   Ageism and the Third Age 12
Aging as a Disease—Another Form of Ageism 12
   Education as an Antidote to Ageism 15
Ageism and Social Policy 16
Conclusion 18

CHAPTER 2 *Theories and Methods* 20

Learning Objectives 20
Introduction 21
Theory in the Study of Aging 22
   Two Levels of Theory 22
   Three Theoretical Perspectives 23
The Life Course and Social Context 29
   Non-Normative Events 29
   History-Graded Events 29
   Normative Age-Graded Events 30
Research Issues and Methods 34
   Research Issues 34
   Types of Research Methods 38
   Ethical Issues in Research 39
Policy and Programs as the Outcome
  of Research 40
   Large-Scale Gerontology Research in Canada 41
The Future of Gerontological Theory
  and Methods 42
Conclusion 42

PART 2 SOCIAL CHANGE 45

CHAPTER 3 *Aging in Canada and the World Today* 45

Learning Objectives 45
Introduction 46
Aging in the World Today 46
   Aging in the Least Developed Nations 47
   Aging in the Less Developed Nations 50
   Summary of Aging in Least and Less Developed Regions 52
   Aging in the Developed Nations 53
   Summary of Aging in the World Today 53
Canada Comes of Age 54
   Immigration 55
   Death Rates 57
   Birth Rates 57
   Baby Boom and Baby Bust 59
   Prospective Aging: A New Way to Think About Population Aging 60
   Summary of Population Aging in Canada 62
Aging in Canada Today 63
   The Aging of the Older Population 63
   Ethnicity 64
   Geographic Mobility 66
   Increased Numbers and Proportions of Older Women 67
The Impact of Population Aging 69
   The Dependency Ratio and the Cost of an Aging Population 69
Conclusion 72

CHAPTER 4 *Aging and Ethnicity* 75

Learning Objectives 75
Introduction 76
Concept of Ethnicity 76
   Ethnic and Cultural Diversity 77
   Theoretical Perspectives on Ethnicity and Aging 78

Ethnocultural Diversity of Seniors in Canada 79
   Visible Minority Seniors 79
Ethnocultural Diversity in Experiences of Aging 80
   Ethnic Identity and Cultural Practices 80
   Intergenerational Relationships 82
   Living Arrangements and Family Life 84
   Community Life 85
   Economic Security 86
   Health and Healthcare 87
   Caregiving 90
Conclusion 91

PART 3 MATURATIONAL CHANGE 94

CHAPTER 5 *Personal Health and Illness 94*

Learning Objectives 94
Introduction 95
Seniors' Health Status 96
   New Patterns of Health and Illness 96
Limits on Activity Due to Physical Decline 98
Coping with Physical Change 102
   Changes in the Environment 104
   Improvements in Technology 105
   Changes in Lifestyle 109
   Falls: An Example of Successful Healthcare
     Management 116
The Compression of Morbidity Hypothesis 122
Successful Aging 124
   The Rowe and Kahn Model
     of Successful Aging 124
   The SOC Model of Successful Aging 125
The Impact of Income and Health
   on Quality of Life 125
Healthy Aging: A Canadian Perspective 128
Final Thoughts 129
Conclusion 129

CHAPTER 6 *The Psychology of Aging 131*

Learning Objectives 131
Introduction 132
Normal Changes in Psychological
   Functioning 132
   Memory and Intelligence 132
   Laboratory Studies 133
   Physical Change as the Source of Mental
     Decline 134

New Approaches to the Study of Mental
   Function 135
Plasticity and Cognitive Reserve 136
The Limits of Laboratory Research
   on Memory 137
The Contextual Approach 137
Training the Mind for Improved
   Performance 140
Physical Exercise and the Brain 142
Summary of Findings on Aging and Mental
   Potential 142
Intelligence 143
   Intelligence as Multidimensional 143
   New Models of Mental Ability:
     Wisdom in Later Life 144
Creativity 145
   Creativity as Measured by Great Works 145
   Creativity as Personal Expression 147
Psychological Disorders: Abnormal Aging 148
   Organic Brain Disorders 148
   The Causes of Dementia 151
   Concern about an Increase in Dementia 151
   Functional Disorders 155
   The Stigma of Mental Disorder 158
Conclusion 160

PART 4 INSTITUTIONAL CHANGE 164

CHAPTER 7 *Healthcare 164*

Learning Objectives 164
Introduction 165
Three Models of Healthcare 165
   The Medical Model 165
   The Social Model 166
   The Health Promotion Model 166
The Origins of the Canadian Healthcare
   System 167
Challenges to the Healthcare System Today 168
   Wait Times: An Ongoing Controversy and
     Challenge to the System 170
The Cost of Healthcare Today 171
   Population Aging and Healthcare Costs 173
The Healthcare System and Older People's
   Healthcare Needs 175
   Hospital Care 175
   Long-Term Institutional Care 177
   Models of Quality Institutional Care 178

The Need for Change 179
Long-Term Care: New Approaches to
   Community Care 180
   Typical Community Care Programs 181
   Geriatric Day Hospitals 182
   Adult Daycare 183
   Assisted Living and Home Care 183
   Summary of the Social Model 186
Health Promotion 187
   The Future of Health Promotion 188
Issues for the Future 189
   Availability 189
   Accessibility 190
   Coordination 191
Conclusion 192

CHAPTER 8 *Finances and Economics 195*
Learning Objectives 195
Introduction 196
Historical Developments in Canada's Pension
   System 198
The Canadian Retirement Income
   System Today 201
   Tier One: Government Transfers 201
   *Tier Two: The Canada Pension Plan and the
      Quebec Pension Plan 204*
   *The Challenge to the CPP in the
      Future 206*
   *Tier Three: Private Pensions, Savings,
      and Work 207*
   *Defined Benefit and Defined Contribution
      Pension Plans 207*
   Registered Retirement Savings Plans 210
   *Private Pensions—Registered Pension
      Plans (RPPs) 211*
   *Summary of Income Security and Replacement
      in Retirement 212*
Inequality in Later Life 213
   Immigrants and Pensions 214
   Women and Pensions 214
   Widows 217
   Women and Pensions in the Future 218
Pension Reform 218
The Future Cost of Reform 219
Conclusion 221

CHAPTER 9 *Retirement and Work 223*
Learning Objectives 223
Introduction 224
Retirement as a Social Institution 224
   The Origins of Retirement 224
Why Do People Retire? 225
   Mandatory Retirement 226
   *Will an End to Mandatory Retirement Lead
      Older Workers to Stay on the Job? 227*
   *Forced Retirement: Age Discrimination in the
      Workplace 228*
   Early Retirement 230
   *Changing Patterns of Retirement: The Trend
      toward Later Retirement 231*
Alternatives to a Fixed Retirement Age 234
   Flexible Retirement 234
   Part-Time Work 236
   Second Careers 237
   Involuntary Retirement 238
Women and Retirement 239
Personal Experience of Retirement 241
Conclusion 242

CHAPTER 10 *Leisure, Recreation,
               and Service 244*
Learning Objectives 244
Introduction 245
What Do Older People Do? 245
A Variety of Activity Patterns 247
   Sport Participation 248
Expanding Leisure Activity 249
New Activities in Old Age 250
   Fitness and Health 250
Seniors' Centres 252
   *Spirituality and Religion: The Search for Meaning
      in Later Life 253*
Education 254
   Educational Alternatives 256
The Use of Technology by Older People 258
Community Service Through Volunteer Work 260
Conclusion 263

CHAPTER 11 *Housing And Transportation 265*
Learning Objectives 265
Introduction 266

An Ecological Model of Housing 267
Living Arrangements 269
    The Decision to Live Alone 270
Types of Housing 271
    Single-Family Houses 271
    Tax and Home Maintenance Programs 272
    Home Adaptation 272
    Reverse Mortgages 273
    Apartment Living 274
    Supportive and Enriched Housing 275
    Housing in Rural Communities 276
Alternative Ideas in Housing 277
    Garden Suites 277
    Naturally Occurring Retirement
        Communities 278
    Planned Retirement Communities 278
Homelessness 279
    The Future of Housing for Seniors 281
Transportation 281
    Public Transportation 281
    Private Transportation 283
    New Transportation Needs and Programs 285
The Future of Housing and Transportation 286
Conclusion 288

PART 5 THE EXPERIENCE OF AGING 291

CHAPTER 12 Family Life 291
Learning Objectives 291
Introduction 292
Marital Status in Later Life 293
    Marriage 293
    Common-Law Unions 296
    Divorce 297
    Remarriage 298
    Lifelong Singlehood 298
    Widowhood 299
    Gender and Widowhood 299
    Dating in Later Life 301
Sexuality and Aging 301
    Adaptations in Sexuality Due to Aging 303
    HIV/AIDS and Sex in Later Life 304
    Sexuality in Long-Term Care Settings 305
    Gay and Lesbian Older Adults 306
Older People as Contributors to Family Life 308
    Daily Help Given by Older People 308
    Financial Support 309

Emotional Support and Being a Role
    Model 309
Grandparenting 310
Grandparenting and New Family Structures 313
Future Research on Family Life 313
Conclusion 314

CHAPTER 13 Social Support 317
Learning Objectives 317
Introduction 318
Informal Supports for Older People 318
    Children as a Source of Informal Support 323
    Sources of Informal Support for Childless Older
        People 324
    Other Sources of Informal Support: Friends,
        Siblings, and Technology 325
    Technology 327
    Dementia and Caregiver Burden 328
    Gender and Spousal Caregiving 332
    Caregiving to Parents and Grandparents 333
    Care for the Caregiver 334
    The Future of Informal Support 335
    Elder Abuse and Mistreatment 336
    Canadian Research Findings 336
    Policy Issues 338
    Future Issues in the Mistreatment of Older
        Persons 339
Future Research on Social Support 340

CHAPTER 14 Dying, Death,
                and Bereavement 342
Learning Objectives 342
Introduction 343
Defining Dying and Death 343
Experiencing Dying and Death in Old Age 344
    Death in Old Age 344
    Seniors' Views of Dying and Death 345
    The Good Death 346
    Existential, Spiritual, and Religious Issues 347
Stages of Dying 349
    Bereavement, Grief, and Mourning
        in Old Age 350
    Loss of a Spouse in Old Age 350
    Ethical Issues in the Treatment of the Dying
        Person 352
    Informed Consent 352

Allowing a Patient to Die 352

Advance Directives 353

Changes in the Treatment of Dying: Hospice and Palliative Care 355

Dying at Home 356

Medical Assistance in Dying: Assisted Suicide and Active Euthanasia 357

Cultural Diversity in End-of-Life Care 359

Cultural Diversity in Funerary Rituals 360

Conclusion 361

Glossary 363

References 370

Index 422

PREFACE

Many changes have taken place in Canadian gerontology since the seventh edition of this textbook was published. New researchers have entered the field of aging. The government has released many reports that summarize studies of health, housing, and pension policies. And consortia of researchers and research centres have published the results of their studies. This body of knowledge will shape social policy in the future. We have used these sources and many others, including academic journals, books, and online reports, to update this text.

As the 21st century unfolds, the study of aging will increase in importance. Canada's population will have more older people than ever before. These seniors will make new demands on Canada's healthcare, retirement income, and housing resources. They will also bring new interests, skills, and approaches to later life. People young and old will need to understand the realities of aging in this new age.

This text presents a full picture of aging—problems and all. But it also emphasizes the opportunities and advantages of later life to illustrate its underlying theme: successful aging. This theme makes more sense today than ever before. Longer life and more years of activity and good health have changed the landscape of old age. Late old age still brings physical decline. But better health and nutrition at every stage of life, along with advances in medicine, extend the active years of middle age. The sayings "60 is the new 40" and "70 is the new 50" may have begun as clever remarks, but they describe the reality of aging today for more and more people. Relatively few older people today (age 65 and over) fit the stereotypical image of the poor and decrepit senior.

Better pension plans, better health, and more opportunities for personal expression and social engagement—all have transformed later life. This text documents that transformation.

French gerontologists use the term *le troisième âge* (the third age) to describe this new stage of life. This phrase defines a time of life between adulthood (the second age) and old age (the fourth age). It refers to the healthy active years after retirement, before old age sets in. This stage may begin in the 50s and go on to age 80 or more.

Two phenomena led to the emergence of the Third Age today. First, demography. More people than ever before live in the Third Age. And as the Baby Boom generation ages, it will swell the older population. Baby Boomers will look and act more like people in middle age than like the stereotypical older person. Second, longevity. People on average live longer today than ever before. And they will live these added years, sometimes called the "longevity bonus," in better health than past generations. Add to this changes in technology that allow people to stay productive longer, opportunities to stay engaged through volunteer work, and the practice of lifelong learning, and all of these changes mean that Third-Agers will remain active and engaged in second careers, leisure, and social service. They will redefine the concept of retirement and of later life.

The old model of aging no longer fits the complexity of the Third Age. Technological change, a globalized economy, unstable work careers, demographic change, convergence of male and female career opportunities—all call for new models of aging to fit new patterns of social experience.

The existence of the Third Age as a large-scale phenomenon causes some rethinking of assumptions about aging. In the past, older people who took part in athletic events seemed like odd specimens. Today, large numbers of people in their 50s and older run marathons, take up surfing, and enjoy extreme sports. A 101-year-old great-great-grandmother quite recently set a paragliding tandem record that won her a place in the *Guinness World Records*. She did this in order to keep up with her 75-year-old son who pursued the sport. Erdman Palmore, a renowned gerontologist, celebrated his birthday every year by bicycling the number of miles that equalled his age. These Third-Agers shatter the stereotype of old age.

Social institutions, such as business and industry, will adapt to this new population of older people. As Baby Boomers retire from the workplace, they will leave behind a labour shortage. The smaller age groups behind them will provide fewer workers to the labour force. This will change the way that business views retirement and the retiree. Some companies will rehire retirees, others will give people incentives to delay retirement.

On the campus of one of the authors, an interim president came out of retirement for two years to manage the campus while the university searched for a new leader. The campus then hired the administrative vice-president, who delayed retirement, to serve as the new president. He then brought back a retired senior administrator to serve as vice-president to manage a troublesome unit. These administrators all had many years of successful experience. They quickly assumed their new roles and brought stability to the campus. This pattern of older workers, who delay retirement or re-enter the workforce, will occur more and more often in varied industries and institutions in the years ahead.

Third-Agers will engage in activities that express their interests and passions. In some cases, they will create institutions to meet these needs. These will include lifelong learning institutes and new volunteer opportunities.

This edition of this text links the generations through the life course perspective. The emergence of the Third Age demands this approach, as it blurs the meaning of retirement and old age. It asks for a view of aging that looks at the whole of adult life—the discontinuities (e.g., retirement) and the continuities (e.g., lifelong learning). A life course perspective shows where and how a person's life has continuity. It also shows how the generations depend on one another. Many Baby Boomers will play the role of caregiver to their aging parents and will give support to their adult children and grandchildren. At the same time, they will deal with their own retirement and health issues. Older people will affect the younger generations through their use of services, their social contributions, and their ability to improve society as they age.

Finally, as Baby Boomers enter the Third Age, they will put pressure on existing programs and services. The Canadian pension system, workplace pension programs, and the healthcare system will have to adapt to this large number of older people. In general, these systems and others may shift the cost of programs and services to the individual. This marks a change from the way that programs and services developed during the 20th century. During the past century, government and corporate programs increased benefits to older people. The 21st century will ask people to take more responsibility for their own pension planning and healthcare costs. This text reports on these changes in social policy and their impact on older people.

The eighth edition of this book has the same goals as the first seven editions. First, we want a readable book—one that students can read without stumbling over social science jargon and dense academic prose.

Second, we want a text that presents aging in the context of Canada's history and social life. In the past, gerontology instructors had to use U.S. texts in their aging courses. But Canada has its own geographic regions, social policies, and mix of cultures and ethnic groups. Canadian students should first learn about aging in their own country.

Third, we want a text that describes Canada's social institutions—its healthcare, income, and housing systems, as well as its family and community life. Canadian students should know, for example, that their healthcare system provides free healthcare benefits to all older people and that the retirement income system provides a basic income to older Canadians. These systems create a social safety net for older people and provide the basis for a decent old age today.

Canadian students should also know that older adults face problems in their society. Many Canadians hold negative stereotypes about older people (look at the number of lotions designed to smooth wrinkled skin); the fast pace of modern society often pushes older people to the sidelines (imagine trying to cross a six-lane street if you have arthritis in your legs); and some groups of older people (many of them very old women) still live in poverty. Canadian society needs improvement.

Students need to know what parts of the social system work for older people and what parts work against them. *Aging and Society: Canadian Perspectives* gives students the facts about aging and helps them sort through and understand the issues surrounding aging today.

This new edition has a fourth goal: to improve on the seventh edition. Many instructors and students across the country have used the seventh edition. We, too, have used it in our classes with hundreds of students. Our students and our colleagues have commented on what they liked and did not like about the text. We have used their comments to improve the text and create this new edition.

As in earlier editions, this book refers to classic Canadian studies as well as the most up-to-date facts and figures on aging in Canada. Research findings and other information in each chapter are clearly referenced to make it easy for students to locate the original academic sources. The text also contains exhibits that present examples of older people today and discuss current issues in the field. This edition also has some new sections that reflect new research in the field of aging. For example, this edition makes reference to the growing impact of technology on seniors' lives. The chapter on healthcare, for example, describes the use of digital technology to diagnose and treat illness. Computers now allow seniors to keep in touch with family members and to join online communities.

FEATURES IN THIS EDITION

Throughout this eighth edition of *Aging and Society: Canadian Perspectives*, we further examine the gendered experience of growing old in Canada and, in particular, assess when gender tends to matter and when it doesn't for older men and older women in Canada.

Chapter 1 contains new material on ageism and the Third Age. This chapter also shows the different effects of aging on men and women. It includes new material on older men. The theme of gender difference appears throughout the book.

Chapter 2 includes information on current research activity in Canada. It provides new material on the life course and life events. It includes new information on cumulative advantage and disadvantage theory. This topic examines the effects of inequality throughout the life course. The chapter also discusses the relationship of research to social policy and the emergence of evidence-based practice.

Chapter 3 contains up-to-date demographic facts and new material on aging in other societies. It also contains thoroughly updated information and statistics based on the latest Canadian data. This chapter puts aging in Canada into the context of aging around the world.

Chapter 4 focuses on aging and ethnicity in Canada. Canada has an ethnically diverse population. Some older ethnic group members arrived in Canada in old age. Others (such as Indigenous elders) have lived here all or most of their lives. This chapter expands on the topics of collectivism, familism, and individualism as they affect older people. It also looks closely at ethnic seniors' family and community life.

Chapter 5 looks at how physical activity, health promotion, and self-care can improve health and well-being in later life. It contains expanded sections on the influence of early health conditions on health in later life. The chapter includes many new charts and exhibits that look at specific topics such as disability in later life, exercise, diabetes, and activity guidelines for seniors. This chapter also describes the effects of culture and poverty on health in old age.

Chapter 6 contains new information on the psychology of aging. This includes recent research on developmental and intellectual disability. This chapter now includes a discussion of the 3Ds that cause psychological distress—delirium, depression, and dementia. The chapter explores the concepts of cognitive reserve and neuroplasticity in later life. This chapter also looks at recent research on mental improvement through training and the link between physical activity and mental performance.

Chapter 7 discusses the healthcare system, its history, and the need for healthcare reform. It documents the continuing increase in home care and the growing need for long-term care. This chapter also discusses the challenge of wait times for healthcare treatment—one of the long-standing criticisms of the Canadian healthcare system. It also includes a section on models of long-term care, new institutional settings, and community-based approaches to long-term care. The chapter introduces the concept of age-friendly cities.

Chapter 8 contains material on the history of the Canadian pension system as well as the latest information on pensions in Canada. It continues to show that financial inequality exists between single women (many of them widows) and men in later life. It also documents the shift in responsibility for pension savings from companies to individuals.

Chapter 9 describes the ongoing redefinition of retirement. Many people now delay retirement. Others move in and out of the workforce after retirement from their midlife careers. This has blurred the lines between work and the traditional meaning of retirement as an end to work. A growing percentage of seniors say they plan to never retire. But many seniors, who want to work, face discrimination in the workplace. Programs now exist to help older workers stay engaged.

Chapter 10 updates information on how older people spend their time. It documents the many leisure activities that now occupy seniors' time. In particular, this chapter shows the growth of interest in active living. It presents information on volunteer opportunities for seniors and also raises questions about volunteering among seniors in the future. Will Baby Boomers take up community service in retirement? Or will they choose to spend their time on personal leisure pursuits?

Chapter 11 contains many new charts and exhibits to provide examples of housing for seniors. This chapter presents information on homeless seniors, a discussion of supportive and enriched housing, and more material on housing for rural seniors. The chapter expands on the topic of age-friendly communities and age-friendly cities. The chapter also looks at issues related to gender and driving a car in later life. It discusses the challenges older people face when they must stop driving.

Chapter 12 contains new information on family life. It includes discussions of the unique option of polyamory in later life (having more than one partner at the same time). The chapter also looks at remarriage and challenges that older couples face in late-life marriage. The chapter contains discussions of life as a single senior, aging as a gay or lesbian senior, HIV/AIDS, and sexuality in long-term care settings.

Chapter 13 discusses social supports in later life. It contains detailed information on gender and caregiving by spouses and adult children. It also presents information on social support for childless older people. The chapter contains added material on elder mistreatment and abuse.

The final chapter, Chapter 14, discusses the experience of dying and death in old age. Canada's ethnic diversity leads to many different religious and cultural views of death and dying. This chapter expands the discussion of attitudes toward death held by various religions. It also expands the discussion of palliative care and recent developments in medical assistance in dying.

This edition, like those before it, documents the aging of Canadian society. It shows the issues that occupy our thinking and it shows the ways that society and individuals have adapted to aging. The first edition of this book, published more than 30 years ago, laid down many of the issues discussed here. That edition looked to the future and saw a growing number of older people. It saw that Canada would have to reshape its policies and programs to meet their needs. Later editions tracked the changes that took place as Canadian society aged.

This edition continues that tradition. But the projected issues of the past exist as real challenges today. Canada has become an older society. Income inequality, early retirement, community-based healthcare, the importance of active living, and caregiver burden affect more people than ever before. The first Baby Boomers have begun to enter old age. This generation as it ages will make new demands on society and this will call for new responses. The eighth edition of *Aging and Society: Canadian Perspectives* points to some of the emerging issues in aging and to the challenges that lie ahead.

ORGANIZATION

This book begins by describing large-scale (macroscopic) changes in society. It then shows how these changes affect people and social institutions. It concludes by showing how individuals respond to these changes and how individuals' actions give new direction to society. The structure of the book reflects a dialectical model of social change.

Part 1, Gerontology Today (Chapters 1 and 2), introduces students to the field of aging. It shatters many of the myths people have about aging and shows the range of topics that gerontologists study. It also describes the theories and methods gerontologists use when they study aging.

Part 2, Social Change (Chapters 3 and 4), looks at the changes in Canada's history and demographic structure that led to population aging (the increased proportion of older people in the population). It also places aging in Canada into a world context. This section looks in depth at the effect of ethnicity on aging. Canada's multicultural population makes this an important topic.

Part 3, Maturational Change (Chapters 5 and 6), looks at individual aging—the physical, psychological, and developmental changes that come with age.

Part 4, Institutional Change (Chapters 7 through 11), examines Canada's institutions—the healthcare, social security, retirement, leisure, and housing and transportation systems.

Part 5, The Experience of Aging (Chapters 12 through 14), looks at the older person in relation to family and friends. The study of death and dying (the last chapter) explores how older people think about and experience dying. It also explores the intimate experiences of widowhood/widowerhood, bereavement, and loss that accompany old age.

PEDAGOGICAL FEATURES

The text contains valuable pedagogical features that enhance learning:

LEARNING OBJECTIVES

After reading this chapter, you will

LO1   Know the three main areas of gerontological study.

LO2   Be able to name and describe the three major theoretical perspectives used in the study of aging.

LO5   Understand how age, period, and cohort (APC) effects influence research findings and how researchers try to disentangle these effects.

LO6   Be able to discuss the difference between cross-sectional and longitudinal research and understand the usefulness and limitations of each type of study.

LEARNING OBJECTIVES
Each chapter begins with a set of learning objectives to set the stage for what follows.

RUNNING GLOSSARY
The text includes a running glossary of key terms that students can use to review and test their knowledge.

stereotypes an exaggerated and often prejudiced view of a type of person or group of people

elderspeak simplified speech like baby talk that some people use when they speak to older people; it stems from stereotyping older people as slow-witted

AGING IN GLOBAL PERSPECTIVE
This text includes "Aging in a Global Perspective" boxes that will challenge students to think about aging as it is experienced and viewed from a global perspective. Each box also includes questions for discussion.

EXHIBIT 10.3   AGING IN A GLOBAL PERSPECTIVE
What a Senior Moment. Canuck Marathon Man, 74, Smokes His Rival, 71

More than 50 minutes after Jimmy Muindi sweeps smoothly to victory in the Rotterdam Marathon, in an impressive time of 2:07:50, the cold and rain of an April day by the North Sea have scattered his welcoming party. The city's smiling mayor, Burgemeester Ivo Opstelten, last seen presenting flowers to the top three finishers—Kenyans to a man—is nowhere to be seen. Nor are the jostling photographers who fought to capture the final sprint. Now the halt, the lame, the crumpled over with dry heaves or diarrhea, and the just plain also-ran, stagger across the finish line.

it. Obviously I have a competitive streak, but I'd have been very upset if I felt people had any reason to think I hadn't run well.

As for the future, there's the anticipated rematch with Ruter at September's Toronto Waterfront Marathon. Shrugging off age and possible injury, Whitlock's sure it will take place. "Joop said he'd come, and so did I. Besides, I said I'd take him to Niagara Falls."

Whitlock also competes on the track, where he currently (2012) holds 15 world age group records ranging in distance from

EXHIBIT 7.1   *The Medical Model and the Social Model in*

Medical Model	Social Model
Patient	Resident, consumer
Acute patients	Chronic clients
Physicians and hospitals	Community settings and

EXHIBITS
We present examples, charts, and graphs to illustrate points in the text. These exhibits engage students in questions that probe their understanding. Many exhibits ask students to reflect on their personal views on a topic.

TIME TO REVIEW
Each chapter includes "Time to Review" questions within the text to help students assess their learning as they go along.

TIME to REVIEW

Give an example from the research of how ageism leads to discrimination in the job market.

Give an example of how a company or service has adapted its product or service to attract older consumers.

Summary

1.   The growth of the older population in Canada h n ade aging a major social issue—one that will affe

SUMMARY
Each chapter concludes with a series of main points that summarize the text.

STUDY QUESTIONS
Each chapter concludes with a list of study questions to help students assess their knowledge of the main concepts covered in the text.

STUDY QUESTIONS

1.   Give three reasons why students should know about aging in Canada.

2.   State three common myths about aging. Explain why

GENERAL ACKNOWLEDGMENTS

Leanna MacLean, publisher, guided us through the early stages of this project. Lisa Peterson, the Content Manager on this project, contacted instructors throughout the country for comments on the seventh edition and worked diligently to get this edition out on time. Jennifer Hare served as production project manager, and Natalie Barrington coordinated the book's text and photo permissions. June Trusty capably handled copyediting. We thank all of these people for their support.

The librarians at the Martin Luther King Memorial Library at San Jose State University helped with database searches. We thank them all for their support.

Canadian colleagues in the field of gerontology contributed to the core knowledge assembled in this text. We cannot thank them all here, but we want to acknowledge that they helped make this a better text.

We would like to thank the reviewers for their valuable feedback:

Michele Green, Seneca College
Michael Corman, Mount Royal University
Pria Nippak, Ryerson University
Silvia Bartolic, University of British Columbia
Parin Dossa, Simon Fraser University
Alice Barron, St. Clair College
Christina Nielsen, Northern College

AUTHORS' ACKNOWLEDGMENTS

MARK NOVAK

It has been a pleasure working with Lori Campbell and Herb Northcott, my co-authors. I enjoyed sharing ideas with them as we went along. They are both careful scholars and hard workers. They brought many new insights and resources to the text. Students will benefit from their knowledge and their sensitivity as scholars and teachers.

I owe special thanks to my mentor and close friend, Hans Mohr. His intellectual integrity inspires all of my work. I can never repay him, only thank him for his support and friendship.

I want to thank my family for their support—my wife, Mona, and my sons, Christopher, Jonathan, Sean, and Daniel. I have some new family members who deserve mention—my daughters-in-law, Shona, Judy, and Elsa, and my grandchildren, Tobin, Shea, Scarlett, Charles, Lena, and Lucas (in birth order). All of them deserve credit for lightening my spirits with their good humour and love.

I never imagined, when I started this text more than 30 years ago, that I'd write the grandparent section of this text based, in part, on my own experience. I hope this book will guide my children and grandchildren as they age and will help them give exceptional care to their aging parents and grandparents.

HERBERT C. NORTHCOTT

I am grateful to Mark Novak for the opportunity to contribute to the eighth edition of Aging and Society: Canadian Perspectives. This book has been Mark's "baby" for over 30 years now. During that time I have given students in my Sociology of Aging course the opportunity to read each of the previous editions. Students have rated this book highly, and I am pleased to be associated with this eighth edition.

I am also grateful to the University of Alberta. The university has given me something meaningful to do and a place to do it in for over 40 years. I could not have asked for more.

LORI CAMPBELL

I wish to thank Mark Novak for all his kindness, generosity, and support. It has been a privilege to work with him over the many years I have been involved with this book. And my thanks to Herb Northcott. His contributions as co-author bring added depth and richness to the text.

My love and gratitude to my family—my siblings, my dearest "2Ps," Payton and Paris, and my truly wonderful husband, Michael Carroll. And in loving memory of my parents, Leon and Dorothy Campbell, who taught me by example what it means to live and age with compassion, humour, and strength of spirit.

INSTRUCTOR RESOURCES

The **Nelson Education Teaching Advantage (NETA)** program delivers research-based instructor resources that promote student engagement and higher-order thinking to enable the success of Canadian students and educators.

The following instructor resources have been created for this eighth edition of *Aging and Society*. *Access* these ultimate tools for customizing lectures and presentations at retail.tophat.com.

NETA TEST BANK

This resource was edited by Daniel Novak, California State University. It includes over 700 multiple-choice questions written according to NETA guidelines for effective construction and development of higher-order questions. Also included are short answer and essay questions.

NETA POWERPOINT

Microsoft® PowerPoint® lecture slides for every chapter have been created by Markus Schafer, University of Toronto. There is an average of 40 slides per chapter, many featuring key figures, tables, and photographs from *Aging and Society*. Slides also include notes with additional content, teaching suggestions, discussion questions, activities, references, and resources. NETA principles of clear design and engaging content have been incorporated throughout, making it simple for instructors to customize the deck for their courses.

IMAGE LIBRARY

This resource consists of digital copies of figures, short tables, and photographs used in the book. Instructors may use these jpegs to customize the NETA PowerPoint or create their own PowerPoint presentations. An Image Library Key describes the images and lists the codes under which the jpegs are saved.

Used by over three million students, Top Hat's all-in-one teaching platform lets you connect with instructors and peers and engage deeply with learning materials inside and outside the classroom.

With Top Hat, you're in charge of your own learning. Check your understanding of course concepts by participating in interactive class presentations and get real-time feedback when completing homework assignments and course readings on your own. Plus, taking tests on Top Hat means you can do everything you need to complete your course in one place.

The Top Hat platform works on both mobile devices and laptops and lets you access everything you need, right in the cloud. So it's easy for you to learn anywhere, anytime.

STUDENT ANCILLARIES

Used by over three million students, Top Hat's all-in-one teaching platform lets you connect with instructors and peers and engage deeply with learning materials inside and outside the classroom.

With Top Hat, you're in charge of your own learning. Check your understanding of course concepts by participating in interactive class presentations and get real-time feedback when completing homework assignments and course readings on your own. Plus, taking tests on Top Hat means you can do everything you need to complete your course in one place.

The Top Hat platform works on both mobile devices and laptops and lets you access everything you need, right in the cloud. So it's easy for you to learn anywhere, anytime.

ABOUT THE AUTHORS

MARK NOVAK

Dr. Mark Novak received his bachelor's degree in sociology from Rutgers University in New Jersey and his Ph.D. degree in sociology from York University in Toronto. He specializes in the study of adult development, adult education, and aging. Dr. Novak taught and conducted research at the University of Winnipeg and the University of Manitoba for more than 20 years. Dr. Novak has written many articles for professional journals in Canada and abroad. He has written several books, including a general interest study in Canada entitled *Successful Aging* and several texts in the field of gerontology. Dr. Novak is currently Dean of the Extended University Division, California State University, Bakersfield.

HERBERT C. NORTHCOTT

Dr. Herbert C. Northcott was born in Brandon, Manitoba, and grew up in Winnipeg. He attended United College (now the University of Winnipeg) and the University of Manitoba, graduating with a B.A. in 1970. He earned a master's degree in sociology in 1971 from Brigham Young University in Provo, Utah. He received a Ph.D. in sociology in 1976 from the University of Minnesota. In 1976, he joined the Department of Sociology at the University of Alberta in Edmonton where he continues to work. He has taught over 11,000 students. He has taught courses in the sociology of aging, health and illness, and dying and death, and has published extensively in these areas. He is married to Laura West and together they have three amazing children and seven wonderful grandchildren.

LORI CAMPBELL

Dr. Lori Campbell is currently the associate dean (academic) in the Faculty of Social Sciences at McMaster University, and an associate professor in the Department of Health, Aging and Society and the Department of Sociology. Dr. Campbell's primary research interests centre on family and aging. She has published research on sibling ties in middle and later life, intergenerational family transfers, and men's experience in filial caregiving. She is currently lead investigator on a qualitative study exploring the experience and meaning of inheritance within families. Dr. Campbell taught the first year Aging and Society introductory course for many years, as well as upper-year courses on theories of aging, men and families, gendered aging, and family relationships across the life course.

CHAPTER 1

AGING TODAY

Polka Dot/Thinkstock

LEARNING OBJECTIVES

After reading this chapter, you will

LO1 Understand the role of gerontology in Canadian society.

LO2 Know some of the myths that give rise to negative stereotypes about older people.

LO3 Recognize the many sources of ageism in Canadian society.

LO4 Understand the effects of ageism on older people's experience.

LO5 Understand that a good old age can take many forms.

LO6 Appreciate the role that education plays in combating ageism.

LO7 Appreciate the role of public policy in bringing about a good age for older Canadians.

LO8 Gain an optimistic view of aging in Canada today and in the future.

INTRODUCTION

Everyone needs to know about aging. First, all of us are getting older. While some of us are over 65 already, most adults not yet 65 will become part of the older population between now and 2040. We will want to make old age as good a time of life as it can be.

Second, when those of you who are younger students reach middle age, your parents, aunts, uncles, neighbours, and older friends will have grown old. You will want to know about aging so that you can help them live the best old age possible.

Third, more people work with the elderly than ever before, and more will find themselves working with the elderly in the future. In 2011, Canada had 4.95 million people age 65 and over (Statistics Canada, 2014a). Older Canadians made up 14.8 percent of the population in that year, and experts predict that this proportion will grow to 9.8 million people, or 24.5 percent of the population, by 2036 (Population Reference Bureau, 2010). Nurses, social workers, teachers, family counsellors, and even travel agents will have more and more older people as clients.

An older population will also put new demands on Canada's social structures. Sociologists define a **social structure** as a relatively stable pattern of social interactions. The family, the education system, and the healthcare system all fit this definition, and they will change in the following ways as Canadian society ages:

- More Canadians will live in three- and four-generation families. And many people will become grandparents while they are still active in their careers.

- Schools and universities will attract more older students than ever before. These students will want flexible schedules. They will also need different kinds of teaching methods and different courses.

- The healthcare system will also change. The current system favours the treatment of acute (short-term) illness, but older people tend to have chronic ailments such as arthritis, hearing problems, and diabetes. An aging society needs to prevent illness before it occurs.

Gerontology is the discipline that systematically studies aging. It looks at the subject from two points of view: how aging affects the individual and how an aging population will change society. This chapter describes (1) myths and realities of aging, (2) stereotyping and attitudes toward aging, and (3) ageism and social policy.

MYTHS AND REALITIES OF AGING

Jessie Taylor called for a cab and headed downtown for her last appointment of the day. She works for the provincial office on aging. She monitors nursing home standards and teaches staff ways to improve patient care. Jessie is 63 years old. She has a sturdy figure, a pixie grin, and a mop of grey hair. As she got out of the cab, the driver got out, too. He grabbed her elbow, ushered her across the street, and deposited her on the sidewalk. "You can't be too careful crossing the street these days," he said, then smiled and waved goodbye. Jessie says that when she goes to her local supermarket, the cashier often asks other customers to wait a moment while she checks Jessie's items through. Then one of the workers helps her to her car with her groceries.

All of this used to surprise Jessie. After all, she works at a job like everyone else, drives her own car, and serves as a leader in her profession. Yet sometimes people treat her like a frail old woman. People see her kind face, grey hair, and wrinkles, and they want to help her. They assume that she needs help doing simple things because of her age. I asked Jessie whether she ever told people that she didn't need their help. She said that sometimes she does, but she doesn't want to discourage these people from helping someone in the future who may need it, so often she goes along with it and grins to herself.

Jessie knows about stereotyping and **prejudice** toward older people.[1] She knows about it first-hand, and she observes it every day in her work. She also knows that stereotypes can be useful. They help us get along in a complex world where we know only a fraction of the people we see and meet every day. But stereotypes can lead to problems.

Stereotypes can lead us to misjudge people, to treat them inappropriately, and, in the case of older people, to assume that they are weak and need help. Stereotyping can also lead to prejudice, a negative attitude toward a

---

1   The terms old, elderly, aged, and senior in this text refer to people age 65 and over unless another age is given.

---

social structure a relatively stable pattern of social interactions

gerontology the discipline that systematically studies aging

prejudice being biased against someone or something; a negative judgment formed beforehand without knowledge of the facts

person, and to discrimination, unfair treatment based on prejudice rather than merit.

Gerontology has two goals. First, scholars and researchers work to produce accurate knowledge about aging. Second, professionals who work with older people apply this knowledge to create a better life for their clients. Academic gerontologists try to decrease prejudice and stereotyping by presenting the facts about aging.

Studies have shown that many people hold incorrect views of aging today. Researcher Erdman Palmore (1977) first devised a "Facts on Aging Quiz (FAQ)" to study knowledge about aging. By the start of this century, more than 150 studies reported the use of the original and later versions of the "FAQ." (See Exhibit 1.1 for a Canadian adaptation of Palmore's "FAQ.")

Researchers and educators have used this quiz with people from a variety of backgrounds. Studies have reported that factual knowledge of aging improves with education (Palmore, 2005). People with a high school education or less, for example, averaged 57 percent correct. Undergraduates did somewhat better, averaging 64 percent. Gerontology students and faculty on average scored 83 percent (Palmore, 1998).

Unwin and colleagues (2008; also Snyder & Zweig, 2010) used the "FAQ" to compare Palmore's findings with results from a study of first-year medical school students 30 years after Palmore's original study. The researchers found that "negative perceptions of aging have persisted and that some attitudes toward elderly people have possibly worsened" (p. 2163). They concluded that medical professionals need more information about older people.

Ruiz and colleagues (2015) found implicit age bias in a sample of 103 medical school students. They also found that bias differed by gender. Female medical students showed less ageism and less anti-aging bias. Compared to male students, they reported a stronger intent to work with older people. The researchers suggested that medical schools use "bias-reduction strategies in undergraduate medical curricula" to combat ageism and stereotyping (p. 73). Other studies have supported this conclusion. Researchers have found that students have a more realistic picture of aging if schools teach students the facts about old age (Birkenmaier, 2009; Eskildsen, 2009; Zucchero, 2011).

Consider the following myths and the facts that gerontologists have found to replace them.

---

discrimination unfair treatment of a person or group based on prejudice

---

EXHIBIT 1.1   *Facts on Aging Quiz*

Try the following quiz to see how much you know about aging in Canada. The answers follow the list of key terms near the end of this chapter. You will find the facts to support these answers throughout this book.

True or False?

1. At least 15 percent of the aged in Canada are living in long-stay institutions (e.g., nursing homes, mental hospitals, homes for the aged).

2. British Columbia has a higher proportion of older people in its population than any other province.

3. Older people today have less contact with their families than older people had in the past.

4. Older people stand a higher risk of criminal victimization than people in other age groups.

5. Memory declines with age.

6. A decline in sexual vigour in older men is usually due to hormone deficiencies.

7. Retirees more often feel depressed, bored, and ill than those who keep working.

8. Most older people in rural areas depend on public transportation to get around.

9. The body's systems go into a steady decline from age 40 on.

10. The majority of older people have incomes below the poverty level (as defined by the federal government).

Source: Adapted from Matthews, Tindale, and Norris, "Facts on Aging Quiz: A Canadian Validation and Cross-Cultural Comparison," *Canadian Journal on Aging*, Vol. 3, Issue 4, pp. 165–174. Reproduced with permission of Oxford University Press.

Myth: People feel lost in retirement. They often get sick and die shortly after they retire.

Reality: Few people feel sick or lost due to retirement. Canada's 2013 *General Social Survey* found that 28 percent of volunteers in Canada were age 55 or older (up from 23 percent in 2004) (Statistics Canada, 2015a). Seniors sat on boards and committees. They also donated to charitable causes. These findings show that seniors stay engaged in later life.

Genoe and Singleton (2006) conducted in-depth interviews with a group of male retirees (age 72 to 86) in eastern Canada. The men in the study said they found meaning in life through volunteering. They also said that activities like acting, dancing, and playing cards kept them in touch with their community. The Canadian Community Health Survey (Ramage-Morin, Shields, & Martel, 2010) found that 56 percent of people age 65 and over reported good health. And even up to age 85, at least half of the population reported good health.

Some people retire because of poor health, and this may account for the myth that retirement causes illness. In most cases, retirement has little, if any, effect on health, social activity, life satisfaction, or happiness. And in some cases the health of workers improves when they retire. Many retirees start new careers, take up volunteer work, or go back to school. Some even return to work.

Myth: Most older people feel depressed and bored.

Reality: Older people form a diverse group. Some people have psychological problems, while others report high life satisfaction. "Apart from dementia," researcher Steven Zarit (2009) wrote, "older people have lower rates of mental disorders than other adult age groups and generally report higher emotional well-being. This is a finding supported by virtually every epidemiological survey." Zarit concluded that "older people may, in fact, be somewhat better off—happier, less depressed, and even less lonely than the other adult age-groups" (pp. 675–676).

Based on results from the Statistics Canada *General Social Survey*, *Maclean's* magazine (Editors, 2011) reported that Canadians age 55 to 64 feel less stress in their lives than people in their middle years (age 35 to 44). Some people in later life no longer have to care for children and have more time to relax. Another Statistics Canada report found that 79.2 percent of women age 65 and over and 77.4 percent of men in that age group said they felt "happy and interested in life" (Milan & Vézina, 2011). Nearly the same proportion of people age 75 and over reported these feelings.

Myth: People in older age groups face a higher risk of criminal victimization than people in younger age groups do.

Reality: Older people face a lower risk of criminal victimization than any other age group. Ogrodnik (2007) reported that "according to the 2004 *General Social Survey*, seniors were three times less likely than non-seniors to experience victimization in the 12 months preceding the survey (10% versus 31%)" (p. 6).

A 2009 report by Statistics Canada (Perreault & Brennan, 2010) found similar results. Young people age 15 to 24 experienced the highest rates of violent crime victimization for assault, sexual assault, and robbery. They had a rate of 284 per 1,000 persons in 2009. People age 65 and over had a rate of only 19 incidents per 1,000 persons in that year (a rate almost 15 times lower than for the youngest age group). Victimization for violent crime decreased steadily with each older age group. The same trend applied to personal property theft (Statistics Canada, 2010a).

The Government of Canada (2011) reported that in cases of violent crime, 70 percent of older victims knew their attacker—most often a family member, friend, or acquaintance engaged in the criminal act. Violence against an older person can occur, for example, when a caregiver becomes frustrated and angry. Still, only one-third of victimized older people experienced a physical injury due to victimization.

The 2004 *General Social Survey* found that nearly all seniors (92 percent) reported feeling satisfied with their safety from crime (Ogrodnik, 2007). A small percentage of older people (17 percent) reported fear of crime during their time alone in the evenings, and 21 percent felt very or somewhat worried about walking alone in their neighbourhoods. Ogrodnik found that compared with younger people, older people tended to stay home because they feared crime.

Older people do face relatively high rates for certain kinds of crimes. For example, compared with younger people, they run a higher risk of being victims of fraud. A government report (Federal/Provincial/Territorial Ministers, 2010) calls fraud "the number one crime against older Canadians" (p. 2).

Home repair con artists, for example, target older people. They look for homes that need repairs—loose shingles or a broken downspout. The swindler then knocks on the older person's door and offers to estimate the cost of repairs. The crook gives a low estimate and says that the older person will have to pay for the work right away to get this deal. The con artist usually asks for cash payment before any work is done.

Some crooks even drive the older person to the bank to withdraw the money. Once the crook has the money, the work may never get done or it is done poorly with cheap material. Con artists of this type may come back again and again to do more repairs. They may even try to borrow money from the older person once they have a relationship.

A number of conditions create a higher risk of fraud among older people. These include lack of information, social isolation, and lack of wariness in business relations. Complex technology and the Internet provide new channels for crooks to play on older people's ignorance of electronic media. Money offers from Nigerian sources often come as email messages. They promise to transfer large amounts of money to a person's bank account. But after the person has agreed to accept the transfer, further letters demand money for transfer fees and other expenses.

Project PhoneBusters, a national program in Canada, handles complaints of mass marketing fraud. This includes scams such as West African fraud and Identity theft (Canadian Anti-Fraud Centre, 2011). The Government of Canada (2011) reported that in 2009, people age 60 and over made up about one-third of the total dollars lost to telephone fraud. The total of money lost to scam artists came to more than $1 million. On average, seniors lost $4,475.35, about 40 percent more than the average for the 20 to 59 age group. A volunteer group called Senior-Busters works with Project PhoneBusters to advise and support senior victims of fraud (Canadian Anti-Fraud Centre, 2014).

Myth: Older people often commit suicide and have the highest suicide rate in Canada.

Reality: Older people have some of the lowest suicide rates in Canada (9.9 per 100,000 for people age 65 and over). Middle-aged Canadians have some of the highest rates (people age 50 to 54 have the highest rate of all—16.6 per 100,000) (Navaneelan, 2012; Statistics Canada, 2014b).

But simple statistics tell only part of the story. For example, compared to older women, older men have higher suicide rates in every age group. Older men age 80 and over, for example, have some of the highest rates among any age or gender group (over 19.4 per 100,000). Older women, age 80 and over by contrast have the lowest suicide rates of all adults (3.4 per 100,000) (Statistics Canada, 2014b).

Also, compared to younger people, older people tend to succeed in their attempts at suicide. Younger people as a group make more than 200 attempts for every successful suicide. The general population makes more than 100 attempts for every success. People age 65 and over make 2 to 4 attempts for every success. Older people seem more deliberate in their attempts. Many older people live alone, so these people have a smaller chance of being found after an attempt. Also, compared to younger people, older people tend to use more lethal means in their attempts (e.g., firearms) (Centre for Suicide Prevention, 2014).

The risk of suicide increases when people feel alone and isolated, feel that they burden others, and feel that they no longer contribute to society. Finally, if a person with these feelings has the means to commit suicide (e.g., drugs or firearms), the likelihood of an attempt increases.

Baby Boomers have had a higher suicide rate than older people in the past. Baby Boomers make up one of the largest age cohorts in Canada. Higher rates for this group could mean an increase in the number of suicides among older people in the future (Centre for Suicide Prevention, 2014).

These studies show that, while relatively few older people kill themselves, some groups of older people face a high risk of suicide.

Myth: Sexual activity and interest in sex decline in later life.

Reality: Studies show that a stereotype of the sexless older person has little basis in fact. Most older people express an interest in sex throughout their lives. And, if conditions permit, older people can (and do) have sexual relations into old age (Fisher, 2010). Gerontologist and sex researcher Alex Comfort said that people give up sex in old age for the same three reasons they stop riding a bicycle: (1) they think it looks silly; (2) they have arthritis and can't get on; and (3) they don't have a bicycle. The lack of a partner often spells the end of sexual relations for widows. But older people with a partner (in or out of marriage) tend to continue an active sex life.

More education about sexual relations in later life would correct the myth of sexual decline. Snyder and Zweig (2010) studied attitudes toward older people and knowledge of sexuality in later life. They found that less than one-fifth of the medical school students in their study (19 percent) said they had "quite a bit" of coursework or lectures related to aging. Some 45 percent said they "rarely or never" attended a class, lecture, or symposium on sexuality in later life. Of the psychology doctoral students in this study, 44 percent said they "rarely or never" attended a class, lecture, or symposium on sexuality in later life. More exposure to information during their studies would increase these professionals' knowledge about sexuality in old age. The general public could learn more about aging and sexuality through accurate portrayals of older people in the media.

TIME TO REVIEW

Recall at least two myths about aging and present two or three facts that refute each of those myths.

ATTITUDES TOWARD OLD AGE

People hold many stereotypes about old age. Sociologists define a stereotype as an exaggerated and often prejudiced view of a type of person or group of people. People who hold a stereotype do not check to see if it is true. If they meet someone who does not fit the stereotype, they think he or she is an exception. Stereotypes often have some basis in truth, but they exaggerate and distort the truth. Often they lead to discrimination.

When it comes to old age, we hold both positive and negative stereotypes: the wise old farmer and the dirty old man, the kindly grandmother and the sex-starved spinster. Hummert (2011) said, "the number of negative stereotypes exceeds that of positive stereotypes" (p. 251).

Many of our stereotypes consist of negative views of older people and old age. Sometimes the stereotype leads from prejudice (an attitude) to discrimination (an action taken against someone). In a classic study, Page (1997) had an elderly woman call to rent an apartment. He then had a young woman and a young man each make a similar call. In a fourth case, a young man called on behalf of an older woman. Page found that the elderly woman and the young man calling on behalf of an elderly woman got three to four times more negative responses than the two younger people did. He concluded that "persons identified as elderly still face the prospect of rejection" (p. 59).

Lineweaver, Berger, and Hertzog (2009) found that older adults showed just as strong an age bias as did younger adults. They tested older and younger adults' predictions of memory decline in a series of cases. They found that younger people *and* older people in the study predicted memory decline with age. Older people predicted a later age of decline but a more extreme decline. Studies (Hummert, 2011) found that "age stereotypes lead to negative attitudes and biased behaviour toward older persons, even from members of the older age group" (p. 254).

Hummert (2011) said that older people who stereotype other seniors display the "black sheep effect." This "occurs when group members derogate in-group members whose characteristics threaten positive perceptions of the group" (p. 253). In an earlier study, Hummert and colleagues (1997) found that, when compared with younger participants, older participants applied more negative stereotypes when shown the faces of very old people. The researchers said that the very old faces threatened the older participants' positive view of themselves.

Thornton and Light (2006) described a way of talking that they called elderspeak. Elderspeak refers to "a specialized speech register resembling baby talk in

addressing older adults" (p. 276). This form of speech uses few clauses, shorter phrases, more filler phrases (e.g., "like," "you know"), words with fewer syllables, slower speech, and longer pauses. Elderspeak also includes the use of words like *dearie*, *cutie*, and *sweetie* (Kennedy, 2012).

Institutional workers may use words like these to address residents. The speaker assumes that the older person has low mental ability or some other impairment. Elderspeak has a negative effect on the older person; it creates low self-esteem, reduces a person's ability to communicate effectively, decreases the quality of interaction, and reduces the older person's sense of control (Thornton & Light, 2006).

Writer Malcolm Cowley (1980) described the effects of ageism on his self-image: "We start by growing old in other people's eyes," he says, "then slowly we come to share their judgment." He recalled the time he backed out of a parking lot and nearly collided with another car. The driver got out, ready to fight. "Why, you're an old man," the driver said after seeing Cowley. Then he got back in his car and drove away. Cowley bristled when he remembered the event.

Some years later, he said, "A young woman rose and offered me her seat in a Madison Avenue bus. That message was kind and also devastating. 'Can't I even stand up?' I thought as I thanked her and declined the seat. But the same thing happened twice the following year, and the second time I gratefully accepted the offer, though with a sense of having diminished myself. 'People are right about me,' I thought. All the same it was a relief to sit down and relax" (pp. 5–6).

Cowley's story shows that a person can internalize ageist beliefs. Ageism can affect a person's self-image and self-confidence. Horton, Baker, and Deakin (2007) reported that age stereotypes can also affect an older person's performance. For example, older people who looked at a newspaper story that contained negative stereotypes showed poorer memory performance than a control group. Horton and colleagues said that "the relationship between explicit negative stereotypes and decreased performance has been established in research across numerous populations and wide-ranging conditions" (p. 1027). The researchers said that people who

---

stereotypes an exaggerated and often prejudiced view of a type of person or group of people

elderspeak simplified speech like baby talk that some people use when they speak to older people; it stems from stereotyping older people as slow-witted

accept ageist stereotypes tend to exercise less and risk poor health as they age.

Grignon, Spencer, and Wang (2010) reported that ageist behaviour in medical settings can have life-threatening consequences. They studied the treatment of older patients for acute myocardial infarction (AMI) or heart attack in Ontario acute care hospitals from 1995 to 2005. They found "treatment rates that would seem to put elderly patients at a disadvantage, as compared to younger ones" (p. 317). For example, nearly all AMI patients admitted to a hospital get therapeutic treatment. This usually means drugs given to remove a blockage and restore blood flow. The medical staff then decide whether they will proceed with more invasive procedures (e.g., coronary artery bypass grafting) or other options for further treatment (e.g., angioplasty).

Grignon and colleagues (2010) found that younger male patients (under age 40) got bypass grafting at three times the rate of older male patients (age 80 and over). For women, the younger group got this more aggressive treatment at four times the rate of older patients. The researchers found a similar pattern for other more active treatments. They concluded that "older patients were more likely to have only therapeutic treatment and hence less likely to have had more invasive treatments" (p. 327).

The researchers gave two reasons for this situation. First, older patients and their families may choose not to have the more invasive procedures. Second, doctors "can use age as a tool to ration care (a phenomenon sometimes described as bedside ageism)" (p. 327). Doctors may use age as a way to limit the use of expensive treatments. They may feel that younger patients have more years to benefit from this care.

The researchers concluded (after controlling for other conditions) "that the age pattern in Ontario resulted at least partly from age-based rationing." Although more research needs to be done to prove this point, they said that age "seems to be used systematically as a rationing tool." The researchers said that if rationing goes on, as their study suggested, the criteria for rationing "should at least be made explicit and discussed" (p. 331).

TIME TO REVIEW

According to gerontologists' research, how do prejudice and discrimination affect older people?

Give an example of how discrimination leads to poor health-care treatment of older people.

Compared with how they might treat a younger patient, why might some doctors treat an older patient's illness less aggressively?

Dr. Robert Butler, the first director of the National Institute on Aging, coined the term *ageism* (1969). **Ageism** refers to prejudice against older people. The Ontario Human Rights Commission (2015) defines ageism as "a socially constructed way of thinking about older persons based on negative attitudes and stereotypes about aging and a tendency to structure society based on an assumption that everyone is young." Bennett and Gaines (2010) called ageism "the third great 'ism' in our society, after racism and sexism" (p. 435).

Butler said that ageism comes about because the young and the middle-aged feel distaste for aging. They see old age as a time of weakness, sickness, and dying. Ageism also comes about because people know little about old age and what they do know is based on myth and fear.

A Canadian study (Revera, 2012) called ageism "the most tolerated form of social prejudice in Canada." This study surveyed 1,501 Canadians ranging from 18 years old to age 75 and over. Revera found that six in ten Canadians age 66 or older reported that they had been "treated unfairly or differently because of their age"; more than one-third of Canadians admit to ageist behaviour; 71 percent agree older people are less valued in our society than younger generations; and one in five Canadians (21 percent) say "older Canadians are a burden on society" (p. 5).

People in Revera's study faced three common forms of discrimination (p. 20):

1. 41 percent of the older people said they had been "ignored or treated as though they were invisible."
2. 38 percent said they were treated as if they had "nothing to contribute."
3. 27 percent said that people assume "older adults are incompetent."

The *Canadian Special Senate Committee on Aging Final Report* (2009; also Ontario Human Rights Commission, 2015) took a stand against ageism. The report says, "There is no place for ageism in a progressive country like Canada" and it recommends that the federal government "move immediately to take steps to promote active aging and healthy aging and to combat ageism" (pp. 9–10).

In Canadian society today, people learn to be prejudiced against the old. These negative views come from many sources. Henneberg (2010) studied the image of old women in children's literature. "Once literary grandmothers are moved center-stage," she said, "they are generally locked into one of three types: the wicked old witch,

---

ageism prejudice against older people

the selfless godmother, or the demented hag" (p. 128). Classic stories like *Hansel and Gretel* and *Rapunzel* present old women as witches: "ugly, bitter, and dangerous." Henneberg said that "women in children's classics fare badly [often they get killed off early in the story], but old women do even worse" (p. 125).

Gilbert and Ricketts (2008) reviewed the literature on children's attitudes toward old people. They reported that "language, humour, and various forms of media, particularly book[s] and television," provide children with views of older people (p. 571). Children begin to hold negative views toward older adults as early as age five. By age eight, these views have become firmly set.

Psychological learning theory (Bandura, 2001) said that early exposure to social information may influence how a child will think about aging and getting older. And this early exposure may carry on into adulthood. Hollis-Sawyer and Cuevas (2013) studied the portrayal of older women in children's picture books. They chose a sample of 90 books. They found that older people appeared in only about one-third of the books. And the books that did include older women generally portrayed them negatively in the text and in images. The books portrayed older women as witches, or crazy, or alone. The authors concluded that "aging-related and gender stereotypes are pervasive in what is presented to children, from fairy-tales

---

EXHIBIT 1.2 AGING IN A GLOBAL PERSPECTIVE
Traffic Signs: A Source of Implicit Ageism

A U.K. traffic sign presents elderly people as feeble or disabled.
Aquir/Shutterstock

A Namibian traffic sign presents a more capable-looking and even energetic image of an elderly person.
Nelson Education Ltd.

These two signs present two different images of older people. The sign from the United Kingdom "portrays a silhouette of a man with a flexed posture using a cane and leading a kyphotic woman" (Gale et al., 2003, p. 1456). It presents older people as frail, feeble, and disabled. It implies that they experience "vertebral collapse" and the need for mobility aids. The Namibian sign presents a more neutral image of the older person. The

figure appears capable and even energetic in a forward-moving posture.

The U.K. sign sparked a controversy in 2008. The advocacy group Age Concern called the sign "outmoded." It called for the removal of the signs and their replacement by reduced speed limit signs. Millward (2008) reported (without apparent irony) that the U.K. sign "was a winning entry in a children's competition in 1981."

Questions

1. Do you notice expressions of ageism in your environment?

2. Do you notice expressions of positive support for older people?

Sources: Gale, R.P., Gale, C.P., Roper, T.A., and Mulley, G.P. "Depiction of Elderly and Disabled People on Road Traffic Signs: International Comparison." *British Medical Journal*, 327: 1456–1457; Millward, D. "Pensioner Groups Demand Elderly Road Sign Change." *The Telegraph*, http://www.telegraph.co.uk/news/newstopics/howaboutthat/2585801/Pensioner-groups-demand-elderly-road-sign-change.html.

to cartoons." They went on to say that from a "life course perspective, the earlier we understand aging in a realistic way, the more educated our decisions will be throughout life" (p. 909).

Calasanti (2008) described the overt and subtle ageism she found in the classroom. Students in response to her questioning would admit that they thought of older people as "slow drivers" or people who wear "unfashionable clothes." Calasanti also uncovered ageism in the language used by gerontologists— scholars who want to rid society of this prejudice. She noted that she (and other gerontologists) used the term *older adults* rather than *old adults* to "soften students' rejection of old people...." (pp. 154–155). Her writing points to the many overt and subtle faces of ageism.

Thompson and colleagues (2014), in a summary of research on attitudes toward sexual expression in later life, said that "young adults appear to hold the most negative views of sexuality in older adults compared to children and middle-aged adults" (p. 259). In their study of 134 students age 18 to 24, they found that students reported explicit positive attitudes toward sexuality in later life. But on further examination, they found that students held implicit (covert) negative attitudes. Their study also found a moderate implicit general bias against older adults.

Sometimes ageism hides as humour. At a conference a few years ago, a sales representative gave one of the authors a page of comments about getting older. The page had the sales rep's name and phone number in the outside margins. Perhaps he thought that people would pass this page along to colleagues so that they could share this bit of humour and know it came from him. The page said:

You know you're getting old when ...

- Everything hurts and what doesn't hurt doesn't work.
- Your pacemaker makes the garage door go up every time a pretty girl walks by.
- Your back goes out more often than you do.
- The last time you helped a little old lady across the street it was your wife.

The author has read these lines to many audiences and classes of students, and people find them funny. But at the risk of ruining the fun, the author suggests that all of these jokes foster ageism. For one thing, they all make older people seem physically and psychologically weak. They also make older people seem less able to do things. Or they imply that older people cannot control their bodily functions.

The man who gave the author this list saw no harm in the humour, and since then the author has received copies of this list from other sources. One copy of this list appeared in *Reader's Digest*. Imagine that a similar list had a racial or ethnic bias. Would you pass it along to your customers or show it to your professor? Would it be published in a national magazine? Few people see these jokes as ageist at first. All of us have grown up with the stereotype of older people as run-down and decrepit.

EXHIBIT 1.3 *What Is It Like to Be Old?*

We cannot know the answer to this question until we reach old age ourselves. But Professor Paul Baker of the University of Victoria set out, at age 33, to learn about aging first-hand. In the story that follows, he described his experiment with old age.

"You're too young to be a gerontologist. How can somebody who's only 33 know what it's like to be 83?" This reaction from one of the few older students in my course on the sociology of aging bothered me. My first instinct was to haul out my academic/scientific defenses and claim that you don't have to be an X to study Xs (be they old, female, black, or handicapped).

But I was left with the uncomfortable feeling that maybe she was right, maybe I was missing some of the more subjective and emotional aspects of aging by working only with "hard," "objective" data. Then I ran across John Griffin's classic book, *Black Like Me*, written in 1961. Griffin dyed his skin and passed as a black man in the southern United States for a month. His book showed how different the world was for a black man, and made a lot of white people realize what racism meant at the human level.

So, how could I become old? The answer was obvious: the same kind of makeup that turned Dustin Hoffman old in *Little Big Man* might work for me, and, with the help of a makeup artist in Vancouver, plus some old clothes, a cane, and a grey wig, I made the transformation. The makeup took several hours to apply, and hurt like hell going on and coming off, but it worked.

My main interest was in experiencing society's reactions to an old man. I walked around in Victoria and Vancouver about a dozen times, in different places, at night and during the day. And what I found was pretty much what I expected; a few people go out of their way to help the old, a few turn their backs, and most people simply ignore them.

One "young" woman (my own age) waited patiently for me as I struggled up the stairs at the Victoria Institute of Gerontology, held the door open, and said, "Have a nice day." I felt very uncomfortable: I was really a young, healthy male but was masquerading as a decrepit old man; I actually felt like I was a "burden" and almost told her I could open doors for myself, even if I was old.

(continued)

On the other hand, I was shoved off the sidewalk in front of the Empress Hotel by a large, noisy bunch of tourists. It may have been accidental, but I felt angry and frustrated. On crowded streets I could no longer stride along and know that other people would move aside. I had to be on the defensive, anticipating others' moves. Crossing busy streets became a totally different experience. I hung back so that the crowds could bolt across as soon as the light changed, and then I shuffled along, keeping my eye on the cars, which seemed like racehorses just itching for the gates to open. The lights always started flashing "DON'T WALK" before I was across. What was I supposed to do, the bunny hop?

I experimented with getting in and out of cars and using buses. The basic lesson I learned was that the world gets bigger and faster for an old man, and I became acutely aware of this dramatic change because I was really young, and hadn't gradually accepted the inevitable changes of aging.

I discovered a sense of comradeship of the old, who had the time to sit and talk. I also found a subtle difference between old Victoria and big Vancouver: it seemed easier to be old here, partly because of the size and pace, but maybe also because in Victoria we have so many old people. I think we have learned to be a little more patient.

Would I do it again? Probably not ... pretending to be old hurt my back, my legs, my feet. It was hard to explain to friends and neighbours what I was doing. I think I'll wait for old age to creep up on me slowly, and, in the meantime, I think I have gained a better understanding for my old friends.

Source: Paul M. Baker, Old before My Time, videotape distributed by the Centre on Aging, University of Victoria, Victoria, BC V8W 2Y2 (1983b). Reprinted by permission of the Estate of Paul Morgan Baker.

Jokes and humour project our own fears about aging onto older people. But do these fears have a basis in fact? Shields (2008) studied community belonging and its relation to self-perceived health. She found that a "strong" or "somewhat strong" sense of community belonging increased with age among adults. The oldest group in the study (65 and over) had the highest proportion of people (71.6 percent) who felt this strong sense of community belonging. People with a strong sense of community belonging reported the highest rates of excellent or very good general health. They also reported the highest rates of excellent or very good mental health. George (2006) reviewed the literature on life satisfaction. She said that in both short-term and long-term studies, life satisfaction in old age remains high.

The study of aging shows that old age has its compensations. Older people in Canada can have guaranteed incomes, subsidized housing, and free medical care. They also get reduced rates on buses and at hotels and car rentals. Other bonuses include tax breaks, free tuition at many universities, and financial support for recreation programs.

Some people in modern society feel ambivalent about aging: ageism exists alongside care and concern for older people (Bousfield & Hutchison, 2010; Hummert, 2011). Research on aging finds that the attitudes of others cause some of the worst problems older people face.

TIME TO REVIEW

What is "elderspeak?"

What is "ageism?"

What are some sources of ageism?

What are some of the benefits of being a senior in Canada?

AGEISM AND DISCRIMINATION IN THE WORKPLACE

Many studies report ageism in the workplace (De Castro, 2008). Chou (2012) surveyed the literature on workplace discrimination. She said employers often think of older workers as "less flexible or creative, less alert, more prone to accidents, in poorer health, unfamiliar with new technologies, more resistant to innovation and technical change, harder to train, lacking in physical strength, less ambitious, less productive, and less financially beneficial" (p. 27).

Chou and Choi (2010) studied micro-aggressive behaviour against older workers. They found that about 80 percent of the people in their study experienced at least one instance of the following experiences in the past year: "being unfairly given undesirable tasks; being watched more closely at the job than others; receiving ethnic, racial, and sexual slurs from boss or coworkers; and being ignored or not taken seriously by boss" (Chou, 2012, p. 28).

Cooke (2006) said some employers view older workers as more expensive and less effective than younger workers. They believe this "despite anti-discrimination laws and evidence that older workers are indeed capable of learning new tasks and tend to have higher loyalty and less absenteeism" (p. 396). Firms that want to retire older workers sometimes do so through "voluntary buy-outs," even where states make mandatory retirement illegal.

Berger (2009) found that many older job hunters (age 45 to 65) concealed their age from employers. They altered their résumés, changed their physical appearance, and altered their language. McMullin and Berger (2006) conducted in-depth interviews with 30 unemployed women and men age 45 to 65. All of these people actively tried to find work and they all reported overt and covert ageism in their job search. "No one will tell you; no one will admit it," one woman told the researchers. "But I have a friend who owns his own company and he said, 'If I interview three people, even though you have the experience, if I think I can get more years out of another one, I would hire another person.' And you know, they don't have to say that, that's just the way it's done (female, aged sixty)" (pp. 211–218).

In answer to a question about age discrimination, one woman made reference to the role that gender plays in age discrimination. "Well definitely because I am a woman and because of my age. They want young, attractive women, not women who are forty-five, fifty or older (female, aged forty-five)." Men in this study also experienced rejection based on their age. One man said, "I went to two interviews there. They finally rejected me … I, as they put it, was 'over-qualified.' … But I couldn't get anyone to hire me (male, aged sixty-two)" (McMullin & Berger, 2006, pp. 211–218).

Rix (2011) said that "age discrimination is all but impossible to document" (p. 202). McMullin and Berger (2006) found throughout their research that employers often used euphemisms in order to reject older workers. Some companies said that they look for someone more junior, they felt the work was too fast-paced for an older worker, instead of saying the person was too old for the job. The authors said that these phrases and excuses try "to avoid charges of ageism and age-based discrimination." Employers "seem to disguise their ageist hiring practices by rejecting older applicants with the use of more age neutral terms" (pp. 211–218).

Employers use years of experience to identify a person's age, and workers find that their strong résumés' may work against them. They indicate the age of the worker, and that alone may eliminate them from consideration. One worker said, "They don't say anything, but you know when there is absolutely no reason why you shouldn't be considered—to just look at my résumé, they know how many years I've been in the business and they can sort of deduce that I'm not thirty-five or forty" (female, aged sixty) (McMullin & Berger, 2006, pp. 211–218).

These workers reported the effects of ageism and (in the case of women) sexism in later life. Ageism in these cases affects more than a person's self-image. It can lead to low wages when a person does find a job (Rix, 2006). This can keep a person from living a decent life.

A NEW VIEW OF OLD AGE

Stereotypes and ageism give a simplistic picture of individual and societal aging. Research shows that older people live rich and complex lives that contradict the stereotypes. For example, many people age 50 to 70 have good incomes, little or no mortgage, and no children to support. They have money to spend, better education than past generations of older people, and active lifestyles. Recreation programs, education, and travel appeal to this group. The corporate world has begun to see older age groups as a market for new goods and services.

The International Longevity Center (2006) said that, "products targeting Baby Boomers are set to become the next big ad category in the coming years" (p. 57, citing Dobrow, 2005). An article in *The Globe and Mail* (2014) made this same point. It described the Baby Boomer market for new cars and concluded that "drivers aged 55 and up are buying more new cars than previous generations…. The pattern has not been lost on car makers, who are marketing more than four-door sedans to image-conscious seniors."

Women make up a large segment of the mid- to later-life market. Nearly 8 million Canadian women comprised the 45-and-over age group in 2011. These women felt satisfied with life, self-confident, and empowered. Milner (2006) said that, to attract this wealthy market segment, companies should focus on the mature woman's desire to look and feel good.

Rozanova, Northcott, and McDaniel (2006) found "successful aging" as a theme in their study of *The Globe and Mail*. They found that many articles described older people as "wealthy, active, healthy, youthful looking, pursuing stay-young activities" (p. 379). An article in *Maclean's* magazine (Editors, 2011, July 28), for example, described an older Canada as "a country that's as cool and calm as a cucumber, and with plenty of time for fun. Suddenly the future is looking … relaxed."

General Social Survey findings reported in this article show that on every measure, Canadians appear less stressed than in 1998 (the comparison year). The survey found that "these declines [in reports of stress in life] may be due to the fact that the 55-plus age group has become a larger part of the Canadian population over the years and in general people of this age tend to feel less stressed by time pressures than their younger counterparts." *Zoomer*, a Canadian magazine originally aimed at the 50-plus audience, now calls itself a "lifestyle" publication aimed at those 45 and over. This shift to a younger demographic suggests the magazine's need to appeal to a broader audience. Still, the stories play to a middle-aged and older demographic.

Some critics believe that this new positive view of later life creates a new stereotype. Studies of the media support this concern. McHugh (2003) studied advertisements that promote retirement in Arizona. These ads portrayed older people as active, energetic, and upper middle-class. But the ads excluded images of disabled or poor older people. These ads subtly distinguish two kinds of older people—haves and have-nots.

A number of authors say that claims of agelessness or youthfulness in spirit deny the uniqueness of later life. Muise and Desmarais (2010) studied Canadian older women, who expressed similar feelings. One woman said she resents "the beauty industry and the media for trying to make women feel they don't measure up if they don't fit the stereotype beauty mould" (p. 134).

A study of magazine and newspaper portrayals of online dating (Wada, Clarke, & Rozanova, 2015, p. 47) found "two distinct ideals of sexuality." Some articles portrayed the decline of sexuality in later life. Others idealized sexual attractiveness for older people. These articles promoted new techniques for achieving sexual pleasure in old age. The authors concluded that "there are multiple ideals of sexuality in contemporary Canadian society."

Gravagne (2013, cited in Outcalt, 2015, p. 113) reviewed current films and found a double message. Films often present a stereotype of the older person (e.g., the grumpy old man) that reinforces ageism, but some films present "counterstories." Films about romance and sexual relationships such as *Something's Gotta Give* and *The Best Exotic Marigold Hotel* confront ageist stereotypes of aging women.

These studies show that views of aging have begun to change. But the media often substitute one stereotype (the ultra-fit, sexually active senior) for another (the aged toothless crone). In part, this complexity reflects the reality of aging today. Older people vary in their gender, health, lifestyles, sexual preferences, income, and age. Writers now describe at least two broad stages of later life: the Third Age (the young-old) and the Fourth Age (late old age).

Ageism and the Third Age

An important distinction helps explain why people in their 60s, 70s, and even 80s say they do not feel "old." This group identifies with the *Zoomer* lifestyle. At the same time, some people in these age groups look and feel "old," either by lifestyle choice (e.g., reclusiveness) or a decline in health. This reflects what writers describe as "the 'destandardization' or 'pluralisation' of the life course." The profusion of terms that exist to describe later life—senior, Baby Boomer, senior citizen, retiree, pensioner—point to the uncertain meaning of later life today (Gilleard and Higgs, 2011, p. 135). And this in turn leaves the individual to define himself or herself in society.

Historian Peter Laslett (1996) identified and named two stages of later life, the "Third Age" and the "Fourth Age." During the Third Age, a person lives in relative affluence, free of work and child-rearing duties, in generally good health, and engaged in fulfilling, socially satisfying activity (Gilleard & Higgs, 2000, 2010). Higgs & McGowan (2013, p. 22) called the Third Age "an aging youth culture." People can be chronologically old, but not act or feel "old."

The category of old age (that a past generation would have applied to a 65-year-old) now fits the Fourth Age. In this last stage of life, people lose their autonomy, their physical health, and their ability to care for themselves. This stage now often comes past the age of 85. The young-old person today may accept the drift into the Fourth Age, attempt to hold on to the relative youthfulness of the Third Age, or waffle between these two options.

The onset of chronic physical disability or dementia often pushes the person from the Third to the Fourth Age of life. Until this occurs, the older person adapts to a shifting social status and mixed messages from society. The media sometimes portray all older people as if they lived in the Fourth Age. Sometimes they promote successful aging that encourages older people to hold on to their Third Age abilities (e.g., sexual performance).

Longer life for nearly everyone has led to a redefinition of old age. The discussion of ageism and of age discrimination hinges in part on the error of mistaking one age category (the Third Age) for another (the Fourth Age). Baby Boomers in the Third Age object to being categorized as Fourth-Agers. The presentation of rock stars as vigorous and youthful, newspaper stories that describe paragliding 90-year-olds, and gyms full of exercising retirees on weekday mornings, provide examples of the Third Age as people live it today.

TIME TO REVIEW

Give an example from the research of how ageism leads to discrimination in the job market.

Give an example of how a company or service has adapted its product or service to attract older consumers.

Describe the difference between life in the Third Age and in the Fourth Age.

AGING AS A DISEASE— ANOTHER FORM OF AGEISM

As you can see, ageism takes many forms. It shows up in literature, advertising, jokes, and attitudes. Even the promotion of health and activity, or "successful aging," in later life can support ageism. This image of later life rejects people with chronic illness, disability, low income, or visual signs of physical decline (grey hair and wrinkles). This view of healthy aging links physical decline to disease—an abnormal state of aging. According to Dillaway and Byrnes (2009), the ideal of successful aging makes normal aging (inevitable physical decline) seem "undesirable and preventable" (p. 706).

Some authors see the current interest in longevity, the increases in surgery to alter the effects of aging, and the desire to act young into old age as a rejection of aging. Calasanti and Slevin (2006) said that successful aging, when it promotes the image of eternal youth "means not aging, not being 'old,' or, at the very least, not looking old." The ideal older woman, according to the ageist stereotype, "is "healthy, slim, discreetly sexy and independent" (p. 3).

Calasanti (2005) said that aging looks avoidable and like a personal failure from this point of view. "To appear unhealthy," she said, "is to have failed and to deserve one's fate; one ought to have changed one's lifestyle or diet" (p. 9). Calasanti said that the older person who shows signs of aging (or even someone who chooses to live a contemplative lifestyle), from this point of view, deserves the poor treatment that person receives. "Not to resist signs of physical decay," she said, "may be perceived as evidence of moral decline" (Calasanti, 2005, citing Jones & Pugh, 2005, pp. 254–255).

Clarke, Griffin, and Maliha (2009) interviewed 36 women age 71 to 93 about their clothing choices. These women used clothing to mask changes in their bodies that signalled aging. They opted for traditional styles and clothing that masked flabby underarm skin (referred to as "bat wings"), wrinkles, pear-shaped bodies, and loose skin at their necks. One woman said she wears turtlenecks because "most women as they get older, they get the turkey wattle here you know, the fat sinks from here, goes to under your chin and you'll find that older women have a bunch of fat hanging down here. I like things with a turtleneck because they hide that ugly part" (p. 718). Their comments hint at the underlying anxiety that affects many older people as they age in North American society.

The **anti-aging industry** cashes in on this denial of aging. A BCC Research report (2013) said that the worldwide market for anti-aging products and services came to $249.3 billion in 2012. The report projected an increase to $345.8 billion by 2018—a compound annual growth rate of 5.7 percent between 2013 and 2018. Products in this market include moisturizers, anti-wrinkle creams, anti-aging injections, skin-tightening devices, hair growth and hair colouring products, and many others, including anti-aging sexual dysfunction drugs. Services include liposuction, facelifts, dermabrasion, hair removal, and many other services, including breast augmentation. The major drug and cosmetics companies (Merck, Novartis, Revlon, Shiseido) all serve this large and growing market.

Men do not escape the effects of aging in social definitions of masculinity. Masculinity "may be defined at its core by certain physical features and an inner sense of being male" (Canham, 2009, p. 90). Ideal characteristics of masculinity include physical strength, independence, restricted emotions, power and control, sexual vigour, aggressiveness, and being non-female. Few men possess all of these idealized traits, but these traits define maleness in Western society.

Few studies have looked at the effect of aging on a man's self-image in later life. Spector-Mercel (2006), for example, said that no masculine equivalent of the *Journal of Women and Aging* exists. This journal includes gender and aging research on women. And yet studies of older men could benefit from more research because older men also struggle with the effects of aging on their self-image (Alex et al., 2008; Canham, 2009; Tannenbaum & Frank, 2011). The growing market for drugs to overcome erectile dysfunction, for example, points to the male quest for youthful performance. And the high suicide rate among older men points to serious psychological challenges that men face as they age.

Baker and Gringart (2009) found that, like older women, older men also express dissatisfaction with their physical appearance as they age. The researchers found that men tended to engage in physical fitness activity to stay in shape. The researchers proposed that men (particularly those under age 70) "engage in physical activity to maintain a certain body-shape ideal" (p. 989). Men at older ages lose this interest in fitness as they age, possibly because they can no longer maintain the ideal of a youthful body. This study found that men become "progressively dissatisfied with their physical appearance" as they age.

Clarke, Bennett, and Liu (2014, p. 27) summarized studies of media portrayals of older men. They found that advertisements portrayed men in competitive, youthful roles. "Older men are seen consuming products and services aimed at sustaining or rejuvenating their virility and sexual engagement, thereby enabling them to age successfully." Still, their research found few images of older men in men's magazines (e.g., *Esquire, GQ,* and *Maxim*).

---

anti-aging industry the multibillion-dollar worldwide market for products that claim to reduce or reverse the effects of aging

The Canadian magazine *Zoomer*, with its focus on people age 50+, had the highest proportion of images of older men (71 percent). Nearly all of these magazines portrayed men positively, with economic, political, and social power. The researchers called this the "dominant cultural messages about masculinity and optimal aging" (p. 32). The researchers concluded that while the magazines surveyed contained many positive portrayals of older men, most men would find these ideals unattainable. For the majority of older readers, they said, "the Fourth Age was increasingly a looming reality" (p. 32). These magazines "contribute to and reflect broader societal narratives about the devaluation and fear of agedness" (p. 33). Baker and Gringart (2009, p. 990) said that "cultural pressures to conform to youthful ideals are experienced by both genders."

Catherine Mayer (2009) coined the term *amortality* to describe the ageless self. Amortals, she said, obey no age norms. "The defining characteristic of amortality," she wrote, "is to live the same way, at the same pitch, doing and consuming much the same things, from late teens right up until death." Amortals deny aging. And in their most extreme pronouncements, they deny death itself—hoping for a scientific breakthrough before they meet the Grim Reaper.

Nora Ephron (2010), in her 70s, wrote, directed, and produced the film *Julie & Julia*. She reflected (with a touch of humour) on the ambivalence she felt about aging in an essay entitled "The O Word" (pp. 127–128):

> *I'm old.*
>
> *I am sixty-nine years old.*
>
> *I'm not really old, of course.*
>
> *Really old is eighty.*
>
> *But if you are young, you would definitely think that I'm old.*
>
> *No one actually likes to admit that they're old.*
>
> *The most they will cop to is that they're older. Or oldish.*
>
> *In these days of physical fitness, hair dye, and plastic surgery, you can live much of your life without feeling or even looking old.*

Bayer (2005) said that "'positive aging' soon equates with anti-aging" (p. 14)—a denial of aging. A study by Hurd Clarke and Griffin (2007) showed that women feel ambivalent about the pressure to look eternally young. And the more anxiety they feel about this pressure, the greater the chance they will buy an anti-aging product (Muise & Desmarais, 2010). Men may also feel pressure

to look younger and more virile, but they less frequently turn to cosmetic solutions.

Calasanti (2007; also see Calasanti & King, 2007) and others (e.g., Hurd Clarke & Korotchenko, 2011; Mitchell & Bruns, 2011) argued that "anti-aging" images in the media form part of a broader system of age discrimination and gender and age inequalities. In an examination of Internet advertisements for anti-aging products, Calasanti (2007) found that these ads reinforce the message that "old people are worthwhile only to the extent that they look and act like those who are middle-aged or younger" (p. 335). The cultural ideal promotes youth, strength, and sexual vigour. For older men, this means maintaining or recapturing their youthful sexual ability; for women, this means maintaining or recapturing their youthful female beauty.

Hurd Clarke and Korotchenko (2011) found that older women often have conflicting feelings about the images of women they see in magazines. Some women believe the "magazine women" are "unnatural"—through air-brushing or other digital enhancements. At the same time, they feel pressured by these images and advertisements "to consume beauty interventions and to work to discipline and alter their bodies so as to appear more desirable" (p. 113).

The medical profession, along with questionable marketers, joins in the attack on the aging body. This has created a new industry in cosmeceuticals, combinations of cosmetics and pharmaceutical substances. Together these substances promise to fight the effects of aging on the skin and in the body. Botox and plastic surgery promise solutions to wrinkles and sagging skin.

Older people today can feel caught in a bind. Society expects people to act young as they age, but an older person might prefer to let the signs of aging show.

Hurd Clarke and Griffin (2007, 2008; also Muise & Desmarais, 2010) found this same tension between societal expectations and personal beliefs. The researchers interviewed 44 women age 50 to 70. They asked the women about their views of beauty in later life. These women viewed natural aging—without the use of hair dye and makeup—as a worthwhile goal. But most of the women engaged in what the researchers call "beauty work." They endorsed the use of cosmetics, anti-wrinkle creams, and even cosmetic surgery to produce a "natural" look as they aged (pp. 132–133). And most of these women used these methods to look young.

The researchers concluded that ageism in Canadian society leads women to cover up the signs of aging. The debate about good aging shows a healthy interest in redefining old age. It captures the diversity of later life, as older people and Canadian society work out new ways to live

EXHIBIT 1.4   *To Dye or Not to Dye: That Is the Question*

"For years I dyed my hair black to cover the grey," my colleague Phyllis confided. "I had it done every three or four weeks. I couldn't stop. If I did, I'd have a line across my head where the dye stopped as the grey hair grew in. I spent a ton of money on this. But what could I do?"

"Then I had a serious illness and the doctors shaved my head. When my hair grew back I let it go grey. But it made me look so old. Now I have black streaks put into the grey. It's a compromise. It doesn't exactly hide my age, but it softens the effect of the grey."

Phyllis, like many women (and men), doesn't want to look old. Our society values youth. Grey hair signals old age and decline. Hair colour hides the effects of aging. But Phyllis feels torn about her decision. She'd rather not colour her hair, but she can't bear to see herself going grey.

A Proctor & Gamble study (Kreamer, 2007) found that 65 percent of women dyed their hair in 2004—a sharp increase from the 1950s. Kreamer said that this "is why going gray has become a difficult ... choice for modern women to make" (p. 72). Grey hair now makes a woman stand out from her age group.

In her book *I Feel Bad About My Neck*, author Nora Ephron (2006) wrote, "There's a reason why forty, fifty, and sixty don't look the way they used to, and it's not because of feminism or better living through exercise. It's because of hair dye.... Hair dye has changed everything, but it almost never gets the credit. It's the most powerful weapon older women have against the youth culture" (p. 36).

But dying your hair doesn't fight against the youth culture (as Ephron probably knew). It reinforces that culture by giving in to the demand that everyone appear young. A woman who dyes her hair gives in to the stereotyped image of youth and beauty that rejects old age and older people.

Will the next wave of aging Baby Boomers dye their hair to appear young? Will they reject this cover-up and shout, "I'm grey and I'm proud?" Will Baby Boomers let their inner grey show?

Questions

1. What do you think about the use of hair dye to hide grey hair? Do you think you will colour your hair when it turns grey?

2. Should people dye their hair to look younger?

3. Does hair colouring marginalize the poorer person who can't afford to pay for hair colouring?

4. Does it reinforce societal ageism?

in the Third Age. Still, more change needs to take place in society and in our attitudes in order to have a more balanced view of later life.

Canada today needs to promote a realistic and diverse presentation of older characters in movies, on television, and in print media. We too often see portrayals that reflect a stereotypical and ageist dichotomy: either angry, grumpy, and frail older people or healthy, active, and youthful older people.

We need to allow for many ways to grow old. Some people want to engage in energetic activities that we associate with youth. Other older people define later life as a time to use their wisdom, share their memories, and offer community leadership. Some people will live vibrant healthy lives into late old age. Others will live with chronic illness. Some will seem youthful to us, others will look old. No single right way to grow old exists. And none of these ways should meet with social rejection.

Education as an Antidote to Ageism

Hess (2006) reviewed the research on attitudes toward older people. He found that people with more knowledge about aging had a more positive view of later life; they could see things from the perspective of the older person. People with more knowledge of aging also felt less anxiety about aging (Allan & Johnson, 2009). Funderburk, Damron-Rodriguez, Storms, and Solomon (2006) reported that people who had personal contact with older adults tended to stereotype less. Negative stereotypes come into play most often when we know little about a person or group.

Some authors (Fletcher, 2007; Gilbert & Ricketts, 2008) say the separation of age groups in modern society perpetuates ageism. Typically, young people and old people spend little time together and know little about one another. Barrett and Cantwell (2007) asked undergraduate students to draw "an elderly person" for a class assignment. They then analyzed the sketches and found that their students' illustrations reflected many of the stereotypes of older people, both negative and positive, prevalent in our society. The negative traits portrayed in the drawings included physical impairment, frailty, ugliness, depression, and social isolation. The positive stereotypes, more common in the drawings of older women than older men, depicted them as "kind, grandmotherly, cookie-baking types" (p. 344).

Many of the sketches showed older people with walking aids (canes were most common), with thinning hair (more likely for older men), and wrinkles (more likely for older women). When the researchers asked the students what they thought shaped their views of older people, the students identified a number of sources. These included infrequent contact with older people, ageist jokes and language, and negative portrayals of older people in the media (television, films, and advertisements).

Studies show that more positive interaction between older and younger people decreases ageism (Bousfield & Hutchison, 2010; Reynolds, 2010). A study at the University of Western Ontario medical school (Diachun et al., 2006), for example, divided students into three groups—a group that learned about aging in the classroom, an experiential group that met older people, and a control group that had neither educational option. The study found that after one year, compared with the control group, both the classroom and the experiential group reported better attitudes toward older people.

Service learning, internships, and field placements offer students a chance to interact with older people. A study of social work students in Canada and the United States asked about their intent to work in a nursing home (Holroyd et al., 2009; Simons & Bonifas, 2009). The researchers found that students who had field placements in a nursing home and those who had worked in a nursing home expressed interest in a nursing home job. Likewise, service learning programs increase students' comfort in working with cognitively impaired older people.

One student said, "... I am doing my senior field placement at a long-term care facility and I love it. I want to become a social worker in either a hospital or long-term care setting." Another student said, "I would very much like to be employed as a social worker in a long-term care facility. I have considerable experience working in long-term care (field placement and summer work placement) and have very much enjoyed this area of social work" (Simons & Bonifas, 2009, p. 309). The researchers concluded that "curricula that place students directly in contact with [nursing home] residents, families, and practitioners would be of great service...." (p. 310).

Service learning programs show the value of interaction between the generations. Knowledge and satisfying contact with older people lead to a more positive view of aging. Karasik (2012) said that experiential activities open students to the possibility of working with older people. Gould, MacLennan, and Dupuis-Blanchard (2012) suggested that nursing students could benefit from work with community-dwelling older people as well as institutionalized seniors. Novice nurses could benefit from "work with experienced nurses who value and enjoy their work with vulnerable older populations" (p. 481). The number of education programs for undergraduates and healthcare professionals has increased in the past few years. These programs will lead to better treatment of older people and a more balanced view of aging in the future.

"One antidote to ageism," Butler (1993) said, "is knowledge, the primary intervention" (p. 77). He reported that knowledge and satisfying contact with older people lead to a more positive view of aging. Butts and Lent (2009) say that "thoughtfully planned intergenerational programs that engage the generations in a purposeful way with clear goals have positive outcomes" (p. 153).

AGEISM AND SOCIAL POLICY

Stereotypes and ageism most often focus on the individual. They exaggerate the physical and mental changes that come with age. But ageism can also focus on population aging. This type of ageism reflects a fear of an aging society. Some commentators have begun to express this form of ageism. They see the new generation of older people as a burden on society. They fear that an increased number and proportion of older people will lead to higher costs for pensions and healthcare. And they fear that this will lead to economic and social collapse.

Geddes (2010) titled a *Maclean's* article "The Health Care Time Bomb: Our Aging Population Will Make Unthinkable Reforms Inevitable." *The National Post* titled a commentary by David Frum (2012) "Grandpa's Free Ride." Frum wrote, "As they age, the pre-1960 cohorts will enjoy more benefits from government than they themselves ever paid for. They will draw more support from the post-1990 cohorts than they themselves paid toward

This young child shares a happy time with her grandmother in a restaurant. Studies show that positive interactions between younger and older people lead to more positive attitudes toward older people.

their elders. And because so many of the benefits for the pre-1960 cohorts have been (and will be) financed by debt, the pre-1960 cohorts will be drawing support from the post-1990 cohorts for years to come."*

Frum (2012, emphasis added) concludes his piece by asking and answering a politically charged question: "Who will bear how much of the burden of adjusting budgets to grim new post-2008 realities? Canadian politicians have been more responsible and more concerned with fairness than most. But even in Canada—and much more in Japan, Europe, and the United States—the answer being heard louder and louder is: *Spare the old, burden the young.*"*

Writers such as these play on the public fear of an aging society. They stereotype the older population as dependent, unproductive, and costly. And they speak in apocalyptic terms, as if population aging will lead to the collapse of society as we know it. One headlines cautioned: "Aging Workforce an Economic Tsunami-in-Waiting" (Hodgson, 2012). Another news story warned of "Canada's Aging Medicare Burden" (Barua & Rovere, 2012; for another example, see Gatehouse, 2010). "In line with this ideology," Rozanova and colleagues (2006, citing Gee & McDaniel, 1993) said, "older adults are stereotyped as unproductive greedy geezers, are blamed for public debt loads, and are portrayed as a threat to the sustainability of public programs" (p. 380).

In spite of these dire predictions by social pundits, the Canadian government has taken a more practical (less extreme) view of population aging. The existence of broad-based social programs in Canada, for example, encourages a response to population aging that serves all age groups. This creates a sense of common interest. For example, Canada's national healthcare system serves people of all ages. For this reason, it tends to unify national concerns around good health regardless of age. Clark's (1993) comment holds true today: "what is interpreted in the U.S. as a crisis is simply seen in Canada as a challenge to good government" (p. 498).

A study by Stone, Rosenthal, and Connidis (1998) shows that influential Canadian researchers take a broad view of intergenerational equity. They look beyond public exchanges of funds (such as Canada's Old Age Security program) to include parent–child exchanges of informal supports. They also look at the mutual exchanges (of money and services) between adult children and their aging parents. And they look at support levels and types of support given and received by many age groups.

A study by Szinovacz and Davey (2012), for example, found that only "20 percent of mothers and 12 percent of fathers received financial help from an adult child" (p. 373). When children did give funds to parents, in most cases they did so for short periods. Studies concluded that *"over the life course, private exchange of supports between parents and children is not balanced. It heavily favours the children"* (Stone et al., 1998, p. 66, emphasis in original). Up to age 70, older people give more support to their children than they receive. And they continue to give to their children throughout their lives.

Federal government statements and reports in general make little reference to intergenerational tensions. Instead they express support for Canada's older population. The Public Health Agency of Canada (2015b) publishes a website called *Age-Friendly Communities*. The site considers "it more important than ever, to support the health and well-being of older Canadians. This way, seniors can lead healthy and active lives and stay involved in their communities." The federal government's Funding: New Horizons for Seniors Program, for example, sponsors projects "led or inspired by seniors." This program promotes volunteerism and seniors' social participation (Human Resources and Skills Development Canada, 2013).

The Canadian government also works to understand and respond to issues that older people face. The government created a National Seniors Council (NSC) in 2007 for this purpose. The NSC keeps the federal government up to date on seniors' needs. Council members meet with representatives of seniors' groups throughout the country. The Council "acts as a voice for older citizens and helps inform Canadian policy."

A background paper written for the Canadian Federal/Provincial/Territorial (F/P/T) Committee of Officials (Seniors) (Edwards & Mawani, 2006) presented a balanced view of intergenerational relations in Canada. The report called for a "society for all ages," a theme endorsed by the Federal/Provincial/Territorial Ministers Responsible for Seniors (p. 10).

---

intergenerational equity a call for balanced support of older and younger people through public policy and public expenditures

society for all ages promotes the well-being and contributions of older people in all aspects of life, recognizes their valuable contributions, and reflects the goals of elimination of ageism in all sectors; a society for all ages has five core principles: dignity, independence, participation, fairness, and security

---

* David Frum, Quebec student riots: Grandpa's free ride, *National Post* (28 April 2012). http://news.nationalpost.com/full-comment/david-frum-on-the-quebec-student-riots-grandpas-free-ride. Used with permission of the author.

This intergenerational approach rejects the growing tendency to isolate different age groups, particularly at the beginning and later stages of life, and encourages intergenerational programs, practices, and policies. These initiatives have become increasingly popular because the benefits to old and young participants are visible and immediate. All of the key informants who were interviewed in the preparation of this background paper recommended increased support for intergenerational activities to enhance healthy aging (p. 10).

This debate over the cost of an older population will continue. And the growing size of the older population will draw attention to the costs of public pensions, healthcare, and other services. But blaming older people for this shift in resources allocation will not lead to a better life for older or younger people. Longino (2005) said that the challenge of an older population "can generate creative answers, many of which are unknowable ahead of time" (p. 83). Gerontologists can provide the public with good information about the costs and the benefits of social policies.

We all have parents and grandparents. We'll all be old someday. We want to live in a society that cares for people at every age.

TIME TO REVIEW

Describe the general pattern of intergenerational relations in Canada.

Support the position that older people deserve their government benefits.

Explain the Canadian government's view of intergenerational relations.

CONCLUSION

In a ranking of countries based on the question: "How well is your government responding to the challenges that an ageing population brings?" Global AgeWatch (2014) placed Canada number four in the world (behind Norway, Sweden, and Switzerland). This should lead to some optimism about the future of aging in Canada.

Canada's government and people have dedicated themselves to the elimination of ageism. However, this goal cannot be achieved through a policy statement, the stroke of a pen, or a speech. Canadians need to understand that people of all ages make up the fabric of a good and just society. And a high quality of life at all ages benefits everyone. The more Canadians understand about

aging, through research and public discussion, the more Canada can realize the vision of a society for all ages.

Gerontology can play an important role in creating a good old age. It can help us understand the facts and the issues related to aging. It can move discussion from fear, stereotype, prejudice, and discrimination to understanding. Gerontology shows that old age forms a normal part of the life cycle. Nearly all of us will enter old age someday, and we'll bring with us the attitudes and experiences of a lifetime. Gerontology can help overcome ageism by presenting a more balanced and accurate view of aging and older people. It can change people's attitudes toward aging and give them more knowledge about their families, their friends, and themselves.

Summary

1. The growth of the older population in Canada has made aging a major social issue—one that will affect us all.

2. Gerontology has two goals: first, to increase our knowledge about old age and, second, to improve the quality of later life. In Canada today, these goals take the form of scholarly research and the practical application of research findings.

3. Canadians have both positive and negative images of aging and older people. Many of these stereotypes have little basis in fact. Negative attitudes can lead to prejudice and discrimination against older people.

4. New images of aging have begun to emerge. These include the image of the ever-youthful person; the active, engaged senior; and the older person who accepts aging and the physical changes it brings.

5. A growing population of healthy and active older people will lead Canadians to rethink their views of aging. Gerontology tries to replace stereotypes with facts, information, and a clearer understanding of later life.

6. Population aging has led to a new form of ageism. Some writers scapegoat the older population and blame older people for rising pension and healthcare costs. Gerontologists refute these claims and present a more balanced view of Canadian society in the future.

7. Education can play an important role in combating ageism. Experiential learning and service learning gives young people a more realistic and positive view of old age.

8. The Canadian government supports the elimination of ageism and the improvement of older people's lives. The government supports a society where people of all ages can get the social support they need—and people can live full and happy lives at every age.

STUDY QUESTIONS

1. Give three reasons why students should know about aging in Canada.
2. State three common myths about aging. Explain why these myths are false.
3. What is ageism? Where do negative attitudes toward aging come from? How can people develop a more positive attitude toward aging?
4. How has the image of the older consumer changed in the past few years? Explain why older consumers have become a force in the marketplace. What types of products do older consumers prefer?
5. What types of education can give younger people a more balanced view of later life?
6. How will an aging population affect social structures like education, healthcare, and the family?
7. Why do some writers predict intergenerational conflict? Do you think this will take place in Canada? Why or why not?
8. What do policymakers mean by "a society for all ages"?

KEY TERMS

ageism (p. 7)
anti-aging industry (p. 13)
discrimination (p. 3)
elderspeak (p. 6)
gerontology (p. 2)
intergenerational equity (p. 17)
prejudice (p. 2)
social structure (p. 2)
society for all ages (p. 17)
stereotypes (p. 6)

ANSWER TO QUIZ IN EXHIBIT 1.1

All 10 statements are false.

Study Tools
CHAPTER 1

Located at retail.tophat.com:

- Review Key Terms with interactive and printable flash cards
- Check Your Comprehension and Think About chapter concepts by completing practice quizzes
- Develop Your Gerontological Imagination with class activities
- Analyze Aging in a Global Perspective with engaging case studies and critical thinking questions
- Demonstrate Your Knowledge of the Concepts by bringing your own experience to personal application questions
- Evaluate Aging in the Media by completing Internet activities with evaluation questions

CHAPTER 2

THEORIES AND METHODS

Robert Kneschke/Shutterstock

LEARNING OBJECTIVES

After reading this chapter, you will

LO1 Know the three main areas of gerontological study.

LO2 Be able to name and describe the three major theoretical perspectives used in the study of aging.

LO3 Understand the strengths and limitations of interpretive, functionalist, and positivist perspectives and theories.

LO4 Appreciate the importance of the life course approach to the study of aging and be able to explain the details of this perspective.

LO5 Understand how age, period, and cohort (APC) effects influence research findings and how researchers try to disentangle these effects.

LO6 Be able to discuss the difference between cross-sectional and longitudinal research and understand the usefulness and limitations of each type of study.

LO7 Know the importance of ethical practices in the conduct of research.

LO8 Appreciate the growth of large-scale research on aging in Canada and its potential for improving social policies and programs for older people.

INTRODUCTION

Thirty-five years ago, the Gerontological Society of America and the Association for Gerontology in Higher Education set out to define the discipline of gerontology (Foundations Project, 1980). They asked 111 scholars, researchers, and professionals in the field to describe a basic education program in gerontology. These experts came from disciplines as different as biomedicine and economics, and their descriptions of the exact content and boundaries of gerontology varied. But they did agree that three broad areas of study should make up the core of a gerontology curriculum: *biomedicine, psychosocial studies*, and *socioeconomic-environmental studies*. Now, more than three decades later, these areas remain central to the study of aging.

The first area, biomedicine, looks at the changes in physiology and health that come with age. This area includes studies of the biochemical causes of aging, studies of reaction time and stress, and studies of Alzheimer's disease and other types of dementia. Experts disagreed least about the curriculum content for this area; this may be due to the long tradition of biomedical research on aging.

The second area, psychosocial studies, examines the changes that take place within individuals and between individuals and groups. This includes studies of memory, learning, and personality, as well as research on family and friendship ties, and recreation and leisure activities of older adults.

The third area, socioeconomic-environmental studies, concentrates on the effects of aging on social structures such as healthcare and education. It also looks at the effects of social structures on the aging individual and includes the study of income policies, healthcare systems, and formal social supports.

Social gerontology includes psychosocial, socioeconomic-environmental, and practice-related research. It looks at aging from the points of view of both the

---

social gerontology a subfield within the wider field of gerontology; it focuses on the social side of aging, while other subfields study the physical and biological aspects of aging

---

EXHIBIT 2.1 *Three Areas of Gerontology Study*

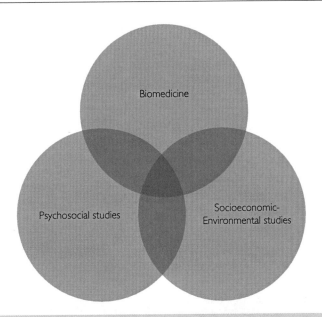

Many research projects today take an *interdisciplinary* perspective. Large studies may include researchers from medicine, physiology, psychology, sociology, statistics, and economics (Oveisgharan & Hachinski, 2010). The *Canadian Study of Health and Aging*, a national study of Alzheimer's disease, for example, included researchers from the social and physical sciences. This study assessed the prevalence of dementia (neuropsychology and epidemiology), the risk factors associated with the disease (medicine and public health), and caregiver burden (social psychology). The overlapping areas of Exhibit 2.1 show where interdisciplinary work would be done.

Sometimes a study takes a *multidisciplinary* approach. In this type of study, researchers from various fields work side by side and share a data set. But they may not integrate their findings into a new way of understanding a research question.

individual and the social system. Social gerontologists often take an interest in physical and healthcare changes that come with age. But the focus of the social gerontologist differs from that of the physiologist or biochemist. When social gerontologists look at biological or physical change in old age, they ask how these changes affect the individual's social life or society as a whole. They want to know how diseases in old age affect hospital costs or how changes in lung capacity affect a person's ability to work.

They also want to know how a social norm such as retirement affects an older person's health, how changes in family life in Canada affect the psychological well-being of older adults, or what counselling methods work best with new retirees. Researchers use a variety of methods to examine these and other questions, and they use gerontological theory to interpret their findings. This chapter will look at (1) the theories that gerontologists use to guide their research and to interpret their findings, (2) the methods researchers use to gather data, and (3) current and future developments in Canadian research on aging.

THEORY IN THE STUDY OF AGING

Sociologists define a theory as a set of statements about how and why facts about the social world relate to one another (Macionis & Gerber, 2010). Some theories make specific predictions about future events. Other theories provide a broad perspective on social life. A good theory helps a researcher choose research methods, questions, and samples. Bengtson and colleagues (2009; also Marshall & Bengtson, 2011) said, "Theories are like lenses. Look at an object through one kind of lens, and the viewer will see one thing; look at it through another lens, and the viewer will be able to see something different" (p. 5). Bengtson and Schaie (1999, p. 5) identify four ways that theory is valuable to researchers. Theory

1. allows for the integration of new knowledge with information that is already known on the topic or issue;
2. provides a framework for the explanation of findings;
3. predicts outcomes in future research;
4. provides practical information for the development of social programs and interventions.

Theories create a structure that explains why things happen the way they do. For instance, research shows that, compared to men, women get more of their retirement income from public pension sources. Why does this difference exist? And is this an important finding or

a trivial fact? Theory offers a framework for explaining research findings and for building knowledge and understanding. Feminist theory, for example, would trace this difference to gender inequalities in the workplace.

Consider the following case. Marianne, age 65, worked as a homemaker for most of her adult life. She raised four children. When they grew up and left home, she retired to a quiet life—gym in the morning, coffee with friends, some shopping in the afternoon, cooking dinner for her husband and herself, then watching TV and reading in the evening. She worked in the labour force for only a year or so before her first child was born. So she did not make enough payments into the Canada Pension Plan to receive benefits in her old age. Instead, she will rely on her husband's benefits as she ages.

Women like Marianne have little or no opportunity to pay into private pension plans during their middle years. This forces them to rely on public pension sources in old age, and it forces some older women to live in poverty. A life course perspective would see the issue differently. It would focus on women's choices and the circumstances they face throughout life. Women, for example, take on home caregiving tasks and this affects their patterns of employment and their pensions.

Theory provides an interpretation of the facts, but no single theory in gerontology can explain all of the facts about aging. And sometimes a researcher will use several theories to explain the results of a study. Authors often select theories to fit their sense of how the world works. If you know the assumptions that underlie a theory, you know the strengths and limitations of using that theory and the biases that each theory brings to the explanation of results. The theory used will guide the collection of data as well as how those data are interpreted.

Social gerontologists have generally used sociological or social-psychological theories in their work. Sometimes they have adapted these theories to fit the study of aging. Theory helps to disentangle the effects of history, biology, and social life on the aging person.

Two Levels of Theory

Theories describe all sorts of human activity and relationships, from individual attitudes to societal structures. The following discussion categorizes theories by placing them into a framework (see Exhibit 2.2). The discussion also gives examples of how gerontologists apply these theories in their work.

Gerontologists often classify theories into two categories or levels of theory: (1) micro level and (2) macro level. But be aware that sometimes these levels overlap and some theories bridge both categories.

EXHIBIT 2.2 *Theories in the Study of Aging*

Levels of Theory		
Micro		**Macro**
individual social interaction		social structures, social processes
Theoretical Perspectives		
Interpretive	**Functionalist**	**Conflict**
how individuals define and create their social world	social order based on cooperation and consensus	society based on conflict between social groups
Theories		
social constructionism	structural functionalism	political economy
symbolic interactionism	age stratification	feminist perspectives
social phenomenology	life course	moral economy
ethnomethodology	disengagement	
social exchange	continuity	
	activity	
	modernization	

This chart presents the most influential theories in the study of aging. It summarizes the discussion in the text.

Micro-level theories focus on individuals and their interactions. They are used to explain phenomena such as the relationship between adult children and their parents, changes in memory with age, and the effect of negative attitudes on an older person's self-image. **Macro-level theories** explain phenomena such as the effect of industrialization on older people's social status, the history and impact of public pensions on poverty rates in later life, and how gender and income affect older people's well-being. Critics of micro-level theories say they focus too much on people's actions and interactions. They ignore or take little account of economic conditions and social policies. Critics of macro-level theories say that this approach tends to minimize people's ability to act and overcome the limits of social structures.

TIME TO REVIEW

Why do gerontologists use more than one theory in their work?

What challenges do researchers face when they try to do interdisciplinary work?

Why is it easier to do multidisciplinary rather than interdisciplinary work?

Why is theory important in the study of aging?

Explain the difference between micro-level and macro-level theories.

Three Theoretical Perspectives

Both micro-level and macro-level theories can take one of three perspectives: (1) the interpretive perspective, (2) the functionalist perspective, or (3) the conflict perspective.

The Interpretive Perspective

The interpretive perspective focuses almost exclusively on the micro level of social life. It looks at how people define situations, how they create their social world, and how they relate to one another in daily life. Historically, social gerontologists have made the least use of this perspective, although interest in this approach has increased significantly in the last few decades. Theories

micro-level theories focus on individuals and their interactions; they are used to explain phenomena such as the relationship between adult children and their parents, changes in memory with age, and the effect of negative attitudes on older people's self-esteem

macro-level theories "examine social structures or structural elements as they influence experiences and behaviors" (Bengtson, Burgess, & Parrott, 1997, p. S76)

interpretive perspective focuses almost exclusively on the micro level of social life; it looks at how people define situations, how they create social order, and how they relate to one another in daily life within this perspective include social exchange theory (Homans, 1961; Liang, Krause, & Bennett, 2001), the symbolic interactionist perspective (Mead, 1934), social phenomenology (Berger & Luckmann, 1966), and ethnomethodology (Garfinkel, 1967). The term social constructionism has come to represent many of these interpretive approaches (Holstein & Gubrium, 2008; Powell & Hendricks, 2009). Nikander (2009) said that social constructionism "recast(s) ageing as a topic to be studied as an interactional, situational and social process" (p. 866). It has its foundations in the early work of Max Weber (1905, 1955) and George Herbert Mead (1934).

Mead, for example, said that objects and events have no meaning in themselves. People give them meaning through everyday interaction. Grey hair can be a sign of wisdom in one society but a sign of decline in another. People give meanings to objects and then base their actions on those meanings. For example, some people refuse to wear a hearing aid because to them it symbolizes decrepitude and weakness. The interpretive perspective views the individual as a creator of social order and organization. This perspective asks the question "How is a recognizable, predictable social order created?" (Berger & Luckmann, 1966; Garfinkel, 1967; Schutz, 1967). The interpretive perspective can give a good understanding of how people interpret their social world, how they interact with one another, and why they do what they do.

Social phenomenologists take a more extreme view. They speak of "the social construction of reality." They view social order as a creation of everyday interaction. Social phenomenologists often look at conversation to find the methods people use to maintain social relations. For example, if I ask, "How are you?" you understand that I don't want to hear about your athlete's foot. You answer, "Fine." We smile and move on.

A doctor who asks this same question wants to know about your health. You give a different answer to this question in a doctor's office. If you answer, "Fine," the doctor may probe and ask some very personal questions. You assume this is part of the doctor's job. A social phenomenologist studies the way that a doctor's conversation builds and creates a social reality that we call "the medical exam."

Interpretive studies that focus on language "can 'give voice' to people as individual informants" (Coupland, 2009, p. 851). For example, a report on conversations with people who live in retirement communities shows how these people understand their own condition (Norrick, 2009). Interviews with older Japanese women (Matsumoto, 2009) and a study of Baby Boom female caregivers in Quebec gave insight into these people's social world.

Schaefer (2010) studied the experience of older adult students who attended college classes. The students' children had grown up, so they no longer needed to spend time on child-rearing. This allowed them to return to school. Schaefer conducted in-depth interviews and used questionnaires to study nine of these students age 50 to 62. She felt that higher education institutions do not necessarily meet the needs of older learners, so she set out to understand these students' experiences in college. She wanted to understand what was "personally meaningful" to them.

This study explored students' past education experiences and their future goals, what brought them to higher education, and what supports they found useful in their program. Schaefer located her study within the tradition of social phenomenology. This allowed her to understand what is "real and meaningful" to the students. Schaefer reported the students' experiences in their own words.

One student said, in explaining her return to school, "I think I went through a big, serious empty nest problem there. It was just this loss—what do I do now?" Another student expressed emotions related to her role as homemaker. "I felt so isolated," she said. "I think that's primarily what it was. I felt so isolated at home day in, day out, taking care of children, taking care of the home, and not getting out in the real world because, you know, he wouldn't let me work either outside the home."

These students discovered a new role for themselves through a return to school. Schaefer also found that the students faced unique challenges. One student said, "This was walking through a whole new door I hadn't been to in years, and things had changed considerably. There was a lot of confusion of what I needed to do to start, the fear of getting started" (pp. 74–86).

These expressions of doubt and uncertainty give a rich understanding of these students' lives as they entered higher education. The interpretive perspective allows us to see and understand the world from the student's point of view. This type of study provides rich information about these students' life transition. Administrators of higher education can use these insights to create more responsive programs for older learners.

The interpretive perspective has weaknesses as well as strengths. For example, it gives only the subjective or individual point of view on social life. It tends to ignore the connections that exist between micro-level social interactions and the larger social forces or structures in society. This means that it cannot answer many of the "big picture" questions that gerontologists ask. The interpretive perspective, for example, cannot tell us about the social forces that kept Schaefer's students from higher education until later life. It also says little about power and conflict between social groups. For example, it cannot explain income inequality between men and women in old age or the effects of ethnicity on social status in later life. Fortunately, the functionalist and conflict perspectives allow gerontologists to examine these questions.

The Functionalist Perspective

The **functionalist perspective** fits within a **positivist worldview**. It holds that social order is based on consensus, cooperation, and shared norms and values. Within this perspective, all parts of society serve a role or function that keeps society in a state of balance or equilibrium. While the interpretive perspective asks, "How do people create their social world through interaction with one another?" the functionalist perspective asks, "What is the structure of the society that people live in and how do the parts of this structure function?"

The structural functionalist theories that grew out of Émile Durkheim's work in 19th-century France best express the traditional functionalist perspective (Parsons, 1937, 1951). Durkheim's studies, such as *The Division of Labor in Society* and *Suicide: A Study in Sociology*, serve as models for this approach. Structural functionalist theories treat society as a system that consists of social institutions such as the family, the military, and schools.

Structural functionalism sometimes draws the analogy between society and a living organism, such as the human body. Just as our bodies adjust to an increase in our blood sugar, so society adjusts to changes in its internal condition. An increase in the number of older people, for example, may lead society to increase funding for health promotion programs or invest more resources in long-term care homes. Structural functionalism predicts that when there is a social change, society will attempt to create an orderly transition to a new stable state.

Structural functionalism also assumes that shared norms and values shape individual behaviour. People conform to these norms through social pressure but also through their belief in society's underlying value system. The values expressed in the commandment "Honour thy father and mother," for example, show up in everyday behaviour and in social policies. Failure to honour or respect a parent may lead to informal sanctions, such as criticism from a sibling or grandparent. Extreme neglect of a parent may lead to the charge of abuse and legal sanctions. Functionalism draws connections between large-scale (macro) social structures and individuals' social roles and actions.

Finally, structural functionalism assumes that society changes or evolves in a positive direction. It explains social problems as dysfunctions, and it proposes to correct these dysfunctions through the use of experts in planning and the helping professions. So, for example, society uses social workers, counsellors, and other experts at shelters and resource centres to address homelessness among older people.

Historically, gerontologists used the functionalist perspective more than any other perspective in their study of aging. Gerontology's most influential early theories—disengagement theory (Cumming & Henry, 1961), activity theory (Neugarten, Havighurst, & Tobin, 1968), continuity theory, and modernization theory (Cowgill & Holmes, 1972)—all rely on structural functionalist assumptions. Riley (1971, 1987; Riley, Foner, & Waring, 1988; Riley, Johnson, & Foner, 1972) also produced a dominant theory based on structural functionalist principles: age stratification theory.

Age stratification theory is also called the "aging and society paradigm" (Riley, 1994; Riley, Foner, & Riley, Jr., 1999). This theory says that lifespan development can be understood as "the process by which human lives are shaped by the social institutions—family, education, work, and leisure—through which they passed on their developmental journey" (Silverstein & Giarrusso, 2011, p. 38). Age stratification theory focuses on the movement of **age cohorts** over the life course. It identifies similarities and differences between and among different age cohorts. Gerontologists define an age cohort as a group of people born in the same period of time. All of the people born between 1950 and 1955, for example, form an age cohort.

---

functionalist perspective holds that social order is based on consensus, cooperation, and shared norms and values, and that all parts of society serve a role or function to keep society in a state of balance or equilibrium; structural functionalism predicts that when there is social change, society will attempt to create an orderly transition to a new, stable state

positivist worldview based on the belief that knowledge is built by studying observable facts and their relationship to one another

age stratification theory focuses on the movement of age cohorts over the life course and on "the role of social structures in the process of individual aging and the stratification by age in the society" (Bengtson, Burgess, & Parott, 1997, p. S81)

age cohort a group of people born in the same period of time; for example, all of the people born between 1950 and 1955 form an age cohort

According to age stratification theory, people in each cohort move or flow through society's predetermined **age grades** as they age. Childhood, adolescence, and young adulthood are all age grades in Canada. As mentioned in Chapter 1, gerontologists now speak of a Third Age that has emerged in Canada. This occurs after retirement but before physical decline and dependence take place in late old age (the Fourth Age).

People born in the same period experience the transitions from one stage to another at roughly the same time. Gerontologists refer to this as "the standardized life course" (Marshall & Bengtson, 2011, p. 23). A tightly standardized life course, for example, has all children in school by age five and moves them through the education system year by year. Likewise, a tightly standardized system has universal retirement at a specific age. A looser system allows for more variability in the life course. We see this today as people choose to retire earlier or later than the traditional age of 65.

Age stratification theorists say that society also changes as people age, so the norms and roles learned by each new cohort change as society changes. The norms of adult behaviour that people learn in their childhood, for example, may no longer fit when these same people reach adulthood. Many older people today were taught in their childhood that sex outside marriage was immoral. Now, due to the death of a spouse or the influence of changing values and lifestyles of their children and grandchildren, many older people have changed their views on sex outside marriage. Similarly, many younger people will rethink their own values as they age and as society changes.

Age cohorts constantly move along as if on an escalator. As one group leaves an age grade, a new group takes its place. Each age grade (childhood, adolescence, young adulthood, and so on) places expectations on its members and offers people new roles. Also, each successive cohort brings new norms and values to its age grade.

This leads to a dialectic between individuals and societal structures. Changes in norms and values bring changes in social organizations. These changes, in turn, shape the process of aging. For example, new cohorts of older people, with interests in travel and lifelong learning, will affect the traditional programs offered in senior centres. Some senior centres will close because they do not meet the demands of these new older adults. Others will remain open by adapting their programs to meet the changing needs and interests of newer cohorts of older people. These changes in programs will also change the way younger and middle-aged people think about later life.

Age stratification theory has a number of strengths. First, it has helped to separate age differences (between cohorts) from age changes over the life course (aging). Second, it highlights the impact of historical and social changes on individuals and cohorts. Third, it shows the relationship between aging and social structures.

This perspective also has its weaknesses. For example, people of the same age do not all experience the world in the same way. An elderly Chinese woman who has just arrived in Canada will see the world differently from an elderly French Canadian man born in Montreal. The age stratification theory overlooks each person's interpretation of the world. It makes little reference to individual control or action. The theory also makes little reference to the tensions and conflicts between social groups in society or to issues of power.

There is also little focus in age stratification theory on how characteristics such as gender, social class, race, and ethnicity create inequalities within age cohorts. For example, it says little about the differences between growing old as a poor black woman compared with growing old as an upper-middle-class white male. Such variations within cohorts may have a greater influence on people's lives and their experiences of aging than the norms and values related to their age grade. A person's race or gender will lead to different behaviours and to different experiences in and responses to sociohistorical events. A person's race or gender will also shape the choices he or she has available. For example, a policy change such as a decrease in government pension payments will have different effects on poor older women and wealthy older men.

Although age stratification theory has its limits, it has made a major contribution to our understanding of aging. It orders many complex phenomena and helps us to see the relationship between the individual and society.

The **life course perspective** has gained prominence among gerontology theorists and researchers (Marshall & Bengtson, 2011; Mayer, 2009). This perspective bridges the micro and macro levels of analysis by incorporating

---

age grades a concept used in age stratification theory to describe periods of life defined by society, such as childhood, adolescence, and young adulthood

life course perspective a functionalist approach that bridges the micro and macro levels of analysis by incorporating social interaction and social structure within its framework; begins with the idea that life unfolds from birth to death in a social, cultural, and historical context; looks at the impact of social institutions, historical periods and events, personal biography, life cycle stage, life events, and resources on the older person social interaction and social structure within its framework. In this way, the life course perspective overcomes some of the limitations of age stratification theory and the functionalist perspective. Researchers use this perspective to explain (1) the continuity and change in individuals' lives over time, (2) age-related and socially recognized life transitions, and (3) the interaction of social life, history, culture, and personal biography (Moen & Spencer, 2006; Settersten, 2006). At the micro or individual level, the life course approach looks at how events and conditions early in life can affect later life.

Life course studies show that experiences compound over time and lead to the outcome we call old age. This applies to physical changes—how much sunscreen a person uses in middle age influences how much their skin wrinkles in old age. It applies to finances—how much a person saves in a pension plan or savings account influences that person's financial well-being in later life. It applies to relationships—a person's choice to marry or stay single will influence that person's family life and social supports in old age.

Hess (1990, p. 12) wrote that the conditions older women face in later life, such as poverty, "are not unique to that life stage but are continuous, with patterned inequalities throughout the life course." The life course approach encourages us to think about the many individual and social forces that affect life in old age. It looks at old age as a unique period, but also as an outcome of earlier stages in life.

Elder and Johnson (2003) describe five principles of the life course perspective:

1. People develop and age at every stage of life.
2. The historical conditions and people's environment influence his or her experiences and opportunities in life.
3. The impact of life transitions (such as marriage or retirement) vary, depending on when they take place in a person's life.
4. People live interdependently. Their lives are influenced by the lives of others in their social network.
5. Individuals shape their lives through action and by making choices.

This perspective recognizes diversity within age cohorts due to differences in race, ethnicity, social class, and gender.

Zarit (2009) gave an example of how a life course perspective helps us understand change in later life. He described how earlier life experiences affect mental disorder in old age. Zarit said that major depressive disorder (MDD) shows up in about 1 to 5 percent of older people.

But research shows that MDD rarely shows up for the first time in old age. New cases, Zarit said, steadily decline after age 30 (with a slight increase after age 75). Anxiety disorders show the same pattern. Most people face anxiety disorder first in adolescence or young adulthood. These mental disorders form a lifelong pattern of disturbance.

Denton, Feaver, and Spencer (2010) used the life course perspective to study involuntary retirement by people with disabilities. Compared with the general population, people with a disability have a much higher rate of involuntary retirement. This study traced involuntary retirement (a later life event) to a person's earlier life—their education, skills, and work history. The study also linked involuntary retirement to historical trends such as globalization and changes in the economy.

"[The life course] perspective," the researchers said, "emphasizes the timing by which individuals and families make their transitions into and out of various roles, such as retirement, in relation to the timing of society. It emphasizes the ... cumulative impact of earlier life events as shaped by historical forces on subsequent events, in other words past experiences matter" (pp. 15–16).

At the macro or societal level, the life course approach shows how social change and historical events can create differences between cohorts (Mayer, 2009). Consider the introduction of personal computers into everyday life. A study of online activities shows the effect of the information technology revolution on different age cohorts. Veenhof and Timusk (2009) compared Internet use by younger and older age groups and found that in 2003, 94 percent of 15- to 24-year-olds used the Internet. In that year, only 28 percent of people age 65 to 74 used the Internet, and only 9 percent of people age 75 and over used the Internet. This study shows the effect of a large-scale social change (the introduction of the Internet) on different age cohorts.

Researchers tend to agree that no unified, systematic approach to the life course exists. Rather, a life course perspective merges theoretical approaches from many disciplines, including sociology, anthropology, and psychology (Settersten, 2003, 2006). The life course approach recognizes variety in life course patterns. It also recognizes diversity within age cohorts due to differences in race, ethnicity, social class, and gender.

This approach takes into account the diversity of roles and role changes across the life course. The life course approach recognizes aging as a lifelong, dynamic, interactive, and multidirectional process. For example, an older person may show some loss of memory over time, but stay physically active and take up new activities in later life. Aging involves both continuity and change—decline in some areas of life, stability or improvement in others.

The life course approach looks at **transitions** and **trajectories**. Transitions refer to changes in social status or social roles (when those changes occur, how long they last, etc.). Transitions include marriage, divorce, remarriage, widowhood, and parenthood. Work-related transitions also occur; for example, getting a first job, changing careers, or retiring.

Trajectories refer to long-term patterns of stability and change. They often include many transitions. One person's marital status trajectory may involve the transition to marriage, a subsequent divorce, then a remarriage, and finally a transition to widowhood. Another person's marital status trajectory may involve only one marriage for life. This latter trajectory involves only the transition to a first marriage and, for one of the couple, the transition to widowhood.

The life course approach has made a number of contributions to the study of aging. First, it bridges the macro and micro levels of analysis by recognizing the importance of social structures and historical context, as well as individual experiences and meanings. It helps us to understand the diversity within and between cohorts. Second, the approach brings together sociological, psychological, anthropological, and historical approaches to the study of aging. Third, the life course approach highlights the interdependence of people's lives over time. It also shows the complexity of individual life paths. Finally, the life course approach understands aging as a dynamic process that takes place throughout life.

The life course perspective appreciates the link between earlier stages of adulthood and later life. Research on topics like diet, health and illness, family life, and work all show the impact of earlier life conditions on old age. For example, women more often than men show an interrupted work history. This leads to lower incomes for women in midlife and also poorer pensions and lower incomes in old age. Likewise, a divorce or the decision to stay single may lead to less in-home support in later life. The decision to have children may mean more available informal support in old age. Poor nutrition in childhood can lead to poor health in old age.

Mayer (2009, p. 416), in a review of life course research, said that life course studies have moved beyond early theoretical formulations. Longitudinal studies that follow cohorts over time now exist in many developed nations (e.g., the United States, Great Britain, Japan). These studies will allow researchers to test theories and explore the connections between earlier and later stages of life. These studies also encourage interdisciplinary research. Studies of health across the life span often apply the life course approach. They trace the effects of later life conditions to health earlier in life. And they point to socioeconomic conditions that lead to different health outcomes in old age.

The life course approach has some limitations. Its broad focus on society, culture, and the individual makes it hard to define as a single theory. Life course long-term studies differ in their findings. Some research shows a strong link between earlier and later life, other research shows only weak links. This raises a question about the general assumption of effects across the life span.

Mayer (2009, p. 416) said that research on and theoretical development of the life course "still has a long way to go." He described four goals for future work on the life course:

1. Large sample studies over time need to study what conditions in early life lead to effects in old age.
2. Studies across countries need to look at the effects of policies and social contexts on the life course.
3. Studies need to look at the interaction of psychological dispositions and life course patterns.
4. Studies need to look at the interaction of individual development and social contexts.
5. Although it has its limits, the life course approach encourages us to think about the many individual and social forces that affect aging.

TIME to REVIEW

What is the difference between a transition and a trajectory?

Explain why the age stratification theory is a functionalist theory.

Explain how the life course perspective extends the insights of the age stratification theory.

What contribution does the life course perspective make to the study of aging?

Can you identify historical or social events that have shaped your life and will influence your experience in old age?

What is an age cohort? Can you identify events or conditions that will influence your cohort as you age?

---

transitions changes in social status or social roles such as marriage, parenthood, divorce, remarriage, and widowhood

trajectories long-term patterns of stability and change that often include many transitions

THE LIFE COURSE AND SOCIAL CONTEXT

Life course researchers study three types of environmental effects: (1) non-normative events (unexpected events such as illnesses, layoffs, and accidents); (2) normative history-graded events (historical events that shape a person's life, such as the Great Depression of the 1930s or World War II); and (3) normative age-graded events (socially sanctioned events that occur most often at a certain age, like marriage or retirement).

Non-Normative Events

Sociologists define norms as shared rules or guidelines that prescribe correct behaviour under certain conditions. Every society has age norms that prescribe how a person of a certain age should act. University students, for example, can travel across the country with backpacks each summer, see Europe by rail, and sleep in hostels or open fields. People accept this behaviour from the young, and they even expect students to take time off to travel. Social scientists call this a normative life event.

People can also go through **non-normative events**, including accidents, sudden changes in health, or the death of a child. Social psychologists call these events non-normative because not everyone experiences them and because people cannot plan for them.

History-Graded Events

Non-normative events describe sudden changes in a person's personal life, but **normative history-graded events** change the lives of many age cohorts. The term cohort describes a group of people born at the same point or within the same period of time (usually five or ten years).

The cohort born between 1945 and 1955 (60- to 70-year-olds in 2015), for example, expect different things from life and from society than do other age cohorts. These people belong to one of the largest cohorts in Canadian history. Canada built elementary schools for them when they were children in the 1950s and 1960s and universities for them in the 1960s and 1970s, and the

private sector built housing for them in the 1980s. They have lived through a relatively peaceful, affluent time in Canada's history, and they expect more from society than do older age groups.

As cohorts age (and members die), cohorts replace one another in society's age structure. Riley, Johnson, and Foner (1972) called this "cohort flow." As cohorts flow through the age structure, they change the size of particular age groups (e.g., the size of the group 20 to 30 years old differed in 1940 and 1970 and 2010). New cohorts also bring new experiences with them as they age. The oldest cohorts of seniors today, for example, have less education than younger cohorts of seniors. The higher educational attainment of young-old cohorts explains this change. These cohorts enter later life with more postsecondary diplomas and university education. Future cohorts will enter later life with even more education (Turcotte & Schellenberg, 2007). Seniors in the future may demand new educational opportunities as they age.

The model of aging used by Riley and her colleagues (1972) omits a few important concepts about aging and age grading. Historical events, for example, also get filtered through the age stratification system, the system of age grades a society uses (e.g., child, adolescent, young adult). The 1920 to 1930 cohort went through the Great Depression of the 1930s in childhood and adolescence. The Depression affected their health (due to poor diet) and their educational opportunities (some had to work at an early age to help support their families).

The Depression also affected the cohort born between 1930 and 1940, but it had a different effect on these people. They lived through the Depression as infants and children. Some of them may not remember the Depression at all; others may simply have accepted the hard times as "the way things are."

Gerontologists use the term *generation* to describe people who share an awareness of their common historical or cultural experiences but who may come from different age cohorts. The Baby Boom generation spans cohorts born between 1945 and the early 1960s; they all lived under the threat of nuclear war, they lived through the turbulent political times of the 1960s, and they lived through a relatively affluent time in Canadian history.

Studies show the effect of social and historical events on individual personality. Like non-normative events, history-graded events happen without warning, and sometimes the changes they bring about do not show up until years later. Society also shapes personality growth more directly through normative age grading.

---

non-normative events unexpected events such as illnesses, layoffs, and accidents

normative history-graded events shape the lives of many age cohorts, such as the Great Depression of the 1930s or World War II

Normative Age-Graded Events

Anthropologists report that all societies move people through a series of age grades, called **normative age-graded events**. Age grades define certain rights and responsibilities for their members. They give order to the life course and help people judge their own development.

Industrialized society today includes the stages of infancy, childhood, adolescence, young adulthood, middle age, and old age. As mentioned earlier, some writers have now added a new stage, the Third Age, after middle age, but before late old age (the Fourth Age) begins. This new stage makes sense in a society where people can expect to live in good health for 15 years or more after age 65.

People internalize the age-grade system and know the proper time for a life event to occur. A Canadian middle-class girl who falls in love today at the age of 14 will feel it is too early to marry. A woman graduate student in her early 20s may also feel it is too early to settle down. A single woman in her late 40s who wants to get married may feel she is late.

Someone for whom major life events come early or late—a teenaged mother or a newlywed octogenarian—may feel out of sync with the age-status system. Gerontologists call this **age-status asynchronization**.

People can be on time in certain ways and late or early in others. They can feel on time when they choose to marry but late in advancing in their profession. Research shows that occupation, ethnic background, and social class affect the timing of life events.

For example, Canadian women with less education tend to marry earlier and have children earlier. Today, many highly educated young women put off marriage and child-rearing in order to start their careers. Women, compared to men, go through different life events. Men typically start a career in their early 20s and stay in the labour force until retirement, but a woman may enter a new phase of life in her late 40s. At that time, her last child leaves home, menopause occurs, and she may re-enter the labour market and begin a new career.

Researchers have increased their interest in life events, life transitions, and life trajectories. This increased interest may reflect recent changes in the timing and sequencing of life events. Women show more diverse patterns of development than ever before, as a result of changing social values, birth control, new career options, more education, and the need for two earners in a family.

The life course model says that a more complete picture of human development requires knowledge of a person's life events and social context. This approach shows that society and history play important parts in shaping individual development.

TIME TO REVIEW

What life events can lead to psychological problems in later life?

What life events can lead to life satisfaction?

How does gender influence a person throughout the life course?

What effect do gender roles have on women and men in later life?

The Conflict Perspective

The conflict perspective holds that society consists of conflicts between dominant and subordinate social groups. Historically, few gerontologists have used the **conflict perspective** in their work. But in recent decades an interest in this perspective has developed. For example, researchers understand that social and structural inequalities experienced earlier in life can lead to poverty and other disadvantages in later life. Also, studies show that women are more likely than men to earn less income, work part-time, or have disrupted work histories due to child care or care of other family members. Public and private pension programs tend to reward those with higher incomes and stable work histories. This means that many women will be financially disadvantaged in their later years.

Researchers who use the conflict perspective study the causes of poverty in later life, women and gender discrimination, the multiple disadvantages facing older ethnic and Indigenous peoples, the ideology of aging as a social problem, and pensions and policies.

The **political economy theory** that grew out of the work of Karl Marx exemplifies the conflict perspective. This theory focuses on conflict and change in social life. It traces this conflict to the struggle between social classes and to the resulting dominance of some

normative age-graded events socially sanctioned events that occur most often at a certain age, like marriage or retirement

age-status asynchronization someone for whom major life events come early or late—a teenaged mother or a newlywed octogenarian—may feel out of sync with the age-status system in Canada.

conflict perspective holds that society consists of conflicts between dominant and subordinate social groups

political economy theory focuses on conflict and change in social life; it traces this conflict to the struggle between social classes and to the resulting dominance of some groups in society and the subordination of others

groups in society and the subordination of others (Kail, Quadagno, & Keene, 2009).

Marxist theory holds, for example, that if managers view older workers as slower and weaker, they will also see these workers as less useful to industry as they age. Therefore, companies will tend to fire or retire older workers and replace them with younger workers who will work faster and for lower wages. Today's information technology (IT) age links youthfulness with technical expertise. As IT workers age, they become marginalized from technical positions (Comeau & Kemp, 2007). It is young workers (typically young males) who are most desirable in the IT industry. As Comeau and Kemp suggested, "these links between youth and computing skills may be the rationale for recruiting young people for technical positions—they are also paid less and have worked more in an environment of competitive global capitalism" (p. 229).

Political economy researchers also study aging in the modern state. They examine the structural conditions in society that create inequality in old age. Gerontologists have looked at such diverse issues as social attitudes toward older people (Gullette, 2007) and income differences between older men and older women (Williams, 2010).

The political economy approach traces the origins of older people's problems to the political and economic structure of capitalist society. This perspective also looks at how social programs and policies for older people serve the interests of middle-aged, middle-class professionals. These programs and policies can reinforce class, gender, and racial inequalities in later life. Estes (2001) called these interlocking systems of oppression. By this she meant that none of these characteristics—gender, race, or social class—is experienced independent of the others. And together they structure opportunities that individuals are given or denied.

The political economy approach looks beyond the individual to understand the forces that shape individual aging today. It broadens gerontologists' understanding of aging and offers another way to interpret the origins and effects of social policies.

Cumulative advantage and disadvantage theory (a type of conflict theory) focuses on the lifelong effects of inequality. This theory says that advantages and disadvantages earlier in life accumulate and are magnified over the life course. "Those who start life with greater resources accumulate more opportunities to increase their resources, while those who start off with less have fewer opportunities for acquiring additional resources and fall further behind" (Prokos & Keene, 2012, p. 599, citing O'Rand, 1996).

Prokos and Keene (2012) tested this theory in a study of grandparents. They looked at a nationally representative sample of U.S. households and used a life course approach to study cumulative disadvantage. In this study, they focused on grandparents who live with and care for grandchildren.

They found that the youngest grandmothers in their study showed the greatest risk of poverty. They traced this finding to the timing of motherhood in grandparents' lives. They call this the "motherhood penalty" (p. 599). Women who had children early in their lives bear a wage penalty, few of them ever recover from this penalty, and the motherhood penalty compounds over time.

The political economy approach emphasizes the impact of history, economics, and the political structure on individuals. It shows how the state and social policies can increase or decrease social inequalities. It also shows how race, ethnicity, social class, and gender can intensify inequality. Further, it looks at different dimensions of powerlessness—social, economic, and political. Marshall and Bengtson (2011) wrote that "a political economy of aging and the life course in this era must extend beyond national boundaries or comparative analysis to develop theory that addresses complex linkages of people and social institutions globally" (p. 27).

Critics of the political economy approach say that it overemphasizes poverty and problems older people face. It also tends to view the individual as the product of political and economic forces and pays little attention to individuals' interpretations of social life. It says little about the ways that individuals shape their world through their interactions with others. This perspective makes the older person seem powerless in the face of uncontrollable and oppressive social forces.

Feminist approaches, within the conflict perspective, bridge the micro and macro levels of theory. Feminist theorists criticize other theories of aging and aging research for not focusing enough on gender relations or

---

interlocking systems of oppression "macro level connections linking systems of oppression such as race, class, and gender" (Estes, 2001, p. 13)

cumulative advantage and disadvantage theory says that advantages and disadvantages earlier in life accumulate and are magnified over the life course

feminist approaches view gender as a defining characteristic in social interaction and life experiences, as well as in the process and experience of aging; gender is seen as socially constructed, with men being more advantaged than women in society

EXHIBIT 2.3 *Betty Friedan*

Betty Friedan published her best-selling book *The Feminine Mystique* in 1963. The book objected to the depiction of women in the media at that time and to their role as homemakers. She argued that this wasted their talents and potential. In October 1966 she co-founded the National Organization for Women (NOW), a civil rights group that sought equality of opportunity for women.

Some people call Friedan the "Mother of the [Feminist] Movement" in the United States. In 1993 Friedan wrote *The Fountain of Age*, where she urged a change in society's view of aging and particularly society's negative view of older women. Friedan herself served as a female model of successful aging. She continued writing into later life and published a memoir, *Life So Far*, at the age of 79.

Betty Friedan (1931–2006): An Early Leader of the Feminist Movement in the United States

Stacy Walsh Rosenstock/Alamy Stock Photo

on women's experiences. They say that gerontologists need to explore women's experiences without constant reference to the experiences of men. In turn, mainstream feminist theory has been criticized for ignoring aging issues and the experiences of older women and older men (Allen & Walker, 2009; Calasanti, 2009; Freixas, Luque, & Reina, 2012). Calasanti and Slevin (2006; also Mitchell & Bruns, 2011) see this as a type of ageism. Feminist research in aging has focused on many unique issues: sexual relations in later life (Connidis, 2006), social activism among older women in Quebec (Charpentier, Queniart, & Jacques, 2008), and identity and the aging body (Clarke, 2008; Slevin, 2006).

The feminist approach has made valuable contributions to the study of aging. First, the feminist approach recognizes the importance of social structure, social interaction, and individual characteristics (primarily gender but also race, ethnicity, and social class) in shaping a person's experience of aging (Freixas, Luque, & Reina, 2012). Second, the feminist approach presents a more inclusive picture of aging and older adults by focusing on the majority of the older population—women—and on issues that are relevant to women's lives. Third, feminist theories of aging challenge the traditional focus on men in research and the ageist biases in "mainstream" feminist theories that ignore issues of age (Calasanti & Slevin, 2006).

TIME TO REVIEW

What are the advantages and disadvantages of taking the conflict perspective?

Explain the concept of "cumulative advantage and disadvantage." How does this help explain poverty among women in later life?

List two contributions that the feminist approach has made to the study of aging.

Why is the feminist approach considered a type of conflict theory?

Further Developments in Gerontology Theory

Theories try to make sense of the complex, multidimensional facts of aging. The theories discussed here show that no single explanation of aging can account for everything we know. But we must have theories in order to understand the mass of detailed information that researchers gather. Bengtson and his colleagues (1997) said, "theory is not a marginal, meaningless 'tacked-on' exercise to presenting results in an empirical paper. Rather, cumulative theory-building represents the core of the foundation of scientific inquiry and knowledge" (p. S84).

What theoretical ideas have emerged in social gerontology in recent years? What approaches will emerge or grow in the years ahead? Many researchers and theorists support the wider use of interpretive frameworks for studying aging. **Narrative gerontology** offers one new framework (Kenyon, Bohlmeijer, & Randall, 2010; Randall & McKim, 2008). This approach seeks to understand aging from the inside. It studies the stories that people tell in order to organize and make sense of their lives. These stories create meaning around their experience of aging.

Stephen Katz (2008), for example, traced his thoughts and feelings about old age to his youth in Toronto's Jewish quarter in Kensington Market. There he identified "old" with "the majority adults; Yiddish; rye bread; barrels of pickled and salted foods...." (p. 141). His warm reflections on his youth showed the roots of his interest in aging today. "Indeed," he said, "if one probes the career of any author or thinker or critic, one will find a narrative of life whose experiences, revelations, and suffering are the voice and soul of their work" (p. 145).

Moral economy theory, a complement to political economy theory, grew out of the work of E.P. Thompson (1971) in England. Political economy theorists and researchers use this perspective to explore issues such as retirement (Moody, 2010). This approach to the study of aging looks at the shared moral assumptions held by members of a society. Studies that use this approach look at values like justice and fairness in society and how they affect social policies. The moral economy theory is concerned with the social consensus that underlies issues like justice between the generations, pension entitlements, and access to healthcare.

Critical gerontology emerged to address limitations in mainstream gerontology theory. It fits within the conflict perspective and "posits that the social order is held together by the dominance of certain interests and groups over others" (Estes, 2011, p. 297). Ray (2008) made the distinction between "theory" and "critical theory." Theory helps to guide research and interpret research findings. Critical theory questions these findings, as well as the structure and method of inquiry. Ray believed the role of critical gerontology is to "cast a critical eye on society and the field of gerontology itself" (p. 97).

Powell and Hendricks (2009) listed four themes, or "conceptual tools," that shape critical gerontology: (1) aging and politics of redistribution; (2) gender and aging; (3) aging, identity, and postmodernism; and (4) ageing and surveillance. These themes highlight the tension between the aging individual and society. Estes (2011, citing Estes & Phillipson, 2007, pp. 330–331) said that critical gerontology provides "alternative theoretical frameworks and emancipatory knowledge, address[ed] toward concerns of social inequalities and social justice" (p. 297).

Post-modern theory contrasts contemporary society with society in the recent past. Where the modern world casts the older person as a "retiree," the older person in the post-modern world can take on many roles at once—worker, caregiver, lover, traveller, student, and so on. The post-modern senior creates the meaning of his or her own old age. Powell and Hendricks (2009) referred to post-modern identity management. Through exercise, diet, plastic surgery, and virtual identities online, the older person can create identity as an ongoing project.

Watkins (2009, p. 6) wrote that

> *In the postmodern world ... [p]ersons may pursue more than one career and experience more than one retirement. Life expectancy based upon statistical averages from previous generations may not describe the current population of older adults and what describes a particular group of senior adults may not be true of another group even in the same city or country. This is not a prediction of the future. It is a description of what is currently taking place all over the world. Aging is not what it used to be and few can adequately explain what it is like now, and none can be certain of what aging will be like in the future.*

The Great Recession of 2008 brought home the uncertainty of modern life that post-modern theory describes. Marshall and Bengtson (2011) referred to the "risk society." This type of society "is one in which social institutions provide less 'insurance' against the vicissitudes of life, such as job loss or loss of one's health, and individuals are expected to assume responsibility to navigate these risks" (p. 24).

---

narrative gerontology seeks to understand the "inside" of aging by examining the narratives or life stories that people tell in order to organize and make sense of their lives, and their experiences of aging

moral economy theory focuses on shared values and social norms that shape popular beliefs in the legitimacy of certain practices and policies; this theory complements political economy theory

critical gerontology theoretical approaches that look "within" theory and research to critically examine and question the underlying and "taken-for-granted" assumptions about aging

post-modern theory contrasts contemporary society with society in the recent past; for example, older people today can take on many roles in retirement, whereas in the past, they had limited options after they retired

Today, a lifetime of pension savings can disappear in a few weeks. In the post-modern world, a plan for retirement at age 55 can suddenly turn into a work career that will last to age 70 and beyond. Instability and uncertainty serve as the dark side of post-modern life. The post-modern world frees a person from fixed, traditional identity. But it also sets the person loose in an uncertain future.

Rosenberg (2009) asked how researchers and theorists should respond to the challenge of the post-modern world: "We in the research community need to consider whether the theories, models, and methods on which research has been predicated in the past have to be adjusted. Or do we need new theories, models, and methods to understand and explain the changes taking place?" (p. 1).

Summary of Gerontology Theories

Researchers predict an increased focus on the political economy perspective, interpretive approaches such as phenomenology and social constructionism, critical and feminist approaches, and life course perspectives. Gans (2009) saw a trend toward novelty across the field of theory in gerontology. He said that theories today differ in their origins, scope, and focus of interest.

Theory will remain central to the study of aging. Bengtson and his colleagues (1999) said, "Theory is the compass with which to navigate through vast seas of data. It is the means by which data are transformed into meaningful explanations, or stories, about the processes and consequences of aging" (p. 18). Gerontological theories offer many explanations of aging. Their variety reflects the complex reality of aging and the many dimensions of gerontology research. Each of these perspectives gives us a different insight into what it means to grow old.

RESEARCH ISSUES AND METHODS

Research Issues

Gerontologists use a number of methods that help them study the process of aging. The proper use of these methods ensures that researchers come up with reliable and valid findings. Improper use can lead to faulty and confusing results. The following discussion will give a glimpse of the methodological issues that gerontologists face in trying to study continuity and change in later life.

Gerontologists generally place changes in old age into one of these three categories—age, period, and cohort effects (sometimes called APC effects) (Yang, 2011):

1. **Age effects** occur due to physical decline. These changes appear with the passage of time. They include an increase in the body's fat-to-muscle ratio, a decline in lung elasticity, and decreases in bone density. They also include environmentally caused changes such as wrinkled skin and cataracts caused by the sun.
2. **Period or environmental effects** occur due to the time of measurement. This category includes social or historical effects on measurement, such as an ongoing war, changes in health habits (for example, increased exercise), or changes in healthcare policies. These effects have different influences on different age cohorts.
3. **Cohort effects** relate to the time of a person's birth. Cohort refers to a group of people born around the same time (usually within a five- or ten-year period). People born in a certain cohort often share a common background and experience of the world. People born just after World War II, for example, are in the cohort that was the first to be exposed to large doses of television. This new technology shaped their entertainment habits and lifestyles. In comparison, those born in the early 1990s spent their youth playing video games, text messaging, and listening to music on their iPods. This technology has shaped entertainment habits and lifestyles that differ from those of their parents' or grandparents' generation.

Gerontologists try to disentangle these effects in order to understand the causes of aging. They use a number of research designs to look at these three effects.

Much of the early research on aging used a **cross-sectional research design**. This method studies

---

age effects on a person's life are related to physical decline or change due to the aging process

period or environmental effects on a person's life are due to the time of measurement; this would include historical, social, or environmental effects, such as an ongoing war, changes in health habits (e.g., better nutrition), or changes in healthcare policies that have different influences on different age cohorts

cohort effects are related to the time of the person's birth

cross-sectional research design studies people from many age groups at one point in time

people from many age groups at one point in time. Early studies done in psychology to study intelligence, for example, found that older age groups, compared with younger age groups, scored lower on intelligence tests. This finding was seen as support for the view that people get "simple-minded" as they get older. But these early studies tended to confuse differences *between age groups* (cohort effects) with *changes due to aging* (age effects). In the 1980s, research by Baltes and Schaie (1982) found that younger people had more education than older people (a cohort effect). This, they said, accounted for some of the differences in younger and older people's test scores.

Most researchers who study aging today still use a cross-sectional design (Neuman & Robson, 2009). This method allows researchers to gather data in a short time at a relatively low cost. It also allows policymakers to assess and meet the needs of different age groups fairly quickly. Researchers in a single study can ask a broad range of questions that give a detailed snapshot of many age groups at one point in time.

Still, this method causes problems. As the early intelligence studies show, cross-sectional studies can confound cohort effects (such as lower education levels in older cohorts) with age changes (such as changes in intelligence due to increasing age). The findings from cross-sectional studies cannot tell us whether aging (maturation) leads to changes in intelligence, health, or any other conditions or behaviours that change over time.

EXHIBIT 2.4 *Types of Research Design*

Date of study	2000	2005	2010	2015	2020
Date of birth					
1935	65	70	75	80	85
1945	55	60	65	70	75
1955	45	50	55	60	65
1965	35	40	45	50	55
1975	25	30	35	40	45
1985	15	20	25	30	35

Age at time of study

Legend:
- Cross-sectional study
- Longitudinal study
- Time-lag study

Cross-sectional study: This type of study takes place at one point in time and looks at many age cohorts. Cross-sectional studies often use survey methods to gather data. This type of study allows for efficient collection of a large amount of data. The U.S. Census Bureau uses this approach when it conducts its national surveys. This type of study captures a snapshot of a population at one point in time, but it cannot analyze the effects of aging over time.

Longitudinal study: This type of study follows one group of people (or several groups) over time. It conducts repeated studies of the same group(s). It can analyze the effects of aging on a single cohort over time. Compared to a cross-sectional study, this type of study takes more time to complete, and it can cost more to conduct.

Time-lag study: This type of study looks at one age group (e.g., 55-year-olds) at several points in time. This type of study can analyze differences in the condition of this age group over time. This type of study can then explore whether external conditions, social policies, health habits, or other influences have led to changes in this age group.

Each of these research designs has advantages and disadvantages. Often practical considerations such as the cost of the research or ease of data collection will determine which method a researcher uses.

Source: Adapted from *Life Span Developmental Psychology: Introduction to Research Methods* by P.B. Baltes, H.W. Reese, and J.R. Nesselroade. (1977). Brooks/Cole Publishing Company, Pacific Grove, CA. 93940. A Division of Thomson Publishing Inc.

Longitudinal research designs attempt to overcome this problem. A longitudinal study looks at a single group of people at two or more points in time. For example, a longitudinal study of how aging affects intelligence might test the same group of people at 10-year intervals. These results give a truer picture of the effects of age on intelligence because this kind of study avoids the problem of trying to compare different cohorts (e.g., people with different educational backgrounds due to the historical conditions in their childhood).

Young and colleagues (2008) asked a research question that only a longitudinal study could answer: Does training over many years reduce the effects of aging on athletes' performance? The researchers used athletes' diaries of their performance in their study. To answer their question, the researchers studied the performance of 45 Masters runners. These runners trained actively for at least 10 years.

The researchers compared the changes in these runners' performance over time with cross-sectional data on running performance. (Cross-sectional trends come from different samples across different age groups. Longitudinal trends come from the same group over time.) Compared with the apparent aging effects seen in the cross-sectional data, Masters athletes showed less decline in performance. This study demonstrates the benefits of exercise over a long time as a way to slow the aging process.

This study shows the benefit of longitudinal research. The researchers could track individual performance over time. They could measure the impact of training on running times for the athletes in their study.

Gerontologists use longitudinal studies when they want to learn about age changes (like the changes in athletes' running times), but this method also creates problems. For example, environmental changes (period effects)—such as historical events, changes in the economy, or changes in political values—can confound changes due to aging. A downturn in the economy, for example, might have influenced these athletes' nutrition or increased their workplace stress, and this might have influenced their running times.

Longitudinal studies involving older people face special problems. These include loss of study participants due to death, illness, and moving; inability to respond due to chronic illness or cognitive decline; and a shift in the sex ratio in the study due to the deaths of more men than women in later life. Subjects in psychological studies can

get better at a test over time through repeated testing. These examples show the kinds of problems gerontologists can face when they search for the causes of change in later life (Ferrer & Ghisletta, 2011).

The *Canadian Longitudinal Study of Aging* (CLSA) tries to overcome some of these limitations through repeated contact with participants over many years. This study follows a random sample of 50,000 men and women from across Canada, age 45 to 85, over a 20-year period. A sub-sample of 30,000 people donate blood and urine and receive in-depth physical exams. The research team includes researchers from the social sciences, psychology, medical and clinical research, population health, and health services (Raina et al., 2009). The study investigates "the complexities of the aging process and improve our understanding of the transitions and trajectories of healthy aging" (p. 222).

The researchers use a public relations campaign (newspapers, radio, the Internet, etc.) to encourage people to join the study. Then the research team arranges brief 20- to 30-minute phone interviews each year "to maintain contact and reduce losses to follow-up" (Raina et al., 2009, p. 225).

The study also plans to offer transportation to data collection sites, free parking, and respite care if needed. Researchers will even visit frail participants in their homes if necessary. The study will keep data collection sites open on Saturdays and at least one evening per week. The study will also send newsletters, birthday cards, and holiday cards to participants to help keep them linked to the study. All of this, the researchers hope, will keep people in the study for 20 or more years.

Large-scale studies such as the CLSA employ multidisciplinary research teams. Lusina et al. (2010) called these "cross-disciplinary" teams. "At their best," the researchers said, "cross-disciplinary research teams provide valuable outcomes that cannot be achieved through single-discipline or single-investigator approaches." The CLSA team will include "more than 160 researchers from 26 universities across Canada" (Raina et al., 2009, p. 222). The study will use similar measures and attempt to set Canadian standards for data collection. This will allow a comparison of results across many age cohorts over time. The scale of the CLSA and its many parts (biological sampling, demographic data gathering, psychological testing, etc.) demand cross-disciplinary teamwork, collaboration, and a large budget (Fortier et al., 2012).

Only government or foundation funding can support this large-scale, complex, and expensive research. Funding needs to continue for decades in order to fulfill the promise of the research program. This will take the

---

longitudinal research designs looks at a single group of people at two or more points in time

commitment of changing political parties under uncertain future economic conditions. Few longitudinal studies have been able to maintain this support for such a long time. Those that have survived for several decades are renowned for their unique contributions to knowledge about aging.

A third method, **time-lag comparison design**, tries to overcome the problems raised by simple cross-sectional and simple longitudinal designs. Time-lag studies look at specific age cohorts at different points in time. A time-lag study, for example, can follow the diabetes rates of more than one cohort (e.g., those born in 1940, 1950, and 1960). This allows researchers to compare different cohorts of the same age (e.g., age 55) at different points in time (e.g., 2000, 2010, and 2020). This type of study tries to measure differences between individuals. It can ask about cohort and period effects "Did the rate of diabetes go up for 50-year-olds over time?" and "What accounts for this change?"

Hou (2010) used a time-lag design to ask two questions: (1) How does Canadians' home ownership change over time as people age? and (2) How has the age profile of Canadian home ownership changed over the course of generations? This requires data on individuals over time. And it requires data that can compare cohorts of homeowners at different points in time. Hou used data from eight Canadian censuses between 1971 and 2006. The study looked at the home ownership tendencies of birth cohorts born in 1910 through the 1970s.

Hou found strong similarities among these cohorts in the pattern of home ownership. Home ownership rates rose quickly through young adulthood to age 40. It then climbed at a slower rate to a plateau near age 65. The rate starts to decline after age 75. But seniors continued to own homes at a high rate at least a decade after age 65.

This study shows continuity in the pattern of home ownership across many age cohorts. It points to the strong tendency of Canadians to own homes over a long period of time. And it points to the link between home ownership and life stage. People tend to own homes as they enter the child-rearing stage. This tendency grows to early old age as family size increases. People tend to stay in their homes into later old age. At that time health and widowhood often lead to a move from a single-family home.

The use of the time-lag series also allowed Hou to compare the home ownership rates of different cohorts (not just individual patterns of home ownership over time). This study found that home ownership rates increased for younger cohorts. For example, at the peak, 73 percent of those born in the 1910s owned homes, but 78 percent of those born during World War II owned homes.

This points to an increase in the tendency to own homes over time in Canada (for similar age cohorts). It supports the idea that home ownership became a stronger desire as the 20th century progressed. And the increase in prosperity in Canada during that century allowed more people to fulfill that desire. It may also point to the effects of government and economic policies (such as tax rebates or interest rates) that encouraged home ownership.

This study allowed Hou (2010) to follow a group of individuals over time to observe their "housing careers" (typically from rental, to first ownership, to owning a larger home, and finally to rental again) (p. 8). It also allowed the comparison of birth cohorts over time to assess the influence of history (war and peace), economics (Canada Pension Plan benefits), and culture (the goal of home ownership) on home ownership tendencies.

Like cross-sectional and longitudinal methods, the time-lag method also presents problems. It confounds cohort effects with environmental ones. If a research study finds that 70-year-olds in 2011 visited doctors less often than 70-year-olds did in 1991, this difference may be because of the better health of 70-year-olds in 2011 (a cohort effect). Or it may be due to a change in the healthcare system, perhaps higher costs to users that kept them from seeing a doctor in 2011 (a period or environmental effect).

Each type of study creates problems when it comes to interpreting results. In addition, longitudinal and time-lag studies pose practical problems. First, they often take many years to complete—years during which researchers must wait before they can show results to granting agencies or to the public. Second, they are expensive to maintain (Neuman & Robson, 2009). The cost can force the researcher to apply for new grants for each wave of the research. The researcher must compete with all other applicants, but cannot tailor sample size or limit the research to fit new funding conditions.

Third, subjects in longitudinal studies drop out (or die), biasing results in later rounds of the study (Alwin, Hofer, & McCammon, 2006). Longitudinal studies of disease face this problem (Vogler, 2006). Those who die during a study leave a healthier, less diseased group behind. This group no longer represents the original sample's characteristics and therefore confounds the study results. (Some studies try to overcome this problem by replacing dropouts with similar types of subjects in order to maintain their sample size.)

---

time-lag comparison design examines different groups of people of the same age at different points in time (e.g., 55-year-olds in 2000, 2010, and 2020)

Fourth, longitudinal studies require institutional support. The time needed to complete a longitudinal study can be so long that researchers themselves may die or move before the study ends. For this reason, some longitudinal studies take place through a research centre or university. The institution can see the study through and provide a home for the data.

Gerontologists have solved some of these problems by turning simple cross-sectional and simple longitudinal designs into **sequential designs**. Researchers create sequential designs by looking at a series of cross-sectional studies during a longer longitudinal study. The cross-sectional studies allow for quick data collection. The longitudinal study provides a check on cross-sectional findings. These two methods together also provide time-lag data on the sampled members of same-aged groups at different times.

The *Aging in Manitoba Longitudinal Study* (AMLS) offers this option to researchers. It provides comparable data on health and healthcare needs for a random sample of older people in Manitoba at different times. In this project, which began in 1971, three independent cross-sectional studies were conducted (in 1971, 1976, and 1983). The groups were then followed over time (1990, 1996, 2001, 2005, and 2006). This method produced both cross-sectional and longitudinal data (within a sequential design). With data now from more than 9,000 participants over 35 years, the *Aging in Manitoba Longitudinal Study* is the longest and most comprehensive, continuous, population-based study of aging in Canada.

This type of study allows researchers to compare the needs of different age groups in a given year (e.g., 66- to 75-year-olds and 76- to 85-year-olds in 2006). It also allows researchers to study the changes in these groups' needs over time (e.g., whether the needs of the sample of 66- to 75-year-olds have changed between 1990 and 2006). The researchers can also see whether social changes have affected all age groups (e.g., whether all groups of older people used hospitals more in 1990 than in 2006). They can then separate period effects—effects due to social conditions at the times of measurement (e.g., new medical care policies)—from effects due to aging—such as the need for more medical care as a person ages.

Salthouse (2006) says that only longitudinal studies allow researchers to assess the long-term effects of interventions. For example, it may take years for an exercise program to affect health in later life. An immediate effect of the exercise program (e.g., an improved self-image) might lessen and disappear over time. Only by following participants over time can researchers assess lasting benefits of the program. Salthouse admits that long-term studies cost a lot and consume time and energy. But they provide the only accurate assessment of an intervention's lasting effect on the process of aging.

These complex designs still do not completely untangle time of measurement, age, and cohort effects, although they do give researchers more information about the group under study. Attempts to neutralize variables take a great deal of time and effort. Without the effort, the researchers could make a fundamental error in understanding. But, even with it, the researcher still has to explain, for example, the specific historical events that led to changes in healthcare use or how these events translated themselves into different behaviours. Whatever method the researcher chooses, logical reasoning and judgment must be used to make sense of research findings.

TIME TO REVIEW

Explain the difference between age, period, and cohort effects. Why do gerontologists try to disentangle these effects?

How do cross-sectional and longitudinal studies differ in their design?

What challenges related to sample membership do longitudinal studies face? How do researchers try to overcome these challenges?

How do longitudinal and time-lag designs try to disentangle the aging, period, and cohort effects? Why is the disentanglement of these effects important in the study of aging?

Why are methods to disentangle these effects often only partly successful?

Types of Research Methods

Gerontologists use psychological tests and surveys to study aging. But they also use other research methods, such as in-depth interviews, participant observation, and content analysis. Researchers in each dimension of aging (biomedical, psychosocial, socioeconomic-environmental) have their preferred methods.

Pharmacologists, chemists, and neurophysiologists use laboratory techniques and controlled experiments to study aging; historians use libraries, archives, diaries, and even paintings; literary scholars use plays, novels, and poetry. Social gerontologists use surveys, personal interviews, focus groups, community-based action research, and case studies. Some studies require more than one

---

sequential designs researchers look at a series of cross-sectional studies during a longitudinal study

method—a questionnaire survey of a large population, for example, may include a psychological test, and an anthropological field study may include the study of a society's literature and history as well as a measurement of the people's physical condition. Research on health service use might involve a mailed survey to community-dwelling older adults as well as face-to-face interviews with a subgroup of that population. Social scientists and health researchers may use qualitative and quantitative methods to better understand an issue (Apesoa-Varano & Hinton, 2013).

Ethical Issues in Research

Research studies on human subjects face ethical challenges. And studies of certain frail or vulnerable groups pose unique problems. Researchers need to recognize the ethical implications of studying vulnerable older people, such as those living with Alzheimer's disease or another cognitive impairment.

Researchers need to consider at least three ethical issues: (1) the need for informed consent, (2) the need to guard subjects against harm or injury, and (3) the need to protect individuals' privacy (Neuman & Robson, 2009).

Informed consent means that the researcher tells the subject the facts about the research and gets written permission from the subjects before they participate in a study. Individuals must freely give their consent without any coercion. They need to understand that they can decide not to answer any questions without explanation. And they need to know that they can withdraw from the study at any time.

Researchers must also guard against doing harm or injury to study participants. This includes physical harm and psychological harm. A person might feel embarrassed or upset at some questions they feel they have to answer. Research questions might force participants to recall events that are unpleasant or traumatic. Researchers need to minimize risk to participants throughout the research process.

Researchers also seek to protect participants from potential harm by protecting their privacy. Researchers can do this by making sure that data analysis cannot reveal an individual's identity. The researcher should also promise to keep personal information confidential. This means securely storing information in a location that only he or she can access.

EXHIBIT 2.5 *The Sheridan Centre for Elder Research*

The Sheridan Centre for Elder Research is located at Sheridan College's Trafalgar Road Campus in Oakville, Ontario. "The goal of the Centre is to identify, develop, test and support implementation of innovative strategies that improve the quality of life for older adults and their families, and to do this through applied research." The centre takes a unique approach to the development of research projects. It includes older people as subjects in its research as you might expect, but it also involves older adults in the community to guide the direction of research. The centre collaborates with business and industry as well as academic leaders.

The centre uses a variety of methods to learn about aging and to turn research findings into practical outcomes. For example, the centre uses focus groups made up of older people in order to guide research directions. Studies also use field observation and laboratory research. Research interests range from studies of the performing arts and their ability to enhance aging, to studies of how business can adapt to an aging society. Studies conducted by the centre include "Horticultural Therapy for Older Adults with Alzheimer Disease and Related Dementias," "Older Adults Embracing Technology—Leave No One Behind," and "Movement Matters: Results of an Introductory Dance Project at the Village of Humber Heights."

The centre also collaborates with many businesses in order to develop and promote products to enhance later life.

iStock/Thinkstock

The centre's Business of Aging Global Network brings together business and industry leaders to share information on products that serve older people. Business partners include healthcare companies and companies that focus on recreation and successful aging.

The Sheridan Centre provides a model of collaboration among researchers, older adults, and the community that leads to direct benefits for older Canadians.

Source: Courtesy of Patricia Spadafora, Sheridan Centre for Elder Research.

EXHIBIT 2.6   *A Question of Method*

Rembrandt van Rijn (1606–1669) began painting self-portraits in the 1620s. He completed his last self-portrait the year of his death, 1669. Here, we see him in late middle age. In all, he painted more than 90 self-portraits. Experts have called his self-portraits a "visual diary." They stand as one of the great achievements in the history of Western art.

Self-Portrait of Rembrandt van Rijn
© Peter Horree/Alamy

Questions

1. Does Rembrandt's self-portrait count as a "research study" of aging? If not, why not? If so, why do you consider it a research study?

2. How does it differ from studies done by social scientists?

3. What do artists discover through their "research"?

4. What can an artist's work teach us about aging?

Older people with Alzheimer's disease or other types of dementia present special challenges in research. For example, they may not be able to give true voluntary informed consent (Neuman & Robson, 2009; Raina et al., 2009). If the mental competency of an individual is in question, the researchers must get written permission from someone who has the legal authority to make such decisions. A family member or staff member in a nursing home may have this authority. Permission from a substitute decision maker allows for research at all stages of the disease. In most provinces in Canada, substitute decision makers can provide permission through court-ordered guardianship, power of attorney, and advance directives.

Universities and other funding agencies have ethics review boards (often called Institutional Review Boards) to evaluate potential risks that participants might face. The ethics review board must approve each study, weigh the potential risks and benefits, and then give permission for research to proceed. This process protects participants from potential harm and ensures that researchers act ethically and responsibly in their research.

POLICY AND PROGRAMS AS THE OUTCOME OF RESEARCH

Research can have more than one purpose. Warner and Sierra (2009), for example, made the case for "basic aging research." The discovery of "biomarkers of aging," they said, could help predict a person's life expectancy, and this could help people live longer, healthier lives. Other studies have a broader social purpose: they want to influence public policy. *Policy*, in this case, refers to government plans or regulations that shape funding and create programs to help older people.

A study of senior immigrants (Stewart et al., 2011), for example, described the challenges and barriers immigrants face in gaining access to services. The study found that financial barriers, language difficulties, and discrimination all kept seniors from getting services they needed. These findings can help policymakers design and implement appropriate, culturally sensitive services.

A study of disability and dependency (Légaré, Décarie, & Bélanger, 2014, p. 215) used micro simulation computer techniques to assess future disability rates in Canada. The researchers said that their results could "establish efficient older-adult programs that correspond to the reality and projections of aging populations."

The health and social service fields now promote **evidence-based practice** as a way to bridge the gap between research and practice (Reinhardt, 2010). Evidence-based practice promotes the use of research findings in the delivery of services to older people. Rahman and Applebaum (2010, p. 8) said that "evidence-based practice was ranked among the fifteen greatest medical milestones since 1840 in 2007."

Andrews, McInerney, and Robinson (2009) applied evidence-based practice in a nursing home setting. The researchers involved staff members of a dementia care unit in an "action research" project. The staff wanted to improve communication with family members of dementia patients. The staff at the start of the project knew little about research that could improve their support of family members. First, staff members located evidence-based information, then they critically assessed the usefulness of the evidence, and finally they developed strategies to better serve family members of their patients. This study showed the value of involving practitioners in the application of research to practice.

These examples show gerontologists' desire to conduct research for practical ends. The Canadian Institutes of Health Research, the Institute of Aging, and the *Canadian Longitudinal Study of Aging* (CLSA) all receive government funding and support. The CLSA research team spent many months gathering financial support from many government agencies. In late 2008, after more than four years of planning, the CLSA had secured $23.5 million to support a five-year implementation phase. This support shows the Canadian government's commitment to research as a basis for policy and program development. Martin-Matthews and Mealing (2009) said these funds established the CLSA "solidly as a national, longitudinal research and data platform" (p. 213).

Large-Scale Gerontology Research in Canada

Gerontology research in Canada has been undergoing some important shifts. For example, attempts have been made to bridge the gap between anglophone and francophone gerontologists in Canada. Further, the past several decades have seen an increase in national studies conducted by interdisciplinary teams. The federal government funded most of these studies and continues to be a major source of funding for research on aging.

An important source of government funding for health-related aging research is the Institute of Aging (IA), a pillar of the Canadian Institutes of Health Research. The IA is a community of researchers from universities and hospitals across Canada. It also includes practitioners, volunteer health organizations, and older adults. They share a common goal: to increase our knowledge about aging, promote healthy aging, and address the challenges of an aging population. The IA studies a broad range of topics, "to support research, to promote healthy aging and to address causes, prevention, screening, diagnosis, treatment, support systems, and palliation for a wide range of conditions associated with aging" (Canadian Institutes of Health Research, 2014). The IA has become a national leader in addressing the health needs of Canada's older population.

These research centres show a trend toward large-scale, interdisciplinary research among Canadian scholars. Collaborative studies save money by pooling researchers' skills and resources. They also create interdisciplinary teams that can carry out sophisticated analyses of large data sets. This research, and the many other studies conducted by researchers throughout Canada, expand our knowledge and understanding of aging. They also help governments, social service agencies, and professionals to plan better programs for older people.

TIME TO REVIEW

What challenges do researchers face as they conduct large-scale (nationwide) research?

What does this research contribute to our understanding of aging in Canada?

What effect can this research have on the development of social policies and programs for older people?

---

evidence-based practice promotes the use of research findings in the delivery of services to older people

THE FUTURE OF GERONTOLOGICAL THEORY AND METHODS

What theories and methods will gerontologists use in the future? First, gerontologists will create new and more sophisticated quantitative methods, including structural equation models, longitudinal factor analysis, and multivariate effects models. As computer power increases and as gerontologists apply methods used in other social sciences, gerontologists will be able to test new and more complex theories.

Second, gerontologists will continue to link the micro and macro levels of theory (Powell & Hendricks, 2009). Age stratification theory, life course approaches, and feminist theories come closest to doing this now. Researchers support the further development of political economy, life course approaches, feminist theories, and interpretive approaches, including phenomenology and social constructionism. These theories allow gerontologists to analyze social processes. These approaches reveal hidden sides of aging and explore ways to create a good old age.

Third, qualitative methods will continue to grow in importance in gerontological research. Qualitative methods can explore the experience of aging at a time when more and more people will want to know about that experience. Neuman and Robson (2009) wrote that "qualitative approaches give a voice to research participants in a way that is not possible in quantitative studies" (p. 348). Qualitative research prizes the richness and diversity of everyday social life. This type of research takes us into the world of older people and their communities. It reveals their experience of later life.

Fourth, technology will continue to expand research opportunities. Laptop computers and tablets allow researchers to enter interview data in the field. Wireless Internet connection gives researchers access to online information from countless locations. Video recording technology allows researchers to observe behaviour without a researcher present. This method allows researchers to gather data throughout the day. A number of researchers can observe and analyze the same data. Researchers have used this technology to study wandering behaviour and the causes of falls in nursing homes.

Fifth, studies in the humanities will add new methods to gerontological research such as linguistic analysis (Nikander, 2009), the study of paintings and photos, life review, autobiographical analysis, and narrative gerontology.

New topics of interest in the future will lead to new approaches in the study of aging. Researchers have an array of options. They will choose the method that best suits their needs and allows them to answer their research questions.

CONCLUSION

Research in gerontology now goes on in many disciplines, including economics, social work, political science, health sciences, psychology, and sociology. Researchers also have access to the latest gerontology research through the use of online databases. Two databases, *AgeLine* and CINAHL (*Cumulative Index to Nursing and Allied Health Literature*), for example, allow researchers to search dozens of journals and to view full-text articles online. The McMaster Optimal Aging Portal (2012) provides "ratings of and links to the best scientific evidence on clinical, public health and health policy questions."

Still, more research on aging in Canada needs to be done. A review of the *AgeLine* database in 2015, for example, found a strong Canadian focus on income, caregiving, and health issues.

Government funding for research on policy-related issues explains in part the concentration on certain topics. But older people and their families also express concern about healthcare and well-being in later life. In 2012 the Canadian Institutes of Health Research's Institute of Aging conducted a nationwide "Speaking of Aging Tour." Researchers met with healthcare workers, policymakers, and industry representatives from across the country to learn how research could help meet the needs of older people. Respondents repeatedly mentioned late-life and end-of-life issues. And yet "late-life care options are little understood and poorly studied" (Joanette et al., 2014, p. 220).

As a result of these consultations, the researchers uncovered new research themes. Topics included the need to assess the effects of medications taken for long periods of time, the management of multiple health problems in older people, and the need to apply research findings to clinical practice.

Researchers also need to study healthy older people because most older people live healthy, active lives. Social gerontologists now see the need to focus on the social conditions that lead to good aging. This will lead to new research questions. For example, what do people of different ethnic backgrounds need as they age? Do the needs of people in rural areas differ from those of people in cities? Do older people have unique educational interests? How do older people learn best? How will early retirees use their time in the future? Researchers have begun to ask these and other questions about aging in Canada.

Summary

1. Three broad areas comprise the field of gerontology: biomedicine, psychosocial studies, and socioeconomic-environmental studies. Social gerontology includes psychosocial and socioeconomic-environmental studies, as well as practice-related research.

2. Gerontologists use theory to guide their research and to interpret their results. Micro- and macro-level theories exist, including interpretive, functionalist, and conflict theories. Each theoretical approach gives a different and valuable insight into aging. The life course perspective bridges micro and macro levels of analysis. It has gained prominence among gerontologists.

3. Gerontologists have developed methods to distinguish age effects (changes due to age) from changes in groups due to differences in cohorts, historical events, and the effects of repeated testing.

4. Longitudinal methods and time-lag designs attempt to overcome the limitations of cross-sectional research. They follow subjects over time in order to disentangle aging effects from cohort differences and historical effects.

5. Gerontologists borrow methods from traditional disciplines such as biology, chemistry, history, philosophy, and anthropology. Researchers have begun to shift their interests as their knowledge grows. New statistical reports now present separate statistics for the oldest age groups. New critical methods of analysis have also emerged as gerontology has grown.

6. Gerontologists use both qualitative and quantitative methods for studying aging and older adults. They use methods that suit their research questions and their discipline. Methods include surveys, face-to-face interviews, focus groups, and case studies, among others.

7. Researchers who study older people often face unique ethical challenges. Those who study frail or cognitively impaired older adults must take special care. They must ensure the willing participation of people in their studies. All researchers must be aware of important ethical concerns: the need for informed consent, the need to guard their participants against harm or injury, and the need to protect participants' privacy.

8. Many Canadian gerontologists take part in large provincial and national studies. These studies, often funded by the government, provide opportunities for multidisciplinary research. These studies take place over long periods of time and allow researchers to conduct individual, cohort, and time-lag analyses. These studies will provide information to guide practitioners and policymakers.

9. Gerontology today is one of the fastest-growing fields of study. It can make old age a better time of life by increasing knowledge about aging. Gerontology research can also help modify and create social structures that meet the needs of older people.

STUDY QUESTIONS

1. What are the three main areas of gerontological study? And what are the three major theoretical perspectives used in gerontological research? What are the strengths and weaknesses of each perspective?

2. What does the life course perspective add to the study of aging? What are three types of life events described by the life course perspective?

3. What do gerontologists mean when they talk about the age, period, and cohort (APC) effects on aging? How do these effects confound one another in research studies? Give an example of how the APC dilemma can confuse the interpretation of research findings. What methods do gerontologists use to disentangle these effects?

4. What is the difference between longitudinal and cross-sectional research? What are the benefits and drawbacks related to each method? What are the pros and cons of using quantitative and qualitative methods?

5. What benefit will Canada see from the implementation of large-scale research projects? What are the pros and cons of this approach?

KEY TERMS

age cohort (p. 25)
age effects (p. 34)
age grades (p. 26)
age-status asynchronization (p. 30)
age stratification theory (p. 25)
cohort effects (p. 34)
conflict perspective (p. 30)
critical gerontology (p. 33)
cross-sectional research design (p. 34)

cumulative advantage and disadvantage theory (p. 31)

evidence-based practice (p. 41)

feminist approaches (p. 31)

functionalist perspective (p. 25)

interlocking systems of oppression (p. 31)

interpretive perspective (p. 23)

life course perspective (p. 26)

longitudinal research designs (p. 36)

macro-level theories (p. 23)

micro-level theories (p. 23)

moral economy theory (p. 33)

narrative gerontology (p. 33)

non-normative events (p. 29)

normative age-graded events (p. 30)

normative history-graded events (p. 29)

period or environmental effects (p. 34)

political economy theory (p. 30)

positivist worldview (p. 25)

post-modern theory (p. 33)

sequential designs (p. 38)

social gerontology (p. 21)

time-lag comparison design (p. 37)

trajectories (p. 28)

transitions (p. 28)

Study Tools CHAPTER 2

Located at retail.tophat.com:

- Review Key Terms with interactive and printable flash cards
- Check Your Comprehension and Think About chapter concepts by completing practice quizzes
- Develop Your Gerontological Imagination with class activities
- Analyze Aging in a Global Perspective with engaging case studies and critical thinking questions
- Demonstrate Your Knowledge of the Concepts by bringing your own experience to personal application questions
- Evaluate Aging in the Media by completing Internet activities with evaluation questions

CHAPTER 3

AGING IN CANADA AND THE WORLD TODAY

Rawpixel.com/Shutterstock

LEARNING OBJECTIVES

After reading this chapter, you will

LO1 Understand the meaning of population aging.

LO2 Be able to explain the impact of population aging on three types of societies: least developed, less developed, and developed societies.

LO3 Be able to state at least three measures of population aging and the usefulness of each.

LO4 Be able to discuss the demographic forces that led to population aging in Canada.

LO5 Understand how the experience of aging differs by gender, ethnicity, and geographic mobility.

LO6 Be able to discuss the aging of the older population and its impact on social and healthcare services.

LO7 Understand the uses and limitations of the concept of a dependency ratio.

LO8 Know some of the responses Canada can make to population aging.

INTRODUCTION

"I have no plans to retire. I have to work as long as I can," Zhao Ruiting, 54, told *The Globe and Mail* (MacKinnon, 2010). Zhao comes from Hebei province, one of China's poorer regions. He sweeps and collects leaves in Beijing's Temple of the Sun Park. Zhao has no pension plan. When he can no longer work he will have to rely on his two sons to care for him. They have jobs in Beijing and know that they will need to support their parents. "It's not fair," Zhao says, "but we will count on them to take care of us because we have no other way."

Many other families in the developing world face a challenge similar to that of Zhao and his family. Rapid increases in the older population in the least developed and the less developed nations have outstripped social supports for older people. In these countries young people may need to support aging relatives. At the same time, the young may struggle to support themselves and their young families.

The developed nations face other challenges due to the large proportion of older people in their populations. An increase in the older population will challenge healthcare and pension systems. These wealthier countries will need to reform social programs and services to meet the needs of an older population. Population aging will affect every social system in all countries, rich and poor.

This chapter will look at (1) aging in the world today, (2) why Canadian society has aged and the population structure of Canada today, and (3) the impact of population aging on Canada's social systems, such as healthcare and government pensions.

AGING IN THE WORLD TODAY

When people think about aging, they think about their family members, friends, or themselves getting older. But societies age, too. For example, from 1921 to 2011, Canada's population grew nearly fourfold. During this same period, the older population grew nearly twelve times, almost three times the rate of the general population. The proportion of people age 65 and over rose from 4.7 percent of the total population in 1921 to 15.7 percent of Canada's population in 2014 (Statistics Canada, 2014c).[1]

This makes Canada's population one of the older populations in the world. By the year 2016, people age 65 and over will outnumber children under age 15, and demographers expect Canadian society to age even more

in the next 50 years. Statistics Canada (2014c) projects that in 2063 one person in four (between 24 percent and 28 percent of the population) will be age 65 and over.

Most of the other countries of the world will also age in the future. The world had nearly 7 billion people in 2010. The United Nations (2011a) reports that in that year the world had 865 million people age 60 years and over—a little more than 12 percent of the world's population. By 2050, the United Nations (2010a; UNDESA, 2013) projects that the world will have more than 2 billion people age 60 and over—the largest number of older people in history.

Two trends account for this worldwide shift to an older population. First, a decline in birth rates. As nations develop and modernize, couples have fewer children. Powell (2011) said that total fertility in the world is expected to decline from 2.82 children per woman in 1995–2000 to 2.15 children per woman in 2045–2050. This is barely above the replacement rate for the world's population. Second, people live longer today than ever before. Worldwide life expectancy is projected to increase from 65 years in 1995–2000 to 76 years in 2045–2050. Powell (2011) wrote that by 2045, for the first time in history, the number of people age 60 and over in the world will surpass the number of children under age 15.

Today, "more than 50 percent of all deaths at the world level occur at ages 60 and over" (United Nations, 2011b, p. 11). The UN calls worldwide **population aging** "unprecedented" (pp. viii–ix). The United Nations (2009) report *World Population Ageing 2009* listed four major findings from its research on population aging:

1. Nearly all countries in the world will experience population aging. The UN called this trend "virtually universal" and "irreversible."
2. Population aging will affect the economy, healthcare, labour markets, and nearly every other social system in countries around the world.
3. The increase in the number of older people (age 60 or over) will take place at the same time as the world sees a decrease in children. By 2045, for the first time in history, the number of older people in the world will be greater than the number of children.
4. Population aging will continue into the future as long as fertility stays low and life expectancy continues to increase. The UN projected an increase in the proportion of people age 60 or over in the world population from 8 percent in 1950 to 22 percent in 2050.

---

[1] Most studies use the population age 65 and over to measure population aging. We will use this figure (unless otherwise noted) to allow for a comparison of different societies, past and present.

population aging demographers, experts who study population change, use at least three measures of population aging: (1) the number of older people in a population, (2) the median age of a population, and (3) the proportion of older people in a population

EXHIBIT 3.1   *Percentage of Population Age 60 or Over*

World and Development Regions, 1950 to 2050

This chart shows that the proportion of older people (age 60 or over) in the world will grow nearly two and a half times (from 8.1 percent to 21.9 percent) over the 100 years projected here. (Figures after 2009 project future population change based on past trends.) The developed nations have the highest proportion of older people in their populations at every period presented here.

One person in three in the developed nations will be age 60 or over by 2050, as projected here. The proportion of older people in the less developed regions will increase more than three and half times from 1950 to 2050. Compared with the more developed regions, the less developed regions will have a smaller proportion of older people in their populations. But the rapid increase in the proportion of older people in all countries will create challenges to social service and healthcare systems to serve older people.

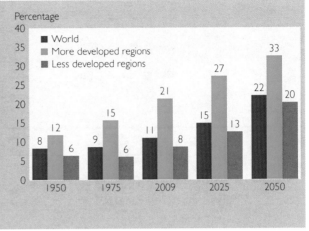

Sources: From *World Population Aging.* Department of Economic and Social Affairs, Population Division, Figure 9, p. 13. © (2010) United Nations. Reprinted with the permission of the United Nations. http://www.un.org/esa/population/publications/WPA2009/WPA2009-report.pdf

The United Nations also predicted an increase in the speed of population aging. The population age 60 and over in the less developed regions increased fivefold from 108 million in 1950 to 554 million in 2013. The number is projected to triple again to 1.6 billion by 2050. The United Nations (2013, p. 13) said that the speed of population aging in the past "will pale in comparison to the ... increase that is about to occur on average in the next 30 years."

The developed nations of North America and Europe took decades and centuries to reach a high proportion of older people in their societies. For example, it took France 115 years, Sweden 85 years, and the United States 69 years to see the 60 or over population grow from 7 percent to 14 percent. The developing nations will need to adapt to an older population in a few decades. China will make that transition in 26 years, Brazil in 21 years, and Columbia in 20 years (Kinsella & Phillips, 2005).

Countries will face specific challenges depending on their level of economic development. The United Nations (2009) divides the world's nations into three categories: **more developed regions** (e.g., Australia, Japan, Canada), **less developed regions** (e.g., China, India, Vietnam), and **least developed regions** (e.g., Haiti, Bangladesh, Ethiopia).[2]

Aging in the Least Developed Nations

The least developed regions face unique challenges due to population aging. These countries often have a low percentage of older people in their populations, but they may have large numbers of older people. High birth rates (demographers define the **birth rate** as the number of live births per 1,000 women in a population) and longer life expectancy account for this situation. These countries need to support a large number of dependent children and a large older population. Middle-aged people in these countries struggle to support the young and the old.

Social change adds to the challenge of aging in the least developed countries. Older people in parts of Africa, for example, face hardships due to rapid urbanization. The young move to the cities for work. This leaves the old behind in villages without traditional family support.

Some countries experience rapid population aging due to HIV/AIDS. The AIDS pandemic in Africa has hit the working-aged population, leading to the loss of middle-aged caregivers for African elders. The *UNAIDS Report on the Global AIDS Epidemic 2010* (United Nations,

---

more developed regions following the UN classification, more developed countries comprise all of Europe and North America, plus Australia, Japan, and New Zealand

less developed regions developing regions and countries are classified as less developed (e.g., China, India, Vietnam)

least developed regions consist of 49 countries with especially low incomes, high economic vulnerability, and poor human development indicators (e.g., Haiti, Bangladesh, Ethiopia)

---

2   The criteria and list of countries, as defined by the United Nations, can be found at www.unohrlls.org/en/ldc. These terms contain no value judgment but refer to the economic development of a country. (Source: Population Reference Bureau, 2010, 2010 *World Population Data Sheet*, p. 18.)

---

birth rate the number of live births per 1,000 women in a population

EXHIBIT 3.2   *Less Developed and Developed Regions of the World: A Comparison of Population Pyramids, 1970, 2013, 2050*

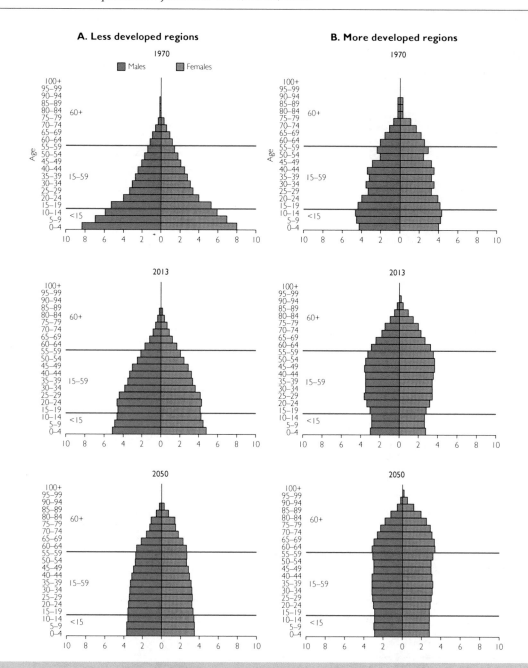

A. Less developed regions

B. More developed regions

These population pyramids show the radical change that will take place in the population structure in the less developed region of the world. The pyramids on the left show a transition from a young society (with large numbers of people at the base of the pyramid) to an older society (with fewer young people and more older people). The pyramids on the right show a similar trend, but a much less dramatic transformation.

Note that the bottom pyramids on the left and right look similar. The less developed nations will have a population structure similar to that of the developed nations, but they lack the wealth and infrastructure to respond in the same way to an older population. The less developed nations will need to find their own methods for meeting the needs of older people and their families.

Source: *World population aging*. Department of Economic and Social Affairs, Population Division, p. 10. © (2013) United Nations. Reprinted with the permission of the United Nations. http://www.un.org/en/development/desa/population/publications/pdf/ageing/WorldPopulationAgeing2013.pdf

EXHIBIT 3.3 AGING IN GLOBAL PERSPECTIVE
The Grandmothers Campaign

Stephen Lewis, a Canadian politician, diplomat, and advocate for social justice, set up the Stephen Lewis Foundation (SLF) in 2003 to support community groups in African nations that work to halt the AIDS epidemic there. The foundation has funded more than 700 projects with 300 organizations in 15 countries.

As part of its mission, the foundation offers support to African grandmothers who care for children orphaned by AIDS. "Grandmothers [in these African nations] are now recognized as community experts and agents of change by governments and international aid agencies. They nurture, feed, and put their grandchildren into school. They work to educate their grandchildren about HIV prevention care and treatment, tend to the sick in their communities, help the recently bereaved, set up support groups, harvest the crops, and advocate for women's rights" (Stephen Lewis Foundation, 2013b).

These women do heroic work in their communities, but they need help. The SLF created the Grandmothers to Grandmothers Campaign in 2006 to raise awareness and mobilize support in Canada for African grandmothers and their orphaned children. The SLF reported that Canada now has 240 grandmother groups who "share ideas, raise awareness, fundraise, advocate and act as ambassadors for their African counterparts." (See "Grandmothers to Grandmothers" at www.grandmotherscampaign.org for more information on this program.)

The Grandmothers Campaign raised more than $12 million in five years. Activities like "Stride to Turn the Tide" in 2010 raised more than $400,000, as 140 grandmothers' groups in Canada walked a collective 12,000 kilometres for this cause.

Stephen Lewis Foundation/Laura Delaney

The Grandmothers Campaign links the hearts and minds of Canadian grandmothers (and in many cases their families and friends) with those of African grandmothers.

Lewis (cited in *Oceanside Grandmothers*, 2013) said that "Against all odds, the Grandmothers Campaign has become a social movement. The Canadian grandmothers have not only raised awareness and huge sums of money (twelve million dollars in five years!), but they have become a force of progressive advocacy at crucial political moments.... The grandmothers' movement has helped to transform international development policy."

2010b) reported that 68 percent of people who have HIV worldwide and 72 percent of people who die of AIDS live in sub-Saharan Africa.

Eke (2004) reported a collapse of the bonds between the generations due to this disease. AIDS has left many older Africans as the sole caregivers for their orphaned grandchildren (Nabalamba and Chikoko, 2011; Oppong, 2006; also Vera-Sanso, 2014). "In some parts of Africa, AIDS is actually called the 'grandmothers' disease'" (AARP, 1998, p. 19).

The Stephen Lewis Foundation (2013a) in Canada says that 40 percent to 60 percent of AIDS orphans in Africa live in grandmother-headed households (see Exhibit 3.3). Botswana, for example, has seen a *decrease* in life expectancy from around 60 years in the 1950s "to a low of 42 years for females and 45 years for males" in the 1990s (Oduaran & Molosi, 2009, p. 123; also Wolff et al., 2009).

Older people in the least developed nations can no longer count on their children for support. Bohman, van Wyck, and Ekman (2009) conducted an ethnographic study of older people in South Africa. Their study showed the impact of modernization on older people. In the past, the old held a valued role in the culture. The young respected them for their wisdom and, in turn, the old could expect support from the young.

Today, South Africans, poor and rich, live in a cash economy. And in many cases the older person, with a South African pension, provides the only cash to the household. The young now rely on the older person for their well-being. This represents a change in the role of the elder. Economic change has led to cultural and social change as older people try to renegotiate their place in the family.

One woman described her situation with some distress (Bohman et al., 2009, p. 451):

If I want to stay with my son and if his wife doesn't need me, doesn't want to live with me, what must I do? I don't know really. I was born here at NN. I stayed with my mother-in-law from 1964 to 1993. I buried her 1993 with no complaints, but if mokoti doesn't love me, what must I do? I don't know.

An adult child in this study said (Bohman et al., 2009, pp. 452–453):

Nowadays there are no patience with the elderly. I do not know why. Young people really do not care for elderly people. In our days we used to have every elderly people. If you see a person that is in the age of your mother/father you consider them as your parents. But nowadays, really life has changed, no respect for elderly.

Ghana provides a good example of the challenges facing the least developed nations. The number of older people (60+) in Ghana will increase from 1.3 million in 2005 to almost 5.6 million people in 2050. During this same time period, people age 80+ will increase six times, from 100,000 to almost 600,000 in 2050. Once people in Africa enter old age, their life expectancy mirrors that of people throughout the world. This means that this large older population will live longer than ever before. But they may live in poverty. Aboderin (2006) said that 45 percent of the people in Ghana live on less than $1 per day, and 79 percent live on less than $2 per day. Under these conditions, the old compete with the young and middle-aged for scarce resources.

One respondent told Aboderin (2006): "In the olden days older people were cared for not just by the children but also by the relatives. Everybody was sharing food and so on but now ... only the children look after the old person" (p. 108). Another respondent said, "if I usually chop (eat) three times a day, (some) days I will chop only once.... So I will force to tighten my belt because *there is nowhere for me to go*" (p. 110, emphasis added by author).

This example shows the challenges that face the least developed nations as their populations age. The older person in the least developed nations has little or no social security. No savings. And only tenuous support from the young. One person told Aboderin (2006): "Right now I can't help my mother how I want because I don't have" (p. 113). This can make old age an uncertain and painful time for many people in the poorest nations.

Age International (2014, p. 8) reported that "80% of older people in developing countries have **no regular income.... Only one in four** older people in low-and middle-income countries **receive a pension**" [emphasis in the original]. At the same time older people in the least developed nations face many of the same physical and mental problems that older people face in developed nations.

Data show increases in diseases such as Alzheimer's disease, angina, osteoarthritis, and diabetes (Nabalamba & Chikoko, 2011; Waters and Gallegos, 2014). Yet few of the least developed nations provide adequate healthcare support to older people. Leive and Xu (2008, cited in Nabalamba & Chikoko) studied healthcare support in 15 African nations. They found that a large proportion of lower-income people must borrow or sell assets to meet healthcare costs. Traditional family structures either do not exist or cannot cope with these chronic healthcare needs.

A study of elder care in Indonesia (Kadar, Francis, & Sellick, 2013, p. 263), for example, reported similar results. Kadar and colleagues said that families traditionally provided support to older people, but today many older people age without family support. In rural areas in particular, "families do not have the financial capacity, understanding and time to provide care for their aged parents." Indonesia offers some support for older people through community health centres. These centres focus on health promotion and disease prevention. But not all centres offer programs for older people, and nurses in these centres "have limited or no specialist skills in caring for the aged in community settings" (p. 267).

A study of older indigenous people in Ecuador (Waters & Gallegos, 2014) found similar issues. Older people experienced declining health, but the formal healthcare system did not meet their needs. Some people in this study could not get to health services, others did not trust the system or could not afford the care. One respondent said that to pay for healthcare, "we have to take out a loan or sell something to go to the health centers. In the [private] clinics, it costs more. I just recently finished paying $500 or $600 for the 2 days that my wife was in the clinic. That's why I don't go anywhere [for health care]. I stay in the house" (p. 380).

Powell (2011, citing Building Blocks, 2004) summarizes the challenge of aging in the least developed nations. "Many older people have had to deal with the loss of their own support while absorbing the additional responsibilities of caring for their orphaned grandchildren. Increasingly, then, it appears that African [and other developing] societies are being asked to cope with population aging with neither a comprehensive formal social security system nor a well-functioning traditional care system in place."

Aging in the Less Developed Nations

The less developed nations have developing economies. They stand between the poorest nations and the developed nations. Nations in this group include India, China, Mexico, and other Latin American nations. The developing nations need solutions that fit their cultures and

Hamady/Shutterstock

This old Masai woman offers decorative beads and earrings for sale in a native Masai village in western Kenya. Developing nations will see a rapid increase in life expectancy and in the number of older people in their populations. Few people in these societies have pensions. Like this woman, they will have to work in old age to earn a living.

current economic conditions. For example, developing nations such as India cannot afford expensive pension programs. India's large population (1.3 billion people, about 37 times that of Canada) and its developing economy challenge its ability to care for people of all ages. More than one-quarter of the population lives below the poverty line. India uses most of its public resources for poverty alleviation, job creation, and food subsidies for the poor.

India's large population, its large uneducated workforce and its developing economy pose challenges to India's older population, especially the poor. Many older people (71 percent) work out of necessity (United Nations, 2012a). Poor people, illiterate older people, and single women often must work to survive. Older women suffer from discrimination, including exclusion from work and healthcare, abuse, and the lack of income and social security.

Older people in India will face many of the challenges faced by elders in the least developed nations. But India's growing economy and increasing middle class will mean improvement for some Indian elders in the future.

China faces challenges similar to those in India. China had a population of about 1.3 billion people in 2010. Wei and Jinju (2009) projected China's population at 1.4 billion by 2030. They projected an increase in the 65-or-over age group from 100 million in 2005 to 200 million in 2026 and 300 million in 2036. In 2029, they said, China's elderly population will exceed that of its children for the first time in history. Retirees at mid-century (people between the ages of 50 and 60 depending on their jobs) will make up about one-third of China's population, or 430 million people (*The New York Times News Service*, 2007).

China began its one-child-per-family policy in 1979. This policy aimed to decrease population growth. The policy decreed that couples could legally have only one child unless they received an exemption. A couple without an exemption could face severe penalties for having additional children. Penalties could be as high as a fee equal to four times the average income of the person's village the previous year. The one-child policy led to a reduced fertility rate from 2.7 children per woman in 1980 to 1.7 children per woman in 2013 (World Bank, 2013). As a side effect, the one-child policy led to an increased proportion of older people in the population and this meant the rapid aging of China's population (Cheng & Rosenberg, 2009).

The one-child policy also challenged the traditional expectation that old people would rely on their children for support. Chinese people now refer to the "4-2-1 problem." This means that one child will need to care for two parents and possibly all four grandparents. This one child will need to support these elders while supporting his or her own family. Gustafson and Baofeng (2014, p. 26) wrote that "As the elderly population grows, the traditional model of co-residence with grown children has been jeopardized by the strict national family planning policies, shrinking family size, increased mobility and the changing role of filial piety."

Longer life expectancy will also add to the number and proportion of older people in China in the future. Better healthcare, for example, led to a decline in mortality. "Based on these trends," Cheng and Rosenberg (2009) said, "the elderly population will increase quickly in the next 50 years, and the speed of population aging will be faster in China than in any other country during this period" (p. 7). Experts call this "one of the greatest demographic changes in history" (French, 2006).

At the current rates of population change, China will get old before it gets rich. It will have to deal with the issues of a developing nation, such as feeding its people, privatizing industry, and growing its economy. At the same time, it will have to deal with issues of a developed society, such as creating pension and healthcare systems to care for its older population.

Huang (2013) says that population aging "has caught Beijing off guard." The country has underdeveloped healthcare and pension systems to serve the old. China put its first pension system in place in 1997 and offers only very low pensions to retirees. People in the countryside have the lowest pensions (as low as $12 per month) and only one-third of the older people outside the cities receive any pension at all. Few healthcare facilities exist for the elderly, even though, Huang reported, 23 percent of older people cannot care for themselves.

Chinese tradition puts the responsibility for care of older people on the family, and the law reinforces this. It states that the old have a legal right to support from their children. Also, older people in China prefer to stay at home and receive support from their families. As a result, today less than 2 percent of China's elderly live in institutions (Huang, 2013). But in urban centres, family support for the elderly can lead to burden and burnout. Zimmer (2005), in a study of Chinese family supports, said that the oldest old "are at a high risk of experiencing chronic and mental health disorders." This decreases their ability to care for themselves and in many cases causes them to rely on family members for support (p. 526). A study in Beijing found that 50 percent of families report financial, emotional, or other hardship in caring for their older relatives. This pressure will grow in the future as small young families care for four to six older relatives.

An increase in the very old population (80+) will put a further burden on the young. The very old population will increase almost sixfold, from 16 million in 2006 to 94 million in 2050 (Johnson, 2006). Li Bengong, the executive deputy director of the China National Committee on Aging, said, "The situation is very serious.... We have weak economic capability to cope with the aging of the population" (Johnson, 2006, p. 20A).

Like other developing nations, China will find it hard to meet the needs of its growing older population. The high cost of building and running long-term care institutions will limit their growth. China has just begun to develop home care options that fit its culture and meet the needs of its aging population. The increased number and proportion of older people in China and their need for support will lead to social change.

The Chinese government recognizes the need for change. Beginning January 1, 2016, China revised its one-child law and now allows parents to have two children. Jiang, Armstrong, and Cullinane (2015) report that "the ruling Communist Party issued the following statement: 'To promote a balanced growth of population, China will continue to uphold the basic national policy of population control and improve its strategy on population development. China will fully implement the policy of 'one couple, two children' in a proactive response to the issue of an aging population.'"

Still, this change in policy will not immediately influence the economy or population aging. Children born under the new policy won't enter the workforce for decades. Tao Wang, chief China economist at UBS (cited in Buckley, 2015) said, "Anything demographic, we always have to think ... of decades in terms of long-term impact."

China's example shows that social policy can accelerate or moderate population aging. But the effects of population policies take place over many years—sometimes with unintended consequences. For example, China will not reap the benefits of this two-child reform for many years to come. In the meantime, couples from the one-child policy era will now have two children to care for in addition to their parents and grandparents.

Summary of Aging in Least and Less Developed Regions

Gerontologists need new theories of aging to explain the changes taking place in developing nations and new plans for social change to fit the needs of an aging world.

Solutions that fit Western developed countries do not necessarily fit developing nations. The Western view of aging does not fit developing nations' needs. For example, the Western, problem-centred approach to aging makes traditional views of old age appear old-fashioned and ineffective.

Western societies evolved away from family-centred supports for older people. Developed countries created pensions and other welfare programs for their older citizens. But this approach requires an economy and political system that supports these programs. In the developing nations of sub-Saharan Africa, for example, family support and family relations in many cases provide the only support for older people (Oppong, 2006).

Developing countries have neither the social services nor the economic resources to help the elderly poor. Nor can these countries afford the housing, health, or welfare services for the old that Western countries have set up. These countries may need a hybrid system that combines family support with government programs. China, for example, has experimented with a variety of pension programs for rural elders. These programs provide small pensions that would replace about 15 percent of the rural retirees' former income. Rural retirees rely for the rest of their income on funds from their children who live and work in urban centres. One plan, started in 2009, provided a pension to parents if their children contributed to the plan. Other countries with other traditions and different resources will find other responses to the challenge of population aging.

Aging in the Developed Nations

The developed nations (such as Sweden, Japan, and Canada) will also have large proportions of older people in their populations. Their populations have grown older over many decades and will continue to get older in the future. In 2010, the five oldest countries in the world (Japan, Italy, Germany, Sweden, and Greece) had more than 18 percent of their populations age 65 or older (Population Reference Bureau, 2010). Europe had a greater proportion of older people than any other continent. One projection estimates that nearly one-third of the United Kingdom's population (29.4 percent) will be age 60 or over in 2025.

In 2010, Japan had the highest percentage of older people in the world (23 percent age 65 and over). A low **fertility rate** (a rate of 1.3 in the early 2000s, while the replacement rate is 2.1) and low death rate will lead to continued population aging in Japan (Monk, 2009, p. 182).[3]

Projections up to 2050 predict that in that year, nearly two of every five people in Japan will be age 65 or older (Maeda, 2009). And Chandler (2006) calls the pace of population aging in Japan "without precedent in the industrial world" (p. 62).

The large increase in the oldest old (age 80+) poses unique problems for Japan. This population will grow to more than 17 million by 2050, a 2.7-fold increase from 2005. Nearly one person in five in Japan will be age 80 and over in 2055. This large increase in the very old will

place heavy demands on government, community, and family support systems.

The Japanese call this *koreika*, or societal aging. A 1995 survey conducted by the Ministry of Health and Welfare in Japan (National Institute of Population and Social Security Research (Japan), 2004) found that 57.3 percent of the respondents considered population aging "a trouble" or "a serious trouble." And 68 percent of the respondents said that Japan should increase its birth rate to slow population aging.

Japan faces challenges similar to those of other developed nations. These challenges include higher costs for pensions, more chronic disease, and the need to rethink healthcare services for an older population. Japan differs from other developed nations in the speed of its transition to an aging society. In only 26 years (1970 to 1996), the Japanese older population grew from 7 percent to 14 percent of the population. By contrast, some European societies took as long as 115 years to see this kind of change. Japan will have to make changes quickly to meet the needs of its aging population and to maintain its standard of living.

The European nations will face challenges similar to those in Japan (although not as extreme). Europeans feel some concern about population aging. The Pew Research Center (Stokes, 2014) reported that 41 percent of Italians saw aging as a major problem. And 52 percent of Spaniards were very worried about the problem. Europeans have lived with gradual population aging for many decades, and they have evolved social and policy responses to their older populations. Despite some recent concerns about European economies, European countries remain among the wealthiest and most politically stable countries in the world. They have the resources and experience to cope creatively with population aging.

Developed nations such as Japan will see increases in healthcare and pension costs. In response they will change pension policies and encourage people to work longer, raise taxes to cover increased costs, or increase the national debt. Whatever approach they choose, developed nations will all have to provide more services to their aging populations.

Summary of Aging in the World Today

Population aging affects nations and people throughout the world. The developed nations will have greater proportions of older people in their populations in the future. They will have the best chance of creating a materially satisfying old age for their people. The least developed

---

3   The fertility rate estimates the average number of live births a woman can be expected to have in her lifetime, based on the age-specific fertility rates of a given year. The total fertility rate equals the sum of single-year age-specific fertility rates (Statistics Canada, 2011a).

---

fertility rate "the average number of children that would be born alive to a woman during her lifetime if she were to pass through all her childbearing years conforming to the age-specific fertility rates of a given year" (Beaujot & McQuillan 1982, pp. 220–221)

Korea has modernized rapidly. Many older people in Korea keep shops. Others sew and sell their goods. They help their extended families with the income, and they stay active in the community.

and the less developed nations will have larger numbers of older people than ever before. They will struggle to provide resources for the old and the young.

Population aging will take place in the context of rapid urbanization, industrialization, globalization, and changes to the environment. We cannot look back. New conditions call for new responses. The large number of older people in the world today, historian Peter Laslett (1976) wrote, "remains irreducibly novel, it calls for invention rather than imitation" (p. 96).

TIME TO REVIEW

What role does the economy and the state of a country's development play in their ability to respond to population aging?

What role does culture play in shaping a society's response?

How do world trends such as global economic activity shape the lives of old and young in the least developed and less developed nations?

CANADA COMES OF AGE

Canada is a relatively young nation compared with European countries. Until the late 1800s, less than 5 percent of the population was age 65 and over. The country then aged gradually through the first part of the 20th century. In 1971, Canada had 8 percent of its population over age 65. By July 1, 2014, 15.7 percent of the population of Canada was age 65 and over (Statistics Canada, 2014d).

By 2036, Canada could have between 9.9 million and 10.9 million older people. The portion of Canada's population age 65 and over at that time could be between 23 percent and 25 percent of the total population (Milan, 2011a; Statistics Canada, 2011b; Turcotte & Schellenberg, 2007). By 2061, Canada could have between 11.9 million and 15.0 million older people. The older population at that time could make up between 24 percent and 28 percent of the population (Statistics Canada, 2014d)—more than five times the proportion of older people in 1901.

CHEN WS/Shutterstock

What caused Canada to age in the 20th century? What will keep it aging in the years ahead? And what effect will population aging have on Canadian society? A look at Canada's population, past and present, will answer these questions.

Demographers, experts who study population change, use at least three measures of population aging: (1) the number of older people in a population; (2) the median age of a population; and (3) the proportion of older people in a population. These measures allow demographers to study change in the composition of a population. They allow studies to compare one group at several points in time or to compare groups with one another. A population ages when any of these measures increase. A society that has a large number of older people and a high proportion of older people is said to be an old or aging society.

Demographers study three conditions that affect a population's size and structure: immigration, death rates, and birth rates. Each of these demographic forces caused the Canadian population to age from the mid-1800s to the present.

Immigration

Of the three demographic forces—immigration, birth rates, and death rates—immigration played the smallest part in the aging of Canada's population. It also affected different parts of Canada in different ways. Waves of immigration in the early 20th century brought new groups of young adults to Canada. Between 1901 and 1911, 1.5 million people arrived in Canada, as many as in the previous 40 years combined. Immigration in the first decade of the 20th century accounted for 44 percent of Canada's total population increase in those years (Statistics Canada, 1981; Statistics Canada, 2012a). Most of these immigrants came to Canada as children or young adults (20 to 34 years old). These young people (and the families they raised) helped keep Canada's population young at the start of this century.

Immigration continued to add to Canada's population until the start of the Great Depression. Between 1901 and 1931, successive waves of immigration brought between 3.5 to 4.5 million people to Canada. These immigrants did more than simply increase the number of people in Canada; they also changed the face of Canadian society. Immigrants before 1900 came mostly from the British Isles, but Leacy (1983) reports that

Canadians of "other European" origin rose from 37 percent of the European-born population in 1881 to 43 percent of the same population in 1911. Germans, Norwegians, Mennonites, Doukhobors, Chinese, and Southern and Eastern Europeans arrived in large numbers. Most of these immigrants were young males.

Many of the Eastern Europeans, along with Icelanders and Mennonites, settled on the prairies. Manitoba in the 1880s and Saskatchewan around 1911 had high birth rates due to the large number of young immigrants in their populations (Henripin, 1972). This large wave of immigration partly explains the drop in the proportion of people over age 65 in Canada from 5 percent in 1901 to 4.7 percent in 1911 and 4.8 percent in 1921. This same group of immigrants increased Canada's older population as they aged. The *Census of Canada* (cited in Turcotte & Schellenberg, 2007) reported that in 2001, 52 percent of all immigrants age 65 and over had arrived in Canada before 1961. Many older immigrants today came to Canada during World War II and the first years after the war (Statistics Canada, 2012a).

Immigration accounted for about 6 percent of Canada's population growth from 1946 to 1978. The proportion of foreign-born people in the older population reached a peak of 38.8 percent in 1961. The proportion of immigrants in the older population then dropped to 28.4 percent by 2001 (Turcotte & Schellenberg, 2007). In part, this reflects a counter-trend to the immigration of older people to Canada. By age 75, Denton and Kusch (2006) said, "net migration is actually negative" (p. 14). This meant that more immigrants in the oldest age groups left Canada than arrived. We know little about why people leave Canada in late old age. They likely return to their home country, probably to enjoy their traditional culture in their old age and to die in their homeland.

Older people comprised only a small percentage of the total immigrant population admitted to Canada in the recent past. They made up between only 2 percent and 4 percent of all immigrants and refugees between 1995 and 2004. Nearly all (91 percent) immigrants age 65 or over today came as family members of Canadian residents (Turcotte & Schellenberg, 2007).

More recent immigration patterns will change the character of Canada's older population in the future. In the period before 1961, most of Canada's immigrants—almost 90 percent—came from the United Kingdom or Europe. This pattern shifted dramatically between 1981 and 2001. The proportion of immigrants from Western and Northern Europe and the United States decreased by almost half (from 45.5 percent to 24.6 percent), while the proportion of immigrants from Asia rose more than

median age half the population is older and half is younger than the median age

EXHIBIT 3.4   *The Aged Population, Canada, 1851 to 2041 (absolute numbers and percentages)*

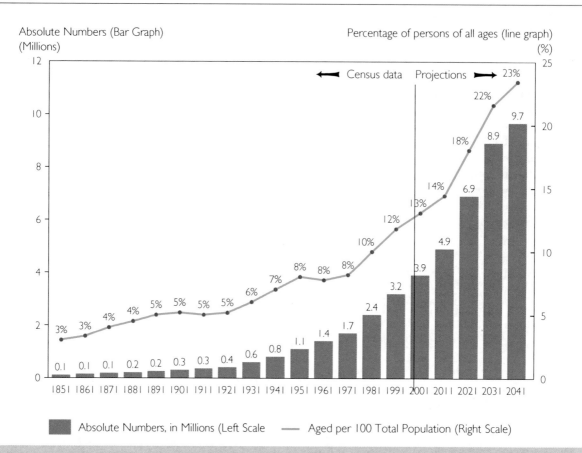

Absolute Numbers (Bar Graph)
(Millions)

Percentage of persons of all ages (line graph)
(%)

■ Absolute Numbers, in Millions (Left Scale）   — Aged per 100 Total Population (Right Scale)

Note that the proportion of people age 65 and over increased from 5 percent of the total population in 1901 to 14.4 percent of Canada's population in 2011 (Health Canada, 2001; Statistics Canada, 2007a, 2011c). This chart projected an increase in the proportion of older people to 23 percent in 2041.

From 1901 to 2011, the number of older people increased more than 16 times (from 0.3 million to 4.9 million people). This chart projects a near doubling of the 2011 number of older people in 2041 (from 4.9 million to 9.7 million people). These figures give a picture of the large increase in the proportion and absolute number of older people in Canadian society in the years ahead.

Sources: 1851–1971: J. A. Norland. *The Age-Sex Structure of Canada's Population,* Statistics Canada, Catalogue No. 99-703 (1976); 1891–1991: Statistics Canada, Age, Sex, and Marital Status (data products: Nation series: 1991 Census of Population), Catalogue No. 93-310 (1992); Statistics Canada, *Canada Year Book 2011,* Catalogue No. 11-402-X (2011c); and Projections: M. Turcotte and G. Schellenberg, *A Portrait of Seniors,* 2006. Statistics Canada, Catalogue No. 89-519-XIE (2007); Statistics Canada, Annual Demographic Estimates Canada, Provinces and Territories, Catalogue No. 91-215-X (2011a). Reproduced and distributed on an "as is" basis with the permission of Statistics Canada.

two and a half times (from 13.9 percent to 36.5 percent) (Caron Malenfant, Lebel, & Martel, 2010; Turcotte & Schellenberg, 2007).

By the early 1990s, the largest portion of immigrants came from the developing countries of Asia, the Caribbean, South America, and Central America. During this period, more than half of immigrants came from East and South Asian countries, including India and China, particularly Hong Kong. Immigrants from mainland China made up the largest number of immigrants in the

1990s (Chui, Tran, & Maheux, 2007). Between 2006 and 2011, the largest percentage of immigrants to Canada (56.9 percent) came from Asia and the Middle East (Statistics Canada 2013a).

Compared with other demographic forces, immigration has little effect on the aging of Canada's population. First, Canada admits relatively few immigrants. A total of only 252,000 people immigrated to Canada in 2006 (a rate of 8 per thousand). In 2009 to 2010, only about 270,000 people immigrated to Canada (Statistics Canada,

2013a). Between 2006 and 2011 a total of only 1.2 million people immigrated to Canada (Statistics Canada, 2013a). If present immigration trends continue, immigration will have little effect on population aging in the future (Chui et al., 2007).

Second, most immigrants are between the ages of 25 and 54. The median age of immigrants who arrived in 2011, for example, was 31.7 years. This came to about six years lower than the median age in Canada that year (37.3 years) (Statistics Canada, 2013a). These people will tend to lower Canada's median age today and will not add to the older population for many years.

Fertility, not immigration, causes population aging or rejuvenation. But immigration does increase the diversity of all age groups, and it creates new challenges for families, communities, and groups that serve older people.

Death Rates

The **death rate** is the number of deaths per 1,000 people in a population. By the late 19th and early 20th centuries, death rates began to drop across Canada. The most reliable figures for this period come from Quebec. Henripin and Peron (1972, cited in Beaujot & McQuillan, 1982) said that the crude death rate in Quebec dropped by half, from 24 per 1,000 in 1871 to 1875 to 12.9 by 1921 to 1925. These figures probably overestimate the drop in death rates for Canada as a whole because historians say that Canada's large cities still suffered from high death rates (Artibise, 1977; Cross, 1983); however, a steady, if not dramatic, decline did take place. Life expectancy at birth rose from 41.9 years for men and 44.2 years for women born in 1851 to 60.0 years for men and 62.1 years for women born in 1931. Life expectancy at age 65 had increased to 78 years for men and 78.7 years for women by 1931. This meant that more people lived longer and that more lived into late old age.

Life expectancy increased steadily for men and women of all ages between 1941 and 2008 (except most recently for women age 85 and over) (Statistics Canada, 2011d). Infants during this time gained the most years in life expectancy. The infant mortality rate (the death rate of children less than one year old) decreased dramatically over the 20th century. By 2008, the **infant mortality rate** had fallen to about 0.5 percent of live births (compared with about 10 percent in 1926) (Martel, 2008; Statistics Canada, 2011e)

Control of childhood disease, better prenatal care, and improved nutrition account for most of this change. Lavoie and Oderkirk (1993) said that in the mid-19th-century epidemics of cholera (in 1832), typhus (in 1846–1849), and smallpox (in 1885–1886) led to high infant and child mortality. Nagnur and Nagrodski (1988) reported that "infectious and parasitic diseases, including tuberculosis, accounted for almost 15% of deaths in 1921; in 1986, however, only about half of one percent of all deaths were the result of these diseases" (p. 26).

From 1920 to 2009/2011 in Canada, life expectancy at birth increased from 59 years for males and 61 years for females to 79.3 years for males and 83.6 years for women (Statistics Canada, 2011d, 2013b). Since 1979, Canada has also seen a drop in the most common causes of death in adulthood—cancer and cardiovascular disease (which includes ischemic heart disease, strokes, arterial disease, hypertension, and rheumatic heart disease) (St-Arnaud, Beaudet, & Tully, 2005; Statistics Canada, 2014e).

People in the oldest cohorts show some of the greatest improvements in life expectancy. Between 1921 and 2007, men age 85 and over showed a 50 percent increase in life expectancy and women showed a 70 percent increase in life expectancy (Milan, 2011b).

Today Canada, along with Japan, Sweden, Denmark, Norway, and the United States, has some of the highest life expectancies in the world. This means that more Canadians than ever before will live to old age.

Birth Rates

The birth rate is the number of births per 1,000 women in a population. A decline in the birth rate is the primary cause of population aging. In the 1700s, for example, Quebec had one of the highest birth rates ever recorded and it had a young population. From 1700 to 1730, women averaged the birth of one child every two years until they reached age 30. Women who reached the age of 50 averaged giving birth to eight or nine children. In the middle of the 18th century, the average was 13 children per woman (Henripin, 1972). During this time, the birth rate ran two to six times higher than the death rate.

Quebec's population grew twentyfold from 1608 to 1765, and by one and a half times again by 1851 (Kalbach & McVey, 1979). Death rates in Quebec began to decline after 1780, but despite this, the province's birth rate was still high and the population stayed young (Henripin, 1972; Kalbach & McVey, 1979).

Frontier regions in Ontario also had high birth rates. McInnis (1977) and Henripin (1972) reported rates similar to Quebec's in rural Ontario in the mid-19th century. A writer of the time reported that children "in Canada

---

death rate the number of deaths per 1,000 people in a population

infant mortality rate the death rate of children less than one year old

EXHIBIT 3.5 *Evolution of Life Expectancy by Age and Sex, Canada, 1921 to 2009/2011*

Year	At Birth		At Age 65		At Age 85	
	Males	Females	Males	Females	Males	Females
1921*	58.8	60.6	13.0	13.7	4.1	4.3
1931[1]	60.0	62.1	13.0	13.7	4.1	4.4
1941*	63.0	66.3	12.8	14.1	4.1	4.4
1951	66.4	70.9	13.3	15.0	4.3	4.7
1961	68.4	74.2	13.5	16.1	4.6	5.0
1971	69.4	76.4	13.8	17.6	5.0	5.9
1981	71.9	79.0	14.6	18.9	5.1	6.5
1991	74.6	80.9	15.7	19.9	5.4	6.9
2001	76.9	81.9	17.0	20.4	5.5	6.8
2009/2011	79.3	83.6	18.8	21.7	6.5	7.7

*The 1921 figures exclude Quebec, and the 1921–1941 figures exclude Newfoundland.

This table shows a steady increase in life expectancy at birth, at age 65, and at age 85 from 1941 to 2009/2011 for both sexes (with one exception: life expectancy at age 85 for women dropped slightly in 2001). Milan (2011b, p. 1) says that these figures show "not only the gains against overall mortality but also the increasing longevity after age 65." Note that women have a longer life expectancy than men at every age and in each time period. This may be due to differences in lifestyles, habits, or the environment (e.g., working conditions).

Recent figures show a change in life expectancy between the sexes. Compared with women, between 1981 and 2009/2011, men at birth and at age 65 gained more years in life expectancy. Changes in work patterns and lifestyles for men and women may account for this change. For example, women have entered the workforce in large numbers. This may add to the stresses they face and this may translate into smaller gains in life expectancy.

Sources: Adapted from M. Turcotte and G. Schellenberg, *A Portrait of Seniors* 2006, Statistics Canada, Catalogue No. 89-519-XIE, Tables 2.1.1 and 2.1.2 (2007). Based on Statistics Canada, Life Tables, Canada, Provinces and Territories, Catalogue No. 84-537-XPB; Canadian Vital Statistics, Birth and Death Databases; and Demography Division (population estimates) and Statistics Canada, Vital Statistics—Death Database; Estimates of Population by Age and Sex for Canada, the Provinces and the Territories; Statistics Canada. 2012d. Canada at a Glance 2012, Catalogue No. 84-518X, p. 5, http://www.statcan.gc.ca/pub/12-581-x/12-581-x2012000-eng.pdf; A. Milan, 2011. *Mortality: Overview*, 2007. Report on the Demographic Situation in Canada. Component of Statistics Canada Catalogue No. 91-209-X. Statistics Canada, Life tables, Canada, provinces and territories 2009 to 2011 (2013 lifetables). Reproduced and distributed on an "as is" basis with the permission of Statistics Canada.

[are a man's] greatest blessing, and happy is that man who has a quiver full of them" (Philpot, 1871, cited in Gagan, 1983a). McInnis (1977) said that Upper Canada at the time "had one of the highest birth rates in the world" (p. 202). Gagan (1983a) estimated that settled Ontario families in Peel County had eight to nine children. New immigrants to Canada before 1830 often had more.

Canada began its **demographic transition** around 1850 as the birth rate decreased. (A population undergoes a demographic transition when it changes from a high birth rate/high death rate condition to a low birth rate/low death rate condition). Henripin (1972) showed that the birth rate in Canada as a whole dropped by about 30 percent from 1851 to 1951 (with a sharp drop during the 1930s). Although

the provinces all showed the same declining trend, their individual rates varied: the Quebec birth rate dropped least, by about 20 percent from 1851 to 1921; Ontario showed a sharp drop of about 50 percent during this same time; Manitoba between 1881 and 1921 showed a drop of more than 60 percent; and Saskatchewan showed a drop similar to Manitoba's between 1901 and 1921 (Henripin, 1972). This drop in the birth rate, more than any other demographic change, led to the aging of Canadian society.

TIME to REVIEW

What role did the death rate play in population aging in Canada? What role will it play in the future?

What role did the birth rate play in population aging in Canada? What role will it play in the future?

demographic transition occurs when a population changes from a high birth rate/high death rate condition to a low birth rate/low death rate condition

Baby Boom and Baby Bust

Two phenomena that affected the birth rate, the **Baby Boom** and the **Baby Bust**, account for the greatest changes in Canadian population from 1946 to the present.

Canada went through the Baby Boom from 1946 to 1964. An explosion in the fertility rate explains this phenomenon. Between those years, the total fertility rate rose from 2.83 to 3.84. The **age-specific birth rate** (the number of births in a given age group per 1,000 women in that age group) nearly doubled for women under 20 years old, going from 30.7 to 59.7 at the height of the Baby Boom in 1959 (Milan, 2011c; Statistics Canada, 1978, cited in Beaujot & McQuillan, 1982). Women averaged more than 3.5 children each at the height of the Baby Boom (Statistics Canada, 2007a). Total births soared from 264,000 in 1941 to almost 476,000 in 1961 (Statistics Canada, 1978, cited in Beaujot & McQuillan, 1982).

Baby Boom the sharp rise in the fertility rate in Canada from about 1946 to the early 1960s (precise dates vary)

Baby Bust the sharp drop in the fertility rate from the mid-1960s on

age-specific birth rate the number of births in a given age group per 1,000 women in that age group

The Baby Boom spanned a 20-year period. The first Baby Boomers (born in 1946) turned 65 in 2011. The youngest Baby Boomers will turn 65 in 2029. At that time, the leading-edge Baby Boomers will be 83 years old.

Foot and Stoffman (1998) said that "Canada's was the loudest baby boom in the industrialized world" (p. 25). Owram (1996) wrote that after World War II, "society seemed to revolve around babies ... sometimes it seemed like everybody was pregnant or had a new baby" (p. 5). Foot and Stoffman traced the Baby Boom to two conditions: a good economy (people felt confident about the future) and a large number of immigrants (many of childbearing age). The Baby Boom reversed not only a general trend of decreased fertility rates that had begun in the 19th century but also a century-long trend in population aging (excluding the years 1911 to 1931) that began in the late 19th century. Statistics Canada (2012c) reported that in 2011, Baby Boomers made up nearly one-third (29 percent) of the Canadian population.

After 1965, Canada went into a baby bust. Foot and Stoffman (1998) trace the baby bust to two trends: the use of the birth control pill and the increased participation of women in the labour force. During the baby bust, the total fertility rate dropped from 3.84 (children per woman) in

---

EXHIBIT 3.6 *The Stages of the Demographic Transition*

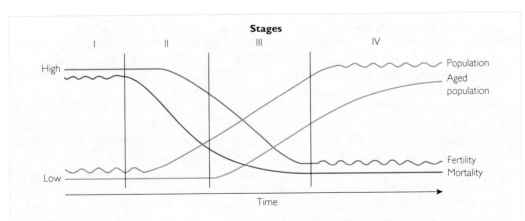

Stage I: High fertility and high mortality. Small population. Slow and varied population growth. High proportion of young people, small proportion of older people.

Stage II: High fertility; mortality begins to decline. Population begins to grow as more children survive. Population explosion may occur and society may get younger. Small proportion of elderly people.

Stage III: Fertility declines and mortality declines further. Population growth begins to level off at larger size. *This is the stage of the transition from a young high-growth to an older low-growth population.* Older population begins to grow as a proportion of the population.

Stage IV: Low fertility, low mortality. Low population growth and large proportion of older people in the population.

Source: Reprinted from "Demography of Aging" by G.C. Meyers, in R.H. Binstock & L.K. George, *Handbook of Aging and the Social Sciences*, 3rd ed. (p. 25). Copyright 1990 Elsevier, with permission.

EXHIBIT 3.7 *Portrait of Generations, Using the Age Pyramid, Canada, 2011*

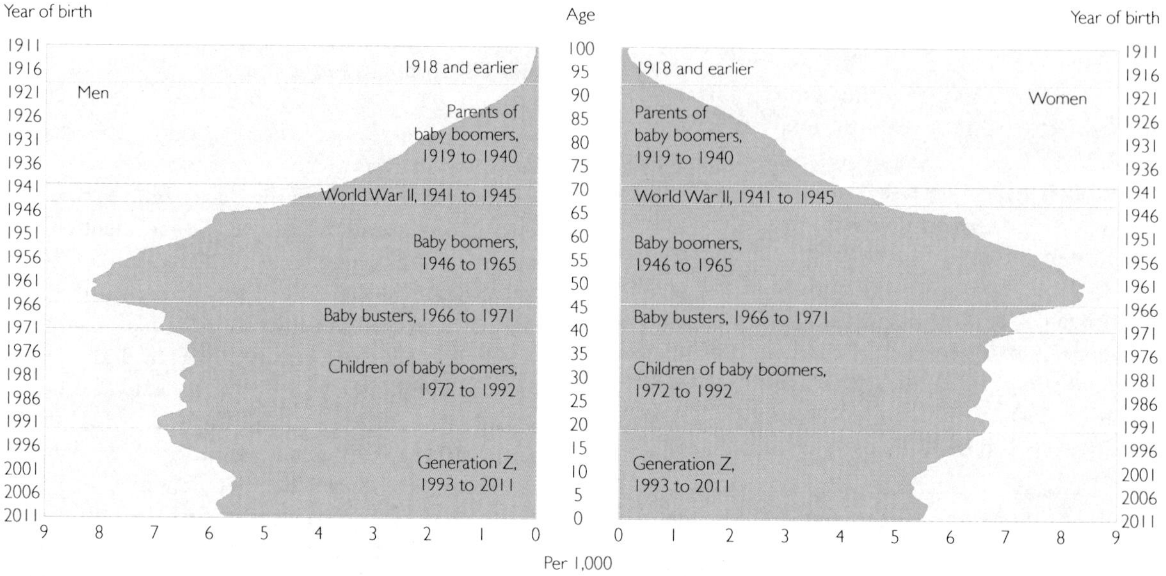

Year of birth | Age | Year of birth

Per 1,000

This chart shows the distribution of Canada's population by generational characteristics in 2011. Note the large size of the Baby Boom generation. Contrast the size of the Baby Boom generation with the size of their parents' generation to get a sense of the "boom" that took place. Note also the small size of recent birth cohorts (born after 2000). The advance of the Baby Boom generation into old age, along with recent small birth cohorts, will lead to rapid population aging in the years ahead.

Source: Statistics Canada, Generations in Canada (2012). Based on 2011 Census of the Population figures, http://www12.statcan.gc.ca/census-recensement/2011/as-sa/98-311-x/98-311-x2011003_2-eng.cfm. Reproduced and distributed on an "as is" basis with the permission of Statistics Canada.

1961 to 2.81 in 1966, a rate below that of 1941. It dropped farther to 1.51 in 2000 (Beaujot & McQuillan, 1982; Denton & Spencer, 2003; Milan, 2011c). Canada's low fertility rate in 2011, at 1.61, fell below the level (2.1) needed to replace the population (Statistics Canada, 2015b).

Low fertility led to a sharp drop in the number of young people in Canada. Between 1976 and 2011, for example, the population of people 0 to 14 years old decreased from 26 percent of the population to 16.7 percent of the population (McKie, 1993; Statistics Canada, 1989, 2012d). Statistics Canada projects a continuing decline in the proportion of the population made up of younger people in the years ahead.

This decrease in the birth rate, especially the sharp drop since the mid-1960s, sped the rate of population aging in Canada. Between 1961 and 2014, the population age 65 and over rose from 7.6 percent to 15.7 percent of Canada's population. The older population is projected to continue to increase as more of the Baby Boom generation moves into old age.

Will an increase in fertility in the years ahead reverse population aging? Statistics Canada considers this unlikely.

Women today marry later and give birth to their last child at a later age than ever before (30.2 years in 2011). And they have fewer children. Statistics Canada (2015b) said, "Many women are having their first child at an older age, compared with several decades ago. They are having fewer children overall, and therefore, are concluding their childbearing in a relatively short time span." The fertility rate of 1.61 children in 2012 would have to increase to 2.1 just to reach a replacement level. To give an idea of where the fertility rate stands today in relation to the past, the rate during the height of the Baby Boom, reached 3.9 children per woman (Statistics Canada, 2007b).

Prospective Aging: A New Way to Think About Population Aging

Canadian demographers use the age 65 as a handy way to mark the start of old age. This makes some sense because Canadian life expectancy averages about 80 years. That creates 15 years or so of healthy old age, and then some years of greater dependence on formal and informal supports.

EXHIBIT 3.8 *Median Age* of the Population, Canada, 1881 to 2056 (excluding Newfoundland)*

Year	Median age	Year	Median age*
1881	20.1	1971	26.2
1891	21.4	1976	27.8
1901	22.7	1981	29.6
1911	23.8	1986	31.6
1921	23.9	1991	33.5
1931	24.7	1996	35.3
1941	27.0	2001	37.6
1951	27.7	2006	39.5
1961	26.3	2011	40.6
1966	25.6	2056	46.9 (projected)

* Half the population is older and half is younger than the median age.

Canada's median age rose 20.5 years from 1881 to 2011. The table shows a jump of 2.3 years in the median age between 1931 and 1941. This reflects the sharp drop in the birth rate during the Depression years. The table also shows a rise in the median age until 1951, followed by a drop from 1952 to 1971. During these years, the rise in the birth rate (the Baby Boom) led to a decrease in the median age by 2.1 years to 25.6 years. In 1976, the median age rose again to above its 1951 high of 27.7. By 1986, more than half the population was over the age of 30. The aging of the Baby Boom cohorts will increase the median age in the years ahead. Statistics Canada projects a continued increase in the median age into the middle of this century.

Sources: Dominion Bureau of Statistics, 1964, Census of Canada (1961 Census), Bulletin 7: 1–4, Ottawa: Queen's Printer; Statistics Canada, 1968, 1966 Census of Canada, Vol. 1 (1–11), Ottawa: Queen's Printer; Statistics Canada, 1973, Census of Canada (1971 Census), Bulletin 1: 2–3, Ottawa: Information Canada; Statistics Canada, 1978, cited in W.E. Kalbach and W.W. McVey, 1979, *The Demographic Bases of Canadian Society*, 2nd ed., Toronto: McGraw-Hill Ryerson, 161, Table 6:3; M.S. Devereaux, 1987, "Aging of the Canadian Population," *Canadian Social Trends*, Winter, 37–38; C. McKie, 1993, "Population Aging: Baby Boomers into the 21st Century," *Canadian Social Trends*, Summer, 2–6; and M.V. George et al., 1994, *Population Projections for Canada, Provinces and Territories 1993–2016*, Ottawa: Ministry of Industry, Science and Technology. Adapted from Annual Demographic Statistics, Cat. No. 91-213, and from Statistics Canada (2002a), 11 Median Age, Canada, 1901–2011, 11. http://www12.statcan.ca/english/census01/Products/Analytic/companion/age/ cdamedaget.cfm, Statistics Canada. July 1, 2006. *The Daily*. http://www.statcan.ca /Daily/English/061026/d061026b.htm; Statistics Canada. 2007. Portrait of the Canadian Population in 2006, by Age and Sex, 2006; Statistics Canada. 2011 Annual Demographic Estimates Canada, Provinces and Territories. Catalogue No. 91-215-X. Ottawa: Minister of Industry. Statistics Canada. 2012. Population by broad age groups and sex, counts, including median age, 1921 to 2011 for both sexes—Canada. http://www12.statcan.gc.ca/census-recensement/2011/dp-pd/hlt-fst/assa/s/highlight.cfm?TabID=1&Lang=E&PRCode=01&Asc=0&OrderBy=6&Sex=1&View=1&tableID=22, Reproduced and distributed on an "as is" basis with the permission of Statistics Canada.

But the use of 65 as shorthand for the start of old age makes less sense for societies with an average life expectancy of, say, 60. In that kind of society, very few people would live into their later 60s and beyond. A person in a less developed society may show physical signs of aging in their 40s—signs that a person in Canada would not show until their 60s or 70s. If the needs of old age begin at age 45, then the use of age 65 as the start of old age may underestimate the older population's need for support.

Demographers have created a measure of old age that takes these societal differences in average life expectancy into account. Demographers refer to this measure as **prospective aging** (Martin, 2011). This measure allows demographers to compare societies with different life expectancies, and to compare one society at different points in time as life expectancy increases. One measure of prospective aging uses the number of years of remaining life expectancy as the start of old age. For example, a defined number of years, say 15 years, subtracted from average life expectancy would serve as the start of old age. This would give a different age for the start of old age in different societies.

The use of prospective aging may lead to a change in Canadian thinking about later life. For example, in 2009/2010 Canadian males had an average life expectancy at birth of 79.3 years and females had an average life expectancy at birth of 83.6 years (Statistics Canada 2011d). Statistics Canada (2010b) projected an average life expectancy at birth in 2036 for males of 84 years and for females, 87.3 years. This higher life expectancy in the

prospective aging allows demographers to compare populations with different life expectancies, and to compare one society at different points in time as life expectancy increases; one measure of prospective aging uses a number of years of remaining life expectancy as the start of old age

EXHIBIT 3.9 *Canada's Oldest Seniors*

Canada has more very old people (age 80 and over) in its population than ever before. Statistics Canada (2011c) reports that 1.38 million Canadians were age 80 and over in 2010. They made up 4 percent of the total population in that year. Projections show that people in this age group could double by the year 2031. And the number of people age 80 and over could quadruple to 5.1 million people by 2061.

Few studies have looked at this age group. The National Advisory Council on Aging (1992) talked with some of Canada's oldest seniors to learn something about their lives and how they see the world. Although this study took place some years ago, the excerpts below show the varied perspectives very old people have on aging and on living in late old age:

It is very peculiar being over 100 ... and fun. I'm a rare breed, a museum piece. They bring people in to look at me. I would say that I have had a very good life. There have been bad times but I am happy now, although my health is slowly deteriorating. Last night, I went to hear my granddaughter and her husband in a Gilbert and Sullivan musical. I was an actress and singer when I was young. They must get it from me. (101-year-old widow living in a long-term care facility)

You shouldn't be congratulated for living too long. It's a question of endurance. Nothing works properly in my body, from teeth to toes.... Old age is a form of punishment. The more you go on, the more you endure. I hate every minute of it. (87-year-old single woman living in a long-term care facility)

I really mourn the loss of my friends. I miss most of all having someone to share news or encounters, reports of the day when I return from shopping or an outing. I sometimes find myself saying "I must tell Mary about that," and then I remember that she is no longer around. We used to be a close group of six and now I am the only one left. (87-year-old widow living in a seniors' housing complex)

I was born blind and have been living here for 40 years. Last year, I married a fellow resident who has cerebral palsy. I am happier than I have ever been in my life because I am so much in love. Life is good to me now. (80-year-old woman living in a long-term facility)

These women report a variety of responses to living into late old age. One has found new love. Another expresses frustration at her physical condition.

Questions

1. How do you think you will feel if you live to a very old age? Does the thought of living 100 or more years appeal to you?

2. Do you think you might agree with some of the comments above? Which ones seem closest to your own imagined view of very old age?

Sources: National Advisory Council on Aging, 1992, *The NACA Position on Canada's Oldest Seniors: Maintaining the Quality of Their Lives*. Ottawa: National Advisory Council on Aging. Courtesy of the National Advisory Council on Aging, Health Canada 2000.

future would raise the societal start of old age. Canadian programs, policies, and researchers might begin to use age 70 as the start of old age in Canada.

To some degree, this adjustment has begun. Canadian social institutions such as government and private pension plans have traditionally defined 65 as the start of old age. Retirement in the past began for most people at age 65. But as Canadians live longer, pension plans (such as the Canada Pension Plan) have begun to adjust the age of full pension eligibility upward. This will begin to shift the start of old age to 70 or later.

Also, many older workers now delay the start of retirement. They realize that longer life expectancy will mean more years of retirement and potentially shrinking fixed pension payments due to inflation. These changes in thinking about old age reflect longer life expectancies and better health in old age in Canada.

The concept of prospective aging can help societies better calculate the start of pension plans and other benefits. In less developed societies (with lower life

expectances), this would mean starting these programs at ages below the traditional age of 65. Developed nations, such as Canada, would start programs for older adults at an age higher than age 65.

Summary of Population Aging in Canada

Canada's demographic transition took place from before 1850 to the present in three stages. In the first stage, before 1850, Canada had both high death and high birth rates and, in Ontario and the Maritimes, a high rate of immigration. These forces kept the average age of Canadians low. In Ontario in the mid-19th century, for example, half the population over the age of 15 was made up of men under the age of 30 (Gagan, 1983b). Statistics Canada data puts the median age of Canadians in 1901 at 22.7 (compared with a median age of 37.3 in 2011).

The second stage of the transition began after 1850, as major declines in birth and death rates occurred. This stage differed from the second stage in Europe's demographic transition, where death rates declined and birth rates stayed high for some time before they dropped to complete the transition. In Canada, both birth and death rates dropped (with some important fluctuations in birth rates) until the present. These changes transformed Canada from a young nation (under 4 percent of the population age 65 and over) in the late 1800s to an older nation (with about 7 percent of the population age 65 and over) by 1950.

Today, in the third stage of the transition, Canada has low death rates, low birth rates, and an aging population. As this century progresses, Canada's population pyramid will change from that of a wide-based, triangular shape to a more rectangular one.

AGING IN CANADA TODAY

Older people differ by age, sex, marital status, and health. They come from different ethnic backgrounds, have lived through varying historical events, and live in all parts of the country. These differences make older people one of the most heterogeneous age groups in Canada.

The Aging of the Older Population

The older population itself has grown older. The population age 80 and over totalled 1.4 million people in 2012, or 4.1 percent of the population. In 1982, this age group made up only 1.9 percent of the population. By 2036, this group is projected to grow to 7.6 percent of the population (nearly double the proportion today and almost four times the proportion of the population in 1982) (Statistics Canada, 2012n).

The 85 or older age group showed a more than five-fold increase in its population from 139,000 in 1971 to 755,000 in 2015. Légaré and colleagues (2015) project an old-old (85+) population of 2.7 million in 2060—3.6 times larger than in 2015. This group now ranks as the largest number of very old people in Canada's history.

Canada also has seen a growth in its oldest-old population—people age 100 and over. Statistics Canada (2011c, 2012f) reported that Canada had 5,825 centenarians in 2011, up from 4,635 in 2006 and 3,795 in 2001 (a 35 percent increase in a decade). Women outnumbered men in this group more than four to one. Statistics Canada said people in this group, born around 1911, had about a 1 percent chance of reaching age 100. Genetics, a good environment, a healthy lifestyle, and good luck account for the long lives of these elders (Statistics Canada, 2007a). Statistics Canada (2011c) projected that the number of people over age 100 could grow to 17,600 by 2031 and 78,300 by 2061—more than a thirteenfold

projected increase between 2011 and 2061. Settersten and Trauten (2010) call old age today "life's longest period, extending three or more decades" (p. 143).

The increase in the oldest-old population will raise new issues. For example, the oldest-old group, compared with people age 65 to 74 (the young-old), shows higher rates for institutionalization, disability, and poor health.

Wister and Wanless (2007) studied 90-year-olds in Canada and reported that this group had high rates of chronic illness and cognitive impairment. Eighty-five percent of 90-year-olds in this study suffered from some functional disability, and the majority of the people had at least one chronic illness. Compared with people under age 85, those age 85 and over show a greater need for daily support. This group will need more institutional support, medical care, household maintenance, and community healthcare services in the future.

At the same time that the oldest cohorts grow in size, the younger cohorts age 65 and over will also become larger. Projections show more than a doubling in the population age 65 to 74 between 1998 and 2041 (Lindsay, 1999). This large number of older Canadians will make new demands on society. The young-old have already begun to change retirement patterns by retiring early or by staying at work past age 65. This group will want more recreational and educational opportunities. Some will want second careers. Services such as job bureaus, schools, and counselling programs will be needed to serve these people.

Programs for older people will cost taxpayers more money. In 2011/2012, for example, Canada spent $39.1 billion on its income security system (compared with $11 billion in 1984) (Service Canada, 2012). More of this money went to older people than to any other age group. The single largest amount of this money went to the **Old Age Security pension** (including the **Guaranteed Income Supplement** and the **Allowance**). If the proportion of older people more than doubles in the next 50 years as expected, will the public be willing to pay out even more of the country's income for older people? Or will the costs lead to resentment and a crisis in Canadian society? We will discuss these issues in more detail later in this chapter under the topic of dependency ratios.

Old Age Security pension Canada's basic retirement income program, which supplements the income of nearly all of the country's older people

Guaranteed Income Supplement an income supplement program for the poorest older people

Allowance an income supplement program for spouses of pensioners who receive only the Old Age Security pension and have a combined income below a set amount

EXHIBIT 3.10   *Population Pyramids by Age Group and Sex, Canada, 1991, 2011, 2031*

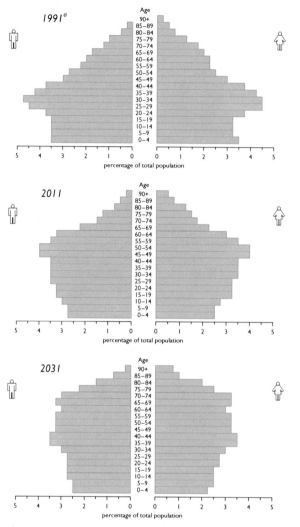

[a]Estimates based on 1991 census; standard projection as of January 17, 2000.

These pyramids show at least three important trends: the dramatic growth in size of the older age cohorts (age 40+); a continued higher proportion of women compared with men in the oldest cohorts; and the movement of the Baby Boom cohorts into old age. The 2031 pyramid is top-heavy, with small younger age groups below a large older population.

Source: Adapted in part from Statistics Canada, Population Projections for Canada, Provinces and Territories, 1993–2016, Catalogue No. 91–520, 1993–2016. Reproduced and distributed on an "as is" with the permission of Statistics Canada.

TIME TO REVIEW

What caused the growth in the very old and oldest populations in Canada?

Why do demographers expect that past trends in population aging will continue in the future?

Ethnicity

Compared with the proportion of immigrants in other age groups, immigrants made up a larger percentage of the older population. Nearly three-quarters of immigrant seniors arrived in Canada before 1976. They moved to Canada for economic reasons or to join their families, and this trend of family reunification continues today

EXHIBIT 3.11 *Number of People Age 80 years and Over in the Canadian Population, 1956 to 2011*

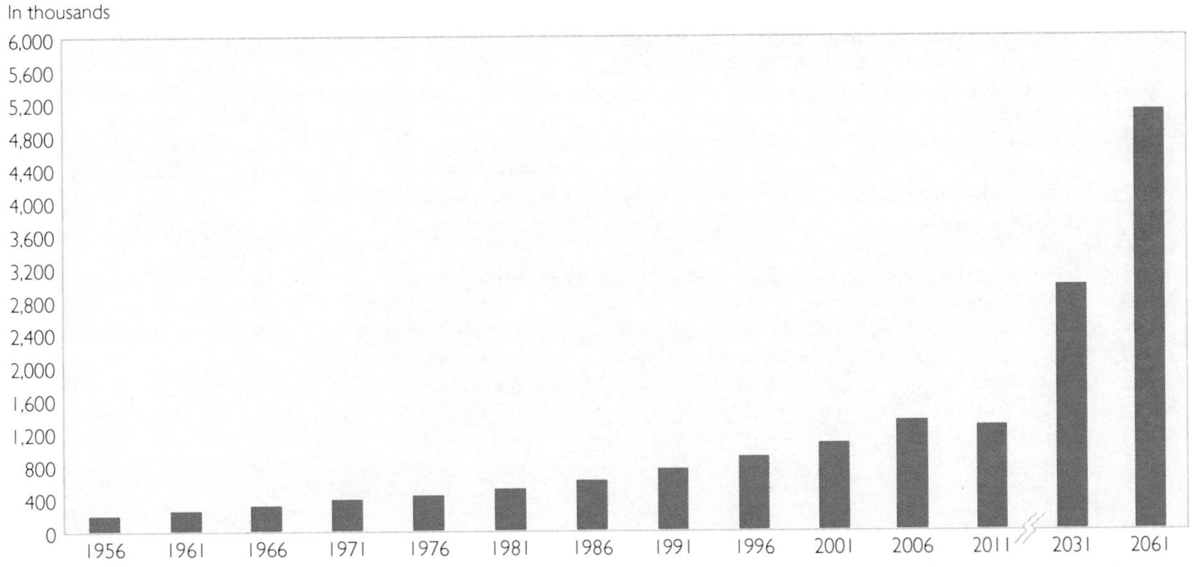

In thousands

This graph shows the rise in the number of people age 80 and over from 1956 to 2061. The growth in this population is projected to dramatically increase in the next 50 years, as the Baby Boom generation reaches late old age.

Sources: Statistics Canada, Portrait. Portrait of the Canadian Population in 2006, by Age and Sex, 2006 Census. Age and Sex, 2006 Census. Census Year 2006. (2007) http://www12.statcan.ca /census-recensement/2006/as-sa/97-551/pdf/97-551-XIE2006001.pdf, Figure 5, p. 10; Milan, A., and Vézina, M. 2011. "Senior Women." Component of Statistics Canada Catalogue No. 89-503-X. *Women in Canada: A gender-based statistical report.* Statistics Canada. Reproduced and distributed on an "as is" basis with the permission of Statistics Canada.

(Citizenship and Immigration Canada, 2011; Ng et al., 2012; Turcotte & Schellenberg, 2007).

Ng and colleagues (2012) reported that in the past, most immigrants age 65 and over came from Europe, but more recent immigrant seniors have come from South Asia, East Asia, and the Middle East. Smaller groups of older immigrants came from the United States, Africa, Central and South America, and the Caribbean. More than half of younger immigrants today (age 25 to 54), who arrived between 2001 and 2006, came from Asia and the Middle East (Statistics Canada, 2006b). This represented a shift in immigration patterns away from Europe and toward Asia and the Middle East. This will lead to larger proportions of non-European seniors in the future.

About 1.4 million people in Canada in 2011 identified themselves as Indigenous. This group has a relatively young population. The median age of the Indigenous population was 28 years in 2011, while non-Indigenous people had a median age of 41 in that year. The Indigenous median age could reach as high as 36.7 years in 2031 (compared with a non-Indigenous age of 43.1 years in 2031). The Indigenous group in 2011 had 83,000 seniors.

They made up 5.9 percent of the Indigenous population (Turner, Crompton, & Langlois, 2013). This came to less than half the proportion of older people found in the non-Indigenous population (14.2 percent). A large proportion of older Indigenous people (34 percent) lived on reserves. Another 43 percent lived in cities.

The Indigenous senior population doubled between 1996 and 2006 (about four times the rate of growth of the non-Indigenous older population). Still, due to high fertility rates and the large number of younger Indigenous people, seniors comprise a relatively small proportion of the Indigenous population. Projections showed that Indigenous elders will make up only about 6.5 percent of the Indigenous population by 2017. At that time, Canada as a whole will have 16.6 percent of its population age 65 and over (Statistics Canada, 2005a, 2006c, 2009).

Indigenous elders continue to play an important role in some communities, serving as keepers of the group's traditions, history, culture, and language. They also pose a challenge to their communities due to Indigenous elders' high rates of chronic illness, such as diabetes and high blood pressure (Turcotte & Schellenberg, 2007). These illnesses require long-term care.

EXHIBIT 3.12   *A Gerontologist Reflects on Late Old Age*

Elaine Brody, at age 86, provided a feature article for The Gerontologist. *Brody is one of the best-known gerontologists of her generation. Among other achievements, she coined the phrase "woman in the middle" to capture the caregiving demands on middle-aged women. In this essay she provides a personal view of late old age. Below you will find some excerpts that focus on her experience*

"My present perspective, then, is that of an 86-year-old woman who, I suppose, was prepared for old age intellectually but not emotionally. Even my children are growing into the stages of life I studied. Common experiences of old age, such as illness and losses, were unexpected, even though expectable.

"I do not remember becoming old. All of a sudden, I was there. Others perceive me as old. Cars stop to let me cross. People offer to help carry my packages. My grandchildren 'check up' on me when my children are out of town and hold my arm when we cross a street. People my age walk more slowly and fatigue more quickly. Our waistlines thicken and our hair thins. Our balance is not great. We develop lots of wrinkles. One of my granddaughters is observant in detecting which of my friends have had what she calls 'a little work done' on their faces (though having such 'work' is by no means limited to the old). Some have had to give up driving—with the accompanying loss of independence and feelings of competence that entails....

"Our perspective on age has changed. One day, three people in succession said to me, 'Did you hear about poor Harold? He was too young to die. He was only 83.' A 92-year-old man died suddenly. Until that moment, he had been a regular member of his Neighbourhood Security Patrol. As comedian Jerry Seinfeld said, 'Who dies at 70 anymore? It's old-fashioned....'"

Source: Adapted from Brody, E.M. (2010), "On being very, very old: An insider's perspective," *The Gerontologist*, 50(1), pp. 2–10, by permission of Oxford University Press.

Most older people in Canada today speak either English or French. A small group of older immigrants, who learned a language other than English in their native countries, continue to use this language at home. For example, 4.5 percent of people age 75 to 84 and 6.1 percent of people age 85 and over could speak neither English nor French, and this proportion has increased since 1981 (Turcotte & Schellenberg, 2007). The increase in numbers of immigrants from non-English speaking countries explains this change in language use. Compared with older immigrant men, older immigrant women tend to have less ability in English and French. Many of these women worked only in the home and spoke only their mother tongue.

This brief look at ethnicity and aging shows that ethnic groups vary in their size, their location, their proportion of older people, and their *institutional completeness*, a term that refers to the amount of community support a group offers its older members. Ethnic diversity means that policies for older people from different types of groups (large, small, rural, or urban) will vary. Planners need to take ethnicity into account, along with socio-economic status and physical mobility, when designing programs for older people. (Chapter 4 provides a more detailed look at ethnicity and aging.)

Geographic Mobility

Older people follow internal migration patterns similar to those of younger people, but they are less mobile (Newbold, 2007). Longino and Bradley (2006) reported that non-retired people in their 50s and 60s who moved around for work tended to make long-distance moves. People with higher education and people whose children had moved a long distance away also tended to make long distance moves.

Still, Northcott and Petruik (2011, 2013) say that most Canadian seniors "age in place." For example, over 70 percent of seniors did not move in the past five years based on 2006 census data. And over 90 percent did not move in the past year. Of the seniors who did move, more than half stayed in the same city, town, or municipality (Northcott & Petruik, 2011).

Many older people prefer to stay in their familiar surroundings. They often own their own homes and prefer to stay there as long as they can. People who live on farms tend to move to a nearby town if they move. Healthcare needs may force a move. Women (many of them widowed), compared with men, show a greater likelihood of making a local move (Northcott & Petruik, 2013).

Only a small percentage (1.2 percent) of older people move between provinces, so interprovincial moves have only a small impact on provincial older populations. British Columbia, for example, with the highest net migration of seniors, increased its number of seniors in 2005 by only 1,184 people (Turcotte & Schellenberg, 2007).

Litwak and Longino (1987; also Newbold, 2007) took a life course perspective in their description of senior mobility. They described three stages of later life when people may choose to move. The first is the retirement stage, when freedom from the need to live near work allows people to move to a more pleasant climate and to have a more relaxed lifestyle. Migration researchers say that retirees often have "'remote thoughts' or daydreams about moving before they make a move. They also gather information about new locations that shape their decision to move" (Longino & Bradley, 2006, p. 77).

Studies in Canada, Great Britain, and the United States have reported that retirees tend to migrate to specific areas. Mobile older people tend to move to places with a mild climate, often by a coast. They also look for places with a reasonable cost of living.

Some senior migrants move out of the country to the U.S. Sunbelt. Others move to Canadian retirement sites like Niagara-on-the-Lake and Victoria, British Columbia. People in good health, with grown children, and with a good income in later life tend to make lifestyle-related moves. Sharma (2013) reported that the probability of an amenity move increases for people without physical limitations, without cognitive problems, who are married, who have a higher income, and have a better education.

Often, migrants have visited a place before. Some have even lived in the place for part of the year in the years before they move. People who plan to move should think about the community life, the culture, and the kinds of services they use (e.g., a library, a hospital, or a theatre).

The census metropolitan areas with highest percentages of the population age 65 years and over in 2010 were Peterborough (19.4 percent), Trois-Rivières (18.7 percent), Kelowna (18.5 percent), and Victoria (18.1 percent) (Charbonneau, Ouellet, & Milan, 2011). These locations attract older people because of the warmer climate and the quality of life older people enjoy there.

Some migrants move temporarily. As many as 80 percent of seasonal migrants never settle permanently in their seasonal homes. This most often applies to Canadian snowbirds who move to the United States. These seniors have a home in Canada and rent or own a home in a warmer climate. Geography plays a role in where Canadian snowbirds settle. For example, Quebec seniors tend to winter on the east coast of Florida. Ontario seniors choose Florida's Gulf coast. Seniors from the Prairies tend to winter in Arizona, Texas, and California. Some people sell their home in Canada but keep a cottage at a lake. Northcott and Petruik (2011) call them "permanent vacationers." They number in the tens of thousands, possibly the hundreds of thousands.

When people's health declines, they make fewer and shorter visits to their seasonal locations. Eventually, they give up their seasonal visits, which leads to the next stage of migration.

In the second, or disability stage, physical limitation may lead the older person to move closer to children or others who can give them help. Statistics Canada reported that, compared with people with no disability, older people who had a long-term illness or disability showed a greater likelihood of moving at this stage (Turcotte & Schellenberg, 2007). The likelihood of this type of move increases with age. Migration due to disability may run counter to amenity migration. People return to locations where they can get care and support from family members (Northcott & Petruik, 2011).

The third stage is the severe disability stage, and it requires the older person to move to a nursing home or other institution.

Migration patterns show a flow of seniors in and out of geographical regions. But some trends do appear. Older people most often say that they move to buy a new home, to change the size of their home, to move to a less expensive home, or to move to a home with special features. Older people also say that they move to be near family or to care for a family member. People move to get more support as they age (Newbold, 2007). Older people tend to move from farms to towns or cities, and most older movers relocate within their local area. Provinces, towns, and neighbourhoods with increased numbers of older people will face new challenges in the future.

Increased Numbers and Proportions of Older Women

The death rates for older women have decreased faster than they have for older men through most of the last century. In 1931, the life expectancy for a 65-year-old woman was 13.7 years; in 1961, it was 16.1 years, and in 2009/2011, it was 21.7 years. For a 65-year-old man, it was only 13.0 years in 1931, 13.6 years in 1961, and 18.8 years in 2009/2011 (Statistics Canada, 2013b). As a result of these changes, the proportion of older women in the population has grown.

Lindsay and Almey (2006) said that women age 65 and over "constitute one of the fastest growing segments of the female population in Canada" (p. 265). Between 1961 and 2010, this group increased from 717,000 to 2.7 million people (nearly a fourfold increase). This has increased the proportion of older women in the female population and the proportion of women in the total older population. In 2010, women made up 56 percent of all older people and 63 percent of people age 80 and over (Milan & Vézina, 2011). Women age 80 and over comprise the fastest-growing segment of the older female population.

The number of senior women will increase even more rapidly in the future due to the aging of the Baby Boomers. Milan and Vézina (2011) project that by 2031, one woman in four will be a senior.

At the same time that the older female population increases, the male older population will also increase. The life expectancy of men has begun to catch up to that of women. At the beginning of the 20th century, there were 105 men for every 100 women age 65 and over, and in the mid-1950s older men still outnumbered older women. But by the 1960s, the pattern reversed.

By 2000, there were 74.9 men for every 100 women age 65 and over. Projections for 2050 showed that the ratio of men to women age 65 and over will increase to 78.6 men per 100 women. In 2051, women will make up 53.2 percent of all people age 65 and over (a decrease from

2004) (Lindsay & Almey, 2006; Milan & Vézina, 2011). Changes in the lifestyles of women, including the stress of the workplace, in part account for these changes.

This convergence of life expectancies will translate into lower rates of widowhood for older married women in the future. And women who experience widowhood in the future will typically do so at a later age. Longer life expectancies for men may mean more social support for women to live at home as they age.

Still, the higher proportion of women in later life and their greater chance of widowhood make old age a different experience for women and men today.

EXHIBIT 3.13   *Population Age 65 and Over, Percentage by Province and Territory, 2011 and 2036 (projected)*

Province	% of Total Provincial/Territorial Population	
	2011	2036*
Newfoundland and Labrador	16.0	31.1
Prince Edward Island	16.3	27.3
Nova Scotia	16.6	28.6
New Brunswick	16.5	29.4
Quebec	15.9	25.1
Ontario	14.6	23.1
Manitoba	14.3	21.4
Saskatchewan	14.9	23.3
Alberta	11.1	21.0
British Columbia	15.7	23.8
Yukon	9.1	19.9
NWT	5.8	20.1
Nunavut	3.3	10.7

*First medium-growth scenario.

This chart shows the number and proportion of older people in each province and territory for 2011. It also shows a projection of the proportion of older people in each province in 2036. Note that by 2036, all provinces and territories will have higher proportions of older people. In many cases, the proportion of older people in a province or territory will double or nearly double. But population aging will occur unevenly across the country.

In 2036, Newfoundland and Labrador, for example, will have nearly one-third of their populations age 65 and over (31.1 percent). Many of the other provinces will have one-quarter or nearly one-quarter of their population age 65 and over. Yukon and the Northwest Territories will have relatively young populations, with one person in five age 65 and over. Nunavut will have the youngest population in the country, with only 10.7 percent of its population age 65 and over in 2036.

Communities with large increases in the proportion of older people will need to shift social and healthcare resources to serve this age group. But in some cases these communities have the fewest economic resources. This could lead to greater disparities in the care of older people between wealthier and poorer communities.

Sources: Adapted from M. Turcotte and G. Schellenberg, *A Portrait of Seniors 2006*, Statistics Canada, Table 1.2, p. 29 (2007); Statistics Canada, Population Projections for Canada, Provinces and Territories 2009 to 2036. Catalogue No. 91-520-X. (2010e). Also, Statistics Canada, Figure 7. Proportion (in percentage) of the population aged 65 and over, Canada, provinces and territories, 2006 and 2011. (2015) Retrieved from https://www12.statcan.gc.ca/census-recensement/2011/as-sa/98-311-x/2011001/fig/fig7-eng.cfm. Reproduced and distributed on an "as is" basis with the permission of Statistics Canada.

Gerontologists call widowhood for women "an expectable life event." Many older women today will need to adapt to a singles lifestyle after a lifetime of marriage. Today, some women have to move to an institution because they have no spousal support at home.

The large size of the older female population means that policies and programs for older people will have a greater impact on women than on men. Most women will live longer than men, so programs for older people will affect them for more years. Also, women in later old age, many of them widows, will need more support and services. The absence or presence of formal or informal social supports will have the greatest impact on older women as a group. This is especially true of healthcare, housing, and income supports. We will study these programs in detail in the chapters ahead. For now, we will look at the overall impact of population aging on Canada's economy.

THE IMPACT OF POPULATION AGING

The Dependency Ratio and the Cost of an Aging Population

Projections of population aging often assume a high dependence of older people on the young. Some authors take this a step further and predict economic decline and social tension due to population aging. A report by the Pew Research Center (Stokes, 2014), for example, began by calling an aging population "a looming economic and social burden." Another study (Eurostat, 2014) said that an older population creates "an increased burden on those of working age." Gee and Gutman (2000) called this extreme view apocalyptic demography. And they said that it distorted the likely effects of population aging.

Gerontologists use a figure called the overall dependency ratio (or rate) to gauge the burden that the old and the young place on people in middle age. Experts arrive at this ratio by adding the number of people age 19 and under to the number of people age 65 and over. They then divide this figure by the number of people 20 to 64.

$$\frac{\text{(Population age 0 to 19)} + \text{(Population age 65+)}}{\text{Population age 20 to 64}}$$

Some writers use the ages 0 to 14 for the youth population. In that case, while the ratio of people age 65 and over to those age 15 to 64 will increase two and a half times from 1996 to 2056, the ratio of young people (age 0 to 14) to those age 15 to 64 will decrease by about one-third. When combined, these projected changes in

the young and old populations result in a lower overall dependency ratio in 2056 compared with the early 1970s.

Denton, Feaver, and Spencer (1986) said that projected overall dependency ratios should calm "those who are concerned about the possible inability of the economy to support its dependent population, young and old, in the decades ahead" (p. 86). But not everyone agrees with this conclusion.

The crude dependency rates, which are based solely on the number of people in each group, tell only part of the story; they do not address the economic burden of an older population.

Scarth (2003), for example, said that it costs more to serve an older population because healthcare for the old costs more than education for the young. Some studies (Robson, cited in Scarth, 2003) say that Canada may need a 3 percent increase in its gross domestic product to finance social security and other programs for older people in the future.

This would lead to an increase in social spending of 87 percent in Canada. This is high compared with predictions of 65 percent for the United States and 40 percent for Japan. It seems as if the apocalyptic demographers have a point when they warn about the crisis due to population aging. But not everyone agrees with these predictions either.

Evans et al. (2001), in an article entitled "Apocalypse No," challenged the prediction of economic crisis. They agreed that "'apocalypse' cannot be definitively ruled out" (p. 162), but they say that the data so far do not support the link between population aging and runaway healthcare costs.

Evans and his colleagues (2001) reviewed economic data from the British Columbia healthcare system. They studied acute hospital use, physicians' services, and drug use. They looked at the impact of population aging on the costs of these services. They found that, in spite of rising numbers of older people in British Columbia, the per capita use rate of hospitals declined from 1969 to the late 1990s. They found that in-patient days per capita decreased because of changes in healthcare practices over the 30-year period. Hospitals tended to send people home sooner and they increased same-day surgical care.

apocalyptic demography the use of demographic facts (such as the aging of the population) to project the high cost of an aging population and predict that population aging will lead to economic and social crisis

overall dependency ratio (or rate) the combined total number of people age 19 and under and people age 65 and over divided by the number of people age 20 to 64.

crude dependency rates are based solely on the number of people in each age group

EXHIBIT 3.14 *Observed and Projected Youth, Senior, and Total Demographic Dependency Ratios, 1971 to 2056*

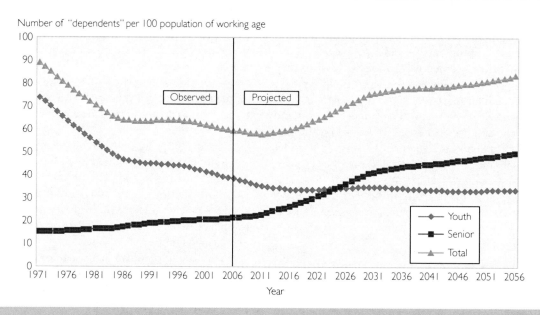

This exhibit illustrates the concept of the elderly and youth dependency ratios. The elderly dependency ratio refers to the number of people age 65 and over divided by the population age 20 to 64. The youth dependency ratio refers to the number of people age 0 to 19 divided by the population age 20 to 64. These ratios show how these two subgroups contribute to the total and overall dependency ratio.

This chart shows an increase in the elderly dependency ratio over the years shown here. It also shows a decrease in the youth dependency ratio. The total dependency ratio decreases through the early years of the 21st century. It then increases but remains below the 1971 level in the years after 2011. These figures suggest that an older population will not necessarily create an undue burden on Canadian society.

Source: Statistics Canada, Dependency Ratio, Healthy People, Healthy Places. Based on CANSIM Tables 051-0001 (1971–2008) and 052-0004 (2009–2056), (2011e), http://www.statcan.gc.ca /pub/82-229-x/2009001/demo/dep-eng.htm. Reproduced and distributed on an "as is" basis with the permission of Statistics Canada.

Evans and his colleagues go on to show that projections for the age 65-and-over population in 1969 should have led to "truly hair-raising" costs—triple the 1969 cost by the end of the 20th century and another doubling for the next 25 years (p. 169). In reality, the researchers found that acute care hospital use rates decreased by half for the age 65-and-over population since 1969. This study shows the danger of projecting costs based on population growth figures alone.

Forces other than population aging, such as the increased cost of new and expensive drugs, account for most of the rise in drug expenditures. Evans and his colleagues (2001) said "the evidence from British Columbia is quite clear.... Changes in the age structure of the overall population have not in the past been major contributors to trends in the per capita utilization of ... three categories of health care services, and they will not be in the future" (pp. 176 and 181).

Researchers may disagree about the specific impact of an aging population on health and public pension resources, but nearly all of them agree that more healthcare and retirement income resources will go to serve older people. And this will cost more money. This shift in resources to the older population will force Canadians to make choices. The next 50 years will see increased debate over this issue and will see some change in the allocation of health and income resources.

Dependency ratios can present a gloomy picture of the future. But dependency ratios tell only part of the story. Even small changes in Canada's economy and social

elderly dependency ratio the number of people age 65 and over divided by the population age 20 to 64

youth dependency ratio the number of people age 0 to 19 divided by the population age 20 to 64

norms could lead to large decreases in the cost of an older population. Linda G. Martin (2011), in a discussion of dependency ratios, cautioned against using dependency ratios to predict the impact of population aging. "Dependency ratios," she said, "are, at best, rough indicators of the extent to which one grouping in a population is dependent on another group" (p. 38). She went on to say that not all young people work for pay, and many older people now choose to work full-time or part-time. In addition, research shows that resources tend to flow from the older to younger generations in a family.

Dependency ratios work best in estimating the impact of population aging on public pensions and healthcare costs. But even here, improvements in health, the postponement of disability until later in life, and more people working past age 65 may all moderate the cost of a large older population (Martin, 2011).

TIME TO REVIEW

What are the pros and cons of using dependency ratios to project future costs in an aging society? Why do some economists urge caution in using these ratios to predict future costs?

What can Canada do now to prepare for an aging society?

Other changes in social policies would also reduce the costs of an older population. For example, most projections of costs for an aging society assume a traditional retirement age of 65 (when people become entitled to Old Age Security payments). But government policies now allow workers to choose a later retirement and many older workers have begun to make this choice.

A change in the age of eligibility for government pensions would reduce pension costs and would encourage workers to stay at work longer. This would increase the number of people who contribute to the pension system and would reduce the number of years they draw a pension.

Also, the Canadian government has taken steps to invest current Canadian Pension Plan (CPP) surpluses in income-generating markets. This is expected to keep the CPP solvent for many years to come without further raises in the cost to workers. Canada can deal with the social "problem" of population aging by redefining pension eligibility and by creating sound policy today.

Dependency ratios also ignore the fact that people save in one part of their lives and use these savings later. Today, many middle-aged workers have private pension plans and savings. And these resources have begun to play an important role in retirees' lives. In the future, compared with pensioners today, retirees will have to rely more on their own resources when they reach old age. In the future, for example, more flexible retirement plans will allow some people to work full- or part-time after age 65. The Canada Pension Plan has changed its rules to make both early and late retirement more attractive. All of these trends will change current dependency patterns and alter projected costs.

A stronger economy would also ease the dependency burden. Even a small improvement in the income of middle-aged people, compared with costs for services to the old, would significantly decrease the cost of an older population to society. In a strong economy, higher costs for services to the elderly may not create a burden for the middle-aged.

Discussions of dependency ratios focus mostly on the costs of an older society. But an older population will also bring benefits, such as a lower crime rate and an increased focus on fitness, diet, and disease prevention. These trends have already begun. Larger numbers of older people may also improve the economy. They will likely spend their savings on travel, restaurants, and professional services. These trends may reduce some of the cost of social resources and create a higher quality of life for people of all ages. They will also create jobs for young and middle-aged workers.

Chappell (2011), in a book review on population aging, said that a focus on dependency ignores the contributions of older people to their families and communities. "The unpaid labour that older adults contribute, particularly to their children and grandchildren, but also their volunteer activities after retirement and their own spending on consumer goods, are not considered" (p. 193).

Creedy and Guest (2009, cited in Cooke, 2011) pointed out some further benefits of an older society. For example, an older population will lead to a mix of skills in the workplace. Young workers bring physical strength and recent training. Older workers bring "experience, reliability, and knowledge" (p. 196). This mix could enhance productivity.

An older population will want different goods and services. This could lead to new investments in technology and products. Increased productivity could "potentially swamp" the effects of increased dependency ratios (p. 197). Cooke concluded (based on Creedy and Guest's research) that the "fears of an ageing crisis are unfounded, and this conclusion is supported by a growing consensus in economics journals" (p. 197).

McDaniel (1986) said that dependency ratios lead to **demographic determinism**. Demographic determinism assumes that population dynamics determine the future of social relations and social institutions. But McDaniel believed that social policies have the greatest effect on the cost of an older population. Martin (2011) put this plainly when she wrote, "Demography is not destiny" (p. 43). And society can do a lot to buffer the negative effects of population aging.

Demographers need to study the connections between demographic facts, political realities, and social change. How much choice do countries have in how they will respond to demographic change? What determines the choices a country makes? Are there models of preferred adaptation to an aging population? Romaniuk (2010) said that societies today with their low fertility rates and low death rates have entered an "unprecedented era in population evolution ... *a new regime of demographic maturity*" (p. 283, emphasis in original). "Not only do we live longer," he said, "but we are also healthier when we reach the upper level of our life span" (p. 286).

Countries such as Sweden, Denmark, and Great Britain could serve as models for Canadian policy. Already, more than 15 percent of the populations of these countries are over age 65, and they have not faced crises as a result (OECD (Organisation for Economic Co-operation and Development), 2011a). Progressive programs have been put in place to serve older people and citizens pay more in taxes to support them. These countries show that the transition to an older society can come about through planning, without social conflict and distress.

TIME TO REVIEW

What is apocalyptic demography?

What is demographic determinism?

Why do demographers use the dependency ratio when they study population aging? What does it tell us about population aging? What is the limitation of this measure? How can the use of this measure mislead the general public and policymakers?

What economic and social changes influence the effect of the dependency ratio on society?

---

demographic determinism the assumption that population dynamics determine the future of social relations and social institutions (e.g., the amount of dependency of the old on the young)

CONCLUSION

Canadian society has its own history, mix of ethnicity, age/sex ratios, economic institutions, and values. Canada also faces its own demographic issues. Canadians now expect to receive a public pension and free or low cost healthcare in old age. Canadian discussions of societal aging often revolve around the costs of these two systems.

Will the Baby Boom generation demand an unaffordable level of social support as it ages? Will the Baby Boomers develop a broader view of their relationship to society and moderate their expectations? Will younger people step up and pay for services to Baby Boomers as part of a social contract? After all, Baby Boomers can claim that they paid into the system all their lives and expect services and programs that meet their needs. This intergenerational debate will continue in the years ahead.

Canada will face unknown political, economic, and social challenges, and it will have to discover its own responses to population aging. An AARP (American Association of Retired Persons) (2007b) study of aging among the G7 nations (Japan, Germany, the United States, the United Kingdom, Italy, France, and Canada) ranked Canada among the nations that can achieve a good old age for its citizens. "Compared to the other G7 countries," the report concluded, "Canada, the U.K. and the U.S. have fewer demographic and labor market challenges and have a number of supportive policies in effect regarding the aging population. The combination of these factors makes these countries well-positioned for the future" (p. 54). The chapters that follow describe the conditions that support this optimistic view.

Preparation for the future will take planning, thought, and creative social action, and all of us will play a part in this societal transformation. The more we know about individual and population aging, the greater the chance that Canada will make a smooth transition to the future.

Summary

1. Societies throughout the world are experiencing population aging today. They have more older people than ever before, the median age of most populations has increased, and the proportion of older people in their populations has increased. These trends will continue in the future for most countries.

2. The United Nations divides nations into three categories: least developed, less developed, and developed. Each of these societies will face population aging. And each type of society will deal with population aging in a different way. Their responses will depend on their respective economic condition and their unique cultures. The developed nations have the most resources to deal with population aging.

3. Canada went through a demographic transition between 1850 and 1950. During this time, immigration increased, the death rate decreased, and, most importantly, the birth rate decreased. Between 1850 and 1950, the older population grew from about 4 percent of the population to almost 8 percent.

4. Canada has a younger population than most of the other developed nations. In 2011, 14.4 percent of its population was age 65 and over. Demographers project that this older population will more than double by 2061 and will equal 25.5 percent of the total population.

5. Canada today has a diverse older population. Older people differ by ethnicity, sex, income, education, and marital status. They also differ by age. Longer life expectancy in old age has given rise to a wide range of age groups within the older population. Large increases in the very old and oldest-old population will place new demands on healthcare and social service resources.

6. Ethnic groups vary in their size, location, proportion of older people, and the amount of community support they offer older people. Researchers and policymakers will have to take ethnicity, socioeconomic status, and geographical mobility into account when designing programs for older people.

7. Women make up a large proportion of the older population. Longer life expectancy for women explains this. The ratio of older men to older women will come closer to equal in the future. Improvements in life expectancy for men in part explain this development.

8. The growth of the older population (and the decrease in the younger population) has led some people to predict an economic crisis due to the large numbers of dependent older people. Gerontologists measure the dependence of young and old people on middle-aged people and call this measure the overall dependency ratio (or rate).

9. Experts look at dependency rates to project the future costs of an aging society. But the effect of future dependency rates will depend on a number of social conditions. A weak economy, low birth rates, low immigration rates, and a rise in costs of services for the old (compared with per capita income for the middle-aged) will increase the burden on middle-aged people.

A strong economy, higher birth rates, more immigration, and a rise in per capita income for middle-aged people (compared with costs in services for the old) will mean less of a burden on middle-aged workers. Changes in social values and retirement ages, as well as better preparation for old age by middle-aged people today, could also decrease the dependence of older people on the young.

10. Dependency rates focus on the costs of an aging society. But an aging society may have a lower crime rate, a lower accident rate, and more concern for lifelong health and fitness. These changes would decrease the waste of social and economic resources and improve the quality of life in Canada.

11. Canada can grow old without upheaval and conflict; most of the developed nations have done so. But the transition to an aging society will take planning, thought, and creative social action.

STUDY QUESTIONS

1. Compare and contrast the challenges facing the developed and developing nations as a result of the increase in the proportion and number of older people in their societies. Discuss some responses each type of society can make to these challenges.

2. What role did each of the three major demographic forces play in the aging of Canada's population from the 1850s to the present? How did each force affect societal aging? Describe the outcome of the demographic transition in Canada in terms of birth rates, death rates, life expectancy, sex ratios, and other current conditions.

3. What effect will population aging have on Canada's social and healthcare services? What changes in Canadian society could buffer an increase in demands on social and healthcare services due to population aging?

4. What do gerontologists mean by the overall dependency ratio? How do gerontologists calculate this ratio? How might a higher percentage of older people affect the economy in the future? Discuss the pros and cons of using the dependency ratio to predict the cost of an aging society in the future?

KEY TERMS

age-specific birth rate (p. 59)
Allowance (p. 63)
apocalyptic demography (p. 69)
Baby Boom (p. 59)
Baby Bust (p. 59)
birth rate (p. 47)
crude dependency rates (p. 69)
death rate (p. 57)
demographic determinism (p. 72)
demographic transition (p. 58)
elderly dependency ratio (p. 70)

fertility rate (p. 53)
Guaranteed Income Supplement (p. 63)
infant mortality rate (p. 57)
least developed regions (p. 47)
less developed regions (p. 47)
median age (p. 55)
more developed regions (p. 47)
Old Age Security pension (p. 63)
overall dependency ratio (or rate) (p. 69)
population aging (p. 46)
prospective aging (p. 61)
youth dependency ratio (p. 70)

Study Tools
CHAPTER 3

{

Located at retail.tophat.com:

- Review Key Terms with interactive and printable flash cards
- Check Your Comprehension and Think About chapter concepts by completing practice quizzes
- Develop Your Gerontological Imagination with class activities
- Analyze Aging in a Global Perspective with engaging case studies and critical thinking questions
- Demonstrate Your Knowledge of the Concepts by bringing your own experience to personal application questions
- Evaluate Aging in the Media by completing Internet activities with evaluation questions

CHAPTER 4

AGING AND ETHNICITY

CP PHOTO/Kevin Frayer

LEARNING OBJECTIVES

After reading this chapter, you will

LO1 Be able to describe the ethnocultural diversity of seniors in Canada.

LO2 Be able to assess the challenges and problems members of certain ethnocultural groups face as they age in Canada (e.g., seniors who are recent immigrants to Canada and Indigenous seniors).

LO3 Understand how membership in an ethnocultural group shapes the experience of aging in Canada.

LO4 Appreciate the changes that lie ahead for Canada's ethnocultural seniors.

INTRODUCTION

A student mentioned that she and her parents had migrated to Canada from Egypt. One of the authors asked if her parents' ethnocultural background influenced their experience of growing old in Canada. She said she would ask her mother. A day later she emailed the author the following message*:

> *Just had my daily talk with mum and when I told her about our conversation, she said that her main concern regarding aging in Canada has to do with how, here [in Canada], the elderly tend to be put in nursing homes and handed off to strangers to be taken care of. That's very rare in Egypt. Elders [in Egypt] have the benefit of maintaining their independence at home and having their kids visit them regularly to look after them (or even temporarily move back in if the parent is ill but not ill enough for hospital care). So, most Egyptians are actually lucky enough to die in the comfort of their own home among loved ones.*
>
> *The few families who do opt for nursing homes or long-term care facilities are looked down upon and considered to be "heartless" or "selfish." It's very shameful because the cultural view is—your parents took care of you from birth when you were unable to look after yourself, therefore it's only fair you do the same when they become unable to look after themselves near death.*
>
> *[The student added] I've never thought of this, really it isn't a question in my mind because I would never put my parents in a nursing home (personal communication, 2012).*

Ethnocultural seniors in Canada have specific expectations about aging based on their culture. For seniors born in Canada, their ethnocultural heritage influences their experiences growing up and growing old. Nevertheless, Canadian society and culture will strongly influence their expectations and experiences as they age.

For seniors who immigrated to Canada, either recently or in their youth, their ethnic culture may have a stronger influence on their experiences as they grow older. For example, a senior who is a recent immigrant will have little access to Canadian Old Age Security and other pension benefits. The recently arrived immigrant senior may have limited English or French language skills. This will restrict their ability to work outside the home. In addition to language problems and financial dependency, seniors who have come to Canada recently may encounter racism. In short, they may face barriers and lack the skills needed to negotiate their new culture. On the other hand, they may find strength and support in their cultural practices, religious beliefs, ethnic identity, family relationships, and participation in their ethnocultural community in Canada.

In contrast, long-time residents who came to Canada earlier in life will have integrated more into Canadian society. They will have access to Canadian Old Age Security and other pension benefits. They will probably have learned to live comfortably in an English- or French-speaking world.

Seniors born in Canada have different ethnocultural backgrounds. These seniors have different degrees of connection with their ethnocultural heritage and varying degrees of integration and assimilation into the Canadian mainstream. While there are differences in lifestyles and experiences in old age *between* ethnocultural groups in Canada, there are also differences among seniors *within* the same ethnocultural group.

Seniors (whether Canadian-born, recent immigrants, or earlier immigrants) tend to view life in Canada through the lens of their ethnicity and cultural background. Furthermore, many seniors hold bicultural identities. Labels such as *Italian Canadian* or *Chinese Canadian*, or *Indo-Canadian* express this bicultural orientation.

This chapter on ethnicity and culture shows the diversity that exists within the senior population in Canada today. It examines (1) what we mean by ethnicity, (2) the ethnocultural diversity of seniors in Canada, and (3) experiences of aging in an ethnically diverse Canada, along with implications for policy and practice.

CONCEPT OF ETHNICITY

The concept of ethnicity has many definitions. The country of birth may define a senior's **ethnicity** or, for the Canadian-born senior, the country or countries of birth of the senior's parents or grandparents may define the senior's ethnicity. Alternatively, citizenship, regardless of country of birth, can define ethnicity. Furthermore, a senior can choose his or her ethnic group identity— the same person, for example, might select Canadian, or French Canadian, or Métis.

While seniors may select their ethnic identity from a range of options derived from their own biography, seniors may also have an ethnic identity imposed on

---

*Reprinted with permission

ethnicity variously defined as country of birth, birthplaces of ancestors, cultural heritage, or self-identification with an ethnocultural group

EXHIBIT 4.1 *My Name Is Sophie and I Am Canadian*

What will it mean to be Canadian in the year 2026? Consider the following hypothetical example. This scenario reflects the increasing diversity of immigrants coming to Canada and the increase in intercultural marriages and unions. Sophie, who is not a real person in this hypothetical scenario, says the following:

> According to the Canadian census, [being Canadian] means: I am third generation Canadian on my mother's side and second generation Canadian on my father's side. My maternal grandparents are Canadian and British. My paternal grandparents are Senegalese. My aunts and uncles come from Canada, Thailand, Senegal and the Ivory Coast. I am Muslim by birth, my father is Muslim and my mother is Roman Catholic. Our family celebrates Aid El-Fitr and Eid Al-Adha, as well as Christmas and Easter. I have multiple citizenships: British, Canadian and Senegalese.

I attended French primary and secondary schools and then went on to university in both English and French. At home I spoke English with my mother and French with my father. I don't remember which language I learned first ... they both came at the same time, I guess. When I was younger I spent my summers between British Columbia, Ontario and Senegal. At the moment, 2026, I divide my time living between Abbotsford and Dubai, while working for three separate companies headquartered in Hong Kong, South Africa and Guatemala. My taxes are paid based on the amount of time I spend in each of my residences. Sometimes I pay four months of taxes to Canada and eight months of taxes to the United Arab Emirates, and other years I may pay more tax to Canada if I have spent longer lengths of time in my Abbotsford residence.

Questions

1. When Sophie retires from the labour force, will she spend her old age in Canada or in another country? Or will she move back and forth between two or more countries?

2. What social policies might influence her choice?

3. What will it mean to Sophie to be Canadian when she reaches old age and retires in 2046?

Source: Policy Horizons Canada, *Super Diversity in Canada 2011*, http://www.horizons.gc.ca/.asp?nm=2011-0072. Reproduced with the permission of the Minister of Public Works and Government Services Canada, 2016.

them by others. For example, a senior may define herself as Canadian but others may define her as Chinese or Asian. Finally, sometimes, a senior's religion serves as an ethnic identifier, as in the case of Jews, Mennonites, or Hutterites.

To highlight the difficulties and ambiguities with the concept of ethnicity, consider the case of a senior whose Jewish parents immigrated separately to Canada from Poland and Austria. Is this person Jewish, Polish, Austrian, European? You may note that your choice of ethnicity for this person may differ from the ethnicity this person chooses for herself. Exhibit 4.1 further illustrates the ambiguities associated with the concept of ethnicity.

Ethnic and Cultural Diversity

Societies tend to privilege some ethnicities and disadvantage others. We refer to the privileged as the dominant or majority group and to the disadvantaged as **minority groups**. In Canada, Canadians originally from northern and western European countries comprise the majority group. Others constitute various minority groups. The term **visible minority** refers to people with non-white skin tones. Indigenous peoples are counted separately

from the visible minority population. The invisibility of whiteness indicates the taken-for-granted advantages of white-skinned groups (Lund & Carr, 2015).

The term **culture** refers to shared language, beliefs, values, customs, and practices. Kaida, Moyser, and Park (2009), for example, examined ethnocultural groups in Canada that emphasized familistic (i.e., family-oriented) cultural values, such as Italians, Chinese, and South Asians. They also studied ethnocultural groups in Canada that emphasized individualistic cultural values, such as the British, Germans, and the Dutch. They found that seniors in Canada from familistic cultures were more likely to live with their adult children than seniors from individualistic cultures.

minority groups in Canada, those ethnocultural groups that have not originated in northern and western European countries

visible minority non-European in origin and/or not white in skin tone; curiously, Canada's official definition of visible minority excludes the Indigenous population (First Nations people, Inuit, Métis)

culture shared language, beliefs, values, customs, and practices

Lai (2012) studied the ethnic identity of older Chinese living in major cities across Canada. He observed that ethnic identity is a concept made up of different dimensions, including personal feelings and observable behaviours. Behaviours included following traditions, speaking an ethnic language, and participating in ethnic organizations. Individuals in the same ethnocultural community vary in the extent to which they identify with the ethnic community, follow cultural customs, and participate in ethnic organizations.

Theoretical Perspectives on Ethnicity and Aging

Gerontologists have applied a variety of theories to the study of ethnicity and aging, including the **multiple jeopardy theory**, buffering theory, and the life course perspective. The multiple jeopardy theory says that old age can add to the disadvantages of race, ethnicity, and gender. The multiple jeopardy perspective says that, compared with a person with only one disadvantage, a person with more than one of these characteristics—for example, a visible minority group member who is female and age 65 or over—will tend to experience greater disadvantage. According to this view, compared with a majority group senior, an ethnic elder may face an increased risk of poverty, discrimination, illness, or death.

Indigenous seniors illustrate the multiple jeopardy theory because they experience the combined effects of being old, Indigenous, and poor. For example, Wilson et al. (2010) showed that older Indigenous persons reported worse health than older non-Indigenous persons in Canada.

Researchers find it hard to measure multiple jeopardy. For one thing, most studies of multiple jeopardy use a cross-sectional method. They look at a minority group at one point in time. This makes it impossible to tell if things have gotten worse for minority members as a result of aging. In other words, does aging add to a person's disadvantage? And if so, by how much? Or does an older minority member simply show the same amount of disadvantage in old age that they experienced throughout life? In spite of these measurement problems, multiple jeopardy theory has some value. It has led researchers to try to separate the effects of age from lifelong effects of inequality.

Lai (2014) noted that the multiple jeopardy perspective may lead us to overlook the contributions of ethnic minority seniors. Many seniors who are thought of as vulnerable and disadvantaged contribute to their families and communities as grandparents, caregivers, and volunteers. They take care of themselves so as not to be a burden. They pass on their experience to the next generations and engage in society to build a better future.

A second perspective, **buffering theory**, states that some groups value seniors and provide meaningful roles for them. These groups can buffer a person from the losses that come with old age. Lai (2009a) describes the buffering effect of Chinese culture. "Chinese tradition and culture," Lai says, "often places strong emphasis on respecting and valuing the contributions of elders and older adults. These common norms and beliefs lead most people to believe that older people are treasured and are seen as important in Chinese culture. This also forms the basis for the older Chinese adults' source of satisfaction and wellness" (p. 244).

Gerontologists have begun to take a broader view of minority group aging: the **life course perspective**. This perspective holds that life unfolds from birth to death in a social, cultural, and historical context. This perspective looks at the impact on the minority older person of social institutions, historical periods and events, personal biography, life cycle stage, life events, and resources. This perspective looks at differences between minority groups, cultural subgroups within a minority group, and age cohorts among minority group members.

The life course perspective looks for continuities and discontinuities within minority groups. For example, it links early life experiences to actions and attitudes in later life. Two Chinese elders will experience aging differently, based on their historical experience. One senior may have arrived in Canada recently after living through the hardships of the Cultural Revolution in China. Another Chinese senior may have lived in a middle-class family in Vancouver her whole life. Historical events will shape these seniors' attitudes toward government, money, and food. These seniors will also come into old age with different health conditions.

The life course perspective also notes that advantages and disadvantages tend to accumulate over a lifetime (Burr, Mutchler, & Gerst, 2010; Kail, Quadagno, & Keene, 2009). Kail and colleagues said that advantages

---

buffering theory holds that a culture that values seniors and provides meaningful roles for them tends to protect them to a degree from losses and social devaluation in later life

life course perspective begins with the idea that life unfolds from birth to death in a social, cultural, and historical context; this perspective looks at the impact of social institutions, historical periods and events, personal biography, life cycle stage, life events, and resources on the minority older person

---

multiple jeopardy theory the hypothesis that there is a compounding of disadvantages associated with age, race, ethnicity, and gender

and disadvantages have "a magnifying or feedback effect" (p. 557). They accumulate and reinforce one another throughout life. For example, membership in a minority group can lead to discrimination and low pay in middle age. This will lead to low pension benefits in retirement and possibly to poverty in late old age.

ETHNOCULTURAL DIVERSITY OF SENIORS IN CANADA

In 2011, 70 percent of Canadian seniors were born in Canada (Statistics Canada, 2016). Canadian-born seniors vary in terms of ethnocultural heritage, mother tongue, religion, and visible minority status. Furthermore, some Canadian-born seniors are the children of immigrants, while some are the grandchildren or great-grandchildren of immigrants. Canadians reported more than 200 ethnic origins in the 2011 census (Statistics Canada, 2013a).

Statistics Canada reported that 30 percent of all seniors in Canada in 2011 were foreign-born. Most foreign-born seniors came to Canada in their youth and grew old in Canada. For example, 75 percent of foreign-born seniors in 2011 had arrived in Canada more than 30 years ago. Another 19 percent came to Canada from 11 to 29 years ago. Only 6 percent had come to Canada within the past 10 years.

Seniors' ethnic diversity shows up most in big cities. For example, 69 percent of seniors in Toronto and 57 percent of seniors in Vancouver in 2011 were foreign-born. Almost six in every ten foreign-born seniors in Canada live in Toronto, Montreal, or Vancouver.

Visible Minority Seniors

Almost 11 percent of seniors in Canada in 2011 reported themselves as members of a visible minority group (Statistics Canada, 2016). Two out of every three visible minority seniors in Canada lived in Toronto or Vancouver. Nearly all visible minority seniors (95 percent) were born outside Canada.

Statistics Canada (2010c, 2011g) estimated that by 2031, visible minority groups including South Asians and Chinese could make up 18 percent of seniors, a substantial increase over the figure of 11 percent reported for Canada in 2011. The diversity of Canada's seniors will also increase in terms of mother tongue (including allophones, who speak neither English nor French) and religion (including non-Christian) (Statistics Canada, 2011g). In short, compared with seniors today, seniors in

---

EXHIBIT 4.2 *Indigenous Seniors: A Unique Canadian Ethnic Group*

The Canadian census includes Indigenous seniors among the Canadian-born. In the 2011 census, a total of 82,690 seniors claimed Indigenous ancestry, although not all identified themselves as Indigenous (Statistics Canada, 2013c). Indigenous seniors are not included in the visible minority population discussed in this chapter.

The Canadian Press

Indigenous woman in Manitoba, 2007

the future in Canada will show more diversity in region of origin, language, and religion.

This diversity will pose challenges for social and healthcare services that traditionally serve a Euro-Canadian senior population. They will need to adapt their services to meet the needs of people who come from different cultural traditions and who may not speak either English or French.

ETHNOCULTURAL DIVERSITY IN EXPERIENCES OF AGING

Seniors' ethnocultural orientations shape their experiences of growing old in Canada. For example, seniors have diverse ethnic heritages and identities that influence their lifestyles and cultural practices. Further, seniors' ethnicity influences intergenerational relationships, living arrangements, family life, and community life. Finally, ethnicity influences seniors' experiences of economic security, health, healthcare, and caregiving.

Ethnic Identity and Cultural Practices

Ethnocultural seniors in Canada differ in terms of their ethnic identity and cultural practices. Ng and Northcott (2010a) reported that South Asian immigrant seniors in Edmonton identified themselves as "more South Asian than Canadian" (59 percent), "equally South Asian and Canadian" (32 percent), and "more Canadian than South Asian" (7 percent). Respondents who had good English-language proficiency and had immigrated to Canada at younger ages were more likely to identify themselves as "equally South Asian and Canadian" or "more Canadian than South Asian."

EXHIBIT 4.3   *Proportion of the Population Belonging to a Visible Minority Group by Age Group, Canada, 2006 and 2031*

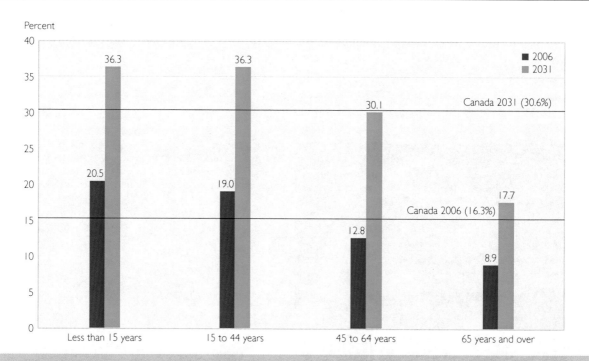

The visible minority population for all age groups in Canada is projected to increase dramatically between 2006 and 2031. Seniors who are visible minorities will double as a proportion of all seniors.

These people will come from Asia (e.g., India, China), the Middle East, the Caribbean, and Latin America. They will bring cultural and linguistic diversity to Canada. The large proportion of visible minority members in the younger age groups will mean a continuing increase in diversity among the older population after 2031.

Source: Statistics Canada. *Projections of the Diversity of the Canadian Population: 2006 to 2031.* Catalogue No. 91-551-X (2010), p. 24. Original source: Statistics Canada, Demography Division. Reproduced and distributed on an "as is" basis with the permission of Statistics Canada.

The elderly East Indian and South Asian Canadian respondents in this study reported that among various cultural practices, they were most likely to continue to speak their native language and practise their religion. Nevertheless, most (68 percent) had become Canadian citizens and most exercised their right to vote in federal, provincial, territorial, and local elections.

Ng and Northcott found that many of the South Asian immigrant seniors in their study kept their ethnic identity as they developed a Canadian identity. A multicultural balancing or blending of ethnic and Canadian identities occurred. Further, those South Asian seniors who had immigrated to Canada at older ages tended to retain their ethnic identity. Those who immigrated to Canada when younger and had grown old in Canada tended to develop a bicultural identity.

Novik (2010) made a similar point in her study of Ukrainian immigrant seniors. Novik interviewed grandmothers (babas) who had migrated to Canada years ago from Ukraine. She noted that being an immigrant in Canada very much influenced their life and identity. As they grew older, these women achieved a bicultural identity and saw themselves in their old age as both Ukrainian and Canadian.

Tieu and Konnert (2015) examined the acculturation and enculturation of older Chinese who had immigrated to Canada. The authors noted that acculturation refers to participation in mainstream Canadian culture, while enculturation refers to participation in a heritage culture. The authors found that older Chinese Canadians retained elements of their cultural heritage and at the same time adopted aspects of mainstream culture. Those who had come to Canada more recently at an older age participated more in their heritage culture, while those who came to Canada years previously at a younger age participated more in mainstream culture. It follows that within each ethnocultural group there is variation in the degree to which each individual follows mainstream and heritage cultural values and practices. In other words, it is a mistake to assume that all members of an ethnocultural group are the same.

Seniors maintain their ethnocultural identity in part by following cultural practices, including eating ethnic foods. For example, many ethnocultural seniors maintain their traditional diets. Exhibit 4.4 describes a Meals on Wheels program for ethnic seniors. Meals on Wheels programs deliver prepared meals to seniors who live in their homes but cannot go grocery shopping or cook for

---

EXHIBIT 4.4 *Langar on Wheels Rolls Out to Punjabi Community*

This article is from The Globe and Mail, *December 17, 2011.*

In January, a program begins that gets ethnically appropriate meals to seniors in Brampton, Milton and Mississauga.

Renu Sodhi can remember very clearly the day she came back from surgery at the hospital. She and her husband Harinder were sitting on the sofa of their Brampton home—both hungry, exhausted and craving some home-cooked Punjabi food.

Mrs. Sodhi suggested they get Indian groceries delivered. "And we got the food, but who was going to make [it]? I was so tired after my operation and [Harinder] can't stand for very long because of his leg problems," she said.

The elderly couple would have signed up for the local Meals on Wheels program, but the idea of eating shepherd's pie or beef stew makes their stomachs squirm. They would rather have their fill of roti with some *sabzi* (vegetables) and *dal* (lentils).

It's a complaint that Nirpal Bhangoo, a case worker with the Punjabi Community Health Services, often hears when she makes her rounds visiting seniors at their homes.

"Many of my clients would prefer eating South Asian food because it's been a part of their diet their whole lives," Ms. Bhangoo said. "You can't really expect them to change that at their age."

The Greater Toronto Area's South Asian immigrant population has grown by about 50 per cent between 2000 and 2006. That's why PCHS is trying to drum up support for Langar on Wheels, a South Asian variation of the Meals on Wheels program, which would likely bring food from the *langar*, the Punjabi word for the communal kitchen in a Sikh house of worship, to the homes of Brampton, Mississauga and Malton seniors. The organizers say Langar on Wheels will be the first of its kind in the GTA and possibly even Canada.

"What this Langar on Wheels program shows us is that we need to rethink the way we give ... that it has to be responsive to the needs of our community," said Eileen MacKenzie, the executive director of the Community Foundation of Mississauga, which provided a $30,000 grant to PCHS in early December. "As our city's demographics change, we need to respond to those needs."

And indeed, cultural variations of Meals on Wheels programs are rising in popularity—with programs for Chinese, Greek, Italian and Indian seniors cropping up all over the world in countries with large immigrant populations, such as the U.K., Australia and the U.S.

As the GTA's demographics changed, Meals on Wheels programs have similarly adapted. Kosher Meals on Wheels was likely the first cultural program when it was launched for Toronto's

(continued)

growing Jewish community in the 1920s, said Inna Dantchenko, who runs the Circle of Care's kosher meals program. Now, volunteers deliver some 82,000 meals along the Bathurst corridor.

And following several waves of Asian immigration to Canada, the Health and Home Care Society of B.C. launched one of Canada's first Chinese Meals on Wheels programs in 1996. The program now serves approximately 150 meals every weekday in Vancouver and Richmond, delivered by Chinese-speaking volunteers. Similar programs have cropped up in Calgary, where it's known as "Chopsticks on Wheels," and Toronto.

PCHS will launch Langar on Wheels in January. The funding the community group has received is earmarked for cooking utensils, consultations with a dietician, providing "culturally appropriate" food free of charge to the 25 seniors who have expressed interest.

Kulbinder Saran Caldwell, the advancement officer at PCHS, says she expects the demand for this kind of Punjabi food delivery to grow.

"There is a lot of stigma when you say you can no longer take care of yourself, that you can't cook for yourself," Ms. Saran Caldwell said. "But I expect that as we get the word out, more seniors will sign on and the demand will explode."

The Sodhis tried to make do with frozen foods and eating at the langar at their *gurdwara*, or temple. But the frozen foods are not healthy or tasty, they say, and Mrs. Sodhi said she felt guilty going daily to the langar, where vegetarian food is provided for free.

"How can we take without giving back? ... It doesn't feel right. We want to be independent," she said.

The concept of a seniors' food program is perhaps odd for South Asians given the norm of *seva*, or care for elderly parents in South Asian culture. But the Sodhis say values inevitably change in Canada. "In India, children selflessly serve their parents. When they are old, they take care of them," Mrs. Sodhi said. "But here, who has the time? All the kids are so busy with their work. It's just different. I feel so guilty asking them for help when I know they don't have time."

Women are also expected to manage the kitchens by themselves in some traditional households, Mr. Sodhi explained, saying his son dutifully brought him food every day while Mrs. Sodhi was in the hospital. But he stopped providing home-cooked meals when Mrs. Sodhi got home, even though she was unable to actually move around the kitchen.

"I don't think we want to suggest that the families of these seniors are uncaring," Ms. Caldwell said. "But there are limited resources available, especially for newcomers who are sometimes trying to hold down multiple jobs or doing shift work to make ends meet. This is a city of immigrants and our seniors are part of the extended South Asian family, so we have to respond to their needs as well."

Source: Baluja, T. Langar on Wheels Rolls Out to Punjabi Community. *The Globe and Mail*, December 17, 2011: M.3. © The Globe and Mail Inc. All Rights Reserved.

themselves. In Canada, these programs increasingly offer unique ethnically diverse diets as they adapt to meet the needs of their emerging ethnic clientele.

TIME to REVIEW

Describe several of the ways that seniors can relate to their ethnic identity.

What do gerontologists mean when they say ethnic seniors may face "multiple jeopardy?"

How can "buffering" help an ethnic senior cope with a new life in Canada?

What trend do demographers see in the proportion of visible minority members in the older population?

What are some of the ways that ethnic seniors maintain their ethnic identity?

Intergenerational Relationships

Some ethnic groups emphasize individualism. Individualism stresses personal independence, privacy, and self-fulfillment (Hossen, 2012). For example, Euro-Canadian seniors typically worry that their adult children will perceive them as a burden, so they try to maintain their independence from their children. For example, they prefer to be institutionalized rather than share a residence with their adult children (Kaida et al., 2009).

Other ethnic groups emphasize the obligations of family members to seniors and prefer collective decision making (Kaida et al., 2009). Collectivistic cultures emphasize interdependence, and loyalty to the group. They sacrifice the interests of the individual for the good of the group (Hossen, 2012). Accordingly, these individualistic and collectivistic orientations lead to different commitments to **filial piety**, the obligations of adult children to their aging parents. Lai (2010) says, "the key elements of filial piety consist of respecting and loving one's parents, not bringing any type of dishonor to one's parents, taking good care of one's parents, obeying one's parents, and worshiping deceased parents and ancestors" (pp. 202–203).

A collectivistic culture, such as the Confucian culture described by Lai, emphasizes the obligations of the young to the old. On the other hand, an individualistic culture expects each generation to look after its own needs. No culture follows these patterns exactly, but cultures tend

---

filial piety the culturally defined obligation, highly valued in Asian cultures, of adult children to their aging parents, requiring adult children to support their parents in their old age

Chinese society values filial piety—respect and love for elders. Life in the North American culture sometimes challenges traditional expressions of respect for elders. Busy lifestyles and single-family homes, for example, make it hard to keep up traditional patterns of family life. Here, a three-generation Chinese family enjoys some time together outdoors. Leisure time and holidays allow parents and grandparents to be together.

to fall to one side or the other of this continuum. These different orientations lead to different intergenerational relationships, living arrangements, and social supports.

Kobayashi and Funk (2010) interviewed older Japanese Canadian parents (*nisei*) and their adult children (*sansei*). Both nisei and sansei generations were born in Canada. These researchers noted that the expectations of both generations regarding the obligations of children to support aging parents (filial piety and filial obligation) had evolved since the grandparent generation of Japanese immigrants (*issei*) had come to Canada.

Nevertheless, expectations of filial piety had endured in modified form. For example, both generations viewed filial obligation as important and had similar expectations of each other. In particular, the expectations of mothers and their children regarding support were most congruent when the mother was widowed and in poor health. In China, filial piety requires sons to support a widowed parent. Nevertheless, Martin-Matthews and her colleagues (2013) observed that for Chinese widows in Canada, it is often daughters who take up this responsibility.

Some immigrant seniors may complain that their children and grandchildren have become too "westernized." For example, some older immigrants from Iran felt that their children were losing their cultural values and identity (Jafari, Mathias, & Baharlou, 2010). They also complained about social isolation and lack of social and family support.

Similarly, Baskin and Davey (2015) observed that Indigenous seniors and elders receive less respect from community members than in the past, especially from younger Indigenous persons living in urban areas. An Indigenous senior living in Toronto said that: "I think sometimes the respect we get as older people is sort of a platitude. You know, sometimes I don't feel that it's genuine" (p. 54). Another Indigenous senior complained about stereotyping saying: "We are not all wise. Every once in a while, someone says to me, 'You have such wisdom in your eyes.' I always say, 'Thanks,' but I don't know what the hell they're talking about!" (p. 55) These Indigenous seniors lamented loss of respect and status and patronizing attempts to praise them. They wished that they be given genuine respect according to traditional cultural values and that this respect be based on a realistic recognition of the seniors for who they are and what they have experienced in life.

Hossen (2012) assessed the experience of South Asian seniors who came to Canada late in life to reunite with their adult children and their grandchildren born in Canada. These seniors experienced cultural shock, having left a familiar way of life to come to a new country and new culture. Hossen (p. 2) noted the "paradox of immigrant life" and asked, "Why do older immigrants so often describe themselves as lonely, isolated, and bored while they appear to be so closely integrated into their kin network?"

Hossen (2012, p. 6) observed that problems include "role emptying" and "role reversal." Instead of the adult children and grandchildren being dependent on the senior, the senior becomes dependent on the children and grandchildren. The seniors tend to live in their children's home (rather than the reverse), are financially dependent on their children, and depend on their children and grandchildren for transportation, language translation, and guidance navigating the new society and culture. Their traditional roles as patriarch, matriarch, teacher and counsellor, are lost. Instead of the children and grandchildren caring for the aging family members, the seniors are often expected to babysit and do household chores. Some find joy in this while others feel overworked and exploited. Furthermore, most perform these duties isolated from the social supports and resources they would have had back home.

Wu and Penning (2015; see also De Jong Gierveld, Van der Pas, & Keating, 2015) studied loneliness reported by older Canadians. They found that older immigrants reported higher levels of loneliness than older persons born in Canada. This was especially true for older immigrants who had come to Canada recently, although it appeared that loneliness declined with increasing length of stay in Canada. Visible minorities also reported higher levels of loneliness. De Jong Gierveld and colleagues observed that

"Immigrants who share both the native language of the receiving country and a similar culture do not differ from native born older adults. Those who share neither have significantly higher mean loneliness scores" (p. 263).

Ng and Northcott (2015) reported that elderly South Asian immigrants living in Edmonton rarely lived alone. Those who did live alone were more likely to say that they felt lonely at least occasionally. Nevertheless, some who lived with family members also reported feeling lonely at times. Those who lived with others were more likely to say that they felt lonely if they were alone for long periods of time each day, and felt that family members were uncaring and disrespectful.

Novik (2010) noted the importance of intergenerational relationships for Ukrainian Canadian seniors' quality of life. Novik interviewed grandmothers who had come to Canada years ago from Ukraine. She also interviewed the grandmothers' daughters and granddaughters. These three generations judged their quality of life by their success in their marital, familial, and community relationships over their lifetime.

The Ukrainian Canadian grandmothers said that marriage and family defined their lives. They emphasized their caregiving roles in raising children and providing end-of-life care to aging parents and dying husbands. In particular, in their old age they valued their roles as grandmothers and their relationships with grandchildren and great-grandchildren.

These women had experienced hard lives. Driven from Ukraine years ago, they experienced harsh conditions in Canada—poverty, prejudice and discrimination, isolation and marginalization, and subordination in a traditional male-dominated culture. Intergenerational relationships cultivated over a lifetime defined these grandmothers' quality of life.

Shankar interviewed older Indo-Fijian women in Edmonton about their intergenerational family relationships (Shankar & Northcott, 2009). These women had grown up in rural Fiji in a traditional male-centred patriarchal family and social structure and had emigrated as adults from Fiji to Canada. Shankar focused on their experiences as grandmothers in Canada.

She noted that traditional Indo-Fijian culture identifies females in terms of their relationships with males: as a father's daughter, a man's wife, a son's mother, and a grandson's grandmother. When a female married, she left her family and became part of her husband's family. In her husband's family she provided care for her husband, their children, and his aging parents. Her mother-in-law had considerable power over the daughter-in-law. In time, the daughter-in-law could hope to become a mother-in-law

herself and achieve the same status, power, and security that her mother-in-law had enjoyed.

In Canada, Shankar found that these Indo-Fijian immigrant women felt at risk in their new environment. They had little education, limited English-language ability, and they lacked skills necessary to work outside the home. As a result they invested heavily in the grandmother role. In particular, they cared for their son's sons in hopes that their grandsons would follow tradition and provide security and support in late old age.

Shankar observed that the grandmother role created problems for older Fijian grandmothers. Compared with life in Fiji, in Canada these grandmothers lived a more isolated life. They had little opportunity to get out of the home and socialize with friends, as was the pattern in rural Fiji. In these families, tension often existed between the older women and their daughters-in-law. These younger women tended to adopt Canadian values and resisted the traditional Indo-Fijian values.

Note that Shankar described a generational phenomenon. The first generation of Indo-Fijian immigrant women she studied invested in their sons and grandsons and in the grandmother role. They did this as a bargain with the traditional patriarchal culture to ensure social and financial security. But this met with resistance from Canadian-born daughters and daughters-in-law, who opposed this traditional model of intergenerational family relations. It appears that the next generation of Indo-Fijian women, like other young women in Canada, tend to become educated, participate in the paid labour force, and demand a more equal bargain within the family.

Living Arrangements and Family Life

Ethnocultural seniors differ in their patterns of living arrangements and preferences for living with adult children and grandchildren. Lee and Edmonston (2014) determined that older persons who had immigrated to Canada were less likely to live independently (alone or with spouse only) than older persons born in Canada. Kaida and her colleagues (2009) found that a collectivistic cultural orientation along with economic disadvantage increased the likelihood of seniors living with their adult children.

Ng and Northcott (2013) found that immigrant seniors who were currently married and who had come to Canada when they were young were more likely to live independently (alone or with a spouse only). However, immigrant seniors who came to Canada recently were most likely to live with their adult children. The motivations for living with adult children included cultural factors and economic necessity. Recently arrived immigrant seniors often do not have their own incomes and have not lived in Canada long enough to qualify for Canada's income support system. They cannot afford to live independently. In addition, Canada's immigration rules require adult children who sponsor their aging parents to provide financial support for a minimum of 10 years.

Kim (2010) noted that immigrant seniors in Canada often find themselves working in their adult child's home. The seniors provide child care and manage the home while their adult children work in the labour force. Some immigrant seniors find meaning and purpose in caring for their grandchildren in Canada. On the other hand, some immigrant seniors expected to be cared for, rather than having to provide care in their old age. Some immigrant seniors feel trapped in the new culture.

Migliore and Dorazio-Migliore (2010) studied the living arrangements of older Italian Canadians living in southern Ontario and the lower mainland of British Columbia. The authors observed a shift among Italian Canadian seniors away from an expectation of living with adult children in old age. The seniors in this study voiced a preference for living independently in their own homes. They did not want to spend their last days in a nursing home or assisted-living facility, even one designed for Italian Canadians, but they would "make do" if necessary.

They did not want to burden their children by living with them. They hoped that their children would not abandon them, but they recognized the difficulties that arise in contemporary Canada when aging parents live with family members who cannot provide intensive care. These immigrants hoped to age independently in their own homes.

TIME to REVIEW

How do cultural and economic factors influence immigrant seniors' decision to live independently or in a multigenerational family?

How does the length of time in Canada affect immigrant seniors' ideas about living with their children or living alone?

What are the advantages and disadvantages of living independently or in multigenerational families?

Community Life

Ethnocultural seniors enjoy associating with each other and engaging in familiar and meaningful activities. Migliore and Dorazio-Migliore (2010), for example, described a prayer group involving elderly Italian

Canadian immigrant women. The daughter of one of the participants in the prayer group said:

> I used to take my mother there [before her mother's death].... They all said the rosary together, and then they had coffee and cake—more of a get together, as well as a prayer group. And, to give ... elderly women who looked after their husbands and families a time-out for themselves.... a time to be together and just enjoy ... what they liked to do, like saying the rosary, enjoying the old hymns ... and songs that they used to sing in their various regions of Italy.... Every Tuesday my mother went, and she looked forward to it. Nothing came in her way to miss this ... outing.... That was number one priority for Tuesday afternoons (p. 77).

Yamada (2013) observed that there are more than 200 support groups serving the Japanese community in Vancouver. Nikkei Place, for example, contains a Japanese cultural centre, a residence for seniors, a nursing home, and a Japanese garden. Tonari Gumi is an organization that mobilizes Japanese volunteers to support Japanese seniors in Vancouver. Services include help with social security documents relating to healthcare and pensions, language translation and advice in legal matters, workshops, lunches, gateball (Japanese croquet), karaoke events, language classes, craft classes, food delivery, and hospital visitation.

Kim, Kang, and Kim (2015) compared Korean immigrant elders living in Toronto and in smaller cities in the southwestern United States. They noted that the Korean community in Toronto is well developed and has many services available in the Korean language. They observed that "an ethnically diverse city like Toronto, Canada, is an immigrant-elder-friendly community and offers good health care access, including transportation, language support, and financial resources, as well as the universal health care the Canadian government offers to residents" (p. 97). As a result, the Korean elders in Toronto reported fewer symptoms of depression than the Korean elders in the smaller cities in southwestern United States.

Ethnocultural seniors may integrate to varying degrees into the cultural mainstream. Alternatively, they may settle in **cultural enclaves** where they cluster together geographically and socially. Cultural enclaves differ in their degree of institutional completeness. **Institutional completeness** refers to the proximity of extended family

---

cultural enclaves areas in a city or region where particular ethnocultural groups tend to congregate geographically and socially

Institutional completeness the presence in a community of a wide range of economic, social, and religious institutions, including the availability of services, agencies, and programs

members; the size of friendship networks; the presence of economic, social, and religious institutions; and the availability of services, agencies, and programs. The more institutionally complete an ethnic enclave or minority group, the more support it can offer to its seniors. An ethnocultural community that offers banking services and healthcare in the language of its members and according to ethnocultural customs illustrates a high degree of institutional completeness. An institutionally complete context provides strong support for the older person.

Portuguese immigrants created the cultural enclave of Little Portugal in west-central Toronto in the 1950s, 1960s, and 1970s (Teixeira, 2010). Teixeira described Little Portugal as an "institutionally complete" community where residents found the social, cultural, commercial, and religious institutions they needed. Residents could bank, shop, work, obtain services, eat out, and go to church in Little Portugal. And they could do so using their Portuguese language. Teixeira observed that integration into Little Portugal made integration into Canadian society relatively unnecessary. Residents, and seniors in particular, lived comfortably in a self-segregated community.

Teixeira (2010) observed that seniors in Toronto's Little Portugal preferred to maintain familiar patterns and relationships despite changes affecting their community. Teixeira noted that Little Portugal has been undergoing **gentrification**. The children of the original Portuguese immigrants tend to move to the suburbs. Over time, homes get sold to non-Portuguese professionals who want to live closer to the city centre where they work. Also, new immigrants from different ethnic groups move in. This drives up home values and property taxes in Little Portugal. As a result, Teixeira observed, some seniors sell their houses and follow their children to the suburbs.

Still, most Portuguese seniors prefer to stay in Little Portugal, where they have lived since coming to Canada. For retired seniors who own their homes and live on modest pensions, the rising property taxes and maintenance costs become a burden. Some people rent parts of their homes to tenants, or they move. The most vulnerable seniors rent a room or an apartment. But rising rental costs tend to displace these seniors. They move against their will to cheaper accommodations, often outside the community where they have spent their lives.

Seniors displaced from Little Portugal may face isolation, although many return to the community for banking, shopping, and services. Teixeira concluded

that seniors in Little Portugal required support to stay in their homes for as long as possible. They also required seniors' institutional housing designed for Portuguese immigrants.

Cultural enclaves with a high degree of institutional completeness have advantages and disadvantages. On the one hand, they provide seniors with a familiar, comfortable, and supportive community. This requires little adaptation. Seniors can easily maintain their language and customs. On the other hand, seniors may feel that they do not need to learn the language and customs of the wider society. This leaves them vulnerable when their cultural enclave undergoes a transition (such as gentrification) and becomes less familiar and less supportive.

Chau and Lai (2011) examined Chinese enclaves in seven major Canadian cities. Contrary to expectations, they found that the physical and mental health of Chinese seniors was better in smaller cities with smaller populations of Chinese seniors than in larger cities. The authors speculated that smaller enclaves of Chinese seniors in smaller cities provided the greatest benefit for the physical and mental health of enclave residents. Smaller enclaves may have stronger internal social bonds and at the same time have better connections and relationships with the dominant external community. In short, the smaller enclaves may provide better access to both "worlds."

TIME to REVIEW

What is "institutional completeness" and how can it help a senior immigrant adjust to life in Canada?

What advantages and disadvantages do seniors experience when they reside in cultural enclaves? And what advantages and disadvantages do seniors experience when they do not reside in cultural enclaves?

Economic Security

The majority of foreign-born seniors in Canada today came to Canada years ago and grew old in Canada. However, some foreign-born seniors came to Canada recently at an advanced age (Northcott & Petruik, 2013). Long-term immigrant seniors have had time to integrate into Canadian society, learn English or French, work in the paid labour force, and earn pension entitlements. Recent immigrant seniors have had less time to adjust to life in Canada and attain economic security.

Analysts generally find that compared with Canadian-born seniors and long-term immigrants, recent immigrant seniors have greater economic disadvantages

---

gentrification in-migration into older urban neighbourhoods by new (often wealthy residents) that tends to drive up property values and displace former residents

in old age. Kaida and Boyd (2011) found that recent immigrant seniors tended to have less access to government pensions and private pensions. Recent immigrant seniors often remained financially dependent on their adult children who sponsored their move to Canada. Kaida and Boyd found that recent immigrant seniors tended to live with family members and that family support helped keep these seniors out of poverty.

Jafari, Mathias, and Baharlou (2010) studied older Iranian immigrants living in British Columbia. These immigrants had come to Canada within the past 10 years. They experienced difficulties in having their work history and credentials recognized in Canada. As a result, they faced unemployment, underemployment, financial hardship, and loss of status in Canada. Some men in this study went back to Iran to work while their families continued to live in Canada.

Grant and Townsend (2010) found that poverty rates for elderly immigrants in Canada were higher than for Canadian-born seniors. About 9 percent of immigrant seniors who resided with one or more family members lived in poverty. This compared to about 3 percent of non-immigrant seniors who lived with family members. Poverty rates were higher for "unattached" immigrant seniors—32 percent for men and 44 percent for women, compared to 27 percent and 37 percent for unattached native-born seniors.

Grant and Townsend (2010; also Ng & Northcott, 2010b) found that, compared with immigrant seniors who had lived in Canada for many years, recent immigrant seniors had higher poverty rates. Further, compared with immigrant seniors who spoke French or English, immigrant seniors who did not speak either language had higher poverty rates. Immigrant seniors from developing nations and those with less education also tended to have high poverty rates.

TIME TO REVIEW

Compare poverty rates for immigrant and non-immigrant seniors and for immigrant seniors who came to Canada recently and years ago.

What conditions lead to poverty for ethnic seniors? What policy changes would help to reduce poverty rates for ethnic seniors?

Health and Healthcare

Ng (2011) reported that younger immigrants who have recently arrived in Canada tend to have better physical health than the general population. This advantage is known as the "healthy immigrant effect." It exists because immigration selection processes screen out the least healthy. In addition, younger immigrants tend to self-select as healthier persons decide to immigrate. Over time, long-term immigrants are exposed to the same environment and adopt the lifestyles of Canadian-born seniors. As a result, the healthy immigrant effect diminishes as immigrants grow older in Canada (Spitzer, 2011).

Older immigrants who have come recently to Canada do not seem to have a health advantage relative to Canadian-born seniors. Indeed, they may have worse physical health than Canadian-born seniors (Kobayashi & Prus, 2010; Northcott & Northcott, 2010). Seniors who have immigrated recently tend to come to Canada to join their children who have immigrated previously. Their children may sponsor their aging parents' immigration to Canada in part because their health has begun to deteriorate in their home country.

Ethnocultural seniors differ in their view of health and their use of various healthcare systems. For example, Indo-Canadian immigrant seniors in Canada may use traditional Ayurvedic medical practices. Chinese Canadian immigrant seniors may rely on traditional Chinese medicine. Seniors in these and other groups will also use Western medicine. Euro-Canadian seniors may rely mostly on Western medicine, but they may also try traditional Indian or Chinese medicine. For example, a Euro-Canadian senior might use a sweat lodge or burn sweet grass, practise yoga, or use acupuncture.

Indigenous seniors often experience problems with formal healthcare services. Problems include language barriers, lack of cultural sensitivity by healthcare workers, and "different concepts regarding the nature of the disease." Indigenous seniors who live on reserves face the high cost of transportation to urban centres for care (Habjan, Prince, & Kelley, 2012, p. 217).

Indigenous seniors pointed out that when an Indigenous person is dying, the community gathers to provide support, share "energy," and perform traditional ceremonies (Hampton et. al., 2010). They reported, however, that hospital policies often prevent culturally appropriate end-of-life care. They noted that hospitals needed to provide large rooms where family and friends can gather, allow the burning of sweet grass, and perform the smudging ceremony. Hospitals could partner with traditional Indigenous healers and allow the dying person to eat traditional foods.

Lanting et al. (2011) realized the importance of culturally appropriate diagnostic measures for health conditions. The researchers held meetings with an Indigenous

Grandmothers Group in Saskatchewan and learned about cultural perceptions of aging and dementia. The grandmothers pointed out that the Indigenous culture views the life cycle as circular. For example, the Indigenous culture views aging and dementia as normal processes that return the aged person back to the "baby stage."

The grandmothers noted the importance of developing culturally appropriate assessment tools. For example, the Cree language in Saskatchewan is rich in visual imagery specific to the ecology of Saskatchewan. The grandmothers pointed out that a test of cognitive ability must use familiar culturally grounded images. This group of grandmothers then helped revise a dementia assessment tool for use with Indigenous peoples in Saskatchewan.

Consistent with the humour prevalent in Cree language and culture, the grandmothers told the following story (Lanting et al., 2011, p. 112). It illustrates the problems that can occur when non-Indigenous healthcare workers interact with Indigenous Canadians.

> *Some nurses they get careless and maybe they are overworked ... and they'll send in a 12 year old boy to translate for grandpa. Like the one who had prostate cancer.... [T]hey told the boy to tell the grandpa that they were going to give him two shots right away and the boy didn't know the words so he told his grandpa that they were going to shoot him twice right now. So the grandpa says that 'I guess there is no hope then'!*

Oliffe et al. (2007) studied the beliefs and health practices of elderly Sikh men who attended a temple in the lower mainland of British Columbia. These men had immigrated to Canada from the Punjab region of India. The Sikh temple offers seniors a place to worship and to meet with other Punjabis. The temple serves three meals each day and includes a wellness clinic next door.

The elderly Sikh men in this study placed a high value on self-reliance and physical work as a way to maintain their strength and health. They also followed dietary prescriptions that they believed led to good health. For example, one man said he drank cold milk to prevent overheating and dehydration when he worked in the hot sun. Further, the meals prepared at the temple were vegetarian because the Sikh religion prohibits the killing of animals. Oliffe and colleagues (2007) observed that religion, spirituality, faith, dietary practices, exercise, and service were intimately intertwined. The men believed that a combination of destiny or luck (kismet) as determined by God, community service (sewa), good deeds (karam), proper diet, and keeping active influenced their health and illnesses.

Oliffe and colleagues (2007) also noted that the elderly Sikh men preferred not to visit a doctor. This continued a pattern that they followed in their earlier years in India. But, in Canada, additional barriers influenced their reluctance to visit a doctor. These men said they didn't know which healthcare services required payment and which were free. The men had their own ideas about the effective use of medicine. And they did not always understand or accept the instructions for taking medicine. Some men preferred traditional remedies.

The Sikh men misunderstood wait lists for elective surgery, for example. In India, payment for services guaranteed immediate and competent care. These men thought that wait times in Canada signalled incompetence. Further, the men had trouble communicating with non-Sikh doctors, even when family members provided translation. The men preferred a Sikh doctor who could understand them "as a person as well as a patient" (Oliffe et al., 2007, p. 231). But the men could not always find a Sikh doctor to care for them. Oliffe and colleagues commented on the importance of providing healthcare that is culturally sensitive. In addition, in the Sikh case, the care needed to respond to gender-specific cultural beliefs and behaviours.

Another study of Punjabi-speaking Sikh older immigrants in British Columbia found that the seniors' views of dental healthcare issues drew heavily on traditional Ayurvedic conceptions and traditional home remedies. Nevertheless, at times these seniors also visited Western dentists for dental care, although they expressed concern about the high cost of that care (MacEntee et. al., 2014).

Interviews with elderly Iranian immigrant women in Toronto found that being socially engaged and involved in the community, and particularly in the Iranian ethnic community, had an influence on individuals' well-being and mental health (Dastjerdi and Mardukhi, 2015). Proficiency in English, adequate finances, proximity to community centres, and access to transportation facilitated community involvement. Those who were not involved in social activities felt isolated.

Culture is a basic element in a person's identity and habitual behaviours. Even dementia patients continue to exhibit cultural patterns and preferences. Kontos (2010) studied elderly residents of an Orthodox Jewish long-term care facility in Ontario. The residents came from Eastern Europe and had moderate to severe dementia.

These dementia patients continued to exhibit humanity, personhood, sociability, and civility, despite their cognitive deficits. Each resident continued to express personal preferences. For example, they differed on where they preferred to sit, on when and how they drank their coffee and tea, and on how they dressed. The residents' ethnicity continued to impact their old age, despite the dementia. For example, residents occasionally used a Yiddish word or phrase. One wore a Star of David around her neck.

Jette and Vertinsky (2011) found that elderly Chinese immigrant women living in Vancouver combined traditional Chinese medicine with Western medicine. However they understood health in terms of Eastern concepts of the unity of mind and body and the importance of "balance." For example, they viewed exercise as an enjoyable activity that contributed to the balance of mind and body.

Lai and Chappell (2007) found that about two-thirds of older Chinese immigrants in Canada used a combination of traditional Chinese medicine (TCM) and Western health services. About one-third used Western health services exclusively. In contrast, only 1 percent used TCM exclusively. Those using TCM were most likely to use Chinese herbs or herbal formulas and consult with a TCM herbalist practitioner. The authors noted that Chinese immigrants shared a common ethnicity but did not necessarily have the same health beliefs. Lai and Chappell said that, "cultural variations do exist within the group and healthcare providers should take this into consideration in health assessment" (p. 62).

Similarly, Chow (2010) wrote that "the Chinese in Canada are a heterogeneous community" and therefore there is a "need for healthcare providers to recognize the diversity within Chinese culture and avoid broad-based assumptions" (p. 62). Some Chinese seniors in Canada speak Mandarin, some Cantonese. Some came to Canada years ago. Some came more recently. Cultural beliefs and practices varied among individuals. In addition, Chow (2012) noted that elderly Chinese Canadians do not adhere to traditional cultural values and practices as much as they used to. Chow found that many Chinese in Calgary lived independently and planned to live in a nursing home when they could no longer live independently. Chow suggested that norms of filial piety have evolved and "taken on a different form" (p. 355).

Tsang, Fuller-Thomson, and Lai (2012) asked older people of Chinese heritage in Canada about sexuality and health. Their study showed an association between satisfaction with sexual activity and good health for older women and an association between frequency of sexual activity, sexual satisfaction, and health for older men.

Tieu, Konnert, and Wang (2010) determined that older Chinese immigrants in Canada are less likely to acknowledge depression and less likely to utilize mental health services than older persons born in Canada. The authors suggested that older Chinese view mental illness as stigmatizing and embarrassing to the family. Further, they typically believe that individuals can solve their mental health problems with self-help initiatives such as exercise and without professional intervention.

Kim and Chen (2011) found that among elderly Korean immigrants in Canada, compared to men, women reported more symptoms of depression. Further, they found that living alone, fewer social activities, poor health, and financial stress were associated with symptoms of depression.

Acharya and Northcott (2007) found that elderly Indo-Canadian women characterized mental distress as negative energy or negative thoughts arising from problematic circumstances in one's life. These women said that they coped first by acknowledging the problem and second by maintaining control over their inner self. They achieved control primarily by "staying busy" and doing their "duties'—meeting personal, family, social, and cultural obligations. They said that staying busy provided self-worth, confidence, meaning, purpose, happiness, and helped to maintain a strong inner self.

These women defined culture as "moral medicine." Acharya and Northcott (2007) noted that culturally prescribed ways of keeping busy were viewed as the best medicine for avoiding or minimizing mental distress. For this reason, these women rarely sought help from either traditional or Western mental health professionals.

Lai and Surood (2008) measured depression in a study of older South Asian immigrants in Calgary. They found that more than one in five persons in the study exhibited at least a mild degree of depression. Older women and those who reported worse physical health tended to report feelings of depression. In addition, those who agreed with South Asian cultural values tended to report depression.

Depressed seniors in this study might have experienced problems adjusting to life in Canada. And they might have felt an incompatibility between their traditional culture and Western culture. Lai and Surood (2008) found that depressed seniors rarely sought professional care. These seniors feared the stigma attached to mental problems and they did not want to embarrass their family members.

Lai and Surood (2010) found a number of barriers that discouraged them from using health services for any kind of health problem. Cultural incompatibility created a barrier for many seniors in their study. Cultural incompatibility included healthcare professionals who do not speak the senior's language and do not understand South Asian cultures. Further, older South Asians avoided healthcare programs they considered culturally insensitive and culturally inappropriate. Lai and Surood (2013) also noted that some seniors felt ashamed and uncomfortable seeking help. They perceived healthcare professionals as "too young." These barriers had a negative effect on physical and mental health for aging South Asian immigrants in Calgary.

In summary, a cultural gap exists between ethnic seniors and the Western healthcare system. This gap exists in the form of language barriers, cultural definitions of health, and cultural preferences for healthcare. These barriers challenge the Canadian healthcare system to provide culturally sensitive and appropriate healthcare for ethnic seniors.

TIME TO REVIEW

Describe some of the differences between Western and non-Western approaches to healthcare.

What barriers do ethnic seniors face when they need healthcare in Canada?

How can the Canadian healthcare system offer culturally sensitive and appropriate healthcare for ethnic seniors?

Caregiving

Family members provide much of the healthcare for aging seniors. This is known as informal care. It complements the formal care provided by doctors, nurses, hospitals, and long-term care facilities.

Suwal (2010) studied caregivers of immigrant seniors who had long-term health conditions. Suwal found that, compared with non-immigrant caregivers, immigrant caregivers' health suffered more from caregiving. At the same time, these caregivers felt that they gave back to the care receiver what they had received. This interpretation helped relieve some of their stress.

Racine (2010) studied the family caregivers of elderly Haitian Canadian seniors. Haitian culture expects men to go to school and become the breadwinner for the family and for women to serve in domestic and caregiving roles. As a result, in the past, women worked in the home and provided care for their husband, children, and aging parents and parents-in-law. Haitian culture does not expect men to participate in domestic or caregiving duties. Accordingly, mothers and grandmothers discouraged men from participating in domestic roles.

Racine (2010) noted that in Canada, Haitian Canadian women typically work outside the home in the paid labour force. But they also work inside the home in domestic and caregiving roles. They may have a triple burden, as they work outside the home, raise children, and care for aging parents. To manage, Haitian Canadian women attempt to renegotiate the traditional division of labour with their male partners. Some men resist doing "women's work," but others assume some domestic and caregiving responsibilities. For example, one older man, age 87, had immigrated to Quebec years ago from Haiti. He provided care for his ill wife. He said, "Oh, you know I have to live with this. I've to get used to it. I cook, do the laundry, the housekeeping.... I manage ... mother's diet because of her [illness]. Each day I change the menu" (p. 345).

Crosato, Ward-Griffin, and Leipert (2007) noted that Indigenous culture emphasized the interrelatedness of senior, caregiver, family, and community in isolated communities in Canada. Cultural norms strongly influenced the delivery of care. For example, Indigenous culture allowed seniors to choose their caregiver and made the chosen caregiver feel honoured to provide care.

Crosato and colleagues (2007) observed that the "circle" recurs as a motif in Indigenous culture. The researchers referred to the seniors' caregivers as the circle of healers. The larger family circle and the encompassing Indigenous community circle provided considerable support to the circle of caregivers. This made caregiving manageable.

Crosato and colleagues noted that the Indigenous community had tenuous relations with the non-Indigenous community. Indigenous caregivers often relied on non-Indigenous medical professionals' expertise. But non-Indigenous professionals needed to respect cultural differences and offer culturally appropriate care. For example, Indigenous care emphasizes interdependence and collectivism "where everyone provides and cares for everyone" (Crosato et al., 2007). In contrast, Euro-Canadian culture emphasizes individualism and self-sufficiency. Furthermore, Indigenous culture emphasizes traditional healing. It incorporates natural foods and notions of balance. The Medicine Wheel (a traditional approach to healing) emphasizes balance and harmony in individual and collective life.

Habjan, Prince, and Kelley (2012) commented on the changing role of Indigenous women caregivers. Indigenous culture assigns the responsibility of care for seniors to women, but many younger and middle-aged women now leave remote communities for urban centres. This has created a shortage of women to provide care for seniors in isolated First Nations communities. One of the Indigenous women interviewed by Habjan and colleagues illustrated the problem:

> My mom is in the hospital right now and she would [be] telling me "I want to die at home", and I started to agree with her but the problem now is who is going to stay with her when she gets out of the hospital? The four of us are working, my brothers and sister. We don't have—like, I don't like to say it, but we don't have the time to be with her because we are all working. But the problem is I can't find anybody to live with her (p. 215).

Habjan and colleagues (2012) said that the shortage of family caregivers increases reliance on paid healthcare workers. But rural and remote First Nations communities often experienced a shortage of professional healthcare workers and support services. Indigenous persons expressed concern about the breakdown of traditional values and family and community networks.

Cultural norms in most collectivistic cultures motivate children to care for their aging parents. Lai (2010) found that caregivers who accept and perform their filial obligations tend to experience caregiving more positively. Still, filial piety did not eliminate the negative effects of caring for elderly family members (see also Suwal, 2010).

Caregiving relationships can be stressful and lead to abuse. Financial dependency of immigrant seniors on their adult children, language barriers, and isolation may also lead to abuse. Lai (2011) determined that 4.5 percent of older Chinese Canadians had experienced abuse in the previous 12 months. The most common forms of abuse included being scolded, yelled at, treated impolitely, or ridiculed. In other words, elder abuse typically involved "disrespect" that violated traditional Chinese cultural norms (Lai, Daoust, & Li, 2014). The abusers of older Chinese Canadians included spouses, sons, daughters, and daughters-in-law.

Walsh and Hassanali (2010; see also Lai, 2011; Lai, Daoust, & Li, 2014) noted that Chinese culture dictates that family honour be preserved and individuals not complain about their problems to outsiders. Accordingly, an abused Chinese elder tends to suffer in silence. It follows that elder abuse may be underreported in the Chinese community.

Caregivers can feel stressed and even suffer illness due to caregiving responsibilities. But caregivers can also find satisfaction in caring for a family member. Ethnic families face challenges as they care for elderly family members in Canada. But most families provide culturally appropriate care to their aging family members.

CONCLUSION

This chapter has examined the ethnocultural diversity of Canada's seniors. Most were born in Canada and offer a rich diversity of cultural orientations. Some Canadian-born seniors are Indigenous peoples. Many foreign-born seniors immigrated from a variety of countries when relatively young and have grown old in Canada. Many of these seniors identify as Canadian or have a bicultural or multicultural identity. Most have adjusted to Canada's mainstream culture. However, some seniors immigrated to Canada recently and are less likely to be integrated into Canadian society and culture. Whether foreign-born or Canadian-born, seniors exhibit diverse cultural beliefs, values, languages, customs, and practices.

Ethnocultural communities provide seniors with identity, direction, purpose, attachment, and support. However, ethnocultural seniors often experience barriers to integration into Canadian society and culture. For example, not knowing English or French constitutes a significant barrier to participation in Canadian social life. Furthermore, communication problems extend beyond simple translation. Communication and understanding involve cultural insight as well as language translation.

Besides problems with language and cultural diversity, Indigenous seniors and recent immigrant seniors experience high rates of poverty. Lack of English or French limits a person's ability to work in the labour force. For immigrant seniors, employment histories in their home country often get little recognition in Canada. Immigrant seniors also get limited entitlement to pensions and governmental income support programs. Seniors need to live in Canada for at least 10 years before they become eligible for these programs.

Indigenous and immigrant seniors receive considerable support from their families. But this support faces challenges as women, who traditionally serve as family caregivers, increasingly participate in the paid labour force. When adult children work outside the home, immigrant seniors may find themselves isolated and without the sociability and support they require.

Finally, ethnocultural seniors often have diverse health beliefs and practices and often combine traditional medicine with Western medicine. They rely on traditional healers and remedies as well as Western healthcare practitioners and treatments. Communication between the ethnocultural seniors, family members, traditional practitioners, and Western practitioners can be problematic. Ethnocultural seniors often prefer to maintain their traditional beliefs and practices. They would like culturally respectful, sensitive, and appropriate care from Western healthcare practitioners and programs.

High rates of immigration to Canada in recent decades have increased the ethnocultural diversity of the Canadian population. The ethnocultural diversity of seniors will continue to increase well into the 21st century as recent arrivals from diverse cultures grow old in Canada.

This chapter reveals a common thread of adaptation, challenge, tension, accommodation, and resistance in the discussion of ethnicity and aging, regardless of the ethnocultural group under consideration. The story of challenge and adaptation is a central theme in the lives of older and younger immigrants, as well as the Canadian-born who are the children and grandchildren of immigrants. The same can be said of Indigenous Canadians.

Throughout this discussion evidence exists of tension between ethnic seniors' earlier life and their current life, their former society and Canadian society, their cultural traditions and Canadian norms and values, their current cultural orientation and the cultural orientation of their parents and grandparents. This tension between past and present, traditional and modern culture, younger and older generations, habits and values of a particular ethnic group and the demands of Canadian society, shows up again and again.

This tension points up the challenges faced by ethnic seniors born in Canada, Indigenous seniors, and elderly immigrants and their families. This tension will continue as immigrants continue to come to Canada from various parts of the world and grow old in Canada. This tension will present opportunities and challenges to Canadian society, as we all grow old together.

Summary

1. Definitions of ethnicity refer to country of birth and/or ancestral heritage.
2. The culture of an ethnic group includes specific beliefs, values, language, customs, and practices.
3. Seniors in Canada exhibit varying degrees of commitment to their ethnocultural heritage and differ in their ethnic identity and cultural practices.
4. Indigenous seniors and seniors who have recently immigrated to Canada may experience multiple jeopardy and disadvantages that cumulate across the life course as a result of the combination of age, race, gender, social class, employment history, and immigration status.
5. Recent patterns of immigration have increased the ethnocultural diversity of seniors in Canada—this trend will continue well into the 21st century.
6. Large metropolitan areas such as Toronto and Vancouver show the most ethnic diversity of seniors.
7. Ethnocultural groups differ along a collectivistic-individualistic continuum. Collectivistic groups emphasize the obligations of family members to seniors and prefer collective decision making. Filial piety, an aspect of collectivistic cultures, refers to culturally defined obligations of adult children to their aging parents.
8. Indigenous seniors and seniors who have immigrated from collectivistic cultures are more likely to live with their adult children and grandchildren.
9. Seniors' involvement in an ethnocultural community can provide social and psychological benefits, but this may also isolate seniors from mainstream culture and society.
10. Indigenous seniors and recent senior immigrants have higher rates of poverty, but they also are more likely to receive family support.
11. Ethnocultural seniors have varying health beliefs and engage in diverse practices to promote health and treat illness. They often use a combination of traditional medicine and Western medicine. Ethnocultural seniors benefit from culturally sensitive healthcare services.
12. Participation in the labour force tends to reduce the ability of family members to provide care for ethnic elders. Still, most ethnic seniors receive care when needed from their family members.

STUDY QUESTIONS

1. Describe some of the ways that an ethnic senior's culture influences his or her life in Canada.
2. Why do gerontologists who study ethnicity focus on Indigenous Canadian seniors, visible minority seniors, and immigrant seniors? Is this focus justified?
3. Does Canada have a duty to accommodate seniors who immigrate from other countries and from other cultures? What forms does accommodation take today? How can Canada better accommodate seniors' needs, given their cultural diversity?

KEY TERMS

buffering theory (p. 78)
cultural enclaves (p. 85)
culture (p. 77)
ethnicity (p. 76)
filial piety (p. 82)
gentrification (p. 86)
institutional completeness (p. 85)
life course perspective (p. 78)
minority groups (p. 77)
multiple jeopardy theory (p. 78)
visible minority (p. 77)

Study Tools
CHAPTER 4

{

Located at retail.tophat.com:

- Review Key Terms with interactive and printable flash cards
- Check Your Comprehension and Think About chapter concepts by completing practice quizzes
- Develop Your Gerontological Imagination with class activities
- Analyze Aging in a Global Perspective with engaging case studies and critical thinking questions
- Demonstrate Your Knowledge of the Concepts by bringing your own experience to personal application questions
- Evaluate Aging in the Media by completing Internet activities with evaluation questions

CHAPTER 5

PERSONAL HEALTH AND ILLNESS

Comstock Images/Stockbyte/Thinkstock

LEARNING OBJECTIVES

After reading this chapter, you will

LO1　Understand patterns of health and illness in old age.

LO2　Understand the link between physical change, chronic illness, and physical capacity as people age.

LO3　Know some of the ways that technology, the environment, and changes in lifestyle can help seniors stay healthy and active.

LO4　Be able to discuss the changes in lifestyle people can make to in order to maintain their health and increase their life satisfaction as they age.

LO5　Be able to explain the differing views on the compression of morbidity hypothesis and the importance of morbidity compression in an aging society.

LO6　Be able to describe the signs of successful aging, explain different models of successful aging, and understand the controversy surrounding this concept.

LO7　Know the effects of gender and income on physical health in later life.

LO8　Be able to discuss the Canadian government's approach to healthy aging.

INTRODUCTION

Gerontologists distinguish between the **maximum life span** (the maximum number of years a member of a species can live) and **life expectancy** (the number of years at birth an average member of a population can expect to live). Scientists think that the maximum human life span of somewhere between 110 and 125 years has stayed the same for the past 100,000 years. Human life expectancy at birth, on the other hand, has increased in the past 2,000 years from an average of 22 years in ancient Rome to around 75 or 80 years today.

Women in Canada have gained more in life expectancy than men in the past century (Milan, 2011b; Statistics Canada, 2012b). A girl born in 2008, for example,

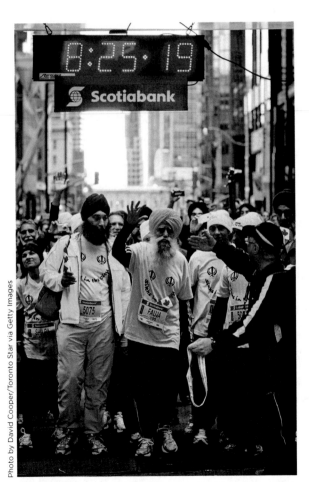

Mr. Fauja Singh, at age 100, finished Toronto's waterfront marathon on October 16, 2011. He finished the race in 8 hours, 11 minutes, and 5.9 seconds. His translator and coach (Mr. Singh speaks only Punjabi) said, "He's absolutely overjoyed. He's achieved his life-long wish." In April 2012, Mr. Singh announced his retirement from long-distance running. He says he will focus on running a faster pace in shorter distances (*CBC News*, 2011b).

can expect to outlive her male peers by about five years. Technology and biomedical science continue to extend life expectancy, and if this trend continues, more and more people will live close to the maximum human life span. This means that more people will live to old age and more will live longer in old age than ever before.

Consider the case of Anne Meeks, age 93, who lives on her own in a two-bedroom condo. She suffers from a number of **chronic health problems** including numbness in her hands, diabetes, and high blood pressure. She lives with chronic pain due to pressure on nerves in her spine and walks with a walker to steady her gait.

She also lacks strength in her arms and at one point couldn't get out of a soft chair in her den. She now wears an emergency call button that can summon help if she falls and can't get up or needs help for any other reason. The button calls an emergency response team that has a key to her home and will come in to rescue her. This has happened two or three times. The emergency button gives Anne and her family peace of mind and it has probably saved her life.

A physiotherapist comes in twice a week to help her develop strength in her legs. "She gets me up on my toes, I stretch." Mrs. Meeks says. "She's a wonderful girl. Very nice and helpful." The therapist also provides a break in Mrs. Meeks' week. She rarely gets out and rarely gets visitors. The therapist provides some social contact as well as physical therapy.

Mrs. Meeks gets support from her daughters and granddaughters who live nearby. But, if her health gets worse, they worry about how long she can live on her own.

A person's health and well-being in old age depend on their habits, income, environment, personal history, and social supports. Long life creates opportunities and challenges for the individual and society. The study of personal health and illness has two goals: to understand changes in the body that come with age and to apply this knowledge to extend and improve human life. This chapter will look at (1) the health of seniors in Canada today, (2) approaches to improving health and preventing illness in later life, and (3) the role of social policy and social organization in creating a good old age.

---

maximum life span the maximum number of years a member of a species can live

life expectancy the number of years at birth an average member of a population can expect to live

chronic health problems long-term illnesses such as arthritis, rheumatism, hypertension, diabetes, and heart disease

SENIORS' HEALTH STATUS

Older Canadians today live relatively healthy lives. Statistics Canada (2015d, 2015e) reports that three-quarters of men and women age 65 to 74 report good to full functional health. Among people age 75 and over, 60.7 percent of men and 55 percent of women report good to full functional health. Even among people age 75 and over, 35 percent of women and 36 percent of men report very good to excellent overall health (Statistics Canada, 2014f; Turcotte, 2011a).

Turcotte went on to report that the proportion of seniors who say they have very good or excellent health increases with education. More than half of senior men with a university degree (55.5 percent) report very good or excellent health. This compares with 35.1 percent of senior men with less than a high school diploma. Women show the same trend: only 30.6 percent of senior women with less than a high school diploma reported very good or excellent health. On the other hand, 55.6 percent of senior women with a university degree reported very good or excellent health.

Turcotte (2011a) predicted increases in the proportion of senior women who report very good or excellent health: "Since growing numbers of women are completing university, it is possible that the proportion of women reporting excellent health will continue to rise in the coming years" (p. 6).

New Patterns of Health and Illness

In spite of this optimistic picture, compared to young people, older people report more chronic illness. The shift from a young to an older population in Canada has led to a change in the pattern of disease. The rate of acute illness (e.g., diphtheria, typhoid, and measles) has decreased during this century. More children now survive infancy, grow to adulthood, and enter old age. This leads to an increase in the rate of non-communicable diseases and chronic illness (e.g., chronic respiratory disease, diabetes,

---

EXHIBIT 5.1   *Self-Perceived Health, by Age Group, Reporting "Very Good" or "Excellent" Health, Canada 2009*

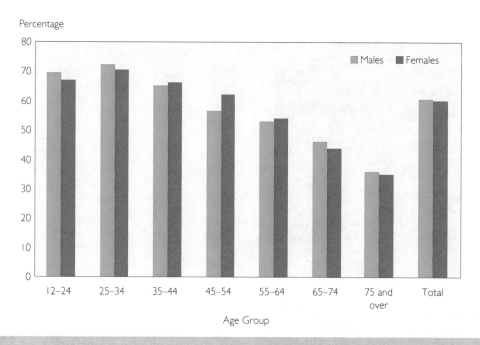

Note that the proportion of men and women who report very good or excellent health decreases from age 25 onward. But also note that a large proportion of senior men and women report very good or excellent health. Even among seniors age 75 and over, more than one-third report very good or excellent health.

Sources: Adapted from Turcotte, M. (2011a). "Women and Health." *Women in Canada: A Gender-based Statistical Report.* Component of Statistics Canada. Catalogue No. 89-503X. Ottawa: Minister of Industry, p. 6. Citing Statistics Canada, *Canadian Community Health Survey,* 2003 and 2009. Also see Ramage-Morin, Shields, and Martel (2010), p. 4. Original data from 2009 *Canadian Community Health Survey—Healthy Aging: 2000/2001 Canadian Community Health Survey.* Reproduced and distributed on an "as is" basis with the permission of Statistics Canada.

and heart disease). The United Nations (2012b) says that these diseases now represent 63 percent of all deaths worldwide, and deaths from these diseases will increase worldwide as populations age. Scientists refer to this society-wide shift from acute illnesses in childhood (e.g., measles, chicken pox) to chronic illness in old age as the **epidemiological transition** (Land & Yang, 2006).

Chronic illness is any long-term illness, such as arthritis, rheumatism, hypertension, diabetes, or heart

---

epidemiological transition the transition a society makes when it moves from a high rate of acute illness (mostly in youth) to a high rate of chronic illness (mostly in old age); Canada has made this transition, as have many developed nations

disease that lasts for at least three months. Denton and Spencer (2009a, 2010) report that 90 percent of Canadians age 65 to 79 have at least one chronic health problem (e.g., high blood pressure). This figure increases to 93.3 percent for people age 80 and over.

One-third of the 65 to 79 age group reported four or more chronic conditions and 7 percent of this age group reported seven or more conditions. Among seniors age 80 and over, 42 percent reported four or more chronic conditions, and 10 percent reported seven or more conditions (Denton & Spencer, 2009a; also Ramage-Morin, Shields, & Martel, 2010). These figures show that the prevalence of chronic conditions and the number of chronic conditions per person increase

---

EXHIBIT 5.2   *Proportion of Population with One or More Chronic Diseases,* by Selected Age Groups, Canada, 2009*

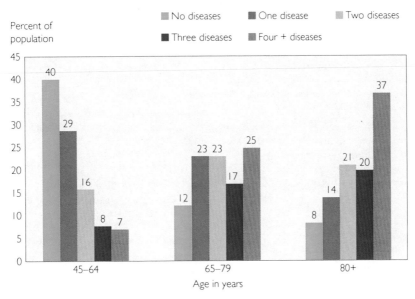

* Note: Diseases include angina, asthma, arthritis or rheumatism, osteoporosis, high blood pressure, bronchitis, emphysema, chronic obstructive pulmonary disease, diabetes, heart disease, cancer, effects of a stroke, Crohn's disease, colitis, Alzheimer's disease, Parkinson's disease, cataracts, glaucoma, thyroid condition, mood disorder, and anxiety disorder.

This chart shows the prevalence of chronic illness in three adult age groups. Note that the proportion of people who report no diseases decreases from 40 percent of the 45 to 64 age group to 8 percent of the 80+ age group. The percentage of people with four or more diseases shows the opposite pattern. Only 7 percent of people age 45 to 64 reported having four or more chronic diseases, but 37 percent of people age 80 and over reported four or more illnesses.

This study took a snapshot of the population in 2009, so we can't conclude that chronic illness increases with age. Only a longitudinal study could show this. But the data here on the middle group age 65 to 79 point to what the future might look like for this age group. The middle group already shows rates of chronic illness above those of the 80-and-over age group in some categories. And it seems likely that, compared with the current group age 80 and over, the 65- to 79-year-olds will show similar or higher rates of chronic illness as they age.

Source: Butler-Jones, D. (2010). *Report on the State of Public Health in Canada 2010: Growing Older—Adding Life to Years*, Figure 3.5, p. 26. Her Majesty the Queen in Right of Canada. Catalogue No. HP2-10/2010E-PDF. http://www.phac-aspc.gc.ca/cphorsphc-respcacsp/2010/fr-rc/pdf/cpho_report_2010_e.pdf. Reproduced and distributed on an "as is" basis with the permission of Statistics Canada.

with age. The use of healthcare resources also increases with age and increases with the number of chronic conditions.

Specific groups among the older population report high rates of chronic conditions. Poor older people, for example, suffer from high rates of chronic illness. Also, compared to men, women have higher rates of many chronic illnesses (Milan & Vézina, 2011). Compared to men, women report higher rates of hypertension, arthritis, and rheumatism, and they are more likely than men to have at least one chronic condition (Lindsay & Almey, 2006). Compared to older men, older women also use more healthcare services, including more physician visits. Health service use may reflect the continuation of a pattern of healthcare use by women during their middle years. The lower usage rate by men may reflect a denial of health problems.

LIMITS ON ACTIVITY DUE TO PHYSICAL DECLINE

Chronic illness can lead to **functional disability**. Functional disability refers to a limitation on a person's ability to perform normal daily activities due to illness or injury. This measure focuses on the effects of illness on a person's everyday life. Functional disability can decrease an older person's quality of life and subjective well-being.

Statistics Canada (2007c) conducted the *Participation and Activity Limitation Survey* (PALS) in 2006. This national survey assessed activity and disability rates among Canadians. The study found that activity

functional disability a limitation in the performance of normal daily activities due to illness or injury

EXHIBIT 5.3   *A Snapshot of Women and Chronic Illness in Old Age*

Women make up a large proportion of the older population and their proportion grows with each older age group. Women tend to live longer than men, but compared to men, older women have more chronic illnesses. Below you will find facts on leading chronic diseases and causes of death for older women. Nearly all of these diseases can be avoided or reduced in severity through exercise, diet, and lifestyle modification.

Nutritional risk: This refers to the risk of poor nutrition due to poor dietary habits (e.g., meal preparation; fruit, vegetable, and fluid consumption). Compared to men age 65 and over, women showed greater nutritional risk. More than one woman in three (36.1 percent) age 65 to 74 faced nutritional risk. Nutritional risk increases with age. Two out of five women age 75 and over (40.6 percent) showed nutritional risk. Women who live alone show some of the greatest risk. Nearly half of these women (48.2 percent) showed nutritional risk (Ramage-Morin & Garriguet, 2013).

Daily activity limitations: Nearly one in five women (18 percent) in their 60s reported a limitation on their daily activities. This figure increases to one in three (35 percent) for women in their 80s or older. Compared to men, a higher proportion of women in all older age groups report an activity limitation (Crompton, 2011).

Overweight and obesity: Compared to women in younger age groups, women age 60 to 79 showed higher rates of obesity. Nearly one woman in three (32 percent) in this age group counted as obese and 35 percent rate as overweight. By comparison, among women in the age group 18 to 39, 18 percent counted as obese and 23 percent as overweight (Statistics Canada, 2013d).

Osteoporosis (thin or brittle bones): In 2009 among people age 50 and over, 19.2 percent of women and 3.4 percent of men had been diagnosed with osteoporosis. Among people age 71 and older, this figure jumped to 31.1 percent for women

and 6.4 percent for men. Older women with osteoporosis risk a bone fracture (often a wrist, spine, upper arm, or hip) as they age. Most fractures result from falls. A fracture can mean the end to an active lifestyle (Garriguet, 2014; Public Health Agency of Canada, 2010a).

Hypertension (high blood pressure): Compared to the proportion of men age 65 and over, a higher proportion of women in this age group had high blood pressure (48.8 percent vs. 45.7 percent). This rate for older women is more than double the rate of the age group of women age 45 to 64 years (20 percent) (Statistics Canada, 2015f).

Diabetes: Compared to women age 65 and over, men had a higher rate of diabetes. Still, in 2014, 465,378 women age 65 and over in Canada (16.2 percent of senior women) had this disease. This represented a 26 percent increase from 2010 (Statistics Canada, 2015e).

Cancer: Men and women differ in their rates of cancer and in the type of cancer they get. Breast cancer is the most common cancer for adult women. Men have high rates of bladder and prostate cancers (Ellison & Wilkins, 2012).

Stress: Seniors were the lowest proportion of people who reported high levels of stress. But, compared to senior men, a higher proportion of senior women reported feeling quite a bit or extremely stressed. Chronic illness and caregiving responsibilities (that often fall to women) partly explain this difference (Statistics Canada, 2014g).

Blood pressure: Blood pressure increases with age. High blood pressure can damage blood vessels and can cause a heart attack or stroke. These rank as leading causes of hospitalization and death in Canada (Statistics Canada, 2014h). In the age group 70 to 79, compared to men, women had higher blood pressure. This puts women at greater risk of a disease such as stroke in later life.

limitation due to disability increases with each older age group. Adults age 15 to 64, for example, report an activity limitation rate of 11.5 percent. This rises to 43.4 percent for people over age 65 and for people age 75 and over, more than half of the population (56.3 percent) reports an activity limitation.

The PALS also found that disability increases dramatically in later old age. The study found that the oldest age group (75 and over) had more than one and a half times the rate of disability of the 65 to 74 age group (33 percent vs. 56.3 percent). Compared with men, women in the 75-and-over age group had a higher disability rate (57.8 percent vs. 54 percent).

Disabilities impair some functions more than others. Older adults with disabilities most often say they have trouble with mobility (e.g., walking from room to room or standing for a long time). They also have trouble with agility (e.g., bending, dressing, or grasping things) and hearing.

Community services, such as transportation by modified vans or buses with wheelchair lifts, can help with some functional problems. But many seniors with disabilities report that they could use more help. For example, older people at all ages report the need for help with everyday housework. And the proportion of people who need this type of help increases with age (from about one person in ten age 65 to 74 who needs help to nearly one person in four age 75 and over who needs help). After age 75, one person in ten needs help with personal care such as washing, eating, dressing, or taking medicine, and 13.2 percent of people age 75 and over need help preparing meals (Lindsay & Almey, 2006).

Gerontologists study the effects of functional disability on **activities of daily living (ADLs)** and **instrumental activities of daily living (IADLs)**. ADLs include bathing, moving from a bed or chair, dressing, getting to and using the toilet, eating, and walking. IADLs refer to home management activities such as using the phone, preparing meals, managing finances, shopping, and doing light housework. Limitations may range from a mild problem such as trouble using the phone to more serious problems such as the inability to eat unassisted or inability to use the toilet. The National Advisory Council on Aging

(2006) *Report Card* found that only about 7 percent of seniors in the community needed help with ADLs, though 22.4 percent needed help with IADLs.

The *Canadian Study of Health and Aging* (CSHA), a study of more than 9,000 community-dwelling seniors, looked at the main causes of disability in older people (Griffith et al., 2010). The study found that five conditions—foot problems, arthritis, cognitive impairment, heart problems, and vision—contributed most to ADL and IADL disability. In particular, a combination of foot problems, arthritis, and heart problems led to the most functional limitations. About 11 percent of the people in this study reported an ADL disability; about 33 percent of people reported an IADL disability. This gives some idea of the prevalence of functional limitations in the older population.

The focus on health problems and disability in later life can give the impression that nearly all older people suffer from a decline in the quality of life. But the CSHA found that two-thirds of older people report no limitation on their daily living. Also, for some seniors, disability comes and goes in later life. The National Population Health Survey in 2002–2003 found that "not all seniors who lose their health do so for good" (Shields & Martel, 2006, p. 17). People who reported leisure physical activity, moderate alcohol use, normal body weight, and non-smoking had the highest odds of recovery.

These findings show that activity limitation and dependency may last only a short time. People can recover from acute injuries such as a strained back, and treatment for chronic problems like arthritis can help people function on their own.

Modern medicine can help older people maintain their physical function. Knee and hip replacement surgery, for example, can give a person many added years of mobility. In 2012–2013, approximately 72,000 Canadians underwent hip and knee replacement surgery (Canadian Institute for Health Information, 2015a). These people gained up to 85 to 90 percent recovery of their mobility (Canadian Orthopaedic Foundation, 2010).

A colleague of one of the authors could barely walk across campus due to a loss of cartilage in his hip. The pain led him to put off meetings in distant offices or cluster meetings to avoid walking more than he had to. He finally decided to have a hip replacement operation. Within two months, he took a trip to Europe and climbed the steps of the Eiffel Tower. Within a year, he was able to hike with a pack in the mountains of Wyoming.

Education programs can help people with less severe physical problems. A Canadian program titled

activities of daily living (ADLs) activities performed daily, such as bathing, moving from a bed or chair, dressing, getting to and using the toilet, eating, and walking

instrumental activities of daily living (IADLs) home management activities such as using the phone, cooking, shopping, managing finances, and doing light housework

EXHIBIT 5.4   *Prevalence of Good Health, by Number of Health-Promoting Factors and Age Group, Household Population Aged 45 or Older, Canada, 2009*

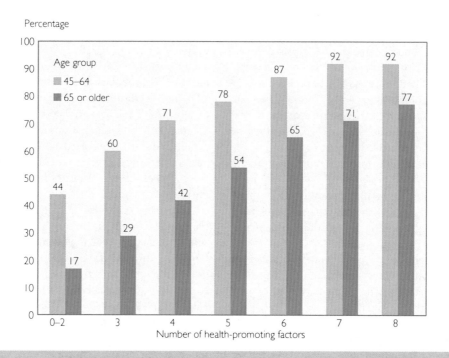

This chart looks at the positive effects of health promotion in later life. The researchers in this study looked at eight factors that measure healthy behaviour: smoking, body mass index (BMI), physical activity, diet, sleep, oral health, stress, and social participation.

This chart shows that for the younger and older age groups, the more health-promoting activity a person engaged in, the greater the likelihood of good health. The chart also shows that health-promoting activity has a cumulative effect. Each additional health-promoting factor significantly increased the proportion of people who reported good health. More than three-quarters (77 percent) of the older people who engaged in eight of the health-promoting factors reported good health.

The researchers said, "The development of chronic conditions is not inevitable. While genetic predisposition plays a role, factors within individuals' control can prevent the development of chronic conditions or limit their severity" (pp. 4–5).

Source: Statistics Canada, *Canadian Community Health Survey*, 2009; Statistics Canada, *Canadian Community Health Survey*, 2000–2001. Reproduced and distributed on an "as is" basis with the permission of Statistics Canada.

"I'm Taking Charge of My Arthritis" led to "fewer functional limitations, less helplessness, and better coping" (Laforest et al., 2012, p. 195; also Laforest et al., 2008). Benefits continued when the researchers maintained contact through phone calls to housebound seniors. Programs such as this along with physical therapy and medication can help older people manage chronic illness and reduce disability.

Disability in later life deserves researchers' and policymakers' attention. First, older people with disabilities need informal and sometimes formal support to maintain a high quality of life. These seniors may rely on the healthcare system for service. An increase in the number of seniors with disabilities will increase costs and will affect the types of resources that the healthcare system needs to provide.

Second, some older people cope well with their disability and some regain their functioning. This group can help us understand how to encourage and rehabilitate other seniors with disabilities. Third, exercise and self-care can prevent, ease, or reverse disabilities. Studies show that even people with chronic illness can improve their functioning.

Ferraro (2006) reports a growth in the use of technology and environmental modification as methods of self-care. But he notes that when a health condition

EXHIBIT 5.5   *Prevalence of Disability by Sex and Age Group, Canada, 2012*

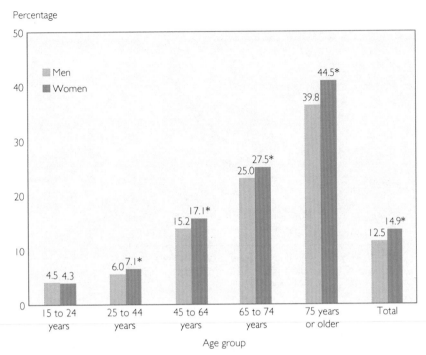

Percentage

*Significantly different from men (p < 0.05)

Over 1.4 million Canadians age 65 and over live with a disability (an impairment that limits their daily activities). This comes to one in three older Canadians. Note that the percentage of people with a disability increases with age. Also, compared with men, at every age from middle age onward, women show a higher rate of disability. People in the oldest age group show the highest rate of disability.

Seniors with a disability report pain, along with flexibility and mobility problems, as the most common types of disabilities. About one in five seniors report one or more of these problems. Seniors also have a high rate of hearing disability (10.4 percent). Rates for specific disabilities also increase with age. For example, less than 1 percent of Canadians age 15 to 24 reported a mobility-related disability. This figure jumps to 27 percent of people age 75 and over. People in the oldest age group often need help to maintain their independence.

Source: Statistics Canada, A profile of persons with disabilities among Canadians aged 15 years or older, 2012, Chart 2. Catalogue No. 89-654-X. http://www.statcan.gc.ca/pub/89-654-x/89-654-x2015001-eng.htm#a1 Reproduced and distributed on an "as is" basis with the permission of Statistics Canada.

becomes serious (e.g., something that might require surgery), people turn to conventional medicine. Most people will combine self-care methods with medical treatment.

Manton, Gu, and Lamb (2006) said they look to improvements in basic medical science and medical care for future declines in disability rates. They predicted an important role for biomedical research and cellular and molecular understanding of chronic diseases. For example, gene therapy in the future may have a profound effect on health and illness in later life.

Gene therapy may allow researchers to replace a defective gene and reverse a state of illness or physical decline. Physicians could use recombinant DNA methods to (1) multiply the gene in a bacterial culture, (2) use a benign virus to place the gene in the host's cell, and (3) allow the gene to produce a needed protein. Scientists may use this technology in the future to cure immune system breakdown, Parkinson's disease, and cancer. In the meantime, a healthy diet, exercise, and self-care play an important role in disease prevention, reduction of symptoms, and in the promotion of well-being in later life.

EXHIBIT 5.6   *Prevalence of Sensory and Physical Disabilities, by Type and Age Group, Canada, 2012*

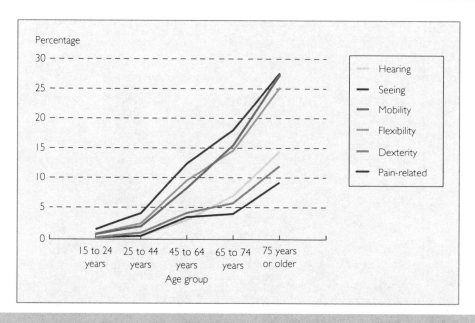

Note that all of the disabilities in this graph increase with age. Pain, mobility, and flexibility are shown as the greatest prevalence among the older population. These three types of disability often occur together. For example, among all adults, 65 percent who reported a pain-related disability also reported a flexibility disability and 61 percent reported a mobility disability.

Some studies project a dramatic increase in disability-related dependency cases (as much as a five-fold increased) between now and 2051 for the 85 and over age group (Légaré, Décarie, & Bélanger, 2014). Older people with one or more disabilities often need support with activities of daily living. An aging population will require an increase in social and healthcare supports.

Source: Statistics Canada, A profile of persons with disabilities among Canadians aged 15 years or older, 2012, Chart 2. Catalogue No. 89-654-X. http://www.statcan.gc.ca/pub/89-654-x/89-654-x2015001-eng.htm#a1 Reproduced and distributed on an "as is" basis with the permission of Statistics Canada.

COPING WITH PHYSICAL CHANGE

Chronic conditions do not always turn into functional disability or the need for assistance with daily activities. Although more than three-quarters of elderly persons have at least one chronic condition, less than one-half experience some functional disability. Even fewer, about one-fifth, require assistance with ADLs. Research has shown that a large majority of older people live without functional handicaps on certain activities. For example, only 6 percent of older men and 7 percent of older women in private households needed help with activities such as bathing or dressing. Even at age 85 or older, only 20 percent of men and 23 percent of women in the community depended on others for ADL help (Gilmour & Park, 2006).

Older people compensate for declines in the senses, muscles, and organs as they age. For example, a person with poor night vision may drive less at night or drive only in his or her neighbourhood. Someone with arthritis may take a yoga class to increase flexibility.

Zimmer, Hickey, and Searle (1997) found that people with arthritis pain tended to cut back on activity (the greater the pain, the greater the tendency to quit activities). But a group of people, called "replacers," added more passive activities to replace activities they had quit. These people often were younger than the "quitters." They also tended to have a spouse, a social network, and fewer mobility problems. These researchers say that professionals should encourage arthritis patients to take up new activities. This study also points to the importance of social supports (a spouse, friends, family) in helping a person stay active and engaged. People who replace their activities will live a higher quality of life.

EXHIBIT 5.7 *What Does It Feel Like to Grow Old?*

What does it feel like to enter late old age—the Fourth Age? Statistical studies and questionnaires only hint at the experience of aging. Laurie Lewis, a woman in her 80s, reflected on the inner experience of aging in an essay for The Globe and Mail. Her story gives an intimate look at the joy, fear, and acceptance that she experiences at this stage of her life.

I arrived last spring at old age. After prancing about merrily at the beginning of my 80s, a small medical situation put me into less prancey territory, and I suddenly felt old.

In my early 80s I still had a kind of pride. I was tough, I looked pretty good, I had moments of verbal clarity, I remembered what I read.

But now, a bare three or four years further along in this voyage, I'm not so feisty. Tiny things have gone wrong, and tiny changes in my being have pushed themselves to my notice.

What is new? What is it that has changed?

Everything takes more effort.

The appearance of attentiveness, which I work to maintain, takes more energy now. I go to the bookshop to hear readings by local authors, or to the university to hear the words of writers from other places delivering lectures and readings. (These things represent one of the perks of living in a university city: There is a lot of free stuff going on, a great advantage for those of us not cushioned by financial security.) I find I must listen closely to follow the reading, the lecture. I make notes in a little red Moleskine. When I read them later, I have no idea what they mean.

There is a sense of some physical insecurity.

Balance? How odd it is, these days, to feel a tiny sense of tottering. I swear it's my new glasses. Perhaps I'm better off without them. Or is it the shoes? I try many different kinds of shoes. Whatever it is, I feel ever so slightly less secure on my feet as I walk on my patio, or down the street. There is, here in my body, a new sense of insecurity. The soles of my feet feel like bubble wrap, unstable. I am particularly careful when I go up or down stairs.

Is it the physical insecurity that leads to the mental/emotional one? Or the other way around?

My mind is shifting. Memory? Yes, that has changed also. I have the sense that all the proper nouns have fled, or are playing hide-and-seek. Names of people, or organizations, or books and journals—these are gone. Well, not gone exactly, but hiding in the wings, just outside my line of sight, my line of thought, outside the memory trace....

Fatigue.

Yes. This, too, is more frequent. I like my afternoon nap, as I have for years, but it feels different now. It's less a real nap and more like a long state of leisure, a bit of floating in space/time.

The face in the mirror.

Weight loss, four or five pounds, has brought with it an epidemic (an epidermis?) of wrinkles. My bony face in the bathroom mirror looks terrified at what it sees. Vanity, vanity. A little fresh paint helps, but not much.

Bones—I have my mother's knee and other body parts.

I seem to have acquired her right knee, the one that turned in slightly, giving a small twist to her torso. I am thinning out. I am weakening. This is not good news. My doctor is worried about my old bones, and therefore I am, too. There's a new treatment that might prevent fractures....

The voice. Oh, the voice.

At one time I had some familiarity with standing in front of a room full of people and speaking out in a good strong voice, being heard, being listened to. I used to be, I say with some chagrin, quite vain in my vigour and quickness, my good posture and strong voice.

Gone. Gone. All of it gone. My voice is full of squeaks and cracks, powerless. It's quite a comeuppance, I tell you.

And yet, something endures, something of the past exists.

Sometimes, waking in the morning without pain, my body will forget itself and think it is young. Under the duvet in the early morning, my old limbs may feel smooth and lithe like those of the girl I used to be. My skin, experienced from the inside, seems supple and rosy.

On the pillow, my hair may be long and blond and gleaming, and there may be eyelashes lacy against my cheeks as I dream-doze, early, before the light, before the morning air, before the thought of coffee, of breakfast.

In that delicious dream state, when words jumble and roll about on the pillow hinting at dreams or poems, I have no age.

Source: Laurie Lewis, *In my early 80s I still had a kind of pride but now, I'm not so feisty.*, Special to *The Globe and Mail* (January 6, 2015). Used with permission of the author.

Other studies of pain due to illness show that pain can cause psychological distress (Gilmour, 2015). The activity reduction model of mental health says that this distress comes from restrictions on daily activities. Pain makes activities such as personal care, social relations, and leisure more difficult (Gilmour, 2015). The greater the intensity of the pain, the less the likelihood that a person would report "flourishing" mental health (p. 18). This study showed the important role activity plays in a person's well-being. Gilmour says that some older people may cope better with activity loss due to pain because they have developed good coping strategies.

People with activity limitations use many methods to cope with their illness. These include keeping a positive attitude toward life, cutting down on household chores, and relying on others for help. Although Litwin (2000) reported that disability negatively affects a person's sense of well-being, he also found that a supportive social network improves well-being. Support from family and friends—the quality of their relationships and the frequency of help—brought older people with disabilities the most satisfaction.

Married people often rely on a spouse for help. A spouse can provide practical help. Spouses also provide

Self-care can take many forms, from exercise, to diet, to environmental modification. Technology can also help a person maintain good health. Here, a woman monitors her blood pressure with a device she uses at home.

social support and social engagement with family and friends (Clouston, Lawlor, & Verdery, 2014). A person without a spouse may need to rely on formal support, such as a homemaker, to help with housework or cooking. Community meal programs can help older people with severe disabilities to eat well. These programs also get people out of their homes and give them a chance to socialize with others.

Three responses to aging can decrease the effects of physiological decline: changes in the environment, improvements in technology, and changes in lifestyle.

Changes in the Environment

Sense thresholds, the points at which a person can begin to perceive a stimulus, begin to increase as early as age 30, and by age 60 most people notice changes in their senses. Turcotte and Schellenberg (2007) reported that 3.4 percent of older people have a hearing problem even with a hearing aid and 2.1 percent have a vision problem

even with corrective lenses. Hearing aids may not help a person follow a conversation because they amplify all sounds, even background noises.

In one case, an elderly man with a hearing aid in a university class showed up to take the course a second time. Surprised, the professor asked him why. The man said that students talking behind him, a bus depot across the street, and a noisy heating system all made his hearing aid useless. Some days he left it at home or shut it off and tried to read the professor's lips. "I only got half of what you said last time," he told the professor. "So I've come back to get the rest." This man needed a quieter classroom.

Changes in the environment—including changes in the way other people speak to or treat an older person—can help that person cope with physical decline. Also, older adults can compensate for a disability by changing their environment. For example, older people who cannot walk stairs may choose to live in a one-floor, ground-level home. Nearly all older people say they would prefer to live in their own home and never move. But few people have a home that can easily adapt to their changing physical needs as they age. Many older people face a dilemma: live in unsuitable housing (e.g., a home with an inaccessible upstairs bedroom) or move and adjust to new housing.

New designs in household products can offer a better quality of life to older residents. New products include a bathroom sink that stops scalding water from reaching the faucet, rubber flooring in the bathroom to prevent slips and falls, window shades with pinholes that let in light with less glare, and lamps that turn on and off with a touch at the base or a voice command.

As the market grows, companies will respond by designing and producing more products for older people. New technologies, like robots that perform simple household tasks, can help a person to live in his or her own home for life. And ever-evolving Internet software applications allow a person in a nursing home to play a card game with a grandchild thousands of miles away.

Some architects and landscape designers have designed special gardens for nursing homes and day centres. Garden designs often include benches for residents and staff to sit with family or clients. A fountain may serve as a destination for short walks. An enclosed loop and coloured walkway can guide people who have cognitive impairment. These gardens can also allow clients or residents to care for some plants of their own.

Gigliotti and Jarrott (2005) started a horticulture therapy program in an adult day service for people with dementia. The day program provides a respite for family caregivers and gives dementia clients a chance to socialize and stay active. The researchers tested the effectiveness of gardening as an activity for dementia clients. Forty-eight clients (average age 80) took part in the study. The dementia clients spent half an hour once a week for nine weeks on horticulture therapy. The researchers compared the results of this program with traditional adult day service programs (exercise, games, crafts, and puzzles). They found that, compared with the time they spent in traditional activities, clients spent more time engaged in horticulture therapy, less time doing nothing, and developed more positive relationships.

Designers find that an enclosed garden offers a safe setting for outdoor activity. Designers can create an environment that matches and enhances the decreased cognitive and physical abilities of the older clients or residents. Staff at one day centre used the garden for calm activities with Alzheimer's clients. A walk in the garden soothed agitated participants (Lovering et al., 2002). Staff members also used the garden for mild physical activity such as bocce and shuffleboard, and to hold group discussions.

One staff member commented about the garden's effect on clients: "It's good for them, it's healthy for them. They enjoy it. I know that people benefit and are healthier from having just 20 minutes of sunlight a day" (Lovering et al., 2002, p. 423). The designers say that "specially designed outdoor spaces" can improve the quality of life of frail and confused older people (p. 417).

Improvements in Technology

In the 18th century, Benjamin Franklin invented bifocals. He cut his glasses in half when he needed to watch the speakers' expressions at the French court. Today, technology helps older people cope with aging in dozens of ways. Some people wear electronic pacemakers to regulate their hearts, people with severe arthritis can have joint replacement surgery, and in some cases, a person can have a childhood problem corrected in old age.

One woman lived her first 60 years with her hipbones outside their sockets. Her muscles and ligaments allowed her to walk, but she limped and tired quickly. As she aged, her muscles weakened and her doctor said she would have to spend the rest of her life in a wheelchair. She searched for and found a doctor who agreed to operate on both of her hips. He warned her that the operation would endanger her life, but she decided to go ahead with the surgery. She now has both hips in place in their sockets and she stands two inches taller than in her youth.

Technological aids to older people range from the simple (e.g., a thick piece of rubber tubing that fits over a wooden spoon handle to help a person with arthritis) to the complex (e.g., a battery-powered tub seat that lowers a person into the tub, reclines at the push of a button, and uses an optional turntable to help the person into and out of the tub). A device such as a bathroom grab bar can prevent falls and injury. Stefanacci and Haimowitz (2014) said that "the most hazardous activities for all ages are bathing, showering and getting out of the tub or shower.... Injuries in or near the bathtub or shower account for more than two-thirds of emergency room visits." Grab bars and rubber mats in the tub can help seniors prevent a fall and serious injury.

A national study of nearly 2,000 Canadian veterans found that 60 percent of them had a grab bar in the bathroom, and almost 80 percent had anti-slip mats in the tub or shower (Speechley et al., 2005). Edwards, Gallagher, and Lockett (2003) estimated that more grab bars in homes could save an estimated $210 million per year in healthcare costs.

People with visual impairment can use technologies such as talking books or computerized reading aids. A person can now control a hearing aid so that the aid adjusts the sound to the environment. The user can filter out high- or low-pitched sounds or reduce background noise. Improvements in technology make coping with disability easier. As prices on these innovations decrease, more people will benefit from their use.

Technology can also allow families to monitor an older relative's activity. Canada Health Infoway (2011) says that technology can report changes in a person's physical condition to a distant healthcare centre. With the parent's permission, some children have arranged to have a camera located in a parent's home. The camera monitors the older person's behaviour and through the Internet will alert the children about any changes that signal danger. For example, the family can program the camera to expect the older person to enter the kitchen in the morning. If this does not happen, the system can alert the children, who can then check for any problems. The older person can turn off the camera at any point. Technology can also detect wandering, can note when a door opens, and can track a person through GPS devices.

These technologies can help older people age in place. Some people appreciate this kind of support, although others find it intrusive. Melenhorst and colleagues (2004) found that older people will tolerate the intrusion if the technology improves their sense of safety and security.

In the future, older people may have access to more exotic aids. For example, computerized robots may help older people with daily chores or help bathe and feed people in nursing homes. Voice-activated robots will pick things up or move them around. Robots may also help patients do passive exercises, help them walk, or bring them something they need. Robots could free nursing home staff from routine work and allow them to spend more time with residents. Voice-activated robots would give an immobilized person a feeling of control over the environment, thereby increasing life satisfaction.

A number of companies see assistive robotics as an emerging market. Companies in Japan and Korea want to create machines that will bring a disabled person food, move them from room to room, or even call a doctor.

A product called My Spoon assists users who need help feeding themselves. A joystick controls a spoon or fork on the end of a mechanical arm. The user can choose a semiautomatic and automatic mode. The robotic arm selects a desired compartment that contains food. The arm then automatically brings the food to the person's mouth.

A robot called the "Care-O-Bot 4" developed in Germany performs household tasks. A touch-screen display or voice command controls the robot. The robot can also support a person while walking, it can deliver food, and it can clean up after a person finishes eating. A database in the robot stores information about the environment and in a semiautomatic mode it can move around a person's home on its own.

Shibata and Wada (2008) reported on a robot named Paro in the shape of a stuffed toy seal. The researchers used the robot to develop a program of "robot therapy" similar to animal therapy for nursing-home residents. The research project explored the use of the robot as a substitute for a live animal. The researchers report that the residents spoke to the robot, stroked it, and hugged it. The study found that Paro improved the residents' moods over a four-month period. The researchers say that "Paro was effective in improving or eliminating depression" among the residents who interacted with the electronic pet (p. 412).

Robots and other assistive technologies will increase in the future. Smart clothing, for example, can monitor a person's heart rate, breath rate, or brain wave patterns 24 hours a day. This creates a "wearable health care system" (Paradiso, Taccini, & Loriga, 2008, p. 687). These products and new ones in development promise to improve the quality of life for older people with disabilities.

Research will have to determine whether robots dehumanize household and institutional settings, whether older people (or institutions) can afford complex machines, and whether people will use high-tech equipment if they have the choice.

The Use of Computers to Enhance Everyday Life

Computers already allow a housebound older person to order groceries, get mail, or play Scrabble with a grandchild across the country. New technologies may make some disabilities less of a problem. Internet banking allows older people with a mobility problem to manage their finances from home. Computer websites allow people to get medical and health promotion information. People with disabilities use computers to communicate with one another. Email, chat rooms, instant messaging, Facebook, Twitter, and video links allow older people to develop and maintain contacts with family members or with a caregiver support group.

Still, older people lag behind the general population in Internet use. Shields and Tremblay (2008a) studied the proportion of screen time people spent using a computer. ("Screen time" refers to the total amount of time spent watching television or using a computer). The proportion of time spent using a computer dropped steadily with age. People age 20 to 24 spent nearly half their screen time (45 percent) on the computer. People age 75 and over spent only 8 percent of their screen time using a computer.

Barriers still exist to widespread computer use by older people. For example, computer use demands physical skill (fine motor coordination to use the keyboard) and mental ability. Scialfa and Fernie (2006) said that computer use taxes verbal and spatial working memory. Computer users need to keep information about search paths and previous Web pages in mind as they browse and search. They also have to contend with pop-up ads and windows that intend to draw attention away from the person's main task. Multiple Web page links, information presented in hard-to-read fonts, and poorly organized websites can make computer use a challenge (at any age). A search on the Internet can quickly lead to confusion as the reader jumps from one link to another.

Socialization and acculturation probably account for some of the difference in computer use by age group. Younger people have grown up with computers. Some writers refer to them as "digital natives." Older people (even those in middle-age) live more as "digital immigrants."

When older people (age 45 and over) use a computer, they often use it to search for health-related information. They search for information about lifestyle choices, specific diseases, symptoms, and drugs or medications (Underhill & McKeown, 2008).

Health-related computer use among this age group differs for men and women. Women, compared with men, tend to look for information on specific diseases and drugs or medications. Compared with women, men tend to look for information on the healthcare system or on healthcare delivery. This reflects the different needs the two sexes have for information at this point in their lives. Women, who serve as caregivers to a spouse or parent, more often provide direct care. Male caregivers tend to manage the delivery of care.

Underhill and McKeown (2008) warned that "the accuracy and reliability of Internet information on any topic can vary widely. Internet sources of health information range from personal accounts of illnesses and patient discussion groups to clinical decision tools and peer-reviewed journal articles." In this case, acting on poor quality or wrong information could lead to life-threatening outcomes.

Czaja and Lee (2006) said that lack of familiarity with computers, lack of training, and hard-to-use systems all present barriers to the use of computers by older people. In addition, some people can't afford a computer or the cost of Internet service. This creates a "digital divide" within the older population. Some people have access to electronic information and social networks while others do not. These differences in computer and technology use, in part, reflect differences in education, ethnicity, and socioeconomic status among seniors (Chang & McCaslin, 2015).

A study of the general population in Canada found a digital divide based on income (Statistics Canada, 2013e). The study found that 98 percent of the wealthiest households had Internet access. But only 58 percent of the poorest households had Internet access. Twenty percent of households without Internet service said the cost of equipment or service kept them from getting access.

Seniors with higher levels of education and higher income will have more access to computer technology. They will also feel more comfortable using computers, the digital divide may close somewhat. In time, an Internet-linked device may seem as normal in an older person's home as a telephone and TV do today.

Many older people struggle to feel comfortable in this new environment. Website designers and manufacturers can design tools that make computer use easier for older people. For example, some websites of interest to older people have buttons that users can click to increase font size. Simple techniques like this encourage older people to use computer technology.

Designers now understand the need to include users in the development of new products. Gandy and colleagues (2008), for example, said, "The first step in the design process is to determine who the target users are." Developing a product for an average user "is a pitfall that results in numerous users whose needs are overlooked" (p. 321). Once researchers have identified a target population, they can then focus on understanding the users' abilities and needs. Sixsmith (2008) calls this "user-centric" analysis and design.

Emerging technologies, like the use of smartphones and tablets as information sources, open worlds of information and social supports to older users. Mobile phones

EXHIBIT 5.8 *Robo-sapiens Rising: Sony, Honda, and Others Are Spending Millions to Put a Robot in Your Home*

In a retirement home, a robot offers its undivided attention to a silver-haired woman sharing stories about her grandkids. Meanwhile, at a hospital, another makes an elderly patient smile with a joke, before reminding him to take his medication. Think of them as high-tech granny and grandpa sitters, fully equipped with interactive webcams to help keep tabs on your favourite seniors. And while not as grand as science-fiction legend Isaac Asimov's robotic future, this is clearly on the way—and coming sooner than you think, courtesy of some of the biggest names in consumer electronics.

Driving this robotic revolution—in healthcare, especially—are global concerns about the greying of the population, a phenomenon already well advanced in Japan, where personal robots have suddenly become all the rage. Robots can now vacuum your house, watch for prowlers, page you at the airport and play with the kids. Advocates say it is only a short step from there to having them monitor shut-ins for signs of distress. This

could allow frail seniors to live independently longer, and it may also bring them peace of mind. "By talking with the elderly," said Norihiro Hagita, whose Kyoto-based team of roboticists at ATR Intelligent Robotics and Communication Laboratories is developing a prototype robot with a touch that feels almost human, "a robot can ease mental stress."

Recognizing a gold mine when they see it, several of the world's largest electronics companies and car manufacturers—brand names such as Sony, Honda, and Toshiba—are pouring hundreds of millions into a field once dominated by super geeks in university labs. And the race to fulfill one of the last great promises of the 20th century—an affordable robo-buddy—is on in a big way. "People don't just want robots like the Roomba," the disc-shaped machine that whips around your home cleaning floors, said Mark Tilden, the Tokyo-based creator of Robo-sapien. "People want their robots to be like Rosie from *The Jetsons*—a wise-cracking New Yorker with an apron."

Questions

1. Do you think older people will accept robotic helpers in their homes?

2. What do you think it will take for people to see robots as just another helpful technological aid?

Source: John Intini, "Robo-sapiens Rising," *Maclean's* (July 15, 2005). Reprinted with permission.

now access the Internet, send instant messages, and download emails. But small screens, tiny words and pictures, and miniscule keyboards all challenge older eyes and fingers. Devices like large-screen smartphones and tablets with touch screens help overcome some of these barriers.

Training can also help older people overcome barriers to the use of new technology (Karmarkar, Chavez, & Cooper, 2008). Effective training increases the older person's confidence and increases the use of computers. Shapira, Barak, and Gal (2007) taught a group of 22 older people (age 70 to 93) how to use the Internet. They compared this group with a control group that received no computer training but took part in recreational activities. The trained group used email, browsed the Web, and took part in forums and virtual communities.

The trained group reported increased well-being and feelings of empowerment. Compared with the control group, they reported less loneliness, less depression, and greater life satisfaction. The untrained group showed deterioration on these measures.

Future generations of older people will face new challenges and new options as new technologies emerge. Good design and training can reduce the lag between innovation and the use of technology by older users.

Assistive Devices

Assistive devices can help people stay active and live safely. Clarke and Colantonio (2005) called assistive devices "a powerful tool to help older adults overcome functional limitations." (p. 192). Statistics Canada (2015g) reported that more than 85 percent of people age 65 to 74 with a disability used an aid or assistive device. This figure increased to 90 percent for people age 75 and over. Assistive devices include a variety of aids, including hearing aids, glasses, walkers, and wheelchairs.

Most people use assistive devices for personal care and in-home mobility. Clarke and colleagues (2009) said that mobility disability tops the list of disabilities. People use canes, walkers, and wheelchairs to cope with mobility problems. These devices support independent living.

Most often people use simple products to make life easier. One woman, for example, bought a mobile phone so she could carry it with her around the house. An older person may use the microwave oven as an assistive device. She can boil water by the cupful in the microwave to avoid lifting a heavy kettle.

For aids to be useful, three things are necessary: (1) people have to know about them, (2) people have to understand their usefulness, and (3) products have to be affordable and accessible. Manufacturers, safety organizations, and the government need to set up norms and standards of safety and suitability for new products for seniors.

Older people will reject devices that make them look different or dependent. Karmarkar and colleagues (2008) describe three types of acceptance of technology: (1) reluctant acceptance, (2) grateful acceptance, and (3) internal acceptance. Designers try to achieve this last type of acceptance. In this case, the device "is considered by users as a medium for overcoming their physical impairments and a replacement for the impaired part of their bodies" (p. 29).

Sometimes a shift in design can overcome resistance to a technology. One woman rejected the use of a motorized wheelchair because it made her feel helpless. But she accepted and even bragged about a motorized scooter that served the same purpose. Designers of devices need to understand how the older person sees the world. They can then design devices that older people will use with confidence.

Current transportation technology helps solve many problems for seniors with disabilities but sometimes the technology does not meet seniors' needs. Seniors report problems travelling through airports, and boarding and leaving planes, long-distance buses, and trains. They also have problems with local transportation, finding it difficult to get to and wait at bus, subway, and streetcar stops.

Some older people who need mobility, visual, and hearing aids do not have them. Thirty percent of people age 65 to 74 and 25 percent of people age 75 and over say they have an unmet need for an assistive device. The more severe the disability, the greater the likelihood that a person will have an unmet need (Statistics Canada, 2015g). People with an unmet need give cost as the main reason for this problem.

Government programs cover the cost of some aids but not others. And government support differs from province to province. An assistive device can help reduce the need for medical care and can help older people stay in the community. This will save the healthcare system money in the long run.

TIME TO REVIEW

Describe some of the technological tools (simple and complex) that can help a person cope with disability.

What barriers exist to the adoption of technology by older people?

How can designers of technology help older people overcome these barriers?

What changes in the environment would help an older person with a disability live a safer and more fulfilling life?

It is important to understand the effect of healthcare aids on a person's social life. A simple self-administered blood sugar test, for example, can cut down on the cost of a nurse's visit. But this cost-saving initiative may remove an important social contact for the older person, who may prefer to see a nurse. We know little about whether technology can have side effects such as social isolation. As well, technology can create dependence. Does an electric wheelchair help a woman who has trouble using a walker or does it put an end to her ability to walk? Researchers have begun to address these and other questions as they look at the impact of technology on older people's lives.

Changes in Lifestyle

Smoking in Later Life

Smoking is one of the leading causes of serious disease and death for older Canadians. One-half of long-term smokers die from diseases related to their smoking. Smoking leads to decreased psychological well-being, poorer subjective health, and reduced levels of physical functioning. Robert Kane, an experienced healthcare researcher, called smoking "the biggest threat to improving our lifestyles…. That trumps everything else" (reported in Buettner, 2010, p. 16).

The economic burden of smoking is immense. Wilkins, Shields, and Roterman (2009) studied "never-daily smokers," "current daily smokers," and "former daily smokers who had quit in the past five years." These last two groups averaged more than twice as many days in the hospital as the never-daily smokers. The smoker and former smoker groups (age 45–74) led to 7.1 million extra hospital days over four years. They accounted for 32 percent of hospital days used by this age group. The Canadian Lung Association (2011) estimated that smoking was costing $4.4 billion each year for direct healthcare costs and $12.5 billion in indirect costs such as long-term disability.

Compared with younger adult age groups, older people showed low rates of smoking (Statistics Canada, 2014i). Less than 10 percent of men and women age 65 and over reported smoking daily or occasionally. Only the 12- to 17-year-old group had a lower proportion of smokers. Nearly two-thirds (61.8 percent) of senior non-smokers said they formerly smoked. Wilkins and colleagues (2009) said that people age 65 to 74 showed the highest proportion of people who had quit for five years or more.

Fortunately, former smokers (especially those who have been non-smokers for 15 years or more) and people who never smoked are more likely to maintain health and to recover from loss of health. Wilkins and colleagues (2009) said, "Former smokers aged 45 to 64 who had quit

for more than five years averaged no more days in hospital than did never-daily smokers." This finding, the researchers said, "underscores the benefit of long-term cessation" (p. 7). Martel, Bélanger, Berthelot, and Carrière (2005) conducted a longitudinal study that compared people over five cycles of the *National Population Health Survey* in Canada. The study looked at health behaviours over an eight-year period from 1994–1995 to 2002–2003. They found that poor health habits like smoking and inactivity in middle age catch up with people as they age. Those who had poor health habits suffered from more chronic disease as they aged.

The researchers concluded that "seniors who started out in good health in 1994–1995 were at a significantly higher risk of losing their health by 2002–2003 if they smoked or quit in the previous 10 years, had inactive leisure-time pursuits, or were in a weight range that was not appropriate for their height." Martel and colleagues said these findings support "the hypothesis that the impacts of healthy habits are cumulative through time. This result reinforces the public health message that healthy habits are profitable throughout the life cycle" (p. 6).

Exercise

Dennis, aged 60, waves as he closes his door and heads out of the office at noon. He's got a gym bag on his shoulder. Along with a group of co-workers, Dennis leaves to do his lunch-hour exercise program. For the next hour, he'll be sweating it out on a treadmill to the sound of the Allman

Rich Legg/iStockPhoto

Exercise slows the effects of aging on the body. It can reverse declines in physical function that have already occurred. Exercise also reduces the risk of chronic illness, improves everyday functioning, and leads to overall feelings of well-being.

EXHIBIT 5.9   *Chronic Obstructive Pulmonary Disease (COPD): A Source of Poor Health in Later Life*

The *epidemiological transition* refers to a decrease in child-hood disease and death from diseases such as smallpox and measles. It also refers to an increase in chronic diseases of old age, including chronic obstructive pulmonary disease (COPD). COPD is the fourth leading cause of death in Canada. Dr. Mark FitzGerald, head of respiratory medicine at the University of British Columbia and Vancouver General Hospital said, "COPD is the number one cause of hospitalizations in Canada, apart from pregnancy" (*Globe and Mail*, 2014).

Chronic diseases have no cure and they can linger for many years. COPD, for example, refers to lung diseases that block airflow. They make breathing difficult and day-to-day living uncomfortable. The Mayo Clinic (2015a) says that emphysema and chronic bronchitis are the two most common ailments in the COPD category. Chronic bronchitis is inflammation of the tubes that carry air to and from the lungs. Airways can swell and produce mucus. Emphysema takes place when air sacs at the end of the lungs' smallest air passage are destroyed.

Medical science cannot reverse COPD damage, but treatment can provide some relief and can prevent further damage. Oxygen therapy, prescription drugs, and even an air conditioner in the home can provide relief. Respiratory educators can help people manage this disease.

Four percent of Canadians age 35 to 79 say that a doctor has diagnosed them with COPD. But studies that use more direct measures of lung function report a rate of 13 percent. The difference between self-reported COPD and measured COPD supports the belief that many people suffer from this illness, but do not have a formal diagnosis.

Statistics Canada (2014j) says that smoking causes the majority of cases. Smoking causes about 80 percent of deaths from COPD.

Individual action can limit or avoid COPD. For example, a smoker can stop smoking. A person can avoid inhaling fumes and other solvents. But a study by the Canadian Lung Association (2010) found that 60 percent of people at risk for COPD "know very little to nothing about the disease." And "there is an overall lack of awareness of the impact of lifestyle choices."

Education could reduce the prevalence of COPD. Also a person's environment influences the likelihood that they will get COPD. People who work in dusty factory conditions, miners, women who inhale smoke while working in poorly ventilated kitchens all risk COPD. A person may have little control over these conditions; in some of these cases, government regulations and public health standards can reduce the risk of COPD.

All of us, rich and poor, breathe the same air. Poor air quality, dangerous work conditions, and second-hand smoke all add to the risk of COPD in the population. An older population will mean more people exposed to COPD risk factors for more years. This makes COPD a public health issue as well as a personal challenge.

Brothers, Luther Allison, or some other high-energy blues band. He'll grab some time in a sauna and hot tub if he has time. He comes back from these sessions energized and ready for an afternoon at his desk.

Beth, aged 59, another Baby Boomer, who works down the hall, belongs to a nearby gym. She has a different routine. She and her staff gather after work for a yoga/Pilates class. They twist, turn, and sweat to relieve the day's stress. "It's not that easy," Beth says. "They work you really hard. It's kind of aerobic yoga." Her 20-year-old niece, who lives in another town, also goes to yoga classes. When Beth visits her niece, she brings her yoga mat and workout clothes and they go to class together.

Alice, aged 45, works as a receptionist. She spends most of her day sitting behind a counter welcoming visitors to an office. She wears a pedometer that counts her steps. She checks it throughout the day and tries to meet the recommended target of 10,000 steps. That sometimes means taking a walk after dinner to reach in her quota.

Millions of Baby Boomers like Dennis, Beth, and Alice now turn to exercise programs, workout videos, and personal trainers to stay fit. Many Baby Boomers realize that they need to develop a new maintenance plan for their bodies. Still, the majority of Baby Boomers and older people today report low levels of physical activity (Statistics Canada, 2012g). And this lack of physical activity adds to the problems caused by poor diet.

Often what people see as unavoidable consequences of aging falls into the category of hypokinesia, or physical problems due to lack of movement. The *Canadian Community Health Survey* in 2011 (Statistics Canada, 2012g) found that, compared with other age groups, people age 65 and over reported the lowest rate of moderate activity in their leisure time.

Statistics Canada (2014k, citing Gilmour, 2007) said "the health benefits of physical activity include a reduced risk of cardiovascular disease, some types of cancer, osteoporosis, diabetes, obesity, high blood pressure, depression, stress and anxiety." Shields and Martel (2006) reported that seniors who engaged in activity three or more times per week reported the best health. Among seniors who exercised infrequently, only 36 percent reported good health. The association between exercise and good health remained after the researchers compared people with similar sociodemographic status and chronic conditions. Shields and Martel (2006) ended their report

hypokinesia physical problems due to lack of movement

EXHIBIT 5.10 *Tax Breaks for Active Seniors: Will This Lead to More Active Lifestyles?*

One method of health promotion may surprise you, and it has stirred some controversy: some governments provide tax incentives to promote physical activity. These incentives include tax exemptions for sports equipment or fitness programs. Von Tigerstrom, Larre, and Sauder (2011) suggest a tax on home entertainment equipment to discourage sedentary behaviour. Tax incentives generally take two forms: tax credits on your annual income tax statement and sales tax rebates. Von Tigerstrom and her associates also report federal and provincial tax credits for physical activity programs and gym memberships. Tax exemptions could include bicycles and other recreation equipment. What do these programs cost? Saskatchewan, for example, spends between $11 million and $18 million each year for its Active Families Benefit program (out of a total tourism department budget of $113 million to $138 million).

Questions

1. Do you think this approach will lead to more physical activity and better health among Canadians?

2. Do you think this is a good use of tax dollars (in this case uncollected tax dollars)?

3. What are some of the reasons this approach might or might not work?

4. Would a 15 percent tax rebate for an exercise program or for equipment lead you to engage in more activity?

5. What about your friends, would they engage in more fitness activity if they got a tax rebate?

6. How would you study these tax programs to assess their benefit?

---

on an optimistic note: "It is always possible to change or improve behaviour….[This] may allow people to spend their senior years without being dependent on others, and with positive perceptions of their physical and mental health" (p. 18).

Benton and Schlairet (2012) studied a group of 23 women, age 40 to 55, in a resistance-training program. They found that resistance training three or four days a week led to better upper and lower body strength and to improved quality of life. Weight-bearing exercise such as weight lifting also increases bone density. This study and others show that exercise can improve health as well as a person's outlook on life.

Researchers find that even the oldest-old people improve muscle mass and strength with weight training. People who took part in a strength-training program in a nursing home (some as old as 98) showed an average strength increase of 174 percent. Some people with disabilities began to walk without the help of a cane. One 93-year-old in the study said, "I feel as though I were 50 again…. The program gave me strength I didn't have before. Every day I feel better, more optimistic. Pills won't do for you what exercise does!" (Haber, 2010, p. 173).

Lovell, Cuneo, and Gass. (2010) conducted a controlled study of healthy older men age 70 to 80. The men worked out on an exercise bicycle for 35 to 40 minutes three times a week. The study found an increase in muscle strength of 21 percent. Because muscle burns more calories than fat, muscle-building exercise can also help a person lose weight.

Studies show that moderate exercise offers as much benefit as vigorous exercise. A study of physical activity and the risk of stroke in women found that vigorous physical activity had no significant effect on stroke risk. But increased walking time and increased pace lowered the risk (Sattelmair et al., 2010). Canada and the World Health Organization recommend at least 150 minutes per week of moderate-to-vigorous exercise (for example, 30 minutes, 5 days per week) (Colley et al., 2011).

Kramer, Fabiani, and Colcombe (2006; also Fallah et al., 2009) report that exercise even improves mental ability. They said that older adults who exercise show improvements in mental tasks and show the greatest improvement in highly complex tasks. Studies on animals find that exercise increases survival of neurons, growth of new neuronal interconnections, and growth of new capillaries in the brain (Cotman & Berchtold, 2002, cited in Kramer et al., 2006; van Praag, 2009).

According to Kramer and colleagues (2006), "The end result of exercise training then is a brain that is more plastic and adaptive to change and more able to survive the vagaries of the aging process. Results suggest that even relatively short exercise interventions can begin to restore some of the losses in brain volume associated with normal aging" (p. 76).

Exercise can reverse or prevent a wide range of illnesses. Colley and colleagues (2011) said regular physical exercise can reduce the "risk of cardiovascular disease, some types of cancer, osteoporosis, diabetes, obesity, high blood pressure, depression, stress and anxiety" (p. 1).

EXHIBIT 5.11   *Canadian Physical Activity Guidelines for Older Adults*
(65 years and older)

■ To achieve health benefits, and improve functional abilities, adults aged 65 years and older should accumulate at least 150 minutes of moderate- to vigorous-intensity aerobic physical activity per week, in bouts of 10 minutes or more.

■ It is also beneficial to add muscle and bone strengthening activities using major muscle groups, at least 2 days per week.

■ Those with poor mobility should perform physical activities to enhance balance and prevent falls.

■ More physical activity provides greater health benefits.

Source: *Canadian Physical Activity Guidelines* © 2011. Used with permission from the Canadian Society for Exercise Physiology, www.csep.ca/guidelines.

Julien et al. (2013) studied the impact on depression of walking outside one's home. They found that those who do not walk outside their home report more depressive symptoms and a greater chance of clinical depression. The researchers said that walking could provide a good intervention in cases of depression. They also suggested improvements in urban environments to make them more walker-friendly.

Aldwin, Spiro, and Park (2006) said that aerobic exercise improves cardiac output, strengthens the heart muscle, lowers bad cholesterol, raises good cholesterol, and increases lung function. Aerobic exercise also improves muscle strength, flexibility, walking, standing, and balance. Weight-bearing exercise increases muscle strength and balance. It also slows calcium loss from bones. People show improvements from exercise even late in life. These improvements lead to better functioning in their homes and greater independence.

Studies show that the more often a person exercises, the better his or her health. Exercise can even buffer other risks created by smoking or by having high blood pressure. Williamson and Pahor (2010), in a review of the research on exercise and aging, said that "physical activity may be the most effective prescription that physicians can dispense for the purposes of promoting successful aging.... Today it is recognized that virtually all of the diseases and conditions that lead to physical disability in older adults has as part of their etiology a component of personal lifestyle choices (e.g., physical inactivity)" (p. 124).

Spinney (2013) looked at older Canadians' preference for aerobic activity. This study compared older Canadians' aerobic activity over four cycles of the *General Social Survey—Time Use* (1992–2010). In the most recent cycle studied (2010) walking, jogging, and hiking ranked first among aerobic activities (a 24.2 percent participation rate). Gardening and grounds maintenance ranked second (a 28.9 percent participation rate). And exercise

ranked next (with an 11.5 percent participation rate). Other activities included home repair, yoga, and travel to and from work. Earlier studies found similar results. The 2000–2001 *Canadian Community Health Survey* ranked walking, gardening, and home exercises as seniors' three most frequently reported activities (Ashe et al., 2009; Statistics Canada, 2014k).

Still, older Canadians can and should be more active. Statistics Canada (2013f) reported a study of the health benefit of aerobic fitness. The study found that 45 percent of people age 60 to 69 rated "needs improvement" on aerobic activity and 33 percent rated "fair." These are the worst ratings of any adult age group. Only 17 percent ranked as "good," and too few people ranked as "very good" or "excellent" to include in the findings.

Spinney's (2013) results give some idea of how to increase aerobic activity among seniors. Spinney found that walking and active transportation (e.g., bicycling) appeal to many seniors. Promotion of these activities would build on already established habits and interests. Mall walking programs, neighbourhood design that promotes walking and bicycling, skiing, skating, and snowshoe trails would all encourage an active lifestyle. Canadian author Margaret Webb, who began an exercise program in her 50s said, "Women like us have discovered that it is as easy to socialize during runs as it is over martinis" (McKinnell, 2014).

Sims-Gould and colleagues (2012) conducted a study of 84 older women (average age 69.6 years) to learn why they joined an exercise program and what kept them coming back. The researchers found that fear of poor health motivated some of the women to join an exercise program.

One woman said that exercise improved her quality of life. "It's so much better," she said, "because I have my balance back." Another woman also joined the program to improve her balance. She found the yoga poses most helpful.

One woman told the researchers: "I was diagnosed with Type 2 diabetes about 11 years ago and the thing they said to me that really impressed me was you've got to exercise aerobically at least three … times a week. It's important because diabetes gets your heart, your liver, everything" (p. 286). Another woman said she felt more confident in her environment now that she exercised. "I committed a great deal more to it," she says, "because I could feel I was becoming stronger. I could feel the change" (p. 289).

Sims-Gould and colleagues say that a life course perspective also explains the commitment of these women to the program. The women in this study experienced a life transition at this time in their lives (between ages 65 and 70). Their move into retirement, for example, encouraged them to rethink their priorities and their sense of self.

One woman said, "I had retired and I didn't like it very much. It was quite an adjustment. I went into a deep depression." At work she enjoyed an active life where she saw people every day. In retirement she missed the camaraderie. "So I saw this ad and I thought, this is going to help me…." (p. 287).

The exercise program they joined supported this transition. It provided them with a new focus on their bodies and their health. It also provided them with a new set of social obligations. The researchers say that commitment to the program, the instructors, the other students, and to their own sense of well-being led the women to stay in the program. The researchers said that "a feeling of membership" led these women to join and stay with a program. "The older women in this study enjoyed a feeling of belonging that came with the commitment to participate" (p. 292).

Designers of fitness programs need to keep this point in mind. People join for many reasons, as this study shows—health, social contact, and a chance to feel more confident. But commitment to others and enjoyment of a support group keeps people engaged.

The spread of unisex fitness centres that offer aerobic and jazzercise classes make exercise more available. These centres bring down at least three barriers to fitness participation for older women: fitness centres offer a safe, clean, and mixed gender environment; they offer activities such as dance aerobics that appeal to women; and they provide equipment that requires little skill or past knowledge to use (e.g., elliptical machines and treadmills).

On the other hand, fitness centres charge a membership fee and sometimes an initiation fee. This can be a barrier to poorer women. Fitness centres and health clubs often locate in suburban shopping centres or other locations far from the inner city. These settings present transportation barriers and may cause cultural (social class) barriers as well for older minority women.

One set of findings puzzles scientists. In 2009, 52.5 percent of adult Canadians said they engaged in moderate activity during their leisure time. But obesity rates have increased in the past 25 years. In 2013, for example, about one older person in five ranked as obese (Statistics Canada, 2014l). Also, muscular strength and flexibility have decreased since 1981. Why would obesity rates increase and physical ability decrease if more than half of adult Canadians get enough exercise? These findings led scientists to use more precise measures of physical activity (Colley et al., 2011).

Colley and colleagues (2011; also Statistics Canada, 2015h) wondered whether people exaggerated their activity in self-reports. The researchers used an accelerometer to study *actual* physical activity in a representative sample of Canadian adults age 20 to 79. (An accelerometer sits above a person's right hip, attached by an elastic belt. The meter records the intensity of a person's activity.) People in the study wore the meter for seven days during their waking hours.

The researchers found that 68 percent of men and 69 percent of women spent the majority of their waking hours on sedentary activity. Men and women age 60 to 79 lived a significantly more sedentary life than younger people in the study. Compared with men and women age 20 to 39, the men and women age 60 to 79 engaged in half the number of minutes of moderately vigorous physical activity (MVPA). This came to 17 minutes on average per day for older men (compared with 33 minutes for men age 20 to 39), and 12 minutes on average per day for older women (compared with 24 minutes for women age 20 to 39).

The researchers used the World Health Organization recommendation of at least 150 minutes of MVPA per week to assess adult Canadians' activity. They found that only 13.1 percent of men and women age 60 to 79 met this standard. Younger adults did only a little better: only 17.4 percent of people age 20 to 39 engaged in more than 150 minutes of MVPA per week and only 14.6 percent of people age 40 to 59 engaged in more than 150 minutes of MVPA per week.

This study helped explain the increase in obesity in Canadian society. People tend to overestimate their level of activity and underestimate their sedentary behaviours. Colley and colleagues' study pointed to the need for more physical activity by Canadian seniors. This study also pointed to potential future health problems in the population as older age groups age.

Shields and colleagues (2010; also Turcotte, 2011a) studied the weight of participants in the 2007–2009 *Canadian Health Measures Survey*. The study examined 3,102 people who lived in private households at the time

---

EXHIBIT 5.12   *Exercise as a Response to Osteoporosis*

Osteoporosis Canada (2011) reported that about 2 million Canadians lived with osteoporosis. One-quarter of women and about 12 percent of men over age 50 in Canada had this disease. For people age 71 and over, 31.1 percent of women and 6.4 percent of men had osteoporosis (Statistics Canada, 2011h). Osteoporosis causes at least 80 percent of fractures in people age 60 and over.

Osteoporosis Canada (2011) estimated that osteoporosis was costing the Canadian healthcare system $1.9 billion a year. Most of this money went to treat fractures. In 2008, each hip fracture cost the healthcare system $21,285 in the first year after hospitalization. In addition to the cost, fractures reduce a person's social contacts, often lead to further illness, and can cause death. Twenty-three percent of people who suffer a hip fracture die in less than a year.

Research shows that exercise can slow the rate of bone loss (Osteoporosis Canada, 2011). Weight-bearing exercise—such as lifting weights—increases bone density. Exercise places a load on the bones and bones respond by forming new bone. Exercise also helps a person maintain the appropriate weight and improve balance. Exercise lubricates the joints and reduces the risk of arthritis. Vitamin D and calcium supplements can also help maintain bone density. All of these methods help prevent fractures and their complications.

---

of the interview (from March 2007 to February 2009). The study took a variety of fitness measures. Three assessments looked at the person's weight and body fat: (1) waist circumference, (2) body mass index, and (3) body composition.

The results confirmed the findings of other studies that found increases in obesity among older Canadians (Shields & Tjepkema, 2006; Tjepkema, 2006). One-third of the men and women age 60 to 69 in this study rated as obese on the BMI. This came to more than double the rate in 1981. Waist circumference is a measure closely associated with a high risk of illness. On this measure more than half of the 60- to 69-year-old men (52 percent) and nearly two-thirds (65 percent) of the women in this age group showed a high risk of illness. "Of particular note," Shields and colleagues (2010) said, "at ages 60 to 69, 75% of males and 82% of females had waist circumference values in the increased- to high-risk range" (p. 8).

Finally, body composition is a combined measure of BMI, waist circumference, and skin fold thickness (Shields et al., 2010). On this measure, 40 percent of men age 60 to 69 and 47 percent of women in this age group scored "fair/needs improvement."

All measures in 2007–2009 (Shields et al., 2010) came out significantly higher (less healthy) than in 1981. Weight circumference, BMI ($30\,\text{kg}/\text{m}^2$ or more), and body composition all at least doubled for men and women age 60 to 69 between 1981 and 2007–2009. In the case of women in this age group, for example, the proportion that rated "fair/needs improvement" grew from 17 percent to 47 percent (or nearly three times).

Middle-aged people in this study showed a similar trend toward obesity ((Shields et al., 2010); also see Navaneelan & Janz, 2014). Men age 40 to 59 showed triple the rate of body composition "fair/needs improvement" scores (11 percent to 33 percent) between 1981 and 2007–2009. And women in this middle-aged group on this measure show a near tripling of their rate, from 13 percent to 36 percent between 1981 and 2007–2009.

What causes this increase in obesity? Inactivity plays a role in obesity. Shields and Tremblay (2008b) studied the activities of people age 20 to 64 as reported in the 2007 *Canadian Community Health Survey*. They looked at the effect of three sedentary behaviours on body weight: watching television, using a computer, and reading. They found no association between reading and obesity for

---

EXHIBIT 5.13   *Biology Is Not Destiny: Attitude Matters*

Osteoporosis can affect a person's social life. Anne Harland's doctor told her that she had low bone density in her right hip and spine. Anne enjoyed dragon boat paddling as a member of the Bosom Buddies Breast Cancer Survivor Dragon Boat Team. Her doctor advised her to give up paddling to avoid a fracture. "The advice was devastating," Anne says.

As a result of her condition, she gave up competitive paddling but she refused to allow osteoporosis to cut her off from her friends. "These changes cannot mar how my 'boat floats,'" she said. "I am more determined to walk and to swim, and I thoroughly enjoy the camaraderie as I sit in the boat with my Buddies on beautiful Lake Banook" (Osteoporosis Canada, 2011). Anne shows that a person's attitude can overcome the social and psychological effects of physical decline.

Source: Reprinted with permission of Anne Harland.

EXHIBIT 5.14   *Percentage at Least Moderately Active in Leisure Time, by Age Group and Sex, Household Population Aged 12 or Older, Canada, 2011*

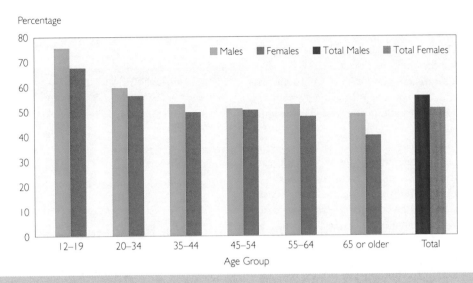

The proportion of men who take part in leisure-time physical activity remains fairly stable from middle age onward. But senior women, compared with middle-aged women, show a significantly lower rate of participation in active leisure (Milan & Vézina, 2011). This, in part, reflects lifelong patterns of participation by men in sports and athletic activity.

It also reflects the male desire to express masculinity. For example, men join 55-plus basketball leagues and hockey leagues for middle-aged and older men. Drummond (2008) said that some older men have begun to engage in weight training. This takes place within the masculine "gym culture" (p. 33). "By engaging together in what is socially and culturally embedded as being masculine," Drummond said, "physical activity and sport offer older men the opportunity to affirm their masculinity in addition to making them feel empowered about engaging in health-related behaviors" (p. 34). Senior women lack this lifelong engagement with sport and athletics.

Will younger generations of women have a more positive attitude toward activity in later life? Will senior women in the future engage in activities that suit their self-image (e.g., aerobics classes or dance?) In your view, does experience with physical activity throughout the life course influence activity in later life?

Source: Statistics Canada, *Physical activity during leisure time*, 2011, Chart 2, http://www.statcan.gc.ca/pub/82-625-x/2012001/article/11667-eng.htm. Reproduced and distributed on an "as is" basis with the permission of Statistics Canada.

either sex. They found a modest association between obesity and computer use for both sexes.

But they found strong evidence of a positive association between time spent watching television and obesity among both men and women. The more television a person watched, the greater the likelihood of obesity. One-quarter of men and women who averaged 21 or more hours a week of television rated as obese on the body mass index. The study controlled for variables such as age, marital status, and household income. Television viewing maintained its association with obesity.

The researchers found that people who watched a lot of television tended toward inactive leisure-time activities. They also ate a high-fat diet and a diet low in fruits and vegetables. But even when they controlled for these items, the hours spent watching television continued their association with obesity. Finally, the researchers propose that the low metabolic rate associated with watching television may account for this link with obesity. The metabolic rate for watching television, they say, scores only slightly above that for sleeping.

A related study by Shields and Tremblay (2008a) looked at the number of hours older people watched television. They found that people age 65 and over watched more hours of television than any other age group. They watched TV nearly twice as many hours on average as people age 20 to 44 (3.2 hours vs. 1.7 hours). The oldest age group age 75 and over reported the highest number of hours watching television.

Television watching may also put a person at risk of an early death. Katzmarzyk and colleagues (2009) studied the relationship between sedentary behaviour (specifically sitting), illness, and death. The researchers studied 17,013 Canadians age 18 to 90 for 12 years. They asked subjects to report their daily pattern of sitting (e.g., almost none of the time, half the time, almost all of the time). The more time a person spent sitting, the higher their rate of illness from all causes (except cancer) and the higher their risk of death. Even people who engaged in leisure-time physical activity showed the negative effects of sitting.

This research shows that too much time spent in front of the TV or computer can even counteract physical activity. The researchers said, "In addition to the promotion of moderate-to-vigorous physical activity and a healthy weight, physicians should discourage sitting for extended periods."

Shields and colleagues (2010) expressed concern that "if these trends [in obesity] continue for another 25 years, half of males and females over the age of 40 years will be obese" with corresponding increases in avoidable costly chronic diseases (p. 9). They said that it may prove easier to have people reduce television viewing than to have them take up exercise.

"Intervention programs aimed at reducing television viewing among both children and adults," they said, "may assist in reducing the prevalence of obesity among adults in the future" (Shields & Tremblay, 2008b, p. 26). Less TV watching could also reduce illness and extend a person's life.

Health promotion programs encourage a more active lifestyle. Chou and Wister (2005) studied the cues that led people to exercise. They found that, compared with people who did not read about their chronic illness, people who read about their illness had twice the likelihood of exercising. Also, knowledge of services, consultations with friends, and visits to a health professional all led to a higher probability of exercising. Chou and Wister said, "Information translates into significant self-care action…." (p. 405) The researchers said that health promotion programs should use reading material and other media to educate clients about exercise.

Health promotion programs for poorer men and women can also help. Ross, Gilmour, and Dasgupta (2010) found that overweight and obesity played a role in the incidence of diabetes. Exercise and weight-loss programs, for example, can improve health, functional ability, and quality of life at every age. But poor older people often lack the opportunity to belong to a fitness club or to attend an exercise class. They may lack the money to join or the transportation to get to a club, and social obligations such as care for grandchildren can make participation in an exercise program a challenge. Ferrucci and Simonsick (2006) noted in an editorial that "we should seriously consider new strategies for reaching out to the frailest and sickest segment of the older population" (p. 1154).

These studies point the way to a new view of aging. Science cannot stop the aging process, but individuals can improve their environment and can delay chronic problems through lifestyle changes and exercise. Millions of people each year would avoid illness and extend their lives by adopting healthier lifestyles.

TIME to REVIEW

What lifestyle practices can improve health and well-being in later life?

What can older people with chronic illness do to maintain the quality of their lives?

What benefits can seniors expect from exercise and fitness?

Falls: An Example of Successful Healthcare Management

Agatha found that as she entered her 60s, her sense of balance decreased. One day she fell backward while holding a pot of hot water; the water spilled on her clothes and scalded her badly. Since then she's fallen on the ice and in her home. "I can't even put on my clothes without holding on for support now," she says. "What really bothers me is that I can't do what I used to do." Agatha works in a day-care centre and fears that she may lose her balance while holding one of the children. Her imbalance may put an end to her work life.

One-third of seniors (34 percent) told Statistics Canada they feel concerned about future falls. Compared to men, a greater proportion of women expressed a concern about falls. The older the group, the greater the perceived risk (Statistics Canada, 2014m).

Falls rank as the most common cause of injuries among seniors in Canada. One in three seniors will fall at least once each year. This came to about 1.7 million Canadian seniors in 2011. Illness, poor balance, medications, and cognitive impairment all increase the risk of a fall. Falls can lead to chronic pain, loss of independence, and even death.

Activities that created little risk in a person's younger years—climbing a ladder, carrying a heavy object, wearing loose-fitting shoes—increase the risk of a fall in later life. Falls make up 85 percent of seniors' injury-related hospital admissions. Most falls that lead to hospitalization take place in the home (Butler-Jones, 2010).

Women make up more than two-thirds (68 percent) of seniors who are injured in a fall. The oldest seniors (75+) show the highest incidence of falls. Ninety-five percent of hip fractures among seniors come from a fall. Falls account for $2 billion in direct healthcare costs in Canada (Public Health Agency, 2015a). Most of this money goes to treat fractures. In 2008, each hip fracture cost the healthcare system $21,285 in the first year after hospitalization.

In addition to the cost, fractures often lead to further illness, and death. Twenty-three percent of people who suffer a hip fracture die in less than a year (Osteoporosis Canada, 2011).

The Centers for Disease Control and Prevention in the United States reported that fall rates differ for men and women age 65 and over. For example, men accounted for 10 percent of emergency room visits due to injuries from falls, while women in this age group accounted for 16 percent of such visits (National Center for Health Statistics, 2013). Butler-Jones (2010) said that "falls can quickly and negatively impact the health status of seniors and their families" (pp. i–ii).

What can seniors and their families do to prevent falls? The Public Health Agency of Canada (2014a, p. iv) called the cause of falls "multifactorial." Seniors can keep paths and driveways clear of ice and snow, their floors clear of slippery rugs and electrical cords. They can avoid excessive alcohol use, maintain good health and diet, and take care in their use of medications. Exercise can help a person maintain good balance and strength. Fall prevention programs can help a person assess risk and take steps to prevent a fall (Maki et al., 2011).

Research shows that fall prevention programs can reduce falls between 11 percent and 27 percent. Stevens and colleagues (2006) said that "the most effective single intervention was exercise which, overall, lowered the risk between 12 percent and 20 percent." Types of effective exercises included Tai Chi, balance and gait training, and strength building. Jenkyn, Hoch, and Speechley (2012) called for an analysis of costs and benefits of fall prevention programs to make the best use of public funds. "By employing effective interventions," Aldwin and Gilmer (2004) said, "we can appreciably decrease the incidence of fall related injuries, improve the health and quality of life of older adults, and significantly reduce healthcare costs." (p. 294)

A program called "Steady As You Go" in Alberta works with healthy mobile seniors to prevent falls. Trained seniors backed by a health professional deliver the program. Participants enrol in two 90-minute sessions. The program discusses footwear, medication side effects, and household hazards. Seniors also learn exercises to strengthen their legs and improve their balance.

A study of the program found that the 235 participants reduced eight out of nine personal risks. A four-month follow-up found that, compared with a control group, participants had a 30 percent lower fall rate. A second program for seniors with low energy and mobility found the same results in a one-year follow-up.

A home exercise program developed and delivered by Action Seniors! in British Columbia reduced falls and injuries from falls by 35 percent (Fall Prevention Clinic, 2011). Other studies showed that balance-training programs worked best at preventing falls. Programs that promote an active lifestyle over the life course also reduce the risk of falls (Butler-Jones, 2010).

These studies show that risk assessment, increased knowledge, and exercise can lower the rate of falls among seniors. Martel, He, and Caron Malenfant (2006) said that "at all ages people with healthy behaviours were at less risk of losing their good health, and the difference became more pronounced with advancing age.... From this result it can be hypothesized that the impacts of healthy habits are cumulative through time" (p. 5).

Programs that teach healthy behaviours could save the healthcare system money and resources. They would also lead to greater safety and a better quality of life for the majority of seniors.

Diet

What should older people eat to stay well and delay the aging process? Consider these facts. First, metabolic rate decreases with age. An older person has to either eat less or exercise more to maintain an ideal weight. Second, older people need to make sure that they get at least minimum adult requirements of basic nutrients. They should also follow general guidelines that apply to people of all ages (e.g., avoid overeating refined sugars and fats). Older men and women in Canada do moderately well on this measure. More than 40 percent of senior women and more than 30 percent of senior men report that they eat fruits and vegetables at least five times a day (Statistics Canada, 2012h).

Third, vitamin supplements may help older people stay in good health. Some older people lose their appetites or find it difficult to chew food. This can lead to vitamin and mineral deficiencies. A vitamin supplement can help ensure that a person gets the nutrients needed.

Kane (in Dan Buettner, 2008) added another important point to these dietary guidelines. "What one is looking for is moderation," he said, "taking in a level of calories that is necessary and balancing those calories

EXHIBIT 5.15   *Diabetes: A Growing Health Concern*

In the 1950s, our family doctor diagnosed my father with diabetes. I remember watching him prepare a large hypodermic needle each morning. He used the needle to give himself his morning dose of insulin by injection. He hated to do this, but this was how he and other diabetics controlled their blood sugar in those days.

As years went by, drug companies developed new methods to control blood sugar. I recall that in his later years he could take oral medication. He also controlled his diet (although my mother at family weddings would catch him "cheating" with a piece of cheesecake or pie). Still the disease took its toll. Cuts healed slowly, his energy level and mood fluctuated with his blood sugar level. He died of kidney failure due to the disease after several months of kidney dialysis.

The Mayo Clinic (2015b) describes Type 2 diabetes (the type most common among older people) as "a chronic condition that affects the way your body metabolizes glucose (sugar)." With this disease, either a person's body resists the effects of insulin or fails to produce enough insulin to regulate blood sugar.

The pancreas secretes insulin (a hormone) into the bloodstream. Insulin allows sugar to enter the body's cells and lowers the amount of sugar in the bloodstream. Insulin secretion from the pancreas decreases as blood sugar drops. The liver stores and releases glucose. This keeps the glucose level (and hence a person's energy level) in balance.

In Type 2 diabetes, this system breaks down. Sugar builds up in the blood. The beta cells in the pancreas produce more insulin, but eventually they become impaired and can't make enough insulin to meet the body's demands.

Too much sugar in the blood can damage organs, blood vessels, and nerves. Complications include chronic kidney disease, lower limb amputation, and eye disease. High blood sugar can lead to blindness, heart attack, stroke, and nerve damage. Diabetes can shorten a person's life expectancy by five to ten years (Canadian Diabetes Association, 2017a).

An aging population in Canada will mean that more older people than ever will suffer from this disease. First, a larger older population will mean more cases of diabetes, even if the rate of illness stays the same. Second, many younger people, due to high rates of obesity, will come into later life with this disease. (Statistics Canada, 2015i).

Today, seniors make up nearly half (48 percent) of all people age 12 and over with diabetes. In 2014, nearly one million older Canadians had diabetes. This came to nearly one person in five age 65 and over. Canada added over 160,000 new cases of diabetes in its older population from 2010 to 2014—a 20 percent increase in less than five years. And an increase in the number of cases as well as the proportion of seniors with this disease will likely occur in the future (Statistics Canada, 2015e).

A number of conditions known as the metabolic syndrome create a high risk of diabetes. These conditions include abdominal obesity (or high waist circumference), elevated triglycerides, low high-density lipoprotein cholesterol (HDL-C), high fasting blood glucose, or high blood pressure (Statistics Canada, 2014n). In 2013, one in four adults age 40 to 59 had metabolic syndrome and two in five adults age 60 to 79 had metabolic syndrome (Statistics Canada, 2014n). Many

of these people will become diabetics. Genetics and lifestyle can also increase the risk of diabetes.

No cure exists for Type 2 diabetes, but a person can manage the condition through diet, exercise, and maintaining a healthy weight. People whose parents and other relatives have diabetes have a higher risk of this disease. Certain ethnic groups have a higher than average risk of diabetes—Indigenous people have three to five times the risk of diabetes compared to the general population. Likewise, seniors of Hispanic, Asian, South Asian, and African descent have a higher than average risk of diabetes.

People cannot change their genetics or their ethnicity, but changes in the diet and habits of older Canadians could lower the prevalence of this disease or at least moderate its severity. The Canadian Diabetes Association (2017a) proposes healthy eating (low in processed carbohydrates and sugars; high in fruits, vegetables, and whole grains), regular physical activity, a healthy body weight, and stress management as ways to manage diabetes. These also serve as good measures for preventing disease in general. We will discuss these methods for maintaining good health in topics that follow.

When diet and exercise cannot control blood sugar, blood sugar monitoring, diabetes medications, or insulin treatment will follow. Diabetics can now monitor and control their blood sugar throughout the day. A doctor may also order periodic A1C testing to obtain a summary of a person's blood sugar over a three-month period. A doctor can also use the A1C test to diagnose diabetes. A range of drugs now exist to treat diabetes. These drugs increase the tissues' sensitivity to insulin, help the body produce more insulin, and influence digestion and blood sugar levels.

In contrast to the crude needle my father used to inject insulin, modern methods use a fine needle and syringe or an insulin pen. Many types of insulin now exist to control diabetes. A person can live a long and healthy life with this disease through modern methods of monitoring and control.

Still, prevention serves as the best response to the risk of diabetes. The Canadian Diabetes Association (2017b) estimates that 5.7 million Canadians age 20 and over had prediabetes in 2015. Prediabetics have higher than normal blood sugar, but not high enough to fit the definition of Type 2 diabetes. The Diabetes Association projects an increase in prediabetics to 6.4 million people age 20 and over in 2025. This would equal almost one in four Canadians (23.2 percent of the population) at that time. The prevalence rate for diabetes was 3.4 million people in 2015. The Diabetes Association projects an increase in diabetes prevalence to 5 million people in 2025 or 12.1 percent of the population at that time. This would be an increase of 44 percent from 2015 to 2015. "The forecast increases are largely due to the aging of the population, the growth in obesity, and the increase in non-white ethnicity.... These individuals can benefit most from early detection and intervention to prevent or delay the onset of type 2 diabetes and its complications" (Public Health Agency, 2011).

The Canadian Diabetes Association (2017c) estimated the cost of this disease could rise to $3.4 billion in 2016 to $5 billion in 2026. Prevention serves as an important approach to moderating these costs. More importantly, prevention can help people avoid the misery associated with this disease.

EXHIBIT 5.16 *Good Nutrition: A Challenge in Our Fast-Food Culture*

Most nutrition experts today have come to similar conclusions about eating habits that lead to good health in later life. They say that an adult past age 50, for example, needs between 2,000 and 3,000 calories per day (the exact number of calories needed depends on a person's weight, gender, unique metabolism, and activities). A woman generally needs fewer calories than a man.

Health Canada (2006) said that "moderating the amount that you eat" is the key to weight management—and this includes portion control. Health Canada advised people to "avoid eating out in places where very large servings or 'all you can eat' are offered" (p. 2).

The trend toward bigger portions with the high sugar and fat content in popular foods in part explains North America's obesity crisis. For example, a meal at Burger King that includes a double beef burger Whopper with cheese, medium fries with salt, a large Coke, and a Dutch apple pie for dessert provides 2,120 calories (Burger King, 2015). That's about the entire daily caloric allowance for an active adult woman, and these calories come mostly from processed sugar, refined starch, and fat.

By comparison, a balanced diet will contain about 40 percent complex carbohydrates, 30 percent low-fat protein, and 30 percent healthy fat (olive oil, fish oil, etc.). An older person will either have to eat less or exercise more (or both) to maintain an ideal weight. As people age, they need to choose foods that give them a balanced diet and get the maximum nutrition from the optimum number of calories.

across carbohydrates, fats, and proteins. Taking in really what you need" (p. 15).

Research findings by Langlois, Garriguet, and Findlay (2009) support this approach. The researchers studied diet and its effect on obesity in a sample of 6,454 Canadians age 18 and over. They found that high calorie intake (whether from fat, carbohydrates, or protein) for women and men increased the odds of obesity. For men, low fibre intake also increased the odds of obesity.

A healthy diet for an older person must take into account the slowing of the system with age, the body's increased sensitivity to extremes (like hot, spicy, and rich foods), and the body's need for high-quality nutrients with a minimum of calories. Volumes of research and study support this simple formula.

Ramage-Morin, Shields, and Martel (2010) summarized the findings on healthy habits from the 2009 *Canadian Community Health Survey—Healthy Aging*. The study found that lifestyle choices influenced the rate of chronic illness and good health. "People who refrained from smoking, walked frequently and were not obese were more likely to be in good health than were those who did not have these characteristics." In addition "social participation, low daily stress, sleeping well, good oral health, and eating fruit/vegetables five or more times a day" all reduced the likelihood of chronic illness (p. 5).

Lengyel, Tate, and Oberik Blatz (2009) gave another reason to eat a healthy diet. They studied the eating habits of 1,211 older Canadian men. They compared men who ate fruits and vegetables rarely with men who ate fruits and vegetables daily. They found that those who ate fruits and vegetables daily had three times the rate of greater life satisfaction. Nicklett and colleagues (2012) studied the diets of 713 women age 70 to 79. They found that, compared to women who ate few fruits and vegetables, women who ate a diet rich in fruits and vegetables (carotenoids) showed an improved survival rate. The researchers said that "Programs and policies to promote longevity should include interventions to improve nutrition and physical activity in older adults" (p. 866).

The World Health Organization (2011) says that to reduce chronic illness: (1) cut down on salt in processed food and cut dietary fat (especially saturated fats);

Group swimming exercises provide people of various ages with a social, low impact form of physical activity that can reduce chronic illness.

Jupiterimages/Thinkstock

EXHIBIT 5.17 *Dietary Restriction and Longevity*

Masoro and Austad (2011) said that "some of the most exciting recent discoveries have to do with one of the oldest observations in the biology of aging, namely that dietary restriction [DR], which is simply reducing the amount of food eaten, can slow aging and extend life in a wide range of species" (p. xiii). According to Sinclair and Howitz (2006), the ability of DR to extend life span "is so remarkable that it took numerous studies to reassure the scientific community that DR is a universal effect" (p. 63).

Other research has found that different types of DR could lead to life extension by different means. Calorie restriction (CR), most often used in studies of mammals, has shown life extension effects. These studies provide all essential nutrients to research animals but reduce calorie intake by 40 percent.

Fontana and colleagues (2011) said that "CR is the only environmental intervention that consistently and strongly increases maximum life span and retards a broad array of indicators of biological aging in many of the laboratory rodents studied so far" (p. 447). Studies that have alternated fasting with feeding (one form of CR) can extend life by as much as 83 percent in rats. Greer and Brunet (2011) said that using more than one method of DR "may allow additive or even synergistic life-span and health-span benefits" (p. 17).

Fontana and colleagues (2011) said that "any intervention that yields an extension of life span without an extension of health span is not successful" (p. 448). They summarized the effect of CR on health-span in two large studies of rhesus monkeys:

> The effect of CR in reducing disease onset was profound. An animal in the control group was three times more likely to have an age-related disease diagnosis than an animal in the CR group.... Additionally, CR conferred a decreased risk of dying from an age-related disease. Specifically, at any point in time, the control animals had three times the rate of death from an age-related cause compared to animals under CR (p. 451).

Long-term studies of CR in humans pose problems of cost and compliance. Some natural experiments point to the good effects of CR on humans. For example, low-calorie diets during wartime in Europe led to a decrease in civilian mortality due to their CR diet. The people of Okinawa show the benefits of CR. They live on a diet about 15 percent less than mainland Japanese. They eat high-nutrient foods such as fresh vegetables, fruits, soy, sweet potatoes, and fish. An older group of Okinawans (age 65 and over) showed lower body fat when compared with mainland Japanese. They also had "markedly lower" rates of death from heart disease; prostate, breast, and colon cancer; and decreased rates of lymphoma (Fontana et al., 2011, p. 452).

Fontana and colleagues (2011) reported that a multicentre controlled study of CR had begun. The two-year CALERIE study showed beneficial effects from CR. The CR subjects showed a decrease in fat mass, a reduced concentration of a marker for inflammation, reduced damage to DNA and RNA, and better heart function. A study that combined CR with exercise showed the best results.

Few Westerners have put themselves on a CR diet. Roy Walford, a researcher active in CR research in the 1980s, tried this diet for himself. He spent two years in Biosphere 2, a futuristic experiment in an artificial environment in Arizona. He lived on two-thirds of the calories for a man his age.*

The other members of the Biosphere team refused to follow Walford's diet. A spokesman for the project observed, "They're not lab rats." But during the experiment, a shortage of food forced all members of the team to reduce their calories by 25 percent to 30 percent for 18 months. The team showed some of the same effects of CR found in rodents, including lower fasting blood sugar and insulin (Walford et al., 2002).

A group called the Calorie Restriction Society, whose members average 12 years on a CR diet, provided further data on humans. This group eats a nutrient-rich diet of vegetables, fruits, whole grains, nuts, egg whites, fish, lean meat, and low-fat milk products. Fontana and colleagues (2011) used physicians' records to study the before-and-after effects of CR. This group showed a decrease in body fat and "profound reductions" in the major risk factors for heart disease, including lower cholesterol and "a remarkable lowering effect on systolic and diastolic blood pressure" (p. 457).

The results of CR studies seem promising. But we know little about the long-term effects of CR on humans. A CR diet without all micronutrients could cause physical damage over time. Fontana and Klein (2007) warned that CR without sound nutrition could lead to bone fractures, infections, low muscle mass, weakness, anemia, stoppage of menstruation, and infertility. Studies need to look at the best diet and the ideal calorie intake to achieve the best effects from CR.

Will large numbers of Canadians take up dietary restriction in the future? Probably not. Most people struggle to eat fewer calories. Our enjoyment of food and its easy availability make adoption of CR unlikely today. Still, studies of DR and CR point the way to a longer and healthier life if a person should choose this route.

---

* Walford died of cancer at age 80 in 2004.

Questions

1. Would you choose a CR diet if you knew it would extend your health and your life expectancy?

2. What foods would you need to give up today to live a CR diet?

3. What would your friends think if you started this diet today? How would it affect your social life?

4. Do you think that social influences (as well as personal preferences) may keep people from adopting this type of diet?

(2) encourage more physical activity; (3) encourage a healthier diet of fruits and vegetables; and (4) stop smoking. These and other health promotion interventions would "reduce the population that is obese, that smokes, and that is physically inactive...." And this "would reduce the numbers with chronic conditions [including heart disease, cancer, and high blood pressure] and the associated need for health services" (Denton & Spencer, 2009a, p. 12; Ramage-Morin, Shields, and Martel, 2010).

Stress Reduction

Stress aggravates or leads to many of the diseases of later life. Selye (1956) coined the term *stress* to refer to the wear and tear on our bodies caused by changes in the environment. A traffic jam can raise your blood pressure. A new job can create excitement and anticipation. Both pleasant and unpleasant situations can cause stress. Pleasant stress, Selye called "eustress" or good stress. A job that involves long hours, sleepless nights, and constant travel will lead to "distress." This can create high blood pressure, heart disease, and stroke—major diseases of later life.

Statistics Canada (2014g) says that stress can lead to "heart disease, stroke, high blood pressure, as well as immune and circulatory complications. Exposure to stress can also contribute to behaviours such as smoking, over-consumption of alcohol, and less healthy eating habits." In 2013, nearly one-quarter (23 percent) of Canadians age 15 or older said they felt "quite a bit" or "extremely stressful." Compared to people with less stress, people who reported high levels of stress also tended to report less life satisfaction. Given the link between stress and illness, methods of stress reduction can play an important role in health promotion and disease prevention.

People can choose from a variety of health promotion and health maintenance methods. These include exercise programs like tai chi, acupuncture, chiropractic treatment, and relaxation therapies. Many tension-reduction techniques exist, from relaxation methods, to meditation practices, to religious retreats.

Rogers, Keller, and Larkey (2010) reviewed 37 studies of meditative movement programs (tai chi and qigong). All programs included community-dwelling participants. Women made up 77 percent of the participants (n = 1435). Most people joined these programs in order to improve their physical function, decrease pain, or promote well-being. Most studies reported physical benefits such as greater mobility and reduced pain. But studies also reported

quantitative improvements in participants' quality of life and improvements in their self-esteem. People in some studies reported a feeling of "wholesomeness" and others reported improved spirit and timelessness. A generation ago, techniques of Chinese or Indian origin such as t'ai chi and yoga would have seemed foreign and strange. Today, many seniors take part in t'ai chi and yoga classes.

Newberg (2011), in a review of the literature on meditative techniques, reported that "meditation, prayer, and other related religious and spiritual practices may have significant effects on the aging brain—positive effects that may help improve memory and cognition, mood, and overall mental health" (p. 83). Studies also show that these methods improve physical health and well-being in later life.

Schneider and colleagues (2009; also Anderson, Liu, & Kryscio, 2008) conducted a randomized controlled study of 201 African American older adults (mean age 58) with coronary artery disease. The experimental group learned and practised transcendental meditation. The control group engaged in a health education program. The study measured survival rates of subjects, as well as the incidence of heart attack and stroke. The study also looked at blood pressure, body mass index, and psychosocial stress, including depression, anger, and hostility in the experimental and control groups.

After five years, the researchers found a 43 percent reduction in risk from all causes of death, including heart attack and stroke. The researchers concluded that "a selected stress-reduction approach may be useful in the secondary prevention of atherosclerotic CVD [cardiovascular disease]." Aldwin, Spiro, and Park (2006) said that "this accords with the growing evidence of the beneficial effect of meditation practice on cardiovascular health" (p. 94).

Lindberg (2005) reviewed the literature on meditation, spirituality, and health in older people. She reviewed 25 years of research and found that, overall, meditation reduced anxiety and depression; improved people's physical, emotional, and spiritual health; and helped people cope with problems, challenges, and stress.

Idler (2006) said that experimental and epidemiological studies showed "direct biological pathways from religious states, particularly those induced by meditation, to health by way of cardiovascular, neuroendocrine, and immune function...." (p. 291) These results and many other studies in the literature showed the value of stress-reduction methods for improving length of life and quality of life.

Disease prevention, health promotion, and stress management should play a role in planning for a successful old age. These activities can reduce the risk of many chronic conditions in later life (anxiety, high blood pressure, and heart disease). They can also reduce the incidence of the three major causes of death in later life: heart disease, cancer, and stroke.

THE COMPRESSION OF MORBIDITY HYPOTHESIS

Canadians have a longer life expectancy today than ever before. Will this mean more years of health and activity with a short period of illness at the end? Or will it mean a slow decline in health with more years of disability? Will we wear out quickly, like Oliver Wendell Holmes's "one-hoss shay" that fell apart in a day? Or will we rust out over many years, like an old Chevrolet? How many people would want to live 120 years if they knew that they would spend their last 30 years in a nursing home with dementia or paralysis due to a stroke?

Researchers have developed two concepts to measure the quality of life in old age. The first, **disability-free life expectancy**, refers to the years of remaining life free of any disability. Researchers compare this with the total number of years of life expectancy. It gives an indication of the quality of life of a person's remaining years. A similar concept, **dependence-free life expectancy**, measures the number of years of remaining life that a person will live in a state free of dependence on others for daily tasks.

Both of these concepts measure the quality of life in old age. As more people live more years in old age, researchers want to know whether people will live these added years in good health and independently or disabled and dependent on others. An active and independent older person will have a higher quality of life. This type of older population will also make fewer demands on the healthcare and social service systems.

About 35 years ago, Fries (1980; see also Fries & Crapo, 1981) gave an optimistic answer to the question of what a longer life would mean. He predicted three things: (1) more people would live a life that approached the hypothetically fixed life span of 110 to 120; (2) longer life would come about primarily through the reduction of chronic illnesses such as heart disease, cancer, and stroke; and (3) severe chronic illness would occur for a short time near the end of life (the **compression of morbidity hypothesis**). Fries believed that healthier habits, training, and health policies could compress morbidity into a few years at the end of life. This would

lead to a **rectangularization**, or **squaring of the survival curve** with less illness in the added years.

Some research supports this belief. Fries (2006) reported on a 21-year-long longitudinal study at Stanford University. The study documented the benefit of vigorous exercise on postponement of disability. The study compared 537 members of a runners' club age 50 and over with 423 people of the same age in a control group. Fries found that the exercise group "delayed the onset of disability *by over 12 years* compared with controls…" (p. 258, emphasis in original).

Fries went on to say that lifetime disability measured in exercisers comes to only one-third to one-half that of people who do not exercise. Fries cites at least five other major studies that support the compression of morbidity hypothesis. He concludes that "both cumulative morbidity and morbidity at the end of life are decreased in those with good health habits. Morbidity is postponed and compressed into fewer years in those with fewer health risks" (p. 258).

This research shows that people have control over their well-being in later life. Good health habits pay off in more disability-free years. Mitnitski and Gubitz (2010) said that "an explosion of … specific prevention strategies, treatments, and rehabilitation options, should lead to decreases in both disease incidence and mortality, resulting in positive trends in life extension and recovery rates" (p. 415).

Fries' work and others that project compression of morbidity describe this as a *possible* outcome of longer life. Those with "good health habits," such as exercisers and runners, may show compressed morbidity. But what about the general population? Does longer life lead to compressed morbidity among the general population (many of whom do not exercise or have good health habits)?

Work by Crimmins and Beltrán-Sánchez (2010) suggested that the general population did not show compression of morbidity. These researchers used data

---

disability-free life expectancy the years of life remaining that are free of any disability

dependence-free life expectancy the number of years of remaining life that a person will live in a state free of dependence on others for daily tasks

compression of morbidity hypothesis the idea that severe chronic illness would occur for a short time near the end of life

rectangularization or **squaring of the survival curve** the change over time in survival curves resulting in a right angle or square shape, leading researchers to conclude that a finite life span exists

EXHIBIT 5.18 *Life Table Survivors by Sex in Canada, 1931 and 2007–2009*

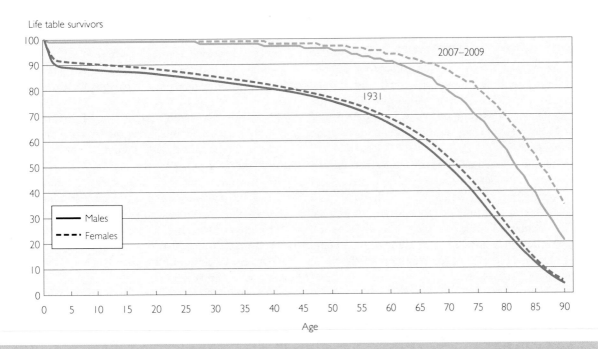

This chart shows the rectangularization of the life curve. It shows the number of people in a cohort (1931 and 2007-2009) who survive over a span of 90 years. The cohorts begin on the left with 100 members. As years go by, the cohort members die off.

Note the sharp drop in the 1931 cohort in the first few years. This cohort faced high rates of infant and child mortality. The 2007-2009 cohort does not show this pattern due to immunization, better nutrition, and better public health. Also note the steady loss of members from the 1931 cohort throughout middle age. By age 65, less than 60 percent of males and 62 percent of females survived in the 1931 cohort (compared with 84 percent of males and more than 90 percent of females age 65 in the 2007-2009 cohort). By age 90, nearly all of the 1931 cohort has died.

Even at age 90 (using 2007-2009 mortality rates), more than 20 percent of men and more than 30 percent of women in the 2007-2009 cohort are expected to be alive. This chart shows the compression of morbidity (illness and ultimately death) to later ages in the 2007-2009 cohort. People will live in relatively good health into late old age and, in the ideal case, will experience a short period of illness before death.

Sources: Martel, L. *Canadian Demographics at a Glance*, Statistics Canada, Catalogue No. 91-003-XIE, p. 17 (2008); Statistics Canada, *Life Tables*, Canada, Provinces and Territories. 2007 to 2009. Table 1a: Complete life tables, males, Canada 2007 to 2009; Table 1b: Complete life table, females, Canada 2007 to 2009. (2012). Reproduced and distributed on an "as is" basis with the permission of Statistics Canada.

from the U.S. *National Health Interview Survey* to look at cardiovascular disease, cancer, diabetes, and mobility. The data spanned an eight-year period—1998–2006. The researchers said the data show "no hint of a declining prevalence of disease over these eight years" (p. 80).

A study of survival curves with and without disease showed "an increase in the life expectancy with disease and a decrease in the years without disease. The same is true for functioning loss, an increase in expected years unable to function and a decrease in years able to function" (p. 81). In other words, this study of the general population in the United States did not show a compression of morbidity. It showed that longer life means more years with chronic illness and disability.

Medical treatment and disease management make it possible for people to live longer with chronic illness. For example, today more people than ever before survive into old age with HIV/AIDS (Roger, Mignone, & Kirkland, 2013). Treatments such as antiretroviral therapy extend the lives of HIV/AIDS patients. They will live more years in old age with this chronic illness. In this way, modern medicine extends life but also extends the years a person will live with an illness.

The work of Crimmins and Beltrán-Sánchez suggested that longer life would mean lower quality of life for more years for more people. But these researchers made a further point. They said, "it is ... the decrease in disease onset due to primary prevention [rather than treatment of disease] that is clearly going to be related to longer disease-free life." This point comes through in all the literature on health in later life. Primary prevention—reduced smoking, more exercise to prevent obesity, and a healthy diet to prevent heart disease—is the key to health in old age. And this puts the compression of morbidity within the reach of everybody. Fries (2006) took an optimistic view of morbidity compression. He said that the variation in ability among seniors shows room for further compression of morbidity. In other words, if some people live morbidity-free lives into late old age, other people can follow this pattern.

Martel and colleagues (2005) concluded that "healthy aging, which contributes to 'successful' aging, does not seem to be reserved to a small group of individuals with a well-kept secret: ... through a combination of personal effort and public will, many people can make it" (p. 6). The potential for further improvement in well-being among older people has led some authors to study the phenomenon of successful aging.

TIME TO REVIEW

Describe three dietary practices that lead to good health in later life.

Describe some of the benefits of stress-reduction practices.

What is the rectangularization of the life curve?

How would personal and social life differ if people, on average, lived for 120 years?

How would this change our ideas about youth, middle age, and old age?

What would society need to do to adjust to a longer life span?

SUCCESSFUL AGING

The Rowe and Kahn Model of Successful Aging

The focus by biologists on intrinsic processes has led to a more precise description of normal aging. But this research does not explain (nor does it try to explain) the differences in function among older people. It does not deal with the influence of the environment, lifestyles, and habits on physical functioning.

Rowe and Kahn (1999) understood the importance of these lifestyle and environmental influences. In a pioneering research study, they developed a model of **successful aging**. They described three signs of successful aging: (1) low chance of disease and disability; (2) high

mental and physical functioning; and (3) active engagement in social relations and productive activity. They proposed that scientists should look at people with these traits. The people to be studied "demonstrate little or no loss in a constellation of physiologic functions ... [and] would be regarded as more broadly successful in physiologic terms" (Rowe & Kahn, 1999). The research would focus on understanding the reasons for these people's success.

Joseph Baker et al. (2009) used Rowe and Kahn's criteria to assess successful aging in a sample of more than 12,000 Canadian seniors. One-fifth of the seniors in the study (20.7 percent) scored as "active" on a Physical Activity Index. But more than half the seniors in this study (54.6 percent) scored as "inactive." The index found that in their daily lives, active seniors used more than twice the average energy of inactive seniors. The study found that compared with inactive seniors, physically active seniors showed more than twice the likelihood of aging successfully.

A moderately active group, compared with inactive seniors, showed one and a half times the likelihood of successful aging. The researchers said that their study confirmed "the importance of physical activity in promoting successful aging as defined by Rowe and Kahn" (Baker et al., 2009, p. 232).

A number of gerontologists (Dillaway & Byrnes, 2009; Martinson & Minkler, 2006; Rudman, 2006) criticize the Rowe and Kahn model of successful aging. Critics say that this model excludes older people with physical disabilities who live satisfying lives. It also excludes the poor, the disadvantaged, immigrant seniors, and others who lacked the opportunity to age "successfully."

The Rowe and Kahn model of successful aging assumes that "individuals can control whether they contract disease, their risk of disease, their mental health and well-being, and their level of engagement with others" (Dillaway & Byrnes, 2009, p. 706). Many of these outcomes depend on genetics, the socioeconomic status of a person's family, life course events, and accident. This model, critics say, subtly blames the "unsuccessful" older person for his or her condition. "Unsuccessful" older people appear as failures compared with their successful age mates.

George (2006) raises a further problem with this model—it doesn't take into account a person's subjective view of life. Someone with a chronic illness or disability can still feel fulfilled and happy.

---

successful aging characterized by a low chance of disease and disability, high mental and physical functioning, active engagement in social relations and productive activity

A study based on the *Canadian Study of Health and Aging* asked 2,783 Canadian seniors what they thought led to a long and healthy life (Bassett, Bourbonnais, & McDowell, 2007). The study recorded seniors' responses in their own words and analyzed the results. The study found that most older people considered a good age their own responsibility. Even in the face of illness, they felt that they had the power to overcome their problems. People mentioned that a good and long life depended on a positive attitude ("take things as they come, don't worry"), self-care ("take care of yourself, don't take risks"), planning and financial control ("keep busy, work hard"), and individual autonomy ("if you can't do that [retain autonomy], it's the beginning of the end" (Bassett, Bourbonnais, & McDowell, 2007, pp. 116–121).

In general, respondents emphasized the importance of monitoring their health, staying active, and keeping busy. They also recognized the need to adjust to changes in health, ability, and circumstances as they aged. The researchers concluded that for this group "successful aging is about maintaining control and order in the face of decline" (Bassett, Bourbonnais, & McDowell, 2007, p. 124). These findings give insight into how older people themselves view successful aging, and how they attempt to make it a reality.

The SOC Model of Successful Aging

Researchers Paul and Margaret Baltes and their colleagues, who created the Berlin Aging Study, explained that a person with chronic illness or disability can live a successful age. They described a process called selective optimization with compensation (SOC) (Baltes & Carstensen, 2003; George, 2006). These researchers viewed successful aging as a response to life's challenges.

The researchers found that people often face losses or physical distress as they age, but those who aged successfully used the SOC method. They *selected* activities that *optimized* their ability. When they could no longer engage in an activity, they *compensated* for losses by setting new priorities. For example, they dropped less important activities and relationships and focused on more important ones, or they substituted one activity for another. A person who could no longer travel due to disability might attend travelogue sessions at a local seniors' centre. Someone who could no longer drive at night might focus on daytime social events.

The SOC model recognizes that aging brings change, but it also shows that people can adapt to changes and improve their mental ability as they age. Riediger, Li, and Lindenbergert (2006) said, "People themselves influence their development within the range of available opportunities" (p. 296). They referred to this as "active life management" (p. 300).

An older person may act with more caution—aware that a decrease in motor coordination increases the risk of a fall. They may also simplify an action by breaking it down into smaller parts. For example, a younger person may mount a bike by standing on one pedal, pushing off, and swinging on to the seat. An older person may get on a bicycle from a stationary position. An older person may get up from a bus seat early in order to make their way to the door. A younger person might wait until the last minute to exit. In this case, the older person's actions may look like the younger person's, but the older person has consciously or unconsciously compensated for decreased reaction time and planned a smooth exit from the bus.

Clearly a model of successful aging must allow for a person to cope with chronic illness, disability in late old age, and genetic diseases. Successful aging based on the SOC model encourages people, at whatever age or physical condition, to make the most of their abilities. This model supports the attempt by anyone—in whatever physical condition—to live a full and engaged life. It should also encourage professionals who work with older people to help each older person reach his or her maximum potential.

TIME TO REVIEW

Give some examples of how people adjust their behaviour to cope with physical changes due to aging.

Why do some gerontologists feel uncomfortable using the concept of successful aging?

What are the limitations or dangers associated with the use of the concept of successful aging?

How does the research on successful aging expand our thinking about human potential in later life?

THE IMPACT OF INCOME AND HEALTH ON QUALITY OF LIFE

McIntosh et al. (2009) noted that among adults in Canada, some health differences exist due to differences in income. The lower a group's income, for example, the higher the

---

selective optimization with compensation (SOC) those who age successfully use the SOC method: they select activities that optimize their ability, and when they can no longer engage in an activity, they compensate for losses by setting new priorities

group's mortality rate. In this study, "the proportion expected to survive to age 75 also climbed steadily [with income], with 51% of men in the lowest income decile [lowest 10 percent] expected to reach age 75, compared with 75% of those in the highest decile [highest 10 percent]" (pp. 58–59). Health-adjusted life expectancy (a measurement of the seniors' quality of life) showed this same trend. The poorest people experienced fewer years of good health in old age.

St. John, Montgomery, and Tyas (2013) studied the effect of social position (socioeconomic status or SES) on frailty in later life. They found a direct relationship between a person's social position (as measured by education, home ownership, and several income variables) and frailty (e.g., dependence on others, incontinence, and dementia). The researchers say "regardless of the measure of social position used, there was a strong association evident between social position and frailty" (p. 235). The researchers found this effect for men and women and in all age groups studied. "The effect of social position was large, robust, and seen in all surrogate measures of social position we examined" (p. 255).

Other studies have found a similar relationship between socioeconomic status and health in later life. Hart and Watt (2015) studied hospital use by 4,407 women age 80 and over in western Scotland. They found that women with a lower occupational class had higher rates of admission and bed-days for coronary heart disease, stroke, and cancer. Compared to people from the highest occupational class, those from the lowest class had higher rates of mental health (dementia) admission. Antonelli-Incalzi and colleagues (2007) found similar results in a study of hospital admissions in Rome, Italy. They found more admissions and longer length of hospital stay for people with lower socioeconomic status. Many other studies (Ross, Gilmour, & Dasgupta, 2010; Sanmartin & Gilmore, 2008) have documented the link between low SES and poor health.

Poorer people also show a higher risk of obesity, a precursor to diabetes. Le Petit & Berthelot (2006) studied the risk of becoming obese among a Canadian sample of over 3,000 people. The people in the lowest income category in this study had the highest risk of becoming obese. Compared to people in the lowest income group, men and women in the middle and upper-middle income categories had 40 percent less risk of obesity. Kaplan and Ross (2008) used data from the *Canadian National Population Health Survey* to study the sources of good health. The study followed 2,432 Canadians age 65 to 85 over a decade. The study looked at what conditions led to "thriving" (exceptional good health with no or only

mild disability) among older people. The study found that higher income predicted exceptionally good health in this sample. Lower income led to poorer health.

People with low education, people with low income, the unemployed, and unskilled workers are more likely to report poor health. "Without exception," McIntosh and colleagues (2009) said, "all of the health indicators ... [in their study] showed steady improvement with increasing levels of education" (p. 59). Low-income seniors have less money for quality food, they may live in substandard housing, and they lack the funds for uninsured healthcare expenses (Butler-Jones, 2010).

Gerontologists have looked at the reasons for this link between social position and health. Matthews and Gallo (2011), for example, conducted a review of the literature to explore the link between SES and health. They said people with low SES are "less educated, have lower-status jobs, and earn less or no income." Studies find links between low SES and minor as well as serious illnesses (e.g., headaches, heart disease, and early death).

The researchers found that people with low SES reported fewer psychological and social resources, including less perceived control, social support, and social integration. Studies that looked at older subjects found a link between social support, income, and health. Likewise, low SES subjects with a low sense of control (e.g., helplessness, poor problem solving ability) had higher rates of illness.

Dogra and colleagues (2015, p. 180) looked at the effect of "aging expectations" on physical participation and health among low SES adults. Previous studies (Wardle & Steptoe, 2003, cited in Dogra et al., 2015) found that, compared to higher SES older adults, those with lower SES had worse expectations of living a long life, worse health habits, and a weaker belief in personal control. Dogra and colleagues studied 160 low SES participants in t'ai chi classes in Toronto. The researchers found a positive link between SES, good aging expectations and physical participation, good self-rated health, social functioning, energy and vitality, and good mental health. People with low SES tended to have low aging expectations and poorer health.

Compared to people with higher SES, people with low SES face more environmental stressors. These include poor-quality housing, poor diet, and in some cases a dangerous environment. These conditions lead to a depletion of a person's resources, making them less able to maintain good health. The researchers call this a "reserve capacity" model of response to stress. Repeated stress, according to this model, makes a person vulnerable to disease and illness. A test of this model by Matthews and colleagues (2008) found that lower levels of education led to metabolic syndrome (a group of conditions that increase the risk of diabetes, heart disease, and stroke) due to lower levels of reserve capacity.

A number of studies link health in later life to a person's education. Clouston, Lawlor, and Verdery (2014), for example, found that each year of education led to an increase in physical performance (grip strength). People typically complete their education early in life, so the effect of education on health in old age acts across many decades. Statistics Canada (2015g) found that people with a university certificate, diploma, or a bachelor's degree reported significantly lower rates of disability.

Mirowsky and Ross (2008) said that a low level of education leads to cumulative advantage or disadvantage over time and influences health in old age. This theory says that education creates "abilities, habits, and attitudes" that provide access to higher social status (p. 95). These abilities lead to avoidance of health risks and better ability to manage health problems when they occur. Higher social status buffers a person from environmental insults and stress.

Mirowsky and Ross (2008) took a life course approach and looked at the effect of early life experiences on health in old age. They studied a national sample of 2,592 households in the United States. The study found support for the cumulative advantage theory—compared to those with less education, better-educated people in this sample showed a slower deterioration in health with age. The study also found a stronger effect of education on health in more recent cohorts. In another study these researchers found that as cohorts aged, the gap in health between lower and better educated subjects increased (Mirowsky & Ross, 2005).

What accounts for this link between education (often completed in youth) and health in later life? Mirowsky and Ross (1998) found support for three links between education and health in later life: (1) education leads people to create a healthy lifestyle; (2) education gives people a sense of control over their lives that leads to healthy choices; and (3) educated parents serve as role models and encourage their children to live a healthy lifestyle. They found that more educated people created a lifestyle—a set of habits such as exercise, diet, and stress management—that promotes good health.

Mirowsky and Ross (1998) said that "Compared to those with little schooling, well-educated persons are more likely to exercise, are more likely to drink moderately rather than abstain or drink heavily, and are less likely to smoke or be overweight" (citing Ross and Wu, 1995). This work points to the "rising importance" of education in determining health in old age (Mirowsky & Ross, 2008, p. 105; also Mirowsky & Ross, 2005). It also points to the effects of social structures (such as education or family economic status) on a person throughout life.

A number of researchers trace health in old age to childhood and a lifetime of good or bad health. O'Rand (2006, pp. 154–155), for example, said that poverty in early childhood leads to a "chain of life course 'insults.' ... Early

---

EXHIBIT 5.19   AGING AND HEALTH FROM A LIFE COURSE PERSPECTIVE

The Dutch "Hunger Winter": Genetic Links Found Between Childhood Conditions and Health in Old Age

The Dutch experienced the "Hunger Winter of 1944–45." During this time, the Nazis occupied Holland and blocked all food supplies to the west of the country. Scientists wondered whether children conceived during this time would show the effects of famine later in life. They began the *Dutch Hunger Winter Families Study* to explore this question. Schulz (2010) says the "Dutch Hunger Winter study ... provides an almost perfectly designed, although tragic, human experiment in the effects of intrauterine deprivation on subsequent adult health" (p. 16757).

This project produced many studies that link conditions before birth and in childhood to health conditions in later life. Studies report that famine led to high lipid profiles, increased cardiovascular disease, and impairment in selective attention for people in their late 50s.

Researchers from Leiden University and Columbia University studied the genetic makeup of 60-year-olds conceived during this time. They compared a gene on the DNA of these people with this same gene on the DNA of their brothers and sisters. The scientists found that the older people conceived during the famine had a different molecular setting for a gene that influences growth. It appears that the lack of food during his time altered the genetic material in the embryos.

Scientists think that this change in the DNA could adapt the person to a shortage of food. Dr. B.T. (Bas) Heijmans of the Leiden University Medical Centre in the Netherlands said, "It could be that the metabolism of children of the Hunger Winter has been set at a more economical level...." This could explain why these children, now in old age, show high rates of obesity and cardiovascular disease. Their bodies, set for a time of hunger, respond poorly to the modern high-calorie Western diet.

Studies such as this one show the effect of the environment on the physiology even before birth. These early effects then shape a person's health many years in the future.

Sources: Lumey, L.H., Stein, A.D., Kahn, H.S., van der Pal-de Bruin, K., Blauw, G.J., Zybert, P.A., and Susser, E.S. 2007. "Cohort Pro The Dutch Hunger Winter Families Study." *International Journal of Epidemiology*, 36(6): 1196–1204; University of Leiden. 2010. "Traces of Dutch 'Hunger Winter' In Genetic Material." News & Events, http://www.news.leiden.edu/news/dutch-hunger-winter.html; Schulz, L.C. 2010. "The Dutch Hunger Winter and the Developmental Origins of Health and Disease." *Proceedings of the National Academy of Sciences of the United States* (PNAS), 107(39): 16757–16758. http://www.pnas.org/content/107/39/16757.full.

and sustained poverty has been shown repeatedly to predict higher rates of disability and mortality in later life." Studies now link cardiovascular diseases to childhood stress, illness, and poverty (Leon & Ben-Schlomo, 1997, cited in O'Rand, 2006). Research on the "early origins" of disease takes a life course approach to health (Carson et al., 2007; Ferraro, 2006; Singh-Manoux et al., 2004).

Matthews and Gallo (2011) said that low SES family life exposes members to "conflictual interactions, ... recurrent episodes of anger and aggression, and deficient nurturing." Young people in such a setting may lack affection and feel a chronic sense of threat. They may also lack role models for healthy behaviours. "To the extent that these experiences occur repeatedly, they are believed to lead to poor health later in life" (Matthews & Gallo, 2011).

Ferraro (2006, pp. 245 and 248) said that "a good start in life aids the chances for a good finish.... It is hard to overstate the influence of early disadvantages." Matthews and Gallo (2011) said, "It is clear that lower SES in childhood has a long-lasting influence into adulthood, even if the factors underlying these trends remain unclear." Clouston, Lawlor, and Verdery (2014, p. 414) said, "socioeconomic status is a persistent and common cause of health and functioning over the entire life course."

The Centers for Disease Control (2013b, p. 5) supports this comment and promotes the need for healthy behaviours early in life:

> *Although the risk of developing chronic diseases increases as a person ages, the root causes of many of these diseases often begin early in life. Practicing healthy behaviors from an early age and getting recommended screenings can substantially reduce a person's risk of developing chronic diseases and associated disabilities.*

The practice of yoga has caught on among older people. It provides a gentle method of stretching muscles and bending joints. Yoga can improve balance, increase flexibility, and stimulate circulation.

Socioeconomic differences throughout life mean that some older people will suffer from the effects of early health disadvantage. Other older people will build on the good health and income that they enjoyed throughout their lives. Life course studies of health make the case for public policies that improve health in childhood and middle age (e.g., health education, welfare programs, income security, child care, and public health programs). Torres and Wong (2013, p. 335) proposed "greater urgency to public policy efforts ... that seek to improve childhood conditions."

HEALTHY AGING: A CANADIAN PERSPECTIVE

Along with non-profit organizations and researchers, the Canadian government has turned its attention to healthy aging. Discussions on this topic have resulted in a Canadian vision of healthy aging. This definition takes a comprehensive view of health that includes physical, mental, social, and spiritual well-being (Edwards & Mawani, 2006).

The federal government sponsors national health promotion programs to support healthy aging. Programs offer exercise, fitness, and dietary advice. The Canadian Health Network, for example, provides information through its website on active living, a healthy diet, and many other health promotion topics. The federal government also sponsors a home adaptation program. This program offers up to $3,500 in forgivable loans to people age 65 and over who need to modify their homes to live comfortably (Canada Mortgage and Housing Corporation, 2015a). This program provides for installation of grab bars in bathrooms, handrails, and easy-to-reach storage cupboards.

The government provides support for healthy aging for at least two reasons. First, the people of Canada want to have programs that improve the lives of older people. Second, health promotion can delay and in some cases decrease the use of expensive healthcare services. For this reason, everyone has an interest in supporting a good and healthy old age.

Wister (2005, p. 192) summarizes the literature on healthy aging:

> *One of the most simple but powerful messages [in the literature] is that infusing balance in one's lifestyle is pivotal to good health; that balancing stress and relaxation, activity, diet and eating habits, body and mind, individual responsibility, and awareness of barriers to changing health behaviours are all part of a healthy lifestyle. Such an approach is not automatic; it is learned and relearned through various interpersonal and institutional channels as we age.*

FINAL THOUGHTS

This chapter has focused on methods of achieving a healthy old age. Many of the methods presented here come down to individual lifestyle choices. This emphasis on personal choice seems appropriate in a chapter on personal health. But personal choice takes place in a social context. We all live within constraints imposed by others and our social systems. For example, not everyone has access to a fitness centre or even the space to exercise. An inner city neighborhood may pose dangers to a woman who wants to begin a walking routine. The office of one of the authors sits in the inner city near a park with signs that say "Drug-free zone." The women in our office must walk in groups for their safety. Someone in this neighborhood, who has no group to walk with, will face danger if they want to jog or walk each day.

The Centers for Disease Control (2013b, p. 5) in the United States sums up the findings on how to improve health in later life:

> *If a meaningful decline in chronic diseases among older adults is to occur, adults at younger ages, as well as our nation's children and adolescents, need to pursue health-promoting behaviors and get recommended preventive services. Communities can play a pivotal role in achieving this goal by making healthy choices easier and making changes to policies, systems, and environments that help [people] of all ages take charge of their health.*

We all live in an environment that includes air, water, and food. These basics play a vital role in our health at every age. Public health measures, government regulations, and professional societies can help ensure a safe and life-supporting environment for people of all ages. The study of personal health shows the deep connection between health behaviours and healthy conditions at every stage of life.

CONCLUSION

People have tried to reverse or stop the process of aging at least since Ponce de Leon set out to find the fountain of youth. Drug companies have looked into the effects on aging of animal glands, sex hormones, and chemical therapies. Salons now offer Botox injections to erase facial wrinkles and other methods to create smoother-looking skin. These methods can make the skin softer or temporarily smooth out wrinkles, but they do nothing to increase life expectancy or reverse aging.

Still, the search goes on. Scientists have explored many methods for increasing life expectancy and extending youth. They have found that certain drugs, calorie-restricted diets, and lowered body temperatures (during hibernation) extend the lives of some animals in the laboratory.

Will any of these methods lead to longer, healthier lives for humans in the near future? Most biological researchers predict a slow increase in life expectancy in the next few years due to better healthcare, healthier lifestyles, and new medical technology.

But any of the following changes could increase the length of life and increase well-being in old age: the discovery and use of gene therapy, the use of stem cell technology, or genetic postponement of aging through natural selection. These changes would both extend life expectancy and increase the number of healthy years people live.

Studies of people age 100 years or older throughout the world give some clue about what a long-lived society would look like. Vogler (2006; also Suh et al., 2008) said that centenarians serve as "a useful human model of disease-free or disease delayed aging" (p. 47). These studies reported that long-lived people have good genes, a purpose in life, physical activity, independence, close family ties, friends, good hygiene, a simple balanced diet, low stress, good self-esteem, and religious faith. In other words, centenarians live balanced lives in supportive social settings.

These findings suggest that we should place the search for a full life where it belongs: within the power of each of us and the society we live in. We can and will extend life expectancy in Canada through scientific research and positive changes in our lifestyle and environments. But life extension will only put off the deeper question: Can we give meaning and purpose to those added years?

Summary

1. Chronic health problems increase with age. Although women live longer than men, they also suffer from more chronic conditions and higher rates of disability. These conditions include hypertension, arthritis, and rheumatism.

2. Changes in health lead to changes in a person's ability to function on his or her own. A decrease in physical ability can lead to the need for help with activities of daily living (ADLs and IADLs). Social and healthcare

supports as well as a more supportive environment can help older people maintain their independence.

3. Technology can help people cope with declines in health. Simple objects such as spoons can be adapted for people with arthritis, computers can increase a person's contact with others, and in the future, robots and computers may help people bathe, exercise, and perform daily tasks. The use of technology will improve the quality of life for people with disabilities.

4. Older people today and in the future risk increased illness due to obesity. Obesity increases the risk of diabetes, heart disease, and other chronic and life-threatening illnesses. A sensible diet and exercise offer the best ways to combat this problem. Stress reduction can play a role in creating successful aging. All of these methods can improve physical function and mental alertness.

5. Research shows that changes in smoking cessation, exercise, diet control, and stress reduction can slow the aging process. People can even improve their lung capacity and bone density through exercise. This can lead to a longer and healthier life.

6. The rectangularization of the life curve points to longer life expectancy for future cohorts of older people.

7. The compression of morbidity hypothesis says that people will live longer and have more disability-free years in the future. Researchers disagree on whether morbidity compression has actually occurred. But scientific research and modern medicine work to increase the number of years older people live disability-free.

8. Many older people stay healthy and active as they age. They live without physical handicap and without special help. Studies of successful aging show that people can extend the number of years they live in good health. Several theories of successful aging exist. The SOC model includes healthy active older people as well as people with chronic illness and disability.

9. A lifetime of inequality can lead to poor health in later life. The life course model of aging studies the connection between health early in life (as early as childhood) and health in old age. Those with good income and health earlier in life generally live a healthier old age.

10. Many Baby Boomers want to live active lives as they age. They will face new challenges as they place new demands on their aging bodies. Studies show that a good old age depends on a balanced lifestyle that includes activity, a good diet, stress release, and social support.

STUDY QUESTIONS

1. How do men and women differ in the physical changes they experience with age? How does income influence a person's health and well-being in later life?

2. How can environmental, technological, and lifestyle changes help older people cope with physical changes? Give some examples of how diet control, exercise, stress reduction, and technology can reduce the incidence of illness and/or help a person cope with physical change.

3. Explain the compression of morbidity hypothesis and the rectangularization of the life curve. How would the compression of morbidity influence healthcare system costs and services in the future? How do men and women differ in life expectancy and in the prevalence of chronic illness?

4. Review the Rowe and Kahn definition of successful aging. Why do some gerontologists dislike this concept? Explain how the SOC model overcomes some of the criticisms of the Rowe and Kahn model. How does the life course model expand our thinking about successful aging?

5. What policies and programs in Canada exist to buffer the effects of inequality on health in later life?

KEY TERMS

activities of daily living (ADLs) (p. 99)
chronic health problems (p. 95)
compression of morbidity hypothesis (p. 122)
dependence-free life expectancy (p. 122)
disability-free life expectancy (p. 122)
epidemiological transition (p. 97)
functional disability (p. 98)
hypokinesia (p. 110)
instrumental activities of daily living (IADLs) (p. 99)
life expectancy (p. 95)
maximum life span (p. 95)
rectangularization or squaring of the survival curve (p. 122)
selective optimization with compensation (SOC) (p. 125)
successful aging (p. 124)

CHAPTER 6

THE PSYCHOLOGY OF AGING

iStock/Thinkstock

LEARNING OBJECTIVES

After reading this chapter, you will

LO1 Be able to explain the achievements and limitations of laboratory research on memory and intelligence.

LO2 Understand the changes in the brain that occur with age and explain the link between these changes and mental performance

LO3 Understand the concepts of cognitive reserve and plasticity as they apply to the older person's brain.

LO4 Be able to describe the research on mental training and physical exercise and their ability to improve mental function in later life.

LO5 Be able to distinguish between different measures of creativity and explain the value of creative expression in old age.

LO6 Understand the difference between normal and abnormal psychological aging and between organic and functional disorders.

LO7 Be able to state the prevalence, causes, and treatment of dementia and depression.

LO8 Be able to explain the issues related to competency and loss of competency for cognitively impaired older people.

INTRODUCTION

A few years ago, one of Canada's leading geriatric specialists gave a talk on memory to a group of seniors. He told the group that, in the absence of disease, changes in an older person's memory should cause no problems in everyday life. Young people and old people both forget things, he said, but older people notice it more because they expect memory loss to come with age. A man stood up at the end of the talk and said, "I respect your views, doctor. But I know my memory has gotten worse with age. What I want to know is what I can do about it."

This response fits with two things research has learned about older people and memory: first, a large proportion of older people believe they have memory problems, and second, memory failure upsets them, even if they forget something unimportant. People fear that memory loss could lead to a loss of independence (Park & Meade, 2006). Some studies report that 40 percent of people age 25 to 75 report memory problems at least once a week (Lachman, 2000). McDougall (2000) says that people fear memory loss more than almost any other effect of aging.

Many people, older people included, accept the stereotype that cognitive decline is a normal part of aging. But recent research on memory, intelligence, and creativity questions this belief. Studies show that people can learn and grow intellectually in old age as well as in youth. On some measures, mental ability may decrease with age, but on other measures, mental ability can improve. Dramatic declines in mental functioning are due to physiological disorders or distress, not to normal aging.

This chapter will look at (1) memory and intelligence in later life, (2) creativity and self-development, and (3) the psychological problems some older people face.

NORMAL CHANGES IN PSYCHOLOGICAL FUNCTIONING

Memory and Intelligence

Psychologists define **memory** as the recall of information after learning has taken place. Most formal measurement of memory takes place in psychology laboratories. Psychologists in the field of aging have spent more time on the study of memory than on any other topic.

Psychologists show a strong interest in memory and aging for a number of reasons. First, popular stereotypes

about aging and early psychological research on memory predict a decline in memory with age. If this is true, studies of memory can trace the causes of this decline. Second, psychologists can study memory in the laboratory under controlled conditions. This makes research on memory relatively easy. Third, studies of memory have produced testable models of how the mind works. These models attempt to explain complex processes such as learning, forgetting, and the storage and retrieval of information. Fourth, new brain imaging techniques allow psychologists to study the chemical and electrical functions of the brain.

Finally, the increasing numbers of people with Alzheimer's disease has led to greater public awareness (and fear) of memory loss. This has led researchers to look for the differences between normal and pathological changes in the brain in later life. Researchers, the public, and policymakers would all like to slow or reverse memory loss in old age. For all of these reasons, the study of memory dominates the study of psychological aging.

Researchers break the process of remembering into a series of steps. Most researchers today use an information-processing model to guide their work. The model includes the following steps: (1) a person perceives information—psychologists call this **sensory memory**; (2) the person acts on this information and transforms it into **short-term memory**; and (3) the person stores the information in **long-term memory**, the storehouse of knowledge that also includes the rules for organizing knowledge.

Take the example of meeting someone at a party. You say hello and you hear them say their name (sensory memory). You repeat their name to yourself a few times (short-term memory). You make a rhyme for their name or associate their name with a physical trait (long-term memory). The greatest mental work goes on when a person moves information into long-term memory.

Hundreds of studies have tried to sort out the effects of age on memory. In particular, the research has focused on differences in learning (acquisition and recall) between younger and older subjects.

Much of the research on memory and aging points to some decline in memory with age. What causes this

memory the recall of information after learning has taken place

sensory memory information perceived through the senses and stored as memory

short-term memory where information is stored temporarily while it is being processed, or for a short time afterward

long-term memory the storehouse of knowledge that also includes the rules for applying knowledge

decline? Research supports the idea of a "common cause" (Hoyer &Verhaeghen, 2006, p. 219). Some studies point to declines in vision and hearing as the source of this decline. Hoyer and Verhaeghen said that "sensory functioning is a strong late-life predictor of individual differences in cognitive function" (p. 219). Other studies show a decline with age in the functional integrity of the brain. Studies that look at processing speed link this general decline to decreased brain function.

Many studies show that older people take longer to learn new information, longer to search for it in memory, and longer to use it when they need it. For example, latency (the length of time a person takes to process information or make a response to a question) increases with age (Braver & West, 2008).

Hundreds of studies have tried to sort out the effects of age on memory. In particular, the research has focused on differences in learning (acquisition and recall) between younger and older subjects. Psychologists believe that acquisition and retrieval are closely related. How someone retrieves information (how they search for and find information in memory) depends on how they acquired it (the methods they used to organize and store the information).

Laboratory studies of memory allow researchers to look at each part of the process.

Laboratory Studies

Laboratory studies find a decline in several types of memory. Decline occurs in non-episodic memory (information with no reference to the time at which it was acquired, such as general knowledge of the world) and in episodic memory (memory acquired at a specific time and place, such as the recall of a vacation in Paris) (Tulving & Szpunar, 2009). Much of the laboratory research on memory looks at episodic memory and this depends largely on recollection (Hoyer & Verhaeghen, 2006).

Controversy exists over when the decline in episodic memory begins. Some researchers believe decline begins in the 20s and 30s. Others say decline begins at later ages (Nyberg & Bäckman, 2011). Episodic memory shows a greater decline with age than other types of memory.

---

latency the length of time it takes for a person to process information or respond to a question

non-episodic memory oriented toward the present or the future, with no reference to the time at which the person stored the memory; includes learned skills through practice or a person's general knowledge of the world

episodic memory oriented toward the past, or acquired at a specific time and place, as in learning in an experimental setting

Some laboratory studies have found deficits in memory in older people due to the way they learn and store information. Zanto and Gazzaley (2010) found that, compared with younger adults, older adults showed a slower speed of encoding (the process whereby a person puts new bits of information together with already stored information). Older adults tend not to think of encoding strategies or they use less elaborate encoding. Encoding, rather than retrieval, may account for the lower recall rate in older adults.

Lustig and Flegal (2008) studied the encoding and retrieval of memorized words by a group of older adults. People who encoded effectively performed best at retrieving memorized words. Successful encoding methods included making a story out of the words, relating the words to their own experience, and combining the words in sentences. Compared to old-old participants in this study (age 76 and older), younger-old people in this study (under age 75) tended to use these strategies.

This shows that work put into encoding (making meaning from random words) leads to better response at recall. This research suggests that memory decline in older adults may be due in part to the use of inefficient processing techniques. For example, older people show deficits in working memory. Working memory stores recent information and also manipulates this information. In addition, it processes new information while temporarily storing other information (Hoyer & Verhaeghen, 2006).

Studies of working memory find that older adults remember less well when irrelevant information comes between two things to be remembered. For example, a change in topics places a greater load on working memory and leads to poorer memory in older people. When a topic changes, older people appear to forget relevant information. Decreased processing efficiency leads to poorer working memory in older people.

Gazzaley et al. (2005) studied the impact of irrelevant information on the working memory of healthy, well-educated younger and older people (age 19 to 30 and 60 to 77, respectively). They presented the subjects with pictures of faces and outdoor scenes. They instructed the groups to ignore the faces or the scenes, or to take a passive approach.

---

encoding the process whereby a person puts new bits of information together with already stored information

working memory where recently acquired information is manipulated and processed at the same time as it is being stored temporarily

The researchers studied the brain activity of the two groups and found that people in the older group had trouble ignoring irrelevant stimuli (faces or scenes). This led to decreased short-term memory of relevant information. The researchers concluded that attention deficit may underlie some of the observed decline in memory.

Bäckman and colleagues (2000) said that this decline in working memory increases in late old age. Craik (2000, p. 82) said, "it is clear that older adults have particular problems in situations where they must hold, manipulate, and integrate moderate amounts of information over short time spans." A study by Kramer, Fabiani, and Colcombe (2006) supported this finding. They found that older people have trouble ignoring irrelevant stimuli (information or sounds), and this leads to decreased mental performance. Darowski and Hambrick (2008; also Rowe, Hasher, & Turcotte, 2008) studied 229 people age 18 to 87. The researchers looked at the effect of distraction on reading time. They found that compared with younger subjects, older subjects showed less ability to control distraction. This led to increased reading time by the older subjects.

The researchers proposed that poor distraction control underlies some of the declines seen in working memory. Waterston (2011) says that the ability to switch from one task to another declines with age. Compared with younger people, older people have more difficulty returning to the original task after a distraction.

Speeded trials appear to increase the learning deficit. More than the young, older subjects miss verbal and pictorial items presented at a rapid rate. They miss late items in a list more than earlier ones, and they encode some items at the expense of others. For example, due to decreased processing speed, an earlier task slows a later activity (e.g., if someone needs to keep some figures in memory, this will inhibit later decision-making speed).

Kramer and colleagues (2006, p. 59) say that processing speed "can often account for a large proportion of age-related variance across a wide assortment of tasks and environments." Slower processing accounts for the loss of information from an earlier task as a person performs a more recent task (e.g., a person may forget figures held in memory while he or she tries to make a decision). The researchers said that slowed processing has a "cascading effect on information processing."

But processing speed alone does not explain age-related changes in mental activity. Hartley (2006) reviewed the research on speed of processing and its effect on mental function in later life. He concluded that research does not support a single cause (like decreased speed of processing) as the explanation for age-related

changes in mental function. At best, he said, a few causes might underlie the changes that psychologists find. These could include changes in executive functions (like switching between tasks or maintaining focus on a task), loss in working memory systems, changes in neurochemistry, or changes in the brain structure (decreases in white matter).

Physical Change as the Source of Mental Decline

Psychologists look at brain structure and function as a source of mental decline in later life. Cerella (1990, p. 201), for example, proposed that deficits in mental functioning (such as memory) may be "distributed throughout the information-processing system rather than being localized in particular stages." He proposed that breakdowns in the older person's neural network lead to slower processing of information. Each breakdown in the network requires the input to travel a greater distance.

The older the person, the greater the neural decay and the slower the processing time. This not only explains the general slowing phenomenon, but also indicates why older people do less well on tests that emphasize speed. It also accounts for why older people may do as well as younger people on skilled tasks. These tasks use well-established neural networks. This model offers a simple explanation that replaces the many explanations related to specific tasks (such as storage and retrieval).

A number of studies support the idea that changes in the brain lead to cognitive decline. Kramer, Fabiani, and Colcombe (2006; Park & Reuter-Lorenz, 2009) reported losses of grey and white matter in the brain. They said that losses in prefrontal grey matter correlate with reduced performance on "frontally mediated executive tasks." Kramer and colleagues concluded that changes in brain structure over time (e.g., atrophy of sections of the brain or loss of dopaminergic receptors) predict declines in cognitive performance (p. 65).

Madden and colleagues (2009) studied the effect of white matter integrity in the brain on cognitive performance. They showed for the first time that a loss in white matter integrity leads to a decline in cognitive performance. Bucur et al. (2008) showed that the loss of white matter integrity led to decreased speed of episodic memory retrieval. These studies support the idea that a loss of brain structure leads to declines in mental function.

Small and colleagues (cited in *Columbia News*, 2008) used magnetic resonance imaging (MRI) technology to map blood flow to the brain and pinpoint the exact location of functional decline. The researchers reported changes in the hippocampus, a part of the brain that serves as a gatekeeper for information. The hippocampus processes information and creates long-term memory. It declines in function with age. Hartley (2006) said that differences in processing speed may be due to "a general reduction in the functional intactness of the central nervous system" (p. 191).

Arnsten (2008) at Yale University focused her research on the chemicals that influence brain function and on the prefrontal cortex, the site of higher brain functions like memory. Arnsten reported that the disruption of chemical pathways, particularly the function of catecholamines—norepinephrine (NE) and dopamine (DA)—leads to declines in prefrontal cortex function. This leads to attention deficits and shows up as a decline in working memory.

Work reported by the *Berlin Aging Study* also points to physical change as a source of cognitive decline. Lindenberger and Baltes (1994; also Hoyer & Verhaeghen, 2006; Park & Reuter-Lorenz, 2009) proposed that sensory decline serves as a measure of brain integrity and has a strong impact on all cognitive abilities. They found that declines in visual and auditory ability explained nearly all age-related declines on a series of psychological tests.

Further research by this team controlled for education, social class, and income. They still found declines in cognition based on sensory decline. They said that this points to a common set of causes that decrease the brain's structural and functional integrity.

Changes in the brain's structure and function explain in part age-related declines in mental performance. But researchers admit that current knowledge has just begun to trace the link between the brain's function and mental ability. The eighth edition of the *Handbook of the Psychology of Aging* (Schaie & Willis, 2016) contains extensive reviews of the literature on brain function and mental performance. Psychologists have also studied genetics, cellular function, and brain physiology to understand mental performance. These studies show the growing interest among psychologists in the effects of biology and physiology on mental functioning.

New Approaches to the Study of Mental Function

Park and Reuter-Lorenz (2009) listed the many changes in mental function and brain structure that come with age, including declines in processing speed, working memory, and long-term memory. They also included decreases in the brain's structure and size and a loss of white matter

integrity (e.g., the presence of neurofibrillary plaques and tangles).

The use of neuroimaging techniques (functional MRI and positron emission tomography [PET] scans) allows researchers to understand how the brain functions in the face of these losses. These techniques revealed an adaptive brain that seeks "to maintain homeostatic cognitive function" (p. 174). Park and Reuter-Lorenz (2009) said, "The brain responds to these neural insults by engaging in continuous functional reorganization and functional repairs that result in self-generated support of cognitive function" (p. 175).

Neuroimaging studies show that the brain compensates for losses. Meade and Park (2009) reported that older adults, compared with younger adults, recruit more parts of the brain to help with mental processing. The researchers said, "The flexibility inherent in this compensation suggests that older adults' neural function is dynamic and that plasticity remains in the neurocognitive system in late adulthood" (p. 37).

Nussbaum (2011; also Park & Bischof, 2011) described the brain as "dynamic, constantly reorganizing, and malleable." This contrasts, he said, "with some traditional ideas of the human brain as a fixed, rigid—and even degenerative—system from early age" (p. 7).

Flexibility in brain function points to a mental reserve capacity. According to this view, high intelligence; education; an active, stimulating lifestyle; genetic makeup; or a physically larger brain provide a reserve capacity. This protects the person from the decline due to aging and from diseases of the brain.

Park and Reuter-Lorenz (2009) said that "Generally, cognitive function declines in parallel across the lifespan with decreasing brain volume, dopamine receptors, and white matter integrity." But not all studies show this effect. "And when they [effects] are observed, they are of a modest magnitude." (p. 179). Some mental processes decline, but the older brain compensates for these losses. This helps explain the variability of cognitive decline among older people (Cosentino, Brickman, & Manly, 2011).

Some older people perform less well than young people on tests and in the lab but other older people outperform the young. Gazzaley and colleagues (2005) studied what happened when they provided irrelevant information to older people in a study of memory. They found, "encouragingly, a subgroup of the older population with preserved suppression [of irrelevant information]." These people, they said, "demonstrated ... the variable impact of the aging process...." This suggests that a cohort of similarly aged older people will vary in their mental ability. And this opens the door to the possibility that older people can improve their mental function in later life.

Plasticity and Cognitive Reserve

For many years scientists and the general public believed that the brain lost neurons with age. This seemed to explain the decline in mental function over time. Finch (cited in Guttman, 2008) said:

> [H]istorically the subject was thought to be very simple: that brain neurons were lost from birth onwards. Now it is really clear that if you don't have a specific disease that causes loss of nerve cells, then most, if not all, of the neurons remain healthy until you die. That's a big change, and it has only come about in the last 10 years.

The most recent research shows that the body not only preserves brain cells, it can create new neurons and new neuronal connections at every age. Scientists call this "neurogenesis."

Cohen (2005) listed four findings from brain research that describe mental growth and development in later life:

1. The brain reorganizes itself in response to new information and experience.
2. Brain cells grow in later life.
3. The brain's emotional centres grow more balanced with age.
4. Compared with younger people, older people use both halves of the brain more equally.

We now know that the brain rewires connections in response to demands. Maguire and colleagues (2000), for example, reported that London cab drivers showed the development of neural links in that part of the brain that makes spatial connections. Older and more experienced drivers showed more brain development. Their experience driving through London's streets leads to brain development in adulthood.

Draganski and colleagues (2006) found that medical students who studied for their qualifying exams increased the volume of their hippocampus and neocortex. Bangert and Schlaug (2006) found that piano players (who make heavy use of both hands) showed enlarged left and right parts of the brain. String players (who make most use of one hand) showed only right-side enlargement. "Structural differences in musicians' brains have been found to be related to early initiation and intensity of long-term instrumental training" (p. 1832). Robert S. Wilson (2011) said, "mental stimulation ... increases the efficiency and adaptability of neural systems" that underlie mental performance (p. 60).

Park and Reuter-Lorenz (2009) developed a Scaffolding Theory of Aging and Cognition to account for these changes in the brain. They said that the brain responds to functional and structural decline by reorganizing itself. They proposed that the brain forms neural scaffolds or protective structures that buffer mental decline. They further proposed that individual experiences can increase neural scaffolding. This means that "new learning, social and cognitive engagement, exercise, and cognitive training could all improve mental function in later life" (Park & Bischof, 2011; also Nussbaum, 2011).

The term **cognitive reserve** originally referred to people with dementia who performed better than expected in everyday life. Stern (2002, 2007) expanded that view. He said, "The concept of reserve should be extended to encompass variation in healthy individuals' performance, particularly when they must perform at their maximum capacity." Stern said that "how we use our brains during our lives influences the amount of cognitive reserve that we have.... [Cognitive reserve] is malleable and changes over the course of our life, depending on innate factors and subsequent exposures" (p. 448).

Education and literacy in particular seem to create a large cognitive reserve. "What we can be sure of," Stern said, "is that over a very long period of time, exposure such as education and leisure activities do contribute to reserve" (cited in De la Vega & Zambrano, 2003; also see Christensen et al., 2008). But he cautioned that research has yet to show what specific activities increase cognitive reserve. We can't say, for example, that a person who takes a photography class or solves Sudoku puzzles will increase their cognitive reserve.

Robert S. Wilson (2011) said a "growth-oriented lifestyle is an important part of maintaining cognitive health in old age. Current research suggests that the activities should be complex and challenging, and because they need to be sustained over a period of time, these endeavors should be engaging and enjoyable" (p. 61).

Some researchers believe that cognitive reserve can protect people from the ravages of Alzheimer's disease. Bennett, Schneider, Aranitakis, and colleagues (2006) conducted a community-based study of people with Alzheimer's disease. They found that some people with Alzheimer's brain pathology continue to function without impairment. The researchers proposed that these people have a "neural reserve." They looked at the backgrounds

---

cognitive reserve refers to exceptional mental performance, particularly when a person has to work at maximum mental capacity; first observed in cognitively impaired people who performed better than expected in everyday life

of these people and found that education and social connections may have created this reserve.

Future research will include more use of neural imaging technology. This technology allows researchers to look directly at changes in brain structure and function. They can see the influence of learning or other activities on the development of brain structures. The use of neural imaging, Park and Bischof (2011) said, "will provide future insights into the malleability and potential of the aging mind" (p. 116).

Willis, Schaie, and Martin (2009) said that the research on **plasticity** (based on experiments and interventions) and the research on cognitive reserve (based on descriptive examples) come to some of the same conclusions: (1) both perspectives emphasize the person's active role in developing a reserve and compensating for losses; (2) both recognize individual differences in reserve capacity; (3) both perspectives recognize that prior conditions in a person's life (e.g., education) influence reserve; (4) both recognize the limits to reserve and plasticity; and finally, (5) both perspectives believe that a person can enhance plasticity and reserve. This last point has led researchers to look outside the laboratory for insights into seniors' mental performance.

TIME TO REVIEW

How does the current research on cognitive reserve and brain plasticity support the need for a life course model of human development?

Based on the research on brain plasticity and cognitive reserve, what are some ways that people could maintain mental function as they age?

The Limits of Laboratory Research on Memory

Other causes besides physical aging account for the differences in memory between older and younger people found in laboratory studies. Differences in educational background and verbal ability, for example, influence results in memory research (Nyberg & Bäckman, 2011).

Test conditions can also influence older subjects' performance on memory tests. Researchers reported that a supportive context improved older subjects' ability to learn paired words. Supports can include guidance on how to encode information, prior knowledge of a topic, practice, or external cues to help learning (Carstensen, Mikels, & Mather, 2006). The design of memory tests, their content, and the use of cross-sectional designs (that

compare older and younger people at one point in time) may all lead to exaggerated findings of memory decline in older people (Nyberg & Bäckman, 2011).

Some studies show that an older person's fear of failure on memory tests leads to poor performance. Researchers call this **stereotype threat** (Hess, 2006; Hummert, 2011; Kang & Chasteen, 2009). For example, test instructions that focus on memory make people aware of declines in mental ability, and this can lower a person's score. Hess reported that "differences in performance were essentially eliminated" when test instructions said positive things about aging and memory (p. 394).

Laboratory studies raise an important question: How well do the results of memory research predict an older person's ability to remember details in everyday life? The answer: Not very well. Memory studies done under laboratory conditions have poor ecological validity (the transferability of knowledge from lab to life). Older people rarely learn or recall well under pressure, and research shows that they remember best when they learn information relevant and useful to them.

The Contextual Approach

The **contextual view of memory** begins with the insight that many conditions influence memory. These include the physical and social context where learning took place, a person's education, their health, and their experience at learning in structured settings (such as a classroom or lab).

In early work done by Charness (1981, 1985), he reported on younger and older chess players' problem-solving abilities. He found that older players had more difficulty than younger players at the same skill level in recalling positions accurately. He attributed this difficulty to older players' poorer retrieval ability. But when Charness evaluated game-playing performance, he found that skill level, not age, determined a player's ability. Older players did as well as younger players of the same skill level.

Charness asked, "Why is there no deficit in molar [overall] problem-solving performance?" (1981, 34–35). Mireles and Charness (2002) in a later study used a neural network model to measure chess performance in the laboratory. They found that in a chess recall task, people with a

---

plasticity the brain's ability to change and adapt over time

stereotype threat an older person's fear of failure on memory tests; this can lead to poor performance

contextual view of memory the idea that many conditions influence memory, including physical, psychological, and social contexts and the knowledge, abilities, and characteristics of the individual, as well as the situation in which the individual is asked to remember

larger knowledge base achieved more accuracy on the recall task. The researchers said that pre-existing knowledge can overcome the effects of systemic slowing due to neural noise. Stine-Morrow and Basak (2011) said that "experts within a domain [such as chess] are ultimately able to perform well the skills they have always practiced" (p. 155).

Work by Phillips, Kliegel, and Martin (2006) supported these earlier studies. Phillips and her colleagues studied two groups of 39 subjects each. One group had a mean age of 24.8. The second group had a mean age of 69.5. The researchers asked each group to engage in two computerized tasks: one, a traditional laboratory task, entailed abstract planning. The second, a planning task, entailed planning a number of errands in a made-up situation with specific constraints.

The researchers found, as expected, a decline in performance based on age for the abstract planning task. But the researchers found no relationship between age and performance on the more ecologically valid errand-planning task. The researchers concluded that a decrease in information processing speed and education accounted for the decrease in performance by the older subjects on the abstract task. They said that task-related knowledge and experience helped older subjects compensate for decreases in processing speed in the errand-planning exercise. In other words, in real-life situations, older people draw on their experience and can perform as well as younger people.

Roring and Charness (2007) found support for this view. They compared chess players with different levels of skill at the start of their careers. Players who had a high skill level at the start of their careers showed a slower rate of decline as they aged. "Expert performance," Morrow (2009) said, "depends on highly organized knowledge structures in long-term memory that enable experts to view problems at an abstract level" (pp. 50–51). Charness and Krampe (2008) said that "having a large vocabulary of patterns linked to plausible moves can compensate for age-related declines in fluid abilities" (p. 248). They said that practice and pattern recognition best explain the performance of experts.

Park and Meade (2006) said that a person who needs to remember to take medication may develop a pattern to help their memory. For example, he or she may take the medication routinely at breakfast or just before bed. Consider Mrs. Harrigan. She puts her vitamin pills near her juice so she'll remember to take them. She builds this into her morning activity. She also wrote a note and posted it on the refrigerator. After a month or so, the pill-taking has turned into a morning routine and she takes the note off the fridge. She's become an "expert" at this task and

no longer needs to keep this in memory. She just follows her new routine.

Nearly everyone makes lists, whether a shopping list or a daily "to do" list for work. This technique takes the load off working memory and frees the mind for other demands. Older people can learn this and other techniques for improving memory and performance.

Allen, Bucur, and Murphy (2006) reported a number of studies that supported a process-specific effect of aging on mental activity. They found that while complex problems led to poorer performance by older workers, this applied to only some tasks. On tasks that have to do with word recognition, for example, older people did as well or better than younger people.

These researchers reported similar findings for math problems—probably because older people have a lifetime of experience with arithmetic. The researchers concluded that some mental processes decline with age, while others remain stable. "The aging process," they said, "is not comprised simply of cognitive decline." Analyses of specific mental processes "opens the possibility for interventions to help older adults compensate in domains that do show age-related decline" (p. 591).

Ackerman (2008) reported on a study of 228 adults between the ages of 21 and 62 with at least a bachelor's degree. The study found that "older adults tended to perform better on most of the knowledge tests, except for those in the domain of physical sciences (e.g., chemistry, physics)" (pp. 476–477). Older adults showed superior results, when compared with younger adults, on knowledge of the humanities (literature, art, music) and civics (government, history, law). A lifetime of accumulated knowledge remains available to older adults. The research concluded that, "age in and of itself is not a particularly important determinant of individual differences in domain knowledge."

Studies of prospective memory (the ability to remember something to be done in the future) find similar results. These studies find that older people can outperform younger people. For example, older people do better at remembering to carry out a task like mailing back a postcard or telephoning the researcher in the future. McDaniel, Einstein, and Jacoby (2008) found that when a person had to remember to do something at a certain time (e.g., take a pill before going to bed), they showed no memory deficit. Hoyer and Verhaeghen (2006) said that after years of experience, older people may use external devices to assist their memory.

Even without the use of memory aids, older people do well at remembering to do things in the future. One study discouraged people from using external memory aids (Kvavilashvili & Fisher, 2007). This study found no age-related declines in time-based memory tasks. The study asked older and younger participants on a Monday to call the researcher on Sunday at a certain time. They found that 81 percent of the older adults called on time. Only 68 percent of the younger adults did. Both groups found that cues throughout the week (e.g., a ringing telephone) reminded them of their task.

Park and Meade (2006) said that studies of everyday memory need to take into account the person, the demands of the task (e.g., is it a new task or a routine task?), and the environment. For example, a question such as "How can I best manage on my current income?" has no right answer. The context will determine the best course of action. Also, as Berg (2008) said "everyday problem solving draws not only on the cognitive abilities of adults but also on their emotional, interpersonal, and physiological regulatory systems" (p. 218).

Solving a problem in everyday life may involve emotion, social sensitivity, and coping with stress. Everyday problems can occur over a long period of time (e.g., how to relate to grandchildren). Also, competence (a person's skill at real-world tasks) can influence performance on mental tasks, and competence can improve with age. Older people often show more competence in real-world tasks than psychological tests measure. Competent older people draw on experience and use strategies (such as selecting only the information they need) to succeed in mental tasks (Smith, 2006). Research on everyday life shows a more optimistic picture of mental performance in later life when compared with laboratory studies (Morrow, 2009).

Some studies have looked directly at what older people remember about the world around them. These studies have found less of the memory deficit reported in laboratory research. Hoyer and Verhaeghen (2006) reported that semantic memory, the store of factual information, showed little decline with age. For example, older and younger people show little difference in general knowledge questions on IQ tests. The more repeated and familiar the knowledge, the better the older person's memory. Older people also have a good memory for past personal events.

Hoyer and Verhaeghen (2006) said that "older adults do not show a deficit on [vocabulary] tasks, but rather an advantage" and that "vocabulary measures probably underestimate the breadth and depth of knowledge and development of word meanings and language

accumulated through years of experience and use" (p. 216). Longitudinal studies support these findings. Only after age 90 do decreases in word knowledge appear. The more automatic the recall (for example, driving a car in a person's own neighbourhood), the better the older person will perform.

The ability to accumulate knowledge and draw on it increases through adulthood. Older people who maintain their cognitive abilities may put more effort into a task, they may call on a past skill, or they may develop a new skill. Carstensen, Mikels, and Mather (2006, p. 344) said that "such expertise can even offset cognitive decline."

The research reported to date should end the stereotyping of older people as forgetful. Studies report compensation for decline, positive effects of physical exercise on memory, and benefits from training. Bugos et al (2007), for example, found that sensory motor training (learning to play the piano) led to significantly improved mental function. Other studies showed that social engagement leads to improved mental ability (Stine-Morrow et al., 2007).

Research also shows that the use of memory aids (such as the use of a notebook) can significantly improve memory performance. Memory aids lead to improved recall. For example, an older person will do better on a multiple-choice test (with all the possible answers displayed) than on a free-recall test with no cues. Supports reduce the amount of mental processing or resource use. In everyday life, this leads to better recall.

Verhaeghen and Cerella (2008) reviewed many studies of mental function in later life. They found at least three different effects of aging on mental function. "Lexical tasks [related to reading and word recognition]," they said, "are largely spared from the ill effects of aging; simple decisions show modest age-related slowing; spatial tasks are slowed to a greater degree.... The picture of cognitive aging that emerges from our analyses," the researchers said, "is both simpler and more positive than that painted in typical review articles: Apart from spatial processes and tasks demanding dual task set maintenance, no cognitive tasks appear to show deficits beyond those seen in simple decisions" (p. 147).

In sum, research supports the idea that causes other than changes in brain structure and function can influence mental performance in older people. Research shows that different types of older people (with more or less education or skill), under a variety of conditions (supportive or non-supportive context), and exposed to varying types of materials to learn (relevant or irrelevant) differ in their ability to perform mental tasks or to remember specific information. Research shows that older people have a reserve mental capacity. And studies show that people

semantic memory the store of factual information

can improve memory performance by using memory cues and by training.

The research on mental potential in later life should end the stereotyping of older people as forgetful. Studies report compensation for decline, positive effects of mental activity, and benefits from training.

Give some examples of how studies of mental performance in everyday life expand our understanding of cognitive ability in later life.

What types of mental ability show the least decline (and in some cases, improvement) in later life?

Training the Mind for Improved Performance

Studies of mental training programs (Draganski et al., 2004, cited in Small & McEvoy, 2008; Nyberg et al., 2003) have reported increased brain activation and grey matter increases. These "studies suggest that focal training can result in changes in the structure and function of the brain" (Small & McEvoy, 2008, p. 582).

Schooler (2009) reported that "doing intellectually challenging things on and off the job is significant and meaningful." Schooler concluded that "even in old age, carrying out self-directed complex tasks has a positive effect on intellectual processes" (p. 31).

Schooler said engagement in complex tasks is similar to mental aerobics. And even in later life, complex tasks "build the capacity to deal with the intellectual challenges that complex environments provide" (p. 32). By contrast, a focus on one activity, for example, working on crossword puzzles, does not lead to general cognitive improvement. These findings open the door to research on training programs that can keep mental functioning strong as we age.

Basak et al. (2008) conducted a controlled experiment to test the effects of training, using video games to improve cognitive function. They chose a group of 40 older adults who said they had not spent any time playing video games in the past two years. Half the group with an average age of 70 got 15 one-and-a-half-hour training sessions with a strategy video game. The training lasted four to five weeks. The other group with an average age of 69 got no training. They served as a control for the experiment.

The experimental group showed improvements when compared to the control group on a number of

psychological functions including task switching, working memory, visual short-term memory, and reasoning. This still leaves the question of whether these results translate into better function in everyday life. But they point in the right direction.

All of these studies showed that the brain needs stimulation and challenge as a person ages. Michael Merzenich (2006) said, "The brain wants to learn. It wants to be engaged as a learning machine." The brain needs new challenges to stay active and to grow. Merzenich said, "The brain requires active continuous learning. It requires change, and that change requires that you acquire new skills and abilities, new hobbies, and activities that require the brain to remodel itself. That's the key."

Schaie (2006) reported on a 14-year longitudinal study of intelligence in older people. The study found that 40 percent of the people in the study who took training showed a reversal in intellectual decline. Another 25 percent showed a reduction in decline. Many other people in the study showed stable performance.

A study done by Kramer, Fabiani, and Colcombe (2006) supported these findings. In a review of studies on cognitive training, they found that in some cases, when compared with younger adults, older adults gain more from formal mental training.

Willis and colleagues (2006) conducted a rigorous test of training on mental function. The National Institute on Aging supported this study with a $15 million grant. For five years, Willis and her colleagues studied 2,802 people with an average age of 73. All of these people lived in the community and all had normal mental ability at the start of the study. The program was called Advanced Cognitive Training for Independent and Vital Elderly, or ACTIVE.

The study randomly divided the participants into four groups. One group received memory training and learned methods for remembering word lists, story ideas, and details. A second group got training on reasoning and learned how to find patterns in a letter or word series. They then learned how to judge the next item in the series. A third group got training on speed of processing information. This group learned to identify objects on a computer screen in short time frames while locating another item on the screen. The fourth group got no training. The people in the training groups got up to 10 one-hour training sessions on a computer. The training took place over five to six weeks. About 700 of the 1,877 people took a 75-minute "booster" session after one year and then after three years beyond the training.

Researchers tested the mental function of participants before the study, just after the training, and yearly for five years. Just after the training, 87 percent of the speed-training group showed improvement, 74 percent of the reasoning group showed improvement, and 26 percent of the memory group showed improvement. These groups showed improvement after five years when compared to the control group.

The reasoning and speed-training groups that got the booster training showed the most benefit. Willis said that "the improvements seen after the training roughly counteract the degree of decline in cognitive performance that we would expect to see over a seven- to 14-year period among older people without dementia."

"After five years, people in each group performed better on tests in their respective areas of training than did people in the control group. The reasoning-training and speed-training groups who received booster training had the greatest benefit" (National Institutes of Health, 2006). They showed the best scores on how quickly and accurately they could do everyday tasks like making change or reading medicine instructions. But only the effect of reasoning training on self-reported performance of daily tasks was statistically significant. In short, the study showed real but modest results in maintaining everyday mental functioning due to training.

This study showed that training can delay or compensate for mental decline. But the study also showed the limitations of short-term training, even with follow-up sessions. The results of this study and others (Small & McEvoy, 2008) suggest that training works best when it targets a specific skill.

Suzman summed up the findings. He said that "relatively brief targeted cognitive exercises can produce durable changes in the skills taught." But, he said, "the main limitation of this type of intervention [ACTIVE] is the lack of transfer from the trained cognitive ability domain to other abilities." Owen and colleagues (2010), for example, trained more than 11,000 people on cognitive tasks. The participants took the training several times a week for six weeks online. The researchers found improvements on all of the tasks but they found no evidence for the transfer of these gains to other tasks. Suzman said that he "would now like to see studies aimed at producing more generalized changes" (cited in National Institutes of Health, 2006).

Computerized training has emerged as one approach to cognitive improvement. Kueider, Parisi, and Rebok (2012) conducted an extensive review of computerized training programs. They said that "there is evidence that computerized cognitive interventions are beneficial ... [but] there is need for future research." Lampit, Hallock, and Valenzuela (2014) conducted a similar review and concluded that the overall effect of computerized training is "positive but small." The review found no effect on executive mental functions or verbal memory.

An industry has emerged in the creation and sale of "digital brain fitness software" (Fernandez, 2011, p. 63). These products claim to improve brain function and to delay or reverse cognitive decline. Fernandez (2010) says this market grew to $295 million worldwide in 2009—a growth of 31 percent since 2005. This industry could grow to an $8 billion business before 2020 as the Baby Boom generation ages (Fernandez, 2011). Industry claims attract customers who worry about current or future mental decline. One ad promises that you will "Think faster, focus better and remember more in 2012" (PositScience, 2012).

A number of companies have enlisted university researchers to test and develop their products. But, Fernandez (2011) said, "the brain fitness software industry is only in its infancy; it is an emerging and largely unregulated market where many products have limited clinical validation and often present confusing claims that make it difficult for consumers to separate wheat from chaff" (p. 64).

Puzzles and games do no harm. But the person who focuses on only one activity does not appear to gain a broader benefit. Hoyer and Verhaeghen (2006) proposed several methods for improving memory as a person ages. These include memory training, an enriched environment, and physical fitness training.

A wider engagement in social life and a challenging environment seem to have the best effect on a person's mental function as they age (Stine-Morrow & Basak, 2011; Robert S. Wilson, 2011). Individuals need social activities that engage their minds. And society needs to provide meaningful roles to keep older people engaged in social life.

Wilson (2011) said that for people to take part in challenging mental activities over a long time, the activities must be "engaging and enjoyable" (p. 61). He proposed acting classes and work with children in schools: "complex activities that are likely to challenge executive control skills." "Eventually," he said, "one may be able to select from a range of cognitive training programs and real-world experiences known to enhance cognitive function and brain reserve" (p. 61).

Stine-Morrow and Basak (2011) summarized the literature on memory and training. They said that in contrast to "stereotypes of inevitable forgetfulness in old age, memory can be improved through intervention" (p. 156). They went on to say that behavioural data and brain research showed that the "mind and brain are well-suited to learn individual skills throughout the life span" (p. 162).

Physical Exercise and the Brain

Exercise increases cardiovascular fitness and endurance. But scientists find that exercise also leads to more connections between brain cells and growth in brain size. A study done at the University of North Carolina—Chapel Hill compared two groups of people age 60 to 76. One group exercised at least three hours per week over 10 years. The other group exercised less than one hour per week. The less active group had fewer small blood vessels in the brain and less predictable blood flow through the brain.

These findings point to the value of regular exercise for brain health. Weinstein and Erickson (2011) said that "physical activity, such as aerobic exercise, might be both an effective prevention and treatment for late-life brain atrophy and cognitive decline. [A]erobic exercise interventions are consistently associated with increased cognitive performance and greater brain volume in older adults" (p. 92).

Poon and Harrington (2006) reported that even mild physical activity, such as playing the fiddle, leads to increased production of brain cells (in this case, the brain cells related to the activity of the left hand). Some evidence suggests that exercise also increases blood flow that brings oxygen to the brain and increases the efficiency of neuronal function. High levels of fitness may lead to more efficient mental processing, especially for complex and demanding tasks (Park & Bischof, 2011).

Aerobic conditioning leads to improvement in simple and complex mental tasks. Colombe and colleagues (2006) found that aerobic exercise increased grey and white matter in the brain. And Erickson and colleagues (2009) found increases in brain volume as well as improved spatial memory due to exercise.

Conditioning improves complex tasks the most. Kramer and colleagues (2006) found that exercise led to improvements in the brain that included neuronal survival, the growth of new connections between neurons, and the growth of new capillaries in the brain. "The end result of exercise training then is a brain that is more plastic and adaptive to change and more able to survive the vagaries of the aging process" (p. 76).

A Canadian study of exercise and the brain compared two groups of older women (a total of 42 women) randomly chosen from the community. One group took part in aerobic exercise; the other group did not. The study measured cardiovascular health, blood flow to the brain at rest, reserve capacity of blood vessels in the brain, and cognitive functions. The active women had better vascular blood flow to the brain and lower blood pressure. Compared with the control group, they also had better cognitive functions (Alberta Heritage Foundation, 2009).

Marc Poulin, the author of the 2009 Alberta Heritage Foundation study, said:

Being sedentary is now considered a risk factor for stroke and dementia. This study proves for the first time that people who are fit have better blood flow to their brain. Our findings also show that better blood flow translates into improved cognition.... The take-home message from our research is that basic fitness—something as simple as getting out for a walk every day—is critical to staying mentally sharp and remaining healthy as we age."

Many studies also show differences between highly fit and less fit people on working memory, reaction time, and reasoning. Etnier (2009) reviewed 11 large-scale studies that looked at the effects of physical activity on cognitive performance and clinical impairment. Nine of the 11 studies showed that exercise led to less risk of cognitive impairment. (The other two studies took place over a relatively short time span, and this may have affected the results.) The studies that showed an effect of exercise on cognitive ability also studied the intensity of the exercise.

Etnier (2009) concluded that "'more is better' and that physical activity intensity is an important component of the dose of physical activity" (pp. 166–167). A review of many other studies led Etnier to conclude that programs that include both strength training and aerobic training best reduce cognitive impairment. She also concluded that activity should take place from 20 to 60 minutes most days.

Researchers continue to study the link between exercise and mental function. For example, researchers do not have a clear idea of how physical activity acts on cognition (Spirduso, Poon, & Chodzko-Zaiko, 2008) or how strong the relationship is. But the research to date points toward the value of living an active lifestyle for good mental function (Stine-Morrow & Basak, 2011).

Summary of Findings on Aging and Mental Potential

A few key points summarize some of the positive findings in the large literature on aging and mental performance:

- Negative stereotypes, test anxiety, and other distractions account for some of the decline we see in lab studies of mental performance.

- Some types of memory and cognitive function show little decline when studied in everyday contexts.

- Compared with younger people, some older people perform as well or better on tests and in everyday life.

- Experts show that practice and pattern recognition in a field can lead to continued high performance.

- Training can improve mental processes, at least for the specific skills trained. Multiple training strategies may have the best chance of skill transfer.

- Physical activity can forestall mental decline and help maintain good mental function. In general, sharp brains tend to stay sharp; cognitive processing may take a little longer, but this is normal aging, not a sign of "senility."

These findings come from a growing literature on mental potential in later life. The increase in the older population, longer life, and the desire of the Baby Boom generation to maintain an active lifestyle will drive more research on mental potential. This research will study ways that older people can maintain and improve their mental functions. Studies in the future may uncover and describe unique mental activities that express themselves only in old age.

INTELLIGENCE

The research on intelligence in old age parallels the research on memory. Early studies assumed that intelligence decreases in old age as the body declines. More recent research questions this simple connection between senescence and intelligence.

Psychologists use at least two definitions of intelligence. First, taking a global view, they refer to it as the "ability to negotiate environmental demands successfully" (Labouvie-Vief, 1985, p. 506). Second, they take a pragmatic view, referring to it as "that which intelligence tests measure" (p. 506) or what a person taking a test can do now. Psychologists most often use this second (more limited) definition when they conduct research on intelligence and aging.

Intelligence as Multidimensional

Current research supports a multidimensional view of intelligence. For example, the Performance Scale scores on IQ tests show a much greater decrease with age than the Verbal Scale scores (40 percent vs. 16 percent decrease). "This classic aging pattern, relative maintenance of function in verbal skills as compared to performance skills, has been seen many times with a variety of different populations" (Botwinick, 1984, p. 254).

A cross-sectional study by Park and colleagues (2002) showed the same results. The study found decreases in working memory, short-term memory, long-term memory, and processing speed in each older age group. But verbal knowledge showed stability across all age groups. People in their 80s, for example, showed scores on verbal knowledge similar to that of 50-year-olds and better than those of 20- and 30-year-olds. These findings support the idea that older people may lose some abilities but remain stable or improve on others.

Horn and Cattell (1966, 1967) developed a model of intelligence, still in use today, that explains these results. They described two types of intelligence—**fluid intelligence** and **crystallized intelligence**. Fluid intelligence refers to reasoning, abstracting, concept formation, and problem solving. It makes little use of knowledge gained through reading, school, or work. Fluid intelligence relies on how well the physical and nervous systems function. Performance tests that demand the use of fluid intelligence ask subjects to manipulate unfamiliar material in new ways mentally, and they sometimes require skill at manipulating objects physically. Studies show a decline in fluid intelligence with age.

Crystallized intelligence refers to the use of stored information, acculturation, and learning. Verbal tests, such as a test of vocabulary or historical events, demand the use of crystallized intelligence. People show stability and even improvement in crystallized intelligence with age.

This two-part model helps explain the empirical results on intelligence. Numerical and verbal skill problems measure crystallized intelligence; spatial and reasoning questions measure fluid intelligence. Fluid intelligence may follow the decline of the biological system from the teen years on, while studies of crystallized intelligence show stable intelligence scores and even increases in scores with age (Kramer, Fabiani, and Colcombe, 2006; Park & Bischof, 2011).

TIME to REVIEW

What effect does age have on a person's intelligence? What type of intelligence stays stable or may even increase with age?

Explain why older people might do better than younger people on tests that emphasize crystallized intelligence.

Why, based on studies of the brain, might older people do worse than younger people on tests of fluid intelligence?

---

intelligence the "ability to negotiate environmental demands successfully" (Labouvie-Vief, 1985, p. 506), "that which intelligence tests measure" (p. 506), or what a person taking the test can do now

fluid intelligence reasoning, abstracting, concept formation, and problem solving, with little use of knowledge gained through reading, schooling, or work

crystallized intelligence depends on stored information, acculturation, and learning

New Models of Mental Ability: Wisdom in Later Life

Traditional models of aging tend to view life as a hill. They assume that ability increases over time, plateaus, and then declines. But this view has begun to change.

First, research shows variability between individuals. In general, younger people outperform older people on memory and intelligence tests. But, on a given measure, some older people perform better than younger people (Ackerman, 2008; McDaniel, Einstein, and Jacoby, 2008).

Second, research finds that most people have unexpressed potential and the ability to gain new mental abilities (Willis, Schaie, and Martin, 2009). Research on decision making supports this view. Marsiske and Margrett (2006) said that older adults think beyond purely rational solutions to a problem. "In the real world, individuals also consider their own preferences, values, and feelings as well as those of their social partners and cultural context" (p. 317). For example, older adults used both emotional and action-oriented coping strategies in problem solving. The researchers say that this attention to the complexity of life shows a higher order of thinking than purely rational problem solving.

Baltes and colleagues set out to study **wisdom** in later life. To do this they set up the *Berlin Aging Study* in 1990. The project defines wisdom as "a highly valued and outstanding expert knowledge about dealing with fundamental—that is, existential—problems related to the meaning and conduct of life" (Kunzmann, 2006, p. 1232). Older people who display wisdom appear more skilled in everyday life. Skills include "life planning, life management, and life review" (Dixon, 2000, p. 32).

Society could use this broad perspective and flexible thinking to redefine problems that escape rational and technical solutions. Baltes and colleagues studied wisdom by asking older people to solve real-life problems. One problem, for example, asked people to respond to a suicidal call from a friend. Another asked respondents to advise a 15-year-old girl who wants to get married immediately. What should she consider and what advice would the older person give (Kunzmann, 2006)?

Scheibe and colleagues (Scheibe, Kunzmann, & Baltes, 2007, cited in Knight & Laidlaw, 2009) listed five criteria of wisdom:

1. a store of factual information about human nature;
2. rich procedural knowledge about handling life's problems;
3. an awareness of life's contexts and how they change over the life span;
4. understanding the relativism of values and tolerance for others; and
5. an understanding of how to deal with uncertainty.

These abilities make wise older people good decision makers and advisers.

Wisdom allows a person to critically view cultural illusions and to act on the basis of universal principles. A series of studies conducted by Grossman and colleagues (2010) compared the responses of younger and older people to conflict situations. In one of the studies, they asked a random sample of 247 younger and older people to read stories about conflicts between ethnic groups in a foreign country. They asked the subjects how they expected the conflicts to develop or be resolved.

Compared with younger subjects, older subjects showed flexibility in their thinking and emphasized the need for multiple perspectives. They saw the value of compromise and the limits of knowledge. The researchers conclude that even though fluid intelligence declines with age, social reasoning improves. They say that older people could play an important role in legal disputes, counselling, and intergroup negotiations.

wisdom "highly valued and outstanding expert knowledge ... related to the meaning and conduct of life" (Kunzmann, 2006, p. 1232)

developmental intelligence the growth of wisdom in later life—an advanced style of cognition

EXHIBIT 6.1 *Some Criteria for Wisdom*

Dr. Gene Cohen described the wisdom that can develop with age. He called the growth of wisdom in later life "developmental intelligence." Cohen said that "our brains never lose the ability to learn ... brain development throughout life increases coordination within the brain. This leads to more complex thinking that we call wisdom."

Cohen considered this an "advanced style of cognition." He described three "styles" that characterize this type of thinking:

1. Relativistic thinking: an awareness that context can affect knowledge and understanding; an awareness that knowledge is not absolute.
2. Dualistic thinking: the ability to suspend judgment while trying to resolve contradictions; the ability to hold mutually exclusive ideas in the mind at the same time.
3. Systematic thinking: the ability to take a broad view of a situation or a system of knowledge.

Source: © 2005. G.D. Cohen, *The Mature Mind: The Positive Power of the Aging Brain*, New York: Basic Books, 36–37. Reprinted by permission of Basic Books, a member of the Perseus Books Group.

Curiously, Baltes and colleagues' later work on wisdom found little empirical support for the unique expression of wisdom by older people. They found that expressions of wisdom could occur from the teen years onward. In a review of the research, Brugman (2006; also Ardelt, 2011) reported that, "in most empirical studies thus far no age differences [between younger and older people] have been found" (p. 449).

Some researchers proposed that wisdom exists as a "potential" in later life, with only some people realizing this potential. Knight and Laidlaw (2009) said that "physical aging, societal ageism, and psychological disorders" can keep someone from developing wisdom in later life (p. 696). These authors said that a person can develop a skill at making wise decisions. An encouraging environment, education, and supportive others can promote wisdom in older people. Ardelt (2011; also Parisi et al., 2009) proposed that intergenerational mentoring might stimulate wisdom in older people. It would also provide young people with wise role models.

It appears that wisdom develops in later life under certain conditions. A person's openness to experience, the presence of role models, and a time of societal transition all foster the development of wisdom. Academic knowledge does not automatically lead to wisdom as Baltes and

his colleagues defined it. But Kunzmann (2006) said, "an interest in understanding and helping others, and social-emotional competencies such as empathic concern seem to be more important" (p. 1233).

CREATIVITY

The bulk of research on psychology and aging has focused on changes in memory and intelligence with age. Comparatively few studies have looked at creativity in later life. The word *creativity*, for example, does not appear in the subject index of the *Handbook of the Psychology of Aging*, 8th edition (Schaie & Willis, 2016). Some studies measure creative achievement by evaluating the greatness of a work or by counting the number of creative works by an individual. Other studies view creativity as a form of personal expression.

Creativity as Measured by Great Works

Lehman (1953, 1968) conducted the classic work in this field. He studied the ages at which scientists, philosophers, mathematicians, painters, inventors, and other creative people produced their greatest works. He selected

---

EXHIBIT 6.2   *Wisdom in Later Life*

In Plato's Republic, Socrates says that he likes to talk to older people because they have gone along a path that all of us will one day follow. So they have a unique perspective on life and aging; some might call it wisdom. Consider the following thoughts on aging by some thoughtful older people.

Art Blake, a retired judge from Jamaica, says that he recently attended the funeral of a friend. He flew back to Jamaica and went directly to the church from the airport. He reached the church before anyone else. "I watched as the people arrived," he says. "Many of them I knew from my childhood, we went to school and grew up together. These are all old people, I thought. Then I thought, I too must look like this. But I couldn't see it in myself. I shave every day and I don't see my age. But I could see it in them.... The mind plays tricks on you."

Art serves as the legal adviser to an education program for older people and sits on the advisory board of a university certification program. "We want to be young," Art says. "We use creams to smooth out the wrinkles. But this is the most natural process. We cannot help but get old."

Bertrand Russell developed new interests as he aged. He began his career as a mathematician, moved on to philosophy, then in late old age he turned to political and social issues. At age 80, he said, "The best way to overcome it [old age]—so at least it

seems to me—is to make your interests gradually wider and more impersonal, until bit by bit the walls of the ego recede, and your life becomes increasingly merged in the universal life. An individual human existence should be like a river—small at first, narrowly contained within its banks, and rushing passionately past boulders and over waterfalls. Gradually the river grows wider, the banks recede, the waters flow more quietly, and in the end, without any visible break, they become merged in the sea and painlessly lose their individual being" (quoted in Puner 1979, p. 270).

John Holt, an educator who wrote about children and their untapped potential, turned to reflect on education for adults later in his career. Holt took up the cello in late middle age. In his book *Never Too Late* (Holt, 1978, p. 185), he wrote about his experience learning the instrument and about his own potential as a person:

If I could learn to play the cello well, as I thought I could, I could show by my own example that we all have greater powers than we think; that whatever we want to learn or learn to do, we probably can learn; that our lives and our possibilities are not determined and fixed by what happened to us when we were little, or by what experts say we can or cannot do.

for his sample people who had already died (because someone still alive could still produce a great work). Lehman found that most past and present scientists produced their greatest creative work between the ages of 30 and 40. Most great writers produced their foremost work before the age of 45, and most poets produced theirs in their late 20s and early 30s. Painters peaked between ages 30 and 45. In most fields, Lehman found that achievement steadily decreased after age 45.

Lehman's research set off a wave of controversy. Dennis (1968), for example, challenged Lehman's conclusions about the decline in creativity with age. Lehman looked at *when a person produced their greatest works*. Dennis studied creative output, *the number of works a person produced*. He too measured the output of artists, scientists, scholars, and dancers. He found that in almost all fields, creativity, as measured by output, peaked between the ages of 40 and 49—about 10 years later than Lehman's findings. Dennis also found that creative output differed by field. Artists peaked earliest in life. Scholars such as historians showed little decline with age. They produced as much in their 70s as in their 40s.

Later studies by Simonton (1977, 1988, 1990) on great composers partly supported the idea that creativity declines with age. Simonton (1990) said, "If one plots creative output as a function of age, productivity tends to rise fairly rapidly to a definite peak and thereafter tends to decline gradually" (p. 322).

Does this mean that creativity ends in middle age? Simonton (2006) modified his view of creativity in a later study. He proposed a **constant-probability-of-success model**. This model states that the ratio of quality works to total works produced during a career stays the same at every stage of the career. An older person may produce fewer masterpieces but will also produce fewer mediocre works. In other words, people can produce great works at every age. Sophocles, Michelangelo, Goethe, Picasso, Winston Churchill, Grandma Moses, and Georgia O'Keefe, to name just a few artists, writers, and politicians, all remained creative past the age of 80.

Why does creativity decline with age in some people? Simonton found that a decline in health, a decrease in energy, changes in a profession, and different goals and motivations later in life all explain the decline in creative output. A person's chosen field will also make a difference. Dancers, gymnasts, and figure skaters, for example, will naturally peak earlier than other creative artists. Painters

and musicians will have longer creative careers. Historians may come into their prime only toward the end of their careers, when their knowledge and experience have ripened.

Cohen (2005) notes that a historian at age 75, for example, could outshine a 25-year-old Rhodes history scholar when it comes to discussing or interpreting history. Arnold Toynbee, the great historian, at age 77 wrote that a historian needs time to develop the expertise necessary for great achievement. Simonton (2006) concluded that past research "may underestimate the creativity of older individuals. The decline may be neither drastic nor inexorable" (p. 270).

Galenson (2006) provided another view of creativity in later life. Galenson's work helps explain why some creative people peak early in their careers, while others show great creativity throughout their lives. Galenson focused on the work of modern artists and writers. He discovered two styles of creativity—experimental innovation and conceptual innovation. Each type of artist and writer approaches creative work differently. And these two approaches show up as creative excellence at different stages in the life cycle.

People can express their creativity at every age. Orchestra conductors, for example, can produce great work late in life. In some fields (music, philosophy, history), it may take a lifetime of experience and reflection to understand the depth of a subject.

---

constant-probability-of-success model states that the ratio of quality works to total works produced during a career stays the same at every stage of the career

Experimental innovators in art focus on presenting visual perceptions. Impressionist artists like Monet and Cezanne fall into this category. They work in a tentative style and paint the same scene or object many times. They use their art to search for perfection in their work. They build their skill and knowledge throughout their careers, and their work improves slowly over time. Cezanne would paint a mountain over and over again in search of a satisfying image. Cezanne said about his art, "I seek in painting."

In contrast to experimentalists, conceptual innovators communicate a specific idea or emotion. They know the goal of each work precisely. They create detailed preparatory sketches and then produce a preconceived image. The great conceptual innovators break with tradition. They develop a new style or approach to art that appears suddenly. Conceptual innovators do not view their work as a search for truth through the production of the work. The conceptual innovator shows in a work of art what he or she has already found. Pablo Picasso, one of the great conceptual innovators, said about his art, "I don't seek; I find." Picasso, like most conceptual innovators, created his most important idea in his early years—he created cubism in his mid-20s.

Galenson showed that the artistic approach of the painter leads to different peak ages in his or her creative output. Experimenters (like Cezanne) peak later because of their approach—a slow, methodical search for their ideal visual presentation. Conceptual artists (like Picasso) produce great works early because they have the end already in mind and they produce sudden breaks with tradition.

Galenson admitted that this simple theory does not capture the many variations in artistic approach. He noted, for example, that some artists show a more extreme version of each approach, others a more moderate version. He also found that artists can change their approach as they arrive at their mature style. Galenson considered the link between artistic styles and the life cycle "not laws, but tendencies" (p. 61). Still, his work showed that the production of great work has as much to do with the artist's personality and approach to art as it does with the artist's age.

The research on creativity showed that it can take place at any age. In some fields, such as physics, mathematics, and sports, young people show the greatest creativity. But in other fields, like history, philosophy, and art, compared with younger people, older people can produce more creative work and greater creative work. The personality of the artist, conceptual or experimental, also determines the amount and quality of an artist's work.

In some fields, it takes a lifetime of learning, thinking, and integrating knowledge to make a great contribution. The most creative people continue to express themselves throughout their lives.

Creativity as Personal Expression

Creativity can refer to a great achievement or a form of personal expression. This last perspective treats creativity as a source of individual satisfaction, regardless of how other people judge the works produced.

Cohen (2005) reported that creativity can improve the health of older adults. One study compared 150 older people involved in community-based arts programs with 150 people not in this kind of program. The arts groups met once a week for 35 weeks. Cohen and his co-researchers found that many of the people in the arts groups showed stable health over a two-year period, and the health of some improved. The study found that, compared with the control group, people in the arts groups reported fewer doctor visits, better mental health, and the use of fewer medications. The group members averaged 80 years old.

Cohen conducted another study of a professionally led choral group (Cohen et al., 2007). This program included 128 people with an average age of 79. The members of the group attended 30 practice sessions and gave 10 public concerts. The researchers used a control group to assess the effect of this program. The researchers found fewer doctor visits, less medication use, less depression, and better morale among the choral group members.

Cohen (2005) said that challenging mental activity and the achievement of control and mastery led to better health and good mental function. Patterson and Perlstein (2011) said, "the benign stress of performance, rehearsal, and the sharing of personally meaningful creative products may stimulate" the protective effects Cohen described (p. 28).

A study of older students in a theatre course (Noice & Noice, 2009) found that participants increased their recall and problem-solving ability. The theatre group, compared with a control group and a visual arts group, reported significantly greater feelings of psychological well-being. The researchers said that theatre training fuses intellectual challenge with social relationships. These features of theatre training lead to better mental performance and better mental health.

Phinney, Moody, and Small (2014) studied the effect of a community-engaged arts program on the physical, emotional, and social lives of participants. The program held weekly workshops in four settings over a three-year period. Artists worked with seniors to produce collective art pieces or performances for the public. The researchers used questionnaires and interviews to assess the impact of program.

An analysis of the results showed that "seniors experienced improvement in perceived overall health, experience of pain, and sense of community" (p. 336). The seniors in the program appreciated the program's structure. One participant said, "[It's given us] a greater sense of mental strength ... a sense of responsibility that say, on a Tuesday, I have something to participate in" (p. 340). Another member said simply, "[It's given me] a reason to get out of bed" (p. 340).

The participants also appreciated the extended commitment they had to make to their project and group. "It's forward looking," one group member said (p. 340). Members in all of the groups described the personal transformation and growth that took place through this program. Finally, the participants spoke about the importance of community and social engagement that they felt. They described a "feeling of belonging" and having a place "within community" (p. 341).

Other studies also show that social engagement leads to improved mental ability (Stine-Morrow et al., 2007). Ristau (2011), in a review of the literature, reported the following good effects on mental potential from social engagement:

- Increased happiness in everyday life (Carstensen, 2009)
- Increased brain reserve (Nussbaum, 2009)
- Increased neuron production (Brown & Park, 2003)
- Reduced or delayed onset of dementia (Crooks et al., 2008)
- Reduced impact of Alzheimer's disease on people with large social networks (Bennett, Schneider, Tang et al., 2006)
- Activation of neural circuits through online social connections (Small & Vorgan, 2008)

Ristau (2011) concluded from the research "that people with regular social ties are significantly less likely to demonstrate cognitive decline when compared to those who are lonely or isolated" (p. 70).

Older people today have more opportunities than ever before to engage in creative and personally and socially rewarding activity (Solan, 2007). This view of creativity makes later life a time of potential discovery and self-renewal rather than a time of decline.

PSYCHOLOGICAL DISORDERS: ABNORMAL AGING

Studies of memory, intelligence, and creativity describe the normal changes that come with aging, but some people show abnormal changes as they age. They may suffer from psychological problems such as paranoia, anxiety neuroses, and schizophrenia. Experts call these *functional disorders* because they interfere with how a person functions. These problems have no clear organic cause, and some older people may have suffered from them throughout their lives.

Other people suffer from organic disorders. At least two different types of organic disorders show up in old age. First, some people enter old age with an existing developmental disability (e.g., Down syndrome). Second, some people develop a disease of the brain or an illness such as Alzheimer's disease or Parkinson's disease. Writers refer to these disorders as *organic brain syndrome, senile dementia,* or *simply dementia.*

Keep in mind that a relatively small number of older people suffer from these disorders. About 69 percent of older people reported very good or excellent mental health in 2011–2012. The *Canadian Community Health Survey* in 2012 found that 80 percent of people age 65 and over had "complete mental health" (Gilmour, 2014). They are flourishing and free of mental illness. Older people have higher rates of "flourishing mental health" than nearly all other age groups (p. 5).

Still, psychological disorders exist and they create distress for some seniors and their families. These disorders also place demands on the formal healthcare system. For this reason, psychological distress in later life affects families and the wider society

Organic Brain Disorders

Intellectual and Developmental Disability (ID/DD)

Intellectual disability refers to disorders that lead to limited mental capacity and problems with daily activities such as managing money and social interaction. This type of disability begins before age 18 and often comes from a physical cause such as autism or cerebral palsy.

---

intellectual disability refers to disorders that lead to limited mental capacity and problems with daily activities such as managing money and social interaction

Developmental disability refers to the effects of diseases such as Down syndrome. These illnesses usually begin at birth and affect a person's function in society throughout his or her life. People with developmental disabilities show limitations in conceptual, social, and practical skills as they age. Developmental disability encompasses intellectual disability, but includes physical disabilities such as blindness from birth (National Institutes of Health, 2013). We will use the term *developmental disability* (DD) to include both types of disability.

Little data exists on the prevalence of developmental disability in Canada. Figures for the United States give some indication of DD prevalence. The U.S. Census Bureau in 2010 reported that 1.2 million adults (0.5 percent of the adult population) had an intellectual disability (such as mental retardation) and 944,000 adults (0.4 percent of the adult population) experienced other DDs, such as cerebral palsy or autism (Brault, 2012, cited in Siberski et al., 2015).

Better treatment and medical care have led to longer life expectancies for people with developmental disabilities. Bittles et al. (2007; also Hirst, Lane, & Seneviratne, 2013) reported that in the last two generations, life expectancy for people with Down syndrome increased from 12 to nearly 60 years of age. This advance has led to an increase in the number of people with developmental disabilities in later life. Many of these people now live in the community, a trend that will increase in the future.

People with developmental disabilities face unique issues as they age. First, they frequently age prematurely. They face an increased risk of earlier-onset Alzheimer's disease, vision impairment, hearing loss, and depression (Krinsky-McHale et al., 2008; Wiseman et al., 2009). In their 40s and 50s, they may need to be supported as if they were 20 or 30 years older (Hirst, Lane, & Seneviratne, 2013). Second, they rarely have children or a spouse to give them support. Third, they will rarely have a pension, savings, or other personal economic resources.

People with a developmental disability also show a tendency toward certain health problems. For example, they show a high rate of gum and dental disease. They show a high rate of death due to respiratory and heart disease. People with Down syndrome show a high rate of cancer. People with DD may experience the start of dementia at an early age (e.g., 40 years old) and people with DD show a high rate of dementia (Hirst, Lane, & Seneviratne, 2013).

People with DD will rely heavily on social services and public support. But social services and government policies often fail to serve their needs. Their relative youth (most need help before age 65) often makes them ineligible for programs open to older people. Also, current housing and recreation options for seniors often fail to meet the needs of a younger person with a developmental disability.

People with developmental disabilities need a wide choice of social support and housing options, including group home living and supported independent living. They also need special programs to support work, leisure, and retirement. These programs should focus on their individual needs and should promote social integration, autonomy, and economic independence.

Janicki and colleagues (2005) found that people with Down syndrome, for example, placed greater hygiene and behaviour demands on staff in group homes. Sparks and colleagues (2000) found a need for training among agencies that provided services to people with a developmental disability. Agencies that served clients with developmental disabilities reported that their staff needed training in general aging and dementia care. Service providers also felt the need for health and medical information. They "expressed concern about the lack of well-trained medical specialists available to serve aging adults with DD" (p. 215). For example, "gerontological nurses need to be aware of the increased risk for specific health conditions for this population, be watchful for these conditions, and ensure periodic monitoring for potential complications" (Hirst, Lane, & Seneviratne, 2013).

Ward, Nichols, and Freedman (2010) studied disparities and inequities in healthcare among people with DD. They conducted focus groups with family members of someone with a DD and healthcare professionals. They found inequities in access to healthcare, knowledge of health issues, communication about healthcare, and the quality of care provided. A study by Kirby and Hegarty (2010) found that nurses who worked with DD patients did not promote breast awareness with this group.

Sparks and his colleagues (2000) proposed a number of actions to better serve adults with developmental disabilities. These include better education for service providers, integration of adults with developmental disabilities into existing programs, and help for clients with developmental disabilities in finding recreation and activities in retirement. This relatively small but growing number of older people will pose challenges to current policies and social services.

Some studies have looked at ways to improve the functioning of people with DD. A study by Siberski and

---

developmental disability a significant impairment in mental ability present at birth or acquired in childhood or adolescence

colleagues (2015) assessed the effects of a training program designed to improve the cognitive ability of people with a developmental disability. The study compared a cognitive training group with two control groups (a computer games group and a wait list group). The study used computer-based training with the experimental group—a novel approach. The cognitive training group worked at a program called "Cognifit." The program provided 21 training tasks on three levels. Tasks mixed visual, auditory, and cross-modality work on "a wide range of cognitive processes" (p. 43).

The study came to several conclusions. First, with supervision, 100 percent of the DD training group and the games group completed the program. Second, the study did not find a statistically significant difference between the training and the control groups. The small sample size, 11 in the training group, 32 in all, possibly explains the lack of statistically significant improvement. In spite of this finding, the researchers said, "The results of the study were encouraging as to the potential of the adult population with ID/DD if only given the opportunity to improve their cognitive functioning...."

A similar study of computerized training (Finn & McDonald, 2011) found a mixture of results. Subjects with DD showed a significant improvement in visual attention when compared to a control group. But the study found no difference on other measures (e.g., visual working memory) and no generalizability of the results to memory in everyday life. This study also used a small sample size and this may account for the lack of significant findings. These studies suggested the need to further refine training methods.

Hirst, Lane, and Seneviratne said that people with DD would benefit from exercise programs, health promotion programs, and programs that screen for certain diseases. But health promotion, treatment studies, and screening programs may not invite these people to participate (Hirst, Lane, & Seneviratne, 2013, citing Davies & Duff, 2001; also Sinai, Bohnen, & Strydom, 2012). Hirst and colleagues said "the implication is that these adults experience aging from a position of vulnerability rather than strength" (p. 43).

Hirst and colleagues also said that people with DD would benefit from health education (including education about physical changes such as menopause). A person with DD will experience changes associated with aging (such as arthritis) in addition to already existing physical problems. Education related to aging would help a person with DD understand these physical changes. Education can also help a person use aids such as eyeglasses or a walker.

Again, staff and healthcare providers play an important role here. Hirst and colleagues (2013) said, "If staff underestimate an individual's potential for social engagement, they are unlikely to encourage the wearing of glasses or a hearing aid" (p. 45). Likewise a person with DD should have the same choices as anyone else with respect to death and dying. This includes decisions about end of life care and palliative care.

Many studies in the literature on older adults and DD refer to the lack of attention this group gets from healthcare and social service providers. Hirst and colleagues (2013) say that people with DD "experience the aging process from different and disadvantageous starting points than the general population" (p. 49). As more people with DD live longer and enter old age, they will make up a larger part of professionals' practice. But ageism combined with stereotyping often limit the support given to a person with DD.

Professional caregivers play an important role in the lives of older DD clients and patients. The person with DD may no longer have living parents or siblings. Decision making then falls to professional caregivers. This makes professional staff knowledge and awareness of DD doubly important. Finally, best practice in the care and treatment of people with DD includes empowering them to make choices about their own care. This requires respect for the individual and appreciation of each person's potential.

Cognitive Impairment in Later Life

Organic brain syndrome, senile dementia, and *dementia* are general terms used to describe a variety of organic brain disorders. Organic disorders lead to confusion and forgetfulness, and may lead to antisocial behaviour. Some individuals with these disorders wander, strike

Women usually serve as family caregivers throughout the life course. They care for children in early adulthood and often care for older family members later in life. Caregiving creates strong family bonds for women at every age, but it also leads to disadvantages for women in the workplace, due to disrupted work careers.

©Dean Mitchell/iStockPhoto

out, or resist help from their caregivers. Dementia cases create stress for both professional care providers and family caregivers. As more people live into late old age, more people will experience dementia. But keep in mind that "Dementia is not a normal part of ageing" (World Health Organization, 2012, p. 4). It is a disease caused by abnormal changes in the brain.

The Causes of Dementia

A variety of illnesses lead to dementia in old age. A decreased blood supply to the brain, for example, causes vascular dementia. This often takes place after a stroke. It shows up as memory loss, confusion, and mood changes. Many other types of dementia can occur in later life. Some, such as Pick's disease and Creutzfeldt-Jakob disease, occur along with other diseases (Mayo Clinic, 2011a).

Alzheimer's disease (about 63 percent of all dementias) stands as the leading cause of dementia in later life. It "is a progressive, degenerative and fatal brain disease, in which cell to cell connections in the brain are lost and brain cells eventually die" (Alzheimer Society, 2010, p. 10). The disease shows up as plaques (clumps of beta-amyloid protein) and tangles (fibrous structures of tau protein). In the case of Alzheimer's disease, plaques and tangles in the brain increase over time. They cause the loss of memory, language, judgment, and a decrease in abstract thinking. Eventually they lead to breakdown in body functions and death.

Concern about an Increase in Dementia

The Alzheimer Society calls the increase in dementia cases in Canada an "epidemic." A background paper for federal, provincial, and territorial officials (Federal, Provincial and Territorial Committee of Officials [Seniors], 2006) called this "one of the greatest public health challenges of the coming generations" (p. 6).

Alzheimer's disease accounts for 64 percent of all dementias (Alzheimer Society of Canada, 2010). The Ontario Alzheimer Society (2010) reported that in 2008 nearly a half million people (480,600), or 1.5 percent of the Canadian population, suffered from dementia. The society projected that in 2038, this figure will more than double to over 1 million people (1,125,200), or 2.8 percent of the population.

The Alzheimer Society of Canada (2010) commissioned a report on the current and future impact of dementia on Canadian society. The report, titled *Rising Tide: The Impact of Dementia on Canadian Society*, poses economic and social challenges to Canadian society. For example, the cost of the increased numbers of dementia cases will grow more than tenfold between 2008 and 2038 (from $15 billion per year to $153 billion per year). This amounts to a cumulative total of $872 billion for this 30-year period. At the same time, the society's report projects that informal care—most of it offered by family members—will increase more than threefold, from 231 million hours in 2008 to 756 million hours in 2038.

The aging of the older population in part explains this increase in dementia cases. The proportion of people age 60 and over with dementia is projected to increase from 7 percent to 9 percent between 2008 and 2038. The proportion of people age 90 and over with dementia will increase from 49 percent to 50 percent for these same years. Longer life for Canadians will mean more people with Alzheimer's disease in the older population and this in turn will mean more need for family, community, and institutional support.

The Alzheimer Society (2010; also Diamond, 2008) report proposed a number of interventions that would buffer the impact of this disease. These include a healthy diet, aerobic exercise, and an active social life. Meade and Park (2009) agreed that social activity can prevent or delay dementia. A Swedish longitudinal study, for example, found that the risk of dementia increased by 60 percent in people with a limited social network.

The Alzheimer Society report also encourages intellectual activity—reading, doing puzzles, and playing chess. These activities appear to develop a cognitive reserve. Snowdon's (2001) classic "Nun Study" supported this approach. He found that, compared with nuns who did physical work in the convent, nuns who engaged in mentally stimulating activity showed less likelihood of getting Alzheimer's disease. The Alzheimer Society's report (2010; also Wierenga & Bondi, 2011) said that "promoting brain health through lifestyle choices is the most effective way of reducing the chances of developing Alzheimer's disease or a related dementia or slowing down the progression of these diseases in people who already have them" (pp. 12–13). The report also supported increased funding for dementia research, increased prevention and early intervention, caregiver supports, case management, and increasing and educating Canada's dementia workforce.

The strategies above would reduce the impact of dementia on Canada's social and economic resources. The report stated that they would save Canadian society hundreds of billions of dollars over the 30 years between 2008 and 2038.

Slaughter and Bankes (2007) report that people in the community with Alzheimer's disease on average lose one functional ability every two months. People in the early stage of the disease will tend to lose instrumental activities of daily living like driving, banking, or cooking. People in the middle and later stages lose activities of daily living abilities like bathing, dressing, or toileting. Slaughter and Bankes said that people with Alzheimer's disease may also suffer from other illnesses (e.g., an infection) or medical complications (e.g., drug interactions). This creates "excess disability"—disability that further decreases a person's daily ability to function.

Physicians often cannot make a certain diagnosis of the disease's presence except after death (Cosentino, Brickman, & Manly, 2011; Wierenga & Bondi, 2011). They first try to rule out other causes of confusion and personality decline such as brain tumours, blood pressure problems, or hyperthyroidism. A patient might have a treatable illness or a problem such as overmedication or infection. Primary care physicians agree on the importance of cognitive assessment, and many carry out these assessments in their practice (Chow et al., 2009; Iracleous

et al., 2010). Still, studies find long delays (as long as two years) between first symptoms and a diagnosis (Morgan et al., 2009).

New tests and assessment tools should help with diagnosis and treatment. Tools include "neuroimaging, such as magnetic resonance imaging (MRI) hippocampal volume measures, and positron emission tomography (PET) scanning...." (Chertkow, 2008) These assessment tools "result in a 90 to 95 per cent accurate diagnosis" of AD today (Diamond, 2008, p. 8).

Tierney and Charles (2002) report on the development of an Alzheimer Predictive Index. Physicians can use this index to assess people who have some memory loss. Research shows that 89 percent of the time the index can predict the onset of Alzheimer's disease within two years. This index and other new methods will lead to quicker diagnosis in the future (Standish et al., 2007). Early diagnosis helps families cope with the disease's progress. Research on early treatment may develop ways to slow or stop the progress of the disease.

EXHIBIT 6.3   *The Stages of Decline Due to Alzheimer's Disease*

Reports often describe the three stages that an Alzheimer's patient goes through. Some people may go through these stages in a few months; for others, it may take years. The changes that come with Alzheimer's disease begin slowly. Often family members recognize the first signs only when they look back over a year or two of caregiving.

Stage I: A person first shows changes in memory. He or she forgets the keys or a wallet more frequently. The person may also forget recent events or forget that he or she did a job around the house. The forgetfulness gets worse over time. The person forgets more often, takes longer to do simple jobs, or begins to recheck work already done.

One woman recalls that her husband, an engineering professor, would spend three or four hours writing a 50-minute lecture that used to take him an hour to write. Another woman recalls that she first became worried when her husband, a physician, lost his way home from work one night. He planned to stop at a patient's house for a short house call around 5 p.m. The patient lived only a few blocks away from their house, so his wife expected him home by 6 p.m. She began to worry at 8 p.m. when she still hadn't heard from him. An hour later he came in exhausted. He had spent the last three hours driving around their neighbourhood looking for their house.

Stage II: The second stage of the disease includes more memory decline, loss of speaking ability, and an end to normal daily activity. The ill person may wander at night, lose control of his or her bowel and bladder, and threaten others. One woman left a knife in her garden after she used it to weed the flowerbed. Her husband picked it up and stalked through the bushes into

a neighbour's yard, saying to the neighbour, "I'm going to kill you." The neighbour ran inside and called the police. When the man's wife came outside to finish weeding, she found the police wrestling her husband into a squad car.

In another case, a man walked into a new car dealership and signed a contract for a $40,000 car. His wife found out only after the salesman called her to check on the financing. The owner of the dealership agreed to void the contract, but only after she pleaded and explained about her husband's illness.

This stage of the disease can put additional stress on the family. Caregivers—most often spouses or children of the ill person—can feel tense, trapped, and exhausted. Family members have to take on new roles: Wives become chauffeurs or nurses; children become parents or police; and husbands become homemakers.

Stage III: The person in the last stage of Alzheimer's disease needs institutionalization and often 24-hour nursing care. The person can no longer speak or communicate. He or she may wander or move constantly unless restrained. Seizures may occur. Death occurs between two and nineteen years after the disease starts. Death often comes from an illness such as pneumonia or heart disease, but death certificates rarely mention Alzheimer's disease as a cause of death, making it impossible to know the exact number of deaths associated with Alzheimer's.

Not all Alzheimer's patients show all the above-mentioned symptoms. Some show other symptoms of confusion such as depression and crying. But these stages give a general picture of the disease. They also give only a faint idea of the stress that Alzheimer's disease puts on the primary caregiver.

EXHIBIT 6.4   *The Social Construction of Dementia*

Social scientists have studied the social construction of mental disorders for many years. Thomas Szasz, for example, spoke of "the myth of mental illness" (1960, 1974). In his work, he described "mental illness" as a medicalization of "problems in living." The medicalization—medical treatment, drug therapy—served a number of purposes, not always for the good of the individual.

Szasz's work set off a controversy that goes on today. It raised questions about the power of the medical establishment to place a label on behaviour. And it brought awareness to the impact of labelling and the agents who benefited from this label. More recent developments in the diagnosis of dementia suggest a movement in this same direction—an "Alzheimerization" of old age.

Dr. Peter Whitehouse, professor of Neurology at Case Western Reserve University, has criticized the diagnostic category "mild cognitive impairment" (MCI). Peterson (2007) defined MCI as "a clinical transitional state between the cognitive changes of aging and the earliest clinical features of dementia." In an interview for the journal *Dementia* (Katz & Peters, 2015), Whitehouse noted that a decline in mental function does occur with age, but he took issue when this natural process became a clinical category or label. In addition, MCI has spawned a new category: pre-clinical AD [Alzheimer's disease] or pre-symptomatic AD that apparently precedes MCI. At this point, normal changes that come with age are trapped in a new net devised by this clinical category. Suddenly, normal aging becomes pre-clinical Alzheimer's disease.

Whitehouse pointed to the interests that drug companies may have in the early clinical labelling of dementia. On the one hand, this appears as a humanitarian goal. Identify the disease early, so treatment can begin early (to better effect). But drug companies have another goal—selling drugs. The earlier the diagnosis, the wider the audience for treatment and the more drugs the company can sell.

Whitehouse raised the question of who benefits from this labelling. He gave the example of two patients who get a diagnosis of MCI. One says, "I'm glad I don't have AD." The other says, "Now I have 10-15 per cent chance of getting AD." In neither case will the person get a clear benefit from drug therapy yet the person now has a label of a mental illness that he or she will have to live with. Whitehouse said, "I think increasingly people who are diagnosed are going to ask what they should be treated with. What is the clinical utility of these tests and labels? I think they're marginal and sometimes negative" (p. 381).

Finally, the focus on a drug-based, medical-model-based "cure" takes attention away from the many things a person can do to promote brain health. These include diet, exercise, having a purpose in life, and feeling a part of a social group.

The Alzheimer Society of Canada report *Rising Tide* (2010) made the following recommendations for a Canadian response to the increase in dementia cases:

1. *Increase the Investment in Dementia Research.* Ultimately, medical science needs to find a cure for Alzheimer's disease and other forms of dementia. The Canadian Institutes for Health Research spends about $21 million per year on dementia research. Ninety-five percent of these funds go to biomedical and clinical research. The Alzheimer Society spends another $3 million on research.

2. *Provide Support for Informal Caregivers.* This can take the form of training, respite programs, and support groups. Care for the caregiver will ensure better care for people with dementia. Ploeg and colleagues (2009) studied a sample of 1,152 adults age 50 and over in Hamilton, Ontario. The researchers asked these people what they knew about supports for adult child caregivers of elderly parents with dementia. About one-third of the sample mentioned each of the following: family doctor, family and neighbours, and home health supports. Only 18 percent of the people in the study mentioned community support services (e.g., adult daycare).

The researchers said, "Efforts should ... be made to increase the awareness of older persons and their caregivers related to available services for parental dementia" (p. 368). Knowledge and use of community supports would help caregivers cope with parental care. The researchers also called on physicians and other healthcare. providers to link family caregivers to dementia care community supports.

3. *Emphasize Prevention and Early Intervention.* Improved methods of detection and diagnosis will allow for early intervention. Some methods such as exercise and diet may delay or prevent some types of dementia.

4. *Build an Integrated System of Care.* This would link home care, respite care, and institutional care. It will allow people with dementia to get the care that suits their family's needs and the stage of the client's illness.

5. *Strengthen and Supplement the Dementia Workforce.* Canada needs to recruit and educate workers who understand the treatment needs of dementia patients. This includes training programs for future workers and on-the-job training for current workers.

EXHIBIT 6.5   *What Does It Feel Like to Have Dementia?*

Few studies before the 1990s reported on the experience of the person with dementia (Alzheimer Society, 2009). Of course, people in the later stages of the disease can't give an account of their experience, but people in the earlier stages can tell us something about how it feels to have this disease. Many studies treat dementia as a social problem, an economic problem, or a challenge to family members. A study by De Witt, Ploeg, and Black (2009) showed the meaning and impact of the disease on people who have the disease and cope with it daily.

The researchers studied eight women in Ontario who lived alone and had mild to moderate cases of dementia. These women described how this disease changed their lives.

One woman, named Leona, told the researchers, "I don't want to do anything wrong ... I don't want to make any big mistakes or anything ... [friend's name] made mistakes and then they would put her in the old people's home" (p. 274).

A woman named Faith spoke about hiding the illness. "[Y]ou want to hide it from people, you don't want people to see you in a way that you don't want to be seen." Another woman said, "[Y]ou hide ... you cover up, you don't admit to yourself, let alone to anybody else what's happening ... you try ... to appear quote unquote normal" (p. 279).

These women feared that someone (a family member? a doctor? a neighbour?) would label them incompetent. Then they might lose their freedom. Many of these women mention being "put in a home" as their greatest fear.

These women also describe the world closing in on them. One woman's children shut off her stove because she forgets that she's cooking. More than once, this set off a smoke detector. Now she can no longer bake. Another woman said that she can't

use her stove without supervision for fear of a fire (she has had two fires already). This makes it hard for her to prepare meals.

One woman lost her ability to drive. "The only thing I have problems with," she says, "is trying to be independent and do [grocery shopping] myself. I can't really get out and I miss the car in that respect" (p. 278). Another woman mentioned her decision not to attend a play. "I thought, what's the point of going? I'm not gonna remember anyways" (p. 282).

The disease distorts these women's relations with others (they need to display competence, to avoid "mistakes," to hide their illness). Dementia narrows their lives and creates paranoia. "You've got to trust and understand the people you're being open with and asking for help," one woman says, "because I have seen too many cases where they overreact, so it's a scary process to, to open up" (p. 279).

Paranoia can also creep in due to forgetfulness. One woman checks and rechecks her doors before going to bed. "You know how you go back to your door time after time after time to make sure it's locked? And that's the way it is now" (p. 283).

This study takes the reader into the world of the person with dementia. These women can still reflect on their condition—although they know they will get worse. They report to us from the early stages of their journey. And what do we learn? The disease affects a person's relations with others. It undermines trust in family and friends. Beneath many of these comments runs a thread of fear, defensiveness, and uncertainty. The tragedy of this disease goes beyond the loss of memory. Clément and colleagues (2009) said that mild cognitive impairment creates a "substantial burden on patients' lives because it diminishes well-being and creates concerns about changing family roles" (p. 148)

Professional caregivers can feel burdened by the demands of dementia patients. In the coming years, service workers will care for more and more clients with these illnesses. They will need to understand the basis of the illness and how to treat these clients. Healthcare workers say they "often feel ill-trained in the field of mental health; they don't know 'what to do' or 'what to say' to help" (Mental Health Commission of Canada, 2014, p. 5). Mental health and other healthcare professionals need ongoing training to support older people with dementia. Training should include communication skills and approaches to treatment.

Practical methods exist to help people manage the disease. A Memory Intervention Program teaches people with mild cognitive impairment strategies for coping with the disease (Baycrest, 2011). For example, the program teaches people to use a day planner to record names and activities. Participants learn about stress, relaxation, and nutrition. Studies show that programs like this delay the progress of the disease.

Roger and colleagues (2012) tested the use of Paro, "a tabletop robotic harp seal," with individuals who had dementia (p. 88). A Japanese company designed Paro to enhance communication and for therapeutic purposes. The designers refer to this as a "social commitment robot," one that develops a social relationship with its owner.

Roger and colleagues in Manitoba conducted a series of pilot studies on Paro's use with nursing home patients and at Deer Lodge Hospital in Winnipeg. The studies found mixed results with patients. One resident hesitated to interact with Paro. Two other residents showed improved mood. Adult children of these residents said their parents enjoyed the interaction and that it helped their parents feel less lonely. Staff seemed positive toward use of social commitment robots. Paro also helped family members communicate and interact with residents. The robot prompted dialogue and led to reminiscences and moments of humour and play.

The interest in the use of social commitment robots with dementia residents has grown internationally. Roger and colleagues report that in 2008, Denmark bought 1,000 Paro robots to use in nursing homes and 20 American nursing homes bought Paro robots for use with residents. The researchers said that, "Depending upon the results of this research, these robots may in the future become an integral part of therapeutic care and an improved quality of life for persons living with dementia" (p. 92).

Several drugs on the Canadian market (Ebixa, Aricept, Exelon, and Reminyl) may delay the decline in mental function for people with mild to moderate symptoms. The drugs may also help control behavioural symptoms (Diamond, 2008; National Institute on Aging, 2009).

Research continues on drugs that may slow the progress of the disease in its mid to later stages. Some drugs (e.g., Namenda) may allow patients to maintain daily functions, such as toileting, a little longer than without medication. This can ease the stress on caregivers.

Drugs, such as sleeping pills and antidepressants, can also control some symptoms. But, at present, nothing can stop the progress of the disease (Wierenga & Bondi, 2011). Scientists continue to work on finding a cure for Alzheimer's disease. Researcher Dr. Mary Tierney, a neuropsychologist and professor at the University of Toronto, studied the effects of menopause (a decrease in estrogen) on memory decline (Oosthoek, 2009). She found that a mix of estrogen—progesterone prevented memory decline in women who did not have dementia. (It had less effect on women who already had the disease.) She suggested that early treatment, before a woman experiences memory problems, could prevent or delay memory loss.

Genetic research and new technologies may lead to a future cure. Vogler (2006; also National Institute on Aging, 2009a) said researchers have found three genes that influence early onset or familial AD. Researchers have found

a fourth gene that influences late onset AD. These results may lead to early diagnosis and treatment of the disease. Stem cell treatment, another line of research, could regenerate brain cells. This approach shows promise, but Diamond (2008) says it may take many decades before stem cell therapy will reach the market.

TIME TO REVIEW

What fears do people express in the early stages of dementia?

What challenges do people with dementia pose for their family caregivers?

What treatments currently exist to help dementia patients and their families cope with this disease?

Why do policymakers and healthcare experts express concern about the potential growth in the number of dementia patients in Canada?

Functional Disorders

Functional disorders disrupt normal life. They include emotional upset, depression, and anxiety. Préville and colleagues (2009) reported that in Quebec, nearly 13 percent of seniors in the community had a mood or anxiety disorder. Many of these people needed mental health services.

Still, the majority of community-dwelling older people today report generally good mental health. In 2009, the *Canadian Community Health Survey* asked a sample of people from across Canada to report on their mental health. Turcotte (2011a; also Gilmour, 2011) found that 70 percent of seniors said they had very good or excellent mental health. Seniors, compared to all other age groups, had the lowest proportion of people (less than 10 percent) who said their days felt "quite a bit stressful or extremely stressful" (p. 8). Retirement from the demands of work probably accounts for this absence of stress.

Depression

Depression refers to a state when a person feels sad, helpless, irritable, and hopeless. Symptoms of depression include lack of interest, feelings of worthlessness, poor ability to concentrate, inability to make decisions, insomnia, loss or gain of weight, and suicidal thoughts. George (2011) called depression "the most prevalent psychiatric disorder in the older population" (p. 149). As many as 44 percent of older people in long-term care

Photo by Dominic Bracco Ii/The Washington Post/Getty Images

Nursing homes in the United States, Japan, Denmark, and Canada use Paro, a "social commitment robot" to enrich the lives of older people in nursing homes.

depression the emotional state of feeling sad, helpless, irritable, and hopeless

homes (nursing homes) had a diagnosis of depression or multiple depressive symptoms (Canadian Institute for Health Information, 2010).

In general, studies have found that the risk of depression decreases in later life. But many cases of depression exist below the level of clinical diagnosis. Préville and colleagues (2009) said that older people tend not to report feelings of depression. So studies may underestimate the actual rate of depression among older people.

Andrew and Rockwood (2007) reviewed data from the *Canadian Study of Health and Aging* and found a 12.6 percent rate of psychiatric illness among community-dwelling older Canadians. Préville and colleagues (2009) reported a similar rate (12.9 percent) of "psychological distress symptoms that met criteria for a DSM-IV

[a manual of psychological disorders] diagnosis" (p. 55). Most of these people reported depression. About 1 percent reported both depression and another psychiatric illness. Other studies reported similar rates of depression among older populations (Knight et al., 2006). Mental distress often accompanies physical illness. For example, Mac-Court, Wilson, and Tourigny-Rivard (2011) reported that about 40 percent of stroke victims experience depression.

People with resources such as social skills, problem-solving ability, and emotional support from family and friends will less likely feel depressed. A person who appraises a situation as non-threatening or who copes actively to improve situations will also show less depression. People with more education, for example, tend to report less psychological distress, and they tend to make

---

EXHIBIT 6.6   *The Three Ds of Psychological Distress: Delirium, Depression, and Dementia*

The three Ds—delirium, depression, and dementia—threaten the well-being of older people, often in late old age. These mental disorders pose problems for clinicians and staff members in nursing homes. Residents may suffer from more than one of these disorders. For example, a person with dementia (a cognitive disorder) may also suffer from depression (a mood disorder). And the symptoms of each disorder can overlap. This makes diagnosis and treatment a challenge for physicians and other healthcare professionals (Gagliardi, 2008).

The descriptions below sort out some of the unique features of each disorder.

Depression

Definition: A person feels sad, helpless, irritable, and hopeless.

Symptoms: Recent unexplained change in mood; lack of interest, insomnia, feelings of worthlessness, poor ability to concentrate, inability to make decisions, insomnia, loss or gain of weight, and suicidal thoughts; slow onset over weeks or months.

Causes/Risk: After a stroke a person may feel sad and depressed. Gagliardi (2008) reported that 25 to 50 percent of stroke patients show major depressive disorder.

Test/Treatment: Geriatric Depression Scale, Mood Disorder Questionnaire, and other instruments designed to assess a person's mental state. Assessment of suicide risk. A physician should also assess a person for any underlying medical illnesses; low mood, no apparent underlying medical condition, and no cognitive impairment suggest depression as a diagnosis; depression responds to treatment.

Delirium

Definition: An acute confusional state; disorganized thinking, disturbed attention. Gagliardi (2008) said that 10 to 30 percent of hospitalized older patients in the United States showed delirium.

Symptoms: Apathy, lethargy, low mood; misperceptions, illusions, emotional outbursts, crying; rapid onset in hours or days.

Causes/Risk: An underlying medical disorder, e.g., a urinary tract infection; medications such as benzodiazepines and narcotic pain medications; other physical disorders.

Test/Treatment: Confusion Assessment Method (a questionnaire screening tool) may signal a medical emergency; treatment should focus on correcting the underlying physical cause of delirium; acute, sudden onset suggests delirium as a diagnosis; delirium responds to treatment;

Dementia

Definition: Progressive cognitive impairment that affects memory, Gagliardi (2008) estimated that 5 percent of people age 71–80 and 37 percent of people age 90 and over in the United States suffered from dementia; language, judgment, and reasoning decline.

Symptoms: Missed appointments, forgetting instructions, accidents, and poor hygiene, in later stages, a person may forget the way home and even forget the names of family members; a person can display changes in mood and may express delusions of persecution or hallucinations.

Causes/Risk: Underlying degeneration of the brain; slow, chronic progression over months and years.

Test/Treatment: Folstein Mini-Mental State Examination, Clock Drawing Test, Addenbrooke's Cognitive Examination—Revised (ACE-R). A physician can help a patient manage symptoms such as depression. Lack of awareness or reporting mental problems such as forgetfulness suggest dementia as a diagnosis; no known treatment exists for Alzheimer's Disease (a common form of dementia).

Sources: Gagliardi, J.P. (2008). Differentiating among depression, delirium, and dementia in elderly patients. *American Medical Association Journal of Ethics*, 10(6), 383–388; Lischka, A.R., Mendelsohn, M., Overend, T., & Forbes, D. (2012). A systematic review of screening tools for predicting the development of dementia. *Canadian Journal on Aging*, 31(3), 295–311; *Toronto Best Practice in LTC Initiative*. (2007). Recognizing delirium, depression and dementia (3Ds). Retrieved from http://rgp.toronto.on.ca/torontobestpractice/ThreeDcomparison.pdf.

more use of mental healthcare services when they need them (Cole et al., 2008). Social as well as psychological conditions influence depression. People who lack education, have a low income, live in poor health or with a disability, and have few social supports show higher rates of depression (George, 2011).

Social support buffers the effect of poor health and protects a person from feeling depressed. Divorced people, people who live alone, and people with few social supports report psychological distress (Préville et al., 2009). Andrew and Rockwood (2007) found that the frailest older people showed the greatest tendency toward depression. The inability to get out and the loss of social supports can also lead to unhappiness or depression.

Gilbart and Hirdes (2000) studied institutionalized older people in Ontario hospitals and found that many of the residents reported sadness and some anxiety. People with the least social engagement reported the least happiness. A decrease in social supports in later life puts the mental health of infirm and isolated older Canadians at risk. Gilbart and Hirdes said that care planning should take a holistic approach, including attention to patients' psychosocial as well as physical needs.

Treatment and Intervention for Functional Disorders

Mental health experts sometimes overlook the needs of older people. Préville and colleagues (2009) said that general practitioners tend to overlook their patients' mental problems—especially mood and anxiety problems. They tend to treat these problems as a normal part of aging and they tend not to send patients for treatment.

Stones and colleagues (2006) said that 40 percent to 55 percent of people in long-term care settings who have depressive symptoms fail to get treatment. Older people may experience depression without displaying sadness (a common symptom in younger people). For this reason, healthcare workers may fail to diagnose it.

Préville and colleagues (2009) found that 57 percent of people in a Quebec study probably needed treatment for mental health problems but did not get treatment. Cole and colleagues (2008) found a similar result when they analyzed data from the *Canadian Community Health Survey* (CCHS). They found that less than one-third of the seniors in this study, who had major depressive symptoms, used a mental health service. The Préville team "concluded that a large proportion of mental health needs in Quebec are potentially not being met" (p. 58). Based on the CCHS study, the same could be said for Canada as a whole.

Rural Canadian seniors face special problems in getting mental health services. Services may not exist in their area, they may live a long distance from services, and they may have trouble getting to services. Indigenous seniors in rural areas often lack diagnostic and mental health services. Rural areas also lack specialists who can make an accurate diagnosis and begin early treatment.

Morgan and colleagues (2009) reported the success of a one-day-per-week memory clinic in rural areas in Saskatchewan. Their study of this clinic compared onsite and telehealth (videoconferencing) for mental health assessment and neurological exams. Patients and caregivers felt high satisfaction with telehealth. Healthcare professionals, through this system, gained the benefit of a team approach to mental healthcare delivery.

A range of treatments can help older people cope with psychological problems. An individual's characteristics (including age), the diagnosis criteria used, the older person's adaptation patterns, and the intervention setting (community or institution) all influence the choice of treatment. For example, some reversible organic brain syndromes can be treated with chemical therapies. Physicians can treat alcoholics in the early stages of Wernicke-Korsakoff dementia (a neurological disease) with large doses of thiamine.

Many therapies exist for older people with functional problems (problems related to a person's personality or social life). Drug therapy, for example, can help older people cope with anxiety and depression. Stones and colleagues (2006) said that long-term care institutions often use drug therapy to treat depression; however, non-drug therapies can also help relieve depression and its symptoms. Behaviour therapy, for example, can help with insomnia, and psychotherapy can help people with personality disorders.

Life review can help with adaptation to loss, and milieu therapy, where a person makes changes to his or her environment, can help a person deal with stress-related problems. Interpersonal therapy focuses on improved responses to grief, interpersonal disputes, role transitions, and interpersonal deficits. These methods show good results with older people (Knight et al., 2006).

Knight and colleagues reported that, compared with psychosocial treatment (e.g., support groups or social activities), psychotherapeutic treatments (e.g., behaviour therapy or psychotherapy) proved more effective. Also, compared with group therapies, individual therapies proved more effective. Cognitive behavioural therapy (CBT) helps people think more positive thoughts and engage in more positive behaviour. This method shows some of the strongest effect in reducing depression.

Nursing home residents could benefit from CBT. Yet, Konnert, Dobson, and Stelmach (2009) said, few studies have looked at alternatives to drug treatment for these people. They conducted a controlled clinical trial of CBT and found significant reductions in depression for residents in their study who took CBT training. In addition, all but one of the residents who responded to a satisfaction question found the training satisfactory. All of these people rated the program as "very helpful in preventing future depression" (p. 294). The researchers conclude that this approach "may be very helpful for preventing depression in nursing home residents" (p. 297).

A policy statement by the Canadian Association on Gerontology (CAG) (MacCourt, Tuokko, & Tierney, 2002) pointed out the need for specialized training for healthcare providers and special services to meet the needs of older people. Special services include day programs, outpatient assessment units, and community outreach programs designed to serve psychogeriatric patients. Lee, Hillier, and Weston (2014) described the development of a multidisciplinary memory clinic in Ontario. This community-based setting brings together a family physician, nurses, social worker, pharmacist, and occupational therapist. The clinic provides high-quality assessment and primary care management. The CAG policy statement supports this type of program. It promotes a multidisciplinary response to older persons' mental health needs.

Zarit (2009) says that prevention offers the best way to ensure good mental health in old age. Preventive methods include maintaining good physical health, developing a web of positive relationships, and engaging in interests that stimulate the mind. A person needs to do these things at every stage of life. In later stages, they may save the person's life.

The Stigma of Mental Disorder

A person with a mental disorder faces many challenges. Activities of daily living such as bathing and eating can pose a challenge. Social relations can break down and leave a person isolated and alone. The stigma of a mental disorder adds to the distress that a person must cope with. Stigma refers to "labeling, stereotyping, status loss, and discrimination" (LeClair & Wilson, 2011 cited in Mental Health Commission of Canada, 2014, p. 2).

The *Canadian General Social Survey* in 2009 (cited in Mental Health Commission of Canada, 2015) asked people whether they experienced discrimination in their lives. More than one-third of Canadians with a mental health condition (37.9 percent) reported discrimination or unfair treatment over the past five years. The stigma of mental disorder can limit a person's access to social and healthcare services. It can keep a person from a job and from housing. The Mental Health Commission (2015, p. 55) called such discrimination "a risk factor for poor mental health."

The Canadian government created and distributed a *Mental Health First Aid Canada* manual to combat stigma. The manual aims to increase mental health literacy and understanding of mental disorders. A training program goes along with the manual. The Mental Health Commission of Canada (MHCC) distributed nearly 140,000 manuals by the spring of 2015. This provides some indication of the number of people who got training through this program. This program makes up part of the MHCC's anti-stigma initiative called "Opening Minds"—designed to "change the attitudes and behaviours of Canadians towards people with a mental health problem or mental illness" (Mental Health Commission of Canada, 2014, p. 4).

Roger et al. (2012) said that people who lose their cognitive ability also risk losing their personhood. The disease can dominate others' perception and treatment of the person. Smith (2012, p. 256) said that a supportive social environment "becomes a crucial aspect of sustaining personhood in dementia." He went on to say that people with dementia have a right to remain active decision makers in their lives. Rogers and colleagues said, "that even those with extreme limitations ought to be viewed as whole persons experiencing contentment, self-worth, self-esteem, purposefulness, peacefulness, and spirituality" (p. 88).

In one case, a group of brothers who golfed together continued to take their oldest brother with them even after he could no longer follow the game due to dementia. They would help him set up his first shot. The ball might go anywhere. The brothers would march down the fairway. After a time they would drop a ball and encourage their oldest brother to take his next shot. He would hit his next shot without any recollection of his earlier one. In this way, the brothers had an enjoyable afternoon out. No one felt frustrated about their oldest brother's loss of memory or his poor golfing skill. They valued his personhood above the problems caused by his disease.

Intuitively this family knew what researchers and healthcare providers now understand in principle. "Personhood," Roger and colleagues said, "has thus come to frame an internationally accepted approach to caring for those with dementia" (p. 88).

The Loss of Competence

Psychological intervention can sometimes protect the older person from harm. It can also lead to making decisions for people who can no longer decide for themselves. A person with a cognitive impairment may lose the ability to understand his or her situation and make decisions. But when should another person step in to make decisions for someone else? This should occur only after a careful assessment of a person's competency.

Legal and clinical professionals use the terms *competency* and *capacity* interchangeably. These terms refer to a person's "cognitive, decisional, affective, and practical abilities to adequately complete a specific task (e.g., drive a car) or make a specific decision (e.g., refuse a medical treatment)" (Moye et al., 2011, p. 368). Wilkins et al. (2009) defined competency as "the ability to understand the relevant information, to appreciate the significance of the information and how it applies to them, to reason the risks and benefits of potential options, and to express a choice" (p. 34).

Generally, Wilkins and colleagues said, a person is assumed to possess decision-making capacity "until there is evidence to the contrary" (p. 34). When necessary, a professional (a physician, psychiatrist, or other recognized expert) formally decides a person's competency through an assessment. An assessment attempts to answer the question of whether a person should lose his or her legal rights based on his or her inability to make a decision.

An assessment should ensure the same assessment standards for everyone and the absence of an assessor's bias. Also, assessment should take place more than once to monitor a person's present and future ability to make decisions. Wilkins and colleagues (2009) proposed "the use of 2 or more psychiatrists in the evaluation, perhaps with a consensus resolution" (p. 38).

Several tools exist to help clinicians make a competency assessment. The MacArthur Competency Assessment Tool for Treatment measures decision-making ability for medical treatment decisions. It also measures overall cognitive ability (Lai & Surood, 2008). Wilkins and colleagues (2009) studied the Hopkins Competency Assessment Test, another diagnostic tool. They found that physicians would prefer to use this test to supplement their assessment of competency. Still, competency assessments can differ from physician to physician (Braun et al., 2009).

No tool can remove the heavy responsibility that comes with an assessment of incompetence. If a person has been assessed as being incompetent, that person's ability to make choices on his or her own behalf is removed. For this reason, experts urge caution in making the judgment.

The Canadian Centre for Elder Law (2011) said that a person's capacity to make decisions may fluctuate "throughout the day or go through longer episodes of reduced or improved capacity" (p. 12). Also, "patients can have capacity to make decisions in one area but not in others" (Maxmin et al., 2009, p. 1367; Whitlatch & Menne, 2009). St-Amant and colleagues (2012) said that a label of incompetence oversimplifies "the decision-making capacity of people with a complex, often unpredictable and varied illness such as dementia" (p. 428).

Competency should rest both on mental ability and on what a person can do. For example, a person may thrive at home but not have the verbal skill to say how he or she manages. Or a person may have lost the ability to manage money but may still have the ability to live alone. In this case, someone else may make decisions for this person on financial issues, but the person keeps the right to make the decision on where to live. Any assessment of a person's decision-making ability should take into account that individual's past decisions, values, and track record.

The issue of competency can often come up in cases of older people at risk. An older person may feel able to live on his or her own, although the individual's children may feel this puts the person in danger. Older people who want to live on their own may minimize risk and hope all goes well (Mast, 2009). But caregivers may fear for a person's safety and magnify the risk (De Witt, Ploeg, and Black, 2009).

The National Advisory Council on Aging (1993, p, 2) presents the following case:

Mrs. X is an 86-year-old widow who has lived alone with the help of home support services for the past ten years. She is an insulin-dependent diabetic with a sweet tooth. During the past two years, she has become increasingly short of memory and confused. She often forgets to eat or eats junk food. Efforts to have her live with her only son and daughter-in-law several miles away have failed. The home care case manager is becoming uncomfortable because, even with the maximum level of home care available, Mrs. X is considered to be at risk. Following a fall, where she fractured her wrist, she was hospitalized. The son, in consultation with home care, decided to institutionalize his mother. Mrs. X is clearly unhappy in the nursing home, objecting to all aspects of her care and continually asking when she can go home.

---

competency the ability to understand information that applies to a decision, the ability to think about the consequences of the decision, and the ability to communicate a decision

Has the son acted in his mother's best interests or in his own? Families struggle with the issue of competency and of removing a person's right to make his or her own decisions. A case manager told St-Amant and colleagues (2012), "Rarely do I find ... there isn't tears and falling apart in caregivers when they are doing that. There is also sometimes, depending on the way the dementia is exhibited ... really severe anger and physical acting out at times and sometimes it's so bad that the people completely withdraw, you know they completely give up" (p. 428).

Family members may consult the family doctor for a competency assessment in order to carry out their own wishes. This assessment may go along with a desire to assume legal guardianship for the older person. But guardianship (where the court appoints someone to make decisions on the older person's behalf) also creates a risk. "Starting from assuredly good intentions [to keep the older person from harm], risk becomes part of an unconscious rhetoric for controlling elderly people" (Silberfeld, 1992, p. 134).

Assessors should be cautious when deciding whether to remove a person's decision-making ability. Moye et al. (2011) said that "capacity evaluation can provide an opportunity to outline [and implement] interventions" (p. 275). For example, a family may doubt an older person's ability to live alone. The family could hire a homemaker to cook and clean for the older person. This would increase the older person's capacity to live alone. The family, the assessor, and the older person should review their assessment after an intervention has had time to work.

Whitlatch and Menne (2009) proposed that families involve a person with dementia in "making daily care decisions for as long as possible" (p. 67). The researchers said that "people in the early and moderate stages of dementia are able to ... voice preferences for care" (p. 69). They can also state whom they would like to make decisions for them when they can no longer decide for themselves.

Browne et al. (2002) said that interference with a person's liberty should take the mildest form necessary to ensure the care receiver's safety. They proposed that in healthcare facilities, for example, staff members should document problem behaviours in writing before placing limits on a person's freedom.

The Canadian Centre for Elder Law (2011) said, "The ability to make decisions is a fundamental human right. All adults have the right to make unwise or risky decisions. The tendency to make damaging choices does not make an older adult incapable. In the absence of a legal declaration of incapacity, all adults retain the right to make choices" (p. 12). This right should be removed only after careful examination and only after scrupulous procedures are followed.

CONCLUSION

Psychological well-being means more than coping with problems, stress, and loss. It means growth, learning, and a sense of purpose. The research on the psychology of aging shows that older people in good health stay alert, intelligent, and able to learn. They face stresses unique to later life, but they can get through these crises, often with the help of others. Sometimes the biggest block to an older person's well-being comes from the prejudices and stereotypes other people have about old age.

The research on the psychology of aging has begun to remove the basis for these stereotypes. Studies explore and describe the positive changes that take place in old age. They have begun to chart human potential in later life.

New models of aging study the talents that develop in later life. These include the older person's heightened ability to use practical knowledge and the expression of wisdom. Many studies focus on abnormal mental changes in later life. The increase in the number of older people and especially the very old will make psychopathology a growing concern. In particular, the number of people with dementia will increase. This will create challenges for individuals, families, and the healthcare system. Research can teach us about the needs of older people with dementia and of the best practices in responding to these needs.

Finally, terms such as *multidimensionality, plasticity,* and *variability* describe the many lifestyles that older people live today. Modern society can recognize the potential in older people, and it can accept and encourage many versions of a good old age.

---

legal guardianship process in which the court appoints someone to make decisions on another person's behalf

EXHIBIT 6.7 *A Comprehensive Mental Health System for Canadian Seniors*

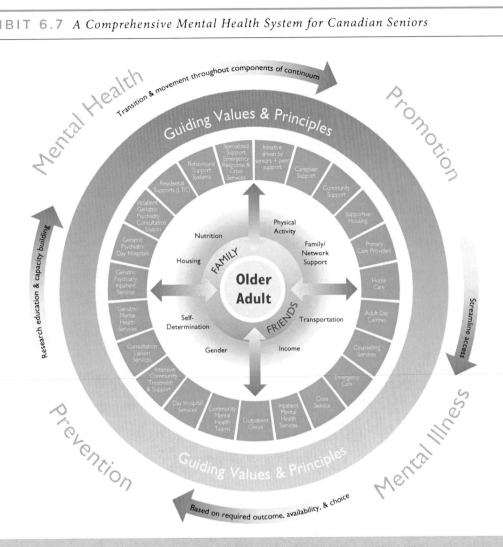

This chart provides an overview of a comprehensive mental health system for seniors. A robust mental health system in Canada can support older people as they age. Such a system would include the promotion of mental health (including successful aging), prevention of mental problems, assessment of problems when they arise, treatment of the person's condition, and support for caregivers.

Source: MacCourt, P., Wilson, K., & Tourigny-Rivard, M-F. (2011). *Guidelines for Comprehensive Mental Health Services for Older Adults in Canada.* Calgary, AB: Mental Health Commission of Canada, (2011), p. 49. Reprinted with permission. Retrieved from http://www.mentalhealthcommission.ca.

Summary

1. The brain changes with age. In general it shrinks, loses neurons, and develops abnormalities. But the brain adapts to these changes. Recent findings show that brain cells can also increase in older people. The brain reorganizes itself over time in response to mental challenges. In most cases, in the absence of disease, people adapt well to changes in brain structure and function. Neuroimaging techniques show that the brain compensates for losses. It adapts to change. Terms like *plasticity* and *cognitive reserve* describe this view of the brain.

2. Psychologists show a strong interest in memory and intelligence. In general, laboratory studies show that memory and intelligence decline with age. But

different types of memory and intelligence show different amounts of change. On some measures of intelligence, older people outperform younger people. And in everyday life, changes in memory have little effect on healthy older people.

3. Studies of memory in real-world (not laboratory) contexts show that older people can compensate for memory declines. Studies of chess masters, for example, find that practice and pattern recognition can reduce deficits in performance. Studies also show that, when compared with younger people, older people's recall of historical and social events showed little or no deficit. Also, performance by older people on real-world tasks shows little decline in mental ability. Training can improve mental performance to some degree.

4. Research on physical exercise shows that it can lead to improved mental function. Increased blood flow to the brain and increased production of brain cells may explain this finding. Exercise can also decrease the risk of stroke and dementia.

5. Psychologists describe two types of intelligence: fluid intelligence and crystallized intelligence. Fluid intelligence includes abstract reasoning and problem solving. This type of intelligence shows the most decline with age. Crystallized intelligence refers to stored knowledge—of history, vocabulary, learned information. This type of intelligence shows little decline and can even improve with age.

6. New models of intelligence have begun to look at human potential in later life. Researchers have begun to study wisdom—a person's good judgment and his or her expert knowledge about life. Older people have the potential to develop wisdom, but this remains a potential that each person needs to fulfill.

7. Creativity can expand in later life. Creativity improves well-being and gives a sense of purpose in life. Some creative work—in fields like history and literature—shows the benefits of lifelong experience. The age of greatest creative activity depends in part on the creative person's approach to his or her field. Some creative people explode on the scene with world-shattering innovations in their youth. Other creative people use their work to discover solutions to creative problems, often producing great work late in their careers.

8. Developmental disability refers to the effects of diseases such as Down syndrome (DS). These illnesses usually begin as a birth defect. People with DS and similar diseases now often live into middle age but their bodies show the effects of age earlier than in most people. This creates problems for them, since they don't fit into service programs designed for people age 65 and over.

9. The number of cases of organic brain disorders such as Alzheimer's disease will increase as more people live to late old age. This will place heavy demands on Canada's social and healthcare services. These disorders also place a heavy burden on families, and people with these diseases often need professional healthcare at the end of their lives.

10. Functional mental disorders (e.g., anxiety and depression) show up less often in old age than people commonly believe. The majority of older people report good mental health. Institutionalized older people show higher than average rates of psychological distress. Older people with functional mental health problems, such as depression, can benefit from drug therapies, psychotherapy, cognitive behavioural therapy, and milieu therapy.

11. Older people can lose competence to manage their lives due to organic or functional problems. Researchers, ethicists, and physicians work to clarify the concept of competency. They want to find a definition and assessment of competency that serves older people's needs and limits restrictions on their rights.

12. The research on the psychology of aging presents a balanced view of aging. Some mental faculties may decline, but others remain stable as long as a person is in good health. More research and knowledge about the process of aging will teach us more about mental potential in later life.

STUDY QUESTIONS

1. What approaches have psychologists taken to the study of memory and intelligence in later life? How do laboratory and contextual studies of memory differ in what they conclude about memory in later life? How do mastery and experience compensate for changes in mental ability?

2. How do the concepts of cognitive reserve and mental plasticity change our way of thinking about the brain and mental potential in later life? What does Baltes' concept of wisdom add to our understanding of intelligence?

3. What do psychologists mean by organic disorders? Why are policymakers and researchers concerned about the future increase in Alzheimer's disease cases? What do psychologists mean by functional disorders? Give some examples. What treatments

do psychologists propose for organic disorders? For functional disorders?

4. What issues do the loss of competence raise for the older person? For the person's physician? For the family? Discuss the tension that exists between an older person's potential need for protection and his or her right to make decisions.

KEY TERMS

cognitive reserve (p. 136)

competency (p. 159)

constant-probability-of-success model (p. 146)

contextual view of memory (p. 137)

crystallized intelligence (p. 143)

depression (p. 155)

developmental disability (p. 149)

developmental intelligence (p. 144)

encoding (p. 133)

episodic memory (p. 133)

fluid intelligence (p. 143)

intellectual disability (p. 148)

intelligence (p. 143)

latency (p. 133)

legal guardianship (p. 160)

long-term memory (p. 132)

memory (p. 132)

non-episodic memory (p. 133)

plasticity (p. 137)

semantic memory (p. 139)

sensory memory (p. 132)

short-term memory (p. 132)

stereotype threat (p. 137)

wisdom (p. 144)

working memory (p. 133)

Study Tools
CHAPTER 6

Located at retail.tophat.com:

- Review Key Terms with interactive and printable flash cards
- Check Your Comprehension and Think About chapter concepts by completing practice quizzes
- Develop Your Gerontological Imagination with class activities
- Analyze Aging in a Global Perspective with engaging case studies and critical thinking questions
- Demonstrate Your Knowledge of the Concepts by bringing your own experience to personal application questions
- Evaluate Aging in the Media by completing Internet activities with evaluation questions

CHAPTER 7

HEALTHCARE

Cultura RM Exclusive/Tim MacPherson/Getty Images

LEARNING OBJECTIVES

After reading this chapter, you will

LO1 Understand the difference between three models of healthcare in use in Canada today.

LO2 Be able to describe the drivers of increased healthcare costs in Canada and how the government might control these costs.

LO3 Be able to discuss the role of long-term care in a healthcare system that meets the needs of older people.

LO4 Be able to analyze the Romanow Report on healthcare in Canada with respect to seniors' healthcare needs.

LO5 Be able to discuss the trends in community healthcare and the importance of community care in an aging society.

LO6 Be able to explain the benefits of health promotion for the individual and society.

LO7 Be able to describe the role that technology will play in the future delivery of healthcare and give examples of the application of technology to seniors' health.

LO8 Appreciate the importance of coordination and integration of healthcare services for the benefit of the individual and for the benefit of the healthcare system.

INTRODUCTION

Mrs. Granovetter, age 72, lives by herself in a three-room apartment. Until six years ago, she worked as a supervisor in a nursing home, but poor health forced her to quit. She says she has an aortic aneurysm that "looks like a bicycle tire with a bubble in it." She also has arthritis, and her joints get so stiff during the night that, she says, it sometimes takes her until noon to get out of bed.

Still, she manages to live on her own. Her daughter, who lives on the other side of town, calls her every day; she talks to or visits with her next-door neighbour daily, and she can still drive. A few times a week, she drives to a nearby shopping centre to sit and watch the people go by. She knows just where to park and how far she has to walk to the nearest bench. Last year, her children took her on a trip to England. She says they didn't get to walk through the castles, but they toured around in the car and she saw the countryside. With help from family and friends, Mrs. Granovetter stays active and enjoys life.

Like Mrs. Granovetter, a majority of older women suffer from arthritis and almost a quarter of them have heart trouble. And, like her, most of them cope well with some help, and they say they have good health. Even among people age 75 and over, nearly three-quarters of those who live outside institutions report good to excellent health (Turcotte & Schellenberg, 2007).

An early Canadian policy statement defined health as "a resource which gives people the ability to manage and even to change their surroundings" (Epp, 1986, p. 3). By this definition, more than 90 percent of people age 65 and over are in good enough health that they can live on their own in the community.

Healthcare system refers to the medical and social services that provide healthcare support to Canadians. The healthcare system provides support that ranges from health promotion, to health maintenance, to long-term chronic care.

This chapter looks at (1) the structure and function of the healthcare system today, (2) how the present system fits the needs of older people, and (3) how the system is changing to meet the needs of an aging society.

THREE MODELS OF HEALTHCARE

Social scientists use models to simplify and describe complex social systems. A model does not perfectly represent the system, but it describes the system's basic structures, functions, and values. Three models of healthcare have shaped the development of the healthcare system in Canada: (1) the medical model, (2) the social model, and (3) the health promotion model.

The Medical Model

The medical model focuses on the treatment of diseases and injuries. Treatment most often takes place in the physician's office, in a hospital, or in other healthcare institutions. The medical model favours surgery, drug therapy, and rehabilitation through physical therapy. Within this model, "the medical history, physical examination, and diagnostic tests provide the basis for the identification

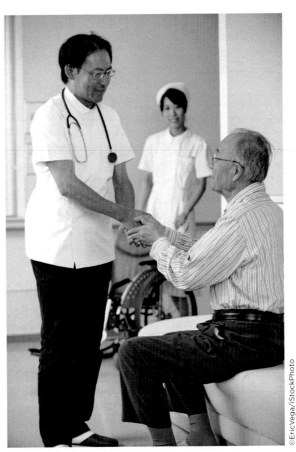

Here, a doctor sees an older patient in a hospital waiting room. In the medical model, healthcare typically takes place in a hospital or doctor's office. The physician oversees medical treatment and prescribes drugs or surgery if necessary. This model can combine with the social model to deliver healthcare in the community.

healthcare system the medical and social services that provide healthcare support to Canadians, support that ranges from health promotion, to health maintenance, to long-term chronic care

medical model a healthcare model that favours surgery, drug therapy, and rehabilitation through physical therapies, with a focus on the treatment of diseases and injuries, usually in the physician's office, a hospital, or other healthcare institutions and treatment of a specific illness. The medical model is thus focused on the physical and biologic aspects of specific diseases and conditions" (Farlex, 2011).

Physicians control both the organization of healthcare and the work of other healthcare professionals within the medical model. They learn this approach to medicine in medical school and often get little training in other forms of healthcare such as counselling or long-term community care. Canada's health insurance system supports the medical model. It funnels most healthcare dollars to doctors and hospitals, and it places the medical profession at the centre of the healthcare system.

The Social Model

The **social model** sees medical care as one part of a complete healthcare system. This model sees personal and family counselling, home care, and adult daycare programs as part of the healthcare system. This model of healthcare tries to keep older people in their own homes. Care often takes place in the community—in a person's home, at a drop-in centre, or in a counsellor's office. In this model, the doctor works as part of a healthcare team that includes nurses, physiotherapists, counsellors, social workers, and other professionals. The social model has grown in importance as more older people need continuing care or long-term care.

Long-term care (LTC) serves people with chronic illnesses and functional disabilities. Long-term care combines medical and nursing care with social and community services. LTC helps people and families cope with the demands of older people who have disabilities or chronic healthcare needs. People with dementia often need LTC until the end of their lives. LTC can take place in a person's home, the community, or a nursing home. Often a person and family will use both community services and home care. LTC gives people as much autonomy as possible. LTC often attempts to keep people out of institutions. Home care, for example, offers a range of services that allow people to stay in their homes. Services include Meals on Wheels, homemaker visits, volunteer visits, and physiotherapy.

Beland and Shapiro (1994) reviewed provincial reports on long-term care. They found a number of policies common to nearly all provinces and territories: (1) decentralized decision making; (2) a coordinated, single-point-of-entry system; (3) a shift from institutional to community services; (4) integration of healthcare and social services; and (5) a continuum of care that includes institutional and community care. The Canadian healthcare system has begun to shift from the medical to the social model of care.

The Health Promotion Model

The **health promotion model** focuses on prevention and self-care. It aims to prevent disease through lifestyle change, increased knowledge about healthy behaviour, and environmental improvement. Programs that promote fitness and those that warn about the dangers of smoking or excessive drinking follow this model. The model also includes actions that most people do not associate directly with healthcare, such as workplace safety regulations, seatbelt legislation, and pollution control for factories.

Each of these models plays a part in the Canadian healthcare system today. The social model has gained acceptance as a possible alternative to institutionalization. The health promotion model may save the healthcare system money in the long run by keeping people healthier longer. Recent decreases in heart disease, for example, may have come about through health promotion programs that encourage low-fat diets and discourage smoking.

Still, the medical model dominates the system today. Canadians spend more money (much of it through taxes and health insurance programs) on physicians and hospital care than on any other kind of healthcare.

TIME TO REVIEW

What does each model of healthcare contribute to the total healthcare system?

Compare and contrast the main approach of each model.

Why do some experts feel that the social and health promotion models especially fit an aging society?

What benefits to older people and to Canadian society would come from a shift toward the social model and health promotion?

---

social model a healthcare model that includes personal and family counselling, home care, and adult daycare programs as part of the healthcare system, and that tries to keep older people in their own homes

long-term care social and medical services, including formal services, home or institutional care, and family care, for people who have functional limitations

health promotion model a healthcare model that focuses on self-care and preventing disease through lifestyle change, increased knowledge about healthy behaviour, and environmental improvement

EXHIBIT 7.1   *The Medical Model and the Social Model in Long-Term Care*

Medical Model	Social Model
Patient	Resident, consumer
Acute patients	Chronic clients
Physicians and hospitals	Community settings and home
Patient fits organization	Organization fits client, changes to fit client if necessary
Rigid system boundaries	Open system boundaries
High priority to short-term need	High priority to long-term need
Serves long-term care if it has excess capacity	Serves long-term care first
Diagnosis/treatment/cure model	Assessment of functional capacity, service needs identified, services delivered
Organizationally inflexible	Organizationally flexible and creative
Institutional care	Community-based care and home care
Excludes people in the community	Includes community members and may include institution
Institution-centred	Person-centred
Makes little use of informal network	Includes informal support
Medical/physical assessment	Multidimensional assessment (physical, psychological, social needs)
Meets patients' medical needs	Helps clients meet their own needs
Patient accepts professional treatment	Client plays role in developing treatment plan
Professional has most power in relationship	Client and professional share power
Hierarchical organization	Flat organization, team approach
Expensive resources	Lower-cost resources
Major share of healthcare budget	Small share of healthcare budget

The table above presents an ideal type of the medical and social healthcare models. Each has a role to play in the Canadian healthcare system. These two approaches see and treat the older person differently. Some critics believe that the system today relies too heavily on the medical model and that an older population needs more services based on social model principles.

Many programs exist as a hybrid between the two approaches. For example, a physician may oversee a team that provides multidimensional health assessment and care delivery. Or a hospital may work closely with a community care program to move a person back into the community.

Source: Adapted from B. Havens, 1995, "Long-Term Care Diversity within the Care Continuum," *Canadian Journal on Aging*, 14(2): 245–262. Reproduced with permission from the *Canadian Journal on Aging*.

THE ORIGINS OF THE CANADIAN HEALTHCARE SYSTEM

In 1957, the Canadian government put in place a hospital insurance system that covered the entire population. In 1968, the government insured physician services, and by 1972, all provinces and territories belonged to a national medical insurance program. These policies reflected the belief that healthcare was "a social good and not merely another purchasable commodity" (Canadian Museum of History, 2010). This view triumphed over the argument that each person should look after his or her own and the family's healthcare. And that the government should support only those who could not afford their own insurance.

The Canada Health Act was proposed in 1984 and it created controversy across the country. Alberta, British Columbia, and Ontario opposed the legislation, as did much of the medical profession. In spite of this opposition, the House of Commons gave the legislation unanimous support. Brian Mulroney, head of the Progressive Conservative Party, called Medicare "a sacred trust which we will preserve" (Hansard, 1983, p.44 cited in the Canadian Museum of History, 2010).

EXHIBIT 7.2   *The "Father of Medicare," Tommy Douglas*

Photo by Barry Philp/Toronto Star via Getty Images

Canadians value their healthcare system and see it as a defining institution in the country. The Canada Health Act of 1984 established the principles of the system, but the system began long before then.

Tommy Douglas (Thomas Clement Douglas) (1904–1986), the premier of Saskatchewan for 18 years (from 1944 to 1961), enacted a provincial version of the medicare system in Saskatchewan in 1962. In 1984, the Canadian federal government created a national medicare system based on Douglas's Saskatchewan model. The federal government agreed to pay half the cost of this system; the provinces and territories would pay the other half. Canadians recognize Douglas as the "father of medicare." For this achievement, in 2004 the nation voted him "The Greatest Canadian."

Yet even after the legislation passed, the medical profession opposed its implementation. Doctors in Ontario staged a 25-day strike in 1986 to show their opposition. Some doctors left the country. The Canadian Medical Association challenged the legislation in the courts. The system today exists because the government held firm and because most Canadians supported a publicly managed healthcare system. Today, the Canadian healthcare system is "an essential component of the Canadian identity" (Canadian Museum of History, 2010).

The Canada Health Act stated that provincial and federal governments would share the costs for the system. The federal government would match provincial contributions to the program dollar for dollar. The Canada Health Act described the principles of the Canadian healthcare system (Canada, 1984; Health Canada, 2010): (1) universal coverage; (2) access to services; (3) portability (people could get the benefits in their new location when they moved); (4) comprehensive services that include outpatient and hospital care;

and (5) administration of the system by a non-profit public agency.

The Act guarantees access to healthcare for all Canadians based on their need, regardless of their ability to pay. This system compares favourably with the U.S. system, where no national system of healthcare exists. Compared with Americans, Canadians have lower mortality rates, better cancer survival rates, and lower rates of obesity, hypertension, diabetes, and respiratory disease. (Exhibit 7.3 compares the Canadian and U.S. healthcare systems).

CHALLENGES TO THE HEALTHCARE SYSTEM TODAY

The Canadian Healthcare Association (2007) studied Canadians' opinions about the healthcare system. The survey polled more than 2,000 respondents, including members of the public, doctors, nurses, pharmacists,

EXHIBIT 7.3 *The Canadian and the U.S. Health Care Systems: A Comparison*

Canada and the United States share an almost 8050-kilometre border, a common language, and similar economic systems. Journalist Trudy Lieberman (2014) lists one other thing Canadians and American have in common, "we don't want each other's health care systems." But, "In truth, most Americans don't know how Canada's system works and Canadians don't know much about the U.S. system." The debate in the U.S. over the Patient Protection and Affordable Care Act (sometimes called "Obamacare") often brought up the spectre of a "Canadian-style" healthcare system. Americans worry about the "socialization" of their healthcare system, although this term hardly captures the uniqueness of the Canadian system.

Canadians and Americans could benefit from knowing more about each other's healthcare systems. Below you will find a point-by-point comparison of the Canadian and U.S. systems. Be aware that the two systems have many subtle differences (in policies, philosophy, implementation) that the points below cannot capture. You will find some suggested readings at the end of this comparative study if you want further details.

Canada bases its healthcare system on the 1984 Canada Health Act. The act has five main principles: public administration; comprehensiveness; universality; portability; and accessibility. The discussion compares the Canadian and U.S. healthcare systems on these principles.

Administration

Canada

- A non-profit public agency administers the system.
- Canada has a single-payer system. The government pays all costs; the system allows no co-pays or user fees.
- Doctors work in the private sector and bill the government for their services. This system sets fees.
- A single-payer system leads to lower administrative costs.
- Canada spends approximately 11 percent of its GDP on healthcare.

United States

- The United States has a multi-payer system.
- Private, for-profit insurance companies compete for customers.
- Doctors work in the private sector and bill insurance companies for their services.
- Multiple-payers lead to more administrative work and higher costs.
- The United States spends approximately 16 percent of its GDP on healthcare.

Comprehensiveness

Canada

- The system covers the full range of medical services from primary care to long-term care.
- The system covers 91 percent of hospital costs and 99 percent of physician costs.

- Long-term care programs and policies differ across the country. The government does not cover all long-term care needs (e.g., respite care or homemaker services).
- Provinces differ in their coverage of drug costs. People often pay some or all long-term care and drug costs out-of-pocket.
- Dental and eye care insurance differs by province. In general individuals pay for these services out of pocket or they carry supplemental insurance.

United States

- Private providers offer a full range of medical services to consumers.
- Payment for a service rests on the individual's ability to pay or on that person's health insurance policy.
- Some employers provide health insurance.
- These policies differ in the services covered, co-pay amounts, and limits on payments.
- The Affordable Care Act also prohibits a company from denying coverage to a person with a prior health condition.

Universality

Canada

- Universal coverage ensures the same level of healthcare for all Canadians, regardless of their ability to pay.

United States

- The population is partially covered.
- Coverage depends on an individual's decision to buy insurance and on the coverage a person buys.
- Some employers provide some amount of health insurance.
- Recent health care legislation requires individuals to buy health insurance or pay a penalty. This will increase coverage but will still leave some people without insurance.
- The Affordable Care Act will lead to health insurance coverage of approximately 90 percent of the non-elderly population. But it will still leave approximately 30 million non-elderly U.S. residents uninsured (CBO, 2015).

Portability

Canada

- The system ensures coverage if a person moves, changes jobs, or moves to another province.
- Canadians who leave the country for a period (e.g., seniors who move south for the winter) keep their coverage.

United States

- The new legislation in the United States provides portability for those who have insurance.
- A person can now change jobs and retain insurance coverage.

Accessibility

Canada

- ■ The system ensures access to a wide range of healthcare services with no user fees.

- ■ The system ensures that healthcare providers receive reasonable payment for their services.

- ■ The system provides some long-term care services.

United States

- ■ Access to service depends on an individual's insurance policy or on out-of-pocket payment to a service provider.

- ■ Coverage depends on how much a person can or will pay for insurance.

- ■ A person can buy long-term care insurance.

These systems show many similarities and also some fundamental differences. People in Canada and the United States have similar healthcare needs and have access to similar healthcare services. The systems differ primarily in the principles that underlie each system (and how those principles express themselves in policies). Put simply, the government in Canada plays a major role in funding healthcare and in creating healthcare policy. The United States treats healthcare as a commodity in the private sector. It allows the market to meet the needs of the public, and it expects individuals to look after their own healthcare needs. The Affordable Care Act, although it introduces an element of government oversight, continues to support the American free-market approach to health care.

Sources: The National Bureau of Economic Research. (2015). *Comparing the U.S. and Canadian Health Care Systems.* Retrieved from http://www.nber.org/bah/fall07/w13429.html; O'Neill, J.E., & O'Neill, D.M. (2007). *Health Status, Health Care and Inequality: Canada vs. the U.S.* NBER [National Bureau of Economic Research] Working Paper No. 13429.

and healthcare managers. The survey reported some disturbing results. Twenty percent of respondents included wait times as an important issue. This topped the list of their concerns—up from 4 percent in 1998. Only 57 percent of respondents in this study felt that Canadians got quality healthcare services. Only 7 percent of those surveyed felt that wait times would decrease and quality would improve "significantly" over the next five years.

Soroka (2007) concluded that Canadians worry that "high-quality health care will be less and less available over time" (p. 20). Canadians feel concerned about costs, access to service, and quality of care.

The Canadian national healthcare system faces some new challenges today. For example, current healthcare reforms have shifted care from institutions to the community. This policy has decreased institutionalization, but it has placed more responsibility on women, families, and communities. Funding has not always followed this shift to community care.

Families will need more community-based and institution-based long-term care as the population ages. Increases in the prevalence of Alzheimer's disease, for example, will lead to more use of community and institutional care. Although most provinces and territories provide some long-term care insurance, the current system does not fully insure LTC. Users often have to pay out of pocket for programs such as adult daycare or homemaker services. Also, the system today emphasizes medical and institutional care, the two most expensive types of services. The healthcare system needs to expand its scope to include more long-term care services in the community.

Wait Times: An Ongoing Controversy and Challenge to the System

Soroka (2007), in a study for the Health Council of Canada, looked at four years of opinion polls in Canada (2002–2006) that asked about attitudes toward the healthcare system. He concludes that "overall … the Canadian public remains firmly committed to universal health care." And he found that Canadians show "overwhelming support for increased spending on health care" (p. 3). But concerns exist about the sustainability of the healthcare system, wait times for service, and the quality of care.

These concerns have a basis in fact. Wait times for some services have increased. For example, "the national median wait time for treatment after consultation with a specialist was 8.0 weeks in 2009 and 9.3 weeks in 2010" (Esmail, 2011, p. 18). This has led to some loss of confidence in the system. The prime minister and the premiers of the provinces and territories responded to long wait times in 2004 with *A 10-Year Plan to Strengthen Health Care.* This plan agreed to focus on five procedures to reduce wait times: cancer, heart, diagnostic imaging, joint replacement, and sight restoration.

Many of these procedures affect older people. They focus on chronic illnesses common in old age. But seven years later, the Canadian Institute for Health Information (CIHI) (2011b) said that wait times "continue to be the focus of intense media coverage and public debate. In a recent survey of 11 countries, respondents from Canada were more likely than those in the other countries to list waits to see a doctor or nurse, difficulty getting after-hours care, and waits for elective surgery as access challenges" (p. 1).

A $5.5 billion Wait Times Reduction Fund (spread over 10 years, from 2004 to 2014) supported improvements in the healthcare system. The government used these funds to reduce unnecessary procedures, set up specialty clinics for some procedures, and track patient needs electronically to respond quickly to emergencies. Findings reported by the CIHI (2011b) should relieve some concerns about wait times. The CIHI found that in 2010–2011 "eight out of 10 patients across Canada received priority procedures within benchmarks" (p. 5).

But the CIHI (2011b) also reported that provinces and territories differed in their ability to meet wait time benchmarks. For example, only Ontario and British Columbia met all priority area benchmarks with 75 percent of the patients who needed care. The ability to meet benchmarks also differed by procedure. A person's ability to get hip and cataract surgery within a preferred time differed by province and territory. Wait times for knee replacement showed few improvements across the country. So, the provinces still need to work at reducing wait times for chronic conditions like knee replacement.

THE COST OF HEALTHCARE TODAY

In 2014, Canada spent $214.9 billion, or about $6,045 per person, on healthcare. This came to 11 percent of its gross domestic product (GDP is the total value of all goods and services produced in the economy), up from 7 percent in 1975 (Canadian Institute for Health Information, 2015b; Statistics Canada, 2004b, 2011b). By comparison, in 2012 the developing nations in the Organisation for Economic Co-operation and Development (OECD) averaged 9.4 percent of GDP. The United States in 2012 in that year spent 16.9 percent of its GDP on healthcare (the highest among all developed nations). Canada in that year spent 11.9 percent of GDP on healthcare ($205.4 billion) (Canadian Institute for Health Information, 2015b).

Hospitals accounted for 30 percent of total healthcare spending in 2014. Physicians accounted for about 15 percent of healthcare costs in that year. Drugs accounted for another 16 percent of spending (Canadian Institute for Health Information, 2015b). Taken together, these three sources of expense come to 61 percent of all healthcare expenditures.

The Canadian Institute for Health Information projects a slower growth in costs in the years ahead due to modest economic growth and government limits on health spending (CIHI, 2015b).

Both private and public spending on healthcare increased each year from 2010 to 2014 both in current and constant (1997) dollars. In those five years, for example, private and public healthcare expenses rose from $193.3 billion to $214.9 billion (Canadian Institute for Health Information, 2014).

These facts show both the strengths and weaknesses of the healthcare system today. Canadian medical and hospital insurance matched the most complete coverage in the world, with almost 100 percent of Canadians covered. Older people, for example, receive free hospital and surgical care as well as free access to a range of programs that include chiropractic and optometric services. Also, all Canadians have access to some form of public support for pharmaceuticals. But in 2012, Canada also ranked among the top OECD nations with the greatest per capita expenditures for healthcare (OECD, 2017). In particular, Canada stood among the top five countries in expenditures for physician services and drugs.

Canada's relatively large older population is partly responsible for this high cost. The CIHI (2014) reported that Canada spends more on seniors' healthcare than it spends on any other age group. Women age 80 and over rank highest in healthcare costs. The CIHI said that older people accounted for 45 percent of all provincial and territorial government health spending in 2012, but seniors made up less than 15 percent of the population in that year. Senior women used 25 percent of healthcare resources. Senior men used 19 percent. The CIHI found "a pronounced increase in per capita spending in the senior age groups" (p. 47).

The CIHI (2011c) compared provincial and territorial healthcare costs for seniors and younger adults. It found that, compared with spending on younger adults, governments spent 4.5 times more per capita on seniors' healthcare ($11,196 compared with $2,494). Why this difference in the cost of seniors' healthcare?

By any standards, older people have more health problems than younger people and use more healthcare services. Roterman (2006) reported that seniors, compared with younger people, see specialists and general practitioners more often. They also have more hospital separations than younger people, and they spend more days in the hospital during each stay.

For example, seniors, compared with other age groups, make disproportionate use of hospital services. People age 65 and over in 2009–2010 used 40 percent of acute hospital stays. But they made up only 13.9 percent of the population. Compared with younger adults, seniors had higher discharge rates for all categories of hospital use, including inpatient, acute, and rehabilitation services.

EXHIBIT 7.4 *Health Expenditure by Use of Funds, Canada, 2014*

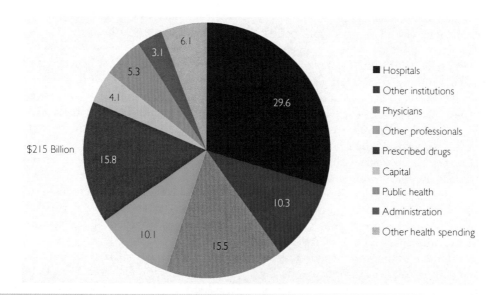

Note that two-fifths of all healthcare funds (39.9 percent) go to hospitals or other institutions. Another 15.5 percent goes to physicians. Drugs add 15.8 percent. Taken together, these three expenses come to more than two-thirds (71.2 percent) of all funds spent on healthcare in Canada in 2014. This figure shows the dominant role of the medical model in the Canadian healthcare system.

Source: Adapted from CIHI (Canadian Institute for Health Information). (2014). *National health expenditure trends, 1975 to 2014*, Table A.2.1, p. 42, Used with permission. Found at https://www.cihi.ca/en/nhex_2014_report_en.pdf.

These rates increased with age. Seniors age 85 and over, compared with seniors age 65 to 74, have more than twice the rate of acute inpatient hospital use and seven times the rate of inpatient complex continuing care. Seniors also tend to stay in the hospital longer than younger adults (e.g., 1.5 times longer for acute inpatient care). And they use more hospital resources during their stay (almost 70 percent more compared with younger adults) (Canadian Institute for Health Information, 2011c).

Compared with younger people, older people show more repeat admissions. The more chronic conditions a person has, the greater the likelihood that he or she will spend time in a hospital. Likewise, seniors who suffered an injury or reported "fair" or "poor" health showed a greater chance of hospitalization (Roterman, 2006).

Seniors also use other healthcare resources at higher rates than younger adults. They make up almost the entire population (95 percent) of people in residential care. They comprise 82 percent of the people who use home care. Compared with non-senior adults, they have almost double the rate of visits to a family doctor. And compared with non-senior adults (age 20 to 64), they use

nearly eight times more government funding for prescription drugs.

Still, it would be wrong to assume that all or even most people age 65 and over use large amounts of healthcare services. The high cost of health services for older people comes from two sources: large expenses in the last years of life and care for chronic illness. The share of healthcare used by seniors has remained stable over more than a decade (from 2000 to 2012) at around 45 percent. During this same period the older population grew from 12.5 percent to 14.9 percent of the Canadian population. This should moderate the concern that an aging population will bankrupt the healthcare system.

TIME TO REVIEW

Compare the healthcare system in Canada with the costs in the United States.

What trend has Canada seen in healthcare costs?

Why does this trend worry policymakers and economists?

EXHIBIT 7.5   *Total Health Expenditure, Canada, 1975 to 2014*

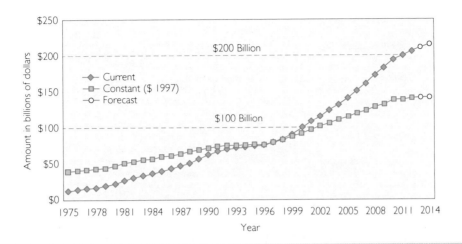

This graph shows projections from the National Health Expenditure Database (Canadian Institute for Health Information, 2015b). "Total health expenditure in Canada, in current dollars was $205.4 billion in 2012 and is forecast to have reached $210.4 billion in 2013 and to climb to $214.9 billion in 2014" (Canadian Institute for Health Information, 2014, p. 20). Inflation accounts for much of this increase. Using constant 1997 dollars and a comparison to Canada's GDP, healthcare expenditures in Canada have stabilized. Total health expenditure was 11.3 percent of GDP in 2012, 11.2 percent of GDP in 2013, and 11.0 percent of GDP in 2014. Per capita expenditures rose modestly from $5,911 in 2012 to $6,045 in 2014.

Source: CIHI. (Canadian Institute for Health Information). (2014). *National health expenditure trends, 1975 to 2014*, p. 21. Used with permission. Original source: CIHI, National Health Expenditure Database, Statistics Canada. Retrieved from https://www.cihi.ca/en/nhex_2014_report_en.pdf.

Population Aging and Healthcare Costs

The cost of Canada's medical care system grows each year. For example, on average, public sector spending grew by 7 percent a year between 2000 and 2010 (Canadian Institute for Health Information, 2014). Cost increases have levelled off since 2010 to about a 2 percent increase per year. Still, costs continue to rise and policymakers, government officials, and the press express concern about the rising cost of healthcare. A *Maclean's* magazine headline (Geddes, 2010) warned of "The Health Care Time Bomb." Stories like this point to population aging as a cause of rising costs. The author subtitles the article: "Our Aging Population Will Make Unthinkable Reforms Inevitable." And this leads to concern about the future sustainability of the healthcare system.

Will an older population lead to a crisis in healthcare spending? Is there a population "time bomb" ready to explode? Population aging does contribute to increased healthcare costs. Compared with younger adults, older people do use more healthcare services. And use increases with age. But "while the Canadian population is aging, it is aging slowly as a whole," said Jean-Marie Berthelot,

CIHI vice-president of programs (CNW, 2017). "Over the past decade, the proportion of health dollars spent on seniors by provincial and territorial governments has remained relatively stable at 44%. This tells us that spending on seniors is not growing faster than spending for the population at large."

Many research studies (Palangkaraya & Yong, 2009; CIHI, 2011c) now show that population change alone does not account for the growth in healthcare use or expenses. Constant et al. (2011) reviewed the literature on population aging and healthcare costs. "Looking at the forecasts provided in these studies," the researchers said, "... experts agree that the effect of both of these cost drivers [population growth and population aging] is small relative to other cost drivers" (p. 8). The Canadian Institute for Health Information (2011a) found that population aging accounted for only 0.8 percent of the total 7.4 percent in projected annual growth in costs. In other words, population aging accounted for about 11 percent of total cost increases.

Recent research supports this conclusion. The CIHI (2011a, 2011c; Lee, 2007) study, *Health Care Cost Drivers: The Facts*, looked at the effect of population aging on healthcare costs. "The common belief is that an aging

---

EXHIBIT 7.6   *Provincial/Territorial Government Healthcare Expenditure per Capita, by Age Group, Canada, 2012*

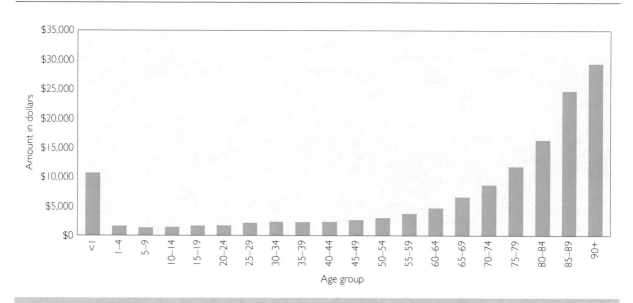

This chart shows the high cost of healthcare at the end of life. Excluding the per capita cost for infants, healthcare costs rise with age. Costs per person remain steady from adolescence to middle age. But costs rise steeply among the older age groups. The per capita healthcare cost for people age 80 and over came to nearly 17 times the per capita cost for children age 1 to 14 and nearly 8 times the per capita cost for healthcare from adolescence through middle age. The increase in the older population, especially the oldest old, raises concerns about the affordability of the healthcare system in the future.

Source: CIHI (Canadian Institute for Health Information). (2014). *National health expenditure trends, 1975 to 2014,* Figure 34, p. 76; also Table E.1.15, p. 171. Used with permission. Retrieved from https://www.cihi.ca/en/nhex_2014_report_en.pdf.

population will lead to greater demands for health care services and accelerated growth in health spending. Contrary to common perception, population aging has been a very modest cost driver overall" (p. vi). The report listed other economic forces that create higher healthcare costs: general inflation, healthcare sector inflation, and other causes (such as changes in technology, increased use of drugs, and doctors' treatment choices). Compared to population aging, these had a greater effect on costs. The CIHI (2014, p.79) calls population aging "a very modest cost driver" of increases in healthcare costs.

Hugh Mackenzie and Michael Rachlis (2010), two of Canada's most respected health and economics experts, studied trends in healthcare costs in Canada. "The data speak clearly," they said. "Based on trends in health care and Medicare spending, *the sustainability crisis does not exist* [emphasis added]. The oft-cited increase in health care spending as a share of total public spending reflects not an extraordinary increase in health care spending, but rather decisions by governments to cut taxes and public spending in areas other than health care" (pp. 8–9).

In other words, the increase in healthcare costs reflects a total decrease in public spending. This makes the proportion of spending on healthcare look artificially larger. Mackenzie and Rachlis explain that when they use the proportion of GDP as a measure of "society's ability to pay … health care costs generally and Medicare costs in particular have been remarkably stable" (pp. 8–9).

The CIHI (2011a) added a further caution when looking at the effects of an aging population on healthcare costs. "Seniors are a diverse group," the report said. "Provincial and territorial government health spending varies among the senior age groups. On average, health care spending per person is highest for those age 80 and older" (p. 16).

Mackenzie and Rachlis (2010) concluded that "the likely impact of the aging of the population on health care costs is overstated.... [O]ver the next 25 years, we can expect to see an increase in health care costs of one percent per year, driven by changes in the age distribution of the population. While the impact of aging is greater than in the recent past (0.8% per year between 2001 and 2010), it does not add up to the looming financial crisis that many are forecasting" (p. 10). They said that "the assertion that Medicare in its current form is not sustainable ... is patently untrue ... the facts do not support the contention that Medicare costs are increasing uncontrollably or unexpectedly" (pp. 13–14). The researchers say that an increase in "productivity and effectiveness in the system" can further buffer the effects of increased costs (p. 56).

Constant and colleagues (2011, p. 21) concluded after a review of research on healthcare cost drivers:

The increase in healthcare expenditures can largely be explained by improvements in medical science and technological innovation, which likely result in greater use of more effective treatments, and changes in patterns of disease (more chronic diseases, mental illnesses), patient behaviours and preferences.

The cost of care in the future will depend on the health of new cohorts of older people, the impact of health promotion and disease prevention, the cost of drugs and technology, and the cost of running and managing healthcare personnel and institutions.

Some critics of the system today question whether older people need more services; others wonder whether older people need the current services offered to them. Some question whether the medical model fits the needs of an aging society. They argue that for the same cost, Canadians could buy care that more closely fits seniors' needs.

Population aging challenges the healthcare system to change. And the direction of change seems clear. Older people, compared with younger people, have different healthcare needs. They need care for chronic illnesses (Canadian Institute for Health Information, 2011d). And these illnesses need long-term care. The effective treatment of chronic illness holds the possibility of controlling healthcare costs as the population ages.

Consider an example of change that would reduce costs. Today, hospital and institutional care for older people with chronic illness drives up the cost of healthcare. Dr. Jeff Turnbull, chief of staff of the Ottawa Hospital, said that home care would come to one-quarter of the $1,100 per day cost of an acute hospital bed (*CBC News*, 2011a). Many of the illnesses of later life can best be treated and cared for in the community.

Kathleen Morris, CIHI's vice president of Research and Analysis, said that governments should spend money on the right services so more seniors can stay at home and out of hospital longer (*CBC News*, 2011a). Home care, adult daycare, and outpatient treatment can buffer the cost of healthcare for seniors. These programs also keep people in their homes—something most older people prefer.

Hospitals will serve a higher proportion of older people in the future. A strong community care system can lead to earlier discharges and fewer days in the hospital for older patients.

"The delivery of appropriate care for those with chronic conditions," McAdam (2008) said, "requires a paradigm shift from episodic, short-term interventions ... to long-term, comprehensive care" (p. 1). A closer look at community-based long-term care and health promotion will show how the system can provide quality care and control costs.

TIME TO REVIEW

What role does population aging play in the increase in healthcare costs?

What are the actual drivers of healthcare cost increases in Canada?

What response to an aging population would moderate healthcare costs and provide appropriate care?

THE HEALTHCARE SYSTEM AND OLDER PEOPLE'S HEALTHCARE NEEDS

Adapting the healthcare system to an aging society can contain costs and provide the kind of care older people want and need. This will mean the integration of the social model of healthcare (home and community care) with institutional treatment.

Hospital Care

The Canadian system has moved toward community-based healthcare services in the past few years. For example, the number of hospital beds in Canada declined from 156,466 beds in 1992 to about 93,525 in

EXHIBIT 7.7 *Selected Nations with Percentage of Population Age 65 and Older and Percentage of Gross Domestic Product (GDP) Spent on Healthcare, 2013.*

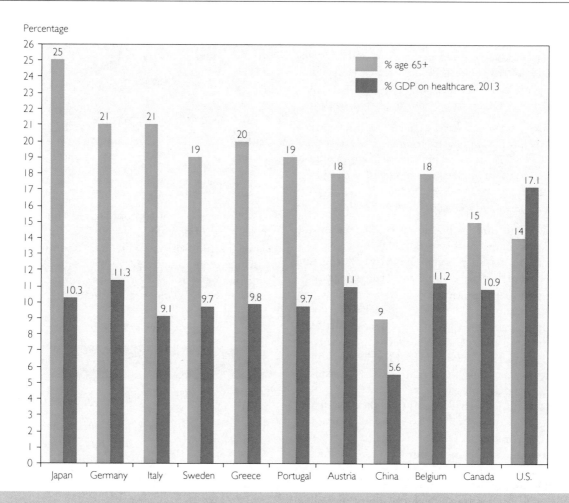

The percentage of GDP spent on healthcare bears no direct relationship to the proportion of older people in a country. This graph shows that the proportion of older people in a country does not explain high healthcare costs. Canada, for example, has the second-youngest population among the developed nations presented here, but ranks among the top five countries in spending (as a percentage of GDP). Public policies that encourage or discourage healthcare use affect how much money gets spent on seniors' healthcare in a country. Doctors' treatment decisions and the increased use of high-tech medical treatment add to costs.

Sources: World Bank. (2015a). *Health expenditure, total (% of GDP)*. World Health Organization Global Health Expenditure database. Retrieved from http://data.worldbank.org/indicator/SH.XPD. TOTL.ZS/countries?order=wbapi_data_value_2013%20wbapi_data_value%20wbapi_data_value-last&sort=desc&display=default; World Bank. (2015b). Population ages 65 and above (% of total). Retrieved from http://data.worldbank.org/indicator/SP.POP.65UP.TO.ZS/countries?display=default.

2012 (OECD, 2015). The Canadian Institute for Health Information (2011e) reported that acute care hospitalizations decreased by 14 percent between 1995–1996 and 2009–2010 (although the rate stabilized after 2001–2002). This has lowered the cost of hospital care.

Finlayson et al. (2005, p. 21) looked at hospital stays in more detail by studying hospital stays for older people in Manitoba between 1985 and 2000. They found "a substantial and consistent decrease" in use of hospitals for inpatient stays during the 16 years of the study (p. 21). They found 53 percent fewer long-stay days and 25 percent fewer short-stay days during this time.

Finlayson and colleagues said that this trend began before the decrease in hospital beds. They suggested that changes in the patterns of practice in the healthcare system (e.g., more home care), in part, account for these changes. Also improvements in technology (e.g., better diagnostic tools) may have led to a decrease in hospital stays. These findings show that changes in the healthcare system can lead to decreases in hospital use and decreases in the cost of hospital care even as the population ages.

Long-Term Institutional Care

Most long-term care institutions house only older people. In 2009–2010, Canada had 2,136 homes for the aged (Statistics Canada, 2011i). These facilities go by a variety of names: "special care facilities, residential care facilities, personal care homes, homes for the aged, nursing homes, lodges for senior citizens, and rest homes" (p. 9). We will use the term nursing home to refer to any institution that is not a hospital and that offers medical care to chronically ill older people. Nursing homes today mostly serve the oldest-old people (age 85 and over).

Statistics Canada (2011i) put the total revenue from nursing homes and residential care facilities in 2009–2010 in Canada at $13.8 billion. The proportion of seniors who live in an institution (primarily a nursing home or hospital) increases with age. Nursing homes now typically house people age 85 and over. Most of these residents have dementia and can no longer live on their own. Also, institutionalization rates vary from province to province. In 2009–2010, British Columbia had the highest percentage of assessed people age 85 and over in residential care at 58 percent. Yukon had the lowest rate at 37 percent (Canadian Institute for Health Information, 2011)

The proportion of older people who live in an institution has declined since 2001. About 5 percent of seniors in Canada (204,008 people) in 2009–2010 lived in a nursing home. This marked a decline in Canada from about 7 percent in 2001. This about equals the United States' rate and the average for the OECD developed nations (OECD, 2011b, 2011c). Better health of older people and more community care explain the decrease in nursing home living.

The Canada Health Act does not include all nursing home care costs in its definition of covered services. So older people have to cover all or part of the cost themselves. The cost of nursing home care varies by province and territory. Fernandes and Spencer (2010) looked at the out-of-pocket cost (to the individual or family) for long-term residential care by province and territory. They found that a non-married senior with average income in New Brunswick would pay $25,550 per year out of pocket in 2008 (the highest in the country). A non-married senior in Quebec would pay only $12,157 per year in 2009 (less than half the New Brunswick rate). Yukon had the lowest out-of-pocket costs for a non-married senior

at $6,395 per year in 2008. In most provinces, seniors with low or very low income pay less than a person with average income or higher.

The poorest older people get support so they can afford nursing home care. The rates charged for the poorest seniors come to less than their combined Old Age Security and Guaranteed Income Supplement. But the difference in cost by province and territory leaves poor older people with more or less extra income, depending on where they live. Very low-income single seniors in Nunavut, for example, would have $13,039 per year to spend from their income after paying their nursing home expenses. But in Prince Edward Island, a very-low-income single senior would have only $20 per month left after paying for care. Similar differences exist for married couples in different provinces. "In sum," Fernandes and Spencer (2010) said, "the private cost for non-married residents of LTC facilities is very uneven across the country" (p. 310). And "such differences across jurisdictions might be regarded as unfair...." (p. 315).

Each province and territory has its own system for classifying institutionalized patients. The government allocates funds to institutions based on the level of care needed by each patient. Most provinces define four levels of nursing home care. In Manitoba, professional staff members assess a senior's need for support before the senior enters a nursing home. Staff members score a person on four ADL abilities (e.g., bathing and dressing), their need for professional help (e.g., oxygen therapy), and behaviour management. A person's ability to live independently and their need for help will determine their level of care. For example, a person in Level 1 care will need minimum support on all six items. A person in Level 4 care will need maximum support on four or more of the items. Very few people get Level 1 care in a nursing home in Manitoba. Most people who enter a nursing home need maximum dependence on one or more of the items assessed (Doupe et al., 2011, p. 34).

A more recent study (Maxwell et al., 2013) looked at what predicted long-term care placement for people in assisted living facilities. Predictors of long-term care placement included older age, poor social relationships, little involvement in activities, cognitive impairment, poor health, recent falls or emergency room visits, and severe incontinence. The people who moved to a LTC facility often had declining health and a need for more healthcare support.

Most people, including government leaders, doctors, nursing home staff, and older people themselves, agree that we should keep older people out of institutions when we can. Provinces use community care programs to keep people in the community as long as possible. Still, institutions play a useful role in the continuum of healthcare services.

LTC institutions can reduce or delay hospitalization and this reduces the cost to the healthcare system. Also, some people need to live in a nursing home. People with Alzheimer's disease, for example, may benefit from institutional care. Institutions can have design features (such as circular hallways, colour-coded walls, or a secure garden) that make life easier for people with memory problems.

All seniors in institutions (regardless of ethnicity) benefit from a pleasant and stimulating environment. Physical activity, for example, encourages good health and engagement with other residents. Benjamin, Edwards, and Caswell (2009) asked nursing home administrators about physical activity in their facilities. All administrators saw physical activity as a good thing for residents. But they also described some of the challenges they faced in promoting physical activity in their institutions, such as funding shortages, staffing shortages, and physical barriers (e.g., limited space).

Administrators tried to overcome these challenges. One administrator used volunteers to help with a walking program. Some facilities improved their structure. For example, they built circular walks in some units for wandering patients to use. Activity can increase the quality and length of patients' lives. Institution administrators need to make physical activity a priority in their facilities.

Canada's long winters, the great distances between some older people and hospitals, the need for constant care, few informal supports, and poverty sometimes make institutional life the only way for people to get the care they need. Institutions can provide a safe and supportive environment for those who need this type of care.

Models of Quality Institutional Care

Quebec launched a relationship-based care (RBC) program in 2002 (Viau-Guay et al., 2013). Between 2005 and 2008, the province implemented this approach in 73 LTC facilities. RBC teaches professional caregivers "theoretical knowledge and practical skills" in order to implement person-centred care (p. 58). Many of these caregivers work with residents who have dementia. These residents may display aggressive physical and verbal behavior. The RBC approach has two main goals: (1) the caregiver provides care that uses communication and touching techniques and (2) the caregiver fosters residents' autonomy and respects the person's preferences. RBC involves massage and touching to relax the person's body and it involves getting the person to stand or at least sit up, even for a

few minutes a day. It also involves a change in caregivers' relationship to the resident. RBC goes beyond physical care and the medical model. It requires sensitivity to the total life experience and abilities of the resident.

Viau-Guay and colleagues studied the effects of RBC training on 420 caregivers who took RBC training. Caregivers one month after training said they found RBC "generally helpful, overall, and that they intended to continue integrating this approach into their care activities" (p.67). Many caregivers in this study appreciated the RBC values of dignity and autonomy for their residents. RBC (and similar person-centred approaches to care) provides caregivers with knowledge and skills that improve their relationships with their clients.

Some groups in institutions have special needs. People with a strong ethnic identity, for example, can benefit from a setting that supports their culture. The Boundary Hospital Community Health Centre in Grand Forks, British Columbia, serves as an example of this cultural sensitivity. The centre houses a 60-bed residential

The creation of a landmark—the Boundary Hospital Community Health Centre in Grand Forks, British Columbia—and a model of good design.

care home. The hospital designed the centre to fit the local culture. The Doukhobors, a religious sect that moved to Canada from Russia, settled in this area in the late 19th century. The health centre reflects the deep roots of this culture in this region. For example, the new two-storey brick entrance looks like a traditional Doukhobor house. The community donated items from the past to decorate the interior. And the designers used colours and materials familiar to residents to make the facility feel more like home. The facility meets modern standards of design and innovation in addition to showing cultural sensitivity.

The Simon K.Y. Lee Seniors Care Home in Vancouver serves Chinese community elders. Residents can speak their own language, and the home respects and supports Chinese culture. It provides contact for residents with plants, animals, and children to allow them as normal a life and environment as possible (S.U.C.C.E.S.S., 2011).

This home adopted a philosophy in institutional care called "the Eden Alternative," founded by Dr. William Thomas in 1991. It works to de-institutionalize nursing homes and other long-term care institutions. The organization has trained more than 17,000 Eden associates. More than 300 Eden Alternative homes now exist in the United States, Canada, Europe, and Australia. The Eden Alternative teaches that "where elders live must be habitats for human beings, not sterile medical institutions." Eden Alternative institutions "are dedicated to eliminating the plagues of loneliness, helplessness, and boredom that make life intolerable in most of today's long-term care facilities" (Eden Alternative, 2009).

The Sherbrooke Community Centre in Saskatoon became the first Eden Alternative home in western Canada. The centre has its own radio station and its own aviary. The bird sanctuary holds budgies, lovebirds, and canaries so that residents can enjoy the birdsong. The centre organizes residents into the "Village," 11 special care homes with nine or ten residents per home.

Nursing homes and other institutions will never take the place of a person's own home or apartment, but the changes suggested here show that a nursing home can be made more comfortable and homelike.

THE NEED FOR CHANGE

Canada's commitment to the medical model accounts for much of the increase in healthcare costs today. But reliance on the medical model can sometimes lead to inappropriate care for older patients.

Roy Romanow, former premier of Saskatchewan, poses with copies of his commission's report, released in November 2002.

These and other issues led the federal government to review the national healthcare system. In April 2001, Prime Minister Jean Chrétien commissioned a study of Canada's healthcare system. He appointed Roy Romanow to chair the Commission on the Future of Health Care in Canada. The prime minister charged the commission to study the current system and propose reforms to meet Canada's future healthcare needs. The commission met with citizens and groups across the country, held televised forums, and received reports from researchers.

The commission handed down its report (often called the **Romanow Report**) in November 2002 (Commission on the Future of Health Care in Canada, 2002). It contained 47 proposals for change. This forms what the report calls a "roadmap for a collective journey by Canadians to reform and renew their health care system." Many of these proposals respond to the needs of older people. Below is a sample of the recommendations that speak to older people's needs.

Recommendation 1: A new Canadian Health Covenant should be established as a common declaration of Canadians' and their governments' commitment to a universally accessible, publicly funded health care system (Commission on the Future of Health Care in Canada, 2002, p. 247).

Recommendation 5: The Canada Health Act should be modernized and strengthened by

Romanow Report The 2002 Canadian federal government report of the Commission on the Future of Health Care in Canada, led by Roy Romanow; the report underscores Canada's commitment to its healthcare system and makes several proposals for improving the delivery of healthcare to seniors

- Confirming the principles of public administration, universality, and accessibility, updating the principles of portability and comprehensiveness, and establishing a new principle of accountability;

- Expanding insured health services beyond hospital and physician services to immediately include targeted home care services followed by prescription drugs in the longer term;

- Clarifying coverage in terms of diagnostic services;

- Including an effective dispute resolution process;

- Establishing a dedicated health transfer directly connected to the principles and conditions of the Canada Health Act (Commission on the Future of Health Care in Canada, 2002, p. 248).

Recommendation 7: On a short-term basis, the federal government should provide targeted funding for the next two years to establish

- A new rural and remote access fund,

- A new diagnostic services fund,

- A primary health care transfer, a home care transfer, and

- A catastrophic drug transfer (Commission on the Future of Health Care in Canada, 2002, pp. 248–249).

Recommendation 26: Provincial and territorial governments should take immediate action to manage wait lists more effectively by implementing centralized approaches, setting standardized criteria, and providing clear information to patients on how long they can expect to wait (Commission on the Future of Health Care in Canada, 2002, p. 251).

Recommendation 34: The proposed new Home Care Transfer should be used to support expansion of the Canada Health Act to include medically necessary home care services in the following areas:

- Home mental health case management and intervention services should immediately be included in the scope of medically necessary services covered under the Canada Health Act.

- Home care services for post-acute patients, including coverage for medication management and rehabilitation services, should be included under the Canada Health Act.

- Palliative home care services to support people in their last six months of life should also be included under the Canada Health Act (Commission on the Future of Health Care in Canada, 2002, p. 252).

Recommendation 35: Human Resources Development Canada, in conjunction with Health Canada, should be directed to develop proposals to provide direct support to informal caregivers to allow them to spend time away from work to provide necessary home care assistance at critical times (Commission on the Future of Health Care in Canada, 2002, p. 252).*

The report concluded by stating that "the immediate priorities must be to strengthen Medicare's legislative and institutional foundations, to stabilize funding, and to address the critical concerns that are eroding Canadians' confidence in the system" (Commission on the Future of Health Care in Canada, 2002, p. 254). These changes will take place over time; the implementation plan extends to 2020.

LONG-TERM CARE: NEW APPROACHES TO COMMUNITY CARE

The Canada Health Act of 1984, the basis of Canada's healthcare system, ensures hospital and physician care for all Canadians. One important benefit of the system is that it protects acute and chronically ill older people from financial ruin in case of a long-term illness.

Within this system, compared with acute care and institutional care, community care gets less funding from the federal government. Older people who need long-term care, including homemaker help, Meals on Wheels, or transportation, must often turn to the social welfare system for help. Some programs and services fall between healthcare and social services, and the availability of these services varies by province and region. Some communities have a wide range of services; others have few. Also, a person may have to pay for these services out of pocket.

New Brunswick has a single-point-of-entry community care program that allows access to all community social and healthcare services from one point in the system. This program serves older people throughout the province. Manitoba has had a similar system for many years. Other provinces and territories also use this approach.

Ontario expanded its commitment to community-based LTC in the late 1990s. It set up **Community Care Access Centres (CCACs)** across the province. Today, Ontario has 14 CCACs. They assess client needs and set up a care plan for each person. Each CCAC contracts for services from providers in their area. Services include physical therapy, occupational therapy, speech therapy, help with activities of daily living, and nursing care (CCAC, 2011; CHCA, 2013).

CCACs award contracts to service providers based on quality and price. For-profit and not-for-profit organizations compete for the contracts. This system creates managed competition among community care providers. The CCACs will feel increasing pressure as the population ages and as budgets remain capped. However, this system has moved community care to a prominent place in the healthcare system.

Quebec integrated its health and social service systems under a single administration in the 1970s. Reforms in 2003 and 2004 created 95 Health and Social Services Centre (HSSC) networks across Quebec, with 12 in Montreal (Kuzmarov, 2009). These networks bring together family doctors, pharmacists, community organizations, and social service agencies. Each network has a health and social service centre (CSSS). Centres combine community service centres, residential and long-term care facilities, hospitals, rehabilitation centres, and child and youth protection centres. Each CSSS integrates services. It ensures "accessibility, case management, follow-up and coordination of services for the population it serves" (Canadian Institute for Health Information, 2011c, p. 91).

The use of regional health boards or councils has spread to other provinces and territories. Regional boards manage and finance institutional and community healthcare services. They control costs at a time when the federal government has cut funds to the provinces, and they are thus responsible for tough decisions about where to cut services. Some of these boards or councils have seniors on advisory committees. Other boards consult with local seniors' groups.

Critics of these boards fear that administrators and healthcare professionals will have most of the power on the boards. Also, community control may lead to unequal access to services and varied standards of service. Supporters of regional boards say they are familiar with local needs and can work for the best interests of the community. Healthcare experts disagree about the value of the boards.

Many provinces intend to shift health services from institutions to community care. But in many cases, the development of community care lags behind hospital bed closings. Community care has grown more technical and demands more knowledge of medical practice as older people leave hospitals sooner. A lack of funding puts more pressure on community services. And in some cases community care simply means more stress for an elderly spouse or an overworked family member caregiver—usually a woman.

TIME to REVIEW

How does the healthcare system benefit from the shift to community care?

How does the individual senior benefit?

What effect does the shift to community care have on family caregivers?

What challenges does the system face as it decreases reliance on institutional care?

Typical Community Care Programs

The social model of healthcare looks for ways to keep people out of institutions. A healthcare system based on the social model of care would provide community care for chronic illnesses and ADL needs. Community care programs include hospitals, nursing homes, doctors' services, and community-based services such as geriatric day hospitals, adult daycare, and home care.

The programs discussed below, beginning with geriatric day hospitals, form a **continuum of care**—from more institutional contact to little or no institutional contact. They show how the Canadian healthcare system has applied some of the principles of the social model of healthcare to meet older people's needs.

Keep three points in mind as you read about these programs. First, in some cases the people who run the programs have done the evaluations of programs presented here, and this could bias their reports. Second, few evaluations use control groups to see what would have happened to a similar group if they had not used this kind of program. A program that claims to save money by keeping people out of institutions should compare its costs to service a similar group of people who were in an institution. Third, evaluation studies often report short-term changes. This makes it difficult to judge the long-term effects of a program.

Community Care Access Centres (CCACs) Ontario's system of community care centres that provide a single point of entry into the healthcare system and services such as in-home care, physiotherapy, and dietetic services

continuum of care the array of services that range from institutional care to little or no institutional contact

EXHIBIT 7.8   *Basic Components of a Sound Continuing Care System*

The list below presents the programs most often used by older people. It is a sample of the mix of services older people use—some medical and some social. This mix can cause confusion for people who need long-term care. Many types of providers offer these services (government, not-for-profit, for-profit); provincial health insurance pays for some services, while other services charge a user fee. Case managers help make sense of this system and can ensure people get the services they need.

Meals on Wheels

Meals on Wheels delivers hot, nutritious meals to a person's home. Volunteers deliver the meals. These programs supplement diet to maintain health.

Adult Daycare

Adult daycare provides personal help, healthcare services, and recreation in a group setting. People attend for half or full days.

Homemaker Services

Non-professionals help with personal care or housekeeping. Services may include help with bathing, housecleaning, and cooking.

Home Nursing Care

A nurse visits someone's home to provide care. This service may cover day and evening care seven days a week and usually requires a doctor's referral.

Community Physiotherapy and Occupational Therapy

Physiotherapists and occupational therapists provide direct treatment and advice on illness prevention, arrange for equipment for home use, and teach family members how to help clients.

Assessment and Treatment Centres and Day Hospitals

Short-term services are available for diagnosing and treating health problems, including physical and psychological assessments, usually in an acute-care hospital.

Nursing Home Care

A nursing home provides institutional care for people who cannot remain at home because of health problems. Nursing homes provide long-term care for chronically ill people.

Chronic Hospital Care

Chronic hospital care is given by an institution that provides special care for people with a chronic illness or functional limit who do not need all of the services of an acute care hospital.

Other Services

Other services include programs that provide people with assistive devices, nutrition counselling, and social workers' services.

Even with these shortcomings, however, evaluations and reports often provide the only available information about new programs. They give some idea of what these programs do and how well they work.

Geriatric Day Hospitals

A **geriatric day hospital** offers a full range of hospital services to people who live in the community. A day hospital will assess an older person's needs and plan a rehabilitation and care program. Khan (2009) said, "Availability of physiotherapist, speech therapist, dietician, pharmacist and occupational therapist under one roof makes the day hospital model ideal to deliver a seamless service" (p. 354). Day hospitals can also keep an eye on older patients at risk in the community and ease older acute care patients back into the community when they leave the hospital.

Khan (2009) reports on the benefits of a day hospital that serves heart failure patients. An outpatient clinic for these patients put heavy demands on their ability. They had to make three or four hospital visits over a six-week period to confirm their diagnosis. They had to walk long hospital corridors to visit many hospital departments. The day hospital put all services for these patients in one facility. Blood work and X-ray services, along with other tests done in one setting, could confirm the diagnosis in one visit. Treatment began immediately. The day hospital also provided rehabilitation services to improve patient health.

A study of a geriatric day hospital program in London, Ontario, by Crilly and colleagues (2005) found that 146 of 151 patients in the program improved while in the program. But a study of these patients from 6 to 18 months after discharge found that nearly 2 in 5 (39 percent) reported deteriorated health. The researchers then compared those who deteriorated with those who maintained their health. They found that the more independent patients—those with less risk of falling, those who live alone, those who got around without an assistive device—tended to maintain their health gains. The frailer older person who lived with someone else and who needed support from the formal care system tended to decline.

---

geriatric day hospital a hospital program that offers a full range of hospital services to older people who live in the community and that assesses individuals' needs before setting up a healthcare plan

The researchers suggested that frailer, more dependent day hospital patients after discharge "may need ongoing input from the system in the form of continued therapy." The researchers said that the healthcare system must integrate geriatric day hospitals into the continuum of care. This needs to include "active intervention in the home after 'discharge'" especially for frail patients (p. 308).

Khan (2009) ended a review of day hospital service on an optimistic note: "The future of [the] geriatric day hospital is bright," he said, "provided its role changes with the changing needs of the elderly population. It should maintain its traditional role but should offer new flexible services for frail elderly patients; the possibilities are endless" (p. 355).

Will geriatric day hospitals save the system money? Only if they can keep people out of nursing homes and in the community. The studies above suggest that they can play this role for many older people who need rehabilitation. The studies also show that people can maintain the benefits they get through day hospital care after they leave the program. But some people may need more intensive and ongoing help in their homes. More research on the effects of geriatric day hospital services will improve their ability to keep people in their homes.

Adult Daycare

Adult daycare programs (ADCs) provide support in the community for people who cannot stay in their homes without it. These programs include hot meals, recreation programs, and a chance for the older person to socialize. The programs also give family caregivers time off to rest, shop, and maintain their own social life. Adult daycare offers fewer medical services and more social and recreational services than day hospitals. Some provinces require that people pay for daycare service themselves, while other provinces include the service as part of the provincial health program.

Research has not shown a conclusive improvement of function or a reduction in the use of other services due to adult daycare (or day hospital care) alone (Lucas, 2006). But studies do report an increase in participants' well-being and their satisfaction with the service. Molzahn, Gallagher, and McNulty (2009) asked ADC users and their families in Victoria, British Columbia, about their satisfaction with their ADC program. Clients and family members said the program improved their quality of life.

The program provided respite to caregivers. It provided clients a chance to socialize with others. One woman said she's a "happier person" because of the day centre.

"I have company over there," she says. "I have someone to talk to." Another client, someone with Alzheimer's disease, said, "I need to not be isolated. I need to be with people who are also struggling with Alzheimer's or dementia. And I get that more from the day program [than from other community-based services]" (p. 40). The ADCs also allowed clients to remain in their homes longer—something the clients and their families preferred.

Assisted Living and Home Care

Assisted living falls somewhere between institutional long-term care and home care on a continuum of healthcare service. (Assisted living also goes by the names *congregate housing or supportive housing*). A person typically moves into an assisted living facility when they can no longer manage at home. The person who chooses assisted living needs more care than home-based health services can provide. People in assisted living most often require help with activities of daily living. In a Manitoba study, almost no people in assisted living had behavioural problems or incontinence (Doupe et al., 2011).

McGrail and colleagues (2013) listed three features of assisted living: (a) staff on-site with 24-hour emergency services; (b) a commitment to resident autonomy, privacy, and choice; and (c) a home-like environment. A typical assisted living arrangement provides a standard bedroom, a private bathroom, and some kitchen facility. Assisted living settings often provide a common-room dining option, a recreation program, help with activities of daily living, central storage of medication, and healthcare clinics (such as foot care or physical rehabilitation). Assisted living settings sometimes offer multiple levels of support so that a person can age in place.

McGrail and colleagues (2013) asked whether assisted living settings saved the healthcare system money? The researchers studied healthcare service use of 1,894 British Columbia seniors. They looked at service use 12 months before and 12 months after admission to assisted living. This study measured residents' health conditions including hypertension, cardiovascular signs and symptoms, and gastrointestinal signs and symptoms. All of the measures decreased in the year after admission to assisted living (with the exception of the use of anti-psychotic medications). The researchers said that healthcare use declined "most substantially for GP visits, medical specialist visits, and hospital care" (p.181).

---

adult daycare programs provide non-institutional support for people who cannot stay in their homes without it

assisted living housing that provides personal care services and other supports to frail seniors to help them live independently in the community

The researchers called the impact of these changes "substantial." They said that "this cohort of 1,894 individuals had more than 800 fewer medical specialist visits in the year after moving to assisted living compared to the year before, more than 8,000 fewer GP visits, and more than 18,000 fewer acute hospital days…. The [economic] effects are not trivial. If we estimate the cost of a day in acute care as $1,000, the move to assisted living appears to be associated with more than $18,000,000 in acute hospital cost avoidance" (pp. 181–182).

This study demonstrates that assisted living can save the healthcare system money. The study also points to the health benefits of assisted living for seniors (e.g., less need for healthcare services). Assisted living often gets a senior out of an unmanageable, sometimes dangerous, and isolated home. It offers the older resident a community, on-the-spot support, and preventive therapy. This combination can delay entry into a nursing home and provide a high quality of life. (See Chapter 11 for more details on this housing option).

Home care is one of the most important parts of a comprehensive healthcare system. Home care includes medical care, such as a visiting nurse, housework, personal care, and meal delivery. Home care blends medical and non-medical care. It helps seniors stay in their homes and provides support to caregivers.

In 1977, the Canadian federal government started the Extended Health Care Services program to support provincial home care programs. In 1984, the Canada Health Act listed home care as an "extended service." This means that the Canadian government recognized the role of home care in a modern healthcare system but does not include it as an insured service covered by the act. To meet these needs, the federal and provincial governments have begun to consider an insured national home care program. Home care may cut healthcare costs and provide quality services to older people.

The Canadian Home Care Association (CHCA) (2013), in its report *Portraits of Home Care in Canada*, defines home care as "an array of services for people of all ages, provided in the home and community setting, that encompasses health promotion and teaching, curative intervention, end-of-life care, rehabilitation, support and maintenance, social adaptation and integration, and support for the family caregivers" (p. xi). The CHCA (2013) said that home care served about 1.4 million people in 2011 through government-funded programs.

On average across the country, 17 percent of seniors benefit from publicly supported home care. Public expense for these programs came to $5.9 billion. Still, home care expenses came to only 4 percent of provincial and territorial healthcare budgets in 2010.

Home care programs differ from province to province, but all of the provinces and territories in Canada have some public home care and nursing services. Some provinces have extensive home care programs that include Meals on Wheels, home repair services, laundry and cleaning help, emergency alert services, friendly visitors, nutrition counselling, and transportation services.

Home care provides support to a large number of older Canadians. And the need for and use of home care increases as a person ages. The greatest increases in the use of home care were by people who live alone (many of them older women). Also, people with chronic conditions and a need for ADL support tend to use home care services (Mitchell, Strain, & Blandford, 2007). Home care use rises dramatically with age. In 2012, 10 percent of people age 65 to 74 received home care. This figure rose to 21 percent of people age 75 to 84, and 45 percent of people age 85 and over (Turcotte, 2014; also Sinha & Bleakney, 2014). Turcotte (p. 2) said, "these percentages may underestimate the number of persons needing help or care."

Compared with seniors who live with someone, a higher proportion of those who live alone use home care. The large majority of home care users got help with housework (89 percent) and other non-medical help. This included personal care (68 percent), meal preparation/delivery (67 percent), and shopping (60 percent) (Carrière, 2006). Some people used home care after discharge from the hospital. These people often lacked informal supports that would allow them to leave the hospital and live at home on their own. Others used home care before nursing home admission to give them support while they waited for placement. Finally, some people used home care before death.

The Canadian Home Care Association (2013) said that the number of people who get home care grew by 55 percent between 2008 and 2011. And the number of people who will use home care will increase in the future. Sims-Gould and Martin-Matthews (2010a) said that home care forms the most rapidly expanding sector of Canada's healthcare system.

The aging of the large Baby Boom generation and the increase in chronic illness among the very old in part explain this projected increase. Governments will turn to home care to save money. And seniors will choose home care because they prefer to stay in their homes (Fraser, Archibald, & Nissen, 2014). The Canadian public

---

home care a range of social and medical services designed to help people live independently in the community

supports the growth of home care. Eighty percent of Canadians in one study agreed that home care and community care programs strengthen the healthcare system (Canadian Healthcare Association, 2007).

A study of home care patient-nurse relationships (Turpin, McWilliam, & Ward-Griffin, 2012) showed the meaning of home care support to the older person. Turpin and colleagues found that patients need the medical help that nurses provide, but patients also valued the relationship with the home care nurse. One client said,

> Well, to me it's really nice if I have somebody I'm very comfortable with, you know? Like after someone has come into your home for 3 or 4 years, you get to know a lot about them. They get to know a lot about you (p. 462).

Another said, referring to her nurse,

> "She's able to talk to you about things and sort of make you feel that there is somebody there looking after you and you don't have to worry because somebody is there, and somebody is coming the next week. And if something is wrong, you can always get in touch with her, too .... I didn't think I would be so at ease" (p. 463).

A compassionate nurse can help a person stay in their home and enjoy a high quality of life in spite of a chronic illness. Turpin and colleagues said that their study underscored the importance of "interpersonal interactions which promote comfort and connectedness, thereby constituting meaningful relationships" (p. 467).

All provincial home care programs assess clients, coordinate services, and manage cases. The Canadian Healthcare Association (2009) called case management the "key to integrated care, especially with complex patients" (p. 40). Egan and colleagues (2009) said case managers serve as a "clinician-broker, combining clinical expertise and information about local services to support patient goals within the context of limited resources" (p. 371).

Private for-profit and non-profit home care agencies also exist. They most often provide help with housework, some nursing care, and palliative care. A wide range of older people use home support and personal care services to maintain themselves in the community. People with dementia and other kinds of cognitive impairment use more home care services than any other group of older people.

Home care clients, seniors, and their caregivers express the need for more home care services. One caregiver client told Fraser, Archibald, and Nissen (2014, p. 255), "It's better with home care. I think it could be better yet. Maybe if we had more home care." Another caregiver told the researchers "I think there should be more funding and more awareness around the issue, and perhaps more supports in place, if possible for people."

Governments funded home care in the belief that it lowered overall healthcare costs. A study by Miller, Hollander, and MacAdam (2008) in Ontario supported this belief. They found that the overall average annual cost for community care ($37,008) came to less than half the average annual institutional cost ($87,376). Compared with community care, institutional care costs the government more at every level of care.

Hollander and Chappell (2007) compared home care and institutional care costs in British Columbia between 1987–1988 and 1996–1997. The researchers found that home care costs came to between 40 percent and 75 percent of institutional cost for the same level of care.

The study also reported that the more stable the person's type and level of care, the better the savings to the system. But the cost of home care for clients who changed levels of care still came to less than the cost of institutional care. Finally, home care clients who died during a given period of the study cost more than people who died in an institution. The more hours of home care used, the closer costs approach those of institutional care.

Hollander and Chappell (2007, p. 160) provided advice and a caution to government officials and policymakers who expect home care to reduce costs:

> Overall, the results presented here lend strong support to the argument that home care can be a lower-cost alternative to residential services, to the extent that actual substitutions can be made. This does not mean that home care is automatically a lower-cost alternative. If monies are not redistributed from long-term institutional care to home care, or if more money is not put into home care while long-term care beds remain constant, that is, if there is no actual substitution then home care will generally not be a lower-cost substitute for residential care.

This comment points to the need for a coordinated and integrated system of care over the full range of healthcare services. Governments need to reduce the amount of institutional care as they ramp up home care services for an aging population.

A move to increase home care will require a change in the funding priorities of the healthcare system. The Romanow Report proposed such a change (Commission on the Future of Health Care in Canada, 2002). It proposed federal funding for home care and makes home

---

EXHIBIT 7.9   *Paid Companions: An Emerging Role in Home Care*

The Canadian healthcare system intentionally limits the development of private sector healthcare options. And yet privatization creeps in. Outcalt (2013, citing Armstrong, Armstrong, & Scott-Dixon, 2008, p. 10) spoke of the "profitization" of healthcare services that takes place when public services contract with private companies to provide services. Armstrong, Armstrong, and Scott-Dixon report that in British Columbia, for example, private companies run some long-term care facilities and receive government funds. For-profit companies often move in where government cutbacks have reduced services.

Outcalt (2013) described the use of "paid companions" as a privatized solution to cutbacks in government spending. These workers provide emotional and social support to older clients. Their services include listening, conversing, and accompanying patients on walks. But their work may easily extend to personal care, cooking, cleaning, and household chores. Few studies have looked at this type of worker.

Outcalt said that companionship work in a person's home resembles other types of home care. But the companion role emphasizes the relationship with the client. "Companions who work in this capacity fulfill a distinct role, providing older adult clients with social and emotional support that stands alone, outside of the task-based services provided by home support workers" (p. 94).

Some of the workers in this study reported a "fictive kin" relationship with their clients.

One worker said,

[Y]ou can't help but bond with the person. You're there day after day, hour after hour through the day. They tell you things they wouldn't even tell their family. They rely on you for everything and me, too,

for them. Because my clients have all been older and wiser, been through life, raised kids—they can give me advice and suggestions that I appreciate, and yeah, I have bonded with him. He's like a second dad in a way, you know (p. 97).

But companionship gets mixed with the paid role of the home care worker. Outcalt referred to the "commodification" of care, where companionship becomes a service a person or family can buy. This role reflects the conditions in modern Canadian life. Often, two adult children in a family work. They have little time to provide care or give personal attention to their aging parent. If the parent suffers from dementia a paid companion can ease the burden on family caregivers. A companion worker put this simply:

[R]eally, it's a reflection of our cultural times that families are spread apart, that we're all working so much to live in this supposedly technologically easier culture, but it takes all of our time. And so, the cost of living—both people working—it's not like you live in an extended family anymore. So it's caring to bring people in. Now it's paid, that's all—it's not extended family: everything is paid (p. 100).

Paid companions solve another problem: they cover over the limited amount of money that governments allocate to home care services. Limited funding and support forces some families to pay for services (such as paid companions) out of pocket. Individuals and families with enough money can buy the extra service. Poorer people make do without the added support. Outcalt says that this solution deepens "the health care divide" (p. 100). It also challenges the Canadian commitment to equitable healthcare for all.

Questions

1. What do you think of paid companions as a private service?

2. Does this service go against the Canadian goal of equal access to healthcare for all?

3. Do you think more adult children in the future will turn to paid companions for their parents?

4. Would you hire a paid companion if your parents or grandparents needed added home care support? Should the government pay for this service?

---

care a legitimate program within the national healthcare system. This may reduce the costs of home care now borne by families. But the report proposes to support home care only for mental healthcare, post-acute care, and palliative care.

In 2013, only four provinces (British Columbia, Manitoba, Ontario, and Prince Edward Island) had legislation that defined and governed home care services. Other provincial governments have begun to recognize the importance of home and community care (Canadian Home Care Association, 2013).

Summary of the Social Model

Roterman (2006) concluded a review of healthcare system use by older people with the following summary: "In relation to their numbers in the population, seniors are heavy users of health care services. This is largely a reflection of the decline in health that often accompanies advancing age" (p. 40). Chronic illness, injury, poor self-perceived health all lead toward more healthcare use—including visits to doctors, hospitalization, drug use, and home care use. The healthcare system has changed over the years to accommodate the needs of Canada's aging population. Although the medical model still dominates the healthcare system, the system has increased the use of home care and other community-based services.

Will increased support for the social model—including home care and community supports—reduce healthcare costs in the future? Chappell and Hollander (2011) said, "The weight of the evidence now clearly indicates that home care, including a major home support component, can be a cost-effective substitute for residential and acute care across time, geographic areas and types of care recipients...." But adding home care to a system that continues to focus on (and increasingly fund) institutional care will only increase costs. Home care and community care must fit into an integrated system of healthcare. This type of system would include assessment of a person's condition and the availability of services that suit an older person's needs.

HEALTH PROMOTION

So far, this chapter has focused on illness rather than health, but there is no other way to talk about the healthcare system. We call it a healthcare system, but it is actually a sickness treatment system. It serves people who are already sick, and it focuses on curing disease. This approach has its limits. Hospitals, doctors, nursing homes, and home care do not prevent disease; they treat illness after it occurs. The health promotion model puts health into a social context.

Marmor and Maioni (2008) said, "The largest payoffs [in healthcare reform] lie not in traditional medical care, but in social investments that improve the average person's capacity to cope and stay well" (p. 28). Further improvements in healthcare for older people will include health promotion and self-care. New generations of older people will come into later life in reasonably good health, live longer than older people in the past, and benefit from programs that help them maintain good health into late old age.

Canada's interest in health promotion dates back to 1974. Marc Lalonde, then the federal minister of health, discussed health promotion in a report called *A New Perspective on the Health of Canadians* (Lalonde, 1974). He proposed the concept of the health field. The health field includes the usual health services, but within it the

healthcare system is one way—not the only way, or even the best way—to improve health. In addition to traditional medical services, the health field includes improvements in human biology (through basic research), improvements in lifestyle, and improvements in the environment as paths to better health.

The health promotion model has gained support since Lalonde first proposed the idea of the health field. Health promotion includes anti-smoking campaigns, better labelling of food products with information about calories and ingredients, increased awareness of the need for exercise, and emission control on cars. This approach makes sense in Canada today. People today live longer than ever before, and they need to age in good health.

Building on the early proposal by Lalonde, governments and agencies throughout the country have begun to offer health promotion programs for seniors. Alberta Health Services, for example, offers a program in Edmonton called Comprehensive Home Option of Integrated Care for the Elderly (CHOICE).

CHOICE promotes good nutrition, exercise, and contact with others. CHOICE staff members go to clients' homes, help people get ready for a day at the CHOICE centre, and help clients home again at night. The centre provides medical, dental, and foot care, as well as rehabilitation aid. Health professionals monitor clients who have

---

health field the realm of health services, including the healthcare system, traditional medical services, improvements in human biology, improvements in lifestyle, and improvements in environment, as envisioned by former federal minister of health Marc Lalonde

chronic conditions to prevent further illness. The centre serves healthy meals and provides activities.

One participant in the CHOICE program, Frank Blackwell, age 85, says the program gives him a better perspective on his health. It also offers respite from his role as caregiver to his wife. He says, "I'm quite happy to get out and meet other people and see that I'm not as sick as I thought I was…. [Also] I am able to get away for a few hours. It's exciting and I'm not worrying about my wife…."

Programs like this provide the kind of services that seniors need to maintain their health and stay in their homes.

The Future of Health Promotion

Older people can benefit from health promotion. Some older people already engage in self-care. They take vitamins, eat breakfast every day, and engage in regular exercise. Improvements in self-care can improve an older person's quality of life. Volumes of studies show that not smoking, maintaining a healthy weight, eating a balanced diet, and exercise all lead to a higher quality of life in old age.

The Public Health Agency of Canada (PHAC) (2009) reported, for example, that t'ai chi (a Chinese form of martial art) can reduce falls in seniors. A program taken twice a week for 15 weeks reduced falls by 47.5 percent among seniors age 70 and older (when compared with a control group). "A 20% decrease in hospitalizations due to falls among seniors could potentially result in over 7,500 fewer hospitalizations." This could lead to 1,800 fewer seniors with permanent disabilities and a saving of $138 million each year in healthcare costs. The PHAC estimates that $1 invested in health promotion yields a return on investment of $6 to $8 in health cost savings.

Will the government support health promotion programs in the future? Support for health promotion programs depends on the political climate, the economy, and the government's belief in the value of health promotion. Consider the case of the federal government's ParticipACTION program.

In 1971, the federal government launched ParticipACTION, a health promotion program that used mass media to raise awareness. Between 1971 and 2000, the program cost a total of $21 million—less than $1 million per year. The program also drew more than $40 million in private-sector funding. Yet, starting in the mid-1990s, Health Canada cut the ParticipACTION budget—most notably in 1999–2000 from $1 million to only $200,000.

The government closed the program at the end of 2001. In 2007, a newly installed federal government reinstated the program with a $5 million budget for two years to help cope with rising obesity rates and declining activity among Canadians. The program continues today. It promotes active living, sponsors health promotion activities, and hosts a website that lists health promotion events. The program gets support from corporate sponsors such as CBC Sports, and Sun Life Financial.

The newly invigorated ParticipACTION program shows a commitment by the government to health promotion. But more can be done to spread the word about programs such as ParticipACTION. Spence and colleagues (2009) studied public awareness of the ParticipACTION program in 2007–2008, nearly 40 years after it began. They asked more than 4,000 Canadians about the program. They found that only 8 percent of the people in their study said they knew about the program with no prompting from the researchers.

After prompting, 82 percent said they knew about the program. People with more education and better income tended to know about the program. People who took part in leisure-time physical activity tended to know about the program. The researchers say that health promotion programs need to use specific strategies to target unique populations (e.g., people with lower levels of education). Programs such as ParticipACTION need more funding to demonstrate their effectiveness.

Health Canada (a federal government agency) supports a number of other health promotion activities. For example, Health Canada produces guides to help older people live an active lifestyle. The handbook *Canada's Physical Activity Guide to Healthy Active Living for Older Adults* prescribes daily and weekly amounts of exercise to maintain good health. In 2005, the Canadian government developed an "Integrated Pan-Canadian Healthy Living Strategy" (Secretariat for the Intersectoral Healthy Living Network, 2005). This strategy focused on reducing chronic disease and obesity through healthy diet and encouraging physical activity. This approach makes sense, given the findings that show the importance of exercise in decreasing obesity.

Disease prevention and health promotion have caught on in Canada among seniors. Canada's *Health Promotion Survey* found that, compared with younger people, seniors less often skipped breakfast, smoked cigarettes, drank alcohol, or used illicit drugs. Nearly half of all seniors (48 percent) said they ate five or more servings of fruit or vegetables each day. Only 39 percent of 25- to 54-year-olds reported this kind of healthy diet. Even among people age 71 and over, about 40 percent said they eat enough fruits and vegetables each day (National Advisory Council on Aging, 2006; Turcotte & Schellenberg, 2007). Some of these health promotion behaviours reflect the values and lifestyles that seniors have brought with them into old age. But in other cases, seniors have responded to health promotion programs.

Seniors also engage in self-care activities that promote and maintain their health. For example, nearly all seniors (97 percent), with at least one chronic condition, who feel in good or better health, say that they could self-manage their medical treatments at home. The large majority (81 percent) of seniors in poor health say they could follow through on medical treatments at home. A large majority of seniors with at least one chronic condition (88 percent) say they know "how to prevent further problems with their health condition" (Canadian Institute for Health Information, 2011d, p. 10). Healthcare providers can engage seniors in setting goals, preparing a treatment plan, and making treatment decisions. Self-care could reduce seniors' use of expensive formal healthcare services.

Today, most writing about healthcare focuses on the obvious drivers of cost—hospitals, doctors, drugs, and nursing homes. Other writing focuses on personal health—diet, exercise, and self-care. But a fuller picture of healthcare would take the environment into account. This would include the air and water quality as well as economic well-being.

A person's housing, their neighbourhood, and their town or city all affect their health. A Canadian program called Healthy Cities works to create an environment that supports health and well-being. For the senior, a healthy city will include "access to recreational, social and community activities." Chapter 11 on Housing and Transportation discusses age-friendly, health-promoting cities in more detail.

> ### TIME TO REVIEW
>
> *What benefits would society and individuals gain from a focus on health promotion in later life? Give some of the research findings that support the health promotion perspective.*
>
> *Why should health promotion focus on economic inequality and the environment a person lives in as well as on personal health?*

ISSUES FOR THE FUTURE

Provincial and territorial long-term care systems differ across the country. The provinces and territories often agree on the same values and principles of long-term care (LTC), but each has its own commitment to services, its own policies on access to care, and its own funding arrangements.

This means that the principle of universality that underlies acute healthcare does not apply as well to LTC. First, clients often must pay out of pocket for long-term care. Government health benefits may not cover day hospital, respite, or homemaker costs. This can leave the poorest older people without help. Second, long-term care can lack coordination. This makes it hard for people to find the help they need. Third, many people fall through the cracks. They may not know about services or may not have access to a service (for example, a religious-based service may serve only people who share that faith). Health professionals refer to this as the **care gap**—the difference between what care could or should be and what care usually is. The care gap leads to missed clinical benefits and higher costs for payers.

The healthcare system of the future will need to respond to these problems in LTC delivery. The present system will have to be revised to meet older people's needs. Improvements need to take place in the availability of services, access to services, and coordination of services.

Availability

The ability to stay in the community depends in part on the availability of services that support a person at home. Some provinces or parts of provinces have a continuum of care—from home care to acute hospital care—for older people. Other parts of the country, such as many rural areas, offer only a few home care options.

Rural areas also show a decline in the number of physicians, bed closures to save money, longer wait times, and less access to medical technologies. This leads to poorer healthcare services for rural seniors. Conde and McDonald (2007; also McDonald & Conde, 2010) studied health service use in rural areas for people age 55 and over. They found that, compared with people in urban centres, rural people tended to see a general practitioner, a specialist, or a dentist less often.

The researchers expressed concern over this finding because regular checkups with a doctor or dentist can prevent serious health problems. The researchers said that long distances to get care and a shortage of doctors lead to infrequent healthcare checkups.

Government policies now make local communities responsible for managing healthcare. This has led rural areas to rely on informal and volunteer home care

---

care gap the difference between what care could or should be and what usual care is; the care gap leads to missed clinical benefits and higher costs for payers

programs. But the aging of rural populations puts pressure on these informal services. Many young people in rural areas leave to find work in cities. Over time, rural communities have more older people and fewer young people to provide volunteer services (Canadian Institute for Health Information, 2011c).

One rural community careworker described the workings of the Meals on Wheels program in her community. She arranges with a local restaurant to pick up a half-dozen to a dozen meals each day at noon, then she delivers them during her lunch hour to people on her caseload. She marvels at the good luck of city-based community workers, who can refer their clients to existing Meals on Wheels programs. Rural parts of Canada need more community care programs.

Accessibility

A program is accessible if an older person can get to it and make use of it. Better access requires better transportation and more home-based care for very old seniors. "For example, in rural communities where there is no public transportation, alternate methods of transportation may be required to ensure older adults can access necessary healthcare services" (Canadian Health Services Research Foundation, 2011, p. 15). Also, specific groups need help gaining access to health services.

Denton and Kusch (2006) reported that new immigrants and seniors from ethnic groups may need special help to get services. Unique dietary requirements, cultural differences, and food preferences can limit ethnic group members' use of community services. Culturally sensitive professionals can help overcome some of these barriers. Sometimes people do not take advantage of the programs that exist.

Ma and Chi (2005) found that many Chinese Canadian elders did not know about services in their community. These seniors also faced a language barrier when it came to using services. Better information for seniors not fluent in English would provide more access to services. Older people would also benefit from multilingual workers trained to work in multicultural settings.

Other inequities exist. Fernandes and Spencer (2010) found that many people in Canada pay for long-term care privately, and these costs differ across the country and even within a province: "A non-married person with average income would pay more than twice as much in the Atlantic provinces as in Quebec, while a couple with one in care would pay almost four times as much in Newfoundland as in Alberta" (p. 307).

Technology will play a growing role in getting healthcare services to rural areas in the future. For example, Alberta began testing the use of technology to control wandering, alert caregivers if a care receiver falls, and help seniors remember to take their medicines. The province invested nearly $2 million over two years (2010–2012) to test these systems. The Alberta minister of health and wellness at the time said, "These technologies are designed to provide seniors with more dignity and independence, while reducing stress on their caregivers" (Government of Alberta, 2011).

Canada has a 50-year history of "telehealth" (sometimes called "telemedicine") that delivers medical diagnoses and consultations through technology. Telehealth includes live videoconferencing, storage of data for later analysis, and remote monitoring of patients in their homes. A study of Canadian telehealth recognized Canada as the world leader in videoconferencing (Canada Health Infoway, 2011).

The use of television and now computer technology brings specialized healthcare to rural and remote communities. In 2009–2010, Canada had 5,710 telehealth systems in place in 1,175 communities across the country. Telehealth allows people with a serious illness to stay in their community rather than risk complications by travelling to a distant health facility. People in remote northern communities make heavy use of telehealth services.

A review of the research on telehealth (Deshpande et al., 2008) found that "real-time telehealth could reduce the number of hospital admissions and mortality rates among patients with chronic conditions such as congestive heart failure" (p. iii). The study also found that telehealth improved communication between patients and healthcare providers, improved the management of chronic diseases, and enhanced older patients' quality of life.

Deshpande and colleagues concluded that, given Canada's aging population and its vast geographic area, telehealth could provide "effective and efficient health services that result in equitable, fair, and sustainable health care delivery." (p. v) Canada Health Infoway (2011) said that telehealth services reduce travel by patients and healthcare providers. They make specialized healthcare available to seniors in remote and rural areas.

New technologies will speed the use of telehealth programs. Widespread Internet access will mean that an older people in a remote setting can get healthcare advice and support in their homes. This can include diagnosis of illness, monitoring health conditions, and specialist consultations. Ontario's program (eHealth Ontario) includes online management of medications to prevent adverse drug reactions, healthcare professionals' online access to a patient's drug history, and an electronic records management system (eHealth Ontario, 2013).

The Canadian Informatics Association (COACH, 2013, p. 11) reported over 195 percent growth in clinical telehealth services between 2006 and 2012. Canada Health Infoway (2011) projected steady growth in telehealth services over the following five to ten years. Technology mediated healthcare can provide home care and also reduce hospital admissions.

Nearly 2,500 patients in Canada got "telehomecare" in 2010 (Canada Health Infoway, 2011). A telehomecare program in New Brunswick called EMPcare@home included daily patient monitoring along with education to support self-management (Seymour et al., 2006). A typical patient was female, age 77, with a history of frequent hospital admissions. The technology collected patients' weight, temperature, and other vital signs. The system stored the data in a central database. The software then coded this data to alert healthcare staff to any warning signs or changes in a person's condition. The staff could then intervene early to prevent complications. The system also provided patients with daily information about their health so they could self-manage their care.

A study of this program found that it reduced hospital and emergency room admissions by 85 percent and led to a 55 percent decrease in emergency room visits after six months. Nearly all (90 percent) of the patients found the system easy to use. One patient told a focus group: "Before I used to go into a panic and off I would go to the hospital ... now I can manage on my own most times...."

Telehealth faces a number of challenges to its growth and adoption. Telehealth programs will at least need (1) a payment schedule to encourage physicians and institutions to use the systems; (2) a training program for health professionals; (3) regular assessment of program outcomes; and (4) government policy and funding support. Advances in technology in the future can help reduce health costs and increase access to healthcare.

Coordination

The healthcare system needs better coordination and integration. Lack of coordination leads to frustration for families and front-line workers. The Special Senate Committee on Aging's Final Report (Carstairs & Keon, 2009,) said, "Health and social service systems are not sufficiently integrated to allow caring professionals and family members to pull together the right basket of services to meet the needs of ailing seniors. Services have to be designed so that people don't fall through the cracks, and so that there are smooth transitions as their needs change" (pp. 33–34).

The need for coordination will increase with the growth of community care because community programs decentralize care. They bring together nurses, social workers, and therapists, who often work for different agencies and whose views on how to care for a client differ. McAdam (2008) conducted a systematic review of the literature on integrated health delivery systems. She found that programs varied in their structure and content but "at a minimum, all successful programs of integrated care for seniors use multidisciplinary care/case management supported by access to a range of health and social services" (p. iv). The best programs also included active involvement by a physician, common planning and assessment tools, and an integrated data system.

A **single-point-of-entry model** best coordinates services for older people. It provides flexibility, continuity, and quality of care for clients. It also controls costs. A single-point-of-entry model gives personalized help to each client. A staff member from a single agency assesses clients' needs, coordinates service delivery, and monitors clients' progress. The staff member may arrange for meal delivery, a visiting nurse, and homemaker help in one case. In another case, the staff member may arrange for respite care and day hospital use. Many provinces, including Manitoba, Alberta, and New Brunswick, already use this approach.

Coordination avoids overlap between services, and integration unites health and social services into one system. Pare (2000, cited in National Advisory Council, 2000) reported on a Montreal program called SIPA (Services integres pour les personnes agees en perte d'autonomie). This program provided an integrated model of coordinated care services for frail seniors. It used hospitals and long-term care settings to serve its clients and it offered nursing services around the clock. Pare reported a 50 percent drop in long-term care admission rates and fewer seniors in hospital beds waiting for care.

Beland and colleagues (2006a, 2006b) used the SIPA program to conduct one of the few randomized control studies of integrated care. The researchers assigned 606 seniors (age 64–104) to SIPA. The SIPA group got care through community-based interdisciplinary teams. A publicly managed and funded system delivered the care. They assigned 624 seniors to a control group (that got usual care for frail seniors in Quebec).

---

single-point-of-entry model a single agency that assesses clients' needs, coordinates service delivery from multiple sources, and monitors clients' progress

The researchers found that the average hospital cost for the SIPA group was \$4,270 less than costs for the control group. But compared with the control group, the average community cost per person came to \$3,394 more for the SIPA group (Beland et al., 2006a). The control group, compared with the SIPA group, had twice the proportion of people waiting for nursing home placement from an acute care hospital. And the SIPA group with disabilities, compared with the control group, cost at least \$4,000 less on average in acute hospitalizations.

In addition, the SIPA group reported greater caregiver satisfaction, no increase in caregiver burden, and no extra out-of-pocket expenses. In other words, the integrated care program provided care that better met the needs of clients and caregivers at no added cost.

What led to these benefits? Integrated services and coordinated planning explains much of SIPA's success. For example, case managers began discharge planning when a patient entered the hospital. They arranged for community resources to meet the patient's needs when the patient returned home. The researchers conclude that "integrated service systems for frail older adults can reduce the use and costs of hospital services and nursing homes without increasing overall health care costs, reducing quality of care, or increasing the burden on older adults and their relatives" (Beland et al., 2006a, p. 25).

Winnipeg Regional Health Authority's Geriatric Program Assessment Teams (GPAT) offer coordinated and integrated healthcare to seniors. The teams visit seniors in their homes to do an assessment of their health and well-being. Members of the teams have training in geriatric care. A team defines a person's needs—home care, help with medications, even home modification. The team then sets out a care plan and forwards the plan to the senior's family physician. GPAT works to reduce emergency department use and to delay institutional care. An audit of the program by the Manitoba Centre for Health Policy found that "Winnipeg had the lowest overuse of medication in the province" (Canadian Institute for Health Information, 2011c, p. 56). Accreditation Canada recognized the program as a leading practice in the country.

The Health Council of Canada (2011) finds an increase in integrated services throughout the country. Approaches to integration differ, but all attempt to "integrate services across an ever-expanding continuum of care to better serve patients (including those in rural and remote regions) and drive efficiencies" (p. 24).

The National Advisory Council on Aging (1995) summed up the value of integrated and coordinated care many years ago and the comments hold true today:

"Health reform means more than controlling costs to achieve an affordable health care system. It means providing appropriate and effective care that is responsive to the changing needs of Canadians" (p. 20). Responding to older people's needs should be the most important goal of a reformed healthcare system.

CONCLUSION

The changes taking place in healthcare today suggest that the healthcare system will look different in the future. Government concerns with efficiency and costs have led to proposals for reform. Healthcare professionals have proposed a shift from a biomedical model to a social, community-based model of healthcare. Closer study of older people's healthcare needs will allow the system to fine-tune programs and treatments. The critique of the medical model and growing interest in social models of healthcare will lead to more community-based services. Also, as the population ages, more people will show an interest in disease prevention and health promotion. More comprehensive models of healthcare, such as the social and health promotion models, will lead to better healthcare for older people as well as better health at all ages.

Summary

1. Healthcare needs for the elderly range from maintenance programs for the well elderly to long-term institutional care for those who have severe health problems.

2. Three models of healthcare exist in Canada today: the medical model, the social model, and the health promotion model. The medical model that dominates the healthcare system today is concerned with the treatment of illness. The social model supports community care and support. The health promotion model focuses on prevention and wellness.

3. The Canadian healthcare system consists of five basic principles: universal coverage, access to services, portability, comprehensive services, and administration by a non-profit public agency. The provincial and federal governments share the cost of this system.

4. Canada has one of the most comprehensive healthcare systems in the world, but it spends proportionately more of its gross national product on healthcare than do some countries with more comprehensive systems.

5. Long wait times for treatment continue to challenge the system. The media and the public focus attention on this issue. The government has addressed this by promising to reduce wait times. Studies show that wait times have improved for some illnesses. But in other cases, wait times remain longer than they should be. Also, wait times differ by province.

6. Research shows that the commitment to the medical model may account for higher than necessary healthcare costs. Complex medical procedures, increased salaries for medical personnel, prescription drug prices, and high institutional costs all lead to increasing healthcare costs.

7. Population aging will have some effect on healthcare costs. But this effect will be modest relative to other causes of increased costs (e.g., increased medication prices). And the effect of population aging will take place gradually over time.

8. Healthcare institutions (e.g., hospitals, nursing homes) serve the needs of many older people, and programs exist that can improve the quality of life of institutionalized patients. But sometimes people enter institutions because they cannot get the support they need to stay in the community.

9. Older people in institutions should lead as normal a life as possible. Models of quality care exist. Seniors need opportunities to socialize, exercise, and maintain as much autonomy as possible. Good design can also improve seniors' quality of life in institutions.

10. The Romanow Report on the Canadian healthcare system proposed reform to the system. The report repeated Canada's commitment to its universal medical care system. It also rejected the use of user fees. Some reforms, such as support for palliative care and long-term care, have taken hold. They will expand in the future and will improve care for older people. Other reform proposals, such as the limitation of home care to post-acute, mental health, and palliative care patients, need expansion to include seniors' needs.

11. The social model of healthcare supports a continuum of services from institutional care to home care. It calls for healthcare programs that help older people stay in their own homes. These programs include geriatric day hospitals, adult daycare programs, and home care.

12. Home care programs tailor services to fit the needs of the older person. They provide families with help to relieve caregiver burden. Home care use has grown in Canada. These programs can save the healthcare system money. But they need to substitute for institutional care in order to reduce costs. Home care

programs allow older people to stay in their homes as long as they can.

13. The health promotion model of healthcare supports healthy lifestyles and a better environment. It takes a broad view of healthcare that recognizes a need for changes in the workplace and improvements in socioeconomic status. Compared with medical and community care programs, health promotion programs tend to get less government financial support.

14. The government will have to deal with three service issues in order to meet the needs of an aging population: availability of services, accessibility of services, and coordination of services.

15. Technologies like telehealth and telehomecare can overcome barriers to healthcare for seniors in remote and isolated communities. This will increase the availability of services and access to services. In particular, technology can bring the diagnosis and treatment of complex conditions to remote areas. Older people can also use technology to monitor and manage chronic disease.

16. Coordination and integration of healthcare services holds a key to quality care and reduced costs. Programs throughout the country use case management and other methods to coordinate services. Integrated services require the cooperation of many types of healthcare professionals.

17. The healthcare system will change in the future and will evolve to meet the needs of older people. This will include more community-based care and more health promotion programs. The system has already begun to make some of these changes.

STUDY QUESTIONS

1. List and describe the three major approaches to healthcare that exist in Canada today.

2. List three of the drivers of increased cost of healthcare in Canada. What impact does population aging have on healthcare costs? How might the government control the drivers of costs? What are three proposals made by the Romanow Report? Why do gerontologists think this report needed to include more reference to older people?

3. Discuss the trends in community healthcare. How will these provide better service to an aging society? Describe at least two community-based healthcare programs that provide high-quality care to seniors.

4. Explain the benefits of health promotion to the individual and to society. Why does health promotion need to look beyond the individual in order to improve health?

5. Discuss three barriers to healthcare that the healthcare system has begun to address. What role will technology play in the future delivery of healthcare?

6. How does coordination and integration of services lead to better healthcare delivery and reduced costs? Describe a program that uses these methods to improve care.

KEY TERMS

adult daycare programs (p. 183)
assisted living (p. 183)
care gap (p. 189)

Community Care Access Centres (CCACs) (p. 181)
continuum of care (p. 181)
geriatric day hospital (p. 182)
healthcare system (p. 165)
health field (p. 187)
health promotion model (p. 166)
home care (p. 184)
long-term care (p. 166)
medical model (p. 165)
Romanow Report (p. 179)
single-point-of-entry model (p. 191)
social model (p. 166)

Study Tools
CHAPTER 7

{

Located at retail.tophat.com:

- Review Key Terms with interactive and printable flash cards
- Check Your Comprehension and Think About chapter concepts by completing practice quizzes
- Develop Your Gerontological Imagination with class activities
- Analyze Aging in a Global Perspective with engaging case studies and critical thinking questions
- Demonstrate Your Knowledge of the Concepts by bringing your own experience to personal application questions
- Evaluate Aging in the Media by completing Internet activities with evaluation questions

CHAPTER 8

FINANCES AND ECONOMICS

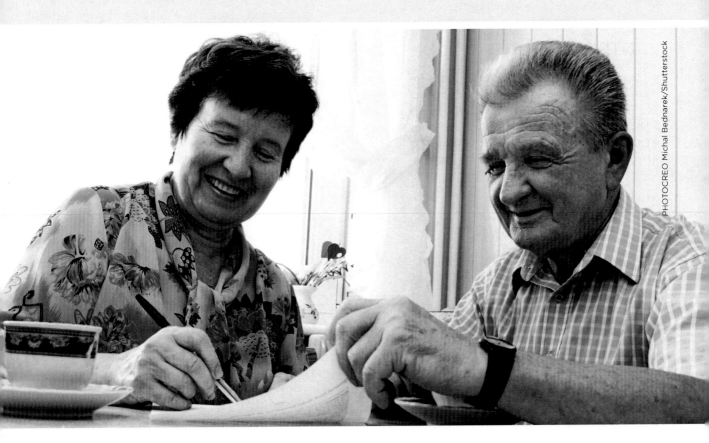

PHOTOCREO Michal Bednarek/Shutterstock

LEARNING OBJECTIVES

After reading this chapter, you will

LO1 Be able to explain the reason for the decline in the poverty rate for older people in Canada.

LO2 Be able to describe some of the flaws in the retirement income system that leaves many older people in poverty.

LO3 Be able to list the three tiers of the Canadian pension system and describe the role that each tier plays in providing seniors with an adequate income.

LO4 Be able to critique each tier of the Canadian pension system and show the need for improvement in each tier.

LO5 Understand why the Canada Pension Plan has changed its policies in response to increased longevity and changing patterns of retirement.

LO6 Be able to explain the reasons that, based on life course experiences, older women, compared with older men, on average have higher rates of poverty and lower incomes.

And describe some of the changes in women's work experience that may lead to improved income for older women in the future.

LO7   Be able to describe the actions taken by the Canadian government to improve each tier of the retirement income system.

LO8   Be able to explain why most Canadians will support improvements to the retirement income system in order to keep it sustainable for the future.

INTRODUCTION

Jack Bruckner, age 63, took early retirement. He gets a pension from his job, a small Canada Pension Plan pension, and an Old Age Security cheque each month. His wife, Betty, age 57, never worked outside the home, so she receives no private pension.

They live in a small, government-subsidized apartment. Last spring, Jack and Betty decided to travel east. Jack knew their old car would never make the trip, so he went to the bank for a car loan. "I never thought they'd give me a loan," he says. "I went in thinking they'd just laugh at the idea. But the bank manager looked at my pension income and approved the loan. I can't believe it—I never thought, with the little we make, that we'd be able to buy a new car."

Like many older people, Jack and Betty do not have much, but they feel satisfied with what they have. Both of them lived through lean times when they first got married. They worry less about money now than in the past and, Jack says, when Betty gets her pension from the federal government in a few years, their financial worries will be over.

Canada's pension system can take most of the credit for the Bruckners' financial well-being. The income of older people, adjusted for inflation, increased faster than that of younger people (age 15 to 64) from the early

EXHIBIT 8.1 *Prevalence of Low Income (After Tax), by Age Group, Canada, 1980 to 2011, Percent*

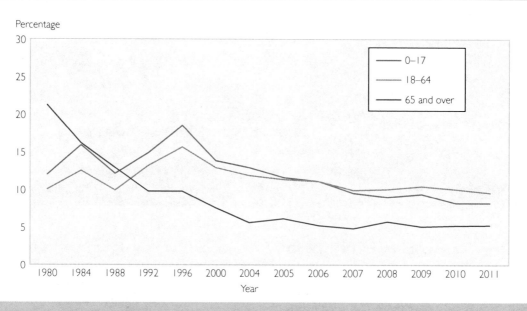

Statistics Canada (2008a) defines low income as an "income level at which families or persons not in economic families [people who live alone] spend 20% more than average of their before-tax income on food shelter and clothing." This graph shows the general downward trend in the poverty rate for all older people. By the early 1990s, seniors' low-income rate had dropped below all other age groups' rates. It continued to decline and hovered around 5 percent from 2006 onward. By 2011, seniors, compared with people age 18 to 64, had about half the low-income rate (5.2 percent vs. 9.7 percent). The decrease in poverty rates holds for all groups of older people, but senior women who live alone still show the highest rates of poverty among older people.

Sources: Statistics Canada. Persons in low income after tax (2006 to 2010), http://www.statcan.gc.ca/tables-tableaux/sum-som/l01/cst01/famil19a-eng.htm. Accessed August 11, 2012. Also, Persons in low income after tax (2001 to 2005), http://www.statcan.gc.ca/tables-tableaux/sum-som/l01/cst01/famil19a-eng.htm, Accessed August 11, 2012. Also, Persons in low income after tax (2007 to 2011), http://www.statcan.gc.ca/tables-tableaux/sum-som/l01/cst01/famil19a-eng.htm?sdi=low%20income. Accessed February 27, 2017. Also, Turcotte, M., & Schellenberg, G. (2007). *A Portrait of Seniors in Canada*, 2006. Statistics Canada. p. 95. Original Source: Statistics Canada, *Survey of Consumer Finances; Survey of Labour and Income Dynamics*. Reproduced and distributed on an "as is" basis with c the permission of Statistics Canada.

1980s to the present. By 2010, the poverty rate for older people had decreased to one-quarter of its 1980 level (see Exhibit 8.1).

Henripin (2009) reported that Canada does especially well in replacing the income of low-income seniors. People with an income at 50 percent of the Canadian national average can expect on average to replace 89.2 percent of their income from government sources. This compares favourably with an average replacement rate from government sources to low-income seniors in 30 developed nations. On average, these nations replace only 83.8 percent of low-income seniors' income.

What about middle- and upper-income earners? Brown (2010a), in a review of Canadian pension plans, said that "the present Canadian system in total (i.e., Social Security plus Private Pension Plans plus RRSPs [registered retirement savings plans]) is, in fact, doing a good job in providing Canadians with retirement income security" (p. 10). Increases in Guaranteed Income Supplement payments (for the poorest seniors), the maturation of the Canada Pension Plan, and more people with employer pensions and RRSPs all lead to better incomes for Canada's seniors. Mo, Légaré, and Stone (2006; Brown, 2010a) say that the Canadian retirement income system encourages investment throughout a person's working life. This leads to more diversified income in retirement and accounts for the relatively high incomes of Canada's seniors today.

Myles (2000), in a review of Canada's pension system, concluded that Canada has one of the best income security systems in the world. And it has one of the lowest rates of seniors' low income among the developed nations. He calls the cost of the public system "modest by international standards." "In short," Myles said, "like Baby Bear's porridge, Canada seems to have gotten it 'just right' when measured against these international benchmarks" (p. 288).

In 2013, for example, senior families had a median after-tax income of $52,500. (Non-senior families in that year had a median income of $77,100.) On average about half of the income in senior families ($26,600) came from government pension plans (Statistics Canada, (2015j). Seniors in 2012 had the lowest proportion of "families in low-income and without wealth" (1 percent). By comparison, 2.6 percent of families with a head age 45 to 54 lived with low income and no wealth (Uppal & LaRochelle-Côté, 2015a).

The Canada pension system in large part explains seniors' generally strong economic position. In 2012 seniors had the lowest proportion of families with debt (42.5 percent). The life cycle hypothesis supports this finding. Compared to middle-aged families (age 45 to 54 with 80.7 percent with debt), many seniors own their own homes and tend to live mortgage-free (Uppal & LaRochelle-Côté, 2015b).

A McKinsey & Company (2015) report debunks the myth that most Canadians will face a crisis in retirement and will have to reduce their standard of living when they retire. McKinsey's research showed that "a strong majority of Canadian households are actually on track to maintain their standard of living in retirement" (p. 2).

The strong financial condition of older people shows up in their relations with their children. Dependency ratios, for example, assume that older people depend on the young for support, but studies of intergenerational family transfers show just the opposite. A study by Metlife in the United States (2009), for example, found that many grandparents set up college funds for grandchildren. They also help with tuition and loans. Swartz (2009) said that parents often provide financial help to grown children in times of trouble, such as during a divorce. Angel and Mudrazija (2011) said that "even poor parents often give substantial gifts to their children...." (p. 169)

Findings from these studies show that money tends to flow from the older to the younger generation. This suggests that many older people can meet their own financial needs and still assist their children and grandchildren. Ploeg et al. (2004) concluded that older parents "wanted to help out of love and commitment to family but, perhaps most importantly, because they were financially able to provide this assistance" (p. S142). Studies and reports like these show that, as a group, older people have better incomes than many people imagine.

Still, the retirement income system has its flaws, some of them serious. While income has risen in the past few years for older people in general, certain groups still have incomes below the poverty line in old age. The McKinsey (2015, p. 3) report on retirement in Canada said that "17 percent of the nation's households [are] financially unprepared for retirement." The report said that two segments of the population face particular challenges: people with low personal savings and people without an employer pension plan.

In addition, older people from lower-income backgrounds, people who cannot speak English or French, people without much education, and people who live in small towns all tend to have lower than average incomes. Very old people, women, and unattached individuals (a term used by Statistics Canada to describe a "person living alone or in a household where he/she is not related to other household members") often live below the poverty line. Older women, compared with older men, also show a greater depth of poverty. In 2011, for example, women age 65 and over had an after-tax low-income rate of 6.4 percent; men had a rate of 3.8 percent. And in that year unattached senior women had the highest rate of low income. They showed an after-tax

EXHIBIT 8.2 *Financial Security among Retirees Age 55 and Over (Percentage)*

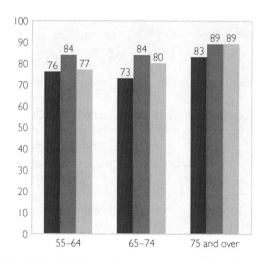

■ Financial situation better and or as expected before retirement

■ Retirement income is sufficient for monthly expenses

■ Keeping up with bills and other financial commitments not a problem

A large majority of every age group in this chart feels financially secure on these measures. The oldest age group shows the highest proportion of people with feelings of financial security. These findings point to the overall success of Canada's retirement income system. But note that in some cases, nearly one-quarter of the people in an age group do not feel financially secure. This points to the need among some older people for better pension support.

Source: Adapted from Marshall, K. (2011). "Retiring with Debt," *Perspectives on Labour and Income*, Statistics Canada, April 12, 2011, p. 8. Reproduced and distributed on an "as is" basis with the permission of Statistics Canada.

poverty rate of 16.1 percent, and men in this age group had an after-tax poverty rate of 12.2 percent (Statistics Canada, 2013g).

Even reports of average family incomes show that, compared with middle-aged people, older people live on lower incomes. For people who earned an average wage before retirement, the Old Age Security (OAS) will make up about 14 percent of their pre-retirement income. The Canada Pension Plan (CPP) will make up another 25 percent. Therefore, the average wage earner will have to find other means to make up lost income in retirement or live on a lower income.

People who earn above the average wage will need to make up even more income in order to maintain their standard of living. And those on fixed pensions (i.e., not indexed to the cost of living) get poorer every year because of inflation. Most people, except the very rich and the very poor, will feel a drop in their income when they retire.

Many individuals and groups, including the federal and provincial governments, the National Council of Women, and the Royal Canadian Legion, have suggested changes to Canada's pension system. Their concerns led to the **great pension debate** in the 1980s and more

recently to debates over the **universality** and sustainability of Canada's public pension system. The results of these debates have begun to influence the retirement income system in Canada and will influence the pensions of future retirees.

This chapter looks at (1) the structure of the Canadian pension system and how it works, (2) the flaws in the system and suggestions for pension reform, and (3) the future of Canada's retirement income system.

HISTORICAL DEVELOPMENTS IN CANADA'S PENSION SYSTEM

In 1889, Germany's Chancellor Otto von Bismarck created the first old-age social insurance program. The program required workers to contribute from their

great pension debate the debate in the 1980s over how to fund public pensions for older Canadians in the future

universality the idea that everyone in Canada has a right to a public pension, regardless of his or her income

pay; employers and the government contributed as well. The system also provided disability benefits and insurance against illness. The German government set age 70 as the retirement age (not age 65 as many people believe). Only in 1916 (nearly two decades after Bismarck's death) did the German system define retirement as age 65.

The United States modelled its Social Security system on the German system but adopted age 65 as its retirement age, independent of the German model. The United States took a practical approach. First, a number of existing state and private pension programs used this age. And second, studies showed that age 65 could lead to a sustainable system without heavy payroll taxes (Social Security, 2015).

Canada followed its own route in setting a retirement age and creating its retirement income system. Until the 1920s, Canadian pension policy reflected the "market ethos" (Bryden, 1974, p. 19). According to this thinking, individuals should take responsibility for themselves in old age and those who need help should get it from their families. Bryden reported that city life and industrialization in Canada made this ethos hard to practise. The *Labour Gazette*, for example, stated in 1924 that "high rents, [and] overcrowding in houses, make it difficult for the poor to provide for their aged parents. It has been the experience of social agencies that many of the old men and women in their districts are suffering from the lack of the necessities of life" (cited in Bryden, 1974, p. 42).

The Canadian federal government decided to act to relieve the poverty among older people. A House of Commons committee issued a report in 1925 that called for a $20 monthly pension to people age 70 or older who passed a residence requirement and a means test (a test of financial need). The committee proposed that the federal government and the provinces should each pay half the cost of pension benefits. The plan did not require pensioners to pay anything into the program. The committee saw the program as a supplement to income more than as a pension.

The Old Age Pension Act became law in 1927, and all of the provinces and the Northwest Territories agreed to the plan by 1936. This plan, for the first time, defined pensions as a right due to all older Canadians. Snell (1993) showed that men, compared with women, had greater access to these pensions. For example, a woman with a younger, employed husband could have her claim rejected because the state expected her husband to support her. Snell traced this decision to the state's assumption about male dominance in families.

In 1951, the federal government passed the Old Age Security Act and the Old Age Assistance Act to replace the Old Age Pension Act. The Old Age Security Act set up a pension plan run solely by the federal government. The new plan paid up to $40 a month at age 70 without a means test. The federal government increased this pension to $55 a month in 1961. The Old Age Assistance Act set up a means-tested pension for people between 65 and 69 years old who could demonstrate financial need. The provinces, territories, and the federal government shared the cost for this program. The plan required no contributions and paid the same pension to all poorer pensioners, including homemakers.

These early programs supplemented the incomes of older people by offering basic income security. The federal government kept payments low so people would have an incentive to provide for their own old age. In the 1960s, the federal government broadened the pension system by setting up the Guaranteed Income Supplement program to supplement Old Age Security. This program was designed to help the poorest older people. In 1966, the federal government and the government of Quebec started the Canada Pension Plan and the Quebec Pension Plan. Today, all wage earners in Canada pay part of their incomes into these plans.

By the 1970s, Canada had two types of programs in place: **income security programs** (the Old Age Security pension and the Guaranteed Income Supplement) and **income maintenance programs** (the Canada Pension Plan and the Quebec Pension Plan). These programs form the basis of the Canadian pension system today. The federal government designed the first type of program to help people meet their basic needs in retirement and the second type to help people maintain their pre-retirement income and lifestyle.

By 1999, federal government transfers (the Old Age Security and the Guaranteed Income Supplement and other transfers paid for from tax revenues) and the Canada Pension Plan (CPP) accounted for 47 percent of older Canadians' retirement incomes (Statistics Canada, 2003a). Federal government transfers and the CPP have made up increasing proportions of seniors' income over the years. Also, by the 1990s, seniors began to get more of their income from occupational pensions and other sources than ever before. These trends led to an overall increase in seniors' income.

income security programs the Old Age Security pension and the Guaranteed Income Supplement are income security programs that help people meet their basic needs in retirement

income maintenance programs the Canada Pension Plan and the Quebec Pension Plan are income maintenance programs that help people maintain their pre-retirement income and lifestyle

EXHIBIT 8.3 *Median Net Worth by Age Group of Major Income Earner, 1999 and 2012, in dollars*

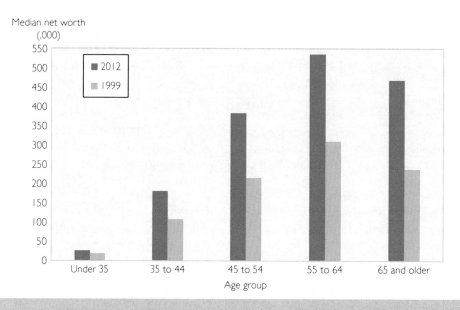

The net worth of all age groups increased between 1999 and 2012. The net worth of the 65 and older age group shows the greatest gain (70.2 percent). These people brought most of these assets with them into old age. They make up the wealthiest generation of older Canadians. Even unattached seniors (a group of seniors with about one-third of the median income of seniors in families) saw an increase in their median net worth of 56.1 percent during these years. Still, variations in wealth exist within this group. Half of this age group have less than this median amount. And some people live at the poorest end of the income spectrum.

Source: Adapted from Statistics Canada. Total and median net worth by age and family type. (2014o). Retrieved from http://www.statcan.gc.ca/daily-quotidien/140225/t140225b001-eng.htm.

A report by Mo, Légaré, and Stone (2006) described the diversification of seniors' income sources from the 1980s to the early 2000s. Income from private pensions, for example, grew from 18 percent of the average senior's income in 1990 to 29 percent in 1999 (Li, 2006, citing Maser, 2003). The researchers said that this diversification of income sources occurred among people in all income levels (not just wealthy people).

The maturation of public and private pension plans in Canada best explains this shift in income sources. The maturation of workplace pension plans also played a role in increasing older people's incomes. Studies show that the more diverse a person's income sources, the better off that person becomes financially. This movement away from government transfers and toward public and private pension income characterizes the Canada pension system's evolution from the 1980s onward. "Thus, on the average," Mo, Légaré, and Stone (2006) said, "the low-income elderly counted tradition-ally on a lower number of income sources to ensure their standard of living; but the situation has improved in recent years" (p. 14).

This diversification of income has also happened among older women living alone. Twenty years ago, this group depended mainly on governmental transfers and on investment income. As they diversified their sources of income, they relied more on private pensions. Public and private pensions still reflect inequalities in the labour market in lifetime work opportunities. Yet, private pensions helped older women move out of poverty (especially single women who live alone) (Stone, 2006).

In sum, Mo, Légaré, and Stone (2006) said, "the elderly count today on improved balance among various sources of income" (p. 18). Any decline in work income or investment income among older people (for example, due to an economic downturn, such as the one in 2008–2009) increases the importance of government and private sources of income—in particular, government transfers and pensions. This makes the study of the Canadian pension system vital to an understanding of old age today.

Describe the historical events that led to the start of public pensions in Canada.

What part(s) of the system promote income security?

What parts help with income maintenance?

Describe the shifts that have taken place in the proportion of seniors' incomes that come from various sources.

THE CANADIAN RETIREMENT INCOME SYSTEM TODAY

Canada's system of pension plans and programs, along with earnings from work, should create a decent old age for all Canadians, but it does not. Some older people still suffer a sharp loss in income and a change in lifestyle when they retire. Almost every tier and subsection of the Canadian pension system needs improvement to address this problem. The following discussion will look at the structure and the limits of the Canadian pension system today.

Tier One: Government Transfers

Canada has a three-tiered pension system shaped like a pyramid. The Old Age Security (OAS), the Guaranteed Income Supplement (GIS), and the Allowance (ALW)—called federal *government transfer programs*—make up the first tier. Nearly all Canadians age 65 or over, rich or poor, get the same OAS pension maximum ($564.87 per month in 2015). But people who earn more than a set amount have to repay their OAS at a rate of 15 cents for every dollar of their income over this amount. So someone with a net income of $117,954 or more in 2015 repaid his or her entire OAS benefit (Service Canada, 2015a). The Guaranteed Income Supplement goes to people with a low income or no income other than the Old Age Security. GIS payments vary by marital status and family income. Poon (2005; Luong, 2009) reported that families who get the GIS have about half the income of non-GIS families. And unattached people who got the GIS had one-sixth the total assets of non-GIS unattached people.

Allowance (ALW) payments go to spouses or common-law partners or survivors of OAS pensioners. The ALW helps survivors age 60 to 64 and couples with only one income. People do not directly contribute to OAS, GIS, or ALW pension funds; the federal government pays them out of tax revenue. Old Age Security Fund payments came to 39.7 percent of all federal transfer payments in 2009 (Statistics Canada, 2011j). The federal government estimates that it spent more than $39.1 billion on government transfers (OAS, GIS, and Allowance) in 2011–2012 (up from $11 billion in 1984) (Service Canada, 2012). This first tier of programs (OAS/GIS/ALW) in 2008 accounted for 15.2 percent of the incomes of older men and 27.2 percent of the incomes

EXHIBIT 8.4 *Canada's Multi-Tiered Pension System*

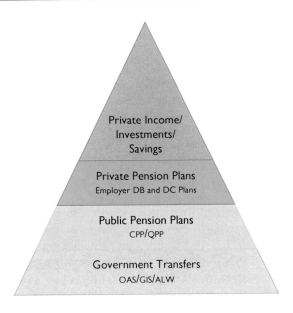

Private Income/
Investments/
Savings

Private Pension Plans
Employer DB and DC Plans

Public Pension Plans
CPP/QPP

Government Transfers
OAS/GIS/ALW

EXHIBIT 8.5   *Sources of Seniors' Income, 2011 (percentage)*

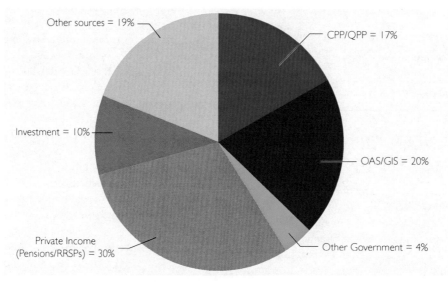

Note: "Other sources" includes employment earnings and other income.

This chart shows the proportion of seniors' income that comes from six major sources. In 2011, almost one-third of seniors' income (29.9 percent) came from private pensions and savings. Almost 38 percent of their income came from public sources (OAS/GIS and CPP/QPP). Investments and other sources of income made up almost a third of seniors' income (29 percent).

This chart presents the average proportion of seniors' income but wide variations exist in income sources within the older population. Wealthier people, for example, will get a higher proportion of their income from private pensions, RRSPs, and investments. Poorer seniors will get most of their income from public sources, primarily the OAS and GIS. Compared with men, women get less of their income from private pensions and work. Women rely more heavily on government pension programs (OAS/GIS/ALW). This, in part, explains their lower incomes in later life.

Source: Statistics Canada, *National Household Survey*, 2011, Income Composition in Canada (2013m), from https://www12.statcan.gc.ca/nhs-enm/2011/as-sa/99-014-x/99-014-x2011001-eng.cfm. Reproduced and distributed on an "as is" basis with the permission of Statistics Canada.

of older women (Canada Mortgage and Housing Corporation, 2015b). These programs protect older people's incomes—especially those of the very poor—from falling below a specified low-income level.

Not surprisingly, poorer people depend on transfers most. These transfers (OAS/GIS/ALW) reduce low-income rates and also decrease income inequality. Compared with older men, older women rely more heavily on government transfers. Older men received more of their income from private pensions (32.4 percent of their income for older men compared with only 26.6 percent of their income for older women). These figures reflect the different work careers of older men and women in the past and today (Canada Mortgage and Housing Corporation, 2015b; Turcotte & Schellenberg, 2007).

In March 2015, the OAS went to 5.5 million Canadians. The federal government indexes OAS payments to the consumer price index or cost of living and adjusts the rate four times a year. But the high cost of the program (almost $35 billion in 2015) makes it an obvious target for federal government cutbacks (Statistics Canada, 2015k).

The GIS goes to the poorest seniors. In March 2015, 1.8 million OAS pensioners (33 percent) received full or partial GIS payments (Statistics Canada, 2015k). GIS benefits in 2015 went to single older people who received less than $17,136 that year from sources other than the OAS, the first $3,500 in employment income, and the GIS. It also went to a spouse or common-law partner of an OAS pensioner in 2015. In this case the spouse or common-law partner had no OAS or GIS income and the OAS pensioner had income of $22,608 or less. The federal government does not tax the GIS, and it indexes GIS payments to the consumer price index so that benefits go up quarterly as the cost of living rises.

A person (or a couple) gets either full or partial GIS payments based on a yearly income test. In the third quarter of 2015, a single person (or a person whose spouse does not get the OAS) could receive a maximum GIS of $765.93 per month, while a partner of an OAS recipient could get a maximum GIS of $507.87 per month (Service Canada, 2015a). Total GIS expenditures in March 2015 came to $815.4 million.

Single pensioners, more often than married pensioners, have incomes low enough to need the GIS. The government also claws back GIS income at the rate of 50 cents for every dollar of income. Registered Retirement Savings Plan (RRSP) income, for example, will reduce a person's GIS income by 50 cents for every $1 withdrawn from an RRSP.

The federal government added the Spouse's Allowance (SPA) program (now called the Allowance (ALW)) to the first tier of the system in 1975. The ALW goes to a low-income pensioner's spouse who is age 60 to 64 years old. It pays an amount equal to the OAS and the maximum GIS at the married rate. This couple gets the same transfer payments as a poor couple with both spouses age 65 and over. If the GIS pensioner dies, the spouse continues to receive payments. When the survivor reaches age 65, the federal government stops ALW payments and the person then gets an OAS/GIS pension.

The vast majority of ALW payments go to women. All widows or widowers age 60 to 64 with low yearly income (below $31,680) can get the ALW. In March of 2015, for example, 80,003 older Canadians got the ALW. The estimate for Allowance payments in March 2015 came to $41.3 million (Service Canada, 2015b). Without GIS and ALW benefits, almost half (47 percent) of all older Canadians would live below the poverty line.

All provinces have provincial or territorial supplement plans to help the poorest seniors. Policies and practices for getting these supplements differ for each province. British Columbia and Ontario, for example, provide supplements automatically to seniors who file their taxes and qualify. Alberta and New Brunswick require that seniors apply for the benefits. Quebec, Nova Scotia, and Prince Edward Island offer other types of aid such as shelter allowance, home renovation credits, and nursing care. The amount of aid also differs by province. Yearly maximum supplements for a single person range from $400 (New Brunswick) to $3,360 (Alberta). All provinces also reduce taxes for older property owners or give rent rebates to seniors. These programs play a further role in keeping very old people and even people with occupational pensions at a decent income level.

Low-income seniors on average get more than three-quarters of their income (77 percent) from the OAS/GIS and other government transfers. They get another 17 percent of their income from the CPP. In other words, nearly all of low-income seniors' income (94 percent on average) comes from government sources. This contrasts with seniors who live above the low-income cut-offs. These people get only 61 percent of their income from government sources. The rest comes from private pensions (26 percent), investments (9 percent), earnings, and other sources (National Seniors Council, 2009).

The National Seniors Council (2009) reported that between 1980 and 2006, low income among seniors decreased from 21.3 percent to 5.4 percent—a rate lower than in most industrialized countries. The council linked this decrease to the effectiveness of the Canadian retirement income system. "Overall," the council said, "today's seniors, while not affluent, are financially secure" (p. 4). Still, Mac-Donald, Andrews, and Brown (2010) said the maximum GIS and OAS together "did not meet the cost of basic needs for an elder living in poor circumstances" (p. 39).

In 2015, for example, the OAS and GIS together guaranteed a single older person a yearly income of $15,969.60. But this leaves many seniors who live in an urban centre (of 30,000 people or more) below the national low-income cut-offs (LICOs). This means that a large proportion of single seniors (most of them unattached women) live in poverty even with government transfers (Statistics Canada, 2011j). Service Canada (2015b) estimates that OAS/GIS/ALW expenditures will come to $46,072 million in 2015–2016.

Some policies weaken the universality of the OAS pension. In 1977, the federal government introduced new residence requirements for government pensions. Until 1977, an older person who had lived in Canada for at least 10 years qualified for an old age pension. After 1977, a person earned one-fortieth of his or her pension for each year in Canada after age 18, and anyone with fewer than 10 years in Canada received no benefits. Many immigrants to Canada will now get less than a full OAS when they turn 65, and others will have to manage without government transfers. This policy will erode the universality of the old age pension system.

Another policy has further weakened the universality of the OAS. The federal budget speech of April 1989 introduced a **clawback** of OAS benefits from wealthier seniors. This measure continues today, and it has turned the OAS into a means-tested pension plan. Myles and Street (1995) concluded that with this policy the "OAS will gradually lose its status as the first tier of the retirement pension system and, along with GIS, become part of the social assistance program for low income seniors" (p. 346).

---

clawback a required repayment of Old Age Security benefits by wealthier seniors to the government

EXHIBIT 8.6   *The Canada Pension System*

Pension	Maximum Benefits per Month (July–September 2015)
Old Age Security	$564.87 (per person)
Requirements and program details: 65 years or over; residence requirement; Canadian citizen or legal resident; non-contributory; indexed quarterly.	
Guaranteed Income Supplement	$765.93 (single)
Requirements and program details: Income below $22,608 combined income per year; non-contributory; indexed quarterly	$1,072.74 (couple, married, or common-law with one OAS pensioner)
Allowance	$1,072.74
Requirements and program details: Equal to the sum of OAS and maximum GIS at married/common-law rate; partner of OAS pensioner who gets GIS; partner between 60 and 64; must satisfy other OAS requirements; non-contributory; indexed quarterly.	
Widowed Partner's Allowance	$1,200.98
Requirements and program details: Paid to any low-income widow or widower (60 to 64 years old); non-contributory; indexed quarterly	
Canada Pension Plan Retirement Pension (max.)	$1,065.00 (monthly, 2015)
Requirements and program details: 9.9 percent of income paid into plan; half by worker, half by employer (minus a basic exemption of $3,500). Up to year's maximum pensionable earnings (2015) – $53,600; indexed yearly.	
Canada Pension Plan Survivor Benefits	$639.00 (CPP 2015 max., partner 65 and over)
	$581.13 (CPP 2015 max., partner under 65)
Canada Pension Plan Death Benefit	$2,500 (CPP, max. lump sum, 2015)
Program details: Paid to estate of deceased contributor.	
Canada Pension Plan Disability Benefit	$1,264.59 (max. 2015)
Program details: Paid to contributors with severe and prolonged disability.	
Canada Pension Plan Children and Orphan Benefits	$234.87 (CPP, 2015)
Program details: Paid to each child of a disabled or deceased contributor.	

This chart shows at a glance the various payments that a senior may receive from a government transfer program. The government adjusts these rates quarterly to reflect increases in the cost of living.

The Old Age Security program goes to nearly all seniors in Canada, regardless of their income (although high-income seniors will pay back all or part of the OAS, depending on their total income). The GIS and Allowance go to specific groups of seniors. The GIS goes to low-income seniors based on their need. The Allowance goes to spouses of OAS pensioners and survivors of OAS pensioners. The Canadian government intends this system to serve as an income security program. It provides a basic income to all seniors in Canada and helps seniors most in need.

Source: Canada Pension Plan/Old Age Security Quarterly Report—Monthly Amounts and Related Figures from July to September 2015. https://www.canada.ca/content/dam/canada/employment-social-development/migration/documents/assets/portfolio/docs/en/statistics/quarterly_report/julsep15.pdf; Employment and Social Development Canada, 2017. Reproduced with the permission of the Minister of Employment and Social Development Canada, 2017.

Tier Two: The Canada Pension Plan and the Quebec Pension Plan

The Canada Pension Plan (CPP) and the Quebec Pension Plan (QPP) form the pension system's second, smaller tier. The CPP allows a province to opt out of the plan. Quebec chose to do so and set up its own plan. The QPP differs from the CPP in a few details, but in most ways it mirrors the CPP. This text will use the term CPP to refer to both plans.

Virtually 90 percent of the labour force between the ages 18 and 70, their employers, and self-employed people paid more than $43.2 billion into the plans in 2015 (Service Canada, 2015b). The CPP paid a maximum retirement benefit in 2015 of $1,065 per month. It paid more than $43.2 billion in 2013–2014 to more than 4.6 million retirees. Service Canada projected a similar expenditure for 2015–2016.

The CPP primarily does two things. First, it ensures that workers have some pension beyond the OAS/GIS/ALW when they retire, and, second, it saves the federal government money in GIS and ALW payments. The CPP combines two types of pension plans: a savings plan and a transfer plan. It works like a savings plan because each worker pays a percentage of his or her salary into it each month. Today the law requires workers to pay 4.95 percent of their wages into the plan; their employers pay a matching amount. Self-employed people paid 9.9 percent of their incomes into the plan. The government expects that investment of the surplus in the plan will allow it to freeze the contribution rate at 9.9 percent for some time. Payments to the CPP are credited to each worker and when he or she retires, their pension will depend on how much they paid into the plan.

The CPP also works like a transfer plan because the money paid in today does not go into a private account for each person; instead, it goes to pay the pensions of retired plan members today. Pension experts also call this a pay-as-you-go plan. Today's workers will receive their CPP pensions from workers' contributions in the future. This type of plan requires that each younger generation pay for the pensions of the older generation.

The CPP does some things well:

1. It protects people from inflation. Personal savings can decrease in value over time, but the CPP promises that a person will get a pension in the future geared to the cost of living at that time.
2. The CPP covers almost all workers, so most workers will enter retirement with some CPP benefits.
3. The plan is a portable pension, which means it moves with workers when they change jobs. In a fluid job market, where people change jobs often, this can mean the difference between having a pension or not.
4. The plan locks in both workers' and employers' contributions from the start. This is called vesting. Workers get credit for their total payments (their own and their employer's contributions) even if they move from one employer to another.
5. The CPP promises to pay workers up to 25 percent of their pre-retirement pensionable earnings (to a maximum of 25 percent of the year's average industrial wage) for life.
6. The plan applies the same rules to men and women. Women pay in at the same rates as men, and the plan entitles them to the same benefits. Some occupational plans (also called employer plans or registered pension plans—RPPs) base benefits on different mortality tables for men and women, so women in some plans get smaller payments because on average they live longer than men.
7. All CPP members get survivor and disability benefits, a vital point because in Canada, women often outlive their husbands and many women today have no pensions of their own.
8. The CPP calculates a person's pension by adjusting pensionable earnings from past years to bring them up to current wage levels. This adjusts for the fact that inflation makes earlier wage levels a poor basis for calculating a pension today and makes the CPP better than occupational plans that use lifetime earnings to calculate pension benefits.
9. The CPP allows contributors to choose early or late retirement. A contributor can receive benefits as early as age 60 or as late as age 70. The CPP, from 2016 on, will decrease a person's benefits by 7.2 percent per year (0.6 percent per month) for each year a person begins receiving benefits before his or her 65th birthday. A person who retires at age 60 would receive 64 percent of the CPP pension he or she would have received if payments began at age 65. The retiree will get this lower rate even after the age of 65.

The CPP, from 2013 on, increased by 8.4 percent per year (0.7 percent per month) for each year a person begins receiving benefits after his or her 65th birthday. A person who retires at age 70 will get a 42 percent larger pension than he or she would have received at age 65 (Service Canada, 2010). These changes discourage early retirement and encourage seniors to retire later. Changes to the CPP also encourage

---

savings plan a payment plan to which each person contributes a percentage of his or her salary each month; in the case of the CPP/QPP, the payments are credited to individual workers and when they retire, their pension will depend on how much they paid into the plan

transfer plan (also called a pay-as-you-go plan) money paid into the plan goes to pay the pensions of retired plan members today; the CPP/QPP also works like a transfer plan

pay-as-you-go plan today's retirees receive their CPP pensions from workers' contributions today; workers today will receive their CPP pensions from workers' contributions in the future; this type of plan requires that each younger generation pay for the pensions of the older generation

portable pension a pension that moves with workers when they change jobs

---

vesting workers with a fully vested pension have credit for their total pension contributions (their own and their employer's contributions) even if they move from one employer to another

workers to save more toward retirement. The new rules allow a person to continue to contribute to the CPP after age 65 if they continue working. This will increase their CPP pension when they retire.

10. The federal government indexes the CPP to the cost of living. It goes up as the cost of living increases, so people do not fall behind each year as they do with a fixed-income pension. In January 2015, the CPP increased pensions by 1.8 percent to account for an increase in the cost of living.

The CPP now pays benefits to more older people than ever before. In 1967, it paid benefits to less than one-half of 1 percent of older people, but in 2011 the CPP retirement benefit went to 89.4 percent of women and 95.3 percent of men age 65 and over (Employment and Social Development Canada, 2015a). The number of people who receive CPP pensions, the size of their pensions, and the total paid out in CPP pensions will all increase in the years ahead.

Still, the CPP has its limits. For instance, it does not help people maintain their pre-retirement income—the second goal of the Canadian pension system. For many older people today—those who never worked for a wage—the CPP offers no help at all, and some people who get the CPP find that it does not pay enough. In 2015, for example, the OAS and CPP together paid a maximum of $19,558.44 to a single person. This left a person below the low-income cut-off (LICO) for a single person in a city of 500,000 or more ($24,328 in 2014). Recipients who receive less than the maximum CPP can fall below the poverty line even in a small town (the LICO was $16,747 for rural areas outside cities in 2014).

These low CPP payments do not replace much of the average person's income. Also, the plan pays low survivor benefits. The CPP paid a survivor age 65 or over $12,780 per year for the maximum survivor benefit plus the CPP pension in 2015 (Service Canada, 2015b). And the poorest older people, who receive the GIS, lose $1 of their benefits for each $2 they receive from the CPP. As a result of these low rates, most people who rely on the OAS/GIS and CPP face a drop in living standards when they retire. People need private pensions or savings to maintain their pre-retirement lifestyles.

The Challenge to the CPP in the Future

Even at the plan's low benefit rate, the CPP could face financial problems in the future. For example, today Canada has five workers to pay the pension of each CPP retiree. By 2030, this will drop to three workers.

Also, an increase in the older population accounts for only about a third of the higher projected increase in CPP costs. About 45 percent of the projected increase in future costs comes from higher payouts for disability and enriched benefits. Higher-than-expected payouts of disability pensions would threaten the CPP reserve fund.

This potential danger led to a variety of proposed reforms in the late 1990s. These included cutting back benefits, better administration of the program, and investment in the stock market. (Battle, 1997; Lam, Prince, & Cutt, 1996; Robson, 1996). Some people at that time proposed raising the retirement age or limiting cost-of-living increases (Brown, 1995; Freeman, 1994).

The government has adopted some of these measures. First, the government responded to this challenge by raising contribution rates (to a total of 9.9 percent of a person's wage). The government expects that this rate increase will be enough to sustain the CPP into the foreseeable future.

Second, in 1998 the Canadian government created the CPP Investment Board to manage CPP surplus revenues. CPP Investment Board former president and CEO David Denison called the reforms of the 1990s "a bold and visionary achievement that has become a model for pension reform around the world." The board exists as a Crown Corporation. It accounts to Parliament and to federal and provincial finance ministers for its actions; however, the board operates independently of the CPP and at arm's length from the government. The board invests "to maximize returns without undue risk of loss" and "to help provide a foundation on which Canadians build financial security in retirement" (CPP Investment Board, 2014, p. 1).

The board began investing current surplus funds in the financial markets in 1999. In March 2014, the fund had assets of $219.1 billion (more than triple the $70 billion of 10 years previously). The board invests CPP funds not used to pay current benefits in a variety of financial instruments and markets. These include emerging market equities, real estate, and utilities. The *2014 Annual Report* stated a 16.5 percent rate of gross investment return for the year 2014 and an 11.7 percent five-year annualized return (CPP Investment Board, 2014, p. 1). The report emphasized its commitment to long-term strategy and growth. Future returns and the investment success of the board will depend in part on the performance of the stock market and the economy in general.

In 2012, the Chief Actuary of Canada considered the CPP "sustainable over a 75-year projection period, and that contributions to the Fund will exceed benefits paid until 2023." The Chief Actuary projected the fund would grow to $500 billion by 2030 (CPP Investment Board, 2014, Introduction).

Prus (2000) underscored the importance of the CPP in the Canadian pension system. He found that income inequality dropped in later life because of the help poorer seniors got from public pensions (CPP and OAS/GIS). Myles (2000) supported this view. He said that even "small proportional increases from all public income sources [including CPP/QPP] tend to reduce inequality" (p. 305). More people than ever before, at every income level, will rely on the CPP to meet their financial needs in later life.

TIME TO REVIEW

How does the CPP function as both a savings plan and a transfer plan?

What role does the CPP play in keeping many older Canadians out of poverty?

What steps has the government taken to ensure the sustainability of the CPP?

Tier Three: Private Pensions, Savings, and Work

Private income makes up the third tier of the Canadian pension system. The OAS/GIS and CPP alone cannot provide a comfortable income for most older people. These sources together still don't lift all seniors out of poverty, and they don't amount to a comfortable income for a middle-class person or family.

Other income received in retirement includes earnings, rent subsidies, and tax exemptions. In 2011, employment income accounted for 20.9 percent of the incomes of men age 65 and over, and 10.3 percent of the incomes of older women (Canada Mortgage and Housing Corporation, 2015b). Also, many organizations offer subsidies to seniors for their goods and services, such as reduced prices on theatre tickets or reduced bus fares for older people. These indirect subsidies add to older people's average total income.

In addition, seniors benefit from subsidized healthcare costs and home care services. Nevertheless, these sources of income cannot make up for the loss of earnings after retirement. Workers need private pensions and savings to make up the difference between federal government pensions and subsidies and their pre-retirement income.

Statistics Canada (2015l) reported that in 2013, more than 6 million workers belonged to more than 19,000 occupational pension plans (registered pension plans—RPPs). Public-sector workers accounted for 51.5 percent of all workers in RPPs. Nearly all public-sector workers (87 percent) (such as government workers, teachers, nurses, people who work for a Crown corporation) belonged to a plan, compared with 25 percent of private-sector workers (people who work for privately owned companies). Most pension plans pay 2 percent of a person's salary times the number of years of service.

Drolet and Morissette (2014) reported a decline in RPP membership for male workers age 15 and over from 52 percent in 1977 to 37 percent in 2011. At the same time, women saw an increase in RPP membership from 36 percent to about 40 percent (Statistics Canada, 2015m). This reflected the entry of women into public-sector jobs that almost always offer an RPP. This trend may change the amount and proportion of income men and women get from an RPP when they retire.

Men more often than women benefit from pension income; 70.3 percent of men compared with only 58 percent of women received occupational pension income in 2011. Occupational pension benefits also make up more of a man's income. In 2011, occupational income made up 32.4 percent of the income of males age 65 and over, but only 26.6 percent of the income of females age 65 and over (Canada Mortgage and Housing Corporation, 2015b). Upper-income workers tended to get the most benefit from private pensions in retirement. For example, occupational pensions made up about half the income of those who earned between $40,000 and $80,000 per year. But occupational pensions made up less than 10 percent of the income of people who earned under $20,000. Poorer people relied on public pensions for most (77 percent) of their income (Li, 2006).

Defined Benefit and Defined Contribution Pension Plans

Employers who want to cut costs and avoid the worry of underfunding have changed the type of pension plan they offer. They moved from **defined benefit (DB) pension plans**

---

defined benefit (DB) pension plans state how much an employee can expect to earn in retirement based on a formula that takes into account years of service and highest salary; the company guarantees the benefit based on this formula

to **defined contribution (DC) pension plans**. A defined benefit plan states how much an employee can expect to earn in retirement based on a formula that takes into account years of service and highest salary. The company guarantees the benefit based on this formula. A defined contribution plan states how much a person will pay into the plan (often matched to some degree by the company). This plan defines the contribution but does not guarantee the outcome. The employee must invest the money, and the outcome in retirement will depend on how well the employee's investments do over time.

In 2013, 71.2 percent of workers with a registered pension plan (RPP) in Canada had a defined benefit plan (Statistics Canada, 2015l). More than 10,000 plans offered defined benefits. They have enrolled 4.4 million workers (mostly unionized workers in the private sector, public-sector employees, and executives) (Statistics Canada, 2015n). Brown (2010b) said that 80 percent of public-sector workers have a DB pension, compared with only 25 percent of private-sector workers.

Among females employees age 25 to 54, one-third belong to a defined benefit plan. Only one in four men belong to this type of plan. This reflects the higher proportion of women, compared to the proportion of men, who work in the public sector—education, healthcare, social assistance, and public administration (Drolet & Morissette, 2014). In 2012, 42 percent of women age 25 to 54 worked in these kinds of jobs, compared to only 17 percent of men.

Compared to young people (age 25 to 34) with a high school diploma, young people with a university degree tend to belong to a defined benefit pension plan. DB plans provide a more dependable retirement income. So, in addition to earning more money than their high school graduate classmates throughout their careers, people with a university education benefit from DB membership. University graduates, compared to high school graduates, also tend to belong to more generous plans (Drolet & Morissette, 2014).

Experts who have studied the occupational pension system in Canada today express worry about the solvency of DB plans. In 2009, for example, 83 percent of RPPs had liabilities (expected costs) greater than their assets. In 2013 Canada Post disclosed a $6.5 billion shortfall in

funding for its pension plan. In that same year, the federal government had over $150 billion in unfunded pension liabilities. These figures create concern about the solvency of pensions for government workers (Fekete, 2013). Longer life expectancy, early retirements, low interest rates, and a sharp fall in stock prices can put these programs under stress.

Brown (2010b) said that a worker "in a private sector SEPP (Single Employer Pension Plan) lives with the risk of the insolvency of the plan.... Once in bankruptcy," he said, "the pension plan and its member have very limited rights to attach to any remaining assets of the plan sponsor" (p. 6). In Ontario in 2010, 25 percent of workers in the private sector belonged to a single-employer pension plan.

The bankruptcy of Air Canada in 2004, for example, led to the discovery of a $1.2 billion shortfall in its pension plan. In 2011, when Air Canada neared bankruptcy again, unfunded liabilities came to more than $2.1 (Markowits, 2011). The company in 2004 had no means to repay the plan; at one point it suggested a 10-year timeline for repaying the shortfall. This provided little comfort to workers on the verge of retirement. Eventually the unions agreed to reduce labour costs and the airline continued to meet its pension obligations. But as the threat of bankruptcy continues into the future, the risk to workers' pensions still exists. To date in Canada, only Ontario has put a government-based pension insurance program in place.

Workers with a pension in the private sector often belong to a defined contribution plan. Members of defined contribution plans in 2013 accounted for 16.8 percent of all RPP members. Nearly all of these workers (86 percent) worked in the private sector (Statistics Canada, 2015l). Many companies (large and small) now opt for defined contribution plans for a number of reasons. First, they find it hard to plan for the costs of defined benefit plans. A company has to make complex and uncertain predictions about workers' life expectancies and about financial markets in the future. Many companies today, in the automobile and airline industries, for example, find it hard to compete because of their pension obligations.

Second, the government regulates defined benefit plans, which gives companies fewer options in how they design and fund these plans. Finally, some companies say that employees prefer defined contribution plans. The programs vest immediately and workers know exactly how much they have in their accounts. Workers who switch jobs may also like these plans. The savings in the plan goes with the worker when he or she moves from one company to another.

---

defined contribution (DC) pension plans state how much a person will pay into his or her pension account (often matched to some degree by the company); this plan defines the contribution but does not guarantee the outcome; the outcome in retirement will depend on how well the employee's investments do over time

EXHIBIT 8.7 *Defined Benefit and Defined Contribution Plans: A Comparison*

Defined Benefit (DB) Plans

These plans offer the most security to workers. A defined benefit plan

- Promises a pension at retirement based on years of service and salary.
- Provides a dependable, guaranteed outcome and makes retirement planning easier.
- In some cases, indexes to inflation.
- Often provides a contribution match by the company.
- Pays out over the lifetime of the worker or last survivor of a married couple.
- Helps retain workers in a competitive employment market because people stay to collect their pension.

But DB plans create some problems for companies. A defined benefit plan

- Creates an uncertain outcome for the company—the company can't know for certain the costs of pension payouts in the future (e.g., due to life expectancy uncertainty and market uncertainty).
- Costs the company money in matching funds and potentially high payout in the future.
- Can lead to financial problems for the firm—companies may lose their competitive edge in the market due to the high costs of pension obligations. Pension obligations can lead to higher costs of goods and services (auto manufacturers and airlines face this problem).

Defined Contribution (DC) Plans

These plans offer the most benefits to the company and some benefits to workers. A defined contribution plan

- Creates certainty for the company—a company may agree to contribute a set amount to a plan during an employee's working years or the company may make no contribution at all.
- Vests immediately; employees own their account and can track the amount in their accounts.

- Richer people gain the most from these plans—they have the extra money to invest in them and they gain the most from the tax advantages.

But these plans create some problems for workers. A defined contribution plan

- Makes the pension payout uncertain—it depends on the amount saved, management fees, and the return on the investment over time. The stock market decline of 2008–2009 showed the weakness of DC pensions. Brown (2010b) says that most people who held individual retirement accounts lost 20 percent to 30 percent of their investments between the summer of 2008 and spring 2009.
- Makes participation optional—this leads to more freedom for the worker, but lower participation than in DB plans.
- Can lead to lower returns because workers don't have investment knowledge. Left on their own, people often make too conservative or too risky investments.
- May encourage investment in the worker's company. This puts retirement at risk because it ties the person's salary and pension to the same firm. If the company closes, workers face a double loss. (Many workers lost their jobs and their entire pension savings in the Enron scandal in the United States that broke in 2001.)
- May lead to low pensions due to poor investments or low rates of savings.
- Allows workers to take their money out and spend it if they switch jobs.
- Often has high management and administrative costs. These costs reduce the pension payout.
- Allows employers to reduce or eliminate matching funds in an economic downturn.
- Allows workers to take a lump sum at retirement and spend the money too quickly.
- Can lead to loss of funds if brokers, companies, or planners take advantage of workers' lack of investment knowledge.

But defined contribution plans load investment risk on the worker. And research shows that most people have little financial knowledge and cannot make informed investment decisions (Schulz & Borowski, 2006). In some cases, for example, workers have invested all of their money in their own company's stock. This will leave them with no job and no pension if the company closes. Also, workers who manage their own funds may choose riskier investments than they should late in their careers.

Many people near retirement lost large amounts of money in the 2008–2009 stock market decline. Some had to postpone retirement to make up for these losses. Shocks in the market demonstrate the risks that individual investments face in an ever-changing economy.

Schulz and Borowski (2006; Gougeon, 2009) concluded that "DC [defined contribution] plans place major risk management burdens on financially unsophisticated individuals." They went on to say that "adequate education in financial affairs is difficult, if not impossible to find (assuming most people would be willing to take the time to learn)" (p. 368).

Gross (2006) said, "It's hard not to conclude that defined benefit pensions are under assault" (p. 10). In 2013, for example, DC membership increased by 0.6 percent; at the same time, membership in DB plans decreased by 0.5 percent. DB plan membership dropped to 71.2 percent of all plan members in 2013 from 84 percent a decade earlier (Statistics Canada, 2015l). This movement away from

DB to DC plans (although gradual in Canada) will have an effect on retiree benefits in the years to come.

Most older people rely on savings to make up lost pre-retirement income. And Canadians tend to prepare well for old age. Investment income in Canada in 2011 made up 10.1 percent of the income of males age 65 and over and 11.1 percent of that of females age 65 and over. These sources ranked as the smallest proportion of income for males and females (Canada Mortgage and Housing Corporation, 2015b).

TIME TO REVIEW

Why have companies moved away from defined benefit pension plans?

Why does the shift from defined benefit to defined contribution plans shift the risk from employers to workers?

How does this shift affect pension planning for workers?

What effect might this shift have on workers' future pension benefits?

Registered Retirement Savings Plans

The shift of responsibility for pension funding to the individual has led to more planning for retirement. Marshall (2011) found that "most Canadians believe they must take an active role in planning for [retirement]" (p. 3). She reports that 81 percent of people age 25 to 64 made some financial plans for their retirement.

The federal government has encouraged this trend. It provides an incentive for retirement savings through **registered retirement savings plans (RRSPs)**. An RRSP is a government plan that allows people to save money without paying income tax on it until they withdraw it in retirement. This defers the taxes to a time when they expect to have a lower income and a lower tax rate. Statistics Canada (2006d) reported that Canadians had invested more in RRSPs than in employer (occupational) pension plans (EPPs).

The maximum contribution to an RRSP for 2017 was set at $26,010 (Canada Revenue Agency, 2015). The

---

registered retirement savings plans (RRSPs) a government plan that allows people to save money for their future pension without paying income tax on the money protected within the RRSP; the savings are taxed when they are withdrawn in retirement; the taxes are deferred to a time when the person has a lower income and is in a lower tax bracket

government adjusts this amount yearly. Individuals who belong to a private pension plan can contribute to an RRSP up to this maximum after adjusting for their contribution to their private pension plan. The number of RRSP members grew from 206,000 in 1969 (2.3 percent of tax filers) to just under 6 million in 2012 (23.7 percent of tax filers) (Statistics Canada, 2011k; Statistics Canada, 2014q). The total contributions to RRSP accounts in 2012 came to $35.7 billion. A Bank of Montreal survey in 2014 found that 64 percent of Canadians had an RRSP account (Marotte, 2014). *CBC News* (2013) reported that Canadians held a total of $775 billion in RRSP accounts.

But not every person or family shares equally in the benefits of RRSP savings. Pyper (2008) reported that older workers (age 45–64) and those in the highest income brackets contributed most to RRSPs. In 2005, only 35 percent of families with a head age 25 to 69 with incomes under $36,500 contributed to an RRSP. But in that year, 89 percent of tax filers who had incomes of $85,000 and over made a contribution. Families with an after-tax income of $85,000 per year or more in 2005 reported RRSP accounts on average of $80,000. "This differs sharply," Pyper (2008) said, "from families with lower incomes (less than $36,500) where only 35 percent of families held RRSPs, with a median value of just $10,000" (p. 6). The wealthiest tax filers also got the highest tax benefit from their contribution due to their high tax rate.

The higher a person's tax bracket, the more they receive through tax deductions when contributing to an RRSP. For instance, a tax filer in the highest tax bracket in Ontario got a tax saving of $464 for an RRSP contribution of $1,000. But a filer in the lowest bracket got a tax saving of only $222 for a $1,000 contribution (Ontario Educational, 2011). The richer person's higher tax rate leads to more tax savings. So, people with more money do better than poorer people under the current system. And wealthier Canadians take more advantage of RRSPs.

Morissette and Ostrovsky (2007) reported that in 2004, the top income earners' savings in RRSPs and RPPs (registered pension plans) came to 9.2 times more than the average savings of the lowest income earners. Any future increase in the limits for RRSP contributions would make them even more attractive to middle- and upper-income earners.

The people with the lowest incomes have the least money to save in RRSPs. But these people also gain less than high-income earners through RRSP savings. For example, low-income people pay little or no tax and so gain little or no tax benefit from the RRSP program. Also, if they do pay into an RRSP, when they withdraw money from the RRSP in their retirement, they may lose income.

EXHIBIT 8.8 *RRSP Contributors as a Percentage of Tax Filers and RRSP Contribution per Tax Filer by Selected Age Groups and Income Groups, 1993–2008 Average*

Age Group	RRSP Contributor as % of Tax Filers	RRSP Contribution per Tax Filer ($)
Under 45 years		
Under $10,000	2.2%	$23
$10,000–$50,000	32.3%	777
$50,000–$100,000	67.8%	3,513
Over $100,000	80.6%	9,426
Age 45 to 65 years		
Under $10,000	3.4%	48
$10,000–$50,000	36.0%	1,119
$50,000–$100,000	66.4%	3,801
Over $100,000	73.9%	9,326

This table shows a clear pattern: the higher the income bracket, the greater the proportion of tax filers who paid into an RRSP. Also, the higher the income bracket, the larger the amounts of money that people in that income bracket held in a plan. Pyper (2008) said, "Family income is related to both the propensity to save and the amount saved. Since families purchase RRSPs (and other investments) out of disposable income, those with higher incomes are more likely to be financially able to invest in RRSPs" (p. 6). Also, those with higher incomes (and higher tax rates) gain the most from the system. Increases in contribution limits will increase the use of RRSPs by wealthier Canadians and will increase the gap between the contributions of the rich and the poor.

Sources: Canada Revenue Agency (various issues); Revenue Canada (1995, 1996, 1997); Canada Revenue Agency (2013). Tax Statistics on Individuals from 1996 to 2000 Tax Year. Special Request to the Statistics and Information Management Directorate, Strategy, and Integration Branch. calculations by authors. Adapted from Lammam, C., Palacios, M., & Clemens, J. (2013). RRSPs and an expanded Canada Pension Plan: A preliminary analysis. Fraser Institute, p. 14. Retrieved from https://www.fraserinstitute.org/sites/default/files/RRSPs-and-an-expanded-canada-pension-plan.pdf.

If they receive OAS/GIS funds or other benefits like subsidized housing, the added income from an RRSP account could lead to a reduction in government benefits. This makes RRSPs most attractive to the relatively well-off.

Private Pensions—Registered Pension Plans (RPPs)

How well does the private pension and savings tier of the retirement income system help most people cope with retirement? Not very well, on three counts.

First, private pension coverage is low: in 2014, only 6.2 million employees, or about 40 percent of all workers, had a registered pension plan (RPP) through their work. This was a decrease from 45 percent in 1991. Less unionization in the private sector, pressure on companies to lower costs, and more workers in low-paid industries accounted for the decrease in RPPs.

These figures included workers in the public sector and workers in the private sector. But where most public-sector employees have an RPP, relatively few private-sector employees do. Most private-sector workers with an RPP work for firms with 1,000 or more employees; smaller firms tend not to offer an RPP. Also, the rate of plan membership for men and women differs in each sector. Women made up more than half (62 percent) of public-sector pension plan members in 2009. But men outnumber women in private-sector RPPs by nearly two to one.

Research points to another problem with the private pension system. Many people don't know whether they have an RPP or not. Morissette and Zhang (2004) found that 4 percent of all full-time permanent employees (390,000 people) "thought they had a retirement plan but didn't" (p. 12). Among recent immigrants (people who arrived in Canada after 1990), 27 percent reported having an employer-sponsored pension plan but didn't. These workers cannot accurately plan for retirement. Workers need a clearer understanding of their pension savings.

People who work part-time, who do seasonal work, who work for small businesses, and at low-paying jobs rarely have an RPP. These workers will need to rely on public pensions and savings. But even people with an RPP can't count on this for a large part of their retirement income. RPPs on average made up only 26.6 percent of senior women's incomes in 2011 and only 32.4 percent of senior men's incomes in that year (Canada Mortgage and Housing Corporation, 2015b).

Second, economic forces can erode the buying power of a private pension. In an inflationary economy, people on a fixed pension—even a good one—become poorer as they age. At 3 percent inflation, a pension will lose about 25 percent of its value over 10 years and nearly half its value after 20 years. Those in the private sector (even workers with defined benefit plans) face the loss of income due to inflation. Workers in the private sector with defined contribution plans face an even greater risk. They depend on market conditions and low inflation rates in order to maintain their income.

An example shows the impact of declining income over time. Robert O'Connor worked as a registrar at a university for 26 years. He and his wife planned for retirement. "We took steps to reduce economic problems as far as we could," he says. "We paid off our mortgage, we bought a new car—anything so we could go into retirement as well equipped as we could."

Still, a drop in their living standard came some years after he retired. "When I was working, I'd say to my wife, 'Well, come on, where will we go for dinner?' Now we don't go out to eat as much. And when we do go, it's more likely we go to a Sizzler's Steak House with a discount coupon than to our favourite restaurant."

"We don't talk much about it. But we've faced a lowering of our social standards. We can't say, 'Let's go back now and look at Scotland.' We say, 'Let's renew our subscription to *Britain in Pictures*.'"

"One of the problems when you retire is to build up a small nest egg, but even relatively fortunate people like myself often watch it disappear. Six weeks ago we had to put a roof on our house. Last week our washing machine broke down. There we had to dip into our bank account. The time is coming when it's not imprudent to contemplate almost the virtual exhaustion of our savings" (personal communication with author).

Third, only a small percentage of people who belong to occupational pension plans ever collect a full pension. Two things account for this: (1) few plans in the past had early vesting (early vesting locks both the employer's and the employee's payments in the plan soon after employment begins); and (2) most plans lack portability. When workers leave a company today, most of them get either a deferred pension (if their money is vested and locked in) or they get their own (but not their employer's) pension contributions back—sometimes with no interest.

The employer's share stays in the fund when workers get their pension contributions back, so a person who moves to a new job loses half of his or her pension savings and has to start again. Even if the whole labour force belongs to occupational pension plans at any time, as long as workers change jobs often (as they do today), only workers with fully vested contributions will ever collect a full pension.

An expansion of private pensions to more workers would provide a better income for more older people. But pension plan expansion seems unlikely at present. Many companies have cut back on pension programs or have shifted to defined contribution plans. This will put more responsibility for retirement savings on individual workers, and it will increase the risk of low retirement incomes for many people. At the least, the government needs to provide oversight of private pensions. This helps ensure that those people who pay into a company pension plan will get a pension when they retire.

Summary of Income Security and Replacement in Retirement

Lafrance and LaRochelle-Côté (2011) said that a person should expect to spend almost as much in retirement as they did in their working years. "Retirement," they say, "is associated with negligible decreases in consumption in most population groups" (p. 6). Their study found that people "in their early 70s consumed 95% of the level measured for the same cohort in its late 40s" (p. 10).

Current groups of retired Canadians, on average, do well. They replace more than 70 percent to 80 percent of their pre-retirement income. Low-income seniors replace as much as 110 percent of their income at age 55 (LaRochelle-Côté, Myles, and Picot, 2010a, 2010b). And when income includes the benefit of owning a home, the replacement rate goes even higher for middle-income earners.

Wealthier seniors replace only about 70 percent of their income in retirement (since they start from a higher income in their middle years). The data show that all Canadian seniors have a financial safety net. Those who enter old age with a history of good incomes maintain a high standard of living in retirement (LaRochelle-Côté et al., 2010a). Those who had lower incomes can rely in part on government pension programs.

Brown (2010a) wonders whether this replacement level will continue for Baby Boomers. He said that

EXHIBIT 8.9 *Social Pensions—A Safety Net for Older People Worldwide*

Pension Watch (2015) tells the story of Krishna, age 75, a farmer in Nepal. He and his wife live with an adult son who has psychiatric problems. His wife has an intestinal illness. Krishna gets a Nepalese government pension of 500 rupees (Cdn$10.00) that he uses to pay his son's and his wife's medical bills.

"Our children send us money when they can," he says. "[This] helps us a great deal." But, he says, "Our pension is a very important source of income to us."

Like many older people in low-income countries, Krishna has few financial resources in old age. The Nepalese government social pension provides a small safety net for Krishna and his family.

Over 100 countries have some social pension program. Social pensions are "non-contributory cash transfers paid regularly to older people" (Pension Watch, 2015). Pension Watch describes three categories of social pensions:

1. **Universal Age Pensions**: This type of pension program bases eligibility solely on age and history of citizenship or residence. Countries as diverse in economic status as New Zealand, Namibia, Netherlands, and Suriname provide this type of pension.

   The Netherlands, a high-income country, provides a pension to 80 percent of the population age 60 and over. The monthly payment comes to Cdn$1,861.41 or 34 percent of average income. Uganda, a low-income country, has a national poverty rate of 52 percent. It provides a pension to only 4 percent of the population age 60 and over. The monthly benefit comes to only Cdn$11.92 per month or 17 percent of average income.

2. **Universal Minimum Pensions**: This type of pension ensures that any person over a certain age will get a pension. But this type of pension includes a "pensions-test." A person may receive a partial pension or no pension depending on their income from other pension sources. Countries as diverse in economic status as Finland, Vietnam, Sweden, and Turkmenistan provide this type of pension. These pensions play a unique role in each country. In countries with little coverage from other pension plans, these plans act as universal age pensions. In countries with other pension plans, this type of pension supplements other pension income.

   Finland, a high-income country, provides this type of pension to 36 percent of the population age 60 and over. The monthly payment comes to Cdn$1,093.25 or 20 percent of average income. Vietnam, a lower-middle-income

country, has a national poverty rate of 21 percent. It provides a pension to 12 percent of the population age 60 and over. The monthly benefit comes to only Cdn$11.92 per month or 5 percent of average income.

3. **Means-Tested Pensions**: This type of pension depends on a person's income or assets. Some programs target specific groups (e.g., the poor) in an attempt to focus scarce pension resources. Pension Watch says that at least 45 countries have means-tested social pensions. Countries as diverse in economic status as Australia, Kenya, the United Kingdom, and Trinidad and Tobago provide this type of pension.

   Australia, a high-income country, provides this type of pension to 51 percent of the population age 60 and over. The monthly payment comes to Cdn$1,890.01 or 26 percent of average income. Kenya, a low-income country, has a national poverty rate of 20 percent. It provides a pension to 3 percent of the population age 60 and over. The monthly benefit comes to only Cdn$30.46 per month or 24 percent of average income.

   Canada's OAS/GIS/ALW system functions as a universal minimum pension and a means-tested pension system. Everyone in Canada is entitled to the OAS. But beyond a certain level of income, whether from a pension or from other income, the government "claws back" OAS income. This allows the system to target pension revenue to benefit the poorest older people. The GIS and ALW supplement OAS payments to the poor.

   Countries differ in their ability to provide pension income to the older population. Lower-income countries can provide pension support to only a small proportion of the population. And they provide only small amounts of income to older people. Older people in these countries must find other means to survive in old age. This can include family support, savings, and work.

   In poor countries, many old people work into old age. In Africa, fewer than one person in ten gets a pension. They have little or no pension and no savings and their families may have no resources to support them. Many older people must still do heavy labour. Social pensions reduce the physical burden on the old and the financial burden on the young. Pension Watch (2015) calls social pensions "one of the most effective tools to reduce old age poverty and invest in human capital development."

"Canadians (either individually or through employer plans) are currently saving far less than they need to save to provide for pensions approaching 70 percent—or even 60 percent—of pre-retirement savings" (pp. 23–24, citing Dodge, Laurin, and Busby, 2010). Future income security will depend, as it does today, on a combination of public and private sources of funds. Workers today need to look ahead and prepare for the quality of life they want in their retirement years.

INEQUALITY IN LATER LIFE

Older people differ by social class, gender, marital status, urban or rural environment, ethnicity, date of immigration to Canada, and a variety of other characteristics. These characteristics all shape a person's income and economic condition in later life.

The political economy perspective looks at the structural reasons for inequality in old age. It points to education and former occupational status as forces that determine income in later life. A person with a high level of education and a high-status occupation stands the best chance of a high income in retirement. These people also stand a good chance of maintaining their status after retirement. Older people who have access to work, investments, and occupational pensions will have higher incomes. These benefits go to people with higher levels of education and higher job status.

Immigrants and Pensions

Some groups face more financial problems than others in old age. The National Seniors Council (2009) said that "a core group of seniors remains vulnerable: the unattached, recent immigrants, those with fewer than ten years in the labour force, and Aboriginal seniors" (p. 9). Membership in a non-European ethnic group, for example, leads to lower income in retirement. Asian, African, or Latin American ethnic group members tend to retire later and have less chance of getting OAS, GIS, or CPP benefits. Minority seniors also have less chance of getting an occupational pension and so have lower incomes.

Trends in public pension policies also lead to lower incomes for immigrants. The Old Age Security pension, for example, goes to any citizen or legal resident age 65 or older who has lived in Canada for 10 years or more after age 18. Recent immigrants have no access to this public pension (Kaida & Boyd, 2011). Recent immigrants (or immigrants who work in low-paying jobs) will have no (or low) Canada Pension Plan income and little or no employment pension income. A language barrier may also keep an older immigrant from getting the social support they need even when they qualify for aid.

Kaida and Boyd (2011) said that in 2006, about 30 percent of senior immigrants who had lived in Canada for less than 20 years had household incomes below Statistics Canada's low-income cut-off. This comes to double the rate of low income for all seniors in that year. Immigrant minority women face some of the greatest disadvantage.

Family support helps older immigrants stay out of poverty or at least helps them make do with their low income. For example, older recent immigrants (many from the Middle East, the Caribbean, and Asia) tend to live with their families. Kaida and Boyd (2011, p. 93) said that low-income rates "would increase by 70 percent to 430 percent (in percentage change) if new-wave immigrants had the same living arrangements distribution

as the Canadian-born of British origins" (i.e., a higher propensity toward independent living). Older immigrant women especially benefit financially from living with kin.

Women and Pensions

Sarah, age 65, worked as a homemaker for most of her adult life. She raised four children. When they grew up and left home, she retired to a quiet life—gym in the morning, coffee with friends, and some shopping in the afternoon. Then she cooks dinner, watches TV, and reads in the evening.

She worked in the labour force for only a year or so before her first child was born. She didn't make enough payments into the Canada Pension Plan to receive benefits in old age. Instead, she will rely on her husband's employment pension and his CPP benefits as she ages.

If her husband dies before Sarah, she will have only the survivor benefit from his employer plan and the CPP survivor benefit. This means that on her husband's death she will see a drop in her income. Her expenses may also decrease at that time, since she will live alone. Still, this drop in income could pose a hardship for her in late old age.

Kaida and Boyd (2011) said that older women in particular "are at higher risks of living in poverty than their male counterparts," especially in later old age. These researchers went on to say that "women are more likely to encounter occupational segregation and pay gaps, and women are often burdened with unpaid work responsibilities at home, suggesting a weaker labor force attachment and less access to work-related pensions (e.g., the CPP/QPPs, occupational pensions) after labor force disengagement" (pp. 84–85).

In 2011, for example, unattached senior men had a mean after-tax income 1.2 times higher than the income of unattached senior women. Men in this group earned on average $34,400 in 2011. Women in that year earned $29,700—a gap of $4,700 (Statistics Canada, 2013h). The low-income rate of all older women after taxes was 6.4 percent in 2011, more than one and a half times the low-income rate of elderly men (3.8 percent). In 2011, unattached older women had a higher after-tax rate of low-income than any other age or family group (16.1 percent) (Statistics Canada, 2013i). Separated and divorced older women, compared with widows, show the highest rates of poverty.

Why do women have such low incomes in old age?

First, traditional expectations about women and work lead women to have different work patterns than men. Women often leave a first job to raise children. Due to family responsibilities, they spend longer than men between jobs, and they tend to work at each job for a shorter time than men (Denton & Plenderleith, 2010).

The traditional expectation that women will place family before career leads to part-time work. Ferrao (2010) reported that in 2009, for example, one in five women age 25 to 54 worked part-time. During that same year, only 1 man in 20 in that age group worked part-time. This keeps women from getting high salaries and from storing up pension credits (Denton & Boos, 2007). When women work outside the home, they often take part-time, low-paying jobs. Many working women say they cannot find a full-time job. Denton and Boos reported that more women than men work fewer than 30 hours per week.

In 2009, for example, 58 percent of senior women employees held part-time jobs. Only 35 percent of working senior men held part-time jobs (Milan & Vézina, 2011). People in part-time jobs risk job loss, have little control of working conditions, rarely belong to a union,

and receive low wages. Part-time workers rarely get pension benefits. For this reason, compared with a man, a woman can work for her entire adult life and still have no pension savings.

Second, the structure of public and private occupational pension plans discriminates against women—sometimes in hidden ways. Women often work for smaller, non-unionized companies with no occupational pension plans and, as mentioned above, they also tend to work part-time. Even among union members, compared with women, a higher proportion of men have employer pensions (19 percent vs.15 percent) (Denton & Boos, 2007). This means that compared with women, men will tend to have more diverse sources of income in retirement, including employment pension income.

Moen and Spencer (2006) say that a person's work career shapes his or her opportunities and choices in retirement. "Health insurance, pensions, unemployment insurance, disability insurance, and Social Security all rest on the edifice of the male lock-step life course" (p. 134).

EXHIBIT 8.10 *Women and Men Age 65 years and Over with After-Tax Low Income, by Family Status, Canada, 1980 to 2011*

Percentage Year	In an Economic Family		Living Alone	
	Women	Men	Women	Men
1980	5.5	6.5	57.1	47
1985	3.6	4.4	42.1	28.7
1990	2.2	2.6	30.5	20.6
1995	1.9	1.9	26.7	12.1
2000	2.5	1.7	21.6	17.6
2005	1.3[1]	1.2[1]	20.3	13.6
2011	1.0E[1]	1.9E[1]	16.1	12.2E[1]

[1]E = Use with caution. Numbers too low for accurate estimate.

Note 1: Statistics Canada low-income cut-off, 1992 base.

Note 2: An economic family is a group of individuals sharing a common dwelling unit who are related by blood, marriage (including common-law relationships), or adoption.

Note that low-income rates dropped for all seniors from 1980 to 2011 (with the exception of women in families in 2000 and men in families in 2011). Note also that, compared with seniors in a family, senior men and women who live alone have significantly higher rates of low income. A decrease in low income among seniors who live alone has closed this gap. But senior women who live alone, compared with women in couples, continue to have 16 times the rate of low income. Among these four groups, senior women who live alone show the greatest improvement in their income. Still, they have higher rates of low income than any of the other groups.

Sources: Milan, A., and Vézina, M. *Women in Canada: A Gender-based Statistical Report.* Senior Women. Statistics Canada. 2011. Component of Statistics Canada Catalogue No. 89-503-X, Table 8, . 25. Original source: Statistics Canada, *Survey of Labour and Income Dynamics, 1980 to 2008.* Also data adapted from Statistics Canada, CANSIM Table 202-0802 and Catalogue No. 75-202-X. Retrieved March 3, 2017, from http://www.statcan.gc.ca/tables-tableaux/sum-som/l01/cst01/famil19a-eng.htm. Reproduced and distributed on an "as is" basis with the permission of Statistics Canada.

EXHIBIT 8.11 *Main Source of Personal Income for Individuals 65 and Older, Canada, 2011*

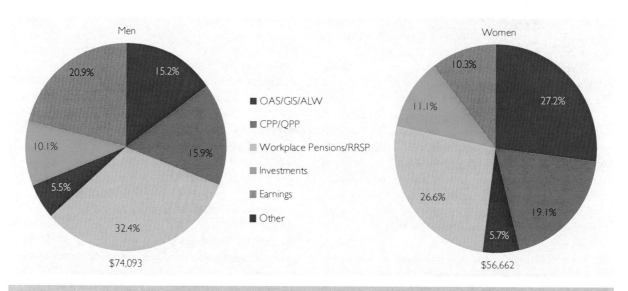

Men

20.9% 15.2%

10.1%

5.5% 15.9%

32.4%

$74,093

■ OAS/GIS/ALW
■ CPP/QPP
■ Workplace Pensions/RRSP
■ Investments
■ Earnings
■ Other

Women

10.3%

11.1% 27.2%

26.6%

5.7% 19.1%

$56,662

Note that, compared to senior women, senior men receive almost twice the proportion of their income from earnings. Senior women, compared to senior men receive almost twice the proportion of their income from public pension sources (OAS/GIS/ALW). Senior men, compared to senior women, also receive a greater proportion of their income from employer pension plans. These differences reflect differences in opportunities for men and women in the workforce in later life, different lifetime employment patterns for men and women, and the fact that women live longer than men and that very old women are not in the labour force.

These differences in the source of income also mean that, compared to senior men, senior women have lower incomes in later life. Reliance on public pension sources means that senior women have relatively small amounts of income from other sources. For example, senior women receive only about 60 percent of the income of senior men from earnings, investment income, and pension plans. Based on the income sources here, senior women receive only 69 percent of the income of senior men.

Milan and Vézina (2011) say that over time the financial picture for older women has improved. Compared with older women in the past, older women today draw less of their income from the OAS/GIS, a sign of their higher total incomes. On the other hand, compared with men, women get a higher proportion of their income from the CPP/QPP. "In 1976," the researchers said, "only 15 percent of the total income of women age 65 and over consisted of retirement income. That proportion steadily increased in the next three decades.... This is attributable to the fact that more of these women held a paid job during their lifetime" (p. 22).

Source: Statistics Canada, National Household Survey, 2011, Statistics Canada Catalogue No. 99-014-X2011034. In Canada Mortgage and Housing Corporation. (2015b). What Are the Trends in Incomes, Wealth and Pensions for Canada's Seniors? Table 8. Retrieved from http://www.cmhc-schl.gc.ca/en/inpr/bude/hoolca/hoolca_vol_001/hoolca_vol_001_005.cfm. Reproduced and distributed on an "as is" basis with the permission of Statistics Canada.

To the extent that a woman's life course differs from this model, women face a disadvantage in retirement.

Third, women in general are paid less than men and hold lower-status jobs. Women, more often than men, work in low-wage jobs that are defined as unskilled and offer little chance for advancement. Women tend to work in sales, service, administration, and health occupations. Men tend to work in management, applied and natural sciences, trades and transportation, and manufacturing. But even in the same field, in professional and non-professional jobs, women earn 56 percent and 85 percent of men's salaries (Williams, 2010).

Statistics Canada (2013j) found that in 2011, women of all ages earned an average of $32,100. Men in that year

earned an average of $48,100. Women's earnings came to 66.7 percent of men's earning in that year. Women showed an increase of 10 percent in their income from 2002 but they still earned only two-thirds of men's incomes (a figure almost unchanged since 1992). Among seniors, men earned on average $30,553 in 2011. Women in that year had a total income on average of $19,961—65 percent of men's income (Canada Mortgage and Housing Corporation, 2015b).

Even in relatively low-paying fields, women find themselves in the poorest-paying jobs. For instance, women tend to work as salaried clerks. Men tend to sell expensive products such as cars or appliances; these jobs often pay a commission in addition to a base salary.

Women work in service jobs, such as a waitress, hairdresser, or child-care worker. Men tend to work at services, such as police officer, security guard, or soldier. Even when women work at the same job as men, they often get lower pay. Low pay also means that, compared with men, women pay a smaller amount into the CPP. This results in a smaller CPP pension when they retire.

The work histories of women lead to lower income in later life and lower overall wealth. A study by Denton and Boos (2007; also Statistics Canada, 2006e) found that work and family roles led to lower asset buildup throughout life. The researchers found that women age 45 and over had a net worth only 64 percent that of men. Women, they said, "have about two-thirds the non-financial assets (including the value of their home) than men do, they have less than half the financial assets (including the value of their pensions and other financial assets)" (p. 12). This leaves older women without a safety net of savings and resources.

Women also tend to save less during their working years (possibly due to low wages). For example, compared to women, men make up a higher proportion of contributors to RRSPs (53 percent vs. 47 percent). And men make nearly two-thirds of all contributions (61 percent) to RRSPs (women made only 39 percent of all contributions). Men contribute on average $3,600 to an RRSP compared with only $2,430 on average for women. Women contribute less to RRSPs and have less to draw on when they retire (Statistics Canada, 2014p).

Divorced and separated women, compared with married women, have less income and wealth in retirement. In addition, women tend to live an average of five years longer than men, meaning that, compared with men, women will have to make their smaller assets last for a longer time period. Denton and Boos (2007) said that the long-term consequences of inequality in the labour force "are that the majority of women will fail to build up the financial assets to provide good incomes for their retirement" (p. 17).

Shippee, Wilkinson, and Ferraro (2012) found that the long-term experience of low income leads to financial strain—a subjective feeling of stress. And they found that financial strain leads to declines in health. They said that "Women's life course patterns place them at distinct risk for financial strain due to their position in the labor force, family roles, and lower earnings compared with men...." (p. 592)

In Canada, poor older women gain some relief from financial strain through the OAS/GIS/ALW programs. The poorest women may see an increase in their income. McIntyre and colleagues (2014) said that the basic income

(OAS/GIS) in Canada "improves the health and mental health of low-income Canadians." Most of them women.

Widows

Widows make up the largest group among women 65 and over, and of all women, they benefit least from Canada's pension system. This shows up in the statistics on low-income seniors. Statistics Canada (2013i) reported that in 2011, unattached senior women (most of them widows) had a low-income rate of 16.1 percent (compared with a rate for unattached senior men of 12.2 percent).

Bernard and Li (2006) found that 72 percent of widows suffered a loss of income after the death of their spouse. And widowhood on average led to a steady decline in income in the five years after the death of the spouse. After five years, widows had an income 15 percent lower than in the year before the spouse's death, and 8.7 percent of widows lived below the government's low-income line.

By contrast, compared with the year before widowhood, widowers (men), on average had a higher income five years after the spouse's death, and only 5.1 percent of widowers fell below the low-income line. After five years, widows entered poverty at twice the rate of widowers. These findings show the dependence of older women on their husbands' earnings and pensions. Senior widows today often have little or no employer pension of their own.

If her husband has an employer pension plan, a widow may find that the plan reduces the benefits when her husband dies. Even when a survivor plan exists, sometimes a woman gets nothing because they opted for higher benefits in retirement while he was alive. This can leave a woman in poverty in the last 15 or 20 years of her life. In addition to these reduced payments in retirement, only 69 percent of members of public-sector plans and 27 percent of members of private-sector plans provided a survivor pension if the plan member died before retirement. Many plans refund only the worker's contributions with interest if a plan member dies before retirement. Some plans return nothing to the surviving spouse.

Private-sector pensions put widows at risk of poverty and the public pension system also lets widows down. The CPP sets the benefits for a surviving spouse age 65 and over at 60 percent of the deceased spouse's pension. The maximum amount payable came to $7,668 a year in 2015.

LaRochelle-Côté, Myles, and Picot (2012a; also 2012b) found that, compared to widowhood, separation/divorce had a greater effect on income replacement in retirement. Higher-income women show the greatest loss of income. They rely most heavily on private pensions and investment income. Lower-income women see less effect on their income due to separation/divorce. They rely more heavily on public pensions. The researchers found that separation/divorce had little effect on the income replacement for older men. Davies and Denton (2002) spoke of the "grave economic situation of women who have experienced a divorce or separation late in life" (p. 487).

TIME to REVIEW

Why do older women, compared with older men, have lower incomes in retirement?

How does the life course view of aging explain the lower incomes of older women?

How has the source of income changed for older women in the past few decades?

What explains this change?

Why do many widows face a drop in income after their husband's death?

Women and Pensions in the Future

Women coming into old age in the future, compared with older women today, will have better incomes. More women today work during their middle years. Women today who leave work to raise a family tend to return to work more quickly than women did in the past. Women with higher education tend to have fewer interruptions in work. Women have also begun to enter male-dominated occupations and more of them belong to private pension plans. Many of these women will get their own CPP pensions in the future.

This trend has already begun. The National Seniors Council (2011) reported nearly a 50 percent increase in the proportion of women's incomes from the CPP/QPP between 1990 and 2005. The council reported more than a doubling of the proportion of women's incomes from workplace pensions and RRSPs between 1990 and 2005. Nevertheless, the large majority of women have no RRSPs, and those who do, compared with men, pay less into their RRSPs and so get less in return.

Denton and Boos (2007) said that current trends will lead older women in the future to have financial supports more similar to those of men. But, they say, "we should not be lulled into a false sense of optimism" (p. 19). In 2003, for example, women age 55 to 64 earned from all sources just over half the income of men in that age group. Women age 35 to 54 earned in total around 60 percent

of men in that age group. This inequality in younger age groups will mean that even in the future, compared with men, women will receive lower CPP pensions (Lindsay & Almey, 2006). Homemakers will have no employer pensions; they will get no CPP pension of their own, and if their husband's pension plan pays no survivor benefits, they will get no pension at all.

The system needs reform to meet the needs of older women. McDonald and Robb (2004) said that "the current pension system does not mirror the complexity of women's lives in terms of their multiple transitions in and out of the labour force, their institutionalized lower earnings, their unpaid work and the changes in individual and family life styles" (pp. 14–15). Women and men need better occupational pension plans, and women need better survivor and homemaker benefits and more help from the OAS/GIS/ALW.

By proposing some changes to the system, the federal government sparked what some people call "the great pension debate" in the early 1980s. The debate was about whether a public pension plan such as the CPP or whether private pension plans would best serve Canadians. More recent debates have been concerned with universality of the OAS and ensuring the solvency of the CPP.

PENSION REFORM

Canada has debated pension reform since the early 1980s. A series of conferences, task forces, and papers at that time all proposed changes in the pension system. And some changes did take place. By the late 1980s, for example, all provinces except British Columbia and Prince Edward Island had some legislation covering occupational pensions. Also, new rules have improved the public pension plan system. What follows are some of the highlights of these reforms.

First, the federal government income security system has made three important improvements over the years: (1) improvements in GIS have led to decreased poverty rates for single older people; (2) as of 1985, all widows and widowers with low incomes get the ALW; and (3) the federal government continues to index the OAS to the rate of inflation, although it has not increased the OAS to bring it closer to the average industrial wage.

Second, beginning in 2012, the CPP allows women and men to deduct some of the years they spent outside the workforce (e.g., for child-rearing or eldercare) from their pensionable years. (Until 1984, these years counted as zero income and lowered a person's average lifetime salary.) People who take time off can now deduct up to 7.5 years (or 16 percent) of their low earnings from their work record. In 2014, this "general drop-out provision" increased to 8 years (or 17 percent of a person's lowest earnings (Service Canada, 2010).

Also, the CPP now provides for **credit splitting** if spouses divorce. Each spouse gets an equal share of the credits accumulated during their time together. This provision, however, includes a hitch: it requires an application for credit splitting.

Third, in May 1985, the federal government announced changes in the Canada Pension Benefits Standards Act. These changes set minimum standards for 1 million federal government workers and workers in federal government industries such as Crown corporations. The federal government asked the provinces and territories to change their rules to meet the new standards:

- Locked-in vesting mandatory after two years in an occupational plan;
- Improved portability by transfer of vested pensions to locked-in RRSPs;
- The right of all full-time workers to join a private plan after two years of work; all part-time workers must have the right to join if they have earned at least 35 percent of the yearly maximum pensionable earnings;
- Payment of survivor benefits worth at least 60 percent of the amount the couple would have received had the contributor lived; these benefits will continue if the survivor remarries;
- Division of pension credits and payments 50-50 if a couple divorces, unless the couple or the courts choose a different option.

Fourth, the federal government and the provinces agreed that all occupational plans will provide a joint life/last survivor benefit. The pension continues even if the survivor remarries. This provision has one drawback: Both spouses must agree to lower pension payments in the present. If the couple chooses a higher pension today, they forgo survivor benefits in the future.

These changes fix some of the inequities in the system. The poorest older people on the GIS benefit from these changes, and so do widows and women who work part-time. Still, many people who could get the GIS do not apply. In 2006, for example, 159,400 people who could get the GIS did not apply (about 10 percent of all eligible

recipients). This led to between $62 million and $95 million in unclaimed funds (Luong, 2009).

Seniors fail to apply for many reasons: "isolation, lack of awareness of the program and its application process, physical or mental health problems, language barriers, low literacy skills, or homelessness" (Luong, 2009, p. 6). Some people fail to apply because they consider the program a type of welfare.

The government wants to see all eligible seniors get the GIS. It increased outreach efforts to find and include these people. As a first step, the government simplified the application process. Seniors no longer have to reapply for the GIS if they increase their income in one year and lose their eligibility. Seniors, who got the GIS in the past, now automatically get reinstated in years when their income drops below the GIS cut-off. Outreach efforts will help more low-income seniors get the benefits they deserve.

In spite of these improvements, the federal government will still have to tackle some tough issues in the future. These include homemakers' pensions, the rising cost of indexed OAS pensions, and **indexation** of private pension plans. Women face many disadvantages in old age that current pension reform only partly addresses. "The whole income-security debate," Neysmith (1984) wrote, "has been defined in terms of pensions that are related to one's track record in the paid-labour force [and] occupationally based pensions by definition cannot meet the needs of most women" (pp. 18–19). Canadian society will need to deal with this larger issue through broader reforms that will have to include increasing opportunities for women in the labour force.

THE FUTURE COST OF REFORM

Changes in private and public pension plans will mean one thing: pensions will cost more money. CPP rates have increased to 9.9 percent of workers' earnings (from 3.6 percent in 1986). Better occupational plans will also cost more. So will better survivor benefits. As Canadian society ages, more people will begin to draw pensions, and younger people will have to pay for most of these costs.

How will people feel about these changes? Will younger people revolt at the high cost of pensions for the older generation? The state of Canada's economy will partly determine how younger people will feel about pension costs. A strong economy and low inflation will make it easier to pay more for pensions; an increased cost

credit splitting a plan by which each spouse of a divorcing couple gets an equal share of pension credits accumulated during their time together

indexation a method of increasing pensions linked to increases in the cost of living

of living and low wages will make it harder. A weaker economy could lead younger people to balk at the high cost.

The vision of economic crisis in the future has led to many reform proposals. One plan would privatize the Canada Pension Plan. Under this proposal, each person would invest CPP funds in private-sector assets, manage his or her own fund, and receive the accumulated money. This plan could serve all Canadians much as the CPP does today.

But this approach has many drawbacks: each worker would bear the risk of a poor investment or of inflation, the plan would include no death or disability benefits, and women would lose child-rearing dropout provisions. Furthermore, based on the experience of other systems, the cost of managing a privatized plan would run about 10 times that of the CPP. Still, some people believe that privatization would solve many future pension plan problems.

Other proposals fit more easily into the current system. They include a later age for retirement. The CPP has already put reforms in place to encourage workers to stay on the job. Reforms include penalties for early retirement and higher pension returns if a person delays retirement. A small increase in the retirement age has a large impact on the cost of retirement benefits. For example, a 10-month increase in the retirement age would lead to a 10 percent cut in the cost of benefits to the system. Workers who delayed retirement would take no money from the national pension system, add to national wealth through their work, and increase government tax revenues.

The retirement of the Baby Boom generation will leave a skill shortage in many industries, so healthier and better-educated workers may choose to stay at work longer. The federal government recognized older workers' interest in staying at work and in 2006 allocated $70 million over two years to start the Targeted Initiative for Older Workers. This program helps older workers who live in vulnerable communities to stay at work. Work opportunities will help many older people maintain their standard of living in retirement.

The federal government began a program in 2012—the Post-Retirement Benefit (PRB)—to give workers a further incentive to stay at work. If people who receive a CPP benefit choose to work, they can choose (if age 65 to 70) to make contributions to the CPP. They will then get a PRB benefit the following year. Each year of work creates an added PRB. These benefits increase with the cost of living. The PRB gets added to a person's CPP pension even if the person receives the maximum pension amount.

Policies in Canada have also put a higher tax on Old Age Security benefits so that wealthier seniors keep less of their payments. The OAS has already evolved from a universal program to a means-tested plan (by taxing back OAS payments from wealthier Canadians). This change fits a trend in government policy (including healthcare policy) to focus programs on people most in need. The clawback of OAS payments to the wealthy begins to achieve what Myles and Teichroew (1991) called "the main project of both the Liberal and Conservative parties throughout the 1980s—to make the welfare state more efficient by targeting scarce transfer dollars to those most in need" (p. 85).

These policies also support the trend to shift responsibility for financial well-being in later life from the state to the individual. Such trends have begun to place pressure on middle-class Canadians to look after their own well-being in old age. The government provides some incentive for this move toward self-support.

A federal government newsletter called *The Latest for Seniors* reported that "Budget 2008 provides the most important federally driven personal finance innovation since the introduction of the Registered Retirement Savings Plan (RRSP): the Tax-Free Savings Account (TFSA)" (Government of Canada, 2008). **Tax-free savings accounts (TFSAs)** allow residents of Canada age 18 or over to put up to $5,500 a year (2017 limit) in after-tax income into a TFSA account. These dollars will be allowed to grow tax-free and will not be taxed when taken out. The government will index this amount to inflation and these funds, when taken out, will not influence eligibility for any other government programs (e.g., OAS/GIS).

The program includes other regulations that make the program flexible (e.g., funds can move from a deceased spouse's account to that of the surviving spouse). The Government of Canada (2015) reported that in 2013, nearly 11 million people had opened a TFSA and nearly 2 million people had contributed the maximum amount in their accounts. The average contribution to a TFSA in 2014 came to $5,426. The value of these accounts in total came to $87.5 billion in 2014 (up from $54.4 billion in 2011). The government hopes the new vehicle will encourage more low- and modest-income people to save more for their retirement. In 2013, for example,

tax-free savings accounts (TFSAs) a program that allows Canadians age 18 or over to put up to $10,000 a year into a savings account; these dollars will be allowed to grow tax-free and will not be taxed when taken out

80 percent of all TFSA holders had incomes of less than $80,000 per year. And half of TFSA holders had income under $42,000 per year.

Canada has developed and maintained a stable and reliable pension system. It needs improvement, but the public has not called for radical change. Beland and Myles (2003) gave four reasons for the stability of the current system. First, Canada spends a relatively modest amount on public pensions (OAS/GIS/ALW). Second, the general revenue rather than payroll taxes supports most of the public pension system. Third, the government has other programs that it can target for spending cuts—for example, healthcare and postsecondary education. Fourth, most of the money spent on public pensions goes to poorer seniors. This approach has broad public acceptance.

Some years ago, Myles (1982) offered two more reasons that Canadians will continue to support a strong public pension system in the future. First, he said, without state support the young would have to help care for their parents themselves, and younger people will prefer to pool their risks through a central pension system. Second, he said, middle-aged people, because they will be old soon themselves, have a self-interest in supporting a strong pension and social security system for the elderly.

In the end, a strong publicly supported pension system—given the longer life expectancy today—makes sense for everyone. As long as taxpayers see this, they will continue to support improvements in Canada's retirement income system.

TIME TO REVIEW

What reforms has the Canadian government put in place to deal with rising current and future pension costs?

What does it mean when experts say that the OAS system has moved from being a universal system to a means-tested plan?

How does this fit with the larger trend toward shifting responsibility for income in retirement away from government and toward the individual?

CONCLUSION

Pension policies over the past 20 years, including the most recent changes in pension laws, have created a dual pension system. (1) The public system in the form of the OAS and GIS will support the most needy older people. This system mostly serves people (many of them women) who work outside the labour market. (2) The private system in the form of RRSPs, TFSAs, and registered pension plans (RPPs) helps maintain the lifestyles of middle- and upper-income earners in retirement. This second system serves government workers, professionals, managers, and other higher-income earners. The CPP falls somewhere between these two systems. The government oversees the program, but it benefits people who have worked in the labour force. Those outside the labour force (e.g., homemakers) benefit little from the CPP.

The shift in policy to self-reliance for middle-income earners may not produce the end product that the government wants. Current and future policies encourage middle-aged, middle- and upper-income earners to save more money in RRSPs and TFSAs. This practice costs the government money in lost taxes and may counteract some of the savings made by cutting OAS payments to middle- and upper-income retirees. A larger retired population will cost society more money one way or another. Policies simply shift the cost of a retired population from one group to another (from young taxpayers to retirees, who have to live on their own resources).

A new view of retirement could help solve this problem. Some studies project a shortage of young workers and a need for older workers in Canada in the future. This shortage could create potential jobs for older workers and reduce the cost of retirement pensions to the state. Also, recent ups and downs in the stock market have reduced pension savings for many people. This has led some people to delay retirement.

Still, most older workers show little interest in staying at work. Workers tend to leave work as early as they can. All of this suggests that Canadian society will continue to debate and reshape its pension program in the years ahead.

Summary

1. Canada's pension system has a sound structure, but the current system needs improvement. Some people—very old women, people in lower-income brackets, people with low levels of education, widows, and homemakers—all run a higher than average risk of low income in old age.
2. Canada has a three-tiered system: the OAS, GIS, and ALW make up tier one, the CPP and QPP make up tier two, and private pensions and savings make up tier three.
3. The Canadian retirement system has two goals: (a) to keep all older people out of poverty; and (b) to replace pre-retirement income. At present, it meets

these goals to some degree, but the system needs improvement.

4. Poorer Canadians, the people who need private savings the most in retirement, have the least chance of having any. Private pension plans cover fewer than half of Canadian workers. The CPP at best replaces only 25 percent of a person's income up to the average industrial wage, and the OAS/GIS/ALW leave the poorest older people in poverty.

5. Registered Retirement Savings Plans (RRSPs) encourage saving for retirement, but wealthier Canadians get the most benefit from this option. They can afford to save the most money in these plans and get the highest tax savings from their investment.

6. Compared with men, women face a higher risk of poverty in old age because unequal coverage by pension plans, lower-paying jobs, and different work patterns due to child-rearing often leave women with lower pensions.

7. Widows run a high risk of poverty in old age. The CPP pays a relatively small survivor pension, and private pension plans offer only about a 60 percent pension to survivors.

8. The federal government has recently made changes to the system. Reforms include higher GIS/ALW payments, a more secure CPP pension system, rules that encourage RRSP and TFSA contributions, and rules that strengthen private pension plans.

9. In 1998, the Canadian government created the CPP Investment Board to manage CPP surplus revenues. The board invests in financial markets. Although this entails some risk, good management of these funds has added to the CPP's ability to meet future demands.

10. Many employers have moved from offering defined benefit pension plans to offering defined contribution pension plans. A defined benefit plan makes the employer responsible for a specific pension for each retiree; a defined contribution plan states how much a worker will pay into the program but does not guarantee a specific income in retirement. This trend has shifted pension risk from the employer to the worker.

11. Proposed reforms to the CPP and to private plans try to ensure that more Canadians, including homemakers, get pension coverage. Better public and private pensions for these people may reduce the costs of federal government transfers in the future. This will save the government money and give more people a better income in retirement.

12. The government will probably reduce its role in providing pensions to middle-income workers in the future. Individuals, families, and the private sector will have to provide retirement income for middle-income earners.

13. Canadians will pay for pension reforms as long as people support the notion that everyone—young and old—gains from a strong pension system.

STUDY QUESTIONS

1. Name and describe the parts of Canada's three-tiered retirement income system. Why do some older people live in poverty today in spite of the drop in poverty rates for older people in general?

2. List two strengths and two weaknesses of the public pension system. Do the same for the private pension system. Why does the private system fail to help most people in retirement?

3. Explain the difference between a defined benefit and a defined contribution pension plan. How does the shift toward defined contribution plans shift the risk from the employer to the worker? What effect will this shift have on pension planning for younger people and on their pensions in the future?

4. How has the Canadian government changed the public pension system to provide better coverage for older Canadians? How will reforms affect middle-class Canadians? How will they affect poorer Canadians? How will reforms affect women?

5. What changes have writers proposed in the current public pension system to provide better retirement incomes for older people in the future? Do you think the public will support reforms to the system? Why or why not?

KEY TERMS

clawback (p. 203)
credit splitting (p. 219)
defined benefit (DB) pension plans (p. 207)
defined contribution (DC) pension plans (p. 208)
great pension debate (p. 198)
income maintenance programs (p. 199)
income security programs (p. 199)
indexation (p. 219)
pay-as-you-go plan (p. 205)
portable pension (p. 205)
registered retirement savings plans (RRSPs) (p. 210)
savings plan (p. 205)
tax-free savings accounts (TFSAs) (p. 220)
transfer plan (p. 205)
universality (p. 198)
vesting (p. 205)

CHAPTER 9

RETIREMENT AND WORK

Monkey Business Images/Shutterstock

LEARNING OBJECTIVES

After reading this chapter, you will

LO1 Understand the origins of retirement in Canada.

LO2 Be able to explain current trends in retirement and the causes of these trends.

LO3 Be able to explain the forces that lead people to retire or stay at work longer.

LO4 Be able to give examples of alternatives to a fixed retirement today.

LO5 Understand the impact of the economy and longer life expectancy on retirement decision making.

LO6 Be able to link the retirement patterns of men and women to their earlier experience in the workforce.

LO7 Be able to show how and why men and women differ in their approach to retirement.

LO8 Appreciate the personal experiences of retirement.

INTRODUCTION

Claude Rioux retired six months after his 65th birthday. He had worked as a warehouseman for an electronic supply company. Claude never thought much about retirement in his middle years. A year or two before he retired, he began to feel he had nothing in common with his co-workers. Most of his friends had retired, and most of his new co-workers had just left high school. They talked about girls and motorcycles and listened to loud music. He had always liked work, but he began to enjoy it less each day.

After he turned 65, his boss came by to ask if he had any retirement plans. Another time, the boss called him into his office and asked him when he planned to leave. "I said I didn't know," Claude says. "Why give him the satisfaction of thinking he could push me out? Hell, I still do a good job. Better than some of the kids who work here now. Oh, I planned to leave in January, but I wouldn't tell him. I thought, 'I'll leave when I'm good and ready.'"

No one forced Claude to retire and he left work just about on schedule. He had little reason to keep working past age 65—he had a small pension from work as well as his Canada Pension Plan (CPP) and Old Age Security (OAS), and he planned to open a small electronics repair shop at home. He stayed on until January only to show that no one could push him around.

Denton and Spencer (2009b) define retirement as a "withdrawal from paid working life" (p. 64). Statistics Canada reports that most Canadians retire at age 65 or earlier. In 2014, for instance, only 17.4 percent of men and 9.1 percent of women age 65 and over continued to work in the labour force (Statistics Canada, 2015m). By age 70 and over, the proportion of workers drops to 6.9 percent for men and only 1.9 percent for women (Turcotte & Schellenberg, 2007). These figures show that retirement has become a normative life event.

But this trend toward retirement at age 65 is changing. With longer life expectancy today, if they retire at age 65, some people will spend a quarter or more of their adult life in retirement. Also, new retirement options in Canada challenge the ideal of a clean break from the labour force at or before age 65.

Denton, Finnie, and Spencer (2011) call retirement "a somewhat fuzzy concept" (p. 3). Today, a person may retire from one job (e.g., teaching), then return to the workforce (e.g., as a real estate broker). A person may retire and re-enter the workforce more than once. A retiree may start a new career, take on part-time work, or, like Claude, open a new business. All of these options and more exist today. This makes retirement a fluid and flexible time of life. Social forces (economic conditions, legal statutes, pension rules) and personal preferences (the desire to leave an unpleasant job or to explore new opportunities) all shape retirement today.

Gerontologists view retirement today from two points of view: first, as a social institution and, second, as a personal experience. This chapter will look at retirement from each of these perspectives. It will look at (1) the origin and role of retirement in modern society, (2) the forces that lead a person to retire or stay at work, and (3) the experience of the person in retirement.

RETIREMENT AS A SOCIAL INSTITUTION

The Origins of Retirement

Myles (1984) traced our idea of old age in Canada today to two developments. The first is the **retirement principle**—the idea that a person leaves work at a fixed age, regardless of mental or physical ability. The second is the **retirement wage**—a pension paid by the state to support older people. Myles said that a new group of people grew out of these two developments: "a population of elders still fit for production who do not engage in economic activity" (p. 7).

Employers and employees have both supported the retirement principle in North America. Industry supported it for two reasons. First, retirement allowed companies to retire older, skilled workers and hire younger, less-skilled workers at lower wages, and second, companies, using a philosophy of "scientific management," sought to speed up production and get more out of their workers. Unions offered to have workers work faster if companies shortened the workday, but a faster pace of work made it hard for older workers to compete with younger workers. Retirement gave older workers a graceful way to leave work.

The Canadian government supported the retirement principle for a number of reasons. Canada's first civil service commissioner, Adam Shortt, said in 1922 that "retirement relieves the government of the embarrassment and extravagance of retaining the services of officers who have outlived their usefulness; creates a proper flow of promotions; renders the service more mobile; deters efficient workers from leaving the public service for private employment [and] in general tends to

---

retirement principle the idea that a person leaves work at a fixed age, regardless of mental or physical ability

retirement wage a pension paid by the state to support all older people

promote efficiency in every way" (quoted in Bolger, 1980, p. 8, cited in Myles, 1984, p. 13).

Canada introduced the Old Age Pension Act in 1927 to promote the goals outlined above and to solve a social problem created by retired workers. Matthews and Tindale (1987) give three reasons for this act. First, more people lived to old age; second, many old people lived in poverty; and third, employers needed to reduce unemployment and increase productivity. The Old Age Pension Act encouraged retirement. It provided a basic income to the poorest older people, and it opened up jobs for the young.

Unions in North America wanted companies to use seniority (first hired, last fired) as a method for deciding layoffs or cutbacks. Seniority gave workers a right to a job, and it gave the oldest workers the most job security. But companies resisted the seniority system because older workers cost them more and seniority rights made it hard for them to fire inefficient older workers. Retirement served both unions and employers: it limited seniority rights to people under the age of retirement and allowed companies to let older workers go. The unions traded the older worker's right to a job for job security in middle age. Snell (1996) said that the new "mandatory, continuing unemployment [program that emerged] would be known by the euphemism 'retirement' " (p. 6).

Still, compared with today, few people retired in the past. First, in Canada many people worked on farms or in small businesses, work settings with no retirement age. Second, and most important, a lack of retirement income kept most people working as long as they could. Only with the increase in public pensions and social supports for older people after World War II did retirement spread (McDonald, 2012).

The U.S. Social Security program led the way for this change. The United States designed Social Security in 1935 as a way to get people to retire (Myles, 1984, p. 16). Until then, governments had given social assistance to older people, but this assistance, like Canada's early old age assistance program, gave only the poorest older people a small amount of money to help them survive. The U.S. government based its program on the English poor law notion of "less eligibility." This rule held that assistance should relieve poverty, but should come to less than the lowest working wage.

In time, Social Security, and later Canada's public pension system, set a new goal for public pensions. They promised to make up for a retiree's lost income. "By 1980, the institution of retirement had been consolidated and old age had become a period in the life cycle defined and sustained by the welfare state" (Myles, 1984, p. 21; also Rix, 2011).

Government now plays the major role in guaranteeing pensions to older retirees. Public pensions and transfer payments act as a deferred wage because people pay into the programs through taxes and payments to the Canada Pension Plan (CPP) and the Quebec Pension Plan (QPP) while they work. In Canada, though, the amount a person gets does not depend only on how much he or she paid in. People today get "a share of the social product over and above any claims they may have possessed in their capacity as wage earners" (Myles, 1984, p. 29). Myles called this a citizen's wage. This wage makes retirement a time of economic security and freedom for many older people.

With government help, retirement has become an option for more people than ever before. Dodge, Laurin, and Busby (2010) showed that a middle-income earner who wanted to replace 70 percent of his or her income in retirement would need to save 17 percent of yearly pre-tax earnings every year in order to retire at age 63. Most people could not or would not save at this rate. Without public pension plans, a large proportion of older people would live in or near poverty. Public pension plans ensure that everyone will have income security in old age.

TIME TO REVIEW

What social forces led retirement to arise in modern society?

What philosophy or perspective supported the development of retirement and made it possible? How do public pension plans support the retirement plans of older workers?

WHY DO PEOPLE RETIRE?

A number of personal conditions lead people to choose retirement. These include a person's expected pension income, early retirement incentives, loss of a job, health, a spouse's decision to retire, and family responsibilities (Pyper, 2006; Statistics Canada, 2006d; Turcotte & Schellenberg, 2007). Social forces can also lead a person to choose retirement. These forces include mandatory retirement rules, better pensions that start at age 65, and a more positive societal attitude toward retirement. Galarneau and colleagues (2015a, 2015b) found that a poor regional economy led workers to retire early. Compared to people in provinces with low unemployment, people in provinces with high unemployment (e.g., Quebec and three of the Atlantic provinces) retire about two years earlier. Layoffs and problems finding new

---

citizen's wage a government pension tied to age

work lead workers in these regions to earlier retirement. These findings show the impact of society-wide economic forces on the individual.

Mandatory Retirement

Mandatory retirement rules play a relatively small role in the pattern of retirement today. No federal law in Canada forces a person to retire at age 65, and no statute requires a worker to leave work at a certain age. The federal public service ended mandatory retirement in 1986.

Still, in cases through the 1990s, the Supreme Court of Canada supported mandatory retirement. As late as 2008, the Supreme Court continued to support this position in limited contexts. In a four-to-three decision, the court upheld mandatory retirement in New Brunswick in cases where an employer has a bona fide retirement pension plan. The Human Rights Act in New Brunswick allows this exception. The New Brunswick Human Rights Commission appealed this exception. Its chair, Gordon Porter, expressed disappointment at the ruling (New Brunswick, 2008). He said at the time: "Mandatory retirement is clearly age discrimination. A person who wants to continue to work should be allowed to do so. It is a question of fairness, and it makes economic sense."

Longer life expectancy, better health among older workers, the change in the type of work people do (less manual labour), and the need for older workers' expertise makes mandatory retirement an outdated policy except in special circumstances. Some provinces, for example, allow

---

EXHIBIT 9.1 *Employment Rates of Women and Men Age 65 Years and Over, Canada, 1976 to 2009*

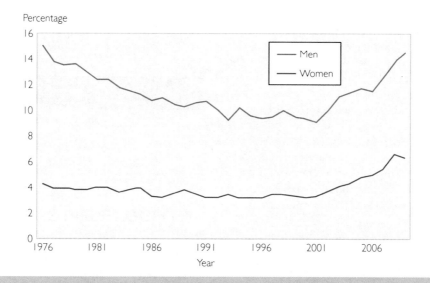

This chart shows three periods of employment participation for senior men and women. The first period (1976–1986) shows a decline in participation. The second period (1986–2001) shows relatively stable employment rates. The third period (2001–2009) shows a rise in employment rates for men and women.

Note that employment rates for men and women show different patterns over this 33-year period. The employment rate for senior men declined until the mid-1990s, then started to rise. By 2009, the proportion of senior men in the labour force had almost returned to the 1976 rate. These figures indicate a trend toward greater labour force participation for older men.

Employment rates for senior women remained relatively stable at around 4 percent of senior women for most of the period shown here. The employment rate for senior women began to rise in the late 1990s and continued to rise to 2009.

By 2009, about 6 percent of senior women took part in the labour force. Note that even with the increased employment rate for older women between 1976 and 2009, their employment rate comes to less than half the rate of senior men. This reflects lifetime patterns of different employment activity for men and women.

What accounts for the increase in labour force participation by older men and women? Some older workers say they enjoy work and don't want to retire. Some women enter the workforce in later life or stay at work longer because they need the income. A widow, for example, may find that her deceased husband's pension no longer provides enough support. A projected labour shortage in the future may lead to more hiring of older workers in some professions, and this may further increase labour force participation for older men and women.

Sources: Uppal, S. "Labour Market Activity among Seniors," *Perspectives*, July 2010: 5–18. Chart source: Milan, A., and Vézina, M. *Senior Women*. Component of *Women in Canada: A Gender-based Statistical Report*. Statistics Canada Catalogue No. 89-503-X, Chart 7, p. 18 (2011). Reproduced and distributed on an "as is" basis with the permission of Statistics Canada.

mandatory retirement for certain jobs, where physical ability effects performance, such as police officers or firefighters. This represents a change from the past where mandatory retirement rules forced many people out of work at age 65.

The government, employers, and employees now favour more flexible retirement options (Rix, 2011). The Canadian Expert Panel on Older Workers (2008) in an article titled "Supporting and engaging older workers in the new economy," recommended "that the federal government eliminate mandatory retirement" throughout Canada. The government acted on this recommendation by amending the Canadian Human Rights Act (p. iii). This removed all exceptions that permit mandatory retirement (except where a legitimate occupational condition would require it).

The end of mandatory retirement comes at an opportune time. Canada may need its older workers to remain on the job (Hicks, 2011). Hering and Klassen (2010) predicted "that labour shortages will be more common in the future...." (p. 10). Fields such as education and healthcare, for example, will soon feel a retirement crunch. MacGregor (2005) said that universities "present a spectacular example" of this retirement wave (p. 29). The Association of Universities and Colleges of Canada (Tibbetts, 2007) said that as many as one-half of the country's 40,000 professors may retire and need to be replaced in the next decade. Healthcare has a little more breathing room. About half the healthcare labour force will reach retirement age in 20 years. In light of this projected labour shortage, the Canadian Standing Senate Committee (2006, cited in Hering & Klassen, 2010, p. 11) said that "workers should have incentives to remain in the labour market and to increase the nature and level of their labour market activity, if they choose."

Will an End to Mandatory Retirement Lead Older Workers to Stay on the Job?

In an analysis of six countries including Canada, Cooke (2006) found that older workers don't tend to stay at work if they have a choice. He said that "despite references to population aging in the mandatory retirement debates in Canada, there is little evidence that banning mandatory retirement has had an effect on labour force participation in other countries" (p. 392). Ontario Ministry of Labour (2006) figures agree. The ministry estimates that the end to mandatory retirement in that province would add only about 4,000 older workers (out of about 100,000 retirees) per year to the labour force.

Employers may favour the release of older workers even in the face of a labour shortage. First, Cooke (2006) says, employers view older workers as more expensive and less effective than younger workers. They believe this "despite anti-discrimination laws and evidence that older workers are indeed capable of learning new tasks and tend to have higher loyalty and less absenteeism" (p. 396). Firms that want to retire older workers will do so through "voluntary buy-outs" even where laws make mandatory retirement illegal.

Second, "there are powerful incentives for older workers to leave the labour force, including public and private pensions" (Cooke, 2006, p. 392). Cooke notes, based on the experience in other countries, "retirement is desirable for many.... Those who can afford to retire because of private pensions or other income may well continue to do so, while those who cannot may look for other routes of exit from paid work" (p. 396). Wannell (2007a) reported that people who retire early (in their 50s) generally leave high-paying jobs. Their retirement income on average comes to about two-thirds of their pre-retirement income, about the amount the pension experts consider necessary to maintain a pre-retirement standard of living.

In other words, as long as public and private pensions offer incentives to retire at age 65 or sooner, an end to mandatory retirement will have little effect on keeping older people at work. "Some people apparently would like to go on working beyond age 65," Townson said (2006), "but most are retiring before then" (p. 149). When asked why they retired, most people said they "really want[ed] to leave their jobs .... individuals simply want to do other things" (Milligan & Schirle, 2008, p. 9).

Townson (2006, citing Policy Research Initiative, 2004) said, "Innumerable surveys have shown that people do not want to work longer if it can be avoided. They might be willing to do so in a job that they liked, but a good many people don't seem to like the jobs they are doing. As one focus group participant [in a Policy Research Initiative study] put it, 'I love to work. It's just that I hate my job.' Reminding these participants that Canadians were living longer and healthier lives, and thus more able to work past retirement, 'had little impact on their view'" (p. 226).

Fourth, several barriers exist that keep retirees from working. Some pension programs (the GIS, for example) clawback a share of retiree earnings. OAS payments start at age 65, as do Guaranteed Income Supplement (GIS) payments and full CPP/QPP payments. A person who works past age 65 will still get these benefits, but will lose a large portion of them through higher taxes. The GIS program, for example, reduces the GIS by $1 for each $2 a single person earns (after an exemption of the first $3,500 earned); a person who earns a provincial supplement loses the other $1 from his or her supplement benefits.

Government policies such as these can result in a large **taxback** on the poorest people (Government of Canada, 2008). Also, the taxback takes money from the older person's income next year for money earned this year. This means that low-income older people who work risk losing next year's income supplements (as well as their salary) if they get sick or lose their job. Also, added income from work may increase a person's tax rate. These rules create a strong incentive for retirement (Wannell, 2007b).

Fifth, better pension plans today make retirement more attractive than ever before. Some workers with good pension plans may have more disposable income in retirement than if they keep on working; taxes and the cost of commuting, clothes, lunches, and other work-related expenses may make work an expensive option. Also, most private pension plans begin to pay full benefits at age 65. These plans provide workers with a strong incentive to retire at 65. In addition, increased leisure and recreational opportunities have changed social attitudes toward retirement (Ekerdt & Sergeant, 2006).

Sixth, inflexible work arrangements give older workers little incentive to stay at work. Uriarte-Landa and Hebert (2009, citing Morissette, Schellenberg, & Silver, 2004) said that more than one worker in four would have stayed at work if they could have found part-time work or if they could have worked shorter or fewer days. A smaller percentage (6 percent) said they would have stayed at work if they had caregiving support. But most employers find it difficult to arrange part-time or flexible work for retirees (Cooke, 2006). Aegon (2014) in its 2014 *Retirement Readiness Survey* reported that only 23 percent of employers have a phased part-time retirement option for employees.

Seventh, a person may retire for personal reasons such as disability, a decline in their health, or caregiving responsibilities (Park, 2010, 2011). Schirle (2010) reported that poor health increases the likelihood of retirement by up to 25 percent.

Clearly, people retire for many reasons, and an end to mandatory retirement will have little effect on current patterns of retirement. Still, an end to mandatory retirement gives older adults the right to remain in their current jobs if they choose. And a trend toward longer work careers suggests that some workers will keep on working.

TIME to REVIEW

Why do people choose to retire?

What social and economic forces lead workers to decide to retire?

What social changes would encourage people to stay at work longer?

Forced Retirement: Age Discrimination in the Workplace

Some seniors retire during an economic downturn if they get laid off. Those who want to work find it hard to get back into the workforce. Brzozowski and Crossley (2010) said that older displaced workers "experience longer jobless spells" (p. 1). And compared with younger displaced workers, older workers lose more earnings (as much as 35 percent of pre-displacement earnings) due to company closure or layoffs (Morissette, Zhang, & Frenette, 2007; also Bonikowska & Schellenberg, 2013).

Older displaced workers may stop looking for work and declare themselves "retired." Age discrimination in part explains the problem older people face when they look for a job. Rix (2006; also Cooke, 2006) said, "Age continues to work against many older jobseekers, as evidenced by the average length of time it takes them to find work, the wage loss many experience upon reemployment, and the size of court awards to victims of discrimination" (p. 3).

A study sponsored by the American Association of Retired Persons (AARP, 2007a) of seven developed nations found that "age discrimination in hiring practices continues to be a serious concern around the world. The level of confidence among workers age 50+ in their ability to find new jobs is much lower than for workers below age 50. Age discrimination is viewed as the single largest barrier to finding jobs for workers over age 50" (p. 59). In this study, 72 percent of Canadians age 50 and over felt that age discrimination would create a barrier to them finding a new job. Twenty-eight percent of people age 50 and over said they had experienced age discrimination. Sixty percent of these people said they experienced age discrimination when looking for a job, and more than 35 percent reported age discrimination in promotion decisions.

---

taxback taxes paid on earnings by recipients of the Guaranteed Income Supplement and provincial supplements that can amount to a 100 percent reduction in supplement payments for the poorest older people who work

In one case, a young entrepreneur, age 24, wrote to a newspaper advice column expressing his concern about hiring older workers for his firm. This CEO worried that an older worker would not fit in with his firm's youth-oriented culture. Misener (2013) responded: "Culture is about norms and values. 'Young' isn't a statement about culture. If the culture is one where people like to have fun at work and who don't take themselves too seriously, there are plenty of people who are not young who want that as well."

This little exchange brings to the surface how some employers stereotype older workers. Misener brought a touch of reality in his response by separating age from style and ability. Older workers bring skills and knowledge to a workplace. And, like people of every age, older workers can and do adapt to the culture and demands of the job. Misener noted that this young firm can hire an older worker who "understands corporate protocols .... together with the credibility, relationships and competence that come with experience." He said the firm would need an experienced executive to lead it to the next level.

Studies of older workers and of firms that hire them overthrow ageist stereotypes. Aon Hewitt (2015), a consulting firm, conducted a national study of older workers for the AARP. The study found that older workers (50+) played a vital role in high-performance businesses. Employers rated older employees high on "experience, professionalism, work ethic, low turnover, and knowledge." Older workers are also keepers of institutional memory.

The study found that leading employers try to recruit and retain older workers through "flexible workplaces, options for transitioning to retirement, and fostering generational diversity and inclusion." Armstrong-Stassen and Schlosser (2011) found that older workers remain loyal to an employer if they get fair treatment and feel valued. Ng and Law (2014), in a review of the literature on older workers, said "there is little link between age and work performance; instead, adaptation and skills acquisition may protect older workers from declining productivity." They used the SOC (selection, optimization, and compensation) model of successful aging to study older workers' adaptation at work. They found that some workers questioned their ability to keep up with change and the demands of work but others adapted to change. One man, age 62, said, "You just find better ways of doing it and .... that's what I've learned" (p. 6). Another man (age 55) said, "I enjoy my work. I'm passionate about it. I like it. It's stimulating. I'm well respected in what I do" (p. 7).

In spite of the studies that show the value and commitment of older workers, Townson (2006) said, "It is widely recognized that age is a barrier for individuals trying to get a job" (p. 192). A number of experimental studies document age discrimination in the workplace. Lahey (2006, cited in Herd, 2009), for example, conducted a study to assess prejudice against older workers. She sent out résumés for equally experienced older and younger workers. The résumés went to 4,000 companies in Florida and Massachusetts. She found that the people presented as younger applicants in their resumes had a 40 percent greater chance of getting called for an interview.

Workers in the Ng and Law (2014) study of older workers expressed their own concerns about their employability. One woman (age 59) said, "I think people look at me and think, well, 'Why would we hire her? She doesn't have many years left'" (p. 5). A career counsellor told another woman (age 56), "the odds of you graduating from, say, a community college program and getting gainful employment aren't all that great" (p. 5). Another woman (age 63) said, "if I take a course and upgrade my skills for a year, I'm 63. Who's still going to hire me?" (p. 6). These women expressed concern about ageism and doubts about their own ability to find work.

A number of companies in developed countries address age discrimination in the workplace. Deutsche Bank developed a task force on age diversity with senior managers in the lead, and the National Health Service in the United Kingdom conducts training on the value of older workers and promotes intergenerational mentoring (AARP, 2007a).

Danny Green, human resources director of Merck Frost in Quebec, said, "Frankly, it's good business for government and employers to make it easier for over-50 employees to continue working. It's a win-win all around—it adds to the GDP of the country" (AARP, 2007a, p. 19). These companies and others recognize the experience and dedication that many older workers bring to their jobs. They also recognize that a company must take a proactive stance to overcome age discrimination in the workplace.

The Expert Panel on Older Workers (2008) called for a "comprehensive and sustained awareness campaign to promote the value and benefits to individuals and employers of continued and active participation in the labour force" (p. ii). This campaign would reduce ageism and remove negative stereotypes about older workers (Bowen, Noack, & Staudinger, 2011).

Age discrimination thrives on stereotyped and prejudiced views of older workers (McDonald, 2012). Eng, a former executive vice president of CARP (a Canadian organization that advocates for financial security and improved healthcare for seniors) (2015) said, "Older workers who lost their jobs in the late 1990s had three times as much difficulty getting new ones as their younger counterparts and they either got jobs within the first two years or not at all." Companies that support older workers with training or new jobs find that older workers perform well. Training and education motivate older workers.

Doug McDonald, a bus driver with the Coast Mountain Bus Company in British Columbia, had 39 years of experience as a driver. He said, "I have my health and I'm still having fun.... What keeps us older workers going, and keeps us coming back to work, is a learning environment" (Expert Panel on Older Workers, 2008, p. 42). Canada could keep older people in the workforce by retraining workers for service-sector jobs and by increasing educational opportunities. At present, few opportunities exist for older worker retraining. Park (2012; also Underhill, 2006) said that "the incidence of training declines with age." For example, in 2007–2008, "45% of workers age 25–54 took at least one job-related course or program compared to 32% of those age 55–64" (pp. 4–6). Only Ontario and Manitoba have training programs for unemployed older workers; the federal government has no policy on training older workers and no training program targeted to them.

This will have to change if Canada wants to keep older workers productive and in the labour force. Bowen, Noack, and Staudinger (2011) said, "Intervention research has shown that adults of all ages can benefit from training" (p. 268). A woman (age 55) in the Ng and Law (2014) study said that after taking a school program, "I just got hired. I'm working part-time learning the job, and then in June when I graduate I have a full time job" (p. 8). This case and others show that older workers have a unique place in the workforce. They bring experience and they adapt to change. Ng and Law (p. 11) concluded "that older workers are in fact much more adaptable than previously portrayed, and that they are actively engaged in strategies to maintain and enhance their work functioning." The Expert Panel on Older Workers (2008; also Rix, 2011) calls for increased training for older workers and continuous learning throughout workers' lives.

Early Retirement

The 2007 *General Social Survey* found that 22 percent of near-retirees (age 45–59) said they planned to retire before age 60. And 25 percent of these workers said they planned to retire between ages 60 and 64. Another 25 percent planned to retire at age 65. This means that nearly three-quarters of older workers planned to leave the labour force either at or before the traditional retirement age. Nearly half of these workers planned on an early retirement (Schellenberg & Ostrovsky, 2008a).

Hering and Klassen (2010), in an essay that supported delayed retirement, admitted that "most workers continue to wish to retire sooner rather than later" (pp. 13–14). From the mid-1990s to 2009, men on average retired at age 62. The average retirement age for women rose from age 61 to 62 (Park, 2011). In 2006, only 15 percent of senior men and 6 percent of senior women remained in the labour force (Uppal, 2010).

Three types of workers tend to take early retirement: workers in poor health, women who retire for personal reasons, and those who expect a good income in retirement (Park, 2010). First, compared with healthy workers, unhealthy workers tend to retire at an earlier age. Park reported that "almost 30% of those who retired between age 50 and 59 indicated health as the reason" (p. 5). Poor health due to heavy drinking, smoking, and obesity predicted early exit from the workforce. Stress at work also leads to early retirement. Compared with women in low-strain jobs, women in high-strain jobs showed twice the tendency to retire early. More generous disability insurance programs today make it easier for workers to retire early if they have a health problem.

Second, in Canada, more women than men retire early for personal reasons. Many women retire because their spouse has retired. Because women often marry older men, they retire at an earlier age on average than men. Also, women, more often than men, retire because of the ill health of a spouse or a family member.

A Statistics Canada study (Turcotte & Schellenberg, 2007) found that family responsibilities ranked third as the most common reason for women to retire. This item barely ranked at all for men. McDonald, Donahue, and Moore (1998, cited in McDonald, 2006a) found that women who retired to give care often worked in marginal jobs, worked irregular schedules, and took voluntary absences. They also tended to have lower personal incomes and were less likely to get benefits from any pension plan or from investments. These findings show the effects of family and personal pressures on women's decisions to retire. These findings also caution against using data based on male retirement patterns to draw conclusions about retirement for women.

Third, good pensions lead workers to retire. Workers in the public sector in 2006–2007 retired on average just over three years earlier than those in the labour force in general. Self-employed workers tended to retire later than other workers (Schellenberg & Ostrovsky, 2008a). These figures support the idea that good pension benefits encourage early retirement (Carrière & Galarneau, 2012b).

As Burtless and Quinn (2001, cited in Myles, 2006) concluded, the "simplest and probably most powerful explanation for earlier retirement is rising wealth" (p. 385). As workers' wealth increased, they tended to buy more years of retirement. Older workers who stay at work often do so because they need the money.

Some private pension plans encourage people to choose early retirement. Many large companies, the government, and universities sponsor early retirement plans. Early retirement allows companies to hire less costly young workers or to leave jobs empty after a retiree leaves.

Canada's Public Service Superannuation Act allows public-service workers to retire as early as age 55 with 30 years' service (the 55/30 pension rule). This makes age 55 the most popular retirement age for public-sector employees. The 2007 *General Social Survey* found that more than three-quarters (76.9 percent) of public-sector workers who planned to retire expected to retire before age 60 (Schellenberg & Ostrovsky, 2008a). Only 18.4 percent of these workers planned to retire at age 65 or older. This pattern differed significantly from that of workers in manufacturing industries.

Private-sector employees tended to stay on until at least age 65. Schellenberg and Ostrovsky (2008a) reported that 49.2 percent of workers in consumer services (e.g., retail sales, food services, recreation) planned to work to age 65 or later. These workers expressed the least certainty about their retirement age. Low wages and the lack of pensions in these jobs means that these workers need to postpone retirement.

Some private-sector pension plans in Canada allow early retirement on a reduced pension. Some private plans even include a special rule allowing early retirement on an unreduced pension after a certain number of years of service or for age plus service. Many defined benefit pension plans allow payment of a full pension at age 50 or 55. These plans provide no incentive for workers to stay at work. More years of work will not make up for the pension payments they can get if they retire early. Workers in these plans tend to leave work before age 65. The RRSP program that allows withdrawal from accounts at any age also supports early retirement.

The CPP allows payments to begin as early as age 60 or as late as age 70. People who retire early get decreases in their basic pension equal to 0.6 percent for each month (7.2 percent per year) between the date the pension begins and the month after their 65th birthday. A person who retires at age 60 will have 64 percent of the pension they would have had if they had retired at age 65. Those who retire at age 70 or later receive an increase of 0.7 percent on their basic pension for every month (8.4 percent per year) between age 70 and the month after their 65th birthday. A person who retires at age 70 will get a 42 percent larger pension than if he or she had retired at age 65. Still, almost 80 percent of workers who get an employer pension before age 60 choose early CPP or QPP benefits at age 60 (Hering & Klassen, 2010). In other words, public and private pension plan policies as well as the RRSP program encourage early retirement.

The desire to leave work, and the existence of public and private pensions, make retirement an attractive goal for many people. But the economic downturn in 2008–2009 forced many older workers to reconsider early retirement. They decided to stay on the job longer to recover from the loss of investment income. This delay in retirement reverses a trend toward early retirement that began in the 1970s. Exhibit 9.2 shows that a stronger economy has once again led workers to plan for an early retirement.

Changing Patterns of Retirement: The Trend toward Later Retirement

In spite of workers' desire for early retirement, studies show an increase in the number of years workers work today (Carrière & Galarneau, 2012a, 2012b; McDonald & Donahue, 2012). Hicks (2011), for example, predicted that over the next 20 years "people are likely to stay in the work force at least five years longer, possible by considerably more" (p. 1). What accounts for this shift in the pattern of retirement? The need for income, an increasing demand for workers, and a more educated workforce all point toward longer work careers.

Workers may hope for an early retirement, but many Canadians cannot afford to retire. Retirement often depends in part on a person's past experience in the workplace and the economic conditions they face throughout life.

Bonikowska and Schellenberg (2013) studied Baby Boomer work patterns over a 28-year period from 1983 to 2010. They studied workers who were age 33 to 38 in 1983. About two-thirds of the workers in their sample had long-term jobs (12 years or more). Many of these workers worked for a single employer for more than 20 years. Long-term job holders fit the traditional pattern of retirement. Long-term job holders (about two-thirds of all workers) tend not to fully retire. Over half the workers age 55 to 64 in their sample returned to work within 10 years. The younger the worker, the greater the likelihood that person would return to work. Men more often than women returned to work.

EXHIBIT 9.2   AVERAGE EXPECTED RETIREMENT AGE

Question: At what age do you think you will finally stop working and be fully retired, if ever?

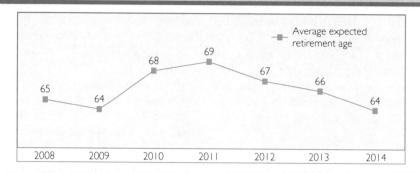

Note that the expected average retirement age reached a peak in 2011 at 69 years. It has since dropped back to the same expected age as in 2008–2009 (age 64). These figures provide insight into the shifting thinking about retirement among working Canadians. They also show the effect of large-scale economic conditions on retirement expectations. The recession of 2008 led many older workers to think about a later retirement age due to the economic downturn and the stock market decline. The economic recovery in recent years has led workers to once again plan for an earlier retirement.

Source: Sun Life Assurance Company of Canada. (2015). *2015 Sun Life Canadian unretirement index report.* Sun Life Assurance Company of Canada, p. 4. Retrieved from http://cdn.sunlife.com/static/canada/sunlifeca/About%20us/Canadian%20Unretirement%20Index/Unretirement%20Index%20tool/2015_Sun_Life_Canadian_Unretirement_Index_Report_en.pdf.

The researchers found that most long-term workers found work fairly soon after their long-term jobs ended. Of those age 60 to 64, for example, 42 percent found work within the same year. Another 21 percent found work the following year. A worker who did not return to work within two years had a lower chance of returning to work. Those who returned to work typically had earnings 18 percent below their long-term job income.

These findings suggest that older workers with strong work records can find work after they leave their long-term job. But about one-third of workers in their 50s have a less stable or very unstable work record and they find re-employment a challenge. About one-quarter of this cohort changed jobs throughout their lives.

Bonikowska and Schellenberg (2013) called these "mobile workers" (p. 22). Compared to long-term job holders, these men and women earned less each year, had lower total earnings, and had fewer years of pensionable service. The researchers found that 12 percent of this sample worked as "marginally attached workers" (p. 22): they worked in short-term positions and they earned and saved little during their work careers.

Many of these workers will have small private pensions, or none at all. The marginal workers may feel no transition to retirement, since they never had a stable long-term job. Many of these workers will need to work into later old age or live on a public pension.

About one-quarter of Canadians age 45 and over said they either didn't know when they would retire or that they would never retire (Schellenberg & Ostrovsky, 2008a). The Canadian Institute of Actuaries (2010) studied pre-retired and retired Canadians age 45 and over. Forty-two percent of the pre-retirees said they were not prepared for retirement. Forty-one percent of pre-retirees said they felt they would face a drop in standard of living in retirement. Sixty-two percent of the pre-retirees said they had concerns about the cost of healthcare and of using up their savings. Many of these people will have to work to maintain their standard of living.

A study conducted for the Sun Life Assurance Company (2015) asked workers age 30–65 what they thought they would be doing at age 66 (one year after the traditional retirement age). About one-quarter of the workers (27 percent) said they would be retired. About one-third (32 percent) said they would still be working full-time (a five-point increase from 2014). Another 27 percent said they would work part-time. In other words, a majority of the 3,000 workers in this sample planned to work past the normal retirement age. Nearly three-fifths (59 percent) of those who plan to keep on working say they need to work for the income.

These facts signal a change in the long-standing trend of early retirement. Gerontologists predict an ongoing increase in retirement age. Age 65 may still define retirement for most workers, and current pension eligibility still makes 65 an attractive age to retire. But many workers may forgo early retirement to ensure

EXHIBIT 9.3 WHAT WORKING CANADIANS EXPECT TO BE DOING AT AGE 66

Question: Thinking about the future, which of the lines in the following graph describes what you think you will be doing at age 66, shortly after the traditional retirement age?

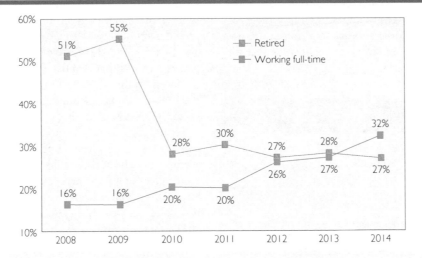

Note that the proportion of workers who plan to work after age 65 doubled between 2008 and 2014 (16 percent vs. 32 percent). During this same period, the proportion of workers who planned to retire dropped almost by half, from 52 percent to 27 percent. These findings point to a major shift in Canadian workers' retirement plans. In part, this change reflects longer life expectancies and the extension of work into the Third Age (the young-old age).

Source: Sun Life Assurance Company of Canada. (2015). *2014 Sun Life Canadian unretirement index report.* Sun Life Assurance Company of Canada, p.3. Base: All respondents in each wave. Retrieved from https://cdn.sunlife.com/static/ca/Learn%20and%20Plan/Market%20insights/Canadian%20Unretirement%20index/2015_Sun_Life_Canadian_Unretirement_Index_Report_en.pdf. Reprinted with permission.

a better pension, increase their savings, and ensure more years of income due to longer life expectancies. And many workers may choose to work after age 65, in part because pension plans like the CPP now provide better pensions to workers who delay retirement. Public policy can and does have an influence on when workers choose to retire.

Also, older women in the workforce will push up the average retirement age. The proportion of older women in the labour force nearly doubled between 1997 and 2010. In 2009, for example, 6.4 percent of senior women held a paid job. This came to double the proportion in 2000 (3.2 percent) (Milan & Vézina, 2011). This signals a return of some women to the labour force later in life and the continuation of work by the large number of women who entered the labour force in their youth.

The 2007 *General Social Survey* found differences in retirement patterns and expectations among different groups of Canadians. Schellenberg and Ostrovsky (2008a) reported that only 44 percent of near-retirees (age 45–59) who immigrated to Canada since 1990 said they felt certain about their retirement plans (compared with 64 percent of Canadian-born people in this age group).

Likewise, compared with 71 percent of Canadian-born near-retirees, only half of immigrants in this age group (50 percent) said they felt confident about their retirement savings. Only 9 percent of immigrant near-retirees, compared with 32 percent of Canadian-born near-retirees, said they expect to retire before age 60.

Recent changes to private pension plan benefits could also lead to fewer early retirements in the future. Defined benefit pension plans pay out a defined amount at a set age according to a formula. These plans encourage retirement at a prescribed age or earlier. But companies have begun to shift from defined benefit to defined contribution plans. For example, more than 100 companies dropped defined benefit plans during 2009 (Callahan, 2009).

This continues a decade-long pattern. Defined contribution plans, an increasingly common option, offer less incentive to retire at a set age. These plans work like a savings account. The longer people work, the more money they add to their plan and the more they will have when they retire. If a person in a defined contribution plan puts off retirement, he or she will have more money to use over fewer years in retirement.

These changes to pension plan rules and policies will affect workers' retirement decisions. Changes to pension rules may make early retirement less attractive. Also, the economic recession in 2008 forced many older workers to postpone retirement (Helman, Copeland, & VanDerhei, 2010; MetLife, 2010a). The trend toward labour force participation for older workers points to a shift away from early retirement, although workers might still prefer this option if they can afford it.

TIME TO REVIEW

Why do some people choose early retirement?

Describe the different reasons that lead men and women to retire.

Why do some people delay retirement?

What effect will delayed retirement have on the labour force? What social conditions today encourage later retirement?

ALTERNATIVES TO A FIXED RETIREMENT AGE

Gendell (2008) divided the post-World War II years into two periods. The first 30 years after the war, he said, favoured early retirement. The second period, from the mid-1980s onward, produced incentives for workers to stay at work. The trend toward workforce participation past traditional retirement ages continues today—and will likely continue into the future.

McDonald (2006a; also Rix, 2011) says that "retirement no longer represents an abrupt transition from work to non-work: it can be gradual, it can involve multiple exits, it is multilayered with other life events and it may never happen" (p. 146). Hardy (2006) said that only about half of retirees today experience retirement as a once-in-a-lifetime break with their past. Many workers, she said, "retire from one job and begin collecting pension benefits as they search for new jobs" (p. 207). Wannell (2007a) said that people with private pension plans "are increasingly finding their way back into paid jobs in their 60s" (p. 19). Today many retirees cycle in and out of retirement—sometimes more than once.

A TD Waterhouse study (TD Bank, 2005, cited in Townson, 2006) found that one-third of the people in the survey planned to work full- or part-time after age 65. Three-quarters of the people who said they would stay at work said they would do so out of choice. Women, more often than men, said they would stay at work because they had to. Novelli and Workman (2006) said that "workers who retire in phases, or steps, are more likely to have a positive view of work and may stay in the workforce longer" (p. 88). Maimaris and colleagues (2010) reviewed the literature on the impact of retirement on mental health. They found that paid and volunteer work beyond retirement can have a good effect on mental health. Work provides a productive social role, income, and social support. They found that people benefit from choosing the pattern of work that best fits their needs.

Many retirees return to work in **bridge jobs**. They work at something new after they retire from their midlife career. Hebert and Luong (2008) found that 9.7 percent of retirees age 50 to 69 worked at a bridge job. Bridge employment ranged from 2 percent for retirees age 50 to 54 to 18 percent for those age 65 to 69. Bridge employment offers many workers an option to full retirement. Studies find that it leads to retirement satisfaction and psychological well-being (Bowen, Noack, & Staudinger, 2011). Options for retirees today include flexible retirement, part-time work, and second careers.

Flexible Retirement

Some workers today choose **flexible retirement**, an option that allows them to slowly cut back the number of hours they work each week.

Older Canadians tend to work if they have occupations that allow for choice in their retirement age and if they can work at their own pace. Many older male workers who continued working tended to work in manufacturing, construction, and transportation industries (Townson, 2006). Farmers (who are mostly self-employed) may need to work in order to earn money and to run the family business.

People who find meaning in work and consider their work important also tend to work after age 65. This applies best to older men who work in managerial jobs, members of the clergy, and university professors (Warman & Worswick, 2010).

Job sharing can serve as an alternative to either retirement or full-time work by spreading the available work for a position over a number of workers. This option fits a trend in the labour force toward more temporary jobs. It allows workers to work part-time in their current positions and this entices some older workers to stay on after retirement age.

Job sharing can benefit employers by giving them more flexibility in responding to labour demands. It also

---

bridge jobs are taken by workers on the path to retirement (often in work outside the individual's former career)

flexible retirement an option that allows workers to slowly cut back the number of hours they work each week

EXHIBIT 9.4 *Targeted Initiative for Older Workers*

Unemployed workers, age 55 to 64, may find it hard to re-enter the workforce. The federal and provincial governments co-sponsored a program for these workers. The Targeted Initiative for Older Workers (TIOW)* assisted these workers with résumé writing, counselling, and skill development.

TIOW focused on communities with a population of 250,000 or less, with high unemployment, company downsizing and closures, unfilled employer demand, and skill mismatches. The examples here give some idea of the program's impact on older workers.

Catherine S. Gemaine worked as a support worker in Ontario for 20 years. The job required a lot of driving. Problems with her vision led her to look for a new job. She enrolled in a TIOW college program in Whitehorse, Yukon. "My dream," she says, "was to find a job working in an office setting where I could be busy and be of assistance to others." Her courses included computer literacy training and conflict resolution, as well as an employment skills workshop. The program also included a one-month job placement. The program led to several casual positions as an administrative assistant, a branch administrative coordinator, and an acting executive assistant to a deputy minister.

Jean Green worked in retail. A program at Southeast Regional College in Moosomin, Saskatchewan, opened a new career option for her. Jean says she came into the program not expecting to gain a lot, but kept an open mind. She says, "The information that I took away from this course is amazing and

the way it was presented ... has had a lasting impression on me." Jean received computer training and CPR and first-aid training, as well as help with her job search. Jean got a job as a post-mistress with Canada Post at the end of her program. She says, "I felt I was the best suited for this [job] as I had learned the skills and confidence building in my [program]...."

Barbara Price and Perri Gorrrara, two unemployed British Columbia women, started a wedding planning business with help from the TIOW program. Barbara needed to find new work after she left a personal assistant/property manager job. Perri worked in the film industry, but had been out of work for six years. Their TIOW program included self-exploration and skill assessment, as well as self-employment training. Barbara says, "It's not just about the job. It's about breaking down mental barriers and assumptions, and living life in a positive way.... You go from thinking 'I can't do anything' to 'I can do anything.' " Barbara and Perri have begun planning their first wedding through their new business.

When an older worker loses his or her job or wants to switch careers, that person faces internal and external challenges—ageism, lack of confidence, and the need to update their skills. But these examples show that older workers come to the market with a willingness to learn a positive attitude. A program such as TIOW helps older workers get over personal and social barriers. This program also helps Canadian society make use of its talented and motivated older workers.

_____
* The TIOW program ended March 31, 2017

Source: Employment and Social Development Canada. *Success Stories: Training Agreements. Older Workers* (2015). Retrieved from http://www.esdc.gc.ca/eng/jobs/training_agreements/stories/index.shtml. Reproduced with the permission of the Minister of Employment and Social Development Canada, 2017.

opens opportunities for people who want part-time or temporary work. In 2004, for example, about one in four men and one in five women age 65 and over in the labour force worked at a temporary job (Turcotte & Schellenberg, 2007). In 2010, men age 55 and over worked on average of 38.6 hours per week (a drop from 40.1 hours in 1997). About 16 percent of men in that year worked part-time (Carriére & Galarneau, 2011).

People who choose partial retirement often choose to work because it provides them with a sense of purpose. They may work at a special project for their former employer, as a consultant, or as a part-time employee. A study conducted for HSBC Insurance Holdings (HSBC, 2006) found that some Canadians "see retirement as a new chapter of life, a time for personal challenges (including work and careers) and taking risks" (p. 7).

Hicks (2011) supported longer work careers and flexible retirement. He said this creates a better "balance between earnings and retirement income sources. Working longer on a part-time, or part-year basis has the additional advantage of maintaining skills and job contacts" (p. 43). A person could then return to work

full-time if they needed to and if the opportunity came up. Delayed retirement also "reduces expenditures and increases revenues [for the CPP], it is the most effective option for responding to the financing pressures generated by population aging" (Hering & Klassen, 2010, p. 19).

Phased retirement can also work well for employers. Some companies see phased retirement as a tool they can use to keep experienced workers on the job (Hewitt Associates, 2008). But rather than create phased retirement policies, companies prefer to work out details with individual retirees. Companies that want to keep their older workers offer flex time, telecommuting, reduced hours without loss of benefits, and adjustment of hours as needed (Pope, 2008). The Agriculture Financial Services Corporation (AFSC), a Crown corporation in Alberta, allows flexible work options. These include shorter work weeks and telecommuting. The AFSC also offers phased retirement options. AFSC ranked as one of Canada's "Top Employers for Canadians Over 40" in 2011. The Bank of Montreal (Commercial Banking) and the Business Development Bank of Canada (BDC) also won this award in part for programs that allow phased retirement.

EXHIBIT 9.5 *Employment Barriers for Older Workers*

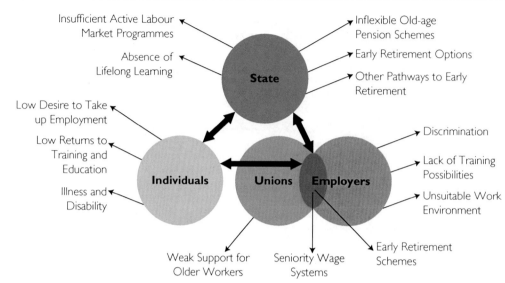

Source: Policy Horizon Canada. (2005). *Encouraging choice in work and retirement: Project report.* Policy Research Initiative. Reproduced with the permission of Policy Horizons Canada, 2017.

Townson (2006) said that "more and more people seem to be interested in phasing into retirement gradually...." (p. 182). Schellenberg, Turcotte, and Ram (2006) found that people in good health, professionals, managers, and technicians showed the greatest likelihood of returning to work. They found that more than half (55 percent) of retirees who returned to work after retirement gave reasons other than money. More than one in five (22 percent) said they didn't like retirement. Another 19 percent said they enjoyed the satisfaction of working.

Dwyer (2015a) told the story of Henry Hems, who works part-time as a shuttle driver for Great Canadian Holidays and Coaches in Kitchener, Ontario. He works about 24 hours per week and gets to travel all over southern Ontario. He doesn't rely on the job for his income. He says the job brings him personal satisfaction. "I wanted to do something different, to get out of the house and be with people."

This interest in flexible retirement has begun to spread throughout the workforce. "It seems almost inevitable," Townson (2006; also Rix, 2011) said "that interest in phased retirement will grow as the population ages" (p. 187).

Part-Time Work

Retired men who work often do so for fewer hours per day than before retirement. In 2009, 35 percent of employed men and 58 percent of employed women age 65 and over

worked part-time (Milan & Vézina, 2011). The proportion of senior men who work part-time has stayed stable since the mid-1990s. But the proportion of senior women who work part-time increased by more than 10 percent.

Professionals and people on the margin of the economy show the greatest tendency to take up part-time work. Many of these people retired due to mandatory retirement or because they could not find a full-time job. Part-time jobs can ease a worker's move to full retirement. Examples of part-time jobs include security guard, hardware store salesperson, and department store clerk. These jobs pay less than the retiree's former salary and the work often has little to do with their former career, but workers take these jobs to stay active and to earn extra money.

Dwyer (2015b) reported the case of Jim Gough, near age 70 and a former information technology worker. Gough found it hard to stay afloat in the shifting IT job market in the early 2000s. Many companies sent their IT work offshore. The dot.com bust after 2000 left him unemployed. Gough left city life in London, Ontario, to move to a family property in Orillia, Ontario.

For his income, Gough draws on a CPP pension, Old Age Security payments, and some savings. He now works part-time at a Home Depot store to supplement his income. Home Depot hires many older workers and trains them as sales associates. Gough got training in electrical supplies. "But the real training," he added, "is when you're on the floor dealing with a customer. I'd always worked

ArtFamily/Shutterstock

Some people choose to work past the traditional retirement age. Some stay at work because they need the income; others want to stay engaged in meaningful activity. Professionals often find it easiest to delay retirement.

in the head office, and never had to go and approach customers. So approaching them, striking up a conversation and interacting with them was new."

Some people, women without pensions or laid-off workers like Jim Gough, work part-time because they need the money. Part-time bridge jobs can help a person transition to a new career in retirement. A study of Canadian workers (AARP, 2007a) found that 30 percent of the workers who planned to work in retirement planned to do so part-time, for a different employer, in a different type of work.

Johnson (2015a) interviewed Sharon Norman, a Vancouver artist who took up part-time work as an insurance agent at age 67. She needed to work for the money at the time she took the job. But, she says, "when I'm painting, I'm by myself. It's wonderful and I love it, but now I have all these people that I meet. I meet grumpy people and people who just want to be really efficient and people who want to tell you their life story. It's neat. Clients come back to say hi. It's a really good thing for me to have that personal contact. I feel very lucky to work at this age...."

Second Careers

Some people retire to a **second career**. Job bureaus for seniors report that former teachers want to work as cabinetmakers, former accountants want to work as painters, and former homemakers want to work in an office or a retail store. These people work at second careers for more than the money; a second career allows them to express

second career work that allows a person to develop skills they did not use in their pre-retirement career

and develop skills they could not use when they worked full-time.

A study conducted by Towers Perrin on behalf of AARP (2007a) asked a random sample of 565 Canadian workers why they would work in retirement. Nearly half of the respondents (45 percent) said they would work for the extra money. Nearly as many (42 percent) said they would work to stay mentally active. And a quarter of the respondents said they planned to work to stay physically active, stay productive, and have something interesting to do. This supports the idea that many older workers see work in retirement as a form of self-development.

Tournier (1972) called a second career a "**free career**" (p. 129). A second career, he said, differs from leisure and from the kind of work a person does in middle age. "It has a goal, a mission, and that implies organization, loyalty, and even priority over other more selfish pleasures—not in the line of duty, since professional obligations are not involved, but for the love of people. It is, therefore, not an escape, but a presence in the world" (p. 130). A second career, Tournier says, grows out of interests that lie dormant or undeveloped in middle age. A saleswoman at a large department store, for example, spent her weekends cooking traditional Ukrainian food for her family. When she retired from work, she served as a volunteer kitchen director at her local seniors' centre. The work gave her a sense of purpose and allowed her to use her talents in a new way.

An organization called Civic Ventures in the United States has developed the idea of a second career further. Civic Ventures sponsors the Experience Corps, a program that recruits older people to serve as tutors and mentors in schools. Civic Ventures also helps community groups develop projects served by older volunteers. It gives awards to older social entrepreneurs to encourage their work and it helps people prepare for new careers in their **Third Age**.

Marc Freedman (2007), founder and CEO of Encore .org, supports what he calls "**encore careers**." An encore career has the following features: first, it takes place after

free career a second career in a field that allows a person to explore previously dormant or undeveloped interests

Third Age the period of life after the period of work and child-rearing in the middle years, but before frailty and dependence set in (the Fourth Age); a period of life created by longer life expectancy and a longer period of good health in later life

encore careers take place after a midlife career ends; they accomplish something important, pay a salary, and allow a person to give back to society

a midlife career ends. Second, it could last as long as 10 or 20 years and accomplishes something important. Third, it pays a salary and offers benefits. Fourth, it allows a person to give back to society.

Freedman said many Baby Boomers will want to work at something meaningful in the second half of life. As an example, consider "someone who—after spending 30 years as a money manager—decides in his or her 60s to become a math teacher or to launch a second career with an environmental organization" (Ruffenach, 2007). This work won't pay as much as a person's midlife job but, Freedman (2007) said that an encore career swaps "income for impact" (p. 5).

Freedman foresees a time when Baby Boomer retirees would take a one- or two-year sabbatical at the end of their midlife career. They would travel, fix up their homes, take up a hobby—the things that people expect to do in retirement. Then they would re-engage in an encore career. Some people would train for this new career; others would use the skills and experience they gathered in their first career.

Ed Speedling went from being a healthcare executive to serving as an advocate for the homeless. "When I walked into St. John's [a homeless shelter]," he says, "it was love at first sight. It was really the fulfilment of a deep desire to work with the poor, to align myself with people who are vulnerable...." As his encore career evolved, Ed went on to do other work with the homeless. He's worked on the streets talking with homeless people and helping them get the services they need. He's also used his first-career skills in the boardroom, advising organization executives. Freedman (2007) used this case to show the power of what he called "the 'experience economy'" (p. 5).

Janet McDonald, age 63, followed her passion for child development when she entered an encore career. Johnson (2015b) interviewed McDonald to learn about her transition to retirement. McDonald worked as an administrator at a children's centre at Capilano University in North Vancouver. She retired in 2011 and, like many middle-class retirees, she worked around the house and travelled. She returned from this mini-sabbatical and went back to work. She now works for a program called StrongStartBC. The program serves as a drop-in and play centre for children age 5 and under. She works half-days during the week and interacts directly with the children and parents.

"I love it," McDonald told Johnson. "I love the children. I love everything about them. I love the ones who are challenging; I love all of them. It doesn't matter what they bring to me, I just work with them to meet their needs and help them do their best."

"It's such a great job," she adds. "Why, if you really love something, do you give it up completely? Why would I stop doing this? I feel like I've been rewarded. I have this little blessing."

McDonald's work in the StrongStartBC program serves as a near-perfect example of an encore career. She gets paid for her work and she does something that she's passionate about—works with children. She moved away from the administrative role she played in the past in order to connect to her earliest love—child development. The StrongStartBC program benefits from her lifetime of experience.

Freedman (2007, p. 22) said encore careers allow society to reap a "windfall of talent." Members of the biggest generation can throw their weight into solving some of society's biggest problems.

Could meaningful work also lead to better health and longevity? A number of other studies point in this direction. Researchers at Johns Hopkins University Medical Centers in the United States, for example, studied seniors who tutored elementary school students in reading. Half the people in the study worked 15 hours a week in Baltimore helping students learn to read. The other half of the group did not work at all. The researchers found improved "physical, cognitive, and social activity" in the tutor group. The study found decreases on these measures in the control group (Freedman, 2007, p. 82). This study and others suggest that work in later life can lead to good health, longer life, and successful aging.

Involuntary Retirement

Involuntary retirement takes place when a worker leaves the workforce unexpectedly (usually before the person's expected retirement age). An accident at work, corporate downsizing, a family crisis can all lead to early exit from the workforce.

The 2006 *Participation and Activity Limitations Survey* (PALS) found that between 2001 and 2006, 39 percent of retirees retired involuntarily. The PALS also found that 65 percent of Canadians age 55 to 64 without a disability worked in the labour force. But only 42 percent of those with a disability in that age group remained at work. Illness or disability rank first as the reason for involuntary retirement. Job loss and caregiving demands can also lead to involuntary retirement (Denton, Plenderleith, & Chowhan, 2010).

The researchers found that involuntary retirees were typically age 55 or less, had less than a high school education, and had a relatively low income. Turcotte and Schellenberg (2007, citing Schellenberg et al., 2005,

p. 13) said that "after holding all other factors constant, involuntary retirees were considerably less likely (38%) than their voluntary counterparts to consider retired life an improvement (53%)." A study of involuntary retirement found that people with low incomes showed the greatest likelihood of post-retirement depression (Gallo et al., 2006).

Denton and colleagues (2010) place involuntary retirement in a life course perspective. Involuntary retirement takes place off-time. It can cause a shock to the worker's self-image and financial condition. Social conditions—the worker's age, education, work history, health—and society's economic conditions all influence the likelihood of involuntary retirement. An older worker who has an accident at work and can no longer do the same job may face involuntary retirement.

Denton and colleagues (2010) proposed supports that would help people with disabilities stay at work. Supports could include the use of technology to make up for physical abilities, changes in the workplace to accommodate workers with disabilities, and an improvement in attitudes toward people with disabilities.

Some workers who retire involuntarily adapt to retirement by working part-time or starting their own businesses. Other workers will try to find new jobs. They will often have to work in lower-status jobs, at low pay, and they may face further job disruptions. Researchers have just begun to study this pattern of retirement.

TIME TO REVIEW

What are some of the options workers now have to traditional retirement?

Why do people choose these options?

How do these options influence a person's decision to stay at work or return to work?

WOMEN AND RETIREMENT

Until recently, relatively few women had a work career that led to retirement. In 1976, for example, 42 percent of senior women said they had never held a job. This figure dropped to only 14 percent in 2009. But even with more women in the labour force, compared with men, women follow different career paths. Some take up careers after raising a family; others work during their child-rearing years; many single women show unbroken work records. McDonald (2006a) called women's retirement "amorphous and fluid" (p. 153).

In 2004, for example, "forty per cent of women's jobs compared with about 29 per cent of men's jobs were considered 'non-standard'" (Stone, 2006, pp. 22–23; Townson, 2006, p. 348). Non-standard jobs include part-time work, seasonal work, and self-employment. This variation in the type of work women do makes it hard to describe a typical pattern of retirement. "The male model of retirement," McDonald (2006b) says, "with its emphasis on individual,

EXHIBIT 9.6 *Events That Push People to Retirement: Retirement Types by Sex, Average Proportions, 1997 to 2009*

Retirement Type	Percentage		
	Both Sexes	Men	Women
Voluntary	77	79	74
Due to economic conditions	12	11	14
Due to health/disability	9	9	9
Due to family responsibilities	2	1	3

Men and women report similar reasons for retirement. More than three-quarters of men and women retire voluntarily. Good pensions and the desire to do something new motivate these workers to retire. Almost one-quarter of workers retire for other reasons. For example, economic conditions such as corporate downsizing or business failure can lead to layoffs. Compared to men, women show a slightly higher rate of retirement for this reason. Compared to men, a higher proportion of women retire due to family responsibilities. But for both genders, family responsibilities push a relatively small percentage of workers to retire.

Source: Carrière, Y. & Galarneau, D. The Impact of Involuntary Breaks in Employment and Level of Education on the Timing of Retirement, Statistics Canada (2012). Original source: Statistics Canada, *Labour Force Survey, 1997 to 2009*. Reproduced and distributed on an "as is" basis with the permission of Statistics Canada.

rational choice, founded on a one-job, continuous work history with pension trade-offs, made no sense for women because it was lopsided. The model ignored gender differences in work and the fact that the majority of men and women live or have lived in some type of family arrangement" (pp. 130–31).

Few studies have looked at how women adjust to retirement or at what retirement means to them. In the past, researchers treated women's retirement as a non-event. Szinovacz (1982) said that until 1975, the annual meetings of the Gerontological Society of America contained almost no discussion of women's retirement. McDonald (2006b) said that the first text on families and retirement came out in 1992. And Denton and Kusch (2006) said, even in 2006, "We know little about women's retirement in Canada" (p. 8).

The studies that have focused on women show diverse patterns among women subjects and large differences between women and men. McDonald (2006a) said women's lives remain bound up with family obligations and traditional gender roles. For this reason, "women's retirement has always been different from men's and will continue to be different for the foreseeable future, despite arguments to the contrary." For one thing, women's multiple entries and exits from the labour force will lead to smaller pensions. So will their "concentration in non-standard and part-time work, their under-representation in unions, their over-representation in the services sector and the continued distribution of their occupations in female employment" (p. 157).

A woman who relies on her husband's pension may fall into poverty if she faces widowhood, divorce, or separation in later life. A divorced woman age 68 told Denton and her colleagues (2004): "I assumed I would be in my house until I died and the house was going to be paid for when my husband retired so I thought we were …. that was going to be our life. We were going to be all set you know, not have to worry about anything" (p. S80). She now lives on a yearly income of less than $20,000. In general, Denton and her colleagues found that women with fewer resources could plan less for retirement. They "were required to 'take life as it comes', living as best they could day to day" (p. S81).

McMullin and Berger (2006) conducted in-depth interviews with 30 unemployed older men and women. One woman in the study said:

I was probably too chicken to get a job. I guess really, I didn't feel confident that I can get a job in my field because I haven't been in it for so many years. I left to raise my kids, and then when I wanted to go back to work I was too afraid (p. 214).

Family responsibilities throughout life shape women's retirement decisions. For example, women more often than men retire because they have family caregiving responsibilities (caring for an infirm parent or spouse). Compared with men, women tend to retire so they can stay at home to provide direct care. Men tend to stay at work to provide financial support to family members. Women, compared with men, more often retire to care for a spouse.

A lifetime of gender differences and discrimination in the workplace also affects women's retirement decisions. Moen and Spencer (2006) said that a person's work career shapes his or her opportunities and choices in retirement. "Health insurance, pensions, unemployment insurance, disability insurance …. all rest on the edifice of the male lock-step life course" (p. 134). To the extent that a woman's life course differs from this model, women face a disadvantage in retirement.

Women's work careers lead to lower pension support. Employer pension plans (EPPs) serve as an important source of retirement income, and 37 percent of Canadians age 25 and over have an EPP. But women "are at a disadvantage in the EPP coverage and accrued value" (Denton & Plenderleith, 2010, p. iii).

Many older women did not work during their middle years. They hold the least value in EPPs. Denton and Plenderleith (2010) said, "The gendering of work and family life puts women at a disadvantage in EPP coverage and the accumulation of wealth in their employer pension plans…. Research has shown that differences in wages, reduced pension contributions, years of job tenure, discontinuous employment and industry appear to account for much of the gender gap in pension wealth" (pp. 3–4).

Part-time and temporary jobs rarely offer a pension. If they do, women contribute only small amounts due to their low pay. Older women often live alone due to divorce or widowhood. They lack the benefit of a spouse's pension plan. The concept of retirement does not apply to these older women.

Denton and Plenderleith (2010) saw some improvement for new cohorts of women who enter later life. But they saw a continuation of this inequality between EPP savings for men and women due to a continuing gap in wages and patterns of work.

A person's job history and their place in the economic order shape their retirement choices. McDonald (2006a) said, "The pension system today, with its emphasis on job tenure in a life-long career, excludes many Canadians who do not match this profile. Specifically, pension policy barely recognizes the burden of institutionalized lower earnings for women or the costs of their unpaid work, and ignores the multiple job changes that women have experienced in the last ten years" (p.158). Women experience cumulative disadvantage throughout their life course. By later life, this disadvantage (e.g., in pay, pension savings, steady work) leads to lower pensions when compared with men.

Pension policies need to reflect the unique work lives of women in Canada. Until they do, older women will face inequality and often poverty in old age even if they spend much of their lives in the labour force. Szinovacz (2006; also Schellenberg, Turcotte, & Ram, 2006) said that retirement studies need to look at the family context to understand women's retirement decisions.

Schellenberg and Ostrovsky (2008b) reported that about 50 percent of two-earner couples say they would prefer to retire together. But "age differences, health conditions, pension eligibility, job loss and career aspirations" often make this difficult (p. 5). Many conditions influence the decision to retire jointly. But if a husband retires due to illness or if a wife has her own pension, the likelihood of joint retirement decreases.

Also, as more women spend more years at work, the likelihood of joint retirement decreases. Future studies of women and retirement need to look at how other family relationships influence women's retirement decisions. For example, researchers need to look at how life changes in the lives of other family members (sickness of a spouse or parent, marriage of children, or widowhood) affect women's careers and retirement patterns.

McDonald (2006b) sums up the need for more research and a new view of women and retirement. "It would seem, therefore," she says, "that the time has come for scholars to go back to the drawing board and address the lack of theoretical progress about gender, families and retirement. At minimum, a life course perspective with revised definitions of retirement that include gender/ family/work linkages would be valuable in reflecting the experiences of people and would lead to policies that would have a better chance for success" (pp. 135–36).

TIME to REVIEW

How does the life course model explain the different retirement options open to men and women in later life?

What trends exist today that could open more options for women?

What do gerontologists mean by "cumulative disadvantage?"

How does this idea explain some of the challenges women face as they plan for retirement?

PERSONAL EXPERIENCE OF RETIREMENT

Dr. Gene Cohen (2005), a pioneer in the study of creative retirement, conducted in-depth interviews with retirees. He found that if people plan for retirement at all, they tend to do financial planning. Few people plan for "how you will be socially engaged, how you will spend your time, what larger goals you want to pursue, and how you can take full advantage of the extra time available in this phase of life" (p. 144).

Ekerdt (1986), in a classic essay, said that many retirees subscribe to what he called "the busy ethic." This ethic values an active life. Retirees who subscribe to this ethic often carry electronic organizers and constantly check their mobile phones so they won't miss messages. Ekerdt said that the busy ethic helps retirees ease into retirement and allows retirees to maintain the same values they held while working—engagement in community affairs, an active social life, and self-development. Retirees legitimate their retirement through "involvement and engagement .... [the busy ethic] esteems leisure that is earnest, occupied, and filled with activity" (pp. 239–240). The busy ethic domesticates or tames retirement. It supports energetic activity and healthful lifestyles—two long-standing North American values. The busy ethic keeps retirement and retirees in the mainstream of life.

But people can do more than just stay busy. People in retirement have a chance to choose what interests and motivates them. Corbett (2007) created the concept of the "life portfolio" to provide focus for a meaningful retirement. A life portfolio consists of a person's commitments to specific activities and relationships. These include family, community service, spiritual development, recreation, and, in some cases, work. Imagine these items placed in a pie chart. The size of each slice will depend on a person's commitment to each activity, group, or individual. A retiree decides how much time and energy he or she will commit to the segments of the portfolio. A portfolio approach gives a person control over his or her future. And it encourages action.

---

cumulative disadvantage occurs as disadvantages, such as low pay and time off work due to family caregiving for women, add up and lead to economic disadvantage in later life

life portfolio consists of a person's commitments to specific activities and relationships, including family, community service, spiritual development, recreation, and, in some cases, work

Corbett (2007) gives an example of an exercise that helps people create their life portfolio. "Think about the dreams, talents, projects, achievements, loves inside of you that would be unexpressed or unrealized if your life ended today. If, at the end of the day you are still alive, and you have done this exercise faithfully, you have the first draft of a portfolio plan" (p. 107). Corbett also encourages people to write a personal mission statement. This statement helps people define what they care most about. From there, they can set goals and begin to take action.

Like the review of a financial portfolio, the life portfolio needs periodic review. If a social activity like a volunteer position ends, a person may want to substitute something new. Part-time work may offer a more satisfying social outlet.

The life portfolio demands reflection—awareness of one's total life experience—and a structure or context for thinking about and anticipating the future. A person may join a non-profit board before retirement, knowing that he or she will retire in a year or so. The continuing board membership will provide a social outlet that will substitute for the social relations that exist at work.

"Life portfolio" sounds like an extension of corporate life—complete with goals and a mission statement. This may appeal to some people, perhaps those who miss the structure of the office. But to others it will sound like an overly structured version of the "busy ethic." Cohen (2005) offered a more modest approach to retirement planning. He advised a balance of active engagement and quiet activity, social time and personal time, short-term projects and long-term commitments.

Moen and Spencer (2006) said that "the emerging third-age concept differentiates retirement, along with the years preceding and following it, from conventional notions of old age" (p. 129). This change reflects longer life expectancy and the better health of retirees today. But it also reflects a different understanding of work and of the life course.

The diversity of retirement experiences today shows that the middle-class-white-male life course no longer describes the complexity of work or retirement. Rapid changes in the economy—mergers, acquisitions, bankruptcies, international trade, outsourcing—make work careers unstable. Even white male middle-aged workers can find themselves unemployed due to any of these forces. Today, the traditional model of retirement exists alongside many other patterns of work and post-work life in the Third Age.

Schulz and Binstock (2006) said, "the notion that most people are forced to retire and suffer in retirement from boredom and psychological distress is a myth" (p. 147). Most people adjust well to retirement. And retirees now have many options. They range from early retirement, to partial retirement, to work at second careers. Moen and Spencer (2006) referred to these activities as "second acts" (p. 132).

CONCLUSION

Moen and Spencer (2006) said that today a person must make "intentional choices about employment, retirement, civic engagement, caregiving, and other behaviours, roles, and relationships" (p. 140). Changes in pension plans (e.g., from defined benefit to defined contribution plans), flexible retirement options, and better health in later life all lead to more choices for the retiree.

Many people will still follow the traditional path from work to a life of leisure. But people in later life today take diverse paths in retirement. A new stage of life now exists beyond the middle years of work, but it is different from the traditional model of retirement. This has turned the trend toward early retirement on its head. More older workers than ever before choose to stay at work longer. And various government policies now encourage a longer work life.

For example, the law now allows a person to partially retire but still accrue pension benefits. Low-income families can now get a tax credit that reduces the loss of OAS income if a person has employment income. Hering and Klassen (2010) propose an increase in the age for full CPP and QPP benefits from 65 to 67. This would encourage workers to stay on the job longer. The CPP already provides an incentive for workers to delay retirement past age 65.

Hicks (2011) predicted a continuation of the trend toward delayed retirement. And he predicted social benefits from longer work careers, including reduced pressure on public pension programs, reduced need for personal savings to ensure a good retirement income, and greater choice in later life. A five-year increase in the retirement age could reduce federal pension spending by between 3 percent and 5 percent of GDP by 2050. "A large retirement-age increase," Hering and Klassen (2010) said, "could by itself solve the problem of [CPP pension] costs rising due to population aging" (p. 20). Hicks (also Hering & Klassen, 2010) said that the public would support increases in the age for a full public pension—as long as small changes took place gradually and public debate explored the issue.

Denton and Spencer (2009b) conducted an extensive review of Canadian and international research on retirement. They find that retirement is a "negative notion" that defines "what people are not doing." But this ignores "what people are actually doing" (p. 74). It ignores productive activity of social value outside the market. People in retirement spend their time in many productive activities. These include volunteer work in hospitals, schools, and service organizations. Retirees also engage in family caregiving.

Guillemard (2006) said that "we are witnessing a real revolution in the social organization of time." She said that the traditional three-stage view of the life cycle—childhood, work, and retirement—is falling apart" (p. 49). Instead, people live more complex lives—they may work, return to school, retire, re-enter the workforce, gain more training, engage in volunteer work, and so on. This new model of later life blurs traditional lines between life stages and it challenges the traditional meaning and experience of later life.

Denton and Spencer (2009b) said that research needs to complement studies of retirement with studies of seniors' activities. This would include studies of productive household activities, caregiving, and volunteering. The study of recreation, leisure, and education in later life provides a complement to the study of retirement.

Summary

1. Most people want to retire, and they retire as early as they can if they have a good pension.
2. Compulsory retirement has ended for most workers in Canada. The government amended the Canadian Human Rights Act to end all mandatory retirement in the country. (Some occupations would still have mandatory retirement [e.g., firefighters and police officers] based on the demands of the job.)
3. Canadians now have more choice about when they retire. Some people leave work before age 65, some take full retirement at age 65, others work part-time, and still others start second careers and encore careers. Some older workers take the option of flexible retirement. They may retire for a while, then return to work—and they may do this more than once. Social conditions (such as the economy, the availability of jobs, or a person's occupation) affect a person's retirement options.
4. A good income gives retirees the most options and the best chance to plan for and enjoy retirement. Professionals and people with good private pensions or savings have the most options. People need to plan for a good retirement, and this should go beyond financial planning to include meaningful activity.

5. The larger number of women in the labour force will lead to new theories of retirement and new research approaches. Women have different work careers than men and often face social-structural barriers (such as low pay and broken work records) that lead to low incomes and few retirement options.
6. Canadian society may need to find ways to keep older workers on the job in order to avoid a labour shortage. Changes to government pension plans will encourage people to stay at work longer, and more flexible work opportunities may attract older workers.
7. Retirement research in the past has focused on how individuals cope with retirement. A broader view of retirement links individual behaviour to social and economic inequities in society. More research needs to be done on the effects of gender, educational background, and socioeconomic status on retirement.

STUDY QUESTIONS

1. Explain how the retirement principle and the citizen's wage give rise to the social institution called *retirement*. What social forces and personal preferences lead people to choose retirement today?
2. Why has mandatory retirement faded as an issue in Canada? What developments have made early retirement possible for older people today?
3. Why do many workers now choose to stay at work longer, some of them after age 65? Give two alternatives to a fixed retirement age.
4. How do men and women differ in their opportunity to retire? What social conditions earlier in their lives shape the retirement decisions of men? Of women?
5. What social forces will shape retirement in the future? How will the economy influence retirement decisions in the future?

KEY TERMS

bridge jobs (p. 234)
citizen's wage (p. 225)
cumulative disadvantage (p. 241)
encore careers (p. 237)
flexible retirement (p. 234)
free career (p. 237)
life portfolio (p. 241)
retirement principle (p. 224)
retirement wage (p. 224)
second career (p. 237)
taxback (p. 228)
Third Age (p. 237)

CHAPTER 10

LEISURE, RECREATION, AND SERVICE

DigitalVision/Thinkstock

LEARNING OBJECTIVES

After reading this chapter, you will

LO1 Understand the changes in use of time throughout the life course.

LO2 Be able to describe how older people differ in their activity patterns by gender, marital status, education level, health, and geography.

LO3 Be able to apply different theories of aging to explain seniors' leisure time activity patterns.

LO4 Be able to describe some of the fitness activities seniors engage in today.

LO5 Understand the role of seniors' centres in Canada and their changing role as Baby Boomers enter old age.

LO6 Understand the many forms that religious belief can take in later life and the importance of spirituality for many people in old age.

LO7 Be able to discuss educational needs and interests of older people and describe some of the programs that serve seniors' emerging educational needs.

LO8 Be able to explain the growth in the use of computer technology by older people and the preferred ways they use technology today.

LO9 Understand the role that community service and volunteering plays in older people's lives and their communities.

INTRODUCTION

Dan Kreske worked as an insurance agent until he retired. He had a good income from his investments, savings, and Canada Pension Plan. He heard about free university classes and started to attend. Now he goes to classes two or three afternoons a week (depending on the courses offered). He has also renewed his interest in athletics. He played golf all through his working years, and he jogged and swam, but in retirement he found he had more time to develop his athletic ability. Several years ago he competed at Lake Placid, New York, in the Masters Division of the North American Speed Skating Championships. He made two third-place and two fourth-place finishes and won 10 points for his team. "I lost to guys 25 years younger than I am—it was one of the greatest thrills of my life," he says.

Many older people, like Dan, continue to develop established skills and talents in retirement. Other older people discover new interests when they retire—they discover a talent for poetry, acting, or art. Still others turn to community service, or they may start to do volunteer work in a hospital or seniors' centre part-time.

Seniors today have more opportunities for self-development and community service than ever before, and many of them have a strong desire to develop themselves and give to others as they age. For many older people, the years after retirement become a time of search, discovery, and fulfillment. This chapter will review some of the programs and activities that help seniors live a satisfying old age in Canada today. This chapter will look at (1) how seniors today spend their time, (2) new personal development programs for seniors (recreation, fitness, and education), and (3) seniors' community involvement.

WHAT DO OLDER PEOPLE DO?

People age 60 to 69 report 7.5 hours of free time per day (Zuzanek, 2009). What do they do with this free time? A number of studies in Canada (Stobert, Dosman, & Keating, 2006; Turcotte & Schellenberg, 2007) have looked at what older people do every day. Studies show that, in the absence of work, older people most often use their time for activities such as housework, shopping, personal care, leisure, and recreation. Older people use their free time to engage in a variety of social activities, including participation in political or charitable organizations or in neighbourhood, community, and school groups.

In retirement, older men and women spend extra time sleeping and resting. Older men and women say they spend seven to eight hours a day on leisure activities (Stobert, Dosman, & Keating, 2006). About half of Canada's 5,780,900 older people (almost 3 million seniors) (CBC News, 2015) say they take part in a religious activity at least once a month (Turcotte & Schellenberg, 2007). But research shows that compared with younger people, seniors spend more of their time on solitary activities and at home. Statistics Canada's *General Social Survey* in 2005 found that, compared with people age 35 to 44, people age 65 and over spent an extra two hours per day on personal care (including sleep) (Stobert, Dosman, & Keating, 2006). Marcum (2013, p. 612) in a study of seniors in the United States found that "age is associated with declines in time spent with others for virtually all types of time use."

Morrow-Howell and colleagues (2014) surveyed the activities of 4,593 people age 55 and over in the United States. They found that nearly all of the respondents (97 percent) reported watching television. In addition to TV, a large majority of respondents took part in other sedentary activities—reading (91 percent), praying/meditating (79 percent), and listening to music (78 percent). A large majority also engaged in personal care activities—housecleaning (80 percent), washing/ironing/mending clothes (69 percent), and meal preparation/clean-up (84 percent). But not everyone engaged in the same bundle of activities.

The researchers found several types of activity profile among the respondents. Those in the low-activity group tended to manage their medical condition and engage in personal leisure. Those in the high-activity group tended to engage in physical exercise, civic/religious activity, and helping others. Poor health and low functional ability in part accounts for the low activity of some respondents. The low-activity group also reported more depressive symptoms. These findings point to physical well-being as a condition for an active lifestyle. Age, self-rated health, depressive symptoms, lower education level, and fewer financial assets all differentiated the high-activity from the low-activity group.

Stobert, Dosman, and Keating (2006) found similar results. They reported two broad types of leisure activity: passive leisure and active leisure. Passive leisure included watching television, listening to the radio, or taking a pleasure drive. Active leisure included going to a movie, playing cards, using the Internet, socializing with friends, and physical recreation. The researchers found that health and life satisfaction played a role in the older person's choice of leisure activities. "Healthy individuals," the researchers said, "spent more on paid work, unpaid work and active leisure.... Less healthy and less satisfied men and women for all age groups consistently spent the most time on passive leisure" (p. 24).

Statistics Canada (2011l) studied social participation among older and younger Canadians. The study found that men and women in all age groups showed high rates of participation in social activities with their family, friends, and community. Participation rates decrease for men and women in the oldest age groups (75 and over). Illness and disability among the oldest old, in part, account for this decrease. Widowhood, the tendency to live alone, and low income also lead to less social engagement (Marcum, 2013; Spinney & Millward, 2014).

The oldest age groups (age 75 and over) showed the lowest rates of participation in sports and physical activity. Participation decreased with each older age group. Only 13.9 percent of women in the oldest age group and 22.1 percent of men in this group took part

in sports or physical activity. Spinney (2013) studied aerobic activity among older Canadians. She found that among the 10 most often reported aerobic activities, older people most often engaged in domestic chores, recreational walking, and active transportation, such as bicycling. Older people report little engagement in sport and leisure activities such as travel related to socializing. Spinney noted that older people preferred unstructured activities that can take place at any time and any location (often near the person's home). This finding holds true for four cycles of the *General Social Survey*, from 1992 to 2010.

People tend to reduce their participation in activities as physical function declines. Women age 65 and over, for example, report a lower rate of physical activity in their leisure time when compared to other

EXHIBIT 10.1 *Leisure Time Physical Activity, by Age Group and Sex, 2010*

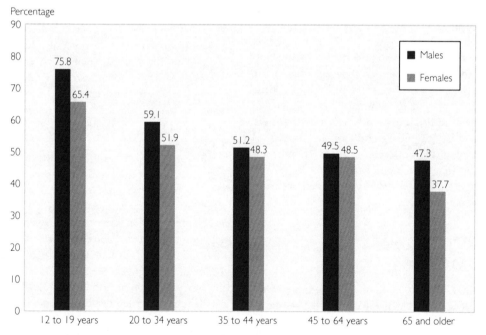

Note: Population age 12 and older who were active or moderately active during leisure time.

Senior men and women show the lowest rate of physical activity of any age group. Poor health and disability among the oldest seniors in part account for this low participation rate. At every age, compared with women, a higher proportion of men take part in leisure time physical activity. For example, compared with senior women, a higher proportion of senior men engage in physical activity (47.3 percent vs. 37.7 percent). In part this reflects a lifelong difference between men and women in physical activity participation. Widowhood also tends to reduce participation in physical activity. Higher rates of widowhood among older women helps explain the low participation rates for older women (the lowest of all age and gender groups).

Source: Adapted from Statistics Canada. Health. *Canada Year Book 2011*. Catalogue No. 11-402-XWE. (2012j). Reproduced and distributed on an "as is" basis with the permission of Statistics Canada.

age groups (Statistics Canada, 2014k). Older people may choose new activities that better fit their ability or they may focus on fewer activities. Statistics Canada (2011l), for example, found that in 2009, pain or discomfort kept one in five seniors (20.6 percent) from taking part in activities. The effects of pain and discomfort differed for men and women. Nearly one-quarter of senior women (23.7 percent) and 16.7 percent of senior men reported that pain or discomfort kept them from activities. Compared with older men, older women reported higher rates of chronic illness. This in part explained senior women's lower participation rate in activities.

Still, health problems only partly explain seniors' inactivity. In many cases, older people simply don't work physical activity into their daily routines. Garriguet and Colley (2012) studied daily patterns of physical activity among Canadians. They found that, compared with younger age groups, the oldest age group in their study (ages 60, 70, and 79) began their moderate-to-vigorous physical activity later in the day (9 to 11 a.m.) and they ended their active period earlier in the day (3 to 5 p.m.). The oldest age group also spent the fewest total minutes on moderate-to-vigorous physical activity.

New generations of older people will enter later life with a better appreciation of active living. Public health organizations, the government, and the media promote active living for all ages. Morrow-Howell and colleagues (2014) said that, even as functional ability declines, "social and physical contexts" can enable engagement. The current social context in Canada supports an active lifestyle from youth onward. Women and men have more access to active living through sports, fitness centres, and community fund-raising events (such as 10K runs or walks to support medical research or a charity). This social context will support active living among seniors in the years ahead.

TIME TO REVIEW

Compare the activities and time use of younger people and seniors.

What accounts for the differences between these age groups?

To what degree do these differences reflect changes due to age?

To what degree do they reflect generational differences in preferred activities?

A VARIETY OF ACTIVITY PATTERNS

Older people as a group show some common approaches to the use of their time. They often engage in socially satisfying, non-demanding, non-strenuous activities. This appears to support the disengagement theory of aging.

Other research questions this conclusion. Marcum (2013) proposed a "life-course respite" hypothesis. This states that older people have more flexibility in how they can spend their time. Middle-aged parents spend much of their leisure time with their young children or in community activities such as the PTA. Young people spend most of their time in school. When older people spend time with others, they often do so in leisure social settings such as at church or a party. Marcum proposed that older people spend time alone, in part, because they feel less social pressure to be with others (something middle-aged parents might envy). From a life course perspective, spending time alone in later life reflects seniors' greater independence and autonomy.

Studies show different activity preferences among different types of seniors. Income, gender, region, and social status all influence what an older person chooses to do. Those with low income and little education and those with high income and a university degree show the lowest involvement in popular culture activities (such as watching TV, listening to music, going to movies, engaging in crafts, and reading newspapers). People with middle incomes and either a high school diploma or some secondary education show the most involvement in popular culture activities. People with university degrees tend to read more books than other groups.

Studies also show that marital status and gender influences activity level. Strain et al. (2002) found that the loss of a spouse (more common for women than for men) led to a decrease in activity over time. Seguin and colleagues (2010) said that few older women do strength training exercises, even though strength training tones the body and preserves vitality. Cousins (2000) found that older women (age 70 and older) had "sensational" negative views of strength and flexibility training. For example, they thought that strength training would lead to serious injury and illness. Cousins said these women felt frail due to inactivity, lacked experience with exercise, and accepted age and gender stereotyping.

Edwards and Mawani (2006) said that older people's activities varied by season. Not surprisingly, cold weather in winter and hot, humid weather in summer led to decreases in outdoor activities. Spinney and Millward (2014) also reported that Canadians spent about 50 percent more minutes on active living in the spring than in the winter. Spinney (2013, p. 449) said that older Canadians may be more "weather sensitive." Canadian winters, in particular, keep older people indoors and inactive.

Social context and local culture can also influence an older person's activities. Witcher (2006) and Witcher et al. (2007) spoke about leisure with older people on Fogo Island, Newfoundland and Labrador. The researchers asked islanders if they'd be interested in leisure time physical activity. One islander named Alex said, "I don't think I would be interested. No. I, I don't think. If it was. I mean, I s'pose I'm past that ... say it that way." Pamela, a woman in the study, said that if people saw an older person engaging in leisure activity, "The older people that's not doing it, well they'd say, 'Well she haven't got anything else to do today?'" (p. 174).

Interviewees thought that at their age they could get little health benefit from leisure physical activity. One participant told the researchers, "We know no matter what we do we're going to get frail." (Witcher et al., 2007, p. 18). Laura, a woman in the study, said, "I mean what do they need ... to do, for older people anyway? 'Cause you ain't gonna live that many more years.... You're going to die, you know, that's for sure, when the time comes.... As long as you can, you know, keep active enough to be able to, ah, you know.... keep about and walk about and you know" (p. 175).

Witcher (2006) said that health promotion approaches in the Fogo Island community needed to recognize the value the local culture placed on productive activity (e.g., woodworking or picking berries). Walking for its own sake or for health benefit got little support here. This community reflected the values of simpler societies, where each member must contribute to the economic life of the community. Witcher said that programs need to understand "how the larger context can affect older adults' participation in leisure-time physical activity...." (p. 3).

Sport Participation

Ramage-Morin and colleagues (2012) said that "despite the highly promoted benefits of physical activity, most Canadians are relatively inactive. Fewer than 15% of adults age 40 or older meet Canada's new physical activity guidelines. An estimated 40% of Canadians age 40 to 59 average more than the recommended 10,000 steps per day; at ages 60 to 79, the figure is 20%" (p. 17). All age groups showed an increase in inactivity between 1994–1995 and 2007–2008. Seniors age 75 and over showed the highest proportion inactive during leisure time (56 percent men and 72 percent of women in 2007–2008).

The researchers said that social norms support inactivity. "Becoming active," Ramage-Morin and colleagues (2012) said, "is contrary to the norm.... Inactive people really tended to remain that way.... Stereotypes of older people as frail and disinclined to make and benefit from lifestyle changes create other barriers to becoming more active" (pp. 25–26).

Canadians show a low level of participation in sports. Ifedi (2008) found that sport participation among Canadians declined for all age groups between 1992 and 2005. People age 55 and over showed the lowest participation rate, 17 percent, down from 25 percent in 1992. "For older non-active Canadians aged 55 and over, 28% indicated that age was the biggest factor for not participating in sport. Almost a quarter of them reported health conditions as the most important reason for nonparticipation. Another quarter of this group cited lack of interest in sport" (p. 61).

EXHIBIT 10.2 *Keeping Active in Spite of Canada's Harsh Winters: Mall Walking*

Canada's winter weather can keep even the avid fitness fanatic indoors. Older people who enjoy walking in their neighbourhood in the warm months can become housebound in the winter. Slippery sidewalks and cold weather keep many people indoors and inactive.

Mall-walking programs can overcome this barrier. A mall provides a safe, well-lit, and comfortable setting for exercise. The West Edmonton Mall, for example, provides more than 6 kilometres of walking space and lays out a walking course for mall walkers. A mall-walking program at the Londonderry Mall in Edmonton has 800 members. Hosler (2007) said that members of one mall-walking program socialize and get discounts at stores in the mall.

This kind of program lowers barriers to physical activity and encourages social contact. Doyle-Baker (2007) conducted a study of 39 mall walkers in Calgary. Participants' ages ranged from 46 to 83 (average age 66.4). Participants in the study improved their walking distance, body mass index, and perceived exertion over time. Culos-Reed et al. (2008) conducted a study of 52 mall-walking seniors. Participants in the eight-week program improved their physical activity and fitness (e.g., resting heart rate). The researchers concluded that "such programs should be considered as part of health-promotion programs, especially for the aging population" (p. 81).

According to Ifedi, nearly all seniors (94.5 percent) saw the physical health benefits of participating in sport and the value of sport as a form of relaxation (95.7 percent). A large majority (73.2 percent) saw the value of sport as a family activity and as a way to make new friends and acquaintances (81.1 percent). A large majority (85 percent) saw sport as a way to gain a sense of achievement. Seniors saw the value of sport participation, but they did not participate in sports themselves.

A difference between men and women shows up in sport participation. Ifedi (2008) reported that at all ages men are more active than women in sports. The low participation in sports by women may reflect the fact that fewer women than men have spouses with whom to share sports activity.

Low participation in sports by women may also point to the lack of past opportunities for women to participate in sports. The difference in activity level between men and women may decrease in the future. Longer life expectancy means that couples will live together and stay active together longer. This could lead to more active lifestyles. Also, more options for an active lifestyle exist today. For example, the growth of fitness clubs and health promotion programs will give women more opportunities to live physically active lives. Lalive, d'Epinay, and Bickel (2003) reported a change in traditional patterns of sport and exercise participation "from one in which sports and physical exercise were a mostly male, urban, and upper- (middle-) class activity, to a more generalized, democratic pattern" (p. 161).

Research shows that health, education, income, and social status all shape leisure in retirement. Older cohorts today may prefer more passive leisure, while younger cohorts of seniors live a more active old age. Each cohort will have its preferred way of spending leisure time, in part based on members' past experience.

EXPANDING LEISURE ACTIVITY

What theory of aging best describes leisure activity in later life? Most of the research on aging and leisure supports the continuity theory of aging. People often keep the leisure preferences in retirement that they had in middle age. People who enjoyed athletic activity, socializing, or travelling will continue to do these things when they retire (unless something such as poor health or economic considerations prevents them from doing so).

Active people tend to stay active, although they may engage in less-strenuous activities. Here, a man plays bocce in a competitive group. A community of active people encourages an active lifestyle.

A study by McGuire, Dottavio, and O'Leary (1987) suggests that we need at least two theories to account for older people's leisure patterns: continuity theory and the lifespan developmental perspective. This second perspective says that people can change, grow, and develop at every age. These researchers looked at data from a nationwide recreation survey in the United States and found two patterns of leisure involvement in older adults. One pattern fits the continuity theory of aging. People who fit this pattern were called **contractors**. This group had stopped at least one outdoor activity in the past year and had not learned any new activity since age 65. A second pattern fits the lifespan developmental perspective. The researchers called the people who fit this pattern

---

contractors people who have stopped at least one outdoor activity in the past year and have not learned any new activity since age 65, in keeping with the disengagement theory of aging

expanders. This group had not stopped any activities in the past year and had added at least one new outdoor activity since age 65.

The study found that contractors continued the same activities they learned in childhood. Expanders, on the other hand, continued to add activities throughout life. The researchers could not predict group membership by the use of income, age, race, or gender, and concluded that leisure service providers should create many options for older adults today. At least one type of older person, the expander, will take advantage of these new opportunities. Can people learn to make better use of their leisure time? These findings show that people can change and expand their repertoire of activities, and they can develop new interests as they age.

Leisure education can help people find new ways to enjoy life in retirement. Research supports the relationship between leisure activity and improved physical and psychological well-being. Leisure activity can also help people cope with stress in later life. Charters and Murray (2006) studied the effects of leisure education on a group of dementia patient caregivers in Dartmouth, Nova Scotia. The program taught caregivers the value of leisure and the ability to plan for leisure. One member in the program said that it helped her to feel less guilty about taking time for herself. Another said the program taught her that she owed herself a break from the demands of caregiving. The program helped the members use leisure as a way to take care of themselves.

NEW ACTIVITIES IN OLD AGE

Fitness and Health

Some decline in physical function is due to aging (for example, the slowdown in cell metabolism or a decrease in lung elasticity). Research shows that aerobic capacity and peak performance decline with age even in trained athletes (Young et al., 2008). But researchers still do not know how much of this decline is due to aging and how much is due to past health problems, past habits, and underuse of the body. Studies of fitness training show that exercise can slow and even reverse some of this decline (Aldwin, Spiro, & Park, 2006; Young et al., 2008).

Exercise can also lead to improvements in memory, intelligence, and cognitive speed (Hogan, Mata, &

This 70-year-old woman maintains an active leisure lifestyle. Here, she snowshoes on Mount Seymour in Vancouver, British Columbia. Research on active leisure shows that it improves mental function as well as physical health.

Carstensen, 2013; Kramer, Fabiani, & Colcombe, 2006). McAuley et al. (2005) studied 174 people age 60 to 75. The researchers exposed them to aerobic exercise activity and stretching/toning activity. They found that after six months, these groups showed increases in well-being and **self-efficacy.** Williamson and Pahor (2010) reviewed the literature on the effect of exercise on physical and mental ability in later life. They concluded that exercise can help maintain mental ability and prevent mental decline. Liu-Ambrose and colleagues (2010) studied the effects of strength training on 155 Canadian women age 65 to 75. Those who closely followed the program's design showed better mental performance.

---

expanders people who have not stopped any activities in the past year and have added at least one new outdoor activity since age 65, in keeping with the lifespan development theory of aging

self-efficacy what people believe they can do; people with a strong sense of efficacy take on more challenging tasks and put out more effort

EXHIBIT 10.3 AGING IN A GLOBAL PERSPECTIVE
What a Senior Moment. Canuck Marathon Man, 74, Smokes His Rival, 71

More than 50 minutes after Jimmy Muindi sweeps smoothly to victory in the Rotterdam Marathon, in an impressive time of 2:07:50, the cold and rain of an April day by the North Sea have scattered his welcoming party. The city's smiling mayor, Burgemeester Ivo Opstelten, last seen presenting flowers to the top three finishers—Kenyans to a man—is nowhere to be seen. Nor are the jostling photographers who fought to capture the final sprint. Now the halt, the lame, the crumpled over with dry heaves or diarrhea, and the just plain also-ran, stagger across the finish line. Then, as the clock ticks ominously closer to three hours—the cut-off point for serious marathoners—Ed Whitlock hoves into view.

At 2:58:40, Canada's unlikeliest star athlete—all five feet, seven inches and 112 lb. of him—crosses the line, sporting his ancient running shoes, shock of white hair and a huge grin. Whitlock, 74, from the Toronto suburb of Milton, is the only man over 70 ever to have broken the three-hour mark. Now he's done it again, for the third time, in the most prestigious race he's ever run. What's more, he's crushed his only serious rival for the over-70 crown, Rotterdam hometown hero Joop Ruter, 71, who arrives 14 minutes later. Back comes Burgemeester Opstelten, with a fresh bunch of flowers, along with an entire Dutch TV crew and several photographers.

Whitlock is a star entry in one of the world's Top 10 marathons—in another first for over-70 runners, organizers paid his way to Rotterdam and reserved an elite starting position for him ahead of the 11,000 ordinary racers. When he finishes, the PA system goes back into operation, trumpeting Whitlock's age and time. "I'm still recovering—it was a tough last k," a disconcertingly relaxed Whitlock tells the media. "I left Joop after about four kilometres. Then I spent much of the race in a large crowd, trying to hide from the wind; I'm a bit of a parasite that way. I was aiming for 2:57, so I lost a minute somewhere," he concludes, a flicker of displeasure momentarily dimming his smile. "But a good result anyway."

Whitlock takes no supplements or vitamins, refuses to stretch before races, trains by running in circles around a local cemetery after a breakfast of tea and bread, and hasn't had a regular physical in 30 years. So that late start in marathon life—which presumably has limited the wear and tear on his body—is observers' best explanation for his success. Whitlock's having none of it, though. "I've been a serious runner my whole life." He will allow for the luck of good genes—his mother died at 91, and an uncle recently passed away at 108. The real answer likely has more to do with his mind. Hours after the marathon, Whitlock declares, "It would have been a disgrace if I had lost to Joop. *I'm* the one with the record time, *he's* the one who should be intimidated by

it. Obviously I have a competitive streak, but I'd have been very upset if I felt people had any reason to think I hadn't run well.

As for the future, there's the anticipated rematch with Ruter at September's Toronto Waterfront Marathon. Shrugging off age and possible injury, Whitlock's sure it will take place. "Joop said he'd come, and so did I. Besides, I said I'd take him to Niagara Falls."

Whitlock also competes on the track, where he currently (2012) holds 15 world age group records ranging in distance from 1500 m to 10,000 m and age groups 65+, 70+, 75+ and 80+, as well as the 3 age group marathon records 70+, 75+ and 80+.

Postscript: Ed Whitlock, at age 82, set another single-age world record in 2013 at the Toronto Waterfront Marathon with a time of 3:41.

THE CANADIAN PRESS/Nathan Denette

Source: Brian Bethune. "What a senior moment. Canuck marathon man, 74, smokes his rival, 71," *Maclean's*, Apr 22, 2005. Reprinted with permission.

An **active leisure lifestyle** does at least two things: it directly benefits health and helps to buffer the influence of life events and illness. Aldwin, Spiro, and Park (2006) reported that physical activity reduces the incidence of diabetes, lowers cholesterol, and increases bone density. These benefits in turn lead to better functioning in daily life for older people. Kramer, Fabiani, and Colcombe (2006) reported that aerobic exercise improves memory, intelligence, and cognitive speed. Edwards and Mawani (2006) said that engaging in physical activity with others creates social connections and builds social networks.

---

active leisure lifestyle a type of lifestyle that directly benefits health and helps to buffer the influence of life events and illness by regular participation in physical activities

What are some of the life events that shape a person's activity in later life?

How do gender roles, education, and health influence a person's activity level?

What policies or programs would encourage seniors to stay active?

SENIORS' CENTRES

Most cities and towns across Canada have seniors' centres. These form the closest thing to a nationwide recreation system for older people. Centres must meet the needs of both frail and active older people in their communities. Most centres offer education programs in arts and the humanities, health services (such as foot care clinics and fitness activities), legal advice, and income counselling. Centres also offer meal and nutrition programs. These serve a number of functions. They provide members with a hot meal once a day or several times a week, they bring people together to socialize, and they allow more able members to volunteer in meal preparation. Meal programs build camaraderie and an informal support network among

members. These centres also link older people to other services in the community.

People drop in to their local centre to socialize, meet other seniors, play cards, take classes, and in some cases get medical help. Some centres offer unique social and healthcare services as well as recreation. The Edmonton Aboriginal Seniors Centre offers drop-in and outreach services. The centre helps participants find affordable housing and holds potluck dinners and craft events. Members of the centre can converse in their native language. Other Indigenous peoples' centres offer help with letter writing, filling out forms, and transportation to activities.

But education programs at universities and colleges now attract many seniors who might once have been satisfied with the programs at a seniors' centre. Also, more mobile, younger seniors may prefer to attend an art gallery or fitness program across town that meets their needs better. This leaves less-well, less-mobile older people to use neighbourhood centres. A concentration of less-healthy seniors in the seniors' centre of the future may move centres more toward the social services agency model.

Milner (2007) asked seniors' centre leaders about the needs of younger people in their programs. She found a shift in programming toward sports, wellness, and more

EXHIBIT 10.4 *Gambling: A Leisure Pastime or a Dangerous Addiction?*

Some older people gamble, whether by passive slot machine play or active poker competition. A look around a casino will find many grey heads. Some people enjoy the thrill of gaming but they keep a close watch on how much they lose. Other people lose themselves in gambling and risk high losses and debt.

Falkowski-Ham et al. (2005) studied the gambling habits of 1,500 adults age 60 and over in Ontario. They found that a large majority (73.5 percent) of the people in their sample engaged in some gambling behaviour in the past year. About half of those who gambled did so through lottery and raffle tickets. Another quarter (23 percent) used electronic machines at casinos, and one in five (19.7 percent) used scratch tickets. Less than 3 percent of the sample gambled weekly. People said they gambled to win money, for excitement or fun, and to socialize. The researchers said that "gambling also appears to serve an important social function, particularly as respondents age and become more isolated (e.g., widowed)."

Research by Tira, Jackson, and Tomnay (2013) supported these findings. The researchers found a single theme that led to late life gambling problems: social isolation. Among the people studied, those who had unresolved losses or those who mismanaged life stresses ran the greatest risk of problematic gambling.

Gambling settings offered these people a sense of belonging or companionship. One person in the study said, "It's

one place you can go ... where you can go in on our own, and you don't have to be with someone. That's a very big factor." (p. 1039) Gambling settings made some of the respondents feel like they belonged to a "young-at-heart" group of older people. Gambling settings gave many of these people a chance to meet other people going through similar life experiences.

McVey (2003) reported that many seniors preferred slot machines. Gamblers in the Tira and colleagues study said they related to the machines as partners. They sometimes talked to the machines and enjoyed being left alone with them. One man commented, "At least you won't get an argument out of the machine there (Frank)" (p. 1041). The design of the games themselves hook lonely people who want stimulation. One woman says, "The colors, noise, vibrancy and features of the games on the screen stayed in my brain like imprints, and seduced and lured me back and back again, hundreds of times." (p. 1041).

Tira, Jackson, and Tomnay (2013; also Zaranek & Chapleski, 2005) put gambling problems into a social context. Retirement, for example, cuts people off from meaningful relations at work. For some problem gamblers, gambling replaced work. Tira and colleagues proposed a number of solutions to gambling problems among seniors: educational programs, more leisure options, and senior-friendly communities. These would offer isolated seniors a chance to meet and socialize with peers without the potentially destructive effects of gambling.

physical activity. Morgan summarized the current and future role of seniors' centres: "Senior centers are constantly evolving from *social centers* to *service centers* to *community centers* and even becoming *entrepreneurial centers* in order to adjust to the changing needs of the seniors they serve." The success of centres in the future will depend on leaders' ability to listen to people in their communities. They can then create "facilities, programs, services and activities that meet the needs of this dynamic market."

Spirituality and Religion: The Search for Meaning in Later Life

A person in later life, having lived many years shaped by social obligations and external goals, may begin an inward journey. Tornstam (2005, 2012) referred to this as "gero-transcendence"—the self begins to expand its boundaries and the person begins to reflect on the meaning of human life.

Gero-transcendence also refers to a shift from materialism and a practical view of life to a more contemplative, cosmic view. It includes "a deepening spirituality, and a greater sense of intergenerational continuity" (Aldwin, Spiro, & Park, 2006, p. 98; also Jewell, 2010). Johnson (2009) said that with gero-transcendence " the individual becomes less self-occupied, becomes more selective about social activities, has a greater affinity with past generations, and takes less interest in superfluous social interaction ... even developing a need for solitary meditation" (p. 669).

This search for fulfillment in later life can take many forms, including religious faith, attendance at religious services, and non-traditional spiritual beliefs. McFadden and Kozberg (2008) said that spirituality brings "meaning and values to life," affirms the person, and connects the person "with someone/something beyond the individual" (p. 7). Atchley (2008) defined spirituality as "an inner, subjective region of life that revolves around individual experiences of being, transcending the personal self, and connecting with the sacred" (p. 12).

The diversity of Canadian life today, with its various ethnic and cultural groups, leads to many different religious and spiritual perspectives. Most Canadians claim Christianity as their religious belief. Forty-three percent of Canadian seniors claim Roman Catholicism as their form of Christianity and 41 percent claim Protestantism (Statistics Canada, 2010d). Other faiths include Judaism,

other Christian sects, Islam, Baha'i, Buddhism, Hinduism, Sikhism, Confucianism, and Taoism.

Idler (2006) said that lifelong membership in a congregation provides continuity in a person's life. A church, synagogue, temple, or mosque may hold collective and individual memories—of births, marriages, and deaths. "For older persons with lifelong religious observances, a thread sews through all these seasons, providing accumulating continuity and deepening memories." Idler goes on to say that in a fast-changing world, religion and religious communities provide continuity. For people who have lived "89, 90, or even 100 years," she said, "it is difficult to name any other aspect of those lives [except religion] that would have changed so little" (p. 294). The oldest age groups in Canada show the highest rates of participation in religious activities. This may reflect the importance of religion in these older people's lives from youth onward.

Compared with other age groups, older Canadians report the highest rate of attendance at religious services (Lindsay, 2008). Thirty-seven percent of seniors report that they engage in religious activity at least once a week. By contrast, only 26 percent of people age 15 to 44 report weekly religious attendance.

Richard and colleagues (2005) studied the quality of later life in urban environments by interviewing older people in Montreal as part of a national study. About half of the groups in their study mentioned spirituality or religion as an important part of aging well. Some people linked quality of life to traditional religious belief. One person said, "I have peace of mind ... because I'm a religious person." Another took a broader view of spirituality. "I'm not really religious," he said, "in the sense of belonging fully to a particular church, although I'm a Catholic. I find interest and solace in the general attitude to the development of the universe." One woman said, "I don't think I could be a survivor without faith. And I talk about spirituality, not religion, because sometimes religion doesn't provide the answers for everyone" (p. 23). These responses illustrate that faith and belief mean different things to different people.

Clark and Schellenberg (2006) created a religiosity index to measure the strength of religious practice and belief among Canadians. This index measures four dimensions of religion: affiliation, attendance, personal practice, and importance of religion. A person could score between 1 and 13 on this index. A person with no affiliation scored zero. Forty-four percent of people age 60 and over scored between 11 and 13 (the highest grouping) on this index—twice the proportion of people age 15 to 29 and one-and-a-half times the proportion of 45- to 59-year-olds.

Gero-transcendence in later life, the self begins to expand its boundaries and reflect on the meaning of human life

Older people face some barriers to religious attendance as they get older. Illness, disability, and transportation problems often limit religious attendance as a person ages. But even with these challenges, 62 percent of people age 60 and over say religion remains very important to them, and 58 percent say they maintain a weekly private religious practice (Clark & Schellenberg, 2006).

This commitment to religion may partly reflect the past experiences of older people. In the past, religion played a bigger role in people's lives than it does today. Lindsay (2008) found that the proportion of Canadians age 15 and over who reported no religion doubled from 11 percent in 1985 to 22 percent in 2005. Low rates of religious attendance and a high proportion of people who report no religion today may lead to a decline in religious participation among older people in the future.

The commitment to religion may also reflect the role that faith can play as health, income, and social supports decline in late old age. Religious belief can help a person

Older members of a community can keep religious traditions alive. Seniors can bring young and old together through holiday rituals and discussions of cultural values. Here, a grandfather performs a Hanukkah ceremony with his young family.

find meaning in the face of despair. Coping methods included prayer, faith in God, and support from clergy and the faith community. McFadden and Kozberg (2008) said that older adults' religious beliefs and practices, and their experiences of spiritual growth and community connections, represent core strengths and resources. Many identify their faith as their most important support for coping with the trials and tribulations of aging. Gilmour (2014) found that people with strong religious or spiritual beliefs in their daily lives tended to have better mental health.

Some people express their spirituality outside traditional religious channels. They may feel oneness with nature or a commitment to the betterment of all life. Some older people turn to Eastern and Western meditation practices to feel a sense of wholeness. Yoga and t'ai chi exercises can create a sense of unity within oneself and with the environment. Studies show that spiritual practices such as these can lead to better health, improved social relations, and increased life satisfaction (Fishman, 2011; Philbin, 2011).

Some people see spirituality as a personal relationship with God. Moore, Metcalf, and Schow (2006) found that spirituality and faith in God gave some people a sense of purpose and enthusiasm. Other people take a more philosophical view. They see God everywhere in the natural world.

Atchley (2008) said that a person's spiritual path can take many forms. Spiritual engagement can take place "through an enduring set of questions used to remain spiritually self-aware; by being committed to regular spiritual practices such as contemplative reading, meditation, or movement practices like yoga or labyrinth walking; by participating in a spiritual community; through workshops or retreats aimed at spiritual growth and peer-support groups aimed at providing social support and opportunities for expression related to the spiritual journey" (p. 13). Spiritual practices, whether formal religious services or quiet reflection on the past, can bring fullness to later life. Researchers and practitioners need to learn about the many expressions of religion and spirituality in later life. They can then apply this understanding to improve their clients' quality of life.

EDUCATION

Most schools today serve the same function they did a century and a half ago when they first began teaching children to become adults and preparing young people for specific jobs in society. This system offers little for the older person, who is already an adult and retired from a job.

Compared with younger learners, older people have less interest in credentials and want shorter, more focused programs. Older people most often take education programs for personal growth rather than career development.

An older person who wants to take a course at a university faces many barriers. First, the older student may face a long walk from a parking lot or bus stop to classes. The cost of parking and bad weather in some regions add to the problem of getting to class.

Second, most classes take place in one- or two-hour time blocks. A person who wants to take one course may have to visit the university three times a week. Even a short commute can add three or more hours of travel to a three-hour-per-week course.

Third, memories of schooling from childhood include competition and fear of failure (Findsen, 2014). An older adult has to overcome these and other internal and external barriers. The American Council on Education (ACE) (Lakin, Mullane, & Robinson, 2007) found a gap in our knowledge of "older adult learners and their postsecondary engagement" (p. 3). Educators need to better understand the older learner and the barriers they face.

Will higher education respond to the needs of the older learner? The ACE study (Lakin et al., 2007) found that more than 40 percent of the institutions in the study said they "did not identify older adult students for purposes related to outreach, programs and services, or financial aid" (p. 3). This may explain why less than 10 percent of older adults make use of higher education programs and services. And only a handful of older adults make use of financial aid. The ACE study said that higher education has not yet defined its role in serving the older learner.

Still, some schools have made an attempt to meet the older learner's needs. Some schools hold classes in convenient locations such as shopping centres, where students can park and get to class easily. They offer courses at convenient times. Single three-hour blocks, weekends, or even week-long courses to better suit older learners' needs. Some instructors use adult education methods in the classroom. Older students have little patience with long lectures. They want to interact with their teachers and classmates. They want to share their knowledge.

Also, the ACE study found that the 65-and-over group shows little interest in degree or diploma programs. Only 0.3 percent took part in this type of education, and only 5 percent of this older group took work-related courses. But 19 percent took personal interest courses. Older people enjoy convenient programs that suit their schedule, income, and learning styles (Robinson, Mullane, & Lakin, 2007).

One new learning opportunity may gain in popularity in the future: online learning. As new cohorts enter later life they will bring the computer skills and confidence that will make online learning more attractive. Many Baby Boomers will have taken classes or gone through an online training program at work. Author Mark Novak's university, for example, offers its driver certification program online (a course required in order to drive university vehicles). Novak took the class in small chunks at his desk when he had some free moments. This substituted for a class that would have used up a morning of his work time. Many similar learning experiences exist in workplaces today.

Adult educators say that the needs of older learners differ from those of younger learners. Older learners most often come back to school for personal development and to find meaning in later life. A study by the American Council on Education (cited in Robinson, Mullane, & Lakin, 2007, p. 14) found that

> [many older adults] are driven to study a subject area that they previously never had the opportunity to learn.... Older adults who have already earned degrees in technical fields, such as engineering and nursing, often take advantage of new opportunities to study liberal arts and other related interests. Older learners ask: Is the knowledge useful? Does it help me make better sense of my life and the world around me? Does it help me live more fully and enjoy my life more?

New generations of older students will require new educational models and new programs to meet their needs. For example, the proportion of people age 25 to 54 with a postsecondary diploma or degree showed a significant increase between 1990 and 2009 (Turcotte, 2011b). These people may want more higher education in later life.

Also, a new educational need has also begun to surface. A growing number of middle-aged people say they intend to work past the normal retirement age. Some will want to change careers in later life. The typical four-year degree or two-year community college program may not suit these students. They want education programs that get them back in the workforce quickly.

Robinson, Mullane, and Lakin (2007) said, "Older adults with an interest in new careers ... want options that quickly transition them to new opportunities. Consequently, many want prior learning assessment, accelerated program formats, improved career counseling, and job placement" (p. 3). Schools will have to rethink their schedules, the location of their classes, and their admissions processes to meet the needs of this growing older population.

EXHIBIT 10.5   *Level of Education, by Age, 2011, Canada*

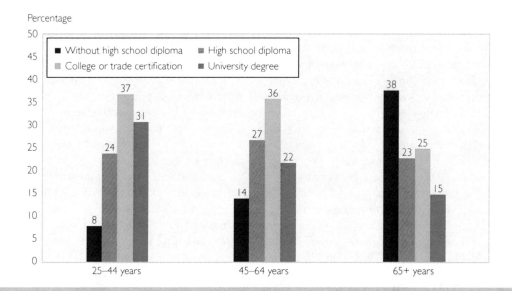

This chart shows the increase in Canadian educational attainment for three age groups. The youngest group (age 25–44) shows the highest level of college and university education (68.4 percent). The oldest age group shows the highest proportion of people (38 percent) without a high school diploma and the lowest level of postsecondary education (39.3 percent). This chart shows the growth in the importance and availability of higher education in Canada over time. The oldest age group had the least opportunity to get a higher education.

And perhaps, in their youth, they felt the least need for higher education in order to enter the workforce and succeed. Today higher education opens the door to income and achievement in the workplace.

Highly educated younger people will enter later life with an interest in education and personal growth. Many of them will have lived their lives as knowledge workers. And all of them will have lived in a knowledge-rich society. This will lead to new approaches to learning in retirement.

Source: Human Resources and Skills Development Canada. "Learning—Educational Attainment." (2012). Found at http://www4.hrsdc.gc.ca/.3ndic.1t.4r@-eng.jsp?iid=29#M_3. Original source: HRSDC calculations based on Statistics Canada. Labour Force Survey (LFS) estimates, by educational attainment, sex and age group, annual (CANSIM Table 282-0004) 2012.

Turcotte and Schellenberg (2007) said that in Canada, "information on [the educational activity of] workers aged 65 or older is not available" (p. 111). The meaning and purpose of education change in later life. Researchers need to understand the many reasons that people want to continue learning in later life. And they need to study the new channels of education that attract seniors today.

Educational Alternatives

Road Scholar

Road Scholar (previously Elderhostel) combines university education with a European hostel experience. David Bianco and Martin Knowlton, a social activist and an educator, respectively, started the program in New Hampshire

---

Road Scholar (previously Elderhostel) a not-for-profit company that promotes lifelong learning by organizing educational and cultural tours aimed at people in their 50s and older (originally based on a combination of university life and the European concept of hostelling)

in 1975. They designed a series of challenging intellectual courses for older people. Then they arranged for the senior students to live on university campuses. The program began with 220 people age 55 and over enrolled in five schools.

Road Scholar has grown stronger and more independent over time. It takes no money from the government, nor does it ask for any. It supports its programs through tuition and donations from alumni and other supporters. The program in 2014 enrolled 97,000 students in 5,500 programs in all 50 U.S. states and 150 countries (Road Scholar, 2014).

Classic Road Scholar programs last one week—from Sunday afternoon until the following Saturday morning. A one-week program typically includes three courses. Road Scholar programs also take place in cities, national parks, and famous locations. Students may stay at a downtown hotel, a retreat house, or other simple lodgings (including safari tents when appropriate). Course choices include such options as whitewater rafting trips, tours of Venice, and African safaris. The program also offers "homestay programs," where students live with a host family in another country. These programs give hostellers a chance to travel, meet new people, and learn things in a variety of settings they might not otherwise visit.

Today a program called Routes to Learning Canada (formerly Elderhostel Canada) offers Road Scholar programs in Canada. Routes to Learning emphasizes environmental and cultural awareness, and programs take place throughout the country and abroad. They range from the strenuous to the sedate. One offered a 10-day Fraser River expedition in voyageur canoes, encouraging grandchildren to attend with their grandparents. Another program offered a weekend at the opera in Toronto and took members backstage to learn about the staging and choreography involved in an opera performance.

Institutes for Learning in Retirement or Lifelong Learning Institutes

Institutes for Learning in Retirement (ILRs), also called **Institutes for Lifelong Learning (LLIs)**, have met with success at a number of Canadian universities. These programs offer a variety of formats from lectures, to seminars, to travel courses. Some programs charge a membership fee and a course registration fee. Others do

Institutes for Learning in Retirement (ILRs) or Lifelong Learning Institutes (LLIs) programs that offer older people a variety of educational formats from lectures, to seminars, to travel courses, with topics usually decided on by the group

not. In most cases, older people decide together on the topics they will study; the ILR model uses peer teachers and group self-management.

ILR courses have no grades or tests, and often take the form of study groups where students teach one another. Students in the ILRs, some of them retired professionals, often lead the classes. But they may teach subjects far from their specialties. A retired engineer might lead a course in Shakespeare, or a professor of adult education might teach a course on French cuisine.

About 200 to 300 people belong to a typical LLI. More than 100,000 people belong to a Road Scholar network-affiliated LLI called the Road Scholar Institute Network (Elderhostel, 2011). Road Scholar estimates that 10 to 20 new institutes start each year. "It is quite clear," Elderhostel (2007) said, "that the future of the learning in retirement movement is very secure and will continue to grow, well into the 21st century."

Each institute has its own culture. Members in some ILRs teach the classes; in other cases an ILR may bring in an expert teacher. Where ILR members teach, the program provides them with an outlet for their intellectual curiosity and talent. It provides the class with insights from a classmate and someone from their generation. This builds esteem for the teacher and creates respect from the students.

Cherem (2010) surveyed 70 members of two senior learning groups. She found two primary motives that led members to lifelong learning: (1) cognitive interest and (2) intellectual stimulation. Secondary motives for learning included feeling a sense of purpose and self-expression.

EXHIBIT 10.6 *A Comparison of Second- and Third-Age Learning*

Second-Age Learning	Third-Age Learning
Work	Leisure
Professional	Amateur
Workforce development/training	Self-development
Social capital	Personal enrichment
Society-subsidized	Individual pays
First career	Second career
Have to know	Want to know
Schooling	Education
Social purpose	Individual purpose
Career preparation	Learning for its own sake

These lists present an ideal type of education at two stages in life (youth/middle adulthood and early old age). Education at each stage of life meets different social and individual needs.

Can you think of other characteristics, like those above, that define education at each of these life stages?

Students will follow a gifted teacher from class to class, telling friends and bringing them along to the lectures or presentations. Groups and courses often grow through this word-of-mouth and the enthusiasm of the members.

Research on social relations in ILRs shows the value and importance of these kinds of relationships in later life. Sociologists refer to these relations as **weak social ties**. These differ from the intimacy of family and friendship ties. Family and friends tend to come from the same social and economic background. But weak social ties like those in an ILR link people from diverse backgrounds. Weak ties expose a person to new views and opinions.

Krause (2006) said that "weak social ties may be an important source of informational support. Having a wider range of views may help older people select the best coping responses during difficult times ... weak ties provide a context in which a person may experiment with new ideas and new behaviors with relatively low levels of accountability" (p. 190). Life course changes such as retirement can remove a person from the weak social ties they enjoyed at work. Education programs can replace this important source of social support.

Findsen (2014) criticized the methods and motives of traditional educational programs (including ILRs). Seen through the lens of the political economy perspective, these programs serve middle-class interests and reproduce social class inequalities. "[T]he middle classes, adept at looking after their own needs reproduce earlier life advantages and translate them to their own benefit in later adulthood" (p. 123). These programs do not address the educational needs of poor people and those from marginalized racial and ethnic groups.

In part, the absence of government funding for lifelong learning explains the middle-class bias of these programs. Road Scholar proudly boasts that it receives no government funding. And ILRs rarely receive government support. This means that these programs must survive on fees paid by students. That skews their membership and content toward people who can afford to pay. Poor and marginalized older people may find these programs unaffordable and perhaps uninteresting. The lack of educational options for poor and marginalized older people will continue as long as society provides little funding for lifelong learning.

Yet, lifelong learning would benefit older people in any income group. Well-designed programs can increase a person's confidence and the ability to do new things. Dr. Gene Cohen (2005) reported on a study of older people in community arts programs. He said that "gaining a sense of mastery in one area can lead to feelings of empowerment that spread to other spheres of life, leading to more confidence, a willingness to take risks, and the energy for trying new things" (p. 179). People in these programs, compared with a control group, remained more socially involved a year into the study. Cohen found that people in the arts programs supported one another socially. They felt a sense of belonging that enhanced their well-being.

Moody and Phinney (2012) studied a "community-engaged arts" program in Vancouver. The researchers asked whether this type of program could foster "social inclusion" among participants. The program took place at a neighbourhood seniors' centre. Twenty people (nineteen women and one man) took part in the program. They ranged in age from 65 to 90 years old. The seniors in this program met each week for two-and-a-half hours from September to June (2007–2008). During each session, the seniors worked on individual art projects with the support of professional artist-volunteers. The program allowed the seniors to display their works at exhibits throughout the year.

This program shows that a well-constructed arts program can create community engagement and personal satisfaction for group members. The program built in opportunities for the artists to display their work. This created a connection between the seniors and their community. This program "demonstrate[s] how community- engaged arts can play a distinctive role in supporting social inclusion for community-dwelling seniors" (p. 63).

TIME to REVIEW

Why do programs like Road Scholar appeal to seniors?

How do the content and structure of its programs meet the needs of people in later life?

How do Institutes for Learning in Retirement or Lifelong Learning Institutes differ from Road Scholar programs?

What benefits do people in these programs report?

THE USE OF TECHNOLOGY BY OLDER PEOPLE

Seals and colleagues (2008; also Rosenthal, 2008) said that computer use can reduce loneliness and isolation. It can help seniors stay in touch with family and friends. Seniors can use the Internet as a source of entertainment, information, and education.

weak social ties these differ from the intimacy of family and friendship ties; weak social ties link people from diverse backgrounds and expose a person to new views and opinions

EXHIBIT 10.7   *Rates of Internet Use from Any Location, by Age Group, 2010 and 2012 (percentage)*

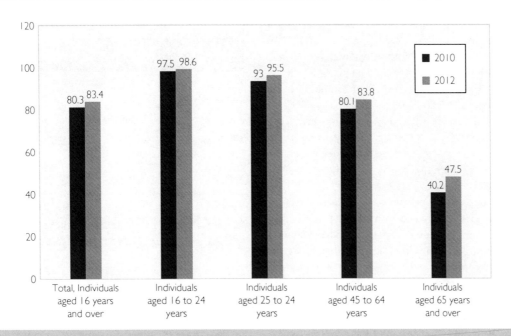

This chart shows a trend toward computer use by older people. The oldest age group shows the smallest proportion of people who use the Internet. But this group shows the greatest proportional increase in Internet use. For people age 65 and over, the rate of use jumped from 40.2 percent to 47.5 percent between 2010 and 2012. This reflects the flow of new cohorts into these age groups as well as increased use by people of all age groups. As cohorts age, they will bring their use of computers and the Internet with them. The digital divide that now exists will shrink. You can see the start of this trend in this chart.

Source: Statistics Canada. Canadian Internet use survey, Internet use, by location of use, household income, and age group for Canada and regions, Table 358-0154 (2013). From http://www5 .statcan.gc.ca/cansim/pick-choisir?lang=eng&p2=33&id=3580154. Reproduced and distributed on an "as is" basis with the permission of Statistics Canada.

Statistics Canada (2011l) said, "Older people are increasingly moving online. Canadians aged 45 and older have accounted for 60% of all new Internet users since 2007." Among the age group 16–24, 98 percent went online in 2009—a slight increase from 2007 (94 percent). But in 2009, 66 percent of people age 45 and older went online. This meant an increase of 10 percentage points from 2007. Jones and Fox (2009) found that people age 70 to 75 showed the greatest proportional increase in Internet users during that time. They also found that the generations differed in their online activities.

Allen (2013) found that younger users tended to download videos and music. In 2010, for example, 87 percent of people age 15 to 24 downloaded music at least once a week. Only 10 percent of seniors age 65–74 downloaded music weekly. Eighty percent of people age 65 and over tended to listen to music on CDs (compared to only 6 percent of people age 15–24 who used CDs). A similar gap existed with the consumption of movies and videos. Nearly 80 percent of young people

(18 to 24) used the Internet to watch videos and movies. Only 10 percent of seniors (65 and over) did so. Allen calls this a "generational divide in Internet use" (p. 2).

A study published by AARP (Koppen, 2010) looked at some of the newer uses of the Internet among people age 50 and over. Among Internet users, nearly two in five (37 percent) used social networking sites. A third (31 percent) used Facebook. Adults age 50 and over mostly used social media to connect to children, grandchildren, and other relatives. This study showed the rapid growth of computer use for social networking among older people.

A Revera (2012a) report on tech-savvy seniors found that 27 percent of people age 75 and over use the Internet (up from 5 percent in 2000). Among these people, more than half said they used social media such as Facebook to keep in touch with family and friends. And among those who went online, 88 percent did so at least once a day. The report also found that one in five online seniors used Skype or Facetime. Seniors also said they posted photos

(20 percent) and sent text messages at least once a week (36 percent) (Revera, 2012b).

Bertha Kronenberg, 88, told the Revera researchers, "The computer is invaluable to me. I don't know what I would do without it.… The Internet is a wonderful record of what's going on in the world." Ms. Kronenberg, who lives in Toronto, uses the computer to stay in touch with family in South Africa. She says she'd be pleased to learn about new technologies. "(You're) never too old to learn anything," she says (Favaro, 2012).

Adrienne Dawson, 91, lives in a long-term care facility. "The other day I took a tour of Italy. I went there when I was younger and loved it. So now I go back on my computer every so often to see how it's changed.… It's like taking a vacation" (Favaro, 2012).

Seventy percent of people age 75 and over told the Revera researchers that technology helps them live in their own homes as long as possible. These seniors said they would use technology to keep socially active (63 percent); keep informed about the news and world issues (69 percent); make their home more secure (49 percent); monitor their healthcare (45 percent); and make their home safer (34 percent) (Revera, 2012b).

By the time you read this, the use of the Internet will have grown even more common and popular among seniors. Veenhof and Timusk (2009) said, "It is likely that people who currently use the Internet will continue to do so, and that differences in utilization rates by age should continue to decline" (p. 25). As new uses for information technology emerge, they will attract people of all ages. This will close the digital divide. But young people and seniors may still use the Internet and technology for different purposes. Different interests and needs dictate the use of technology for different age groups.

Professor Ron Baecker, founder and director of the Technologies for Aging Gracefully Lab at the University of Toronto, said, "Some technology is not easy enough to use. But even more so than the technology, what's required is an ecosystem of support. And that can be family members, friends, grandchildren, training courses" (Favaro, 2012).

One woman found "that speaking to people, customers and employees in computer stores … offers a wealth of information." Another woman said, "Professional help is the best ($50–$75/hour), but it's worth it!" (Rosenthal, 2008, p. 615) These women found ways to overcome the challenges of computer use. Seniors now and in the future will use computers to surf the Internet for sites, including online pharmacies, health advice, and online shopping. Housebound seniors will find these services especially useful. Telehealth services already

monitor the health of people with chronic illnesses. As well, the use of email, Skype, Facebook, chat rooms, and discussion groups will open new social outlets for all older people.

TIME to REVIEW

Compare the use of computers and the Internet by younger and older people.

How do computers help older people stay connected?

What do researchers mean when they talk about a "digital divide" among older people?

What could be done to reduce or eliminate the digital divide?

COMMUNITY SERVICE THROUGH VOLUNTEER WORK

Exercise, recreation, and education lead to increased life satisfaction for older people. So does community service and volunteer work (Bowen, Noack, & Staudinger, 2011).

Hall et al. (2006) found that Canadians engage in at least four types of community service: charitable giving, volunteering through an organization, helping others directly, and membership in an organization. Nearly everyone in this national study (96 percent) said they participated in at least one of these activities in a year.

Turcotte and Schellenberg (2007) said that volunteering "is not only a way of contributing to their communities and to society, but also an effective way to meet people and to avoid social isolation." For example, women who enter rural communities later in life use volunteer activity as a way to meet new people. "We were 'imports' [into the community]," one woman told Rozanova, Dosman, and de Jong Gierveld (2008), "and it was easy to get to know people when we [got] involved [in volunteer work]" (p. 80).

Volunteering also provides people with a sense of purpose and psychological well-being. A man in a rural community told Rozanova and colleagues (2008): "I've been involved in the fire department … for a few years [as a volunteer firefighter].… There's a personal reason we're putting that fire out.…" (p. 79). Rosanova and colleagues point out that the ability to volunteer often depends on available opportunities in a community. This volunteer firefighter had an organization he could join. Volunteers (compared with people who help family members and friends) need formal organizations to support their work.

EXHIBIT 10.8   *Distribution of Volunteers and Total Hours Contributed, by Age Group, 2013*

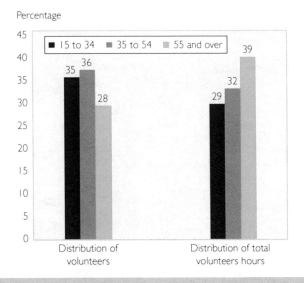

This chart compares three age groups and their volunteer activities. Note that the oldest age group (55 and over) makes up the smallest proportion of volunteers. Health and mobility problems in later old age explain this difference in part. But also note that among those who volunteer, the oldest group provides the greatest proportion of volunteer hours. This reflects the older volunteers' strong commitment to their communities and to the fact that retirees have more time to spend on volunteering.

Source: Turcotte, M. Volunteering and charitable giving in Canada. Spotlight on Canadians: Results from the *General Social Survey*. Statistics Canada. (2015). Retrieved from http://www.statcan. gc.ca/pub/89-652-x/89-652-x2015001-eng.pdf. Original source: Statistics Canada. *General Social Survey on Giving, Volunteering and Participating* (2013). Reproduced and distributed on an "as is" basis with the permission of Statistics Canada.

Benefits of volunteering include good mental health, stronger social networks, and high life satisfaction (Bowen, Noack, & Staudinger, 2011). Cutler, Hendricks, and O'Neill (2011) said that civic engagement also enhances the older person's health. Civic engagement can take the form of paid work, but many older people use their time to volunteer for causes they consider important.

Compared to younger age groups a smaller proportion of people age 65 and over volunteer (38 percent of those age 65 to 74 compared to 42 percent for those age 25 to 34) (Turcotte, 2015). But seniors who do volunteer give more time to volunteering than any other age group. For example, senior volunteers between the ages of 65 and 74 averaged 231 hours of volunteer work each year. Volunteers age 25 to 34 averaged 126 hours (or about half of the seniors' volunteer hours) (Turcotte, 2015). Older people (55+) contributed 39 percent of all volunteer hours in 2013. But they made up only 28 percent of the population of volunteers.

Seniors also have the highest proportion of "top volunteers"—"the people on whom charitable and non-profit organizations rely most heavily. They are the people who are deeply committed and who dedicate the greatest number of hours to their volunteer work" (Vézina &

Crompton, 2012, p. 43). Top volunteers spend at least 161 hours on volunteer work during the year. This equals four weeks of full-time work. Top volunteers accounted for 77 percent of all volunteer hours in 2010. Turcotte (2015) reported that people age 55 and over made up 38 percent of top volunteers in 2013 (compared to 34 percent of those aged 35 to 54).

Will this hold true for Baby Boomers? Cutler, Hendricks, and O'Neill (2011) predicted that "civic engagement likely will expand through the retirement years of the baby boom." They said, "Volunteering is not in steep decline, as some have predicted" (p. 227).

No one can say for sure what seniors will do in the future. Administrators of non-profit agencies will need to adapt volunteer roles to attract Baby Boomers and meet their needs. For example, volunteers age 55 and over tend to focus on specific activities. In 2013, 42 percent of volunteers age 55 and over sat on a committee or a board (only 26 percent of people age 15 to 34 engaged in this activity).

The *General Social Survey* (Turcotte, 2015) found that older volunteers and donors remain strong supporters of volunteer organizations. The proportion of people who volunteer from age 45 onward increased from 2004

EXHIBIT 10.9   *A Passion for Service: Susan Wetmore and CESO*

Reporter Elizabeth Nolan interviewed Susan Wetmore of Salt Spring Island, British Columbia, to learn about her reasons for serving as a CESO volunteer.

As volunteer advisor with CESO (Canadian Executive Service Organization) since 2003, the 63-year-old native of Ontario has directed much of her later years toward development work, an activity she absolutely adores. She's even been featured in the book *Lifeworth* as an example of someone who's created a fulfilling life.

"A life worth living for me is to be able to give to others, to share my interests and skills, to grow with them and to learn with them," she told the book's authors.

When Wetmore applied to CESO, she had a working history full of different career paths and reinventions under her belt, all of which had left her with a wide skill set of practical abilities. She was at times a Corrections Canada social worker dealing with youth sex offenders; a talk show host and producer; the owner of a catering business; and the director of catering at the Hilton Hotel in London.

Although the CESO program has allowed her to travel the world, the places she's visited are among some of the least known to outsiders.

"I'm not going to places that are high on the tourist list," Wetmore observed.

"The countries I go to all vie for the title of poorest in the world—the average income is around $30 a month."

Wetmore mainly works with restaurants and hotels, spending around four weeks at each assignment. Her considerable experience in hospitality makes her an asset to small business owners struggling to make their operations work.

But along with recognizing how to make a cafe and takeout business functional, she's found her other skills are just as useful. The first thing she does during any assignment is spend about a week just getting to know the business owners, learning what they have to offer and what they are hoping to achieve.

"Having been in social work, I've got a good ear for listening, and good observation skills as well," Wetmore said. "I think the key in doing any of this development work is basically how you see the problems—and are you going to give them the fish, or the tools to get the fish.

"I don't do it for them. We give them the tools to do the changing, and they can take our advice or not."

Wetmore's first assignment was in the Ukraine. She has since worked in Armenia, Honduras, Haiti, and Cameroon, among other international projects. National assignments have included working with Aboriginal women in Ontario and Nova Scotia.

Perhaps because CESO knows she likes a challenge and is not afraid to take risks, Wetmore has been put into some situations that most seniors travelling on their own wouldn't touch. Her tri-fold strategy is to live like the locals, avoid carrying valuables and documents, and live without fear—she believes that if you exude fear, someone is sure to pick up on it. "It's interesting ... I don't focus on it," she said.

Although she is not keen on guns or military presence, it's something she's learned to get used to. Once in Burkina Faso, for example, she was travelling through the desert to a famous weekly market when two soldiers hitched a ride. She wound up being sandwiched in the back seat between the two men, one

Driftwood Gulf Islands Media

carrying a full soup pot and the other holding an AK-47 wedged between his legs.

"The whole thing was just one of those moments—if my friends could see me now."

In another, scarier situation in Colombia, a CESO colleague she was travelling with got robbed by phony police. When she was telling the story to an interpreter afterward that person said, "You're lucky they didn't pull a gun on you."

"That was the closest to being scared shitless I've ever become," Wetmore said.

She prefers not to have assignments in former Soviet territories, although she had a surprisingly good experience in Tajikistan. Despite concerns on how a white woman would be received, she bonded closely with the male owner of a bakery, deli and cafe.

At the end of an assignment Wetmore always evaluates her own work to see what could have been done better or more efficiently, but at the same time, she recognizes values that don't fall under traditional markers of success. A relationship established with one person, like the restaurant owner in Tajikistan, can bring about the most meaningful benefits.

"No matter how it turns out they are always grateful you've come and spent that time with them. Getting people to celebrate what they have, build on their strengths and figure out how it will work is the key," she said.

Source: Nolan, E. "A Passion for Service—Susan Wetmore and CESO." Young at Heart/Driftwood Gulf Islands Media, March 21, 2012. Photo and story reprinted with permission.

to 2013. Also, compared to younger donors, older donors tend to give more to charities and non-profit organizations. People age 55 and over made up 47 percent of the total of all charitable donations in 2013, an increase from 39 percent in 2004. As an example of their generosity, older people provided half of all donations to religious organizations (over $2.6 billion) in 2013.

Statistics Canada (2012k) reports that, compared with people age 25 to 34, people age 65 and over donated more than twice as much to charities and other non-profit organizations in 2010 ($2,566.70 vs. $1,165.90). And although seniors made up 16.2 percent of the population of donors, they made 24.2 percent of all donations. Seniors also tend to give large donations. Hall and colleagues (2006) rated 31 percent of people age 65 and over as top donors (those who gave $325 or more). Turcotte (2015) reported that in 2013, people age 75 and over gave the most to charities and non-profit organizations (on average $726). This came to twice the amount on average donated by people age 25 to 34.

These figures point to a growing commitment of older Canadians to volunteering and to financial support for charities. The increase in the size of the older population in the years ahead may mean more volunteer and financial resources available for charitable and non-profit organizations.

Senior volunteers can have a global as well as a local impact. And this might appeal to the Baby Boom generation. The federal government sponsors a program called **Canadian Executive Service Organization (CESO)** (pronounced "kesso"), begun in 1967. It recruits experienced volunteers and assigns them to work in underdeveloped countries in Africa, Asia, the Caribbean, and Central and South America. The program also works with Indigenous groups in Canada. Volunteers, many of whom are retired people between the ages of 60 and 70, give technical and management advice to businesses, undertake feasibility studies, and help train workers and managers. The program now has completed 47,500 assignments in 122 countries including Canada, underdeveloped countries, and new market economies in central Europe (CESO, 2015) (see Exhibit 10.9).

Volunteering, whether at a local school or in a foreign country, can give an older person a sense of purpose in life. Turcotte and Schellenberg (2007) said that older people in the future will have more education and better

health. This will increase the number of potential volunteers. Canadian society needs to match the talents of these seniors with suitable volunteer opportunities.

TIME TO REVIEW

What benefits do older people gain from volunteering?

What challenges do organizations face as they rely more on volunteer help?

Why might an increase in volunteering by older people lead to a withdrawal of government support to social service agencies?

CONCLUSION

In later life people need varied activities to fulfill the ideals of physical, social, and spiritual well-being. A wide range of leisure options creates the best condition for successful aging.

Today, a **structural lag** can exist between the changing lives of older people and the opportunity to live a good old age. For example, many older people say they would like to volunteer more but cannot find suitable volunteer positions. Likewise, agencies sometimes have trouble using the talents of senior volunteers.

Many of the newest programs and activities respond to this mismatch or imbalance. Senior athlete programs, lifelong learning institutes, and innovative volunteer programs all respond to the growing leisure, recreation, and education needs of older people today. More affluence, a better-educated older population, and the desire for a meaningful retirement will call for more creative responses to leisure in the future. New generations of older people will define old age as a time of personal growth and community enrichment.

structural lag a mismatch between changes in the aging process (e.g., better health for older people, more active lifestyles) and the roles and places in the social structure that can meet the needs of this new older person

Summary

1. Some older people spend a great deal of their time on passive media-related activities, such as reading the newspaper and watching television. Older people often spend their time alone, but they also enjoy spending time with others.

Canadian Executive Service Organization (CESO) a federal government program that recruits volunteers, many of whom are retired executives, to serve as advisers and mentors in underdeveloped countries or with Indigenous groups in Canada

2. Income, lifestyle, gender, marital status, social context, and health influence what people do and how active they remain in old age. Compared with older women, older men show higher rates of physical activity and sport participation.

3. Older people in good health tend to stay active into late old age. People with a history of active leisure also stay active in later life. Leisure education can help people stay active as they age.

4. An active leisure lifestyle provides physical, psychological, and social benefits in later life. This leads to better functioning and greater life satisfaction.

5. Seniors' centres across the country offer education, counselling, and recreation for older people. They form the closest thing to a network of recreational programs in Canada. Centre activities will need to change in the future to meet the needs of younger, more active seniors.

6. People with many years of schooling will keep on learning as they age. Traditional university classes often fail to meet seniors' educational needs. Some universities sponsor special programs for seniors. Programs such as Road Scholar and Institutes for Learning in Retirement (ILRs) or Lifelong Learning Institutes (LLIs) offer alternatives to traditional schooling and are designed to fit older people's interests and learning styles. Some seniors will want work-related training in order to stay active in the workforce.

7. Computer technology has attracted the interest of many older people. The Internet, for example, has provided new sources of information to both active and housebound older people. It has begun to change the way older people access new ideas, information, and people. Trends show that seniors' use of computers and the Internet will grow in the future.

8. Many older people volunteer to help others, and studies show that volunteers report an increase in life satisfaction. More older people might offer their skills and services to the community if they had the opportunity. Current trends raise questions about whether Baby Boomers will want to volunteer their services.

STUDY QUESTIONS

1. How do most older people spend their time in retirement, according to studies on leisure activities? What activities do retired people enjoy most?

2. How and why do the lifestyles of older people vary in retirement? How do older people differ in their activity patterns by gender, marital status, education, health, and geography? What early life influences affect a person's activity patterns in later life?

3. Describe some of the programs and services available that can help older people stay active. List some of the physical and psychological benefits of regular exercise and fitness programs for seniors.

4. What special needs must recreational planners consider when they design programs for older people? How can recreational planners attract sedentary seniors to activity programs?

5. What services do seniors' centres provide for older people? What other types of programs compete with seniors' centres for the older person's participation? What future challenges will seniors' centres face as the Baby Boom enters old age?

6. Why do older people attend educational programs? What types of courses do they prefer when they go back to school? How will universities and colleges have to modify their programs if they want to attract older students? List and describe the major educational alternatives that are available to older people today.

7. What trends have emerged in the use of computers by seniors? Describe the uses seniors typically make of the Internet. How has seniors' use of the Internet changed in the past few years? How has home computer use benefited older people?

8. Summarize the major types of activities that lead to increased life satisfaction in later life. Why does volunteer work, in particular, lead to high life satisfaction?

KEY TERMS

active leisure lifestyle (p. 251)
Canadian Executive Service Organization (CESO) (p. 263)
contractors (p. 249)
expanders (p. 250)
gero-transcendence (p. 253)
Institutes for Learning in Retirement (ILRs) or Lifelong Learning Institutes (LLIs) (p. 257)
Road Scholar (p. 256)
self-efficacy (p. 250)
structural lag (p. 263)
weak social ties (p. 258)

CHAPTER 11

HOUSING AND TRANSPORTATION

Flashon Studio/Shutterstock

LEARNING OBJECTIVES

After reading this chapter, you will

LO1 Be able to explain the ecological model of housing.

LO2 Understand the difference between living arrangements and housing options and know the major housing options for seniors.

LO3 Be able to compare the types of housing suitable for seniors at different stages of their lives.

LO4 Appreciate the importance of home adaptation to seniors' feeling of well-being and quality of life.

LO5 See how supportive and enriched housing meshes with the healthcare system.

LO6 Know about alternative ideas in housing, including supports for homeless seniors.

LO7 Be able to compare seniors' interest in the use of public transportation and private transportation.

LO8 Be able to describe some new approaches to meeting seniors' transportation needs.

LO9 Be able to describe the development of age-friendly communities in Canada and the world-wide movement toward age-friendly cities.

INTRODUCTION

Beatrice, age 78, and her husband, Wes, age 83, live in their own home—a one-storey brick house on a quiet residential street. They have lived in this same house for more than 50 years—all of their married life. They raised two children here, a son who now lives on his own in the same city and a daughter who lives about three hours away with her husband and two children. Although Wes has some difficulty getting around, he continues to drive—but only in good weather and only short distances. Bea and Wes live close to a grocery store, a drugstore, their doctor's office, and a bus stop. In good weather, Bea walks for exercise around her neighbourhood. On summer evenings, she and Wes sit on their front porch, watching children play and talking to neighbours out for their evening stroll.

Bea and Wes are known to everyone on the street. But now their children have become concerned about them remaining in their house. At a recent family gathering, their son and daughter brought up the issue of Bea and Wes selling their house and moving in with them. "Mom, Dad," their son said, "Sis and I have been thinking. You don't need a house this big anymore. It requires too much upkeep. You have stairs to cope with when you use the basement laundry room. And you have the yard to mow in the summer and the driveway to shovel in the winter. It is too much for you now. Why not move in with us? You could live half of the year with each of us so you wouldn't have to worry about being a burden on anyone."

"We knew what they were planning," Bea says, "so we were ready. 'This is our house and our home,' I told them. 'We own it. We paid for it. We are happy and comfortable here. And this is where we're going to stay for as long as we possibly can.'"

Beatrice and Wes's house gives them more than just a place to live; it gives meaning to their life. It connects them to friends on the street and to a lifetime of memories. The wall over the TV, for example, holds vacation pictures from trips they took over the years—as a couple, and as a family. In the dining room, the bookshelves Wes built are filled with pictures of their children and grandchildren and their collection of travel souvenirs. Their home connects them to a life—and a neighbourhood— that is familiar, secure, and comfortable

A home allows older people like Beatrice and Wes to feel more independent. Home also means security, comfort, and familiarity. It offers privacy and control. In a home, personal routines and important celebrations become part of the fabric of daily life. For many older people, home is intricately tied to treasured possessions and cherished memories of an earlier life—children growing up or the

early years of marriage. This is often particularly true in widowhood. "I just love it here...." a widowed woman said of the house she and her husband had built together years before (Shenk, Kuwahara, & Zablotsky, 2004, p. 165). For another widowed woman her long-time home "contains many memories and much love" (p. 167).

Not all older people need or want to live in a single-family house. Some older people live in apartments; others live with their children; still others live in supportive or enriched housing (where they can get help with meals and cleaning); and some live in garden suites (portable, self-contained dwellings built beside a family member's permanent home). The kind of housing that an older person needs and can afford depends on their health, marital status, income, and ability.

Canada's housing system today allows older people many choices about where to live. Housing options include private houses, apartments, retirement communities, independent-living lodges, assisted-living facilities, and long-term care homes. All of these housing options

© Stuart Monk/iStockPhoto

Owning a home requires the most ability to manage the environment. Home repairs and maintenance require know-how and physical strength. For this reason, couples tend to live in single-family homes. Widowed and single older women opt for a less-demanding housing option, like apartment living.

have a place in the housing market. Yet not all older people have equal access to these choices—either financially or geographically.

This chapter will look at (1) the housing options available to older people, (2) the programs and policies that exist in Canada to help older people meet their housing needs, and (3) transportation systems that enable older people to keep in touch with their community and use the resources available to them.

AN ECOLOGICAL MODEL OF HOUSING

Lawton and Nahemow (1973) created an **ecological model** that describes the relationship between the older person and his or her environment. Perry, Andersen, and

---

ecological model the Lawton-Nahemow model of interaction between the individual and the environment that holds that a person's ability and the demands of the environment influence that person's life satisfaction and ability to function

Kaplan (2013, p.76) called this one of the key "foundational theories" in the study of seniors' housing. The Lawton–Nahemow model describes the interrelation of two variables: individual capability (competence) and the demands of the environment (**environmental press**). Lawton and Nahemow define capability as "the aggregate of a person's abilities, including health, psychological adjustment, and intelligence." They define environmental demand as "environmental forces that, combined with need, lead a person to make a response" (p. 659).

People feel the most comfortable when their capability matches the demands of the environment and they can fulfill their needs. Too great or too little environmental demand leads to a decreased feeling of well-being and a maladaptive response. A healthy person in a hospital bed, for example, will feel bored and lethargic because the environment demands too little. A person recovering from a stroke may feel fatigued after a 10-minute conversation because the conversation demands too much. The

---

environmental press the demands of the environment on a person

---

EXHIBIT 11.1 *Seniors' Housing: Adding Up the Senior Population, 2011*

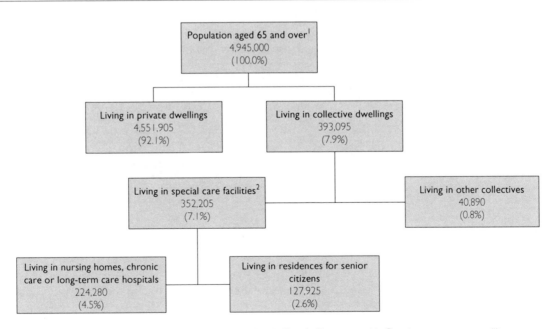

1. Includes all individuals living in private or collective dwellings in Canada. Persons outside Canada on government, military or diplomatic postings are not included.
2. Nursing homes, chronic care, long-term care hospitals and residences for senior citizens.

Note that the large majority of seniors (92.1 percent) live in private dwellings in the community. Only a small percentage of older people live in a collective dwelling (7.9 percent) and an even smaller percentage live in a nursing home or similar dwelling (4.5 percent). The likelihood of living in a collective dwelling increases with age.

Source: Statistics Canada. Living arrangements of seniors. *Census in Brief.* Box 2, p. 7. (2012). Retrieved from http://www12.statcan.gc.ca/census-recensement/2011/as-sa/98-312-x/98-312-x2011003_4-eng.pdf. Reproduced and distributed on an "as is" basis with the permission of Statistics Canada.

EXHIBIT 11.2   *The Lawton-Nahemow Ecological Model*

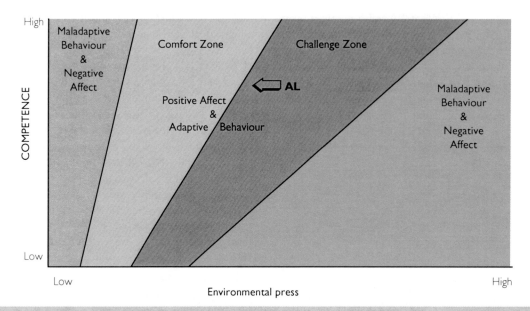

The Lawton-Nahemow ecological model states that "when a person of a given level of competence behaves in an environment of a given press level," the result could be placed on a chart like the one shown here (Lawton, 1980, p. 11). The chart shows the results of the fit between a person's competence and environmental press in terms of the person's behaviour and affect (feeling). The model shows that varied combinations of competence and press can lead to adaptive behaviour and positive affect. Likewise, the model shows that improvement in a person-environment fit can take place in three ways: the person can move to or create a less-demanding environment; the person can improve his or her competence; or the person can do both. The chart also illustrates the following points:

1.   The mid-point of the chart (AL) represents average press at a given level of competence. To the immediate left of the mid-point is the "Comfort Zone," where a person feels most at ease.

2.   As the press increases, adaptation takes place until the press goes beyond the person's ability to adapt (the right diagonal).

3.   If the environmental press decreases below the adaptation level, a person will feel bored and anxious (the left diagonal).

4.   The "Challenge Zone" represents the points where press encourages the maximum use of a person's ability.

5.   The greater the competence, the greater the adaptive ability; the lower the competence, the lower the adaptive ability.

6.   No matter how high the level of competence, at some level of press the person will lose the ability to adapt. And no matter how low the level of competence, the person still has some adaptive ability.

7.   A person with low competence can be easily upset by even a small increase in press. But a person with low competence can benefit from even a small improvement in the environment (Lawton, 1980).

Sources: M.P. Lawton and L. Nahemow, "Ecology and the Aging Process," in C. Eisdorfer and M.P. Lawton, eds., *Psychology of Adult Development and Aging* (1973). Washington: American Psychological Association. Copyright © 1973 by the American Psychological Association. Reprinted with permission.

Lawton-Nahemow model says that people try to find a comfortable fit between what they can do and what they need to do to meet their needs.

Parmelee and Lawton (1990) updated the person-environment model. This revised model redefines the competence dimension as "autonomy" and redefines the environmental press dimension as "security." An autonomous person (one with high competence) can pursue goals with his or her own resources. This person has freedom of choice and action. If a person has some disability, a secure environment (one with little press) can help that person achieve his or her goals. A secure environment offers dependable physical and social resources.

Autonomy and security "form a dialectic that lies at the heart of person-environment relations in late life" (p. 466). An increase in security—for example, a move to a nursing home—puts limits on a person's autonomy. Likewise, greater autonomy, such as driving a car, entails some risk.

Housing and transportation should maximize autonomy, but provide enough security for a feeling of comfort. Loss of a spouse, changes in a person's informal supports, and illness may all lead to changes in a person's autonomy. And this in turn may lead to changes in housing needs. Some people will need help in order to feel secure. Help can include home maintenance, financial aid, and changes that adapt the environment to fit the person's level of autonomy. Housing options offer different balances between autonomy and security. The most suitable choice will depend on the older person's ability, which will also change over time.

The current approach to housing for older people in Canada focuses on **aging in place** (Federal/Provincial, 2012; Government of Canada, 2014a). This policy attempts to provide older people with environmental, social, and economic supports so they can stay in their own homes as they age. Older people, especially those in cities, express a desire to age in place. Older people who live in suburban or rural settings find it more difficult to age in place unless they have access to social services. Planners may need to provide special transportation and services for suburban and rural seniors (Canada Mortgage and Housing Corporation, 2008a).

The philosophy of aging in place responds to many older people's desire to stay out of alternative seniors' housing. Salomon (2010) reports that in a 2005 study, 89 percent of people age 50 and over said they wanted to stay in their homes "indefinitely." If that proved impossible, 85 percent said they wanted to stay in their local community as long as possible. Other studies support this finding (Canada Mortgage and Housing Corporation, 2015c). A survey of seniors' housing preferences in Atlantic Canada found that 34 percent of respondents said, "I want to stay where I am living now" (Weeks et al., 2013, p. 83). For many older people "aging in place means any alternative to moving to a long-term care facility (Canada Mortgage and Housing Corporation, 2015c).

This chapter uses the ecological model to look at the housing and transportation options that exist for older people. An ideal housing system would allow people to match their ability to the environment's demands. It would help them to stay where they are as long as they want to stay there, and it would allow a smooth movement from one setting to another when a change in a person's ability or needs makes a move necessary.

TIME TO REVIEW

State two benefits of the ecological model of seniors' housing.

What does the Lawton and Nahemow model mean by "person-environment fit?"

Give some reasons older people prefer to age in place.

What two ways can people adapt to a situation to improve their "person-environment fit?"

aging in place older people living into late old age in the same place they lived in their middle years

LIVING ARRANGEMENTS

An older person's living arrangement can influence his or her quality of life and well-being. The term *living arrangements* refers to the type of household a person lives in. Living arrangements can include living in an institution; living with a spouse, with grown children, with relatives or non-relatives; or living alone. Older Canadians live in all of these arrangements, but the proportion of people in each type of accommodation differs by age and gender.

Married or common-law couples, who live without children, comprise almost half (47.3 percent) of all senior households. Those who live alone make up 42.7 percent of senior households. About 9 percent of senior couples live with their children or grandchildren (Statistics Canada, 2012l). A small percentage of older adults live with other relatives or non-relatives (Canada Mortgage and Housing Corporation, 2010a).

Three-generation households make up only a small percentage of all households in Canada. Many three-generation households are immigrant households. For example, in a study of older South Asian immigrants in Edmonton, compared with older men, unmarried older women tended to live in a three-generation household (Canada Mortgage and Housing Corporation, 2015c; Ng, Northcott, & Abu-Laban, 2007). Lee and Edmonston (2014) said, "traditional cultural values among some groups [e.g., non-Europeans], particularly immigrants, may translate into a preference for sharing living arrangements with relatives and even non-relatives...." (p. 362).

Older people who live with adult children do so for reasons related to their own needs or the needs of their children. For example, some older people move in with their children to get support and assistance. This can take place after a spouse's death, the loss of a driver's licence, or because of declining health. In other cases, older people live with their children to provide care for a grandchild, or to help an adult child make ends meet. Still, over the past 50 years in Canada, more older people and a greater proportion of older people live on their own in the community. Better incomes among seniors, better health in old age, and more people living into old age as a married couple in part explain this trend. Also, seniors today prefer independent living.

Statistics Canada (2012l) reported that in 2011, 16 percent of men age 65 and over lived alone, compared with 31.5 percent of women in this age group. For those age 85 and over, 21.8 percent of men and 36.6 percent of women lived alone. These figures show that a man will typically live in a family setting throughout his life, but a woman will likely live alone at some point in her later years. This means that men and women have different housing needs as they age.

In 2011, about 7.1 percent of Canadian seniors lived in long-term care institutions or **collective dwellings** (often called *special care facilities*) (Statistics Canada, 2012l). But with increasing age, the likelihood of a person entering an institution increases significantly, particularly for women. So, while about 1 percent of seniors age 65 to 69 live in institutions, this rises to 29.6 percent of seniors age 85 and over (Statistics Canada, 2012l). People age 75 and over make up more than half (51.6 percent) of the people in collective dwellings in Canada. And women make up a large majority of people in collective dwellings—70.4 percent of people age 65 and over and 73.4 percent of people age 75 and over (Canada Mortgage and Housing Corporation, 2011a).

The Decision to Live Alone

Senior women show the greatest tendency to live alone. Three things explain this trend toward women living alone. First, women tend to outlive men, leaving many women widowed in old age. For example, only 11 percent of senior men, compared with 42 percent of senior women, were widowed. And, compared with widowed men, fewer widowed women remarry (Turcotte & Schellenberg, 2007). Second, better government pension plans and subsidized housing make living alone in a private household a viable option for more women today. Community-based healthcare supports also make it possible for older women with health problems to stay in their own homes, rather than move to seniors' care facility.

Third, attitudes and values explains this trend. Most older people say they would rather not live with their children; they prefer the privacy and independence that come with living alone. Widowed women who live alone sometimes benefit from the support of children and grandchildren who live nearby. They also benefit from close connections to friends and neighbours. But most children and their elderly parents today share what Rosenmayr and Kockeis (1963) called "**intimacy at a distance.**"

Parents and children visit each other, help each other, and keep in touch by phone and email, but most do not live together.

This trend toward living alone, particularly among older women, has policy implications. For example, 38 percent of seniors who live alone report trouble affording their housing. Other people who live alone report health problems and isolation. The Canada Mortgage and Housing Corporation (CMHC) (2006a) said many seniors have a **core housing need**. A person has a core housing need if the housing is too small or in poor repair, or if the household spends more than 30 percent of its total income on housing. The CMHC (2010a) reported that among seniors who maintain a household, 8.2 percent of senior men and 22.5 percent of senior women have a core housing need. Among seniors who live alone, nearly a quarter of men and more than a quarter of women (22.5 percent of men and 25.4 percent of women) have a core housing need. Low incomes for senior men and women who live alone lead to core housing need.

Unmarried older people also have smaller support networks than married people, and they rely more on formal healthcare services (such as homecare) than do married couples. Those who live alone may also neglect their health. Single older people who live alone need suitable apartment housing and better public transportation. Many older people who live alone will need housing alternatives such as supportive housing and home-sharing programs.

TIME TO REVIEW

What do gerontologists mean by "living arrangements?"

What challenges are faced by older people who live alone?

What advantages do some older people see in living alone?

Think about the interrelationship of living alone, widowhood, being female, and having low income. What social conditions lead to the tendency for older women to live alone on low income?

---

intimacy at a distance the choice of many older people to live near, but not with, their children

core housing need exists when the housing is too small or in poor repair or the household spends more than 30 percent of its total income on housing

---

collective dwellings these include healthcare facilities; also refers to long-term care institutions

TYPES OF HOUSING

Single-Family Houses

The majority of Canadian families with a head age 65 or older owned their own home (76 percent of people age 65 to 74 and 71 percent of people age 75 and over). And the large majority of these families have no mortgage—71.3 percent of 65- to 74-year-olds and 82.6 percent of people age 75 to 84 (Canada Mortgage and Housing Corporation, 2015c, 2015d). Most homeowners want to stay in their own homes after they retire.

Older homeowners stay put for a number of reasons. First, they enjoy the comfort and familiarity of their homes. Second, selling a home may create an increase in taxes because of an increase in a person's liquid assets. Third, increased liquid assets may make a person ineligible for certain health or income supports. Finally, home ownership (with a paid-up mortgage) can increase household income by 10 to 13 percent for people age 60 to 69. For people age 70 and over, it can increase income by 12 to 15 percent. For many people, staying in their homes makes good financial sense (Brown, Hou, & Lafrance, 2010). Beyond the financial gain, Brown and colleagues said, home ownership provides "an important source of well-being for retirement-age households" (p. 6).

Older men, more often than older women, tend to live in single-family houses (Richards & Rankaduwa, 2008). A woman often has to move out of a single-family home as she ages. First, when her husband dies, she may

have less money to spend on housing. Increased heating costs, maintenance, and taxes can all force a woman to sell her home and move into an apartment. "If I had the money, I would gladly stay here for the rest of my days," a woman in Prince Edward Island said, "but now that he's gone it's going to be a burden" (Hamilton & Brehaut, 1992, p. 19). Another woman said, "I don't heat all the house in the winter. I close all but one bedroom in the winter time and the bathroom. And I don't heat my dining room ... because your oil is so expensive and can't heat it all" (p. 21).

Second, older women give up their homes because they tend to know less about how to care for a home. Older women say they lack knowledge about repairs, lack experience hiring tradespeople, and can't afford to hire people to do the work.

Even though the majority of people prefer to age in place, they do perceive barriers to growing old in their own home. The cost of housing, maintenance, and housing design (e.g., a stairway in a two-storey home) can all create barriers to aging in place.

Compared with people under age 65, seniors tend to downsize when they move. They also tend to move from a house to an apartment or condominium (Canada Mortgage and Housing Corporation, 2011b). Older seniors (those age 85 and over) tend to favour apartments over houses. They choose apartment living to lower maintenance costs and reduce the effort it takes to maintain a single-family home.

EXHIBIT 11.3 *Housing Tenure by Age of Primary Household Maintainer, Canada, 2011*

Age Category	Owners	Owners without Mortgage[*]	Renters
44 years and under	58%	14%	41%
44–54	75%	31%	25%
55–64	77%	53%	23%
65–74	76%	71%	24%
75+	71%	83%	29%
Total	69%	42%	31%

[*]As a percentage of owner households whose mortgage status is known.
Note: Numbers may not add to 100 percent due to rounding.

Home ownership increases to age 55 to 64. It then drops with each older age group. The proportion of people who rent housing shows the opposite trend. The proportion of renters increases from ages 55 to 64 on. Still, the large majority of people age 45 and over own their own homes. And high proportions of those with homes in the oldest age groups live without a mortgage (83 percent for those age 75 and over). This adds to their annual income, since they live rent-free in their own homes. Homeownership in later life makes good financial sense. And, as long as a person can maintain their home, it adds to their sense of well-being.

Source: CMHC (Canada Mortgage and Housing Corporation). Housing for older Canadians—The definitive guide to the over-55 market. Volume 1, *Understanding the Market*, Table 14, p. 21. (2015). Retrieved from http://www.cmhc-schl.gc.ca/odpub/pdf/67514.pdf. Original source: Statistics Canada, *National Household Survey*.

EXHIBIT 11.4   *Structure Type by Age of Primary Household Maintainer,* Canada, 2011*

Dwelling Type	Age		
	55 to 64	65 to 74	75+
Single detached	62%	59%	52%
Apartment 5+ storeys	7%	10%	15%
Apartment < 5 storeys	14%	16%	19%

*Includes all households, regardless of tenure

Note that the proportion of people who live in a single detached home decreases with each older age group (although it remains high even into later old age). Note also that apartment dwelling increases with each older age group. For high-rise apartment complexes, the proportion more than doubles (from 7 percent to 15 percent) from the youngest to the oldest age group.

These trends reflect the greater maintenance demands of single detached household living and in some cases, the greater demands of the physical household structure itself (e.g., stairways in a two-storey house). As the environmental press increases with age, people tend to move to less-demanding apartment living.

Source: CMHC (Canada Mortgage and Housing Corporation). Housing for older Canadians—The definitive guide to the over-55 market. Volume 1, *Understanding the Market*, Table 14, p. 21. (2015). Retrieved from http://www.cmhc-schl.gc.ca/odpub/pdf/67514.pdf. Original source: Statistics Canada, *National Household Survey*.

Tax and Home Maintenance Programs

Older homeowners without mortgages live rent-free, so they should have the most financial assets and they should have the least trouble paying for housing; however, many older people have trouble maintaining their homes. They own large, older houses—most of them single-family, detached—that cost a high proportion of the owner's income to heat and maintain.

The federal government and the provinces help older homeowners through grants, loans, and tax rebates. British Columbia, for example, allows seniors who have lived in the province for at least one year to defer payment of property taxes until they sell their home. At that time, they pay the outstanding taxes with interest (at below-market rates) from the money they get for their home (Government of British Columbia, 2012).

The federal government's **Residential Rehabilitation Assistance Program (RRAP)** offers loans to homeowners of up to $16,000 for people who live in southern Canada and $24,000 for people who live in far northern areas. Landlords can receive between $24,000 and $36,000, depending on a house's location. These loans help homeowners and landlords improve run-down housing. The government will forgive these loans if an owner remains in the home during the "loan forgiveness period" (which can be up to five years) and if a landlord does not increase rent after repairs have been completed (Canada Mortgage

and Housing Corporation, 2013a). This program also provides forgivable loans to convert existing housing into self-contained units. These suites provide housing for low-income seniors or adults with disabilities.

The government also grants forgivable loans to landlords and homeowners to adapt a building to seniors' needs. The loans cover costs up to $3,500. Improvements include additional handrails, lever handles on doors, bathtub grab bars and seats, walk-in showers, and easy-to-reach storage areas. Canada Mortgage and Housing Corporation (2013b) calls this the Home Adaptations for Seniors' Independence (HASI) program. Some provinces also sponsor home repair programs that offer low-interest and forgivable loans to low-income older people. Many provinces also offer older people a rebate or tax credit on school property tax. Programs tend to focus on the neediest cases and on people with health or safety needs. Alternative types of home ownership are also available that can help make housing more affordable for seniors in Canada.

Home Adaptation

Studies show that the proportion of people with disabilities increases with age. Also, the number of disabilities and the severity of disabilities increase with age (Canada Mortgage and Housing Corporation, 2010b). Most older people in private households report some limitations in mobility (walking and carrying) and agility (bending and stretching). Because climbing stairs can become difficult, some people close off the upstairs of their home and live only in the downstairs rooms (others move to housing with only one floor).

Residential Rehabilitation Assistance Program (RRAP) a federal government program offering loans to low-income people to help them improve run-down housing

People who want to age in place may need to adapt their current housing to support independent living. Sometimes a simple change makes a difference. For example, a person can arrange the furniture so that he or she can use a wall for support when walking. Many people add night lights, non-skid strips in the bathtub, and brighter light bulbs. The Canada Mortgage and Housing Corporation (2011c) studied the use of "smart" grab bars for bathtubs. They provide visual and sound cues to users. The study found that, compared with a control group with standard grab bars, seniors who had "smart" grab bars in their homes tended to use them more often. The use of grab bars in tubs could save many seniors from injury.

A study conducted in Ottawa looked at the use of a magnetic "smart voice" fridge door sensor. The sensor lets the senior know that the fridge door has been left open after a pre-programmed interval. The sensor helps prevent food spoilage. It can also alert a remote monitoring site to unusual patterns of behaviour (e.g., a fridge door left open or not opened at all for a long time). This can signal a health problem that needs attention (Canada Mortgage and Housing Corporation, 2011d). This and other "smart" devices will help seniors live safely and independently in the future. Satariano, Scharlach, and Lindeman (2014) reviewed the literature on technological devices for seniors. They reported on software that supports improved health practices, mobile devices that facilitate walking, and assistive devices that help with cooking and cleaning.

But aging in place may entail more extreme changes as people age and their physical conditions change. Sometimes a home will need professional remodelling. Kitchens and bathrooms, for example, may need adaptation to make them accessible (Canada Mortgage and Housing Corporation, 2011e). Home modification can allow people to stay in their homes into late old age. This seems like an increasingly popular way to help older people stay independent (Pynoos, Caraviello, & Cicero, 2009).

Canada Mortgage and Housing Corporation said that private and non-profit housing companies have responded to older people's needs. Housing adaptation now takes many forms. **Universal design**, for example, aims to serve people of all ages. Designers use lever door handles, low-threshold tubs, and temperature limits on hot water tanks to make life easier and safer for older people. These features also meet the needs of children and people with disabilities. Companies use two strategies to adapt homes for older people (Canada Mortgage and Housing Corporation, 2008b): "first, adding assistive devices and other technical equipment and second, modifying rooms and areas such as hallways and entrances" (p. 1).

Housing adaptations can keep a senior in touch with friends and relatives. Older friends, for example, may themselves have mobility challenges. **Visitability** applies only to the first floor of a single-family home. It requires that an older resident or visitor with a disability be able to move barrier-free within the first floor of a single-family house. Pynoos, Cicero, and Nishita (2010; also Canada Mortgage and Housing Corporation, 2011e) listed four features of visitability: "a zero-step entrance, interior doors with a minimum width of 32 inches, an accessible route inside the house, and a half bathroom on the first floor" (p. 332). Visitability provides a welcoming environment for guests who may have mobility limitations. Modifying a home for visitability can cost less than a major home modification. And it can provide the older person with much needed social contact.

Lifespan housing, an approach begun in Norway, puts all essential rooms (the living room, dining room, kitchen, and bathroom) on the ground floor. The United States calls it "universal housing," and the United Kingdom refers to it as "Lifetime Homes." Canada uses the term **FlexHousing** (Canada Mortgage and Housing Corporation, 2008c). This type of housing has no thresholds or steps, provides easy access to all rooms of the house, and can adapt to the needs of a person in a wheelchair. Details include easy-to-reach light switches and sockets, accessible furniture, non-slip flooring, and kitchen cabinets and appliances that can move up and down on a wall bracket as needed.

Reverse Mortgages

Some older homeowners are asset-rich but cash-poor. A person may have $150,000 in equity in his or her home but be unable to pay the gas or water bill. A reverse mortgage allows older homeowners to draw on 20 percent to 30 percent of the equity in their home (Canada Mortgage and Housing Corporation, 2008d). They can use this

---

universal design housing adaptations that serve people of all ages; designers use lever door handles, low-threshold tubs, and temperature limits on hot water tanks to improve housing for older people, as well as children and those with disabilities

visitability requires that an older resident or visitor with a disability be able to move barrier-free within the first floor of a single-family house

FlexHousing a housing concept that designers and builders use to make future changes in housing easy and affordable in order to meet the changing needs of people as they age

money for daily expenses, home repairs, or other needs. Some people choose this option to cover sudden medical expenses or to help a younger family member. Usually the loan and interest on the loan do not have to be repaid until the homeowner sells the house or dies.

Several types of reverse mortgages exist. The most common plan is called the **reverse annuity mortgage (RAM)**. In this plan, an older person uses the house to secure a loan from a bank. The person then buys a lifetime annuity from an insurance company with the loan. The insurance company pays the bank interest on the loan and pays the older person a set amount for life. The older person can stay in the home as long as he or she wants. The bank takes over the house when the last survivor of a couple dies. This plan has at least one major limitation: the interest payments to the bank will increase if interest rates rise, thus reducing the older person's income.

Not everyone will benefit from a reverse mortgage. In one model, for example, a reverse mortgage can add interest charges of 25 percent to 40 percent to the original loan. A $55,000 loan could pay a 70-year-old single man almost $6,000 per year as an annuity (a yearly payment for life). This would amount to about $90,000 over 15 years. But at 11 percent interest, the RAM over 15 years would produce a debt of just over $274,000. The loan company would deduct this money from the sale of the house. In other words, the RAM would cost $274,000 less the $90,000 paid out, or about $184,000.

Some people will agree to this cost, choosing to have more money now. Other people will find the cost too high and may want to leave the full value of their home to their children. Low interest rates today and increased home equity could make RAMs more attractive. Also, a RAM can help a person or couple spend less of their retirement savings. Low returns on investment income push people toward a reverse mortgage. Mclister (2015), reporting for *The Globe and Mail*, predicted that "reverse mortgages will become a vital fallback for hundreds of thousands of Canadians in decades to come ... one in ten senior homeowners may rely on a reverse mortgage within a decade."

Still, many financial advisers believe that reverse mortgages should be used only as a last resort. People need to fully understand the benefits and the costs of RAMs so that they can make informed decisions (Attfield, 2015).

reverse annuity mortgage (RAM) a type of reverse mortgage whereby a person buys a life annuity and gets an income while living in the home; the mortgage company takes over the house when the person dies

Why do older people prefer to live in single-family homes?

What are the challenges single-family homeowners face?

Why do some people have to move out of their homes as they age?

What financial supports and mortgage arrangements can help people stay in their single-family homes longer?

What structural changes to a home can help a person stay in a single-family home?

Apartment Living

Apartment living tends to follow a U-shaped path over time. Adults age 25 and under tend to rent apartments. Then the rental rate drops in middle age and rises again in later life (after age 60 or so) (Canada Mortgage and Housing Corporation, 2006b). The CMHC (2010a) reported that in 2006, 43.4 percent of seniors who lived in senior-led households lived in multiple dwellings (including apartments, semi-detached houses, row houses, and apartments in duplexes). This figure increased to 48.3 percent among people age 75 and over. Older people often choose to move into an apartment when they can no longer care for a house, or when they need improved accessibility because of mobility limitations.

People with good incomes can choose from a wide range of apartments: a high-rise or a low-rise, a two-bedroom suite with a balcony and a view, or an apartment near a bus route and shopping. Begg (2011) says Baby Boomers will want more services and higher quality amenities (e.g., movie rooms, a swimming pool, a gym).

Some older renters, however, have fewer options. Many people move to rental housing because they have low incomes. Canada Mortgage and Housing Corporation (2010a) reported that 31.4 percent of senior renters had a core housing need. Most people with housing affordability problems received government payments as their main source of income. These older people need rent support to ease the burden of housing costs.

Most of the provinces, along with the federal government, offer aid to renters in low-income housing. These programs keep a person's rent at or below 30 percent of his or her income. Some provinces offer **shelter allowances** to older people. British Columbia, for example, sponsors Shelter Aid for Elderly Renters

shelter allowances government allowances that subsidize the person, not the housing project, and allow older people to choose their own apartment

(SAFER), a program that provides help with rent to low- and middle-income seniors age 60 and older (BC Housing, 2008). Shelter allowances subsidize the person, not the housing project. They allow older people to choose their own apartment from those available in the marketplace. This policy frees people from having to move into government housing.

Supportive and Enriched Housing

Most provinces have built supportive housing. Supportive housing goes by other names: retirement villages and hostels (Australia), sheltered housing (United Kingdom), and assisted living (United States). Canada Mortgage and Housing Corporation defines **supportive housing** as "a range of housing options designed to accommodate the needs of seniors through design features, housing management, and access to support services." Supportive housing encompasses many and varied types of housing. It provides a secure, safe, and home-like environment. It offers support services (i.e., housekeeping, meals, etc.) and social and recreational activities. Government, non-profit organizations, and the private sector all provide supportive housing.

One end of the "supportive housing" continuum gives people more social and healthcare support than they get in a normal apartment building. These dwellings suit people who need minimal to moderate support services such as provision of meals, housekeeping, laundry service, monitoring, and emergency response. These support services allow the older person to live independently.

The other end of the continuum includes housing that supports people who otherwise would need nursing home care. This type of supportive housing may include a health clinic on site, 24-hour on-site emergency response, and help with bathing, dressing, and toileting. A study in Ontario estimates that 35 percent of people on a long-term care waiting list "could live in the community with appropriate community supports and an additional 45% could live in supportive housing with case managed services" (Lum et al., 2010, p. 2). Lum and colleagues found that "supportive housing made important contributions to the sustainability of the health care system by anticipating and managing health crises before they occurred, thereby reducing unnecessary hospital admissions, and the number of emergency (911) calls" (p. 3).

The Canada Mortgage and Housing Corporation (CMHC) (2015e) reported that 224,962 seniors lived

These two women share a meal together at home. Home sharing can help seniors with the cost of housing. It also provides single seniors with companionship and live-in support.

in 2,794 seniors' housing complexes in 2015. These settings—from suites to single rooms—offer a range of services including meals. The large majority (87 percent) of people in these settings need a minimum of care. The CMHC survey found that residences added services to attract tenants.

The most popular services desired by seniors included a "24-hour call bell service (95.4 percent), on-site nurse service (50.6 percent), transportation (43.2 percent), exercise rooms (40.4 percent), movie theatres (28.7 percent), on-site pharmacies (9.2 percent), and swimming pools (10.3 percent). A CMHC report said, "In order to appeal to the evolving needs of today's seniors, residences are offering a wide variety of services and amenities.... The key factor in today's market is that seniors are looking more for a lifestyle than just a place to live" (Ladurantaye, 2011).

Williams and Lum (2011) said that supportive housing can help seniors stay in good health and in their own homes. Supportive housing can divert people from nursing homes or hospital care "and may allow for more cost-effective use of resources" (p. 33). The researchers proposed this as a way to cope with the increased healthcare costs due to population aging.

The term **enriched housing** can apply to many types of housing. In Canada, it ranges from converted hotels that offer rooms and hot meals for single men, to campus-like settings with high- and low-rise housing and many levels of healthcare. Sometimes enrichment means only a lounge with a television set in an apartment building. More elaborate enriched housing includes lounges, shops,

---

supportive housing provided for people who need minimal to moderate care and use services such as homemaking, personal care, and social support programs

enriched housing provides services such as meals and cleaning services to help people live on their own

and, in some cases, clinics. Some buildings employ activity workers and program planners, who show films and organize exercise programs and field trips for residents.

Most enriched housing also includes communal facilities such as a dining room and laundry rooms. This type of housing provides social support services, safety, and a sense of community. Even something as simple as being able to see a natural landscape from the apartment window has health benefits for older people (e.g., lowering blood pressure and heart rate) (Tan & Brown, 2005).

At the other end of the supportive housing continuum are housing options and services designed for those with more significant care needs. This type of housing is often referred to as **assisted living**. It provides personal care services to frail seniors to help them live independently in the community. This type of supportive housing is well suited to older seniors (age 75 and over) with moderate to severe disabilities.

Supportive housing can take many forms, from bungalows to high-rise apartments. The CMHC says that supportive housing should have five characteristics: (1) it should look and feel residential; (2) the physical environment should support seniors' needs; (3) it should offer access to needed services; (4) management should have a progressive philosophy; and (5) it should offer choice at a reasonable cost. Supportive housing provides an option between living without supports and living in an institution.

Critics of enriched housing say that it can lead to early dependency by giving people too many services and that it attracts sick or less able people. But studies have found more benefits than drawbacks to this kind of housing. Early work by Lawton (1976) found that people in enriched housing reported high morale and high life satisfaction. He said that proper planning discourages dependence.

Enriched housing allows individuals to live on their own rather than in institutions. For example, an alarm system for each apartment can give residents a sense of security and can save a person's life in an emergency. And something as simple as "I'm okay" signs for doorknobs in apartment buildings encourages neighbourliness. Enriched housing offers an important alternative to people who need support but who do not need the high levels of care given in a nursing home or hospital.

For all its benefits, enriched housing can lead to unique problems. For example, the average age of residents increases over time as residents age in place. Some buildings that began with a mixture of age groups among residents 10 or 15 years ago now house a markedly older group, whose average age is 80 or older. This may compromise the self-government that exists in these buildings. Enriched housing complexes could become high-rise nursing homes over time.

Apartment housing comes in many packages: high-rise, low-rise, public, private, age-segregated, age-integrated, without services, or enriched with services. Older people as a group need this variety because their needs and abilities differ. They also need tax rebates, shelter allowances, and subsidized housing so that they can freely choose the housing that best suits their needs. Appropriate housing design can also help people stay in their apartments or homes even if they lose some abilities.

Housing in Rural Communities

Dandy and Bollman (2008) reported that 33 percent of older people in Canada live in "predominantly rural regions" (p. 3). Some communities serve as destinations for retirees (due to warmer weather or recreation opportunities). Other settings offer rural amenities such as a slower pace of life and a feeling of community. Still other communities grow older because people age in place. Rural areas not near a metro centre showed the fastest growth in their proportions of seniors (largely due to young people moving away).

Whatever the reason, these rural communities have an increased need for affordable housing with services and amenities. But, compared with a person in a city, a person in a rural setting often has fewer housing options. While rural regions have slightly lower costs for housing, they face higher home maintenance, utility, and transportation costs. Rural areas also vary in their proximity to urban centres and in the availability of adequate housing and social services (for example, healthcare services and home care support) (Canada Mortgage and Housing Corporation, 2011e).

While most older people in rural communities (82 percent) own their own home, the small number of older people in these communities limits the variety of housing options available. For example, few rental options exist in rural settings (Canada Mortgage and Housing Corporation, 2011e), and older people who rent their homes often face severe affordability problems.

While rural communities often have support programs and services for frail older people, they lack a

---

assisted living housing that provides personal care services and other supports to frail seniors to help them live independently in the community

range of options for older people who have varied needs for supports.

Keating, Swindle, and Fletcher (2011; also Chappell, Schroeder, & Gibbens, 2008) reported that caregivers in small isolated communities lack community supports such as respite care. These communities also lack places where caregivers can meet, they lack healthcare workers, and they lack public transportation. Overall, rural areas often lack home care services available to urban seniors. Sims-Gould and Martin-Matthews (2008) found that long distances, bad weather, poor road conditions, and high gasoline prices all challenge the delivery of home care services to rural seniors.

One home support worker told the researchers, "It's farther to drive, it's mostly gravel roads, I'm not charging mileage, and I'm thinking if the gas prices go up, I'm going to have to figure out a way to work out some, because I'm going over 40 kilometres to some." Another worker said, "[I]t is a challenge for me charging the same rate as the ones in town, because I just burn so much more gas, everything, going everywhere so" (p. 46).

Communities that age rapidly show some of the greatest shortages in healthcare services for older people. Keating and colleagues (2011) report the lack of availability and access to healthcare services. Rural seniors' homes sometimes lack electricity and running water (Sims-Gould & Martin-Matthews, 2008).

ALTERNATIVE IDEAS IN HOUSING

Garden Suites

Most older people do not want to move in with their children. The design of modern houses may explain part of the reason that older Canadians do not choose to live with their adult children. Most modern houses have no room for another kitchen, bedroom, or bathroom to accommodate an aging parent.

In Australia, the state of Victoria created a housing option for older people that overcomes the problems of modern house design. They call this alternative a **granny flat**. It consists of a portable modular cottage for a parent. The government arranges to move the cottage onto a son's or daughter's property, then the government connects the flat to the electricity, sewer, water, and telephone services of the house. When the older person dies or moves to a

nursing home, or if the family moves, the government takes the cottage away. This plan allows children to care for their parents as long as they can.

Canada developed a version of the granny flat known as the **garden suite**, sometimes called a "secondary suite." These units allow older Canadians to live near, but not with, their children (Canada Mortgage and Housing Corporation, 2014a). In Canada, a garden suite most often exists as a separate building on the adult child's property, although some families convert a garage to serve as a garden suite. This building sits in the backyard and uses the utilities attached to the adult child's home.

A CMHC survey (2008a) found that 23 percent of older homeowners (age 55 and older) would consider installing a garden suite on their property or creating an additional suite in their home to accommodate a family member. More than half of all older Canadians (44 percent of those age 55 and older) would consider living in such accommodations.

There are pros and cons to creating garden suites (Canada Mortgage and Housing Corporation, 2008c). Garden suites cost relatively little; they allow the older person to live independently in the community, with informal support nearby. They also allow an older homeowner to sell his or her house and free up money for living expenses. Garden suites may work best in rural areas where seniors have fewer housing options.

Garden suites need to overcome some barriers before they will gain general acceptance. Some locations put families through a lengthy approval process, and neighbours may object to a garden suite located in the backyard next door. Also, homes with little land make installation a challenge.

Garden suites will suit families only where the adult children own a home with the space to locate the building. When a family does agree to set up a garden suite, the family members—parents and children—need to talk about what they expect from one another. Still, garden suites offer a unique option to older people and their families. The CMHC (2011e) said garden suites "can make it possible for seniors who are interested in downsizing and in living very close to relatives to do so while still maintaining a high level of independence. They are therefore a form of housing that can create new options for seniors and their families and caregivers" (p. 119).

Garden suites and other innovative housing arrangements will lead to new family interdependencies and new challenges to family relations. What will happen if the

---

granny flat part of a house made into a self-contained unit for an elderly relative, or a small, portable cottage or dwelling erected in the garden of an adult child's house

garden suite garden suite a separate building on an adult child's property or part of the adult child's house made into a self-contained unit for an elderly relative; also known as a granny flat

older person's adult child separates from or divorces his or her spouse? What will happen if the adult child moves to another city? Studies of these options will have to show that they make social as well as financial sense, and trial projects can answer only some of these questions; longer-term studies will show whether garden suites can work in Canada.

Naturally Occurring Retirement Communities

The populations in some neighbourhoods and apartment buildings grow older as people age in place. Gerontologists call these **naturally occurring retirement communities (NORCs)**. People in these communities say they like living with their older neighbours. They say this keeps the neighbourhood peaceful and quiet, they share common interests with neighbours, and they find their neighbours friendly and helpful.

Some NORCs offer amenities that keep older people in place and attract others. For example, older people in inner-city neighbourhoods live near the churches, shops, and neighbours they've known for years. This makes the local community an important resource. Older minority group members especially value access to foods and cultural centres that serve their needs. Hwang (2008) found a strong preference for local amenities among Chinese and Korean Canadian seniors. Both groups enjoyed a sense of belonging in their neighbourhoods. Koreans found an "instant network" through their church. The Chinese found community resources through housing and services in Chinatown. Hwang concluded that the neighbourhood provided a support network that extended beyond the family.

Masotti and colleagues (2007; also Fiessel et al., 2013) said, "NORCs can develop in all communities" (p. 86). They can occur on a city block, in an apartment complex, in a group of single-family homes, or in a condominium community. Each NORC and its services respond to local community needs. Masotti et al. (2006, 2007) describe a "Healthy NORC." This type of community provides amenities that support healthy aging. Examples of health-producing amenities include safe places to walk and bicycle; clean, well-lit sidewalks and walking paths; parks that include things to see and do; and good public transport.

Fiessel and colleagues (2013) list five key features of a NORC: (1) coordination of healthcare services; (2) partnerships between residents and service providers, government, and local foundations; (3) responsiveness to seniors' needs; (4) senior governance and social support among members; and (5) filling service gaps.

The growth of the older population in Canada and the desire of older people to age in place will encourage more NORC development. Masotti and colleagues (2007) said we can expect NORCs to become an international phenomenon. They predicted continued growth in "both numbers and proportion of the population" (p. 86) in this housing arrangement.

Planned Retirement Communities

Most **planned retirement communities** come about when a developer builds and sells houses to healthy, active retirees. These communities supply health services, shopping centres, and recreation facilities. People who settle in these communities value the new homes, clean streets, easy access to shopping, and middle-class neighbours. The weather in some of these locations and the relaxed lifestyle appeal to people in these communities. Residents also look for safety and freedom from fear of crime. The new communities often have gates and guards, and teams of residents who watch out for strangers. They also have age restrictions that allow only people age 55 or older to move in.

Life Lease Housing

Life lease housing offers older individuals or couples a lifetime right to live in a housing unit. They neither own nor rent their unit. They have a leasehold interest in their unit defined by a contract.

The person or couple pays an upfront charge to join the community. The fee may reflect the age (life expectancy) of the person or couple or the potential resale value of the unit. A typical upfront cost comes to 50 percent to 90 percent of the cost of buying a similar unit for full value.

Life lease housing often refunds the entry fee when the owner moves out. The sponsor then resells the unit to another senior or senior couple. Life lease owners pay a monthly management and maintenance fee.

Life lease housing usually limits entry to seniors. This creates a community that some seniors prefer. Life lease housing also includes communal services and facilities such as lounges, workshops, and dining rooms. A life lease development in Windsor, Ontario, called Southwinds, for example, includes handicapped access (Canada Mortgage and Housing Corporation, 2012f).

---

naturally occurring retirement communities (NORCs) neighbourhoods that already have many older people; these communities can enhance the experience of current residents

planned retirement communities a developer builds and sells houses to healthy, active retirees; these communities supply health services, shopping centres, and recreation facilities

The CMHC noted that the terms and conditions of life lease housing can confuse buyers. In particular, the refund of the entry fee when a person moves or dies can vary from one housing complex to another. Some buildings will charge a relatively small upfront fee (e.g., 50 percent of the market value) but may pay no redemption at the end of the lease. Other buildings charge near market rates at entry but will pay back the full market value at the time the person leaves the unit (Canada Mortgage and Housing Corporation, 2012g).

A person may not fully understand the choice they make. And different people may prefer different options according to their financial circumstances. The CMHC (2012h) advises a person or couple to see a lawyer who understands this housing option before they purchase a unit.

The CMHC notes that life lease housing cannot meet the need for affordable senior housing. Life lease housing will serve only people who can afford the upfront cost (often funds from the sale of their home).

Continuing Care Retirement Communities

To protect against high long-term care costs, some older people have moved to continuing care retirement communities (CCRCs). "Continuing care retirement communities (CCRCs) or communities offering Life Care are designed to offer active seniors an independent life-style and a private home from which to enjoy it, regardless of future medical needs" (Seniorresource.com, 2010a). "This campus of care concept allows seniors to remain within one facility as the level of care required changes" (Canada Mortgage and Housing Corporation, 2011b, p. 4).

Residents sign a contract with the facility that guarantees them access to housing and defined types of care for the rest of their lives. Helpguide.org (2007) describes three typical contracts:

1. *Life care/extensive contract.* This type of contract assures the resident of unlimited nursing care at no added cost for as long as needed. This contract provides the most insurance—but at the highest cost.
2. *Modified/continuing care contract.* This type of contract provides long-term care or nursing care for a limited time. After that time, the resident pays the cost of care. This contract provides some security, and it costs less than the extensive contract.
3. *Fee-for-service contract.* This type of contract offers no prepaid care. The resident pays for long-term care services as needed. This contract provides no insurance against high long-term care costs in the future, but it costs the least at the start.

People in CCRCs live in private apartments that have kitchens, so residents can make their own meals. Some communities have common dining rooms where residents can eat if they choose. Most CCRCs provide transportation, fitness centres, and social activities. They also offer around-the-clock nursing care in a nursing home wing attached to the main building or in a separate building.

Fees for long-term care services vary, depending on the CCRC's entrance fee and monthly charges. Most communities charge high entrance fees; all charge a monthly fee for rent and some services. Continuing care retirement communities attract older-old people. The typical resident is a single woman around 80 years old. These people want the security of future nursing home care. Helpguide.org (2007) calls CCRCs "the most expensive long-term care solution available to seniors."

Still, there are also some risks associated with CCRCs. First, monthly payments can go up. Second, a person does not own the property. Third, the company that owns the community may go out of business. Older people can lose their investment and their housing if this happens.

In the future, more people will fit the profile of current CCRC residents (single women, 80 and older). They will want protection from crippling long-term care costs. But the high cost of entry into a CCRC will limit the number of people who can move to this type of housing. New types of CCRCs may emerge to meet the needs of a growing market. They may appear in more flexible forms with varied services. Potential residents will attempt to match a community with their assets, their needs, and their expectations about community life.

HOMELESSNESS

In an ideal world, a chapter on housing would not contain a section on homelessness. Homelessness should not exist for any age group. But it does. It affects young people, single people, families, and older people.

Homeless older people stand at the far end of the housing continuum. They often live on the street and use shelters for rest at night and some meals. Some homeless people live in rural communities, although homelessness in rural areas is less visible than in urban centres. Homeless people often experience "accelerated aging" due to poor nutrition, chronic illness, and exposure to weather (Waldbrook, 2013, p. 339). Researchers consider homeless people over age 50 as seniors.

continuing care retirement communities (CCRCs) allow seniors to remain in one facility if the level of required care changes

Waldbrook said that personal issues and systemic barriers lead to homelessness. Personal issues include mental illness, physical illness, unemployment, and family problems. Systemic barriers include a lack of affordable housing, lack of low-income subsidies and benefits, and unemployment. Sudden changes in income, housing, or employment can lead to homelessness in old age. Waldbrook surveyed and interviewed a small sample (N = 15) of formerly homeless women. The women reported a number of health conditions related to their homelessness. One woman (Marie) told Waldbrook, "I know for a fact that I've got chronic bronchitis from sleeping on the street in the winter ... I think it comes from having hypothermia and frostbite from sleeping outside in the wintertime" (p. 347).

Women also reported drug use, alcohol use, and chronic stress during their time on the street. Another woman (Lauren) told Waldbrook, "It's harder on women being homeless ... because women have to do some nasty things to get a roof over their head, ... Sometimes I had to sleep with men to stay with them.... And it's harder to stay on the streets, right? Like it's not nearly as safe" (p. 347). Some women in this study experienced homelessness early in life, others became homeless in old age. In some cases, homelessness worsened already existing problems.

Ploeg et al. (2008) studied a homeless intervention program in Ontario. Their study included 129 clients in the program. They found that half the clients were between 54 and 65 years of age. Half were over age 65. They found that the clients had chronic illnesses, mental health problems, and suffered from substance abuse. Homelessness creates stress and leads to a poor diet and untreated health problems. Homelessness also leads to lower life expectancy.

In a review of the literature, McDonald, Dergal, and Cleghorn (2007) reported that more older men than older women were homeless. Compared with women, older men become homeless earlier in life and so spend more years living on the street. This group includes people with drug addictions and mental illness.

A second group of homeless people became homeless after retirement. The recent recession and loss of jobs forced some older people into homelessness. People near the poverty line and on a fixed income may also fall into homelessness if rents increase. This group lacks the street smarts of long-term homeless people. This exposes them to danger from other residents in shelters and even more danger on the streets.

In a study of 68 older homeless adults in Toronto, McDonald, Dergal, and Cleghorn (2007) compared recent homeless older people (those homeless after the age of 50) with those who were homeless over a longer period of time (homeless before the age of 50). They found that (1) compared with women, more men were homeless; (2) more women than men became homeless after the age of 50; and (3) more than half of the homeless people were immigrants to Canada.

The long-term homeless, on average, became homeless at age 38; the recent homeless at age 57. The recent homeless identified their friends as their social support, while the long-term homeless were more likely to name social services providers as their social contacts. Further, compared with the recently homeless, long-term homeless older people found ways to reduce their presence on the street. This included using more social services and shelters.

Recently homeless older people used fewer services and noted barriers to healthcare service use. "It seems fairly clear," McDonald and her colleagues (2007) said, "that the housing issues vary between the two sub-groups and require different approaches. Certainly, affordable housing is needed to address homelessness in general, but we would argue that interventions to find housing for the recent older homeless should be swift and immediate and would be one of the first priorities of intervention in order to prevent entrenchment in street life" (p. 40).

Shelters for the homeless often don't meet the needs of older homeless people. For example, shelters cannot offer help with daily living activities or the need for bed rest. Also, many shelters cannot meet the needs of people with mobility problems. But the limited number of nursing home and hospital beds leaves shelters as the only option. Many homeless older people also exhibit antisocial behaviour (such as poor hygiene and the use of foul language) that makes it hard to move them to other care settings (Furlotte et al., 2012).

Supportive housing and assisted living programs sometimes serve homeless seniors. These programs provide a room, meal services, recreation, and healthcare programs. They do not offer 24-hour nursing care. The women in Waldbrook's study (2013) valued the support they received once they entered supportive housing. "I have support here," one woman (Maggie) said. "They [the staff] come with us for appointments if we need them. You'll never be alone in supportive housing" (p. 351).

Fairway Woods serves homeless older people in a 32-apartment housing project. The project, in suburban Langford, British Columbia, near Victoria, serves as a model of successful supportive housing for homeless seniors (Canada Mortgage and Housing Corporation, 2007). In 2006–2007, a study of the Fairway Woods site found that 75 percent of the tenants were men, most between the ages of 55 and 64. Tenants at Fairway Woods had previously lived in shelters, a detoxification facility, substandard housing, and other social housing projects. Most of the tenants had multiple physical and mental health problems and addictions.

The majority of the tenants rated their quality of life as good, and their living arrangements as good or excellent. Prior to living at Fairway Woods, many of the tenants said they felt "anxious," "angry," "isolated," and "stuck" most of the time. Since coming to Fairway Woods, they felt they lived more stable lives. While their problems had not all gone, they felt "relieved," "more secure," and "more confident." They also felt better able to cope with life (Canada Mortgage and Housing Corporation, 2007, p. 4).

The Government of Canada recognizes the need to eliminate or reduce homelessness among seniors (Newswire, 2015). The government created a Supporting Homeless Seniors Program to serve homeless and at-risk older people. The program works with the Salvation Army and other community organizations to ensure that homeless older people get CPP and OAS benefits. A Homelessness Partnering Strategy provides government support to 61 communities to prevent and reduce homelessness in Canada. The program includes support to Indigenous, rural, and remote communities.

Waldbrook (2013) said that changes in society—workforce restructuring, reductions in government assistance, and changes in the family—may lead to more homelessness for the Baby Boom generation. The increased numbers of older people in the years ahead will need social and housing supports that keep them off the streets.

The Future of Housing for Seniors

Housing in the future will need to meet the needs of a diverse older population. Some older people will live independently in the community, others will live with family members, still others will live in a variety of supportive housing designed to meet seniors' needs. People in rural settings and people in cities may need different housing solutions. People should be able to age in place, if they choose. But some people will need to move due to changes in health, marital status, and income as they age. Canada's older population needs a variety of options. These will range from single-family detached homes to long-term care facilities. The future will see a blending of housing and services to help older people live as independently as possible.

TIME TO REVIEW

What are some of the alternatives to single-home and normal apartment living that meet older people's unique needs?

What are some of the pros and cons of life lease community membership?

What types of settings lend themselves to a NORC?

What are some of the solutions to homelessness among the older population?

TRANSPORTATION

A home has to suit an older person's abilities and meet his or her needs, but a house or an apartment can become a prison if the older person cannot get to services, friends, and recreation. Transportation gives older people a sense of independence and control over their lives. It allows them to visit friends, attend cultural events, go shopping, and receive healthcare. A lack of transportation can lead to isolation, poor health, and decreased well-being (Wheatley, Carr, & Marottoli, 2014). Women age 85 and over listed transportation problems as "the second most common reason after health problems for not participating in more social, recreational, or group activities (24%). Transportation problems were mentioned by 10% of women aged 75 to 84" (Turcotte, 2012, p. 15).

Older people identify transportation as one of the primary issues that affects their quality of life. They feel that good public transportation can help them avoid loneliness and isolation. Those who live alone, the recently widowed, and people with chronic health problems all benefit from good public transportation. Older people with mobility problems require public transportation to access needed services. Rural, suburban, and urban older people have different transportation options and needs.

Public Transportation

Transportation studies in Canada report that the majority of older people have access to private or public transportation. In 2005, for example, 95 percent of women age 65 to 74 and 98 percent of men the same age had access to a vehicle or to public transportation. Even among seniors age 85 and older, 86 percent had access to a vehicle or public transit. Those who own a vehicle and have a driver's licence, or who can afford to take taxis, have an easier time meeting their transportation needs.

Few seniors use public transit as their main means of transportation. And studies project a future decline in the use of public transit among seniors (Freund & Vine, 2010).

Seniors who take public transportation often report that it does not meet their needs. Mercado and Newbold (2009) say that public transportation is "quite unpopular among the elderly." Among adult age groups "the elderly returned the biggest negative" response to public transportation (p. 4). People with a physical limitation show some of the strongest negative response to public transport. For all seniors, public transport lacks the "reliability, convenience, spontaneity, personal security and flexibility" of the private car (p. 13).

Public transit lacks design features that meet seniors' needs. Clear markings on the edges of stairs on buses and trains, for example, would make for safer entry and exit. And wider aisles would make public buses easier for everyone to use (Hunter-Zaworski, 2008). Hunter-Zaworski suggested handholds and non-slip floor surfaces. Many older people would benefit from transportation services that they could contact on demand, rather than on services that follow a set route and schedule.

Transit needs to be accessible as well as available. Older seniors find that steep steps, long walks to a bus or subway stop, or the challenge of getting on and off a bus all limit their use of public transport. Likewise some people find that bus drivers fail to lower their buses to help them get on board. Other bus drivers simply bypass someone with a walker. Mercado and Newbold (2009, p. 18) said that "in Ontario, where the largest number of elderly Canadians resides, less than 50% of the 55 public transit systems have accessible vehicles and some even have zero accessibility." Planners need to ensure that older people can get to and use transit in their neighbourhoods.

Compared with older men, older women tend to be more disadvantaged in their access to both private and public transportation. For example, Sleightholm and colleagues (2010) found that 79 percent of senior men drove a private vehicle but only 44 percent of women drove. Dupuis, Weiss, and Wolfson (2007) found that older women are three times more likely than older men to have unmet transportation needs. Older women in poor health and with few financial resources report the most transportation problems.

Rural and urban seniors have different transportation problems. Seniors in cities see good public transportation as a necessary link to social networks and recreational activities. They need convenient and safe bus stops and subway stations (Mercado & Newbold, 2009). They also need barrier-free transportation (e.g., buses without high steps, wheelchair access on trains, etc.). People in the suburbs face other problems. Rigid bus routes and schedules make it hard for older people in the suburbs to travel. In the winter, long waits for buses, icy sidewalks, or snow

mounds at bus stops keep people housebound. Rural areas often lack public transportation (Turcotte, 2012).

Alternative public transport programs in rural areas add an option to local bus routes. They include supplemental transportation programs and independent transport networks. They meet special mobility needs. They provide door-through-door service, escorts, and other types of personal support. These and other transport options fill in the gaps left by conventional public transport systems. Communities that offer a "family of services" will best meet the needs of the older population.

People in rural areas rely heavily on cars and trucks. Small towns often lack other forms of transport, and people often live far from friends and shopping. Although more rural seniors own a vehicle and drive, those without a car are particularly vulnerable to mobility problems and social isolation. "Outside cities," Turcotte (2012) said, "alternatives to the car are virtually non-existent as primary means of travel" (p. 12). Older people in rural areas without a car "are particularly at risk for social isolation, as well as difficulty in accessing community and medical services" (Turcotte, 2006, p. 48).

People in rural areas need more options. First, town planners could place seniors' housing close to downtown in small towns. Seniors could then walk to the services and shops they need. Second, small towns' transportation programs might include volunteer-run shuttle buses or car pools for seniors. Freund and Vine (2010) said that technology and the Internet could make these options attractive. Databases, software programs, and social media could make ride-sharing easy and popular. Advanced planning and shared rides, Freund and Vine said, blur the difference between public and private transit. "In this new approach to community transportation, people are finding ways to achieve efficiency by traveling together in private vehicles" (p. 79).

In cities, most seniors do not need special transportation services; instead, they need improvements to existing services. Ninety percent of the transportation disadvantaged said they could use services that already exist if the services changed slightly. Suggested changes include well-lit subway stations, buses that adjust their step height to suit passengers when they enter and leave, and clearer signage. These modifications would help people of all ages.

A report by the CMHC (2008a) said that transportation routes and time schedules best suit the needs of younger, employed people. Also, older people express concerns about the safety of public transit. The National Advisory Council on Aging (2006) reported that 55 percent of older women in Canada felt unsafe using public transportation at night. Better lighting at bus stops and in subway stations would help seniors feel safer when travelling at night. Seniors would benefit from flexible schedules during off-peak hours, door-to-door options with multiple stops, and a "stopping-when-hailed" system outside busy hours and on routes with light traffic.

Limits to mobility (whether due to lack of transport or fear of trouble) can reduce an older person's independence. One woman described her view of mobility independence (Finlayson & Kaufert, 2002, p. 82):

Woman: Well, really a car is independence to me. And independence is important to me because independence is power.

M.F.: How is independence power?

Woman: Because then you do what you want to do. It's doing what you want to do, when you want to do it. And that's power. It's the power to move around when you want to.

Will older people make more use of public transportation and alternative transport methods in the future? Molnar and Eby (2009; also Rosenbloom, 2009) don't think so. First, the use of alternative transportation systems has dropped over time. Second, national data show that, compared with younger people, older people make fewer trips on public transportation. Finally, aging Baby Boomers, who grew up in an automobile culture, will prefer to drive their own cars. Public transportation will play a part in the mix of options for older people. But older people now and in the future will use the private car as their primary means of transportation.

Private Transportation

A birthday card makes reference to the issue of driving in later life. The front of the card says, "At my age I can't see very well, my reaction time is slow, and I don't have much strength in my hands." Open the card and it says, "But thank goodness I can still drive."

The card makes us smile. But it points to a real dilemma. Vehicle use provides older people with mobility and a link to their community. Davidson (2008) said that seniors now see driving "as a 'right' rather than a privilege" (p. 44).

But driving pushes the limits of safety for some older people (and for other drivers on the road). Older drivers feel distracted by difficult situations, take a longer time to read signs, have trouble judging speed, have trouble seeing in low light conditions, and have slower reaction time. Still, Mercado and Newbold (2009) found that physical limitations did not keep people from driving. "Individuals will drive to the extent the severity of their health limitation allows them to. In other words, people will likely curtail driving only if such limitation is severe" (p. 12).

For many older people, their car links them to the world outside their home. For example, compared with seniors who live with others, seniors who live alone show three times the likelihood of driving. Their car allows them to complete daily tasks and keep up their social networks. Weeks and colleagues (2015) found that many drivers (25.5 percent) drove because they didn't like to ask for a ride or didn't have another driver available (17 percent). Few older people (in any living arrangement) would willingly give up their driver's licence.

Mercado and Newbold (2009) said that older people view car driving as a necessity and a measure of freedom. Compared to drivers, people who do not drive or do not live with a driver report more transportation challenges (Weeks et al., 2015). Even people with physical or mental limitations continue to drive. Their study "showed how important license possession and car ownership are to personal mobility" (p. 2). This study also found that older people, like younger people, prefer auto travel to other forms of transportation.

A study in Atlantic Canada by Weeks and colleagues looked at the challenges faced by drivers and non-drivers. About one-quarter of drivers reported weather-related challenges related to driving. Myers, Trang, and Crizzle (2011) studied actual driving patterns in a sample of 46 seniors. They used electronic devices installed in vehicles to monitor driving behaviour. They found that bad weather, more than any other reason, led people to postpone or cancel trips. Still, 69 percent of the people in their study were more likely to drive than not drive on snowy or rainy days. And, compared to women, men showed a greater tendency to drive in bad weather or on bad roads. Men also reported more night-time driving comfort.

Turcotte (2012) said that in 2009, 3.25 million Canadian seniors had drivers licences—"three-quarters of all seniors" (p. 3). About 200,000 senior drivers were age 85 and over. The 2009 *Canadian Community Health Survey—Healthy Aging* (2008–2009) found that nine out of ten seniors with a valid driver's licence drove at least once a week in the month before the study. Sixty percent of the seniors in the study chose the car as their most common form of transportation. Twenty-eight percent of the seniors in the study said they rode as a passenger in a car; only 6 percent used public transportation (Sleightholm et al., 2010).

Compared with older women, older men tend to have a driver's licence and access to a vehicle (Turcotte, 2012). Among drivers 75 to 84 years of age, for example,

EXHIBIT 11.5 *The Most Common Form of Transportation, Seniors Age 65 and Older, Canada, 2009*

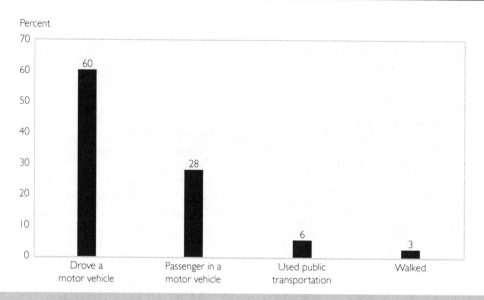

A large majority of seniors drive a motor vehicle as their primary form of transportation. Many studies show a strong preference for use of a car by seniors. Even into late old age, people prefer to drive themselves if they can. And even people with a disability will continue to drive. For example, 54 percent of people with three or more chronic conditions continue to drive. And 47 percent of people in fair/poor health continue to drive. People identify driving with personal freedom. They will drive as long as they can.

Compared with senior women, senior men showed a greater tendency to drive (44 percent vs. 79 percent). Senior women showed a greater tendency to travel as passengers, to use public transport, or walk. Widowed seniors, among all marital groups, showed the least tendency to drive and the greatest likelihood to travel as a passenger, use public transport, or walk.

Sources: Sleightholm, M., Billette, J.-M., Normandin, C., and Hofmann, N. The Use of Transportation by Seniors in Canada. *EnviroStats*, Winter, *4*(4), p. 13. From Statistics Canada, *Canadian Community Health Survey—Healthy Aging* (2009).

86 percent of men, compared with only 57 percent of women, had a driver's licence. And for those 85 years of age and older, 67 percent of men and 26 percent of women had a driver's licence. This gender gap is expected to narrow as the Baby Boomers enter later life because men and women in this generation have a lifetime affection for the private car.

But older people have health problems that may affect their driving. For example, arthritis and rheumatism may limit a person's ability to steer and respond to emergencies. Some older people take multiple medications that may interfere with their driving ability. Physical changes in later life can impair a person's ability to drive. Decreased vision, cognitive impairment, decreased strength and mobility, and slower reaction time all decrease a person's ability to drive safely. Turcotte (2012) said that "seniors' dependence on cars raises safety issues" (p. 3).

Studies disagree on the effects of age on driving ability. Hakamies-Blomqvist (2004, cited in Scialfa & Fernie, 2006), in a study published in the United States,

reported that when judged by miles driven per year, except for very young drivers, older adults have the highest accident rate. Rudman and colleagues (2006) reported that compared with younger or middle-aged drivers, older drivers (age 65 to 75) stand a greater chance of a serious or fatal injury. Compared with drivers age 30 to 59, drivers age 80 and older have death rates 13 times higher per mile driven.

Molnar and Eby (2009) summarized a series of studies that dispute the claim that older drivers have a high accident rate. These studies show that the measure of accidents-per-miles-driven works against older people. Older drivers tend to take shorter trips and drive on city streets. This boosts the risk of accidents. Studies that correct for this bias show similar accident rates for younger and older drivers.

Many older people take their health condition into account when they drive (Davidson, 2008). They may drive less often, avoid night driving, and stay off highways. Lord and Luxembourg (2006) found that some older drivers modify their driving routes, or do their shopping closer to home—"favoring accessibility and proximity over quality of goods and services" (p. 103). Sylvia Cornel, a 90-year-old widow, for example, continues to drive her car in her neighbourhood. But she no longer takes long trips to see her daughter in a mountainous area where she might encounter snow. This kind of accommodation represents a trade-off between mobility and safety.

The decision to stop driving is difficult for older people. The transition to a "life after driving" is also difficult for seniors' families. They often have to convince the older family member that driving is unsafe. Rudman and her colleagues (2006) found that senior drivers (age 65 and older) and pre-senior drivers (age 55 to 64) wanted to continue driving for as long as possible.

Bryanton and Weeks (2014) studied 201 people age 70 and over who had valid driver's licences. Nearly all of these people (96 percent) continued to drive. And of these drivers, 73.4 percent said they never considered retiring from driving. Only a little more than half of the drivers (55.8 percent) said they would take part in an educational program to help them retire from driving. For many older people, the loss of their driver's licence is significantly linked to a loss of self-esteem as well as a loss of independence.

Davidson (2008) pointed to the psychological link between male drivers and their cars. She says that men have a lifelong love affair with the car. "This love affair does not wane with age. If anything, it deepens, but it also evolves: A car is often the means by which a young man constructs masculinity, whereas in old age it may be the means by which he seeks to maintain it" (p. 46). As one senior said about giving up driving, "[i]t's a sign that you're growing old and you're going downhill" (Rudman et al., 2006, p. 68). Another respondent said, "[Y]our vehicle is your magic carpet ride to getting out there in the world. And without it, you're kind of imprisoned in your own home" (p. 69).

Some seniors stop driving before functional problems lead to an accident or injury, but others do not. This has led the Canada Safety Council to set up a program called the **55 Alive Mature Driving Program**. This program helps seniors improve their driving skills and teaches them how aging affects driving.

Some people have suggested special driver's licences for daytime-only drivers and non-highway driving. Smart cars (with automatic guidance systems), head-up instrument displays projected on the windshield, and night

---

55 Alive Mature Driving Program a program that helps seniors improve their driving skills and teaches them how aging affects driving

vision technology make driving easier. Infrared monitors and audio warning systems in cars can help older drivers keep track of other cars, traffic lights, and pedestrians. Research is required to see whether they also reduce accidents.

The rising number of older people with Alzheimer's disease also poses problems. Turcotte (2012) reported that 28 percent of people with a diagnosis of Alzheimer's disease or another form of dementia have a driver's licence. This came to 20,000 people. Turcotte said that 14,600 of them said they had driven in the past month. (About 7,000 people with severe dementia still had a licence.) Wheatley, Carr, and Matolli (2014) reported an increased crash rate for drivers with dementia, when compared to controls. The Champlain Dementia Network of Ottawa produces a Driving and Dementia Toolkit that helps doctors assess a person's ability to drive if he or she has some dementia. It also provides doctors with information about referral centres and other help for families (Byszewski, 2009).

Some provinces monitor the ability of older drivers. Ontario requires that drivers age 80 and over take written and road tests each year. Alberta requires drivers age 75 and over to produce a medical report that says they can drive. Drivers have to renew this medical clearance at age 80 and every two years after that.

Education and training can improve older drivers' abilities. And technology can make roads and cars safer for drivers of all ages. Policies and practices need to balance safety concerns for the older person and the public with the older person's right to drive and his or her need for mobility.

TIME to REVIEW

How could public transportation improve to better serve older people?

What unique public transportation needs do rural seniors have?

What advantages do older people see in private transportation?

How do seniors who drive cope with physical disabilities?

New Transportation Needs and Programs

Transportation needs for older people in the future will go beyond current use patterns. New programs may rely on technological change and on new forms of social organization. Older people will run some of these programs themselves. One program in Edmonton, referred to as a **transportation brokerage**, matches passengers with services that meet their needs. In Moncton and the Acadian peninsula, a **mobility club** helps people in small towns and rural areas. This club formed a non-profit, self-help transport service. People with cars call in to tell a dispatcher about trips they plan to make in the next week or so. People who need rides call a day before they have to take a trip. A dispatcher matches riders with drivers. Drivers also volunteer for one emergency trip per month. Rural communities need to combine these and other special services (e.g., dial-a-ride vans or accessible taxi services) with fixed bus routes to serve older people.

The use of the Uber, Lyft, and other Internet-based transportation systems could benefit older people. These options would provide seniors with the type of on-demand transportation they prefer. These options would serve a dual purpose. Those who need a ride could easily summon one. Those who drive could earn extra income by providing rides to other seniors. This option could work well in urban and rural settings. Baby Boomers who use Uber and similar options in middle age may find this a good fit for their needs as they age.

Mercado and his colleagues (2007) said that Canada needs an improved transit system to prepare for the increased number of older drivers in the future. They said that "an improved transit system now will allow the next waves of elderly population to make an easy transition from car driving and perhaps encourage them to cease driving earlier than they do at present" (p. 17).

transportation brokerage a program that matches passengers with transportation services that meet their needs

mobility club a volunteer group of older people who provide rides to other seniors

THE FUTURE OF HOUSING AND TRANSPORTATION

What will the future of Canadian housing for seniors look like? No one can say for sure, but current trends suggest some new developments in seniors' housing.

First, members of the Baby Boom generation will redefine seniors' housing needs as they enter old age. This group, unlike past generations of seniors, will enter old age

---

EXHIBIT 11.6   *In an Aging Society, Driving with Dementia May Be the New Impaired Driving*

Writers Julian Sher and Moira Welsh presented the following case study. It shows the emotions that older people can feel when they lose their ability to drive a car.

It is half a century old, but the photograph of a teenage soldier sitting on his British Cromwell tank gives a shot of pride to the old man he has become.

"It was a rather splendid tank," says Alan Burridge, 75, of Woodstock. "Driving that gave me an incredible feeling of power."

That feeling, from driving race cars to the family sedan, was a natural part of Burridge's life until last September, when his licence was suspended by Ontario's Ministry of Transportation.

Diagnosed in 2011 with early Alzheimer's disease, Burridge was encouraged by his doctor to take a $550 on-road driving test from a private company to see how his incipient mental decline was affecting his driving skills. Burridge failed the test, got angry, took it a second time, and failed again.

The final word on his driver's licence, the plastic card that can be key to a person's independence, arrived in a letter from the transportation ministry.

"Although you may be disappointed," the suspension letter read, "this decision has been reached to ensure both your own safety and that of other road users...."

Woodstock's Burridge was fuming when he lost his licence.

"I've driven tanks and race cars," he said. "I've been driving for decades and now they say I can't drive?"

After he left the British Army in 1957, Burridge delighted in the rapid acceleration of the Aston Martin, much like the early James Bond. Later, when he moved from England to Ontario, he'd take a friend's supercharged Lotus for laps around the Drummondville racetrack. He was a mechanical engineer who understood these machines and their power.

Last year, when his doctor asked him to take DriveABLE's on-road test, he was accompanied by an occupational therapist and a driving instructor who he felt critiqued him on minor points and exaggerated the concern he expressed about driving a test car he was not accustomed to.

They allowed him to take the $550 test a second time, for free, but he still failed.

"I've lost my independence," he says.

That is going to be the case for more and more senior drivers. As medical and safety experts point out, the difference between the alcohol-impaired driver and the medically impaired one is that there is a chance the drunk driver may sober up.

"There is an element of choice with drunk driving," says B.C.'s Stephanie Melvin. "But we're all going to age. We all have those 'where did I leave my keys?' moments and it's going to be difficult for families to deal with an aging relative who drives."

Source: Sher, J., and Welsh, M. "In an aging society, driving with dementia may be the new impaired driving." *Toronto Star* (10 Feb. 2012), http://www.thestar.com/news/canada/article/1129358--in-an-aging-society-driving-with-dementia-the-new-impaired-driving.

with pensions and housing equity. They have already surprised housing pundits; people expected Baby Boomers to downsize their housing (to condominiums and townhouses) as they aged. But many of them have taken the equity from their midlife homes and bought bigger houses. Likewise, many have bought vacation homes that may serve as their retirement homes in the future.

Perks and Haan (2010) predict that seniors will continue to age in place in the years ahead. These researchers predict that more than 80 percent of seniors in the future will live in the community until past age 80. Shaun Hildebrand, senior vice president of Urbanation, said that in the future, many seniors will "either downsize into other ownership options or exit the ownership market in general, and move into seniors' residences" (Begg, 2011). Perks and Haan supported this prediction. They said that "roughly 2 million individuals who were 55 to 75 in 2002 are expected to leave general community living by 2022. This will either be due to mortality or moving into an alternative dwelling, possibly with nursing care" (p. 459).

If these futures come about, Canada will see an increase in the number of people who will need supportive housing and nursing home care. People with social supports (e.g., a spouse) will tend to live in the community. Older, widowed, or unhealthy older people will need more supportive housing. Haan and Perks (2008) found that social supports, more than health condition or wealth, predict whether a person will live in a home that they own as they age.

Second, new technology will improve housing for older people and allow more people to age in place. New technologies include low-tech solutions such as countertops that can move up and down to suit the user and barrier-free floor plans. More sophisticated technologies include robotic arms that respond to a user's voice. They can take food out of a cupboard, pour a drink, or put food on the table. Other countries have developed houses with electric door openers and locks, remote-control window shades, and voice-activated appliances. Some of these devices already exist in Canadian homes and may become standard in the future.

Estrada (2011) offered the following advice to creators of home technology for seniors: "Make it easy to use. Make it hard to break. And make sure you have nice, quality technical support if it does." She sees tablets and TVs as the primary screens in older adult households in the immediate future.

Third, new types of housing options have begun to emerge. FlexHousing, for example, provides a multigenerational option. FlexHousing designs "adapt to changes in a family's lifestyle with rooms that can change in size and function (adjustable) with fixtures to suit everyone's needs" (Canada Mortgage and Housing Corporation, 2014b). With FlexHousing "as the needs of the household occupants change, ideally the floor plan, amenities and services of the home can be easily, and cost-effectively adapted" (Canada Mortgage and Housing Corporation, 2015f). The home would adapt easily to the changing physical needs of residents. This type of home has barrier-free access, wide doorways, and reinforced bathroom walls to support grab bars at a later stage of life. Other options such as a prefabricated apartment that fits into a garage may offer alternatives to multigenerational living.

Fourth, researchers propose a safer pedestrian environment. Adams and colleagues (2012) found that neighbourhood characteristics either supported or limited walkability. Walkable neighbourhoods included relatively short walks to a grocery store, a restaurant, a post office, and other amenities. Walkable neighbourhoods also rated high in safety and pleasing surroundings categories. A Belgian study (Van Holle et al., 2014) found that walkable environments led to more physical activity. Seniors integrated walking into their daily routines when they could make short trips to shops and services on foot.

Pynoos, Cicero, and Nishita, (2010) say that elder-friendly communities should provide quality living spaces that benefit people of all ages. The Public Health Agency of Canada (2014b; World Health Organization, 2007, 2009) says that **age-friendly communities** have safe neighbourhoods, pleasant outdoor spaces, and opportunities for seniors to volunteer or work. The Canadian government offers a guide, *Pan-Canadian Age-Friendly Communities Milestones* to help communities plan and develop an age-friendly environment.

Research shows that the structure of the environment influences an older person's choice of an active or sedentary lifestyle. Larsen, El-Geneidy, and Yasmin (2010, p.17), for example, found that cycling distance decreased with age from age 45 onward. They proposed "measures to improve the sense of security for these more vulnerable users of the road. Age-friendly environments empower older Canadians to remain independent for as long as possible, allowing them to remain active members of society" (Canadian Health Services Research Foundation, 2011, p. 8).

---

age-friendly communities have safe neighbourhoods, pleasant outdoor spaces, and opportunities for seniors to volunteer or work

EXHIBIT 11.7   *Age-Friendly City Topic Areas*

Age-friendly cities integrate services and the built environment to support older residents. The petals in this diagram show some of the components of an age-friendly city. An age-friendly city promotes activity, social connections, and healthy aging.

How well does your town or city serve as an age-friendly city? Can you find examples in your town or city for the items on these petals?

Source: Reprinted from Global age-friendly cities: A guide. World Health Organization, page 9, Copyright 2007. Retrieved from http://www.who.int/ageing/publications/Global_age_friendly_cities_Guide_English.pdf.

CONCLUSION

Housing for older people in the future will recognize the needs of a diverse older population. Older people of all ages prefer to age in place and in their community. This will mean one thing for the active Baby Boomer and another for the frail 85-year-old. Oberlink (2008) said that housing and transport should create a livable community—"one that has affordable and appropriate housing, supportive community features and services, and adequate mobility options. Together these facilitate personal independence and the engagement of residents in civic and social life."

Housing and transport needs will range from more long-term care beds, to new types of housing developments with integrated services, to modified homes to allow people to stay in their homes longer, to new communities for active Baby Boomers. The continuum of housing and transportation for older people will expand in the future and will include more options than ever before.

Summary

1. Research on housing and transportation shows that older people enjoy old age most when they feel in control of their environment. People can maintain this control by changing their environment (for example, moving to an apartment from a single-family home or modifying their existing home so they can remain there).

2. A good match between a person's ability and environmental demand leads to high life satisfaction. An ideal housing system offers older people a range of housing choices because people's needs differ. People should be able to move from one type of housing to another—from a house to an apartment, or from an apartment to enriched housing—as their needs change. Or they should be able to get support to help them stay where they are.

3. Most older people want to stay in the kind of housing they now occupy and "age in place." Government policies and programs—such as rent subsidies, tax rebates, and repair loans—help older people stay where they are. Other programs—such as loan guarantees, new building programs, and shelter allowances—allow older people to move to the kind of housing that suits their needs.

4. Canada offers older people a wide range of housing options. These include single-family homes, apartments and condominiums, retirement communities, and long-term care homes. New types of housing—like garden suites and multigenerational housing—will increase seniors' housing options in the future.

5. More older people than ever before, especially women, live alone. Today, relatively few older people live with family members. For some older people, living alone reflects their financial ability to live independently. But for others, living alone leads to trouble affording their housing, and can lead to social isolation.

6. A number of government programs, including tax benefits and home maintenance programs, aim to keep people in their homes. Home adaptation, for example, can extend the years a person can live in a single-family home. Reverse mortgages can help older people draw funds from the value of their home in order to cover their cost of living. This, too, extends the years of home ownership.

7. Apartment living offers many types of housing for older people. Apartments range from luxury buildings with swimming pools and other amenities to subsidized apartments that offer safe and clean housing to low-income seniors. Supportive apartment housing provides seniors with social and healthcare supports in a community setting.

8. Housing poses unique challenges for seniors in rural communities. People who own their own homes face high costs for utilities and maintenance. They may also face isolation due to the lack of suitable transportation.

9. Many housing alternatives exist for seniors today. They range from garden suites, naturally occurring retirement communities (NORCs), planned retirement communities, life lease housing, and continuing care retirement communities (CCRCs).

10. Homeless older people often live on the street and use shelters for overnight rest and meals. Some homeless seniors have lived that way for years. Others became homeless recently. These two groups have different needs.

11. Good transportation links older people to their communities—to services, recreation, and friends. But both urban and rural transportation systems need improvement. Older people in cities could use the transportation that exists if it was modified to suit their needs.

12. Rural seniors often have no available public transportation. But new programs in rural settings include bus services shared by a number of small towns, volunteer bus services, and people who pool their resources to help one another get around.

13. Older people, like younger people, prefer auto travel to other forms of transportation. Older men are more likely than older women to have a driver's licence and a car. The ability to drive changes with age. Seniors with disabilities or cognitive impairment may find driving difficult and dangerous. But older people resist giving up their driver's license. They link the loss of a driver's licence to a loss of independence. Programs exist to help seniors drive safely.

14. Good housing and transportation lead to high life satisfaction for older people. An environment that fits the person's abilities helps keep the person safe, satisfied, active, and in touch with the community.

15. Canada now promotes the development of age-friendly communities. This fits with the World Health Organization's world-wide promotion of age-friendly cities.

STUDY QUESTIONS

1. Describe the ecological model of housing. When does a person feel the most comfortable according to this model?

2. Explain "aging in place." Describe some housing strategies and actions that help older people age in place. What types of housing suit older people at different stages of later life?

3. Define the term *living arrangement*. What types of living arrangements are available to older Canadians? Why do many older women opt to live alone rather than with other family members? What conditions make this trend possible?

4. What are reverse annuity mortgages (RAMs)? What are the pros and cons of seniors using RAMs?

5. List and describe some of the new alternative types of housing that older people can choose to live in today.

6. Explain some of the different housing and transportation needs of rural seniors compared with seniors living in urban centres. What unique housing and transportation challenges do older people in rural

settings face? What housing and transportation solutions exist in rural settings today? What housing and transportation needs still exist in rural settings for older people?

7. Describe the transportation preferences of older people. Describe the major transportation issues raised by an increase in senior drivers. Describe two programs now available to help older people meet their transportation needs.

8. Describe the characteristics of an age-friendly city and an age-friendly community. Give some examples of age-friendly cities in Canada and describe what they have done to create a more supportive environment for older people.

KEY TERMS

55 Alive Mature Driving Program (p. 285)
age-friendly communities (p. 287)
aging in place (p. 269)
assisted living (p. 276)
collective dwellings (p. 270)
continuing care retirement communities (CCRCs) (p. 279)
core housing need (p. 270)
ecological model (p. 267)
enriched housing (p. 275)
environmental press (p. 267)
FlexHousing (p. 273)
garden suite (p. 277)
granny flat (p. 277)
intimacy at a distance (p. 270)
mobility club (p. 286)
naturally occurring retirement communities (NORCs) (p. 278)
planned retirement communities (p. 278)
Residential Rehabilitation Assistance Program (RRAP) (p. 272)
reverse annuity mortgage (RAM) (p. 274)
shelter allowances (p. 274)
supportive housing (p. 275)
transportation brokerage (p. 286)
universal design (p. 273)
visitability (p. 273)

Study Tools
CHAPTER 11

Located at retail.tophat.com:

- Review Key Terms with interactive and printable flash cards
- Check Your Comprehension and Think About chapter concepts by completing practice quizzes
- Develop Your Gerontological Imagination with class activities
- Analyze Aging in a Global Perspective with engaging case studies and critical thinking questions
- Demonstrate Your Knowledge of the Concepts by bringing your own experience to personal application questions
- Evaluate Aging in the Media by completing Internet activities with evaluation questions

CHAPTER 12

FAMILY LIFE

Monkey Business Images/Shutterstock

LEARNING OBJECTIVES

After reading this chapter, you will

LO1 Be able to give the facts about the variety of family and friendship relationships older people have in later life (e.g., marriage, common-law union, living together apart, lifelong singlehood).

LO2 Understand the challenges older people face in their relationships as they cope with changes such as divorce, widowhood, and remarriage.

LO3 Be able to speak about the role of sexual relations and its importance in later life for people with various sexual orientations.

LO4 Understand the lives of older lesbian, gay, bisexual, and transsexual older people and the challenges they face as they age.

LO5 Appreciate the informal supports that older people give to their children and other family members, including daily help, emotional support, financial support, and help with child-rearing.

LO6   Be able to explain the charm of grandparenting and the challenges that some grandparents face when they have to raise their grandchildren.

LO7   Be able to discuss the issues related to visiting rights that can arise for grandparents if their adult child's marriage breaks up.

LO8   Be able to explain the future directions in family research as the family evolves and new research questions emerge.

INTRODUCTION

Families have changed. Rising divorce rates, blended households, and high residential mobility all point to major changes in the structure of the modern family. Add to this the fact that people live longer and more older people live alone than ever before, and you might think that families have abandoned their aging members. More than 35 years ago, gerontologist Ethel Shanas (1979) called this the "hydraheaded myth" of family breakdown. Yet people continue to believe this myth today, even though studies show over and over again that it is not true.

Families in the past had a typical structure. They had a large number of children, a moderate-sized middle generation, and few elders. This description fit family structure until recently in Canada and most of the world. Today, a decreased birth rate and longer life expectancy has created a new family structure. Wu (2014, p. 351) in a guest editorial for the *Canadian Journal on Aging* said, "families now resemble a beanpole, with fewer people in the younger generations and large numbers in the older generations." Wu went on to say that beanpole families (1) have smaller numbers of people in each generation, (2) have increased interaction and more years of interaction across generations, and (3) have a larger number of generations that coexist.

The family of one of the authors now has four generations alive at the same time—his mother-in-law and three generations of children, grandchildren, and great-grandchildren. Gerontologists speak of convoys of relatives who travel together for many years. His mother-in-law, for example, has seen her children grow old and retire. And she has seen her grandchildren set up families of their own.

This change in family structure created many of the topics and issues that gerontologists study today—from widowhood, to grandparenting, to caregiving. This change in family structure also raises questions about the definition of the family. The nuclear family of parents and children, who live together in a single household, now coexists with other family forms. Single parents, gay and lesbian couples with and without children, three-generation households, all count as families. Also, high

rates of divorce, remarriage (sometimes more than once), children and grandchildren from multiple marriages also create new meanings of family.

Wu (2014, p. 352) pushed the meaning of family further and said, "it is shared experiences, not just legal or biological ties, that define kin group membership." Some seniors create "fictive kin." They feel as close to certain friends, neighbours, or caregivers as they do to their biological relatives. "Exchanges of social support," Wu (2014, p. 352) said, "are not just about reciprocity but are also about the creation of affective ties." McDaniel and Gazso (2014, p. 400: italics in the original) said people (especially in low-income families) "in order to survive—choose flexible, sometimes novel, social-support relations, including kin and non-kin: these are *aging families by choice*."

All of these family forms (nuclear, extended, blended, created, invented) exist in Canada today. Add to this Canada's many ethnic and racial groups, with their own cultural preferences in family structure, and you get some idea of the diversity of family life in Canada. Older people play an important role in the evolving, changing structure of Canadian families. And with the increase in life expectancy, older people will play a part in family life for more years than ever before.

Consider the following case.

Meema, the name her grandchildren and great-grandchildren call her, turned 93 last year. She stands about 155 centimetres. She's free with advice and free to tell you she doesn't like something if she doesn't.

A photo taken of Meema at a grandson's wedding a few years ago shows her sitting in the front row. Around her stand a crowd of her offspring—her daughters, their husbands, their children, her grandchildren, and in her lap her newest great-grandchild.

All of these family members support her in one way or another. Those farthest away call regularly and visit when they can. Those who live nearby remain in daily or weekly contact with her.

Meema speaks to her closest daughter, Sarah, every day. In the summer, Sarah picks her up to take her to their cottage. She has three granddaughters within driving distance. Now she has five great-grandchildren less than an hour away. Someone drives her to see them or they visit with her every few weeks. She's immersed in an ongoing series of birthday parties, graduations, and holiday celebrations.

This year she'll go to her oldest granddaughter's house for Thanksgiving, where the whole tribe will gather. She also has a daughter on the West Coast, four grandchildren in other parts of the country, and six great-grandchildren who live out West. Meema lives in a complex web of loving relationships.

Her family monitors her health and well-being and supports her when she needs help. But support in her family flows both ways. She has provided babysitting services for decades, she helped one daughter financially when she needed to refurbish her home, and she serves as the matriarch of the family. She's held in respect and treated with care and concern by all—even though the clan quarrels, argues, and often disagrees. It's never quiet at a family gathering.

Research shows that older people, like Meema, keep in contact with their families, they turn to family members for help when they need it, and they themselves provide support to family members (Connidis, 2010; Lee & Gardner, 2010). Through help with child-rearing, financial support, and good advice, older people enrich family life.

This chapter looks at (1) marital status in later life (including marriage, widowhood, divorce, remarriage, and lifelong singlehood), (2) sexuality and aging (including research on gay and lesbian older adults), and (3) the contributions old people make to their families (including grandparenting).

MARITAL STATUS IN LATER LIFE

The life course perspective takes a dynamic view of family life and social relations. It shows how events and conditions that occur early in life affect roles and relationships in later life. This perspective sees family life as a scene of both stability and change. For example, some people marry young and stay married to the same spouse throughout their life. They experience the continuity of marriage. But many of these same people experience changes in their sex lives, in their relationship with their spouse, and in the development of new roles within their marriage.

Gerontologists view some of these changes, such as grandparenthood or widowhood, as normative or expected life events. Other changes, such as divorce, are less predictable and affect fewer people. Changes in

marital status often lead to change in a person's social status and a change in that individual's social network. The following sections focus on life events and issues related to marital status in later life: marriage, common-law unions, divorce, remarriage, lifelong singlehood, and widowhood.

Marriage

Nearly all Canadians will marry at least once in their lifetime. In 2011, 46.4 percent of Canadians age 15 and over were legally married (Milan, 2013). More than 60 percent of those who marry stay married to the same person and celebrate their 30th wedding anniversary (Clark & Crompton, 2006). Among seniors age 65 to 74 in 2011, 21 percent of women and 10 percent of men said they had been married (to one or more spouses) for at least 50 years. For seniors age 75 and over, this figure rose to 74 percent (Milan, 2013).

In 2011, among seniors living in private households, 76 percent of senior men and 49 percent of senior women lived in a couple (either as a spouse or common-law). Men are more likely than women to be married in later life (Statistics Canada, 2014q). This in part reflects a tendency for older men to remarry in late old age. Among the oldest seniors (age 85 and over), 46.2 percent of men and only 10.4 percent of women lived with a spouse or in a common-law relationship (Statistics Canada, 2012l). Older women are more likely to be widowed.

Some seniors remarry after the death of a spouse or a divorce. In 2011, 14 percent of seniors had married more than once. When statistics include common-law relationships, 19 percent of seniors had more than one relationship in their lifetime. Milan, Wong, and Vézina (2014) said that "many seniors still want to be part of a couple ... " [and] "marriage remains the preferred option of seniors who engage in another union" (p. 7).

The chart in Exhibit 12.1 shows the marital status of older Canadians by gender and age group.

Married older adults have some advantages over their unmarried peers. First, older married couples tend to have more financial resources than older unmarried people. Compared with older people who are unmarried, older couples tend to be younger, and often one or both members of the couple are working. Even among people the same age, married couples have more money (Turcotte & Schellenberg, 2007). This may be because they had a higher lifetime income than unmarried people, more savings, and a family home.

Second, compared with older people who live alone or in other living arrangements, older married people report higher life satisfaction, better health, and greater

EXHIBIT 12.1   *Proportion of the Older Population in Couples by Age Group and Sex, Canada, 2011*

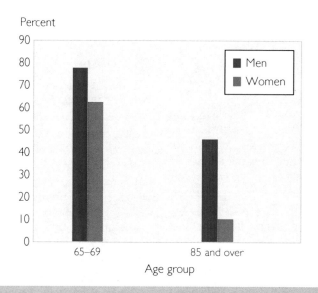

Percent

Compared with older men, older women as a group experience a sharp drop in the proportion who live with a partner. The proportion of women who live as part of a couple drops from ages 65–69 to ages 85 and over. By late old age (age 85 and over), men, compared with women, show more than four times the proportion who live with a partner. Women in the oldest age groups face the prospect of widowhood and the likelihood that they will live alone.

Source: Statistics Canada. Living arrangements of seniors, Census Brief No. 4. (2012). Reproduced and distributed on an "as is" basis with the permission of Statistics Canada.

happiness (Proulx, Helms, & Buehler, 2007; Prus, 2011; Turcotte & Schellenberg, 2007; Umberson & Kroeger, 2016). Lawler and colleagues (2013) studied 852 community-dwelling older people. They found that compared to non-married people, married people said they had a **confidant** (91.9 percent vs. 77.8 percent). A confidant led to higher well-being scores, less illness, and higher health-related quality of life.

In a study of 355 adults age 20 to 78, Villar and Villamizar (2012, p. 128) found that "comments about the positive quality of the relationship were ... more frequent in the two oldest groups" [age 50 and over]. Satisfaction in marriage tends to be higher for those recently married and those in long-term marriages. It tends to be lower among those in their child-rearing years. Researchers talk about this as the "U-curve" of marital satisfaction—higher satisfaction at both ends of the marriage continuum, with a dip in the middle years. Older spouses, particularly men, are more likely than younger couples to feel increased satisfaction with their marriage over time.

Affection and companionship, rather than emotional intensity, often become more important in later-life marriage (Schafer, Mustillo, & Ferraro, 2013). One woman, in an in-depth study of marriage after widowhood, expressed the importance of companionship. She said, "You miss having somebody that is special." Women in this study also valued romance and intimacy in their marital relations (Watson, Bell, & Stelle, 2010, p. 306). Lodge and Umberson (2012) found that later life couples (age 70–86) valued emotional intimacy over sex. And they felt satisfied as a couple with this view. Watson and colleagues called romance a "counter narrative." It expands the "master narrative" of later life relationships that emphasizes practical benefits such as financial support, companionship, and caregiving.

"Empty nest" couples often enjoy a new freedom in later life. They tend to spend more time together and to disagree less about issues such as parenting and household chores (Shiota & Levenson, 2007). They live adult-centred lives that allow them to travel, visit with friends, share work at home, and do things together. Couples in this stage of life focus more time and energy on themselves and each other.

confidant someone in whom one confides

Third, research shows that married people tend to adjust better than non-married people to aging. A good marriage gives the couple intimacy, mutual support, and high life satisfaction (Proulx, Helms, & Buehler, 2007). A good marriage includes an active sex life (Galinsky & Waite, 2014). But it also provides a sense of security and emotional stability. Marriage is linked to longer life and better health, especially for men. In a study of adults age 50 and over, for example, widowed men had the highest risk of stroke compared with married men and women (Maselko et al., 2009). Married partners monitor each other's health. Marriage also helps reduce emotional loneliness and provides social support (Schlesinger & Schlesinger, 2009).

People who report a close relationship in their marriage also report reduced depression and anxiety and higher self-esteem. Mancini and Bonanno (2006) said that "marital closeness is a vital resource in old age" (p. 606). Married people also stand the best chance of staying out of nursing homes if they get sick because they have someone to care for them. Marriage ideally gives a person a live-in support system. Older married couples tend to rely more on each other than on outside social supports. They also report a greater likelihood than non-married older adults of having sexual relations.

Although high marital satisfaction is common among older couples, individuals also face challenges and disappointments in later-life marriages. A relationship that includes bickering, fighting, and abuse, for example, may only get worse with age. The researchers found that disagreements over household concerns (where to live and home repairs) and health problems (often related to a spouse's declining health and caregiving) showed up more often in unhappy marriages.

Most couples in long-term marriages report high life satisfaction. With the kids grown and out of the house, married couples can enjoy their time together. This married couple displays the fulfillment that many older couples report.

Dundanim/Shutterstock

Dissatisfaction in a marriage can lead to depression and illness (Choi & Marks, 2008).

Couples in happy marriages were more likely to report fewer problems (or no problems) than were those in unhappy marriages. Koppen and Anderson (2008) say that the number of problems older couples face may not be as important as the types of problems husbands and wives identify. Studies need to look at the quality of a marriage to understand its impact on well-being.

Henry, Miller, and Giarusso (2005) interviewed 105 older couples who had been married an average of 42 years. The couples talked about difficulties, disagreements, and disappointments they dealt with in their marriage over the previous few years. The three most common issues were (1) leisure activities, (2) intimacy, and (3) financial matters.

Leisure issues involved a lack of sharing or interest in the other spouse's hobbies and activities; travel disagreements (for example, one spouse wanting to travel, the other wanting to stay home, or a difference in the desired destination); or disappointment with the lack of "quality time" together.

Intimacy challenges included both physical and emotional issues. There were "roadblocks to physical intimacy" for some couples because of changes in sexual desire or disagreements over sexual practices. Emotional intimacy challenges tended to centre on communication problems—a spouse's lack of communication or that person's negative style of communication.

Disagreements over spending habits tended to be the most common financial issue identified by these married people. Typically this involved either a spouse not wanting to spend money or spending too much money.

Some couples in Henry and colleagues' (2005) study felt their relationship did not have any problems (the fourth most common theme), or at least, as one wife said, "Not enough of anything to count" (p. 252). Other less common problems included personality differences, intergenerational relationships, personal habits, health problems, and work/retirement issues.

Men and women reported about the same number of challenges in their marriage. But men and women reported different challenges. Compared with men, women more often reported health issues. Men more often reported financial issues. Men, more often than women, reported no problems with their marriage.

Calasanti and Kiecolt (2007) summed up the findings on long-term marriages: "Among couples married at least 50 years," they wrote, "most express high marital satisfaction, regardless of whether they share interests and values or lead more independent lives" (p. 11).

Common-Law Unions

The number of people in Canada choosing to live in common-law relationships increased over the three decades between 1981 and 2011. A common-law relationship means that a couple lives together without being legally married. In 2011, about one-fifth (19.9 percent) of all couples lived as common-law partners. In 1981, only 6.3 percent of couples lived common-law (Milan, 2013). This is one of the most significant demographic changes in Canada in the past 40 years (Turcotte & Schellenberg, 2007). More younger people than older people choose this form of relationship. But increasing numbers of older people choose to live together and not marry.

In particular, the group age 40 and over shows a growth in this alternative to marriage (Martel & Caron-Malenfant, 2008; Milan, 2013). In 2011, 6 percent of Canadians age 65 and older with a spouse or partner lived in a common-law relationship. This represents 166,025 Canadian seniors (Statistics Canada, 2012m). The number of people age 65 to 69 in a common-law relationship increased by 66.5 percent between 2006 and 2011 (Milan, 2013). This increase outpaced all other age groups. Milan, Wong, and Vézina (2014) said that "even if seniors living in common-law unions are still relatively rare, their numbers are bound to increase in the coming years" (p. 7).

What explains the increase in common-law unions among the older population? First, many Baby Boomers live in common-law unions. The aging Baby Boomers have contributed to increased numbers across all marital groups—including common-law unions—simply due to the number of people in their age cohorts. Second, common-law unions have become more socially accepted among older people. Third, many cohabiting older couples entered these common-law unions at younger ages (perhaps in their 20s or 30s) and simply "aged in place" in those relationships. Fourth, people who experience separation, divorce, or widowhood often opt for cohabitation over remarriage. These older people desire a close and intimate relationship, but not necessarily one within marriage (Wu, Schimmele, & Ouellet, 2014).

Older adults now and in the future will have greater choice in the type of intimate relationships they form. For example, today many unmarried couples live in long-term committed relationships while they maintain separate households. These non-resident couples are known as LAT (living apart together) couples. A British study (Duncan & Phillips, 2008) found that 13 percent of people age 55 to 64, who lived apart, said they had a LAT relationship.

Turcotte (2013b) looked at data from the 2001 and 2011 *Canadian General Social Survey* family module to learn about LAT couples. Young people age 20 to 24 showed the greatest tendency to live as an LAT couple (31 percent). In 2011, only 2 percent of people age 60 and over lived as an LAT couple (a slight increase from 2001). And the likelihood of living as an LAT couple generally decreases with age. (The data show a slight increase among people age 70 and over. This reflects people who live apart due to a partner's health (e.g., the partner lived in a nursing home).

Turcotte (2013b) found that most LAT relationships lasted on average 7.5 years for people age 60 and over. Two-thirds of this group said they lived in this type of relationship by choice. Often the motives for choosing a LAT relationship, particularly for women, revolve around autonomy. Turcotte reported that two-thirds (37 percent) of the older group said they chose this option in order to remain independent. LAT partners want a home of their own and the freedom from duties typically involved in a marriage. They can have independent relationships with their children, grandchildren, and friends at some times and meet with family and friends as a couple at other times.

Forty-two percent of the people age 60 and over, who lived as an LAT couple by choice, said they did not intend to live with their partner in the future. Turcotte called these "non-transitional" relationships (2013b, p. 5). Given the rate of widowhood in later life, Turcotte said "LAT relationships could be a source of emotional support and contribute to the wellbeing of some seniors who do not necessarily want to enter into another couple relationship and live together" (p. 5). LAT relationships among older people add to the diversity of modern family life

Will a large number of seniors choose the LAT option in the future? Turcotte said that Baby Boomers show a greater tendency to live in LAT relationships than earlier

---

LAT (living apart together) couples have a committed relationship but maintain separate households

EXHIBIT 12.2 *Polyamory—A Growing Trend among Seniors?*

What is polyamory? Polyamory means having more than one partner in an open relationship. Some seniors (a small number at this point) come into later life with a polyamorous lifestyle. They may have lived a heterosexual or LGBT life with several partners and lovers at the same time. They will enter later life with a preference for this kind of relationship. One senior writes, "For some of us seniors discovering polyamory is not a change of lifestyle, it's discovering there is now a narrative for who we already are" (Sandstory, 2015).

Other seniors may find that polyamory fits their needs as a widow/widower. Ken Haslam, 80, speaks and writes on polyamory. He says that polyamory can meet the needs of a spouse who cares for an institutionalized partner who has Alzheimer's disease. He says, "I think that polyamory is a way of approaching this problem, of being there for a failing partner but still getting your own needs met" (Haslam, 2015).

Polyamory proposes an option to monogamous relationships such as conventional marriage or common-law partnering. Seniors who want to explore this option can find blogs and podcasts on the Internet to advise and guide them. These sites also provide opportunities for seniors to share their concerns and experiences with like-minded others (Matthews, 2014). The Internet provides an opportunity to share a lifestyle option that in the past would have kept people isolated and feeling guilty. Consider this posting on a senior dating site called *Polyamorous Passions*:

> A senior couple ages 59 (male) and 51 (female) seek "another lady to join our family." He stays home and she drives an 18-wheel truck. She is 6 days on the road and home for two. The couple requests someone slightly overweight "since we are not Ken and Barbie we do not look for perfection."

Until November 23, 2011, Canadian law (Section 293 of the Criminal Code of Canada) made polyamory illegal. On that date the British Columbia Supreme Court ruled that this law does not apply to "unformalized polyamorous relationships." The Canadian Polyamory Advocacy Association (CPAA) says that this "effectively makes polyamory legal in Canada where a person is not married in a ceremony" (Canadian Polyamory Advocacy Association, 2015). This interpretation of the law clears the way for more seniors to openly live a polyamorous lifestyle.

Questions

1. Will more seniors adopt a polyamorous lifestyle in the years ahead?

2. Will Baby Boomers bring an open approach to relationships in later life (as they did in their youth)?

3. How would you feel if a senior relative of yours adopted a polyamorous lifestyle? What issues would this raise in your family?

4. Would you consider adopting this lifestyle in later life? Why or why not?

generations of seniors. He projected an increase in this option for future generations of seniors, although he said, "the number of senior LAT couples remains low" (p. 5).

Divorce

Divorce rates in Canada have increased significantly since the early 1970s. Nguyen (2012) calls these "silver separations." The liberalization of divorce laws, particularly the 1986 amendment to the Divorce Act, in part, explains this increase. Lambert (2009; Statistics Canada, 2008b) reported that 38 percent of married couples could expect to divorce before celebrating their 30th anniversary.

In 2011, 12 percent of seniors reported that they were divorced (up from 4 percent in 1981) (Milan, Wong, & Vézina, 2014). Even among people age 85 and over, 4 percent reported divorce or separation (compared to only 1 percent in 1981). Research also shows that divorce rates for men and women in later life have increased (from 2 percent in 1981 to 12 percent in 2011) (Statistics Canada, 2006f). This represents a shift toward greater acceptance of divorce among older people. The number of divorced older people will likely increase in the future as younger cohorts, many of whom will already be divorced, enter later life. Brown and Lin (2012) call this the "gray divorce revolution."

The reasons for late-life divorce are often different than for divorce at younger ages. For younger couples, interpersonal disputes often lead to divorce. Late-life couples often divorce because the marriage can no longer support the changing roles, needs, or desires of the individuals (Wu & Schimmele, 2007). Other reasons for divorce are similar for younger and older couples. They include problems of abuse, alcohol or drug addiction, and infidelity. Most people who divorce in middle or later life do not remarry, but more divorced older men than women remarry.

Divorce in later life often means economic insecurity, particularly for women. Deborah O'Connor, a University of British Columbia professor who studies the effect of divorce on seniors, said, "Financially, it's devastating" (Nguyen, 2012). A 61-year-old woman, separated from her common-law partner, expressed concern about her future. The couple had been together for 21 years. She said, "One of the things that I found shocking was that I expected my retirement to be with my partner, and that sets you up for many different assumptions.... Now I've been disabused of all those assumptions and illusions, it changes the horizon and the landscape significantly" (Attfield, 2014).

This study supports other research that finds very high rates of poverty among older unmarried women (Meyer & Parker, 2011). And because divorced older women are unlikely to remarry, they often feel the economic effects of divorce throughout their later years. Men in the LaRochelle-Côté, Myles, and Picot study (2012a) felt less effect on their finances from widowhood or divorce.

Longer life expectancies in the future could increase the number of marriages that last 50 years or more, but researchers also predict a higher divorce rate and more divorced older people in the future. This will make the economic well-being, mental health, and family life of divorced older people an ongoing concern.

Remarriage

Remarriage in later life is relatively uncommon. It is also more likely to occur for men than for women, and for divorced older adults than for the widowed. The motivations to remarry in later life include loneliness (especially for men) and financial security (particularly for women) (Calasanti & Kiecolt, 2007; Watson, Bell, & Stelle, 2010). One man said that after the death of his wife, loneliness was "the worst feeling.... We were married for 38 years.... The need for companionship is important" (Schlesinger & Schlesinger, 2009, pp. 35–36).

Widowed women are often disinclined to remarry because of the loss of freedom, increased domestic chores, and potential spousal care in the future. A woman told the Schlesingers (2009): "I want my independence. I have the resources, why do I want him to get sick, and I'll have to care for him. I don't need a man. Today, many of my friends are single. We can travel, have companionship, don't want to be caregivers, been there, done that!" (pp. 42–43).

The Schlesingers (2009) also asked the men and women in their sample to compare their first marriages with their remarriage experiences. They found that men had a hard time making this comparison. But a number of women in the study reported happier second marriages. One woman said, "My first husband was very different. Looking back now, I see he was not a nice person, bitter, sour. While he was a good man, I thought I loved him, but now I realize I never liked him. He always put me down, we never had fun" (p. 41).

Another woman said, about her second marriage: "Very different. My second partner is older, more cultured, sure of himself, is secure in himself. He is into fitness, walks, trips. My first was anxious, always had to prove himself, needed to be reassured, needed me all the time. My partner is strong, my first was weak."

A number of factors contribute to the satisfying second-marriage experience for these older women. First, the greater maturity of these women and the insights they gained from their first marriage helped them select a more compatible partner. Second, without child-rearing responsibilities (and, in the case of retirees, work commitments), these couples had more time to invest in their relationship. They could also share domestic chores.

TIME TO REVIEW

Why do people divorce in later life?

What effect does divorce have on a person's psychological and social well-being?

What effect does divorce have on women's economic well-being?

How do men and women differ in their ideas about remarriage?

Lifelong Singlehood

A small proportion of older Canadians, about 3 percent, have never married or lived common-law (5.3 percent of older men and 5.5 percent of older women), down from just over 8 percent in 1981 (Milan, Wong, & Vézina, 2014; Turcotte & Schellenberg, 2007). The proportion of older singles increases with age, from 5.2 percent for people age 65 to 74 to 6.7 percent for people age 85 and over (Turcotte & Schellenberg, 2007). This may reflect the different social and historical conditions that people in each of these older age groups lived through (e.g., coming of age during World War II). Among people age 55 to 64, about 4 percent have never married or lived common-law.

Many singles have made unique adaptations to aging. They play vital and supportive roles in the lives of siblings, older parents, and others. They form friendships and other social relationships to provide themselves with supporters, confidants, and companions.

Little research exists on the lives and social relationships of lifelong single older people (Carr & Moorman, 2011). Older singles often face the stereotypes of aging as well as those associated with people who are seen as "unmarriageable." One common and enduring belief is that older never-married people live lonely, socially isolated lives, disconnected from family. But most older singles, particularly single women, develop strong and diverse social networks and have active ties with siblings, friends, and other family members (McDill, Hall, & Turell, 2006).

Overall, never-married older people report that they lead active lives and feel happy, are in good health, and feel satisfied with their standard of living. In general, single women are more satisfied with their lives than single men. Older single women see their independence, their ability to control their own finances, and their freedom to arrange their own social activities as benefits of singlehood (Band-Winterstein & Manchik-Rimon, 2014).

People who remain single often develop unique relationships with other family members. Never-married older people, compared with married and widowed older people, tend to rely more on siblings and friends for social support (Connidis, 2010).

Carol, a colleague in the office of one of the authors, remained single into old age. She lived with her parents and cared for them in the family home until they died. She also looked after and supported two of her aunts. She took them for doctors' appointments and shopping. These relationships kept her busy and engaged in family life.

She also kept a close relationship with her sister, although they lived in different cities. She visited her sister often and stayed with her during holidays. She bought her sister's daughter toys and clothes. As her niece grew up, they became good friends. Carol and her niece go shopping and attend yoga classes together. After Carol retired, she bought a home in her sister's town and moved there. She works part-time for her brother-in-law in his business. Although single, Carol developed and maintained a network of close relationships throughout her life. Single older women, like Carol, compared to divorced and widowed older women, report less "single strain" (fewer chronic stressors associated with being single) (Pudrovska, Schieman, & Carr, 2006).

Still, never-married older people lack spousal and child support in later life. And never-married seniors without children report reduced household support (Penning & Wu, 2014). As a result, compared with married older people, single seniors may use more formal supports.

Researchers project an increase in the number of older single people as Baby Boomers enter later life. As they age, these singles may play a significant role in helping to change societal attitudes about permanent singlehood. Future studies should look at the coping strategies that never-married people use to maintain their high quality of life.

Widowhood

In 2015, there were almost 1.5 million widowed Canadians age 65 and older. This came to 25 percent of all older Canadians—13 percent of men and 43 percent of women. Rates of widowhood increase with age for both men and women, but women have a higher rate of widowhood at all ages. Among seniors there are more than four times as many widowed women as widowed men (Statistics Canada, 2006f, 2015o). This means that most older men, particularly those younger than age 85, can expect to end their lives with a spouse. Older women, particularly those age 75 and older, are more likely to live their final years in widowhood.

Widows outnumber widowers for three reasons: (1) women live longer than men; (2) women tend to marry older men; and (3) men, more than women, tend to remarry after widowhood. Widowhood for women is now an "expectable life event"—one that creates a great deal of stress. For example, many widows report that widowhood stripped them of their identity. Widowhood signals the end of a woman's former identity (as a wife) and it begins the need to build a new identity.

Widowhood can lead to lower income, the loss of social support, loss of intimacy, and loneliness (Cornwell, 2011). But responses to widowhood vary. Some widowed women move on in life and establish new relationships with a male partner. Other widows reorganize their lives and live alone. Some widowed women find or establish meaning in their lives through holding on to memories of their role as wife and mother. They continue personal rituals and routines as mother and homemaker. And they keep their attachment to their marital home and possessions. Cornwell's work on social networks finds that widowhood tends to increase a person's involvement in the community and this provides new sources of social support.

Gender and Widowhood

Most studies of widowhood in the past focused on women, but more recent studies look at how loss of a spouse affects each gender (Bennett, 2007; Dahlberg & Lennartsson, 2015; Lee & DeMaris, 2007). Studies of family supports, friendship, and confidants show that, compared with a married person, a widowed person is less likely to have a confidant (Ha, 2008). However, support from children, friends, and other relatives tends to increase after widowhood. Research finds that widowed women have more social supports than widowed men.

Most older men spent their lives focused on their careers, while older women spent their lives focused on

EXHIBIT 12.3   *Marital Status for Population Age 65 and Over, Canada, 2011*

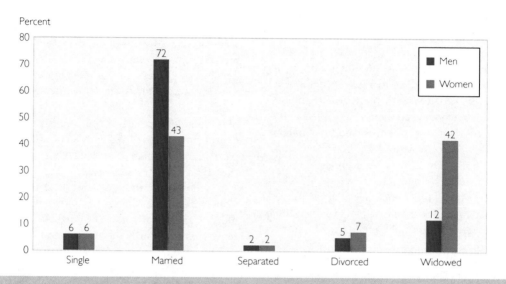

Men and women in this table show similar rates of being never married, separated, and divorced. But women, compared with men, show three times the rate of widowhood (42 percent vs. 12 percent) and a much lower marriage[1] rate (43 percent vs. 72 percent). The different marriage and divorce rates of men and women lead to different experiences in later life. These differences include a higher proportion of older women who live alone, a higher proportion of older women with low income, and a higher proportion of older women who lack spousal support in case of illness.

[1]Note: The married category in Canada includes same-sex marriage. It does not include common-law relationships.

Sources: Statistics Canada. Census of Canada, Legal Marital Status (6), Common-law Status (3), Age Groups (17), and Sex (3) for Population 15 Years and Over of Canada, Provinces, Territories, Census Divisions and Census Agglomerations, 2006 Census—100% Data Catalogue No. 97–5562-XCB2006007. (2006); Statistics Canada, CANSIM Table 051-0042, Estimates of population, by marital status or legal marital status, age and sex for July 1, Canada, provinces and territories annual (persons) (2012), found at http://www5.statcan.gc.ca/cansim/a47 Reproduced and distributed on an "as is" basis with the permission of Statistics Canada.

relationships. As a result, women have more close social ties than men in old age. Because men have fewer supports than women, they more often experience loneliness after their spouse dies. They may also experience a decline in their social functioning and mental health status.

Social support holds the key to life satisfaction for widowers. Women, more often than men, say they have close relationships with family and friends besides their spouses. They often name these friends, relatives, and children as their confidants, and they keep up these relationships when their husband dies. A widower loses a wife, a companion, and his link to other family and social ties.

This may explain why many men seek another partner soon after they lose a spouse. Research shows that widowed men, compared with women, find it harder to make new friends or to join self-help groups. Studies show that widowers suffer from isolation and loneliness after the loss of their spouse (Calasanti & Kiecolt, 2007). This in part reflects their low involvement in relationships outside marriage over the life course.

Relatively few widows remarry. This, in part, reflects the larger number of eligible women compared with

older men. Those who do remarry say they want companionship and the feeling that they add to another person's happiness. Those who remarry tend to be younger, worry less about finances, and have a higher household income than widowed women who remain single (Moorman, Booth, & Fingerman, 2006).

Many older widows report an interest in men, but not necessarily an interest in remarriage (Carr & Moorman, 2011; Moorman et al., 2006). Some widows report negative attitudes toward remarriage and an increased enjoyment in their independence. Older women may want to avoid the role of caregiver in a new marriage, or even having to arrange their lives around a new partner. Research finds that women stay socially active in mother and grandmother roles after their husbands die. Many women also hold on to their wife role. They remain committed to being a wife—or to the memory of being a wife—many years after the death of their husband.

Older women's longer life expectancy and the tendency to remain widowed lead to many of the problems that older women face. These often include financial difficulties. Inflation, for example, will eat away at a survivor's pension, if the widow has one. A widow also runs a greater risk of institutionalization than a married person because she will lack spousal support if she gets sick. Widowhood, in spite of good social supports, can put a woman at greater risk as she ages. Supportive relationships with family and friends help widowed women deal with the challenges they face.

More research needs to look at the social lives of widows and widowers to understand how their needs differ. In particular, researchers need to include more men in their studies. This will create a more balanced view of widowhood. Researchers also need to look at how age, gender, race/ethnicity, social class, financial status, the quality of their marital relationship, and social support affect the experience of widowhood.

TIME to REVIEW

Why are there more widowed women than widowed men in later life?

What different effects does widowhood have on men and women in later life?

How do men and women differ in their response to widowhood?

Dating in Later Life

Men tend to remarry after widowhood and women tend to stay single, but studies report little about how widows and widowers form new intimate relationships (Connidis, 2006). Studies of dating in later life look at how single older people develop social and, in some cases, sexual relationships.

Older people say they date for several reasons. Some people want to find a marital partner. Others want to stay socially active. Older women say it increases their prestige. They believe that other women envy them for dating. Men say they date in order to talk about their personal concerns, but also for sexual satisfaction (Calasanti & Kiecolt, 2007). Dating can act as a starting point for romance, sex, and love (Watson, Bell, & Stelle, 2010).

New approaches to dating arrived with the spread of the Internet and social networking. An American Association of Retired Persons (AARP) (Fisher, 2010) study of sexual activity among Americans age 50 and over found that, compared with the past, more older singles in 2010 used dating services. This approach may relieve some of the tension and mismatching that occurs when people meet face to face for the first time.

Zimmerman (2013) reported that 60 percent of single Americans age 50 and over take advantage of online dating. A study of online personal ads supports this idea. Alterovitz and Mendelsohn (2009) studied 600 personal ads from Yahoo! Personals. These ads provided information to prospective dating partners. The researchers found that men looked for younger partners. The older the group of men, the larger the age gap between themselves and their desired partners.

Young adult men looked for women about their same age. The oldest group of men (age 75 and over) looked for women nearly 10 years younger. Women showed the opposite of this pattern. Women sought older men as they aged. Only after age 75 did women seek younger men.

This study confirms some stereotyped differences between men and women throughout the life course. For example, compared with women, men tended to provide information about their social status. And compared with men, women tended to seek out this information. Men, compared with women, tended to seek physical attractiveness. Men showed a greater willingness to re-partner. Women showed more selectivity and a willingness to wait for the right man.

Vic Kragen, a retired insurance executive, became a widower in his late 60s. He travelled on his own after he retired, but he soon felt the need for companionship. He surfed the Web through a couples matching service and contacted a woman in a nearby city. She seemed compatible with his interests and they got along well on a first date. After some time, they decided to take a cruise together. When one of the authors asked, "Will you be sharing a room on the cruise?" "Of course," Vic answered (personal communication with author).

The trend toward the use of online connections by older people has just begun. Some older people already use social media to screen potential partners. Others use Facebook and Twitter to maintain a large network of friends and acquaintances. Almost every Baby Boomer can tell a story about a reconnection with a high school friend or lost relative. The use of social media may bring down some of the barriers to dating in later life. New seniors with a lifetime of experience using the Internet will feel comfortable with these new online options.

SEXUALITY AND AGING

Wurtele (2009) asked 1,340 undergraduate students in a class on late adulthood to create an "Older Adults" survey. She wanted to know what students would include in the survey. She noted "the infrequent inclusion of sexual activities" in the students' surveys (p. 1029). She concluded that students hold a stereotyped view of older adults' activities and their sex lives.

Yet studies show that the stereotype of the sexless older person has little basis in fact. For example, most older people have an interest in sex throughout life, and given good health and a partner, older people can (and do) have sexual relations into late old age (Elliott & Umberson, 2008; Fisher, 2010; Watson, Bell, & Stelle, 2010). Older people who experience barriers to sexual activity—due to the lack of a partner or poor health—tend to place less importance on sex.

Syme and colleagues (2013, p. 323) in a review of the literature on sexuality in later life said that, "older adults consistently identify sexual well-being as integral to overall quality of life." They went on to list the benefits of a satisfying sex life in old age: cardiovascular health, increased feelings of relaxation, less depression, increased psychological well-being, high overall quality of life, and high self-esteem.

Syme and colleagues used the *Wisconsin Longitudinal Study* of the life course to explore sexuality among 10,317 people. The sample ages ranged from 63 to 67, with most people age 64. Women made up 51.6 percent of the sample. Two-thirds of the people in this sample said they had sex at least once a month. Still, half the people in the sample said they had problems maintaining their sexual activity. Compared to men in this study, significantly more women reported a lack of sexual satisfaction related to issues with their partner. Syme and colleagues found that diabetes and fatigue interfered with sexual satisfaction and performance.

Compared with women, men in good or excellent health report the most interest in sex, the most active sex lives, and high-quality sex lives. The gap between men and women on these measures widened with age. For example, most sexually active men reported a good-quality sex life, but only half of sexually active women reported a good-quality sex life. And, compared with women, men had a longer "sexually active life expectancy" (Hyde et al., 2010; Lindau & Gavrilova, 2010, p. 1).

Women tend to stop having sexual relations earlier than men. This reflects the higher rates of widowhood for women in old age. Whether a woman maintains an active sex life or not depends on good health and the presence of an active sexual partner. Being married is key to older women's continued sexual activity. Widowhood or a husband's decision to stop having sex often puts an end to a woman's sexual activity.

Many older couples say that sex is more satisfying now than when they were younger. They feel more experienced, more relaxed, and enjoy the closeness with their partner. Sexual expression often evolves with age to include other forms of intimacy beyond just sexual intercourse, such as touching, hugging, and holding hands (Hurd Clarke, 2006). Emotional closeness and companionship often take on greater importance for older couples. Older people can have a satisfying marriage without an active sex life. But research supports the idea that continued sexual activity leads to happiness and well-being for older couples (Watson, Bell, & Stelle, 2010).

An AARP survey *Sex, Romance, and Relationships* (Fisher, 2010) looked at the sex lives of middle-aged and older adults. Fisher and a team of researchers surveyed 1,670 adults age 45 and over in 2009 (a representative sample of the U.S. population). The study asked about the frequency of sexual activities, including intercourse, kissing and hugging, self-stimulation, oral, and anal sex.

The study found that people with a partner but not married had sex more often and with more satisfaction than married people.

People in the Fisher study reported satisfaction in a sexual relationship if (1) they had a sexual partner, (2) they had frequent sexual intercourse (more than once a week), (3) the partners had good health, (4) the partners felt low levels of stress, and (5) the partners felt no financial worries.

A high proportion of men and women in this study reported kissing/hugging and sexual touching/caressing at least once a month. This fits with the stereotype of older people as less active in more intimate forms of sexual activity. But this study also showed that among younger age groups of men and women, a high proportion continued to engage in sexual intercourse at least once a month (42 percent for men and 32.3 percent for women). At age 70 and over, one in five men (21.7 percent) continued to have sexual intercourse at least once a month. And one woman in ten (10.5 percent) reported at least monthly sexual intercourse. This lower rate for women reflects the high rate of widowhood among very old women who lack a partner. Sexual activity declined for men and women in the oldest age group. But this study shows that younger women (age 60–69) continue to engage in a variety of sexual activities.

The Fisher study reported one surprising finding. Compared to married people, people with a partner, but not married, said they had sex more often and with more satisfaction. Pepper Schwartz, professor at the University of Washington and adviser to this study, said that, "long-term married couples may get a little less interested [in sex].... Older people in nonmarried relations work harder at it and enjoy it more."

Watson, Bell, and Stelle (2010) conducted in-depth interviews with eight white, middle-class, heterosexual women who remarried late in life. Their ages ranged from 64 to 77. Seven of the eight experienced widowhood, one was divorced. Widows in this study reported a reawakening of their sexuality. Most of the women had resigned themselves to an asexual life in widowhood. Some women expressed surprise at their new interest in and enjoyment of sex.

One woman said sex "wasn't that important ... I guess that's the word, and were both, I guess, surprised that it was as good as it was. Well, mmmm, I mean, it's just a great part of marriage. It's not THE most important part at all, but it is great, and our sex life is great" (p. 306). This comment expressed the importance of sex within older marriage. One woman expressed the emotional closeness she enjoys as a part of the sexual experience. "There is a sweeter emotional kind of flavor to it ... there is even sort of a spiritual realm to it" (p. 306).

This expression of sexual interest and awakening goes against the stereotypical view of relationships in later life that play down sexuality and emphasize companionship. Older people themselves may accept the myth of the asexual relationship or the relationship where sexual interest has lessened with age. The women in this study also accepted this myth. "To their surprise," Watson and colleagues (2010, p. 309) said, "all of that changed when they married. The sexuality in the relationship, and the romance, became important in addition to the companionship."

These women expressed a resistance to the accepted cultural narrative of marriage in later life. They also gave a glimpse into the real-life experience of older women. The researchers said that these women wanted to "break the silence" and tell someone about their relationships. The researchers also cautioned that their small sample of eight white middle-class women has limits. Women from other social classes with other racial/ethnic backgrounds might (and probably would) tell a different story. But this research challenges the myth of an asexual old age and offers a fresh view of marriage and intimacy in later life. Research on other groups of older women would add to this insider's view of marriage and sexuality.

Adaptations in Sexuality Due to Aging

Sexually active older people have to adjust to changes in their bodies as they age. As he ages, a man takes longer to get an erection, takes longer to feel ready for intercourse again, and may have shorter, less intense orgasms. A woman may find that her vagina loses elasticity and opens less fully, and that she may have shorter orgasms (Mayo Clinic, 2011b). Older couples may need to use

vaginal lubrication. Hypertension (high blood pressure) can interfere with sexual performance in both men and women (Woolston, 2009). Many books and videos exist that can help couples explore ways to adapt to these changes.

People can accept changes in their bodies as they get older—changes in strength, the senses, and athletic ability. But a change in sexual function can often damage a person's self-concept and psychological well-being. Sexual performance remains an integral part of what it means to be "manly" or "womanly" in our society. Many older men equate sex with sexual intercourse and, therefore, see their ability to "perform" as central to sexual activity as well as their own sense of self.

Impotence can significantly challenge a man's self-identity, particularly for men in the young-old age group (those in their 60s). For older men (in their 70s and 80s), erectile dysfunction is more likely to be seen as part of normal aging and, therefore, less challenging to their masculinity. But erectile dysfunction can lead a man to define himself as old. Women do not appear to have a comparable sexually related trigger that self-defines them as "old." In fact, many women feel growing older is sexually liberating.

Butler and Lewis (1976, 2002) talked about a **second language of sex** that could overcome the negative feelings that come with changes in sexual functioning. This language focuses on responsiveness, caring, and affection. Some older women see sexual intercourse as "the icing on the cake" (Hurd Clarke, 2006). They emphasize cuddling and companionship more. As one remarried older woman said, "What is important is that we cuddle up, and then if there is sex on top of it, that's extra good" (p. 136).

Drugs (such as Viagra) now exist to restore or enhance sexual performance in older men. Marshall (2008) talked about "a new cultural consensus on sexuality and aging" (p. 21). In the Viagra era, people expect to stay sexually active in later life. An AARP survey of people age 45 and over in the United States found that, compared with men, women have fewer resources to use if they feel a drop in their sexual interest or performance. The AARP study found that 10 percent of the men in the study, but none of the women, used "medications to improve sexual functioning" (Fisher, 2010, p. 16).

Many men who use Viagra say it increases their sexual enjoyment (Vares et al., 2007). Marshall (2008) says the medicalization of male sexuality creates a new market for performance-enhancing drugs, including testosterone

---

second language of sex the "language of sex" that develops in a long-term intimate relationship and focuses on responsiveness, caring, and affection

treatment. Marshall views the use of drugs as a form of age denial and as a move by the pharmaceutical industry to boost profits, even though treatments like testosterone come with health risks. Barnett, Robleda-Gomez, and Pachana (2012) said that drugs such as Viagra, that overcome erectile dysfunction (ED), make "normal ageing" look "dysfunctional." These researchers called for more research on the "social, psychological and emotional" impact of ED drugs on men and their partners (p. 84).

Older men in the future will likely turn to these drugs to enhance and maintain their sexual performance. Marshall notes that even younger men (age 45 to 65) now use these drugs to increase their sexual function. The desire to continue an active sex life into old age will lead to active sex lives among older adults in the future.

HIV/AIDS and Sex in Later Life

The Canadian Public Health Association (n.d.) begins an article on HIV/AIDS in later life with the following story and some advice:

> *Françoise was infected with HIV (human immuno-deficiency virus) at the age of 67. She had just begun a relationship with a man, a few years after the death of her husband. It had not occurred to Françoise to protect herself from HIV/AIDS. She never thought that it could happen to her.* [*]
>
> *Francoise was wrong. No matter what your age, you need to take steps to protect yourself from HIV.*

Few people think of seniors when they think of HIV or AIDS (acquired immunodeficiency syndrome). HIV/AIDS usually brings to mind young people who have unprotected sex, members of the gay and lesbian community, or drug users who share needles. But as Baby Boomers move into later life, HIV/AIDS may show up more often among seniors. Two things account for this.

First, some seniors will have contracted HIV/AIDS earlier in life. A person can live with HIV for many years without showing signs of AIDS. And new therapies allow people to live longer with the disease. These people will bring this illness with them into old age (Roger, Mignone, & Kirkland, 2013).

Second, the Public Health Agency of Canada (PHAC) counts sexual contact as the major HIV/AIDS risk for seniors. Divorce, widowhood, and drugs to correct erectile dysfunction will lead to more

sexually active seniors with new partners. If these seniors have unprotected sex, they risk getting HIV/AIDS (LeBlanc, 2011).

Post-menopausal women who have unprotected sex run a very high risk. Sperm stay in a woman and infected sperm contain high concentrations of HIV. Also, older women have a drier vagina and thinner vagina walls. This can lead to small lesions that admit HIV entry into the blood stream (Canadian Public Health Association, n.d.). Ross, Humble, and Blum (2013) asked 186 heterosexual women age 50 and over about their knowledge of sexuality and HIV/AIDS. These women on average answered almost 50 percent of the questions on HIV/AIDS incorrectly. The researchers said that "These results suggest a lack of understanding of how the virus can be spread" (p. 174; also Roger, Mignone, & Kirkland, 2013). The researchers called for more "social awareness and education in this group regarding ... HIV/AIDS" (p. 165). Awareness of HIV/AIDS and its link to sexual contact might lead to more cautious behaviour by seniors.

The Public Health Agency of Canada (PHAC) (2010b) reported that at the end of 2008 "12.4% (2,644) of all reported AIDS cases [from 1979 to 2008] occurred in people 50 years of age or older." Older men (age 50 and over) face the greatest risk of getting this disease. Men accounted for nearly all AIDS cases in the older population (90.2 percent) from 1979 to 2008. Heterosexual contact accounts for about one-quarter to one-third of reported AIDS cases among older Canadians. But 61.3 percent of men with AIDS during these years reported having sex with another man. The PHAC said that lack of knowledge about HIV infection later in life among older people and among healthcare and policy experts increases the risk of HIV/AIDS.

People age 50 and over with HIV/AIDS face unique problems as they age. Doctors, for example, may misdiagnose HIV/AIDS in older patients. They don't expect to see this disease in an older person. Also, healthcare providers often fail to discuss sexual behaviour with older adults (Mairs & Bullock, 2013). Nearly 70 percent of people age 50 and over with HIV/AIDS received a late diagnosis. Some of these people continued with unprotected sex (Brennan et al., 2013).

Roger and colleagues (2013, p. 301) said, "it is likely that older adults living with HIV/AIDS face even more discrimination, fear of contagion, lack of support, and fear of rejection." And this can lead to decreased quality of life and social isolation. Furlotte and colleagues (2012) found that stigma associated with HIV/AIDS led to fear about the future for people with this disease.

The researchers conducted an in-depth study of nine men and two women diagnosed with HIV/AIDS who lived in Ottawa. The people in this study expressed

---

[*] **Source:** Canadian Public Health Association, Seniors and HIV/AIDS: it's time to start talking, found at http://www.cpha.ca/en/programs/portals/hiv/fundamentals/sex-health/s06/s06a.aspx Used with permission.

worry about finding supportive housing. One woman (age 61) said, "I do sometimes think that someday I will be in a residential area for older people and I do wonder, will they let people in who are HIV positive? Will I be able to go to a residential area?" (p. 42). Many worried that established long-term care and housing settings wouldn't meet their needs as they age. The researchers called for more research to understand the needs and best practices to serve this population.

Brennan and colleagues (2013, p. 41) said, "training for professionals may be needed, given the inevitable increase in the number of PHAs [people who are living with HIV/AIDS] who are growing older." Furlotte and colleagues' (2012) study also points to the need to train health and social service workers in caring for older people with HIV/AIDS. Both of these studies and others call for more research to understand the challenges that older people with HIV/AIDS face.

Sexuality in Long-Term Care Settings

People in institutional settings face unique challenges to the expression of their sexuality. The structure of life in a long-term care facility allows people little privacy and little control over their time and activities. The views of the staff and facility policies can limit a person's sexual activity.

Rheaume and Mitty (2008) said that "in most long-term care settings, staff members tend to view resident's attempts at sexual expression as 'problem' behavior" (p. 342). Even married couples who share a room can feel inhibited (Kemp, 2008). Moss and Moss (2007) said that men who live in long-term care facilities may find it difficult to express their sexuality. And this can lead to a loss of their sense of masculinity.

Mahieu, Van Elssen, and Gastmans (2011) reported that the desire for sexual intimacy remains for many residents, including those with cognitive impairment. But many staff members and administrators feel uncomfortable when cognitively impaired residents express their sexuality. They also fear that the sexual intimacy of cognitively impaired residents may not be consensual. And this could lead to legal action against the facility. Staff members need to assess a cognitively impaired resident's ability to consent to sexual relations. At the same time, staff members need to protect dementia patients from sexual exploitation or abuse (often by other residents) (Rosen, Lachs, & Pillemer, 2010).

EXHIBIT 12.4   *AIDS Case Reports among Older Canadians, Number and Proportion (percentage), 1999 to 2008*

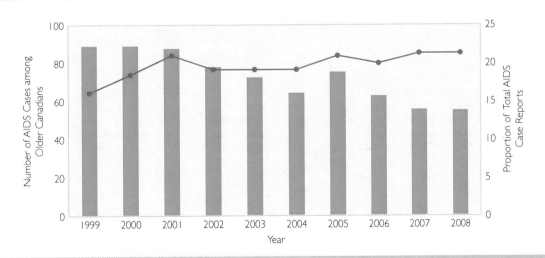

The line in this chart shows an increase in the proportion of total AIDS cases attributable to older Canadians. The proportion grew from 15.9 percent in 1999 to 21.6 percent in 2008—a 35.8 percent increase. During this same period, the number of AIDS cases among older Canadians (the bar chart) decreased from about 90 in 1999 to less than 60 in 2008, with some variation over time. This means that while the number of AIDS cases among seniors has dropped, seniors now make up a higher proportion of all AIDS cases.

Research supports the need for more formal training programs that teach workers about the sexual needs and feelings of older residents. A number of studies (Benbow & Beeston, 2012; Mahieu, Van Elssen, & Gastmans, 2011) called for programs that (1) give staff members information about sexuality in later life, (2) examine staff members' attitudes toward sexuality in later life, and (3) provide skill training so that staff members can work effectively with residents. Administrators can also encourage staff members to talk about issues and institutional policies (Rheaume & Mitty, 2008).

Staff members need to consider residents' need for privacy and to recognize other barriers to sexual expression that residents face. These include adverse effects of medication, physical limitations, and attitudes of staff and families.

Attitudes of staff and older people toward sexuality will continue to change as new cohorts of people enter old age. Younger and midlife cohorts today have more open and accepting attitudes to sex. If they bring these attitudes with them into institutional settings, this will affect staff attitudes and policies. Training can heighten staff members' understanding of sexuality in later life. More knowledge can improve their ability to deal with sexual relations in their institution.

Gay and Lesbian Older Adults

Most studies of sexuality in later life have focused on married or single heterosexuals. Few studies report on older gay and lesbian adults, often referred to as LGBT (lesbian, gay, bisexual, or transsexual) individuals or couples (Humble, 2013). Do older gays and lesbians adapt better or less well than heterosexuals to sexual changes with age?

As is true of heterosexuals, many older gays and lesbians have committed and enduring relationships and close ties to family and friends. Typically, the younger the individual, the more likely he or she will be in a relationship. The legalization of gay marriage in Canada in 2005 removed legal barriers and some of the stigma associated with an LGBT orientation. In 2012 "three in five Canadian adults felt that same-sex couples should have the right to marry" (Humble, 2013, p. 132, citing Angus Reid, 2012).

About 2 percent of Canadians (346,000 adults) between the ages of 18 and 59 consider themselves gay, lesbian, or bisexual (Statistics Canada, 2011m). The 2011 Canadian census reported that from 2006 to 2011, the number of same-sex couples grew from 7,500 to 21,000. The proportion of married same-sex couples (compared to all same-sex couples) nearly doubled between

---

EXHIBIT 12.5   *Whose Life Is It Anyway? Sexuality in a Nursing Home Setting*

Author M.C. White presented the following example of the complex issues that confront family members and administrators when dealing with sex in a nursing home.

Bob and Dorothy have dementia. Dorothy lost her husband sixteen years ago to a heart attack, and Bob has outlived three previous wives. Before Dorothy moved into the nursing home, many women were vying for Bob's attention. But the manager of the nursing home could tell that once Bob met Dorothy, "it was love." When Bob saw Dorothy, he would light up "like a young stud seeing his lady for the first time." Bob and Dorothy soon were spending all of their free time together.

They continued their love affair until Bob's son realized that their relationship had become sexual. Bob's son assumed that his father was being taken advantage of—that due to his dementia, he could not adequately understand the relationship and that Dorothy's advances might "be hard on his father's weak heart." Bob's son insisted that his father be transferred to a different nursing home and refused the nursing home manager's request to let Dorothy say goodbye. For a while, Dorothy stopped eating. She lost over twenty pounds and was treated for depression. In a twisted turn of events, her doctor believes that her Alzheimer's may have saved her life. [The loss might have killed her if its memory hadn't faded so mercifully fast.]

Questions

1. Do people with dementia in an institutional setting have the right to conduct sexual relationships without interference?

2. Was Bob's son right in trying to protect his father?

3. Did Bob's son and the nursing home manager act in Bob's best interest? In Dorothy's best interest?

4. How could this have been handled differently?

Source: White, M.C. 2010. "NOTE: The Eternal Flame: Capacity to Consent to Sexual Behavior among Nursing Home Residents with Dementia," *The Elder Law Journal*, 18: 133. The above source is a paraphrase by M.C. White of the original source: Henneberger, M. 2008. "An Affair to Remember," *Slate*, June 10, 2008, http://www.slate.com/articles/life/family/2008/06/an_affair_to_remember.html (names changed in original).

2006 and 2011. The number of same-sex marriages nearly tripled. Men made up more than half these couples (54.5 percent). Nearly half of all same-sex couples (45.6 percent) lived in three cities—Toronto, Montreal, and Vancouver. Seniors make up a small proportion (about 6.24 percent) of people in same-sex couples (Statistics Canada, 2012m).

Lee (1987) conducted the first study of gay aging men in Canada. He found that men who had partners in the past—a wife, lovers, or a combination of both—reported high life satisfaction even if they now lived alone. Lee found that gay men with a partner tend to report high life satisfaction, but he also reported that having a lover in later life "is not easy to achieve" (p. 147).

Lee also found that men who preferred other gay men as friends, those who knew an older gay man as a role model, and those involved in a gay social life showed higher life satisfaction. Lee's findings showed that older gay men get satisfaction from many of the same things as heterosexual men—companionship, sexual fulfillment, and friendship. They also have unique sources of satisfaction and face unique challenges as they age. Lee's study showed that gay men can adapt to the changes that come with age and that, as he said, "it is possible to achieve happiness alone or by sharing life with a lover, even one found late in life" (p. 151).

Current research supports Lee's findings. Many gays and lesbians have strong, committed relationships and active social networks. For example, one-quarter of same-sex female couples have children in the home (Statistics Canada, 2011m). This represents a sign of these couples' commitment to one another.

But some concerns of older gay and lesbian adults grow out of the stigma associated with their sexual orientation, including worrying about discrimination in healthcare, housing, and long-term care. Leung (2014), for example, reported on discrimination that one woman, Paulette Kupnicki, faced in a seniors' housing complex. "She put up flyers on the building's bulletin board, advertising a seniors' games group and an upcoming play about LGBT (lesbian, gay, bisexual, transgender) issues, in which she was involved. The games group flyer was left in place, but her notice about the play was anonymously taken down. Its removal set Kupnicki's heart pounding: The thought that some residents did not welcome same-sex couples filled her with dread." According to Leung, many LGBT seniors worry that they will have to "re-closet" if they move into a long-term care facility. They fear they will face discrimination and receive poor treatment because of their sexual orientation.

One theme appears in nearly all the studies of homosexuality in later life. Societal attitudes toward homosexuality have shaped and continue to shape the lives of gay and lesbian older people. A study of 394 undergraduate students (Wright & Canetto, 2009), for example, found that students held stereotypical views of gay and lesbian older people. Students believed that older lesbians expressed traits similar to heterosexual men and gay men showed traits similar to heterosexual women.

The double social stigma of being gay and being old may increase the challenges that older gays and lesbians face in later life. For example, societal homophobia has led many gay and lesbian older people to hide their homosexuality. They fear that exposure might cost them their jobs or their sense of belonging in their local communities.

Van Wagenen, Driskell, and Bradford (2013) said, "LGBT people face significant adversities throughout their lives. Members of the LGBT community face social exclusion, discrimination, and pressure to change their sexual orientation. Averett, Yoon, and Jenkins (2011, p. 216) spoke of a triple threat that older lesbians face: "ageism, heterosexism, and sexism." These researchers studied 394 gay women. They found that the women underutilized services for lesbians as well as programs and services for all older people. Abatiell and Adams (2011, p. 881) said that LGBT older people "have tremendous difficulty finding appropriate support."

LGBT seniors in a MetLife and American Society on Aging (2010) study said they feared that the medical profession would not treat them with respect if they had a serious illness. Twelve percent of the lesbian respondents, for example, said, "They have absolutely no confidence that they will be treated respectfully." For this reason, friends often provide support and serve as surrogate families or "chosen families." Nearly half of the women in the Averett, Yoon, and Jenkins (2011) study (47.1 percent) said they relied on partners and family members to care for them if they get sick.

Other research supports this statement. Fredriksen-Goldsen and Muraco (2010, p. 398) said, "Older LGB adults report feeling skeptical of health care professionals and reluctant to rely on a system that has historically discriminated against them and pathologized their communities.... Because of past negative experiences ... older LGB adults identify the need for service providers to receive training and education to ensure sensitive and appropriate treatment."

The MetLife and American Society on Aging study found that adaptations to a hostile society may improve an LGBT person's ability to cope with the challenges of aging. Three-quarters of the people in the study said their sexual orientation helped prepare them for aging. And just over one-quarter (29 percent) said that coping with discrimination in particular helped them prepare for aging. People said that their sexual orientation led to greater resilience and to the development of stronger support networks. More than one-third of respondents (39 percent) said that their sexual orientation led to greater self-reliance.

Like older heterosexual adults, older gays and lesbians need a broad range of social supports and services. Researchers report that gays and lesbians can best meet healthcare and social services needs by planning and implementing programs for their community. This includes participation in non-heterosexual clubs, groups, or organized networks.

Living in a homophobic and hostile environment causes some of the greatest stress for gay men and lesbians of any age. Canadian law supports gay marriage. But many people oppose giving gay couples the same rights and recognition as heterosexual married couples. Older gay men and lesbians have suffered under this attitude for a lifetime. Self-help groups, more research on gay and lesbian aging, and more societal acceptance will all lead to a better life for older gay men and lesbians in the future.

Research on homosexuality in later life has only begun, and a number of research topics still need study. These include the longitudinal study of aging gay and lesbian couples, ethnic and cultural diversity among gays and lesbians, the special concerns of older gays and lesbians, and caregiving for older gays and lesbians (Brotman et al., 2007). Researchers also need to study the relationships between gay older parents and their adult children and grandchildren. Studies of gay and lesbian aging show that societal influences and past experiences shape a person's life in old age. They also show that sexuality plays an important part in homosexual as well as heterosexual aging.

Ruth Weg (1983, p. 76), a pioneer in the study of aging and sexuality, said something that is still true today:

> There is no one way to love or to be loved; there is no one liaison that is superior to another. No one life-style in singlehood or marriage, heterosexual or homosexual, will suit all persons. Self-pleasuring, homosexuality, bisexuality, celibacy, and heterosexuality are all in the same human sexual repertoire.... In a social climate that is more open and accepting, the reality of numbers is helping to return the "old" to the mainstream of living and sexuality to the elderly.

TIME to REVIEW

What challenges and needs do LGBT seniors share with heterosexual seniors?

What special challenges do LGBT seniors face due to their sexual orientation?

Why do some LGBT seniors express reluctance to use formal supports?

What effect might this have on their informal support systems?

OLDER PEOPLE AS CONTRIBUTORS TO FAMILY LIFE

Most of the writing on older people in families focuses on their needs and on what other people do for them. But older people also give help to their families. Early work by Shanas (1967) found that, contrary to the belief that older parents are passive recipients of their children's support, reciprocal help was given in the form of household chores, financial aid, and assistance during illness and other crisis situations. These findings remain true today. Older parents also provide child-care assistance. Research finds that reciprocity within supportive family relationships leads to well-being and higher morale in later life. In cases where the grandparent lives with their children and grandchildren, "exchanges of support—emotional, practical, financial, or a combination of these factors—may flow between generations to various degrees. Grandparents sharing a home with grandchildren may provide an important resource for one or both generations—as well as for the middle generation, if present" (Milan, Laflamme, & Wong, 2015).

Older people give at least three kinds of support. First, they help their spouses and children with healthcare and daily chores; second, they give their children financial support; and third, they provide emotional support and serve as role models for younger family members.

Daily Help Given by Older People

Contrary to what many people believe, younger seniors (under age 75) tend to provide more assistance to younger relatives than they receive (Turcotte & Schellenberg, 2007). For example, older parents may provide a home for unmarried, divorced, or unemployed adult children. In this way they provide "capital" or resources to their children (Putney, Bengtson, & Wakeman, 2007). Research shows that economic support most often flows from the older to the younger generation (Silverstein, 2006).

Older people give varied forms of help to younger people. For example, older people help others with housework or yardwork; most of this help goes to their children, to a friend, or to a neighbour. Also, older people provide child-care help with grandchildren. And child-care support provided by older people to their grandchildren increases their children's economic status. Some older parents provide daily and lifelong care to children with disabilities.

Many parents also share their home with adult children who delay leaving home or return home in adulthood (Beaupre, Turcotte, & Milan, 2006a, 2006b). Adult children who live with older parents often do so because they have no spouse, attend school, or have no job. The number of adult children (those in their 20s and 30s) who live with parents has increased since the 1980s. What accounts for this change? First, more children remain home for more years in adulthood. Some delay leaving home in order to finish school. Others remain home after they get their first job in order to save money.

Second, **boomerang children** return to their parents' home after having moved out at an earlier point in time. Statistics Canada (2011o) reported that in 2011, 42.3 percent of young adults age 20 to 29 lived in their parents' home. Some never left their parents' home. But many of these young adults were boomerang kids.

Stone, Rosenthal, and Connidis (1998) studied different kinds of help given by older parents to their children. These included financial support, child care, and help with daily chores. The researchers found that overall support from older parents to adult children peaks between ages 55 and 64, with 47 percent of these parents saying that they give help. Still, a quarter of parents age 65 to 74 give medium or high levels of help. And even at age 75 and older, nearly one-fifth (18 percent) of parents say they give some help to their children.

These researchers said that older parents age 45 to 74 probably give most of their support as unpaid work, such as child care. Later in life (age 75 and over), parents may offer more financial support as their own physical ability declines. These researchers suggested that parents give the most support to the children they feel have the most need. The authors find that the give-and-take of support remains relatively balanced between parents and children until around age 70. Then children begin to give more help than they receive.

These researchers and others (Turcotte & Schellenberg, 2007; also Suitor et al., 2011) find that although support within families flows both ways, over a lifetime parents give more support than they receive. Stone, Rosenthal, and Connidis (1998) said that "if we had included the monetary value of services provided informally by one generation to another we would increase markedly the relative size of the figure for flows that benefit the young" (p. 24). Older people also pass on possessions, money, and property to younger generations through inheritance bequests (Eckerdt, Addington, & Hayter, 2011).

Research finds differences in the types of help that older men and women provide to others (Turcotte & Schellenberg, 2007). Men are more likely to help with home maintenance, outside chores, and transportation. They also tend to help with practical advice. Older women are more likely to provide emotional support or child care. Older people, compared with those who are younger (25 to 54 years of age), are also more likely to provide help to a neighbour. These findings show that most older people live interdependently with family, neighbours, and friends. They give and receive help with practical activities and finances. They exchange emotional support throughout their lives.

Financial Support

Older people often give younger members of their family financial support. The amount and kind of support given differs by social class and ethnic group, but studies show that even middle-aged people think of their parents as givers.

A study by MetLife (2009) in the United States found that grandparents gave money to their grandchildren for many reasons. Two in five grandparents said they gave "general support." One-quarter (26 percent) helped financially with education. Grandparents also provided money to help their grandchildren with personal life events, medical bills, and rent. This broad range of support shows that grandparents stay engaged with their families.

Emotional Support and Being a Role Model

Research shows that adult children rely on their parents as role models throughout their lives. Many adult children turn to their parents for emotional support and help during and after a divorce. Parents can also act as role models for their adult children as they experience important later-life transitions such as grandparenthood, widowhood, and retirement.

Older family members derive great satisfaction from the help they give to their children and to other younger

---

boomerang children adult children who return to their parents' home after having moved out at an earlier point in time family members. Some older people help younger family members find jobs; they give advice (as when a grandmother advises a daughter on how to handle a crying baby); they may head the family; or they may serve as **kin keepers**, who keep family members in touch with one another.

Kin keepers often hold on to treasured family possessions and pass them on to the next generation (Adler, 2008, citing Clift, n.d.). Women generally occupy the kin keeper role. Families with kin keepers tend to get together more often. Men in families with kin keepers benefit by having stronger ties to their siblings.

Older parents bring their families together on special occasions, which increases contact among family members. Older women may serve as advisers and confidants to their widowed daughters. Older men often give financial help to their children and grandchildren. Family roles can give meaning and purpose to an older person's life. Research finds that older people have the highest emotional well-being when they give as well as receive support. Reciprocity makes older people feel useful, independent, and worthwhile. Older people's supportive roles can strengthen intergenerational ties and create more fulfilling relationships between parents and their children, as well as their grandchildren.

TIME to REVIEW

What are some of the sources of support older people give to their families?

What benefits do families gain from the support of their older members?

How does support from older family members strengthen family bonds?

Grandparenting

Grandparenthood is a common experience for older Canadians. More people will take on the grandparent role today than ever before, and many of them will assume this role in late midlife. In 2010, there were about 700,000 grandparents age 45 and over in Canada (Turcotte & Schellenberg, 2007). Sixty percent of people age 55 to 64 were grandparents. This jumps to 87 percent of those age 65 to 74, and 94 percent for people age 75 and over (Milan, Laflamme, & Wong, 2015).

Women make up 80 percent of grandparents, reflecting the fact that, compared with men, more women

kin keepers the people in a family who keep family members in touch with one another; women generally occupy this role

live into old age. On average, grandparents have between four and five grandchildren (Milan, Laflamme, & Wong, 2015). And most grandparents have regular contact with at least one grandchild. The number of grandchildren per grandparent will probably decrease in the future as couples have fewer children. But, Uhlenberg (2009) says, grandparents will have more time and energy in the future to focus on their grandchildren.

With increased longevity, many grandparents will live to see their grandchildren grow into adults with children of their own. Uhlenberg, using U.S. data, said that "by 2020 almost half of all 10-year-olds are expected to have all grandparents alive. Indeed, we anticipate that 80% of those reaching age 30 in 2020 will still have at least one living grandparent" (p. 493).

Grandparents now play complex roles in the lives of their grandchildren. Some grandparents feel that they do enough by simply being present, but others play a more active role as family arbitrators, watchdogs, or family historians. Grandparents often look out for the well-being of younger relatives, help them when they can, and create links between family members. Grandparents in an AARP study (Lampkin, 2012) said they shape their grandchildren's values and help them develop morally and spiritually. The grandparent role offers older people one of the most satisfying and enjoyable ways to give to other family members.

Research shows that grandchildren value their grandparents. Grandparents provide adult grandchildren with a view into the past—to their childhood, their family history, and historical events. As one 29-year-old grandson said of his relationship with his grandparents: "It is very important for knowing your roots and for family history and for knowing where you came from....

Grandparents take great joy in the achievements of their grandchildren. Grandparents reinforce family values—such as the value of education. Some grandparents provide grandchildren with funds to help with school tuition.

EXHIBIT 12.6 *Grandparents Who Live with Their Grandchildren*

Some grandparents involve themselves in the daily lives and care of their grandchildren. In 2011, 4.8 percent of children in Canada age 14 and under lived in multigenerational households with at least three generations (grandparents, parents, and grandchildren) (Statistics Canada, 2012m). About 8 percent of all grandparents live with their grandchildren. People age 45 and over with Indigenous identity and those who report "a Traditional Indigenous Spirituality" had a larger proportion of grandparents who live with their grandchildren. Traditional adoption practices in Indigenous culture in part explain this tendency. Also, housing shortages in northern communities may force three generations to live together.

Likewise Sikh, Hindu, and other immigrant populations showed a higher proportion of grandparents living with their grandchildren (Milan, Laflamme, & Wong, 2015). Cultural preferences explain part of this decision. But also, recent immigrant elders often live with their children. The Canadian Family Reunification Program requires that a sponsor (for example, an adult child) take financial responsibility for the new immigrant (an elderly parent). In sum, grandparents of Indigenous or South Asian background make up a high proportion of grandparents who live with grandchildren.

A small number of grandparents in Canada (less than 1 percent) live with grandchildren without the presence of the middle generation. In 2011, about 0.5 percent of children age 14 and under lived in this type of household (Statistics Canada, 2012m). Most of these children (57.8 percent) live with a grandparent couple. Researchers call these arrangements skip-generation households. Grandparents in these households "may assume a parental role, providing a valuable emotional and/or financial resource for their grandchildren" (Milan, Laflamme, & Wong, 2015, p. 3). Most of these grandparents (80 percent) pay something toward household expenses, although this differs by ethnic group.

Grandparents often care for their grandchildren because their own children can't provide the care. One grandparent told the AARP (Lampkin, 2012): "[My] daughter and granddaughter had no place to go. I felt I had to [take them in]. If not, I would not see them again [or they would be] homeless" (p. 16). This can occur because of divorce or separation, mental health difficulties, substance abuse, or the death of an adult child. Grandparents often feel rewarded when they raise their grandchildren, but they also face challenges. These can include worries about their own health, problems with social isolation, and financial difficulties.

At a period when older people expect more time and freedom in their retirement years, these grandparents take on unanticipated child-care responsibilities, often with high-risk grandchildren. Caring full-time for a grandchild can create a close emotional bond, particularly for grandmothers, but it can also increase grandparents' stress (Dolbin-MacNab & Keiley, 2009).

Dolbin-MacNab (2006) said that skip-generation grandparents could benefit from parent education and training. This would build on their parenting experiences. But it would also help grandparents deal with the new challenges of parenting grandchildren. Support groups, peer counselling, and respite services would also buffer grandparents' stress.

It's like a key" (Kemp, 2005, p. 168). Grandchildren feel respect for their grandparents. They admire their strength and resilience in surviving the hardships and struggles of their younger years. Grandchildren also worry about the present-day health challenges their grandparents face (Boon & Shaw, 2007).

The grandparent–grandchild relationship has become more common in the lives of adult grandchildren. The majority of young adults in Canada have at least one living grandparent (70 percent of adults in their 20s and 32 percent of adults in their 30s) (Kemp, 2003). Life course transitions within the family, such as divorce or death, can often bring grandparents and adult grandchildren closer together. With people living longer, adult grandchildren have the opportunity to get to know their grandparents as "real people" and as friends.

Grandparents can introduce grandchildren to the wonders of the natural world by taking hikes or going camping in natural surroundings. Grandparents can have fun and don't have to abide by the rational rules that parents sometimes need to enforce. Grandparents and grandchildren can provide support and enjoyment for one another.

Novelli and Workman (2006) said grandparents can serve as role models and mentors. "There's not much kids can't learn from grandparents," they said, "including strong moral values. Grandchildren will be the first to agree. They say their grandparents have taught them good manners, respect for others, and a strong work ethic" (p. 69). Barnett and colleagues (2010) found that grandparents who had good relationships with their own children in adolescence and adulthood showed more involvement with their grandchildren. This especially held true for grandparents who had good relations with their daughters.

Gender can also influence the quality of the grandparent–grandchild relationship, with closer ties in general for female family members. For example, grandchildren tend to be closer to their maternal grandparents. Grandparents are closer to granddaughters than to grandsons, and grandmothers have closer and more active ties with

---

skip-generation households grandparents living with grandchildren without the presence of the middle (parent) generation

Longer life expectancy and better health in later life will mean that several generations will live together for many years. Some people will live to see their great-grandchildren grow to adulthood.

Blend Images/Shutterstock

both granddaughters and grandsons than do grandfathers (Monserud, 2011). What a grandparent makes of the grandparent role depends on the older person's gender, age, marital status, geographic proximity, and relationship with his or her adult children. Proximity can influence emotional closeness in grandparent–grandchild relationships (Monserud, 2008), but living nearby does not guarantee a close bond.

Little research exists on grandfather–grandchild relationships (Bates, 2009). Some researchers say that the importance of grandfathers has been underestimated (Mann, 2007; Stgeorge & Fletcher, 2014). Bates and Taylor (2012) ranked grandfathers as involved, passive, or disengaged. They found that, compared with disengaged grandfathers, involved grandfathers had fewer depressive symptoms and a more positive attitude. The researchers concluded that grandfathers' involvement with grandchildren leads to good mental health. (But it may also be true that grandfathers with good mental health enjoy engagement with their grandchildren.) Stgeorge and Fletcher (2014, p. 354) said that as grandfathers age "family connections will become increasingly salient goals and ... the meaning of these relationships will be packed with concern, commitment and action." Reitzes and Mutran (2006) report that the grandparent role leads to good self-esteem.

Research findings suggest that aging and decreased activity may lead to decreases in grandparents' influence on their grandchildren. Grandparents may focus their energy on some of their closer or more personable grandchildren.

In general, research shows that while the bond between adult grandchildren and their grandparents

remains high across the life course, the relationship involves continuity and change over time. This can mean continued closeness over time, closer ties with grandmothers and less close ties to grandfathers, or a gradual decline over time with some increased closeness in the grandparents' later years. Illness and decreased activity, for example, may lead to decreases in grandparents' involvement with their grandchildren. For both generations, the tie is often seen as "an unconditional latent reserve of support" or a "safety net" of support, should it be needed (Kemp, 2005, p. 173).

Monserud (2011) said that "grandparents and adult grandchildren are potential sources of mutual assistance" (p. 426). They can provide emotional, practical, and financial support for one another. Adult grandchildren can even serve as caregivers if a grandparent's health deteriorates.

Studies show that feelings between grandparents and grandchildren depend on the relationship between the grandparents and the parents (Ben Shlomo et al., 2010; Monserud, 2008, 2011). The closer the relationship between the parent and grandparent, the closer the tie between grandparents and grandchildren. The quality of the grandparents' relationship with their children-in-law may be of particular importance in influencing the quality of the grandparent–grandchild tie.

Gladstone (1989) studied 110 grandparents in Canadian families where parents had split up. He found that adult children and children-in-law act as mediators between grandchildren and grandparents. They can obstruct or arrange visits. Children-in-law can inhibit contact by keeping the former spouse from seeing children. This would, in turn, keep the grandparents from seeing the children. Contact with grandchildren of divorced or separated children depends on the grandparents' relationship to the former child-in-law, whether the child or the child-in-law has custody of the grandchild, and geographical closeness.

A self-help group with chapters across the country called **GRAND (Grandparents Requesting Access and Dignity)** helps grandparents who cannot get access to their grandchildren. The group, started in 1983, provides education and support, and lobbies for changes in laws to protect grandparents' access to their grandchildren. After GRAND collected 10,000 names on a petition to change the Divorce Act, members presented the petition to the House of Commons. The petition asked that the act

GRAND (Grandparents Requesting Access and Dignity) a group that helps grandparents who cannot get access to their grandchildren

include a statement such as the one in the Quebec Civil Code. It says, "In no case may a father or mother, without serious cause, place obstacles between the child and grandparents." This petition, however, was not successful. The federal Divorce Act does allow for access applications from people other than parents but does not explicitly identify grandparents.

Grandparents who go to court risk increasing the tension with their children or children-in-law. Today, grandparents have to show the courts why they should have access to their grandchildren and that denying access would be harmful to grandchildren. A change in the law would guarantee grandparents' rights of access.

Manitoba, for example, provides a website with information related to grandparent–grandchild access issues (Manitoba Justice, 2017). The site lists services such as family conciliation and "a free, child-focused information program, *For the Sake of the Children*, for parents, grandparents and other interested people. It includes information on resolving disputes, children's needs and communicating for the benefit of children."

Grandparenting and New Family Structures

Some older people manage a complex system of relationships due to the marriage and remarriage of their children. These complexities increase as children marry and divorce, sometimes more than once.

High divorce rates among children lead to new relationships for older people. A grandmother, for example, may stay in touch with her former daughter-in-law after her son's divorce in order to keep in contact with her grandchildren. She may even develop a close personal friendship with her former daughter-in-law. If her former daughter-in-law remarries, she may meet and get to know a new family of grandparents and children from this new marriage. This will expand her kinship and social network.

Grandparents may include step-grandchildren in their list of grandchildren. Today we have nuclear, extended, blended, lesbian and gay families, as well as broken families. One of the authors and his wife recently attended a dinner at a friend's home. Our friend arranged the dinner to introduce us to his son and daughter-in-law, who were visiting from out of town. The young couple had six parents around the table. The son's two parents, the daughter-in-law's mother with her second husband, and the daughter-in-law's father with his male partner. A grandchild in this family will have six doting

grandparents—one set in a long-term traditional marriage, a second set in a second marriage, and a third set in a gay relationship.

Things get more complicated if both parents in a second marriage have grandchildren—from children in former marriages and from their own marriage. Likewise, if any of these children divorce and remarry, they may have children from more than one marriage. How will the parents relate to this collection of grandchildren—some distant in relation to them and some very close? Many older people will find themselves in these complex family structures. No rulebook exists to help sort out the right way to grandparent under these conditions.

What are some of the pleasures that grandparents report in their relations with their grandchildren?

What challenges does divorce in a family create for some grandparents, and what are some responses they can make to these challenges?

What do gerontologists mean when they talk about a skip-generation family? What challenges does this family structure cause for grandparents?

FUTURE RESEARCH ON FAMILY LIFE

The family has shown resilience throughout history. It has changed in size and structure over the past centuries. And it will change in the future. Yet it remains the primary emotional and practical support system for individuals young and old.

Researchers will study new family forms and their impact on older adults and their families. Consider some of the directions research will take in the future.

First, for many years research on the family and social supports in later life focused on the "normal" family. These studies looked at the typical crises faced by a white, Anglo-Saxon widow and grandmother. Researchers studied the supports that this typical family needed.

Researchers now believe that this image takes too narrow a view of family life. The literature idealizes marriage, but it says little about the dysfunctions that marriage can create. Married couples may argue about money, intimate relations, and changing feelings toward each other.

When spouses rely on each other for support, they can lose contact with friends and relatives. This situation can lead to feelings of burden, isolation, and depression for both spouses. More research on marriage in later life should focus on both the benefits and the problems that marriage can bring. Studies need to look at marital history and individuals' views of marriage.

Second, the structure of the family has changed significantly over the past decades. Sociodemographic changes in family size and structure, patterns of marriage and divorce, changing roles for women, increased life expectancy, and greater diversity in the timing of life course events and transitions mean that more families will include older family members.

Many older people today have living siblings, adult children, and grandchildren. Families have more generations alive at one time than ever before. This means that older people today have large social networks. We know little about the lives and relationships of older people in these new family structures. Researchers should also continue to study the needs and experiences of older gay and lesbian couples and individuals.

Third, research on older people's family life has paid little attention to the lives of certain types of people. Little research has been done on never-married older people (Pudrovska, Schieman, & Carr, 2006), divorced older people (Lin, 2008; Wu & Schimmele, 2007), or the childless elderly (Dykstra & Hagestad, 2007; Penning & Wu, 2014). We also know little about gender differences in the social support needs of different marital status groups, including those who remarry in later life.

Fourth, few studies have compared the family life of older people from different cultural and ethnic backgrounds. More research on ethnicity in old age should look at family relations, informal supports, and the use of social services by different ethnic groups. Kobayashi (2000) looked at intergenerational support in Japanese Canadian families. She found that filial obligation (the obligation to care for a parent) led adult children to provide emotional support to parents. But it did not affect the amount of financial or service support children gave. She said that researchers need to study ethnicity and parent–child exchanges and the differences in support given by sons and daughters.

Fifth, research in the past several decades focused mostly on older women. Few studies on family and social relations looked at older men. Researchers need to look at male friendships, lone-father families, widowers, grandfathering, gay men as they age, men's remarriage, as well as men involved in caregiving to family members—sons and older husbands (Calasanti & Bowen, 2006). Studies that have described men show that they face special challenges in old age.

Sixth, some researchers suggest that marriage is becoming increasingly fragile. Current low-marriage rates among younger people, increases in common-law and living apart together (LAT) relationships, high divorce rates, and fewer remarriages in middle and later life will lead to new and more diverse patterns of family life for older people. These trends may produce more unmarried older people, both men and women. And the future may see more older people with children from multiple marriages.

Seventh, new patterns of family life have begun to emerge: serial monogamy (multiple marriages in a lifetime), remarriage, and polyamory. These all lead to more complex family structures in later life (Milan, Wong, & Vézina, 2014; Putney, Bengtson, & Wakeman, 2007; Treas & Marcum, 2011). Gillis (2015) said that second, third, and non-traditional families could lead to contested wills and fights over inheritance. A 1996 law in British Columbia allowed "second spouses and half-siblings to contest wills on the basis that they're not adequately provided for." This led to a spike in disputed wills in that province.

Some grandparents will have grandchildren from several marriages of their children. They will have multiple in-laws from these marriages. Their grandchildren may in turn have several marriages. Older people themselves may have children, grandchildren, and great-grandchildren from their own multiple marriages. This will create rich, complex, and diverse family structures. We don't even have names for many of these relationships. Researchers will need to identify and study these new family patterns.

Will family (blood) bonds hold families together in the future? Or will people choose as relatives the people they like best? Will people invent new family structures to suit their needs? Or will people try to maintain traditional family structures? Who will feel obligated to support whom in the future? What will motivate older and younger people to care for one another? The answers to these questions lie ahead of us. But one thing seems certain: the changing family today will challenge all of us to rethink family relations in the future.

CONCLUSION

Older people give as much to their families as they receive. And they serve as role models for the young. Old age is a time of change—the death of a spouse, for example, creates one of life's greatest stresses. But research shows that most older people cope with the challenges of aging and experience satisfying and rewarding family lives.

Summary

1. The myth persists that middle-aged children abandon their elderly parents, but studies show again and again that children maintain contact with their parents, provide them with help, and get help and support from them when they need it.

2. A good marriage provides support for both partners as they age. Married older people use less formal care, rely less on children and friends for support, and have a lower institutionalization rate than unmarried older people. Older women run a higher risk than older men of losing this support due to widowhood.

3. Older adults now and in the future will have greater choice in the type of intimate relationships they wish to form. These will include common-law and living apart together (LAT) relationships for those older people who want a close and intimate relationship but not necessarily one within marriage.

4. Older divorced men are more likely than older divorced women to remarry. Being divorced in later life often means economic insecurity, particularly for women, and loss of social contact with children for men. There has been a significant increase in the number of divorced older people.

5. Never-married older adults play vital and supportive roles in the lives of siblings, older parents, and others. They also form friendships and other social relationships to provide themselves with supporters, confidants, and companions.

6. Widowhood has become an expected life event for women in Canada, although it still creates stress in a woman's life. Researchers disagree about the impact of widowerhood on men. Some studies show that widowers have fewer social supports and that they suffer from isolation, loneliness, and a high risk of suicide. More recent studies suggest that men may need less social support than women and that they adapt in different ways to widowerhood.

7. Single older people form new relationships through dating. Some people find this stressful; others find it a good way to meet people. Online dating services make finding a partner a simple process. And many older people use these services to arrange dates with compatible partners. Single Baby Boomers will feel comfortable using the Internet to chat and meet with potential mates.

8. Older people have an interest in sex throughout life. Most people will need to adjust their expectations about sexual performance in later life. But, given good health and a willing partner, older people can enjoy sexual relations into late old age. New attitudes toward sexuality and the use of drug therapies for men may encourage more sexual activity in later life. An increase in cases of HIV/AIDS among older people points to the need for more education for seniors about this disease.

9. LGBT seniors have the same concerns as heterosexual seniors—health, finances, caregiving. They also face prejudice, stereotyping, and discrimination due to their sexual orientation. Long-term relationships with a committed partner can provide older gay men and lesbians with companionship, acceptance, and support. Other social network ties with family members and friends also serve an important social support function in their lives.

10. Most older people keep up social contacts with relatives and friends as they age. They give support to family and friends as well as receive it. They help their children socially, financially, and emotionally. They help their peers by acting as confidants. Older people, like younger people, get esteem and a sense of purpose from helping others.

11. Grandparenting offers older people one of the most enjoyable roles in old age. Older people can shape the role to suit their personality, lifestyle, and interests. Some grandparents raise their grandchildren in skip-generation households. Grandparents and grandchildren form a unique bond that satisfies both generations. With increased longevity, many grandparents will live to see their grandchildren grow into adults with children of their own.

12. Many gaps still exist in the literature on family life in old age. Research on atypical groups of older people—for example, older gay men and lesbians, permanently single and divorced older people—will increase our understanding of family and intimate relations in later life.

STUDY QUESTIONS

1. What are the benefits of marriage in old age? How does divorce affect people in old age? Why do some older people choose to live in common-law or living apart together (LAT) relationships?

2. What types of people form the social support networks of older divorced and never-married people? Compare and contrast the networks of divorced and never-married people.

3. Explain why widows outnumber widowers in the aging population. Why do men seem to suffer more than women socially and psychologically when they lose a spouse?

4. Describe the differences in sexuality in later life for men and women. Consider the different physical changes men and women experience as well as social-psychological differences. What challenges do LGBT older people face?

5. Discuss the role that grandparents play in the lives of grandchildren. What are the benefits of the grandparent–grandchild tie for grandparents? Explain the different styles of grandparenting. Why do some grandparents go to court in order to gain the right to see their grandchildren?

6. Why do some gerontologists believe that researchers should expand the scope of studies on aging and the family? What types of issues and trends should future research address?

KEY TERMS

boomerang children (p. 309)
confidant (p. 294)
GRAND (Grandparents Requesting Access and Dignity) (p. 312)
kin keepers (p. 310)
LAT (living apart together) couples (p. 296)
second language of sex (p. 303)
skip-generation households (p. 311)

Study Tools
CHAPTER 12

{

Located at retail.tophat.com:

- Review Key Terms with interactive and printable flash cards
- Check Your Comprehension and Think About chapter concepts by completing practice quizzes
- Develop Your Gerontological Imagination with class activities
- Analyze Aging in a Global Perspective with engaging case studies and critical thinking questions
- Demonstrate Your Knowledge of the Concepts by bringing your own experience to personal application questions
- Evaluate Aging in the Media by completing Internet activities with evaluation questions

CHAPTER 13

SOCIAL SUPPORT

Dmitry Kalinovsky/Shutterstock

LEARNING OBJECTIVES

After reading this chapter, you will

LO1 Understand the types and sources of informal support older people receive.

LO2 Be able to explain some of the models researchers use in trying to describe informal supports.

LO3 Be able to discuss the link between informal and formal care and describe how these two types of care supplement one another.

LO4 Appreciate the importance of informal social supports for well-being and happiness in later life.

LO5 Understand the experience of caregivers, including the satisfaction that comes with caregiving and the challenges faced by caregivers of older people with dementia.

LO6 Be able to explain the positive and negative effects of caregiving on different types of caregivers (e.g., spouses, children, siblings, friends).

LO7 Know the facts about elder abuse and mistreatment in Canada and some of the policies and practices that can reduce elder abuse and mistreatment.

LO8 Be able to consider the future of informal supports due to demographic and social change.

INTRODUCTION

Dr. Joe sat in the armchair, staring into space. He held an ice cream cone in his right hand. The ice cream began to drip onto his wrist, but he didn't notice. Molly, his wife, wiped his hand and helped him move the cone to his mouth. He sucked on the ice cream. It left a vanilla circle around his lips. Molly wiped this away too. Molly spoke to Joe of family events they had shared in the past. His face showed little sign of recognition. After some time, an attendant came to take Joe back to his room. Molly and I walked to our cars in silence.

Molly had invited me to visit Joe with her in his nursing home. Joe was in the final stages of Alzheimer's disease, a disease that robs the person of their memory, their relationships, and finally their life. Joe had worked as a family physician for more than 30 years. In his late 50s, his memory began to fail. One day he came home at 9 p.m., several hours after his usual dinnertime. Molly had begun to worry. *But,* she thought, *I suppose he's gotten delayed at the office.* In fact, he'd circled the neighbourhood for nearly two hours, looking for their home. He came home distressed and frightened. Molly reports this as one of the first dramatic signs of Joe's illness.

Had he shown signs of dementia before? Probably. Molly played over and over again the years before Joe's illness became apparent. She searched for signs of Joe's growing forgetfulness. Forgotten keys, a missed appointment, a forgotten name or place. But always these seemed like simple mistakes. Only as his illness progressed did it become obvious that Joe had a progressive dementia.

Finally it became impossible to care for Joe at home. His wandering at night kept Molly sleepless and constantly on edge. One winter night toward the end of Joe's time at home, he found the car keys and quietly left the house. He drove for miles outside the city until the car ran out of gas. He saw the lights of a distant farmhouse and walked through the snow to the front door. The startled farm family let him in and called the police. The police found the car, traced it to his home address, and called Molly. She knew that she couldn't care for Joe at home any longer.

But her life as a caregiver didn't end when Joe entered a nursing home. Molly visits often, even though Joe no longer recognizes her. Like many spouses of Alzheimer's patients, she lives in limbo—between the life she and Joe shared together and the time that she will live alone after Joe's death. Still, she feels an obligation to ensure Joe's well-being. Caregivers can feel a sense of achievement as they look after their care receivers. But caregivers can also experience stress and sometimes illness due to their caregiving responsibilities. Many studies now document the pros and cons of informal support.

This chapter looks at (1) the informal support older people receive from family members and friends, (2) family caregivers and the challenges they face, and (3) abuse and mistreatment of older people.

INFORMAL SUPPORTS FOR OLDER PEOPLE

Life course events and sociocultural conditions influence the quality of life in old age, but they do not determine it. Older people can and do respond actively to the changes that aging brings. Their response depends on their personality, past experience, and social resources, including social supports. **Social support** refers to help and assistance we give to and receive from others. Social support helps older people cope with aging and improves their quality of life and well-being.

Researchers study two types of social support: formal and informal. Keefe (2011, citing Carrière, 2006) reported that about 1.2 million people in Canada (most of them age 65 and over) use formal home care services. **Formal support** refers to help given by professional caregivers such as doctors, nurses, and social workers as well as paid homemakers and other healthcare services. People pay for formal supports either from their own resources or through their taxes. Studies find that few older people who need help with daily chores or healthcare use only formal care. More often people use informal supports for everyday help.

Informal support refers to the unpaid help given by friends, neighbours, and family. Informal support includes everyday help such as rides to the doctor or to a shopping centre, help with housecleaning or yardwork, or just a visit from a neighbour. Informal supporters can also help an older person cope with a personal crisis, adjust to a change in health, or locate a formal service. It is estimated that 70 percent to 80 percent of informal support received by older adults comes from family and friends (Keefe, 2011).

Spouses tend to provide the most care. Sinha and Bleakney (2014) report that spouses provide a median of 9 hours of care each week (two hours more than that of family and friends). After a spouse, children are the most important source of social support for older family

---

Social support the help and assistance people give to one another

Formal support paid support from professional caregivers such as doctors, nurses, social workers, and home care workers

Informal support unpaid support from family members, friends, neighbours, and others in the community

members. Older women, in particular, tend to receive support from their adult children (Choi et al., 2014).

Gerontologists refer to the amount of resources available to a person, including social support, as their *life course capital* or *social capital*. The amount of social capital available to a person changes over time and differs for each individual.

In 2012, more than 4.5 million Canadians age 45 and older reported providing some type of care or assistance to an older family member or friend, an increase of 20 percent over 2007 (Cranswick & Dosman, 2008; Sinha, 2013b). In 2013, caregivers age 45 and over spent a median of three hours caring for a family member or friend. Women provide the majority of informal support, especially in cases of high-intensity care. Older care recipients are also more likely to be women.

Seniors age 65 and over spend the most hours giving care. Nearly a quarter of seniors (23 percent) spent 20 hours or more per week on caregiving. Care for a spouse largely accounts for the long hours spent by seniors on caregiving. Senior caregivers may feel especially strained by caregiving, since some of them have health and mobility limitations (Sinha, 2013b).

Social policies now favour a mix of informal and formal care. Sims-Gould and Martin-Matthews (2010b) said that when this works well it leads to a "trusting relationship between paid and unpaid carers" (p. 416). "Family caregivers describe various ways in which they care 'with' the home support workers. Either by working together to accomplish a task or by setting the stage for one another's care, the caring work is inextricably linked" (p. 420).

Studies show that people usually turn to the formal system only after the informal system no longer meets their needs. Formal care use also tends to increase with age. But even people who make extensive use of formal care services still rely on their informal care network. Bookman and Harrington (2007, cited in Gonyea, 2009) said that family caregivers act as "geriatric case managers, medical record keepers, paramedics, and patient advocates to fill dangerous gaps in a system that is uncoordinated, fragmented, bureaucratic, and often depersonalizing" (p. 1005).

Informal caregivers provide about two-thirds of all care. People continue to get support, especially from the nuclear family, even after they face a healthcare crisis. Informal supports can also buffer stress from life events such as widowhood or illness. A greater proportion of older women, compared with older men, get emotional support from children or friends (Connidis, 2010). Older men, compared with older women, have smaller support networks.

EXHIBIT 13.1 *Informal Caregivers. People Who Provided Care, by Age and Sex, 2012*

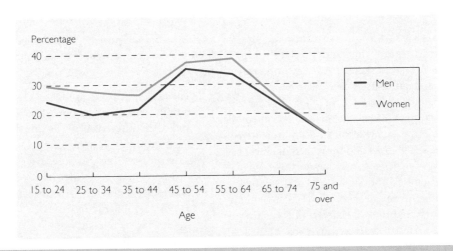

Note that the age groups 45 to 64 have the highest proportion of caregivers. About half of caregivers age 45 to 54 gave care to a parent. Parents often need help due to aging and frailty. Caregiving peaked in the 55 to 64 age group for women, with nearly 4 in 10 women and more than 3 in 10 men providing care. These caregivers provided care to aging parents, but also to their spouse. About one-quarter of caregivers age 65 to 74 gave care to a spouse. Nearly half of caregivers age 75 and over gave care to a spouse. Note that at every age before age 74, compared to men, a higher proportion of women serve as caregivers.

Source: Turcotte, M. Family caregiving: What are the consequences? Statistics Canada (2013), p. 2. Retrieved from http://www.statcan.gc.ca/pub/75-006-x/2013001/article/11858-eng.pdf. Original source: Statistics Canada, *General Social Survey* (2012). Reproduced and distributed on an "as is" basis with the permission of Statistics Canada.

EXHIBIT 13.2   *Seniors Receive More Formal Care as They Age and Lose Social Networks*

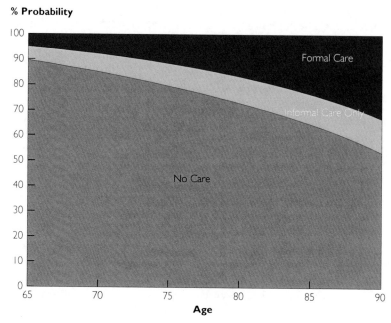

Note: Probabilities are calculated for the typical senior, where age varies but all other variables in the model are held constant.

Note that the older the person, the more formal care they need and use. The loss of informal supports explains this increase in informal supports. Note also that with age, people need more of both formal and informal supports. By age 90, almost half of older people need some care—most of it formal support.

Source: Kelly Cranswick and Derrick Thomas, "Elder care and the complexities of social networks," *Canadian Social Trends*, Summer 2005. Statistics Canada, Catalogue No. 11-008; p. 12. Chart on p. 12 of article. Reproduced and distributed on an "as is" basis with the permission of Statistics Canada.

Caregiving networks vary significantly in size, proximity, and composition—by gender, relationship, and age. These network characteristics explain variations in the types and amounts of care older people get. Older adults may not get enough care when they have small networks, networks with mostly male non-relatives, and networks with members who live far away. Research also finds that social networks and living arrangements can influence the informal and formal support that older people receive. Cranswick and Thomas (2005) say that "the size, quality and proximity of people's social networks are arguably among the things that determine whether seniors receive formal care delivered by professionals, rely on informal care provided by family and friends or, indeed, receive no care at all" (p. 10). Overall, very few older people who live in the community are without some close supportive ties.

Studies have looked at how older people choose their informal supporters out of their potential group of supporters. Studies have also looked at the tasks informal supporters perform. Four models describe the way people use informal supports: the task specificity model, the hierarchical compensatory model, the functional specificity of relationships model, and the convoy model:

1.   The **task specificity model** says that different groups (family, friends, neighbours) have different abilities and offer different types of support (Litwak, 1985). Each group plays a specific role in supporting the older person. For example, a spouse might provide companionship, while adult children provide everyday support, and friends act as confidants.

2.   The **hierarchical compensatory model** of support states that people choose all types of support first from their inner family circle. This typically means

task specificity model contends that different groups (of family, friends, neighbours) have different abilities and offer different types of support, each playing a specific role

hierarchical compensatory model contends that people choose their supports first from their inner family circle and then move outward to get support from less-intimate people as they need more help

their spouse and children. They then move outward to get support from less-intimate people if more intimate ties are not available or are unable to meet their needs. This model says that a married older person will get help first from a spouse, while a widow or widower will get help first from a child (most often a daughter) (Peckham et al., 2014). The older person will then turn to friends, siblings, or other family members, then to neighbours, and then to formal supports, in that order.

Sinha and Bleakney (2014) used data from the 2012 Canadian *General Social Survey* and found support for this model. They reported that family and friends provide most social support for people at home. A spouse or common-law partner most often provided support followed by grown children. Extended family members, siblings, friends, and neighbours served least often as caregivers.

3. The **functional specificity of relationships model** (Simons, 1983–1984) recognizes that a relationship, say between a son and mother, can lead to different kinds of support. In one case, the son may play an active role in support, for example, by visiting and running errands. In another case, the son may manage formal care for his mother. This model says that people negotiate their relationships and support based in part on the history of their relationship. Gender, marital status, parenthood, and proximity of helpers all influence the amount and type of support a person will get.

4. The **convoy model of support** sees people as having a dynamic network of close ties with family and friends (Antonucci, Birditt, & Akiyama, 2009). This model uses concentric circles to position close relationships around the individual, with the closest ties in the closest circle. Outer circles show ties that are less close. These ties form a "convoy" that travels with individuals throughout life, exchanging social support and assistance. The nature of this convoy can grow and change over time with changing life circumstances.

Penning (1990; also Penning and Wu, 2014) compared the ability of the task specificity model and the hierarchical compensatory model to explain older people's use of informal supports. She found only limited support for each model. Older people tended to use a variety of formal and informal supports at the same time and not in a specific hierarchical order. She also found that groups did a variety of tasks that overlapped. For example, relatives and neighbours both helped with household tasks. Sinha (2013b) reported that 71 percent of informal caregivers (in this case age 15 and over) help with two or more tasks. Nearly all caregivers (88 percent) provided emotional support as well as instrumental help.

Penning (1990; also Penning & Wu, 2014; Rutherford & Bowes, 2014) said that "it is unlikely that assistance is provided routinely and uniformly on the basis of a set order of preference." She concluded that "the issue of who provides assistance to whom, of what type, and under what conditions is complex" (p. 227).

Campbell, Connidis, and Davies (1999) found some support for the functional specificity of relationships model. They found that siblings provide a range of social support for certain groups, including single women, the childless, single men, and widowed women. But siblings provide little support for divorced and married men. In general, siblings give support when they live nearby. Siblings also tend to serve as companions and confidants, and they more often provide practical support to sisters than to brothers. These findings show that particular groups of older adults develop supportive ties with siblings "not as substitution or compensation for lost ties but based on a lifetime of negotiating unique ties with siblings" (p. 144).

Haines and Henderson (2002) assessed the convoy model of social support. They found that while the model helps to identify significant supportive relationships, not all strong ties provide support. They also found that weak ties, typically ignored in the convoy model of support, can and do provide instrumental support, emotional support, and companionship. Sims-Gould, Martin-Matthews, and Rosenthal (2008; also Rutherford & Bowes, 2014) reported that often a network of individuals provide support. But, they say, current models don't look at how multiple care providers assist one another in their work.

Other research findings add another dimension to this complexity of social support. An older person's living arrangement, whether or not an older person lives with someone, strongly influences the type of support he or she gets. If an older person lives with someone, that person will likely give him or her support for the activities necessary for daily living. Shared living arrangements (between siblings or friends) may help widowed or childless older people live in the community. For example,

---

functional specificity of relationships model contends that a family or friendship tie may provide one type of support or a broad range of support, depending on the particular relationship between the caregiver and the care receiver

convoy model of support describes social support as a network of close family and friends who travel together throughout life, exchanging social support and assistance

caregivers who live with an older parent often provide daily help with meal preparation and household chores (Pezzin, Pollak, & Schone, 2015).

Turcotte and Sawaya (2015) studied the effect of different housing conditions on caregiving responsibilities. They found that in 2012, a majority of caregivers (62 percent) lived in a private household apart from their care receivers. Sixteen percent of caregivers lived with their care receiver. The other care receivers lived in a care facility or supportive housing.

More than a quarter (29 percent) of caregivers who live with their care receiver and one-third (33 percent) of those who give care to a care receiver in an institution reported a strain on family relationships. One-quarter of caregivers, who care for someone in an institution, cared for someone with Alzheimer's disease or dementia. This, along with the poor health of seniors in institutions, accounts for the high proportion of these caregivers who report family strain.

Two conditions lead to the use of formal supports along with informal supports. First, some older people have incomplete informal networks and need specific kinds of help (such as someone to shop for them or clean their home). Second, some older people who have intact networks have high healthcare needs. For example, compared with other caregivers, those who care for older family members with dementia use more personal care services and in-home services. Sinha and Bleakney (2014) found that 9 out of 10 people who got care at home relied on family and friends. But about half of these people also got help from professionals. Families sought professional help most often for medical care. People with Alzheimer's disease or dementia tended to use professional help. In these cases, informal supporters may find their resources stretched to the limit.

Ideally, the informal and formal systems work together in these cases to share the overall load. Social policies often speak of partnerships between state programs and informal supports. Sims-Gould and Martin-Matthews (2010b) found that both formal and informal care providers perform physical and emotional care work. Sinha and Bleakney (2014) reported that informal caregivers tend to provide help with transportation, indoor household tasks, and outdoor maintenance. Informal supporters tended to help with more than one task. Formal supports focused on medical care such as changing bandages and performing medical tests (e.g., a blood pressure test). Formal care also provided help with household tasks (e.g., meal preparation) and personal care (e.g., bathing).

Harlton, Keating, and Fast (1998) found that older people and policymakers differed in their view of care of older people. Policymakers often believe that family and neighbourhood (informal) supports give older people more control over their lives. But many older people feel that family support makes them more dependent and a burden on their families. They do not feel that family members should provide housing, financial support, or personal care.

The seniors in this study preferred state-funded supports, believing that these supports give them the most control over the services they receive. Also, a number of researchers ask whether caregiving by family members will simply shift the burden of care from formal caregivers to family members. The emphasis on family and community care can place a burden on **informal caregivers** (Peckham, Williams, & Neysmith, 2014).

Policymakers need to learn more about the views of older clients and their families in order to create programs that meet older people's needs. They must also recognize that family caregivers face significant personal costs—financial and health-related—in their caregiving role. The policy to shift care to "the community" often means placing more responsibility on middle-aged women. For example, Sinha (2013b) reported that women made up 54 percent of caregivers (age 15 and over). Compared to men, they reported a greater likelihood of caregiving 20 or more hours per week. But many middle-aged women (traditional caregivers) have entered the labour force in large numbers. Many now have to juggle child care, work responsibilities, and care for older parents. This added demand leads to stress, absenteeism, and sometimes withdrawal from work (Noelker & Browdie, 2012).

The government may serve families best when it assists family caregivers with programs and resources to support family care (Keefe, Légaré, & Carrière, 2007). Sinha (2013b) reported that in 2012, only 7 percent of caregivers (age 15 and over) got financial help from a government program. And only 5 percent received federal tax credits.

TIME TO REVIEW

How do informal supports differ from formal supports?

State some of the ways that family members interact with the formal support system.

What causes caregivers to feel stressed by their caregiving responsibilities?

Describe some of the impacts that caregiving has on caregivers' social, work, and family lives.

informal caregivers unpaid care providers with a tie of kinship or affection toward the care receiver

EXHIBIT 13.3 *Non-Economic Social and Physical Costs of Caregiving*

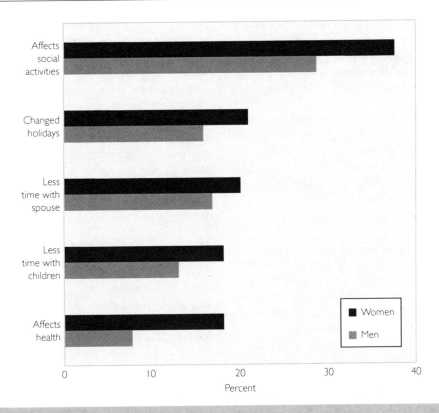

Caregivers give support to family members out of love, respect, and duty. They often say they feel good about caregiving and want to see their family member thrive. But caregiving can also take a toll on a person's health and well-being. This chart shows the personal and social costs of caregiving.

Note that, compared with men, women report a greater impact of caregiving on their lives. Women take on more personal care, such as bathing and meal preparation, that puts demands on their time. This type of care offers less flexible scheduling. Men tend to take on more administrative tasks such as arranging for home repair or a visiting nurse. This may account for the higher proportion of women who report the toll caregiving takes on their social and family lives.

In particular, compared with men, more than twice the proportion of women (18 percent vs. 8 percent) report an effect of caregiving on their health. Compared with men, a higher proportion of women report that caregiving feels "a bit stressful" or "quite a bit stressful" (not shown in this chart).

Source: Keefe, J. Supporting caregivers and caregiving in an aging Canada. IRPP Study No. 23. (2011), p. 9. Reproduced with permission of IRPP.org, http://irpp.org/wp-content/uploads/assets/research/faces-of-aging/supporting-caregivers-and-caregiving-in-an-aging-canada/IRPP-Study-no23.pdf. Original source: Statistics Canada, *General Social Survey*, 2007.

Children as a Source of Informal Support

Adult children tend to stay in touch with their parents. Daughters (more than sons) tend to serve in the caregiving role. Pillemer and Suitor (2014), in a study of caregiving for elderly mothers, found that, compared to sons, daughters had twice the odds of becoming a caregiver. Other studies reported that daughters, compared with sons, spend more time caring for parents (Fingerman et al., 2010). Even working daughters with children at home spend more than twice as much time as working sons providing care to an older parent (29 hours per month vs. 13 hours per month) (Williams, 2005).

Caregiving can create stress in adult children's lives. One caregiving daughter told Garity (2006): "I use a lot of energy to keep everything balanced. When something happens [to my parent] post-placement like feeding or behavioral problems I let that structure my life as opposed to my having control over the things that I want to do." Another said, "My husband [who works out of town during the week] has said we'd probably be divorced if he were at home because my father ... takes a lot of my time right now" (p. 45).

The marital status of adult children influences their level of involvement with older parents (Sarkisian & Gerstel, 2008). Married sons and daughters are less likely than their single or divorced counterparts to stay in touch with parents. Married children less often provide parents with financial support, emotional support, or practical help. They are also less likely to receive these types of assistance from parents. The marital status of the parent can also influence his or her relationship with adult children, including the support received. For example, adult children provide about the same support to divorced or widowed mothers but provide the least support to divorced fathers (Lin, 2008).

Adult children provide much of the support needed by their parents. Merz and Consedine (2009) report that strong feelings of attachment to a parent and recognition of past help lead to caregiver well-being. Pillemer and Suitor (2014) reported that physical proximity predicts entry into the caregiving role. And, years before they need care, parents often have an idea of which child will become a caregiver.

Studies show that adult children and their parents see the amount of support provided by the children differently. Many studies report that older people feel they receive less support than their children say they give. Early work by Bengtson and Kuypers (1971) referred to this as differences in the **developmental stake**, or (more recently) **generational stake** (Birditt et al., 2012). Compared with their children, older people have a greater stake in the parent–child relationship. They have invested more in the relationship and they have more to lose if it fails. So older people tend to emphasize the existence of family harmony and solidarity.

Older people's positive interpretation of the relationship allows them to maintain a feeling of generational continuity within the family. They may de-emphasize the amount of support they receive in order not to see themselves as a burden on their children (Kim et al., 2011). This difference in perception can create tensions in the family. Adult children may feel that their parents do not appreciate how much they do for them, even though the children may feel they do as much as they can.

Generational stake theory looks at how the generations provide support for one another and negotiate family solidarity. Recent research describes a second theoretical approach. It focuses on the potential for conflict and estrangement between parents and adult children. This approach sees parent–adult child relations as a simultaneous mix of positive and negative emotions. Researchers refer to this as "generational ambivalence" (Lüscher & Hoff, 2013). Gilligan and colleagues (2015)

found that negative feelings in particular lead to feelings of depression for mothers and adult children. These negative feelings led to psychological distress for both generations, even in the presence of positive feelings. Studies of generational ambivalence point to the complexity of parent and adult child relationships. These relationships develop over a lifetime and feelings developed at an earlier time can influence relationships many years later.

Research shows that intergenerational interaction has grown in intensity and complexity in recent years. Older people and their children live longer lives and spend more years interacting with one another. Today, people spend more years as an adult child of living parents than as parents of young children. This trend will continue in the future. In some cases, caregivers of very old parents will need support themselves as they grow older.

Sources of Informal Support for Childless Older People

Adult children are a primary source of support and well-being for older parents. But who provides this support to older adults who are without children? Studies find that childless older people create a network of supportive family and friends.

Those who have chosen to remain childless report high life satisfaction and happiness (Connidis, 2010). They have about the same satisfaction with life as married older people who have close relations with their children, and higher satisfaction than parents with distant ties to children. Compared with older people who have no children due to circumstances beyond their control, those who remain childless by choice have higher life satisfaction.

Plotnick (2009) reported that compared with older people with children, childless older couples and individuals have more income and more wealth. Older unmarried childless women, compared with older unmarried mothers, have 12 percent to 31 percent more income and 33 percent more wealth. This study points to the high cost of raising children for unmarried mothers. This cost shows up as lower income and less wealth in later life. Connidis (2010) said, "Having children is not essential to having a satisfying old age. Childless old persons are engaged with the social world and negotiate smaller but active social networks of family and friends.... [M]ost older childless persons see advantages to their situation" (p. 185).

Childless older people who report disadvantages point to a lack of companionship, missed experiences, a feeling of incompleteness, and lack of care in old age (Connidis, 2010). Widows may face a disadvantage if

---

developmental stake or generational stake the idea that, compared with their children, older people have a greater investment in the relationship with their children.

Here, a group of friends share a cup of tea at a local coffee shop. Friends from the same age cohort share a lifetime of experiences. Friends will recall the same music, films, and historical events that shaped their lives. Friendship leads to increased quality of life in old age.

they have no children. They may lack informal support and may need to rely on formal support. Compared with older people with children, they also face a greater risk of institutionalization.

Garland (2015) reports the case of Linda Wiesman, 67, who has no children. She has begun to experience physical limitations due to two knee replacements. She wonders who will care for her in later old age. She said, "I worry about dementia and longevity because they run in the family" (p. 2). She may need to turn to her three nieces for help. Garland said that, on the financial front, a childless older person should put together a professional advisory team (e.g., an accountant, lawyer, geriatrician). This team can provide a financial safety net and protect the older person from financial abuse.

Research often ignores childless adults or views their lives "through a lens of deficiency" or as the "other" category (in contrast to parents) (Dykstra & Hagestad, 2007, p. 1291). As a result, compared with what we know about seniors with children, we know less about the social networks and relationships of childless older people. We also know less about the varied responses people make to childlessness.

Chang, Wilber, and Silverstein (2010) said that the literature on caregiving and popular belief assumes that childless older people feel lonely and lack support. Chang and colleagues looked at this issue in detail. They studied 1,456 people age 75 and over who had a disability and lived in the community. The study compared parents with childless older people in the sample. The study found that, compared to parents, childless older people did not differ in feelings of depression or well-being. The researchers conclude "there were no significant differences between parents and childless older

adults in psychological well-being, personal care use, or assistive device use. Thus, whether or not one had offspring was not related to either depression or positive well-being" (p. 717).

The researchers suggested that childless older people "have strong and durable family ties with siblings, cousins, nieces, and nephews.... Childless individuals may also receive support from children of siblings, neighbors, and close friends" (p. 717). This study and others rejected the stereotype of the childless older person as lonely and without social support.

Penning and Wu (2014) looked closely at the effect of childlessness on social support. They found that childlessness led to less support only in the cases of widowed and never-married people. And this affected only extra household domestic support. Dykstra and Hagestad (2007) said that for some people, "life without children can have particular advantages, in others it can have disadvantages, and in yet others, no effects at all." They said that research should explore "when childlessness matters and when it does not" (p. 1301).

Other Sources of Informal Support: Friends, Siblings, and Technology

Friends

Friends can be an important source of support in later life. Studies find that people enjoy friends most in youth and in old age. High-quality friendships in later life lead to high life satisfaction and well-being. Studies show that many older people get more enjoyment out of visits with friends than with family. Researchers say that people in a family may visit one another as a matter of routine or because they feel obliged to see one another. But when older people see their friends, they do so out of choice. Most older people choose friends from their own age group. Older people may have more in common with their friends than with younger family members. Shared interests and experiences lead to greater warmth and good feelings (Blieszner, 2014; Carr & Moorman, 2011). Blieszner said that friends also provide practical help with shopping and transportation, and with emotional support.

Friends support a person's self-worth. But relations with family members don't always have this effect. Compared with family, friends have this effect because the older person chooses friendship ties voluntarily. Friends provide a support that family cannot give. Blieszner (2014) said that "Friends, rather than relatives, tend to have a greater effect on feeling happy and having a positive outlook" (p. 26). For example, friends provide companionship and "may facilitate and encourage self-expression, thereby helping people feel productive in late life" (Krause, 2006, p. 190).

Moremen (2008a) asked older women in her study to choose the person they felt closest to and explain how that person contributed to their health. Half of the women named friends as their closest confidants. Female friends were more likely to be named as confidants than were male friends or daughters. Many of these women said that they would turn to their friend to discuss physical health concerns or when they felt sad or lonely. But they did not feel comfortable sharing concerns about mental health issues or financial problems. And they didn't call on their friends for personal care. These women felt their close confidants kept them healthy. They provided diet and exercise advice, provided meals and transportation, shared fun and laughter, and helped them feel good about themselves.

Friends help older people cope with widowhood and loss. They also serve as confidants. Statistics Canada's *General Social Survey* in 2013 asked Canadians about their friend and family relations. More than half of the

people in the survey (51 percent) said they had five or more close friends. But responses differed by age. When asked about "other" friends, beyond family and close friends, people under age 25 on average said they had 24 close friends. This drops to only 10 "other" friends for people age 65 and over.

While friends can play a vital role in the support network of older people, friendships in later life can also involve tensions and disappointments. Moremen (2008b) said that friendship can have its downside. Some of the women in Moremen's study reported "disruptions" in their friendships when friends did not share their interests, habits, and other friends. A loss of trust in the relationship, dishonesty, or exploitation could strain the friendship. Also a decline in health can make friendship too demanding. Carr and Moorman (2011) said that older adults "selectively choose to maintain relatively fewer, but higher quality, relationships" (p. 153).

In spite of potential problems, friendships help older people overcome distress caused by lost work roles or widowhood. "Having at least one friend can

---

EXHIBIT 13.4   *Median Number of Close Family, Friends, and Other Friends/Acquaintances, by Age, 2013*

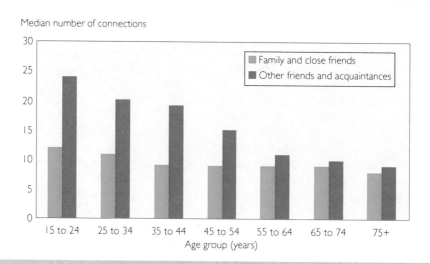

This chart shows that the median number of family/close friends decreases to middle age, then levels off and drops slightly in the oldest age group (age 75+). Family relations and close friendships tend to remain stable throughout adulthood. They provide a base of support into old age. But the median number of other friends/acquaintances decreases steadily with age. This reflects changes in life circumstances from youth onward. In middle age, a person may have less time for other friends and acquaintances. In old age, declines in health, the loss of friends through death, and decreased mobility in late old age all lead to a reduced network of friends and acquaintances.

Source: Sinha, M. Canadians' connections with family and friends, Spotlight on Canadians: Results from the General Social Survey (2013), p. 7. Retrieved from http://www.statcan.gc.ca/pub/89-652-x/89-652-x2014006-eng.pdf. Original source: *General Social Survey* (2013). Reproduced and distributed on an "as is" basis with the permission of Statistics Canada.

reduce isolation, as [a person's] social circle shrinks with the deaths of family members and friends, the loss of a spouse or partner, a move to a care facility, or activity limitations attributable to poor health" (Statistics Canada, 2010e, p. 367).

Friends who are the same age often share the same physical limits, the same interests, and the same historical background. Lifelong friends also share cherished experiences and memories. Research shows the importance of close and supportive friendships in the lives of older adults (Pilkington, Windsor, & Crisp, 2012). A variety of relationships, including friendships, create a full and satisfying support network.

Siblings

Siblings are also an important source of social support for older people. Eighty percent of older adults have at least one living sibling (brother or sister). The sibling bond often lasts throughout a lifetime, but its importance often gets overlooked. The supportive role of a sibling will vary by individual need and circumstance. For example, a married older person with many children nearby may make little use of sibling support. A single older person will make the most use of sibling support.

Most adults report having frequent contact with and positive feelings about their siblings (Spitze & Trent, 2006). In general, compared with older men, older women tend to have more active sibling ties, with ties between sisters stronger than ties between brothers or a brother and sister (Connidis, 2010). In Spitze and Trent's study of adult sibling ties in two-child families, sisters exchanged advice and kept in touch by phone more often than did other pairs of siblings. Their closeness rests, in part, on their shared experience of aging. Older sisters, for example, may have experienced widowhood. They often form close friendship bonds and provide emotional support to one another. Compared with men, women more often report that they help a sibling with child care. They also tend to get help with home repairs (usually from a brother)

Geographic closeness influences some types of sibling support but not others. People need to live near one another to spend time together. Siblings who live across the country from one another may get together only once a year or less. They can't depend on one another for everyday support, such as shopping.

But email, Skype, and inexpensive phone service makes regular contact easy today. Siblings now can share personal information and family activities via Facebook and other social networking sites. This will not substitute for an intimate face-to-face talk with a confidant over coffee. But, for siblings who want to stay in touch, the Internet allows for more sharing over distance than ever before.

Technology

The Internet opens a world of opportunity for family members to get support and information. For example, a study found that 25 percent of caregivers used the Internet to get information on their care receiver's condition, on available services, and on healthcare facilities (National Alliance for Caregiving, 2009). People who use these supports find that they reduce caregiver strain.

Research also shows the value of online support groups in providing support and relieving caregiver stress. Many caregivers cannot get to a face-to-face support group. Caregivers in rural or remote settings, for example, may lack the time and transportation to get to a support group. Nearly all caregivers of dementia care receivers find it difficult to get away to a support group. These caregivers can benefit from Internet-based support groups. Caregivers in these groups share strategies for managing stress and they support one another in times of crisis (Alzheimer Society, 2009). The Internet allows caregivers to give and get support at a time convenient to them and from their own home.

Future generations of older people will feel more comfortable using the Internet. Digital forms of communication already bridge time and space barriers between family and friends. Grandparents, for example, interact with grandchildren through real-time video connections. The following is a real-world example of this.

While writing this section, one of the authors received a call on the Skype system from his son in Santa Fe, New Mexico. They connected via video and the author had a chance to visit with him and his family. His son's wife stopped by the computer to say hello as she went about her chores. His two grandchildren, Tobin and Shea, shared their schoolwork and their latest craft projects with him. They were able to look together at the pictures and videos from their recent Christmas vacation.

This might not seem like "social support." But it is. The use of technology enriches the author's life and keeps him in close touch with family members far away. He and his wife continually get updates on family members through regular Facebook posts. He expects that technology will play an important role in family life in the years ahead. Improvements in technology and lower costs will make family contacts like this easier for everyone in the future.

TIME TO REVIEW

Children, other family members, and neighbours can provide support to an older person. How do these various supporters differ in the kinds of support they offer?

What are some ways the formal healthcare system supports family caregivers?

How does technology serve as a support for older people?

Dementia and Caregiver Burden

The 2007 *General Social Survey* focused on social support and caregiving in Canada. The survey found that 2.7 million Canadians age 45 and over gave care to a senior with long-term health problems. Women made up more than half (57 percent) of these caregivers. People under age 65 (mostly adult children) made up three-quarters of these caregivers. Close family members (spouses and children) made up 70 percent of caregivers (Cranswick & Dosman, 2008; Milan, Keown, & Urquijo, 2011).

St-Amant and colleagues (2012, citing Smetanin et al., 2009) said that hours of unpaid care are projected to triple to 756 million hours by 2038. The increase in the older population, in part, accounts for this increase in the need for unpaid care. But the projected increase in cases of dementia (in most cases, Alzheimer's disease) add to the demands on unpaid caregivers.

Harris and colleagues (2011), for example, conducted in-depth interviews on caregiving with 10 couples. The couples had been married at least 30 years. One woman, who cared for a husband with dementia, told the researchers "in the last few months when I have tried to talk to him about should we do this and should we do that, he'll say 'I just don't know, you're just going to have to decide.' ... I'm not used to that, you know. It's a different role. Become more of the decision-maker and more assertive ... " (p. 954).

The disease forces readjustment for both members of the couple. This woman expresses concern, fear, and perhaps some relief that she can move forward with choices she needs to make. Studies of caregivers describe the uncertainty and distress that comes with defining a new role in relation to their spouse.

Another woman in this study expressed her frustration with day-to-day chores and the tension this brings to their relationship: "He demands everything he wants," she said, "and I don't like anyone demanding that I get up and do something." She said, "Now if you were paralyzed I wouldn't mind all of this and here comes the names, that's where it starts." (p. 955).

Harris and colleagues (2011) said that in the case of Alzheimer's disease (ADRD: Alzheimer's disease and related disorders), the spousal caregiver feels emotional turmoil. Caregivers who felt trust, respect, and a strong bond felt less hostile and angry toward their care receiver. Still, Derouesne and colleagues (1996) reported that a diagnosis of ADRD affected the sexual intimacy of 80 percent of couples in their study. And between 40 percent and 47 percent reported sexual problems due to the illness. One woman told Harris and colleagues (2011, p. 958), "Physical intimacy and sexuality? There is none ... he shows no interest. I just don't talk about it. It's just part of it that you accept and go on...." (p. 958).

Some women weather the stress of caregiving better than others. Good marital relations and a strong bond of intimacy can buffer caregiver burden. Harris and colleagues (2011, p. 959) said, "high levels of couple intimacy pre-diagnosis seemed to be a necessary ingredient of high levels of intimacy post-diagnosis...." Prior intimacy allows some caregivers to feel good about their caregiving role. They feel a duty toward their care receiver and see their work as an expression of love. Caregivers feel less burden if they have good family supports, if they have a care receiver with milder cognitive impairment, if they use formal services, and if they take care of themselves.

Caregivers often report that they need home healthcare, in-home respite care, and adult day-away programs. They also report a need for support groups, homemaker services, and transportation services. One caregiver remarked on the importance of adult day care. "The Day Center is great, I couldn't survive without them. We would be looking at a long-term care facility. You know, it gives me the time to go out and conduct the family business, run the home, without having to worry that he's safe" (MacCourt, Wilson, & Tourigny-Rivard, 2011, p. 54).

When a care receiver's behaviour becomes too difficult to handle, even the best family supports and community care cannot relieve the caregiving burden. Family caregivers risk burnout unless they get some relief. As a daughter caring for her father-in-law emphasized: "I have found by going through this that my husband closes up and it really affects our home and family life.... No freedom, always a commitment, all of the time. It really has torn our family apart" (Dupuis & Smale, 2005, p. 2).

Studies report that even after a spouse enters an institution, family and friends continue to give personal care and in some cases medical care. Cranswick and Dosman (2008) said that "almost one-half of their family and friend caregivers helped out by ensuring that the requisite formal care was in place" (p. 52). As a result, many community-dwelling spouses feel some stress even after a spouse enters a care facility.

Turcotte and Sawaya (2015; also Turcotte, 2013a) found that caregivers who cared for nursing home patients reported high levels of stress. Twenty-two percent of these caregivers said they felt depressed. Caregivers with a care receiver in an institution often spent long hours on care, provided personal care, and cared for care receivers with dementia. These caregivers also reported a decline in their health and reduced time with family and friends. The more impaired the family member, the greater the risk of **caregiver burden**.

---

caregiver burden problems and stress due to caregiving

Russell (2007), a social worker who counsels caregivers, says that coping with a chronic illness "becomes the center of existence—for both caregiver and care recipient" (p. 64). He describes his own experience as a caregiver when his wife got sick (pp. 64–65):

As a caregiver myself, the realization of sudden and complete change stands out as a singular point in time, the moment I realized that things would never be the same. After what was supposed to have been a routine surgery for my wife, the surgeon informed me with few words that she had cancer—ovarian cancer, stage four. Tough, nasty stuff. My feelings of stress were immediate and pronounced. I ceased to sleep well, had difficulty focusing on teaching and writing,

---

EXHIBIT 13.5 *A Profile of Caregivers (Age 45 and Over) for Seniors with Long-Term Health Conditions*

Age	% Distribution Downward[1]
45 to 54 years	43
55 to 64 years	32
65 to 74 years	16
75 years and over	8
Gender	
Men	43
Women	57
Marital Status	
Single	7
Married or common-law	76
Widowed	7
Divorced	10
Work Status	
Working at a paid job	57
Retired	31
Other[2]	12

[1]Due to rounding, totals might not add up to 100.

[2]Other work status includes such activities as looking for work, going to school, caring for children, household work, and long-term illness.

Note that three-quarters of caregivers are between the ages of 45 and 64. Most of these people care for older family members. Compared with men, a higher proportion of women serve as caregivers. Three-quarters of these caregivers are married or live in a common-law relationship. More than half of them (57 percent) work at a paid job. Many caregivers juggle multiple roles and responsibilities—spouse, parent, and employee.

Cranswick and Dosman (2008) say that in this study "the majority of caregivers who were not coping well were married women. One in three of burdened caregivers had at least one child at home.... Two-thirds were caring for a parent. The difficulty coping may be because of the role conflict that occurs, especially for women, as they attempt to manage the many facets of their lives" (p. 53).

Source: Cranswick, K. and Dosman, D. "Eldercare: What We Know Today." *Canadian Social Trends*, 86: 48–56 (2008), p. 49. Statistics Canada, General Social Survey 2007.

and felt angry most of the time. In sixty years of life, there had been many changes, but this change was not part of any plan....

There are changes that are not welcomed, changes I resent and for which I am angry. Ultimately, though, I share the sentiment that we are in the next stage of a long life together, a stage unlike any before, yet one in which emotional and affective bonds remain strong and meaningful.

Russell followed a pattern of caregiving common among men. He took a managerial approach. He calls it "a 'let's get busy' coping reaction" (p. 64). And he rarely talked about his feelings or his situation with others, even with other men who also cared for their wives. He considers this the "'no talk' maxim of masculinity" (p. 65).

Chappell, Dujela, and Smith (2014) reported a contradictory finding. Their study found that compared to spouses, adult children reported greater feelings of burden. After one year in this study, adult children's burden decreased, while spousal scores remained the same. Still, compared to spouses, adult children reported significantly more burden at both time periods. The researchers say that "adult children are more likely to have multiple demands of home, interests, work, and caregiving roles which all contribute to their burden" (p. 469).

Both spouses and adult children felt burdened in part because they felt their resources were strained (e.g., they lacked family support and felt lonely due to caregiving). Spouses, in particular, felt burdened by their care receiver's condition (e.g., sleep problems and agitation). Spouses typically lived with their care receivers and this

Many middle-aged women find themselves in the role of caregiver to their parents. Caregivers can feel conflicting emotions. They feel love for their parents, but they also feel the stress of caregiving. For example, a cognitively impaired parent may act out physically and may not recognize the adult child. The adult child may find roles reversed as the impaired parent becomes the cared-for person in the relationship. A parent with dementia creates unique physical and emotional challenges.

may account for the impact of caregiving on their lives. The researchers said that their study showed that different conditions lead to burden for each type of caregiver.

Lai (2007, 2009a) examined the effects of culture on caregiver burden in a Chinese Canadian community. Despite a strong Chinese tradition of caring for older family members, these caregivers felt caregiver burden. Caregivers with health problems, those who faced greater care demands, and those who had fewer financial resources all report greater caregiver burden. Recent immigrants, people with a religious belief, and people who felt less committed to filial piety all felt a greater burden. Lai cautioned, though, that while strong feelings of filial piety may ease caregiver burden, they do not make caregiving easy. In fact, strong filial piety may keep caregivers from using the outside help and resources they need.

O'Connor (1999) reported that many spouse caregivers, regardless of ethnicity, refuse to use outside help. They feel an obligation to their spouse and they feel that they can give the best care. People who care for someone with dementia experience an extra layer of burden. The Canada Mortgage and Housing Corporations (2015g) says that caregivers who live with a person with dementia provide 75 percent more care compared to other caregivers. And they experience 20 percent higher levels of stress.

MacLean (2008) conducted in-depth interviews with older wives whose husbands with dementia were waiting for placement in a long-term care setting. The study looked at how wives cope with caregiving while awaiting placement. The study found that wives experience multiple "layers of loss." First, wives talked about the loss of communication with their husbands. Women missed having a partner to talk to about household finances or other everyday issues. They even missed simple dinner conversations. They felt that their husband's "true self" had gone.

Second, wives identified the loss of their marriage partnership. In taking on the physical care of their spouse, as well as his household tasks and responsibilities, these women felt their relationship was no longer a "give-and-take" partnership. One woman said, "Well, granted, I'm still his wife, but he's not like my husband ... my husband isn't there" (p. 53).

Third, many of the women felt a loss of personal freedom. This involved the loss of contact with friends or the inability to attend social activities. They missed the everyday freedoms like running down to the mailbox to mail a letter or going shopping. As one woman described it: "I feel I'm sort of tied down. I'm pretty well trapped" (p. 53).

Most of these women just tried to get through the day—one day at a time. As MacLean explained, "with this simple and primary goal, these women demonstrated their clear understanding that longer term goals are inappropriate when caregiving for a person whose illness experience changes minute to minute, hour to hour, and day after day" (p. 104).

Even after a spouse enters an institution, a caregiver spouse feels caregiver burden. One wife told Gladstone (1995): "When you're apart after never being apart it has an effect on you. You seem to be in a turmoil. We'd known each other since we were 14 years old so we were together a long, long time" (p. 56).

Rosenthal and Dawson (1991) identified the concept of **quasi-widowhood**. This term describes married individuals who "feel widowed" because their spouse lives apart in a long-term care setting. These people have lost the physical presence of their spouse and the emotional support and companionship of a partner. Ross, Rosenthal, and Dawson (1994) studied 40 wives who had placed their husbands in nursing homes. These women said that they felt relief after placement but also felt failure, "anger, guilt, sadness, depression and grief" (p. 40).

A study of wives and children who oversaw placement of a care receiver in a long-term care facility found the experience disturbing. They recalled the experience as "heartbreaking," "devastating," and "the worst thing [they] ever had to do" (Sussman & Dupuis, 2012, p. 399). One caregiver in a Swedish study told Johansson and colleagues (2014, p. 3) "'It feels terrible, actually a bit frightening. You feel steam-rollered, with no options. It was just hard facts and next a room was offered, take it or leave it.'"

---

quasi-widowhood experiencing feelings of grief, depression, and loss after a spouse is placed in a nursing home

---

EXHIBIT 13.6   *Till Death Do Us Part? The Challenge to Spouses of an Institutionalized Partner*

Most religious traditions forbid sex outside of marriage and call this adultery. The institutionalization of a spouse brings up an issue that many people silently struggle with each day. Is it permissible for the healthy spouse to have a sexual relationship with a new partner? The increase in cases of dementia in our aging society will raise this question for more people than ever before.

Rabbi Richard F. Address (2011) tells the following story of a person (fictional in this case but based on his experiences) who seeks spiritual counsel for this dilemma:

[T]he person sits down and looks anxiously into the eyes of the priest, minister, rabbi, or imam. Slowly, the story unfolds.

"You know," the person says, "I love my spouse and visit almost every day. And when our kids come home they visit, too. Last year, when the stress of working and caregiving became too much, my kids gave me a trip and on that trip I met someone who, coincidently, lives near here, and we became friendly. So when we got home, we exchanged e-mails and then we met and our friendship grew. It became very important, as I was feeling alone, and gradually the friendship evolved into something more and, to tell you the truth, we have become intimate."

[The person goes] on. "And I am overwhelmed with conflicting feelings. I cannot talk about this with my children. I am uncomfortable talking about this with our friends with whom we shared years of dinners, engagements, trips, and the like. I need to know if I am doing something wrong. My spouse hardly knows who I am. I am a healthy seventy-year-old, I go to work several days a week and have my life, and I am lonely and have needs. So tell me, am I wrong? Am I committing adultery?"

Rabbi Address captures the pain and confusion that a person can feel in this situation. Our religious traditions don't prepare people for this. And religious leaders differ in their advice depending on their tradition and their reading of the scriptures.

Rabbi Address ends his essay with a question. "The attempt to redefine adultery in light of Alzheimer's disease and related dementias presents the religious community with an interesting challenge. How do you try and reinterpret one's tradition in light of such a new reality?"

Many individuals and families will confront this situation in the future.

Questions

1. How do you feel about a spouse who has a sexual relationship while caring for an institutionalized spouse with dementia? Do you consider this immoral?

2. Are there situations that call for a reinterpretation of religious and cultural norms?

3. How would you advise a member of your family who faced this dilemma?

Source: Address, R.F. 2011. "Till Death Us Do Part? A Look at Marriage Rituals When a Partner Has Alzheimer's Disease," Reprinted with permission from *Generations* 35:3: 52–56. Fall 2011. Copyright © 2011. American Society on Aging, San Francisco, California. www.asaging.org.

Most women over time adapt to their spouse living in an institution. Some women accept the loss of their spouse as a friend and companion and restructure their lives outside the institution. Other spouses keep close ties to the institution. Johansson and colleagues (2014) found that family caregivers tried to stay connected to their care receiver after nursing home placement. Active visitors took on a variety of tasks, including planning birthday parties, personalizing their husband's room, and bringing in special foods. Overall, active visitors provided care as a way to maintain their attachment to their husbands and as a way to maintain their role as a wife and supporter. Wives felt most satisfied if they felt useful. But Ross, Rosenthal, and Dawson (1994) found that active visitors felt more depressed at the end of nine months and felt dissatisfied with the care their husbands got.

This study by Ross and colleagues suggests that wives who give up the caregiver role do better after their husbands are institutionalized. The researchers found that about two-thirds of spouses gave up some of their caregiving responsibility. They visited less and allowed staff to take on the job of caring. This group began what the researchers call "embracing new realities." They felt less depressed and they felt "sort of like a widow" (p. 29). But healing began to take place as they gained distance from the caregiver role.

Gender and Spousal Caregiving

Compared with older women, older men more often get care from a spouse. Still, husbands play a significant role in caring for their wives in later life. Men make up about 40 percent of spousal caregivers. Research suggests that husbands often see caregiving as a "new career" or a continuation of their authority in the marital relationship (Ribeiro, Paul, & Nogueira, 2007). Husbands often bring problem-solving strategies from their work role to their care role (Russell, 2007).

Some men feel uncomfortable providing care that involves "traditionally female" tasks, such as domestic work and personal care. Many men are not prepared for the caregiving role and need to learn new and unfamiliar skills. Still, they feel satisfaction and a sense of accomplishment in being able to provide care to their spouse (Connidis, 2010).

Calasanti (2006) studied the different experiences of 22 husband and wife caregivers (9 men [average age 72] and 13 women [average age 67]). She found that husbands and wives did similar caregiving tasks, but they thought of their tasks differently. Calasanti spoke of different "caregiving styles" (p. 276).

One husband told Calasanti: "I hated making meals, but I have gotten used to that. It's more routine.... I didn't think I could handle incontinence, but I guess I can. So on you go." Another husband talked about the problem he faces when he has to clean up his wife's bowel movements: ... and then you have to ... fix it, you know" (p. 283).

Men, she says, approached caregiving by "rationally identifying and mastering tasks." One husband likened his caregiving work to a job. Men, she found, took great pleasure in successfully completing their work. Men distanced themselves emotionally from their caregiving tasks. One husband described how he learned to do caregiving work: "You just have to pick it up like you do a trade. Like laying brick or finishing concrete" (Calasanti, 2006, p. 277; Calasanti & King, 2007).

Men took a problem-solving approach to unpleasant tasks like toileting. This distanced them emotionally from the task. Women took a more empathic approach to their work. They performed tasks similar to those of men, but they defined their work as nurturing. Freedman, Cornman, and Carr (2014) found that wives felt a sense of happiness when providing care to their husbands. The researchers proposed that "women may derive a greater sense of meaning and accomplishment from providing care than do men emotionally from the task. Women took a more empathic approach to their work [than carrying out chores]" (p. 867).

Calasanti (2006, p. 277) calls this "emotion work." Wives tried to smooth over tensions and unpleasantness. They wanted to make their husbands happy. Wives linked their caregiving to their earlier role as mothers. One woman considered herself a caregiver at heart. Another woman put this simply: she said she was "a mom."

Family, friends, and the broader society often praise men for taking on care work, particularly tasks typically performed by women. Ribeiro, Paul, and Nogueira (2007) called this "perceived social honour." Yet, Russell (2007) found that while men were praised for special care tasks, they got little recognition for "unheroic" daily caregiving chores. Many husbands felt their spousal care was invisible and that others around them did not appreciate how much of their lives was consumed by the demands of caregiving. "For many [men], the locus of care work, the home, represented a location in which they became as invisible as the work they performed" (Russell, 2007, p. 311). This invisibility contributed to an increased sense of social isolation.

Compared to husbands, wives show a stronger negative association between a spouse's illness and marital satisfaction. In general, compared to husbands, wives experience and report a stronger impact of spousal health problems on marital satisfaction. Korporaal and colleagues (2013, p. 1281) said, "wives are more sensitive to communicative and other qualitative aspects of the marital relationship." Older caregiving wives report more burden than older caregiving husbands. Especially when the wife is relatively healthy and the husband needs care.

Son and daughter caregivers show many of the same gender-related approaches to caregiving as do spouses. Studies find that sons will get involved in care primarily in the absence of a female caregiver. But sons, compared with daughters, get less involved in their parents' emotional needs and less often get involved in routine household work. They seem better at setting limits on how much help they give. They also feel less guilty about setting these limits. Male caregivers rely more on formal help for their care receivers. Studies of caregiving husbands and sons as well as wives and daughters show that gender roles influence caregiving activities.

Caregiving to Parents and Grandparents

Along with spouses, adult children provide most of the informal care to older family members. Caregiving children often feel intense pressure as they try to meet the demands of work, their children, and caregiving. Caregiving can cause declines in the caregiver's health. A respondent in one study of middle-aged children said, "I have looked after both parents for twenty-seven years and they have become very dependent on me. We are very tied down and I don't know how much more my nerves and health can stand" (Marshall, Rosenthal, & Synge, 1983, pp. 267–268). In another study, a woman said, "[Mother] has been getting more and more forgetful and confused and can't be alone at all. I'm depressed, and I don't sleep well. How can I go to work when she needs constant supervision?" (Brody, 1990, p. ix).

Long-distance caregivers (those who live a long distance from their care receiver) often experience guilt or worry. Even caregivers who live nearby say they feel they could do more and do better at giving care. Keefe (2011) concluded that "the majority of caregivers experienced feelings of guilt" (p. 10).

Caregiving can bring up the inherent tension between the adult child's personal autonomy and his or her interdependence within a family. Caregivers sometimes use vacation time from work to manage their caregiving tasks. Sometimes they need to decrease their work hours, leave work early, or turn down job opportunities. Caregiving can disrupt social and holiday plans as well as sleep patterns.

long-distance caregivers live a significant distance from the care recipient

Caregivers report feelings of shame related to others' perception of their care receiver (Werner et al., 2012).

Caregivers report conflicts between family and work responsibilities. For women and men, this shows up as job dissatisfaction, absenteeism, and lost job opportunities. Some caregivers, typically adult daughters, may quit their jobs to take care of parents. Many caregivers report that they feel disappointment, resentment, and frustration.

Lee and colleagues (2015) conducted a longitudinal study in Canada to explore the impact of caregiving on work for men and women. They found "a negative impact of caregiving on employment among female caregivers" (p. 21). Caregiving often led to labour force withdrawal. They found that for men "providing parent care did not affect their participation in the labour force" (p. 22). The researchers trace this finding to the different caregiver patterns for each gender. Women tend to provide hands-on personal care to a parent. Men tend to manage care and may hire others to provide help.

The researchers concluded that "gender is a key factor in shaping the transitions between employment and caregiving. Men tend to remain in the labour force in the face of elder care responsibilities, whereas women caregivers tend to lose work as well as its rewards, both intrinsically and extrinsically" (p. 23).

Adult children often need to negotiate parent care within their sibling network. Connidis and Kemp (2008) found that, in general, adult children with fewer family and work responsibilities, and greater proximity to their parents, most often get selected by their siblings to serve as caregiver. Sisters more often than brothers serve in this role. Hequembourg and Brallier (2005) found that caregiving roles among siblings get divided like the domestic tasks in a traditional marriage. Sisters—like wives—assume the role of "care coordinator."

TIME TO REVIEW

What do gerontologists mean by "caregiver burden?" What causes feelings of burden?

How do men and women differ in their caregiving activities?

What unique challenges does each gender face in the role of caregiver?

How do children and spouses differ in their activities as caregivers?

How do children and spouses differ in their feelings about caregiving?

How do sons and daughters differ in their caregiving activities and in their feelings about caregiving?

Care for the Caregiver

Many caregivers report feelings of satisfaction and accomplishment. Caregivers said they enjoyed helping their care receiver feel better. They also felt duty and love toward the person receiving the care (Starr et al., 2015).

Still, many family members pay an emotional and psychological price when they take on informal caregiving. Caregivers of cognitively impaired older people, particularly those caring for relatives with Alzheimer's disease or other forms of dementia, feel the most stress (MacLean, 2008).

Rutherford and Bowes (2014) found that caregiving depended on caregivers' good health. They said, "Deterioration in the carer's health would have serious implications for their partners who depended on them for care, and they were aware of this" (p. 479). Stress in the caregiver's life, in the form of illness or exhaustion, can lead to a crisis in care for the care receiver. This research shows the importance of caregiver well-being for the care receiver.

Respite services in the community can give caregivers a break from the demands of caregiving. Russell (2007), based on his own experience and research, said, "Respite from caregiving responsibilities is essential to health and well-being of caregivers" (p. 66). Noelker and Browdie (2012) called respite "a vital support service for caregivers" (p. 103). Respite services range from friendly visitors who stay with the care receiver for a few hours, to full-day adult daycare, to longer institutional respite. Institutional respite programs can last from several days to several weeks, allowing caregivers to take vacations, deal with personal needs such as medical treatment, or simply rest.

Many family caregivers say they value and want respite. One caregiver, who got in-home respite, said, "I kept my sanity. I could breathe again, and I wasn't spinning in circles. I was more patient, happier, and more caring" (Chappell, 1997, p. 26). Carstairs and Keon (2009) say that "respite services and access to information and education on caregiving should form significant components of a national caregiver strategy" (p. 122).

Researchers suggest that the meaning of respite differs among professionals and caregivers (Noelker & Browdie, 2012). Almost half of the caregivers in a study by Chappell, Reid, and Dow (2001) defined respite as "stolen moments"—activities or situations that for a short time took them away from the worries of caregiving. None of the caregivers in the study talked about respite in terms of services.

Chappell, Schroeder, and Gibbens, (2008) said respite should be seen as an outcome defined by the caregiver. And this can take many forms. Dupuis (2000), for example, found that caregiving daughters who experienced "leisure moments" in the institution-based caregiving context felt more enjoyment in caregiving. These stolen or leisure moments may provide caregivers with a form of respite that is more a state of mind than a tangible service. Respite must respond to a specific caregiver's need. "Whether a caregiver receives a break depends on their frame of mind ... it is a feeling that they are not trapped, that they have options'" (p. 61).

Elder care programs at work can also help family caregivers cope with the demands of work and caregiving.

A MetLife Mature Market (2010b) study found that, compared to non-caregiving workers, employees who gave elder care reported fair or poor health. Among women age 50 and over, who worked outside the home, 17 percent reported fair or poor health (compared to 9 percent of non-caregivers). Caregiving employees also reported less attention to health promotion and preventive care. They also tended to report "depression, diabetes, hypertension, or pulmonary disease" (p. 5).

The pressures of caregiving and work force some women into retirement and may lead to poor health (Office of Women's Health, 2012). Proulx and Le Bourdais (2014) found that women who work full-time, care for an aging parent, and have older children tend to leave work due to caregiving. They say that their life stage (having grown children) allows them the option of leaving the workforce. Women with younger children, although "sandwiched," tend to remain at work in spite of the stress they feel.

Kim, Ingersoll-Dayton, and Kwak (2013) studied the effects of caregiving on work performance in a sample of 652 employed caregivers. They found that work interruptions led to lower performance appraisals. The study also found that a supportive supervisor led to fewer work interruptions and better performance at work. The researchers proposed workplace training for supervisors that includes an understanding of workers who care for older relatives.

Company responses to employee caregiving demands can include geriatric care management services (offered mostly by large corporations for complex long-distance caregiving). More often companies offer 800 numbers or Employee Assistance Programs (EAP) where employees can get information. EAPs then refer employees to local resources in the community. Some companies offer paid or unpaid family leave, telecommuting options, and flexible schedules.

All of these options grow from the recognition that caregiving puts a heavy demand on employees (Lee et al., 2015) and the recognition that elder care supports help the company retain good workers, maintain productivity, and help keep employees healthy. Companies often see elder care programs as part of their focus on employee wellness and well-being. A MetLife Mature Market study (2010b, p. 5) concluded that, "eldercare benefits and wellness programs can provide not only the needed support to working caregivers, but also a vehicle to directly reduce employee health care costs, with resulting bottom-line benefits to the employer."

Good programs and other interventions cannot completely do away with feelings of burden, nor should they be expected to. Spouses and children feel loss, anger, and frustration as they see a person close to them suffer through an illness. These feelings reflect a legitimate response to a parent's or spouse's suffering. But interventions can help caregivers know more about caregiving; they can help caregivers cope with the everyday demands of care; and they can give caregivers social and emotional support.

Most of the research on caregiving documents caregiver stress and burden. But some studies have looked at the positive effects of caregiving. For example, people who seek help or who have a strong support network feel less stress. Caregivers in some studies say they feel glad that they can give back to their care receiver. Other caregivers speak of caregiving as an opportunity for personal growth (Carbonneau, Caron, & Desrosiers, 2010; Peacock et al., 2010; Yap et al., 2010). A study titled "Receiving While Giving" expresses this well (Savundranayagam, 2014). This study found that social support, especially emotional support, buffers stress among spouses. And it leads to positive views of caregiving. Some studies report that work provides social contact and a break from caregiving demands (Arksey & Glendenning, 2008). It provides a type of respite. In addition it provides financial resources to support caregiving costs (Orzeck et al., 2014).

Few of the proposals to ease caregiver burden address the large-scale issues of gender inequality or the changing role of women in the labour force. For example, current programs and policies that encourage community care put the burden on female family members. Too often help for caregivers comes into play only when family care breaks down. The rhetoric about family care suggests that the state would like to shift more caregiving to family members. But practitioners and policymakers must move to a more community-oriented approach to caregiving. In this model, families serve as only one of many available resources.

The Future of Informal Support

Informal supports play a vital role in the well-being of older people. But the availability of informal supports may decrease in the years ahead. At least two changes in Canadian society point in this direction.

First, demographic changes may decrease the amount of informal support older people will get in the future. Keefe (2011) projects that the number of older Canadians who will need support will double in the next 30 years. But family size has shrunk, so older people in the future will have fewer children to call on for help. A decrease in the availability of nuclear family supports will increase the risk of institutionalization. Also, the number of children over the age of 65 who care for their parents will increase in the future as more people live longer. Some of these children will be unable to care for their parents, and some may need healthcare help themselves. Keefe (2011) predicted an increase in the need for formal home care in the future.

Informal and formal support services will need to work together to provide care to a large older population. Ploeg and colleagues (2009) asked adults age 50 and over in Hamilton, Ontario, what supports they would use in the case of parental dementia. Most of the respondents said they would turn to a physician (37 percent) or family and friends (33 percent). Only a third (31 percent) mentioned home health services. The researchers found this "troubling, given that the very purpose of these services is to help people retain social function and quality of life in the community" (p. 369). They proposed that family doctors and other health professionals help families find and use the supports they need.

Second, as people live longer, their support networks suffer loss from the death of a spouse and cohort attrition. Peers die off over time, leaving members of some support networks without help. This makes children a vital source of support for older people as they age. This could put future pressure on the children of the Baby Boom. In the third and later decades of this century, middle-aged children may find themselves challenged by their parents' care needs. For those without children, or with geographically distant children, the need for formal support services will also increase.

These trends suggest potential problems with the availability of informal supports in the future. Gaymu and colleagues (2010) said that "policy and programs will need to prepare for a greater number of elderly spouses providing care and in Canada ... a significant increase in the number that will rely on formal services" (p. 57).

But other trends might lead to stronger informal supports. First, because of longer life expectancy, more spouses will live together longer than ever before. This increased longevity will give married couples more informal support as they age.

Second, greater longevity will mean the parent–child relationship can endure long into the adult child's middle and later years. This may strengthen the bond within these relationships and increase social support.

Third, current trends in health promotion (better diet, exercise, and a decrease in smoking) may lead to better health in old age. If these trends continue, older people in the future may need less long-term healthcare support than older people need today.

Fourth, new types of groups based on the mutual needs of older people may develop. These groups fall between the informal (voluntary) support structures of the family and the formal (professionalized) structures of the health and social service systems. These semi-formal structures include car pools, groups of people in the same building who shop together, friendly visitors, or "daily hello" phone calls. These supports and relationships do not rely on kinship, friendship bonds, or the fee-for-service bond of formal supports. Instead, they are based on a bond of reciprocity and on the fact that they bring mutual benefit to users. More of these groups in the future could make up for losses in older people's social networks.

Both trends—the decrease in informal supports and the increase in alternative forms of support (including home care and semi-formal structures)—could increase in the future. The well-being of older people in the future will depend on how well alternatives to traditional supports meet their needs and on how well these different sources of support form an integrated system.

Researchers caution that current trends in policy may lead to future problems in long-term care. Current policy supports a shift in responsibility for care of older adults from institutions and professionals to "the community." This most often means a shift to the family and, typically, to the middle-aged or older woman. Women, as well as men, who choose to care for older family members need support at work, good community supports, and institutional care when their care receiver needs it. Fewer institutional beds will leave families without this option.

Rosenthal (1994) said that formal support should play the central part in social support for seniors. Families (very often middle-aged women) could then decide how much or how little of this support they need. "We should not overestimate the availability or quality of family care," Rosenthal said. "Some older people do not have family members who are able to provide care" (p. 421). Others may have family members who do not have the time or energy to give more than emotional support. Still others may prefer professional help to family care.

TIME to REVIEW

What causes gerontologists to worry about the future availability of social supports?

Why are some gerontologists critical of the shift from formal support to "community support?" What role do semi-formal structures play in the mix of social supports for older people?

How might the collaboration of formal and informal supports create a strong system of support in the future?

Elder Abuse and Mistreatment

Most older people get support and comfort from their families, but some people face exploitation and abuse. No single definition of mistreatment against older persons exists. But a broad definition refers to abuse and neglect as "any action or inaction by ANY person, which causes harm to the older or vulnerable person" (Council Against Abuse of Older Persons, 2008, emphasis in the original).

Mistreatment of older persons includes physical abuse, psychosocial abuse, financial abuse, neglect (active or passive), institutional abuse, and domestic violence. Rosen (2014, p. 76 citing LoFaso, 2013) wrote that "Elder abuse can have devastating, long-lasting effects on older adults. Depression and anxiety can consume their days and leave them emotionally and physically frail."

Research shows that most abuse against older persons comes from family members (Lindenbach et al., 2012). In this situation, many abused older people suffer in silence, making the rate of abuse hard to estimate and harder to eliminate. A number of studies of abuse against older persons in Canada discuss research findings, policy issues, and best practice.

Canadian Research Findings

Most Canadian research on abuse against older persons has used convenience samples, sometimes with low response rates. This makes it hard to generalize from the findings. Podnieks and colleagues (1990) conducted Canada's first random-sample survey on abuse against older persons. The researchers conducted telephone interviews with a sample of 2,008 people age 65 and over who lived in private households. These people presented a statistically reliable picture of the 91 percent of seniors who lived on their own in the community. The survey asked about abuse carried out by family members and other intimates.

Podnieks and her colleagues (1990; Turcotte & Schellenberg, 2007) found that female victims of abuse outnumber male victims by almost two to one. Also, some types of people faced a higher risk for some types of abuse than for others. For example, people who reported material abuse tended to live more isolated lives and to have poor health. These people faced abuse from varied sources, including spouses, friends, children, and distant relatives.

Neglect can arise from unresolved conflict in a family, bad feelings about a divorce or remarriage, or emotionally distant ties with adult children or stepchildren. These fractured relationships can lead to withdrawal and, ultimately, neglect by children and other family members. Women who report neglect also have poor health, low morale, and a dependence on others for functional help. They faced abuse from spouses, children, and non-family caregivers. Compared with older women, older men run a high risk of abandonment (the most extreme form of neglect) (Stratton & Moore, 2007).

Employment and Social Development Canada (2013) estimated that between 4 percent and 10 percent of older people in Canada had experienced abuse. Most of these cases involved passive, verbal, emotional, and financial abuse rather than physical violence or neglect. Sinha (2013b), for example, reports that seniors had the lowest rate of family violence of all age groups (though senior women had a 25 percent higher rate than senior men). These figures count only the most serious and obvious cases. Because of this, researchers caution that percentages probably underestimate the number of abused older people.

Adult children make up 42 percent of police-reported crimes of family violence (Sinha, 2013b). Research has often focused on cases where an adult child caregiver abuses an older person he or she cares for. But studies show that often the abusing child relies on the abused person for housing or financial support (Podnieks, 2008). Financial dependence can lead to resentment, anger, and abuse. Often the non-payment of bills in the long-term care facility signals possible financial abuse (Ealey, 2014). When community-dwelling seniors suffer financial abuse, it is often at the hands of someone (a family member, friend, or neighbour) they had trusted to do their banking or pay their bills.

People who report chronic verbal abuse and physical violence have some things in common. They tend to be married, and they report that the abuse came from their spouse. Sinha (2013b) reported that husbands made up one-third (32 percent) of family violence cases reported by senior women to police. Police reports show assault and verbal threats as the most common forms of family violence against older women. Most violent behaviour against senior women in the family involved threats (18 percent) or use of physical force (64 percent). Abusive husbands can use feelings of jealousy as a pretext for their violent and coercive behaviour (Beaulaurier et al., 2007).

Work by Sinha (2011), using police-reported data, supported these findings. The police reported almost 7,900 senior victims of violent crime in 2009. In about a third of the cases (35 percent) a member of the victim's family committed the violence. In another 35 percent of cases, a friend or acquaintance committed the violence. A stranger committed the violence in 29 percent of the cases.

Compared with senior men, senior women fell victim to more incidents of family violence. Family members (often a spouse or child) committed 41 percent of all victimizations against senior women. Family members (most often a grown child) committed only 23 percent of victimizations against senior men. Senior men more often faced victimization from an acquaintance or stranger. Family violence for senior men and women most often occurred as common assault (53 percent of cases) or verbal threat (21 percent of cases). Most incidents involved physical force or verbal threats (but no weapon).

Sinha (2011) said that these figures probably underestimated the extent of violence against seniors. The 2009 Canadian *General Social Survey*, for example, found that seven in ten cases of violence against seniors don't get reported. The people in these cases didn't feel the incident was important enough to report or they dealt with the incident in some other way (Perreault & Brennan, 2010). Also, rates of violence drop in older age groups. Some people in the oldest age group (aged 85 and over) live away from their families in institutional settings. And seniors with cognitive impairment may be unable to report cases of violence.

Salari (2011) referred to an "ecological iceberg of elder mistreatment" (p. 417). She said that most of the mistreatment of older adults goes unreported and unmeasured. Some abused older people who live in isolation or who have disabilities or cognitive impairment never come to the attention of authorities. An abuser may also ensure that his or her behaviour goes undetected by keeping the older person confined at home.

Researchers have developed several theories to explain the causes of abuse against older persons. One theory holds that caregiver stress leads to abuse. A second theory says that abuse exists as part of a larger pattern of violence in some families. Family members who suffered abuse or who witnessed abuse in childhood become abusers themselves. A third theory sees abuse against older persons within marriage as a continuation of earlier spousal abuse into later life. Finally, some theorists say that abuse against older persons fits into a larger societal pattern of ageism and the devaluation of older people (Canadian Network for the Prevention of Elder Abuse, 2009; Kosberg, 2014).

Aronson, Thornewell, and Williams (1995) took a feminist approach to the study of abuse against older persons. They said that the term *elder mistreatment* masks the link between abuse against older women and the relative powerlessness of women throughout life. They prefer the term *wife assault in old age* to describe the physical abuse of older women. Feminist scholars see elder mistreatment "as one of the consequences of family patriarchy, which is identified as one of the main sources of violence against women in society" (Employment and Social Development, 2013). Beaulieu, Gravel, and Lithwick (1999) supported this point. They found that in 40 percent of domestic violence cases, the violence had gone on for more than 25 years. Aronson and her colleagues say that studies of abuse against older women must link current abuse to structured social inequalities.

TIME to REVIEW

What is the most common form of elder mistreatment?

How do rates of mistreatment differ by gender?

Why do many cases of elder abuse go unreported?

Policy Issues

Policy refers to regulations and guidelines on how to deal with abuse against older persons. Abuse policies attempt to help the older abused person. Policies can include criminal court action, mandatory reporting, guardianship and power of attorney, and mediation to resolve disputes. These methods use public means (by a social worker or police) to improve a family relationship. But this course of action often fails.

The law assumes that two people in a dispute have only a limited relationship to each other, but an abused spouse or parent often has a long-term relationship with

his or her abuser and he or she may want to maintain this relationship (sometimes at personal risk). Immigrant seniors sponsored by their families, for instance, rely on their families for their well-being. But this dependency can lead to an imbalance of power in the family. If family income declines or the older person's health declines, stress within the family may lead to abuse. Legal action may do little to improve the abused person's life. A legal outcome, such as removing the abused person from a setting, may cause more stress to the abused person.

Likewise, the abused person may reject legal remedies such as jailing an abusing child or spouse on whom he or she depends for help. Sinha (2013b) found that in 18 percent of cases of police-reported family violence, the victim requested that no charges be laid. Many abused older people were afraid to report the abuse because they feared reprisal from the abuser (Beaulaurier et al., 2007). The National Seniors Council (2007) recommended "social solutions" (e.g., counselling and education) in addition to support from the legal community.

A study in Manitoba on reporting of abuse found that many older respondents did not favour mandatory reporting (Roger & Ursel, 2009). Twenty-two percent of the older adults in this study said they "disagreed somewhat" with mandatory reporting. Another 22 percent said they neither "agreed" nor "disagreed." Nearly everyone supported mandatory reporting in cases of an older adult with an illness or dementia.

The question of mandatory reporting shows that no simple solution to elder mistreatment exists. This is especially true when abuse takes place in a family setting where the abused person and the abuser rely on each other for support.

Researchers support the need for intervention strategies for both the abused older people and their abusers. Nahmiash and Reis (2000) examined the effectiveness of intervention strategies in cases of abuse in

---

EXHIBIT 13.7 *Government Action to Minimize Abuse*

In December of 2012 the Canadian Parliament amended Paragraph 718.2(a) of the Criminal Code by passing the Protecting Canada's Seniors Act. The act adds to subparagraph (iii), the following: (iii.1) evidence that the offence had a significant impact on the victim, considering their age and other personal circumstances, including their health and financial situation (Government of Canada, 2012). This act "helps ensure consistently tough penalties for those who take advantage of elderly Canadians" (Government of Canada, 2014b).

In June 2015, the Canadian Parliament passed the Canada Digital Privacy Act 2015 (DPA). The DPA says that

a person's consent to release data will be valid only "if it is reasonable to expect that an individual to whom the organization's activities are directed would understand the nature, purpose and consequences of the collection, use or disclosure of the personal information to which they are consenting." The DPA will provide added protection to seniors by requiring organizations to "simplify their consent documentation and online terms when receiving data from less sophisticated individuals in order to ensure consents are valid" (Cooper, 2015).

Canada. The most successful strategies involved concrete help from nurses and other medical professions as well as homemaking services.

Other successful interventions helped to empower older people. These included support groups, volunteers who acted as advocates, and information about a person's rights and available resources. Individual counselling to reduce caregiver stress as well as education and training also proved helpful.

Barriers exist to implementing these changes. For example, Wolf (2001) found that many victims of family violence refuse to join a support group. She suggested that a successful support group should have an older group leader or co-leader, someone familiar with issues these older people face. Other research (Lithwick et al., 1999) found that many abused older people refuse services that might reduce stress. These included medical services, home care assistance, daycare centres, and respite programs. Beaulaurier and colleagues (2007) said staff members at shelters need to recognize and understand the special needs and concerns of elderly abuse victims.

Tam and Neysmith (2006) said that the Western definition of elder abuse does not include abuse as defined by other cultures. The researchers interviewed Chinese home care workers who provided services to Chinese seniors and their families in Toronto. The researchers found that "disrespect" of older family members was the primary type of elder abuse in the Chinese community. Disrespect involves actions and attitudes that violate traditional Chinese norms or values. The home care workers in their study said that disrespect could include family members being overly bossy or rude, abrupt commands, unnecessary scolding, or dismissive comments.

Older people felt disrespected if family members restricted the older person's space or mobility; for example, some older family members were made to stay in their rooms. In some cases, the family kept the older relative from eating meals with the family or kept them from taking part in the dinner conversation. Home care workers said these older people showed signs of loneliness and depression because they felt socially isolated.

Older people in Asian cultures may face other issues if they experience abuse. They may hesitate to report the abuse for fear of bringing shame to the family, they may rely on their children to navigate Western culture, and they may accept mistreatment if they fear deportation (Bennett, 2014).

Tam and Neysmith (2006) recommended that "researchers be cautious about applying elder abuse categories derived from a Western cultural perspective to understand or account for abuse in other cultures" (p. 149). This recommendation extends to policymakers as well.

Future Issues in the Mistreatment of Older Persons

Mistreatment of older persons has existed throughout history. What then accounts for the relatively sudden interest in abuse and neglect? Four social changes account for this interest: (1) the growth of the older population, (2) the increased political power of older people, (3) the women's movement and a critical analysis of the family, and (4) the state's willingness to intervene in family life.

Today, professionals, on behalf of the state, work to protect vulnerable minorities such as children and seniors. Through this process, abuse against older persons has become a legitimate social problem. The identification of abuse as a problem is the first step in creating social policies to protect abused older people.

The research on abuse against older persons supports the idea that older people suffer from varied forms of mistreatment. Some subgroups may have a higher-than-average risk of abuse and may need special attention. This includes older women, those who are physically or cognitively frail, and those who depend on their abuser for financial security or caregiving.

Professionals need more education about abuse and they need tools to assess and detect abuse. Lindenbach and colleagues (2012), for example, proposed the use of a screening instrument to aid detection. A screening "provides for systematic and objective documentation of the phenomenon" (p. 236). A number of instruments exist that focus on specific issues such as risk factors (e.g., isolation or dependency) or actual signs of abuse.

Staff and community professional training can play a role in the prevention and detection of abuse and mistreatment. The Public Health Agency of Canada (2010c) proposed the use of social media networks as a way to increase awareness of elder abuse and mistreatment among professionals. The agency proposed that blogs, Facebook, and Twitter can build professional communities of practice. These media allow professionals to "communicate, collaborate and share information."

Healthcare and social service workers in rural and remote communities will find these media especially useful. They lack a community of other professionals and can feel isolated. Blogs such as *Exploring the Space Between* allows front-line workers to post and share their concerns and experiences. CHNET-Works! (2012) provides in-service education to "researchers, decision-makers and practitioners from across Canada." The system offers weekly webinars that share leading-edge research and approaches to practice. Professionals can view these webinars and other educational programs at no cost.

Future studies can explore policies and practices that help ensure the safety of a growing and diverse older population. Abused older people need support and attention, but keep in mind that the vast majority of older people do not experience abuse. Research findings should make us more aware of abuse but also help keep the issue of abuse in perspective.

FUTURE RESEARCH ON SOCIAL SUPPORT

Many older people live rich social lives. They interact with family members, friends, and neighbours, as well as with their spouses. Most older people rely on these networks of family and friends for social, emotional, and healthcare support.

Some trends, such as cohort attrition for very old people and smaller families for Baby Boomers, suggest that informal supports will decline in the future. Other trends, such as longer life expectancy for spouses, suggest that older people will still rely on informal supports in the years ahead. These two trends may counterbalance each other. Also, older people in the future may develop new types of social supports. Seniors might rely more on **fictive kin**. This term refers to close relationships with non-relatives such as friends, neighbours, and home care workers (Penning & Wu, 2014). These and other new relationships need further study.

---

fictive kin the close relationships that an older person develops with non-relatives such as friends, neighbours, and home care workers

Summary

1. Older people often depend on informal support networks for emotional and healthcare support, but informal support can place a burden on family members (particularly women). These burdened caregivers may lose their income from work, their pensions, and even their health due to caregiving demands.
2. Older people also get support from friends, siblings, and technology. These supports provide help to older people with children and to childless older people.

Each of these sources provides a unique support to the older person.
3. Adult children, most often daughters, provide most of the informal support needed by their older parents. Research shows that strong feelings of attachment to a parent lead to caregiving, and feelings of closeness between parents and children lead to satisfaction and happiness. Older adults, particularly those without a spouse or children, receive support from siblings and friends as well.
4. Caregivers can experience caregiver burden, especially in cases where a senior suffers from dementia. Caregiving can place a strain on the caregiver's health, marital relationship, and work. Studies show the complex feelings of love, obligation, anger, frustration, guilt, and satisfaction that caregivers experience.
5. Even after a care receiver enters an institution, caregivers can continue to feel burdened. Counselling, support groups, respite programs, and elder care programs can moderate feelings of burden.
6. Abuse against older people is most often committed by family members. Abuse most often takes the form of material abuse and chronic verbal aggression. A smaller proportion of older people face physical aggression and neglect. Education for police, counsellors, family members, and older adults themselves may help reduce the incidence of abuse. Legal services, mental health services, and shelters could help older people to cope with the aftermath of abuse.
7. Some trends, such as cohort attrition for very old people and smaller families for Baby Boomers, suggest that informal supports will decline in the future. Other trends, such as longer life expectancy for spouses, suggest that older people will still rely on informal supports in the years ahead. These two trends may counterbalance each other. Also, older people in the future may develop new types of social supports.

STUDY QUESTIONS

1. Explain the difference between formal and informal support. What kind of support do most older people give to their families? What kind of support do they get from their families? How do older people choose their potential support groups?
2. What are the major difficulties that arise when people take on the role of caregiver to their aged

parents? What satisfaction do caregivers derive from their role? What is caregiver burden? What resources exist to help family members cope with the stress of caregiving?

3. Why do demographers think that the availability of informal supports may decrease in the future? In the absence of informal support, what other types of support are available to the older population?

4. What are the different types of abuse against older persons? How common is this abuse? Who is often responsible for abusing an older person?

5. Suggest some ways that abuse against older persons can be prevented, both in the community and in institutions.

KEY TERMS

caregiver burden (p. 329)
convoy model of support (p. 321)
developmental stake or generational stake (p. 324)
fictive kin (p. 340)
formal support (p. 318)
functional specificity of relationships model (p. 321)
hierarchical compensatory model (p. 320)
informal caregivers (p. 322)
informal support (p. 318)
long-distance caregivers (p. 333)
quasi-widowhood (p. 331)
social support (p. 318)
task specificity model (p. 320)

Study Tools
CHAPTER 13

Located at retail.tophat.com:

- Review Key Terms with interactive and printable flash cards
- Check Your Comprehension and Think About chapter concepts by completing practice quizzes
- Develop Your Gerontological Imagination with class activities
- Analyze Aging in a Global Perspective with engaging case studies and critical thinking questions
- Demonstrate Your Knowledge of the Concepts by bringing your own experience to personal application questions
- Evaluate Aging in the Media by completing Internet activities with evaluation questions

CHAPTER 14

DYING, DEATH, AND BEREAVEMENT

susico/Shutterstock

LEARNING OBJECTIVES

After reading this chapter, you will

LO1 Understand the meaning of dying and death in old age.

LO2 Recognize that seniors who are dying "live while dying."

LO3 Appreciate the individual senior's experience of dying, death, and bereavement.

LO4 Be able to describe the social response to dying, death, and bereavement in old age.

LO5 Be able to explain end-of-life issues, including palliative care and medical assistance in dying.

LO6 Appreciate cultural diversity with respect to dying, death, and bereavement in Canada.

INTRODUCTION

How do you feel about dying and death? Draw a line across a piece of paper. Put a dot at each end of the line. Put the word *birth* at the left end of the line. Put the word *death* at the right end of the line. Now add a dot for to-day's date. Put the date of your birth under the *birth* dot. Now put the date you project for your *death* under the dot that says *death*.

How did you feel about fixing a date for your death? How did you come up with a date? Do you look forward to your next birthday? Or do you think about how few years you have left to do the things you want to do? Do people of different ages think the same way about death? How do older people feel about death?

The 92-year-old mother of one of the authors talked openly about her eventual death. She acknowledged that she might die at any time, and regularly reviewed her plans for her funeral. Nevertheless she intended to live to at least 100. As she reviewed her life story, she spoke of times earlier in her life when she almost died in childbirth, when her sister died as a young woman in the 1940s from polio, and her father died from a heart attack. Death for her had always been a part of her life. Still, even at age 92, she thought of her death as distant rather than imminent.

Seniors, like the author's mother (and like most younger people), focus on living their lives. They typically view death as a distant event. But the awareness and experience of death does differ for older people. For one thing, older people witness the deaths of friends and relatives. Many older people experience the loss of a spouse and cope with widowhood or widowerhood and personal loss.

Finally, seniors often contemplate their own dying experience. They may wonder: Will death come suddenly? Or will it come after a long illness? Will it be painful? Will I ask for life support? Or will I ask for a "do not resuscitate" order or medical assistance in dying? Older people may wonder about all these things even as they go about their normal routines.

This chapter looks at death in old age. It focuses on (1) definitions of dying and death; (2) the individual senior's experience of dying, death, and bereavement, including attitudes toward death; and (3) preferences for where death takes place, ethical issues, and cultural diversity.

DEFINING DYING AND DEATH

When do we begin to die? When we take our last breaths? When our doctor tells us that we have a terminal illness? Some people argue that we begin to die at birth or even at conception. Nevertheless, young people typically think of themselves as living, and even seniors who know they have a terminal illness typically see themselves as "living while dying" (Leming & Dickinson, 2016).

The older person, family members, and healthcare professionals have different views of the dying person. Seniors define themselves as dying, or not, depending on their assessment of their health. Seniors may assess their health realistically or in overly optimistic or overly pessimistic terms. They may initially deny dying and later come to accept impending death. Sometimes, seniors suspect or recognize that they have a terminal illness before anyone else does.

The dying grandmother of one of the authors brushed off her middle-aged daughter who had come to offer care and support. She became frustrated with the daughter's unrealistic and overly optimistic stance. She brought her daughter down to earth when she said emphatically and with exasperation: "I am dying, dearie. I'm dying." Her death was indeed imminent and she knew it, although her grown-up daughter denied, or at least pretended to deny, its reality.

Family members may deny impending death. Alternatively, family members may perceive their elderly family member as dying long before the senior does.

Finally, the senior's physician may make a terminal diagnosis and later inform family members when death is imminent. Remember that even after a terminal diagnosis, a senior may live well in many respects. So when does dying begin? We conclude that the experience of dying remains ambiguous and depends on one's point of view.

The concept of death also has its ambiguities. In the past, we defined death as the cessation of cardiac and respiratory function. In more recent decades we typically define death in terms of the cessation of brain function, so-called "brain death" (Leming & Dickinson, 2016). Nevertheless, brain death, coma, persistent vegetative state, minimal consciousness, and life on a life-support machine make the assessment of life versus death difficult today. For example, a person in a coma will appear unawake and unaware, while a person in a persistent vegetative or minimally conscious state will appear awake but unaware or inconsistently aware (DeSpelder & Strickland, 2011).

To further complicate matters, gerontologists (who specialize in the study of old age) and thanatologists (who specialize in the study of dying and death) distinguish physical death from social death (Northcott & Wilson, 2017). **Social death** refers to the perception or behaviour of others when they perceive or treat a person as if physically dead, when the physical body has not yet died.

---

social death refers to the perception or behaviour of others that indicates that they perceive or treat a person as if physically dead when the physical body has not yet died

Photo by Chris Jackson/Getty Images

Girls in face paint in Real del Monte on the Day of the Dead on November 2, 2014, in Hidalgo, Mexico.

With respect to seniors, social death often describes socially marginalized elderly persons, including the very old, the frail elderly, the isolated and ignored senior, the senior with dementia, the senior abandoned in a nursing home, the poor senior, a racial minority, or a recent immigrant. In these cases when society overlooks or ignores seniors, social death precedes physical death.

In a curious twist, physical death sometimes precedes social death. For example, in some cultures that require elaborate funerals, a family may define a physically dead elderly family member as alive until they have saved enough money for the funeral. The family and the community do not acknowledge the death until the funeral takes place, even though a year or more may have passed since the actual physical demise (Leming & Dickinson, 2016).

Furthermore, we often keep the dead alive in our minds, memories, and rituals. We can imagine the dead as living, we have conversations with the dead in our minds, and we may engage in rituals designed to bring the dead and the living together, for a moment at least. Consider the Mexican tradition of the annual Day of the Dead festival (DeSpelder & Strickland, 2011).

TIME TO REVIEW

Compare and contrast the different views of dying and death held by family members, physicians, and older people.

What do gerontologists mean by "social death"? How does this differ from physical death?

EXPERIENCING DYING AND DEATH IN OLD AGE

The individual senior experiences dying and death as intensely personal; nevertheless, culture and society shape that experience (Northcott & Wilson, 2017). Societal

perspectives toward death fall on a continuum. Some societies see death as an enemy, something we fight with all our power. Other societies welcome death and even see it as a transition to a better, even blissful, world. Still others see death as a mystery (Leming & Dickinson, 2016).

In the ancient past, people saw death as a mysterious transition and created myths and stories to explain death. The Greek Hades, the Christian Heaven or Hell, and the Muslim Paradise all show humans grappling with the meaning of death (Kastenbaum, 2012).

For some societies, death meant an eternity of darkness and shadow. For others, as Dante describes in his *Inferno*, it could mean punishment for an evil life. And for Muslims, death means a life of ease and pleasure for believers. The power of stories about life after death and their central role in religion and culture tell us that people have always wondered about death.

But times have changed and we have a new view of dying and death (although one that coexists with some of our traditional views). Science and technology extend life and push dying and death to late old age. We rarely have a direct experience of death. We see graphic scenes of violence and death in the movies or on TV, but these images have little impact on our daily lives.

Today, death challenges our moral and ethical codes. Our legal system grapples with the issue of medical assistance in dying, our healthcare system deals with the long trajectory toward death that we call long-term care, and families cope with institutions such as hospitals and nursing homes, where death most often occurs. Death may still fill us with fear but more often it confronts us with practical choices: To die in an institution or at home? To continue or end treatment? To request medical assistance in dying or continue to live with illness? To opt for burial, cremation, or freezing of the body until science finds a cure? Discussions of dying and death today often focus on dying and death in old age.

Death in Old Age

In the past, high infant mortality rates, childhood diseases, and high female death rates during child-bearing years made death in all age groups a common event. Today, most infants will live to old age. Life expectancy at birth in Canada in 2009–2011 stood at 79.3 years for males and 83.6 years for females. Even in old age, life expectancy has increased. A man age 65 in 2009–2011 could expect to live another 18.8 years (to an average age of 83.8 years); a woman at age 65 could expect to live another 21.7 years (to an average age of 86.7 years) (Martel, 2013).

Longer life expectancy today means that most people die of the diseases of old age—cancer, heart disease, stroke, chronic lung disease, Alzheimer's disease, diabetes, and influenza and pneumonia. In 2011, seniors accounted for 79 percent of all deaths in Canada. In that year, cancer caused 28 percent of deaths in old age. Heart disease caused another 21 percent of deaths and stroke, 6 percent (calculated from Statistics Canada, 2014r).

The **trajectory of dying** (for example, a slow, lingering death from cancer or a sudden death from an acute illness, heart attack, stroke, or accident) differs today from dying trajectories in the past. In the past, people died at a younger age and they often died quickly of an acute illness (e.g., pneumonia) or accident. Nearly one-third of deaths (29 percent) in 1926 occurred in infants and children under age five. Today, less than 1 percent of deaths occur in young children (Statistics Canada, 2011n), and most deaths occur in old age following a long period of illness and decline.

Carstairs (2010) noted that only about 10 percent of deaths have a sudden-death trajectory. She pointed out that the remaining 90 percent of deaths would benefit from care designed to improve the quality of life while dying, either at home, in a hospital, or in long-term care. Note that trajectories of dying affect where a person will die. A long drawn-out dying trajectory is more typical of persons who are very old and frail and is associated with death in a long-term care facility, such as a nursing home. A shorter dying trajectory is associated with death either at home or in hospital (Northcott & Wilson, 2017).

***

trajectory of dying the pattern or course of dying over time, for example, sudden death or slow decline

Nevertheless, a person with cancer has the greatest chance of dying at home, because cancer patients and their families can often plan for death. The healthcare system (including home care) has adapted to the demands of this illness. A person with dementia, on the other hand, will likely die in a nursing home or hospital. A person with a major acute illness will probably die in a hospital. While a senior is most likely to die in a hospital today, the percentage of deaths occurring in a hospital in Canada has been declining since the 1990s. Seniors are increasingly likely to die in a long-term care facility or at home (Northcott & Wilson, 2017).

Death in later life today usually comes slowly and predictably. People often experience a decline in function and health over time, along with periodic intense crises that may lead to death. Dying can include pain, delirium, swallowing problems, loss of mental function, and other forms of discomfort (Northcott & Wilson, 2017). Dying in old age makes special demands on healthcare providers, family members, and older people themselves.

Seniors' Views of Dying and Death

Only a small number of studies have looked at how older people feel about death. And major theories of aging do not address the subject. According to activity theory, people want to stay active throughout their lives and substitute new roles and activities for ones that they lose as they age. When people retire, activity theory says, they have the highest life satisfaction if they find new things to do. This theory says nothing about death,

EXHIBIT 14.1 *The Seven Leading Causes of Death at Age 65 or Older by Sex, Canada, 2011 (percentage of total deaths)*

	Women	Men
Malignant neoplasms (cancer)	24.8	31.3
Heart diseases	20.7	21.9
Cerebrovascular diseases (stroke)	7.2	5.3
Chronic lower respiratory diseases	5.2	5.6
Alzheimer's disease	4.3	2.2
Diabetes	2.9	3.3
Influenza and pneumonia	2.9	2.6

Note that cancer and heart disease accounted for about half of the deaths of older people in 2011. Compared with women, men tend to have a higher rate of death by cancer. In particular, men have a higher rate of lung cancer. In contrast, women have higher rates of death by stroke and Alzheimer's disease. This may reflect the fact that more women live into later old age.

Source: Calculated from Statistics Canada (2014). Leading causes of death, total population, by age group and sex, Canada. CANSIM Table 102-0561, www5.statcan.gc.ca/cansim/a47. Reproduced and distributed on an "as is" basis with the permission of Statistics Canada.

EXHIBIT 14.2   *The Last Goodbye*

I approached the front door feeling a little nervous. Did he know that I was coming to say goodbye? I glumly wondered if, when you are dying, it makes you feel better, or worse, to suddenly have a pilgrimage of people visit you at home. Especially a person like me, who somehow had not found the time in the past several years during one of my visits home to stop by to see him and just say hello.

My apprehension melted when he and his wife answered the door. The joy on his face and his insistence on giving me a huge hug made it clear that I was a welcomed visitor. Knowing how sick he was, I did not want to stay and wear him out. I handed over a small gift and indicated that I merely wanted to drop it off and express my love and support. His face fell. "I thought you were going to stay and visit a while." At that, I gladly allowed myself to be ushered into the familiar sitting room.

As our visit began, he was reflective but joyfully so. He spoke of watching me grow up with his kids, and he fondly recounted adventures we had all shared. He expressed gratitude that he had "so many good memories."

The conversation turned, at his direction, to his health. Openly, he discussed the extreme pain, nausea, and weakness he was battling. He was not complaining, just explaining. He stated simply that the doctor at the hospital had told him that "it was bad." He said he came home initially unwilling or unable to read about the diagnosis. However, after about three days, he read all the materials he could, and with a wry grin, he said, "That *really* scared me."

He continued, "I know the doctor had said it was bad, but…." That sentence was left unfinished. Emotion brimmed in his eyes and those of his wife. He told me that the aggressive treatment he was undergoing was not a cure. He added, "There is no cure." Our eyes met. Simply, he stated, "It's okay now." I glanced at his wife, who avoided eye contact, and I thought of how her daughter had told me his wife kept saying that she was not ready to live without her husband.

While he seemed to accept his situation, his children seemed to be in complete denial. Had he been as frank with them as he was with me?

When it came time for me to leave, he again gave me a tight hug. He stood at the door, waving as I got into the car and pulled away. I feared that this was our last goodbye.

Source: Anonymous (2012).

although it would support living life to the fullest, even while dying.

Disengagement theory says that people want to disengage from social roles as they age. This theory says that retirement and withdrawal from social responsibilities lead to high life satisfaction. According to this theory, an awareness of impending death starts the process of disengagement. People know that they will die soon, so they ease their way out of social life.

Disengagement produces a smooth transition of power and responsibility from one generation to the next. This theory says that death disrupts society less if older people disengage from social roles as they age. This theory focuses on the social effects of dying, but it says little about death as a personal experience or about how older people feel about death.

Erikson's theory of ego development (1963, 1982) claims that the last stage of life leads to a life review. A person looks over his or her life, achieves acceptance of the life lived, and prepares for death. Erikson describes this as ego integrity. People in this stage often feel a deep concern for others and for the culture they will leave when they die. As these theories show, older people respond to death in various ways: Some people deny it, some accept it, and some embrace it.

Compared with younger people, older people think about death more. But compared with younger people, seniors are less afraid of death (Leming & Dickinson, 2016). Seniors today typically express more concern about the process of dying than about death itself. For example, a long and difficult process of dying often leads a dying senior to express a welcoming preference for death. When death finally comes, others often speak of that death as a "blessing" (Northcott & Wilson, 2017).

Seniors commonly state that they do not want to be a burden on others. And dying seniors in particular have concerns about being or becoming a burden on family members who provide care. As a result, dying seniors tend to focus on the needs of their caregivers, minimize their own needs, and plan for their deaths.

The Good Death

As noted above, the dying senior may welcome death as an end to suffering. Similarly, the bereaved may see their loved one's death as a blessing when it ends suffering. In other words, people often perceive dying as more problematic than death itself. How would you prefer to die?

---

life review a dying person looks over his or her life, seeks a conviction that one's life has had meaning and purpose, ties up loose ends, achieves acceptance of the life lived, and prepares for death

ego integrity the acceptance of the notion that one's life cycle is something complete and unique

What constitutes the ideal death from your point of view? What would you accept as a "good enough" death? What do you think defines a bad death?

As you can see from Exhibit 14.3, the good or the bad death depends on a number of criteria. Dying from a heart attack that occurs in one's sleep at home or dying with loved ones near are versions of what most people consider to be a good death. Dying in the hospital in pain, without dignity, and surrounded by strangers following a long, agonizing struggle with cancer would be considered by most people a bad death.

Note that what constitutes a good or a bad death depends on one's point of view. From the point of view of the dying senior, the criteria for a good death include a lack of pain during the dying process, a quick death, dying at home surrounded by loved ones, maintaining a sense of dignity, having a sense of control, and being prepared to die. From the point of view of the dying person's significant others, death may be viewed as good when it relieves family members of the burden of care or minimizes financial costs to family members. From the point of view of society as a whole, death may be viewed as good when it makes minimal demands on social resources and facilitates the transfer of authority, power, and wealth.

TIME TO REVIEW

Compare the causes of death in the past with the causes of death today. What changes in society explain this difference in the causes of death?

What do gerontologists mean when they refer to a "trajectory of dying?" Give an example of a trajectory of dying for an older person.

Existential, Spiritual, and Religious Issues

Existential issues for dying seniors involve finding meaning in the life one has lived and in one's dying and death. Dying and death can become a spiritual quest, whether in religious or non-religious terms (Northcott & Wilson, 2017).

Religion plays a smaller role in Canada today than in the past, but people often turn to religious leaders and institutions at the time of death. Church groups, for example, arrange visits to dying church members. Religious leaders spend time with dying people at their bedsides and lead religious services after a person has died.

People with different religious beliefs differ in their attitudes toward death. Most religions teach that people get the kind of afterlife they deserve. Studies show that people with mild or uncertain religious belief fear death most, while those with strong religious beliefs or no belief at all deal with death best (Leming & Dickinson, 2016). Religious people follow the social rules of their religion and accept conventional religious explanations of the afterlife. People who hold traditional religious beliefs, but do not practise their religion, may accept enough of religion to believe in an afterlife, but not enough to feel they will have a good one.

Some religions, such as Christianity and Islam, teach that the individual lives on after death, is reunited with loved ones who have died previously, and can look forward to reunion with loved ones who will die at some time in the future. Christianity and Islam teach that the individual is judged by God and that one's actions in life influence one's circumstances in the afterlife.

Some seniors and dying persons tend to engage in a life review in order to achieve ego integrity. While

EXHIBIT 14.3 *"Good Death" versus "Bad Death"*

Each culture defines a "good" and a "bad" death. Below, Northcott and Wilson (2017) offer an ideal type of a good and a bad death as defined by modern Western culture.

Criteria	Good Death	Bad Death
What	Heart attack, "natural" death	Cancer, AIDS, ALS, Alzheimer's disease
How	Quick, painless	Slow, agonizing, without dignity
Where	At home, in bed	In hospital, in intensive care unit
With whom	With loved ones	Alone or with strangers
When	During old age, timely, prepared	In very old age, untimely, unprepared
Why	Meaningful, expected, accepted	Meaningless, senseless

Source: Summarized from Northcott, H.C., & Wilson, D.M. (2017). *Dying, Death, and End-of-Life Care in Canada*, 3rd ed. Toronto: University of Toronto Press.

EXHIBIT 14.4 *Attitudes toward Death: A Questionnaire*

Sonia Duffy and colleagues (2006) created the questionnaire below to better understand people's different attitudes toward death and dying. Responses to these hypothetical situations can *clarify* feelings about death and the dying process. People draw on personal, religious, and cultural resources in their responses. Consider your responses to these "scenarios." How would your classmates respond, your friends, your family members? What was the basis for your responses (or those of your family and friends)?

End-of-life trade-off scenarios

Imagine that you have just been diagnosed with a terminal illness and have been told that you are expected to live only six more months. During this time, you will be faced with several difficult choices to make about your care. A series of choices will be presented to you. [Consider] what your choices would be and why. [Try answering these questions again after reading this chapter. Have any of your answers changed? Why or why not?]

Scenario 1: Dying at home versus being a burden to family

You are being discharged from the hospital but require a great deal of personal care. Would you rather go home knowing that your care would be difficult for your family or would you rather go to a nursing home or hospice?

Scenario 2: Disclosure versus non-disclosure of information to the patient

You have been diagnosed with a terminal illness, but your doctor has not told you yet. Would you want to be informed and make your own decisions or would you want your family to be told and be responsible for the decisions?

Scenario 3: Pain control versus being mentally alert

You are experiencing extreme pain, but when you take pain medication you are no longer alert. Would you rather take pain medication and be pain-free if it meant sleeping most of the time?

Scenario 4: Antibiotics versus extending the dying process

Sometimes antibiotics are given to patients to fight infection. Would you want to take antibiotics to extend your life knowing that it would prolong the dying process?

Scenario 5: Intensive care even if no hope of recovery

You have the chance to stay in intensive care and have everything done to prolong your life as long as possible or go home and spend your remaining days spending time with your family. Which would you rather do?

Scenario 6: CPR versus no chance of recovery

You have an unexpected allergic reaction to a medication. The reaction causes your heart to stop. Would you want to be resuscitated even though you have only six months left to live?

Scenario 7: Respirator (short- or long-term)

You are having trouble breathing and have the choice of spending your remaining days on a respirator or dying within several days. Which would you rather do?

Scenario 8: Feeding tube (short- or long-term)

You are no longer able to eat. Your doctor offers to put in a feeding tube into your stomach. Would you want to be kept alive with a feeding tube and prolong the dying process or die within a couple of weeks without a feeding tube?

Scenario 9: Dialysis (short- or long-term)

You have kidney disease, which requires you to go to the hospital three times a week for half a day to have your blood cleaned by dialysis. Would you want to continue this even though you only have six months to live?

Scenario 10: Withdrawing treatment versus prolonging suffering

You are in a great deal of pain and your pain medication is not working. You have been placed on a respirator. Would you want to remain on a respirator and prolong your life temporarily, or would you want life support removed?

Source: Adapted from Duffy, S., Jackson, F., Schim, S., Ronis, D., and Fowler, K. (2006). "Cultural Concepts at the End of Life." *Nursing Older People.* September, 18(8) 2006, pp. 10–14, www.nursingolderpeople.co.uk. Reprinted with permission.

this process may be viewed in secular and psychological terms, it can also be viewed from a religious perspective. People who achieve ego integrity have accepted their life as they have lived it, made peace with humanity and with God, sought forgiveness and redemption for shortcomings, and gained hope for a good afterlife (Leming & Dickinson, 2016).

Some religions, such as Hinduism and Buddhism, teach that the individual is required to live repeatedly in an ongoing cycle of life, death, and rebirth. Each life that an individual lives is influenced by lives that person has lived previously. One seeks to live in such a way that one's next life will be favourable. The ultimate goal is to live well enough to escape the cycle of life and death altogether, to die and not be reborn.

In short, religions focus on how one should live life in the face of death. They present an account of what one can expect after death, whether reward or punishment, or the continuation or the extinction of the conscious self (Leming & Dickinson, 2016).

The ancient Chinese believed in an afterlife. This terracotta army, buried more than 2,000 years ago, was found and unearthed in Xi'an, China. Like the pharaohs of Egypt, the first emperor of the Qin Empire in China was buried with his worldly possessions—in this case, a replica of his army. The army was thought to serve and protect the emperor in the afterlife.

STAGES OF DYING

Dr. Elizabeth Kubler-Ross (1969) developed one of the first descriptions of the dying process from the point of view of the modern patient. She did this by speaking with patients who faced death from cancer. Kubler-Ross described five stages that her patients went through before they died.

First, she said, people deny that they are dying. They say, "Not me." They may believe that the doctor has the wrong X-rays or someone else's tests. They may go from specialist to specialist looking for a new diagnosis. They may not even hear the doctor tell them they have a fatal illness.

Second, she said, people feel angry. They begin to believe that they will die. "Why me?" they ask. At this point, people blame the doctors or their spouse or God for their illness.

Third, they begin to bargain. They say, "Yes, me, but ..." and try to make deals with the hospital staff. They may promise to be a good patient and to follow doctor's orders, if only they will get better. They may bargain with God, promising to go to religious services or to live a more pious life. They may bargain with God for one more summer at the cottage, or for enough time to see a child married, a grandchild born, or to have their next birthday.

Fourth, they feel depressed. Their illness gets worse, and they know they will die. They say, "Yes, me," and they feel a great sadness. Kubler-Ross said that depression has two stages. In the first stage, people mourn present losses—the loss of family, career, and the things they love, such as a home, car, or cottage. In the second stage, they mourn future losses—the loss of good times to come, the chance to see children or grandchildren grow up, and other future events. People begin to say goodbye in this stage.

Fifth, people accept death. They say, "My time is close now ... it's okay." They say goodbye to family and friends and die in peace.

Kubler-Ross said that at every stage, a person holds on to hope. At first, a person may hope the doctor made a mistake; later they may hope for a remission (if the person has cancer, for example), and still later they may hope for a painless death.

Some writers have been critical of Kubler-Ross's model of the dying process and question the number of her stages or their order (Leming & Dickinson, 2016). Kubler-Ross herself says that patients can skip stages, stages can overlap, and people can go back over the same stage many times. Some responses, such as anger, come up again and again.

Some people have used this model to tell people how they should die. But dying people do not appreciate being told that they should die in neat, linear steps. Furthermore, different illnesses create different trajectories of death and different patterns of response. Kubler-Ross based her model on cancer patients in a hospital. People with other illnesses show other trajectories. Sometimes, a cancer patient can have long plateaus between times of decline. But someone who dies shortly after an auto accident may not go through any of these stages. Northcott and Wilson (2017) said that the dying process depends on many things, including a person's age, illness, will to live, beliefs and values, social supports, and the treatments used to fight or manage the disease.

All sides of this debate share one thing: they have brought discussion and thinking about death into the open. People who have to cope with dying and death—patients, their families, first responders, and medical staff—now have a number of ways to think and talk about death. This has helped free many people from the silence that surrounded dying and death only a short time ago.

TIME TO REVIEW

What role can religion play in helping a person cope with dying?

How do stage theories of dying help us to better understand the dying process?

Why do some gerontologists criticize stage theories of dying?

Bereavement, Grief, and Mourning in Old Age

Seniors who reach very old age often observe that they have outlived their friends. The mother of one of the authors of this book frequently noted at age 89 that "all my friends are gone." She also observed that her husband and all of his brothers and sisters (there were seven) and their spouses "are gone" and that "I am the last one left." She would then list them in a ritualistic review.

Bereavement resulting from the death of a loved one causes **grief**, defined as a sense of profound loss and the experience of deep sorrow. Society and culture impose rules on the bereaved to guide and control the bereaved person's private grieving and public **mourning**. Mourning expresses grief in public. It typically involves social conventions (Kastenbaum, 2012).

Society does not always acknowledge an individual's grief. For example, society may not acknowledge grieving that occurs in the case of social death. Consider a woman whose husband has advanced dementia and resides in a nursing home. She may think of herself as a widow even though society neither recognizes her as a widow nor considers her bereaved. She may grieve for the loss of her husband as he once was and exhibit **anticipatory grief** (Kastenbaum, 2012) in expectation of his eventual physical death. But society does not allow her to grieve officially or

---

bereavement the state of having recently experienced the death of a loved one

grief a sense of profound loss and the experience of deep sorrow

mourning the public expression of grief, typically following social and cultural rules

anticipatory grief experienced prior to and in anticipation of the death of a loved one

Cris Kelly/Shutterstock

Here, a man expresses grief privately in a cemetery. Society allows only a short time for public grieving at a funeral. But grief at the loss of a loved one can go on long after a funeral takes place.

---

define herself as a widow until he is physically dead. The literature labels this a case of **disenfranchised grief**.

In the past, most theories of grieving assumed that grief began at the time of a loved one's death and proceeded over the span of a year or two. The bereaved person was supposed to feel less and less grief over time and end in a final resolution. Researchers today note that grief, while it typically declines in intensity and becomes less disruptive, does not necessarily come to an end. Grief often remains a recurring experience and is never truly over (Northcott & Wilson, 2017). For example, a person may feel the return of grief during the holiday season in December, on a wedding anniversary date, or as a random occurrence.

Seniors who experience grief may feel disbelief, shock, numbness, sadness, and/or guilt. A person can also feel abandoned, isolated, angry, and depressed. People who have problems with grieving may turn to alcohol and drugs. Still, only a small percentage of people go through **morbid grieving**.

Northcott and Wilson (2017) said that the pattern of grieving depends on how a loved one dies, on whether the death takes place suddenly or over time, on the age of the bereaved person, on the age of the deceased, and on the relationship that the bereaved had with the deceased. Forewarning about the impending death of a beloved spouse, for example, may allow a person to work through some grief and to plan for the future, easing adjustment into losing the spouse.

Loss of a Spouse in Old Age

Widowhood and widowerhood are expected in later life (Martin-Matthews, 2011). Most long-term marriages come to an end with the death of an elderly spouse. Because women have a longer life expectancy than men, and because women tend to marry men who are a few years older, a man typically expects to die before his wife. Widows outnumber widowers by a considerable margin.

Northcott and Wilson (2008) said "the death of spouse in old age … jeopardize[s] a lifestyle that depends on two person[s] cohabitating and assisting each other in managing life in old age…. The loss of a spouse [undermines] shared identity and transforms the life of the surviving spouse. Furthermore, the social status of the surviving spouse is devalued, even stigmatized to a degree." Still,

---

disenfranchised grief defined by society as illegitimate grief and therefore unacknowledged because society defines the relationship between the grieving person and the deceased as insignificant`

morbid grieving also known as complicated or pathological grieving, refers to a pattern or duration of grieving that society considers abnormal and problematic

widows and widowers adjust and some even "come to see widowhood as an opportunity for growth and a time of autonomy, independence, and freedom" (p. 164).

Widows and widowers face some common problems. For example, widowhood signals the end of a woman's former role and identity as a wife and requires the creation of a new identity. Similarly, van den Hoonaard (2010) said that widowerhood threatens a man's identity by undermining his sense of masculine competency. This leads him to protect his masculinity. For example, he may minimize efforts to (learn to) cook or clean house. He may consider re-partnering with a new woman. Both widowers and widows indicate that they no longer feel comfortable or welcome around couples and find their social lives transformed as a result.

The *Changing Lives of Older Couples* study in the United States included more than 1,500 people before widowhood (Mancini & Bonanno, 2006). The researchers then conducted a three-wave longitudinal study at 6, 18, and 48 months after the death of a study participant's spouse. This study, for the first time, detailed the frequency and variety of reactions to a spouse's death. Because it looked at pre-loss mental health, the study could assess the effect of loss on psychological well-being.

The study found five responses to the loss of a spouse:

1. chronic grief (defined as low pre-loss depression, high post-loss depression after 6 to 18 months);
2. common grief or recovery (low pre-loss depression and high post-loss depression at 6 months with improvement at 18 months);
3. resilience (low pre- and low post-loss depression at 6 and 18 months);
4. depressed-improved (high pre-loss depression and low post-loss depression at 6 and 18 months); and
5. chronic depression (high pre-loss depression and high post-loss depression at 6 and 18 months).

Only a small group (about 15.6 percent) showed chronic grief—low pre-loss depression but high post-loss depression. This study distinguished these people from those who showed chronic depression—high pre- and high post-loss depression. The chronic depression group made up 7.8 percent of the study population. The largest group in this study (45.7 percent), the resilience group, reported low pre- and low post-loss depression after 6 to 18 months. This result may surprise some people. It shows that those in good mental health before a spouse's death cope reasonably well with their grief.

Some people, the depressed-improved group, felt less depressed after their spouse's death. These people may have suffered through an unpleasant marriage or a long, stressful period of caregiving. The spouse's death may have come as a relief. The study found that many spouses either recovered from their grief after 6 to 18 months (10.7 percent) or coped well with their grief and showed low depression at 6 to 18 months (45.7 percent).

Compared with men, a smaller proportion of women remarry after their spouse dies. This, in part, reflects the smaller number of eligible men compared with eligible women in later life. Also, men tend to remarry younger women. Women who do remarry say they want a companion and the feeling that they add to another person's happiness. Many older widows report an interest in men, but they also report negative attitudes toward remarriage and an increased enjoyment of their independence (van den Hoonaard, 2010). Some women, for example, experience widowhood as a release, allowing them to rediscover parts of their identities they had lost in marriage. One woman said she would not marry again (for the fourth time). "I'm tired of taking care of sick old men," she said. "I want to enjoy myself for a while" (personal communication).

Another woman, a student about 75 years old, stated that she had loved her husband, loved being a wife and mother, but now that her husband was deceased, she said: "Why would I want to be married again? I am enjoying my freedom!" Martin-Matthews (2011) warns us to resist the tendency to view widowhood and widowerhood as overly problematic. While some people have great difficulty coping with the death of their spouse, most people adjust reasonably well.

Spouses who have died continue to influence the living in many ways. People sometimes talk to dead spouses, ask them for advice, or try to imagine what they would do in a situation now faced by the surviving spouse. One woman said she felt her husband lie down next to her in bed some months after his funeral. Widows or widowers will sometimes decide against remarriage because of the close tie that still exists with their dead spouse. More research on bereavement in old age will show how this experience differs from bereavement in younger people. Indeed, there is some evidence that older widows adjust to widowhood with less difficulty than younger widows (Northcott & Wilson, 2017).

TIME to REVIEW

Discuss the relationship between grief and mourning.

What do gerontologists mean by "disenfranchised grief"?

What are some of the conditions that determine the experience of grieving?

Compare and contrast the experience and behaviour of men and women after the death of a spouse.

Ethical Issues in the Treatment of the Dying Person

Contemporary approaches to the treatment of dying patients raise a variety of ethical questions. For example, is it ethical to stop actively treating a person's illness? Does the decision not to resuscitate a person whose heart has stopped or not to put someone on a respirator hasten a person's death? Or does it simply recognize the inevitability of death and the futility of further treatment?

Other ethical questions come up again and again in literature on dying and death. First, how much information should healthcare providers give a dying person about his or her condition and treatment? Second, when should a doctor allow a person to die? Third, should society and the legal system allow a person to choose to die and be helped to die?

Informed Consent

Several decades ago, experts debated whether to tell dying patients about their condition or keep this knowledge from them. At that time, physicians usually informed family members about a terminal diagnosis, but they typically withheld this information from dying patients. Today, Western society supports the dying patient's right to be informed about the likely outcome of their illness. They have a right to know their physician's suggested choice of treatment, possible alternative treatments, and the option of choosing no treatment. While patients must give their consent to be treated, they do not have the right to demand treatment that the healthcare system does not approve, even if the patient believes the treatment will extend life (Northcott & Wilson, 2017).

Allowing a Patient to Die

Doctors face other ethical conflicts when they treat dying patients. Medical ethics say that a doctor should try to cure patients, but the Hippocratic Oath also says that a doctor should first "do no harm." What should a doctor do when machines, surgery, or drugs that extend a person's life also prolong suffering? What should a doctor do when a patient asks to die? Family members may not want to end artificial life support. When does a family or a doctor have the right or the obligation to take someone off these machines, stop treatment, and allow death to occur?

Today, death often follows the decision of the family and the healthcare provider to cease treatment and allow the patient to die (Northcott & Wilson, 2017). Physicians inform family members when a patient is brain dead or when aggressive treatment is judged to be futile. A doctor may explain when a treatment will prolong suffering.

In these situations, physicians typically recommend the withdrawal of life-prolonging care so that the patient can die a natural death. Physicians give the

---

EXHIBIT 14.5 *Conflict over the Treatment of a Dying Man*

The following story appeared on CBC News online. It shows that conflict can arise when the values of modern medicine and the values of a family collide.

Doctors offer to treat dying Winnipeg man after colleagues refuse: Family's religious beliefs conflict with medical opinions

A doctor in Winnipeg has agreed to treat a dying 84-year-old man amid a legal and medical row between his family and physicians who say keeping him alive is unethical, a published report said Wednesday.

Three doctors at the city's Grace Hospital have refused to continue providing care to the elderly patient, Samuel Golubchuk, who they say has no brain function and should not be kept physically alive on a ventilator.

But other doctors have come forward and agreed to provide care, said Heidi Graham, spokeswoman for the Winnipeg Regional Health Authority.

"Our regional critical care program and hospital have developed a plan that involves having one attending physician of record for the patient in question," Graham told CBC News on Wednesday morning.

"This physician will be supported by two other physicians. These three physicians have already agreed to this, and this situation will allow the other physicians in the Grace intensive care unit to continue with their scheduled rotations if they so desire."

Graham also confirmed that discussions are under way that could result in the return of some of the doctors who refused to care for Golubchuk.

"When a person is born, it's written down when they're going to die. So it's God that decides this, not the doctors," said Miriam Gellar, Golubchuk's daughter.

Gellar said her father still makes eye contact with her and is able to squeeze her hand. She believes he could still recover and that the doctors who refuse to treat her father are "misguided" and have "no compassion."

"We feel he knows we're there with him. We gave him his card on Father's Day and his eyes lit up," she said. "Give the person a chance to recover and, you know, to live out their life the way they're supposed to. We're speaking for him. This is his choice."

Last month, in a letter to the Winnipeg health authority, Golubchuk's original attending physician, Dr. Anand Kumar, said he would no longer work in Grace Hospital's critical care unit because it meant providing medical service to his former patients that were "grotesque."

(continued)

Golubchuk had developed bedsores, Kumar wrote, and doctors were having to trim infected flesh from his body to prevent the infection from spreading.

"To inflict this kind of assault on him without a reasonable hope of benefit is an abomination," Kumar's letter said. "I can't do it."

Kumar advised the family to remove Golubchuk's ventilator and feeding tube, but they went to court instead and obtained a temporary order to continue treatment until the case can be heard fully in September.

Earlier this week, two doctors who had been maintaining Golubchuk's life support treatment also withdrew from the case.

"This week, I have come to the 'ethical line in the sand' that I had previously said I would never cross," Dr. David Easton said in a letter on June 17.

"Do potential legal consequences and threat of 'jail' take precedence over my duty to not inflict further harm to the patient? I have been, and am, extremely conflicted in all this.

"I had perhaps naively thought that by having my own institution 'strongly suggesting' me to act against my will

and provide said care, that I would somehow be absolved of these issues internally, but in fact this has further compounded them and increased my degree of conflict to an indescribable degree."

Arthur Schafer, a medical ethicist at the University of Manitoba, said the physicians were correct to follow their conscience once they'd formed a professional opinion on Golubchuk's case.

"They did morally the right thing," Schafer said. "As every first-year medical student learns, the basic principle of medical ethics is 'do no harm.'"

But Percy Golubchuk, the patient's son, said it's all about being able to trust that a medical team will provide the care that's needed to preserve life.

A person, he said, "should not be afraid when you go into a hospital that you might not come out because a doctor thinks your life is not worth living."

[Percy] Golubchuk's father was put on life support late last year when he was being treated in hospital for injuries suffered in a fall.

Source: CBC News. "Doctors offer to treat dying Winnipeg man after colleagues refuse. Family's religious beliefs conflict with medical opinions" (18 June 2008), http://www.cbc.ca/news/canada/story/2008/06/18/winnipeg-doctor.html?ref=rss]. Reprinted with permission by CBC Licensing.

family time to come to terms with the situation and to make decisions. Once the family makes the decision to cease care, healthcare professionals may turn off life-sustaining machines, take out a feeding tube, and replace aggressive care with palliative care designed to make dying comfortable. The family and healthcare professionals allow the patient to die.

Persons lacking the mental competence to refuse treatment (for example, patients in a coma) must rely on someone else to decide and act for them. Family members, a friend, or a medical doctor often must make end-of-life decisions for the patient. Experts encourage people to state in writing their healthcare preferences for the end of their life. This allows a person's voice to be heard and respected even if they can no longer speak for themselves. These "advance directives" can help family members and healthcare workers make difficult medical decisions.

Advance Directives

Advance directives go by a number of names. They may be called a personal directive, a healthcare directive, a living will, or a continuing (or enduring or durable) power of attorney. An advance directive states a person's

healthcare wishes and other preferences for the end of their life. It may designate a decision maker to implement the writer's wishes. A person writes this directive in advance in case they become incompetent and can no longer make personal decisions.

An advance directive gives specific information to family members and healthcare providers about the kind and amount of treatment the person prefers. It states who has the right to make end-of-life decisions for the writer of the directive. For example, a person may request that, if in a coma and dying from a terminal disease, no resuscitation takes place if his or her heart stops. This request may lead the dying person's physician to place a **do-not-resuscitate (DNR) order** on the patient's medical care chart.

Advance directives allow the person to maintain some control and to provide consent (in advance) for treatment, withdrawal of treatment, and withholding of treatment. **Power of attorney** gives someone (e.g., a lawyer, spouse, adult family member, or friend) the right to make decisions on behalf of the person, if the person loses his or her mental capacity.

advance directives (including a personal directive, healthcare directive, living will, and continuing power of attorney) a precise statement of the desired treatment and care, including what medical actions are to be taken under what conditions, and a declaration of who has the right to decide in the situation where the writer of the advance directive is no longer able to express his or her wishes

do-not-resuscitate (DNR) order a person may request that, if dying from a terminal disease, resuscitation not be attempted if the dying person's heart stops; this request may lead the dying person's physician to place a do-not-resuscitate (DNR) order on the patient's medical care chart

power of attorney a legal document that gives someone, usually a lawyer, adult family member, or friend, the right to make decisions on behalf of the ill person if the person loses his or her mental capacity

Advance directives help family members and healthcare practitioners make timely healthcare decisions, avoid contention, and even avoid court intervention in decision making. Note that advance directives cannot request treatment that is illegal in Canada. And an advance directive cannot obligate a family member or healthcare professional to do something they oppose for personal or professional reasons (Northcott & Wilson, 2017). Nevertheless, advance directives have become an effective means of stating one's preferences for end-of-life care that healthcare practitioners increasingly

welcome. Indeed, when the mother of one of the authors was hospitalized in 2014 at the age of 92, a staff member from the hospital telephoned and strongly suggested that his mother meet with a lawyer to have a personal directive and power of attorney drawn up. Clearly, the hospital wanted an advance directive in place to facilitate decision making about the end-of-life care that they anticipated.

Most people have heard of advance directives, but relatively few people have them. People tend to put off making an advance directive because they don't want to think about poor health, dying, and death.

EXHIBIT 14.6 *A Personal Directive*

The following is an example of a personal directive. While this example is written by John Doe, of course it could be written by Jane Doe instead. Further, this example refers to the Province of Alberta's *Personal Directives Act*; however, most provinces and territories have similar legislation. The relevant legislation could be referenced depending on where Jane or John Doe live at the time their personal directive is created.

John Doe
{put city and province}
(hereinafter referred to as "the Maker")

1) Cancel Previous Advance Health Care Directive

1.1 I cancel all Personal Directives, Advance Health Care Directives or Living Wills that I have already given.

2) Appoint an Agent

2.1 I APPOINT my wife, Jane Smith, to be my Agent and in the event of death or refusal or inability of my wife, Jane Smith, to continue to act, I APPOINT my son, Jim Doe to be my Agent in accordance with the *Personal Directives Act* for Alberta (hereinafter referred to as my "Agent").

3) Come into effect

3.1 This directive will have effect only when I lack capacity to make decisions about my personal matters.

3.2 I will lack capacity when two medical practitioners authorized to carry on practice in the Province of Alberta or authorized to carry on practice in whatever jurisdiction I may be residing declares that I lack capacity to make decisions about my personal matters.

4) Personal decision

4.1 My Agent has authority to make personal decisions on my behalf.

4.2 In this directive, "personal decisions" means any matter of a non-financial nature that relates to my person and without limitation includes:

4.2.1 my health care;

4.2.2 my accommodation;

4.2.3 with whom I may live and associate;

4.2.4 my participation in social, educational and employment activities;

4.2.5 legal matters that do not relate to my financial affairs.

5) Agent's Authority

5.1 My Agent must instruct my health care service providers based on the following guidelines:

5.1.1 In general, I do not wish my life to be prolonged by artificial means when I am in a coma or a persistent vegetative state and, in the opinion of my physician and other consultants, have no known hope of regaining awareness and higher mental functions, no matter what is done. In this circumstance, I wish to be kept comfortable and free from pain. This means that I may be given pain medication even though it may dull consciousness and indirectly shorten my life.

5.1.2 Further decisions regarding my care at the end of life should be guided by my Agent's knowledge of my wishes, beliefs and values (see attached document)

6) Dated, signed and witnessed

I make this Personal Directive on the day of ___ __ , 20 __ , at {City, Province}.

_____   _____
WITNESS   John Doe

People tend to believe that they have lots of time to prepare for death, which they view as a distant event. Education about advance directives can increase a person's knowledge about end-of-life options and increase use of these documents. Further, people who have an advance directive need to discuss their end-of-life preferences with their preferred surrogate (e.g., a spouse, sibling, adult child, or friend). People need to make their wishes clear to the person they designate as their surrogate decision maker.

Family members and physicians sometimes differ in their judgment of a person's will to live and the person's end-of-life preferences. This potential for conflict supports the need for an advance directive. An advance directive allows a person to think about his or her preferences while in a sound state of mind. The patient or the patient's relatives or friends need to make healthcare professionals aware of the advance directive and what it says.

Advance directives can ensure that older persons get the care they want. However, advance directives can pose problems. First, in some cases people may change their minds as they near death, but they may not get a chance to change their advance directive. Second, subtle forms of coercion may influence an older person's instructions in an advance directive. Older people may propose an end to treatment because they feel that they will burden others with their care. It follows that it is important to have good communication between dying people and their caregivers.

TIME TO REVIEW

What challenges do professionals face when they want to get informed consent from someone with dementia? What solutions can help overcome these challenges?

Under what conditions can a physician allow a person to die?

How do advance directives help physicians and family members make life-and-death decisions about a patient?

Changes in the Treatment of Dying: Hospice and Palliative Care

The idea of the **hospice** dates back to at least the Middle Ages in Europe. Hospices at that time took in travellers who needed food, shelter, and care. Hospices today meet the special needs of dying patients. Dame Cicely Saunders opened the first modern hospice, St. Christopher's, in London, England, in 1967. St. Christopher's offers **palliative care**. Palliative care does not attempt to extend life in the face of a terminal illness. Instead, palliative care tries to relieve symptoms and help patients enjoy their last days.

People fear death for many reasons, but often they fear the pain that may accompany death more than death itself. A hospice attempts to control pain and other symptoms. Pain relief ensures that the person will die in comfort, thus relieving much of the person's fear and anxiety. St. Christopher's pioneered pain-relief techniques now used by hospices and palliative care programs around the world.

Medical staff base pain control on two techniques: first, they adjust drug dosage until it relieves a patient's pain. Second, the nurses give the next dose before the previous one has worn off. This erases the memory, anticipation, and fear of pain. Patients cared for by this method need lower dosages to maintain a pain-free state because the drug does not have to overcome pain that has begun. Lower dosages mean that patients stay more alert.

A hospice allows a person to die with a minimum of technological intervention. The hospice does not use respirators or resuscitators to keep people alive. Staff members make dying a part of life. Patients also know they have a say in their treatment; they can ask for medication when they feel they need it, and they can ask to die at home. St. Christopher's (and other hospices) agree to readmit patients whenever the patient or the family needs more support.

A hospice gives people love and care. Staff members focus on the comfort of the patient. The hospice also helps patients do as much as they can for themselves; this increases patients' well-being by giving them a sense of control over their treatment. The family members of dying patients also receive care and support.

Initially, the hospice existed separately from the hospital. However, hospitals have adopted the idea of

hospice a place or program of care designed to meet the special needs of dying patients

palliative care directed toward improving the quality of life for the dying, including symptom control and spiritual support as well as bereavement support and education for the family members of dying patients

hospice palliative care and created palliative care units within the hospital. In Canada, the first palliative care units opened in the mid-1970s and today many hospice palliative care programs exist across the country. Palliative care can also take place in a nursing home or in a person's home. Workers in palliative care programs include physicians, nurses, physiotherapists, psychologists, and volunteers.

Palliative care challenges some core beliefs that people hold today. People believe in the curative power of modern medicine. As a result they may feel that palliative care gives up on the patient. They may feel guilty about choosing palliative care for a dying parent or spouse. As a result, the dying, their healthcare providers, and their family members may not agree on when to shift the emphasis of care from maintaining life to facilitating dying.

Gawande (2010, p. 38), a physician, reports the following case:

> [A woman] in her eighties, with end-stage respiratory and kidney failure, had been in the unit for two weeks. Her husband had died after a long illness, with a feeding tube and a tracheotomy, and she had mentioned that she didn't want to die that way. But her children couldn't let her go, and asked to proceed with the placement of various devices: a permanent tracheotomy, a feeding tube, and a dialysis catheter. So now she just lay there tethered to her pumps, drifting in and out of consciousness.

Gawande showed that physicians and family members often have difficulty agreeing on end-of-life treatment and decisions (see also Tan & Manca, 2013). This is understandable given the ambiguity that exists in many dying trajectories. Some who are thought to be dying, recover and live on. Some who are thought to be recovering, die unexpectedly. If the time of impending death were certain and obvious, then it would be easier for family members and healthcare workers to agree on end-of-life care decisions.

Family members who have difficulty accepting that their loved one is dying sometimes prolong the dying trajectory. Healthcare workers are often uncertain as to whether or not death is imminent and inevitable. Consequently, they continue to provide unnecessary care and initiate hospice palliative care only when death is apparent, often within a very short time preceding death (Cable-Williams and Wilson, 2014).

Northcott and Wilson (2017) called for the gradual use of palliative care measures as a person approaches death. An abrupt change from a treatment plan to a death plan is difficult for dying persons and their families. Palliative care should be introduced early in all serious illnesses, mainly for the relief of pain and suffering. The focus on palliative care can then grow if the disease worsens and death becomes obvious. This may avoid the appearance that treatment has ended and palliative care has begun.

Dying at Home

Some families try to care for their dying relative at home. Dying at home generally requires the support of family members, often assisted by healthcare professionals who provide hospice palliative home care services. In the typical case, one family member—usually a spouse or an adult child— assumes the role of primary caregiver.

Still, many older people will have no one at home to provide palliative care. Older widows, for example, often lack someone to look after them. Also, multiple pathologies in an older patient may make pain control more complex. Caregivers of dying older people who use palliative home care may need the use of a temporary hospital or hospice bed or a day hospital to provide some relief from the demands of caregiving.

Edwards, Olson, Koop, and Northcott (2012) studied primary caregivers and persons dying at home from advanced cancer. They examined the process of decision making as the dying trajectory unfolded. These researchers noted that family caregivers go to great lengths to follow the wishes of their dying family members. But over time, caregivers of dying persons engaged in a "dance" where the lead shifted from the dying person to the caregiver. While the caregiver initially assumed a supportive and then a managing role, the caregiver eventually took over care and decision making completely. Still, the caregivers tried their best to follow the patient's wishes. Dying at home can place a great deal of stress on the family and on the primary caregiver in particular.

TIME to REVIEW

Discuss the role of the advance directive in end-of-life care.

Describe the treatment that a dying person gets in a hospice or palliative care unit in a hospital. How does this differ from the treatment of a dying person in a typical hospital?

What challenges face the family and dying person if they choose to die at home?

Medical Assistance in Dying: Assisted Suicide and Active Euthanasia

People often confuse assisted suicide and active euthanasia. If you commit suicide, you kill yourself. If you ask for euthanasia, you ask someone else to kill you. The confusion arises when you ask someone to help you commit suicide. For example, you might ask your doctor to prescribe a lethal dose of medicine. If you take this medicine yourself, then the term **assisted suicide** applies, or more accurately **physician-assisted suicide**.

Alternatively, if the doctor injects this medicine into your vein causing your death, then the term **active euthanasia** applies. Who kills you, whether you do it or your physician, makes all the difference. Increasingly, people are using the term **medical assistance in dying** when a physician hastens a patient's death either by euthanasia or by helping the patient to commit suicide.

Modern medicine has become very successful in prolonging life and delaying death. Some critics of medical assistance in dying argue that we should not hasten death. There is some irony in the term "hasten death" in that the term often refers to ending the delay of death.

In 2013, Dr. Donald Low, who was dying of brain cancer at the age of 68, posted a video on YouTube. In this video, he issued a heart-rending and passionate appeal for the legalization of physician-assisted suicide in Canada. He died a few days later. In the video, Dr. Low said he thought it would take Canada a long time to legalize physician-assisted suicide.

Twenty years previously, the Supreme Court of Canada had ruled against Sue Rodriguez's petition to legalize physician-assisted suicide. The Supreme Court argued that if Canada developed effective hospice palliative care, the dying would have no need for physician-assisted suicide. Dr. Low would have been pleasantly surprised at the Supreme Court's decision in 2015 stating that the Criminal Code should not prevent physician-assisted death and should be revised accordingly. The Supreme Court gave the Government

of Canada a year to determine the guidelines for implementing physician-assisted death. In June 2016, the Government of Canada legislated guidelines for medical assistance in dying (see Exhibit 14.7).

Note that the Supreme Court removed the prohibition against both physician-assisted suicide and active euthanasia. This is a dramatic development. Only a few jurisdictions had legalized physician-assisted suicide and fewer had gone on to legalize euthanasia. Canada, with the Supreme Court decision of 2015, jumped to the forefront of the Death with Dignity and Right to Die movements. The Province of Quebec had taken a similar step in 2014, independently of the Supreme Court of Canada.

Note that before the Supreme Court's landmark decision, a physician in Canada could not legally assist you to commit suicide. Nor could a physician directly cause your death if you asked to be euthanized. Canadian law had previously defined both assisted suicide and active euthanasia as illegal. Nevertheless, a physician could withhold or withdraw treatment at a patient's request, or administer palliative care, even if doing so hastened the death of the patient (Northcott & Wilson, 2017). That is, prior to the Supreme Court's decision, a physician could not legally cross the line from **passive euthanasia** (allowing death) to active euthanasia (causing death).

The *Globe and Mail* newspaper conducted an online poll in Canada in March 2009. The paper asked readers, "Would you support making assisted suicide available to terminally ill patients?" Fifty-five percent of almost 20,000 readers favoured this proposition. Nevertheless, many groups and individuals oppose euthanasia and physician-assisted suicide. They see this as a move toward unregulated killing of old and disabled people. Others say that with proper regulation, physician-assisted death can end suffering for thousands of people who choose to end their lives.

Some people support assisted suicide and active euthanasia on humanitarian grounds. They focus on suffering and quality of life as key issues. Other people see the choice of assisted suicide and active euthanasia as a right in modern society. Some people support these options on economic grounds, given the high cost of healthcare at the end of life. Still others oppose assisted suicide and active euthanasia, fearing a "slippery slope" that will lead to more extreme and potentially abusive practices.

assisted suicide made possible with the help of someone

physician-assisted suicide a physician provides a patient with advice about how to commit suicide or with the technical means (e.g., lethal medications) to commit suicide

active euthanasia intervening actively to end a person's life

medical assistance in dying (or physician-assisted death) a physician helps a person to die either by assisting the patient's suicide or by euthanasia

passive euthanasia withholding or ceasing treatment of someone who is ill or injured and not expected to recover

EXHIBIT 14.7 *Guidelines for Medical Assistance in Dying*

The Government of Canada (2016) posted on its website guidelines for medical assistance in dying in Canada. Following are excerpts from that posting.

Medical assistance in dying

[Medical assistance in dying] can only be legally provided by physicians and nurse practitioners (depending on the province or territory where you live).

There are 2 types of medical assistance in dying available to Canadians. They include where a physician or nurse practitioner:

1. directly administers a substance that causes death, such as an injection of a drug
   - this is commonly called voluntary euthanasia
2. gives or prescribes a drug that is self-administered to cause death
   - this is commonly known as medically-assisted suicide

Who is eligible for medical assistance in dying

In order to be eligible for medical assistance in dying, you must meet all of the following conditions. You must:

- be eligible for health services funded by the federal government, or a province or territory
- generally, visitors to Canada are not eligible for medical assistance in dying
- be at least 18 years old and mentally competent (this means capable of making health care decisions for yourself)
- have a grievous and irremediable medical condition
- make a request for medical assistance in dying which is not the result of outside pressure or influence
- give informed consent to receive medical assistance in dying. This means you have consented to medical assistance in dying after being given all of the information needed to make your decision, including information about:
  - your medical diagnosis
  - available forms of treatment
  - available options to relieve suffering, including palliative care

Grievous and irremediable medical condition

To be considered as having a grievous and irremediable medical condition, you must meet all of the following conditions. You must:

- have a serious illness, disease or disability
- be in an advanced state of decline that cannot be reversed
- be suffering unbearably from your illness, disease, disability or state of decline
- be at a point where your natural death has become reasonably foreseeable, which takes into account all of your medical circumstances

You do **not** need to have a fatal or terminal condition to be eligible for medical assistance in dying.

Mental illness

People with a mental illness are eligible for medical assistance in dying as long as they meet all of the listed conditions.

However, you are not eligible for this service if:

- you are suffering only from a mental illness
- death is not reasonably foreseeable when considering all the circumstances of your medical condition
- a mental illness reduces your ability to make medical decisions

Informed consent

You must be mentally competent and capable of making decisions at the time that the service is provided. This is because the physician or nurse practitioner will ask you to confirm your choice right before administering medical assistance in dying. You are able to withdraw your consent at any time.

Protecting the right of providers to act according to their beliefs and values

Not all health care providers will be comfortable with giving or helping to provide medical assistance in dying. The practice may not be consistent with a provider's beliefs and values. The legislation does not force **any person** to provide or help to provide medical assistance in dying.

Countries vary with respect to their laws regarding assisted suicide and active euthanasia (Tiedemann, Nicol, & Valiquet, 2011). A few countries have legalized physician-assisted suicide (Kastenbaum, 2012; Tiedemann et al., 2011) and even fewer have legalized euthanasia.

The Netherlands has been a leader in the assisted death movement. The Netherlands has for several decades allowed physician-assisted suicide within specific guidelines. In 2002, the Netherlands passed the Termination of Life on Request and Assisted Suicide (Review Procedures) Act. Under this law, both physician-assisted suicide and active euthanasia are legal if a series of conditions are met.

For example, the patient's suffering must be unbearable and the patient must have no hope for improvement. The person must make an informed choice. And a second doctor must agree with the first doctor's assessment. Doctors have to report a case when they have assisted with a death.

In 2009, doctors in the Netherlands reported a total of 2,636 cases of physician-assisted suicide. In 80 percent of these cases, people died at home after their doctors provided a lethal dose of drugs. This compares to 2,331 reported deaths by euthanasia in 2008 (a 10 percent increase over 2007) (Caldwell, 2010). This may indicate a rise in actual numbers or a greater willingness of doctors to report cases.

The neighbouring countries of Belgium, Luxembourg, and Switzerland have followed the Netherlands's lead. Switzerland allows residents of other countries to come to Switzerland to purchase an assisted suicide. Some people refer to this as "suicide tourism."

The legalization of physician-assisted death, especially in the form of euthanasia, is a recent phenomenon. Those persons taking advantage of the legalization of physician-assisted suicide and physician-assisted death have been a relatively small percentage of all deaths. The annual report from Oregon for 2014 (*Death with Dignity Act Annual Report*, 2014) stated that 155 persons sought a lethal prescription from their doctors and 105 died using this medicine. Oregon had legalized physician-assisted suicide in 1998, the first state in the United States to do so.

Not all who seek a lethal prescription commit suicide. Having a lethal prescription in hand gives a person a choice. A report in 2009 about physician-assisted suicide in Oregon (Oregon, 2009) found that from 1997 to 2009, most of the patients who committed physician-assisted suicide died at home (98.3 percent) and most enrolled in hospice care (91.5 percent). From 1997 to 2010, a total of 526 persons in Oregon died by physician-assisted suicide. In Oregon in 2010, about 2 in every 1,000 deaths were physician-assisted suicides (Tiedemann, Nicol, and Valiquet, 2011).

TIME TO REVIEW

What is the difference between physician-assisted suicide and active euthanasia?

What does Canadian law say about a physician's ability to engage in either of these activities? How does passive euthanasia differ from the two approaches named above?

Describe how the state of Oregon and the Dutch in Europe legally view physician-assisted suicide and euthanasia.

Cultural Diversity in End-of-Life Care

Some cultures prefer that the physician *not* tell dying patients about their prognosis. This creates a dilemma for physicians in Canada, who must obtain informed consent from the patient in order to provide or withdraw treatment (Durst, 2010; MacLean et al., 2010).

Yeo (2009) said that contemporary Western end-of-life approaches, such as open discussions of death and discussions about stopping aggressive care, may not suit minority cultures. She said that healthcare professionals need to take cultural differences into account. Yeo said that family members in Asian cultures, for example, may demand that everything be done to keep an older parent alive. The values of filial piety and a belief in the will of God require this. Similarly, the beliefs of Orthodox Jews may demand that life be prolonged as long as possible, even though physicians may say that such care is futile.

Members of some North American Indigenous cultures and of Chinese cultures may not feel comfortable discussing death. These cultures take the position that if a person knows that they are dying, they will give up

EXHIBIT 14.8 *Assisted Suicide and Euthanasia: Some Terms and What They Mean*

Assisted suicide involves providing the means for someone to commit suicide (e.g., supplying prescription drugs) knowing that the person intends to commit suicide.

Euthanasia, sometimes referred to as mercy killing, is a term that comes from the Greek word for *good death*. It means causing a person's death on the assumption that the person wants to die and/or faces intolerable suffering. Because euthanasia involves one person causing the death of another, opponents argue that euthanasia is a euphemism for murder.

Passive euthanasia means withholding or stopping treatment of someone who is thought to be terminally ill, for example, turning off life-support systems and allowing a person to die "naturally."

Active euthanasia means intervening actively to end a person's life, for example, administering a lethal dose of sedatives to someone with a terminal illness.

Voluntary euthanasia means that a person who is competent to make his or her own decisions has asked a physician or someone else to cause his or her death.

Non-voluntary euthanasia means that the person lacks the competence to give consent. A person in a coma falls into this category. Someone else makes the decision to end this person's life.

Involuntary euthanasia means a competent patient has not sought euthanasia but had euthanasia imposed without consent. The term *murder* appropriately comes to mind.

EXHIBIT 14.9 *Physician-Assisted Death Comes to Canada*

Gloria Taylor challenged Canada's law prohibiting physician-assisted suicide. Sue Rodriquez had attempted to do this in the early 1990s but the Supreme Court of Canada ruled in 1993 against her petition. Gloria Taylor's campaign also reached the Supreme Court of Canada, but with a different outcome. The Supreme Court's ruling in 2015 dramatically changed end-of-life care in Canada. Gloria's story follows.

Gloria Taylor was a pioneer. She was the first person in Canada to win the right to die with the help of a doctor. And she led the charge to make the right to a peaceful death a reality for the rest of us.

Gloria was born and raised in Castlegar, British Columbia, and lived most of her life in Westbank, not far from Kelowna. In her professional life, she worked as a postal worker and a residential care worker. Ever outspoken and free-spirited, she volunteered as a health advocate and spent evenings and weekends riding motorbikes with her friends and family.

Gloria was 61 years old when her doctor told her she had ALS. The doctor told Gloria that the disease would likely paralyze her within six months, and would kill her within a year. Gloria outlived that—she survived three additional years.

During that time, she waged a public fight to die on her own terms. She was the lead plaintiff in the *Carter v. Attorney General of Canada* case, suing the government to give grievously ill patients the right to end their lives with the help of a physician.

With the help of the BC Civil Liberties Association, Gloria became the first Canadian ever to win the right to ask a doctor for help in dying....

"I am dying," she said in a statement to the press. "I do not want to, but I am going to die; that is a fact. I can accept death because I recognize it as a part of life. What I fear is a death that negates, as opposed to concludes, my life."

In the end, Gloria did not have to ask a doctor for help to die peacefully. She died suddenly and unexpectedly from an infection in 2012. Her family members, including her mother, Anne Fomenoff of Castlegar and her eldest son, Jason Taylor, of Kelowna, British Columbia, carried on Gloria's work in her honour....

In 2014, the Supreme Court of Canada agreed to hear arguments in *Carter v. Canada.* And on Feb. 6, 2015, it made history by striking down the Criminal Code prohibition on physician-assisted dying.

Source: Used with permission of Dying with Dignity Canada, http://www.dyingwithdignity.ca/gloria_taylor.

hope. Accordingly, the family may ask the physician not to inform a dying elder about his or her condition.

Modern medicine can feel proud of recent advances in end-of-life care. But, as Yeo (2009) cautioned, minority cultural values may clash with the latest thinking in Western medicine. The ethnic and racial diversity of the older population in Canada requires sensitivity to cultural differences. Healthcare workers, in particular, need sensitivity to an older person's ethnic, religious, and cultural background.

Yeo (2009) proposed that healthcare settings bring in people from ethnic populations to provide more culturally and linguistically appropriate services. These people can serve as guides and associates to healthcare professionals. Respected clergy, educators, clan leaders, and interpreters can all serve in this role. They can bridge the cultural gap between minority patients and the healthcare setting. And healthcare settings need to provide training and continuing education to non-minority healthcare professionals. This will increase professionals' awareness of patients' diversity and their cultural preferences.

Cultural Diversity in Funerary Rituals

Howarth (2007) argued that the social construction and response to dying, death, and bereavement changed from traditional to modern times. Most recently, dissatisfaction with science, medicine, and materialism has led to an increasing personalization of dying, death, and bereavement. The psychologist, grief counsellor, and funeral director have displaced the physician and priest. Emphasis has shifted from the body and soul to the psychological "self." In addition, the secular memorial service has replaced the religious funeral service. Finally, while the body used to be present at the funeral, with burial following, increasingly, the memorial service takes place without the body present and after the body has been buried or cremated.

Today in Canada, no single response to dying, death, and bereavement exists. Canadians display a mix of traditional, religious, medical, scientific, individualistic, and personal responses to the end of life. Canadians today may choose from a range of options, including a traditional religious funeral or a contemporary secular memorial service. The bereaved can purchase an earth burial, a cremation, or perhaps even a "green" burial (Smith, 2007). (For details about green burials, go to www.naturalburialassoc.ca.)

Funeral practices and rituals structure the grieving process. They prescribe what mourners should say, what they should wear, and how they should behave. Mourners in some cultures wear black; in others they wear white. Some societies value silent, unemotional grieving; others encourage displays of emotion at the funeral. Christians prefer earth burial; Hindus and Buddhists favour cremation. The Christian burial may take place several days after death while the Islamic burial occurs as soon as is possible.

Jewish tradition requires that the family sit shiva for seven days after a funeral. According to this custom, mourners tear their clothes, sit on low chairs to deny themselves physical comfort, cover the mirrors in their home, and light a candle that burns for one week. The mourning family accepts visitors throughout the week, and 10 men gather at the house each day for prayer. Mourning continues in less intense stages for a year until the unveiling of a commemorative stone on the grave of the deceased.

Each culture has its own funeral rituals and mourning practices, but all have a common purpose: to help the bereaved family cope with grief and re-establish community bonds after the loss of a community member. Regardless of which culture a person belongs to or the type of funeral he or she attends, each bereaved person has to work through personal feelings of grief.

TIME to REVIEW

Describe some of the cultural differences that exist in the care and treatment of the dying person. Compare the modern medical approach with the approach of some traditional cultures.

Describe some of the different funeral rituals that different cultures engage in.

CONCLUSION

This chapter has touched on some of the complex issues related to dying and death. Each culture and religion has its own views on issues such as euthanasia, funeral practices, and mourning. Each culture shapes its members' beliefs about the meaning of death, about life after death, and about care for the sick and dying. While people respond in unique ways to their own death and to the deaths of people they know and love, society and culture shape those personal responses.

Today, changes in technology, developments in the management of terminal illness, and new meanings assigned to death raise questions about dying, death, and bereavement. The study of dying and death can help people understand these issues and make better choices for themselves. An incident in the life of the lead author of this book, Mark Novak, made this clear to him:

> After my father's funeral, my mother, my sister, my father's brothers, and I got into a rented limousine and drove to the cemetery. The funeral director stopped the cars in the funeral procession at the cemetery gate. We saw the hearse pull ahead and stop a hundred yards away. I turned around to talk to one of my uncles in our car. A few minutes later, the director waved all the cars on. We stopped behind the hearse and got out. It was empty.
>
> The director led us to the graveside. We stood close to the grave, but we could not see the coffin or any earth. A blanket of fake grass covered the earth that had come from the grave. Another blanket covered the coffin. Relatives and friends gathered to the side and behind us. The director said some prayers and a few kind words. My mother, my sister, and I stood and stared at the fake grass.
>
> I think we were supposed to leave. But I motioned to the director to pull the grass back. He looked surprised. I told him to pull the grass back. He did. We saw the corner of the coffin and the corner of the grave, and we started to cry.
>
> I tell this story because my knowledge of death and dying gave me the confidence to act. I felt I should do something, and I knew what I had to do.

Those of us in the field of aging use our knowledge of aging each day. We use it to better understand our families and friends, and we use it to understand the changes we go through as we age. Knowledge about aging allows us to plan for our future with less fear and denial. The study of aging can make old age a better time of life for each of us and for the people we love.

Summary

1. We live even while dying. We should not think of living and dying as mutually exclusive. When we discuss dying, we discuss living. When we discuss end-of-life issues, we discuss living as good a life as possible, even as death approaches.

2. Today's technology can keep people alive artificially, prolonging life and delaying death. This raises questions about the definition of death, the boundary between life and death, and appropriate end-of-life care.

3. Death occurs more often in old age today than in the past. Cancers, heart disease, and stroke cause the majority of deaths occurring in old age in Canada today. Few people experience sudden death; most experience a long dying trajectory. Most people die in the hospital or in a long-term care facility.

4. Attitudes toward dying, death, and bereavement vary by age, religion, and culture. Older people generally

accept death more than younger people. Seniors often fear the process of dying more than death itself and hope to have a "good" death. Like younger people, older people say they want to continue living if they feel their life has meaning.

5. People with either no religious belief or a very strong one seem to cope with death best.

6. Elisabeth Kubler-Ross reports five stages of dying. Not everyone goes through all of these stages in the order Kubler-Ross describes. But her writings encouraged a more open discussion of dying and death when they first appeared.

7. The death of a loved one defines bereavement. The bereaved person typically experiences deep sorrow, grieves privately over his or her loss, and mourns publicly following social conventions. In some situations, society disallows grief. While some have difficulty coping with the death of a spouse in old age, most adjust reasonably well.

8. Dame Cicely Saunders opened the first modern hospice in England in 1967. St. Christopher's Hospice offered an alternative to hospital care for the dying and started the hospice palliative care movement. Hospices offer pain control and a home-like setting for death.

9. Palliative care units in hospitals offer the same comfort and care as a hospice. Some of these units along with palliative home care programs help patients die in their own homes. They also assure patients that they can return to the hospital at any time.

10. Most Western experts and patients prefer an open discussion about dying and end-of-life care options. They agree that patients have a right to know about the choice of treatment the physician has made and about alternative treatments, including the choice of no treatment. Doctors today need to understand their own feelings about death and dying so they can give their patients the kind of care their patients prefer.

11. Doctors say that proper pain control can end the fear that leads people to ask for euthanasia or help committing suicide. The law in Canada today does not require doctors to take heroic measures to keep a terminally ill patient alive. Doctors and patients can decide to withdraw or withhold treatment or ask for medical assistance in dying.

12. Advance directives indicate patients' wishes for end-of-life care in case a patient can no longer make his or her wishes known. Advance directives state who has the right to make decisions on behalf of the patient.

13. Canadian law before 2016 prohibited assisted suicide and active euthanasia, preferring the development of palliative care instead. In 2016, following a ruling from the Supreme Court of Canada in the previous year, Canada changed the law and developed guidelines to allow for medical assistance in dying.

14. Death leads to grief and mourning for survivors. Culture and religion help people cope with feelings of grief and provide guidelines for mourning. Funerals bring the community together and give mourners support. Still, each person has to work through feelings of grief in his or her own way.

STUDY QUESTIONS

1. How do people in the 21st century make sense of aging, dying, and death?

2. What does research show about seniors' attitudes toward dying and death? How does this differ from younger people's attitudes?

3. How does society influence our attitudes toward dying and death?

4. How do different ethnic groups differ in their views of dying and death?

5. Explain the difference between physician-assisted suicide, euthanasia, and palliative care.

6. Why is medical assistance in dying a controversial issue? Why have some groups opposed and some accepted this method of ending life?

KEY TERMS

active euthanasia (p. 357)
advance directives (p. 353)
anticipatory grief (p. 350)
assisted suicide (p. 357)
bereavement (p. 350)
disenfranchised grief (p. 350)
do-not-resuscitate (DNR) order (p. 353)
ego integrity (p. 346)
grief (p. 350)
hospice (p. 355)
life review (p. 346)
medical assistance in dying (p. 357)
morbid grieving (p. 350)
mourning (p. 350)
palliative care (p. 355)
passive euthanasia (p. 357)
physician-assisted suicide (p. 357)
power of attorney (p. 353)
social death (p. 343)
trajectory of dying (p. 345)

GLOSSARY

55 Alive Mature Driving Program a program that helps seniors improve their driving skills and teaches them how aging affects driving (p. 285)

active euthanasia intervening actively to end a person's life (p. 357)

active leisure lifestyle a type of lifestyle that directly benefits health and helps to buffer the influence of life events and illness by regular participation in physical activities (p. 251)

activities of daily living (ADLs) activities performed daily, such as bathing, moving from a bed or chair, dressing, getting to and using the toilet, eating, and walking (p. 99)

adult daycare programs provide non-institutional support for people who cannot stay in their homes without it (p. 183)

advance directive (including a personal directive, healthcare directive, living will, and continuing power of attorney) a precise statement of the desired treatment and care, including what medical actions are to be taken under what conditions, and a declaration of who has the right to decide in the situation where the writer of the advance directive is no longer able to express his or her wishes (p. 353)

age cohort a group of people born in the same period of time; for example, all the people born between 1950 and 1955 form an age cohort (p. 25)

age effects on a person's life are related to physical decline or change due to the aging process (p. 34)

age-friendly communities have safe neighbourhoods, pleasant outdoor spaces, and opportunities for seniors to volunteer or work (p. 287)

age grades a concept used in age stratification theory to describe periods of life defined by society, such as childhood, adolescence, and young adulthood (p. 26)

ageism prejudice against older people (p. 7)

age-specific birth rate the number of births in a given age group per 1,000 women in that age group (p. 59)

age-status asynchronization someone for whom major life events come early or late—a teenaged mother or a newlywed octogenarian—may feel out of sync with the age-status system (p. 30)

age stratification theory focuses on the movement of age cohorts over the life course and on "the role of social structures in the process of individual aging and the stratification by age in the society" (Bengtson et al., 1997, p. S81) (p. 25)

aging in place older people living into late old age in the same place they lived in their middle years (p. 269)

Allowance an income supplement program for spouses of pensioners who receive only the Old Age Security pension and have a combined income below a set amount (p. 63)

anti-aging industry the multibillion-dollar worldwide market for products that claim to reduce or reverse the effects of aging (p. 13)

anticipatory grief experienced prior to and in anticipation of the death of a loved one (p. 350)

apocalyptic demography the use of demographic facts (such as the aging of the population) to project the high cost of an aging population and predict that population aging will lead to economic and social crisis (p. 69)

assisted living housing that provides personal care services and other supports to frail seniors to help them live independently in the community (pp. 183, 276)

assisted suicide made possible with the help of someone (p. 357)

Baby Boom the sharp rise in the fertility rate in Canada from about 1946 to the early 1960s (precise dates vary) (p. 59)

Baby Bust the sharp drop in the fertility rate from the mid-1960s on (p. 59)

bereavement the state of having recently experienced the death of a loved one (p. 350)

birth rate the number of live births per 1,000 women in a population (p. 47)

boomerang children adult children who return to their parent's home after having moved out at an earlier point in time (p. 309)

bridge jobs are taken by workers on the path to retirement (often in work outside the individual's former career) (p. 234)

buffering theory holds that a culture that values seniors and provides meaningful roles for them tends to protect them to a degree from losses and social devaluation in later life (p. 78)

Canadian Executive Service Organization (CESO) a federal government program that recruits volunteers, many of whom are retired executives, to serve as advisers and mentors in underdeveloped countries or with Indigenous groups in Canada (p. 263)

care gap the difference between what care could or should be and what usual care is; the care gap leads to missed clinical benefits and higher costs for payers (p. 189)

caregiver burden problems and stress due to caregiving (p. 329)

chronic health problems long-term illnesses such as arthritis, rheumatism, hypertension, diabetes, and heart disease (p. 95)

citizen's wage a government pension tied to age (p. 225)

clawback a required repayment of Old Age Security benefits by wealthier seniors to the government (p. 203)

cognitive reserve refers to exceptional mental performance, particularly when a person has to work at maximum mental capacity; first observed in cognitively impaired people who performed better than expected in everyday life (p. 136)

cohort effects are related to the time of the person's birth (p. 34)

collective dwellings these include healthcare facilities; also refers to long-term care institutions (p. 270)

Community Care Access Centres (CCACs) Ontario's system of community care centres that provide a single point of entry into the healthcare system and services such as in-home care, physiotherapy, and dietetic services (p. 181)

competency the ability to understand information that applies to a decision, the ability to think about the consequences of the decision, and the ability to communicate a decision (p. 159)

compression of morbidity hypothesis the idea that severe chronic illness would occur for a short time near the end of life (p. 122)

confidant someone in whom one confides (p. 294)

conflict perspective holds that society consists of conflicts between dominant and subordinate social groups (p. 30)

constant-probability-of-success model states that the ratio of quality works to total works produced during a career stays the same at every stage of the career (p. 146)

contextual view of memory the idea that many conditions influence memory, including physical, psychological, and social contexts and the knowledge, abilities, and characteristics of the individual, as well as the situation in which the individual is asked to remember (p. 137)

continuing care retirement communities (CCRCs) allow seniors to remain in one facility if the level of required care changes (p. 279)

continuum of care the array of services that range from institutional care to little or no institutional contact (p. 181)

contractors people who have stopped at least one outdoor activity in the past year and have not learned any new activity since age 65, in keeping with the disengagement theory of aging (p. 249)

convoy model of support describes social support as a network of close family and friends who travel together throughout life, exchanging social support and assistance (p. 321)

core housing need exists when the housing is too small or in poor repair or the household spends more than 30 percent of its total income on housing (p. 270)

credit splitting a plan by which each spouse of a divorcing couple gets an equal share of pension credits accumulated during their time together (p. 219)

critical gerontology theoretical approaches that look "within" theory and research to critically examine and question the underlying and "taken-for-granted" assumptions about aging (p. 33)

cross-sectional research design studies people from many age groups at one point in time (p. 34)

crude dependency rates are based solely on the number of people in each age group (p. 69)

crystallized intelligence depends on stored information, acculturation, and learning (p. 143)

cultural enclaves areas in a city or region where particular ethnocultural groups tend to congregate geographically and socially (p. 85)

culture shared language, beliefs, values, customs, and practices (p. 77)

cumulative disadvantage occurs as disadvantages for women, such as low pay and time off work due to family caregiving, add up and lead to economic disadvantage in later life (p. 241)

cumulative advantage and disadvantage theory says that disadvantages earlier in life accumulate and are magnified over the life course (p. 31)

death rate the number of deaths per 1,000 people in a population (p. 57)

defined benefit (DB) pension plans state how much an employee can expect to earn in retirement based on a formula that takes into account years of service and highest salary; the company guarantees the benefit based on this formula (p. 207)

defined contribution (DC) pension plans state how much a person will pay into his or her pension account (often matched to some degree by the company); this plan defines the contribution but does not guarantee the outcome; the outcome in retirement will depend on how well the employee's investments do over time (p. 208)

demographic determinism the assumption that population dynamics determine the future of social relations and social institutions (e.g., the amount of dependency of the old on the young) (p. 72)

demographic transition occurs when a population changes from a high birth rate/high death rate condition to a low birth rate/low death rate condition (p. 58)

dependence-free life expectancy the number of years of remaining life that a person will live in a state free of dependence on others for daily tasks (p. 122)

depression the emotional state of feeling sad, helpless, irritable, and hopeless (p. 155)

developmental disability a significant impairment in mental ability present at birth or acquired in childhood or adolescence (p. 149)

developmental intelligence the growth of wisdom in later life—an advanced style of cognition (p. 144)

developmental stake or **generational stake** the idea that, compared with their children, older people have a greater investment in the relationship with their children (p. 324)

disability-free life expectancy the years of life remaining that are free of any disability (p. 122)

discrimination unfair treatment of a person or group based on prejudice (p. 3)

disenfranchised grief defined by society as illegitimate grief and therefore unacknowledged because society defines the relationship between the grieving person and the deceased as insignificant (p. 350)

do-not-resuscitate (DNR) order a person may request that, if in a coma and dying from a terminal disease, resuscitation not be attempted if the dying person's heart stops; this request may lead the dying person's physician to place a do-not-resuscitate (DNR) order on the patient's medical care chart (p. 353)

ecological model the Lawton–Nahemow model of interaction between the individual and the environment that holds that a person's ability and the demands of the environment influence that person's life satisfaction and ability to function (p. 267)

ego integrity the acceptance of the notion that one's life cycle is something complete and unique (p. 346)

elderly dependency ratio the number of people age 65 and over divided by the population age 20 to 64 (p. 70)

elderspeak simplified speech like baby talk that some people use when they speak to older people; it stems from stereotyping older people as slow-witted (p. 6)

encoding the process whereby a person puts new bits of information together with already stored information (p. 133)

encore careers take place after a midlife career ends; they accomplish something important, pay a salary, and allow a person to give back to society (p. 237)

enriched housing provides services such as meals and cleaning services to help people live on their own (p. 275)

environmental press the demands of the environment on a person (p. 267)

epidemiological transition the transition a society makes when it moves from a high rate of acute illness (mostly in youth) to a high rate of chronic illness (mostly in old age); Canada has made this transition, as have many developed nations (p. 97)

episodic memory oriented toward the past, or acquired at a specific time and place, as in learning in an experimental setting (p. 133)

ethnicity variously defined as country of birth, birthplaces of ancestors, cultural heritage, or self-identification with an ethnocultural group (p. 76)

evidence-based practice promotes the use of research findings in the delivery of services to older people (p. 41)

expanders people who have not stopped any activities in the past year and have added at least one new outdoor activity since age 65, in keeping with the lifespan development theory of aging (p. 250)

feminist approaches view gender as a defining characteristic in social interaction and life experiences, as well as in the process and experience of aging; gender is seen as socially constructed, with men being more advantaged than women in society (p. 31)

fertility rate "the average number of children that would be born alive to a woman during her lifetime if she were to pass through all her childbearing years conforming to the age-specific fertility rates of a given year" (Beaujot & McQuillan, 1982, pp. 220–221) (p. 53)

fictive kin the close relationships that an older person develops with non-relatives such as friends, neighbours, and home care workers (p. 340)

filial piety the culturally defined obligation, highly valued in Asian cultures, of adult children to their aging parents, requiring adult children to support their parents in their old age (p. 82)

FlexHousing a housing concept that designers and builders use to make future changes in housing easy and affordable in order to meet the changing needs of people as they age (p. 273)

flexible retirement an option that allows workers to slowly cut back the number of hours they work each week (p. 234)

fluid intelligence reasoning, abstracting, concept formation, and problem solving, with little use for knowledge gained through reading, schooling, or work (p. 143)

formal support paid support from professional caregivers such as doctors, nurses, social workers, and home care workers (p. 318)

free career a second career in a field that allows a person to explore previously dormant or undeveloped interests (p. 237)

functional disability a limitation in the performance of normal daily activities due to illness or injury (p. 98)

functionalist perspective holds that social order is based on consensus, cooperation, and shared norms and values, and that all parts of society serve a role or function to keep society in a state of balance or equilibrium; structural functionalism predicts that when there is social change, society will attempt to create an orderly transition to a new, stable state (p. 25)

functional specificity of relationships model contends a family or friendship tie may provide one type of support or a broad range of support, depending on the particular relationship between the caregiver and the care receiver (p. 321)

garden suite a separate building on an adult child's property or part of their adult child's house made into a self-contained unit for an elderly relative; also known as a granny flat (p. 277)

gentrification in-migration into older urban neighbourhoods by new (often wealthy residents) that tends to drive up property values and displace former residents (p. 86)

geriatric day hospital a hospital program that offers a full range of hospital services to older people who live in the community and that assesses individuals' needs before setting up a health-care plan (p. 182)

gerontology the discipline that systematically studies aging (p. 2)

gero-transcendence in later life, the self begins to expand its boundaries and reflect on the meaning of human life (p. 253)

GRAND (Grandparents Requesting Access and Dignity) a group that helps grandparents who cannot get access to their grandchildren (p. 312)

granny flat part of a house made into a self-contained unit for an elderly relative, or a small, portable cottage or dwelling erected in the garden of an adult child's house (p. 277)

great pension debate the debate in the 1980s over how to fund public pensions for older Canadians in the future (p. 198)

grief a sense of profound loss and the experience of deep sorrow (p. 350)

Guaranteed Income Supplement an income supplement program for the poorest older people (p. 63)

healthcare system the medical and social services that provide healthcare support to Canadians, support that ranges from health promotion, to health maintenance, to long-term chronic care (p. 165)

health field the realm of health services, including the healthcare system, traditional medical services, improvements in human biology, improvements in lifestyle, and improvements in environment, as envisioned by former federal minister of health Marc Lalonde (p. 187)

health promotion model a healthcare model that focuses on self-care and preventing disease through lifestyle change, increased knowledge about healthy behaviour, and environmental improvement (p. 166)

hierarchical compensatory model contends that people choose their supports first from their inner family circle and then move outward to get support from less-intimate people as they need more help (p. 320)

home care a range of social and medical services designed to help people live independently in the community (p. 184)

hospice a place or program of care designed to meet the special needs of dying patients (p. 355)

hypokinesia physical problems due to lack of movement (p. 110)

income maintenance programs the Canada Pension Plan and the Quebec Pension Plan are income maintenance programs that help people maintain their pre-retirement income and lifestyle (p. 199)

income security programs the Old Age Security pension and the Guaranteed Income Supplement help people meet their basic needs in retirement (p. 199)

indexation a method of increasing pensions linked to increases in the cost of living (p. 219)

infant mortality rate the death rate of children less than one year old (p. 57)

informal caregivers unpaid care providers with a tie of kinship or affection toward the care receiver (p. 322)

informal support unpaid support from family members, friends, neighbours, and others in the community (p. 318)

Institutes for Learning in Retirement (ILRs) or **Lifelong Learning Institutes (LLIs)** programs that offer older people a variety of educational formats from lectures to seminars, to travel courses, with topics usually decided on by the group (p. 257)

institutional completeness the presence in a community of a wide range of economic, social, and religious institutions, including the availability of services, agencies, and programs (p. 85)

instrumental activities of daily living (IADLs) home management activities such as using the phone, cooking, shopping, managing finances, and doing light housework (p. 99)

intellectual disability refers to disorders that lead to limited mental capacity and problems with daily activities such as managing money and social interaction (p. 148)

intelligence the "ability to negotiate environmental demands successfully" (Labouvie-Vief, 1985, p. 506), "that which intelligence tests measure" (p. 506), or what a person taking the test can do now (p. 143)

intergenerational equity the call for balanced support of older and younger people through public policy and public expenditures (p. 17)

interlocking systems of oppression "macro level connections linking systems of oppression such as race, class, and gender" (Estes, 2001, p. 13) (p. 31)

interpretive perspective focuses almost exclusively on the micro-level of social life; it looks at how people define situations, how they create social order, and how they relate to one another in daily life (p. 23)

intimacy at a distance the choice of many older people to live near, but not with, their children (p. 270)

kin keepers the person in a family who keeps family members in touch with one another; women generally occupy this role (p. 310)

LAT (living apart together) couples have a committed relationship but maintain separate households (p. 296)

latency the length of time it takes for a person to process information or respond to a question (p. 133)

least developed regions consist of 49 countries with especially low incomes, high economic vulnerability, and poor human development indicators (e.g., Haiti, Bangladesh, Ethiopia) (p. 47)

legal guardianship process in which the court appoints someone to make decisions on another person's behalf (p. 160)

less developed regions developing regions and countries are classified as less developed (e.g., China, India, Vietnam) (p. 47)

life course perspective (1) a functionalist approach that bridges the micro and macro levels of analysis by incorporating social interaction and social structure within its framework (p. 26); (2) begins with the idea that life unfolds from birth to death in a social, cultural, and historical context; looks at the impact of social institutions, historical periods and events, personal biography, life cycle stage, life events, and resources on the minority older person (p. 78)

life expectancy the number of years at birth an average member of a population can expect to live (p. 95)

life portfolio consists of a person's commitments to specific activities and relationships; these include family, community service, spiritual development, recreation, and, in some cases, work (p. 241)

life review a dying person looks over his or her life, seeks a conviction that one's life has had meaning and purpose, ties up loose ends, achieves acceptance of the life lived, and prepares for death (p. 346)

long-distance caregivers live a significant distance from the care recipient (p. 333)

longitudinal research design looks at a single group of people at two or more points in time (p. 36)

long-term care social and medical services, including formal services, home or institutional care, and family care, for people who have functional limitations (p. 166)

long-term memory the storehouse of knowledge that also includes the rules for applying knowledge (p. 132)

macro-level theories "examine social structures or structural elements as they influence experiences and behaviors" (Bengtson, Burgess, & Parrott, 1997, p. S76) (p. 23)

maximum life span the maximum number of years a member of a species can live (p. 95)

median age half the population is older and half is younger than the median age (p. 55)

medical assistance in dying or physician-assisted death a physician helps a person to die either by assisting the patient's suicide or by euthanasia (p. 357)

medical model a healthcare model that favours surgery, drug therapy, and rehabilitation through physical therapies, with a focus on the treatment of diseases and injuries, usually in the physician's office, a hospital, or other healthcare institutions (p. 165)

memory the recall of information after learning has taken place (p. 132)

micro-level theories focus on individuals and their interactions; they are used to explain phenomena such as the relationship between adult children and their parents, changes in memory with age, and the effect of negative attitudes on older people's self-esteem (p. 23)

minority groups in Canada, those ethnocultural groups that have not originated in northern and western European countries (p. 77)

mobility club a volunteer group of older people who provide rides to other seniors (p. 286)

moral economy theory focuses on shared values and social norms that shape popular beliefs in the legitimacy of certain practices and policies; this theory complements political economy theory (p. 33)

morbid grieving also known as complicated or pathological grieving, refers to a pattern or duration of grieving that society considers abnormal and problematic (p. 350)

more developed regions following the UN classification, more developed countries comprise all of Europe and North America, plus Australia, Japan, and New Zealand (p. 47)

mourning the public expression of grief, typically following social and cultural rules (p. 350)

multiple jeopardy theory the hypothesis that there is a compounding of disadvantages associated with age, race, ethnicity, and gender (p. 78)

narrative gerontology seeks to understand the "inside" of aging by examining the narratives or life stories that people tell in order to organize and make sense of their lives, and their experiences of aging (p. 33)

naturally occurring retirement communities (NORCs) neighbourhoods that already have many older people; these communities can enhance the experience of current residents (p. 278)

non-episodic memory oriented toward the present or the future, with no reference to the time at which the person stored the memory; includes learned skills through practice or a person's general knowledge of the world (p. 133)

non-normative events unexpected events such as illnesses, lay-offs, and accidents (p. 29)

normative age-graded events socially sanctioned events that occur most often at a certain age, like marriage or retirement (p. 30)

normative history-graded events shape the lives of many age cohorts, such as the Great Depression of the 1930s or World War II (p. 29)

Old Age Security pension Canada's basic retirement income program; it supplements the income of nearly all of the country's older people (p. 63)

overall dependency ratio (or rate) the combined total number of people under age 19 and people aged 65 and over divided by the number of people aged 20 to 64 (p. 69)

palliative care directed toward improving the quality of life for the dying, including symptom control and spiritual support as well as bereavement support and education for the family members of dying patients (p. 355)

passive euthanasia withholding or ceasing treatment of someone who is ill or injured and not expected to recover (p. 357)

pay-as-you-go plan today's retirees receive their CPP pensions from workers' contributions today; workers today will receive their CPP pensions from workers' contributions in the future; this type of plan requires that each younger generation pay for the pensions of the older generation (p. 205)

period or environmental effects on a person's life are due to the time of measurement; this would include historical, social, or environmental effects, such as an ongoing war, changes in health habits (e.g., better nutrition), or changes in healthcare policies that have different influences on different age cohorts (p. 34)

physician-assisted suicide when a physician provides a patient with advice about how to commit suicide or with the technical means (e.g., lethal medications) to commit suicide (p. 357)

planned retirement communities a developer builds and sells houses to healthy, active retirees; these communities supply health services, shopping centres, and recreation facilities (p. 278)

plasticity the brain's ability to change and adapt over time (p. 137)

political economy theory focuses on conflict and change in social life; it traces this conflict to the struggle between social classes and to the resulting dominance of some groups in society and the subordination of others (p. 30)

population aging demographers, experts who study population change, use at least three measures of population aging: (1) the number of older people in a population, (2) the median age of a population, and (3) the proportion of older people in a population (p. 46)

portable pension a pension that moves with workers when they change jobs (p. 205)

positivist worldview based on the belief that knowledge is built by studying observable facts and their relationship to one another (p. 25)

post-modern theory contrasts contemporary society with society in the recent past; for example, older people today can take on many roles in retirement, whereas in the past they had limited options after they retired (p. 33)

power of attorney a legal document that gives someone, usually a lawyer, adult family member, or friend, the right to make decisions on behalf of the ill person if the person loses his or her mental capacity (p. 353)

prejudice being biased against someone or something; a negative judgment formed beforehand without knowledge of the facts (p. 2)

prospective aging allows demographers to compare populations with different life expectancies and to compare one society at different points in time as life expectancy increases; one measure of prospective aging uses a number of years of remaining life expectancy as the start of old age (p. 61)

quasi-widowhood experiencing feelings of grief, depression, and loss after a spouse is placed in a nursing home (p. 331)

rectangularization, or squaring of the survival curve the change over time in survival curves resulting in a right angle or square shape, leading researchers to conclude that a finite life span exists (p. 122)

registered retirement savings plans (RRSPs) a government plan that allows people to save money for their future pension without paying income tax on the money protected within the RRSP—the savings are taxed when they are withdrawn in retirement; the taxes are deferred to a time when the person has a lower income and is in a lower tax bracket (p. 210)

Residential Rehabilitation Assistance Program (RRAP) a federal government program offering loans to low-income people to help them improve run-down housing (p. 272)

retirement principle the idea that a person leaves work at a fixed age, regardless of mental or physical ability (p. 224)

retirement wage a pension paid by the state to support all older people (p. 224)

reverse annuity mortgage (RAM) a type of reverse mortgage whereby a person buys a life annuity and gets an income while living in the home; the mortgage company takes over the house when the person dies (p. 274)

Road Scholar a not-for-profit company that promotes lifelong learning by organizing educational and cultural tours aimed at people in their 50s and older (originally based on a combination of university life and the European concept of hostelling) (p. 256)

Romanow Report the 2002 Canadian federal government report of the Commission on the Future of Health Care in Canada, led by Roy Romanow; the report underscores Canada's commitment to its healthcare system and makes several proposals for improving the delivery of healthcare to seniors (p. 179)

savings plan a payment plan to which each person contributes a percentage of his or her salary each month; in the case of the CPP/QPP, the payments are credited to individual workers and when they retire, their pension will depend on how much they paid into the plan (p. 205)

second career work that allows a person to develop skills they did not use in their pre-retirement career (p. 237)

second language of sex the "language of sex" that develops in a long-term intimate relationship and focuses on responsiveness, caring, and affection (p. 303)

selective optimization with compensation (SOC) those who age successfully use the SOC method: they select activities that optimize their ability, and when they can no longer engage in an activity, they compensate for losses by setting new priorities (p. 125)

self-efficacy what people believe they can do; people with a strong sense of efficacy take on more challenging tasks and put out more effort (p. 250)

semantic memory the store of factual information (p. 139)

sensory memory information perceived through the senses and stored as memory (p. 132)

sequential designs created by researchers by looking at a series of cross-sectional studies during a longitudinal study (p. 38)

shelter allowances government allowances that subsidize the person, not the housing project, and allow older people to choose their own apartment (p. 274)

short-term memory where information is stored temporarily while it is being processed, or for a short time afterward (p. 132)

single-point-of-entry model a single agency that assesses clients' needs, coordinates service delivery from multiple sources, and monitors clients' progress (p. 191)

skip-generation households grandparents living with grandchildren without the presence of the middle (parent) generation (p. 311)

social death refers to the perception or behaviour of others that indicates that they perceive or treat a person as if physically dead when in fact the physical body has not yet died (p. 343)

social gerontology a subfield within the wider field of gerontology; it focuses on the social side of aging, while other subfields study the physical and biological aspects of aging (p. 21)

social model a healthcare model that includes personal and family counselling, home care, and adult daycare programs as part of the healthcare system, and that tries to keep older people in their own homes (p. 166)

social structure a relatively stable pattern of social interactions (p. 2)

social support the help and assistance people give to one another (p. 318)

society for all ages promotes the well-being and contributions of older people in all aspects of life, recognizes their valuable contributions, and reflects the goals of elimination of ageism in all sectors; a society for all ages has five core principles: dignity, independence, participation, fairness, and security (p. 17)

stereotypes an exaggerated and often prejudiced view of a type of person or group of people (p. 6)

stereotype threat an older person's fear of failure on memory tests; this can lead to poor performance (p. 137)

structural lag a mismatch between changes in the aging process (e.g., better health for older people, more active lifestyles) and the roles and places in the social structure that can meet the needs of this new older person (p. 263)

successful aging characterized by a low chance of disease and disability, high mental and physical functioning, and active engagement in social relations and productive activity (p. 124)

supportive housing provided for people who need minimal to moderate care and use services such as homemaking, personal care, and social support programs (p. 275)

task specificity model contends that different groups (of family, friends, neighbours) have different abilities and offer different types of support, each playing a specific role (p. 320)

taxback taxes paid on earnings by recipients of the Guaranteed Income Supplement and provincial supplements that can amount to a 100 percent reduction in supplement payments for the poorest older people who work (p. 228)

tax-free savings accounts (TFSAs) a program that allows Canadians age 18 or over to put up to $5,500 a year (2017 limit) into a savings account; these dollars will be allowed to grow tax-free and will not be taxed when taken out (p. 220)

Third Age the period of life after the period of work and child-rearing in the middle years, but before frailty and dependence set in (the Fourth Age); a period of life created by longer life expectancy and a longer period of good health in later life (p. 237)

time-lag comparison design examines different groups of people of the same age at different points in time (e.g., 55-year-olds in 2000, 2010, and 2020) (p. 37)

trajectories long-term patterns of stability and change that often include many transitions (p. 28)

trajectory of dying the pattern or course of dying over time; for example, sudden death or slow decline (p. 345)

transfer plan (also called a pay-as-you-go plan) money paid into the plan goes to pay the pensions of retired plan members today; the CPP/QPP also works like a transfer plan (p. 205)

transitions changes in social status or social roles such as marriage, parenthood, divorce, remarriage, and widowhood (p. 28)

transportation brokerage a program that matches passengers with transportation services that meet their needs (p. 286)

universal design housing adaptations that serve people of all ages; designers use lever door handles, low-threshold tubs, and temperature limits on hot water tanks to improve living for older people, as well as children and those with disabilities (p. 273)

universality the idea that everyone in Canada has a right to a public pension regardless of his or her income (p. 198)

vesting workers with a fully vested pension have credit for their total pension contributions (their own and their employer's contributions) even if they move from one employer to another (p. 205)

visible minority non-European in origin and/or not white in skin tone; curiously, Canada's official definition of visible minority excludes the Indigenous population (First Nations people, Inuit, Métis) (p. 77)

visitability requires that an older resident or visitor with a disability be able to move barrier-free within the first floor of a single-family house (p. 273)

weak social ties these differ from the intimacy of family and friendship ties; weak social ties link people from diverse backgrounds and expose a person to new views and opinions (p. 258)

wisdom "highly valued and outstanding expert knowledge . . . related to the meaning and conduct of life" (Kunzmann, 2006, p. 1232) (p. 144)

working memory where recently acquired information is manipulated and processed at the same time as it is being stored temporarily (p. 133)

youth dependency ratio the number of people aged 0 to 19 divided by the population aged 20 to 64 (p. 70)

REFERENCES

AARP (American Association of Retired Persons). (1998). *Aging Everywhere*. Washington, D. C.: American Association of Retired Persons.

AARP (American Association of Retired Persons). (2007a). Now hear this: Name game. *AARP Bulletin*, July–August, 8.

AARP (American Association of Retired Persons). (2007b). AARP profit from experience: Perspectives of employers, workers and policymakers in the G7 countries on the new demographic realities. Retrieved February 25, 2017, from http://assets.aarp.org/rgcenter/econ/intl_older_worker.pdf.

Abatiell, P., & Adams, M. (2011). LGBT aging: A question of identity. *The Gerontologist, 51*(6), 880–884.

Aboderin, I. (2006). *Intergenerational support and old age in Africa*. New Brunswick, NJ: Transaction Publishers.

Acharya, M. P., & Northcott, H. C. (2007). Mental distress and the coping strategies of elderly Indian immigrant women. *Transcultural Psychiatry, 44*(4), 614–636.

Ackerman, P. L. (2008). Knowledge and cognitive aging. In F. I. M. Craik & T. A. Salthouse (Eds.). *The handbook of aging and cognition*, 3rd ed. (pp. 445–489). New York: Psychology Press.

Adams, M. A., Sallis, J. F., Conway, T. L., Frank, L. D., Saelens, B. E., Kerr, J., Cain, K. L., & King, A. C. (2012). Neighborhood environment profiles for physical activity among older adults. *American Journal of Health Behavior, 36*(96), 757–769.

Address, R. F. (2011). Till death us do part? A look at marriage rituals when a partner has Alzheimer's disease. *Generations, 35*(3), 52–56.

Adler, L. (2008). *Our treasured belongings: Ties that bind*. University of Kentucky: Cooperative Extension Service. Retrieved from http://www.ca.uky.edu/hes/fcs/factshts/hhf-lra-170.pdf.

Aegon. (2014). The changing face of retirement. *The Aegon retirement readiness survey*, 2014. The Hague. Retrieved from http://cicero-group.com/wp-content/uploads/2015/03/Aegon-Retirement-Survey-2014.pdf.

Age International. (2014). Facing the facts: The truth about ageing and development. London: Age International.

Alberta Heritage Foundation for Medical Research. (2009). Research finds older women who are physically fit have better cognitive function: Want to stay sharp as you age? Then get moving! Retrieved http://www.aihealthsolutions.ca/press/2009-01-08.php.

Aldwin, C. M., & Gilmer, D. F. (2004). *Health, illness, and optimal aging: Biological and psychosocial perspectives*. Thousand Oaks, CA: Sage.

Aldwin, C. M., Spiro, A., & Park, C. L. (2006). Health, behavior, and optimal aging: A life span developmental perspective. In J. E. Birren & K. W. Schaie (Eds.), *Handbook of the psychology of aging*, 6th ed. (pp. 85–104). Burlington, MA: Elsevier Academic Press.

Aléx, L., Hammarström, A., Norberg, A., & Lundman, B. (2008). Construction of masculinities among men aged 85 and older in the north of Sweden. *Journal of Clinical Nursing 17*, 451–459.

Allan, L. J., & Johnson, J. A. (2009). Undergraduate attitudes toward the elderly: The role of knowledge, contact and aging anxiety. *Educational Gerontology, 35*, 1–14.

Allen, K. R., & Walker, A. J. (2009). Theorizing about families and aging from a feminist perspective. In V. L. Bengtson, M. Silverstein, M. M. Putney, & D. Gans (Eds.), *Handbook of theories of aging* (pp. 517–528). New York: Springer.

Allen, M. K. (2013). Consumption of culture by older Canadians on the Internet. Statistics Canada. Retrieved from http://www.statcan.gc.ca/pub/75-006-x/2013001/article/11768-eng.htm.

Allen, P. A., Bucur, B., & M. D. Murphy. (2006). Information-processing theory. In R. Schulz, L. S. Noelker, K. Rockwood, & R. L. Sprott, (Eds.), *The encyclopedia of aging*, 4th ed. (pp. 588–591). New York: Springer.

Alterovitz, S., & Mendelsohn, G. (2009). Partner preferences across the life span: Online dating by older adults. *Psychology and Aging, 24*(2), 513–517.

Alwin, D. F., Hofer, S. M., & McCammon, R. J. (2006). Modeling the effects of time integrating demographic and developmental perspectives. In R. H. Binstock & L. K. George (Eds.), *Handbook of aging and the social sciences*, 6th ed. (pp. 20–38). Burlington, MA: Academic Press.

Alzheimer Society of Canada. (2009). *Enhancing quality of life for people living with dementia*. Alzheimer Society of Canada.

Alzheimer Society of Canada. (2010). *Rising Tide: The Impact of Dementia on Canadian Society*. Based on a study conducted by RiskAnalytica and written by Scott Dudgeon, Chief Executive Officer of the Alzheimer Society of Canada from November 2007 until June 2009. Alzheimer Society of Canada.

Alzheimer Society of Ontario. (2010). *Fact sheet: Rising tide— The impact of dementia on Canadian society*. Retrieved from http://alzheimerontario.org/English/Rising_Tide_January_2010_Fact_Sheet/default.asp?s=1.

Anderson, J. W., Liu, C., & Kryscio, R. J. (2008). Blood pressure response to transcendental meditation: A meta-analysis. *American Journal of Hypertension, 21*(3), 310–316.

Andrew, M. K., & Rockwood, K. (2007). Psychiatric illness in relation to frailty in community-dwelling elderly people without dementia: A report from the Canadian study of health and aging. *Canadian Journal on Aging, 26*(1), 33–38.

Andrews, S., McInerney, F., & Robinson, A. (2009). Realizing a palliative approach in dementia care: Strategies to facilitate aged care staff engagement in evidence-based practice. *International Perspectives on Dementia Education Training and Knowledge Transfer, 21*(Suppl. S1). Retrieved from http://journals.cambridge.org/action/displayAbstract;jsessionid=52C85F2814B7FB904CD32B61539F13FC.journals?fromPage=online&aid=5218132.

Angel, J. L., & Mudrazija, S. (2011). Aging, inheritance, and gift-giving. In R. H. Binstock & L. K. George (Eds.), *Handbook of aging and the social sciences*, 7th ed. (pp. 163–174). London: Academic Press (Elsevier).

Angus Reid. (2012). *Australians support same-sex marriage more than Americans and Britons*. Retrieved July 27, 2012, from http://www.angus-reid.com/wp-content/uploads/2012/03/2012.03.12_SameSex.pdf.

Antonelli-Incalzi, R., Ancona, C., Forastiere, F., Belleudi, V., Corsonello, A., & Perucci, C. A. (2007). Socioeconomic status and hospitalization in the very old: A retrospective study. *BMC Public Health, 7*, 227.

Antonucci, T. C., Birditt, K. S., & Akiyama, H. (2009). Convoys of social relations: An interdisciplinary approach. In V. L. Bengtson, M. Silverstein, M. M. Putney, & D. Gans (Eds.), *Handbook of theories of aging* (pp. 247–260). New York: Springer.

Aon Hewitt (2015). A business case for workers age 50+: A look at the value of experience 2015. Retrieved from http://www.aarp.org/research/topics/economics/info-2015/business-case-older-workers.html?intcmp=AE-BL-IL-DOTORG.

Apesoa-Varano, E. C., & Hinton, L. (2013). The promise of mixed-methods for advancing Latino health research. *Journal of Cross Cultural Gerontology, 28*, 267–282.

Ardelt, M. (2011). Wisdom, age, and well-being. In K. W. Schaie & S. L. Willis (Eds.), *Handbook of the psychology of aging*, 7th ed., (pp. 279–291). London: Academic Press (Elsevier).

Arksey, H., and Glendinning, C. (2008). Combining work and care: Carer's decision-making in the context of competing policy pressures. *Social Policy and Administration, 42*(1), 1–18.

Armstrong, P., & H. Armstrong. (2001). *The double ghetto: Canadian women and their segregated work*, 3rd ed. Don Mills, ON: Oxford University Press.

Armstrong, P., Armstrong, H., & Scott-Dixon, K. (2008). *Critical to care: The invisible women in health services*. University of Toronto Press.

Armstrong-Stassen, M., & Schlosser, F. (2011). Perceived organizational membership and the retention of older workers. *Journal of Organizational Behavior, 32*(2), 319–344.

Arnsten, Amy. (2008). Arnsten lab: Yale University department of neurobiology. Retrieved from http://info.med.yale.edu/neurobio/arnsten/Research.html.

Aronson, J., Thornewell, C., & Williams, K. (1995). Wife assault in old age: Coming out of obscurity. *Canadian Journal on Aging, 14*(Suppl. 2), 72–88.

Artibise, A. (1977). *Winnipeg: An illustrated history*. Toronto: Lorimer.

Ashe, M. C., Miller, W. C., Eng, J. J., & Noreau, L. (2009). Older adults, chronic disease and leisure-time physical activity. *Gerontology, 55*, 64–72.

Atchley, R. C. (2008). Spirituality, meaning, and the experience of aging. *Generations, 32*(2), 12–16.

Attfield, P. (2014). Single at 60—A fork in the road to retirement. *The Globe and Mail*, December 1. Retrieved from http://www.theglobeandmail.com/globe-investor/retirement/single-at-60-a-fork-in-the-road-to-retirement/article21834326.

Attfield, P. (2015). Home Finance: Cash-poor but house-rich retiree? The pros and cons of reverse mortgages. *The Globe and Mail*, January 3. Retrieved from http://www.theglobeandmail.com/globe-investor/personal-finance/household-finances/cash-poor-but-house-rich-retiree-the-pros-and-cons-of-reverse-mortgages/article22170702.

Averett, P., Yoon, I., & Jenkins, C. L. (2011). Older lesbians: Experiences of aging discrimination and resilience. *Journal of Women & Aging, 23*, 216–232.

Bäckman, L., Small, B. J., Wahlin, A., & Larson, M. (2000). Cognitive functioning in very old age. In F. I. M. Craik & T. A. Salthouse (Eds.), *The handbook of aging and cognition*, 2nd ed., 499–558. Mahwah, NJ: Lawrence Erlbaum Associates.

Baker, J., Meisner, B. A., Logan, A. J., Kungl, A-M, & Weir, P. (2009). Physical activity and successful aging in Canadian older adults. *Journal of Aging and Physical Activity, 17*, 223–235.

Baker, L., & Gringart, E. (2009). Body image and self-esteem in older adulthood. *Ageing & Society, 29*, 977–995.

Baltes, M. M., & Carstensen, L. L. (2003). The process of successful aging: Selection, optimization, and compensation. In U. M. Staudinger & U. Lindenberger (Eds.), *Understanding human development: Dialogues with lifespan psychology* (pp. 81–104). Dordrecht, Netherlands: Kluwer Academic Publishers.

Baltes, P. B., & Schaie. K. W. (1982). Aging and IQ—The myth of the twilight years. In Steven H. Zarit (Ed.), *Readings in aging and death: Contemporary perspectives*, 2nd ed. (pp. 97–101). New York: Harper and Row.

Bandura, A. (2001). Social cognitive theory: An agentic perspective. *Annual Review of Psychology, 52*, 1–26.

Band-Winterstein, T., & Manchik-Rimon, C. (2014). The experience of being an old never-married single: A life course perspective. *International Journal of Aging and Human Development, 78*(4), 379–401.

Bangert, M., & Schlaug, G. (2006). Specialization of the specialized in creatures of external human brain morphology. *European Journal of Neuroscience 24*, 1832–1834.

Barnett, M. A., Saramella, L. V., Neppl, T. K., Ontai, L., & Conger, R. D. (2010). Intergenerational relationship quality, gender, and grandparent involvement. *Family Relations, 59*(1), 28–44.

Barnett, Z. L., Robleda-Gomez, S., & Pachana, N. A. (2012). Viagra: The little pill with big repercussions. *Aging and Mental Health, 16*(1), 84–88.

Barrett, A. E., & Cantwell, L. E. (2007). Drawing on stereotypes: Using undergraduates' sketches of elders as a teaching tool. *Educational Gerontology, 33*, 327–348.

Barua, B., & Rovere, M. (2012). Canada's aging medicare burden. *Fraser Forum*. Retrieved from http://search.proquest.com.libaccess.sjlibrary.org/abicomplete/indexingvolumeissuelinkhandler/43138/Fraser+Forum/$N/$N/$N?accountid=10361.

Basak, C., Boot, W. R., Voss, M. W., & Kramer, A. F. (2008). Can training in a real-time strategy video game attenuate cognitive decline in older adults? *Psychology and Aging, 23*(4), 765–777.

Baskin, C., & Davey, C. J. (2015). Grannies, elders, and friends: Aging Aboriginal women in Toronto. *Journal of Gerontological Social Work, 58*(1), 46–65.

Bassett, R., V. Bourbonnais, & I. McDowell. (2007). Living long and keeping well: Elderly Canadians account for success in aging. *Canadian Journal on Aging, 26*(2), 113–126.

Bates, J. S. (2009). Generative grandfathering: A conceptual framework for nurturing grandchildren. *Marriage & Family Review, 45*, 331–352.

Bates, J. S., & Taylor, A. C. (2012). Grandfather involvement and aging men's mental health. *American Journal of Men's Health, 6*(3), 229–239.

Battle, K. (1997). Pension reform in Canada. *Canadian Journal on Aging, 16*(3), 519–552.

Baycrest. (2011). *Memory intervention program*. Retrieved from http://www.baycrest.org/care-programs-57.php.

Bayer, K. (2005). Cosmetic surgery and cosmetics: Redefining the appearance of age. *Generations, 29*(3), 13–18.

BC Housing. (2008). Shelter aid for elderly renters. Retrieved from http://www.bchousing.org/programs/SAFER.

BCC Research. (2013). *Aging Products and Services: The Global Market*. Retrieved February 27, 2014, from http://www.bccresearch.com/market-research/healthcare/antiaging-products-services-hlc060b.html.

Beaujot, R., & McQuillan, K. (1982). *Growth and dualism: The demographic development of Canadian society*. Toronto: Gage.

Beaulaurier, R. L., Seff, L. R., Newman, F. L., & B. Dunlop. (2007). External barriers to help seeking for older women who experience intimate partner violence. *Journal of Family Violence, 22*, 747–755.

Beaulieu, M., Gravel, S., & Lithwick, L. (1999). Older adult mistreatment: Dynamics in personal relationships. *Gerontology Research Centre News* (Simon Fraser University), February.

Beaupre, P., Turcotte, P., & Milan, A. (2006a). Junior comes back home: Trends and predictors of returning to the parental home. *Canadian Social Trends* (Winter), 28–34. Statistics Canada Cat. No. 11-008. Ottawa: Minister of Industry.

Beaupre, P., Turcotte, P., & Milan, A. (2006b). When is Junior moving out? Transitions from the parental home to independence. *Canadian Social Trends* (Winter), 9–15. Statistics Canada Cat. No. 11-008. Ottawa: Minister of Industry.

Begg, R. (2011). Trends in seniors' housing: Market analysis. *Healthcare Facility Management*. Retrieved from http://www.healthcarefacilitymanagement.ca/VReport1August2011.aspx.

Beland, D., & Myles, J. (2003). *Stasis amidst change: Canadian pension reform in an age of retrenchment*. SEDAP Research Paper No. 111. Hamilton, ON: McMaster University.

Beland, F., Bergman, H., Lebel, P., Dallaire, L., Fletcher, J., Tousignant, P., & Contandriopoulos, P. (2006a). Integrated services for frail elders (SIPA): A trial of a model for Canada. *Canadian Journal on Aging, 25*(1), 25–42.

Beland, F., Bergman, H., Lebel, P., Clarfield, A., Tousignant, P., Contandriopoulos, A., & Dallaire, L. (2006b). System of integrated care for older persons with disabilities in Canada: Results from a randomized controlled trial. *Journals of Gerontology: Series A: Biological Sciences And Medical Sciences, 61*(4), 367–373.

Beland, F., & Shapiro, E. (1994). Ten provinces in search of a long term care policy. In V. Marshall & B. McPherson (Eds.), *Aging: Canadian perspectives* (pp. 245–267). Peterborough, ON: Broadview Press.

Benbow, S. M., & Beeston, D. (2012). Sexuality, aging and dementia. *International Psychogeriatrics, 24*(7), 1026–1033.

Bengtson, V. L., Burgess, E. O., & Parott, T. M. (1997). Theory, explanation, and a third generation of theoretical development in social gerontology. *Journals of Gerontology: Series B: Psychological Sciences and Social Sciences, 52*(2), S72–S88.

Bengtson, V. L., Gans, D., Putney, N. M., & Silverstein, M. (2009). Theories about age and aging. In V. L. Bengtson, M. Silverstein, M. M. Putney, & D. Gans (Eds.), *Handbook of theories of aging* (pp. 3–23). New York: Springer.

Bengtson, V. L., & Kuypers, J. A. (1971). Generational differences and the developmental stake. *International Journal of Aging and Human Development, 2*, 249–260.

Bengtson, V. L., Rice, C. J., & Johnson, M. L. (1999). Are theories of aging important? Models and explanations in gerontology at the turn of the century. In V. L. Bengtson & K. W. Schaie (Eds.), *Handbook of theories of aging* (pp. 3–20). New York: Springer.

Bengtson, V. L., & Schaie, K. W. (Eds.). (1999). *Handbook of theories of aging.* New York: Springer.

Benjamin, K., Edwards, N., & Caswell, W. (2009). Factors influencing the physical activity of older adults in long-term care: Administrators' perspectives. *Journal of Aging and Physical Activity, 17,* 181–195.

Bennett, A. E. (2014). Cultural standards for Asian Americans weigh heavily on both young and old. *Victimization of the Elderly and Disabled, September/October,* 37–47.

Bennett, D. A., Schneider, J. A., Aranitakis, Z., Kelly, J. F., Aggarwal, N. T., Shah, R. C., & Wilson, R. S. (2006). Neuropathology of older persons without cognitive impairment from two community-based studies. *Neurology, 66*(12), 1837–1844.

Bennett, D. A., Schneider, J. A., Tang, Y., Arnold, S. E., & Wilson R. S. (2006). The effect of social networks on the relation between Alzheimer's disease pathology and level of cognitive function in old people: A longitudinal cohort study. *Lancet Neurology, 5*(5), 406–412.

Bennett, K. M. (2007). No "sissy stuff": Towards a theory of masculinity and emotional expression in older widowed men. *Journal of Aging Studies, 21,* 347–356.

Bennett, T., and Gaines, J. (2010). Believing what you hear: The impact of aging stereotypes upon the old. *Educational Gerontology, 36,* 435–445.

Ben Shlomo, S., Taubman-Ben-Ari, O., Findler, L., Sivan, E., & Dolizki, M. (2010). Becoming a grandmother: Maternal grandmothers' mental health, perceived ghosts, and personal growth. *Social Work Research, 34*(1), 45–57.

Benton, M. J., & Schlairet, M. C. 2012. "Improvements in quality of life in women after resistance training are not associated with age." *Journal of Women & Aging, 24*:59–69

Berger, E. D. (2009). Managing age discrimination: An examination of the techniques used when seeking employment. *The Gerontologist, 49*(3), 317–332.

Berger, P. L., & Luckmann, T. (1966). *The social construction of reality.* New York: Doubleday.

Bernard, A., & Li, C. (2006). *Death of a spouse: The impact on income for senior men and women.* Statistics Canada. Ottawa: Minister of Industry.

Birditt, K. S., Tighe, L. A., Fingerman, K. L., & Zarit, S. H. (2012). Intergenerational relationship quality across three generations. *Journals of Gerontology, Series B: Psychological Sciences and Social Sciences,* 1–12. Retrieved from http://psychsocgerontology.oxfordjournals.org.libaccess.sjlibrary.org/content/early/2012/05/23/geronb.gbs050.full.pdf.

Birkenmaier, J. (2009). Social work knowledge of facts on aging: Influence of field and classroom education. *Educational Gerontology, 35* (9), 784–800.

Bittles, A. J., Bower, C., Hussain, R., & Glasson, E. J. (2007). The four ages of Down syndrome. *European Journal of Public Health, 17*(2), 221–225.

Blieszner, R. (2014). The worth of friendship: Can friends keep us happy and healthy? *Generations, 38*(1), 24–30.

Bohman, D. M., van Wyck, N. C., & Ekman, S-L. (2009). Tradition in transition—Intergenerational relations with focus on the aged and their family members in a South African context. *Scandinavian Journal of Caring Sciences, 23*(3), 446–455.

Bolger, Joe. (1980). Bill C-12 and the debate over public service pension indexing. Unpublished master's essay. Ottawa: Carleton University.

Bonikowska, A., & Schellenberg, G. (2013). An Overview of the Working Lives of Older Baby Boomers. Statistics Canada, Social Analysis Division. Ottawa: Minister of Industry.

Bookman, A., & Harrington, M. (2007). Family caregivers: A shadow workforce in the geriatric health care system? *Journal of Health Politics, Policy & Law, 32,* 1005–1041.

Boon, S. D., & Shaw, M. J. (2007). Grandchildren's perceptions of grandparents' health: Worries and impact on their own lives. *Journal of Intergenerational Relationships, 5*(1), 57–78.

Botwinick, J. (1984). *Aging and behavior,* 3rd ed. New York: Springer.

Bousfield, C., & Hutchison, P. (2010). Contact, anxiety, and young people's attitudes and behavioral intentions towards the elderly. *Educational Gerontology, 36,* 451–466.

Bowen, C. E., Noack, M. G., & Staudinger, U. M. (2011). Aging in the work context. In K. W. Schaie & S. L. Willis (Eds.), *Handbook of the psychology of aging,* 7th ed. (pp. 263–277. London: Academic Press (Elsevier).

Brault, M. W. (2012). Americans with disabilities 2010. Economics and Statistics Administration, United States Bureau of the Census; 2012. http://www.census.gov/prod/2012pubs/p70-131.pdf. Accessed June 13, 2013.

Braun, M. M., Gurrera, R. J., Karel, M. J., Armesto, J. C., and Moye, J. (2009). Are clinicians ever biased in their judgments of the capacity of older adults to make medical decisions? *Generations, 33*(1), 78–81.

Braver, T. S., & West, R. (2008). Working memory, executive control, and aging. In F. I. M. Craik & T. A. Salthouse (Eds.), *The handbook of aging and cognition,* 3rd ed. (pp. 311–372). New York: Psychology Press.

Brennan, D. J., Emlet, C. A., Brennenstuhl, S., Rueda, S., & OHTN Cohort Study Research Team. (2013). Socio-demographic profile of older adults with HIV/AIDS: Gender and sexual orientation differences. *Canadian Journal on Aging, 32*(1), 31–43.

Brody, E. M. (1990). *Women in the middle: Their parent-care years.* New York: Springer.

Brotman, S., Ryan, B., Collins, S., Chamberland, L., Cormier, R., Julien D., Meyer, E., Peterkin, A., & Richard, B. (2007). Coming out to care: Caregivers of gay and lesbian seniors in Canada. *The Gerontologist, 47*(4), 490–503.

Brown, J., Cooper-Kuhn, C. M., Kempermann, G., Van Praag, H., Winkler, J., Gage, F. H., & Kuhn, H. G. (2003).

Enriched environment and physical activity stimulate hippocampal but not olfactory bulb neurogenesis. *European Journal of Neuroscience, 17*(10), 2042–2046.

Brown, R. L. (1995). Security for social security—Raise the age of entitlement? In E. M. Gee & G. M. Gutman (Eds.), *Rethinking retirement* (pp. 69–73). Vancouver: Gerontology Research Centre, Simon Fraser University.

Brown, R. L. (2010a) *Economic security in an aging Canadian population.* SEDAP Research Paper No. 268. Hamilton, ON: McMaster University.

Brown, R. L. (2010b). *Retirement 20/20: Innovation in Pension Design.* SEDAP Research Paper No. 267. Hamilton, ON: McMaster University.

Brown, S. C., & Park, D. C. (2003). Theoretical models of cognitive aging and implications for translational research in medicine. *The Gerontologist, 43,* 57–67.

Brown, S. L., & Lin, I-F. (2012). The gray divorce revolution: Rising divorce among middle-aged and older adults, 1990–2010. *Journals of Gerontology. Series B: Psychological Sciences and Social Sciences, 67*(6), 731–741.

Brown, W. M., Hou, F., & Lafrance, A. (2010). *Incomes of retirement-age and working-age Canadians: Accounting for home ownership.* Statistics Canada. Economic Analysis (EA) Research Paper Series. Ottawa: Minister of Industry.

Browne, A., Blake, M., Donnelly, M., & Herbert, D. (2002). On liberty for the old. *Canadian Journal on Aging, 21*(2), 283–293.

Brugman, G. M. (2006). Wisdom and aging. In J. E. Birren & K. W. Schaie (Eds.), *Handbook of the psychology of aging,* 6th ed. (pp. 445–476). Burlington, MA: Elsevier Academic Press.

Bryanton, O., & Weeks, L. E. (2014). Informing the development of educational programs to support older adults in retiring from driving. *Educational Gerontology, 40*(10), 756–766.

Bryden, K. (1974). *Old age pensions and policy-making in Canada.* Montreal: McGill-Queen's University Press.

Brzozowski, M., & Crossley, T. F. (2010). *Understanding the outcomes of older job losers.* SEDAP Research Paper No. 264. Hamilton, ON: McMaster University.

Buckley, C. (2015). China ends one-child policy, allowing families two children. *The New York Times, October 29.* Retrieved February 25, 2017, from https://www.nytimes.com/2015/10/30/world/asia/china-end-one-child-policy.html?_r=0.

Bucur, B., Madden, D. J., Spaniol, J., Provenzale, J. M., Cabeza, R., White, L. E., & Huettel, S. A. (2008). Age-related slowing of memory retrieval: Contributions of perceptual speed and cerebral white matter integrity. *Neurobiology of Aging, 29*(7), 1070–1079.

Buettner, D. (2008) *The blue zones.* Washington, DC: National Geographic.

Buettner, D. (2010). *The blue zones: Lessons for living longer from the people who've lived the longest.* Washington, DC: National Geographic Society.

Bugos, J. A., Perlstein, W. M. McCrae, C. S. Brophy, T. S., & Bedenbaugh, P. H. (2007). Individualized piano instruction enhances executive functioning and working memory in older adults. *Aging and Mental Health, 11*(4), 464–471.

Building Blocks. (2004). Africa-wide briefing notes—supporting older carers. HIV AIDS Alliance and HelpAge International.

Burger King. (2015). Burger King USA nutritionals: Core, regional and limited time offerings, July 2015. Retrieved from https://www.bk.com/pdfs/nutrition.pdf.

Burr, J. A., Mutchler, J. E., & Gerst, K. (2010). Public policies and older populations of color. In R. B. Hudson (Ed.), *The New Politics of Old Age Policy,* 2nd ed. (pp. 160–182).

Burtless, G., & Quinn, J. (2001). Retirement trends and policies to encourage work among older Americans. In P. Budetti, R. Burkhauser, J. Gregory & H. Allan Hunt (Eds.), *Ensuring health and income security for an aging workforce* (pp. 375–416). Kalamazoo, MI: Upjohn Institute.

Butler, R. N. (1969). Ageism: Another form of bigotry. *The Gerontologist, 9,* 243–246.

Butler, R. N. (1993). Dispelling ageism: The cross-cutting intervention. *Generations, 17*(2): 75–78.

Butler, R. N., & Lewis, M. I. (1976). *Sex after 60: A guide for men and women for their later years.* New York: Harper and Row.

Butler, R. N., & Lewis, M. I. (2002). *The new love and sex after 60.* New York: Ballantine.

Butler-Jones, D. (Chief Public Health Officer Canada). (2010). *Report on the state of public health in Canada 2010: Growing older—Adding life to years.* Cat No. HP2-10/2010E-PDF. Ottawa: Her Majesty the Queen in Right of Canada. Retrieved from http://www.phac-aspc.gc.ca/cphorsphc-respcacsp/2010/fr-rc/pdf/cpho_report_2010_e.pdf

Butts, D. M., & Lent, J. P. (2009). Better together: Generational reciprocity in the real world. In R. B. Hudson (Ed.), *Boomer bust? Economic and political issues of the graying society. The boomers and their future,* Vol. 2 (pp. 145–165). Westport, CT: Praeger.

Byszewski, A. (2009). *The driving and dementia toolkit,* 3rd ed. The Champlain Dementia Network. Retrieved from http://www.champlaindementianetwork.org/uploads/Resources/kitjune09.pdf.

Cable-Williams, B. E., & Wilson, D. M. (2014). Awareness of impending death for residents of long-term care facilities? *International Journal of Older People Nursing, 9,* 169–179.

Calasanti, T. (2005). Ageism, gravity, and gender: Experiences of aging bodies. *Generations, 29*(3), 8–12.

Calasanti, T. (2006). Gender and old age: Lessons from spousal care work. In T. M. Calasanti & K. F. Slevin (Eds.),

Age matters: Realigning feminist thinking (pp. 269–294). New York: Routledge Taylor & Francis.

Calasanti, T. (2007). Bodacious berry, potency wood and the aging monster: Gender and age relations in anti-aging ads. *Social Forces, 86*(1), 335–355.

Calasanti, T. (2008). A feminist confronts ageism. *Journal of Aging Studies, 22*, 152–157.

Calasanti, T. (2009). Theorizing feminist gerontology, sexuality, and beyond: Intersectional approach. In V. L. Bengtson, M. Silverstein, M. M. Putney, & D. Gans (Eds.), *Handbook of theories of aging* (pp. 471–485). New York: Springer.

Calasanti, T., and Bowen, M. E. (2006). Spousal caregiving and crossing gender boundaries: Maintaining gendered identities. *Journal of Aging Studies 20*, 253–263.

Calasanti, T., & Kiecolt, K. J. (2007). Diversity among late-life couples. *Generations, 31*(3), 10–17.

Calasanti, T., & King, N. (2007). Taking "women's work" like a man: Husbands' experiences of care work. *The Gerontologist, 47*(4), 516–527.

Calasanti, T., & Slevin, K. F. (Eds.). (2006). *Age matters: Realigning feminist thinking*. New York: Routledge.

Caldwell, S. (2010, June 20). Euthanasia cases in Holland rise by 13 per cent in a year. *The Telegraph*. Retrieved from www. telegraph.co.uk/news/worldnews/europe/netherlands/7841696/Euthanasia-cases-in-Holland-rise-by-13-per-cent-in-a-year.html.

Callahan, J. J. (2009). New challenges for old warriors. *Aging Today, 30*(3), 3–4.

Campbell, L. D., Connidis, I. A., & Davies, L. (1999). Sibling Ties in Later Life: A Social Network Analysis. *Journal of Family Issues, 20*(1), 114–148.

Canada. (1984). *Canada Health Act*, R. S. C. 1985, c. C-6. Ottawa: Queen's Printer. Retrieved from http://www.laws.justice.gc.ca/en/C-6/index.html.

Canada Health Infoway. (2011). *Telehealth benefits and adoption: Connecting people and providers across Canada*. Retrieved from https://www2.infoway-inforoute.ca/Documents/telehealth_report_summary_2010_en.pdf.

Canada Mortgage and Housing Corporation (CMHC). (2006a). 2001 Census Housing Series: Issue 10. Aging, residential mobility and housing choices. *Research Highlights*. SocioEconomic Series 06-001. Retrieved from http://www.cmhc-schl.gc.ca/odpub/pdf/64992.pdf.

Canada Mortgage and Housing Corporation (CMHC). (2006b). Senior housing for seniors: A feasibility study. *Research Highlights*. Socio-Economic Series 06-023. Retrieved from http://www.cmhc-schl.gc.ca/odpub/pdf/65308.pdf.

Canada Mortgage and Housing Corporation (CMHC). (2007). Supportive housing for homeless and hard-to-house seniors: An in-depth case study. *Research Highlights*. Socio-Economic Series 07-017. Retrieved from http://www .cmhc-schl.gc.ca/odpub/pdf/65672.pdf.

Canada Mortgage and Housing Corporation (CMHC). (2008a). Impacts of the aging of the Canadian population on housing and communities. *Research Highlights*. SocioEconomic Series 08-003. Retrieved from http://www.cmhc-schl.gc.ca/odpub/pdf/65913.pdf.

Canada Mortgage and Housing Corporation (CMHC). (2008b). Adapting homes to extend independence. *Research Highlights*. Socio-Economic Series 08-009. Retrieved from http://www.cmhc-schl.gc.ca/odpub/pdf/66004.pdf.

Canada Mortgage and Housing Corporation (CMHC). (2008c). Designing flexible housing. Retrieved from http://www.cmhc-schl.gc.ca/en/inpr/afhoce/tore/afhoid/cohode/deflho/index.cfm.

Canada Mortgage and Housing Corporation (CMHC). (2008d). Reverse mortgages. Retrieved from http://www.cmhc-schl.gc.ca/en/inpr/afhoce/tore/afhoid/fite/remo/index.cfm.

Canada Mortgage and Housing Corporation (CMHC). (2008e). About your house—General Series: Garden suites. Retrieved from http://www.cmhc.ca/en/co/renoho/refash/refash_026.cfm.

Canada Mortgage and Housing Corporation (CMHC). (2010a). 2006 Census Housing Series: Issue 10. The housing conditions of Canada's seniors. *Research Highlights*. Socio-Economic Series 10-021. Retrieved from http://publications.gc.ca/collections/collection_2011/schl-cmhc/NH18-23-110-021-eng.pdf.

Canada Mortgage and Housing Corporation (CMHC). (2010b). 2001 Participation and Activity Limitation Survey: Issue 8. Profile of the housing conditions of seniors with disabilities. *Research Highlights*, July.

Canada Mortgage and Housing Corporation (CMHC). (2011a). 2006 Census Housing Series: Issue 15. Seniors in collective dwellings. *Research Highlights*, October.

Canada Mortgage and Housing Corporation (CMHC). (2011b). Seniors' housing report: British Columbia. *Housing Market Information*. Retrieved from http://www.cmhc-schl.gc.ca/odpub/esub/66231/66231_2011_A01.pdf.

Canada Mortgage and Housing Corporation (CMHC). (2011c). Smart grab bars: A potential initiative to encourage bath grab bar use in community-dwelling older adults. *Research Highlight*, May. Retrieved from http://www.cmhc.ca/odpub/pdf/67275.pdf.

Canada Mortgage and Housing Corporation (CMHC). (2011d). Smart technologies in affordable seniors housing. *Research Highlights*, September.

Canada Mortgage and Housing Corporation (CMHC). (2011e). Seniors' housing. *Canadian Housing Observer, Chapter 8*. Retrieved from http://www.cmhcschl.gc.ca/en/ corp/about/cahoob/upload/Chapter_8_EN_W.pdf.

Canada Mortgage and Housing Corporation (CMHC). (2012f). Life leases. Retrieved from http://www.cmhc-schl.gc.ca/en/inpr/afhoce/tore/afhoid/fite/lile/index.cfm.

Canada Mortgage and Housing Corporation (CMHC). (2012g). Life leases: How the strategy works. Retrieved from http://www.cmhc-schl.gc.ca/en/inpr/afhoce/afhoce/afhostcast/afhoid/fite/lile/lile_001.cfm.

Canada Mortgage and Housing Corporation (CMHC). (2012h). Life leases: Advantages and issues. Retrieved from http://www.cmhc-schl.gc.ca/en/inpr/afhoce/tore/afhoid/ fite/lile/lile_002.cfm.

Canada Mortgage and Housing Corporation. (2013a). Homeowner Residential Rehabilitation Assistance Program—Homeowner RRAP. Retrieved: http://www.cmhc-schl. gc.ca/en/co/prfinas/prfinas_001.cfm.

Canada Mortgage and Housing Corporation. (2013b). Home Adaptations for Seniors' Independence (HASI). Retrieved http://www.cmhc-schl.gc.ca/en/co/prfinas/prfinas_004.cfm.

Canada Mortgage and Housing Corporation (CMHC). (2014a). Garden suites. About your house. Retrieved from http://www.cmhc-schl.gc.ca/odpub/pdf/65009.pdf?fr=1441901300719.

Canada Mortgage and Housing Corporation. (2014b). FlexHousing checklist. Homes that adapt to life's changes. Retrieved from http://www.cmhc-schl.gc.ca/odpub/pdf/61943.pdf?fr=1421086550208.

Canada Mortgage and Housing Corporation. (2015a). Home Adaptations for Seniors' Independence (HASI)—Francesca Grossi. Retrieved from http://www.cmhc-schl.gc.ca/en/inpr/afhoce/afhoce/vi/vi_076.cfm.

Canada Mortgage and Housing Corporation. (2015b). What Are the Trends in Incomes, Wealth and Pensions for Canada's Seniors? Retrieved from http://www.cmhc-schl.gc.ca/en/inpr/bude/hoolca/hoolca_vol_001/hoolca_vol_001_005.cfm.

Canada Mortgage and Housing Corporation. (2015c). Housing for older Canadians—The definitive guide to the over-55 market. Volume 1, *Understanding the Market*. Retrieved from http://www.cmhc-schl.gc.ca/odpub/pdf/67514.pdf.

Canada Mortgage and Housing Corporation. (2015d). Do seniors want to rent or buy housing? Retrieved from http://www.cmhc-schl.gc.ca/en/inpr/bude/hoolca/hoolca_vol_001/hoolca_vol_001_010.cfm,

Canada Mortgage and Housing Corporation. (2015e) Seniors' housing report. Canada Highlights. Retrieved from https://www03.cmhc-schl.gc.ca/catalog/productDetail.cfm?cat=160&itm=31&lang=en&sid=Sp4S5v3wW74oAQkLOJAJ9yiLgNaFxdilSthPkEyCKt1nOnAxSc6wMjh2TtpnfLcs&fr=1445183910749.

Canada Mortgage and Housing Corporation. (2015f). What Is FlexHousing? Retrieved from http://www.cmhc-schl.gc.ca/flex/en/lemo.cfm.

Canada Mortgage and Housing Corporation (CMHC). (2015g). Housing options for people living with dementia. Volume 2. CMHC: Ottawa.

Canada Revenue Agency. (2015). MP, DB, RRSP, DPSP, and TFSA limits and the YMPE. Retrieved from http://www.cra-arc.gc.ca/tx/rgstrd/papspapar-fefespfer/lmts-eng.html.

Canadian Anti-Fraud Centre. (2011). Mass marketing fraud & ID fraud activities. *Quarterly Statistical Report*, April-June 2011. Retrieved from http://www.antifraudcentre centreantifraude.ca/english/documents/QuarterlyStatistical Report_Apr-Jun2011.pdf.

Canadian Anti-Fraud Centre. (2014). *Senior support unit.* Retrieved from http://www.antifraudcentre-centreanti-fraude.ca/english/cafc-seniorbusters.html

Canadian Centre for Elder Law. (2011). A practical guide to elder abuse and neglect law in Canada. Vancouver: British Columbia Law Institute. Retrieved February 26, 2017, from http://www.bcli.org/sites/default/files/Practical_Guide_English_Rev_july_2011.pdf.

Canadian Coalition for Seniors' Mental Health. (2009). *Suicide prevention among older adults: A guide for family members.* Toronto: Author.

Canadian Diabetes Association. (2017a). Living with Type 2 diabetes. Retrieved February 25, 2017, from http://www.diabetes.ca/diabetes-and-you/living-with-type-2-diabetes.

Canadian Diabetes Association. (2017b). Diabetes Statistics in Canada. Retrieved February 25, 2017, from http://www.diabetes.ca/how-you-can-help/advocate/why-federal-leadership-is-essential/diabetes-statistics-in-canada.

Canadian Diabetes Association. (2017c). Diabetes in Canada. Retrieved February 25, 2017, from https://www.diabetes.ca/getmedia/513a0f6c-b1c9-4e56-a77c-6a492bf7350f/diabetes-charter-backgrounder-national-english.pdf.aspx.

Canadian Healthcare Association. (2007). *10th annual health care in Canada survey* Retrieved from http://www.cha.ca/documents/pa/2007_hcic.pdf.

Canadian Healthcare Association. (2009). *Home care in Canada: From the margins to the mainstream.* Ottawa: Author. Retrieved from http://www.cha.ca/documents/Home_Care_in_Canada_From_the_Margins_to_the_Mainstream_web.pdf.

Canadian Health Services Research Foundation (CHSRF). (2011). *Better with age: Health systems planning for the aging population: Synthesis report.* Retrieved from http://www.chsrf.ca/Libraries/Aging_roundtable_reports/CHSRF_Toronto_Roundtable-Web.sflb.ashx.

Canadian Home Care Association (CHCA). (2013). *Portraits of home care in Canada.* Retrieved from http://www.cdnhomecare.ca/media.php?mid=3394.

Canadian Institute for Health Information (CIHI) (2010). Depression among Seniors in Residential Care. Ottawa, ON: CIHI.

Canadian Institute for Health Information (CIHI). (2011a). *Health care cost drivers: The facts.* Ottawa: CIHI.

Canadian Institute for Health Information (CIHI). (2011b). *Wait times in Canada: A comparison by province, 2011.* Retrieved from http://secure.cihi.ca/cihiweb/products/Wait_times_tables_2011_en.pdf.

Canadian Institute for Health Information (CIHI). (2011c). *Health care in Canada, 2011: A focus on seniors and aging.* Ottawa: CIHI.

Canadian Institute for Health Information (CIHI). (2011d). *Seniors and the health care system: What is the impact of multiple chronic conditions?* Retrieved from https://secure.cihi.ca/free_products/air-chronic_disease_aib_en.pdf.

Canadian Institute for Health Information (CIHI). (2011e). *Highlights of 2009-2010 inpatient hospitalizations and emergency department visits.* Retrieved from http://secure.cihi.ca/cihiweb/products/quickstats_dad_nacrs_2009_10_highlight_en.pdf.

Canadian Institute for Health Information (CIHI). (2014). National health expenditure trends, 1975 to 2014. Retrieved from https://www.cihi.ca/en/nhex_2014_report_en.pdf.

Canadian Institute for Health Information. (2015a) Quick stats. Types of primary hip replacements, CJRR, 2012-2013 and types of primary knee replacements, CJRR, 2012-2013. Retrieved from https://www.cihi.ca/en/quick-stats.

Canadian Institute for Health Information (CIHI). (2015b). Spending. Retrieved from https://www.cihi.ca/en/spending-and-health-workforce/spending.

Canadian Institute of Actuaries. (2010). *Government facilitated retirement income plans* (White Paper). Ottawa.

Canadian Institutes of Health Research. (2014). Institute of Aging. Retrieved from http://www.cihr-irsc.gc.ca/e/8671.html.

Canadian Lung Association. (2010). Exploring self-awareness levels of major lung disease risk factors among Canadians most at risk. Retrieved from https://www.lung.ca/lung-health/lung-info/lung-statistics/lung-disease-statistics.

Canadian Lung Association. (2011). Smoking in Canada backgrounder. Retrieved from http://extras.newswire.ca/smr/SmokingbackgroundrFINAL.pdf.

Canadian Museum of History. (2010). *Making Medicare: The History of Health Care in Canada, 1914-2007.* Retrieved from http://www.historymuseum.ca/cmc/exhibitions/hist/medicare/medic01e.shtml.

Canadian Network for the Prevention of Elder Abuse. (2009). *Abuse of older men.* Retrieved from http://www.cnpea.ca/abuse_of_older_men.htm.

Canadian Orthopaedic Foundation. (2010). FAQ for total joint replacements. Retrieved from http://www.canorth.org/en/patientresources/Default.aspx?pagename=FAQ%20for%20Total%20Joint%20Replacements.

Canadian Polyamory Advocacy Association (CPAA) (2015). Status. Retrieved from http://polyadvocacy.ca.

Canadian Public Health Association. (n.d.). Seniors and HIV/AIDS: It's time to start talking. Retrieved from http://www.cpha.ca/en/portals/hiv/article03.aspx.

Canadian Special Senate Committee on Aging. (2009). *Canada's aging population: Seizing the opportunity. Special Senate Committee on Aging—Final Report.* Ottawa: The Senate.

Canadian Standing Senate Committee on Banking Trade and Commerce. (2006). The demographic time bomb: Mitigating the effects of demographic change in Canada. Ottawa: Queen's Printer.

Canham, S. L. (2009). The interaction of masculinity and control and its impact on the experience of suffering for an older man. *Journal of Aging Studies, 23,* 90–96.

Carbonneau, H. L. N., Caron, C., & Desrosiers, J. (2010). Development of a conceptual framework of positive aspects of caregiving in dementia. *Dementia 9,* 327–353.

Caron-Malenfant, E., Lebel, A., & Martel, L. (2010). *Projections of the diversity of the Caadian population.* 2006 to 2031. Statistics Canada Cat. No. 91-551-X. Ottawa: Minister of Industry

Carr, D., & Moorman, S. M. (2011). Diversity and family relations in an aging society. In R. A. Settersten, Jr., & J. L. Angel (Eds.), *Handbook of sociology of aging* (pp. 145–160). New York: Springer.

Carrière, G. (2006). Seniors' use of home care. *Health Reports, 17*(4), 43–47. Statistics Canada Cat. No. 82-003-XIE. Retrieved from http://www.statcan.gc.ca/pub/82-003-x/2005004/article/9498-eng.pdf.

Carrière, G., & Sanmartin, C. (2010). Waiting time for medical specialist consultations in Canada, (2007). *Health Reports, 21*(2), 1–8.

Carrière, Y, & Galarneau, D. (2011). Delayed retirement: A new trend? *Perspectives on Labour and Income,* October 26, 3–16.

Carrière, Y., & Galarneau, D. (2012a). How many years to retirement? Statistics Canada. Ottawa: Minister of Industry.

Carrière, Y., & Galarneau, D. (2012b). The Impact of Involuntary Breaks in Employment and Level of Education on the Timing of Retirement. Statistics Canada. Ottawa: Minister of Industry.

Carson, A. P., Rose, K. M., Catellier, D. J., Kaufman, J. S., Wyatt, S. B., et al. (2007). Cumulative socioeconomic status across the life course and subclinical atherosclerosis. *Annals of Epidemiology, 17*(4), 296–303.

Carstairs, S. (2010). *Raising the bar: A roadmap for the future of palliative care in Canada.* Ottawa: The Senate of Canada.

Carstairs, S., & Keon, W. J. (2009). *Canada's aging population: Seizing the opportunity. Special Senate Committee on Aging—Final Report.* Ottawa: The Senate. Retrieved from http://www.parl.gc.ca/Content/SEN/Committee/402/agei/rep/AgingFinalReport-e.pdf.

Carstensen, L. L. (2009). *A long bright future.* New York: Broadway Books.

Carstensen, L. L., Mikels, J. A., & Mather, M. (2006). Aging and the intersection of cognition, motivation, and emotion. In J. E. Birren & K. W. Schaie (eds.), *Handbook of the psychology of aging*, 6th ed. (pp. 343–362). Burlington, MA: Elsevier Academic Press.

CBC News. (2008, June 18). Doctors offer to treat dying Winnipeg man after colleagues refuse. Family's religious beliefs conflict with medical opinions. Retrieved from http:// www.cbc.ca/news/canada/story/2008/06/18/ winnipeg-doctor.html?ref=rss.

CBC News. (2011a). Seniors in hospital beds costly for health system. Retrieved from http://www.cbc.ca/news/health/ tory/2011/12/01/seniors-hospital-beds-health-care.html=.

CBC News. (2011b). 100-year-old sets record with marathon finish. Retrieved February 25, 2017, from http://www.cbc. ca/news/canada/toronto/100-year-old-sets-record-with-marathon-finish-1.1091974.

CBC News. (2015. More Canadians are 65 and over than under age 15, StatsCan says. September 29. Retrieved from http://www.cbc.ca/news/business/statistics-canada-seniors-1.3248295 March 2, 2017.

CBO (Congressional Budget Office). (2015). Insurance Coverage Provisions of the Affordable Care Act—CBO's January 2015 Baseline. Retrieved from http://www. cbo.gov/sites/default/files/cbofiles/attachments/43900-2015-01-ACAtables.pdf.

Centers for Disease Control and Prevention. (2013). *The State of aging and health in America 2013*. Atlanta, GA: Centers for Disease Control and Prevention, U.S. Department of Health and Human Services. Retrieved January 25, 2014, from http://www.cdc.gov/aging/pdf/state-aging-health-in-america-2013.pdf

Centre for Suicide Prevention. (2014). *Centre for Suicide Prevention toolkit*. Retrieved from http://suicideinfo.ca/ LinkClick.aspx?fileticket=cmFwRL4DMJw=.

Cerella, J. (1990). Aging and information-processing rate. In. J. E. Birren & K. W. Schaie, eds. *Handbook of the psychology of aging*, 3rd ed., 201–222. San Diego: Academic Press.

CESO. (2015). About Us. Retrieved from http://www.ceso-saco. com/About.aspx.

Chandler, C. (2006, September 18). Changing places. *Fortune*, 62.

Chang, E., Wilber, K. H., & Silverstein, M. (2010). The effects of childlessness on the care and psychological well-being of older adults with disabilities. *Aging & Mental Health*, 14(6), 712–719.

Chang, J., & McCaslin, R. (2015). Correlates of, and barriers to, Internet use among older adults. *Journal of Gerontological Social Work*, 58(1).

Chappell, N. L. (1997). *National Respite Project: Evaluation report*. Victoria: Centre on Aging, University of Victoria.

Chappell, N. L. (2011). The age of aging: How demographics are changing the global economy and our world: A book review. *Canadian Studies in Population*, 38(1–2), 191–193.

Chappell, N. L., Dujela, C., & Smith, A. (2014). Spouse and adult child differences in caregiving burden. *Canadian Journal on Aging*, 33(4), 462–472.

Chappell, N. L., & Hollander, M. J. (2011). An evidence-based policy prescription for an aging population. *Healthcare-Papers*, 11, 8–18. Retrieved from http://www.longwoods. com/content/22246.

Chappell, N. L., Reid, R. C., & Dow, E. (2001). Respite reconsidered: A typology of meanings based on the caregiver's point of view. *Journal of Aging Studies*, 15(2), 201–216.

Chappell, N. L., Schroeder, B., & Gibbens, M. (2008). Respite for rural and remote caregivers. In N. Keating (Ed.), *Rural ageing: A good place to grow old?* (pp. 53–62). Bristol, UK: The Policy Press. University of Bristol.

Charbonneau, P., Ouellet, G., & Milan, A. (2011). Age and sex structure: Subprovincial, 2010. *Report on the demographic situation in Canada*. Component of Statistics Canada Cat. No. 91-209-X. Ottawa: Minister of Industry.

Charness, N. (1981). Aging and skilled problem solving. *Journal of Experimental Psychology: General*, 110(10, 21–38.

Charness, N. (1985). Aging and problem-solving performance. In N. Charness (Ed.), *Aging and human performance* (pp. 225–259). Chichester, U. K.: John Wiley & Sons.

Charness, N., & Krampe, R. T. (2008). Expertise and knowledge. In S. M. Hofer & D. F. Alwin (Eds.), *Handbook of cognitive aging: interdisciplinary perspectives* (pp. 244–258). Los Angeles: SAGE Publications.

Charpentier, M., Queniart, A., & Jacques, J. (2008). Activism among older women in Quebec, Canada: Changing the world after age 65. *Journal of Women & Aging*, 23(3/4), 343–360.

Charters, J., & Murray, S. B. (2006). Design and evaluation of a leisure education program for caregivers of institutionalized care recipients. *Topics in Geriatric Rehabilitation*, 22(4), 334–337.

Chau, S., & Lai, D. W. L. (2011). The size of an ethno-cultural community as a social determinant of health for Chinese seniors. *Journal of Immigrant and Minority Health*, 13, 1090–1098.

Cheng, Y., & Rosenberg, M. W. (2009). *Financial security of elders in China*. SEDAP Research Paper No.241. Hamilton, ON: McMaster University.

Cherem, B. F. (2010). What sustains learning in the later years? *The LLI Review, Fall*, 104–111.

Chertkow, H. (2008). Diagnosis and treatment of dementia: Introduction. Introducing a series based on the Third Canadian Consensus Conference on the Diagnosis and Treatment of Dementia. *Canadian Medical Association Journal*, 178(3), 316–321. Retrieved from http://www. ecmaj.ca/content/178/3/316.short.

CHNET-Works! (2012). What is CHNET-Works!? Retrieved from http://www.chnet-works.ca.

Choi, H., & N. F. Marks. (2008). Marital conflict, depressive symptoms, and functional impairment. *Journal of Marriage and Family, 70*(2), 377–390.

Choi, H., Schoeni, R. F., Langa, K. M., & Heisler, M. M. (2014). Spouse and child availability for newly disabled older adults: Socioeconomic differences and potential role of residential proximity. *Journals of Gerontology*, Series B: Psychological Sciences and Social Sciences, 70(3), 462–469.

Chou, P. H. B., & Wister, A. V. (2005). From cues to action: Information seeking and exercise self-care among older adults managing chronic illness. *The Canadian Journal on Aging, 24*(4), 395–408.

Chou, R. J. (2012). Discrimination against older workers: Current knowledge, future research directions and implications for social work. *Indian Journal of Gerontology, 26*(1), 25–49.

Chou, R. J. & Choi, N. G. (2010). Prevalence and correlates of perceived workplace discrimination among older workers in the United States. Copy on file with author.

Chow, H. P. H. (2010). Growing old in Canada: Physical and psychological well-being among elderly Chinese Immigrants. *Ethnicity and Health, 15*(1), 61–72.

Chow, H. P. H. (2012). Health care service needs and correlates of quality of life: A case study of elderly Chinese immigrants in Canada. *Social Indicators Research, 106*, 347–358.

Chow, T. W., Binder, C., Smyth, S., Cohen, S., & Robillard, A. (2009). 100 years after Alzheimer: Contemporary neurology practice assessment of referrals for dementia. *American Journal of Alzheimers Disease & Other Dementias, 23*(6), 516–527.

Christensen, H., Anstey, K. J., Leach, L. S., & Mackinnon, A. J. (2008). Intelligence, education, and the brain reserve hypothesis. In F. I. M. Craik & T. A. Salthouse (Eds.), *The handbook of aging and cognition*, 3rd ed. (pp. 133–189). New York: Psychology Press.

Chui, T., Tran, K., & Maheux, H. (2007). Immigration in Canada: A portrait of the foreign-born census year 2006. Statistics Canada. Ottawa: Minister of Industry.

Citizenship and Immigration Canada. (2011). *Canada facts and figures: Immigration overview permanent and temporary residents, 2010.* Minister of Public Works and Government Services Canada. Retrieved from http://www.cic.gc.ca/english/pdf/research-stats/facts2010.pdf.

Clark, P. G. (1993). Moral discourse and public policy in aging: Framing problems, seeking solutions, and "public ethics." *Canadian Journal on Aging, 12*(4), 485–508.

Clark, W., & Crompton, S. (2006). Till death do us part? The risk of first and second marriage dissolution. *Canadian Social Trends* (Summer), 24–34.

Clark, W., & Schellenberg, G. (2006). Who's religious? *Canadian Social Trends* (Summer), 2–9.

Clarke, L. H. (2008). Visible and invisible ageing: Beauty work as a response to ageism. *Ageing and Society, 28*(5), 653–674.

Clarke, L. H., Bennett, E. V., Liu, C. (2014). Aging and masculinity: Portrayals in men's magazines, *Journal of Aging Studies, 31*, 26–33.

Clarke, L. H., Griffin, M., & Maliha, K. (2009). Bat wings, bunions, and turkey wattles: Body transgressions and older women's strategic clothing choices. *Ageing and Society, 29*, 709–726.

Clarke, P., Chan, P., Santaguida, P. L., & Colantonio, A. (2009). The use of mobility devices among institutionalized older adults. *Journal of Aging and Health, 21*, 611–627.

Clarke, P., & Colantonio, A. (2005). Wheelchair use among community-dwelling older adults: Prevalence and risk factors in a national sample. *Canadian Journal on Aging, 24*(2), 191–198.

Clément, F., Belleville, S., Bélanger, S., & Chasse, V. (2009). Personality and psychological health in persons with mild cognitive impairment. *Canadian Journal on Aging, 28*(2), 147–156.

Clift, E. M. (n.d.). *Kin keeping.* Trigg County Extension Agent for Family and Consumer Science.

Clouston, S. A., Lawlor, A., & Verdery, A. M. (2014). The role of partnership status on late-life physical function. *Canadian Journal on Aging, 33*(4), 413–425.

COACH: Canadian Health Informatics Association. (2013). Retrieved from https://www.coachorg.com/en/communities/resources/TeleHealth-Public-FINAL-web-062713-secured.pdf.

Cohen, G. D. (2005). *The mature mind: The positive power of the aging brain.* New York: Basic Books.

Cohen, G. D., Perlstein, S., Chapline, J., Kelly, J., Firth, K. M., & Simmens, S. (2007). Impact of professionally conducted cultural programs on the physical health, mental health, and social functioning of older adults—2-year results. *Journal of Aging, Humanities and the Arts, 1*(1–2), 5–22.

Cole, M. G., McCusker, J., Sewich, M., Ciampi, A., & Dyachenko, A. (2008). Health services use for mental health problems by community-living seniors with depression. *International Psychogeriatrics, 20*, 554–570.

Colley, R. C., Garriguet, D., Janssen, I., Craig, C. L., Clarke, J., & Tremblay, M. S. (2011). Physical activity of Canadian adults: Accelerometer results from the 2007 to 2009 *Canadian Health Measures Study. Health Reports, 22*(1), 1–8.

Colombe, S. J., Erickson, K. I., Scalf, P. E., Kim, J. S., Prakash, R., McAuley, E., et al. (2006). Aerobic exercise training increases brain volume in aging humans. *Journals of Gerontology: Medical Sciences, 61*(11), 1166–1170.

Columbia News. (2008). New MRI approach can identify sources of memory loss in humans and mice. Retrieved from http://www.columbia.edu/cu/news/00/12/MRI.html.

Comeau, T. D., & Kemp, C. L. (2007). Intersections of age and masculinities in the information technology industry. *Ageing and Society, 27*(2), 215–232.

Commission on the Future of Health Care in Canada. (2002). *Building on values: The future of health care in Canada: Final report* (Romanow Report). Ottawa: Government of Canada. Retrieved from http://www.hc-sc.gc.ca/english/pdf/care/romanow_e.pdf.

Conde, H., & McDonald, J. T., (2007). The health services use among older Canadians in rural and urban areas. Social and Economic Dimensions of an Aging Population. SEDAP Research Paper No. 178. Hamilton, ON: McMaster University.

Connidis, I. A. (2006). Intimate relationships: Learning from later life experiences. In T. M. Calasanti & K. F. Slevin (Eds.), *Age matters: Realigning feminist thinking* (pp. 123–153). New York: Routledge.

Connidis, I. A. (2010). *Family ties and aging*, 2nd ed. Los Angeles: Pine Forge Press.

Connidis, I. A., & Kemp, C. L. (2008). Negotiating actual and anticipated parental support: Multiple sibling voices in three-generation families. *Journal of Aging Studies, 22*, 229–238.

Constant, A., Petersen, S., Mallory, C. D., & Major, J. (2011). *Research synthesis on cost drivers in the health sector and proposed policy options.* Canadian Health Services Research Foundation. Ottawa: CHSRF.

Cooke, M. (2006). Policy changes and the labour force participation of older workers: Evidence from six countries. *Canadian Journal on Aging, 25*(4), 387–400.

Cooke, M. (2009). Population ageing, pensions and growth: Intertemporal trade-offs and consumption planning. *Canadian Studies in Population, 38*, Spring/Summer, 195–197.

Cooke, M. (2011). A book review of J. Creedy and R. Guest. (2009). Population ageing, pensions and growth: Intertemporal trade-offs and consumption planning. In *Canadian Studies in Population, 38*(1–2), 195–197. Retrieved February 25, 2017, from http://www.canpopsoc.ca/CanPopSoc/assets/File/publications/journal/2011/CSPv38n1-2p195.pdf.

Cooper, D. (2015). Highlights of the Canada Digital Privacy Act 2015. Retrieved from http://www.insideprivacy.com/international/canada/highlights-of-the-canada-digital-privacy-act-2015.

Corbett, D. (with R. Higgins). (2007). *Portfolio life.* San Francisco: John Wiley & Sons.

Cornwell, B. (2011). Independence through social networks: Bridging potential among older women and men. *The Journals of Gerontology. Series B: Psychological Sciences and Social Sciences. 66*(6), 782–794.

Cosentino, S. A., Brickman, A. M., & Manly, J. J. (2011). Neuropsychological assessment of the dementias of late life. In K. W. Schaie & S. L. Willis (Eds.), *Handbook of the psychology of aging*, 7th ed. (pp. 339–352). London: Academic Press (Elsevier).

Cotman, C. W., & Berchtold, N. C. (2002). Exercise: A behavioral intervention to enhance brain health and plasticity. *Trends in Neuroscience, 25*, 295–301.

Council Against Abuse of Older Persons. (2008). *What is abuse?* Retrieved from http://www.caaop.com/en/what_is_abuse.php.

Coupland, J. (2009). Discourse, identity and change in mid-to-late life: Interdisciplinary perspectives on language and ageing. *Ageing & Society, 29*(6), 849–861.

Cousins, S. O. (2000). "My health couldn't take it": Older women's beliefs about exercise benefits and risks. *Journals of Gerontology Series B 55*(5), P283–P294.

Cowgill, D. O., & Holmes, L. D. (Eds.). (1972). *Aging and modernization.* New York: Appleton-Century-Crofts.

Cowley, M. (1980). *The view from 80.* New York: Viking Press.

CPP Investment Board. (2014). 2014 annual report. Retrieved from http://cppib.com/content/dam/cppib/Our%20Performance/Financial%20results/CPPIB_F2014_Annual%20Report_English.pdf.

Craik, F. L. M. (2000). Age-related changes in human memory. In D. C. Park & N. Schwarz (Eds.), *Cognitive aging: A primer*, 75–92. *Philadelphia: Taylor & Francis.*

Craik, F. I. M., & Salthouse, T. A. (Eds.). (2008). *The handbook of aging and cognition*, 3rd ed. New York: Psychology Press.

Cranswick, K., and Derrick, T. (2005). Elder care and the complexities of social networks by *Canadian Social Trends*, Summer 2005. Statistics Canada—Catalogue No. 11-008; pp. 10–15. Charts on p. 12 of article. Reprinted with permission.

Cranswick, K., & Dosman, D. (2008). Eldercare: What we know today. *Canadian Social Trends, 86*, 48–56.

Cranswick, K., & Thomas, D. (2005). Elder care and the complexities of social networks. *Canadian Social Trends*, Summer. Statistics Canada Cat. No. 11-008.

Creedy, J., & Guest, R. (2009). Population ageing, pensions and growth: Intertemporal trade-offs and consumption planning. United Kingdom: Edward Elgar Publishing.

Crilly, R. G., Lytwynec, S., Kloseck, M., Smith, J. M., Olsen, T., Gold, B., & Masse, S. (2005). Patient outcomes after discharge from a geriatric day hospital. *Canadian Journal on Aging, 24*(3), 305–310.

Crimmins, E. M., & Beltrán-Sánchez, H. (2010). Mortality and morbidity trends: Is there a compression of morbidity? *Journal of Gerontology: Social Sciences, 66B*(1), 75–86.

Crompton, S. (2011). *Women with activity limitations*. A component of *Women in Canada: A gender-based statistical report*. Ottawa: Statistics Canada.

Crooks, V. C., Lubben, J., Petitti, D. B., Little, D., & Chiu, V. (2008). Social network, cognitive function, and dementia incidence among elderly women. *American Journal of Public Health, 98*(7), 1221–1227.

Crosato, K. E., Ward-Griffin, C., & Leipert, B. (2007). Aboriginal women caregivers of the elderly in geographically isolated communities. *Rural and Remote Health, 7*, 796.

Cross, D. S. (1983). The neglected majority: The changing role of women in nineteenth-century Montreal. In P. W. Ward (Ed.), The social development of Canada: Readings. Richmond, BC: Open Learning Institute.

Culos-Reed, S. N., Stephenson, L., Doyle-Baker, P. K., & Dickinson, J. A. (2008). Mall walking as a physical activity option: Results of a pilot project. *Canadian Journal on Aging, 27*(1), 81–87.

Cumming, E., & Henry, W. E. (1961). *Growing old: The process of disengagement*. New York: Basic Books.

Cutler, S. J., Hendricks, J., & O'Neill, G. (2011). Civic engagement and aging. In R. H. Binstock & L. K. George (Eds.), *Handbook of aging and the social sciences*, 7th ed. (pp. 221–233). London: Academic Press (Elsevier).

Czaja, S. J., & Lee, C. C. (2006). Human factors engineering. In R. Schulz, L. S. Noelker, K. Rockwood, & R. L. Sprott (Eds.), *The encyclopedia of aging*, 4th ed. (pp. 549–552). New York: Springer.

Dahlberg, L., & Lennartsson, C. (2015). Predictors of loneliness among older women and men in Sweden: A national longitudinal study. *Aging and Mental Health, 19*(5), 409–417.

Dandy, K., & Bollman, R. D. (Statistics Canada). (2008). Seniors in rural Canada. *Rural and Small Town Canada: Analysis Bulletin, 7*(8).

Darowski, E. S., & Hambrick, D. Z. (2008). Age-related differences in cognition: The role of distraction control. *Neuropsychology, 22*(5), 638–644.

Dastjerdi, M., & Mardukhi, A. (2015). Social factors affecting well-being and mental health of elderly Iranian immigrant women in Canada. In N. Khanlou & F. B. Pilkington (Eds.), *Women's Mental Health: Resistance and Resilience in Community and Society* (pp. 83–95). Switzerland: Springer International Publishing.

Davidson, K. (2008). Declining health and competence: Men facing choices about driving cessation. *Generations, 32*(1), 44–47.

Davies, N., & Duff, M. (2001). Breast cancer screening for older women with developmental disability living in community group homes. *Journal of Developmental Disability Research, 45*, 253–257.

Davies, S., & Denton, M. (2002). Economic well-being of older women who became divorced or separated in mid- or later life. *Canadian Journal on Aging, 21*(4), 477–493.

Death with Dignity Act Annual Report. (2014). Retrieved from https://public.health.oregon.gov/ProviderPartner Resources/EvaluationResearch/DeathwithDignityAct/ Documents/year17.pdf.

Decady, Y., & Greenberg, L. (2014). Ninety years of change in life expectancy. *Health at a Glance*. Statistics Canada. Minister of Industry. Retrieved from http://www.statcan. gc.ca/pub/82-624-x/2014001/article/14009-eng.pdf

De Castro, A. B., Gee, G. C., & Takeuchi, D. T. (2008). Workplace discrimination and health among Filipinos in the United States. *American Journal of Public Health, 98*(3), 520–526.

De Jong Gierveld, J., Van der Pas, S., & Keating, N. (2015). Loneliness of older immigrant groups in Canada: Effects of ethnic-cultural background. *Journal of Cross-Cultural Gerontology, 30*(3), 251–268.

De la Vega. R., & Zambrano, A. (2003). Topic interview: Professor Yaakov Stern, cognitive reserve [online]. *La Circun-valaci6n del hipocampo, September*. Retrieved from http:// www.hipocampo.org/entrevistas/ystern.asp.

Delisle, M. A. (1988). What does solitude mean to the aged? *Canadian Journal on Aging, 7*, 358–371.

Dennis, W. (1968). Creative productivity between the ages of 20 and 80 years. In B. L. Neugarten (Ed.), *Middle Age and Aging* (pp. 106–114). Chicago: University of Chicago Press.

Denton, F. T., Feaver, C. H., & Spencer, B. G. (1986). Prospective aging of the population and its implications for the labour force and government expenditures. *Canadian Journal on Aging, 5*, 75–98.

Denton, F. T., Feaver, C. H., & Spencer, B. G. (2010). Cohort working life tables for older Canadians. *Canadian Studies in Population, 37*(1–2), 175–206.

Denton, F. T., Finnie, R., & Spencer, B. G. (2011). *The age pattern of retirement: A comparison of cohort measures*. SEDAP Research Paper No. 283. Hamilton, ON: McMaster University.

Denton, F. T., & Spencer, B. G. (2003). Population change and economic growth: The long-term outlook. SEDAP Research Paper No. 12. Hamilton, ON: McMaster University.

Denton, F. T., & Spencer, B. G. (2009a). Chronic health conditions: Changing prevalence in an aging population and some implications for the delivery of health care services. *Canadian Journal on Aging, 29*(1), 11–21.

Denton, F. T., & Spencer, B. G. (2009b). What is retirement? A review and assessment of alternative concepts and measures. *Canadian Journal on Aging, 28*(1), 63–76.

Denton, F. T., & Spencer, B. G. (2010). Chronic health conditions: Changing prevalence in an aging population and some implications for the delivery of health care services. *Canadian Journal on Aging, 29*(1), 11–21.

Denton, M., & Boos, L. (2007). The gender wealth gap: Structural and material constraints and implications for later life. *Journal of Women and Aging, 19*(3/4), 105–120.

Denton, M., Kemp, C. L., French, S., Gafni, A. Joshi, A., Rosenthal, C. J., et al. (2004). Reflexive planning for later life. *Canadian Journal on Aging, 23*(Supplement1), S71-S82.

Denton, M., & Kusch, K. (2006). *Well-being throughout the senior years: An issues paper on key events and transitions in later life.* SEDAP Research Paper No. 165. Hamilton, ON: McMaster University.

Denton, M., & Plenderleith, J. (2010). *Employer pension plan inequality in Canada.* Research Institute for Quantitative Studies in Economics and Population. QSEP Research Report No. 438. Hamilton, ON: McMaster University. Retrieved from http://socserv.mcmaster.ca/qsep/p/qsep438.pdf.

Denton, M., Plenderleith, J., & Chowhan, J. (2010). *Retirement decisions of people with disabilities: Voluntary or involuntary.* SEDAP Research Paper No. 271. Hamilton, ON: McMaster University.

Derouesne, C., Guigot, J., Chermat, V., Winchester, N., & Lacomblez, L. (1996). Sexual behavioral changes in Alzheimer's disease. *Alzheimer's Disease and Associated Disorders, 10*, 86–92.

Deshpande, A., Khoja, S., McKibbon, A., & Jadad, A. R. (2008). *Real-time (synchronous) telehealth in primary care: Systematic review of systematic reviews.* Canadian Agency for Drugs and Technologies in Health. Ottawa: CADTH.

DeSpelder, L. A., & Strickland, A. L. (2011). *The last dance: Encountering death and dying,* 9th ed. New York: McGraw-Hill.

De Witt, L., Ploeg, J., & Black, M. (2009). Living on the threshold: The spatial experience of living alone with dementia. *Dementia, 8*(2), 263–291.

Diachun, L. L., Dumbrell, A. C., Byrne, K., & Esbaugh, J. (2006). . . . But does it stick? Evaluating the durability of improved knowledge following an undergraduate experiential geriatrics learning session. *Journal of the American Geriatrics Society, 54*(4), 696–670. Retrieved from http://www.sc.gc.ca/seniors-aines/nfa-cnv/pdf/aging_e.pdf.

Diamond, J. (2005, 2008). *A report on Alzheimer's disease and current research.* Toronto: Alzheimer Society of Canada. Retrieved from http://www.alzheimer.ca/docs/ASLayBookletEng%204.pdf.

Dillaway, H. E., & Byrnes, M. (2009). Reconsidering successful aging: A call for renewed and expanded academic critiques and conceptualizations. *Journal of Applied Gerontology, 28*, 702–722.

Dixon, R. A. (2000). Concepts and mechanisms of gains in cognitive aging. In D. C. Park & N. Schwarz (Eds.), *Cognitive aging: A primer* (pp. 33–41. Philadelphia: Taylor and Francis.

Dodge, D. A., Laurin, A., & Busby, C. (2010, March 18). *The piggy bank index: Matching Canadians' saving rates to their retirement dreams.* C. D. Howe Pension Papers.

Dogra, S., Al-Sahab, B., Manson, J., & Tamim, H. (2015). Aging expectations are associated with physical activity and health among older adults of low socioeconomic status. *Journal of Aging and Physical Activity, 23*, 180–186.

Dolbin-MacNab, M. L. (2006). "Just like raising your own?" Grandmothers' perception of parenting a second time around. *Family Relations, 55*, 564–575.

Dolbin-MacNab, M. L., & Keiley, M. K. (2009). Navigating interdependence: How adolescents raised solely by grandparents experience their family relationships. *Family Relations, 58*(April), 162–175.

Douglas, S. (2013). Ed Whitlock runs 3:41 marathon at age 82. *Runner's World, October 21.* Retrieved from http://www.runnersworld.com/newswire/ed-whitlock-runs-341-marathon-at-age-82

Doupe, M., Fransoo, R., Chateau, D., Dik, N., Burchill, C., Soodeen, R-A., Bozat-Emre, S., & Guenette, W. (2011). *Population aging and the continuum of older adult care in Manitoba.* University of Manitoba, Faculty of Medicine, Manitoba Centre for Health Policy. Retrieved from http://mchp-apps-erv.cpe.umanitoba.ca/reference/LOC_Report_WEB.pdf.

Doyle-Baker, P. K. (2007). Mall walking: A new strategy for physical activity among older adults. *WellSpring, 18*(1).

Draganski, B., Gaser, C., Busch, V., Schuierer, G., Bogdahn, U., & May, A. (2004, January 22). Changes in gray matter induced by training. *Nature, 427*, 311–312.

Draganski, B., Gaser, C., Kempermann, G., Kuhn, H. G., Winkler, J., Buchel, C., & May, A. (2006). Temporal and spatial dynamics of brain structure changes during extensive learning. *Journal of Neuroscience, 26*(23), 6314–6317.

Drolet, M., & Morissette, R. (2014). New facts on pension coverage in Canada. Statistics Canada. Minister of Industry. Retrieved from http://www.statcan.gc.ca/pub/75-006-x/2014001/article/14120-eng.pdf.

Drummond, M. (2008). Sport, aging men, and constructions of masculinity, *Generations, 32*(1), 32–35.

Duffy, S., Jackson, F., Schim, S., Ronis, D., & Fowler, K. (2006). Cultural concepts at the end of life. *Nursing Older People, 18*(8), 10–14.

Duncan, S., & Phillips, M. (2008). New families? Tradition and change in partnering and relationships. In A. Park, J. Curtice, K. Thomson, M. Phillips, M. Johnson, & E. Clery (Eds.), *British social attitudes: The 24th report.* London: Sage.

Dupuis, J., Weiss, D. R., & Wolfson, C. (2007). Gender and transportation access among community-dwelling seniors. *Canadian Journal on Aging, 26*(2), 149–158.

Dupuis, S. L. (2000). Institution-based caregiving as a container for leisure. *Leisure Sciences 22*(4), 259–280.

Dupuis, S. L., & Smale, B. (2005). The dementia supportive environment framework: Implications for recreation and leisure. Paper presented at the Eleventh Canadian Congress on Leisure Research, May 17–20, 2005, Nanaimo, BC. Retrieved from http://lin.ca/Uploads/cclr11/CCLR11-31.pdf.

Durst, D. (2010). Cultural diversity in long-term care: Confusion with cultural tensions. In D. Durst & M. MacLean (Eds.), *Diversity and aging among immigrant seniors in Canada: Changing faces and greying temples* (pp. 187–204). Calgary: Detselig.

Dwyer, A. (2015a). Forced out of a job at 52, Henry steers a new course. *The Globe and Mail,* February 23.

Dwyer, A. (2015b). Part-time work past 65: A necessary reality for Jim. *The Globe and Mail, February 2.*

Dykstra, P. A., & Hagestad, G. O. (2007). Roads less taken: Developing a nuanced view of older adults without children. *Journal of Family Issues, 28*(10), 1275–1310.

Ealey, T. (2014). Protect residents from financial abuse. *Long-Term Living,* September, 26–27.

Eckerdt, D. J., Addington, A., & Hayter, B. (2011). Distributing possessions: Personal property can become a social matter. *Generations, 35*(3), 34–40.

Eden Alternative. (2009). About the Eden Alternative. Retrieved from http://www.edenalt.org/about-the-eden-alternative.

Editors. (2011, July 28). If demographics is destiny, the future looks relaxing. *Maclean's.* Retrieved from http://www2.macleans.ca/2011/07/28/if-demographics-is-destiny-the-future-looks-relaxing/.

Edwards, N., Gallagher, E., & Lockett, D. (2003). Steady as you go (SAYGO): A falls-prevention program for seniors living in the community. *Canadian Journal on Aging, 22*(2), 207–216.

Edwards, P., & Mawani, A. (2006). *Healthy aging in Canada: A new vision, a vital investment from evidence to action.* A Discussion Brief prepared for the Healthy Aging and Wellness Working Group of the Federal/Provincial/Territorial (F/P/T) Committee of Officials (Seniors). Retrieved from http://www.phac-aspc.gc.ca/seniors-aines/publications/public/healthysante/vision/vision-bref/index-eng. php [November 15, 2010].

Edwards, S. B., Olson, K., Koop, P. M., & Northcott, H. C. (2012). Patient and family caregiver decision making in the context of advanced cancer. *Cancer Nursing,* May/June, 35(3), pp 178–186, doi: 10.1097/NCC.0b013e31822786f6.

Egan, M., Wells, J., Byrne, K., Jaglal, S., Stolee, P., Chesworth, B. M., & Hillier, L. M. (2009). The process of decision making in home-care case management: Implications for the introduction of universal assessment and information technology. *Health and Social Care, 17*(4), 371–378.

eHealth Ontario. (2013). Your health connection. Retrieved from http://www.ehealthontario.on.ca/en.

Eke, B. (2004). Intergenerational impact of the AIDS pandemic in Nigeria. *Journal of Intergenerational Relationships, 2*(3–4), 39–52.

Ekerdt, D. J. (1986). The busy ethic: Moral continuity between work and retirement. *The Gerontologist, 26*(3), 239–244.

Ekerdt, D. J., & Sergeant, J. F. (2006). Retirement. In R. Schulz, L. S. Noelker, K. Rockwood, & R. L. Sprott (Eds.), *The encyclopedia of aging,* 4th ed. (pp. 1032–1037). New York: Springer.

Elder, G. H., Jr., & Johnson, M. K. (2003). The life course and aging challenges, lessons, and new directions. In R. A. Settersten, Jr. (Ed.), *Invitation to the life course: Toward new understandings of later life,* 49–81. Amityville, NY: Baywood Publishing Company.

Elderhostel. (2007). *The learning in retirement movement.* Retrieved from http://www.elderhostel.org/ein/learning_na.asp.

Elderhostel. (2011). *2010 annual report.* Retrieved from http://www.roadscholar.org/support/EH_AnnualReport_Feb11_NoDonors.pdf.

Elliott, S., & D. Umberson. (2008). The performance of desire: Gender and sexual negotiation in long-term marriages. *Journal of Marriage and Family 70,* 391–406.

Ellison, L. F., & Wilkins, K. (2012). Canadian trends in cancer prevalence. *Health Reports, 23*(1), 7–16.

Employment and Social Development Canada. Government of Canada. (2013). Elder abuse modules. Retrieved from http://www.esdc.gc.ca/eng/seniors/funding/pancanadian/elder_abuse.shtml

Employment and Social Development Canada (ESDC). (2015a). Financial security—retirement income. Retrieved from http://well-being.esdc.gc.ca/misme-iowb/.3ndic.1t.4r@-eng.jsp?iid=27.

Employment and Social Development Canada. (2015b). *About the New Horizons for Seniors program.* Retrieved from http://www.esdc.gc.ca/eng/seniors/funding/about/index.shtml

Eng, S., (2015). Top 10 Dumb Things People Say About Pensions. Retrieved from http://join.carp.ca/pension-reform.

Ephron, N. (2006). I feel bad about my neck. New York: Knopf Publishing Group.

Ephron, N. (2010). *I remember nothing and other reflections.* New York: Alfred A. Knopf.

Epp, J. (1986). Achieving health for all: A framework for health promotion. Statistics Canada Cat. No. H-39-102/1986E. Ottawa: Minister of Supply and Services.

Erikson, E. H. (1963). *Childhood and society,* 2nd ed. New York: W. W. Norton.

Erikson, E. H. (1982). *The life cycle completed.* New York: W. W. Norton.

Erickson, K. I., Prakash, R. S., Voss, M. W., Chaddock, L., Hu, L., Morris, K. S., et al. (2009). Aerobic fitness is associated with hippocampal volume in elderly humans. *Hippocampus, 19*(10), 1030–1039.

Eskildsen, M. A. (2009). A multimodal aging and dying course for first-year medical students improves knowledge and attitudes. *Journal of the American Geriatrics Society, 57*(8), 1492–1497.

Esmail, N. (2011). Leaving Canada for medical care. *Fraser Forum*, March, 19–21.

Estes, C. L. (2001). Political economy of aging: A theoretical framework. In C. L. Estes (Ed.), *Social policy and aging: A critical perspective* (pp. 1–22). Thousand Oaks, CA: Sage Publications.

Estes, C. L. (2011). Crises and old age policy. In R. A. Settersten, Jr., & J. L. Angel (Eds.), *Handbook of sociology of aging.* (pp. 297–320). New York: Springer.

Estes, C. L., & Phillipson, C. (2007). Critical gerontology. In J. E. Birren (Ed.), *Encyclopedia of gerontology: Age, aging, and the aged,* 2nd ed. Vol. A–K (pp. 330–336). San Diego, CA: Academic Press.

Estrada, S. (2011). Prognostications about great gadgets. *Aging in Place Technology.* Retrieved from http://www.agein placetech.com/blog/prognostications-about-great-gadgets.

Etnier, J. L. (2009). Physical activity programming to promote cognitive function. Are we ready for prescription? In W. Chodzko-Zajko, A. F. Kramer, & L. W. Poon (Eds.). *Enhancing cognitive functioning and brain plasticity* (pp. 159–175). Champaign, IL: Human Kinetics.

Eurostat. (2014). Population structure and ageing. For current information, go to http://ec.europa.eu/eurostat/statistics-explained/index.php/Population_structure_and_ageing.

Evans, R. G., McGrail, K. M., Morgan, S. G., Barer, M. L., & Hertzman, C. (2001). Apocalypse no: Population aging and the future of health care systems. *Canadian Journal on Aging, 20*(Suppl. 1), 160–191.

Expert Panel on Older Workers. (2008). *Supporting and engaging older workers in the new economy.* Retrieved from http://www.hrsdc.gc.ca/eng/publications_resources/lmp/eow/2008/older_workers_2008.pdf.

Falkowski-Ham, A., Mun, P., Single, E., & Wiebe, J. (2005). *Gambling and problem gambling among older adults in Ontario.* Report. Responsible Gambling Council. Retrieved from http://www.gamblib.org/catalogue/article/gambling-and-problem-gambling-among-older-adults-i.

Fallah, N., Mitnitski, A., Middleton, L., & Rockwood, K. (2009). Modeling the impact of sex on how exercise is associated with cognitive changes and death in older Canadians. *Neuroepidemiology, 33,* 47–54.

Fall Prevention Clinic. (2011). *Action seniors!* Falls Prevention Clinic. Retrieved from http://fallclinic.com/research.

Farlex. (2011). Medical model. *The Free Dictionary.* Retrieved from http://medical-dictionary.thefreedictionary.com/medical+model.

Favaro, A. (2012). Tapping into technology helps seniors stay sharp. *CTV News. Health.* Retrieved from http://www.ctvnews.ca/health/health-headlines/tapping-into-technology-helps-seniors-stay-sharp-1.851670.

Federal, Provincial and Territorial Committee of Officials (Seniors). (2006). Healthy aging in Canada: A new vision, a vital investment. From evidence to action. A background paper. Retrieved February 26, 2017, from http://www.health.gov.bc.ca/library/publications/year/2006/Healthy_Aging_A_Vital_latest_copy_October_2006.pdf.

Federal/Provincial/Territorial Ministers Responsible for Seniors Forum. (2010). *What every older Canadian should know about frauds and scams.* Cat. No.: HS64-12/8-2010. Retrieved from http://dsp-psd.pwgsc.gc.ca/collections/collection_2010/rhdcc-hrsdc/HS64-12-8-2010-eng.pdf.

Federal/Provincial/Territorial Ministers Responsible for Seniors. (2012). Thinking about aging in place. Retrieved from http://www.seniors.gc.ca/eng/working/fptf/pdf/place.pdf.

Fekete, J. (2013). Canada Post's $6.5-billion shortfall just a fraction of more than $150 billion in unfunded federal pension liabilities. *National Post*, December 16. Retrieved from http://news.nationalpost.com/news/canada/canada-posts-6-5-billion-shortfall-just-a-fraction-of-more-than-150-billion-in-unfunded-federal-pension-liabilities.

Fernandes, N., & Spencer, B. G. (2010). The private cost of long-term care in Canada: Where you live matters. *Canadian Journal on Aging, 29*(3), 307–316.

Fernandez, A. (2010). *Transforming brain health with digital tools to assess, enhance and repair cognition across the lifespan: "State-of-the-market" report.* San Francisco, CA: SharpBrains.

Fernandez, A. (2011). The business and ethics of the brain fitness boom. *Generations, 35*(2), 63–69.

Ferrao, V. (2010). Paid work. *Women in Canada: A gender-based statistical report.* Statistics Canada Catalogue No.89-503-X. Ottawa: Minister of Industry.

Ferraro, K. F. (2006). Health and aging. In R. H. Binstock & L. K. George (Eds.), *Handbook of aging and the social sciences,* 6th ed. (pp. 238–256). Burlington, MA: Academic Press.

Ferrer, E., & Ghisletta, P. (2011). Methodological and analytical issues in the psychology of aging. In K. W. Schaie & S. L. Willis (Eds.), *Handbook of the psychology of aging,* 7th ed. (pp. 25–39). London: Academic Press (Elsevier)

Ferrucci, L., & Simonsick, E. M. (2006). A little exercise. *Journal of Gerontology Series A: Biological Sciences and Medical Sciences, 61,* 1154–1156.

Fiessel, W., Kulyk, M. R., Peel, B., Pfeifer, S., Robert, J-A., Statler, K. (2013). Aging in place: A Saskatchewan perspective. Retrieved from http://www.uregina.ca/cce/assets/docs/pdf/career-development/sihl/aging-place.pdf

Findsen, B. (2014). Learning in later life: Issues and educational responses. In C. J. Boden-McGill & K. P. King (Eds.), *Developing and sustaining adult learners*, pp.119–131. Charlotte, NC: Information Age Publishing.

Fingerman, K. L., Pitzer, L. M., Chan, W., Birditt, K., Franks, M. M., & Zarit, S. (2010). Who gets what and why? Help middle-aged adults provide to parents and grown children. *Journal of Gerontology: Social Sciences*, 66B(1), 87–98.

Finlayson, M., & Kaufert. J. (2002). Older women's community mobility: A qualitative exploration. *Canadian Journal on Aging, 21*(1), 75–84.

Finlayson, M., Lix, L., Finlayson, G. S., & Fong, T. (2005). Trends in the utilization of specific health care services among older Manitobans: 1985 to 2000. *Canadian Journal on Aging*, 24(Suppl.1), 15–27.

Finn, M., & McDonald, S. (2011). Computerised cognitive training for older persons with mild cognitive impairment: A pilot study using a randomised controlled trial design. *Brain Impairment*, 12(3), 187–199.

Fisher, L. L. (2010). Sex, romance, & relationships: AARP Survey of midlife and older adults. Washington, DC: AARP. Retrieved from http://assets.aarp.org/rgcenter/ general/srr_09.pdf.

Fishman, L. (2011). Foreword. *Topics in Geriatric Rehabilitation*, 27(2), 93.

Fletcher, S. K. (2007). Intergenerational dialogue to reduce prejudice: A conceptual model. *Journal of Intergenerational Relationships*, 5(1), 7–19.

Fontana, L., Colman, R. J., Hollaszy, J. O., & Weindruch, R. (2011). Calorie restriction in nonhuman and human primates. In E .J. Masoro & S. N. Austad (Eds.), *Handbook of the biology of aging*, 7th ed. (pp. 447–461). London: Elsevier (Academic Press).

Fontana, L., & Klein, S. (2007). Aging, adiposity, and calorie restriction review. PubMed PMid:173417. *Journal of the American Medical Association*, 297(9), 986–994.

Foot, D. K., & Stoffman, D. (1998). Boom, bust, and echo 2000: Profiting from the demographic shift in the new millennium. Toronto: Macfarlane Walter & Ross.

Fortier, I., Doiron, D., Wolfson, C., & Raina, P. (2012). Harmonizing data for collaborative research on aging: Why should we foster such an agenda? *Canadian Journal on Aging*, 31(1), 95–99.

Foundations Project. (1980). Foundations for gerontological education. *The Gerontologist, 20*, Part II.

Fraser, K., Archibald, M., & Nissen, C. (2014). Uncovering the meaning of home care using an arts-based and qualitative approach. *Canadian Journal on Aging*, 33(3), 246–258.

Fredriksen-Goldsen, K. I. & Muraco, A. (2010). Aging and sexual orientation: A 25-year review of the literature. *Research on Aging, 32*(3), 372–413.

Freedman, Marc. (2007). *Encore: Finding work that matters in the second half of life*. New York: PublicAffairs.

Freedman, V. A., Cornman, J. C., & Carr, D. (2014). Is spousal caregiving associated with enhanced well-being? New evidence from the panel study of income dynamics. *Journals of Gerontology, Series B: Psychological Sciences and Social Sciences, 69*(6), 861–869.

Freeman, A. (1994, April 21). CPP dips into surplus fund. *The Globe and Mail*, B1–2.

Freixas, A., Luque, B., & Reina, A. (2012). Critical feminist gerontology: In the back room of research. *Journal of Women & Aging, 24*, 44–58.

French, H. W. (2006, June 30). As China ages, a shortage of cheap labor looms. *The New York Times*. Retrieved from http://www.nytimes.com.

Freund, K., & Vine, J. (2010). Aging, mobility, and the Model T: Approaches to smart community transportation. *Generations*, 34(3), 76–81.

Fries, J. F. (1980). Aging, natural death, and the compression of morbidity. *New England Journal of Medicine, 303*, 130–36.

Fries, J. F. (2006). Compression of morbidity. In R. Schulz, L. S. Noelker, K. Rockwood, & R. L. Sprott (Eds.), *The encyclopedia of aging*, 4th ed. (pp. 257–259). New York: Springer.

Fries, J. F., & Crapo, L. M. (1981). *Vitality and aging.* San Francisco: W. H. Freeman.

Frum, D. (2012, April 28). David Frum on the Quebec student riots: Grandpa's free ride. *National Post*. Retrieved from http://fullcomment.nationalpost.com/2012/04/28/david-frum-on-the-quebec-student-riots-grandpas-free-ride.

Funderburk, B., Damron-Rodriguez, J. A. Storms, L. L., & Solomon, D. (2006). Endurance of undergraduate attitudes toward older adults. *Educational Gerontology*, 32(6), 447–462.

Furlotte, C., Schwartz, K., Koornstra, J. J., & Naster, R. (2012). 'Got a room for me?': Housing experiences of older adults living with HIV/AIDS in Ottawa. *Canadian Journal on Aging*, 31(1), 37–48.

Gagan, D. (1983a). Land, population, and social change: The 'critical years' in rural Canada West. In P. W. Ward (Ed.), *The social development of Canada: Readings*. Richmond, BC: Open Learning Institute.

Gagan, D. (1983b). Geographical and social mobility in nineteenth-century Ontario: A microstudy. In P. W. Ward (Ed.), *The social development of Canada: Readings*. Richmond, BC: Open Learning Institute.

Gagliardi, J. P. (2008). Differentiating among depression, delirium, and dementia in elderly patients. *American Medical Association Journal of Ethics*, 10(6), 383–388.

Galarneau, D., Turcotte, M., Carrière, Y., & Fecteau, E. (2015a). The local unemployment rate and permanent retirement. Statistics Canada. Catalogue No. 75-006-X. Ottawa: Minister of Industry.

Galarneau, D., Turcotte, M., Carrière, Y., & Fecteau, E. (2015b). Impact of the local unemployment rate on permanent retirement. Statistics Canada.

Gale, R. P., Gale, C. P., Roper, T. A., & Mulley, G. P. (2003). Depiction of elderly and disabled people on road traffic signs: International comparison. *British Medical Journal, 327,* 1456–1457.

Galenson, D. W. (2006). *Old masters and young geniuses: The two life cycles of artistic creativity.* Princeton: Princeton University Press.

Galinsky, A. M., & Waite, L. J. (2014). Sexual activity and psychological health as mediators of the relationship between physical health and marital quality. *Journal of Gerontology: Series B: Psychological Sciences and Social Sciences, 69*(3), 482–492.

Gallo, W. T., Bradley, E. H., Dubin, J. A., Jones, R. N., Falba, T. A., Teng, H.-M., & Kasl, S. V. (2006). The persistence of depressive symptoms in old workers who experience involuntary job loss: Results from the health and retirement survey. *Journal of Gerontology: Social Sciences, 61*(4), S221–S228.

Gandy, M., Westeyn, T., Brashear, H., & Starner, B. (2008). Wearable systems design issues for aging or disabled users. In A. S. Helal, M. Mokhtari, & B. Abdulrazak (Eds.), *The engineering handbook of smart technology for aging, disability, and independence* (pp. 317–338). Hoboken, NJ: Wiley.

Gans, D. (2009). The future of theories of aging. In V. L. Bengtson, M. Silverstein, M. M. Putney, & D. Gans (Eds.), *Handbook of theories of aging* (pp. 723–737). New York: Springer.

Garfinkel, H. (1967). *Studies in ethnomethodology.* Englewood Cliffs, NJ: Prentice-Hall.

Garity, J. (2006). Caring for a family member with Alzheimer's disease: Coping with caregiver burden postnursing home placement. *Journal of Gerontological Nursing, 32*(6), 39–48.

Garland, S. B. (2015). A safety net for childless seniors. *Kiplinger's Retirement Report, 22*(7), 2–5.

Garriguet, D. (2014). Bone health: Osteoporosis, calcium and vitamin D. *Health Reports, 22*(3), 7–14.

Garriguet, D., & Colley, R. C. 2012. Daily patterns of physical activity among Canadians. *Health Reports, 23*(2), 1–6.

Gatehouse, J. (2010, December 6). Generation war: What the boomers are leaving their children: Fewer jobs. Lower pay. Higher taxes. Bleaker futures. Now the screwed generation is starting to push back. *Maclean's, 123*(47), 54.

Gawande, A. (2010, August 2). Letting go. *The New Yorker,* 36–49.

Gaymu, J., Busque, M. A., Légaré, J., Décarie, Y., Vézina, S., & Keefe, J. (2010). What will the family composition of older persons be like tomorrow? A comparison of Canada and France. *Canadian Journal on Aging, 29*(1), 57–71.

Gazzaley, A., Cooney, J. W., Rissman, J., & D'Esposito, M. (2005). Top-down suppression deficit underlies working memory impairment in normal aging. *Nature Neuroscience, 8*(10), 1298–1300.

Geddes, J. (2010, April 12). The health care time bomb: Our aging population will make unthinkable reforms inevitable. *Maclean's.* Retrieved from http://www2.macleans.ca/2010/04/12/the-health-care-time-bomb.

Gee, E. M., & Gutman, G. M. (Eds.) (2000). The overselling of population aging: Apocalyptic demography, intergenerational challenges, and social policy. Don Mills, ON: Oxford University Press.

Gee, E. M., & McDaniel, S. A. (1993). Social policy for an aging society. *Journal of Canadian Studies, 28*(1), 139–153.

Gendell, M. (2008). Older workers: Increasing their labor force participation and hours of work. *Monthly Labor Review,* (January), *42.* Retrieved from www.bls.gov/opub/mlr/2008/01/art3full.pdf.

Genoe, M. R., & Singleton, J. F. (2006). Older men's leisure experiences across their lifespan. *Topics in Geriatric Rehabilitation 22*(4), 348–56.

George, L. K. (2006). Perceived quality of life. In R. H. Binstock & L. K. George (Eds.), *Handbook of aging and the social sciences,* 6th ed. (pp. 320–336). Burlington, MA: Academic Press.

George, L. K. (2011). Social factors, depression, and aging. In R. H. Binstock & L. K. George (Eds.), *Handbook of aging and the social sciences,* 7th ed. (pp. 149–162). London: Academic Press (Elsevier).

Gigliotti, C. M., & Jarrott, S. E. (2005). Effects of horticulture therapy on engagement and affect. *The Canadian Journal on Aging, 24*(4), 367–377.

Gilbart, E. E., & Hirdes, J. P. (2000). Stress, social engagement, & psychological well-being in institutional settings: Evidence based on the minimum data set 2.0. *Canadian Journal on Aging, 19*(Suppl. 2), 50–66.

Gilbert, C. N., & Ricketts, K. G. (2008). Children's attitudes toward older adults and aging: A synthesis of research. *Educational Gerontology, 34,* 570–586.

Gilleard, C., & Higgs, P. (2000). *Cultures of ageing: Self, citizen, and the body.* London, UK: Pearson Education.

Gilleard, C., & Higgs, P. (2010). Aging without agency: Theorizing the fourth age. *Aging & Mental Health, 14*(2), 121–128.

Gilleard, C., & Higgs, P. (2011). Ageing abjection and embodiment in the fourth age. *Journal of Aging Studies, 25*(2), 135–142.

Gilligan M., Suitor, J. J., Feld, S., & Pillemer, K. (2015). Do positive feelings hurt? Disaggregating positive and negative components of intergenerational ambivalence. *Journal of Marriage and the Family, 77*(1), 261–276.

Gillis, C. (2015). The inheritance wars. *Macleans* (March 9). Retrieved from http://www.macleans.ca/society/life/the-inheritance-wars.

Gilmour, H. (2007). Physically active Canadians. *Health Reports, 18*(3), (August), 45. Statistics Canada Cat. No. 82-003. Retrieved from http://www.statcan.gc.ca/pub/82- 003-x/2006008/article/phys/10307-eng.pdf.

Gilmour, H. (2011). Cognitive performance of Canadian seniors. *Health Reports, 22*(2), 1–5.

Gilmour, H. (2015). Chronic pain, activity restriction and flourishing mental health. *Health Reports, 26*(1), 15–22.

Gilmour, H., & Park, J. (2006). Dependency, chronic conditions and pain in seniors. *Supplement to Health Reports, 16*: 21–31. Statistics Canada Cat. No. 82–003.

Gilmour, J. (2014). Positive mental health and mental illness. *Health Reports, 25*(9), 3–9. Retrieved from http://www.statcan.gc.ca/pub/82-003-x/2014009/article/14086-eng.pdf.

Gladstone, J. W. (1989). Grandmother–grandchild contact: The mediating influence of the middle generation following marriage breakdown and remarriage. *Canadian Journal on Aging, 8*: 355–365.

Gladstone, J. W. (1995). The marital perceptions of elderly persons living or having a spouse living in a long-term care institution in Canada. *The Gerontologist 35*(1), 52–60.

Global AgeWatch. (2014). Global rankings table. Retrieved from: http://www.helpage.org/global-agewatch/population-ageing-data/global-rankings-table/

Globe and Mail [The]. (2014). Campaign aims to advance bold, national lung health strategy. Retrieved from http://www.theglobeandmail.com/partners/philanthropy1114/campaign-aims-to-advance-bold-national-lung-health-strategy/article21539783.

Gonyea, J. G. (2009). Multigenerational bonds, family support, and baby boomers: Current challenges and future prospects for eldercare. In R. B. Hudson (Ed.), *Boomer Bust? Economic and political issues of the graying society. The boomers and their future*, Vol. 2. (pp. 213–232).

Gougeon, P. (2009). Shifting pensions. *Perspectives*, May, 16–23. Statistics Canada Cat. No. 75-001-X.

Gould, O. N., MacLennan, A., & Dupuis-Blanchard, S. (2012). Career preferences of nursing students. *Canadian Journal on Aging, 31*(4), 471–482.

Government of Alberta. (2011). New technologies bring more independence to seniors. Alberta Health Services. Retrieved from http://alberta.ca/home/NewsFrame.cfm?ReleaseID=/acn/201102/29884107B7B2F-04CE-2F97-D410400C4690A575.html.

Government of British Columbia. (2012). Property tax deferment. Retrieved from http://www.sbr.gov.bc.ca/individuals/property_taxes/property_tax_deferment/about.htm.

Government of Canada. (2008) The latest for seniors. Changes to seniors' benefits, 2008. Retrieved May 7, 2009, from http://www.seniors.gc.ca/content.jsp?lang=enandauxPageID=142#3.

Government of Canada. (2011). Seniors as victims of crime in Canada. National Victims of Crime Awareness Week. Retrieved from http://www.victimsweek.gc.ca/res/r54.html.

Government of Canada. (2012). Protecting Canada's Seniors Act. *Justice Laws Website.* Retrieved from http://laws-lois.justice.gc.ca/eng/annualstatutes/2012_29/page-1.html#h-2.

Government of Canada. (2014a). *Action for seniors.* Retrieved from http://www.aines.gc.ca/eng/report/pdf/action_report_for_seniors.pdf.

Government of Canada. (2014b). Harper government introduces the Digital Privacy Act, which will provide added protection for seniors against financial abuse. Employment and Social Development Canada. Retrieved from http://news.gc.ca/web/article-en.do?nid=836829.

Government of Canada. (2015). Tax-Free Savings Account Statistics, 2015 Edition (2013 tax year). Retrieved March 4, 2017, from http://open.canada.ca/data/en/dataset/be1860c7-06a1-450d-af15-21c1669b2bc6.

Government of Canada. (2016). Medical assistance in dying. http://www.healthycanadians.gc.ca/health-system-systeme-sante/services/end-life-care-soins-fin-vie/medical-assistance-dying-aide-medicale-mourir-eng.php. Accessed December 22, 2016.

Grant, H., & Townsend, J. (2010). The incidence of poverty among Canada's elderly immigrants. In D. Durst & M. MacLean (Eds.), *Diversity and Aging among Immigrant Seniors in Canada: Changing Faces and Greying Temples.* Calgary: Detselig.

Gravagne, P. H. (2013) *The becoming of age: Cinematic visions of mind, body and identity in later life.* Jefferson, NC: McFarland.

Greer, E., & Brunet, A. (2011). The genetic network of life-span extension by dietary restriction. In E. J. Masoro & S. N. Austad (Eds.), *Handbook of the biology of aging*, 7th ed. (pp. 3–23). London: Elsevier (Academic Press).

Griffith, L., Raina, P., Wu, H., Zhu, B., & Stathokostas, L. (2010). Population attributable risk for functional disability associated with chronic conditions in Canadian older adults. *Age and Ageing, 39*(6), 738–774. Retrieved from http://ageing.oxfordjournals.org/content/39/6/738.full. pdf+html.

Grignon, M., Spencer, B. G., & Wang, L. (2010). Is there an age pattern in the treatment of AMI? Evidence from Ontario. SEDAP Research Paper No. 278. Hamilton, ON: McMaster University.

Gross, D. (2006). The big freeze. *AARP Bulletin*, March.

Grossman, I., Na, J., Varnum, M. E. W., Park, D. C., Kitayama, S., & Nisbett, R. E. (2010). Reasoning about social conflicts improves into old age. *Proceedings of the National Academy of Sciences*. Retrieved from http://www.pnas.org/content/early/2010/03/23/1001715107 and http://www.pnas.org/content/suppl/2010/03/24/1001715107.DCSupplemental/pnas.201001715SI.pdf.

Guillemard, A. M. (2006). What age for employment? The need for a new social organization of the working age. In L. O. Stone (Ed.), *New frontiers of research on retirement* (pp. 49–64). Statistics Canada Cat. No. 75-511-XIE. Ottawa: Minister of Industry.

Gullette, M. M. (2007). What exactly has age got to do with it? My life in critical age studies. *Journal of Aging Studies*, *22*(2), 189–195.

Gustafson, K., & Baofeng, H. (2014). Elderly care and the one-child policy: Concerns, expectations and preparations for elderly life in a rural Chinese township. *Journal of Cross Cultural Gerontolgy*, *29*, 25–36.

Guttman, M. (2008). The aging brain. Retrieved from http://www.usc.edu/hsc/info/pr/hmm/01spring/brain.html.

Ha, J. (2008). Changes in support from confidants, children, and friends following widowhood. *Journal of Marriage and Family*, *70*(2), 306–318.

Haan, M., & Perks, T. (2008). The housing careers of older Canadians: An investigation using cycle 16 of the *General Social Survey*. *Canadian Studies in Population*, *35*(2), 223–242.

Haber, D. (2010). *Health promotion and aging: Practical applications for health professionals*, 5th ed. New York: Springer.

Habjan, S., Prince, H., & Kelley, M. L. (2012). Caregiving for elders in First Nations communities: Social system perspective on barriers and challenges. *Canadian Journal on Aging*, *31*(2), 209–222.

Haines, V. A., & Henderson, L. J. (2002). Targeting social support: A network assessment of the convoy model of social support. *Canadian Journal on Aging*, *21*(2), 243–256.

Hakamies-Blomqvist, L. (2004). Safety of older persons in traffic. In *Transportation in an aging society: A decade of experience*. Washington, DC: National Academy of Sciences, Transportation Research Board.

Hall, M., Lasby, D., Gumulka, G., & Tryon, C. (2006). *Caring Canadians, involved Canadians: Highlights from the 2004 Canada Survey of Giving, Volunteering and Participating.* Statistics Canada. Ottawa: Minister of Industry.

Hamilton, K., & Brehaut, T. (1992). Older women: A study of the housing and support service needs of older "single" women. A Report for the Canada Mortgage and Housing Corporation. Charlottetown: Renaissance Communications.

Hampton, M., Baydala, A., Bourassa, C., McKay-McNabb, K., Placsko, C., Goodwill, K, et al., (2010). Completing the circle: Elders speak about end-of-life care with Aboriginal families in Canada. *Journal of Palliative Care, 26*(1), 6–14.

Hansard. (1983). Canada, House of Commons Debates. December 9.

Hardy, M. (2006). Older workers. In J. E. Birren & K. W. Schaie (Eds.), *Handbook of the psychology of aging*, 6th ed. (pp. 201–218). Burlington, MA: Elsevier Academic Press.

Harlton, S. V., Keating, N., & Fast, J. (1998). Defining eldercare for policy and practice: Perspectives matter. *Family Relations, 47*(3), 281–288.

Harris, S. H., Adams, M. S., Zubatsky M, & White, M, (2011). A caregiver perspective of how Alzheimer's disease and related disorders affect couple intimacy. *Aging & Mental Health, 15*(8), 950–960.

Hart, C. L., & Watt, G. C. M. (2015). Occupational class differences in later life hospital use by women who survived to age 80: The Renfrew and Paisley prospective cohort study. *Age and Ageing, 44*(3), 515–519.

Hartley, A. (2006). Changing role of the speed of processing construct in the cognitive psychology of human aging. In J. E. Birren & K. W. Schaie (Eds.), *Handbook of the psychology of aging*, 6th ed. (pp. 183–207). Burlington, MA: Elsevier Academic Press.

Haslam, K. (2015). Poly and aging. *Polyamory in the News! . . . by Alan*. Retrieved from http://polyinthemedia.blogspot.com/2015/04/poly-and-aging.html.

Health Canada. (2001). Canada's seniors. No. 1: A growing population. Retrieved from http://www.hc-sc.gc.ca/seniors-aines/pubs/factoids/2001/ no01_e.htm.

Health Canada. (2006). Obesity. *It's your health*. Minister of Health Cat. No. H13-7/20-2006E-PDF. Retrieved from http://www.healthcanada.gc.ca/iyh

Health Canada. (2010). *Canada Health Act—Annual report 2009–2010*. Ottawa: Minister of Health. Retrieved from http://www.hc-sc.gc.ca/hcs-sss/pubs/cha-lcs/2010-cha-lcs-ar-ra/index-eng.php.

Health Council of Canada. (2011). *Progress report 2011: Health care renewal in Canada*. Toronto: Health Council of Canada.

Hebert, B.-P., & Luong, M. (2008). Bridge employment. *Perspectives on Labour and Income*, November, 5–12.

Helman, R., Copeland, C., & VanDerhei, J. (2010). *The 2010 retirement confidence survey: Confidence stabilizing, but preparations continue to erode*. Employee Benefit Research Institute, Issue Brief, No. 340. Washington, DC: Employment Benefit Research Institute.

Helpguide.org. (2007). *Continuing care retirement communities (CCRCs)*, www.helpguide.org/elder/continuing_care_retirement_communities.htm.

Henneberg, S. (2010). Moms do badly, but grandmas do worse: The nexus of sexism and ageism in children's classics. *Journal of Aging Studies, 24*(2), 125–134.

Henneberger, M. (2008, June 10). An affair to remember. *Slate*. Retrieved from http://www.slate.com/articles/life/family/2008/06/an_affair_to_remember.html.

Henripin, J. (1972). *Trends and factors of fertility in Canada*. Ottawa: Statistics Canada (Dominion Bureau of Statistics).

Henripin, J. (2009). Aging and the necessity of a radical reform of the Canadian pension system. *Canadian Studies in Population, 36*(1–2), 17–36.

Henripin, J., & Y. Peron. (1972). The demographic transition of the province of Quebec. In D. Glass & R. Revelle (Eds.), *Population and social change* (pp. 213–231). London: Edward Arnold.

Henry, R. G., Miller, R. B., & Giarrusso, R. (2005). Difficulties, disagreements, and disappointments in late-life marriages. *International Journal of Aging and Human Development, 61*(3), 243–264.

Hequembourg, A., & Brallier, S. (2005). Gendered stories of parental caregiving among siblings. *Journal of Aging Studies, 19*: 53–71.

Herd, P. (2009). The two-legged stool: The reconfiguration of risk in retirement income security [Part of a special issue: The Great Recession: Implications for an aging America]. *Generations, 33* (3), 12–18.

Hering, M., & Klassen, T. R. (2010). *Strengthening fairness and funding in the Canada Pension Plan: Is raising the retirement age an option?* SEDAP Research Paper 263. Hamilton, ON: McMaster University.

Hess, B. B. (1990). Gender and Aging: The Demographic Parameters. *Generations, 14*(3), 12–15.

Hess, T. M. (1990). Aging and cognition: Knowledge organization and utilization. Amsterdam: North-Holland.

Hess, T. M. (2006). Attitudes toward aging and their effects on behavior. In J. E. Birren & K. W. Schaie (Eds.), *Handbook of the psychology of aging*, 6th ed. (pp. 379–406). Burlington, MA: Elsevier Academic Press.

Hicks, P. (2011). *The surprisingly large policy implications of changing retirement durations*. SEDAP Research Paper No. 284. Hamilton, ON: McMaster University.

Higgs, P., & McGowan, F. (2013). Aging, embodiment and the negotiation of the Third and Fourth Ages. In A. Kampf, B. L. Marshall, & A. Petersen (Eds.), *Aging Men, Masculinities and Modern Medicine* (pp. 21–34). New York: Routledge

Hirst, S. P., Lane, A., & Seneviratne, C. (2013). Growing old with a developmental disability. *Indian Journal of Gerontology, 27*(1), 38–54.

Hodgson, G. (2012, July 11). Aging workforce an economic tsunami-in-waiting. *The Vancouver Sun*, A.11.

Hogan, C. L., Mata, J., & Carstensen, L. L. (2013). Exercise holds immediate benefits for affect and cognition in younger and older adults. *Psychology and Aging, 28*(2), 587–594.

Hollander, M., & Chappell, N. L. (2007). A comparative analysis of costs to government for home care and long-term residential care services, standardized for client care needs. *Canadian Journal on Aging, 26* (Suppl 1), 149–161.

Hollis-Sawyer, L. & Cuevas, L. (2013) Mirror, mirror on the wall: Ageist and sexist double jeopardy portrayals in children's picture books. *Educational Gerontology, 39*(12), 902–914.

Holroyd, A., Dahlke, S., Fehr, C., Jung, P., & Hunter, A. (2009). Attitudes toward aging: Implications for a caring profession. *Journal of Nursing Education, 48*(7), 374–380.

Holstein, J. A., & Gubrium, J. F. (Eds.) (2008). *Handbook of constructionist research*. Guilford, NY: Guilford Press.

Holt, J. (1978). *Never too late: My musical life story*. New York: Delacorte Press.

Homans, G. C. (1961). *Social behaviour: Its elementary forms*. New York: Harcourt Brace Jovanovich.

Horn, J. L., &. Cattell, R. B. (1966). Age differences in primary mental ability factors. *Journal of Gerontology, 21*(2), 210–220.

Horn, J. L., & Cattell, R. B. (1967). Age differences in fluid and crystallized intelligence. *Acta Psychologica, 26*(2), 107–129.

Horton, S., Baker, J., & Deakin, J. M. (2007). Stereotypes of aging: Their effects on the health of seniors in North American society. *Educational Gerontology, 33*, 1021–1035.

Hosler, I. (2007). Stepping out: Mall walking and older adults. *WellSpring, 18*(1).

Hossen, A. (2012). Social isolation and loneliness among elderly immigrants: The case of South Asian elderly living in Canada. *Journal of International Social Issues, 1*(1), 1–10.

Hou, F. (2010). *Homeownership over the life course of Canadians: Evidence from Canadian censuses of population*. Statistics Canada. Economic Analysis (EA) Research Paper Series. Ottawa: Minister of Industry.

Howarth, G. (2007). *Death and dying: A sociological introduction*. Cambridge, UK: Polity Press.

Hoyer, W. J., & Verhaeghen, P. (2006). Memory Aging. In J. E. Birren & K. W. Schaie (Eds.), *Handbook of the psychology of aging*, 6th ed. (pp. 209–232). Burlington, MA: Elsevier Academic Press.

HSBC Insurance Holdings, Ltd. (2006). *The future of retirement in a world of rising life expectancies*. Retrieved from http://www.hsbc.com/1/PA_1_1_S5/content/assets/retirement/hsbc_future_of_retirement.pdf.

Huang, Y. (2013). Population aging in China: A mixed blessing. *The Diplomat*. Retrieved from http://thediplomat.com/2013/11/population-aging-in-china-a-mixed-blessing.

Human Resources and Skills Development Canada. (2013). "Approved Funding Projects: New Horizons for Seniors." Retrieved from http://www.hrsdc.gc.ca/eng/seniors/funding/approved/index.shtml.

Humble, A. M. (2013). Moving from ambivalence to certainty: Older same-sex couples marry in Canada. *Canadian Journal on Aging, 32*(2), 131–144.

Hummert, M. L. (2011). Age stereotypes and aging. In K. W. Schaie & S. L. Willis (Eds.), *Handbook of the psychology of aging*, 7th ed. (pp. 249–262). London: Academic Press (Elsevier).

Hummert, M. L., Garstka, T. A., & Shaner, J. L. (1997). Stereotyping of older adults: The role of target facial cues and perceiver characteristics. *Psychology and Aging, 12*, 107–114.

Hunter-Zaworski, K. M. (2008). Accessible public transportation services in America. In A. S. Helal, M. Mokhtari, & B. Abdulrazak (Eds.), *The engineering handbook of smart technology for aging, disability, and independence* (pp. 519–534). Hoboken, NJ: Wiley.

Hurd Clarke, L. (2006). Older women and sexuality: Experiences in marital relationships across the life course. *Canadian Journal on Aging, 25*(2), 129–140.

Hurd Clarke, L., & Griffin, M. (2007). The body natural and the body unnatural: Beauty work and aging. *Journal of Aging Studies, 21*(3), 187–201.

Hurd Clarke, L., & Griffin, M. (2008). Visible and invisible aging: Beauty work as a response to ageism. *Ageing and Society, 28*: 653–674.

Hurd Clarke, L., & Korotchenko, A. (2011). Aging and the body: A review. *Canadian Journal on Aging, 30* (3), 495–510.

Hwang, E. (2008). Exploring aging-in-place among Chinese and Korean seniors in British Columbia, Canada. *Ageing International, 32*: 205–218.

Hyde, Z., Flicker, L., Hankey, G. J., Almeida, O. P., McCaul, K. A., Chubb., S. A. P., & Yeap, B. B. (2010). Prevalence of sexual activity and associated factors in men aged 75 to 95 years: A cohort study. *Annals of Internal Medicine, 153*(11), 693–702.

Idler, E.. (2006). Religion and aging. In R. H. Binstock & L. K. George (Eds.), *Handbook of aging and the social sciences*, 6th ed. (pp. 277–300). Burlington, MA: Academic Press.

Ifedi, F. (2008). *Sport participation in Canada, 2005. Culture, Tourism and the Centre for Education Statistics Research papers*. Ottawa: Ministry of Industry. Retrieved from http://www.statcan.gc.ca/pub/81-595-m/81-595-m2008060-eng.pdf.

International Longevity Center. (2006). *Ageism in America*. New York: Author. Retrieved from http://www.ilcusa.org/media/pdfs/Ageism%20in%20America%20-%20The%20ILC%20Report.pdf.

Iracleous, P., Nie, J. X., Tracy, C. S., Moineddin, R., Ismail, Z., Shulman, K. I., & Upshur, R. E. G. (2010). Primary care physicians' attitudes toward cognitive screening: Findings from a national postal survey. *International Journal of Geriatric Psychiatry, 25*: 23–29.

Jafari, S., Mathias, R., & Baharlou, S. (2010). Socio-cultural determinants of mental health among elderly Iranian immigrants. In D. Durst & M. MacLean (Eds.), *Diversity and aging among immigrant seniors in Canada: Changing faces and greying temples* (pp. 285–300). Calgary: Detselig.

Janicki, M. P., Dalton, A. J., McCallion, P., Baxley, D. D., & Zendell, A. (2005). Group home care for adults with intellectual disabilities and Alzheimer's disease. *Dementia, 4*(3), 361–385.

Jenkyn, K. B., Hoch, J. S., & Speechley, M. (2012). How much are we willing to pay to prevent a fall? Cost-effectiveness of a multifactorial falls prevention program for community-dwelling older adults. *Canadian Journal on Aging, 31*(2), 121–137.

Jette, S., & Vertinsky, P. (2011). "Exercise is medicine": Understanding the exercise beliefs and practices of older Chinese women immigrants in British Columbia, Canada. *Journal of Aging Studies, 25*, 272–284.

Jewell, A. (2010). The importance of purpose in life in an older British methodist sample: Pastoral implications. *Journal of Religion, Spirituality and Aging, 22*(3), 138–161.

Jiang, S., Armstrong, P., & Cullinane, S. (2015). China unveils two-child policy. CNN, Retrieved from http://www.cnn.com/2015/12/27/asia/china-two-child-policy.

Joanette, Y., Gutman, G., McElhaney, J., Upshur, R., & Muscedere, J. (2014). Exploring the many facets of research in late-life issues. *Canadian Journal on Aging, 33*(2), 220–225.

Johansson, A., Ruzin, H. O., Graneheim, U. H., & Lindgren, B-M. (2014). Remaining connected despite separation—Former family caregivers' experiences of aspects that facilitate and hinder the process of relinquishing the care of a person with dementia to a nursing home. *Aging and Mental Health, 18*(8), 1029–1036.

Johnson, G. (2015a, February 28). On the job past 70—for Sharon it's the 'new normal.' *The Globe and Mail.*

Johnson, G. (2015b, February 11). Retiree Janet follows her passion—back to working with kids. *The Globe and Mail.*

Johnson, M. L. (2009). Spirituality, finitude, and theories of the life span. In V. L. Bengtson, M. Silverstein, M. M. Putney, & D. Gans (Eds.), *Handbook of theories of aging.* (pp. 659–674). New York: Springer.

Johnson, T. (2006, December 13). China fears aging population will strain benefits system. *San Jose Mercury News*, 20A.

Jones, J., & Pugh, S. (2005). Ageing gay men: Lessons from the sociology of embodiment. *Men and Masculinities, 7*(3), 248–260.

Jones, S., & Fox, S. (2009). *Generations online in 2009*. Retrieved from www.pewinternet.org/Reports/2009/Generations-Online-in-2009.aspx.

Julien, D., Gauvin, L., Richard, L., Kestens, Y., and Payette, H. (2013). The role of social participation and walking in depression among older adults: Results from the VoisiNuAge study. *Canadian Journal on Aging, 32*(1), 1–12.

Kadar, K. S., Francis, K., & Sellick, K. (2013). *Ageing in Indonesia—Health status and challenges for the future. Ageing International, 38*, 261–270.

Kaida, L., & Boyd, M. (2011). Poverty variations among the elderly: The roles of income security policies and family co-residence. *Canadian Journal on Aging, 30*(1), 83–100.

Kaida, L., Moyser, M., Park, S. Y. (2009). Cultural preferences and economic constraints: The living arrangements of elderly Canadians. *Canadian Journal on Aging, 28*(4), 303–313.

Kail, B. L., Quadagno, J., & Keene, J. R. (2009). The political economy perspective of aging. In V. L. Bengtson, M. Silverstein, M. M. Putney, & D. Gans (Eds.), *Handbook of theories of aging* (pp. 555–571). New York: Springer.

Kalbach, W. E., & McVey, W. W. (1979). *The demographic bases of Canadian society*, 2nd ed. Toronto: McGraw-Hill Ryerson.

Kang, S. K., & Chasteen, A. L. (2009). The moderating role of age-group identification and perceived threat on stereotype threat among older adults. *International Journal of Aging and Human Development, 69*(3), 201–220.

Kaplan, M. S., & Ross, N. (2008). Prevalence and factors associated with thriving in older adulthood: A 10-year population-based study. *Journals of Gerontology: Series A: Biological Sciences and Medical Sciences, 63*(10), 1097–1104.

Karasik. R. J. (2012). Engaged teaching for engaged learning: Sharing your passion for gerontology and geriatrics, *Gerontology & Geriatrics Education, 33*(2), 119–132.

Karmarkar, A., Chavez, E., & Cooper, R. A. (2008). Technology for successful aging and disabilities. In A. S. Helal, M. Mokhtari, & B. Abdulrazak (Eds.), *The engineering handbook of smart technology for aging, disability, and independence* (pp. 29–48). Hoboken, NJ: Wiley.

Kastenbaum, R. J. (2012). *Death, Society, and Human Experience.* 11th ed. Boston: Pearson.

Katz, S. (2008). Thinking of age: Personal reflections on critical gerontology. *Journal of Aging Studies, 22*(2), 140–146.

Katz, S., & Peters, K. R. (2015). Interview with Dr. Peter Whitehouse, 23 July 2012. *Dementia, 14*(3), 370–382.

Katzmarzyk, P. T., Church, T. S., Craig, C. L., & Bouchard, C. (2009). Sitting time and mortality from all causes, cardiovascular disease, and cancer. *Medicine & Science in Sports & Exercise, 41*(5), 998–1005. Retrieved from http://www.ncbi. nlm.nih.gov/pubmed/19346988?ordinalpos=2&itool= EntrezSystem2.PEntrez.Pubmed.Pubmed_ResultsPanel. Pubmed_DefaultReportPanel.Pubmed_RVDocSum.

Keating, N., Swindle, J., & Fletcher, S. (2011). Aging in rural Canada: A retrospective review. *Canadian Journal on Aging, 30*(3), 323–338.

Keefe, J. (2011). *Supporting caregivers and caregiving in an aging Canada.* IRPP Study No. 23. Retrieved from http://www. irpp.org/pubs/irppstudy/irpp_study_no23.pdf. Original Source: Statistics Canada, *General Social Survey,* 2007.

Keefe, J., Légaré, J., & Carrière, Y. (2007). Developing new strategies to support future caregivers of the aged in Canada:

Projections of need and their policy implications. *Canadian Public Policy, 33*(suppl.), S66–S80.

Keefe, J., & Rajnovich, B. (2007). To pay or not to pay: Examining underlying principles in the debate on financial support for family caregivers. *Canadian Journal on Aging, 26*(supplement 1), 77–90.

Kemp, C. L. (2003). The social and demographic contours of contemporary grandparenthood: Mapping patterns in Canada and the United States. *Journal of Comparative Family Studies, 34*(2), 187–212.

Kemp, C. L. (2005). Dimensions of grandparent–adult grandchild relationships: From family ties to intergenerational friendships. *Canadian Journal on Aging, 24*(2), 161–178.

Kemp, C. L. (2008). Negotiating transitions in later life: Married couples in assisted living. *Journal of Applied Gerontology, 27*(3), 231–251.

Kennedy, J. (2012, May 26). Don't call me "dear." *The Ottawa Citizen,* B.6.

Kenyon, G. M., Bohlmeijer, E., & Randall, W. (Eds.). (2010). *Storying later life: Issues, investigations, and interventions in narrative gerontology.* New York: Oxford University Press.

Khan, S. A. (2009). The geriatric day hospital: Past, present and future. *Age and Ageing, 38*(3), 354–355.

Kim, A. H. (2010). Filial piety, financial independence, and freedom: Explaining the living arrangements of older Korean immigrants. In D. Durst & M. MacLean (Eds.), *Diversity and aging among immigrant seniors in Canada: Changing faces and greying temples* (pp. 387–408). Calgary: Detselig.

Kim, J., Ingersoll-Dayton, B., & Kwak, M. (2013). Balancing eldercare and employment: The role of work interruptions and supportive employers. *Journal of Applied Gerontology, 32,* 347–369.

Kim, K., Zarit, S. H., Eggebeen, D. J., Birditt, K. S., & Fingerman, K. L. (2011). Discrepancies in reports of support exchanges between aging parents and their middle-aged children. *Journals of Gerontology, Series B: Psychological Sciences and Social Sciences, 66*(5), 527–537.

Kim, W., & Chen, Y. (2011). The social determinants of depression in elderly Korean immigrants in Canada: Does acculturation matter? *International Journal of Aging and Human Development, 73*(4), 283–298.

Kim, W., Kang, S., and Kim, I. (2015). Depression among Korean immigrant elders living in Canada and the United States: A comparative study. *Journal of Gerontological Social Work, 58*(1), 86–103.

Kinsella, Kevin and David R. Phillips (2005). Global ageing: The challenge of success. *Population Bulletin,* Vol. 60, No. 1. Washington, D. C.: Population Reference Bureau.

Kirby, S., & Hegarty, J. (2010). Breast awareness within a developmental setting. *European Journal of Oncology Nursing, 14,* 328–336.

Knight, B. G., Kaskie, B., Shurgot, G. R., & Dave, J. (2006). Improving the mental health of older adults. In J. E. Birren & K.W Schaie (Eds.), *Handbook of the psychology of aging*, 6th ed. (pp. 407–424). Burlington, MA: Elsevier Academic Press.

Knight, B. G., & Laidlaw, K. (2009). Transitional theory: A wisdom-based model for psychological interventions to enhance well-being in later life. In V. L. Bengtson, M. Silverstein, M. M. Putney, & D. Gans. (Eds.). *Handbook of theories of aging* (pp. 693–703). New York: Springer.

Kobayashi, K. M. (2000). *The nature of support from adult sansei (third generation) children to older nisei (second generation) parents in Japanese Canadian families*. SEDAP Research Paper No. 18. Hamilton, ON: McMaster University.

Kobayashi, K. M., & Funk, L. (2010). Of the family tree: Congruence on filial obligation between older parents and adult children in Japanese Canadian families. *Canadian Journal on Aging, 29*(1), 85–96.

Kobayashi, K. M., & Prus, S. G. (2010). *Examining the gender, ethnicity, and age dimensions of the healthy immigrant effect: Implications for health care policy*. SEDAP Research Paper No. 274. Hamilton, ON: McMaster University.

Konnert, C., Dobson, K., & Stelmach, L. (2009). The prevention of depression in nursing home residents: A randomized clinical trial of cognitive-behavioral therapy. *Aging & Mental Health, 13*(2), 288–299.

Kontos, P. C. (2010). Embodied selfhood: Ethnographic reflections, performing ethnography, & humanizing dementia care. In J. E. Graham & P. H. Stephenson (Eds.), *Contesting aging and loss* (pp. 125–152). Toronto: University of Toronto Press.

Koppen, J. (2010). *Social media and technology use among adults 50+*. Washington, DC: AARP.

Koppen, J., & Anderson, G. (2008). *Retired spouses: A national survey of adults 55–75*. Washington, DC: AARP, Knowledge Management.

Korporaal, M., Broese van Groenou, M. I., & van Tilburg, T. G. (2013). Health Problems and Marital Satisfaction among Older Couples. *Journal of Aging and Health, 25*(8): 1279–1298.

Kosberg, J. I. (2014). Rosalie Wolf memorial lecture: Reconsidering assumptions regarding men as elder abuse perpetrators and as elder abuse victims. *Journal of Elder Abuse and Neglect, 26*(3), 207–222.

Kramer, A. F., Fabiani, M., & Colcombe, S. J. (2006). Contributions of cognitive neuroscience to the understanding of behavior and aging. In J. E. Birren & K. W. Schaie (Eds.), *Handbook of the psychology of aging*, 6th ed. (pp. 57–83). Burlington, MA: Elsevier Academic Press.

Krause, N. (2006). Social relationships in late life. In R. H. Binstock & L. K. George (Eds.), *Handbook of aging and the social sciences*, 6th ed. (pp. 181–200). Burlington, MA: Academic Press.

Kreamer, A. (2007). Going gray: What I learned about beauty, sex, work, motherhood, authenticity, and everything else that really matters. New York: Little, Brown and Co.

Krinsky-McHale, S. J., Devenny, D. A., Gu, H., Jenkins, E. C., Kittler, P., Murty, V. V., Schupf, N., Scotto, L., Tycko, B., Urv, T. K., Ye, L., Zigman, W. B., Silverman, W., & Taylor, S. J. (2008). Successful aging in a 70-year-old man with Down syndrome: A case study. *Intellectual and Developmental Disabilities, 46*(3), 215–228

Kubler-Ross, E. (1969). *On death and dying*. New York: Macmillan.

Kueider, A. M., Parisi, J. M., Gross, A. L., Rebok, G. W. (2012). Computerized cognitive training with older adults: a systematic review. *PLoS One, 7*(7). Retrieved from http://journals.plos.org/plosone/article?id=10.1371/journal.pone.0040588.

Kunzmann, U. (2006). Wisdom. In R. Schulz, L. S. Noelker, K. Rockwood, & R. L. Sprott (Eds.), *The encyclopedia of aging*, 4th ed. (pp. 1230–1234). New York: Springer.

Kuzmarov, I. W. (2009). The Quebec government's approach to the vulnerable aging population. *The Aging Male, 12*(1/2), 37–40.

Kvavilashvili, L., & Fisher, L. (2007). Is time-based prospective remembering mediated by self-initiated rehearsals? Effects of incidental cues, ongoing activity, age and motivation. *Journal of Experimental Psychology: General, 136*, 112–132.

Labouvie-Vief, G. (1985). Intelligence and cognition. In J. E. Birren & K. W. Schaie (Eds.) *Handbook of the psychology of aging*, 2nd ed. (pp. 500–530). New York: Van Nostrand Reinhold.

Lachman, M. E. (2000). Promoting a sense of control over memory aging. In L. Bäckman, R. D. Hill, & A. Stigsdotter-Neely (Eds.), *Cognitive rehabilitation in old age* (pp. 106–120). New York: Oxford University Press.

Ladurantaye, S. (2011, July 5). Seniors housing vacancy stays above 10 per cent. Retrieved from http://www.steveladurantaye.ca/seniors-housing-vacancy-stays-10-cent.

Laforest, S., Nour, K., Gignac, M. A. M., Gauvin, L., & Parisien, M. (2012). The role of social reinforcement in the maintenance of short-term effects after a self-management intervention for frail housebound seniors with arthritis. *Canadian Journal on Aging, 31*(2), 195–207.

Laforest, S., Nour, K., Parisien, M., Griskan, A., Poirier, M. C., & Gignac, M. (2008). "I'm taking charge of my arthritis": Designing a targeted self-management program for frail seniors. *Journal of Physical and Occupational Therapy in Geriatrics, 26*(4), 45–66.

Lafrance, A., & LaRochelle-Côte. (2011). Consumption patterns among aging Canadians. *Perspectives on Labour and Income*. Component of Statistics Canada Cat. No 75-001-X. Retrieved from http://www.statcan.gc.ca/pub/75-001-x/2011002/pdf/11417-eng.pdf.

Lahey, J. (2006). *Age, women, and hiring: An experimental study.* Work Opportunities for Older Americans Series Working Paper No. 4. Chestnut Hill, MA: Center for Retirement Research at Boston College.

Lai, D. W. L. (2007). Cultural predictors of caregiving burden of Chinese-Canadian family caregivers. *Canadian Journal on Aging, 26*(supplement 1), 133–148.

Lai, D. W. L. (2009a). From burden to depressive symptoms: The case of Chinese-Canadian family caregivers for the elderly. *Social Work in Health Care, 48,* 432–449.

Lai, D. W. L. (2009b). Older Chinese' attitudes toward aging and the relationship to mental health: An international comparison. *Social Work in Health Care, 48,* 243–259.

Lai, D. W. L. (2010). Filial piety, caregiving appraisal, and caregiving burden. *Research on Aging, 32*(2), 200–223.

Lai, D. W. L. (2011). Abuse and neglect experienced by aging Chinese in Canada. *Journal of Elder Abuse and Neglect, 23*(4), 326–347.

Lai, D. W. L. (2012). Ethnic identity of older Chinese in Canada. *Journal of Cross-Cultural Gerontology, 27,* 103–117.

Lai, D. W. L. (2014). Uncovering the hidden treasures and strengths: Contributions of aging Chinese in Canada. *International Journal of Sociology of the Family, 40*(1), 71–96.

Lai, D. W. L., & Chappell, N. (2007). Use of traditional Chinese medicine by older Chinese immigrants in Canada. *Family Practice, 24,* 56–64.

Lai, D. W. L., Daoust, G. D., & Li, L. (2014). Understanding elder abuse and neglect in aging Chinese immigrants in Canada. *The Journal of Adult Protection, 16*(5), 322–334.

Lai, D. W. L., & Surood, S. (2008). Predictors of depression in aging South Asian Canadians. *Journal of Cross-Cultural Gerontology, 23,* 57–75.

Lai, D. W. L., & Surood, S. (2010). Types and factor structure of barriers to utilization of health services among aging South Asians in Calgary, Canada. *Canadian Journal on Aging, 29*(2), 249–258.

Lai, D. W. L., & Surood, S. (2013). Effect of service barriers on health status of aging South Asian immigrants in Calgary, Canada. *Health and Social Work, 38*(1), 41–50.

Lakin, M. B., Mullane, L., & Robinson, S. P. (2007). *Framing new terrain: Older adults and higher education. First report: Reinvesting in the third age: Older adults and higher education.* Washington, DC: American Council on Education (ACE)

Lalive d'Epinay, C. J., & Bickel, J. F. (2003). Do 'young-old' exercisers feel better than sedentary persons? A cohort study in Switzerland. *Canadian Journal on Aging, 22*(2), 155–165.

Lalonde, Marc. (1974). *A new perspective on the health of Canadians.* Ottawa: Minister of Supply and Services.

Lam, N., Prince, M. J., & Cutt. J. (1996). Restoring the Canada Pension Plan: Simulating the future and stimulating the social policy debate. In J. B. Burbridge et al. (Eds.), *When we're 65: Reforming Canada's retirement income system* (pp. 129–170). Toronto: C. D. Howe Institute.

Lambert, A.-M. (2009). *Divorce: Facts, causes, and consequences.* 3rd ed. Ottawa: Vanier Institute of the Family. Retrieved from http://www.vanierinstitute.ca/include/get.php?nodeid=190.

Lampit, A., Hallock, H., & Valenzuela, M. (2014). Computerized cognitive training in cognitively healthy older adults: A systematic review and meta-analysis of effect modifiers. *PLoS Medicine, 11*(11). Retrieved from http://www.ncbi.nlm.nih.gov/pmc/articles/PMC4236015.

Lampkin, C. L. (2012.) *Insights and spending habits of modern grandparents.* Washington, DC: AARP.

Land, K. C., & Yang, Y. (2006). *Morbidity, disability, and mortality.* In R. H. Binstock & L. K. George (Eds.), *Handbook of aging and the social sciences,* 7th ed. (pp. 41–58). London: Academic Press (Elsevier).

Langlois, K., Garriguet, D., & Findlay, L. (2009). Dietary composition and obesity among Canadian adults. *Health Reports, 20*(4), 1–11. Statistics Canada Cat. No. 82-003.

Lanting, S., Crossley, M., Morgan, D., & Cammer, A. (2011). Aboriginal experiences of aging and dementia in a context of sociocultural change: Qualitative analysis of key informant group interviews with Aboriginal seniors. *Journal of Cross-Cultural Gerontology, 26,* 103–117.

LaRochelle-Côte, S. (2010). Self-employment in the downturn. *Perspectives on Labour and Income, 11*(3), 5–13. Statistics Canada Cat. No. 75-001-X. Retrieved from http://www.statcan.gc.ca/pub/75-001-x/2010103/pdf/11138-eng.pdf.

LaRochelle-Côte, S., Myles, J., & Picot, G. (2010a). Income security and stability during retirement in Canada. Statistics Canada Cat. No. 11F0019M—No. 306. Analytical Studies Branch Research Paper Series. Ottawa.

LaRochelle-Côte, S., Myles, J., & Picot, G. (2010b). Replacing family income during the retirement years: How are Canadians doing? Statistics Canada Cat. No. 11F0019M—No. 328. Analytical Studies Branch Research Paper Series. Ottawa. Retrieved from http://www.statcan. gc.ca/pub/11f0019m/11f0019m2010328-eng.pdf.

LaRochelle-Côté, S., Myles, J., Picot, G. (2012a). Income Replacement Rates among Canadian Seniors: The Effect of Widowhood and Divorce. Social Analysis Division and Labour Statistics Division,Analytical Studies Branch Research Paper Series.

LaRochelle-Côté, S., Myles, J., Picot, G. (2012b). What Are the Impacts of Late-Life Widowhood or Divorce on Income Replacement Rates? *Economic Insights Series, 10.* Retrieved from http://papers.ssrn.com/sol3/papers.cfm?abstract_id=2094472.

Larsen, J., El-Geneidy, A., & Yasmin, F. (2010). Beyond the quarter mile: Examining travel distances by walking and cycling, Montreal, Canada. *Canadian Journal of Urban*

Research: Canadian Planning and Policy (supplement), *19*(1), 70–88.

Laslett, P. (1976). Societal development and aging. In R. H. Binstock & E. Shanas (Eds.), *Handbook of aging and the social sciences*. New York: Van Nostrand.

Laslett, P. (1996). *A Fresh Map of Life: The Emergence of the Third Age*, 2nd ed. London, UK: Macmillan Press.

Lavoie, M., & Oderkirk. J. (1993). Social consequences of demographic change. *Canadian Social Trends* (Winter), 2–5.

Lawler, F. H., Mold, J. W., & McCarthy, L. H. (2013). Do older people benefit from having a confidant? An Oklahoma Physicians Resource/Research Network (OKPRN) Study. *Journal of the American Board of Family Medicine, 26*(1), 9–15.

Lawton, M. P. (1976). The relative impact of enriched and traditional housing on elderly tenants. *The Gerontologist, 16*, 237–242.

Lawton, M. P. (1980). *Environment and aging*. Monterey, CA: Brooks/Cole.

Lawton, M. P., & Nahemow, L. (1973). Ecology and the aging process. In C. Eisdorfer & M. P. Lawton (Eds.), *The psychology of adult development and aging* (pp. 619–674). Washington, DC: American Psychological Association.

Leacy, F., (Ed.). (1983). *Historical Statistics of Canada*, 2nd ed. Ottawa: Minister of Supply and Services.

LeBlanc, A. J. (2011). Aging with HIV/AIDS. In R. A. Settersten, Jr., & J. L. Angel (Eds.), *Handbook of sociology of aging* (pp. 495–512). New York: Springer.

LeClair, K., & Wilson, K. (2011). Conceptualizing Stigma with Older Adults, unpublished model adapted from Link and Phelan. Toronto: CCSMH.

Lee, G. R., & DeMaris, A. (2007). Widowhood, gender, and depression. *Research on Aging, 29*(1), 56–72.

Lee, J. A. (1987). The invisible lives of Canada's gray grays. In V W. Marshall (Ed.), *Aging in Canada*, 2nd ed. (pp. 138–55). Toronto: Fitzhenry and Whiteside.

Lee, L., Hillier, L. M., & Weston, W. W. (2014). Ensuring the success of interprofessional teams: Key lessons learned in memory clinics. *Canadian Journal on Aging, 31*(1), 49–59.

Lee, M. (2007). *How sustainable is medicare?* Ottawa: Canadian Centre for Policy Alternatives.

Lee, M., & Gardner, J. E. (2010). "Grandparents' involvement and support in families with children with disabilities. *Educational Gerontology, 36*(6), 467–499.

Lee, S. M., & Edmonston, B. (2014). Residential independence of elderly immigrants in Canada. *Canadian Journal on Aging, 33*, 359–377.

Lee, Y., Tang, F., Kim, K. H., & Albert, S. M. (2015). Exploring gender differences in the relationships between eldercare and labor force participation. *Canadian Journal on Aging, 34*(1), 14–25.

Légaré, J., Décarie, Y., & Bélanger, A. (2014). Using microsimulation to reassess aging trends in Canada. *Canadian Journal on Aging, 33*(2), 208–219.

Légaré, J., Décarie, Y., Deslandes, K., & Carrière, Y. (2015). The oldest old: A new reality in Canada's population. Policy Brief No. 20. *Population Change and Life Course Strategic Knowledge Cluster*. Retrieved February 25, 2017, from http://ir.lib.uwo.ca/cgi/viewcontent.cgi?article=1045&context=pclc_rpb.

Lehman, H. C. (1953). *Age and achievement*. Princeton, NJ: Princeton University Press.

Lehman, H. C. (1968). The creative production rates of present versus past generations of scientists. In B. L. Neugarten (Ed.), *Middle age and aging* (pp. 99–105). Chicago: University of Chicago Press.

Leive, A., & Xu, K. (2008). Coping with out-of-pocket health payments: Empirical evidence from 15 African countries. *Bulletin of the World Health Organization, 86*(11).

Leming, M. R., & Dickinson, G. E. (2016). *Understanding Dying, Death, and Bereavement*, 8th ed. Stamford, CT: Cengage Learning.

Lengyel, C. O., Tate, R B., & Oberik Blatz, A. K. (2009). The relationships between food group consumption, self-rated health and life satisfaction of community-dwelling Canadian older men: The Manitoba follow-up study. *Journal of Nutrition for the Elderly, 28*, 158–183.

Leon, D., & Ben-Shlomo, Y. (1997). Preadult influences on cardiovascular disease and cancer. In N. D. Kuh & Y. Ben-Shlomo (Eds.), *A life course approach to chronic disease epidemiology* (pp. 45–77). New York: Oxford University Press.

Le Petit, C., & Berthelot, J-M. (2006). Obesity—A growing issue. *Health Reports, 17*(3), 43–50.

Leung, W. (2014). Coming out all over again: Why the first gay-rights generation faces familiar challenges in old age. *The Globe and Mail, October 9*. Retrieved from http://www.theglobeandmail.com/life/relationships/coming-out-all-over-again-why-the-first-gay-rights-generation-faces-familiar-challenges-in-old-age/article21006378.

Li, J. (2006). Separation, linkage and blurring in the public and private pillars of Canada's retirement income system. In L. O. Stone (Ed.), *New frontiers of research on retirement*, 95–111. Ottawa: Ministry of Industry. Statistics Canada. Cat. No. 75-511-XIE.

Liang, J., Krause, N. M., & Bennett, J. M., (2001). Social exchange and well-being: Is giving better than receiving? *Psychology and Aging, 16*, 511–23.

Lieberman, T. (2014). Comparing U.S., Canadian health care systems. January 13. Retrieved from http://healthjournalism.org/blog/2014/01/comparing-u-s-canadian-health-care-systems.

Lin, I-Fen. (2008). Consequences of parental divorce for adult children's support of their frail parents. *Journal of Marriage and Family, 70*(1), 113–128.

Lindau, S. T., & Gavrilova, N. (2010). Sex, health, and years of sexually active life gained due to good health: Evidence from two U.S. population-based cross-sectional surveys of ageing. *British Medical Journal*. Retrieved from http://www.ncbi.nlm.nih.gov/pmc/articles/PMC2835854.

Lindberg, D. A. (2005). Integrative review of research related to meditation, spirituality, and the elderly. *Geriatric Nursing, 26*(6), 372–377.

Lindenbach, J. M., Larocque, S., Lavoie, A-M., & Garceau, M-L. (2012). Older adult mistreatment risk screening: Contribution to the validation of a screening tool in a domestic setting. *Canadian Journal on Aging, 31*(2), 235–252.

Lindenberger, U., & Baltes, P. B. (1994). Sensory functioning and intelligence in old age: A strong connection. *Psychology and Ageing, 9*, 339–355.

Lindsay, C. (1999). *A portrait of seniors in Canada*, 3rd ed. Statistics Canada Cat. No. 89-519-XPE. Ottawa: Statistics Canada.

Lindsay, C. (2008). Canadians attend weekly religious services less than 20 years ago. *Matter of Fact, No. 3*. Component of Statistics Canada Cat. No. 89-630-S. Ottawa: Statistics Canada, Minister of Industry.

Lindsay, C., & Almey, M. (2006). Senior women. In *Women in Canada: A gender-based statistical report*, 5th ed. (pp. 265–290). Statistics Canada Cat. No. 89-503-XIE. Social and Aboriginal Statistics Division. Ottawa: Minister of Industry.

Lineweaver, T. T., Berger, A. K., & Hertzog, C. (2009). Expectations about memory change across the life span and impacted by aging stereotypes. *Psychology and Aging, 24*, 169–176.

Lischka, A. R., Mendelsohn, M., Overend, T., & Forbes, D. (2012). A systematic review of screening tools for predicting the development of dementia. *Canadian Journal on Aging, 31*(3), 295–311.

Lithwick, M., Beaulieu, M., Gravel, S., & Straka, S. M. (1999). Mistreatment of older adults: Perpetrator–victim relationships and interventions. *Journal of Elder Abuse and Neglect, 11*(4), 95–112.

Litwak, E. (1985). *Helping the elderly: The complementary roles of informal networks and formal systems*. New York: Guilford Press.

Litwak, E., & Longino, C. F., Jr. (1987). Migration patterns among the elderly: A developmental perspective. *The Gerontologist, 27*, 266–272.

Litwin, H. (2000). Activity, social network and well-being: An empirical examination. *Canadian Journal on Aging, 19*(3), 343–362.

Liu-Ambrose T., Nagamatsu, L. S., Graf, P., Beattie, B. L., Ashe, M. C., & Handy, T. C. (2010). Resistance training and executive functions: A 12-month randomized controlled trial. *Archives of Internal Medicine, 170*(2), 170–178.

Lodge, A. C., & Umberson, D. (2012). All shook up: Sexuality of mid- to later life married couples. *Journal of Marriage and Family, 74*(3), 428–443.

LoFaso, V. (2013). The role of the primary physician in assessing and treating the mental health concerns of elder abuse victims." *NYC Elder Abuse Center eNewsletter*, March/April, nyceac.com/wp-content/uploads/2013/03/Exploring-the-Intersection-of-Elder-Abuse-and-Mental-Health_eNewsletter.pdf. Retrieved October 20, 2014.

Longino, C. F., Jr. (2005). The future of ageism: Baby boomers at the doorstep. *Generations 29*(3), 79–83.

Longino, C. F., Jr., & Bradley, D. E. (2006). Internal and international migration. In R. H. Binstock & L. K. George (Eds.), *Handbook of aging and the social sciences*, 6th ed. (pp. 7963). Burlington, MA: Academic Press.

Lord, S., & Luxembourg, N. (2006). Mobility of elderly residents living in suburban territories: Mobility experiences in Canada and France. *Journal of Housing for the Elderly, 20*(4), 103–121.

Lovell, D. I., Cuneo, R., & Gass, G. C. (2010). Can aerobic training improve muscle strength and power in older men? *Journal of Aging in Physical Activity, 18*, 14–26.

Lovering, M. J., Cott, C. A., Wells, D. L., Schleifer Taylor, J., & Wells, L. M. (2002). A study of a secure garden in the care of people with Alzheimer's disease. *Canadian Journal on Aging, 21*(3), 417–427.

Lucas, J. A. (2006). Adult day care. In R. Schulz, L. S. Noelker, K. Rockwood, & R. L. Sprott (Eds.), *The encyclopedia of aging*, 4th ed. (pp. 17–20). New York: Springer.

Lum, J., Williams, A. P., Sladek, J., & Ying, A. (2010). Balancing care for supportive housing final report. Retrieved from http://www.crncc.ca/knowledge/related_reports/pdf/Balancing%20Care%20for%20Supportive%20Housing%20Final%20Report.pdf.

Lund, D. E., & Carr, P. R. (Eds.). (2015). *Revisiting the Great White North? Reframing Whiteness, Privilege, and Identity in Education. Second Edition*. Rotterdam: Sense Publishers.

Luong, M. (2009). GIS update. *Perspectives*, July 5-13. Statistics Canada Cat. No. 75-001-X.

Lüscher, K., & Hoff, A. (2013). Intergenerational ambivalence: Beyond solidarity and conflict. Pp. 39–64. In I. Albert & D. Ferring (Eds.), *Intergenerational relations: European perspectives in family and society*. Bristol: Policy Press.

Lusina, S. J., Langton, N., Sims-Gould, J., & Khan, K. M. (2010). Considering the team in research teams: Enhancing the quality of health research for aging Canadians. *Canadian Journal on Aging, 29*(2), 281–286.

Lustig, C., & Flegal, K. E. (2008). Targeting latent function: Encouraging effective encoding for successful memory training and transfer. *Psychology of Aging, 23*(4), 754–764.

Ma, A., & Chi, I. (2005). Utilization and accessibility of social services for Chinese Canadians. *International Social Work, 48*, 148–160.

MacCourt, P., Tuokko, H., & Tierney, M. (2002). Editorial: Canadian Association on Gerontology policy statement on issues in the delivery of mental health services to older adults. *Canadian Journal on Aging, 21*(2), 165–174.

MacCourt, P., Wilson, K., & Tourigny-Rivard, M-F. (2011). Guidelines for Comprehensive Mental Health Services for Older Adults in Canada. Calgary, AB: Mental Health Commission of Canada. Retrieved from http://www.mentalhealthcommission.ca.

MacDonald, B. J., Andrews, D., & Brown, R. L. (2010). The Canadian elder standard—Pricing the cost of basic needs for the Canadian elderly. *Canadian Journal on Aging, 29*(1), 39–56.

MacEntee, M. I., Wong, S. T., Smith, A., Beattie, B. L., Brondani, M., Bryant, S. R., Graf, P., & Soheilipour, S. (2014). Oral healthcare challenges for older Punjabi-speaking immigrants. *Canadian Journal on Aging, 33*(2), 196–207.

MacGregor, D. (2005). The ass and the grasshopper: Canadian universities and mandatory retirement. *Time's up! Mandatory retirement in Canada*. Toronto: James Lorimer and Company.

Macionis, J. J., & Gerber, L. M. (2010). *Sociology 7th Canadian Edition*. Upper Saddle River, New Jersey: Pearson Education, Inc.

Mackenzie, H., & Rachlis, M. (2010). *The sustainability of medicare*. Ottawa: The Canadian Federation of Nurses Unions.

MacKinnnon, M. (2010, November 4). Census to detail rapid greying of China. *The Globe and Mail*. Retrieved from http://www.theglobeandmail.com/news/world/asia-pacific/census-to-detail-rapid-greying-of-china/article1786390/page2.

MacLean, E. (2008). *Getting through the day: A coping process of drawing upon resources while caring for a spouse with dementia awaiting long term care placement*. Master's thesis, School of Nursing. Hamilton, ON: McMaster University.

MacLean, M., Novik, N., Ram, K., & Schmidt, A. (2010). End-of-life care for immigrant seniors. In D. Durst & M. MacLean (Eds.), *Diversity and aging among immigrant seniors in Canada: Changing faces and greying temples* (pp. 169–186). Calgary: Detselig.

Madden, D. J., Spaniol, J., Costello, M. C., Bucur, B., White, L. E., Cabeza, R., Davis, S. W., Dennis, N. A., Provenzale, J. M., & Huettel, S. A. (2009). Cerebral white matter integrity mediates adult age differences in cognitive performance. *Journal of Cognitive Neuroscience, 21*(2), 289–302.

Maeda, D. (2009). Japan. In E. Palmore, F. Whittington, & S. Kunkel (Eds.), *The international handbook on aging* (3rd ed.) (pp. 321–329). Santa Barbara, CA: ABC-CLIO.

Maguire, E. A., Gadian, D. G., Johnsrude, I. S., Good, C. D., Ashburner, J., Frackowiak, R. S., et al. (2000). Navigation-related structural change in the hippocampi of taxi drivers. *Proceedings of the National Academy of Sciences of the United States of America, 97*(8), 4398–4403.

Maguire, E. A., Woollett, K., & Spiers, H. J. (2006). London taxi drivers and bus drivers: A structural MRI and neuropsychological analysis. *Hippocampus, 16*(12), 1091–1101.

Mahieu, L., Van Elssen, K., & Gastmans, C. (2011). Nurses' perceptions of sexuality in institutionalized elderly: A literature review. *International Journal of Nursing Studies, 48*(9), 1140–1154.

Maimaris, W.M, Bchir, B. M., Hogan, H., & Lock, K. (2010). The Impact of Working Beyond Traditional Retirement Ages on Mental Health: Implications for Public Health and Welfare Policy. *Public Health Reviews, 32*(2), 532–548.

Mairs, K., & Bullock, S. L. (2013). Sexual-risk behaviour and HIV testing among Canadian snowbirds who winter in Florida. *Canadian Journal on Aging, 32*(2), 145–158.

Maki, B., Sibley, K. M., Jaglal, S. B., Bayley, M., Brooks, D., Fernie, G. R., Flint, A. K., et al. (2011). Reducing fall risk by improving balance control: Development, evaluation and knowledge-translation of new approaches. *Journal of Safety Research, 42*(6), 473–485.

Mancini, A. D., & Bonanno, G. A. (2006). Marital closeness, functional disability, and adjustment in late life. *Psychology and Aging, 21*(3), 600–610.

Manitoba Justice. (2017). Grandparent and Family Access—Dealing with Child Access Issues. Retrieved March 11, 2017, from http://www.gov.mb.ca/justice/family/law/grandparentaccess.html.

Mann, R. (2007). Out of the shadows?: Grandfatherhood, age and masculinities. *Journal of Aging Studies, 21*, 281–291.

Manton, K. G., Gu, X., & Lamb, V. (2006). Change in chronic disability from 1982 to 2004/2005 as measured by long-term changes in function and health in the U.S. elderly population. *Proceedings of the National Academy of Sciences of the United States of America, 103*(48), 18374–18379.

Marcum, C. S. (2013). Age differences in daily social activities. *Research on Aging, 35*(5), 612–640.

Markowits, R. (2011). Air Canada and unionized workers endured a year of frustration in 2011. *The Canadian Press—Online Edition*. Retrieved from http://www.winnipegfreepress.com/business/breakingnews/air-canada-and-unionized-workers-endured-a-year-of-frustration-in-2011-135116623.html.

Marmor, T. & Maioni, A. (2008). Health care in crisis: The drive for health reform in Canada and the United States. Woodrow Wilson International Center for Scholars. The Canada Institute. Issue nine.

Marotte, B. (2014). Fewer Canadians plan to contribute to RRSPs, citing lack of funds. *The Globe and Mail*, January 10. Retrieved from http://www.theglobeandmail.com/globe-investor/

personal-finance/retirement-rrsps/fewer-canadians-plan-to-contribute-to-their-rrsp-citing-lack-of-funds/article 16268931.

Marshall, B. L. (2008). Older men and sexual health: Post-Viagra views of changes in function. *Generations, 32*(1), 21–27.

Marshall, K. (2011). Retiring with debt. *Perspectives on Labour and Income*, April 12, 3–12.

Marshall, V. W., & Bengtson, V. L. (2011). Theoretical perspectives on the sociology of aging. In *Handbook of sociology of aging* (pp. 17–33). New York: Springer.

Marshall, V. W., Rosenthal, C. J., & Synge, J. (1983). Concerns about parental health. In E. W. Markson (Ed.), *Older women: Issues and prospects*, 253–273. Lexington, MA: D. C. Heath.

Marsiske, M., & Margrett, J. A. (2006). Everyday problem solving and decision making. In J. E. Birren & K. W. Schaie (Eds.), *Handbook of the psychology of aging*, 6th ed. (pp. 315–342). Burlington, MA: Elsevier Academic Press.

Martel, L. (2008). *Canadian demographics at a glance*. Statistics Canada. Cat. No. 91-003-XIE. Ottawa: Minister of Industry.

Martel, L. (2013). Mortality: Overview, 2010 and 2011. Component of Statistics Canada Catalogue no. 91-209-X. Ottawa: Minister of Industry. Accessed 26 November 2015 at www.statcan.gc.ca.

Martel, L., Bélanger, A., Berthelot, J-M., & Carrière, Y. (2005). Healthy aging. Healthy today, Healthy tomorrow? Findings from the *National Population Health Survey*. Ottawa: Statistics Canada.

Martel, L., & Caron-Malenfant, E. (2008). Portrait of the *Canadian population in 2006: Findings*. Statistics Canada, 2006 Census Analysis Series. Retrieved from http://www12.statcan.ca/english/census06/ analysis/popdwell/index.cfm.

Martel, L., He, J., & Caron-Malenfant, E. (2006). Report on the demographic situation in Canada 2003 and 2004. *Statistics Canada Demography Division*. Ottawa: Minister of Industry.

Martin, L. G. (2011). Demography and aging. In R. H. Binstock & L. K. George (Eds.), *Handbook of aging and the social sciences*, 7th ed. (pp. 33–45). London: Academic Press (Elsevier).

Martin-Matthews, A. (2011). Revisiting widowhood in later life: Changes in patterns and profiles, advances in research and understanding. *Canadian Journal on Aging, 38*(3), 339–354.

Martin-Matthews, A., & Mealing, L. (2009). Editorial: Realizing the vision. The Canadian longitudinal study on aging as a strategic initiative of the Canadian Institutes of Health Research. *Canadian Journal on Aging, 28*(3), 209–214.

Martin-Matthews, A., Tong, C. E., Rosenthal, C. J., & McDonald, L. (2013). Ethno-cultural diversity in the experience of widowhood in later life: Chinese widows in Canada. *Journal of Aging Studies, 27*, 507–518.

Martinson, M., & Minkler, M. (2006). Civic engagement and older adults: A critical perspective. *The Gerontologist, 46*, 318–324.

Maselko, J., Bates, L. M., Avendano, M., & Glymour, M. M. (2009). The intersection of sex, marital status, and cardiovascular risk factors in shaping stroke incidence: Results from the *Health and Retirement Study. Journal of the American Geriatric Society, 57*, 2293–2299.

Maser, Karen. (2003). An introduction to *Canada's retirement* income programs. *Canada's Retirement Income Programs: A Statistical Overview (1990–2000)*. Statistics Canada Cat. No. 74-507-XIE.

Masoro, E. J. & Austad, S. N. (2011). Preface. In E. J. Masoro & A. N. Austad (Eds.), *Handbook of the biology of aging* (7th ed., pp. xiii–xiv). London: Elsevier (Academic Press).

Masotti, P., Fick, R., Johnson-Masotti, A., & MacLeod, S. (2006). Healthy naturally occurring retirement communities: A low-cost approach to facilitating healthy aging. *American Journal of Public Health, 96*(7), 1164–1170. Retrieved from http://www.ncbi.nlm.nih.gov/pmc/articles/PMC1483864.

Masotti, P., Fick, R., Johnson-Masotti, A., & MacLeod, S. (2007). The aging population and naturally occurring retirement communities (NORCs): Local government, healthy aging, and healthy NORCs. *Alaska Medicine, 49*(2 Suppl), 85–88.

Mast, B. T. (2009). Uncertainties in dementia: What do people with dementia experience? *Generations, 33*(1), 30–36.

Matsumoto, Y. (2009). Dealing with life changes: Humor in painful self-disclosures by elderly Japanese women. *Ageing and Society, 29*(6), 929–952.

Matthews, A. M., & Tindale, J. A. (1987). Retirement in Canada. In K. S. Markides & C. L. Cooper (Eds.), *Retirement in industrialized societies: Social, psychological and health factors* (pp. 43–75). Toronto: John Wiley and Sons.

Matthews, H. (2014). 11 Best polyamory blogs of 2014. *Dating Advice.com*. Retrieved from http://www.datingadvice.com/for-men/11-best-polyamory-blogs-of-2014

Matthews, K. A., & Gallo, L. C. (2011). Psychological perspectives on pathways linking socioeconomic status and physical health. *Annual Review of Psychology, 62*, 501–530. Retrieved from http://www.ncbi.nlm.nih.gov/pmc/articles/PMC3121154.

Matthews, K. A., Räikkönen, K., Gallo, L., & Kuller, L. H. (2008). Association between socioeconomic status and metabolic syndrome in women: Testing the reserve capacity model. *Health Psychology,27*(5), 576–583.

Maxmin, K., Cooper, C., Potter, L., & Livingston, G. (2009). Mental capacity to consent to treatment and admission. *International Journal of Geriatric Psychiatry, 24*, 1367–1375.

Maxwell, C. J., Soo, A., Hogan, D. B., Wodchis, W. P., Gilbart, E., Amuah, J., Eliasziw, M., Hagen, B., & Strain, L. A. (2013). Predictors of nursing home placement from assisted living settings in Canada. *Canadian Journal on Aging, 32*(4), 333–348.

Mayer, C. (2009, March 12). Ten ideas changing the world right now: 5. Amortality. *Time*. Retrieved from www.time.com/time/specials/packages/article/0,28804,1884779_1884782_1884758,00.html.

Mayer, K. U. (2009). New directions in life course research. *Annual Review of Sociology, 35*, 413–433.

Mayo Clinic. (2011a). Dementia: Causes. Retrieved from http://www.mayoclinic.com/health/dementia/DS01131/DSECTION=causes.

Mayo Clinic Staff. (2011b). Sexual health. Retrieved from http://www.mayoclinic.com/health/sexual-health/HA00035.

Mayo Clinic. (2015a). COPD. Retrieved from http://www.mayoclinic.org/diseases-conditions/copd/basics/definition/con-20032017.

Mayo Clinic. (2015b). Type 2 diabetes: Treatments and drugs. Retrieved from http://www.mayoclinic.org/diseases-conditions/type-2-diabetes/basics/treatment/con-20031902.

McAdam, M. (2008). *Frameworks of integrated care for the elderly: A systematic review.* Ontario: Canadian Policy Research Networks. Retrieved from http://www.cssnetwork. ca/Resources%20and%20Publications/MacAdam-Frame-works%20for%20Integrated%20Care%20for%20the%20 Frail%20Elderly.pdf.

McAuley, E., Elavsky, S., Jerome, G. J., Konopack, J. F., & Marquez, D. X. (2005). Physical activity-related well-being in older adults: Social cognitive influences. *Psychology and Aging, 20*(2), 295–302.

McDaniel, M. A., Einstein, E. O., & Jacoby, L. L. (2008). New considerations in aging and memory: The glass may be half full. In F. I. M. Craik & T. A. Salthouse (Eds.). (2008). *The handbook of aging and cognition,* 3rd ed. (pp. 251–309). New York: Psychology Press.

McDaniel, S. (1986). *Canada's aging population.* Toronto: Butterworths.

McDaniel, S., & Gazso, A. (2014). Liminality and low-income aging families by choice: Meanings of family and support. *Canadian Journal on Aging, 33*(4), 400–412.

McDill, T., Hall, S. K., & Turell, S. C. (2006). Aging and creating families: Never married heterosexual women over forty. *The Journal of Women and Aging, 18*(3), 37–50.

McDonald, J. T., & Conde, H. (2010). Does geography matter? The health service use and unmet health care needs of older Canadians. *Canadian Journal on Aging, 29*(1), 23–37.

McDonald, L. (2006a). Gendered retirement: The welfare of women and the 'new' retirement. In L. O. Stone (Ed.), *New frontiers of research on retirement* (Chapter 10, 137–164). Statistics Canada. Cat. No. 75-511-XIE. Ottawa: Minister of Industry.

McDonald, L. (2006b).Gender and family—Major dimensions of retirement research. In L. O. Stone (Ed.), *New frontiers of research on retirement* (Chapter 9, pp. 129–136). Statistics Canada Cat. No. 75-511-XIE. Ottawa: Minister of Industry.

McDonald, L. (2012). *The evolution of retirement as systematic ageism.* SEDAP Paper No. 292. Hamilton, ON: McMaster University. Retrieved from http://socserv.mcmaster.ca/sedap/p/sedap292.pdf.

McDonald, L., Dergal, J., & Cleghorn, L. (2007). Living on the margins: Older homeless adults in Toronto. *Journal of Gerontological Social Work, 49*(1/2), 19–46.

McDonald, L., & Donahue, P. (2012). *Retirement lost?* SEDAP Research Paper No. 291. Hamilton, ON: McMaster University.

McDonald, L., Donahue, P., & Moore, B. (1998). *The economic casualties of retiring to caregive.* Program for Research on the Independence and Economic Security of the Older Population. Research Paper No.28. McMaster University.

McDonald, L., & Robb, A. L. (2004). The economic legacy of divorce and separation for women in old age. *Canadian Journal on Aging, 23*(Suppl. 1), S83–S97.

McDougall, G. J. (2000). Memory improvement in assisted living elders. *Issues in Mental Health Nursing, 21*(2), 217–233.

McFadden, S., & Kozberg, C. (2008). Religious and spiritual supports for late-life meaning. *Generations, 32*(2), 6–11.

McGrail, K. M., Lilly, M. B., McGregor, M. J., Broemeling, A-M., Salomons, K., Peterson, S., McKendry, R., & Barer, M. L. (2013). Health care services use in assisted living: A time series analysis. *Canadian Journal on Aging, 32*(2), 457–469.

McGuire, F. A., Dottavio, F. D., & O'Leary, J. T. (1987). The relationship of early life experiences to later life leisure involvement. *Leisure Sciences, 9*: 251–257.

McHugh, K. (2003). The 'Ageless Self'? Emplacement of identities in sun belt retirement communities. *Journal of Aging Studies, 14*, 103–115.

McInnis, R. M. (1977). Childbearing and land availability: Some evidence from individual household data. In R. Lee (Ed.), *Population patterns in the past* (pp. 201–227). New York: Academic Press.

McIntosh, C. N., Fines, P., Wilkins, R., & Wolfson, M. C. (2009). Income disparities in health-adjusted life expectancy for Canadian adults, 1991–(2001). *Health Reports, 20*(4), 55–64.

McIntyre, L, Emery, J. C. H., Fleisch, V. C., Dutton, D. J. (2014). Impact of Basic Income program on Canadian seniors' health and mental health. American Public Health Associarion. Retrieved from https://apha.confex.com/apha/142am/webprogram/Paper298550.html.

McKie, C. (1993). Population aging: Baby boomers into the 21st century. *Canadian Social Trends* (Summer), 2–6.

McKinnell, J. (2014). Can you get fitter at 50 than you've ever been in your life? *Maclean's* magazine, November 6.

McKinsey & Company. (2015). Building on Canada's strong retirement readiness. Retrieved March 3, 2017, from https://www.google.com/#q=McKinsey+%26+company+2015+canada+retirement&*.

Mclister, R. (2015). Decoding the mortgage market: Will you die with a mortgage? 10 reasons why more people will. *The Globe and Mail,* April 8. Retrieved from http://www.theglobeandmail.com/globe-investor/personal-finance/mortgages/will-you-die-with-a-mortgage-a-growing-number-of-canadians-likely-will/article23776003.

McMaster Optimal Aging Portal. (2012). Retrieved from http://www.mcmasteroptimalaging.org.

McMullin, J. A., & Berger, E. D. (2006). Gendered ageism/ag(ed) sexism. In T. M. Calasanti & K. F. Slevin (Eds.), *Age matters: Realigning feminist thinking* (pp. 201–223). New York: Routledge.

McVey, W. (2003). *Seniors who gamble: A summary review of the literature 2003.* Department of Sociology, University of Alberta. Retrieved from http://www.uofaweb.ualberta.ca/abgaminginstitute/pdfs/ Munro_Seniors.pdf, September 2, 2010.

Mead, G. H. (1934). *Mind, self and society: From the standpoint of a social behaviorist.* Chicago: University of Chicago Press.

Meade, M. L., & Park, D. C. (2009). Enhancing cognitive function in older adults. In W. Chodzko-Zajko, A. F. Kramer, & L. W. Poon (Eds.), *Enhancing cognitive functioning and brain plasticity* (pp. 35–47). Champaign, Ill.: Human Kinetics.

Melenhorst, A., Fisk, A., Mynatt, E., & Rogers, W. (2004). Potential intrusiveness of aware home technology: Perceptions of older adults. *Proceedings of the Human Factors and Ergonomics Society, 48,* 266–270.

Mental Health Commission of Canada. (2014). Eliminating stigma: A focus on seniors' mental health. Ottawa, ON: Author.

Mental Health Commission of Canada. (2015). *Informing the Future: Mental Health Indicators for Canada,* Ottawa, ON: Author.

Mercado, R. G., & Newbold, K. B. (2009). Car driving and public transit use in Canadian metropolitan areas: Focus on elderly and role of health and social network factors. SEDAP Research Paper No. 243. Hamilton, ON: McMaster University.

Mercado, R. G., Páez, A., & Newbold, K. B. (2007). Policy areas impinging on elderly transportation mobility: An explanation with Ontario, Canada, as example. SEDAP Research Paper No. 187. Hamilton, ON: McMaster University.

Merz, E. M., & Consedine, N. S. (2009). The association of family support and wellbeing in later life depends on adult attachment style. *Attachment & Human Development, 11(2),* 203–221.

MetLife. (2009). *2009 grandparents: Generous with money, not with advice. A MetLife QuickPOLL of American grandparents.* Westport, CT: MetLife Mature Market Institute. Retrieved from www.metlife.com/assets/cao/mmi/publications/quick-facts/mmi-grandparents-gener-ous-money-not-advise.pdf.

MetLife. (2010a). *8th annual study of employee benefits trends. Findings from the national survey of employers and employees.* Westport, CT: MetLife Mature Market Institute. Retrieved from www.metlife.com/assets/institutional/services/insights-and-tools/ebts/Employee-Benefits-Trends-Study.pdf.

MetLife Mature Market. (2010b). *Working caregivers and employer health care costs.* Westport, CT: MetLife Mature Market Institute. Retrieved from http://www.metlife.com/assets/cao/mmi/publications/studies/2010/mmi-working-caregivers-employers-health-care-costs.pdf.

MetLife and American Society on Aging. (2010). *Still Out, Still Aging: The MetLife Study of Lesbian, Gay, Bisexual, and Transgender Baby Boomers.* Retrieved November 11, 2010, from http://www.metlife.com/assets/cao/mmi/publications/studies/2010/mmi-still-out-still-aging.pdf.

Meyer, M. H., & Parker, W. M. (2011). Gender, aging, and social policy. In R. H. Binstock & L. K. George (Eds.), *Handbook of aging and the social sciences,* 7th ed. (pp. 323–335). London: Academic Press (Elsevier).

Migliore, S., & Dorazio-Migliore, M. (2010). 'La buona vecchiaia': Aging and well-being among Italian Canadians. In J. E. Graham & P. H. Stephenson (Eds.), *Contesting aging and loss* (pp. 63–84). Toronto: University of Toronto Press.

Milan, A. (2011a). Age and sex structure: Canada, provinces and territories, 2010. *Report on the demographic situation in Canada.* Component of Statistics Canada Cat. No. 91-209-X). Ottawa: Minister of Industry.

Milan, A. (2011b). Mortality: Overview, 2007. *Report on the demographic situation in Canada.* Component of Statistics Canada Cat. No. 91-209-X. Ottawa: Minister of Industry.

Milan, A. (2011c). Fertility: Overview, 2008. *Report on the demographic situation in Canada.* Component of Statistics Canada Cat. No. 91-209-X. Ottawa: Minister of Industry.

Milan, A. (2013). Marital status: Overview, 2011. Statistics Canada. Ottawa: Minister of Industry. Retrieved from http://www.statcan.gc.ca/pub/91-209-x/2013001/article/11788-eng.pdf

Milan, A., Keown, L.-A., & Urquijo, C. R. (2011). Families, living arrangements and unpaid work. *Women in Canada: A gender-based statistical report.* Component of Statistics Canada Cat. No. 89-503-X. Ottawa: Minister of Industry.

Milan, A., Laflamme, N., & Wong, I. (2015). Diversity of grandparents living with their grandchildren. *Insights on Canadian Society.* Statistics Canada. Retrieved from http://www.statcan.gc.ca/pub/75-006-x/2015001/article/14154-eng.htm.

Milan, A., & Vézina, M. (2011). Senior women. *Women in Canada: A gender-based statistical report.* Component of Statistics Canada Cat. No. 89-503-X. Ottawa: Minister of Industry.

Milan, A., Wong, I., & Vézina, M. (2014). Emerging trends in living arrangements and conjugal unions for current and future seniors. *Insights on Canadian Society*. Statistics Canada. Retrieved from http://www.statcan.gc.ca/pub/75-006-x/2014001/article/11904-eng.pdf.

Miller, J. A, Hollander, M., & MacAdam, M. (2008). *The continuing care research project for Canada and the Government of Ontario: Synthesis report.*

Milligan, K., & Schirle, T. (2008). Working while receiving a pension: Will double dipping change the elderly labour market? Conference paper prepared for the John Deutsch Institute Conference on Retirement Policy Issues in Canada, held in Kingston, ON, October 25–26, 2007.

Millward, D. (2008, August 19). Pensioner groups demand elderly road sign change. *Telegraph*, Retrieved from http://www.telegraph.co.uk/news/newstopics/howaboutthat/2585801/Pensioner-groups-demand-elderly-road-sign-change.html.

Milner, C. (2006). Marketing successfully to age 40-plus women. *Journal on Active Aging 5(4)*, 22–26.

Milner, J. (2007). Recreation and the age wave. *Journal on Active Aging, 6(2)*, 72–77.

Mireles, D. E., & Charness, N. (2002). Computational explorations of the influence of structured knowledge on age-related cognitive decline. *Psychology and Aging, 17(2)*, 245–259.

Mirowsky, J., & Ross, C. E. (1998). Education, personal control, lifestyle and health. *Research on Aging, 20(4)*, 415–449.

Mirowsky, J., & Ross, C. E. (2005). Education, cumulative advantage, and health. *Ageing International, 30(1)*, 27–62.

Mirowsky, J., & Ross, C. E. (2008). Education and self-rated health: Cumulative advantage and its rising importance. *Research on Aging, 30(1)*, 93–122.

Misener, D. (2013). Young firm worries about cultural fit with older hire. *The Globe and Mail,* February 13. Retrieved from http://www.theglobeandmail.com/report-on-business/small-business/sb-growth/the-challenge/young-firm-worries-about-cultural-fit-with-older-hire/article8483286.

Mitchell, L. A., Strain, L. A., & Blandford, A. A. (2007). Indicators of home care use in urban and rural settings. *Canadian Journal on Aging, 26(3)*, 275–280.

Mitchell, V., & Bruns, C. M. (2011). Writing one's own story: *Women, aging, and the social narrative. Women & Therapy 34*, 114–128.

Mitnitski, A. B. & Gubitz, G. J. (2010). *Trends in survival and recovery from stroke and compression of morbidity.* American Heart Association. Retrieved from http://stroke.ahajournals.org/content/41/3/415.full.pdf.

Mo, L., Légaré, J., & Stone, L. (2006). The diversification and the privatization of the sources of retirement income in Canada. EDAP Research Paper No. 159. Hamilton, ON:

McMaster University. Initially in L. O. Stone (Ed.), New frontiers of research on retirement (pp. 407–428). Statistics Canada Cat. No. 75-511-XIE.

Moen, P., & Spencer, D. (2006). Converging divergences in age, gender, health, and well-being: Strategic selection in the third age. In R. H. Binstock & L. K. George (Eds.), *Handbook of aging and the social sciences* (6th ed., pp. 127–144). Burlington, MA: Academic Press.

Molnar, L. J., & Eby, D. W. (2009). Getting around: Meeting boomers' mobility needs. In R. B. Hudson (Ed.), *Boomer bust? Economic and political issues of the graying society. The boomers and their future*, Vol. 2 (pp. 189–211). Westport, CT: Praeger.

Molzahn, A. E., Gallagher, E., & McNulty, V. (2009). Quality of life associated with adult day centers. *Journal of Gerontological Nursing, 35(8)*, 37–46.

Monk, C. (2009). Review of the book *The political economy of Japan's low fertility,* edited by F. M. Rosenbluth. Stanford, CA: Stanford University Press, (2007). *Canadian Studies in Population, 36*, 178–182.

Monserud, M. A. (2008). Intergenerational relationships and affectual solidarity between grandparents and young adults. *Journal of Marriage and Family, 70*, 182–195.

Monserud, M. A. (2011). Changes in grandchildren's adult role statuses and their relationships with grandparents. *Journal of Family Issues, 32(4)*, 425–451.

Moody, E., & Phinney, A. (2012). A community-engaged art program for older people: Fostering social inclusion. *Canadian Journal on Aging, 31(1)*, 55–64.

Moody, H. R. (2010). The moral erconomy of retirement. *Generations, 33(3)*, 27–33.

Moore, S. L., Metcalf, B., & Schow, E. (2006). Quest for meaning in aging. *Geriatric Nursing, 27(5)*, 293–299.

Moorman, S. M., Booth, A., & Fingerman, K. L. (2006). Women's romantic relationships after widowhood. *Journal of Family Issues, 27(9)*, 1281–1304.

Moremen, R. D. (2008a). Best friends: The role of confidantes in older women's health. *Journal of Women & Aging, 20(1–2)*, 149–167.

Moremen, R. D. (2008b). The downside of friendship: Sources of strain in older women's friendships. *Journal of Women and Aging, 20(1/2)*, 169–187.

Morgan, D. G., Crossley, M., Kirk, A., D'Arcy, C., Stewart, N., Biem, J., Forbes, D., Harder, S., Basran, J., Dal Bello-Haas, V., & McBain, L. (2009). Improving access to dementia care: Development and evaluation of a rural and remote memory clinic. *Aging & Mental Health, 13(1)*, 17–30.

Morissette, R., & Ostrovsky, Y. (2007). *Pensions and retirement savings of families. Perspectives on Labour and Income, 19(4)*, 5–18.

Morissette, R., Schellenberg, G., & Silver, C. (2004). *Retaining older workers. Perspectives on Labour and Income, 5(10)*, 15–20.

Morissette, R., & Zhang, X. (2004). Retirement plan awareness. *Perspectives on Labour and Income*, 5(1), 11–18.

Morissette, R., Zhang, X., & Frenette, M. (2007). Earnings losses of displaced workers: Canadian evidence from a large administrative database on firm closures and mass layoffs. *Analytical Studies Branch Research Paper Series*, No. 291. Cat. No. 11F0019MIE. Ottawa: Statistics Canada.

Morrow, D. G. (2009). A contextual approach to aging and expertise. In W. Chodzko-Zajko, A. F. Kramer, & L. W. Poon (Eds.), Enhancing cognitive functioning and brain plasticity (pp. 49–60). Champaign, IL: Human Kinetics.

Morrow-Howell, N., Putnam, M., Lee, Y. S., Greenfield, J. C., Inoue, M., & Chen, J. (2014). An investigation of activity profiles of older adults. *Journals of Gerontology, Series B: Psychological Sciences and Social Sciences*, 69(5), 809–821.

Moss, S. Z., & Moss, M. S. (2007). Being a man in long term care. *Journal of Aging Studies*, 21(1), 43–54.

Moye, J., Marson, D., Edelstein, B., Wood, S., & Saldivar, A. (2011). Decision making capacity. In K. W. Schaie & S. L. Willis (Eds.), *Handbook of the psychology of aging*, 7th ed. (pp. 367–379). London: Academic Press (Elsevier).

Muise, A., & Desmarais, S. (2010). Women's perceptions and use of 'anti-aging' products. *Sex Roles*, 63, 126–137.

Myers, A. M., Trang, A., & Crizzle, A. M. (2011). Naturalistic study of winter driving practices by older men and women: Examination of weather, road conditions, trip purposes, and comfort. *Canadian Journal on Aging*, 30(4), 577–589.

Myles, J. (1982). Social implications of a changing age structure. In G. Gutman (Ed.), *Canada's changing age structure: Implications for the future*. Vancouver: Simon Fraser University Publications.

Myles, J. (1984). Old age in the welfare state: The political economy of public pensions. Boston: Little Brown.

Myles, J. (2000). The maturation of Canada's retirement income system: Income levels, income inequality, and low income among older persons. *Canadian Journal on Aging*, 19(3), 287–316.

Myles, J. (2006). From pension policy to retirement policy: Towards a new social agenda? In L. O. Stone (Ed.) *New frontiers of research on retirement* (pp. 65–82). Statistics Canada Cat. No. 75-511-XIE. Ottawa: Minister of Industry.

Myles, J., & Street, D. (1995). Should the economic life course be redesigned? Old age security in a time of transition. *Canadian Journal on Aging*, 14(2), 335–359.

Myles, J., & Teichroew, L. (1991). The politics of dualism: Pension policy in Canada. In J. Myles & J. Quadagno (Eds.), *States, labor markets, and the future of old-age policy* (pp. 84–104). Philadelphia: Temple University Press.

Nabalamba, A., & Chikoko, M. (2011). Aging population challenges in Africa. *AFDB Chief Economist Complex*, 1(1), 1–19.

Nagnur, D., & Nagrodski, M. (1988). Cardiovascular disease, cancer and life expectancy. *Canadian Social Trends* (Winter), 25–27.

Nahmiash, D., & Reis, M. (2000). Most successful intervention strategies for abused older adults. *Journal of Elder Abuse and Neglect*, 12(3–4), 53–70.

National Advisory Council on Aging (NACA). (1992). *The NACA position on Canada's oldest seniors: Maintaining the quality of their lives*. Ottawa: Minister of Supply and Services Canada.

National Advisory Council on Aging (NACA). (1993). Freedom and responsibility: Home alone. *Expression*, 9(2), 2.

National Advisory Council on Aging. (1995). The NACA position on community services in health care for seniors: Progress and challenges. Ottawa: NACA.

National Advisory Council on Aging. (2000). SIPA success. *Expression*, 14(1), 9.

National Advisory Council on Aging. (2006). *Seniors in Canada 2006 Report Card*. Ottawa: Minister of Public Works and Government Services Canada. Retrieved from http://intraspec.ca/rc2006_e.pdf.

National Alliance for Caregiving. (2009). *Caregiving in the U.S. 2009*. Washington, DC: NAC and AARP.

National Center for Health Statistics. (2013) *Health, United States, 2012: With special feature on emergency care*. Hyattsville, MD. 2013.

National Institute of Population and Social Security Research (Japan). (2004). *Key learning from the 2nd public opinion survey on population issues in Japan*. Retrieved from http://www.ipss. go.jp/English/pospi_2nd/chosa.html.

National Institute on Aging. (2009). *Alzheimer's disease medications fact sheet*. Retrieved from http://www.nia.nih.gov/Alzheimers/Publications/medicationsfs.htm.

National Institutes of Health. (2006). Mental exercise helps maintain some seniors' thinking skills. Retrieved from http://www.nia.nih.gov/newsroom/2006/12/mental-exercise-helps-maintain-some-seniors-thinking-skills.

National Institutes of Health. (2013). Intellectual and developmental disabilities. Retrieved from http://report.nih.gov/nihfactsheets/ViewFactSheet.aspx?csid=100.

National Seniors Council. (2007). *Report of the National Seniors Council on elder abuse*. Ottawa: Government of Canada.

National Seniors Council. (2009). Report of the National Seniors Council on low income among seniors. *Survey of Labour and Income Dynamics*. Cat. No.: HS1-9/2008. Gatineau, Quebec: Government of Canada. Retrieved from http://www.seniorscouncil.gc.ca/eng/research_publications/low_income/2009/hs1_9/hs1_9.pdf.

National Seniors Council. (2011). *National Seniors Council*. Online brochure. Retrieved from http://www.seniorscouncil.gc.ca:80/eng/research_publications/working_for_seniors/index.shtml.

Navaneelan, T., & Janz, T. (2014). *Adjusting the scales: Obesity in the Canadian population after correcting for respondent bias.* Statistics Canada.

Neugarten, B. L., Havighurst, R. J., & Tobin, S. (1968). Personality and patterns of aging. In B. L. Neugarten (Ed.) *Middle Age and Aging* (pp. 173–177). Chicago: University of Chicago Press.

Neuman, W. L., & Robson, K. (2009). *Basics of social research: Qualitative and quantitative approaches,* Canadian ed. Toronto, ON: Pearson Education Canada.

Newberg, A. B. (2011). Spirituality and the aging brain. *Generations, 35*(2), 83–91.

Newbold, K. B. (2007). *Return and onwards migration among older Canadians: Findings from the 2001 Census.* SEDAP Research Paper No. 171. Hamilton, ON: McMaster University.

New Brunswick. (2008). New Brunswick Human Rights Commission. Supreme Court issues decision on mandatory retirement case (08/07/22). Communications New Brunswick. News Release. Retrieved from http://www. gnb. ca/cnb/news/hrc/2008e1074hr.htm.

New York Times News Service. (2007, March 23). China faces economic dilemma as boomers near early retirement. Wire-International, A3. LexisNexis Academic.

Newswire. (2015). Government of Canada working hard to support homeless seniors. Retrieved from http://www.newswire. ca/news-releases/government-of-canada-working-hard-to-support-homeless-seniors-518424531.html.

Neysmith, S. M. (1984). Poverty in old age: Can pension reform meet the needs of women? *Canadian Woman Studies, 5,* 17–21.

Ng, C. F., & Northcott, H. C. (2010a). The ethnic and national identity of South Asian immigrant seniors in Edmonton, Canada. *Canadian Ethnic Studies, 41/42,* 131–156.

Ng, C. F., & Northcott, H. C. (2010b). South Asian immigrant seniors living in Edmonton: Diverse experiences. In D. Durst & M. MacLean (Eds.), *Diversity and aging among immigrant seniors in Canada: Changing faces and greying temples* (pp. 301–325). Calgary: Detselig.

Ng, C. F., & Northcott, H. C. (2013). Living arrangements of South Asian immigrant seniors in Edmonton, Canada: An assessment of the economic, cultural, health, and availability of kin explanations. *Journal of Housing for the Elderly, 27*(1–2), 1–27.

Ng, C. F., & Northcott, H. C. (2015). Living arrangements and loneliness of South Asian immigrant seniors in Edmonton, Canada. *Ageing and Society, 35*(3): 552–575, doi:10.1017/ S0144686X13000913.

Ng, C. F., Northcott, H. C., & Abu-Laban, S. M. (2007). Housing and living arrangements of South Asian immigrant seniors in Edmonton, Alberta. *Canadian Journal on Aging, 26*(3), 185–194.

Ng, E. (2011). *The healthy immigrant effect and mortality rates.* Ottawa: Statistics Canada. Retrieved from http://www. statcan.gc.ca/pub/82-003-x/2011004/article/11588-eng. htm.

Ng, E., Lai, D. W. L., Rudner, A. T., & Orpana, H. (2012). What do we know about immigrant seniors aging in Canada? A demographic, socio-economic and health profile. *CERIS Working Papers 88-90.* Retrieved from http://www.eldera-buseontario.com/wp-content/uploads/2014/03/What-do-we-know-about-immigrant-seniors-aging-in-Canada.pdf

Ng, E. S. W., & Law, A. (2014). Keeping Up! Older Workers' Adaptation in the Workplace after Age 55. *Canadian Journal on Aging, 33*(1), 1–14.

Nguyen, L. (2012). Rising 'grey divorce' rates create financial havoc for seniors. *The Globe and Mail, September 19.* Retrieved from http://www.theglobeandmail.com/news/politics/ rising-grey-divorce-rates-create-financial-havoc-for-seniors/article4553219.

Nicklett, E. J., Semba, R. D., Xue, Q-L, Tian, J., Sun, K., Cappola, A. R., Simonsic E. M., Ferrucci, L, and Fried, L. P. (2012). "Fruit and vegetable intake, physical activity, and mortality in older community-dwelling women." *Journal of the American Geriatrics Society,* 60:862–868.

Nikander, P. (2009). Doing change and continuity: Age identity and the micro-macro divide. *Ageing & Society, 29,* 863–881.

Noelker, L., & Browdie, R. (2012). Caring for caregivers: Developing models that work. *Generations, 36*(1), 103–106.

Noice, H., & Noice, T. (2009). An arts intervention for older adults living in subsidized retirement homes. *Aging, Neuropsychology, and Cognition, 16,* 56–79.

Norrick, N. (2009).The construction of multiple identities in elderly narrators' stories. *Ageing and Society, 29*(6), 905–921.

Northcott, H. C., & Northcott, J. L. (2010). Integration outcomes for immigrant seniors in Canada: A review of literature 2000–2007. In D. Durst & M. MacLean (Eds.), *Diversity and aging among immigrant seniors in Canada: Changing faces and greying temples* (pp. 37–57). Calgary: Detselig.

Northcott, H. C., & Petruik, C. R. (2011). The geographic mobility of elderly Canadians. *Canadian Journal on Aging, 30*(3), 311–322.

Northcott, H. C. & Petruik, C. R. (2013) "Trends in the residential mobility of seniors in Canada, 1961–2006." *The Canadian Geographer, 57*(1): 43–55, doi:10.1111/j.1541-0064.2012.00449.x.

Northcott, H. C., & Wilson, D. M. (2008). *Dying and death in Canada,* 2nd ed. Peterborough, ON: Broadview Press.

Northcott, H. C., & Wilson, D. M. (2017). *Dying, Death, and End-of-Life Care in Canada,* 3rd ed. Toronto: University of Toronto PressToronto: University of Toronto Press.

Novelli, B., & Workman, B. (2006). *50+: Igniting a revolution to reinvent America.* New York: St. Martin's Press.

Novik, N. (2010). An exploration of the factors impacting upon elderly Ukrainian immigrant women. In D. Durst & M. MacLean (Eds.), *Diversity and aging among immigrant seniors in Canada: Changing faces and greying temples* (pp. 363–386). Calgary: Detselig.

Nussbaum, P. D. (2009). *Your brain health lifestyle.* Tarentun, PA: Word Association Publishers.

Nussbaum, P. D. (2011). Brain health: Bridging neuroscience to consumer application. *Generations, 35*(2), 6–12.

Nyberg, L., & Bäckman, L. (2011). Memory changes and the aging brain: A multimodal imaging approach. In K. W. Schaie & S. L. Willis (Eds.), *Handbook of the psychology of aging,* 7th ed. (pp. 212–231). London: Academic Press (Elsevier).

Nyberg, L., Sandblom. J., Jones, S., Stigsdotter Neely, A., Petersson, K. M., Ingvar, M., et al. (2003). Neural correlates of training-related memory improvement in adulthood and aging. Proceedings of the National Academy of Sciences, USA, *100,* 13728–13733.

Oberlink, M. R. (2008). *Opportunities for creating livable communities.* Washington, DC: AARP.

Oceanside Grandmothers to Grandmothers. (2013). *Turning the tide.* Retrieved from http://oceansideg2g.ca/SLF-Connection.php.

O'Connor, D. (1999). Living with a memory-impaired spouse: (Re)cognizing the experience. *Canadian Journal on Aging, 18*(2), 211–235.

Oduaran, A., & Molosi, K. (2009). Botswana. In E. Palmore, F. Whittington, & S. Kunkel (Eds.), *The international handbook on aging,* 3rd ed. (pp. 119–129). Santa Barbara, CA: ABC-CLIO.

OECD (Organisation for Economic Co-operation and Development). (2011a). *Elderly population by region. OECD Factbook 2011.* Retrieved from http://www.oecd-ilibrary.org/docserver/download/fulltext/3011041ec012.pdf?expires=1342373226&id=id&accname=freeContent&checksum=7CB066062A6118FA4DEFEBE068C7CA64.

OECD (Organisation for Economic Co-operation and Development). (2011b). Key findings: Canada. *Health at a Glance 2011: OECD Indicators.* Retrieved from http://www.oecd.org/dataoecd/13/0/49084244.pdf.

OECD (Organisation for Economic Co-operation and Development). (2011c). *Canada. Long-Term Care.* Retrieved from http://www.oecd.org/dataoecd/60/56/47877490.pdf.

OECD (Organisation for Economic Co-operation and Development) Stat. (2015). *Health Care Resources: Hospital Beds.* Retrieved from https://stats.oecd.org/Index.aspx?DataSetCode=HEALTH_REAC.

OECD (Organisation for Economic Co-operation and Development) Stat. (2017). *Health expenditure and financing.* Retrieved March 1, 2017, from http://stats.oecd.org/Index.aspx?DataSetCode=SHA.

Office of Women's Health. (2012). Caregiver stress fact sheet. Retrieved February 15, 2014, from http://www.womenshealth.gov/publications/our-publications/fact-sheet/caregiver-stress.html#b.

Ogrodnik, L. (2007). *Seniors as victims of crime 2004 and 2005.* Canadian Centre for Justice Statistics. Statistics Canada Cat No. 85F0033MIE. Ottawa: Ministry of Industry.

Oliffe, J. L., Grewal, S., Bottorff, J. L., Luke, H., & Toor, H. (2007). Elderly South Asian Canadian immigrant men: Confirming and disrupting dominant discourses about masculinity and men's health. *Family and Community Health, 30*(3), 224–236.

Ontario Educational Credit Union Limited. (2011). *RRSP tax calculator.* Retrieved from http://www.oecu.on.ca/tools/rrsptax_calc.htm.

Ontario Human Rights Commission. (2015). Ageism and age discrimination (fact sheet). Retrieved from http://www.ohrc.on.ca/en/ageism-and-age-discrimination-fact-sheet.

Ontario Ministry of Labour. (2006). *Facts and figures: Mandatory retirement.* Retrieved from http://www.labour.gov.on.ca/english/news/2006/06-126b_2.html.

Oosthoek, S. (2009). Pointing the way toward lowering dementia risk in women. *Current Research.* Alzheimer Society. Retrieved from http://www.alzheimer.ca/english/research/Mary_Tierney.htm.

Oppong, C. (2006). Familial roles and social transformations: Older men and women in sub-Saharan Africa. *Research on Aging, 28*(6), 654–668.

O'Rand, A. M. (1996). The precious and the precocious: Understanding cumulative disadvantage and cumulative advantage over the life course. *The Gerontologist, 36,* 230–238.

O'Rand, A. M. (2006). Stratification and the life course: Life course capital, life course risks, and social inequality. In R. H. Binstock & L. K. George (Eds.), *Handbook of aging and the social sciences,* 6th ed. (pp. 145–162). Burlington, MA: Academic Press.

Oregon. (2009). *2009 summary of Oregon's Death with Dignity Act.* Retrieved from www.oregon.gov/DHS/ph/pas/docs/year12.pdf.

Orzeck, P., Brotmam, S., Drummond, J. D., Silverman, M., Shiller, I., & Barylak, L. (2014). Caregivers in the healthcare workplace. *Les cahiers du CREGÉS,* numéro 2014, vol. 1.

Osteoporosis Canada. (2011). Frequently asked questions. Retrieved from http://www.osteoporosis.ca/index.php/ci_id/5506/la_id/1.htm *and* http://www.osteoporosis.ca/index.php/ci_id/7702/la_id/1.htm.

Outcalt, L. (2013). Paid companions: A private care option for older adults. *Canadian Journal on Aging, 32*(1), 87–102.

Outcalt, L. (2015). The becoming of age: Cinematic visions of mind, body and identity in later life by Pamela H. Gravagne (review). *Canadian Journal on Aging 34*(1), 113–114.

Oveisgharan, S., & Hachinski, V. (2010). Hypertension, executive dysfunction, and progression to dementia. The Canadian study of health and aging. *Archives of Neurology*, 67(2), 187–192.

Overdorf, J. 2010. "Aging in India: Not the same old story." *Global Post*, June 13. Retrieved: May 5, 2013, http://www.globalpost.com/dispatch/health/100604/retirement-communities-india

Owen, A. M., Hampshire, A., Grahn, J. A., Stenton, R., Dajani, S., Burns, A. S., Howard, R. J., & Ballard, C. G. (2010). Putting brain training to the test. *Nature*, 465, 775–778.

Owram, D. (1996). *Born at the right time: A history of the baby-boom generation*. Toronto: University of Toronto Press.

Page, S. (1997). Accommodating the elderly: Words and actions in the community. In L. A. Pastalan (Ed.), *Shelter and service issues for aging populations: International perspectives*, 55–61. New York: Haworth.

Palangkaraya, A., & Yong, J. (2009). Population aging and its implications on aggregate health care demand: Empirical evidence from 22 OECD countries. *International Journal of Health Care Finance & Economics*, 9(4), 391–402.

Palmore, E. B. (1977). Facts on aging: A short quiz. *The Gerontologist*, 18, 315–320.

Palmore, E. B. (1998). Facts on aging quiz (2nd ed.). Springer: New York.

Palmore, E. B. (2005). Three decades of research on ageism. *Generations*, 29(3), 87–90.

Paradiso, R., Taccini, N., & Loriga, G. (2008). Textile sensing and e-textiles (smart textiles). In A. S. Helal, M. Mokhtari, & B. Abdulrazak (Eds.), *The engineering handbook of smart technology for aging, disability, and independence* (pp. 673–692). Hoboken, NJ: Wiley.

Pare, I. (2000, October 27). Des projets-pilotes prometteurs en sante. *Le Devoir*.

Parisi, J. M., Rebok, G. W., Carlson, M. C., Fried, L. P., Seeman, T. E., Tan, E. J., et al. (2009). Can wisdom of aging be activated and make a difference societally? *Educational Gerontology*, 35, 867–879.

Park, D. C., & Bischof, G. N. (2011). Neuroplasticity, aging, and cognitive function. In K. W. Schaie & S. L. Willis (Eds.), *Handbook of the psychology of aging*, 7th ed. (pp. 109–119). London: Academic Press (Elsevier).

Park, D. C., Lautenschlager, G., Hedden, T., Davidson, N. S., Smith, A. D., & Smith, P. K. (2002). Models of visuospatial and verbal memory across the adult life span. *Psychology and Aging*, 17, 299–320.

Park, D. C., & Meade, M. L. (2006). Memory: Everyday. In R. Schulz, L. S. Noelker, K. Rockwood, & R. L. Sprott (Eds.), *The encyclopedia of aging*, 4th ed. (pp. 744–747). New York: Springer.

Park, D. C., & Reuter-Lorenz, P. (2009). The adaptive brain: Aging and neurocognitive scaffolding. *Annual Review of Psychology*, 60, 173–196. Retrieved from http://www.annualreviews.org/doi/pdf/10.1146/annurev.psych.59.103006.093656.

Park, J. (2010). Health factors and early retirement among older workers. *Perspectives on Labour and Income*, June 5–13.

Park, J. (2011). Retirement, health and employment among those 55 plus. *Perspectives on Labour and Income*, January 31, 3–12.

Park, J. (2012). Job-related training of older workers. *Perspectives on Labour and Income*, 24(2), 1.

Parmelee, P. A., & Lawton, M. P. (1990). The design of special environments for the aged. In J. E. Birren and K. W. Schaie (Eds.), *Handbook of the psychology of aging*, 3rd ed. (pp. 464–488). San Diego: Academic Press.

Parsons, T. (1937). *The structure of social action*. New York: McGraw-Hill.

Parsons, T. (1951). *The social system*. New York: Free Press.

ParticipACTION. (2013). Canadian physical activity guidelines for adults 65 years and older. Retrieved from http://www.participaction.com/get-started/physical-activity-guidelines/guidelines-for-adults/guidelines-for-adults-65-years-and-older.

Paterson, D. H., Jones, G. R., & Rice, C. L. (2007). Ageing and physical activity: Evidence to develop exercise recommendations for older adults. *Applied Physiology, Nutrition, and Metabolism*, 32(S2E). Retrieved from http://www.nrcresearchpress.com/doi/full/10.1139/H07-1112011.

Patterson, M. C., & Perlstein, S. (2011). Good for the heart, good for the soul: The creative arts and brain health in later life. *Generations*, 35(2), 27–36.

Peacock, S., Forbes, D., Markle-Reid, M., et al. (2010). The positive aspects of the caregiving journey with dementia: Using a strengths-based perspective to reveal opportunities. *Journal of Applied Gerontology*, 29, 640–659.

Peckham, A., Williams, A. P., & Neysmith, S. (2014). Balancing formal and informal care for older persons: How case manages respond. *Canadian Journal on Aging*, 33(2), 123–136.

Penning, M. J. (1990). Receipt of assistance by elderly people: Hierarchical selection and task specificity. *The Gerontologist*, 30, 220–227.

Penning, M. J., & Wu, Z. (2014). Marital status, childlessness, and social support among older Canadians. *Canadian Journal on Aging*, 33(4), 426–447.

Pension Watch: Social Protection in Older Age. (2015). About social pensions. Retrieved from http://www.pension-watch.net/pensions/about-social-pensions/about-social-pensions/social-pensions-around-the-world.

Perks, T., & Haan, M. (2010). The dwelling-type choices of older Canadians and future housing demand: An investigation using the aging and social support survey (GSS16). *Canadian Journal on Aging*, 29(3), 445–463.

Perreault, S., & Brennan, S. (2010). Criminal victimization in Canada, 2009. *Juristat, 30*(2). Statistics Canada Cat. No. 85-002-X. Ottawa. Retrieved from http://www.statcan.gc.ca/pub/85-002-x/2010002/article/11340-eng.pdf.

Perry, T. E., Andersen, T. C., & Kaplan, D. B. (2013). Relocation remembered: Perspectives on senior transitions in the living environment. *The Gerontologist, 54*(1), 75–81.

Peterson, R. C. (2007). Mild cognitive impairment. *Continuum: Lifelong Learning in Neurology, 13*(2), 15–38.

Pezzin, L. E., Pollak, R. A., & Schone, B. S. (2015). Bargaining power, parental caregiving, and intergenerational coresidence. *Journals of Gerontology B, Psychological Science and Social Science, 7*(6), 969–980.

Philbin, K. A. (2011). Mourning and body memory: A sensory, integrative approach to psychological health and healing. *Topics in Geriatric Rehabilitation, 27*(2), 127–133.

Phillips, L. H., Kliegel, M., & Martin, M. (2006). Age and planning tasks: The influence of ecological validity. *International Journal of Aging and Human Development, 62*(2), 175–184.

Philpot, H. J. (1871). *Guide book to the Canadian dominion containing full information for the emigrant, the tourist, the sportsman and the small capitalist.* London: E. Stanford.

Phinney, A., Moody, E. M., & Small, J. A. (2014). The effect of a community-engaged arts program on older adults' well-being. *Canadian Journal on Aging, 33*(3), 336–345.

Pilkington, P. D., Windsor, T. D., & Crisp, D. A. (2012). Volunteering and subjective well-being in midlife and older adults: The role of supportive social networks. *The Journals of Gerontology, Series B: Psychological Sciences and Social Sciences, 67*(2), 249–260.

Pillemer, K., & Suitor, J. J. (2014). Who provides care? A prospective study of caregiving among adult siblings. *The Gerontologist, 54*(4), 589–598.

Ploeg, J., Campbell, L, Denton, M., Joshi, A., & Davies, S. (2004). Helping to build and rebuild secure lives and futures: Financial transfers from parents to adult children and grandchildren. *Canadian Journal on Aging, 23*(Suppl), S131–S144.

Ploeg, J., Denton, M. Tindale, J., Hutchison, B., Brazil, K., Akhtar-Danesh, N., Lillie, J, & Plenderleith, J. M. (2009). Older adults' awareness of community health and support services for dementia care. *Canadian Journal on Aging, 28*(4), 359–370.

Ploeg, J., Hayward, L., Woodward, C., & Johnston, R. (2008). A case study of a Canadian homelessness intervention programme for elderly people. *Health & Social Care in the Community, 16*(6), 593–605.

Plotnick, R. D. (2009). Childlessness and the economic well-being of older Americans. *Journal of Gerontology: Social Sciences, 64*(6), 767–776.

Podnieks, E. (2008). Elder abuse: The Canadian experience. *Journal of Elder Abuse & Neglect, 20*(2), 126–150.

Podnieks, E., Pillemer, K. Nicholson, J. P., Shillington, T., & Frizzel, A. (1990). *National survey on abuse of the elderly in Canada.* Toronto: Ryerson Polytechnic Institute.

Policy Research Initiative. (2004). *Views on life-course flexibility and Canada's aging population.* Ottawa: PRI Project: Population Aging and Life-Course Flexibility.

Polyamorous Passions. (2015). Senior Dating Site. Retrieved from http://www.polyamorouspassions.com/seniors.

Poon, L., & Harrington, C. A. (2006). Commonalities in aging- and fitness-related impact on cognition. In L. W. Poon, W. Chodzko-Zajko, & P. D. Tomporowski (Eds.). *Active living, cognitive functioning, and aging,* Vol 1. (pp. 33–50). Champaign, IL: Human Kinetics.

Poon, P. (2005). Who's missing out on the GIS? *Perspectives on Labour and Income, 6*(10), 5–14.

Pope, E. (2008). *Highlights and implications. Staying ahead of the curve: The AARP work and career study.* Washington, DC: AARP Knowledge Management.

Population Reference Bureau. (2010). *2010 world population data sheet.* Retrieved February 25, 2017, from http://www.prb.org/pdf10/10wpds_eng.pdf.

PositScience. (2012). Save 50% on PositScience brain fitness programs. Retrieved from http://www.positscience.com.

Poulin, Marc. (2009). Study Title. City: Alberta Heritage Foundation.

Powell, J. L. (2011). Aging in Africa. *Sincronia,* Spring. Retrieved from http://www.globalaging.org/health/world/2011/African%20report.pdf.

Powell, J. L., & Hendricks, J. (2009). The sociological construction of ageing: Lessons for theorizing. *The International Journal of Sociology and Social Policy, 29*(1/2), 84–94.

Préville, M., Vasiliadis, H.-M., Boyer, R., Goldfarb, M., Demers, K., Brassard, J., Beland, S.-G., & Scientific Committee of the ESA Study. (2009). Use of health services for psychological distress symptoms among community-dwelling older adults. *Canadian Journal on Aging, 28*(1), 51–61.

Prokos, A. H., & Keene, J. R. (2012). The life course and cumulativee disadvantage: Poverty among grandmother-headed families. *Research on Aging, 34*(5), 592–621.

Proulx, C., Helms, H., & Buehler, C. (2007). Marital quality and personal well-being: A meta-analysis. *Journal of Marriage and Family, 69*(3), 576–593.

Proulx, C., & Le Bourdais, C. (2014). Impact of providing care on the risk of leaving employment in Canada. *Canadian Journal on Aging, 33*(4), 488–503.

Province of Manitoba (2008). *Grand relations.* Retrieved from http://www.gov.mb.ca/index.html.

Prus, S. G. (2000). Income inequality as a Canadian cohort ages: An analysis of the later life course. *Research on Aging, 22*(3), 211–237.

Prus, S. G. (2011). Comparing social determinants of self-rated health across the United States and Canada. *Social Science*

& *Medicine, 73*(1), 50–59. Retrieved from http://www.sciencedirect.com.falcon.lib.csub.edu/science/article/pii/S0277953611002474

Public Health Agency of Canada. (2009). *Overview of the issue.* Ottawa, ON: Author. Retrieved from http://www.phac-aspc.gc.ca/seniors-aines/publications/pro/healthy-sante/workshop-atelier/injury/injury2-eng.php#evidence.

Public Health Agency of Canada. (2010a). What is the impact of osteoporosis in Canada and what are Canadians doing to maintain healthy bones? Retrieved from http://www.phac-aspc.gc.ca/cd-mc/osteoporosis-osteoporose.

Public Health Agency of Canada. (2010b). HIV/AIDS among older Canadians. *HIV/AIDS Epi Update.* Retrieved from http://www.phac-aspc.gc.ca/aids-sida/publication/epi/2010/6-eng.php.

Public Health Agency of Canada. (2010c). Social Media in Elder Abuse Prevention. Retrieved March 11, 2017, from http://www.phac-aspc.gc.ca/ea-ma/EB/eb-Sept-2010-eng.php.

Public Health Agency of Canada. (2011). Diabetes in Canada: Facts and figures from a public health perspective. Chapter 4: Reducing the risk of type 2 diabetes and its complications. Retrieved from http://www.phac-aspc.gc.ca/cd-mc/publications/diabetes-diabete/facts-figures-faits-chiffres-2011/chap4-eng.php.

Public Health Agency of Canada. (2014a). *Seniors' falls in Canada. Second report.* Ottawa: Minister of Health.

Public Health Agency of Canada. (2014b). Age-friendly communities. Retrieved from http://www.phac-aspc.gc.ca/seniors-aines/afc-caa-eng.php.

Public Health Agency of Canada. (2015a). Seniors' falls in Canada—Infographic. Retrieved from http://www.phac-aspc.gc.ca/seniors-aines/publications/public/injury-blessure/seniors_falls-chutes_aines/infographic-infographie_2015-eng.php.

Public Health Agency of Canada. (2015b). *Age-friendly communities.* Retrieved from http://www.phac-aspc.gc.ca/seniors-aines/afc-caa-eng.php.

Pudrovska, T., Schieman, S., & Carr, D. (2006). Strains of singlehood in later life: Do race and gender matter? *Journal of Gerontology: SS 61*(6), S315–S322.

Puner, M. (1979). *Vital maturity.* New York: Universe Books.

Putney, N. M., Bengtson, V. L., & Wakeman, M. A. (2007). The family and the future. In R. A. Pruchno & M. A. Smyer (Eds.), *Challenges of an aging society: Ethical dilemmas, political issues* (pp. 117–155). Baltimore: Johns Hopkins University Press.

Pynoos, J., Caraviello, R., & Cicero, C. (2009). Lifelong housing. Retrieved from http://www.bankofcanada.ca/rates/ related/inflation-calculator.

Pynoos, J., Cicero, C., & Nishita, C. M. (2010). New challenges and growing tends in senior housing. In R. B. Hudson (Ed.), *The new politics of old age policy,* 2nd ed. (pp. 3–20). Baltimore: Johns Hopkins University Press.

Pyper, W. (2006). Aging, health and work. *Perspectives on Labour and Income, 7*(2), 5–15.

Pyper, W. (2008). RRSP investments. *Perspectives on Labour and Income, 20*(1), 5–11.

Racine, L. (2010). Caring for older Haitian parents: The impact of immigration on family dynamics and caring activities on family caregivers. In D. Durst & M. MacLean (Eds.), *Diversity and aging among immigrant seniors in Canada: Changing faces and greying temples* (pp. 341–362). Calgary: Detselig.

Rahman, A., & Applebaum, R. (2010). What's all this about evidence-based practice? The roots, the controversies, and why it matters. *Generations, 34*(1), 6–12.

Raina, P. S., Wolfson, C., Kirkland, S. A., Griffith, L. E. Oremus, M., Patterson, C., Tuokko, H., Penning, M., Balion, C. M., Hogan, D., Wister, A., Payette H., Shannon, H., & Brazil, K. (2009). The Canadian longitudinal study on aging (CLSA). *Canadian Journal on Aging, 28*(3), 221–229.

Ramage-Morin, P. L., Bernier, J., Newsom, J. T., Huguet, N., McFarland, B. H., & Kaplan, M. S. (2012). Adopting leisure-time physical activity after diagnosis of a vascular condition. *Health Reports, 23*(1), 17–29.

Ramage-Morin, P. L., & Garriguet, D. (2013). Nutritional risk among older Canadians. *Health Reports, 24*(3), 3–13.

Ramage-Morin, P. L., Shields, M., & Martel, L. (2010). Health-promoting factors and good health among Canadians in mid- to late life. *Health Reports, 21*(3), 1–9.

Randall, W., & McKim, E. (2008). *Reading our lives: The poetics of growing old.* New York: Oxford University Press.

Ray, R. E. (2008). Coming of age in critical gerontology: Introduction. *Journal of Aging Studies, Special Issue 22*(2), 97–100.

Reinhardt, J. P. (2010). Research methods in evidence-based practice: Understanding the evidence. *Generations, 34*(1), 36–42.

Reitzes, D. C., & Mutran, E. J. (2006). Self and health: Factors that encourage self-esteem and functional health. *Journal of Gerontology, 61*(1), S44–S51.

Revera. (2012a). Tech-savvy seniors bridging the digital divide: Revera Report. Retrieved from http://www.reveraliving.com/about-revera/news/publications/docs/tech-savvyseniorsrelease-_june20.

Revera. (2012b). Backgrounder: Revera report on tech-savvy seniors. Retrieved from http://www.rever-aliving.com/about-revera/news/publications/docs/backgroundertech-savvyseniors_june20.

Reynolds, L. (2010). Aging disability awareness training for drivers of a metropolitan taxi company. *Activities, Adaptation, and Aging, 34,* 17–29.

Rheaume, C., & Mitty, E. (2008). Sexuality and intimacy in older adults. *Geriatric Nursing, 29*(5), 342–349.

Ribeiro, O., Paul, C., & Nogueira, C. (2007). Real men, real husbands: Caregiving and masculinities in later life. *Journal of Aging Studies, 21*, 302–313.

Richard, L., LaForest, S., Dufresne, E., & Sapinski, J. P. (2005). The quality of life of older adults living in an urban environment: Professional and lay perspectives. *Canadian Journal on Aging, 24*(1), 19–30.

Richards, J.-L., & Rankaduwa, W. (2008). Housing Canada's oldest-old: Correlates of their residential status. *Journal of Housing for the Elderly, 22*(4), 376–403.

Riediger, M., Li, S.-C., & Lindenberger, U. (2006). Selection, optimization, and compensation as developmental mechanisms of adaptive resource allocation: Review and Preview. In J. E. Birren & K. W. Schaie (Eds.), *Handbook of the psychology of aging*, 6th ed. (pp. 289–313). Burlington, MA: Elsevier Academic Press.

Riley, M. W. (1971). Social gerontology and the age stratification of society. *The Gerontologist, 11*, 79–87.

Riley, M. W. (1987). On the significance of age in sociology. *American Sociological Review, 52*, 1–14.

Riley, M. W. (1994). Aging and society: Past, present and future. *The Gerontologist, 34*, 436–446.

Riley, M. W., Foner, A., & Riley, J. W., Jr. (1999). The aging and society paradigm. In V. L. Bengtson and K. W. Schaie (Eds.), *Handbook of theories of aging* (pp. 327–43). New York: Springer Publishing.

Riley, M. W, Foner, A., & Waring, J. (1988). Sociology of age. In N. Smelser (Ed.), *Handbook of sociology*. Beverly Hills: Sage.

Riley, M. W., Johnson, M. E., & Foner, A. (Eds.) (1972). *Aging and society. Vol. 3: A sociology of age stratification.* New York: Russell Sage Foundation.

Ristau, S. (2011). People do need people: Social interaction boosts brain health in older age. *Generations, 35*(2), 70–76.

Rix, S. (2006). *Update on the aged 55+ worker: 2005.* Washington, DC: AARP Public Policy Institute. Retrieved from http://assets.aarp.org/rgcenter/econ/dd136_worker.pdf.

Rix, S. E. (2011). Employment and aging. In R. H. Binstock & L. K. George (Eds.), *Handbook of aging and the social sciences*, 7th ed. (pp. 193–206). London: Academic Press (Elsevier).

Road Scholar. (2014). The Road Scholar online press room. Retrieved from http://www.roadscholar.org//press/factsheet.asp.

Robinson, S. P., Mullane, L., & Lakin, M. B. (2007). *Framing new terrain: Older adults and higher education.* Washington, DC: American Council on Education. Retrieved from http://www.acenet.edu/Content/NavigationMenu/ProgramsServices/CLLL/Reinvesting/Reinvestingfinal.pdf.

Robson, W. B. P. (1996). Ponzi's pawns: Young Canadians and the Canada Pension Plan. In J. B. Burbridge et al. (Eds.), *When we're 65: Reforming Canada's retirement income system* (pp. 27–56). Toronto: C. D. Howe Institute.

Roger, K. S., Guse, L., Mordoch, E., & Osterreicher, A. (2012). Social commitment robots and dementia. *Canadian Journal on Aging, 31*(1), 87–94.

Roger, K. S., Mignone J., & Kirkland, S. (2013). Social aspects of HIV/AIDS and aging: A thematic review. Research note. *Canadian Journal on Aging, 32*(3), 298–306.

Roger, K. S., & Ursel, J. (2009). Public opinion on mandatory reporting of abuse and/or neglect of older adults in Manitoba, Canada. *Journal of Elder Abuse & Neglect, 21*, 115–140.

Rogers, C., Keller, C., & Larkey, L. K. (2010). "Perceived benefits of meditative movement in older adults." *Geriatric Nursing, 31*(1): 37–52.

Romaniuk, A. (2010). Fertility in the age of demographic maturity: An essay. *Canadian Studies in Population, 37*(3–4), 283–295.

Roring, R. W., & Charness, N. (2007). A multilevel model analysis of expertise in chess across the lifespan. *Psychology and Aging, 22*, 291–299.

Rosen, A. L. (2014). Where mental health and elder abuse intersect. *Generations, 38*(3), 75–79.

Rosen, T., Lachs, M. S., & Pillemer, K. (2010). Sexual aggression between residents in nursing homes: Literature synthesis of an underrecognized problem. *Journal of the American Geriatrics Society, 58*(10), 1970–1979.

Rosenberg, M. (2009). Editorial: The times they are a-changin'. *Canadian Journal on Aging, 28*(1), 1.

Rosenbloom, S. (2009). Meeting transportation needs in an aging-friendly environment. *Generations, 33*(2), 33–43.

Rosenmayr, L., & Kockeis, E. (1963). Propositions for a sociological theory of aging and the family. *International Social Science Journal, 15*: 410–426.

Rosenthal, C. J. (1994). Editorial: Long-term care reform and 'family' care: A worrisome combination. *Canadian Journal on Aging, 13*(3), 419–27.

Rosenthal, C. J., & Dawson, P. (1991). Wives of institutionalized elderly men. *Journal of Aging and Health, 3*(3), 315–334.

Rosenthal, R. L. (2008). Older computer-literate women: Their motivations, obstacles and paths to success. *Educational Gerontology, 34*:610–626.

Ross, C. E., & Wu, C. 1995. The links between education and health. *American Sociological Review, 60*, 719–745.

Ross, M. M., Rosenthal, C. J., & Dawson, P. (1994). The continuation of caregiving following the institutionalization of elderly husbands. In National Advisory Council on Aging, *Marital disruption in later life* (pp. 23–32). Cat. No. H71-3/17-1994E. Ottawa: Minister of Supply and Services.

Ross, N. A., Gilmour, H., & Dasgupta, K. (2010). 14-year diabetes incidence: The role of socio-economic status. *Health Reports, 21*(3). Retrieved from http://www.diabeseducation.ca/images/socio_economic_status_and_diabetes.pdf.

Ross, P., Humble, A. M., & Blum, I. (2013). Sexuality and HIV/ AIDS: An exploration of older heterosexual women's knowledge levels. *Journal of Women & Aging, 25,* 165–182.

Roterman, M. (2006). Seniors' health care use. *Supplement to Health Reports, 16,* 33–45. Statistics Canada Cat No. 82–003.

Rowe, G., Hasher, L., & Turcotte, J. (2008). Age differences in visuospatial working memory. *Psychology and Aging, 23*(1), 79–84.

Rowe, J. W., & Kahn, R. L. (1999). *Successful aging.* New York: Dell Publishing.

Rozanova, J., Dosman, D., & de Jong Gierveld, J. (2008). Participation in rural contexts: Community matters. In N. Keating (Ed.), *Rural ageing: A good place to grow old?* (pp. 75–86). Bristol, UK: The Policy Press. University of Bristol.

Rozanova, J., Northcott, H. C., & S. A. McDaniel. (2006). Seniors and portrayals of intra-generational and inter-generational inequality in *The Globe and Mail. Canadian Journal on Aging 2*(4), 373–386.

Rudman, D. L. (2006). Positive aging and its implications for occupational possibilities in later life. *Canadian Journal of Occupational Therapy, 73,* 188–192.

Rudman, D. L., Friedland, J., Chipman, M., & Sciortino, P. (2006). Holding on and letting go: The perspectives of pre-seniors and seniors on driving self-regulation in later life. *Canadian Journal on Aging, 25*(1), 65–76.

Ruffenach, G. (2007, November 17–18). In search of a purpose. *The Wall Street Journal,* wsj.com. Retrieved from http:// online.wsj.com/article/SB119515599441894584.html.

Russell, R. (2007). The work of elderly men caregivers: From public careers to an unseen world. *Men & Masculinities, 9*(3), 298–314.

Russell, R. (2008). Their story, my story: Health of older men as caregivers. *Generations, 32*(1), 62–67.

Rutherford, A., & Bowes, A. (2014). Networks of informal caring: A mixed-methods approach. *Canadian Journal on Aging, 33*(4), 473–487.

Salari, S. (2011). Elder mistreatment. In R. A. Settersten, Jr., & J. L. Angel (Eds.), *Handbook of sociology of aging* (pp. 415–430). New York: Springer.

Salomon, E. (2010). *Housing policy solutions to support aging in place. Fact sheet 172.* Washington, DC: AARP Public Policy Institute. Retrieved from www.hebrewseniorlife.org/work-files/HSL/AAPRaging-in-place.pdf.

Salthouse, T. A. (2006). Theoretical issues in the psychology of aging. In J. E. Birren and K. W. Schaie (Eds.), *Handbook of the psychology of aging,* 6th ed. (pp. 3–13). Burlington, MA: Elsevier Academic Press.

Sandstory. (2015). Now a word for seniors. *Reddit.* Retrieved from https://www.reddit.com/r/polyamory/comments/3jqr0i/now_a_word_for_seniors.

Sanmartin, C., & Gilmore, J. (2008). Diabetes: Prevalence and care practices. *Health Reports, 19*(3). Statistics Canada Cat. No. 82-003-X. Ottawa: Statistics Canada.

Sarkisian, N., & Gerstel, N. (2008). Till marriage do us part: Adult children's relationships with their parents. *Journal of Marriage and Family, 70*(2), 360–376.

Satariano, W. A., Scharlach, A. E., & Lindeman, D. (2014). Aging, place, and technology: Toward improving access and wellness in older populations. *Journal of Aging and Health, 26*(8), 1373–1389.

Sattelmair, J. R., Kurth, T., Buring, J. E., & Lee, I.-M. (2010). Physical activity and risk of stroke in women. *Stroke, 41,* 1243–1250. Retrieved from http://stroke.ahajournals.org/ cgi/content/abstract/41/6/1243.

Savundranayagam, M. Y. (2014). Receiving while giving: The differential roles of receiving help and satisfaction with help on caregiver rewards among spouses and adult-children. *International Journal of Geriatric Psychiatry, 29,* 41–48.

Scarth, W. (2003). *Population aging, productivity, and growth in living standards.* SEDAP Research Paper No. 90. Hamilton, ON: McMaster University.

Schaefer, J. L. (2010). Voices of older baby boomers students: Supporting their transitions back into college. *Educational Gerontology, 36* (1), 67–90.

Schafer M. H., Mustillo, S. A., & Ferraro, K. F. (2013). Age and the tenses of life satisfaction. *Journals of Gerontology, Series B: Psychological Sciences and Social Sciences, 68*(4), 571–579.

Schaie, K. W. (2006). Intelligence. In R. Schulz, L. S. Noelker, K. Rockwood, & R. L. Sprott (Eds.), *The encyclopedia of aging,* 4th ed. (pp. 600–602). New York: Springer.

Schaie, K. W., & Willis S. L. (Eds.) (2016). *Handbook of the psychology of aging,* 8th ed. London: Academic Press (Elsevier).

Scheibe, S., Kunzmann, U., & Baltes, P. B. (2007). Wisdom, life longings, and optimal development. In J. A. Blackburn & C. N. Dulmas (Eds.), *Handbook of gerontology: Evidence-based approaches to theory, practice, and policy* (pp. 117–142). Hoboken, NJ: John Wiley & Sons.

Schellenberg, G., & Ostrovsky, Y. (2008a). The retirement plans and expectations of older workers. 2007 *General Social Survey* Report. *Canadian Social Trends.* Component of Statistics Canada Cat. No. 11-008-X.

Schellenberg, G., & Ostrovsky, Y. (2008b). Retiring together, or not. *Perspectives on Labour and Income, 9*(4), 5–11.

Schellenberg, G., Turcotte, M., & Ram, B. (2005). What makes retirement enjoyable? *Canadian Social Trends,* Fall, 12–14.

Schellenberg, G., Turcotte, M., & Ram, B. (2006). The changing characteristics of older couples and joint retirement in Canada. In L. O. Stone (Ed.), *New frontiers of research on retirement* (pp. 199–218). Statistics Canada Cat. No. 75-511-XIE. Ottawa: Minister of Industry.

Schirle, T. (2010). Health, pensions, and the retirement decision: Evidence from Canada. *Canadian Journal on Aging, 29*(4), 519–527.

Schlesinger, B., & Schlesinger, R. A. (2009). Canadian-Jewish seniors: Marriage/cohabitation after age 65. *Journal of Gerontological Social Work, 52*(1), 32–47.

Schneider, R., Nidich, S., Kotchen, J. M., Kotchen, T., Grim, C., Rainforth M. et al. (2009). Effects of stress reduction on clinical events in African Americans with coronary heart disease: A randomized controlled trial. *Circulation, 120*, S461. Retrieved from http://circ.ahajournals.org/cgi/content/meeting_abstract/120/18_MeetingAbstracts/S461-a

Schooler, C. (2009). The effects of the cognitive complexity of occupational conditions and leisure-time activities on the intellectual functioning of older adults. In W. Chodzko-Zajko, A. F. Kramer, & L. W. Poon (Eds.). *Enhancing cognitive functioning and brain plasticity* (pp.15–34). Champaign, IL: Human Kinetics.

Schulz, J. H., & Binstock, R. H. (2006). *Aging nation: The economics and politics of growing older in America*. Westport, CT: Praeger.

Schulz, J. H., & Borowski, A. (2006). Economic security in retirement: Reshaping the public-private pension mix. In R. H. Binstock & L. K. George (Eds.), *Handbook of aging and the social sciences*, 6th ed. (pp. 360–379). Burlington, MA: Academic Press.

Schulz, L. C. (2010). The Dutch hunger winter and the developmental origins of health and disease. *Proceedings of the National Academy of Sciences of the United States (PNAS), 107*(39), 16757–16758. Retrieved from http://www.pnas.org/content/107/39/16757.full.

Schutz, A. (1967). The phenomenology of the social world. [Tr. by G. Walsh & F. Lehnert.] Evanston, IL: Northwestern University Press.

Scialfa, C. T., & Fernie, G. R. (2006). Adaptive technology. In J. E. Birren & K. W. Schaie (Eds.), *Handbook of the psychology of aging*, 6th ed. (pp. 425–4441). Burlington, MA: Elsevier Academic Press.

Seals, C. D., Clanton, K., Agarwal, R., Doswell, F., & Thomas, C. M. (2008). Lifelong learning: Becoming computer savvy at a later age. *Educational Gerontology, 34*, 1055–1069.

Secom. (2017). "Meal-assistance robot: My Spoon." Accessed February 21, 2017, at http://www.secom.co.jp/english/myspoon.

Secretariat for the Intersectoral Healthy Living Network in partnership with the F/P/T Healthy Living Task Group and the F/P/T Advisory Committee on Population Health and Health Security (ACPHHS). (2005). *The integrated pan-Canadian healthy living strategy*. Ottawa: Minister of Health. Retrieved from http://www.phac-aspc.gc.ca/hl-vs-strat/pdf/hls_e.pdf.

Seguin, R. A., Economos, C. D., Palombo, R., Hyatt, R., Kuder, J., & Nelson, M. E. (2010). Strength training and older women: A cross-sectional study examining factors related to exercise adherence. *Journal of Aging and Physical Activity, 18*(2), 201–218.

Selye, H. (1956). *The stress of life*. New York: McGraw-Hill.

Seniorresource.com. (2010a). *Housing choices*. Retrieved from www.seniorresource.com/house.htm#ccrc.

Service Canada. (2010). *Changes to the Canada Pension Plan*. Retrieved from http://www.servicecanada.gc.ca/eng/isp/pub/factsheets/ISPB-348-11-10_E.pdf.

Service Canada. (2012). *Income security programs information card*. Retrieved from http://www.servicecanada.gc.ca/eng/isp/statistics/rates/janmar12.shtml.

Service Canada. (2015a). Old Age Security payment amounts. Retrieved from http://www.servicecanada.gc.ca/eng/services/pensions/oas/payments/index.shtml.

Service Canada. (2015b). Quarterly report of Canada Pension Plan and Old Age Security monthly amounts and related figures—July to September 2015. Retrieved from http://www.servicecanada.gc.ca/eng/services/pensions/infocard/julsep15.shtml.

Settersten, R. A. (2003). Propositions and controversies in life-course scholarship. In R. A. Settersten (Ed.), *Invitation to the life course: Toward new understandings of later life* (pp. 15–45). Amityville, NY: Baywood.

Settersten, R. A. (2006). Aging and the life course. In R. H. Binstock & L. K. George (Eds.), *Handbook of aging and the social sciences*, 6th ed. (pp. 3–19). Burlington, MA: Academic Press.

Settersten, R. A., & Trauten, M. E. (2010). On time and ties: Why the life course matters for old age policies. In R. B. Hudson (Ed.), *The new politics of old age policy*, 2nd ed. (pp. 41–159). Baltimore: The Johns Hopkins University Press.

Seymour, A., Hagerman, V., De Jong, C., & Wilson, J. (2006). Evaluation demonstrates telehomecare reduces need for hospital care. *Canadian Healthcare Technology*. October. Retrieved from http://www.rivervalleyhealth.nb.ca/en/programs/patient/Canadian_Healthcare_Technology.pdf.

Shanas, E. (1967). Family help patterns and social class in three societies. *Journal of Marriage and the Family 29*: 257–66.

Shanas, E. (1979). The family as a social support system in old age. *The Gerontologist, 19*: 169–174.

Shankar, I., & Northcott, H. (2009). Through my son: Immigrant women bargain with patriarchy. *Women's Studies International Forum, 32*: 424–434.

Shapira, N., Barak, A., & Gal, I. (2007). Promoting older adults' well-being through Internet training and use. *Aging & Mental Health, 11*(5), 477–484.

Sharma, A. (2013). The chain is only as strong as the weakest link: Older adult migration and the first move. *Research on Aging, 35*(5), 507–532.

Shenk, D., Kuwahara, K., & Zablotsky, D. (2004). Older women's attachments to their home and possessions. *Journal of Aging Studies, 18,* 157–169.

Shibata, T., & Wada, K. (2008). Robot therapy and elder care institutions: Effects of long-term interaction with seal robots. In A. S. Helal, M. Mokhtari, & B. Abdulrazak (Eds.), *The engineering handbook of smart technology for aging, disability, and independence* (pp. 405–418). Hoboken, NJ: Wiley.

Shields, M. (2008). Community belonging and self-perceived health. *Health Reports, 19*(2), 1–10.

Shields, M., & Martel, L. (2006). Healthy living among seniors. *Supplement to Health Reports, 16,* 7–20. Statistics Canada. Cat. No. 82-003.

Shields, M., & Tjepkema, M. (2006). Trends in adult obesity. *Health Reports, 17*(3), 53–9. Statistics Canada Cat. No. 82-003.

Shields, M., & Tremblay, M. S. (2008a). Screen time among Canadian adults: A profile. *Health Reports, 19*(2), 31–43. Statistics Canada Cat. No. 82-003.

Shields, M., & Tremblay, M. S. (2008b). Sedentary behaviour and obesity. *Health Reports, 19*(2), 19–30. Statistics Canada, Catalogue 82-003.

Shields, M., Tremblay, M. S., Laviolette, M., Craig, C. L., Janssen, I., & Gorber, S. C. (2010). Fitness of Canadian adults: Results from the 2007–2009 *Canadian Health Measures Survey. Health Reports.* Statistics Canada. Retrieved February 25, 2017, from http://www.statcan.gc.ca/pub/82-003-x/2010001/article/11064-eng.pdf.

Shiota, M. N., & Levenson, R. W. (2007). Birds of a feather don't always fly farthest: Similarity in big five personality predicts more negative marital satisfaction trajectories in long-term marriages. *Psychology and Aging, 22*(4), 666–675.

Shippee, T. P., Wilkinson, L. R., Ferraro, K. F. (2012). Accumulated financial strain and women. *Journals of Gerontology Series B: Psychological and Social Sciences, 67*(5), 585–594.

Shringarpure, R., & Davies, K. J. A. (2009). Free radicals and oxidative stress in aging. In V. L. Bengtson, M. Silverstein, M. M. Putney, & D. Gans (Eds.), *Handbook of theories of aging,* (pp. 229–244). New York: Springer.

Siberski, J., Shatil, E., Siberski, C., Eckroth-Bucher, M., French, A., Horton, S., Loefflad, R. F., & Rouse P. (2015). Computer-based cognitive training for individuals with intellectual and developmental disabilities: Pilot study. *American Journal of Alzheimer's Disease & Other Dementias, 30*(1), 41–48.

Silberfeld, M. (1992). The use of 'risk' in decision-making. *Canadian Journal on Aging, 11*(2), 124–36.

Silverstein, M. (2006). Intergenerational family transfers in social context. In R. H. Binstock & L. K. George (Eds.), *Handbook of aging and the social sciences,* 6th ed. (pp. 165–180). Burlington, MA: Academic Press.

Silverstein, M., & Giarrusso, R. (2011). Aging individuals, families, and societies: Micro-meso-macro linkages in the life course. In R. A. Settersten, Jr., & J. L. Angel (Eds.), *Handbook of sociology of aging* (pp. 35–49). New York: Springer.

Simons, K., & Bonifas, R. (2009). Social work student interest in nursing home employment: A North American study. *Journal of Gerontological Social Work, 52,* 294–314.

Simonton, D. K. (1977). Creative productivity, age, and stress: A biographical time-series analysis of 10 classical composers. *Journal of Personality and Social Psychology, 35*(11), 791–804.

Simonton, D. K. (1988). Age and outstanding achievement: What do we know after over a century of research? *Psychological Bulletin, 104,* 251–267.

Simonton, D. K. (1990). Creativity and wisdom in aging. In J. E. Birren & K. W. Schaie (Eds.), *Handbook of the psychology of aging,* 3rd ed., (pp. 320–329). San Diego: Academic Press.

Simonton, D. K. (2006). Creativity. In R. Schulz, L. S. Noelker, K. Rockwood, & R. L. Sprott (Eds.), *The encyclopedia of aging,* 4th ed. (pp. 269–270). New York: Springer.

Sims-Gould, J., & Martin-Matthews, A. (2008). Distance, privacy and independence: Rural homecare. In N. Keating (Ed.), *Rural ageing: A good place to grow old?* (pp. 43–51). Bristol, UK: The Policy Press. University of Bristol.

Sims-Gould, J., & Martin-Matthews, A. (2010a). Strategies used by home support workers in the delivery of care to elderly clients. *Canadian Journal on Aging, 29*(1), 97–107.

Sims-Gould, J., & Martin-Matthews, A. (2010b). We share the care: Family caregivers' experiences of their older relative receiving home support services. *Health and Care in the Community, 18*(4), 415–423.

Sims-Gould, J., Martin-Matthews, A., & Rosenthal, C. J. (2008). Family caregiving and helping at the intersection of gender and kinship: Social dynamics in the provision of care to older adults in Canada. In A. Martin-Matthews & J. E. Phillips (Eds.), *Aging and caring at the intersection of work and home life* (pp. 65–84). New York, NY: Psychology Press.

Sims-Gould, J., Miran-Khan, K., Haggis, C., & Liu-Ambrose, T. 2012. "Timing, experience, benefits, and barriers: Older women's uptake and adherence to an exercise program." *Activities, Adaptation & Aging, 36:* 280–296.

Sinai, A., Bohnen, I., & Strydom, A. (2012). Older adults with intellectual disability. Current *Opinions in Psychiatry, 25*(5), 359–364.

Sinclair, D. A., & Howitz, K. T. (2006). Dietary restriction, hormesis, and small molecule mimetics. In E. Masoro, J. Edward, & S. N. Austad (Eds.), *Handbook of the biology of aging* (6th ed., pp. 63–104). Burlington, MA: Elsevier.

Singh-Manoux, A., Ferrie, J. E., Chandola, T., & Marmot, M. (2004). Socioeconomic trajectories across the life course and health outcomes in midlife: Evidence for the accumulation hypothesis. *International Journal of Epidemiology, 33*(5), 1072–1079.

Sinha M. (2011). Police-reported family violence against seniors, 2009. In Statistics Canada (Ed.), *Family violence in Canada-A statistical profile* (pp. 27–31). Statistics Canada Cat. No. 85-224-X. Ottawa: Statistics Canada.

Sinha, M. (2013a). Portrait of Caregivers, 2012. Spotlight on Canadians: Results from the *General Social Survey*. Statistics Canada. Retrieved from http://www.statcan.gc.ca/pub/89-652-x/89-652-x2013001-eng.pdf.

Sinha, M. (2013b). Family violence in Canada: A statistical profile, 2011. *Juristat*. Statistics Canada. Ottawa: Minister of Industry. Retrieved from http://www.statcan.gc.ca/pub/85-002-x/2013001/article/11805-eng.pdf.

Sinha, M. (2015). Canadians' connections with family and friends, 2013. *Spotlight on Canadians: Results from the General Social Survey*. Retrieved from http://www.statcan.gc.ca/pub/89-652-x/89-652-x2014006-eng.pdf.

Sinha, M., & Bleakney, A. (2014). Receiving care at home. *Spotlight on Canadians: Results from the General Social Survey*. Statistics Canada. Retrieved from http://www.statcan.gc.ca/pub/89-652-x/89-652-x2014002-eng.pdf.

Sixsmith, A. (2008). Modeling the well-being of older people. In A. S. Helal, M. Mokhtari, & B. Abdulrazak (Eds.), *The engineering handbook of smart technology for aging, disability, and independence* (pp. 569–584). Hoboken, NJ: Wiley.

Slaughter, S., & Bankes, J. (2007). The functional transitions model: Maximizing ability in the context of progressive disability associated with Alzheimer's disease. *Canadian Journal on Aging, 26*(1), 39–48.

Sleightholm, M., Billette, J.-M., Normandin, C., & Hofmann, N. (2010). The use of transportation by seniors in Canada. *EnviroStats, 4*(4), 12–15. Retrieved from http://www.statcan.gc.ca/pub/16-002-x/16-002-x2010004-eng.pdf.

Slevin, K. F. (2006). The embodied experiences of older lesbians. In T. M. Calasanti & K. F. Slevin (Eds.), *Age matters: Realigning feminist thinking* (pp. 247–268). New York: Routledge.

Small, B. J., & McEvoy, C. L. (2008). Does participation in cognitive activities buffer age-related cognitive decline? In S. M. Hofer & D. F. Alwin (Eds.), *Handbook of cognitive aging: Interdisciplinary perspectives* (pp. 575–586). Los Angeles: SAGE Publications.

Small, G., & Vorgan, G. (2008). *iBrain: Surviving the technological alteration of the modern mind*. New York: HarperCollins.

Smetanin, P., Kobak, P., Briante, C., Stiff, D., Sherman, G., & Ahmad, S. (2009). *Rising tide: The impact of dementia in Canada 2008 to 2038*. RiskAnalytica: The Alzheimer's Society of Canada.

Smith, A. (2012). Broadening the dementia debate: Toward social citizenship (review). *Canadian Journal on Aging, 31*(2), 255–256.

Smith, A. D. (2006). Cognitive Processes. In R. Schulz, L. S. Noelker, K. Rockwood, & R. L. Sprott (Eds.), *The encyclopedia of aging*, 4th ed. (pp. 229–232). New York: Springer.

Smith, D. (2007). Big death: Funeral planning in the age of corporate deathcare. Halifax: Fernwood.

Snell, J. G. (1993). The gendered construction of elderly marriage, 1900–1950. *Canadian Journal on Aging, 12*(4), 509–523.

Snell, J. G. (1996). The citizen's wage: The state and the elderly in Canada, 1900–1951. Toronto: University of Toronto Press.

Snowdon, D. (2001). *Aging with grace: What the nun study teaches us about leading longer, healthier, and more meaningful lives*. Bantam Books, New York, NY.

Snyder, R. J., & Zweig, R. A. (2010) Medical and psychology students' knowledge and attitudes regarding aging and sexuality. *Gerontology & Geriatrics Education*, 31:3, 235–255.

Social Security. (2015). Otto von Bismarck. *Social Security History*. Retrieved from http://www.ssa.gov/history/ottob.html.

Solan, K. (2007). Over-60 innovators energize social changes. *Where to Retire, 16*(6), 66.

Soroka, S. N. (2007). *Canadian perceptions of the health care system*. A Report to the Health Council of Canada. Toronto: Health Council of Canada. Retrieved from http://www.queensu.ca/cora/_files/PublicPerceptions.pdf.

Sparks, B., Temple, V., Springer, M., & Stoddart, K. P. (2000). Service provision to older adults with developmental disabilities: A survey of service providers. *Canadian Journal on Aging, 19*(2), 210–222.

Spector-Mersel, G. (2006). Never-aging stories: Western hegemonic masculinity scripts. *Journal of Gender Studies, 15*(1), 67–82.

Speechley, M., Belfry, S., Borrie, M. J., Jenkyn, K. B., Crilly, R., Gill, D., McLean, S., Stolee, P., Vandervoort, A. A., & Jones, G. R. (2005). Risk factors for falling among community-dwelling veterans and their caregivers. *Canadian Journal on Aging, 24*(3), 261–274.

Spence, J. C., Brawley, L. R., Craig, C. L., Plotnikoff, R. C., Tremblay, M. S., Bauman, A., Faulkner, G. E. J., Chad, K., & Clark, M. I. (2009). ParticipACTION: Awareness of the ParticipACTION campaign among Canadian adults—Examining the knowledge gap hypothesis and a hierarchy-of-effects model. *International Journal of Behavioral Nutrition and Physical Activity, 6*. Retrieved from http://www.ncbi.nlm.nih.gov/pmc/articles/PMC2795738/?tool=pmcentrez.

Spinney, J. E. L. (2013). Aerobic activity preferences among older Canadians: A time-use perspective. *Canadian Journal on Aging, 32*(4), 443–451.

Spinney, J. E. L., & Millward, H. (2014). Active living among older Canadians: A time-use perspective over 3 decades. *Journal of Aging and Physical Activity, 22*, 103–113.

Spirduso, W. W., Poon, L. W., & Chodzko-Zajko, W. (2008). Conclusions and future research directions. In W. W. Spirduso, L. W. Poon, & W. Chodzko-Zajko (Eds.), *Exercise and its mediating effects on cognition* (pp. 211–219). Champaign, IL: Human Kinetics.

Spitze, G., & Trent, K. (2006). Gender differences in adult sibling relations in two-child families. *Journal of Marriage and Family*, 68(4), 977–992.

Spitzer, D. L. (Ed.). (2011). *Engendering migrant health: Canadian perspectives.* Toronto: University of Toronto Press.

St-Amant, O., Ward-Griffin, C., DeForge, R. T., & Oudshoorn, A. (2012). Making care decisions in home-based dementia care: Why context matters. *Canadian Journal on Aging*, 31(4), 423–434.

Standish, T. I. M., Molloy, D. W., Cunje, A., & Lewis, D. L. (2007). Do the ABCS 135 short cognitive screen and its subtests discriminate between normal cognition, mild cognitive impairment, and dementia? *International Journal of Geriatric Psychiatry*, 22(3), 189–194.

St-Arnaud, J., Beaudet, M. P., & Tully, P. (2005). Life expectancy. *Health Reports*, 17(1), 43–47. Statistics Canada Cat. No. 82-003.

Starr, E., Ball, J., Williams, A. P., Morton-Chang, F., Warrick, N., & Snyder, D. (2015). Housing options for people living with dementia. Canada Mortgage and Housing Corporation.

Statistics Canada. (1978). *Vital statistics.* Vol. III: Births-Deaths, 1975 and 1976. Cat. No. 84-204. Ottawa: Health Division, Vital Statistics and Diseases Registry Section, Statistics Canada, Ministry of Supply and Services.

Statistics Canada. (1981). *Canada year book*, 1980–81. Ottawa: Minister of Supply and Services.

Statistics Canada. (1989). *Canada year book*, 1990. Cat. No. 11-402E/1990. Ottawa: Minister of Supply and Services.

Statistics Canada. (2003a). *Canada's Retirement Income Programs: A Statistical Overview (1990–2000).* Minister of Industry.

Statistics Canada. (2004a). The people: Hospitals. *The Canada e-Book.* Retrieved from http://www43.statcan.ca/02/02b/02b_008a_e.htm.

Statistics Canada. (2005a). *Projections of the Aboriginal populations, Canada, provinces and territories: 2001 to 2017.* Cat. No. 91-547-XIE. Ottawa: Minister of Industry.

Statistics Canada. (2006a). Canada's population by age and sex. *The Daily*, October 26. Retrieved from http://www.statcan.ca/Daily/English/061026/d061026b.htm.

Statistics Canada. (2006b). *Census of population.* Cat. No. 97-557-XCB2006019. (Canada, Code01). Retrieved from http://www12.statcan.gc.ca/census-recensement/2006/dp-pd/tbt/Rp-eng.cfm?tabid=1&lang=e&apath=3&detail=0&dim=0&fl=a&free=0&gc=0&gk=0&grp=1&pid=89447&prid=0&ptype=88971,97154&s=0&showall=0&sub=0&temporal=2006&theme=72&vid=0&vnamee=&vnamef=.

Statistics Canada. (2006c). Aboriginal peoples in Canada in 2006: Inuit, Métis and First Nations. *2006 Census.* Retrieved from http://www12.statcan.gc.ca/census-recensement/2006/as-sa/97-558/p2-eng.cfm.

Statistics Canada. (2006d). *The wealth of Canadians: An overview of the results of the survey of financial security, 2005.* Cat. No. 13F0-026MIE—No. 001. Ottawa: Minister of Industry.

Statistics Canada. (2006e). *Net worth of family units, by selected family characteristics (by sex and age).* Retrieved from http://www40.statcan.ca/l01/cst01/famil112a-eng.htm.

Statistics Canada. Census of Canada. (2006f). Legal Marital Status (6), Common-Law Status (3), Age Groups (17), and Sex (3) for Population 15 Years and Over of Canada, Provinces, Territories, Census Divisions and Census Agglomerations, 2006 Census—100% Data Catalogue Number 97-5562-XCB2006007. Ottawa, ON: Statistics Canada.

Statistics Canada. (2007a). Portrait of the Canadian population in 2006, population and dwelling counts. *2006 Census.* Ottawa: Minister of Industry.

Statistics Canada. (2007b). *2001 Census.* Retrieved from http://www12.statcan.ca/english/census01/release/release5.cfm.

Statistics Canada. (2007c). *Participation and activity limitation survey.* Retrieved from http://www.statcan.ca/english/freepub/89-628-XIE/2007003/series1-en.htm.

Statistics Canada. (2008a). *Low income before tax cutoffs (LICO-BT).* Retrieved from http://www12.statcan.ca/census-recensement/2006/ref/dict/fam020-eng.cfm.

Statistics Canada. (2008b). Divorces in Canada, 2005. *The Daily*, November 18.

Statistics Canada. (2009a). Aboriginal peoples in Canada in 2006: Inuit, Métis and First Nations. *2006 Census.*

Statistics Canada. (2010a). Criminal victimization in Canada, 2009. *General Social Survey, 2009.* Retrieved from http://www.statcan.gc.ca/pub/85-002-x/2010002/article/11340/tbl/tbl4-eng.htm.

Statistics Canada. (2010b) Population projections for Canada, provinces and territories, 2009 to 2036. Cat. No. 91-520. Retrieved from http://www12.statcan.gc.ca/census-recensement/2011/as-sa/98-311-x/2011003/fig/fig3_1-1-eng.cfm.

Statistics Canada. (2010c). *Projections of the diversity of the Canadian population: 2006 to 2031.* Cat. No. 91-551-X. Ottawa: Minister of Industry.

Statistics Canada. (2010d). Religion (13) and age groups (8) for population, for Canada, provinces, territories, Census metropolitan areas and Census agglomerations, *2001 Census*—20% sample data. Retrieved from http://www12.statcan.ca/english/census01/products/standard/themes/RetrieveProductTable.cfm?Temporal=2001&PID=68339&APATH=3&GID=431515&METH=1&PTYPE=55430&THEME=56&FOCUS=0&AID=0&PLACENAME=0&PROVINCE=0&SEARCH=0&GC=0&GK=0&VID=0&VNAMEE=&VNAMEF=&FL=0&RL=0&FREE=0.

Statistics Canada. (2010e). Seniors. *Canada year book, 2010.* Retrieved from http://www.statcan.gc.ca/pub/11-402-x/2010000/pdf/seniors-aines-eng.pdf.

Statistics Canada. (2011a). *Births, 2008.* Catalogue No. 84F0210X. Health Statistics Division. Ottawa: Minister of Industry.

Statistics Canada. (2011b). Health. *Canada year book 2011.* Cat. No. 11-402-XWE. Ottawa: Minister of Industry. Retrieved from http://www.statcan.gc.ca/pub/11-402-x/2011000/pdf/health-sante-eng.pdf.

Statistics Canada. (2011c). *Annual demographic estimates* Canada, provinces and territories. Cat. No. 91-215-X. Ottawa: Minister of Industry.

Statistics Canada. (2011d). *Life expectancy at birth, by sex, by province.* Retrieved from http://www40.statcan.ca/l01/cst01/health26-eng.htm.

Statistics Canada. (2011e). *Infant mortality rates, by province and territory. Both sexes.* Retrieved from http://www40.statcan.ca/l01/cst01/health21a-eng.htm.

Statistics Canada. (2011f). Dependency ratio. *Healthy people, healthy places.* Based on CANSIM Tables 051-0001 (1971-2008) and 052-0004 (2009-2056). http://www.statcan.gc.ca/pub/82-229-x/2009001/demo/dep-eng.htm, accessed October 28, 2011.

Statistics Canada. (2011g). Ethnic diversity and immigration. *Canada year book 2011.* Cat. No. 11-402-XWE. Ottawa: Minister of Industry. Retrieved from http://www.statcan.gc.ca/pub/11-402-x/2011000/pdf/ethnic-ethnique-eng.pdf.

Statistics Canada. (2011h). Study: Osteoporosis, calcium and vitamin D. *The Daily,* July 20. Retrieved from http://www.statcan.gc.ca/daily-quotidien/110720/dq110720b-eng.htm.

Statistics Canada. (2011i). Residential care facilities, 2009/2010. Cat. No. 83-237-C. Ottawa: Minister of Industry. Retrieved from http://www.statcan.gc.ca/pub/83-237-x/83-237-x2012001-eng.pdf.

Statistics Canada. (2011j). *Government transfer payments to persons.* Retrieved from http://www40.statcan.gc.ca/l01/cst01/govt05a-eng.htm.

Statistics Canada. (2011k). *Income tax ... by the numbers.* Retrieved from http://www42.statcan.ca/smr08/2011/smr08_154_2011-eng.htm.

Statistics Canada. (2011l). *Canada year book 2011.* Cat. No. 11-402-XWE. Ottawa: Minister of Industry. Retrieved from http://www.statcan.gc.ca/pub/11-402-x/2011000/pdf-eng.htm.

Statistics Canada. (2011m). *Gay pride ... by the numbers.* Retrieved from http://www42.statcan.ca/smr08/2011/smr08_158_2011-eng.htm.

Statistics Canada. (2011n). *Leading causes of death in Canada, 2008.* Cat. No. 84-215-XWE. Ottawa: Minister of Industry. Retrieved from http://www.statcan.gc.ca/pub/84-215-x/2011001/tbls-eng.htm.

Statistics Canada. (2011o), Living arrangements of young adults aged 20 to 29. Retrieved from http://www12.statcan.gc.ca/census-recensement/2011/as-sa/98-312-x/98-312-x2011003_3-eng.cfm.

Statistics Canada. (2012a). Population growth in Canada: From 1851 to 2061. Population and dwelling counts, 2011 Census. *Census Brief.* Cat. No. 98-310-X2011003. Ottawa: Minister of Industry.

Statistics Canada. (2012b). *Canada at a Glance 2012.* Cat. No. 84-518X. Retrieved from http://www.statcan.gc.ca/pub/12-581-x/12-581-x2012000-eng.pdf.

Statistics Canada. (2012c). *Generations in Canada.* Retrieved from http://www12.statcan.gc.ca/census-recensement/2011/as-sa/98-311-x/98-311-x2011003_2-eng.cfm.

Statistics Canada. (2012d). 2011 Census: Age and sex. *The Daily,* May 29. Component of Cat. No. 11-001-X).

Statistics Canada. (2012e). *Population by broad age groups and sex, counts, including median age, 1921 to 2011 for both sexes—Canada.* Retrieved from http://www12.stat-can.gc.ca/census-recensement/2011/dp-pd/hlt-fst/as-sa/Pages/highlight.cfm?TabID=1&Lang=E&PRCode=01&Asc=0&OrderBy=6&Sex=1&View=1&tableID=22.

Statistics Canada. (2012f). *Number of centenarians by sex, Canada, 2001 to 2061.* Censuses of population, 2001, 2006 and 2011; and (2010).

Statistics Canada. (2012g). Physical activity during leisure time, 2011. *Health Fact Sheets.* Retrieved from http://www.statcan.gc.ca/pub/82-625-x/2012001/article/11667-eng.htm. Original source: *Canadian Community Health Survey, 2011.*

Statistics Canada. (2012h). Fruit and vegetable consumption, 2011. *Health Fact Sheets.* Retrieved from http://www.statcan.gc.ca/pub/82-625-x/2012001/article/11661-eng.htm. Original source: *Canadian Community Health Survey,* 2011.

Statistics Canada. (2012i). *Persons in low income after tax (2006 to 2010).* Retrieved from http://www.statcan.gc.ca/tables-tableaux/sum-som/l01/cst01/famil19a-eng.htm.

Statistics Canada. (2012j). Health. *Canada Year Book 2011.* Catalogue No. 11-402-X. Retrieved from http://www.statcan.gc.ca/pub/11-402-x/2012000/pdf/health-sante-eng.pdf.

Statistics Canada. (2012k). *Caring Canadians, involved Canadians: Tables Report, 2010.* Ottawa: Ministry of Industry. Retrieved from http://www.statcan.gc.ca/pub/89-649-x/89-649-x2011001-eng.pdf.

Statistics Canada. (2012l). Living arrangements of seniors. *Census in Brief.* Retrieved from http://www12.statcan.gc.ca/census-recensement/2011/as-sa/98-312-x/98-312-x2011003_4-eng.pdf

Statistics Canada. (2012m). Portrait of families and living arrangements in Canada. Families, households and marital status. *2011 Census of Population.* Cat. No. 98-312-X2011001. Ottawa: Minister of Industry.

Statistics Canada. (2013a). Immigration and ethnocultural diversity in Canada. *National Household Survey*, 2011. Retrieved from http://www12.statcan.gc.ca/nhs-enm/2011/as-sa/99-010-x/99-010-x2011001-eng.pdf.

Statistics Canada. (2013b). Life tables, Canada, provinces and territories 2009 to 2011. Retrieved from http://www.statcan.gc.ca/pub/84-537-x/84-537-x2013005-eng.htm.

Statistics Canada. (2013c). Aboriginal peoples in Canada: First Nations people, Métis and Inuit. *National Household Survey*, 2011. Catalogue No. 99-011-X2011001. Ottawa: Minister of Industry.

Statistics Canada. (2013d). Body composition of Canadian adults, 2009 to 2011. Retrieved from http://www.statcan.gc.ca/pub/82-625-x/2012001/article/11708-eng.htm.

Statistics Canada. (2013e). Canadian Internet use survey, 2012. *The Daily*, November 26. Retrieved from http://www.statcan.gc.ca/daily-quotidien/131126/dq131126d-eng.htm.

Statistics Canada. (2013f). Aerobic fitness of Canadians, 2009 to 2011. Retrieved from http://www.statcan.gc.ca/pub/82-625-x/2012001/article/11711-eng.htm.

Statistics Canada. (2013g). Persons in low income after tax (in percent, 2007 to 2011). Retrieved from http://www.statcan.gc.ca/tables-tableaux/sum-som/l01/cst01/famil19a-eng.htm?sdi=low%20income.

Statistics Canada. (2013h). Average income after tax by economic family types (2007 to 2011). Retrieved from http://www.statcan.gc.ca/tables-tableaux/sum-som/l01/cst01/famil21a-eng.htm

Statistics Canada. (2013i). Persons in low income after tax (percentage, 2007 to 2011). Retrieved from http://www.statcan.gc.ca/tables-tableaux/sum-som/l01/cst01/famil19a-eng.htm?sdi=low%20income.

Statistics Canada. (2013j). Average earnings by sex and work pattern (all earners) Retrieved from http://www.statcan.gc.ca/tables-tableaux/sum-som/l01/cst01/labor01a-eng.htm.

Statistics Canada. (2013k). Canadian Internet use survey, Internet use, by location of use, household income and age group for Canada and regions. occasional (percent). Table 358-0154. Retrieved from http://www5.statcan.gc.ca/cansim/pick-choisir?lang=eng&p2=33&id=3580154.

Statistics Canada. (2013m). *National Household Survey*, 2011. Income Composition in Canada. Retrieved March 3, 2017, from https://www12.statcan.gc.ca/nhs-enm/2011/as-sa/99-014-x/99-014-x2011001-eng.cfm.

Statistics Canada. (2014a). *The Canadian population in 2011: Age and sex*. Retrieved from http://www12.statcan.ca/census-recensement/2011/as-sa/98-311-x/98-311-x2011001-eng.cfm.

Statistics Canada. (2014b). Suicide and suicide rates, by sex and by age group. Retrieved from http://www.statcan.gc.ca/tables-tableaux/sum-som/l01/cst01/hlth66d-eng.htm.

Statistics Canada. (2014c). Canada's population estimates: Age and sex, 2014. *The Daily*, September 26. Retrieved from http://www.statcan.gc.ca/daily-quotidien/140926/dq140926b-eng.htm.

Statistics Canada. (2014d). Canada's population estimates: Age and sex, 2014. *The Daily*, September 26. Retrieved from http://www.statcan.gc.ca/daily-quotidien/140926/dq140926b-eng.htm.

Statistics Canada. (2014e). Causes of death, 2010 and 2011. Retrieved from http://www.statcan.gc.ca/daily-quotidien/140128/dq140128b-eng.htm.

Statistics Canada. (2014f). Perceived health, 2013. Retrieved from http://www.statcan.gc.ca/pub/82-625-x/2014001/article/14022-eng.htm.

Statistics Canada. (2014g). Perceived life stress, 2013. Retrieved from http://www.statcan.gc.ca/pub/82-625-x/2014001/articles/14023-eng.htm. Statistics Canada.

Statistics Canada. (2014h). Blood pressure of adults, 2012 to 2013. Retrieved from http://www.statcan.gc.ca/pub/82-625-x/2014001/article/14101-eng.htm.

Statistics Canada. (2014i). Smoking 2013. Retrieved from http://www.statcan.gc.ca/pub/82-625-x/2014001/article/14025-eng.htm.

Statistics Canada. (2014j). Chronic obstructive pulmonary disease in adults, 2012 to 2013. Retrieved from http://www.statcan.gc.ca/pub/82-625-x/2014001/article/14103-eng.htm.

Statistics Canada (2014k). Physical activity during leisure time, 2013. Retrieved from http://www.statcan.gc.ca/pub/82-625-x/2014001/article/14024-eng.htm.

Statistics Canada. (2014l). Overweight and obese adults (self-reported), 2013. Retrieved from http://www.statcan.gc.ca/pub/82-625-x/2014001/article/14021-eng.htm.

Statistics Canada. (2014m). Study: Understanding seniors' risk of falling and their perception of risk, 2008 and 2009. Retrieved from http://www.statcan.gc.ca/daily-quotidien/141001/dq141001a-eng.htm.

Statistics Canada. (2014n). Metabolic syndrome in adults, 2012 to 2013. Retrieved from http://www.statcan.gc.ca/pub/82-625-x/2014001/article/14123-eng.htm.

Statistics Canada. (2014o). Total and median net worth by age and family type. Retrieved from http://www.statcan.gc.ca/daily-quotidien/140225/t140225b001-eng.htm.

Statistics Canada. (2014p). Registered retirement savings plan contributions, 2012. *The Daily*. Retrieved from http://www.statcan.gc.ca/daily-quotidien/140325/dq140325b-eng.htm.

Statistics Canada. (2014q). Study: Emerging trends in living arrangements and conjugal unions for current and future seniors, 1981 to 2011. *The Daily*, February 24. Retrieved from http://www.statcan.gc.ca/pub/75-006-x/2014001/article/11904-eng.htm.

Statistics Canada (2014r). Leading causes of death, total population, by age group and sex, Canada. CANSIM Table 102-0561. Accessed November 26, 2015, at www5/statcan.gc.ca/cansim/a47.

Statistics Canada. (2015a). *General Social Survey*: Giving, volunteering and participating, 2013. *The Daily*. Retrieved February 18, 2017, from http://www.statcan.gc.ca/daily-quotidien/150130/dq150130b-eng.htm.

Statistics Canada. (2015b). Fertility: Fewer children, older moms. *Canadian Megatrends*. Retrieved from http://www.statcan.gc.ca/pub/11-630-x/11-630-x2014002-eng.htm.

Statistics Canada. (2015c). Figure 7. Proportion (in percentage) of the population aged 65 and over, Canada, provinces and territories, 2006 and 2011. Retrieved from https://www12.statcan.gc.ca/census-recensement/2011/as-sa/98-311-x/2011001/fig/fig7-eng.cfm.

Statistics Canada. (2015d). *Canadian Community Health Survey*: Combined data, 2013/2014. Table 4 Canadians reporting good to full functional health, by age group and sex, household population age 12 and older, 2013/2014. *The Daily*. Retrieved from http://www.statcan.gc.ca/daily-quotidien/150624/t004b-eng.htm.

Statistics Canada. (2015e). CANSIM Table 105-0501. Health indicator profile, annual estimates, by age group and sex, Canada, provinces, territories, health regions and peer groups. Occasional. Retrieved from http://www5.statcan.gc.ca/cansim/a26?lang=eng&id=1050501.

Statistics Canada. (2015f). High blood pressure, by age group and sex. Retrieved from http://www.statcan.gc.ca/tables-tableaux/sum-som/l01/cst01/health03b-eng.htm.

Statistics Canada. (2015g). A profile of persons with disabilities among Canadians aged 15 years or older, 2012. Catalogue Number 89-654-X. Chart 4.Retrieved from http://www.statcan.gc.ca/pub/89-654-x/89-654-x2015001-eng.htm#a1.

Statistics Canada. (2015h). Directly measured physical activity of adults, 2012 and 2013. Retrieved from http://www.statcan.gc.ca/pub/82-625-x/2015001/article/14135-eng.htm.

Statistics Canada. (2015i). Diabetes, by age group and sex. Retrieved from http://www.statcan.gc.ca/tables-tableaux/sum-som/l01/cst01/health53a-eng.htm.

Statistics Canada. (2015j). *The Daily*. Canadian income survey, 2013. Retrieved from http://www.statcan.gc.ca/daily-quotidien/150708/dq150708b-eng.htm.

Statistics Canada. (2015k). Quarterly report of Canada Pension Plan and Old Age Security monthly amounts and related figures—July to September 2015. Retrieved from http://www.servicecanada.gc.ca/eng/services/pensions/infocard/julsep15.shtml.

Statistics Canada. (2015l). Pension plans in Canada, as of January 1, 2014. Retrieved from http://www.statcan.gc.ca/daily-quotidien/150722/dq150722b-eng.htm.

Statistics Canada. (2015m). Labour force characteristics by age and sex (Estimates). Retrieved from http://www.statcan.gc.ca/tables-tableaux/sum-som/l01/cst01/labor20a-eng.htm.

Statistics Canada. (2015n). Registered pension plans (RPPs) and members, by type of plan and sector. (Total public and private sectors). Retrieved from http://www.statcan.gc.ca/tables-tableaux/sum-som/l01/cst01/famil120a-eng.htm.

Statistics Canada. (2015o). Table 051-0042. Estimates of population, by marital status or legal marital status, age and sex for July 1, Canada, provinces and territories, annual (persons). Retrieved from http://www5.statcan.gc.ca/cansim/a26?lang=eng&id=510042.

Statistics Canada. (2016). 2011 *National Household Survey*: Data Tables. Catalogue No. 99-010-X2011030. Accessed February 10, 2016.

Stefanacci, R. G., & Haimowitz, D. (2014). Bathroom assistances. *Geriatric Nursing*, 35(2), 151–153. Retrieved from http://www.gnjournal.com/article/S0197-4572(14)00052-4/abstract.

Stephen Lewis Foundation. (2013a). Grandmothers. Retrieved from http://www.stephenlewisfoundation.org/what-we-do/areas-of-work/grandmothers.

Stephen Lewis Foundation. (2013b). Grandmothers campaign. Retrieved from http://www.stephenlewisfoundation.org/get-involved/grandmothers-campaign.

Stern, Y. (2002). What is cognitive reserve? Theory and research application of the reserve concept. *Journal of the International Neuropsychological Society, 8*, 448–460.

Stern, Y. (Ed.). (2007). *Cognitive reserve: Theory and applications.* New York: Taylor and Francis.

Stevens, J. A., Corso, P. S., Finkelstein, E. A., & Miller, T. R. (2006). The costs of fatal and non-fatal falls among older adults. *Injury Prevention 12*, 290–229.

Stewart, M., Shizha, E., Makwarimba, E., Spitzer, D., Khalema, E. N. and Nsaliwa, C. D. (2011). Challenges and barriers to services for immigrant seniors in Canada: "You are among others but you feel along." *International Journal of Migration, Health and Social Care, 7*(1), 16–32. Retrieved from http://www.emeraldinsight.com/journals.htm?articleid=1949673&show=abstract.

Stgeorge, J. M., & Fletcher, R. J. (2014). Men's experiences of grandfatherhood: A welcome surprise. *International Journal of Aging and Human Development, 78*(4), 351–378.

Stine-Morrow, E. A. L., & Basak, C. (2011). Cognitive Interventions. In K. W. Schaie & S. L. Willis (Eds.), *Handbook of the psychology of aging,* 7th ed. (pp. 153–171). London: Academic Press (Elsevier).

Stine-Morrow, E. A. L., Parisi, J. M., Morrow, D. G., Greene, J., & Park, D. C. (2007). Engagement Model of Cognitive Optimization through Adulthood. *Journals of Gerontology: Series B: Psychological Sciences and Social Sciences, 62*(Special Issue 1), 62–69.

St. John, P. D., Montgomery, P. R., & Tyas, S. L. (2013). Social position and frailty. *Canadian Journal on Aging, 32*(3), 250–259.

Stobert, S., Dosman, D., & Keating, N. (2006). *Aging well: Time use patterns of older Canadians.* Statistics Canada Cat. No. 89-622-XIE, No. 2. Ottawa: Minister of Industry.

Stokes, B. (2014). The countries that will be most impacted by aging population. Fact Tank. Retrieved from http://www.pewresearch.org/fact-tank/2014/02/04/the-countries-that-will-be-most-impacted-by-aging-population.

Stone, L. O. (Ed.) (2006). *New frontiers of research on retirement.* Statistics Canada Cat. No. 75-511-XIE. Ottawa: Minister of Industry.

Stone, L. O., Rosenthal, C. J., & Connidis, I. A. (1998). *Parent–child exchanges of supports and intergenerational equity.* Statistics Canada Cat. No. 89-557-XPE. Ottawa: Ministry of Industry.

Stones, M. J., Clyburn, L. D., Gibson, M. C., & Woodbury, M. G. (2006). Predicting diagnosed depression and antidepressant treatment in institutionalized older adults by symptom profiles: A closer look at anhedonia and dysphoria. *Canadian Journal on Aging 25*(2), 153–59.

Strain, L. A., Grabusic, C. C., Searle, M. S., &. Dunn, N. J. (2002). Continuing and ceasing leisure activities in later life: A longitudinal study. *The Gerontologist, 42*(2), 217–223.

Stratton, D. C., & Moore, A. J. (2007). Fractured relationships and the potential for abuse of older men. *Journal of Elder Abuse and Neglect, 19*(1/2), 75–97.

S. U. C. C. E. S. S. (2011). Simon K. Y. Lee senior care home. Retrieved from http://www.successbc.ca/eng/component/option,com_mtree/task,listcats/cat_id,93/Itemid.

Suh, Y., Atzmon, G., Cho, M. O., Hwang, D., Liu, B., Leahy, D. J., et al. (2008). Functionally significant insulin-like growth factor I receptor mutations in centenarians. Proceedings of the National Academy of Sciences of the United States of America, *105*, 3438–3442.

Suitor, J. J., Sechrist, J., Gilligan, M., & Pillemer, K. (2011). Intergenerational relations in later-life families. In R. A. Settersten, Jr., & J. L. Angel (Eds.), *Handbook of sociology of aging* (pp. 161–178). New York: Springer.

Sun Life Assurance Company of Canada. (2015). *2015 Sun Life Canadian unretirement index report.* Sun Life Assurance Company of Canada. Retrieved from http://cdn.sunlife.com/static/canada/sunlifeca/About%20us/Canadian%20Unretirement%20Index/Unretirement%20Index%20tool/2015_Sun_Life_Canadian_Unretirement_Index_Report_en.pdf.

Sussman, T., & Dupuis, S. (2012). Supporting a relative's move into long-term care: Starting point shapes family members' experiences. *Canadian Journal on Aging, 31*(4), 395–410.

Suwal, J. V. (2010). Health consequences to immigrant family caregivers in Canada. *Canadian Studies in Population,37*:107–124.

Swartz, T. T. (2009). Intergenerational family relations in adulthood: Patterns, variations, and implications in the contemporary United States. *Annual Review of Sociology, 35,* 191–212.

Syme, M. L., Klonoff, E. A., Macera, C. A., & Brodine, S. K. (2013). Predicting sexual decline and dissatisfaction among older adults: The role of partnered and individual physical and mental health factors. *Journals of Gerontology Series B: Psychological Sciences and Social Sciences, 68*(3), 323–332.

Szasz, T. S. (1960). The myth of mental illness. *American Psychologist, 15*(2), 113–118.

Szasz, T. S. (1974). The myth of mental illness. New York: HarperCollins.

Szinovacz, M. E. (1982). Introduction: Research on women's retirement. In M. Szinovacz (Ed.) *Women's retirement.* Beverly Hills, CA: Sage.

Szinovacz, M. E., & Davey, A. (2012). Stability and change in financial transfers from adult children to older parents. *Canadian Journal on Aging, 31*(4), 367–378.

Tam, S., & Neysmith. S. (2006). Disrespect and isolation: Elder abuse in Chinese communities. *Canadian Journal on Aging, 25*(2), 141–151.

Tan, A., and Manca, D. (2013). Finding common ground to achieve a "good death": Family physicians working with substitute decision-makers of dying patients. A qualitative grounded theory study. *BMC Family Practice* 14:14.

Tan, J. W., & Brown, R. D. (2005). Effect of viewing a landscape on physiological health of elderly women. *Journal of Housing for the Elderly, 19*(3–4), 187–202.

Tannenbaum, C., & Frank, B. (2011). Masculinity and health in late life men. *American Journal of Men's Health, 5*(3), 243–254.

TD Bank Financial Group. (2005). Retirement, what retirement? According to TD Waterhouse RSP Poll 1/3 Canadians plan to keep on working. Toronto: TD Bank. Retrieved from http://www.tdassetmangement.com/Content/InvResources/PressRoom/p_LibraryItem.asp?LIID=351&CAT=30.

Teixeira, C. (2010). Gentrification, displacement, and resistance: A case study of Portuguese seniors in Toronto's "Little Portugal." In D. Durst & M. MacLean (Eds.), *Diversity and aging among immigrant seniors in Canada: Changing faces and greying temples* (pp. 327–340). Calgary: Detselig.

Thompson, A. E., O'Sullivan, L. F., Byers, E. S., & Shaughnessy, K. (2014). Young adults' implicit and explicit attitudes towards the sexuality of older adults. *Canadian Journal on Aging 33*(3), 259–270.

Thompson, E. P. (1971). The moral economy of the English crowd in the eighteenth century. *Past and Present, 50,* 76–136.

Thornton, R., & Light, L. L. (2006). Language comprehension and production in normal aging. In J. E. Birren & K. W. Schaie (Eds.), *Handbook ofthe psychology of aging,* 6th ed. (pp. 261–267). Burlington, MA: Elsevier Academic Press.

Tibbetts, J. (2007, December 9). Fewer grad students leading to professor shortage. CanWest News Service. Retrieved from http://www2.canada.com/ottawacitizen/news/story.html?id=ffd41b3e-4a47-47c4-bbdc-2b910bd97a4b&k=36637.

Tiedemann, M., J. Nicol, & D. Valiquet. (2011). *Euthanasia and assisted suicide: International experiences.* Library of Parliament Background Paper No. 2011-67-E. Ottawa: Canada, Library of Parliament.

Tierney, M. C., & Charles, J. (2002). The care and treatment of people with dementia and cognitive impairment: An update. In Writings in gerontology: Mental health and aging (pp. 97–112). Ottawa: National Advisory Council on Aging.

Tieu, Y., & Konnert, C. (2015). Measuring acculturation and enculturation among Chinese Canadian older adults. *Canadian Journal on Aging, 34*(1), 36–46.

Tieu, Y., Konnert, C., & Wang, J. (2010). Depression literacy among older Chinese immigrants in Canada: A comparison with a population-based survey. *International Psychogeriatrics, 22*(8), 1318–1326.

Tira, C., Jackson, A. C., & Tomnay, J. E. (2013). Pathways to late-life problematic gambling in seniors: A grounded theory approach. *The Gerontologist, 54*(6), 1035–1048.

Tjepkema, M. (2006). Adult obesity. *Health Reports, 17*(3), 9–25. Statistics Canada Cat. No. 82-003.

Tornstam, L. (2005). *Gerotranscendence: A developmental theory of positive aging.* New York: Springer.

Tornstam, L. (2012). The theory of gerotranscendence. In Gibson, J. J., & Singleton, M. F., *Leisure and aging: Theory and practice.* Leeds: Human Kinetics.

Toronto Best Practice in LTC Initiative. (2007). Recognizing delirium, depression and dementia (3Ds). Retrieved from http://rgp.toronto.on.ca/torontobestpractice/ThreeDcomparison.pdf.

Torres, J. M., & Wong, R. (2013). Childhood poverty and depressive symptoms for older adults in Mexico: A life-course analysis. *Journal of Cross Cultural Gerontology, 28*, 317–377.

Tournier, P. (1972). *Learning to grow old.* London: SCM Press.

Townson, M. (2006). New vulnerable groups and living standards in the retirement years. In L. O. Stone (Ed.), *New frontiers of research on retirement* (pp. 345–354). Statistics Canada Cat. No. 75-511-XIE. Ottawa: Minister of Industry.

Treas, J., & Marcum, C. S. (2011). Social relations and aging. In R. A. Settersten, Jr., & J. L. Angel (Eds.), *Handbook of sociology of aging* (pp. 131–141). New York: Springer.

Tsang, A. K. T., Fuller-Thomson, E., & Lai, D. W. L. (2012). Sexuality and health among Chinese seniors in Canada. *Journal of International Migration and Integration, 13*(4), 525–540.

Tulving, E., & Szpunar, K. K. (2009). Episodic memory. *Scholarpedia, 4*(8), 3332.

Turcotte, M. (2006). Seniors' access to transportation. *Canadian Social Trends, 82*, 43–50.

Turcotte, M. (2011a). Women and health. *Women in Canada: A gender-based statistical report.* Component of Statistics Canada Cat. No. 89-503X. Ottawa: Minister of Industry.

Turcotte, M. (2011b). Women and education. In *Women in Canada: A gender-based statistical report.* Statistics Canada. Ottawa: Minister of Industry.

Turcotte, M. (2012). Profile of seniors' transportation habits. *Canadian Social Trends, 93*, 3–16. Statistics Canada Cat. No. 11-008.

Turcotte, M. (2013a). Family caregiving: What are the consequences? Statistics Canada. Retrieved from http://www.statcan.gc.ca/pub/75-006-x/2013001/article/11858-eng.pdf.

Turcotte, M. (2013b). Living apart together. *Insights on Canadian Society.* Statistics Canada. Retrieved from http://www.statcan.gc.ca/pub/75-006-x/2013001/article/11771-eng.pdf.

Turcotte, M. (2014). Canadians with unmet home care needs. *Insight on Canadian Society.* Statistics Canada. Retrieved from http://www.statcan.gc.ca/pub/75-006-x/2014001/article/14042-eng.pdf.

Turcotte, M. (2015). Volunteering and charitable giving in Canada. Spotlight on Canadians: Results from the *General Social Survey.* Statistics Canada. Ottawa: Minister of Industry. Retrieved from http://www.statcan.gc.ca/pub/89-652-x/89-652-x2015001-eng.pdf.

Turcotte, M., & Sawaya, C. (2015). Senior care: Differences by type of housing. Statistics Canada. Retrieved from http://www.statcan.gc.ca/pub/75-006-x/2015001/article/14142-eng.pdf.

Turcotte, M. & Schellenberg, G. (2007). *A portrait of seniors in Canada: 2006.* Statistics Canada Cat. No. 89-519-XIE. Ottawa: Minister of Industry.

Turner, A., Crompton, S., & Langlois, S. (2013). *Aboriginal peoples in Canada: First Nations people, Métis and Inuit. National Household Survey,* 2011. Retrieved from http://www12.statcan.gc.ca/nhs-enm/2011/as-sa/99-011-x/99-011-x2011001-eng.pdf.

Turpin, L. J., McWilliam, C. L., & Ward-Griffin, C. (2012). The meaning of a positive client–nurse relationship for senior home care clients with chronic disease. *Canadian Journal on Aging, 31*(4), 457–469.

Uhlenberg, P. (2009). Children in an aging society. *Journal of Gerontology, 64*(4), 489–496.

Umberson, D., & Kroeger, R. A. (2016). Gender, marriage, and health for same-sex and different-sex couples: The future keeps arriving. In S. M. McHale, V. King, J. Van Hook, & A. Booth (Eds.), (pp.189–213).*Gender and Couple Relationships. National Symposium on Family Issues.* Volume 6. Springer.

Underhill, C. (2006). Training through the ages. *Perspectives on Labour and Income, 7*(10), 17–27.

Underhill, C., & McKeown, L. (2008). Getting a second opinion: Health information and the Internet. *Health Reports*, *19*(1), 1–5.

UNDESA (2013). Population Division, World Population Prospects: the 2012 Revision, 2013.

United Nations. (2009). *World population ageing (2009)*. Department of Economic and Social Affairs. Population Division. New York: United Nations.

United Nations. (2010a). Population age 60 years or over. *Population Aging and Development 2009.*

United Nations. (2010b). *UNAIDS report on the global AIDS epidemic.* Retrieved February 25, 2017, from http://www.unaids.org/globalreport/documents/20101123_GlobalReport_full_en.pdf.

United Nations. (2011a). World population prospects, the 2010 revision. Department of Economic and Social Affairs. Retrieved from http://esa.un.org/unpd/wpp/Excel-Data/population.htm.

United Nations. (2011b). World mortality report 2009. New York. Retrieved from http://www.un.org/en/development/desa/population/publications/pdf/mortality/worldMortalityReport2009.pdf.

United Nations. (2012a). Population Fund. Report on the status of elderly in select states of India, 2011. Retrieved from http://countryoffice.unfpa.org/india/drive/AgeingReport_28Nov2012_LowRes-1.pdf#page=1&zoom=auto,0,846.

United Nations. (2012b). Population ageing and the non-communicable diseases. *Population facts, 2012/1.* Retrieved from http://www.un.org/esa/population/publications/popfacts/popfacts__2012-1.pdf.

United Nations. (2013). World population aging. Retrieved from http://www.un.org/en/development/desa/population/publications/pdf/ageing/WorldPopulationAgeing2013.pdf.

Unwin, B. K., Unwin, C. G., Olsen, C., & Wilson, C. (2008). A new look at an old quiz: Palmore's Facts on Aging Quiz turns 30. *Journal of the American Geriatric Society, 56*(11), 2162–2163.

Uppal, S. (2010). Labour market activity among seniors. *Perspectives on Labour and Income, July,* 5–18.

Uppal, S., & LaRochelle-Côté, S. (2015a). Changes in wealth across the income distribution, 1999 to 2012. *Insights on Canadian Society*. Statistics Canada. Minister of Industry.

Uppal, S., & LaRochelle-Côté, S. (2015b). Changes in debt and assets of Canadian families, 1999 to 2012. *Insights on Canadian Society*. Statistics Canada. Minister of Industry.

Uriarte-Landa, J., & Hebert, B-P. (2009). Work–life balance of older workers. *Perspectives on Labour and Income*, October, 17–28.

van den Hoonaard, D. K. (2010). *By himself: The older man's experience of widowhood.* Toronto: University of Toronto Press.

Van Holle, V., Van Cauwenberg, J., Van Dyck, D., Deforche, B., Van de Weghe, N., & Bourdeaudhuij, I. (2014). Relationship between neighborhood walkability and older adults' physical activity: Results from the Belgian Environmental Physical Activity Study in Seniors (BEPAS Seniors). *International Journal of Behavioral Nutrition & Physical Activity, 11*(1), 1–18\.

Van Praag, H. (2009). Exercise and the brain: Something to chew on. *Trends in Neurosciences, 32*(5), 283–290.

Van Wagenen, A., Driskell J., & Bradford, J. (2013). 'I'm still raring to go': Successful aging among lesbian, gay, bisexual, and transgender older adults. *Journal of Aging Studies, 27*, 1–14.

Vares, T., Potts, A., Gavey, N, & Grace, V. M. (2007). Reconceptualizing cultural narratives of mature women's sexuality in the Viagra era. *Journal of Aging Studies, 21*, 153–164.

Veenhof, B., & Timusk, P. (2009). Online activities of Canadian boomers and seniors. *Canadian Social Trends*, 25–34. Component of Statistics Canada Cat. No. 11-008-X.

Vera-Sanso, P. (2014). Are older people a burden? Challenging the myths. Facing the facts: The truth about ageing and development. *Age International* (pp. 21–23). London: Age International.

Verhaeghen, P., & Cerella, J. (2008). Everything we know about aging and response time. *Handbook of cognitive aging: Interdisciplinary perspectives*, 134–150.

Vézina, M., & Crompton, S. (2012). Volunteering in Canada. *Canadian Social Trends*, April 16. Component of Statistics Canada Cat. No. 11-008-X.

Viau-Guay, A., Bellemare, M., Feillou, I., Trudel, L., Desrosiers, J., & Robitaille, M. J. (2013). Person-centered care training in long-term care settings: Usefulness and facility of transfer into practice. *Canadian Journal on Aging, 32*(1), 57–72.

Villar, F., & Villamizar, D. J. (2012). Hopes and concerns in couple relationships across adulthood and their association with relationship satisfaction. *International Journal of Aging and Human Development, 75*(2), 115–139.

Vogler, G. P. (2006). Behavior genetics and aging. In J. E. Birren & K. W. Schaie (Eds.), *Handbook of the psychology of aging*, 6th ed. (pp. 41–55). Burlington, MA: Elsevier Academic Press.

Von Tigerstrom, B., Larre, T., & Sauder, J. (2011). Improving uptake of essential services: Using the tax system to promote physical activity: Critical analysis of Canadian initiatives. *Government, Politics, and Law, 101*(8), 10–16.

Wada, M., Clarke, L. H., & Rozanova, J. (2015). Constructions of sexuality in later life: Analyses of Canadian magazine and newspaper portrayals of online dating. *Journal of Aging Studies, 32*, 40–49.

Waldbrook, N. (2013). Formerly homeless, older women's' experiences with health, housing, and aging. *Journal of Women & Aging, 25*, 337–357.

Walford, R. L., Mock, D., Verdery, R., & MacCallum, T. (2002). Calorie restriction in Biosphere 2: Alterations in physiologic, hematologic, hormonal, and biochemical parameters in humans restricted for a 2-year period. *Journals of Gerontology, Series A, Biological Sciences and Medical Sciences, 57*(6), B211–B224.

Walsh, C. A., & Hassanali, S. (2010). Elder abuse: Perspectives in the Chinese-Canadian community. In D. Durst & M. MacLean (Eds.), *Diversity and aging among immigrant seniors in Canada: Changing faces and greying temples* (pp. 251–268). Calgary: Detselig.

Wannell, T. (2007a). Young pensioners. *Perspectives on Labour and Income 8*(2), 5–14.

Wannell, T. (2007b). Public pensions and work. *Perspectives on Labour and Income, 8*(8), 12–19.

Ward, R. L., Nichols, A. D., & Freedman, R. I. (2010). Health care inequalities among adults with intellectual and developmental disabilities. *Health Social Work, 35*(4), 280–290.

Wardle, J., & Steptoe, A. (2003). Socioeconomic differences in attitudes and beliefs about healthy lifestyles. *Journal of epidemiology and community health, 57*(6), 440–443.

Warman, C., & Worswick, C. (2010). Mandatory retirement rules and the retirement decisions of university professors in Canada. *Labour Economics, 17*(6), 1022–1029.

Warner, H. R., & Sierra, F. (2009). Canadian Institutes of Health Research-Institute of Aging: Profiles: The longevity dividend: Why invest in basic aging research? *Canadian Journal on Aging, 28*(4), 391–394.

Waters, W. F., & Gallegos, C. A. (2014). Aging, health, and identity in Ecuador's indigenous communities. *Journal of Cross Cultural Gerontolgy, 29,* 371–387.

Waterston, M. L. (2011). The techno-brain. *Generations, 35*(2), 77–82.

Watkins, D. R. (2009). Spiritual formation of older persons in a postmodern context. *Journal of Religion, Spirituality and Aging, 22*(1–2), 1–11.

Watson, W. K., Bell N. J., & Stelle, C. (2010). Women narrate later life remarriage: Negotiating the cultural to create the personal. *Journal of Aging Studies, 24,* 302–312.]

Weber, M. (1905/1955). The Protestant ethic and the spirit of capitalism. New York: Charles Scribner's Sons.

Weeks, L. E., Shiner, D., Stadnyk, R., MacDonald, D. J. (2013). What should we build when they are ready to come? Developing evidence-based housing for older adults. *Senior Housing & Care Journal, 21*(1), 69–85.

Weeks, L. E., Stadnyk, R., Begley, L., & MacDonald, D. J. (2015). The influence of driving status on transportation challenges experienced by older adults. *Journal of Applied Gerontology, 34*(4), 501–517.

Weg, R. B. (1983). The physiological perspective. In R. B. Weg (Ed.), *Sexuality in the later years: Roles and behavior* (pp. 39–80). New York: Academic Press.

Wei, C., & Jinju, L. (2009). Future population trends in China: 2005–2050. Center for Policy Studies and the Impact Project. General Paper No.G-191. Retrieved from http://www.monash.edu.au/policy/ftp/workpapr/g-191.pdf.

Weinstein, A. M., & Erickson, K. I. (2011). Healthy body equals healthy mind. *Generations, 35*(2), 92–98.

Werner, P., Mittelman, M. S., Goldstein, D., & Heinik, J. (2012). Family stigma and caregiver burden in Alzheimer's disease. *The Gerontologist, 52*(1), 89–97.

Wheatley, C. J., Carr, D. B., & Marottoli, R. A. (2014). Consensus statements on driving for persons with dementia. *Occupational Therapy In Health Care, 28*(2), 132–139.

White, M. C. (2010). The eternal flame: Capacity to consent to sexual behavior among nursing home residents with dementia. *The Elder Law Journal, 18,* 133.

Whitlatch, C. J. & Menne, H. (2009). Don't forget about me! Decision making by people with dementia. *Generations, 33*(1), 66–73.

Wierenga, C. E., & Bondi, M. W. (2011). Dementia and Alzheimer's disease: What we know now. *Generations, 35*(2), 37–45.

Wilkins, K., Shields, M., & Rotermann, M. (2009). Smokers' use of acute care hospitals-A prospective study. *Health Reports,20*(4), 1–9. Statistics Canada Cat. No. 82-003-XPE.

Wilkins, K. M., Lund, B. C., McAdams, J. D., & Yates, W. R. (2009). Clinical utility of the Hopkins Competency Assessment Test on an Inpatient Geropsychiatry Unit. *American Journal of Alzheimer's Disease and Other Dementias, 24,* 34–39.

Williams, A. P., & Lum, J. M. (2011). Chicken Little? Why the healthcare sky does not have to fall. *HealthcarePapers, 11*(1), 52–58.

Williams, C. (2005). The sandwich generation. *Canadian Social Trends,* Summer. Statistics Canada Cat. No. 11-008.

Williams, C. (2010). Economic Well-Being. *Women in Canada: A gender-based statistical report.* Component of Statistics Canada Cat. No. 89-503-X. Minister of Industry. Retrieved from http://www.statcan.gc.ca/pub/89-503-x/2010001/article/11388-eng.pdf.

Williamson, J., & Pahor, M. (2010). Evidence regarding the benefits of physical exercise. *Archives of Internal Medicine, 170*(2), 124–125.

Willis, S. L., Schaie, K. W., & Martin, M. (2009). Cognitive plasticity. In V. L. Bengtson, M. Silverstein, M. M. Putney, & D. Gans (Eds.), *Handbook of theories of aging* (pp. 295–322). New York: Springer.

Willis, S. L., Tennstedt, S. L., Marsiske, M., Ball, K., Elias, J., Koepke, K. M., et al. (2006). Long-term effects of cognitive training on everyday functional outcomes in older adults: The ACTIVE Study. *Journal of the American Medical Association, 296,* 2805–2814. Retrieved from http://www.nia.nih.gov/Alzheimers/ResearchInformation/NewsReleases/Archives/PR2006/PR20061219ACTIVE.htm.

Wilson, K., Rosenberg, M. W., Abonyi, S., & Lovelace R. (2010). Aging and health: An examination of differences between older Aboriginal and non-Aboriginal people. *Canadian Journal on Aging, 29*(3), 369–382.

Wilson, R. S. (2011). Mental stimulation and brain health: Complex, challenging activities can support cognitive health in older adults. *Generations, 35*(2), 58–62.

Wiseman, F. K., Alford, K. A., Tubulewicz, V. L. J., & Fisher, E. M. C. (2009). Down syndrome—Recent progress and future prospects. *Human Molecular Gemnetics, 18*(Review Issue 1), R75–R83.

Wister, A. V. (2005). Baby Boomer health dynamics. How are we aging? Toronto: University of Toronto Press.

Wister, A. V., & Wanless, D. (2007). A health profile of community-living nonagenarians in Canada. *Canadian Journal on Aging 26*(1), 1–18

Witcher, C. S. G. (2006). Designing health-promotion messages for older adults in rural areas. *WellSpring, 17*(2), 1–4.

Witcher, C. S. G., Holt, N. L., Spence, J. C., & Cousins, S. O. (2007). A case study of physical activity among older adults in rural Newfoundland, Canada. *Journal of Aging and Physical Activity, 15,*166–183.

Wolf, R. S. (2001). Support groups for older victims of domestic violence. *Journal of Women & Aging, 13*(4), 71–83.

Wolff, S. J., Kabunga, E., Tumwekwase, G., & Grosskurth, H. (2009). 'This is where we buried our sons': People of advanced old age coping with the impact of the AIDS epidemic in a resource-poor setting in rural Uganda. *Ageing and Society,29*(Part 1), 115–134.

Woolston, C. (2009). Sex and high blood pressure: Ills and conditions. Retrieved from www.ahealthyme.com/topic/bpsex.

World Bank. (2013). *Fertility rate, total (births per woman).* Retrieved from http://data.worldbank.org/indicator/SP.DYN.TFRT.IN/countries.

World Bank. (2015a). *Health expenditure, total (% of GDP).* World Health Organization Global Health Expenditure database. Retrieved from http://data.worldbank.org/indicator/SH.XPD.TOTL.ZS/countries?order=wbapi_data_value_2013%20wbapi_data_value%20wbapi_data_value-last&sort=desc&display=default.

World Bank. (2015b). Population ages 65 and above (% of total). Retrieved from http://data.worldbank.org/indicator/SP.POP.65UP.TO.ZS/countries?display=default.

World Health Organization. (2007). *Global age-friendly cities: A guide.* Retrieved 23 May 2012 from http://www.who.int/ageing/publications/Global_age_friendly_cities_Guide_English.pdf.

World Health Organization. (2009). *WHO Global network of age-friendly cities.* Retrieved 22 May 2012 from http://www.who.int/ageing/Brochure-EnglishAFC9.pdf.

World Health Organization. (2011). Global strategy on diet, physical activity and health: Chronic disease risk factors. Retrieved from http://www.who.int/dietphysicalactivity/publications/facts/riskfactors/en/index.html.

World Health Organization. (2012). *Dementia: A public health priority.* Retrieved from http://apps.who.int/iris/bitstream/10665/75263/1/9789241564458_eng.pdf?ua=1.

Wright, S. L., & Canetto, S. S. (2009). Stereotypes of older lesbians and gay men. *Educational Gerontology, 35,* 424–452. Retrieved from www.lung.ca/_resources/Backgrounder_smoking.doc.

Wu, Z. (2014). Editorial: Introduction to special issue on aging families. *Canadian Journal on Aging, 33*(4), 351–354.

Wu, Z., & Penning, M. (2015). Immigration and loneliness in later life. *Ageing and Society, 35,* 64–95.

Wu, Z., & Schimmele, C. M. (2007). Uncoupling in later life. *Generations, 31*(3), 41–46.

Wu, Z., Schimmele, C. M., & Ouellet, N. (2014). Repartnering after widowhood. *Journals of Gerontology, Series B: Psychological Sciences and Social Sciences, 70*(3), 496–507.

Wurtele, S. K. (2009). Activities of older adults' survey: Tapping into student views of the elderly. *Educational Gerontology, 35*(11), 1026–1031.

Yamada, C. (2013). Achieving dreams in one's post-retirement "second life": A study of seniors' migration from Japan to Canada. *Senri Ethnological Studies, 80\,* 81–95.

Yang, Y. (2011). Aging, cohorts, and methods. In R. H. Binstock & L. K. George (Eds.), *Handbook of aging and the social sciences,* 7th ed. (pp. 17–30). London: Academic Press (Elsevier).

Yap, P., Luo, N, Ng, W. Y., Chionh, H. L., Lim, J., & Goh, J. (2010). Gain in Alzheimer Care Instrument—A new scale to measure caregiving gains in dementia. *American Journal of Geriatric Psychiatry, 18,* 68–76.

Yeo, G. (2009). How will the U.S. healthcare system meet the challenge of the ethnogeriatric imperative? *Journal of the American Geriatrics Society, 57*(7), 1278–1285\.

Young, B. W., Weir, P. L., Starkes, J. L., & Medic, N. (2008). Does lifelong training temper age-related decline in sport performance? Interpreting differences between cross-sectional and longitudinal data. *Experimental Aging Research,34*(1), 27–48.

Zanto, T. P., & Gazzaley, A. (2010). Delays in neural processing during working memory encoding in normal aging. *Neuropsychologia, 48*(1), 13–25.

Zaranek, R. R., & Chapleski, E. E. (2005). Casino gambling among urban elders: Just another social activity. *Journal of Gerontology, Series B: Psychological sciences and social sciences, 60*(2), 74–81.

Zarit, S. H. (2009). A good old age: Theories of mental health and aging, In V. L. Bengtson, M. Silverstein, M. M. Putney, & D. Gans (Eds.), *Handbook of theories of aging* (pp. 675–690). New York: Springer.

Zimmer, Z. (2005). Health and living arrangement transitions among China's oldest-old. Research on Aging, *27*(5), 526–555.

Zimmer, Z., Hickey, T., & Searle, M. S. (1997). Pattern of change in leisure activity behavior among older adults with Arthritis. *The Gerontologist, 37*(3), 384–392.

Zimmerman, H. (2013). Dot-com dating. *AARP The Magazine, 56*(2A), 64.

Zucchero, R. A. (2011). A co-mentoring project: An inter-generational service-learning experience. *Educational Gerontology, 37*(8), 687–702.

Zuzanek, J. (2009). Time use research in Canada—2015History, critique, perspectives. *Electronic International Journal of Time Use Research, 6*(2), 178–192. Retrieved from http://www.eijtur.org/pdf/volumes/6-2-zuzanek-time-use-research-in-canada.pdf.

INDEX

55 Alive Mature Driving Program, 285

A

AARP (American Association of Retired Persons), aging
    among G7 nations, 72
Abnormal aging, 148–160
    dementia, 150–155
    functional disorders, 155–158
    organic brain disorders, 148–155
    stigma of mental disorder, 158–160
Abuse and mistreatment. *See* Elder abuse and
    mistreatment
Accessibility of healthcare, 190–191
ACE (American Council on Education), 255
Action Seniors! 117
ACTIVE (Advanced Cognitive Training for Independent
    and Vital Elderly) program, 140
Active aging, promotion of, 11–12
Active euthanasia, 357, 359
Active Families Benefit program, 111
Active leisure lifestyle, 245, 251
    See also Leisure and recreation
Activities of daily living (ADLs), 99
Activity levels, 11–12, 98–102
Activity patterns
    in leisure time, 115
    of older people, 245–248
Activity theory, 23, 25
Address, Richard F., 331
Adult daycare programs, 182, 183
Advance directives, 353–355
Advanced Cognitive Training for Independent
    and Vital Elderly (ACTIVE) program, 140
Aerobic exercise, 112–113
Africa
    HIV/AIDS and population aging, 47, 49
    immigration to Canada from, 65
Age cohorts
    age stratification theory, 25–26
    cohort effects, 34
    defined, 25
    history-graded events, 29
    rectangularization of life curve, 123
Age effects, 34
Age-friendly communities, 287–288
Age-Friendly Communities (PHAC), 17
Age grades
    defined, 26
    history-graded events, 29
    normative age-graded events, 30

Ageism
    aging as disease, 12–16
    decrease through positive interaction between older
        and younger people, 16
    defined, 7
    education as antidote to, 15–16
    in educational system, 8–9
    effects on self-image and self-confidence, 6–7, 11
    Fourth age, 12
    in healthcare system, 7
    in humour, 9–10
    social policy and, 16–18
    sources of, 7–9
    Third age, 12
    in workplace, 10–11, 228–230
Age International, 50
Age stratification theory, 23, 25–26
Age-specific birth rates, 57, 59
Age-specific fertility rates, 53
Age-status asynchronization, 30
Aging, 2–19
    abnormal aging, 148–160
    attitudes toward, 6–10
    in Canada today, 54–69
    Canadian perspective on, 17–18
    coping with physical change, 102–122
    dependency ratio and cost of, 69–72
    as disease, 12–16
    experience of, 103
    healthy aging, 128–129
    myths and realities of, 2–5
    new view of, 11–12
    quiz on facts of, 3
    social policy and, 16–18
    successful aging, 124–125
    terminology when referring to older population, 9
    in world today, 46–54
Aging in Manitoba Longitudinal Study (AMLS), 38
Aging in place, 269
AIDS, 47, 49, 304–305
Alberta
    CHOICE (Comprehensive Home Option of Integrated
        Care for the Elderly), 187–188
    driving tests, 285
    opposition to Canada Health Act, 167
    pension supplements, 203
    proportion of older people, 68
    "Steady As You Go" program, 117
    telehealth services, 190
Allowance (ALW), 63, 201–204
Alzheimer Predictive Index, 152

Alzheimer Society of Canada, 153
Alzheimer's disease
    caregiving, 318, 328–332
    causes of, 151
    cognitive reserve, 136
    driving ability and, 285, 286
    ethical issues in research, 40
    increase in, 151–155
    social construction of, 153
    stages of decline, 152
American Association of Retired Persons (AARP), aging
        among G7 nations, 72
American Council on Education (ACE), 255
AMLS (Aging in Manitoba Longitudinal Study), 38
Amortality, 14
Anti-aging industry, 13–15
Anticipatory grief, 350
Anxiety
    about aging, 14
    life course perspective and, 27
Apartment living, 274–275
Apocalyptic demography, 69
Asian ethno-cultural seniors
    ethnic identity and cultural practices, 80–82
    as visible minority, 79–80
Asian immigration to Canada, 55–56, 65
Assessment and treatment centres, 182
Assisted living, 183–186, 276
Assisted suicide, 357–359, 360
Assistive devices, 108–109
Association for Gerontology in Higher Education (AGHE), 21
Australia
    granny flats, 277
    means-tested pensions, 213
Austria, healthcare spending in, 176
Autonomy in housing, 268–269
Availability of healthcare, 189–190

B
Baby boomers, 59–60
    common-law unions, 296
    encore careers, 238
    exercise, 110
    hair dye, 15
    online learning, 255
    products targeting, 11
    retirement, 231
Baby busters, 59–60
Bad death, 347
Baecker, Ron, 260
Baker, Paul, 9–10
Bankruptcy of private pension plans, 208
"Beanpole families," 292
Beauty and personal appearance
    aging as disease, 12–15
    hair dye, 15

Belgium
    assisted suicide, 359
    healthcare spending in, 176
Bereavement, 350
    See also Death and dying
Berlin Aging Study, 144
The Best Exotic Marigold Hotel (film), 12
Bhangoo, Nirpal, 81
Bicultural orientation, 76
    See also Ethno-cultural seniors
Biomedicine, 21
Birth rates
    age-specific, 57, 59
    baby boom and baby bust, 59–60
    defined, 47
    effects on aging population in Canada, 57–58
Black Like Me (Griffin), 9
"Black sheep effect," 6
Blackwell, Frank, 188
Blake, Art, 145
Blood pressure, 98
Boomerang children, 309
Boredom, myth about aging and, 4
Botswana, population aging in, 48
Brain
    cognitive impairment, 150–155
    exercise and, 142
    new approaches to study of mental function, 135–136
    organic brain disorders, 148–155
    physical change as source of mental decline, 134–135
    plasticity and cognitive reserve, 136–137
    training for improved performance, 140–141
Bridge jobs, 234
British Columbia
    Action Seniors! 117
    foreign-born seniors, 79
    geographic mobility, 66
    healthcare system, ethno-cultural seniors and, 88
    home care, 186
    opposition to Canada Health Act, 167
    pension supplements, 203
    per capita use rate of hospitals, 70
    proportion of older people, 68
    shelter allowances, 274–275
Brody, Elaine, 66
Buffering theory, 78
Burridge, Alan, 286
"Busy ethic," 241
Butler, Robert, 7

C
Calasanti, Toni, 13–14
Caldwell, Kulbinder Saran, 82
Calorie restriction (CR), 120
Cameras, 105

Canada
    baby boom and baby bust, 59–60
    birth rates, 57–58
    challenges to the healthcare system, 168–171
    comparison with U.S. healthcare system, 169–170
    death rates, 57
    effects of older population on social structures, 2
    elder abuse and mistreatment, 336–338
    ethnicity, 64–66
    geographic mobility, 66–67
    healthcare costs, 171–176
    healthy aging, 128–129
    history of pension system, 198–200
    HIV/AIDS, 305
    immigration, 55–57
    increased numbers and proportions of older women,
        67–69
    intergenerational relationships, 17–18
    large-scale gerontology research in, 41
    life expectancy, evolution of, 57–58
    marital status of older population, 300
    means-tested pensions, 213
    median age of population, 61
    need for change in healthcare system, 179–180
    number of foreign-born seniors, 79
    oldest-old population, 62–65
    origins of healthcare system, 167–168
    percentage reporting incidents of ageism, 7
    perspective on aging, 17–18
    population aging in, 54–69
    population growth, 46
    population pyramids by age group and sex, 64
    proportion of population belonging to visible minority
        groups, 80
    prospective aging, 60–62
    quiz on aging in, 3
    size of older population, 2, 46, 54, 56
    wait times in healthcare system, 170–171
Canada Digital Privacy Act (DPA), 338
Canada Health Act of 1984, 167–168
Canada Mortgage and Housing Corporation (CMHC), 270,
    273, 275
Canada Pension Benefits Standards Act of 1985, 219
Canada Pension Plan (CPP), 204–207
    as citizen's wage, 225
    early retirement, 71
    future challenges to, 206–207
    late retirement, 71
    origin of, 199
    reform to, 218–221
*Canada's Physical Activity Guide to Healthy Active Living for
    Older Adults*, 188
Canadian Diabetes Association, 118
Canadian Executive Service Organization (CESO), 262, 263
Canadian Federal/Provincial/Territorial Committee of
    Officials, 17

Canadian Home Care Association (CHCA), 184
Canadian Informatics Association (COACH), 191
Canadian Longitudinal Study of Aging (CLSA), 36, 41
Canadian Polyamory Advocacy Association (CPAA), 297
Canadian Special Senate Committee on Aging Final Report, 7
Canadian Study of Health and Aging (CSHA), 99
Cancer, 57, 98
Cardiovascular disease, 57
Care gap, 189
Caregiver burden, 328–332
Caregiving
    Alzheimer's disease, 318, 328–332
    care for caregiver, 334–335
    ethno-cultural seniors, 90–91
    gender and, 332–333
    informal caregivers, 319–320
    Internet use by caregivers, 327
    to parents/grandparents, 333
    social and physical costs of, 323
    See also Social support
Care-O-Bot, 4, 106
Caribbean countries
    caregiving, 90
    immigration to Canada from, 65
CBT (cognitive behavioural therapy), 157–158
Census of Canada, 55
Central America, immigration to Canada from, 65
CESO (Canadian Executive Service Organization), 262
Changing Lives of Older Couples study, 351
Charitable donations, 261, 263
CHCA (Canadian Home Care Association), 184
Childless older people, informal supports for, 324–325
Children
    caregiving to parents/grandparents, 333
    financial help from parents, 197
    Hunger Winter Study, 127
    as informal supports, 323–324
China
    afterlife, 349
    healthcare spending in, 176
    immigration to Canada from, 56
    one-child policy, 51–52
    population aging, 46, 51–52
China National Committee on Aging, 52
Chinese ethno-cultural seniors
    accessibility of healthcare, 190
    caregiving, 91, 330
    community life, 86
    elder abuse and mistreatment, 339
    healthcare, 87, 89
    intergenerational relationships, 82
    life course perspective, 78
Chinese Meals on Wheels program, 82
CHOICE (Comprehensive Home Option of Integrated
    Care for the Elderly), 187–188
Chrétien, Jean, 179

Chronic health problems, 96–98
  defined, 95
  proportion of population with, 97
  women and, 98
  See also Personal health and illness
Chronic hospital care, 182
Chronic obstructive pulmonary disease (COPD), 110
Citizen's wages, 225
  See also Pension system
Civic engagement, 260–263
Civic Ventures, 237
Clawback, 203
Clothing, 13
CLSA (Canadian Longitudinal Study of Aging), 36, 41
CMHC (Canada Mortgage and Housing Corporation), 270, 273, 275
COACH (Canadian Informatics Association), 191
Cognifit, 150
Cognitive behavioural therapy (CBT), 157–158
Cognitive impairment, 150–155
  new approaches to study of mental function, 135–136
  physical change as source of, 134–135
  See also Dementia
Cognitive reserve, 136–137
Cohen, Gene, 144, 241, 258
Cohort effects, 34
Cohort flow, 29
Collective dwellings. *See* Long-term care (LTC) facilities (collective dwellings)
Common-law unions, 296–297
Community belonging, 10
Community care, 180–186
  adult daycare programs, 183
  assisted living and home care, 183–186
  geriatric day hospitals, 182–183
Community Care Access Centres (CCACs), 181
Community life, 85–86
Community service through volunteer work, 260–263
Companionship
  in marriage, 294
  paid companions, 186
Competency
  defined, 159
  loss of, 159–160
Comprehensive Home Option of Integrated Care for the Elderly (CHOICE), 187–188
Comprehensive mental health system for seniors, 161
Compression of morbidity hypothesis, 122–124
Computers, 106–108
Conceptual innovation, 146–147
Confidant, 294
Conflict perspective, 23, 30–32
Congregate housing. *See* Assisted living
Constant-probability-of-success model, 146
Contextual view of memory, 137–140

Continuing care retirement communities (CCRCs), 279
Continuity theory, 23, 249–250
Continuum of care, 181
Contractors, 249
Convoy model of support, 321
Coordination of healthcare, 191–192
COPD (chronic obstructive pulmonary disease), 110
Core housing need, 270
Cornel, Sylvia, 285
Cosmeceuticals, 14
Cost. *See* Finances and economics
Cowley, Malcolm, 6
CPAA (Canadian Polyamory Advocacy Association), 297
CPP. *See* Canada Pension Plan (CPP)
Creativity
  as measured by great works, 145–147
  as personal expression, 147–148
Credit splitting, 219
Criminal victimization, 4–5
Critical gerontology, 33
Cross-disciplinary research teams, 36
Cross-sectional research design, 34–35
Crude dependency rates, 69
Crystallized intelligence, 143
CSHA (Canadian Study of Health and Aging), 99
Cultural enclaves, 85–86
Cultural incompatibility, 90
Culture, 77
  See also Ethnicity and culture; Ethno-cultural seniors
Cumulative advantage and disadvantage theory, 241
  defined, 31
  quality of life and, 127

D
Daily activity limitations for women, 98
Daily living support given by older people, 308–309
Dating, 301
Dawson, Adrienne, 260
Day hospitals, 182, 182–183
Day of the Dead festival, 344
Death and dying, 342–362
  advance directives, 353–355
  allowing patients to die, 352–353
  assisted suicide and active euthanasia, 357–359
  attitudes toward, 348
  bereavement, 350
  conflicts over treatment, 352–353
  cultural diversity, 359–361
  defining, 343–344
  dying at home, 356
  ethical issues, 352–355
  existential, spiritual, religious issues, 347–348
  good death, 346–347
  hospice and palliative care, 355–356
  informed consent, 352

Death and dying (*continued*)
    last goodbye, 346
    leading causes of, 345
    loss of spouse in old age, 350–351
    in old age, 344–345
    seniors' views of, 345–346
    stages of, 349
Death rates, 57
Defined benefit (DB) pension plans, 207–210
Defined contribution (DC) pension plans, 207–210
Delirium, 156
Dementia, 150–155
    caregiving, 328–332
    causes of, 151
    cognitive reserve, 136
    defined, 156
    driving ability and, 285, 286
    ethical issues in research, 40
    experience of, 154
    gardening and, 104–105
    increase in, 151–155
    loss of competence, 159–160
    policy and programs as outcome of research, 41
    social construction of, 153
Demographic determinism, 72
Demographic transitions, 58–59
Denison, David, 206
Dependence-free life expectancy, 122
Dependency ratios. *See* Support (dependency) ratios
Depression, 155–157
    defined, 156
    in ethno-cultural seniors, 89
    myth about aging and, 4
Developmental disability, 148–150
Developmental intelligence, 144
Developmental stake, 324
Diabetes, 98, 118
Diet and food
    ethno-cultural seniors, 81–82
    lifestyle changes, 117–121
Dietary restriction (DR), 120
Digital divide, 107
Disabilities
    compression of morbidity hypothesis, 122–124
    intellectual and developmental disabilities,
        148–150
    involuntary retirement due to, 27, 238–239
    limits on activity due to physical decline, 98–102
    prevalence of, 101, 102
Disability-free life expectancy, 122
Discrimination
    defined, 3
    against LGBT older adults, 307–308
    stigma of mental disorder, 158–160
    in workplace, 10–11, 228–230
    See also Ageism

Disease
    aging as, 12–16
    patterns of, 96–98
Disenfranchised grief, 350
Disengagement theory of aging, 23, 25, 247, 346
Distress, 121
Diversification of income, 200
The Division of Labor in Society (Durkheim), 25
Divorce, 297–298, 312–313
Do-not-resuscitate (DNR) order, 353
Douglas, Tommy, 168
Doukhobors, 179
Down syndrome, 149
DPA (Canada Digital Privacy Act), 338
Driving ability, 283–285, 286
Duffy, Sonia, 348
Durkheim, Emile, 25
Dying at home, 356
    See also Death and dying

E
EAP (Employee Assistance Programs), 334
Early retirement, 230–231
Easton, David, 353
Ecological model of housing, 267–269
Economics. *See* Finances and economics
Ecuador, population aging in, 50
Eden Alternative homes, 179
Edmonton Aboriginal Seniors Centre, 252
Education
    ageist behaviour in system, 8–9
    alternatives, 256–258
    as antidote to ageism, 15–16
    college attendance among older adults, 24
    effects of older population on, 2
    knowledge of aging and level of, 2
    for leisure and recreation, 254–258
    levels by age, 256
    quality of life and, 127
    Second-age versus Third-age learning, 257
Ego integrity, 346
Egyptian ethno-cultural seniors, 76
Elder abuse and mistreatment, 336–340
    Canadian research findings on, 336–338
    caregiving and, 91
    future issues in, 339–340
    policy issues, 338–339
Elderhostel (Road Scholar) program, 256–257
Elderly dependency ratio, 70
Elderspeak, 6
Emotional support given by older people, 309–310
EMPcare@home program, 191
Employee Assistance Programs (EAP), 334
Employment. *See* Workplace and employment
"Empty nest" couples, 294

Encoding, 133
Encore careers, 237–238
End-of-life care. *See* Death and dying
Enriched housing, 275–276
Environment, changing to cope with effects of aging, 104–105
Environmental (period) effects, 34
Environmental press, 267
Ephron, Norah, 14, 15
Epidemiological transition, 97, 110
Episodic memory, 133
Erectile dysfunction, 303–304
Erikson's theory of ego development, 346
Ethical issues
    in death and dying, 352–355
    in gerontology, 39–40
Ethics review boards, 40
Ethnicity and culture
    aging in Canada, 64–66
    caregiving, 330
    concept of, 76–79
    culture, defined, 77
    diversity of, 77–78
    elder abuse and mistreatment, 339
    in end-of-life care, 359–360
    ethnicity, defined, 76
    in funerary rituals, 360–361
    in long-term care settings, 178–179
    multigenerational households, 311
    theoretical perspectives on aging and, 78–79
Ethno-cultural seniors, 75–93
    accessibility of healthcare, 190
    in Canada, 79–80
    caregiving, 90–91
    community life, 85–86
    diet and food, 81–82
    economic security, 86–87
    ethnic identity and cultural practices, 80–82
    health and healthcare, 87–90
    intergenerational relationships, 82–84
    living arrangements and family life, 84–85
    number of foreign-born in Canada, 79
    visible minority seniors, 79–80
Ethnomethodology, 23
European ethno-cultural seniors, intergenerational relationships, 82
European immigration to Canada, 55, 65
European nations, population aging in, 53
Eustress, 121
Euthanasia, 357–359
Evidence-based practice, 41
Exercise. *See* Fitness and exercise
Existential issues in dying, 347–348
Expanders, 250
Experience Corps, 237
Experimental innovation, 146–147
Extended Health Care Services program, 184

F
Fairway Woods, 280–281
Falls, reducing, 116–117, 188
Family life, 291–316
    caregiving, 90–91
    changing family structure, 292–293
    common-law unions, 296–297
    contributions to, 308–313
    dating, 301
    divorce, 297–298
    effects of older population on, 2
    future research on, 313–314
    grandparenting, 310–313
    intergenerational relationships, 82–84
    lifelong singlehood, 298–299
    living arrangements, 84–85
    marriage, 293–295
    multigenerational households, 311
    remarriage, 298
    sexuality, 301–308
    widowhood, 299–301
The Feminine Mystique (Friedan), 32
Feminist perspectives, 23, 31–32
Fertility rates
    age-specific, 53
    baby boom and baby bust, 59–60
    defined, 53
    total, 53, 60
Fictive kin, 186, 292, 340
Fijian ethno-cultural seniors, 84
Filial piety, 82, 91
Film industry, stereotypes in, 12
Finances and economics, 195–222
    diversification of income, 200
    of divorce, 297–298
    economic position of seniors in pension system, 196–198
    economic security and immigration, 86–87
    effects on quality of life, 125–128
    financial security among retirees, 198, 212–213
    government transfer programs, 201–204
    healthcare costs, 171–176
    history of pension system, 198–200
    inequality, 213–218
    of long-term institutional care, 177
    in marriage, 295
    median net worth by age group, 200
    pension reform, 218–221
    prevalence of low income, 196
    reverse mortgages, 273–274
    social pensions worldwide, 213
    sources of income, 202
    support given by older people, 309
    women and, 214–218
    See also Pension system
Finland, universal minimum pensions, 213
First Nations communities. *See* Indigenous peoples

Fitness and exercise
    brain and, 142
        for leisure and recreation, 250–251
        lifestyle changes, 109–116
        marathon running, 251
        See also Leisure and recreation
FitzGerald, Mark, 110
FlexHousing, 273, 287
Flexible retirement, 234–236
Fluid intelligence, 143
Fomenoff, Anne, 360
Food. *See* Diet and food
Forced retirement, 228–230
Formal support
    defined, 318
    informal care and, 319–320, 322
The Fountain of Age (Friedan), 32
Fourth age, 12, 26, 30, 103
Franklin, Benjamin, 105
Fraud, 4–5
Free career, 237
Freedman, Marc, 237–238
Friedan, Betty, 32
Friends as informal supports, 325–327
Frum, David, 16–17
Functional disability, 98
Functional disorders
    defined, 148
    depression, 155–157
    treatment and intervention for, 157–158
Functional specificity of relationships model, 321
Functionalist perspective, 23, 25–28
Funding: New Horizons for Seniors Program, 17
Funerary rituals, 360–361
Future
    CPP challenges, 206–207
    elder abuse and mistreatment issues, 339–340
    of family life research, 313–314
    of gerontology, 42
    of health promotion model, 188–189
    healthcare issues, 189–192
    of housing for seniors, 281, 286–288
    of informal supports, 335–336
    of social support research, 340
    transportation needs, 285–286
    women and pensions, 218

G
Gambling, 252
Garden suites, 277–278
Gardening, dementia and, 104–105
Gay and lesbian older adults, 306–308
GDP (gross domestic product), healthcare spending and, 176
Gellar, Miriam, 352
Gemaine, Catherine S., 235

Gene therapy, 101
General Social Survey (GSS)
    charitable donations, 261, 263
    criminal victimization, 4
    stress, 11
    See also Statistics Canada
Generational stake, 324
Generations, 29
Gentrification, 86
Geographic mobility (migration), 66–67
Geriatric day hospitals, 182–183
Geriatric Program Assessment Teams (GPAT), 192
Germany
    healthcare spending in, 176
    history of pension system, 198–199
Gerontological Society of America (GSA), 21
The Gerontologist, 66
Gerontology, 21–42
    areas of study in, 21
    defined, 2
    ethical issues in, 39–40
    future of, 42
    goals of, 3
    large-scale research in Canada, 41
    policy and program development as outcome of, 40–41
    research issues in, 34–40
    social, 21–22
    theory in, 22–34
    types of research methods, 38–39
Gero-transcendence, 253
Ghana, population aging in, 50
GIS program. *See* Guaranteed Income Supplement (GIS)
        program
Golubchuk, Percy, 353
Golubchuk, Samuel, 352–353
Good death, 346–347
Gorrrara, Perri, 235
Gough, Jim, 236–237
Government transfer programs, 201–204
    See also Allowance (ALW); Guaranteed Income
        Supplement (GIS) program; Old Age Security (OAS)
        program
GPAT (Geriatric Program Assessment Teams), 192
Grab bars, 105
Graham, Heidi, 352
GRAND (Grandparents Requesting Access and Dignity), 312
Grandmothers Campaign, 49
Grandparenting, 310–313
Granny flat, 277
Great pension debate, 198
Greece, healthcare spending in, 176
Green, Danny, 229
Green, Jean, 235
Grief, 350
Griffin, John, 9
Gross domestic product (GDP), healthcare spending and, 176

GSS. *See* General Social Survey (GSS); Statistics Canada
Guaranteed Income Supplement (GIS) program, 201–204
    defined, 63
    origin of, 199

H

Hagita, Norihiro, 107
Hair dye, 15
Haitian ethno-cultural seniors, 90
Harland, Anne, 114
Harm or injury to study participants, 39
Haslam, Ken, 297
Health. *See* Healthcare; Personal health and illness
Health benefits of marriage, 295
Health Canada, 188
Health Council of Canada, 192
Health field, 187
Health promotion model of healthcare, 100, 111, 116, 166,
    187–189
Health Promotion Survey, 188
Healthcare, 164–194
    ageist behaviour in system, 7
    apocalyptic demography and use of, 69–70
    challenges to the healthcare system, 168–171
    community care, 180–186
    comparison of Canadian and U.S. healthcare systems,
        169–170
    cost of, 171–176
    effects of older population on, 2
    ethno-cultural seniors, 87–90
    future issues in, 189–192
    health promotion model, 166, 187–189
    healthcare system, defined, 165
    HIV/AIDS, 304
    hospital care, 175–177
    Indigenous peoples, 78
    infant mortality rates and improvements in, 57
    long-term institutional care, 177–179
    medical model, 165–166, 167
    mental disorders among older population, 4
    need for change in, 179–180
    origins of Canadian system, 167–168
    social model, 166, 167
    wait times, 170–171
    See also Personal health and illness
Healthy immigrant effect, 87
Hems, Henry, 236
Hierarchical compensatory model, 320
History of pension system, 198–200
History-graded events, 29
HIV/AIDS, 47, 49, 304–305
Holt, John, 145
Home adaptation, 272–273
Home care, 183–186
    defined, 184
    telehealth services, 191

Home nursing care, 182
Home ownership, 266–267, 271
Home repair fraud, 4–5
Homelessness, 279–281
Homemaker services, 182
Hong Kong, immigration to Canada from, 56
Hospices, 355–356
Hospital care, 175–177
Housing, 265–281
    apartment living, 274–275
    bias in, 6
    core housing need, 270
    ecological model of housing, 267–269
    enriched housing, 275–276
    future of, 281, 286–288
    garden suites, 277–278
    home adaptation, 272–273
    home ownership, 37, 266–267
    homelessness, 279–281
    living alone, 270
    living arrangements, 84–85, 269–270
    naturally occurring retirement communities
        (NORCs), 278
    planned retirement communities, 278–279
    reverse mortgages, 273–274
    in rural communities, 276–277
    single-family houses, 271
    supportive housing, 275–276
    tax and home maintenance programs, 272
Humour, ageism masquerading as, 9–10
Hunger Winter Study, 127
"Hydraheaded myth," 292
Hypertension, 98
Hypokinesia, 110

I

I Feel Bad About My Neck (Ephron), 15
IA (Institute of Aging), 41
Illness. *See* Healthcare; Personal health and illness
ILRs (Institutes for Learning in Retirement), 257–258
Immigration
    barriers to services, 41
    effects on aging population in Canada, 55–57
    ethnicity and aging population, 64–65
    healthy immigrant effect, 87
    language use at home, 66
    multigenerational households, 311
    pension system, 214
    retirement patterns, 233
    See also Ethno-cultural seniors
Impotence, 303–304
Income. *See* Finances and economics
Income maintenance programs, 199
    See also Canada Pension Plan (CPP); Quebec Pension
        Plan (QPP)

Income security programs
    defined, 199
    economic position of seniors in pension system,
        196–198
    See also Guaranteed Income Supplement (GIS) program;
        Old Age Security (OAS) program
Indexation, 219
India
    immigration to Canada from, 56
    population aging in, 51
Indian ethno-cultural seniors
    ethnic identity and cultural practices, 81
    healthcare, 87–89
    intergenerational relationships, 84
Indigenous peoples
    caregiving, 90–91
    healthcare, 87–88
    intergenerational relationships, 83
    median age of, 65
    multigenerational households, 311
    multiple jeopardy theory, 78
    not counted as visible minority, 77
    number of, 79
    population aging, 65
    senior centres, 252
Indonesia, population aging in, 50
Inequality in pension system, 213–218
Infant mortality rates, 57
Informal caregivers, 322
    See also Caregiving
Informal supports, 318–327
    care for caregiver, 334–335
    for childless older people, 324–325
    children as, 323–324
    defined, 318
    friends as, 325–327
    future of, 335–336
    siblings as, 327
    technology as, 327
    See also Caregiving
Informed consent, 39–40, 352
Institute of Aging (IA), 41
Institutes for Learning in Retirement (ILRs), 257–258
Institutes for Lifelong Learning (LLIs), 257–258
Institutional care. *See* Long-term care (LTC) facilities
        (collective dwellings)
Institutional completeness, 66, 85–86
Instrumental activities of daily living (IADLs), 99
"Integrated Pan-Canadian Healthy Living Strategy," 188
Intellectual disability, 148–150
Intelligence, 143–145
Intergenerational equity, 17
Intergenerational relationships, 17–18, 82–85
    See also Family life
Interlocking systems of oppression, 31
International Longevity Center, 11

Internet
    caregiver use of, 327
    for leisure and recreation, 258–260
    online dating, 301
    scams involving, 5
    transportation options, 286
    usage by age group, 259
    use by older adults, 27, 106–108
Interpretive perspective, 23–25
Intimacy. *See* Sexuality and intimacy
Intimacy at a distance, 270
Inuit seniors. *See* Indigenous peoples
Involuntary euthanasia, 359
Involuntary retirement, 27, 238–239
Iranian ethno-cultural seniors, 83
Italian ethno-cultural seniors, 85
Italy
    healthcare spending in, 176
    population aging in, 53

J
Japan
    healthcare spending in, 176
    population aging in, 53
Japanese ethno-cultural seniors, 83, 85
Job sharing, 234–235
Journal of Women and Aging, 13
Judaism
    ethno-cultural seniors and healthcare, 88
    Kosher Meals on Wheels program, 81

K
Katz, Stephen, 33
Kenya, population aging in, 51
Kin keepers, 310
Korean ethno-cultural seniors, community life, 85
Koreika (societal aging), 53
Kosher Meals on Wheels program, 81
Kragen, Vic, 301
Kreske, Dan, 245
Kronenberg, Bertha, 260
Kubler-Ross, Elizabeth, 349
Kumar, Anand, 352–353

L
Labour. *See* Workplace and employment
Labour Gazette, 199
Lalonde, Marc, 187
Langar on Wheels program, 81–82
Languages
    ethno-cultural seniors, 76
    spoken in home, 66
    visible minority seniors, 79

Laslett, Peter, 54
Last goodbye, 346
LAT (living apart together) couples, 296
Latency, 133
Later retirement, trend toward, 231–234
The Latest for Seniors, 220
Lawton–Nahemow ecological model of interaction, 267–269
Least developed regions
    defined, 47
    population aging in, 47–50
Legal guardianship, 160
Leisure and recreation, 244–264
    activity patterns, 115, 245–248
    community service through volunteer work, 260–263
    education, 254–258
    fitness and health, 250–251
    gambling, 252
    mall-walking programs, 248
    in marriage, 295
    religion and spirituality, 253–254
    senior centres, 252–253
    sports, participation in, 248–249
    technology usage, 258–260
    theories on, 249–250
    See also Fitness and exercise
Lesbian, gay, bisexual, or transsexual (LGBT) older adults, 306–308
Less developed regions
    defined, 47
    population aging in, 50–53
    population pyramids by age group and sex, 48
    proportion of older people in, 47
Lewis, Laurie, 103
Lewis, Stephen, 49
LGBT (lesbian, gay, bisexual, or transsexual) older adults, 306–308
Li Bengong, 52
Lieberman, Trudy, 169
Life course approach (life-span developmental perspective), 23, 26–30
    future goals of, 28
    leisure activity patterns, 249–250
    minority group aging, 78
    principles of, 27
    quality of life and, 127
    social context and, 29–30
Life course capital, 319
Life expectancy
    at birth, 57, 61
    compression of morbidity hypothesis, 122–124
    defined, 95
    evolution in Canada, 57–58
    of men, 68
    prospective aging, 60–62
    of women, 67
Life lease housing, 278–279

Life portfolio, 241–242
Life review, 346
Life satisfaction
    community belonging and, 10
    retirement and, 4
Life So Far (Friedan), 32
Life-course respite hypothesis, 247
Lifelong Learning Institutes (LLIs), 257–258
Lifelong singlehood, 298–299
Life-span developmental perspective. *See* Life course approach (life-span developmental perspective)
Lifespan housing, 273
Lifestyle changes, 109–122
    exercise, 109–116
    falls, reducing, 116–117
    smoking in later life, 109
    stress reduction, 121–122
Lifeworth, 262
Literary depictions of elderly, 8
Little Big Man (film), 9
Living alone, 270
Living arrangements, 269–270
LLIs (Lifelong Learning Institutes), 257–258
Loneliness
    older immigrants, 83–84
    remarriage and, 298
    retirement and, 4
Long-distance caregivers, 333
Longevity, dietary restriction and, 120
Longitudinal research designs, 35–37
Long-term care
    community care, 180–186
    continuing care retirement communities (CCRCs), 279
    defined, 166
    future issues in, 189–192
Long-term care (LTC) facilities (collective dwellings), 177–179
    defined, 166
    elderspeak by workers in, 6
    models of quality, 178–179
    proportion of older people in, 270
    sexuality in, 305–306, 331
    students' field placement in, 16
Long-term memory, 132
Low, Donald, 357
Low income, prevalence of, 196
LTC facilities. *See* Long-term care (LTC) facilities (collective dwellings)
Luxembourg, assisted suicide, 359
Lyft, 286

M
MacArthur Competency Assessment Tool for Treatment, 159
MacKenzie, Eileen, 81
Mackenzie, Hugh, 174
Macro-level theories, 22–23

Major depressive disorder (MDD), 27
Mall-walking programs, 248
Mandatory retirement, 226–228
Manitoba
    access to grandchildren in divorce, 313
    birth rates, 58
    elder abuse and mistreatment, 338
    home care, 186
    immigration, 55
    proportion of older people, 68
Marathon running, 251
Marital status
    common-law unions, 296–297
    dating, 301
    divorce, 297–298
    lifelong singlehood, 298–299
    marriage, 293–295
    remarriage, 298
    widowhood, 299–301
Marketing to older population
    cosmeceuticals, 14
    targeting baby boomers, 11–12
Marriage, 293–295
Martin, Linda G., 71
Marx, Karl, 30–31
Masculinity, 13
Maximum life span, 95
Mayer, Catherine, 14
McDonald, Doug, 230
McDonald, Janet, 238
MCI (mild cognitive impairment), 153
MDD (major depressive disorder), 27
Mead, George Herbert, 24
Meals on Wheels programs, 81–82, 182, 190
Means-tested pensions, 213
Media
    men in, 13–14
    portrayals of sexuality, 12
Median age
    in Canada, 61
    defined, 55
    of Indigenous peoples, 65
Medical assistance in dying, 357–359
Medical model of healthcare, 165–166, 167
Meditation, 121
Meeks, Anne, 95
Melvin, Stephanie, 286
Memory, 132–143
    cognitive reserve, 136–137
    contextual view of, 137–140
    defined, 132
    encoding, 133
    episodic, 133
    exercise and, 142
    laboratory studies of, 133–134
    latency, 133

limits of laboratory studies, 137
long-term, 132
new approaches to study of mental function, 135–136
non-episodic, 133
physical change as source of mental decline, 134–135
plasticity, 136–137
prospective, 138
semantic, 139
sensory, 132
short-term, 132
training for improved performance, 140–141
working, 133
Memory Intervention Program, 154
Men
    caregiving, 330, 332–333
    defined benefit (DB) pension plans, 208
    driver's licences, 283–284
    elder abuse and mistreatment, 337
    employment rates for seniors, 226
    erectile dysfunction, 303–304
    gay older men, 306–308
    as grandfathers, 312
    health status of seniors, 96
    homelessness, 280
    leading causes of death, 345
    life expectancy, 68
    loss of spouse in old age, 350–351
    low income, 215
    marriage in later life, 293–295
    masculinity, defined, 13
    normative age-graded events, 30
    part-time work, 236
    personal appearance, 13–14
    prevalence of disabilities, 101
    private pension plans, 207
    public transportation, 282
    reasons for retirement, 239
    remarriage, 298
    sexuality, 301–308
    sibling bonds, 327
    single-family houses, 271
    source of personal income, 216
    stopping driving, 285
    widowhood, 299–301
Mental health
    abnormal aging, 148
    benefits of marriage, 295
    comprehensive system for seniors, 161
    depression, 155–157
    exercise and, 111
    functional disorders, 155–158
    pain and, 103
    stigma of mental disorder, 158–160
    See also Intelligence; Memory; Psychology of aging
Mental Health Commission of Canada (MHCC), 158
Mental Health First Aid Canada, 158

Metabolic syndrome, 118
Métis seniors. *See* Indigenous peoples
MetLife and American Society on Aging study, 307
MHCC (Mental Health Commission of Canada), 158
Micro-level theories, 22–23
Middle East, immigration to Canada from, 56, 65
Middle Eastern ethno-cultural seniors, 76
Migration (geographic mobility), 66–67
    See also Immigration
Mild cognitive impairment (MCI), 153
Ministry of Health and Welfare in Japan, 53
Minority groups, 77
    See also Ethno-cultural seniors
Mobile workers, 232
Mobility club, 286
Modernization theory, 23, 25
Moral economy theory, 23, 33
Morbid grieving, 350
More developed regions
    defined, 47
    population aging in, 53
    population pyramids by age group and sex, 48
    proportion of older people in, 47
Morris, Kathleen, 175
Motherhood penalty, 31
Mourning, 350
Mulroney, Brian, 167
Multidimensional view of intelligence, 143
Multigenerational households, 311
Multiple jeopardy theory, 78
My Spoon, 106

N
Namibia, traffic signs in, 8
Narrative gerontology, 33
National Advisory Council on Aging (NACA)
    coordination of healthcare, 192
    oldest-old population, 62
National Organization for Women (NOW), 32
National Seniors Council (NSC), 17
Naturally occurring retirement communities (NORCs), 278
Nepal, social pensions, 213
Netherlands
    assisted suicide, 358–359
    Hunger Winter Study, 127
    universal age pensions, 213
Neuroimaging techniques, 135
Never Too Late (Holt), 145
New Brunswick
    community care, 180
    mandatory retirement, 226
    pension supplements, 203
    proportion of older people, 68
    telehealth services, 191
A New Perspective on the Health of Canadians (Lalonde), 187

Newfoundland and Labrador, proportion of older people, 68
Nikkei Place, 85
Nolan, Elizabeth, 262
Non-episodic memory, 133
Non-normative events, 29
Non-voluntary euthanasia, 359
Norman, Sharon, 237
Normative age-graded events, 30
Normative history-graded events, 29
Northwest Territories, proportion of older people, 68
Nova Scotia
    pension supplements, 203
    proportion of older people, 68
Novak, Mark, 361
NOW (National Organization for Women), 32
Nunavut, proportion of older people, 68
Nursing home care, 182
    See also Long-term care (LTC) facilities (collective
        dwellings)
Nutrition. *See* Diet and food
Nutritional risk for women, 98

O
OAS program. *See* Old Age Security (OAS) program
Obesity, 98, 113–116
    childhood hunger and, 127
    diet and, 119
    poverty and, 126
Occupational therapy, 182
O'Connor, Robert, 212
Old Age Assistance Act of 1951, 199
Old Age Pension Act of 1927, 199, 225
Old Age Security Act of 1951, 199
Old Age Security (OAS) program, 63, 201–204
Oldest-old population, 62–65
One-child policy (China), 51–52
Online dating, 301
Online learning, 255
Ontario
    ageist behaviour in medical settings, 7
    birth rates, 57–58
    community care, 181
    driving tests, 285
    foreign-born seniors, 79
    home care, 186
    opposition to Canada Health Act, 167–168
    pension supplements, 203
    proportion of older people, 68
    seasonal migration, 67
    supportive housing, 275
    telehealth services, 190–191
Ontario Human Rights Commission, 7
Organic brain disorders, 148–155
Osteoporosis, 98, 114
Osteoporosis Canada, 114

Overall dependency ratio (or rate), 69
Overweight, 98

P
Paid companions, 186
Pain, mental health and, 103
Palliative care, 355–356
Palmore, Erdman, 3
PALS (Participation and Activity Limitation Survey), 98–99, 238
Pan-Canadian Age-Friendly Communities Milestones, 287
Parents
     caregiving to, 333
     children as informal supports, 323–324
     daily living support given by, 308–309
     financial help for children, 197
     as role models, 309–310
Paro, 106, 154–155
ParticipACTION health promotion program, 188
Participation and Activity Limitation Survey (PALS),
          98–99, 238
Part-time work, 236–237
Passive euthanasia, 357, 359
Passive leisure lifestyle, 245
Pay-as-you-go plan, 205
Pension system
     Canada and Quebec Pension Plans, 204–207
     as citizen's wage, 225
     defined benefit and defined contribution plans, 207–210
     early retirement, 231
     economic position of seniors, 196–198
     government transfer programs, 201–204
     history of, 198–200
     immigrants and, 214
     inequality, 213–218
     private pension plans, 207
     reform to, 218–221
     registered pension plans (RPPs), 211–212
     registered retirement savings plans (RRSPs), 210–211
     social pensions worldwide, 213
     subsidies, 207
     tiers of, 201
     women and, 214–218, 240–241
     See also Retirement
Period (environmental) effects, 34
Personal appearance
     men's choices, 13–14
     women's choices, 13
Personal expression, creativity as, 147–148
Personal health and illness, 94–130
     assistive devices, 108–109
     compression of morbidity hypothesis, 122–124
     coping with physical change, 102–122
     diet, 117–121
     dietary restriction and longevity, 120
     environmental changes in, 104–105

exercise, 109–116
     falls, reducing, 116–117
     fitness and exercise, 250–251
     health status of seniors, 96
     healthy aging, 128–129
     impact of income and health on quality of life, 125–128
     lifestyle changes, 109–122
     limits on activity due to physical decline, 98–102
     patterns of disease, 96–98
     stress reduction, 121–122
     successful aging, 124–125
     technological changes and, 105–109
Personality, history-graded events and, 29
Personhood, 158–159
PHAC (Public Health Agency of Canada), 188, 304
Physical activity
     decline in, 245–247
     guidelines, 112
     sports, participation in, 248–249
     tax incentives, 111
     See also Fitness and exercise
Physical death, 343–344
Physician-assisted suicide, 357, 360
Physiotherapy, 182
Planned retirement communities, 278–279
Plasticity, 136–137
Policy. *See* Social policy
Political economy theory, 23, 30–31
Polyamorous Passions, 297
Polyamory, 297
Population aging
     ageism and social policy, 16–18
     aging of older population, 62–65
     birth rates and, 57–58
     in Canada, 54–69
     death rates and, 57
     defined, 46
     dependency ratio and cost of, 69–72
     ethnicity and, 64–66
     geographic mobility and, 66–67
     healthcare costs and, 173–175
     immigration and, 55–57
     increased numbers and proportions of older women, 67–69
     in least developed regions, 47–50
     in less developed regions, 50–53
     in more developed regions, 53
     prospective aging, 60–62
     on world scale, 46–54
Portable, 205
Portraits of Home Care in Canada, 184
Portugal, healthcare spending in, 176
Portuguese ethno-cultural seniors, community life, 86
Positivist worldview, 25
Post-modern theory, 33–34
Post-Retirement Benefit (PRB) program, 220
Poverty. *See* Finances and economics

Power of attorney, 353
Prejudice
    defined, 2
    against LGBT older adults, 307–308
    sources of, 7–9
    stereotypes and, 6
    See also Ageism
Price, Barbara, 235
Prince Edward Island
    home care, 186
    pension supplements, 203
    proportion of older people, 68
Privacy, 39–40
Private pension plans, 207
    bankruptcy of, 208
    defined benefit and defined contribution plans, 207–210
    early retirement, 231
    registered pension plans (RPPs), 211–212
    registered retirement savings plans (RRSPs), 210–211
    women and, 240
    See also Retirement
Private transportation, 283–285
Proctor & Gamble, 15
Project PhoneBusters, 5
Prospective aging, 60–62
Prospective memory, 138
Protecting Canada's Seniors Act, 338
Psychology of aging, 131–163
    abnormal aging, 148–160
    comprehensive mental health system for seniors, 161
    creativity, 145–148
    intelligence, 143–145
    memory, 132–143
Psychosocial studies, 21
Public Health Agency of Canada (PHAC), 17, 188, 304
Public Service Superannuation Act of 1985, 231
Public transportation, 281–283

Q
QPP (Quebec Pension Plan). *See* Quebec Pension Plan (QPP)
Qualitative methods, 42
Quality of life, effects of income and health on, 125–128
Quantitative methods, 42
Quasi-widowhood, 331
Quebec
    birth rates, 57
    community care, 181
    death rates, 57
    foreign-born seniors, 79
    pension supplements, 203
    proportion of older people, 68
    relationship-based care (RBC) programs, 178
    seasonal migration, 67
Quebec Pension Plan (QPP), 199, 204–207, 225
    See also Canada Pension Plan (CPP)

R
Rachlis, Michael, 174
RBC (relationship-based care) programs, 178
Recreation. *See* Leisure and recreation
Rectangularization, 122
Registered pension plans (RPPs), 207, 211–212
Registered retirement savings plans (RRSPs), 210–211
Relationship-based care (RBC) programs, 178
Religion and spirituality
    death and dying, 347–348
    as ethnic identifier, 77
    ethno-cultural seniors and healthcare, 88–89
    participation in, 253–254
    visible minority seniors, 79
Religiosity index, 253
Remarriage, 298
Rembrandt van Rijn, 40
Research in gerontology
    elder abuse and mistreatment, 336–338
    future of, 42, 313–314
    issues in, 34–40
    methods of, 38–39
    policy and program development as outcome of, 40–41
Residential Rehabilitation Assistance Program (RRAP), 272
Respite services, 334
Retirement
    age of eligibility, 71
    alternatives to fixed retirement age, 234–239
    average age, 232
    defined, 224
    early, 230–231
    financial security among retirees, 198, 212–213
    flexible, 234–236
    forced, 228–230
    geographic mobility, 67
    involuntary, due to disability, 27, 238–239
    later retirement, trend toward, 231–234
    mandatory, 226–228
    myths and realities of, 4
    origins of, 224–225
    part-time work, 236–237
    personal experience of, 241–242
    reasons for, 225–234, 239
    second careers, 237–238
    women and, 239–241
    See also Finances and economics; Pension system
Retirement principle, 224
Retirement wage, 224
    See also Pension system
Reverse annuity mortgage (RAM), 274
Reverse mortgages, 273–274
Rioux, Claude, 224
Rising Tide (Alzheimer Society of Canada), 153
"Risk society," 33–34
Road Scholar (Elderhostel) program, 256–257

Road Scholar Institute Network, 257
Robots, 105–106, 107, 154–155
Role emptying, 83
Role loss, 2
Role models, older relatives as, 309–310
Role reversal, 83
Romanow, Roy, 179
Romanow Report, 179–180
Routes to Learning Canada, 257
Rowe and Kahn model of successful aging, 124–125
Rural communities
    housing in, 276–277
    public transportation, 282
Russell, Bertrand, 145
Ruter, Joop, 251

S

SAFER (Shelter Aid for Elderly Renters) program,
    274–275
Saskatchewan
    Active Families Benefit program, 111
    birth rates, 58
    immigration, 55
    proportion of older people, 68
Saunders, Dame Cicely, 355
Savings plan, 205
Scaffolding Theory of Aging and Cognition (STAC), 136
Schafer, Arthur, 353
Schwartz, Pepper, 302
Seasonal migration, 67
Second careers, 237–238
Second language of sex, 303
Second-age learning, 257
Security in housing, 268–269
Selective optimization with compensation (SOC), 125
Self-efficacy, 250
Self-image and self-confidence
    effects of ageism on, 6–7
    men and, 13
    women and, 11
Self-perceived health, 96
Semantic memory, 139
Senior centres, 252–253
Sensory memory, 132
Sequential designs, 38
Services intégrés pour les personnes âgées en perte
    d'autonomie (SIPA) program, 191–192
Sex, Romance, and Relationships (AARP), 302
Sexuality and intimacy, 301–308
    adaptations due to aging, 303–304
    changes in values, 26
    HIV/AIDS, 304–305
    LGBT older adults, 306–308
    in long-term care settings, 305–306, 331
    in marriage, 294–295
    media portrayals of, 12

    myths and realities of, 5
    polyamory, 297
Shanas, Ethel, 292
Shelter Aid for Elderly Renters (SAFER) program, 274–275
Shelter allowances, 274
Sher, Julian, 286
Sherbrooke Community Centre, 179
Sheridan Centre for Elder Research, 39
Shortt, Adam, 224
Short-term memory, 132
Siblings as informal supports, 327
Sikhism, healthcare and, 88
Simon K.Y. Lee Seniors Care Home, 179
Singh, Fauja, 95
Single-family houses, 271
Singlehood, lifelong, 298–299
Single-point-of-entry model, 191
SIPA (Services intégrés pour les personnes âgées en perte
    d'autonomie) program, 191–192
Skip-generation households, 311
SLF (Stephen Lewis Foundation), 49
Smart clothing, 106
Smoking, 109
SOC (selective optimization with compensation), 125
Social capital, 319
Social constructionism, 23, 24
Social death, 343–344
Social engagement, creativity and, 147–148
Social exchange theory, 23
Social gerontology, 21–22
Social model of healthcare, 166, 167
    community care, 180–186
    summary of, 186–187
Social pensions worldwide, 213
Social phenomenology, 23, 24
Social policy
    ageism and, 16–18
    in China, 51–52
    elder abuse and mistreatment, 338–339
Social psychology. *See* Psychology of aging
Social Security program (U.S.), 225
Social spending
    apocalyptic demography and, 69–70
    change in age of eligibility, 71
Social structures, 2
Social support, 317–341
    care for caregiver, 334–335
    caregiving, 328–333
    for childless older people, 324–325
    children as informal supports, 323–324
    defined, 318
    elder abuse and mistreatment, 336–340
    formal support, 318
    friends as informal supports, 325–327
    future of informal supports, 335–336
    future research on, 340

informal supports, 318–327
    siblings as informal supports, 327
    technology as, 327
Society for all ages, 17
Socioeconomic status, quality of life and, 125–128
Socioeconomic-environmental studies, 21
Sodhi, Harinder, 81–82
Sodhi, Renu, 81–82
Something's Gotta Give (film), 12
South Africa, population aging in, 49–50
South America, immigration to Canada from, 65
Spain, population aging in, 53
Special care facilities. *See* Long-term care (LTC) facilities
    (collective dwellings)
Speedling, Ed, 238
Spirituality. *See* Religion and spirituality
Sports, participation in, 248–249
Spouse's Allowance (SPA) program, 203
    See also Allowance (ALW)
Squaring of the survival curve, 122
St. Christopher's (hospice), 355
STAC (Scaffolding Theory of Aging and Cognition), 136
Standardized life course, 26
Statistics Canada
    baby boomers, 59
    charitable donations, 263
    criminal victimization, 4
    foreign-born seniors, 79
    life expectancy at birth, 61
    living arrangements, 269–270
    oldest seniors, 63–65
    prevalence of low income, 196
    registered pension plans (RPPs), 207
    size of older population, 46
    stress, 4
    visible minority seniors, 79–80
    See also General Social Survey (GSS)
"Steady As You Go" program, 117
Stephen Lewis Foundation (SLF), 49
Stereotype threat, 137
Stereotypes
    among fellow seniors, 6
    defined, 6
    in film industry, 12
    in healthcare system, 7
    new, 12
    positive and negative, 6
    problems caused by, 3
    in workplace, 228–230
    See also Ageism
Strength training, 111
Stress
    caregiver burden, 328–332
    declines in, 11–12
    reducing, 121–122
    women and, 98

StrongStartBC, 238
Structural functionalism, 23, 25
Structural lag, 263
Subsidies for seniors, 207
Successful aging, 124–125
Suicide
    assisted, 357–359
    myths and realities of, 5
Suicide: A Study in Sociology (Durkheim), 25
Support (dependency) ratios
    in China, 51–52
    oldest-old population and economy, 63–64
    of population aging, 69–72
Supporting Homeless Seniors Program, 281
Supportive housing, 275–276, 280–281
    See also Assisted living
Sweden, healthcare spending in, 176
Switzerland, assisted suicide, 359
Symbolic interactionism, 23
Szasz, Thomas, 153

T
T'ai chi, 121, 188, 254
Targeted Initiative for Older Workers (TIOW)
    program, 235
Task specificity model, 320
Tax incentives
    for home maintenance, 272
    for physical activity, 111
Taxback, 228
Tax-free savings accounts (TFSAs), 220
Taylor, Gloria, 360
Taylor, Jason, 360
Taylor, Jessie, 2–3
Technology
    accessibility of healthcare, 190–191
    coping with physical change through, 105–109
    home adaptation, 273
    information technology work, 31
    Internet use by seniors, 27
    for leisure and recreation, 258–260
    for mental training, 140–141
    online learning, 255
    research opportunities and, 42
    as social support, 327
Telehealth services, 190–191
Telephone fraud, 5
Television, obesity and, 115–116
A 10-Year Plan to Strengthen Health Care, 170
Theories in gerontology, 22–34
    conflict perspective, 30–32
    functionalist perspective, 25–30
    interpretive perspective, 23–25
    on leisure and recreation, 249–250
    micro- and macro-level, 23–24

Theory of ego development (Erikson), 346
Third age, 12, 26, 30, 237, 257
    See also Retirement
Thomas, William, 179
Thompson, E. P., 33
Three-generation households, 269
Tilden, Mark, 107
Time-lag comparison design, 37–38
TIOW (Targeted Initiative for Older Workers) program, 235
Tonari Gumi, 85
Total fertility rate, 53, 60
Toynbee, Arnold, 146
Traditional Chinese medicine, 89
Traffic signs, 8
Trajectories, 28
Trajectory of dying, 345
Transfer plan, 205
Transitions, 28
Transportation, 281–288
    common forms of, 284
    future needs, 285–286
    private, 283–285
    public, 281–283
Transportation brokerage, 286
Turnbull, Jeff, 175

U
Uber, 286
Uganda, universal age pensions, 213
Ukrainian ethno-cultural seniors
    immigration to Canada, 81
    intergenerational relationships, 84
UN (United Nations), 46–47
UNAIDS Report on the Global AIDS Epidemic 2010 (UN), 47
United Kingdom, traffic signs in, 8
United Nations (UN), 46–47
United States
    assisted suicide, 359
    Civic Ventures, 237
    comparison with Canadian healthcare system, 169–170
    developmental disability in, 149
    healthcare spending in, 176
    history of pension system, 199
    immigration to Canada from, 65
    migration to, 67
    Social Security program, 225
Universal age pensions, 213
Universal design, 273
Universal minimum pensions, 213
Universality, 198

V
Vesting, 205
Viagra, 303–304

Vietnam, universal minimum pensions, 213
Visible minority groups, 79–80
    defined, 77
    proportion of population belonging to, 80
Visitability, 273
Voluntary euthanasia, 359
Volunteer work, community service through, 260–263
Von Bismarck, Otto, 198

W
Wait times in healthcare system, 170–171
Walford, Roy, 120
Weak social ties, 258
Weber, Max, 24
Weg, Ruth, 308
Weight training, 111
Welsh, Moira, 286
Wetmore, Susan, 262
White, M.C., 306
Whitehouse, Peter, 153
Whitlock, Ed, 251
Widowhood, 299–301
    economic inequality, 217–218
    loss of spouse in old age, 350–351
Wiesman, Linda, 325
Wife assault in old age, 338
    See also Elder abuse and mistreatment
Wilson, Robert S., 136
Winnipeg Regional Health Authority (WRHA), 192
Wisconsin Longitudinal Study, 302
Wisdom, 144–145
Women
    ageism in literature, 8
    ageism in workplace, 11
    Allowance (ALW) payments, 203
    caregiving, 328–333
    chronic health problems, 98
    defined benefit (DB) pension plans, 208
    driver's licences, 283–284
    early retirement, 230
    elder abuse and mistreatment, 337–338
    employment rates for seniors, 226
    feminist perspectives, 23, 31–32
    financial consequences of divorce, 297–298
    health status of seniors, 96
    HIV/AIDS, 304–305
    homelessness, 280
    increased numbers and proportions of older women, 67–69
    Indigenous peoples and caregiving, 91
    leading causes of death, 345
    lesbian older women, 306–308
    life expectancy, 67
    living alone, 270
    loss of spouse in old age, 350–351
    low income, 215
    marriage in later life, 293–295

motherhood penalty, 31
normative age-graded events, 30
as part of mid- to later-life market, 11
part-time work, 236
pension system, 214–218
personal appearance, 13, 14–15
prevalence of disabilities, 101
private pension plans, 207
public transportation, 282
reasons for retirement, 239
remarriage, 298
retirement, 239–241
sexuality, 301–308
sibling bonds, 327
single-family houses, 271
source of personal income, 216
sports, participation in, 249
widowhood, 299–301
Working memory, 133
Workplace and employment
ageism in, 10–11, 228–230
barriers for older workers, 236

caregiving and, 334–335
employment rates, 226
in home of adult children, 85
information technology work, 31
part-time work, 236–237
second careers, 237–238
See also Pension system; Retirement
World Population Ageing 2009 (UN), 46
WRHA (Winnipeg Regional Health Authority), 192

Y
Yoga, 121, 254
Youth dependency ratio, 70
Yukon, proportion of older people, 68

Z
Zarit, Steven, 4
Zhao Ruiting, 46
Zoomer Canada magazine, 11, 14
Zoomer lifestyle, 12